FREUD

A Life for Our Time

BOOKS BY PETER GAY

Schnitzler's Century:
The Making of Middle-Class Culture, 1815–1914 (2001)

The Bourgeois Experience: Victoria to Freud
Education of the Senses (1984)
The Tender Passion (1986)
The Cultivation of Hatred (1993)
The Naked Heart (1995)
Pleasure Wars (1998)

Reading Freud: Explorations and Entertainments (1990)

Freud: A Life for Our Time (1988)

A Godless Jew:
Freud, Atheism, and the Making of Psychoanalysis (1987)

Freud for Historians (1985)

Freud, Jews and Other Germans:
Masters and Victims in Modernist Culture (1978)

Art and Act: On Causes in History—Manet, Gropius, Mondrian (1976)

Style in History (1974)

Modern Europe (1973), with R. K. Webb

The Bridge of Criticism: Dialogues on the Enlightenment (1970)

The Enlightenment: An Interpretation
Vol. II: The Science of Freedom (1969)

Weimar Culture: The Outsider as Insider (1968)

A Loss of Mastery: Puritan Historians in Colonial America (1966)

The Enlightenment: An Interpretation
Vol. I: The Rise of Modern Paganism (1966)

The Party of Humanity: Essays in the French Enlightenment (1964)

Voltaire's Politics: The Poet as Realist (1959)

The Dilemma of Democratic Socialism:
Eduard Bernstein's Challenge to Marx (1952)

FREUD

A Life for Our Time

PETER GAY

W · W · NORTON & COMPANY / NEW YORK · LONDON

FOR

BILL AND SHIRLEY KAHN
DICK AND PEGGY KUHNS

First published as a Norton paperback 1998
Copyright © 1998, 1988 by Peter Gay
Printed in the United States of America.

———————————

The text of this book is composed in Avanta, with display type set in Walbaum.
Composition and manufacturing by The Haddon Craftsmen, Inc.
Book design by Antonina Krass.

———————————

Ornament, depicting Oedipus solving the riddle of the Sphinx, is adapted
from an ancient Greek vase painting.

Library of Congress Cataloging-in-Publication Data

Gay, Peter, 1923–
Freud: a life for our time / Peter Gay.
p. cm.
Bibliography: p.
Includes index.
1. Freud, Sigmund, 1856–1939. 2. Psychoanalysts—Austria—
Biography. 3. Psychoanalysis—History. I. Title.
BF173.F85G377 1988
150.19'52—dc19 87-20454

ISBN 0-393-31826-5 pbk.

W. W. Norton & Company, Inc.
500 Fifth Avenue, New York, N.Y. 10110
www.wwnorton.com

W. W. Norton & Company Ltd.
Castle House, 75/76 Wells Street, London W1T 3QT
2 3 4 5 6 7 8 9 0

There is no one so great that it would be a disgrace for him to be subject to the laws that govern normal and pathological activity with equal severity.

—Freud, "Leonardo da Vinci and
a Memory of His Childhood"

FOREWORD TO THE NORTON
PAPERBACK EDITION

When I first published my biography of Freud in 1988, he was beset by controversy, as he had been through his long and combative life. He had grimly predicted that he would disturb the sleep of mankind and, to mankind's mixed feelings, he succeeded. Today, ten years later, he is more controversial than ever, so his life is still a life for our time. Then, as now, he was under sustained attack from several quarters, religious and secular alike, but today his life and work (the two, of course, are inextricably interwoven) rouse even more spirited criticism and no less spirited defense than only a decade ago. No major player on the stage of modern European culture has had more obituaries than Freud, yet, astonishingly, his vital signs appear to be in good order. If they were not, the vehement, often vicious assaults on him would not have to be reiterated so insistently.

Nor have these postmortems been the monopoly of hostile psychologists, skeptical psychiatrists, or enraged former admirers. The press has followed, and in its way generated, these vicissitudes of Freud's reputation with leering attention. *Time* wondered in a lead article whether Freud was dead, and rather thought he was; *New York* magazine put a well-drawn portrait of Freud with a solitary tear running down his cheek on its cover; the *New York Review of Books,* with its impressive circulation and educated readership a powerful cultural force, has given generous room to the repeated, and repetitive, harangues of Frederick Crews, who has made the destruction of Freud and all his works a personal crusade. For three decades now, psychoanalysis, which could do no wrong in the 1950s, has not been able to do anything right. And since Freud is the sole begetter of psychoanalysis, attacks on it have often been attacks on him. I may not be the one to say so, but to my mind Freud's exposed position makes a reliable biography all the more necessary.

What role, if any, will Freud and his ideas play in the general psychology of the future? The widely advertised rival therapies (not all of them from California), the spectacular emergence of medication to alleviate certain types of mental distress, and, with that, the proliferation of biological approaches to the mind at work, make the survival value of Freud's ideas highly problematic. But speculation about the obsolescence of those ideas remains hazardous in the extreme. It is not widely known that in his last book, *An Outline of Psychoanalysis*, which he did not live to finish, the aged Freud—he was then eighty-two—held out the prospect of replacing psychoanalytic treatment with still undiscovered chemical substances. In other words, the Founder himself saw nothing incompatible between his psychoanalytic perspective and neuropsychiatry. It seems possible, certainly imaginable, that these two ways of looking at the mind, its functioning and its failures, may be synthesized into one grand, comprehensive theory. But that synthesis will require a thinker as original and as bold as Freud.

AS THE NOTES to this text should make plain, I was fortunate to have researched this biography at a time when it was possible to secure access to full sets of Freud's correspondence, which had been used, and in many ways abused, in earlier publications. In his great three-volume life, Ernest Jones prudently omitted some of the most interesting passages in his exchange of letters with Freud, and was remarkably discreet about the way that Freud died—or, rather, was put to death at his own request. At the urging of Anna Freud, Jones even corrected her father's nearly flawless English. Published collections of Freud's correspondence with Karl Abraham, Oskar Pfister, and Lou Andreas-Salomé were scandalously expurgated. And of the important exchange of letters between Freud and Sándor Ferenczi, only a few specimens were available in print. Being able to go beyond these fragmented, at times falsified, publications and consult the originals greatly served the purposes of this biography. In consequence, I was able to publish around 2,000 passages, some new, some corrected, for the first time.

I was grateful, though not excessively so. The stonewalling of which I complained ten years ago kept me from material that would have helped me to round out my portrait of Freud the man and of the world in which he lived. It was only after I had published my biography that I was permitted to read correspondence between Freud and his sister-in-law Minna Bernays, and even that collection turned out to be sadly truncated; a number of these letters, dating from the turn of the century—the years when, if ever, they might have carried on an affair—though promised to me, were in the end withheld.

I should note parenthetically that the much-canvassed question, Did Freud and Minna Bernays have an affair? is really of modest significance. Readers of this book may recall that, judging by whatever evidence I had, I thought that there was nothing to the story. But I declared myself perfectly willing to change my mind if new material warranted it. Some among Freud's most implacable critics have made this issue a kind of litmus test of psychoanalysis, as though Freud's adultery, if documented, would drag all his theory into the abyss with him. But that strikes me as preposterous: as I have assumed throughout this book, Freud's ideas stand, or fall, on their own.

Some blank spots on the record still remain, but only one of them promises to be of any real significance: the so-called Brautbriefe, the correspondence between Freud and his fiancée. They were engaged for five years, rarely together, and writing nearly every day. Their correspondence promises to make both Freud and, even more, Martha Bernays more vivid than ever. Over a hundred of Freud's letters to his fiancée (though none of her letters to him, except for the few fragments I managed to discover and publish) have been published in full and in part, and they whet the appetite for the hundreds more that still await the light of day. I doubt that they will contain sensational revelations, but they should enlarge our grasp of Freud's inner life. When they are published (or otherwise made available to scholars) there will be time for another edition.

IF I WERE writing this biography today, what would I do differently? Not much, I think. I would say more about Freud the psychoanalyst as politician, and I would recast my comments on the Schreber case, which continues to be hotly debated. For the rest, I think I can stand by the text. After all, when it appeared ten years ago, this biography had a gratifying reception. It sold well, and even became a bestseller in the United States, France, and Brazil. It was reviewed appreciatively and translated into nine languages. Yet, naturally, it had its denigrators who, as it were, lobbed shells at me from the extreme right and the extreme left. Some treated me as nothing better than an apologist for the Freudian establishment, as an adorer of my idol, Freud; others, fanatical Freudians, excoriated me for daring to disagree with the Master and treating him as a mere human being. These hostile reviewers comforted me; they involuntarily assured me that I had done something right. I imagine that this new paperback edition will generate a few new obituaries of Freud but also, I trust, discredit them.

Peter Gay
May 1998

CONTENTS

Twelve · *To Die in Freedom* · 588

THE POLITICS OF DISASTER · 588   DEFIANCE AS IDENTITY · 597   FINIS
AUSTRIAE · 611   DEATH OF A STOIC · 629

PREFACE

In April 1885, in a much-quoted letter, Sigmund Freud announced to his fiancée that he had "almost completed an undertaking which a number of people, still unborn but fated to misfortune, will feel severely." He was referring to his biographers. "I have destroyed all my notes of the last fourteen years, as well as letters, scientific extracts, and manuscripts of my works. Among letters, only family letters have been spared." With all the stuff he had scribbled piling up about him, he felt like a Sphinx drowning in drifting sands until only his nostrils, he wrote, were sticking up above the heaps of papers. He was pitiless about those who would be writing his life: "Let the biographers labor and toil, we won't make it too easy for them." He already looked forward to seeing how wrong they would be about him. Researching and writing this book, I have often visualized this scene: Freud the Sphinx freeing himself from mountains of paper that would have helped the biographer immeasurably. In later years, Freud repeated this destructive gesture more than once, and in the spring of 1938, preparing to leave Austria for England, he threw away materials that an alert Anna Freud, abetted by Princess Marie Bonaparte, rescued from the wastebasket.

Freud also found other ways of discouraging his future biographers. Indeed, some of the comments that Freud made about the writing of lives must give pause to anyone writing *his* life. "Biographers," he noted in 1910, in his paper on Leonardo da Vinci, "are fixated on their hero in a quite particular way." They choose that hero in the first place, Freud thought, because they feel a strong affection for him; their work is in consequence almost bound to be an exercise in idealization. A quarter century later, under the impress of old age, ill health, and the Nazi menace, he was more caustic still. "Whoever turns biographer," he wrote to Arnold Zweig, who had proposed to write Freud's life, "commits himself to lies, to concealment, to hypocrisy, to embellishments, and even to dissembling his own lack of understanding, for biographical truth is not to be had, and, even if one had it, one could not use it." In short, Freud had little faith in the biographical enterprise.

Exploring undiscovered regions of the mind, however, Freud stood ready to use himself as a guinea pig. His metaphor of the Sphinx is telling, but usually he saw himself rather as her conqueror, Oedipus, the hero who alone mastered that mysterious and lethal creature by answering her question. As he ruefully observed more than once, few humans have disclosed their feelings, their ambitions and wicked wishes, with such sublime disregard for their reputation. He reported and closely analyzed some of his most revealing dreams; he recorded some embarrassing memories of his early years. On the other hand, he dammed the stream of self-disclosure the moment he felt it threatening to wash away his cherished secrets. "Whoever is quick to reproach me for such reserve," he wrote, reasonably enough, after abruptly terminating the interpretation of his famous dream of Irma's injection in mid-revelation, "should himself try to be more candid than I." As a fearless researcher, he exposed most of his innermost being to public scrutiny; as a good bourgeois, he valued his privacy, immensely.

Freud left tantalizing autobiographical hints on which students of his life have seized with understandable and uncritical enthusiasm. Writing to his friend Wilhelm Fliess in 1900, he said of himself, "I am not a man of science at all, not an observer, not an experimenter, not a thinker. I am nothing but a conquistador by temperament, an adventurer if you want to translate this term, with all the inquisitiveness, daring, and tenacity of such a man." But this pronouncement, like others of the sort, has only misled those who would understand him. There is no point in distorting his spirit by obeying his letter. It is one thing to treat Freud's self-appraisals with respect; a responsible biographer can do no less. It is quite another thing to treat his pronouncements as gospel. As will appear more than once in these pages, Freud was not his own best judge.

ALL THE PASSION that has greeted Freud's ideas, and the partial, often highly subjective manner of Freud's self-revelations and self-estimates, have made it natural for every dimension of his life to invite conflicting interpretations. Despite decades of research and scores of studies, he remains puzzling and intensely controversial. Freud has been called genius, founder, master, a giant among the makers of the modern mind, and, no less emphatically, autocrat, plagiarist, fabulist, the most consummate of charlatans. Every worshiper who has hailed him as a Columbus has been matched by a detractor who has derided him as a Cagliostro. His life has provided inexhaustible fodder for innuendo, speculation, and mythmaking: one American fundamentalist pastor has denounced him in a venomous anti-Catholic leaflet as "a Jew who

converted to Roman Catholicism" and "well-known as the world's foremost pervert." Psychoanalysts for their part, though they would scoff at such rubbish, have only too often treated Freud as though he were indeed the pontiff of his faith and his words unchallengeable papal pronouncements. No reconciliation of such extremes seems possible. Nor would it be desirable; the truth about Freud is not likely to lie in the middle.

These storms over Freud should surprise no one. After all, it was his fate, as he put it with rather quizzical satisfaction, to "agitate the sleep of mankind." The fundamental task of psychoanalysis, he once wrote the novelist Stefan Zweig, was to "struggle with the demon"—the demon of irrationality—in a "sober way." But, he added, this very sobriety, which reduces that demon to "a comprehensible object of science," only made his ideas about the nature of human nature seem all the more dismaying, all the more unacceptable. No wonder that mankind has for the most part defended itself against Freud's message with angry denials. It is a commonplace that we all speak Freud today whether we recognize it or not. We casually refer to repression and projection, neurosis and ambivalence and sibling rivalry. A historian calls our time an age of narcissism and everyone professes to understand what he means. But such glib verbal endorsements have often been more damaging than the most vehement rejection. They are an attempt, more or less conscious, at robbing Freud's thought of its tough-minded realism. Freud said more than once that he could deal with his enemies; it was his friends who worried him.

The heated disputes over Freud's character have proved, if anything, even more virulent than those over his theories. Freud himself contributed to the atmosphere in which rumor can flourish by making memorable but misleading aphorisms and leaving behind inaccurate appraisals of his own work. This is paradoxical: Freud's creation, psychoanalysis, is after all committed to the most unsparing inquiry; it presents itself as the nemesis of concealment, hypocrisy, the polite evasions of bourgeois society. Indeed, Freud took considerable pride in being the destroyer of illusions, the faithful servant of scientific veracity. "The truth," he wrote to Sándor Ferenczi in 1910, "is for me the absolute aim of science." Two decades later, he said it again, to Albert Einstein: "I no longer count as one of my merits that I always tell the truth as much as possible; it has become my métier."

WE KNOW A GREAT deal about Freud. He conducted a vast correspondence, most of which I have read; in both its formal and its intimate guise, it discloses many important truths about him. He produced a copious body of work, some of which is openly, some of it covertly, autobiographical. His letters and his publications contain passages that can be trusted to appear in all biographies of Freud—including this one: I have tried to be accurate rather than startling. Even so, considering how closely he has been scrutinized, and how many telling clues he left, sizable areas on the map of his life remain blank and require further exploration. Was Freud's father married twice or three times? Did Freud have a love affair with his sister-in-law Minna Bernays, or is this the sheer fantasy of a hostile contemporary, or of an ingenious detective-biographer? Why did Freud think it advisable to psychoanalyze his daughter Anna when his papers on technique frown severely on the analyst's being close to his analysand? Did Freud plagiarize and then excuse his illicit borrowings by pleading a poor memory, or are such charges honest misunderstandings of his procedure or perhaps malicious slanders against a conscientious researcher? Was Freud addicted to cocaine and did he produce his psychoanalytic theories under its influence, or was his use of cocaine moderate and in the end innocuous?

There are more questions still. Was Freud the scientific positivist he claimed to be, or was he, rather, principally indebted to the cloudy speculations of the romantics or to Jewish mysticism? Was he as isolated in the medical establishment of his time as he liked to complain? Was his oft-declared detestation of Vienna actually a pose, in fact the most Viennese trait in him, or an authentic distaste? Is it true that his academic preferment was slowed down because he was a Jew, or is this a legend spawned by the kind of overly sensitive grievance collectors who profess to detect anti-Semitism everywhere? Was his abandonment, in 1897, of the so-called seduction theory of neuroses an instance of remarkable scientific courage, an act of filial piety, or a craven retreat from a generalization that made him unpopular with his colleagues? How far-reaching were what he called his "homosexual" feelings for his intimate friend of the 1890s, Wilhelm Fliess? Was he the self-appointed chieftain of a tight and submissive clan of disciples, a Louis XIV of psychology, proclaiming *La psychanalyse, c'est moi*, or a genial, if sometimes severe, guide to the hidden laws of the mind who freely acknowledged the contributions of colleagues and predecessors? Was he vain enough to have himself photographed in a group portrait standing on a box lest he be dwarfed by taller men—or is this too, perhaps, the fantasy of a biographer in search of material that will discredit Freud?

Such biographical controversies, though absorbing in themselves, are of more than biographical interest. They impinge upon the largest question that his work raises: Is psychoanalysis a science, an art, or an imposture? They impinge upon it because, unlike other great figures in the history of Western culture, Freud seems to stand under the obligation to be perfect. No one acquainted with the psychopathology of Luther or Gandhi, Newton or Dar-

win, Beethoven or Schumann, Keats or Kafka, would venture to suggest that
their neuroses damaged their creations or compromised their stature. In sharp
contrast, Freud's failings, real or imagined, have been proffered as conclusive
evidence for the bankruptcy of his creation. It has become a common tactic
to strike at psychoanalysis by striking at its founder, as though the successful
blackening of his character would encompass the ruin of his work. Granted,
a discipline as candidly autobiographical as Freud's depth psychology, and as
subjective in its materials, is bound to display traces of the founder's mind.
Yet surely the validity of psychoanalytic propositions does not depend on
what we uncover about their originator. One could easily imagine a Freud
the perfect gentleman propagating a fundamentally flawed psychology, or a
Freud riddled with defects, even vices, as the most significant psychologist
in history.

To be sure, there is no reason why Freud should be immune from psychoanalytic scrutiny, why his writings and his memories, whether accurate or
distorted, should not be made to yield biographical information. It seems only
just: Freud, after all, aimed at a general psychology that would explain not
just a handful of neurotic contemporaries but all humans everywhere—including himself. Indeed, Freud himself has pointed the way. "It should not
be a matter of indifference or without significance," he wrote in his paper
on Goethe, "which details of a child's life had escaped the general amnesia."
Adult conduct invites this kind of deep attention no less. "He who has eyes
to see and ears to hear," he wrote in a famous passage, "becomes convinced
that mortals can keep no secret. If their lips are silent, they gossip with their
fingertips; betrayal forces its way through every pore." Freud offered this
reflection in his case history of "Dora," but it applies to him as much as to
his analysands. In the course of a long and unrivaled career as the archeologist
of the mind, Freud developed a body of theories, empirical investigations, and
therapeutic techniques which, in the hands of a scrupulous biographer, may
uncover his wishes, anxieties, and conflicts, a sizable repertory of motives that
remained unconscious yet helped to shape his life. Hence I have not hesitated
to employ his discoveries, and as much as possible his methods, to explore his
own life's history. Yet I have not allowed them to monopolize my attention.
As a historian, I have placed Freud and his work within their various environ-
ments: the psychiatric profession he subverted and revolutionized, the Austrian culture in which he was compelled to live as an unbelieving Jew and
unconventional physician, the European society that underwent in his lifetime the appalling traumas of war and totalitarian dictatorship, and Western
culture as a whole, a culture whose sense of itself he transformed out of all
recognition, forever.

I HAVE WRITTEN this book neither to flatter nor to denounce but to understand. In the text itself, I do not argue with anyone: I have taken positions on the contentious issues that continue to divide commentators on Freud and on psychoanalysis, but have not sketched the itinerary leading to my conclusions. For readers interested in the controversies that make investigation into Freud's life so fascinating, I have appended an extensive and argumentative bibliographical essay, which should enable them to discover the reasons for the stands I have taken, and to find materials presenting rival opinions.

One interpreter of Freud with whom I disagree is Freud himself. He may have been literally correct, but was essentially misleading, when he called his life "externally quiet and without content," to be "disposed of with a few dates." To be sure, Freud's life superficially looks like that of many another highly educated, intelligent, and active nineteenth-century physician: he was born, he studied, he traveled, he married, he practiced, he lectured, he published, he argued, he aged, he died. But his internal drama is gripping enough to command any biographer's unflagging attention. In the famous letter to his friend Fliess that I have quoted, Freud called himself a conquistador. This book is the history of his conquests. It will turn out that the most dramatic of those conquests was, however incomplete, that of himself.

—PETER GAY

A Note on Usage and Citations

Virtually all translations are my own. But since this book is addressed to an English-speaking audience, I have also cited, for convenience, the places in the English-language versions of Freud's writings and correspondence where the reader may find the passages I have quoted.

As I also note in the text, I have reproduced Freud's English—excellent, though on occasion slightly stilted and inaccurate—precisely as he wrote it, mistakes, coinages, and all, without encumbering the quotations with intrusive comments. Thus, when readers encounter "intellegible" or "Prussianity," they have authentic Freud before them.

For the sake of euphony, and to avoid clumsy locutions like "his/her" or, worse, "s/he," I have used the traditional masculine form to apply to both sexes.

FOUNDATIONS

1856–1905

ONE

A Greed for Knowledge

 On November 4, 1899, the house of Franz Deuticke, Leipzig and Vienna, published a substantial volume by Sigmund Freud, *Die Traumdeutung.* But the date on the title page of *The Interpretation of Dreams* was 1900. While on its face this inconsistent bibliographical information reflects nothing more than a publishing convention, in retrospect it aptly symbolizes Freud's intellectual patrimony and eventual influence. His "dream book," as he liked to call it, was the product of a mind shaped in the nineteenth century, yet it has become the property—cherished, reviled, inescapable—of the twentieth. The title of the book, especially in its laconic German, "Dream Interpretation," was provocative enough. It evoked the kind of cheap brochure, aimed at the credulous and the superstitious, that catalogues dreams as predictions of calamities or good fortune to come. He had "dared," Freud commented, "against the objections of severe science, to take the part of the ancients and of superstition."

But for some time *The Interpretation of Dreams* proved of little general interest: in the course of six years, only 351 copies were sold, and a second edition was not called for until 1909. If, as Freud came to believe, it was indeed his fate to agitate the sleep of mankind, that would be years later. It is sobering to contrast this tepid, yawning reception with that of another revolutionary classic shaping modern culture, Charles Darwin's *Origin of Species.* Published on November 24, 1859, forty years almost to the day before Freud's dream book, its entire first edition of 1,250 copies was sold out by evening, and new, revised editions followed rapidly. While Darwin's book was subversive, it stood at the storm center of a great debate about the nature of the human animal and had been eagerly awaited. Freud's book, which proved no less subversive, at first seemed only esoteric and eccentric, food for a handful of specialists. Whatever hopes he harbored for quick and wide acceptance proved unrealistic.

Freud's labor had been long, almost rivaling Darwin's decades of silent preparation; his interest in dreams reached as far back as 1882, and he had begun to analyze them about 1894. However slowly *The Interpretation of Dreams* would make its way, it is the centerpiece of Freud's life. In 1910, he observed that he considered the book his "most significant work." If, he added, "it should find recognition, normal psychology, too, would have to be put on a new basis." In 1931, in his preface to the third English edition, Freud again paid the dream book his considered homage. "It contains, even according to my present-day judgement, the most valuable of all the discoveries it has been my good fortune to make. Insight such as this falls to one's lot but once in a lifetime."

Freud's pride was not misplaced. Despite the inevitable false starts and no less inevitable detours of his early researches, all his discoveries of the 1880s and 1890s flowed into *The Interpretation of Dreams.* More: much that he would discover afterwards, and not about dreams alone, was implicit in its pages. With its copious, immensely revealing autobiographical material, the book can claim unrivaled authority for Freud's biographer. It sums up all he had learned—indeed, all he was—right back to the maze of his complicated childhood.

FOOD FOR MEMORIES

Sigmund Freud, the great unriddler of human enigmas, grew up among enough conundrums and confusions to pique the interest of a psychoanalyst. He was born on May 6, 1856, in the small Moravian town of Freiberg, the son of Jacob Freud, a generally impecunious Jewish wool merchant, and his wife Amalia. The names his father inscribed for him in the family Bible, "Sigismund Schlomo," did not survive Freud's adolescence.

He never used "Schlomo," his paternal grandfather's name, and after experimenting with "Sigmund" during his later years at school, adopted it some time after he entered the University of Vienna in 1873.*

The Freuds' Bible also records that Sigismund "entered the Jewish covenant"—in short, was circumcised—a week after his birth, on May 13, 1856. This much is dependable; most other information is far less certain. Freud thought he had "reason to believe" that his father's family had "lived for a long time on the Rhine (in Cologne), fled east as a result of a persecution of the Jews in the fourteenth and fifteenth century, and in the course of the nineteenth century migrated back from Lithuania through Galicia into German Austria." Freud was relying on a family tradition here: one day the secretary of the Jewish community at Cologne had met his father by chance and spelled out for him the Freuds' descent, all the way back to its fourteenth-century roots in Cologne. The evidence for Freud's ancestry may be plausible, but it is slender.

The course of Freud's emotional evolution was shaped far less by this actuarial detail and historical lore than by the bewildering texture of familial relationships he found very hard to sort out. Tangled domestic networks were fairly common in the nineteenth century, when early death from disease or in childbirth was only too familiar and widows or widowers often remarried promptly. But the riddles confronting Freud were intricate beyond the ordinary. When Jacob Freud married Amalia Nathansohn, his third wife, in 1855, he was forty, twenty years older than his bride. Two sons from his first marriage—Emanuel, the elder, married and with children of his own, and Philipp, a bachelor—lived nearby. And Emanuel was older than the young, attractive stepmother whom his father had imported from Vienna, while Philipp was just a year younger. It was no less intriguing for Sigismund Freud that one of Emanuel's sons, his first playmate, should be a year older than he, the little uncle.

Freud would recall this nephew John as his inseparable friend and "companion in my misdeeds." One of these (among Freud's earliest memories invested in retrospect with an erotic emotional power it probably did not have at the time) was perpetrated when he was about three years old: Sigismund and John fell upon John's sister Pauline in a meadow where they had been picking flowers, and cruelly snatched away her bunch. At times the two boys,

*He continued to vacillate even then: in 1872, still at school, he had signed one of his letters "Sigmund," but three years later, while he was studying medicine at the University of Vienna, he inscribed "Sigismund Freud, stud. med. 1875" in his copy of Darwin's *Die Abstammung des Menschen,* a German translation of *The Descent of Man.* Since he never commented on his reasons for shortening his first name, all conjectures about its significance for him must remain purely speculative.

as intense in enmity as they were in friendship, turned their aggressions against one another. One pugnacious episode that entered the store of family legends about Freud occurred when he was not yet two years old. One day, Freud's father asked him why he had hit John, and Freud, thinking if not yet speaking clearly, ably conducted his own defense: "I beated him 'cause he beated me."

Twisting the intricate pattern of Freud's family relations further, his handsome young mother seemed to him far better matched with his half brother Philipp than with his father, yet it was with the father that Amalia Freud shared a bed. In 1858, before he was two and a half, this problem attained particular poignancy: his sister Anna was born. Recalling these years, Freud thought he had realized that his little sister had come out of his mother's body. What had seemed harder to fathom was how his half brother Philipp had somehow taken his father's place as competitor for his mother's affections. Had Philipp perhaps given his mother that hateful new little rival? It was all very confusing and somehow as necessary to know about as it was dangerous.

Such childhood conundrums left deposits that Freud repressed for years and would only recapture, through dreams and laborious self-analysis, in the late 1890s. His mind was made up of these things—his young mother pregnant with a rival, his half brother in some mysterious way his mother's companion, his nephew older than himself, his best friend also his greatest enemy, his benign father old enough to be his grandfather. He would weave the fabric of his psychoanalytic theories from such intimate experiences. When he needed them, they came back to him.

Some salient family realities Freud did not find it necessary to repress. "My parents were Jews," he noted succinctly in his brief "Autobiographical Study" of 1925. Visibly scornful of coreligionists who had sought protection from anti-Semitism in the haven of baptism, he added: "I, too, have remained a Jew." It was a Judaism without religion. Jacob Freud had emancipated himself from the Hasidic practices of his ancestors: his marriage to Amalia Nathansohn was consecrated in a Reform ceremony. In time, he discarded virtually all religious observances, mainly celebrating Purim and Passover as family festivals. His father, Freud recalled in 1930, "allowed me to grow up in complete ignorance of everything that concerned Judaism." Yet, though striving for assimilation, Jacob Freud was never ashamed of, never sought to deny, his essential Jewishness. He continued to read the Bible at home, in Hebrew, for his edification, and "spoke the holy language," Freud believed, "as well as German or better." Thus, Jacob Freud established an atmosphere in which the young Freud acquired an enduring fascination with "biblical history," that is to say, the Old Testament, when he had "barely acquired the art of reading."

But as a little boy, Freud was not surrounded by Jews alone, and this, too, brought complications. The nursemaid who took care of him until he was about two and a half was a devout Roman Catholic. Freud's mother remembered her as elderly, ugly, and clever; she fed her charge pious stories and dragged him to church. "Then," Freud's mother told him, "when you got home, you would preach and tell us what God Almighty does." That nurse did more, though precisely how much remains obscure: she acted, Freud hinted somewhat obliquely, as his teacher in sexual matters. She was sharp with the precocious little boy and very demanding, but, Freud thought, he had loved her none the less for that.

It was a love rudely cut off: during his mother's confinement with his sister Anna, his half brother Philipp had the nursemaid arrested for petty theft and she was sent to prison. Freud missed her sorely. Her disappearance, coinciding with his mother's absence, generated a vague, disagreeable memory that Freud managed to clarify and to interpret only many years later. He recalled desperately searching for his mother, howling all the while. Then Philipp had opened a cupboard—in Austrian, a *Kasten*—to show that she was not imprisoned there. This did not calm Freud; he was not soothed until his mother appeared in the doorway, "slim and beautiful." Why should Philipp show Sigismund an empty cupboard in reply to his cry for his mother? In 1897, as his self-analysis was at its most intense, Freud found the answer: when he had asked his half brother Philipp where his nursemaid had gone to, Philipp had replied that she was *eingekastelt*—"boxed in"—a joking reference to her being in jail. Evidently Freud had feared that his mother, too, had been boxed in. Childish rivalry with an older brother who had presumably given his mother a child, no less childish sexual curiosity about babies who come out of bodies, and a sad sense of deprivation at the loss of his nurse, agitated the boy too young to grasp the connections but not too young to suffer. That Catholic nursemaid, old and unprepossessing as she was, had meant much to Freud, almost as much as his lovely mother. Like some figures who were to engross his fantasy life later—Leonardo, Moses, to say nothing of Oedipus— the young Freud enjoyed the loving ministrations of two mothers.

For all the care extended to little Sigismund, Jacob and Amalia Freud were poor. At Freud's birth in 1856, they occupied a single rented room in a modest house. Their town, Freiberg, was dominated by the tall, slim steeple of its Catholic church, with its famous chimes, rising above some substantial houses and many more modest dwellings. Its principal attractions, apart from the church, were a handsome market square and inviting surroundings that boasted stretches of fertile farmlands, dense woods, and gentle hills, with the Carpathian Mountains rising in the shimmering distance. In the late 1850s, the town had over 4,500 inhabitants; about 130 of them were Jews. The Freuds lived at Schlossergasse 117, a plain two-story house, above the owner, Zajík, a blacksmith. There, above a smithy, Freud was born.

THE FREUDS DID not remain in Freiberg much longer. They moved first briefly to Leipzig, in 1859, and then, the year after, to Vienna. To recall his family's poverty seems to have been painful to Freud; in a disguised autobiographical passage he inserted in a paper of 1899, he described himself as "the child of originally well-to-do parents who, I believe, lived in that provincial hole comfortably enough." This hyperbole is a mild instance of what Freud would later call the "family romance," the widespread disposition to find one's parents more prosperous or more famous than they are in reality, or perhaps even to invent a distinguished parentage. Freud was simplifying his family's motives for leaving Freiberg and prettifying their existence there. After a "catastrophe in the industrial branch in which my father was engaged," he wrote, "he lost his fortune." In the end, Jacob Freud never wholly secured what he had never really enjoyed. For some time, in fact, though gradually their situation improved, the Freuds' move to Vienna brought them little relief: "Then came long hard years," Freud wrote later; "I think nothing about them was worth remembering."

The precariousness of their financial situation was not alleviated by Amalia Freud's fertility. Jacob Freud and his wife had come to Vienna with two children, Sigismund and Anna—one son, Julius, had died in Freiberg in April 1858, at seven months. Now, in rapid succession, between 1860 and 1866, Freud was presented with four sisters—Rosa, Marie, Adolfine, and Pauline— and the youngest, his brother Alexander.* In 1865 and early 1866, the harshness of these years was exacerbated by the indictment, conviction, and imprisonment of Josef Freud, Jacob Freud's brother, for trading in counterfeit rubles. The catastrophe was traumatic for the family. Freud did not care for his uncle Josef, who invaded his dreams, and recalled in *The Interpretation of Dreams* that the calamity made his father's hair turn gray with grief in a few days. Probably Jacob Freud's grief was mingled with anxiety: there is evidence that he and his older sons, who had emigrated to Manchester, were implicated in Josef Freud's schemes.

Economic hardship and family disgrace were not the only reasons why

---

*There is a family tradition reported by Freud's sister Anna that the name "Alexander" was chosen at a family council, and was suggested by the ten-year-old Freud in recall of Alexander's magnanimity and his prowess as a military leader. (See *Jones* I, 18. For this and all other short forms and abbreviations, see p. 653.)

Freud found his first years in Vienna unworthy of recall. He was in mourning for Freiberg, especially for the lovely countryside in which it was embedded. "I never felt really comfortable in the city," he confessed in 1899; "I now think that I have never got over the longing for the beautiful woods of my home, in which (as a memory remaining from those days attests), scarcely able to walk, I used to run off from my father." When in 1931 the mayor of Příbor unveiled a bronze tablet at Freud's birthplace, Freud—then seventy-five—in a letter of thanks briefly rehearsed the vicissitudes of his life and singled out one secure relic from his distant past: "Deep within me, covered over, there still lives that happy child from Freiberg, the first-born son of a youthful mother, who had received the first indelible impressions from this air, from this soil." This is more than casual palaver or social politeness; the rhythmic rhetoric—"from this air, from this soil"—carries its own validation. It reaches down to the most secret layers of Freud's mind, bespeaking his never-quenched thirst for the days when he loved his young, beautiful mother and ran away from his old father. It is not surprising that Freud could never overcome his mixed feelings about Vienna.

FREUD'S SON MARTIN has suggested that his father's vocal, often reiterated detestation of Vienna was really a covert declaration of love. Is it not the signature of the authentic Viennese to delight in finding fault with his adored city? To be sure, for someone who hated Vienna as fiercely as Freud told everyone he did, he proved uncommonly resistant to leaving it. He had excellent English, good foreign connections, repeated invitations to settle abroad, but he stayed until he could stay no longer. "The feeling of triumph at liberation is mingled too strongly with mourning," he wrote, a very old man, just after his arrival in London in early June 1938, "for one had still very much loved the prison from which one has been released."

Evidently his ambivalence ran deep; however beloved Vienna may have been, it had become a prison. But Freud scattered his declarations of hate across his correspondence long before the Nazis marched into his country. There is nothing self-conscious, nothing of the pose, about them. "I will spare you any reference to the impression that Vienna made on me," he wrote at sixteen to his friend Emil Fluss after returning from Freiberg. "It was disgusting to me." Later, writing to his fiancée Martha Bernays from Berlin, he confessed, "Vienna oppresses me—perhaps more than is good," good for him, he meant. St. Stephen's Cathedral, which dominates the Vienna skyline, he told her, was to him only "that abominable steeple." He recognized that something carefully buried was emerging in these shafts of hostile commentary. His hatred of Vienna, he thought, bordered on the personal, "and, in contrast to the giant Antaeus, I gather fresh strength as often as I lift my foot from the hometown soil." Vienna never wholly ceased to be for him the theater of hardship, repeated failure, prolonged and hateful solitude, unpleasant incidents of Jew-hatred. That Freud should spend his vacations in the mountains and on long country walks also hints at his feelings. Vienna was not Freiberg.

This diagnosis has its implausible side. Nothing appears more desperately urban than psychoanalysis, that theory and therapy invented by and for citified bourgeois. Freud, too, was the quintessential city dweller, laboring in his consulting room all day and his study all evening, taking his daily walks through the modern Vienna being built while he was a student and a young physician. Most observers have in fact seen psychoanalysis, like its founder, not just as an urban but as a specifically Viennese phenomenon. Freud vehemently demurred: when the French psychologist Pierre Janet suggested that psychoanalysis could have sprung only from the sensual atmosphere of Vienna, Freud treated this insinuation as a malicious and at bottom an anti-Semitic slander. In truth Freud could have developed his ideas in any city endowed with a first-rate medical school and an educated public large and affluent enough to furnish him with patients. Obviously Freud, who never forgot the forests around Freiberg, was not some itinerant rustic caught by fate in the constricting city. But the Vienna that Freud gradually constructed for himself was not the Vienna of the court, the café, the salon, or the operetta. Those Viennas did very little to advance Freud's work. It is not for nothing that his bride should have been from Hamburg, his favorite adherents from Zurich, Budapest, Berlin, London, and even more far-flung places, his psychological theories formed in an intellectual universe large enough to embrace all of Western culture.

STILL, IT WAS in Vienna that Freud settled and stayed on. His father was not the man to make things easier. An incurable optimist at least on the surface, he was a small merchant with insufficient resources to cope with the industrializing world around him. He was likable, generous, open to pleasure, firmly persuaded of his son Sigismund's singular gifts. Every member of the family, his grandson Martin Freud recalled, loved him; he was "terribly nice with us small children," bringing presents and telling amusing stories. Everyone "treated him with great respect." But to his son Sigmund, Jacob Freud would be far more problematic than that.

The appealing youthfulness and striking good looks of his mother did not make the young Freud's emotional task any easier. Later he would recapture a childhood experience, one of those "significant details" that he rescued from the pervasive amnesia which mantles everyone's earliest years. The memory came back to him in October 1897, in the midst of his self-analysis, while discoveries about his unconscious life were tumbling out at him with dizzying profusion. Sometime between the ages of two and two and a half, he told his close friend Wilhelm Fliess, his "libido toward matrem had awakened" on an overnight railway journey from Leipzig to Vienna, a trip on which he had had the "opportunity of seeing her nudam." Immediately after unpacking this tantalizing recollection, Freud remembered that he had welcomed the death of his infant brother Julius, born some seventeen months after him, with "malevolent wishes and genuine childish jealousy." This brother, and Freud's nephew John, a year older than himself, "now determine what is neurotic, but also what is intense, in all my friendships." Love and hate, those elemental forces struggling over human destiny, forces that were to loom large in Freud's mature psychological writings, were confronting one another in this recall.

At times Freud made telling mistakes in remembering his childhood past, and here is one: he was actually nearly four, not just over two, on the occasion of the glimpse of his naked mother—he was bigger, stronger, more capable of voyeurism and explicit desire than he consciously allowed himself to be in retrieving the memory of seeing *matrem nudam.* It is no less telling that even at forty-one, already the most unconventional of explorers in the forbidden realms of sexuality, Freud could not bring himself to describe this exciting incident without lapsing into safe, distancing Latin.

Whatever the exact nature of the episode, it would be his doting, energetic, and domineering mother, far more than his pleasant but somewhat shiftless father, who equipped him for a life of intrepid investigation, elusive fame, and halting success. Her ability to overcome a lung ailment—Freud's youngest daughter, Anna, called it a "tuberculous illness"—for whose sake she went to spas for several summers, is a tribute to her vitality. In the end, Freud never fully worked through the meaning of his passionate unconscious ties to that commanding maternal figure. While many of his patients were women and he wrote much about them, he liked to say all his life that Woman had remained a dark continent to him. It seems most likely that some of this obscurity was self-protective in origin.*

Freud's equivocal feelings about his father were far closer to the surface. Another of his crucial childhood memories, pathetic rather than arousing, attests to that. The recollection at once troubled and fascinated him. "I may have been ten or twelve years old when my father began to take me along on his walks," and to talk about the world he had known. One day, to show how radically life had improved for Austria's Jews, Jacob Freud told his son this story: "When I was a young fellow, one Saturday I went for a walk in

---

*For that dark continent, Woman, see pp. 501–22.

the streets in your birthplace, beautifully decked out, with a new fur cap on my head. Along comes a Christian, knocks off my cap into the muck with one blow, and shouts, 'Jew, off the sidewalk!' " Interested, Freud asked his father, "And what did you do?" The composed reply: "I stepped into the road and picked up my cap." His father's submissive response, Freud recalled soberly, perhaps a little ungenerously, "did not seem heroic to me." Was his father not a "big strong man"?

Stung by the spectacle of a cowardly Jew groveling to a gentile, Freud developed fantasies of revenge. He identified himself with the splendid, intrepid Semite Hannibal, who had sworn to avenge Carthage no matter how mighty the Romans, and elevated him into a symbol of "the contrast between the tenacity of Jewry and the organization of the Catholic Church." They would never find *him*, Freud, picking up his cap from the filthy gutter.* This was the boy who, at fourteen, spoke the part of Brutus, a monologue in Friedrich Schiller's revolutionary play *The Robbers*. From his childhood days on, an assertive display of intellectual independence, controlled rage, physical bravery, and self-respect as a Jew coalesced into a highly personal, indestructible amalgam in Freud's character.

If Freud's feelings about his parents were intricate, their faith in him seemed to be absolute. On his thirty-fifth birthday, his father gave his "dear son" his Bible, with a Hebrew inscription. "It was in the seventh year of your age," it began, "that the spirit of God began to move you to learning." Actually, for the Freuds, happy portents of future fame long antedated their son's precocious passion for reading. In his *Interpretation of Dreams*, seeking to account for one of his dreams of ambition, Freud recalled a tale "which I so often heard tell in my childhood." It seems that at his birth, "an old peasant woman had prophesied to my mother, happy over her first-born, that she had given the world a great man." Freud cynically commented that "such prophecies must occur very frequently; there are so many mothers full of

---

*Freud had, I suspect, still another reason for choosing as his favorite hero the immortal commander who had nearly conquered hated, and hateful, Rome against all the odds, a reason of which Freud was probably not aware. Just as, in naming his youngest brother Alexander, he had celebrated a conqueror greater than his father, Philip of Macedonia—who was, in his own right, a great man—so he could with Hannibal imaginatively identify with another mighty figure whose fame had grown more resounding than that of his own father, Hamilcar—who was, like Philip of Macedonia, a statesman and military leader of historic stature. In his *Psychopathology of Everyday Life*, Freud himself connected his choice of Hannibal with his father: in *The Interpretation of Dreams*, he had made a curious slip, calling Hannibal's father Hasdrubal instead of Hamilcar, and he thought that this somehow related to his dissatisfaction with Jacob Freud's conduct toward anti-Semites. (See *Psychopathology of Everyday Life*, *SE* VI, 219–20.) But there was also most probably an oedipal element in Freud's choices: he could show himself superior to his father—which is to say, win the oedipal struggle—without having to demean that father too much. Hence Freud could be, at home, victorious while respecting his "enemy." (See also p. 132.)

joyous anticipations and so many old peasant women or other crones whose power in the world has passed and who therefore have turned to the future. Nor will it have been to the loss of the prophetess." Yet his skepticism was only halfhearted: he was not disinclined to put some trust in this pleasing forecast. And he speculated that the climate in a household which told and retold such anecdotes could only feed his longing for greatness.

Another episode, which he remembered quite precisely, reinforced his parents' conviction that they were harboring a genius. He was eleven or twelve, sitting with his parents in one of the restaurants in the Prater, Vienna's famous park. A strolling poetaster was wandering from table to table, improvising for a few coins little verses on any theme proposed to him. "I was sent off to ask the poet to our table and he showed himself grateful to the messenger. Before inquiring for his topic, he dropped a few verses about me and, inspired, declared it probable that some day I would become ⸥ a cabinet minister." In the liberal mood dominating Austria in the 1860s, the prophecy seemed no more than sensible. Looking back, Freud attributed his plan to study law to impressions of this sort.

IT WAS ONLY NATURAL that this immensely promising young man should be the declared family favorite. His sister Anna testifies that he always had a room of his own, no matter how straitened his parents' circumstances. When the Freuds arrived in Vienna, they moved to the traditional Jewish district, Leopoldstadt, stretching across the northeastern edge of the city. It had once been Vienna's ghetto, and, absorbing an ever-increasing influx of Jewish immigrants from eastern Europe, it was rapidly turning into something of a ghetto once again. Nearly half of the 15,000 Jews living in Vienna around 1860 clustered in the district. Leopoldstadt was not just a slum; a number of prosperous Jewish families chose to live there. But the majority huddled in badly overcrowded, unprepossessing quarters. The Freuds were with that majority.

After a time, Jacob Freud began to enjoy a modicum of affluence, most likely subsidized by his more fortunate two older sons, who, once settled in Manchester, had done very well there. Yet even after he could afford servants, a painting of his seven young children, expeditions to the Prater, and more spacious living quarters, he and his family made do with six rooms. This apartment, to which they moved in 1875, when Freud was a university student, was scarcely lavish for the sizable family. Alexander, the youngest, Freud's five sisters, and their parents crowded into three bedrooms. Freud alone had his "cabinet" for his private domain, a room "long and narrow, with a window looking on the street," more and more crammed with books, the adolescent Freud's only luxury. This is where he studied, slept, and often ate his meals by himself to save time for reading. And this is where he received his school friends—his "study mates," his sister Anna called them, not his playmates. He was an attentive but somewhat authoritarian brother, helping his brother and sisters with their lessons and lecturing at them about the world: his didactic streak was marked from his school days on. He also acted as a rather priggish censor. When she was fifteen, his sister Anna remembered, he frowned on her reading Balzac and Dumas as too risqué.

The family accepted Freud's boyish imperiousness with equanimity and fostered his sense of being exceptional. If Freud's needs clashed with those of Anna or the others, his prevailed without question. When, intent on his school books, he complained about the noise that Anna's piano lessons were making, the piano vanished never to return. It was much regretted by his sister and his mother alike, but without apparent rancor. The Freuds must have been among the very few middle-class Central European families without a piano, but that sacrifice faded in face of the glorious career they imagined for the studious, lively schoolboy in his cabinet.

IN THE VIENNA of Freud's youth, despite the social disabilities under which Austrian Jews still labored, high aspirations for talented Jewish youngsters were far from utopian. Since 1848, the year of revolutions across the Continent and the accession of Emperor Franz Josef, the sluggish multinational Habsburg empire had been dragged toward political reform; resisting with all its might, it was being forcibly propelled into the nineteenth century. Beginning in 1860, the year the Freuds settled in Vienna's Leopoldstadt, a series of edicts designed to shore up traditional authority had the unintended consequence of liberalizing the state. Together, the unshackled press and the fledgling political parties struggling for power schooled Austrians in the risky rhetoric of public combat as election campaigns grew ever more venomous; the new Reichsrat, established to exercise only advisory functions, blossomed into a real legislature initiating laws and voting the budget. Despite all these daring experiments in representative government, the political public remained a small minority of the population. Even the electoral reforms of 1873, hailed as a great step forward, retained steep walls of property qualifications: electing the people's spokesmen remained the privilege of a mere 6 percent of adult males. Limited autocracy, in short, gave way to limited constitutionalism.

The most spectacular-looking tinkering proved in the end little better than cosmetic. In an age of rabid nationalism, the Habsburg regime barely held quarreling political interests and hostile ethnic groups in check; whatever solutions Austrian politicians might devise could be only provisional at best. "Within two decades," as the historian Ilsa Barea has aptly summed it up, no fewer than "eight Austrian constitutions were launched, retracted, revised, experimenting with federalism and centralism, indirect and direct franchise, authoritarian and representative government." The showy glitter of the monarchy and high society barely concealed the general bankruptcy of ideas or the stalemate of irreconcilable forces. Imprudent wars and disastrous diplomatic initiatives competed for the public attention with progressive social legislation.

For some years, however, those wagering on continued improvement in politics, economics, and social relations had some persuasive evidence on their side. In the late 1860s, the imperial cabinet was dominated by civilized, dedicated middle-class bureaucrats and politicians: it was not called the "bourgeois ministry" for nothing. Under this *Bürgerministerium* and its immediate successors, the government transferred control over education and marriage to the secular authorities, opened the way to interdenominational marriages, and introduced a humane criminal code. In tandem with these forays into liberalism, Austrian commerce and banking, industry, transport, and communications took impressive strides: the industrial revolution came to Austria-Hungary late, but it came. Yet all was thrown into doubt by the stock market crash of May 9, 1873, "Black Friday," which cast its shadow over these many accomplishments. Mass bankruptcies and bank failures ruined imprudent speculators, hapless depositors, unlucky businessmen, artisans, and farmers. "The Austrians," wrote one astute German visitor in June, "have lost all their money or, rather, have discovered that they never had any money."

Confronted with the sudden loss of their savings or their investments, and in search of a scapegoat, the Austrians permitted themselves an orgy of anti-Semitic outbursts. Journalists held the "machinations" of Jewish bankers responsible for the collapse; popular cartoonists depicted hook-nosed and curly-haired brokers gesticulating wildly in front of the Vienna stock exchange.* It is not without reason that Freud should date his particular Jewish self-awareness to his years at the university, where he began his studies in the fall of 1873.† But the exacerbated tone of anti-Semitic propaganda was not the only menacing ingredient in the extremist political rhetoric of the day.

---

*Actually, Austrian Jews suffered as much as anyone else under the "Big Crash." Arthur Schnitzler's father, for one, "with so many other innocent victims, lost all he had saved so far." (Arthur Schnitzler, *Jugend in Wien* [1968], 48.)

†Recalling those days in a letter to J. Dwossis, his Hebrew translator in Jerusalem, in 1930, Freud wrote pointedly of "German anti-Semitism." (Freud to Dwossis, December 15, 1930. Freud Museum, London.) And indeed there had been in the early 1870s a very similar surge in Germany, employing the same bigoted rhetoric. But the Austrian variant did not need any impulse from its northern neighbor, any more than it did later.

That had already been inflamed by ferocious partisan factionalism, an emerging working-class consciousness, and the unappeasable discontent of national minorities, the Poles and Czechs and others. The fragile achievements of the 1860s were very much in danger.

Nevertheless, for Austria's Jews this remained a time of promise. Since 1848 the legal position of Jews in the Habsburg lands had been steadily improving. The year of revolution had brought the legalization of Jewish religious services, the end of special onerous and humiliating taxes, and equality with Christians in the right to own real property, enter any profession, assume any public office. The 1850s saw the fall of such galling monuments to bigotry as the laws forbidding Jewish households to employ gentile servants and gentile households to employ Jewish midwives. By 1867 practically all remaining pockets of legal discrimination had been wiped out. For Jews at least, the results of these legal reforms were exhilarating.

What is more, in 1860 a liberal faction had captured Vienna and inaugurated a reign in which solid burghers among Jews could count on social acceptance and even political preferment. Indeed, after the Compromise of 1867, the *Ausgleich*, which transformed the sprawling Habsburg domains into the dual monarchy of Austria-Hungary, several members of the "bourgeois ministry" were Jewish. This was the time when Freud and his parents encountered the poet-prophet in the Prater restaurant, a time, he later wrote in *The Interpretation of Dreams*, when "every diligent Jewish boy carried a minister's portfolio in his satchel."

There is something a little pathetic about Freud paraphrasing in the late 1890s Napoleon's memorable revolutionary dictum that each soldier carries a marshal's baton in his knapsack. The handsome, extraordinarily popular demagogue Karl Lueger, who made anti-Semitism a plank in his opportunistic political platform, had become Vienna's powerful mayor in 1897. Jew-hatred had been an ingredient in Viennese politics for some time: in 1885 Freud reported to his fiancée that on election day, June 1, there had been "riots and anti-Semitic demonstrations." But Lueger became the catalyst for the new politics of the 1890s. While he had Jewish friends and was far more genial with Jews in private than in the histrionic facade he presented to his adoring public, many among his supporters were more rabid than their leader and quite consistent in their anti-Semitism. His advent therefore sealed the bankruptcy of Austrian liberalism with irrevocable finality. But for more than thirty-five years—while Freud grew up, studied, married, had his family, and struggled toward the propositions of psychoanalysis—liberalism had been a prominent, if more and more tattered, strand in Viennese politics. It was the kind of atmosphere in which Freud had felt at home. Harking back to those heady decades in old age, he called himself "a liberal of the old school."

During the 1860s and beyond, in fact, liberalism was for Vienna's Jews a stance at once principled and prudent: the alternatives of Zionism and Socialism had not yet emerged on their horizon. Like many others among his emancipated brethren, Freud became a liberal because the liberal world view was congenial to him and because, as the saying goes, it was good for the Jews. Freud was a pessimist about human nature and hence skeptical about political panaceas of all kinds, but he was not a conservative. As a self-respecting bourgeois he was impatient with arrogant aristocrats and, even more, with repressive clerics. He viewed the Church of Rome and its Austrian minions as the principal obstacles in the way of full Jewish integration into Austrian society. Even as a schoolboy, we know, he had formed elaborate and agreeable fantasies in which he took imaginary revenge against every anti-Semite in the book. The luxuriant growth of populist racial anti-Semitism provided him with new targets of hate, but he never forgot the old enemy, Roman Catholicism. For Freud and other assimilated Jews, Austrian liberals stood as a most encouraging contrast to demagogues and priests alike.

One can see why. It had been the liberals, after all, who had granted Austria's Jews full civic rights in 1867. It is telling that the *Neue Freie Presse*, Vienna's only newspaper with an international reputation, should find it necessary to remind its readers in 1883, on the occasion of an anti-Semitic demonstration, that "the first dogma of liberalism" is "that citizens of all confessions enjoy equal rights." Not surprisingly, the *Neue Freie Presse* was Freud's daily fare; it espoused the liberal views he cherished.

By the time the young Freud awoke to these political realities, these views were commonplaces among Austria's Jews. In the midst of the election campaign of 1879, Adolf Jellinek, the chief rabbi of Vienna, declared that "in line with their most vital interests, the Jews of Austria must adhere to the constitution and to the forces of liberalism." The publicist and rabbi Joseph Samuel Bloch recited a very catalogue of liberalism's virtues: more than a doctrine, more than a convenient principle, it was the Jew's spiritual asylum, his haven of rescue, his franchise of liberty, his protecting goddess, the queen of his heart. And Austria's Jews put their votes where their heart was: their allegiance to liberal candidates was overwhelming. Freud voted for them whenever he could.* Clericalism, ultramontanism, a federalism that favored the non-German elements in the Austro-Hungarian empire—these were the Jews' enemies. Freud's political passions did not run very high, but the very paucity of critical comment in his letters of the liberal decades

---

*On June 2, 1885, Freud wrote to his fiancée, Martha Bernays, "The elections were yesterday, a very excited day for Vienna. The liberal party lost four seats; in Mariahilf and the Badner district, anti-Semites were elected." (By permission of Sigmund Freud Copyrights, Wivenhoe.)

suggests his general satisfaction, his essential agreement with Jellinek, with Bloch, with the *Neue Freie Presse*. From the late 1890s on, when Lueger and his cronies governed the city, he would have more to say.

THE ADVENT OF LIBERALISM in politics and culture meant more than a club of like-minded politicians in office. Its emblems were everywhere. In the train of other nineteenth-century capitals—Berlin, Paris, London—Vienna was growing and changing with dazzling rapidity. In 1860, it had about half a million inhabitants; twenty years later, when Freud was completing his medical studies, there were more than 700,000 Viennese, many of them, like the Freuds, born elsewhere. Much like Paris, which the energetic, imaginative, and ruthless prefect Baron Haussmann rebuilt almost beyond recognition, Vienna in these two decades changed its face forever. In 1857, Franz Josef had authorized the razing of the old fortifications around the inner city; seven years later, most of them were gone, and the Ringstrasse, a vast angular horseshoe of an avenue, was taking shape. In 1865, the year the nine-year-old Freud entered the Leopoldstädter Kommunal-Real- und Obergymnasium, the emperor and empress formally inaugurated that great boulevard. Public building after public building, punctuated by massive apartment houses, arose on either side, celebrating liberal culture and liberal constitutionalism. The new opera house was ready in 1869; two vast ornate museums a dozen years later; the neoclassical House of Parliament and the neo-Gothic Town Hall, expensive and expressive architectural statements of the liberal ideology, were both open for their important business in 1883.

It was all very impressive and all very precarious. Many years later, seeking to capture the essence of the Dual Monarchy, the Austrian essayist and novelist Hermann Broch recalled in a much-quoted phrase "the gay apocalypse around 1880." The apocalypse was well disguised, decked out in self-protective sentimental effusions about the beautiful blue Danube, the effervescence of high culture, and the festive sound of waltzes. Broch had hindsight to guide his vision, but there were a few critical spirits even then—not Freud, for he was busy with medicine and love—who thought the Danube muddy, the champagne stale, and the waltz a desperate dance on the rim of a growling volcano.

Vienna through these decades remained a favorite refuge for Jewish immigrants from the east. They kept coming, in far greater numbers than to any German city, because even if the signals from Austria were mixed, the situation elsewhere was worse. By the late nineteenth century, Vienna's Jews made up a diverse group: old settled families; immigrants from abroad, mainly Russia; newcomers from the Habsburg lands of Galicia, Hungary, or (like the

Freuds) Moravia. It was also a fluctuating one; just as thousands of Jews thronged to the city as a refuge from persecution and a haven of opportunity, many left it to settle in Germany or overseas. There were to be moments in the 1880s and 1890s when Freud, too, thought of emigrating, perhaps to the United States, more probably to the England he had loved since his youth.

THE IMPACT OF the Jewish invasion, as anti-Semites of all stripes liked to call it, put Vienna's assimilated Jews before a dilemma that their fellows elsewhere, in Berlin or London, also faced in these years, though less acutely. A measure of sympathy for poverty-stricken, often traumatized refugees from a benighted Eastern Europe was often overborne by a defensive rejection of their habits and appearance. Freud was not exempt from such sentiments. As a sixteen-year-old, returning from a visit to his native Freiberg, he encountered on a train a "highly honorable old Jew and a corresponding old Jewess complete with melancholic, languishing little daughter and an impudent, promising son," and he described his revulsion to his friend Emil Fluss, Jewish like himself. He found their company "more intolerable than any other" and thought he recognized the old man as a well-known type from Freiberg. "So was the son, with whom he was talking about religion. He was of the kind of wood from which fate carves the swindler when the time is ripe: crafty, mendacious, encouraged by his dear relatives in the belief that he has talent, but without principles or a view of life." A professional Jew-baiter could hardly have expressed it more forcefully.*

Many of the immigrants from the miserable villages of the east dressed and spoke and gestured in ways alien and disagreeable to the Viennese; they were too exotic to be familiar and not exotic enough to be charming. They came as peddlers and small shopkeepers, but many of their sons entered callings vulnerable to bigoted criticism and easy slander: banking, or wholesale trading, or journalism. By the 1880s, at least half of all Viennese journalists, physicians, and lawyers were Jews. Freud at Gymnasium contemplating either a legal or a medical career was being perfectly conventional. That is what many young Jews in Vienna did. Demonstrating their proverbial appetite for learning, they poured into Vienna's educational institutions and, concen-

---

*In the absence of more evidence, this supercilious description remains somewhat mysterious. It may just have been the snobbery a well-educated, German-speaking Jew might share with his close friends. But since Freud's mother also had undeniably Eastern European speech, one must wonder whether Freud either denied his mother's origins or, more subtly and less consciously, was in rebellion against her.

trated as they were in a few districts, clustered in a few schools until their classes resembled extended family clans. During the eight years that Freud attended his Gymnasium, between 1865 and 1873, the number of Jewish students there increased from 68 to 300, rising from 44 to 73 percent of the total school population.

Feeling beleaguered by this ever-growing Jewish presence, Austrian gentiles worried over it in humor magazines, social clubs, and political meetings. They made anxious jokes, pleaded for the assimilation of the "alien" invaders, or, some of them, issued strident calls for their expulsion. In 1857, when Freud was a year old, the census showed slightly more than 6,000 Jews in Vienna, just over 2 percent of the population; ten years later, what with favorable legislation and improving economic chances, Jews had moved to the city in large waves: they now numbered 40,000, or 6 percent. In 1872 Jacob Burckhardt, the great Swiss historian of the Renaissance, who detested the haste and nervousness of modern civilization and saw Jews as its supreme embodiment, grimly charged during one of his visits that the Jews were running Vienna. With evident approval, he noted "the growing aversion to the all-powerful Jews and their thoroughly venal press." Yet the invasion was not yet over; by 1880, when they had grown to over 72,000, one in every ten inhabitants of Vienna was a Jew. When Burckhardt returned to the city in 1884, he found it thoroughly "judaized"—*verjudet*. It is a repulsive term that was to enjoy an ominous career in Freud's lifetime. Certainly it expressed a widespread perception.

The nineteenth century, then, though the age of Jewish emancipation all across Europe, proved an uneasy interlude between the old anti-Semitism and the new. Emancipation itself was cause for reaction. The Jew, the arrogant, self-elected God's favorite and Christ-killer, became the Jew, the unscrupulous speculator and corrosive cosmopolitan. Naturally enough, children echoed their parents, and anti-Jewish talk overflowed from public demagogy and family prejudices into the daily banter of schoolmates. In the upper classes of his Gymnasium, Freud, too, began to recognize "the consequences of being descended from an alien race." As the "anti-Semitic agitation among my school comrades admonished me to take a position," he identified all the more closely with that hero of his youth, the Semite Hannibal.

At the same time, the opportunities beckoning emancipated Austrian Jews spread beyond financial profit or professional advancement. Jews participated prominently in the life of Vienna's culture as its makers and its middlemen: they were publishers, editors, gallery owners, theatrical and musical promoters, poets, novelists, conductors, virtuosos, painters, scientists, philosophers, and historians.* Names like Arthur Schnitzler, Karl Kraus, Gustav Mahler, only hint at the diversity in this formidable array of talents. In the bureaucracy of the Dual Monarchy and in its army, Jews made careers largely after being converted to Catholicism, but some achieved high ranks without baptism. A number of Jewish families were ennobled, for their wealth or their service to the state, without denying, let alone renouncing, their origins.

Arthur Schnitzler, six years Freud's junior, physician, psychologist, novelist and playwright, recalled this ambiguous situation in his autobiography: "In those days—the late-blossoming period of liberalism—anti-Semitism existed, as it had always done, as an emotion in the numerous hearts so inclined and as an idea with great possibilities of development, but it did not play an important role politically or socially. The word hadn't even been invented, and those who disliked Jews were called, derisively, 'Jew devourers' "—*Judenfresser*. Schnitzler could think of only one such type in his class, and he was unpopular for being dandified, snobbish, and stupid. The anti-Semitism of those years was, Schnitzler thought, neither respectable nor dangerous. Yet it made him anxious and bitter. Jew-hatred was a nuisance becoming more disagreeable, more threatening, with the years. Another educated Viennese witness, Dr. Valentin Pollak, born in 1871, remembered: "In my early youth, it was still only dumb hate." It was "not accepted by good society, but we felt it badly," having to ward off brutal ambushes by adolescent hooligans. Austria's Jews had hoped for something better. But until the full deployment of racial anti-Semitism in the late 1890s, optimism fought down gloomy premonitions. This was a time when Jewish schoolboys, Freud and others, caressed in their fantasies a general's uniform, a professor's lectern, a minister's portfolio, or a surgeon's scalpel.

*Recalling his stay in Vienna at the end of the century, the German Jewish novelist Jakob Wassermann stressed that, in marked contrast to Germany, "nearly all the people with whom I came into intellectual or cordial contact were Jews. . . . I soon recognized that all public life was dominated by Jews. The banks, the press, the theater, literature, social functions, all was in the hands of Jews." Since the Austrian aristocracy had no truck with such pursuits, they were left to a few nonconformists—and to Jews. (Jakob Wassermann, *Mein Weg als Deutscher und Jude* [1922], 102.)

THE LURE OF RESEARCH

 Ambitious, outwardly self-assured, brilliant in school and voracious in his reading, the adolescent Freud had every reason to believe that he had a distinguished career before him, one as distinguished as sober reality would allow him to pursue. "At the Gymnasium," he tersely summed up his record, "I was first in my class for seven years, held a privileged position, was scarcely ever examined." The report cards he preserved repeatedly pay tribute to his exemplary conduct and his outstanding work in class. His parents naturally predicted great things for him, and others, like his religion teacher and paternal friend Samuel Hammerschlag, gladly substantiated their fond and extravagant expectations.

BUT BEFORE SETTLING down to fulfilling his parents' hopes, and his own, Freud underwent an adolescent rite of passage: first love. In 1872, when he was sixteen, he returned to Freiberg for a visit. One of his traveling companions was Eduard Silberstein, his most intimate friend of those years. The two had formed an exclusive secret "Spanish Academy" which had no other members, playfully addressed one another by the names of two dogs in one of Cervantes's tales, and exchanged confidential letters in Spanish as well as carrying on their more expansive German correspondence. In one emotional communiqué, Freud confessed to an "agreeable, wistful feeling" at his friend's absence and to his "longing" for some "heartfelt" talk. Another of his confidential messages to his "Queridisimo Berganza!" bears the caution, "May no other hand touch this letter"—*No mano otra toque esa carta.* This was the letter in which Freud poured out his most private amorous feelings to his friend.

The ostensible object of Freud's attachment was Gisela Fluss, a year younger than he, the sister of another school friend, also from Freiberg. He was much taken with this "half-naive, half-cultivated girl," but had kept his feelings to himself, blaming his "nonsensical Hamlet-dom" and timidity for his failure to give himself the pleasure of conversation with her. He continued to refer to Gisela Fluss, as he had for some months, by a learned pun on her name, "Ichthyosaura": *Fluss* means "river" in German, and Ichthyosaurus was a river creature, suitably extinct. But his "first rapture," as he called it, never amounted to much more than shy allusions and a few poignant encounters.

Freud's confession to his friend Silberstein in fact strongly suggests that the whole experience was essentially a belated oedipal infatuation: he dwelled at length and enumerated with delight the charms of Gisela's mother, an affluent Freiberg matron—her intelligence, her cultivation, her versatility, her invariable cheerfulness, her gentle way with her children, and her cordial show of hospitality, not least to him. Frau Fluss, then, far more than her daughter Gisela, was the true target of his taciturn, fleeting adolescent passion: "It seems," he acknowledged, intuitively anticipating the kind of perception to which he would devote his life, "that I have transferred respect for the mother to friendship for the daughter."

But Freud soon had graver things on his mind. He was about to attend the university, and his choice of career, like his hope for fame, was not free from inner conflicts and painful, well-remembered setbacks. In his *Interpretation of Dreams,* he recorded a humiliating incident dating from his seventh or eighth year. One evening, he had urinated in his parents' bedroom, in their presence. Freud the psychoanalyst would later explain why boys might want to do such a thing. Exasperated, Jacob Freud had told his son that he would never amount to anything. The memory of this episode pursued the young Freud for years. It had been a "terrible blow to my ambition," and he continued to replay it in his dreams. Perhaps the incident did not happen quite this way. But since distorted memories are no less, possibly even more, revealing than accurate ones, this memory appears to encapsulate his desires and his doubts. Whenever he recalled it, Freud confessed, he quickly recited his successes, as though to show his father, triumphantly, that he had amounted to something after all.* If he did urinate in his parents' bedroom, that must have been a rare moment in the Freuds' household: the self-possessed boy yielding to a momentary if irresistible impulse, the affectionate father exploding in fleeting irritability. In general, the Freuds' golden boy could do no wrong—and did no wrong.

The impulses animating Freud's search for greatness—from which the need for revenge and self-vindication cannot be excluded—were far from transparent. Hence the motives dictating his choice of medicine, and the course he would follow once he had made his decision, are hard to unravel. Freud's account, though precise, requires interpretation and elaboration. He

---

*Freud recounted this scene as part of his interpretation of his Count Thun dream. As commentators have rightly pointed out, there are complexities beyond complexities. It seems possible that Freud invaded his parents' bedroom out of sexual curiosity, and then urinated in his excitement. More to the point here, in 1914 Freud added the comment that bed-wetting, to which he was at times susceptible when he was two years old, and which he closely associated with the bedroom scene, is related to the character trait of ambition. (See *Interpretation of Dreams, SE* IV, 216.) For the best summary, see Didier Anzieu, *Freud's Self-Analysis* (2d ed., 1975; tr. Peter Graham, 1986), 344–46.

records his conflicts but cavalierly simplifies their resolution. "Under the powerful influence of a friendship with a somewhat older Gymnasium colleague who later became well-known as a politician, I too wanted to study law and become socially active." That school friend was Heinrich Braun, who ended up as one of Austria's most prominent Social Democratic political leaders and editors. "However, the doctrines of Darwin, then topical, powerfully attracted me because they promised an extraordinary advancement in our understanding of the world; and I know that the recital of Goethe's beautiful essay 'On Nature,' in a popular lecture by Professor Carl Brühl shortly before my final school examinations, decided me to inscribe myself in medicine."

The story bears the mark of mythmaking or, at least, of excessive compression. Carl Bernhard Brühl, a prominent comparative anatomist and professor of zootomy at the University of Vienna, was a gripping popular lecturer. The fragment that changed Freud's mind is an emotional and exclamatory hymn celebrating an eroticized Nature as an embracing, almost smothering, ever-renewed mother. It may have given the final impulsion to a decision that had been ripening in Freud's mind for some time. He said so more than once. But it was by no means a sudden revelation. Too much had gone before to permit the fragment in Goethe's style the significance that Freud would bestow on it. After all, it was not even by Goethe.

Whatever the precise course of Freud's ruminations, in mid-March 1873 he informed his friend Emil Fluss, in a tone he self-consciously described as oracular, that he "could report some news, perhaps the most important of my paltry life." Then he hesitated, in a teasing, ambivalent mood quite uncharacteristic of him. The matter was not yet ripe for decision and discussion: "I did not want to pass off something unfinished as a fact, only to have to take it back later." It took Freud until May 1 to wrestle his way to full clarity. "If I lift the veil, won't you be disappointed?" he asked Fluss. "Now, try it: I have determined to become a natural scientist." He would leave the law behind. But, keeping up the lighthearted vein, Freud retained the legal vocabulary, as if to suggest some lingering affection for the career he was abandoning: "I will examine the millennia-old documents of nature, perhaps personally eavesdrop on its eternal lawsuit, and share my winnings with everyone willing to learn." This is brisk, even witty, but it hints at the obstinacy of conflicts overcome or, rather, resolutely set aside. In August of that year, in fact, Freud enclosed in a letter to Silberstein a printed visiting card that read: "Sigismund Freud/stud. jur." It may have been a joke, but a joke hinting at regrets.

Writing in 1923, Fritz Wittels, a Viennese physician who became one of Freud's maverick followers and his first biographer, shrewdly speculated that Freud's claim for the place of the fragment "On Nature" in his life sounds like a screen memory, the kind of innocuous recall concealing behind its spurious clarity some graver, less unequivocal past experience. The maternal vision conjured up by the fragment Brühl had read out loud, with its promise of fond protection, embracing warmth, and never-exhausted nourishment, may have appealed to Freud, then an impressionable adolescent. But whatever its impact may have been, "On Nature" fell on fertile soil.

At all events, it is highly improbable that earnest, practical parental advice made medicine more alluring than the law: Freud took care to assert in print that although his family "lived in very straitened circumstances, my father insisted that in choosing my profession I should follow my inclinations alone." If Freud's memory of hearing "On Nature," then, really was a screen memory, it must have concealed not prudential but emotional motives. While he chose medicine freely, he wrote in his "Autobiographical Study," he "felt no particular partiality for the position and activity of a physician in those early years, nor, by the way, later. Rather, I was moved by a sort of greed for knowledge." This is among the most suggestive autobiographical passages Freud ever published. Freud the psychoanalyst would later point to the sexual curiosity of youngsters as the true source of scientific inquisitiveness. It is a reasonable speculation to see the episode in his parents' bedroom at seven or eight as a straightforward, rather coarse expression of such curiosity, later refined into research.

THE STUDY OF MEDICINE promised Freud psychological rewards beyond the sublimation of his primitive appetite for knowledge. As a young man, he later noted, he had not yet grasped the uses of observation (which implies distance and objectivity) for his insatiable curiosity. Not long before his marriage, he sketched a little self-portrait for his fiancée that suggests this same lack of cool distance: he felt like the heir of "all the passions of our ancestors when they defended their temple." But, powerless, unable to express his "ardent passions with a word or in a poem," he had always "suppressed" himself. When, many years later, his biographer Ernest Jones asked him how much philosophy he had read, Freud replied, "Very little. As a young man I felt a strong attraction toward speculation and ruthlessly checked it." In the last year of his life, he still spoke in the same vein of "a certain reserve in face of my subjective propensity to concede too much to the imagination in scientific inquiry." No doubt Freud found it essential to hold his scientific imagination on a loose rein, especially during the years of discovery. But his self-appraisals—in letters, confessional scientific papers, and recorded conversations—echo with a certain fear of losing himself in a morass of speculation, and with a powerful wish for self-control. As late as his third year at the university, in 1875, Freud was still thinking of "acquiring a doctorate of philosophy based on philosophy and zoology." But medicine won out in the end, and his turn to medicine, a study rigorous, meticulous, empirical, responsible, was a way not of embracing loving, suffocating Mother Nature, but of fleeing her, or at least of holding her at arm's length. Medicine was part of Freud's self-conquest.

Even before he graduated from Gymnasium, with distinction, in June 1873, Freud recognized that the nature he most eagerly wanted to understand was human nature. His greed for knowledge, he observed in retrospect, was "directed more at human affairs than at natural objects." He precociously demonstrated this disposition in letters to his closest friends, replete with unabashed inquisitiveness and psychological perceptions. "It gives me pleasure," he wrote to Emil Fluss in September 1872, when he was all of sixteen, "to apprehend the thick texture of connecting threads that accident and fate have woven around us all." Young as he was, Freud already found merely superficial communications highly suspect. "I have noticed," he complained to Eduard Silberstein in the summer of 1872, "that you have only let me have a selection from your experiences, but have kept your thoughts wholly to yourself." He was already looking for deeper revelations. Reporting on the international exhibition held in Vienna in the spring of 1873, he said he thought it pleasant and pretty but far from overwhelming. "I fail to find a large, coherent picture of human activity, as little as I can discover the traits of a landscape in a herbarium." The "grandeur of the world," he went on, rests on the multiplicity of possibilities, but, unfortunately, "it is not a firm basis for our self-knowledge." These are the words of a born psychologist.

FREUD'S AMBIVALENCE ABOUT practicing medicine was not pronounced enough to cripple his desire to heal, or his pleasure in cures. In 1866, a ten-year-old schoolboy, he had already energetically displayed humanitarian inclinations, imploring his teachers to organize a campaign to supply bandages for Austrian troops wounded in the war against Prussia. Nearly a decade later, in September 1875, after he had been enrolled in the medical faculty for two years, he confessed to Eduard Silberstein, "I now have more than one ideal. To the theoretical one of my earlier years a practical one has now been added. Last year, asked what my greatest wish might be, I would have answered: a laboratory and free time, or a ship on the ocean with all the instruments the researcher needs." Clearly his admired Darwin, who had spent such fruitful years on the *Beagle*, was on Freud's mind as he elaborated his fantasy. But the discovery of scientific truths was not Freud's only wish. "Now," he went on, "I vacillate about whether I should not rather say: a large hospital and plenty of money, to curtail some of the evils which befall our bodies, or to remove them from the world." This desire to tilt at illness would erupt periodically. "I arrived at my patient's today quite at a loss how I could muster the necessary sympathy and attention for him," he wrote his fiancée in 1883, "I was so weary and apathetic. But as he began to complain," Freud's lethargy "vanished as I noticed that I had a task here, and significance."

But the most consistent sublimation of his childish curiosity ran to scientific investigations, to the riddles of mind and of culture. Looking back in 1927, he insisted that he had never properly been a physician and had found his way back to his real vocation after an extended and circuitous journey. Again, in his final autobiographical retrospect, written in 1935 when he was nearly eighty, he charted the "regressive development" he had followed after a "lifelong detour through the natural sciences, medicine and psychotherapy," to return to "those cultural problems that had once fascinated the youth, scarcely awakened to thinking." The detour, we will find, was less diversionary than Freud's phrasing would suggest. All, as the psychoanalysts say, was grist for his mill.

EARLY ON AT the University of Vienna Freud encountered the irritant of anti-Semitism, infuriating and memorable enough to find a prominent place in his autobiography half a century later. He made a point of noting that he had responded with defiance, even truculence. Typically, he turned rage to advantage. Gentile fellow students impertinently expected him "to feel inferior" and a stranger to the Austrian people—*nicht volkszugehörig*—"because I was a Jew." But he "resolutely" rejected this invitation to humility: "I never understood why I should be ashamed of my descent or, as one was beginning to say, my race." With the same self-respect, "without much regret," he abandoned the dubious privilege of belonging, sensing that his isolation would serve him well. To be condemned to the opposition fed his bent, he thought, "for a certain independence of judgment." Recalling the honest and courageous Dr. Stockmann in Ibsen's *Enemy of the People*, Freud professed to have relished being strictly excluded from the "compact majority."*

He was not just boasting after the fact. Freud's moral and physical courage are on record. In early 1875 he told Eduard Silberstein that his trust in what is generally accepted had dwindled and his "secret disposition toward minor-

---

*Around Christmas 1923, Freud read an advance copy of Fritz Wittels's biography of him, and annotated it freely. Speaking of Freud's early years, Wittels had written, "His fate as a Jew in the German cultural area made him sicken early with the feeling of inferiority, which no German Jew can escape." Freud's marginal comment was "!"—his way of expressing strong disagreement. It is possible that Freud's emphatic claim to having been spared the feeling of inferiority was an indirect response to Wittels's characterization. (See pp. 14–15 in Freud's copy of Wittels, *Sigmund Freud*. Freud Museum, London.)

ity opinions grown." This attitude sustained him in his confrontations with the medical establishment and its entrenched opinions. But he reserved a special fury for anti-Semites. In 1883, on a train journey, he encountered several of them. Angered by his opening the window for some fresh air, they called him "miserable Jew," commented scathingly on his un-Christian egotism, and offered to "show" him. Apparently unperturbed, Freud invited his opponents to step up, yelled at them, and triumphed over the "rabble." In the same vein, his son Martin recalled that in 1901, in the Bavarian summer resort of Thumsee, Freud routed a gang of about ten men, and some female supporters, who had been shouting anti-Semitic abuse at Martin and his brother Oliver, by charging furiously at them with his walking stick. Freud must have found these moments gratifying contrasts to his father's passive submission to being bullied.

These displays of pugnacity were in the future; university life of the 1870s was not yet disfigured by anti-Semitic student riots, as it would be later. For the present, moral courage alone was what Freud needed—and a direction. He launched on his university career early, at seventeen; he finished it late, in 1881, when he was twenty-five. His sweeping curiosity and his preoccupation with research kept him from obtaining his medical degree in the usual five years. Freud's catholicity was programmatic. "As to the first year at the university," he announced to his friend Silberstein, "I shall spend it entirely in studying humanistic subjects, which have nothing at all to do with my future profession, but which will not be useless to me." He vowed that if asked for his plans, he would refuse to give "a definite reply and say merely— oh, a scientist, a professor, something like that." However critical he was coming to be of philosophy and of those, like Silberstein, who had "yielded to philosophy from despair," Freud read a good deal of philosophy himself in these years. It is significant, though, that the thinker he read with the greatest profit should have been Ludwig Feuerbach. "Among all philosophers," he informed Silberstein in 1875, "I worship and admire this man the most."

AN HEIR OF THE eighteenth-century Enlightenment like Freud was bound to find much to admire in Feuerbach, intellectually the most robust among the left-wing Hegelians. Feuerbach had cultivated a style free of the arid abstractions marring German academic prose, and a pugilistic manner that charmed, or appalled, his readers as he took up arms against the "silly and perfidious judgments" of his detractors. He had much to teach Freud, in substance as in style: he regarded it as his assignment to unmask theology, to uncover its all-too-mundane roots in human experience. Theology must become anthropology. Strictly speaking, Feuerbach was not an atheist, being more intent on rescuing the true essence of religion from the theologians than on destroying it all. But his teaching, and his method, were calculated to make atheists. The point of his work on religion, he wrote in his most famous book, *The Essence of Christianity*, first published in 1841, was fundamentally "the destruction of an *illusion*," an *"utterly pernicious"* illusion at that. Freud, who came to see himself as a destroyer of illusions, found this stance most congenial.

Feuerbach was congenial to Freud in still another way: he was almost as critical of most philosophy as he was of theology. He offered his own way of philosophizing as the very antithesis, the "dissolution," of *"absolute, immaterial, self-satisfied* speculation." In fact, he acknowledged (or, rather, advertised), much as Freud would do later, that he lacked a talent for the "formal philosophical, the systematic, the encyclopedic-methodological." He was in search not of systems but of reality, and even denied his philosophy the name of philosophy, and himself the title of philosopher. "I am nothing but an *intellectual researcher into nature"*—a *geistiger Naturforscher.* That was a name Freud could appropriate for himself.

Freud's philosophical explorations as a young university student propelled him into the refreshing and seductive ambiance of the philosopher Franz Brentano; he attended no fewer than five courses of lectures and seminars offered by this "damned clever fellow," this "genius," and sought him out for private interviews. Brentano, an ex-priest, was a plausible exponent of Aristotle and of empirical psychology. A stimulating teacher who believed in God and respected Darwin at the same time, he made Freud question the atheist convictions he had brought to the university with him. "Temporarily," Freud confessed to Silberstein when Brentano's influence was at its peak, "I am no longer a materialist, also not yet a theist." But Freud never became a theist; at heart he was, as he informed his friend late in 1874, "a godless medical student and an empiricist." After he had worked his way through the persuasive arguments with which Brentano had overwhelmed him, Freud returned to his unbelief and remained there. But Brentano had stimulated and complicated Freud's thinking, and his psychological writings left significant deposits in Freud's mind.

All this intellectual activity appears rather remote from the study of medicine, but Freud, seemingly adrift, was an apprentice explorer rooting about. His lifelong reservations about the specialized study of medicine were a legacy of these years.* Apart from the opportunities it gave him for hearing memorable lecturers and for doing research that fascinated him, Freud found his medical education, beyond doubt, an uncertain blessing. Yet his professors

---

*This attitude was to be a prominent ingredient in his defense of lay analysts. See pp. 489–500.

were all he could have asked for. During his time at the University of Vienna as student and researcher, the medical faculty was a superb, highly select fraternity. Most of its members had been imported from Germany: Carl Claus, who headed the Institute of Comparative Anatomy, had recently been acquired from Göttingen; Ernst Brücke, the famous physiologist, and Hermann Nothnagel, who headed the Division of Internal Medicine, had both been born in northern Germany and trained in Berlin; Theodor Billroth, a celebrated surgeon, gifted amateur musician, and one of Brahms's closest friends, had been lured to Vienna after holding chairs in his native Germany and in Zurich. These professors, luminaries in their fields, lent an air of intellectual distinction and cosmopolitan breadth to parochial Vienna. It is no accident that during those years the medical school attracted scores upon scores of students from abroad—from other parts of Europe and from the United States. In his informal and informative *Guide to American Medical Students in Europe,* published in 1883, the American neurologist Henry Hun gave Vienna the highest commendation: "Besides its medical advantages," he wrote, "Vienna is a delightful city to live in." He praised its "café life," its opera and its public gardens, and its people for being "kind-hearted, handsome, and devoted to pleasure."

Freud would have demurred at much of this lavish praise. He had had less than pleasant experiences with the Viennese, did not much frequent cafés, and rarely went to the opera. But he would have cheerfully subscribed to the description of Vienna's medical faculty as a body of distinguished men with international reputations. His professors had still another virtue in his eyes: they had no use for the anti-Semitic agitation spreading across Vienna's culture like a stain. Their liberalism confirmed Freud's sense of himself as someone better than a pariah. Nothnagel, in whose division Freud began to work not long after he had obtained his medical degree, was an outspoken champion of liberal causes. An inveterate public lecturer, he became, in 1891, a founder of the Society for Combating Anti-Semitism; three years later, his lectures were disrupted by rowdy anti-Semitic students. Brücke, as civilized as Nothnagel if less of a joiner, had Jewish friends and, moreover, was a professed political liberal, which meant that he shared Freud's hostility to the Church of Rome. Freud had sound political as well as scientific reasons, then, for recalling his professors as men he could "respect and take as models."

IN THE EARLY SUMMER of 1875, Freud put some distance between himself and that abominable steeple of St. Stephen's. He went to visit his half brothers in Manchester, a trip long promised and long postponed. England had occupied his fantasies for years; he had been reading, and greatly enjoying, English literature ever since his boyhood. In 1873, two years before he saw the country for the first time, he had informed Eduard Silberstein, "I am reading English poems, writing English letters, declaiming English verse, listening to English descriptions, and thirsting after English views." If this were to keep up, he joked, he would catch "the English disease."* Thoughts about his future continued to preoccupy him after the visit to his English family no less than before. His cordial reception in Manchester, and his impressions of England in general, made him wonder whether he might not settle there. He liked England far better than his homeland, he told Silberstein, for all of its "fog and rain, drunkenness and conservatism." The visit remained unforgettable: seven years later, in an emotional letter to his fiancée, he recalled the "ineffaceable impressions" he had taken home with him, the "sober industriousness" of England and "its generous devotion to the public weal," to say nothing of the prevalent "stubbornness and sensitive feeling for justice of its inhabitants." The experience of England, he told her, had had "a decisive influence" on his life.

Freud's excursion sharpened the focus of his interests. English scientific books, he wrote to Silberstein, the writings of "Tyndall, Huxley, Lyell, Darwin, Thomson, Lockyer, and others," would always keep him a partisan of their nation. It was their consistent empiricism, their distaste for grandiose metaphysics, that most impressed him. "I am," he added immediately as an afterthought, "more distrustful than ever of philosophy." Gradually, the teachings of Brentano were fading into the background.

In fact, Freud would have little need of philosophy for some time. Upon his return, he began to concentrate on his work in Carl Claus's laboratory, and Claus, among Darwin's most effective and prolific propagandists in the German language, soon gave Freud an opportunity to distinguish himself. He had been brought to Vienna to modernize the department of zoology and bring it up to the level of other divisions at the university, and had managed to secure funds to establish an experimental station for marine biology in Trieste. Part of the endowment went for grants to a few favored students who would do closely circumscribed research there. Freud, clearly in Claus's good books, was among the earliest he chose to go, and in March 1876 Freud set out for Trieste. This gave him a first glimpse of the Mediterranean world, which he would so diligently explore in later years, summer after summer, with unwearied delight. He went with an assignment that reflected Claus's long-standing interest in hermaphroditism: to test the recent assertion of a Polish researcher, Simone de Syrski, that he had observed gonads in eels. This was an astonishing discovery—if it could be substantiated. For, as Freud laid out the issue in his report, there had been "innumerable efforts through the

---

*"The English disease"—*die englische Krankheit*—was the German nickname for rickets.

centuries" to find the eel's testes, and all had failed. If Syrski was right, the traditional view of the eel as hermaphroditic would be shown to be baseless.

Freud's first efforts were futile. "All the eels I have cut open," he confided to Silberstein, "are of the tenderer sex." But not all his reports were pure science; Freud allowed himself to be interested not only in the eels but also in the young women of Trieste. The interest, his letters suggest, was distant, downright academic. Betraying a certain anxiety before the lures of the sensual "Italian goddesses" he noticed on his walks, Freud commented on their appearance and their cosmetics, and kept aloof from them. "Since it is not permitted to dissect humans," he wrote, humor covering a certain timidity, "I have in fact nothing at all to do with them." He did better with the eels: after two stays at Trieste and after dissecting some four hundred specimens, Freud could partially, inconclusively, confirm Syrski's claim.

It was a commendable contribution, but when he later recollected his early ventures into rigorous research, Freud spoke of them with some disdain.* In assessing the career of his mind, he could be quite unjust to himself. His search for the gonads of the eel helped to school Freud in patient and precise observation, the kind of concentrated attention he would later find so indispensable as he listened to his patients. Whatever his reasons—and some obscure antipathy cannot be excluded—Freud's references to his work with Claus breathe a certain discontent, with himself no less than with others. It is striking that Freud should find no place for Claus's name in his autobiographical writings.

Freud's feelings about his next mentor, the great Brücke, are in radical contrast. "In the physiological laboratory of Ernst Brücke," he wrote, "I found rest and full satisfaction at last." He felt free to admire—and strove to imitate—"Master Brücke himself," as well as Brücke's assistants. One of these, Ernst von Fleischl-Marxow, a "dazzling personality," he came to know well. Freud also found in Brücke's circle a friend whose share in the making of psychoanalysis was to be decisive: Josef Breuer, a successful, affluent, highly cultivated physician and eminent physiologist fourteen years his senior. The two men were soon on the best of terms; Freud adopted Breuer as one in a succession of fatherly figures, and became a regular in the Breuer household,

---

*When, in 1936, the Swiss psychiatrist Rudolf Brun asked Anna Freud to send him some of her father's "early neurological writings," she replied that he held these researches in low esteem. "He thinks that you will be disappointed if you occupy yourself with them." (Anna Freud to Rudolf Brun, March 6, 1936. Freud Collection, B1, LC.)

It has long been tempting to see Freud's search for the eel's testicles as an early instance of his interest in sexuality. But that conjectural reconstruction of his inner biography is on a par with the claim that there is some deep meaning in the fact that Freud, the discoverer of the Oedipus complex, was asked in his final examination at the Gymnasium to translate thirty-three verses from Sophocles's *Oedipus Rex*. Both, after all, were assignments.

in some ways as good a friend to Breuer's charming and maternal wife Mathilde as to Breuer himself. This was not the only dividend Freud derived from Brücke. For six years, between 1876 and 1882, he worked in his laboratory, solving the problems his revered professor set for him, to Brücke's evident satisfaction—and his own. Unraveling the puzzles of the nervous system, first of lowly fishes, then of humans, meeting his exacting teacher's demands and expectations, Freud was singularly happy. In 1892, just after his mentor had died, Freud named his fourth child Ernst, after Brücke. It was the most heartfelt tribute at his command. Brücke was for Freud, and remained, "the greatest authority that worked upon me."

Freud's attachment to Brücke seems filial, nothing less. It is true that Brücke was almost forty years Freud's elder, nearly the age of Freud's father. It is true, too, that the act of investing one human being with the attributes and importance of another can entail leaps far more improbable than that of Sigmund Freud's putting Ernst Brücke in the place of Jacob Freud. "Transference," as Freud the psychoanalyst would call this shift of intense feelings, is athletic and ubiquitous. But much of Brücke's irresistible appeal to Freud was precisely that he was *not* Freud's father. His authority over Freud was earned rather than bestowed by the accident of birth; and at this critical juncture, when Freud was training himself to become a professional investigator into human mysteries, such authority was necessary to him. Jacob Freud was genial and good-humored; soft, yielding, he virtually invited rebellion. Brücke, in contrast, was reserved, precise to the point of pedantry, an intimidating examiner and exacting chief. Jacob Freud liked to read and had a measure of Hebrew erudition. Brücke was nothing if not versatile: a gifted painter with a lifelong, far from amateurish interest in aesthetics and a civilizing influence on his pupils.* In one facial feature, his eyes, he strikingly resembled not Freud's father but Freud himself; all of Freud's acquaintances, however widely they might differ in the rest of their description, would comment on Freud's keen, probing eyes. Brücke had eyes like that, and they memorably entered Freud's dreams. In one of them, the so-called *"Non vixit"* dream which he analyzed in detail in *The Interpretation of Dreams,* Freud annihilates a rival with a "piercing look." This proved in self-analysis to be the distorted memory of a very real experience in which it was Brücke, not Freud, who had done the annihilating: "Brücke had discovered that a few times I had come late to the students' laboratory," where Freud was then a demonstrator. "So, one day he came promptly at the opening time and waited

---

*"Doing his daily rounds at the laboratory" in Vienna, Erna Lesky, the historian of the Vienna medical school, has observed, "Brücke considered himself not only a teacher of physiology, but the representative of a general cultural idea." (Erna Lesky, *The Vienna Medical School of the 19th Century* [1965; tr. L. Williams and I. S. Levij, 1976], 231.)

for me. What he said was concise and to the point; but it was not the words that mattered. The overwhelming thing was the terrible blue eyes with which he looked at me and before which I melted away." Anyone, Freud went on, who remembered "the great master's eyes, marvelously beautiful into his old age, and who has ever seen him in anger, will easily empathize with the emotions of the one-time youthful sinner." What Brücke gave Freud, the young sinner, was the ideal of professional self-discipline in action.

Brücke's philosophy of science was no less formative for Freud than his professionalism. He was a positivist by temperament and by conviction. Positivism was not an organized school of thought so much as a pervasive attitude toward man, nature, and styles of inquiry. Its votaries hoped to import the program of the natural sciences, their findings and methods, into the investigation of all human thought and action, both private and public. It is characteristic for this cast of mind that Auguste Comte, the early-nineteenth-century prophet of positivism in its most extreme form, should have thought it possible to put the study of man in society on a dependable basis, invented the term "sociology," and defined it as a kind of social physics. Born in the eighteenth-century Enlightenment, rejecting metaphysics only marginally less decisively than theology, positivism had prospered in the nineteenth century with the spectacular triumphs of physics, chemistry, astronomy—and medicine. Brücke was its most eminent representative in Vienna.

He had imported his confident and ambitious scientific style from Berlin. There, in the early 1840s, still a medical student, he had joined his brilliant colleague Emil Du Bois-Reymond in solemnly consigning to the rubbish heap of superstition all pantheism, all nature mysticism, all talk of occult divine forces manifesting themselves in nature. Vitalism, the romantic philosophy of nature then current among natural scientists, with its loose, poetic talk of mysterious innate powers, aroused their resistance and their talents for spirited polemics. Only "the common physical-chemical" forces, they argued, are "active in the organism." Inexplicable phenomena must be approached by the "physical-mathematical method" alone, or by assuming that if there are "new" forces "inherent in matter," they must be "reducible to components of attraction and repulsion." Their ideal investigator was, in Du Bois-Reymond's words, the natural scientist unhampered by "theological preconceptions." When that nineteenth-century Renaissance man Hermann Helmholtz, on his way to acquiring world fame for his contributions to an astonishing range of fields—optics, acoustics, thermodynamics, physics, biology—joined Brücke and Du Bois-Reymond, the "school" was complete. Its influence spread rapidly, irresistibly; its members and followers occupied prestigious chairs in leading universities and set the tone in the scientific journals. When Freud studied in Vienna, the positivists were in control.

Near the end of 1874, Freud formed the plan of going directly to the source and spending the winter semester in Berlin, where he would attend the lectures of Du Bois-Reymond, Helmholtz, and the celebrated pathologist—and political progressive—Rudolf Virchow. The prospect, he wrote Silberstein, made him "glad as a child." In the end, nothing came of it, but Freud could draw from the fountainhead right at home. In that very year, Brücke outlined his principles, lucidly and at length, in a course to be published in 1876 as *Lectures on Physiology.* They incarnated medical positivism in its most materialist form: all natural phenomena, Brücke argued, are phenomena of motion. Freud heard these lectures as a matter of course, and with assent. Indeed, his commitment to Brücke's fundamental view of science survived his turn from the physiological to the psychological explanations of mental events. When in 1898, four years after Helmholtz's death, Freud's friend Wilhelm Fliess sent him the two-volume set of Helmholtz's lectures as a Christmas present, he knew that they would mean a great deal to Freud.* That Freud would apply his mentor's principles in ways Brücke could not have easily foreseen, and would not have wholeheartedly applauded, does not lessen Freud's debt to him. To Freud, Brücke and his brilliant associates were the chosen heirs of philosophy. Freud's forceful disclaimer that psychoanalysis has no world view of its own, and could never generate one, was his way of paying tribute to his positivist teachers years later: psychoanalysis, he summed up the case in 1932, "is a piece of science and can adhere to the scientific world view." In short, psychoanalysis is, like all the sciences, devoted to the pursuit of truth and to the unmasking of illusions. It might have been Brücke speaking.

The self-assurance of Brücke and his band of like-minded colleagues was buttressed by their reliance on the epoch-making work of Darwin. In the early 1870s, though it had secured many influential supporters, the theory of natural selection remained controversial; the intoxicating aroma of a sensational and dangerous innovation still clung to it. Darwin had undertaken to place man firmly in the animal kingdom and had ventured to explain his emergence, survival, and divergent development on wholly secular grounds; the causes operating to effect changes in the natural order of living beings that Darwin had spread out before an astonished world did not need to be referred to a deity, however remote. All was the work of blind, clashing,

*It is a significant indication of Freud's essential attitudes toward Judaism that the gift should have been for Christmas.

profane forces. Freud the zoologist studying the gonads of eels, Freud the physiologist studying the nerve cells of crayfish, Freud the psychologist studying the emotions of humans, engaged in a single enterprise. In the rigorous histological work on the nervous system that Freud did for Brücke, he was participating in the vast collective effort of demonstrating the traces of evolution. For him, Darwin never ceased to be "the great Darwin," and biological investigations charmed Freud more than tending patients. He was preparing himself for his calling, he wrote to a friend in 1878, by choosing to "maltreat animals" rather than "torture humans."

He was pursuing his researches to good purpose. Some of Freud's earliest published papers, written between 1877 and 1883, detail findings that are far from trivial. They substantiate evolutionary processes revealed in the nervous structures of the fish he was examining under his microscope. What is more, it becomes clear in retrospect that these papers form the first link in the chain of ideas leading to the draft of a scientific psychology he would attempt in 1895. Freud was working toward a theory specifying the ways that nerve cells and nerve fibrils function as a unit. But he moved on to other investigations, and when, in 1891, H. W. G. Waldeyer published his epoch-making monograph on the "neuron" theory, Freud's pioneering research was ignored. "It was not the only time," Ernest Jones has noted, "that Freud narrowly missed world fame in early life through not daring to pursue his thoughts to their logical—and not far-off—conclusion."

STILL LIVING AT home but with his mind on his work, Freud flourished in Brücke's laboratory and under Brücke's supervision. In 1879 and 1880, he was forced to take a year out for compulsory military service. This obligation largely meant tending a few sick soldiers and being bored. But his officers' praise of Freud's conduct was extravagant. They assessed him as "honorable" and "cheerful," as "very eager" and dutiful, and described his character as "firm"; they thought him "very reliable" as well as "very considerate and humane" with his patients. Freud, though, finding this enforced interlude tedious in the extreme, beguiled long stretches of idle time by translating four essays from John Stuart Mill's collected works. The editor of the German edition of Mill, Theodor Gomperz, an eminent Austrian classical scholar and historian of Greek thought, had been seeking to enlarge his stable of translators, and Freud's association with Brentano provided this welcome diversion: Brentano had recommended him to Gomperz.

Yet it was his fascination with research, far more than his military service, that slowed Freud down; he did not take his medical degree until the spring of 1881. His new dignity actually changed little in his mode of life: still hoping to secure fame through medical investigations, he remained with

Brücke. Hence he took until the summer of 1882 before he brought himself, on Brücke's advice, to leave the sheltering environment of the laboratory at last and take a very junior post in Vienna's General Hospital. The official reason for this move was his poverty. That was part of the story, but only part. His poverty bothered him now as it never had bothered him before. In April 1882, he had met Martha Bernays, who was visiting one of his sisters at his house. The visitor was slender, lively, dark and rather pale, with expressive eyes—decidedly attractive. Freud fell in love quickly, as he had fallen in love ten years before. But Martha Bernays was different. She was reality, not fantasy, not another Gisela Fluss inviting mute adolescent adoration. She was worth working for, worth waiting for.

FREUD IN LOVE

Having seen Martha Bernays, Freud knew what he wanted, and his masterful impetuosity carried her with him. By June 17, 1882, only two months after their first meeting, they were engaged. The two were well aware that this was not a prudent move. Her widowed mother, powerful and opinionated, had doubts about Freud's suitability. Not without reason: Martha Bernays had social prestige but no money; Freud had neither the one nor the other. He was undeniably brilliant but, it seemed, condemned to long years of impecuniousness, with no immediate prospects for a grand career or for some scientific discovery that would make him famous and (which mattered far more now) make him prosperous. He had nothing to expect from his aging father, who needed financial assistance himself. And he was too self-respecting to let himself become permanently dependent on the support of his fatherly friend Josef Breuer, who would at times give him money in the transparent guise of loans. The logic of his situation was compelling; Brücke only said out loud what Freud must have thought. Private practice was the only road to the substantial income necessary for founding the middle-class household on which he and Martha Bernays insisted.

To prepare for medical practice Freud had to gather clinical experience with patients, experience he could never amass by listening to lectures or experimenting in laboratories. For one as passionately preoccupied as Freud was with research, becoming a clinician required painful sacrifices; only the prize in the offing reconciled him to making them. In fact, the engagement tested the couple's endurance to the utmost. If it did not founder, that was a tribute to Freud's single-minded perseverance and, even more, to Martha Bernays's tact, forbearance, and sheer emotional staying power. For Freud proved a stormy lover.

He wooed Martha Bernays in the ways approved in his class and his culture: kisses and embraces were all the couple permitted themselves. During their engagement her virginity remained intact. Freud, too, may have been celibate all this time; there is no firm evidence to the contrary. But those more than four interminable years of waiting left their imprint on the formation of Freud's theories about the sexual etiology of most mental ailments; when in the 1890s he theorized about the erotic travail attendant upon modern life, he was writing in part about himself. He was immensely impatient. Now almost twenty-six, he expended all his highly charged, largely suppressed emotions, his rage little less than his love, on a single object.

Martha Bernays, five years his junior, popular with young men, was supremely desirable to Freud. He courted her with a fierceness that almost frightened him and called out all her resources of good sense and, in critical moments, her ability to stand by cherished attachments threatened by his possessiveness. To exacerbate matters, during most of their frustrating engagement, she was living with her mother in Wandsbek, near Hamburg, and he was far too poor to visit her often. Ernest Jones has calculated that the couple were apart for three of the four and a half years between their first meeting and their marriage. But they wrote to each other practically every day. In the mid-1890s, when they had been married for a decade, Freud reported in passing that his wife was suffering from a writer's block. She surely showed no traces of that symptom during her engagement. But their separations were not calculated to make things calm between them. Probably the gravest area of tension was religion: Martha Bernays had grown up in a strictly observant Orthodox Jewish family and accepted its pieties, while Freud was not just an indifferent unbeliever but a principled atheist determined to win his bride away from all that superstitious nonsense. He was unyielding, quite imperious, in his repeated, often angry demand that she abandon what she had not questioned for a moment so far.

In fact, Freud left Martha Bernays in no doubt that he meant to be the head of his household. Commenting to her in November 1883 on an essay about the enfranchisement of women which he had translated during his stint in the army, he praised John Stuart Mill for his ability to transcend "common prejudices," but immediately fell into common prejudices of his own. Mill, he complained, lacked "a sense for the absurd." The absurdity Mill had defended was that women can earn as much as men. This, Freud thought,

overlooked domestic realities: to keep a household in order, to superintend
and to educate children, is a full-time occupation which virtually precludes
a wife's employment outside the home. Like other conventional bourgeois of
his day, Freud made much of the difference between the sexes, "the most
significant thing about them." Women are not, as Mill's essay claimed,
oppressed as though they were black slaves: "Any girl, even if with no right
to vote or legal competence, whose hand a man kisses and for whose love he
dares all, could have set him straight." To send women out into the struggle
for existence was a "stillborn" idea; to think of her, Martha Bernays, his
"tender, dear girl," as a competitor struck Freud as sheer foolishness. He
conceded that the day might come when a different educational system would
make for new relationships between men and women, and that law and
custom might grant women rights now withheld from them. But full emancipation would mean the end of an admirable ideal. After all, he concluded,
"nature" has destined woman, "through beauty, charm, and sweetness, for
something else." No one could have guessed from this faultlessly conservative
manifesto that Freud was on his way to the most subversive, disturbing,
unconventional theories about human nature and conduct.

FREUD'S CORRESPONDENCE WITH Martha Bernays shows him in an unaccustomed role, that of romantic lover. He was fond and confidential, by turns
impulsive, exigent, exalted, depressed, didactic, gossipy, dictatorial, and at
rare moments repentant. Already an entertaining and energetic correspondent, Freud now became prolific in a genre he had never practiced before, the
love letter. Hectoring, inconsiderate in his frankness, unsparing with her
feelings and even more with his own, he filled his letters with circumstantial
reports of conversations and candid vignettes of colleagues and friends. As he
analyzed his feelings in his letters to Martha Bernays, so he analyzed her
letters to him, with an attention to minutiae worthy of a detective—or a
psychoanalyst. Some subtle detail, some suspect omission, spoke to him of a
bout of illness left unreported, or perhaps of her inclination for another man.
But though his love letters are often aggressive and void of flattery, they rise
on occasion to an affecting lyricism.

These love letters, indeed, add up to a veritable autobiography of Freud
in the early 1880s. He withheld very little from his fiancée. In addition to
recording, openly, his feelings about his work, his often unsatisfactory associates, his unslaked ambitions, he poured out his longing for her. He was
preoccupied with all the kisses he could not give her because she was so far
away. In one letter he justified his addiction to cigars by her absence: "Smoking is indispensable if one has nothing to kiss." In the fall of 1885, during

his stay in Paris, he clambered up one of the towers of Notre Dame, and evoked his yearning by counting his way to the top: "One climbs up three hundred steps, it is very dark, very lonely, on every step I could have given you a kiss if you had been with me, and you would have reached the top quite out of breath and wild." She responded to her "beloved treasure" less volubly, less imaginatively, less passionately perhaps, but sweetly enough, sending him greetings and kindly kisses in return.

At times, seeking to mold Martha Bernays, Freud turned pedagogue. He would lecture her gently on the physician's need to keep his emotional distance from all patients, even from friends: "I could well imagine how painful it was for you to hear how I sit by a sickbed in order to observe, how I treat human suffering as an object. But my girl, it can't be done any other way and must look different to me than to others." Yet, quickly abandoning this slightly superior tone, he added that there was one human being, only one, whose sickness would make him forget his objectivity: "I don't need to name her to you, and therefore I want to have her well always." He was, after all, writing love letters.

Being in love subverted Freud's self-confidence. His intermittent bouts of jealousy at times bordered on the pathological in their intensity, their sheer irrational anger. Forty years later, Freud would analyze mild jealousy as an "affective state," similar to mourning, which one might well call "normal"; its marked absence, he thought, is bound to be a symptom of deep repression. But Freud's jealousy went beyond the understandable resentment a lover might harbor against rivals. Martha Bernays must not call a cousin familiarly by his first name, but, formally, must use his last name. She must not show such a palpable predilection for two of her admirers, one a composer and the other a painter: as artists, Freud wrote glumly, they had an unfair advantage over a mere scientist like himself. Above all, she must forsake all others. But these intrusive others included her mother and her brother Eli, who was shortly to marry Freud's sister Anna, and Martha Bernays refused to countenance his jealous demands that she break with them. This generated strains that took years to dissipate.

More self-observant than ever, Freud had some inkling of his precarious state. "I am so exclusive where I love," he told Martha Bernays two days after they had become engaged. He acknowledged, ruefully, "I certainly have a disposition to tyranny." But this flash of self-recognition did not make him less tyrannical. It is true enough that Martha Bernays had already refused one offer and was likely to get others. But Freud's effort to monopolize the young woman he loved attests less to realistic perils than to a wavering self-esteem. The unresolved repressed conflicts of his childhood, where love and hate had been confusingly intertwined, now came back to haunt him as he wondered whether he was really worthy of his Martha. She was, he told her over and over, his princess, but he often doubted that he was a prince. For all that he was his mother's golden Sigi, he behaved like a beloved only child whose position is being undermined by the arrival of a sibling.

In the end, Freud did not permit credulous wrath and frowning jealousy to poison his attachment; he was not Othello. He never doubted his choice and often took unmixed pleasure in it. The prospect of domesticity delighted him, and he cheerfully took the time to list the requisites for what he called their hoped-for "little world of happiness." They were to have a pair of rooms, some tables, beds, mirrors, easy chairs, rugs, glasses and china for ordinary use and for festive occasions, hats with artificial flowers, big bunches of keys, and lives filled with meaningful activity, kind hospitality, and mutual love. "Shall we hang our hearts on such small things? As long as a grand destiny does not knock at our peaceable door—yes, and without misgivings." Freud's imagination usually dwelt on his grand destiny, but he could entertain with evident relish fantasies that he shared with untold numbers of undistinguished, unmemorable bourgeois of his time.

To realize these fantasies meant that Freud could not evade Brücke's advice, and six weeks after he had committed himself to Martha Bernays, he joined the General Hospital in Vienna. He stayed for three years, sampling a variety of medical specialties by moving from department to department— surgery, internal medicine, psychiatry, dermatology, nervous diseases, and ophthalmology in turn. Freud worked purposefully, his eye on advancement for the sake of his ultimate goal, marriage. Yet he had to be realistic, at least a little; the ladder of preferment in the Austrian medical profession was steep and had many rungs. Freud began in the lowliest possible position available at the General Hospital, as an *Aspirant*, a kind of clinical assistant, and rose to *Sekundararzt* in May 1883, when he joined Theodor Meynert's psychiatric clinic. He had to climb other steps; in July 1884, he became Senior *Sekundararzt*, and more than a year later, he attained after some setbacks the coveted rank of *Privatdozent*. * It was a position that provided prestige but no salary, desirable mainly as the first glimpse of a professorship beckoning in the distant future. But it provided no basis for marriage. Not surprisingly, Freud found himself entertaining hostile fantasies, not excluding death wishes, against colleagues standing in his way. "Wherever in the world there

---

*The "Referat" recommending Freud for his promotion to *Privatdozent* in the strongest possible terms was submitted to the faculty on February 28, 1885, and signed "E. Brücke, Meynert, Nothnagel." But the appointment was not confirmed by the ministry until September. (Photocopy of the handwritten four-page "Referat." Freud Museum, London.)

is rank order and promotion," he later mused about these days, "the way for wishes requiring suppression lies open."

FREUD DID NOT remain content with wishes. In October 1882, he successfully applied to Hermann Nothnagel, who had recently taken over the prestigious Chair of Internal Medicine, for a place in his department. Nothnagel became, with Brücke, one of his staunchest supporters as Freud slowly advanced toward public recognition and a modest measure of solvency. Freud described the great man after the first meeting as quite alien to him: "Uncanny to see such a man who has so much power over us and over whom we have no power at all. No," he added, "the man is none of our race. A Germanic woodsman. Totally blond hair, head, cheeks, neck." Still, he found Nothnagel gracious and gratifyingly willing to help advance his career. In time, the famous professor piqued Freud's ambition and provided him with a standard for invidious comparisons: "Under favorable circumstances," Freud boasted to his fiancée in February 1886, "I could achieve more than Nothnagel, to whom I feel myself far superior."

This was a strictly private contest. With the brain anatomist and psychiatrist Theodor Meynert, no less distinguished than Nothnagel, Freud would eventually clash in public. He had transferred to Meynert's department after half a year with Nothnagel, and found "the great Meynert" as much rival as protector. Things had been different at one time. Meynert's work and personality had impressed Freud while he was still a medical student. Indeed, Meynert's philosophical posture could only serve Freud as confirmation and stimulus. Tough-minded, aspiring to a scientific psychology, Meynert was a strict determinist who dismissed free will as an illusion; he saw the mind as obeying a fundamental hidden order and awaiting the sensitive, penetrating analyst. Almost from the beginning of their association, though, Freud complained that Meynert was hard to work with, "full of crotchets and delusions"; he "won't listen to you or understand you." In the 1890s, the two would feud over very real issues, hypnotism and hysteria.

RESENTMENT AND RAGE that developed on another occasion during this period, this time rage against himself, lay dormant for years before it surfaced, instructively distorted, in Freud's self-portrait four decades later: "I may here recount, looking back, that it was my fiancée's fault if I did not become famous in those early years." It is the story of a great opportunity not grasped: Freud almost made a spectacular contribution to the practice of surgery. In the early spring of 1884, he reported to Martha Bernays that he had become interested in the properties of cocaine, then a little-known drug, which a

German army physician had been employing to bolster his men's physical endurance. It might or might not amount to anything, he told her, but he planned to experiment with its possible uses in alleviating heart trouble and cases of nervous exhaustion, such as the "miserable condition" attendant upon the withdrawal of morphine. Freud's interest had a personal dimension. He hoped that cocaine might help his associate Ernst von Fleischl-Marxow, who was suffering from the agonizing consequences of an infection, to shed his addiction to morphine, which he had been taking as a painkiller. But late that summer Freud indulged himself in one of his rare visits to Wandsbek after being separated from his fiancée for a year. His loneliness must have been extreme, even in retrospect: he would speak of not having seen Martha Bernays for "two years" or even "more than two years"—two touching symptomatic slips.

His impatience led Freud to hurry his researches. He completed a technical paper, "On Coca," a fascinating compound of scientific reporting and strenuous advocacy, in June, and published it in a Viennese medical journal the following month. Early in September, Freud went off to see Martha Bernays, but not before mentioning his work with cocaine, and its properties at once soothing and stimulating, to his friend Leopold Königstein, an ophthalmologist. When Freud returned to Vienna after this interlude, he discovered that not Königstein, but another associate, Carl Koller, "to whom I had also spoken about cocaine, had performed the decisive experiments upon the eyes of animals and had demonstrated them at the ophthalmological congress at Heidelberg." As Freud remembered it, he had run into a colleague complaining of intestinal pains and had prescribed a 5 percent solution of cocaine, which had produced a peculiar feeling of numbness on lips and tongue. Koller had been present on this occasion, and this, Freud was sure, had been his "first acquaintance" with the anesthetic properties of the drug. Even so, Freud judged, "Koller rightly counts as the discoverer of local anesthesia with cocaine, which has become so important in minor surgery," notably in operations on the eye. "But I have borne my fiancée no grudge for my negligence at the time"*—which is to say that he both did and did not blame her, a little.

Such an ingenious way of burdening someone else with one's own failure to follow through is rare in Freud. It suggests that even from the safe vantage point of remote hindsight, cocaine held some uncomfortable, not wholly acknowledged meaning for him. The facts were even clearer than his painful

*"The cocaine business," Freud wrote his sister-in-law Minna Bernays on October 29, 1884, "has indeed brought me much honor, but the lion's share to others." (By permission of Sigmund Freud Copyrights, Wivenhoe.)

recollections would intimate. If Freud recognized from the outset that Koller fully deserved his instant celebrity, it rankled that he had missed by a hairs-breadth the royal road to fame and, with that, to marriage. Worse, his lyrical plea for cocaine as a panacea for pain, exhaustion, low spirits, and morphine addiction proved to be sadly misplaced. Freud himself began taking the drug as a stimulant to control his intermittent depressed moods, improve his general sense of well-being, help him relax in tense social encounters, and just make him feel more like a man.* He recommended it recklessly, even sending moderate quantities to Martha Bernays when he thought her indispositions warranted it. In June 1885—this was not the only time—he mailed to Wandsbek a vial of cocaine holding about half a gram and suggested that she "make for yourself 8 small (or 5 large) doses from it." She acknowledged the shipment promptly, thanked him warmly, and told him that, even though she did not need any, she would divide up the shipment and take some of the drug. There is no evidence, though, that she (or for that matter, her fiancé) ever acquired the habit.

Freud's prescriptions of cocaine to his friend Fleischl-Marxow did not prove so innocuous. If he could only succeed in relieving his pains! Freud wistfully exclaimed to his fiancée early in 1885. His fervent wish was not realized. Fleischl-Marxow, slowly, miserably dying, was if any-thing more enthusiastic about the curative properties of cocaine than Freud himself and ended up taking large amounts daily. Unfortunately, the remedy only exacerbated his sufferings: in the course of his treatments, Fleischl-Marxow became addicted to cocaine as he had been, before, to morphine.

Certainly Freud's experimentation with drugs at first did him little harm in what he sardonically called "the chase after money, position, and reputa-tion." His paper on coca and the papers he published soon after gave him something of a name in Viennese medical circles and even abroad, and it took some time for the possibly addictive character of cocaine to emerge. But there was no denying that Koller had reaped most of the prestige derived from the discovery of cocaine as a local anesthetic, and Freud's strictly limited success had, for him, the smell of failure. Moreover, his ill-advised though wholly well-meant intervention in Fleischl-Marxow's case, to say nothing of his equally ill-advised recommendation that cocaine be administered by means of injection, saddled him with residual feelings of guilt. Reality gave Freud good grounds for self-criticism. There was nothing anyone could have done

---

*Thus on June 2, 1884, he playfully threatened Martha Bernays that he would show himself stronger than she, "a big wild man with cocaine in his body," when next they met. (*Jones* I, 84.)

to relieve Fleischl-Marxow's agony, but other physicians experimenting with cocaine found that the drug, subcutaneously injected, could have the most unfortunate side effects.*

This misadventure remained one of the most troubling episodes in Freud's life. His dreams disclose an enduring preoccupation with cocaine and its consequences, and he continued to use it in modest quantities at least until the mid-1890s.† No wonder he was intent on minimizing the effects of the affair upon him. When Fritz Wittels declared in his biography that Freud had "thought long and painfully just how this could have happened to him," Freud denied it: "False!" he wrote in the margin. No wonder, too, that unconsciously he found it useful to shift responsibility for the whole matter to the very person for whose sake he had intensified his perilous search for fame.

YEARNING FOR HIS fiancée in far-off Wandsbek, Freud filled empty hours by rereading *Don Quixote;* it made him laugh, and he warmly commended the book to Martha Bernays, even if some of it was rather "coarse" and hardly proper reading for his "little princess." This was the poverty-stricken young physician who bought more books than he could afford and who read classic works into the night, deeply moved and no less deeply amused. Freud sought out teachers from many centuries: the Greeks, Rabelais, Shakespeare, Cervantes, Molière, Lessing, Goethe, Schiller, to say nothing of that witty eighteenth-century German amateur of human nature Georg Christoph Lichtenberg, physicist, traveler, and maker of memorable aphorisms. These classics meant more to him than that intuitive modern psychologist Friedrich Nietzsche. Freud had read him as a young student and spent good money on his collected works in early 1900, the year of Nietzsche's death. He hoped, he told his friend Fliess, "to find the words for much that remains mute in me." Yet Freud treated Nietzsche's writings as texts to be resisted far more than to be studied. It is symptomatic that after reporting the purchase of Nietzsche's works, he immediately added that he had not yet opened them: "For the time being too indolent."

---

*This is a complicated issue: Fleischl-Marxow injected himself with cocaine, and Freud did not at the time object to this procedure. Later, Freud turned away from it, and denied that he had ever advocated it.

†See above all the important dreams of Irma's injection and of the botanical monograph, analyzed in *The Interpretation of Dreams.* (*SE* IV, 106–21, 169–76.) In reporting the former, dreamt and analyzed in 1895, Freud noted that he had recently used cocaine to reduce some nasal swellings. (Ibid., IV, 111.)

Freud gave as his principal motive for this kind of defensive maneuver an unwillingness to be diverted from his sober work by "an excess of interest"; he preferred the clinical information he could glean from the analytic hour to the explosive insights of a thinker who, in his idiosyncratic way, had anticipated some of Freud's most radical conjectures.* Freud would insist that he had never made any claims to priority—a denial too unequivocal to be wholly accurate—and would single out the psychological writings of the German physicist and philosopher Gustav Theodor Fechner as the only ones he had found useful. They had clarified the nature of pleasure for him. Much as he liked and profited from reading, Freud liked and profited from experience even more.

In the early 1880s, while he was in training for private practice, Freud's principal concerns were professional rather than theoretical. But the mysteries of the human mind were absorbing his attention more and more. Early in 1884, he quoted to his "sweet little princess" one of his favorite poets, Friedrich Schiller, just a little sententiously: "Hunger and love: that, after all, is the true philosophy, as our Schiller has said." Years later, Freud would resort to this line more than once to illustrate his theory of the drives: hunger stood for the "ego drives" which serve the survival of the self, while love, of course, was a polite name for the sexual drives, which serve the survival of the species.

To see Freud as a budding psychoanalyst in the 1880s would be anachronistic. He kept up his researches in anatomy, especially cerebral anatomy. But he was beginning to concentrate on psychiatry, with an eye to the income. "From a practical perspective," he later wrote bluntly, "brain anatomy was certainly no advance over physiology. I took material considerations into account by starting the study of nervous diseases." It was then a little practiced branch of medicine in Vienna; not even Nothnagel had much to offer him in this field. "One had to be one's own teacher." His appetite for prestige and prosperity grew with what it fed on, and so did his urge to know. He needed more than Vienna could give. "In the distance," in Paris, he wrote forty years later, recapturing all the vividness of a fresh experience, "there shone the great name of Charcot."

---

*"Lacking talent for philosophy by nature," he wrote in 1931, looking back, "I made a virtue of necessity"; he had trained himself to "convert the facts that revealed themselves to me" in as "undisguised, unprejudiced, and unprepared" a form as possible. The study of a philosopher would inevitably enforce an unacceptable predetermined point of view. "Hence I have rejected the study of Nietzsche although—no, because—it was plain that I would find insights in him very similar to psychoanalytic ones." (Freud to Lothar Bickel, June 28, 1931. Typescript copy, by permission of Sigmund Freud Copyrights, Wivenhoe.)

IN MARCH 1885, while his appointment as *Privatdozent* was still some months away, Freud applied to his faculty for a travel grant. It provided only a meager stipend and a no less meager six months' leave of absence, but Freud had his mind set on it and kept up a running commentary on his prospects in his letters to Martha Bernays. "Ah, I am not contented at all," he wrote her early in June, in his typical analytical manner; "I am so insuperably lazy, and also know the reason for it: expectations always make us humans neglect the present." Every applicant needed a protector on the commission that would deal out the stipends. "For me it is Brücke, a very honorable but hardly energetic advocate." Freud apparently underestimated Brücke;* Fleischl-Marxow, who had reason to know, told Freud that the situation "had been extremely unfavorable for you, and the success that today's session brought you can be ascribed only to Brücke's going to bat for you, and his downright passionate championship of you, which has made a great stir." Certainly the testimonial of Brücke was positive enough, but Freud had the award in his pocket only in mid-June, after committee wranglings worthy of a more munificent prize. He never had a moment's hesitation about how he would divide his time: he would visit his fiancée and her family first, before going on to Paris. After a six-week visit to Wandsbek, where he finally and fully disarmed Frau Bernays's lingering objections to him, Freud arrived in Paris in mid-October.

As soon as he was settled, he explored the city, gathering first impressions: the streets, the churches, the theater, the museums, the public gardens. The reports he sent off to Martha Bernays are alive in satisfying detail: his astonishment at the "real obelisk from Luxor" in the Place de la Concorde, the elegant Champs-Élysées, free of shops but filled with carriages, the noisy, plebeian Place de la République, and the tranquil Tuileries gardens. Freud took particular delight in the Louvre, where he lingered over the antiquities, a "host of Greek and Roman statues, gravestones, inscriptions, and debris. A few extremely beautiful things, ancient gods represented any number of times; I have also seen the famous Venus de Milo without arms," as well as impressive busts of Roman emperors, and "Assyrian kings—as tall as trees, holding lions in their arms like lap dogs, winged man-animals with beautifully done hair, cuneiform inscriptions as neat as though they had been done yesterday, bas-reliefs painted in Egypt in burning colors, veritable colossi of kings, real sphinxes, a world as in a dream." He knew he would want to visit

---

*Not surprisingly, Freud's later public account did not perfectly, or completely, reproduce his private feelings; instead, it indicated that he had obtained his stipend through the "warm plea of Brücke." ("Selbstdarstellung," *GW* XIV, 37/"Autobiographical Study," *SE* XX, 12.)

the Assyrian and Egyptian rooms again, a number of times. "For me," he commented, "these things have more historical than aesthetic value." But his excitement betrays more than academic interest; it foreshadows a predilection for ancient statuary from the Mediterranean and the Near East to which he would give way once he could afford the space and the cash.

But in 1885, in Paris, he had little time—and very little money. When he went to the theater, it was to see the marvelous Sarah Bernhardt, a well-made drama by Victorien Sardou, which he thought boastful and trivial, or Molière comedies, which he found brilliant and used as "French lessons." In general he made do with cheap seats, at times with *"quatrième loge de côté,* really shameful pigeon-hole loges," for one franc fifty. He was living on loans and felt compelled to be stingy with mundane items like matches and stationery. "One always drinks wine which is very cheap, a deep red, and otherwise tolerable," he reported to Minna Bernays, Martha's sister, shortly after his arrival. "As far as food is concerned, one can get it for 100 fr. or for 3 fr., one must only know where." Lonely at first, he was inclined to be censorious and a little self-righteous. He was also patriotic: "As you see, my heart is German, provincial, and in any case did not come along with me." The French, he thought, were immoral seekers after sensations, "the people of psychological epidemics, of historical mass convulsions."

At times, he confided certain prudential stratagems to Martha Bernays, not without trepidation. In late 1885, he was making weekly visits, perhaps not wholly necessary, to a bored Austrian woman patient, his family physician's wife—"with not very fortunate manners, terribly affected"—because "it is a matter of good sense to get oneself on good terms with a Viennese colleague." But such manipulative conduct made him uneasy; earlier, confessing to his "rage for work," he had told his fiancée that he must take good care to do nothing in his "urge for work and for success" that might be interpreted as "dishonest."

But more important, from the beginning Freud was dazzled by Jean Martin Charcot. For some six weeks, he worked on the microscopic study of children's brains in Charcot's Pathological Laboratory at the Salpêtrière; some extensive publications on cerebral paralysis in children and on aphasia would later testify to his continuing, if gradually fading, interest in neurological research. Yet the powerful presence of Charcot propelled him away from the microscope in a direction in which he had already shown some telling signs of going: psychology.

Charcot's scientific style and personal charm overpowered Freud even more than his specific teachings. He was "always stimulating, instructive, and splendid," Freud told Martha Bernays, "and I will miss him terribly in Vienna." Reaching for expressions that would do justice to his exaltation in

Charcot's presence, he resorted to religious—or at least aesthetic—language: "Charcot," he confessed, "who is one of the greatest physicians, a genius and a sober man, simply uproots my views and intentions. After some lectures I walk away as from Notre Dame, with a new perception of perfection." Only the charged rhetoric of generation would convey his emotions; Freud, so fiercely intent on his independence of mind, was only too ready to be impregnated by this brilliant scientist and no less brilliant performer: "Whether the seed will one day bring forth fruit, I do not know; but that no other human being has ever acted on me in this way I know for certain."

Charcot was no doubt theatrical; lucid always, usually serious but sometimes humorous to drive his points home. Every one of his "fascinating" lectures, Freud thought, was "a little work of art in construction and composition." Indeed, Freud noted, "he never appeared greater to his listeners than after he had made the effort, by giving the most detailed account of his train of thought, by the greatest frankness about his doubts and hesitations, to reduce the gulf between teacher and pupil." As lecturer and advocate, Freud, who skillfully exploited his own uncertainties, would proceed no differently.

Watching these performances at the Salpêtrière, Freud took intense pleasure in the intellectual excitement that animated Charcot as he diagnosed and identified particular mental ailments; these proceedings recalled to Freud the myth of Adam distinguishing and naming the animals. Freud, the unsurpassed nomenclator who would act as the Adam of psychoanalysis, was in this as in so much else Charcot's disciple. Discriminating mental illnesses from one another, and from physical ailments, was a rare art in those days: this was the time when Freud, still quite ignorant of the neuroses, could diagnose the chronic headaches of a neurotic as meningitis, and when "greater authorities than I in Vienna were in the habit of diagnosing neurasthenia as a brain tumor."

Charcot was far more than an actor. At once medical luminary and social lion, enjoying unmatched prestige, he had diagnosed hysteria as a genuine ailment rather than the malingerer's refuge. What is more, he had recognized that it afflicts men—all traditional notions to the contrary—no less than women. Even more daring, Charcot had rescued hypnosis from mountebanks and charlatans for the serious purposes of mental healing. Freud was amazed and impressed to see Charcot inducing and curing hysterical paralyses by means of direct hypnotic suggestion.*

Hypnosis was not a complete revelation to the Freud of 1885. As a medical student he had already persuaded himself that, for all its unsavory reputation,

---

*For some years after his return to Vienna, he tried out the technique on his patients—with, some striking successes apart, rather indifferent results.

the hypnotic state was an authentic phenomenon. But it was gratifying to have Charcot confirm what he already largely believed, and impressive to see what happened to Charcot's patients during and after their hypnoses. In the words of Pierre Janet, Charcot's most famous pupil, they developed a "magnetic passion" for the hypnotist—a loving feeling, whether filial, maternal, or downright erotic in nature. This passion, Freud found out not long after, had its inconvenient side; one startling day in Vienna one of his early patients, freed from hysterical pains after a hypnotic session, threw her arms around her healer's neck. This embarrassing experience, Freud recalled, gave him a clue to the "mystical element" hidden in hypnosis. Later, he would identify this element as an instance of transference and employ it as a powerful instrument of psychoanalytic technique.

ONCE SETTLED IN his routine, Freud ceased to think of his stay in Paris as a confused, not always pleasant, dream and concentrated fiercely on his researches—fiercely enough to think it necessary to reassure his fiancée: she still reigned supreme over his feelings. "If you would like to order declarations of love from me," he wrote her in December, "I could scribble full fifty sheets like this, but you are after all so good and don't demand it." But he promised her that he had "now overcome the love for science in so far as it stood between us, and that I want nothing but you." Yet thoughts of his poverty never quite left him alone. He described himself to Martha Bernays, a little pathetically, as "a poor, young human being tormented by burning wishes and gloomy sorrows," filled with "scrounger's hopes"—*Schnorrerhoffnungen*—concretely, with the hope that one of his affluent friends would lend him money.

But his work prospered and so, after a time, did his social life. In January and February 1886, he was invited to receptions at Charcot's palatial house. Feeling awkward and uncertain of his spoken French, he fortified himself with a dose of cocaine, dressed formally, and went with pulses beating. His reports to his fiancée attest to his anxiety and to his relief at not making himself ridiculous in Charcot's presence. One late evening in February, just back from a reception at the great man's house, he wrote his "beloved sweet treasure" after midnight. "Thank God, it's over." It had been "dull to bursting, only that bit of cocaine kept me from it. Just think: forty or fifty people this time, of whom I knew three or four. Nobody was introduced to anybody else, everyone was left to his own devices to do what he wanted." He thought he had spoken badly, worse than usual. But he did get into a political discussion, in which he identified himself as "neither Austrian nor German," but as a "*juif.*" Then, close to midnight, he had drunk a cup of chocolate. "You must not think that I am disappointed, one cannot expect anything else from a *jour fixe;* I only know that we will not set one up for ourselves. But do not tell anyone how boring it was." Still, while Freud might find such social occasions tedious or his French inadequate, Charcot singled him out for particular attention. This cordiality only made Charcot all the more available as a model.

What mattered most to Freud was that his model was obviously prepared to take his patients' outlandish behavior seriously, and no less prepared to entertain strange hypotheses. Paying the most careful and penetrating attention to his human materials, Charcot was an artist, on his own testimony a *visuel*—"a man who sees." Trusting what he saw, he defended practice over theory; an observation he once threw out burned itself into Freud's mind: *La théorie, c'est bon, mais ça n'empêche pas d'exister.* Freud never forgot this *bon mot,* and in later years, unsettling the world with incredible facts, never tired of repeating it: theory is all very well, but that does not prevent facts from existing. This was the principal lesson Charcot had to impart: the scientist's submissive obedience to facts is not the adversary, but the source and servant, of theory.

ONE CONCRETE QUESTION that Charcot did not resolve to Freud's complete satisfaction, and one he agitated for some years, concerned the nature of hypnosis. Even for its supporters, even in France, hypnosis was far from uncontroversial. Charcot and his pupils defined the hypnotic state as "an artificially produced morbid condition—a neurosis"—in short, a nervous disease, specifically hysteria, with unmistakable organic components. And, Charcot argued, the hypnotic state can be produced only in hysterics. But a rival school in Nancy, inspired by Ambroise Auguste Liébeault, an obscure private physician, and by his active and prolific follower Hippolyte Bernheim, took a different line: hypnosis is purely a matter of suggestion; hence almost everyone must be susceptible to it. For a few years, Freud vacillated. With superb impartiality, he translated a volume of Charcot's *Lectures on the Diseases of the Nervous System* in 1886, and, two years later, Bernheim's major treatise, *On Suggestion and Its Applications to Therapy.* He continued to lean toward Charcot's views, but when he called on Bernheim in Nancy in 1889, he found his visit, undertaken to improve his technique of hypnotic suggestion, one of the most profitable excursions in his life. Psychoanalysis, as Freud developed it in the mid-1890s, was an emancipation from hypnosis. But a handful of papers and reviews of the early 1890s lay bare its roots in hypnotic experimentation, and in fact hypnosis remained in Freud's repertory for some years.

Once Freud was back in Vienna, after a stopover in Berlin to study children's diseases, the issue for him was not which French school to follow, but how to deal with the incredulous medical establishment. His preface to Bernheim's book clearly mirrors his discontent with local colleagues: "The physician," he wrote, the recalcitrant Viennese physicians very much in mind, "can no longer remain aloof from hypnotism." Once known, it will "destroy" the prevalent belief that "the problem of hypnosis is still surrounded, as Meynert asserts, by a halo of absurdity." Freud insisted that Bernheim and his associates in Nancy had shown the manifestations of hypnotism, far from being eccentric, actually linking up "with familiar phenomena of normal psychological life and of sleep." Hence the serious study of hypnosis and hypnotic suggestion brings to light "the psychological laws" governing the mental life of "the majority of healthy people." Hectoring his colleagues a little, Freud concluded that "in matters of natural science, it is always experience alone and never authority without experience that brings about the final decision" on whether an idea is to be accepted or rejected.

One instrument of persuasion ready to Freud's hand was the report he submitted to his medical faculty at Easter, 1886. Dwelling on the intellectual debts he had incurred in Paris, he was unfailingly enthusiastic in his account: since German (or, for that matter, Austrian) scientific workers have only sparse contacts with the French, the findings of French neuropathology, "partly highly remarkable (hypnotism), partly important in practice (hysteria)" have found little recognition in German-speaking lands. He confessed himself strongly attracted by Charcot's "liveliness, cheerfulness, and perfect eloquence, which we are accustomed to ascribe to the national character of the French," and by his "patience and love of work, which we as a rule claim for our own nation." Having enjoyed close "scientific and personal intercourse" with him, Freud now made himself Charcot's advocate. The most exhilarating and enduring message Freud had brought home with him concerned the vista Charcot had opened of the neuropathologist's next assignment. "Charcot used to say that by and large anatomy has finished its work and the theory of the organic diseases might be called complete; now the time of the neuroses has come." Freud's superiors found these words unpalatable, but they are a dim forecast of his future.

As that future drew closer, he kept his memories of Charcot very much alive. Freud made him into another Brücke, an intellectual father he could look up to and try to emulate. Even after he had come to question aspects of Charcot's teachings, Freud continued to pay him every homage at his command: in addition to translating Charcot's lectures into German, he kept on propagating Charcot's ideas and quoting him as an authority on suitable occasions. Freud had acquired an engraving of André Brouillet's painting *La Leçon clinique du Dr Charcot*, which shows Charcot demonstrating a female hysteric to a rapt audience in the Salpêtrière; later, after moving to Berggasse 19, he hung it up proudly in his consulting room, over a glassed-in bookcase crammed with small antique sculptures. More: in 1889, Freud named his first son, Jean Martin, known as Martin, after Charcot, a tribute the master acknowledged with a brief courteous reply and "all my congratulations."* When Charcot died in 1893, Freud wrote for the *Wiener Medizinische Wochenschrift* an affectionate obituary article which, without being self-referential, must rank among Freud's autobiographical fragments, an indirect testimonial to his own scientific style.

ALL THIS CAME some years later. In the spring of 1886, Freud's prospects looked as uncertain as they ever had. Once back in Vienna, though, he recognized that his months in France had been more than a leave; they were an ending. He resigned from the General Hospital, and on Easter Sunday, April 25, the morning edition of the *Neue Freie Presse* carried in its local news a small item: "Herr Dr. Sigmund *Freud*, Docent for Nervous Diseases at the University, has returned from his study trip to Paris and Berlin and has consulting hours at [District] I, Rathhausstrasse No. 7, from 1 to 2:30." Breuer and Nothnagel sent him patients, some of them paying ones, and while he continued to do research in Meynert's new anatomical laboratory, his main concern was making a living. He was not very sanguine about winning "the battle for Vienna," and floated the idea of emigration. Perseverance won out; he found some of the nervous sufferers he treated scientifically interesting, while some of his other patients, more boring, rewarded him by paying their bills. His impecuniousness was painful; he confessed that there were times when he could not afford to take a cab to make house calls.

At rare moments, when his income seemed solid enough to bring marriage within reach, Freud enjoyed flashes of euphoria. It did not help matters that he should find himself battling his professional peers. Freud's enthusiasm for French innovations only reinforced the skepticism he had begun to arouse with his championship of cocaine. Lecturing in the fall of 1886 to the Vienna society of physicians on male hysteria, and proposing psychological etiologies for it, he received a mixed hearing. One old surgeon, whom he never forgot, objected to Freud's thesis—brought back from Paris—that men can be hysterics: did not the name "hysteria" itself, from the Greek word for "womb," make it plain that women alone could suffer from hysteria? Other physicians were more receptive, but with his exasperated sensitivity, Freud chose to

---

*Charcot's message is brief and allusive: he expressed the hope that "the Evangelist and the generous centurion" whose names Freud's son bore might "bring him good fortune." Plainly, Charcot expected Freud to understand his references to the Evangelist John and to the pagan knight Martin who had handed a beggar his cloak and ended up a Christian saint.

interpret his colleagues' attitude as sheer, obtuse rejection. From now on, he thought, he stood in opposition to the establishment. Even Meynert, after all, long one of his most vocal supporters, had decided to break with him.

By this time, however, he also had good reasons for contentment. Freud's own meager, steadily dwindling savings, added to his fiancée's modest legacies and dowry, wedding presents in cash from her family, and, above all, generous loans and gifts from wealthy friends, finally enabled him to marry Martha Bernays. The civil wedding took place in Wandsbek on September 13. But unanticipated legal complications necessitated a second ceremony. While the civil marriage on which Freud had insisted was sufficient in Germany, a religious ceremony was required by Austrian law. And so on September 14, Freud, the sworn enemy of all ritual and of all religion, was compelled to recite the Hebrew responses he had quickly memorized to stamp his marriage valid. Once married, Freud got his revenge or, at least, his way: "I remember very well her telling me," a cousin of Martha Bernays, now Martha Freud, recalled, "how not being allowed to light the Sabbath lights on the first Friday night after her marriage was one of the more upsetting experiences of her life." On issues of such importance as the religious—or, rather, irreligious— style of his household, Freud adamantly asserted his authority.

After a year of marriage, he had splendid news for his family. On October 16, 1887, he conveyed it exuberantly to Frau Bernays and Minna Bernays in Wandsbek: "I am terribly tired and still have to write so many letters, but writing to you comes first. You already know from a telegram that we have a little daughter," Mathilde. "She weighs three thousand four hundred grams," some seven and a half pounds, "which is very respectable, is terribly ugly, has sucked on her right hand from her first moment, otherwise seems very good-humored and behaves as though she is really at home." Five days later, he had discovered good grounds for changing his tune: everyone was telling him that little Mathilde "looks strikingly like *me*," and in fact "she has already grown much prettier, sometimes I think already quite pretty." He had named the child after his good friend Mathilde Breuer—"naturally." Just a month later, he met in her husband's circle a visitor from Berlin, Wilhelm Fliess, who was to become the most fateful friend in his life.

TWO

The Theory in the Making

A NECESSARY FRIEND — AND ENEMY

 "An intimate friend and a hated enemy have always been necessary requirements of my emotional life," Freud confessed in *The Interpretation of Dreams*. "I always knew how to provide myself with both over and over." There were times, he added, when the two were united in the same person. In his early childhood, that double role had been played by his nephew John. After his marriage, and during the decade of discoveries, Freud made Wilhelm Fliess into that necessary friend and, later, enemy.

Fliess, an ear, nose, and throat specialist from Berlin, had come to Vienna in the fall of 1887 for further study. Taking Breuer's advice, he had attended some of Freud's lectures on neurology, and late in November, after he returned home, he received a heartfelt overture from Freud. "While my letter of today has a business motive," Freud wrote, "I must introduce it with the confession that I entertain the hope of continuing the relationship with you, and that you have left a deep impression on me." This was at once more formal and more emotional than Freud's usual style, but then his friendship with Fliess would be unique in his experience.

In developing the theory of psychoanalysis, Freud was to have more enemies, and fewer friends, than he wanted. Failure was probable; hostility and ridicule were virtually certain. Fliess was precisely the intimate he needed: audience, confidant, stimulus, cheerleader, fellow speculator shocked at nothing. "You are the only Other," Freud would tell him in May 1894, "the alter." In the fall of 1893, Freud had admitted to Fliess, voicing an insight he would refuse to follow up for another seven or eight years, "You really spoil my critical faculties." Such utter credulity in a man like Freud, proud of being a hardheaded man of science, calls out for interpretation.

That credulity seems all the more striking because Fliess is now regarded as a crank and pathological numerologist. But the decline in his reputation came later. His pet theories in fact sound bizarre in the extreme: Fliess singled out the nose as the dominant organ, which spreads its influence over all of human health and sickness. He was, moreover, enslaved to a scheme of biorhythmic cycles of 23 and 28 days, to which males and females were seen to be subject and which, he believed, would permit the physician to diagnose all sorts of conditions and ailments. Yet around the turn of the century, these ideas, now almost wholly discredited, found a sympathetic hearing and even a measure of support from respectable researchers in several countries. His credentials were after all impeccable: Fliess was a reputable specialist with a solid practice extending far beyond his home base in Berlin. Besides, the ideas Freud was playing with appeared at the outset no less outlandish than Fliess's notions. And Breuer had recommended him, which was to the Freud of the late 1880s a virtual guarantee of intellectual probity.

Fliess's scientific learning was wide-ranging and his scientific ambition vast; he impressed others, less needy than Freud, with his appearance, his cultivation, his erudition. As late as 1911, long after Fliess and Freud had parted in bitterness, Freud's loyal follower Karl Abraham, a sober observer, found Fliess amiable, keen, original—perhaps the most valuable acquaintance, he thought, he "could have made among Berlin physicians." Freud had felt precisely that way when he and Fliess first met. Their isolation as medical subversives only made them all the more congenial to one another. "I am pretty much alone here with the clearing up of the neuroses," Freud would write to Fliess in the spring of 1894. "They pretty much consider me a monomaniac." Their correspondence must have seemed to Freud and Fliess a conversation of two monomaniacs in possession of deep, still unacknowledged truths.

Fliess displayed a firm grasp of Freud's theorizing and supplied him with ideas as much as with support. He was a diligent and perceptive reader of Freud's manuscripts. He gave Freud an understanding of the essential unity of all human culture and the evidentiary value of all human manifestations: "You have taught me," Freud told him gratefully in June 1896, "that a bit of truth lurks behind every popular lunacy." He helped Freud to focus his attention on jokes as useful material for psychoanalytic scrutiny. Again, Fliess speculated about infantile sexuality in his published writings of the mid-1890s, years before Freud was willing to make so scandalous an idea consistently his own. While Freud seems to have been the first to insist that some sexual malaise lies at the heart of all neuroses, Fliess in turn sponsored the idea of human bisexuality and watched Freud elaborate it into a cardinal principle.

All this said, the ultimate irrationality of Fliess's fanciful notions and of his efforts at proof should have become obvious much earlier than they did, especially to Freud. To be sure, one could make a case for Fliess's high-flying attempt to ground biology in mathematics. Nor was there anything inherently ridiculous in the proposition that one particular bodily organ casts its shadow over the others. A psychoanalyst might well be expected to take a wry interest in the nose, so reminiscent of the male genitalia in its shape and of the female sexual apparatus in its tendency to bleed. The idea of displacement from one part of the body to another, not merely of thoughts but of symptoms, was to become a mainstay of psychoanalytic diagnosis. A scientist of the mind, like Freud on the verge of postulating erogenous zones shifting in the course of human development, might find merit in a theory claiming that "genital places" located in the nose influence the course of menstruation and of childbirth. What should have given Freud pause, even before later researches made nonsense of Fliess's obsessions, was Fliess's dogmatism, his inability to recognize the wealth and the baffling complexity of causes ruling human affairs. But as long as Fliess's praise was "nectar and ambrosia" to him, Freud was not about to raise, or even think of, inconvenient doubts.

The same willed blindness controlled Freud's play with Fliess's biomedical numbers game. The idea of male sexual cycles was, in view of female menstrual rhythms, not implausible. Significantly, Havelock Ellis, that enthusiast and romantic among sex researchers, devoted a long chapter to "the phenomena of sexual periodicity" in a volume of his *Studies in the Psychology of Sex*, virtually contemporary with Freud's *Interpretation of Dreams*. An indefatigable collector of relevant and recondite materials on sexual matters from many countries, Ellis had read Fliess's work on sexual periods and found it interesting if, in the end, not persuasive, certainly not as far as male rhythms were concerned: "Although Fliess brings forward a number of minutely observed cases I cannot say that I am as yet convinced of the reality of this 23 days' cycle." He supposed with his characteristic generosity that "these attempts to prove a new physiological cycle deserve careful study and further investigation," but concluded that while "the possibility of such a cycle should be borne in mind," at the present time "we are scarcely entitled to accept it." Ellis recognized that Fliess's way of manipulating his key numbers 23 and 28, their intervals and their totals, allowed him to demonstrate anything whatever. Later researchers were more impatient with Fliess than Ellis had been, and would profess themselves wholly unconvinced.

Freud, though, remained convinced for some years, and diligently contributed material to Fliess's collection of probative numbers: the intervals of his migraine headaches, the rhythms of his children's ailments, the dates of his wife's menstrual periods, the length of his father's life. Something other than flattery, something more than sheer neediness, was involved in this lapse into unscientific naiveté. Freud, the great rationalist, was not wholly free from superstition, especially number superstition. It is true that in 1886, he and his new bride had moved into the apartment house built on the site of Vienna's Ring-Theater which had burned down with more than four hundred fatal casualties five years before: it was precisely his defiance of superstition that allowed Freud to set aside common fears. But certain numbers raised anxieties in him. For years he harbored the haunting belief that he was destined to die at the age of fifty-one, and later, at sixty-one or sixty-two; he felt pursued by these fateful ciphers as reminders of his mortality. Even the telephone number he was assigned in 1899—14362—became confirmation: he had published *The Interpretation of Dreams* at forty-three, and the last two digits, he was convinced, were an ominous monition that sixty-two was indeed to be his life's span. Freud once analyzed superstition as a cover for hostile, murderous wishes, and his own superstitions as a suppressed desire for immortality. But his self-analysis did not completely free Freud from this bit of irrationality, and this residue of what he called his "specifically Jewish mysticism" made him susceptible to Fliess's wildest speculations.

There was much that bound Freud to Fliess beyond professional self-interest. The two were simultaneously insiders and outsiders: highly trained professional physicians working at, or beyond, the frontiers of acceptable medical inquiry. What is more, they were Jews confronting almost identical problems and prospects in their society, propelled into intimacy with the ease of brothers in a persecuted tribe. Emotionally speaking, Fliess was Breuer's successor: Freud's involvement with the former intensified as his dependency on the latter began to wane. That Breuer should have been the one to bring Freud and Fliess together is a piquant irony.

It may be stretching the term beyond its legitimate province, but in important ways, Freud imposed on Fliess a role akin to that of psychoanalyst. Freud's prolonged failure, his virtual refusal, to appraise his intimate friend realistically hints that he was caught in a severe transference relationship: Freud idealized Fliess beyond measure and endowed him with the most admirable qualities of Brücke or Charcot. Freud even wanted to name a son after Fliess, only to be frustrated, in 1893 and 1895, by the birth of daughters, Sophie and Anna. He poured out his innermost secrets to his Other in Berlin on paper and, during their carefully prearranged, eagerly anticipated "congresses," in person. Beginning in late 1893, he confided to Fliess that he was suffering from chest pains and arrhythmia, a troubling and worrisome heart condition that Fliess attributed to Freud's smoking habit. Fliess was the only one to know: in April 1894, reverting to that disagreeable topic, Freud warned him that his wife was "not a confidante of my death deliria." The previous summer, he had disclosed to Fliess that Martha Freud was enjoying a feeling of "revival," since "for the present, for a year, she does not have to expect a child." He spelled it out explicitly: "We are now living in abstinence." This is the sort of thing a decent bourgeois would confess only to his analyst. Fliess was the man Freud could tell everything. And he did tell Fliess everything, more than he told anyone else about his wife or his wife about himself.

INDEED, ONE REASON why Freud found Fliess so indispensable in the 1890s was that his wife was not his confidante in the investigations to which he was devoting his concentrated attention. Overborne by his dazzling presence, Martha Freud makes a rather shadowy figure. While he bequeathed, somewhat against his will, a most profuse record to posterity, her surviving or accessible traces are sparse. The casual comments of visitors, and some of her husband's, can be read to intimate that she was simply a model *Hausfrau*, managing the household, providing the meals, superintending the servants, raising the children. But her contribution to family life was far more than dutiful, unpaid, essential drudgery. The family revolved around Freud. It is not without interest that he should have been the one to name their six children—after *his* friends, *his* mentors; when his second son was born in 1891, Freud named him after *his* admired Oliver Cromwell. But the Freuds' eldest son, Martin, recalled his mother as being at once kind and firm, effective and thoughtful about the all-important domestic details and no less important travel arrangements, capable of reassuring self-control, never rattled. Her insistence on punctuality (a quality which, her son Martin observed, was rare in casual Vienna), gave the Freud household its air of dependability—even, as Anna Freud would later complain, of obsessive regularity. Max Schur, Freud's last physician, who came to know her well in her last years, thought that many had underestimated her; he learned to like her greatly even if she would regularly object to his sitting on the bed, and mussing it up, when he was examining her husband.

As such a vignette suggests, Martha Freud was the complete bourgeoise. Loving and efficient with her family, she was weighed down by an unremitting sense of her calling to domestic duty, and severe with lapses from middle-class morality.* When she was an old lady in London, she described reading as her only "diversion," but quickly added, at once apologetic and amused, "however, only at night in bed." She would begrudge herself this pleasure during the day, held back by her "good upbringing." Freud intimated to Fliess that his wife was extremely reserved and slow to warm up to strangers. But though generally undemanding, she could be persistent once she had set her mind on a wish she thought reasonable. To judge from hints in Freud's letters and from her photographs, she soon traded her slender youthfulness for a neat, just slightly drab, middle age; she did little to resist the then accepted style of aging, which relentlessly turned the young wife into a stately matron.† From the beginning of their engagement, Freud had candidly told her that she was not really beautiful in the literal sense, but that her appearance marked her as "sweet, generous, and reasonable." Once married, she took little time to attend to whatever beauty she possessed.

Her continuing, merciless pregnancies must have taken their toll: the Freuds had six children in nine years. Just before her marriage, she had dreamt of having three. It would have been easier. "My poor Martha has a tormented life," her husband observed in February 1896, when their last, Anna, was a little over two months old. Most onerous of all, Martha Freud had to manage, over and over, one child's ailment after another. Freud would lend a hand, listen to his children's woes, or, on the summer vacations, lead expeditions gathering mushrooms in the mountains. He was an active father when he had time, and concerned. But the principal burdens of domesticity fell on his wife.

For all her love of books when she allowed herself to indulge it, Martha Freud was not a companion for her husband on his long and lonely progress toward psychoanalysis. She assisted Freud in ways natural to her by presiding over a domestic setting in which he could be at ease, partly by letting him take most of it for granted. Responding to a letter of condolence after Freud's death, she took it as "a feeble consolation that in the 53 years of our marriage, there was not a single angry word between us, and that I always tried as much as possible to remove the *misère* of everyday life from his path." She felt it a privilege to have been able to look after "our dear chief" for all these

---

*She never forgave Stefan Zweig, despite his miserable end (he committed suicide in Brazil in 1942 after long bouts with depression), for leaving his wife Friderike for a younger woman, whom he then married. She could not understand, she told Friderike Zweig, "our friend's infidelity to you!" Even his death, she added, did not mitigate her resentment. (Martha Freud to Friderike Zweig, August 26, 1948. Freud Collection, B2, LC.)

†To be sure, standards of what constitutes middle or old age were rather different then. Freud could in the 1890s speak of an "aging spinster (about thirty)." (Freud to Fliess, Draft H, enclosed in letter of January 24, 1895. *Freud–Fliess*, 107 [108].)

decades. This meant a great deal to him, but it was not everything. His wife virtually made Fliess necessary.

In his reminiscences of the Freuds, the French psychoanalyst René Laforgue, who knew them in the 1920s, praised Martha Freud as "a practical woman, marvelously skillful in creating an atmosphere of peace and *joie de vivre.*" She was, he thought, an excellent, hard-working housewife who did not hesitate to help out in the kitchen and who "never cultivated that sickly pallor fashionable with so many female intellectuals." But, he added, she thought her husband's psychoanalytic ideas "a form of pornography." In the midst of a lively, crowded household, Freud was alone. On December 3, 1895, he announced to Fliess the birth of little Annerl, reporting that mother and infant, "a nice and complete little female," were doing well. In the very next letter, only five days later, he rejoiced at the sight of Fliess's handwriting, which allowed him to "forget much loneliness and privation." The association is pathetic; Freud cherished his family and would not have done without it. But the family did not assuage his dismaying sense of isolation. That was Fliess's task.

FREUD'S FRIENDSHIP WITH Fliess ripened with fair speed, rather uncharacteristic for an age in which intimacy was usually slow to develop and sometimes resisted decades of close association. Freud's first letter to Fliess in November 1887 serves as an eloquent hint at the eruptive emotionality that he did his utmost to master. There he addressed Fliess as "Esteemed friend and colleague!"—*Verehrter Freund und Kollege!* By August 1888, Fliess had become "Esteemed friend!"—*Verehrter Freund!*" And two years later, he was on occasion a "dear" and even a "dearest" friend—*Liebster Freund!* This remained Freud's preferred mode of address until the summer of 1893, when he raised the pitch to "Beloved friend!"—*Geliebter Freund!* By that time, the two had been addressing one another with the intimate *du* for more than a year, while Freud continued to address Frau Fliess, more distantly, with *Sie.*

It was during this opening phase of Freud's dependence on his Other from Berlin that he became increasingly dissatisfied with available techniques for handling neurotic patients. "In the time span of 1886 to 1891," Freud recalled, "I did little scientific work and published almost nothing. I was occupied in finding my way in my new profession and in securing material subsistence for myself and my rapidly growing family." This is being unduly harsh to a time of incubation: Freud was laying the groundwork for a revolution. His translation of Bernheim's book on hypnotism and suggestion, and his visit to Nancy in 1889, were steps in his self-education as a psychotherapist.

Even his study of aphasia, his first book, published in 1891 and dedicated to Breuer, subtly points to Freud's growing engagement with psychology. *On the Conception of the Aphasias: A Critical Study* is a distinguished monograph in neurology, but among his abundant, thoroughly informed citations of authorities, Freud significantly scattered citations of philosophers like John Stuart Mill and psychologists like Hughlings Jackson. Criticizing dominant views of this strange family of speech disorders, he described himself, a little self-consciously, as "fairly isolated." He was beginning to make this sense of solitude into his signature. In fact *On the Aphasias* is, in its technical if lucid way, a revisionist work. Freud's "attempt to shake a convenient and engaging theory of language disturbances" amounted to the introduction of a psychological element into the clinical picture. In tune with the tendency of the time to ascribe mental events to physical causes, other specialists had little doubt that aphasic impairments in speech or understanding must be due to particular, localized lesions in the brain. Freud on the contrary pleaded for recognition that "the significance of the element of [physiological brain] localization has been overestimated in aphasia, and that we are right to concern ourselves once again with the functional conditions of the language apparatus." Surrounded by neurologists, Freud was beginning to seek out psychological causes for psychological effects.

More or less halfheartedly, he continued to employ hypnotic suggestion to relieve his patients of their symptoms and in the winter of 1892, published a short case history detailing one of his therapeutic successes. "If one wanted to make a living from the treatment of patients with nervous ailments," he later commented dryly, "one obviously had to do something for them." He found the conventional treatment of neurasthenics—electrotherapy, which he also tried on his patients—far more unsatisfactory even than hypnotism, and in the early 1890s, he "shoved the electrical apparatus aside," with an obvious sigh of relief.

Freud's letters of those years hint at more far-reaching innovations, especially at a virtually unprecedented alertness to the probable impact of sexual conflicts on neurotic illness. By early 1893, he had translated his conjectures into firm assertions. In one of the extensive memoranda he sent Fliess for comment across the years, Freud put the matter flatly—after warning Fliess to keep the manuscript out of his young wife's hands: "It may be taken as well known that neurasthenia is a frequent consequence of an abnormal sexual life. The assertion, however, which I should like to make and test with observations is that neurasthenia can in fact *only* be a sexual neurosis." Freud did not rule out hereditary disposition as a cause, but he was beginning to insist that "acquired neurasthenia" had sexual instigators: exhaustion caused by masturbation, or *coitus interruptus*. Women, of whose

underlying sensuality Freud had no doubt, seemed comparatively unsuscepti-
ble to neurasthenia; but when they suffered from it, its origins were the same
as in men. The conclusion Freud drew was that neuroses are completely
preventable and completely incurable. Hence "the physician's task is wholly
shifted into prophylaxis."

The whole memorandum shows Freud at his most self-confident, and
reflects his interest in the social implications of nervous illness: he already saw
himself at this early date as physician to society. Healthy sexuality, he argued,
calls for the prevention of venereal diseases and, as an alternative to masturbation, for "free sexual intercourse" between unmarried young men and
women. Hence there is need for a contraceptive superior to the condom,
which is neither safe nor palatable. The memorandum reads like a rapid
incursion into enemy territory; in the monograph that Freud was then preparing with Breuer, *Studies on Hysteria,* the erotic dimension was to retreat into
the wings once more. From that book, Freud would note later, with unconcealed sarcasm, "it would have been hard to guess what significance sexuality
has for the etiology of the neuroses."

THOUGH *Studies on Hysteria* was published only in 1895,* the earliest case
discussed in the book, Breuer's historic encounter with "Anna O.," dates back
to 1880. It ranks as the founding case of psychoanalysis: it impelled Freud
more than once to attribute paternity to Breuer instead of himself. Certainly
Breuer deserves a commanding place in the history of psychoanalysis; in
confiding to his young friend Freud the fascinating story of Anna O., he
generated more unsettling ideas in Freud than he himself was willing to
entertain. One of these confidential sessions took place on a stifling summer
evening in 1883. The scene, as Freud reconstructed it for his fiancée, displays
the unforced intimacy of the two friends and the high level of their professional gossip. "Today was the hottest, most agonizing day of the whole season;
I was already childish from exhaustion. I noticed that I had need of some
uplift and was therefore at Breuer's, from whom I have just come so late. He
had a headache, poor fellow, and was taking salicyl. The first thing he did
was to chase me into the bathtub, from which I emerged rejuvenated. As I
accepted this moist hospitality, my thought was, if little Martha were here,
she would say, that is how we want to organize things, too." It might take
years before they could do so, he mused, but it would happen, if only she kept
on liking him. "Then"—Freud returned to his report—"we took our evening
meal upstairs in our shirt sleeves (I am now writing in a more pronounced

---

*A "Preliminary Communication," jointly written by Breuer and Freud, appeared in 1893. It was
reprinted in 1895 as the first chapter of *Studies on Hysteria.*

negligé), and then came a long medical conversation about 'moral insanity,' and nervous illnesses and strange cases." The two men became more and more personal in their talk as they discussed Martha's friend Bertha Pappenheim "once again." This was the patient whom Breuer would lend immortality under the pseudonym Anna O.

Breuer had begun treating this interesting hysteric in December 1880, and stayed with the case for a year and a half. In mid-November 1882, Breuer told Freud about Anna O. for the first time. Then, on that hot midsummer night of 1883, Freud informed his fiancée, Breuer had revealed "some things" about Bertha Pappenheim that "I am supposed to repeat only 'once I am married to Martha.' " When he went to Paris, Freud tried to interest Charcot in this remarkable case, but "the great man," probably persuaded that his own patients were extraordinary enough, showed indifference. Yet Freud, intrigued by Anna O. and disappointed by the therapeutic effects of hypnotic suggestion, made Breuer talk to him about her again. When the two nerve specialists put together their studies on hysteria in the early 1890s, Anna O. took pride of place.

One reason why Anna O. was so exemplary a patient is that she did much of the imaginative work herself. Considering the importance that Freud would learn to attribute to the analyst's gift for listening, it is only fitting that a patient should contribute almost as much to the making of psychoanalytic theory as did her therapist, Breuer, or for that matter the theorist, Freud. Breuer rightly claimed a quarter century later that his treatment of Bertha Pappenheim contained "the germ cell of the whole of psychoanalysis." But it was Anna O. who made consequential discoveries, and it would be Freud, not Breuer, who assiduously cultivated them until they yielded a rich and unsuspected harvest.

There are contradictions and obscurities in successive versions of the case, but this much is more or less beyond dispute: In 1880, when Anna O. fell ill, she was twenty-one. She was, in Freud's words, a young woman of "exceptional cultivation and talents," kindly and philanthropic, given to works of charity, energetic and at times obstinate, and exceedingly clever. "Physically healthy," Breuer noted in his case report, "menstruates regularly. . . . Intelligence considerable; excellent memory, astonishingly acute [gift for] combinations and keen intuition; hence attempts to deceive her always fail." He added that her "strong intellect" could "also digest solid nourishment," but while she needed that nourishment, she had not received it since she left school. And so, condemned to a dull existence amidst her strait-laced Jewish family, she had long been inclined to escape into "systematic daydreaming," into what she liked to call her "private theater." Breuer was sympathetic as he watched her domestic predicament. "Very monotonous life, wholly restricted to her family," his report goes on in its telegraphic style, "substitute is sought in passionate love for her father, who spoils her, and indulgence in highly developed poetic-fantastic talent." She was, Breuer thought (as Freud recalled with astonishment and wry disbelief) "sexually astonishingly undeveloped."

The event that precipitated her hysteria was the fatal illness of her father, to whom she was, as Breuer had not failed to observe, greatly attached. Until the last two months of his life, when she became too ill to take care of him, she had nursed him devotedly, tirelessly, to the detriment of her own health. During these months of being his nurse, she had developed increasingly incapacitating symptoms: weakness induced by loss of appetite, a severe nervous cough. By December, after half a year of her exhausting regimen, she was afflicted with a convergent squint. Up to this time, she had been an energetic, vital young woman; now she became the pathetic victim of disabling ailments. She suffered from headaches, intervals of excitement, curious disturbances of vision, partial paralyses and loss of sensation.

Early in 1881, her symptomatology grew still more bizarre. She experienced mental lapses, long somnolent episodes, rapid shifts of mood, hallucinations about black snakes, skulls, and skeletons, mounting difficulties with her speech. At times, she regressed in her syntax and grammar; at times, she could speak only English, or French and Italian. She developed two distinct, highly contrasting personalities, one of them extremely unruly. When her father died in April, she responded with shocked excitement which died away to a stupor, and her array of symptoms became more alarming than before. Breuer visited her daily, at evening, while she was in a condition of self-induced hypnosis. She would tell stories, sad, at times charming, and, as she and Breuer discovered together, this talking out temporarily relieved her symptoms. Thus began an epoch-making collaboration between a gifted patient and her attentive physician: Anna O. described this procedure, felicitously, as her "talking cure," or, humorously, as "chimney sweeping." It proved cathartic as it awakened important memories and disposed of powerful emotions she had been unable to recall, or express, when she was her normal self. When Breuer took Freud into his confidence about Anna O., he did not neglect to tell him about this process of catharsis.

The turning point in her talking cure came during the hot spring of 1882, when Anna O. underwent a spell resembling hydrophobia. Though parched with thirst, she was unable to drink until one evening, during her hypnotic state, she told Breuer she had seen her English lady-companion—whom she disliked—letting her little dog drink out of a glass. Once her suppressed disgust came out into the open, the hydrophobia disappeared. Breuer was impressed, and adopted this unorthodox mode of securing relief. He hypnotized Anna O. and observed that she could, under hypnosis, trace each of her symptoms in turn to the occasion that had given rise to it during her father's illness. In this way, Breuer reported, all of her various symptoms, her paralytic contractions and her anesthesias, her double and distorted vision, her various hallucinations, and the rest, were "talked away"—*wegerzählt.* Breuer granted that this talking away had proved far from easy. Anna O.'s recollections were often hazy, and her symptoms reappeared with painful vividness precisely while she was sweeping the chimney of her mind. But her participation in the talking cure grew more and more energetic—Breuer praised it a dozen years later with unfeigned admiration. Her symptoms turned out to be residues of feelings and impulses she had felt obliged to suppress. By June 1882, Breuer noted in conclusion, all of Anna O.'s symptoms were gone. "Then she left Vienna for a trip, but still needed a good deal of time before she wholly regained her mental balance. Since then she has enjoyed complete health."

Questions about Breuer's case history arise at this point. The truth is that at the conclusion of the treatment, Breuer referred Anna O. to Dr. Robert Binswanger's highly regarded Swiss sanatorium Bellevue, at Kreuzlingen. In mid-September 1882, three months after her symptoms had presumably disappeared, Anna O. made a brave attempt to give an account of her condition. She was still at Kreuzlingen and, she reported in her near-perfect English, was "totaly deprived of the faculty to speak, to understand or to read German." In addition, she was suffering from "strong neuralgic pain" and from "shorter or longer absences," which she called "timemissing." No doubt she was much better. "I only get realy nervous, anxious and disposed to cry, when the but too well motived fear to lose the German language for longer again, takes possession of me." Even a year later, she was by no means well, and was suffering recurrent relapses. Her subsequent career was remarkable: she became a pioneering social worker, an effective leader in feminist causes and Jewish women's organizations. These achievements testify to a substantial measure of recovery, but Breuer, in *Studies on Hysteria,* compressed with little warrant a difficult, often disrupted time of improvement into a complete cure.

Writing up Anna O. in 1895, Breuer casually noted that he had "suppressed a large number of quite interesting details." They were, as we know from Freud's correspondence, more than just interesting: they constitute the reasons why Breuer had been so reluctant to publish this case in the first place. It was one thing to recognize hysterical conversion symptoms as the meaningful response to particular traumas, and the neurosis as not simply a flowering of some hereditary disposition but a possible consequence of a stifling environment. It was quite another thing to admit that the ultimate origins of hysteria, and some of its florid manifestations, were sexual in nature. "I confess," Breuer wrote later, "that the plunging into sexuality in theory and practice is not to my taste." The full story of Anna O., to which Freud had alluded with veiled phrases here and there, was erotic theater that Breuer found exceedingly disconcerting.

Many years after, in 1932, writing to Stefan Zweig, one of his most impassioned advocates, Freud recalled "what really happened with Breuer's patient." This, he reported, is what Breuer had told him long ago: "On the evening of the day that all her symptoms had been brought under control, he was called to her once more, found her confused and writhing with abdominal cramps. Asked what was the matter, she replied, 'Now comes Dr. B.'s child.'" At that moment, Freud commented, Breuer held "the key in his hand," but, unable or unwilling to use it, "he dropped it. With all his great mental endowment he had nothing Faustian about him. In conventional horror he took to flight and left the patient to a colleague." It is most likely that Breuer had been hinting at this hysterical pregnancy that July evening in 1883, when he had told Freud things he could repeat only after Martha Bernays had become Martha Freud.

THE CASE OF Anna O. did more to divide Freud and Breuer than to bring them together; it speeded the sad decline and eventual collapse of a long-standing, rewarding friendship. As Freud saw it, he was the explorer who had had the courage of Breuer's discoveries; in pushing them as far as they would go, with all their erotic undertones, he had inevitably alienated the munificent mentor who had presided over his early career. Breuer once said of himself that he was ridden by the "demon 'But,'" and Freud was inclined to interpret such reservations—*any* reservations—as craven desertion from the field of battle. No doubt quite as irritating, Freud owed Breuer money that Breuer did not want him to repay. His disagreeable grumbling about Breuer in the 1890s is a classic case of ingratitude, the resentment of a proud debtor against his older benefactor.

For over a decade, Breuer had supplied Freud unstintingly with much-needed, and for years warmly appreciated, encouragement, affections, hospitality, and financial support. Freud's characteristic gesture of naming his first child after Frau Breuer, an appealing, attractive friend to the penniless and aspiring young doctor, was a cheerful acknowledgment of the thoughtful patronage coming his way. That had been in 1887. Yet as early as 1891, relations between the two men had begun to change. That year Freud was deeply disappointed with Breuer's reception of *On the Aphasias,* which, as we know, Freud had dedicated to him. "Hardly thanked me," Freud reported to his sister-in-law Minna, a little bewildered, "was very much embarrassed and said all sorts of incomprehensibly bad things about it, remembered nothing good; at the end, to mollify me, [he offered] the compliment that the writing is excellent." In the following year, Freud reported some "battles" with his "companion." By 1893, as he and Breuer were publishing their joint preliminary report on hysteria, he was growing impatient and thought that Breuer was "standing in the way of my advancement in Vienna." A year later he reported that "scientific contacts with Breuer have ceased." By 1896, he was avoiding Breuer and professed that he no longer needed to see him. His idealization of his old friend, doomed as such idealizations are to disappointment, had generated some vitriolic reactions in him. "My anger at Breuer receives ever new nourishment," he wrote in 1898. One of his patients had reported that Breuer was telling people he had "given up his contacts" with Freud because "he cannot agree with my style of life and the management of my finances." Freud, who was still in Breuer's debt, qualified this as "neurotic insincerity." Avuncular, perhaps misplaced, friendly concern would have been a better name for it.

After all, Freud's debt to Breuer was more than pecuniary. It was Breuer who had been instrumental in teaching Freud about catharsis and had helped to free him from the futile mental therapies current in his day; it was Breuer who had been willing to tell Freud in the most suggestive detail about Anna O., a case to which Breuer, after all, looked back with mixed emotions. Besides, Breuer's scientific procedure could serve Freud as a generally admirable model: Breuer was both a fertile generator of scientific hunches and a close observer, even if at times his fertility outran his observation—as did Freud's. Indeed, Breuer was only too aware of the gap often yawning between conjecture and knowledge; in *Studies on Hysteria,* he quoted Theseus in *A Midsummer Night's Dream* on tragedy, "The best in this kind are but shadows," and expressed the hope that there might be at least some correspondence between the physician's idea of hysteria and the real thing.

Nor did Breuer deny the influence of sexual conflicts on neurotic suffering. But Anna O., it seems, with her youthful attractions, her charming helplessness, and her very name, Bertha, reawakened in Breuer all his dormant oedipal longings for his own mother, also called Bertha, who had died as a young woman when he was three. There were moments in the mid-1890s when Breuer professed himself a convert to Freud's sexual theories, only to be overpowered by his ambivalence, by his demon "But." Then he would retreat to a more conservative posture. "Not long ago," Freud reported to Fliess in 1895, "Breuer gave a big speech about me" to the Vienna society of physicians, "and introduced himself as a *converted* adherent to the sexual etiology" of the neuroses. "When I thanked him for this in private, he destroyed my pleasure by saying, 'I don't believe it all the same.'" The retraction baffled Freud: "Do you understand this? I don't." Five years later, only a little less baffled, Freud told Fliess about a woman patient whom Breuer had referred to him, and with whom he had had, after severe frustrations, a stunning analytic success. When she confessed her "extraordinary improvement" to Breuer, he "clapped his hands and exclaimed over and over, 'He is right after all, then.' " But Freud was not inclined to appreciate this belated tribute, even though Breuer had obviously shown his confidence in him by sending this difficult patient; he wrote it off as coming from "a worshiper of success." By this time, with Freud's memories of his friend's loyal services wiped out, Breuer could do no right. Freud could see Breuer more judiciously only after his self-analysis had taken hold, some of his emotional storms had abated, and his friendship with Fliess was decaying. "I have not despised him for a long time," he told Fliess in 1901; "I have felt his strength." It is surely not without significance that Freud was now, after several years of self-analysis, in a position to make this discovery. Yet for all his strength, Breuer had come to see the case of Anna O. as excessively demanding and downright embarrassing. "I vowed at the time," he recalled, "that I would not go through such an ordeal again." It was a case he never forgot, but not a case from which he could ever really profit. When Freud's biographer Fritz Wittels intimated that Breuer had managed to dispose of the memory of Anna O. after some time, Freud tartly commented in the margin, "Nonsense!" The psychoanalytic process is a struggle with resistances, and Breuer's rejection of the elemental, shocking truths that this process may uncover is a plain instance of such a maneuver. Fliess, Freud's necessary friend, had proved much more receptive.

HYSTERICS, PROJECTS, AND EMBARRASSMENTS

 Freud had his own resistances to battle and overcome, but judging from the cases he presented in *Studies on Hysteria,* he made learning from his patients a kind of program. He was a willing, highly self-conscious apprentice: in 1897, writing to Fliess, he called his analysand "Frau Cäcilie M." his "instructor"—*Lehrmeisterin.* No doubt, Cäcilie M., really Baroness Anna von Lieben, had been one of Freud's most interesting, probably the most time-consuming, of his early patients. She was his "principal client," his "prima donna." Rich, intelligent, sensitive, literary, belonging

to a sizable clan of eminent Austrian Jewish families Freud came to know well, she had been plagued for years by a variety of extraordinary and puzzling symptoms—hallucinations, spasms, and the strange habit of converting insults or criticisms into severe facial neuralgias, virtual "slaps in the face." Freud had sent her to Charcot and, in 1889, had taken her with him when he went to Nancy on a study-visit to the hypnotist Bernheim. Across the years, she had taught him much about the meaning of symptoms and about therapeutic technique. But his other hysterics, too, had been Freud's instructors. He would look back in long retrospect at his early ventures into psychological analysis with marked disdain. "I know," he wrote in 1924, recalling his report on "Frau Emmy von N.," "that no analyst can read this case history without a pitying smile." But this was being too harsh and wholly anachronistic. Freud's treatment of Emmy von N. and the others was, to be sure, primitive work from the perspective of fully developed psychoanalytic technique. But the significance of these analysands for the history of psychoanalysis derives from their capacity to demonstrate to Freud some of its most important rudiments.

The hysterics Freud treated in these heroic days displayed an astonishing assemblage of conversion symptoms, from painful legs to chilly feelings, depressive moods to intermittent hallucinations. Freud was not yet prepared to eliminate the element of heredity, the "neuropathic" legacy, from his diagnoses. But he now preferred to look for early traumatic experiences as clues to these hidden sources of his patients' odd disabilities. He was becoming persuaded that his neurotics' secrets were what Breuer called *secrets d'alcôve*, sexual conflicts hidden from the sufferers themselves. This was, at least, what he thought they were telling him, if often in the most oblique ways.

Listening became, for Freud, more than an art; it became a method, a privileged road to knowledge that his patients mapped out for him. One of the guides to whom Freud remained grateful was Emmy von N., really Baroness Fanny Moser, a wealthy middle-aged widow whom Freud saw in 1889 and 1890 and treated with Breuer's hypnoanalytic technique. She was afflicted with convulsive tics, spastic speech inhibitions, and recurrent, terrifying hallucinations about dead rats and writhing snakes. In the course of the treatment, she produced traumatic, to Freud highly interesting, memories—a girl cousin being taken away to an insane asylum, her mother lying on the floor after a stroke. But even better, she became a vocal object lesson for her physician. When Freud insistently questioned her, she grew annoyed, "pretty surly," and demanded that he stop "asking her where this or that came from, but let her tell me what she had to say." He had already recognized that, tedious and repetitive as her recitals were, he gained nothing by interrupting her, but had to hear her stories out to the end, point after laborious point. Emmy von N., as he told her daughter in 1918, also taught him something else: "Treatment by means of hypnosis is a senseless and worthless proceeding." This was a decisive moment; it impelled him "to create the more sensible psychoanalytic therapy." If there was ever a physician poised to convert his mistakes into sources of insight, it was Freud.

In allowing him to see that hypnosis is in fact "senseless and worthless," Emmy von N. helped Freud to free himself from Breuer. In their joint "Preliminary Communication" of 1893, Freud and Breuer had stated in a memorable sentence that "the hysteric suffers mainly from reminiscences." Down to the early 1890s, Freud had attempted to elicit in Breuer's manner, by means of hypnosis, the significant memories that his patients were reluctant to produce. The scenes thus brought to mind often had a cathartic effect. But some patients were not hypnotizable, and uncensored talking struck Freud as a far superior investigative device. In his gradual abandonment of hypnosis Freud was not just making a virtue out of a defect; the shift amounted, rather, to the momentous adoption of a new mode of treatment. The technique of free association was in the making.

Freud celebrated the brilliant results that this new technique could produce by lingering over the case history of "Fräulein Elisabeth von R.," whom he hypnotized only briefly at first. His report on this patient, who came to him in the fall of 1892, demonstrates how systematically he was now cultivating his gift for close observation. The first clue to a diagnosis of Elisabeth von R.'s neurosis was her erotic arousal as he pressed or pinched her thighs during a physical examination. "Her face," Freud noticed, "assumed a peculiar expression, one of pleasure rather than of pain; she cried out—somewhat, I could not help thinking, as with a voluptuous tickling—her face flushed, she threw back her head, closed her eyes, her trunk bent backward." She was experiencing the sexual pleasure that she denied herself in conscious life.

It was talk, though, rather than observation, however perceptive, that proved the key to her cure. In this analysis, "the first full-length analysis of a hysteria I undertook," Freud and Elisabeth von R. "cleared away" the "pathogenic psychological material." It was a procedure "we liked to compare to the technique of excavating a buried city." Freud encouraged his patient to associate freely. When, during her silences, he asked her what was going on in her head, and she replied, "Nothing," he refused to accept this for an answer. Here was another significant psychological mechanism that his cooperative (or, rather, uncooperative) patients were demonstrating to him: Freud was learning about resistance. It was resistance that kept Elisabeth von R.

from talking; it was her willful forgetting, he thought, that had produced her conversion symptoms in the first place. The only way to get rid of her pain was to talk it away.

The case flooded Freud with ideas. Elisabeth von R.'s symptoms began to "put in a word, too": they flared up at the moment their onset was being talked out, and subsided once she had told her story in full. But Freud also had to absorb the harder lesson that the cure was not a melodramatic explosion of insights. A single recital was rarely enough; traumas had to be "worked through." The final ingredient in Elisabeth von R.'s recovery was an interpretation of the evidence that Freud offered and that she vehemently resisted for some time: she loved her brother-in-law and had repressed wicked longings for her sister's death. Her acceptance of this immoral wish put an end to her suffering. "In the spring of 1894," Freud reported, "I heard that she was going to a private ball, to which I managed to secure access, and I did not let the opportunity escape me of seeing my former patient flying by in a brisk dance."

Later, talking to her daughter, Elisabeth von R., who had been born Ilona Weiss in Budapest in 1867, discounted Freud's resolution of her neurotic symptoms. She described Freud as "just a young, bearded nerve specialist they sent me to." He had tried "to persuade me that I was in love with my brother-in-law, but that wasn't really so." Yet, her daughter adds, Freud's account of her mother's family history was substantially correct, and her mother's marriage was happy. The patient may have chosen, more or less unconsciously, to repress Freud's interpretation of her troubles. Or Freud may have read unacceptable passions into her free, uninhibited stream of eloquence. In any event, here was one of his former patients—a hysteric who had often suffered severe pains in her legs when she was standing or walking—dancing the night away. Freud the physician-researcher, ambivalent about his career in medicine, could take satisfaction in her restored vitality.

BY 1892, WHEN "Miss Lucy R." came into treatment with Freud, he had recognized the value of his purposeful attentiveness. Her most obtrusive symptom, which he managed to dissolve after working with her for nine weeks, was a sensation of the offensive smell of burnt pudding, associated with feelings of depression. Instead of minimizing this rather peculiar olfactory hallucination, Freud let it guide him to the origins of Miss Lucy's malaise. The lawfulness of the mind and the picturesque language of symptoms were becoming clear to him: there had to be a real and sufficient reason why a particular smell should be linked to a particular mood. But that link, he recognized, would become visible only if this distraught English governess could recapture relevant memories. Yet she would do so only if she "let her criticism rest"—if she allowed her thoughts to meander without controlling them with rational objections. Freud thus continued to apply with Lucy R. what he had been practicing with Elisabeth von R.: free association. At the same time, Lucy R. made it plain to Freud that humans are only too unwilling to let criticism rest; they are apt to reject their associations on the ground that they are trivial, irrational, repetitious, irrelevant, or obscene. During the 1890s, Freud remained a most active, almost aggressive listener; he interpreted his patients' confessions rapidly and skeptically, probing for deeper levels of distress. But the alert passivity of the psychoanalyst, which Freud would later call "evenly suspended" or "evenly hovering" attention, was beginning to enter his repertory. He owed Elisabeth von R. and Lucy R. and his other hysterics a great deal. By 1892, Freud had assembled the outlines of psychoanalytic technique: close observation, apt interpretation, free association unencumbered by hypnosis, and working through.

Freud had still another lesson in store for him, one that would preoccupy him throughout his career. In a charming vignette, recording a kind of single-session analysis, he describes the case of "Katharina," an eighteen-year-old country girl who had served him at an Austrian mountain inn. "Not long ago," he informed Fliess in August 1893, "I was consulted by the innkeeper's daughter on the Rax; it was a beautiful case for me." Having noticed that Freud was a physician, Katharina ventured to confide to him her nervous symptoms—shortness of breath, dizziness, a frightful choking feeling—and to ask his advice. Freud, on holiday, eager to escape his neurasthenics and find refreshment in a climbing excursion on the Rax, instead found himself back practicing his profession. Neuroses seemed to crop up everywhere. Resigned and intrigued, Freud led his "patient" through a straightforward interview. She disclosed (so he reported) that when she was fourteen, an uncle had made several coarse but unsuccessful attempts to seduce her and that about two years later, she had seen him lying on top of a girl cousin. That is when her symptoms had begun. An innocent and inexperienced girl at fourteen, she had found her uncle's attentions most unwelcome; but it was only when she had seen him on top of her cousin that she had connected them with intercourse. The memory disgusted her and had generated an anxiety neurosis compounded by hysteria. Her artless recital helped to discharge her feelings, her moody manner gave way to sparkling, healthy liveliness, and Freud hoped that she would derive some lasting benefit from this conversation. "I have not seen her again."

But he thought of her: three decades later, Freud added to *Studies on Hysteria* a confessional footnote in which he dispensed with discretion and confessed that the man who had tried to molest Katharina was not her uncle, but her father. Freud was severe with himself. There are better ways to disguise a patient's identity: "A distortion like the one I undertook in this instance should be definitely avoided in a case history." No doubt the twin aims of psychoanalysis—to provide therapy and to generate theory—are usually compatible and interdependent. But at times they clash: the rights of the patient to privacy may conflict with the demands of science for public discussion. It was a difficulty Freud would confront again, and not with his patients alone; as his own most revealing analysand, he found self-disclosure at once painful and necessary. The compromises he engineered were never wholly satisfactory, either to him or to his readers.

With all their problems, cases like this, whether beautiful like Katharina's or not, advanced technique and theory alike: by 1895, in *Studies on Hysteria* and in his confidential communications to Fliess, Freud was moving toward some far-reaching generalizations. Accumulating and ordering pieces of the great puzzle that is mind, he was evolving the psychoanalytic ideas, and the psychoanalytic vocabulary, that would become canonical by the end of the century. He kept Fliess fully informed as his ideas developed and changed, sending to Berlin a barrage of case vignettes, aphorisms, dreams, not to forget the "drafts," those rehearsals for papers and monographs in which he recorded his findings and experimented with ideas—drafts on anxiety, on melancholia, on paranoia. "A man like me," Freud told Fliess the year *Studies* was published, with the panache of a researcher obsessed, "cannot live without a hobby horse, without a dominating passion, without—to speak with Schiller—a tyrant, and he has come my way. And in his service I now know no moderation. It is psychology."

HOWEVER EXIGENT, FREUD's tyrant invaded but did not compromise his domestic tranquility. His private life was as settled and serene as he would let it be. In the fall of 1891, the Freuds had moved to Berggasse 19, to an apartment in a scarcely distinguished but, it turned out, most convenient neighborhood. The house remained his headquarters for forty-seven years. Though busy and preoccupied, Freud did not slight the family's claims on him. In October 1895, he ran a birthday party, "20 individuals strong," for Mathilde, then eight, and he took time for other cheerful domestic occasions. When, in the spring of 1896, his sister Rosa married, he found his daughter Sophie, then just three, with "curled hair and a wreath of forget-me-nots on her head," the "most beautiful thing" at the wedding. Freud was visibly fond of his "chicks," and, for that matter, of his "hen."

The "second generation" in particular was steadily on Freud's mind. In his letters he often interrupted the flow of abstruse conjectures or clinical histories with news about his brood. He reported to Fliess some of Oliver's beguiling sayings: when an "enthusiastic" aunt asked the little boy what he wanted to become, he answered, "In February, aunt, five years." Freud's gloss on this comment, and on his children in general: "In their multifariousness, they are very amusing." With the same amusement, Freud told Fliess about his youngest, Anna, whose aggressiveness, somewhat precocious at the age of two, he found endearing: "Not long ago, Annerl complained that Mathilde had eaten all the apples, and demanded that someone slit open her belly (as in the fairy tale of the little goat). The child is developing charmingly." As for "Sopherl," she had entered, "at three and a half, the stage of beauté," and, one might add, remained there. Perhaps the child who provided Freud with the most consistent entertainment was Martin, who started writing little verses at an early age, called himself a poet, and intermittently suffered attacks of "harmless *poet*itis." Perhaps half a dozen of Martin's childhood productions figure in Freud's letters to Fliess. The first to be reported runs, in its entirety:

> Says the doe, "Hare,
> Is your throat when you swallow still sore?"*

Martin was then not yet eight. The following year, his mind (like that of many Central European children) running on the fox, that clever, unscrupulous, and hence most popular animal of folk tale and fables, he perpetrated some verses on the "seduction of the goose by the fox." In Martin Freud's version, the fox's declaration of love ran:

> I love you,
> Through and through,
> Kiss me, do!
> Among all the rest
> Of the beasts I could like you the best.

"Don't you find the structure remarkable?" Freud genially inquired.†

All too often, though, Freud's pleasure in his children was punctured by anxiety. "Much joy could be had from the little ones," he wrote, "if there were not so many scares." The principal, almost monotonous, serial drama in his close-knit household centered on the children's recurrent ailments—all of them duly reported to Fliess, himself the father of young children. Freud's children had a way, only too well-known to large families, of passing on their

---

*" 'Hase,' spricht das Reh, / 'Tut's Dir beim Schlucken im Halse noch weh?' " (Freud to Fliess, May 16, 1897. *Freud–Fliess*, 260 [244].)

†"Ich liebe Dich, / herzinniglich, / komm, küsse mich, / Du könntest mir von allen / Tieren am besten gefallen." (Freud to Fliess, March 24, 1898. Ibid., 334 [304].)

illnesses to their siblings. Freud came to face the never-ending bouts of stomach upsets and catarrhs and chicken pox with an experienced father's equanimity or, as a long string of bulletins to Fliess attests, an anxious father's alarm.

Fortunately, the good domestic news outweighed the bad. "My little Annerl is well again," runs one characteristic report, "and the other animals, too, are again growing and grazing properly." Financially, too, things were going better—some of the time. Long condemned to husband his florins, Freud enjoyed welcome intervals of affluence. Late in 1895, he had the satisfaction of seeing himself "beginning to dictate my fees." This, he commented sturdily, was how it should be: "One cannot do without people who have the courage to think new things before they can demonstrate them." Yet even toward the end of the century he was still not out of debt; even after he became a prominent specialist, he would sometimes find his consulting room empty. Then he would brood on his children and their financial future.

One indispensable ingredient in Freud's domestic arrangements was his sister-in-law Minna. During his engagement to Martha Bernays, he had written Minna intimate and affectionate letters, signed himself "Your Brother Sigmund," and called her "My Treasure." In those years, she too had been engaged, to Ignaz Schönberg, one of Freud's friends. But Schönberg died young, in 1886, of tuberculosis, and after his death, Minna Bernays apparently resigned herself to spinsterhood. She grew heavier, more jowly, becoming exceedingly plain; she looked older than her sister Martha, though she was in fact four years younger. Long a welcome visitor at Berggasse 19, she became a permanent fixture there in the mid-1890s. She was the intellectual sister, known for her witty remarks and capable of following Freud's imaginative flights at least some of the way. In the pioneering years, Freud thought her his "closest confidante," along with Fliess.* She remained close to him; in summer, the two occasionally visited Swiss resorts or Italian cities alone.† At all times, she was an integral member of the household, helping to manage Freud's youngsters and taking them to resorts.

WHILE BY THE mid-1890s, his domestic life and, somewhat less securely his medical practice, seemed stable and settled, Freud's scientific prospects were still hard to predict. He was publishing papers on hysteria, obsessions and

*In the 1890s, as Freud told Marie Bonaparte many years later, it had been Fliess and Minna Bernays alone who had believed in him. (Marie Bonaparte to Ernest Jones, December 16, 1953. Jones papers, Archives of the British Psycho-Analytical Society, London.)

†The rumor, launched by Carl G. Jung, that Freud had an affair with Minna Bernays lacks convincing evidence. (For a detailed discussion of this issue, see the bibliographical essay for this chapter.)

phobias, anxiety neuroses—all in their exploratory way reports from the battlefields of psychology. Despite the reassurance provided by Fliess's continued friendship and support, Freud often felt engulfed by indifference, silence, hostility. When *Studies on Hysteria* received a mixed, quizzical, but far from dismissive review from the eminent neurologist Adolf von Strümpell, Freud characterized it, with exaggerated sensitiveness, as "mean." Admittedly, the review was unbalanced, somewhat perfunctory; Strümpell gave his readers no inkling of the case histories and expended unnecessary space worrying over the use of hypnotism in the treatment of hysterics. But at the same time, Strümpell welcomed the book as "pleasing proof" that the perception of hysteria as essentially psychogenic was gaining ground. To call such a review *niederträchtig* was to display a tenderness to criticism that was threatening to become a habit with Freud.

His tensions emerged in bouts of depression and distressing physical symptoms—some of them doubtless psychosomatic. Two or three times, beset by nasal catarrh, he reluctantly gave up his beloved cigars on Fliess's orders. For Fliess to outlaw cigars was only too easy; his one defect, Freud thought, was that he did not smoke. But Freud could not sustain the prohibition for long and, in a mood of defiance, soon lapsed. "I am not observing your ban on smoking," he told Fliess in November 1893; "do you think it's such a glorious fate to live many long years in misery?" He needed his cigars for his work. As it was, even while he was smoking, his moments of euphoria, evanescent bursts of joy, were subverted by intervals of hesitation and gloom. His condition, as he summed it up, was "in turn proud and blissful, embarrassed and miserable." His letters to Fliess chart the roller-coaster ride of his emotions. "Wild, isn't it, my correspondence?" he exclaimed one October day in 1895. "For two weeks I was in a writing fever, thought I had the secret already, now I know I don't have it yet." Still, he insisted, he was not losing heart.

Nor was he. "Now keep listening," he greeted Fliess a few days later. "During a diligent night the previous week, burdened with that measure of pain which produces the optimum for my brain activity, the barriers suddenly lifted, the covers dropped, and from the details of the neuroses to the determinants of consciousness all had become transparent." Only eleven days later, Freud was no longer so confident. He was "dead tired," managed to produce one of his migraine attacks, and reported that "the pleasure-pain explanation of hysteria and obsessional neurosis, announced with so much enthusiasm, has become dubious to me." He had "rebelled" against his "tyrant," psychology, he told Fliess, felt "overworked, irritated, confused," beaten and disillusioned, and wondered why he had troubled Fliess with his ideas at all. Something, he thought, was still missing. But he kept working. The symptoms he was so desperately trying to understand were, in part, his own; in the midst of his periodic headaches, he sent Fliess a memorandum on migraine. One can see why Freud craved reassurance.

THE VENTURE THAT triggered in Freud the most wildly oscillating fantasies of fame and failure was an ambitious project for a scientific psychology, which he had conceived in the early spring of 1895. He planned nothing less than "to investigate what form the theory of mental functioning assumes if one introduces the quantitative point of view, a sort of economics of nerve forces; and, second, to extract from psychopathology a gain for normal psychology." This was the psychology that had beckoned to him from afar for so long.

His "Psychology for Neurologists," as he had called it to Fliess in April, "tormented" him. "I have devoted every free minute in the past weeks, spent the night hours from eleven to two with such fantasizing, translating, and guessing," he wrote in May. He was so overworked that he could no longer muster any interest in his ordinary practice. On the other hand, his neurotic patients gave him "great pleasure," because they had so much to contribute to his researches: "Almost everything is confirmed daily, new things are added, and the certainty of having the heart of the matter in hand does me good." The Freud of these years might describe himself as middle-aged, but he had the buoyant endurance and, in face of intermittent disappointments, the hardy resilience of a young researcher.

He needed all the concentrated energies he could command. Either of Freud's two scientific aims—to introduce the quantitative viewpoint, or to compel psychopathology to inform general psychology—would have been far-reaching enough. Together, they constituted a utopian enterprise. During September and early October 1895, after one of his "congresses" with Fliess, in a rush of feverish creativity, he put his "Psychology for Neurologists" on paper. On October 8, he sent it off to Fliess for criticism. His self-imposed task made him suffer. In the travail of composition, he likened his investigations to an exhausting mountain climb, with peak after successive peak leaving him breathless. By November, he could no longer understand "the mental state in which I hatched the Psychology." He felt the way an explorer must feel who has staked his all on a promising trail that in the end leads nowhere. Freud found the immediate rewards for his hectic labors diffuse and insubstantial. He never took the trouble to finish the project and studiously ignored it in his autobiographical retrospects. Yet if it is a failure, it is a magnificent one. The "Psychology" does not precisely read like an early draft of psychoanalytic theory, but Freud's ideas on the drives, on repression and defense, on the mental economy with its contending forces of energies, and on the human animal as the wishing animal, are all adumbrated here.

FREUD'S INTENTION, AS he announced it at the start of his massive memorandum, was "to furnish a natural-scientific psychology, that is, to represent psychical processes as quantitatively determined states of specifiable material particles, and thus make those processes graphic and consistent." He wanted to show how the mental machinery works, how it receives, masters, and discharges excitations. Outlining the project in a burst of optimism, he told Fliess, "Everything seemed to mesh, the gear mechanism fitted together, one got the impression the thing now really was a machine that would shortly go by itself. The three systems of neurons; the free and bound states of quantity; the primary and secondary processes; the principal tendency and the compromise tendency of the nervous system; the two biological rules of attention and defense; the indications of quality, reality, and thought; the condition of the psychosexual group—the sexual determination of repression; finally, the factors of consciousness as a function of perception—all that was right and is still right today! Naturally, I can't contain myself for sheer pleasure."

Freud's mechanistic metaphors and his technical vocabulary—"neurons," "quantity," "biological rules of attention and defense," and the rest—were the language of his world, of his medical training and Vienna's General Hospital. His attempt to establish psychology as a natural science on the solid basis of neurology fits the aspirations of the positivists with whom Freud had studied, and whose hopes and fantasies he now worked to realize. He never abandoned his ambition to found a scientific psychology. In his *Outline of Psychoanalysis*, the final summing up which he wrote in London during the last year of his life and left, like the project, unfinished, Freud claimed flatly that the stress on the unconscious in psychoanalysis enabled it "to take its place as a natural science like any other." In the same meaty fragment he speculated that in the future, psychoanalysts might "exercise a direct influence, by means of particular chemical substances, on the amounts of energy and their distribution in the mental apparatus." The formulation echoes his program of 1895 almost word for word.

With much justice, Freud's project has been called Newtonian. It is Newtonian in its effort at subjecting the laws of mind to the laws of motion, something psychologists had been trying to do since the middle of the eighteenth century. It is Newtonian, too, in seeking propositions open to empirical verification. Its very admissions of ignorance echo Newton's scientific style, his celebrated philosophical modesty. While Newton had frankly conceded that the nature of gravitation remained a mystery, he had insisted at the same time that this should not prevent the scientist from recognizing its force and measuring its action. Adopting the same agnostic stance, Freud argued, in 1895 and long after, that even though psychologists had not grasped the secrets of mental energies, they need not give up observing their workings and reducing them to law. In 1920, borrowing his phrasing from Newton directly, Freud still firmly maintained that "we do not feel justified in framing any hypotheses" on the "excitatory processes" in the mind. Yet within these carefully demarcated constraints, Freud was certain that much could be understood about mental functioning.

But the difficulties were daunting. Some of the animating principles governing the mental machinery seemed to Freud fairly clear. The mind is under the sway of the constancy principle, which dictates that it discharge unsettling stimuli which invade it either from within or from without. "This is the principle of neuronal inertia," to use Freud's own technical formulation: "neurons tend to divest themselves of Quantity." They do so because the state of quiescence, of calm after the storm, gives pleasure, and the mind courts pleasure or (which is often much the same thing) evades pain. Yet "flight from the stimulus" alone cannot account for all mental activity; the constancy principle is broken through at point after point. Memories, which played such a prominent role in Freud's thinking then and later, accumulate in the mind as it stores stimuli. More: the mind in search of satisfactions tries to secure them by acting on the real world—perceiving it, reasoning about it, and modifying it to make it yield to persistent wishes. Hence a scientific psychology aiming to account for all of mental life must explain memory, perception, thought, planning, quite as much as the satisfaction of relaxation after the discharge of stimuli.

One way Freud thought to do justice to this diversity of mental work was to postulate three types of neurons, those suitable for receiving stimuli, those transmitting them, and those carrying the contents of consciousness. He was speculating, though not wildly and in the company of other reputable psychologists. But there was much required by his scheme, notably an understanding of the nature and activities of consciousness, that defeated Freud, just as difficulties with similar conjectures were defeating his colleagues. In any event, Freud's ideas, even as he was jotting down his "Psychology," were beginning to move in a very different direction. He was on the verge, not of a psychology for neurologists, but of a psychology for psychologists. The physiological and biological substrata of the mind never lost their importance for Freud, but for several decades they faded into the background as he explored the domains of the unconscious and its manifestations in thought and act—slips, jokes, symptoms, defenses, and, most intriguing of all, dreams.

SOMETIME DURING THE night of July 23–24, 1895—probably, he thought, early in the morning—Freud dreamt a historic dream. It would enter psychoanalytic lore as the dream of Irma's injection. More than four years later, in *The Interpretation of Dreams,* Freud gave it exceptional stature, using it as a paradigm for his theory that dreams are wish fulfillments. At the time he dreamt it, he was hard at work on the project, but was agreeably housed in relaxing surroundings—at Bellevue, the resort villa in a Vienna suburb to which the Freuds often repaired for holidays. The place and time were ideal, not so much for dreaming—Freud dreamt profusely all through the year— but for reflecting on his dreams at leisure. This was, he noted later, the first dream he had "submitted to a detailed interpretation." But though painstaking, meticulous, apparently exhaustive, his report on that interpretation is fragmentary. After tracing each dream element separately to its springs in his recent and remote experience, Freud broke off: "I will not claim that I have completely uncovered the meaning of this dream or that its interpretation is without gaps. I could dwell on it for a long time still, derive further elucidations from it, and discuss new riddles it throws up. I myself know the passages from which further trains of thought could be pursued; but considerations that arise with every dream of one's own restrain me from the work of interpretation." Some of what Freud publicly confessed sounded in fact far from creditable to him; hence a modicum of privacy would seem no more than his due. Freud stood ready to claim it: "Let him who has a rebuke for my reserve ready at hand try to be more candid than I." True enough; few, even the most uninhibited, would have been willing to reveal so much about themselves.

Curiously, Freud's letters to Fliess, normally an inexhaustible resource, only compound the mystery of his selective candor. On July 24, a few hours after he had dreamt his momentous dream, Freud sent an unusually laconic message to his friend in Berlin, addressing him (perhaps a little ambiguously) as his "daimon"—his fate, his inspiration. He wondered why Fliess had not written lately and whether Fliess still cared about his work, asked after Fliess's own ideas, his health, and his wife, and mused on whether the two were destined to be friends only in times of misfortune. In the manner of one good friend writing to another, he closed a little irrelevantly, commenting that he and his family were "living very contentedly" in Bellevue. Not a word about "Irma" or about the work of interpretation that must have engrossed him that day.

In August, Freud hinted to Fliess that he had after long intellectual travail managed to understand "pathological defense and, with that, many important psychological processes." This reads like an oblique allusion to the ideas thrust up by his analysis of the Irma dream. When he met Fliess in Berlin early in September, he may well have canvassed that dream with him. But not until June 1900, almost five years later, did Freud emphatically recall that triumphant moment to Fliess's mind. He was again at Bellevue. After chatting about family news and about the pleasures of a late, flower-scented spring, he asked Fliess rhetorically, "Do you really believe that some day, on this house, one will read on a marble tablet: 'Here revealed itself, on July 24, 1895, the secret of the dream to Dr. Sigm. Freud'?" It was a rhetorical, darkly untrusting question.

Complex messages, betokening much beyond Freud's yearning for fame, crowd into this frequently quoted fantasy. Its cheerful tone seems to conceal a subtle reproach, a belated hint that as Freud solved his dream on that summer day in 1895, he was preoccupied with Fliess's radical defects. Sherlock Holmes would have understood that Freud's long silence was, like the dog that did not bark in the night, weighty with significance. What Freud did not tell Fliess on July 24, 1895, or the readers of *The Interpretation of Dreams,* was that the dream of Irma's injection was a carefully constructed, highly intricate scenario designed at least in part to rescue Freud's idealized image of Fliess in defiance of some damning evidence. A fuller, less protective interpretation of this dream than the one Freud published leads to what must be the most dismaying episode in his life.

The Irma dream that Freud remembered upon awakening is, like most of his dreams, opulent and pellucid. On the surface it is a mixture of family news and professional concerns. There is a large hall in which the Freuds are receiving many guests, among them "Irma," whom Freud identified as a friend of the family, "a young lady I had been treating psychoanalytically." Freud takes her aside to reproach her for not accepting his "solution" and tells her, addressing her with the familiar *du,* that if she still has pains, "it is really your fault." She replies that the choking pains in her throat, stomach, and abdomen are more severe than he knows. Taken aback, Freud studies Irma and wonders if he has not perhaps overlooked some organic ailment. He looks down her throat, and after she hesitantly opens her mouth properly, sees a white patch and some grayish scabs formed like the turbinal bones of the nose. The dream scene then grows crowded with physician-friends of Freud's, all of them in suitable disguise: Oscar Rie, pediatrician to Freud's children; Breuer, that eminence in Vienna's medical circles; and Fliess, too, in the garb of a knowledgeable specialist with whom Freud is on the best of terms. Somehow these doctors—all but Fliess!—prove to have been responsible for Irma's persistent pains. Indeed, Freud dreams that his friend "Otto"—Oscar Rie—has thoughtlessly given Irma an injection. "A propyl preparation, propyls . . . ," Freud stutters, "propionic acid . . . trimethylamin," and "probably with a syringe that was not clean."

In a discussion prefacing his interpretation, Freud disclosed that Irma's hysterical anxiety symptoms had improved in the course of her analysis, but her somatic pains were still troublesome. The day before, Freud had met Rie, who (it seemed to Freud) had obliquely criticized him for not curing Irma entirely; seeking to justify himself, Freud had written out an account of the case for Breuer. While Freud did not trouble to say so, it is obvious that tense as the relations between the two had become, Breuer remained an authority for Freud, someone whose judgment he continued to value and whose criticism he feared.

That was the background Freud offered to account for the dream's origins and for the wish it distorted and dramatized. He interpreted the dream image by image, speech by speech: the reception of guests recalled a comment by his wife anticipating her birthday party; the chemical trimethylamin, his friend Fliess's theories about sexual chemistry; the unclean syringe, his pride in the way he carefully kept *his* syringes clean as he administered two daily morphine injections to an elderly patient. As he followed up one trace after another, Freud's thoughts ramified. They went back to a tragic case in which a drug he had prescribed in good faith and on good authority had led to a patient's death; to another case in which his intervention had exposed a patient to needless risks; to his wife, who had been bothered by her veins during pregnancy and who (as he did not make clear to the reader) was pregnant now. Freud interpreted all, or most, of these memories as associations centering on his proficiency as a healer. The burden of the wish the dream portrayed was, then, that Irma's sufferings should be truly seen as not his fault but the fault of others. "In short, I am conscientious." Conveniently enough, the very friend who seemed to have criticized the sensitive Freud was in the dream an irresponsible and untrustworthy physician. Thus Freud chose to read the dream of Irma's injection as a dream of revenge and of self-reassurance: when all its ideas were brought together they could be labeled, he concluded, "worry over health, one's own and that of others, and a doctor's conscientiousness."

Freud mentioned some additional themes woven into the fabric of this dream—an illness of his eldest daughter, Mathilde, was one of them—while taking care to evade others in his ingenious interpretation. Freud pressing his solution on his patient, Irma refusing to open her mouth properly, to say nothing of the dirty syringe his friend Otto had used, all invite the psychoanalytically inclined reader to reflect on Freud's sexual fantasies. But there was also an omission more important and less visible than these, for Freud's reading constitutes a massive displacement: the doctor whose conscientiousness he wished to establish with this dream was far less himself than Fliess.

The key to this interpretation is the complex identity of Irma herself. Like most central figures in dreams, she was, as Freud insisted, a *Sammelperson,* a "composite." Freud most probably borrowed her chief features from Anna Lichtheim, daughter of his religion teacher Samuel Hammerschlag, a young widow and one of Freud's favorite patients. In unmistakable ways, though—

her youth, her widowhood, her hysteria, her work with Freud, her association with the Freud family, probably her physical symptoms—Anna Lichtheim closely resembled another of Freud's patients, Emma Eckstein. And it was Emma Eckstein who figured as the principal in a medical melodrama of early 1895 in which Freud, and far more, Fliess, played unenviable roles. In Freud's unconscious, making up his dream, the figure of Emma Eckstein and that of Anna Lichtheim seem to have merged to become Irma.

In addition to her hysterical anxiety symptoms, Emma Eckstein suffered severely from pains in, and bloody secretions from, her nose. While he thought her nosebleeds psychogenic, Freud had asked Fliess to examine his patient, lest in searching for the roots of her psychological malaise he overlook a physical ailment. In the Irma dream he worries precisely about making such a faulty diagnosis. Accordingly, Fliess had come to Vienna and operated on Emma Eckstein's nose. But the operation had brought no relief: her pains did not abate, and were exacerbated by abundant hemorrhages and a fetid smell. Alarmed, Freud called in Viennese surgeons, and on March 8, 1895, he related to Fliess what had happened. His old school friend Ignaz Rosanes, a reputable specialist, had met Freud at Emma Eckstein's apartment. She was bleeding from the nose and mouth, and the "fetid odor was very bad." Rosanes "cleaned the surroundings of the opening, pulled out adhesive blood clots, and suddenly pulled at something like a thread, kept pulling." Before he, and Freud, could stop for reflection, "a good half meter of gauze had been taken out of the cavity. The next moment a flood of blood followed, the patient turned white, with bulging eyes and without pulse." Rosanes acted quickly, packing the cavity with fresh gauze, and the bleeding stopped. The whole thing had taken half a minute, but it was enough to make Emma Eckstein "unrecognizable." Freud grasped in an instant just what had happened; confronted with calamity, he felt sick. After her nose had been packed, he "fled" to the next room to drink a bottle of water, and thought himself pretty pathetic. A little glass of cognac restored him to himself. As he returned, "a little tottery," to her side, Emma Eckstein greeted him with the "superior" remark: "So this is the strong sex."

Freud protested that it had not been the blood that unmanned him but, rather, "the pressure of emotions." We can guess what they were. Yet even in his first letter, written under the impress of this disconcerting episode, Freud was eager to protect Fliess from the obvious charge of careless, almost fatal malpractice. "So we had been unjust to her," he conceded. Emma Eckstein was perfectly normal; her nosebleeds had not been hysterical in origin but had been caused by "a piece of iodoform gauze that had got torn off as you were pulling it out and was left in for two weeks." Freud took the burden onto himself and exculpated his friend: he should not have urged

Fliess to perform an operation in a foreign city, where he could not follow up. "You did it as well as one can." The accident with the gauze was one "that happens to the luckiest and most circumspect of surgeons." This was the kind of defensive excuse that Freud the psychoanalyst would soon call denial. But not yet. He cited another specialist as confessing that it had once happened to him, and added reassuringly, "Naturally no one is reproaching you."

Actually, as Freud delicately intimated in a letter of early April, one Viennese specialist, like Fliess an ear, nose, and throat man, had intimated that Emma Eckstein's profuse, recurrent bleeding was caused by Fliess's disastrous intervention, of which his forgetting the gauze in her nose was only the worst consequence. Fliess appears to have been offended, but Freud tried to soothe him: whatever all these experts might think, "for me you remain the physician, the type of man into whose hands one trustingly puts one's life and that of one's family." But Freud was not satisfied merely to reassert his full confidence in Fliess's skills and attentiveness; he made Emma Eckstein responsible for the whole catastrophe. In late April, in a letter to his "Dear Magician," he referred to his patient, now gradually improving, as "my incubus and yours." A year later, he returned to the subject, reporting to Fliess "a quite surprising solution of Eckstein's hemorrhages—which will please you very much." Freud thought he could prove that Fliess had been right all along, that "her bleeding was hysterical, happened from *longing.*" He sent flattering word: "Your nose has once again smelled right." Emma Eckstein's bleedings were "wish-bleedings."

That she should be doing "brilliantly" only eased Freud's task of finding an ironclad alibi for his friend. He maintained tactful silence about the awkward question of whether Fliess's decision to operate had been at all reasonable, tactful silence about the strip of gauze Fliess had allowed to fester. It was all Emma Eckstein's fault. She positively liked to bleed, for the symptom allowed her to demonstrate her various ailments to be real rather than imaginary, and this gave her a claim to the affection of others. Freud, to be sure, adduced some clinical evidence that she had probably been profiting from her bleeding for years. But that could not absolve Fliess; Freud's evasiveness is blatant. What really mattered was not whether his inconvenient incubus engineered her ailments in order to be loved, but whether her clumsy surgeon was as lovable as Freud needed him to be. Even if Freud modeled Irma largely on Anna Lichtheim, the striking resemblance of the two women made it quite inevitable that Emma Eckstein too would invade the Irma dream. Fliess made only a fleeting appearance in the dream as Freud reported it, and Freud himself wondered, "Should not this friend, who plays such a large role in my life, appear further in the dream's context of thought?" The answer is that he did. The dream of Irma's injection discloses, among other things, Freud's anxiety to conceal his doubts about Fliess not just from Fliess but from himself.

It is a paradox: here was Freud, struggling toward the laws of unconscious mental operations, exculpating the guilty and maligning the innocent, all for the sake of retaining his necessary illusion. In the years that followed, Freud would establish beyond cavil that inconsistency is, though not the desirable, the inescapable lot of man. He liked to quote a line from one of his favorite writers, the Swiss poet Conrad Ferdinand Meyer, about "man with all his contradictions." He came to recognize the hold of ambivalence—the tense coexistence of love and hate—over the human mind. Some of his earliest patients had taught him that humans can know and not know at the same time, understand intellectually what they emotionally refuse to accept. More psychoanalytic experience was to offer overwhelming clinical support for Shakespeare's observation that the wish is father to the thought. A favorite way of dealing with inconvenient complications, no matter how obtrusive, is to wish them away. This is what happened to Freud during the spring and summer of 1895.

All through this time, and beyond, Fliess continued to be Freud's irreplaceable Other. "Look at what happens," Freud wrote him as late as 1899, shortly after one of their meetings. "Here I live morosely and in darkness until you come; I scold myself, kindle my flickering light at your calm one, feel well again, and after your departure, I have again got eyes to see, and what I see is beautiful and good." There was no one else, in Vienna or anywhere, who could perform this service for Freud, not even his witty, intelligent sister-in-law Minna Bernays. Yet the Fliess who thus realized Freud's design for the perfect listener was partly of Freud's own making.

One reason why his idealized portrait remained inviolate for so long was that Freud took some years to recognize, and work through, the erotic ingredient in his dependency. "The company of the friend, which a special— perhaps feminine—side demands," Freud once confessed to Fliess, "no one can replace for me." That was late in their friendship, in 1900. A year later he returned to this point, a note of reproach creeping into his matter-of-fact autobiographical comment: "I do not share your contempt for friendship between men, probably because I am to a high degree party to it. In my life, as you well know, woman has never replaced the comrade, the friend." Freud wrote this self-appraisal when his intimacy with Fliess had declined and he could afford to be clear-sighted. In 1910, looking back on the whole fateful attachment, Freud bluntly told several of his closest disciples that his attachment to Fliess had contained a homosexual element.* But in 1895 and 1896, Freud fought down his doubts about Fliess. It would take him five years or more to work his way clear of his thralldom.

SELF-ANALYSIS

By the late spring of 1896, Emma Eckstein had virtually vanished from Freud's correspondence with Fliess, though not from his life.† He had more pressing things on his mind: his loquacious patients, his professional isolation, his dizzying forays into psychological theorizing. "On the whole," he reported to Fliess in April 1896, "I am getting ahead very well on the psychology of the neuroses, have every reason to be satisfied." Again, a month later: "I am working on psychology, sturdily and alone." He was also laboring over a monograph on infantile cerebral paralysis for Nothnagel's prestigious encyclopedic *Special Pathology and Therapy*. Driven by his search for the secrets of the neuroses, he fulfilled his assignment in neurology with a great show of reluctance. "I am wholly mired in infantile paralyses, which do not interest me at all," he lamented to Fliess late in 1895. A year later, he denigrated the "Nothnagel work" as "repellent"; when he published *Infantile Cerebral Paralysis* in early 1897, he wholly failed to value the substantial scholarly text, on which most other physicians would have been glad to rest their reputation.‡

But in the spring and summer of 1896, his father was dying, and this was far more absorbing for Freud than his neurological chores, even more absorb-

---

*See pp. 274–77.

†She remained a friend of the family and became a colleague; a letter from Freud to Fliess on December 12, 1897, discloses that she had begun to psychoanalyze patients of her own. (See *Freud–Fliess*, 312 [286].)

‡The Swiss neurologist Rudolf Brun noted in 1936, "Freud's monograph is the most thorough and complete exposition that has yet been written on the cerebral paralyses of children. . . . One gets an idea of the superb mastery of the enormous clinical material here brought together and critically worked through from the fact that the bibliography alone occupies fourteen and a half pages. It was a superb achievement and alone would suffice to assure Freud's name a permanent place in clinical neurology." (Quoted in *Jones* I, 219.)

ing than the neuroses. "My old father (81 years old)," he informed Fliess in late June 1896, "is in Baden," a resort half an hour from Vienna, "in the wobbliest condition, with heart failures, paralysis of the bladder, and the like." All of Freud's summer plans, including a meeting with Fliess, were thrown into doubt. "I really believe," he wrote two weeks later, "that these are his final days." He longed to meet Fliess and "once again live with head and heart together," but did not dare leave the neighborhood. His father's impending death moved Freud but did not depress him. "I don't begrudge him the well-earned rest, as he himself wishes it. He was," Freud added, using the mournful past tense while Jacob Freud was still breathing, "an interesting human being, inwardly very happy," and now was going "with decency and dignity." August saw some temporary remission, a last flickering of the embers, and Freud could take time out for a brief holiday. But on October 23, Jacob Freud died, bearing himself "valiantly to the end, as he was in general a far from common human being." This was no time for sober critical appraisals; the man who had picked up his cap from the gutter and had failed to make a good living in Vienna was affectionately forgotten. For a time, Freud was only proud of his father.

But the inevitable reaction set in; he found it difficult even to write letters. "Through some of those dark paths behind the official consciousness," he wrote, thanking Fliess for his condolences, "the old man's death has moved me very much. I had esteemed him highly, understood him very exactly, and he had effected much in my life with his characteristic mixture of deep wisdom and fantastic lightheartedness." His father's death, Freud added, had reawakened all of the past in his inmost self. "I now have a quite uprooted feeling." This was hardly a characteristic response for a middle-aged son contemplating the end of an aged father who had "long outlived himself"; Freud's mourning was exceptional in its intensity. It was exceptional, too, in the way he put it to scientific use, distancing himself somewhat from his loss and at the same time gathering material for his theories.

One phenomenon he observed in himself, and named, during these sorrowful days was survivor guilt.* He confirmed its existence dramatically a few years later, in 1904. Visiting Greece for the first time, he had a curious feeling of derealization. Was the Acropolis really as he had learned about it in school? Was not his presence there too good to be true? Much later, analyzing this experience, which long puzzled him, he referred it back to a feeling of guilt: he had surpassed his father, and that was somehow forbidden. Freud found

---

*Freud wrote in one letter of the "self-reproach that appears regularly among the survivors." (Freud to Fliess, November 2, 1896. *Freud–Fliess*, 214 [202].)

in his self-analysis that it is as perilous to win one's oedipal battles as it is to lose them. The roots of his recognition went back to the days just after his father's death when he translated his feelings into theory. The charge that Freud was always working has some merit.

THE DEATH OF his father, then, was a profound personal experience from which Freud drew universal implications; it acted like a pebble thrown into a still pond, making successive rings of unsuspected magnitude. Reflecting on the event in 1908, in the preface to the second edition of his *Interpretation of Dreams,* he commented that for him the book had a powerful "subjective" meaning which he had "been able to understand only after its completion." He had come to see it as "a piece of my self-analysis, my reaction to my father's death, that is, the most significant event, the most decisive loss, of a man's life."

This entanglement of autobiography with science has bedeviled psychoanalysis from its beginnings. Freud's famous confessional remark about the unrivaled significance of a father's death is no less remarkable for what it omits than for what it says: should it really be true that a mother's death is any the less poignant? Freud's mother, self-possessed and commanding, lived on to 1930, to the age of ninety-five, exacting fealty from her brood, including her first-born favorite golden son. It was almost as though her active long life enabled her psychoanalyst son to skirt the full implications of the oedipal combat to which he had been, after all, the first to call attention. It matters to the history of psychoanalysis that Freud was very much his father's son, dreaming and worrying more about paternal than about maternal relations, and unconsciously eager to leave some of his ambivalence about his mother unanalyzed.

In general, Freud was sensitive to the peculiar nature of his evidence. It struck him as odd, he wrote a little defensively in 1895, reporting on Elisabeth von R., "that the case histories I write read like novellas, and that they, so to speak, lack the serious stamp of scientific method." He reassured himself that it is "the nature of the subject, rather than my predilection, that is evidently to be held responsible for this result." But the accusation that Freud was inclined to take his own pulse to guess at the general climate of opinion was not to be disarmed by such easy consolation. As early as 1901, heading the vanguard in an army of doubters, Fliess attacked Freud on the ground that "the thought-reader reads in others only his own thoughts."

Since then, the objection that Freud simply—and illegitimately—translated his own psychological traumas into so-called laws of the mind has not been stilled. One can see how it arose and why it has persisted. Many of Freud's most unsettling ideas drew on acknowledged, or covert, autobiographical sources. He exploited himself freely as a witness and made himself into the most informative of his patients. In the strict natural sciences, such observant subjectivity presents no problem. The motives or neurotic difficulties of a physicist or biologist are of interest solely to his family and friends— and to his biographer. The validity of his conclusions can be determined by objective tests, by the replication of his experiments or the recalculation of his chains of mathematical reasoning. Ideally, with psychology the same austere procedure should hold. What must matter to the student of psychoanalysis is ultimately not whether Freud had (or imagined) an Oedipus complex, but whether his claim that it is the complex through which everyone must pass can be substantiated by independent observation or ingenious experiments. Freud did not regard his own experiences as automatically valid for all humanity. He tested his notions against the experiences of his patients and, later, against the psychoanalytic literature; he spent years working over, refining, revising, his generalizations. His famous case histories eloquently reflect his simultaneous commitment to individuality and generality; each depicts an unduplicable patient who at the same time belongs to a category of cases.

Freud recognized, then, that no one, not even he himself, is Everyman. But with due caution, allowing for the variations that make each individual just that—an individual—Freud was prepared to read his own mental experience the better to grasp that of his fellow humans. Though intent on maintaining his privacy and averse to disclosing his inner life to strangers, he yielded to the pressure, for the sake of his science, to be indiscreet about himself. He was simply one more source of material. Freud expected to rest his case on the sheer weight of psychoanalytic evidence and on the explanatory power of his formulations. If he found the loss of his father the most decisive loss he could sustain, the impact of such a tragedy must differ, and might differ drastically, in other mourners. But the private provenance of his convictions would not inhibit Freud from developing a theory about mourning and, even more broadly, a theory about the ubiquitous family drama with its ever-varied yet largely predictable plot of wishes, gratifications, frustrations, and losses, many of them unconscious.

HIS FATHER'S DEATH in October 1896 provided Freud with a powerful impetus toward building the structure he was beginning to make into his life's work. But before he could fully profit from his grievous loss, he had to repair a serious misstep which had dominated his thinking in the mid-1890s. He had to jettison his so-called seduction theory, the claim that all neuroses are the result of a brother's, a servant's, a father's, sexual abuse of a child.* The seduction theory in all its uncompromising sweep seems inherently implausible; only a fantasist like Fliess could have accepted and applauded it. What is astonishing is not that Freud eventually abandoned the idea, but that he adopted it in the first place.

Yet its appeal to him is apparent. Throughout his life, Freud's theoretical thinking oscillated fruitfully between complexity and simplicity—this, as we have just seen, becomes apparent in his case histories. The recognition of complexity did justice to the stunning multifariousness of human experience, richer by far than psychologists concentrating on the conscious mind could ever know.† In contrast, Freud also cherished the ideal of simplicity; the reduction of apparently dissimilar mental events to a few well-defined categories was his aim in scientific research. In his clinical experience, Freud had witnessed many things that his Viennese medical colleagues found unrespectable, indeed largely incredible: the mysterious effects of hypnotism, the amorous advances of patients, the talking away of hysterical symptoms, the hidden work of sexuality. In fact, he was perfectly prepared to believe things even more incredible than these. Moreover, in the mid-1890s, still in search of a reputation for original scientific contributions that had so far eluded him, Freud could welcome the seduction theory as a neat generalization that would explain a range of medical disorders as results of one kind of savage act— incestuous seduction or rape.

Given Freud's idea that "neurasthenia" is largely due to sexual problems, the inferential step needed to make such a theory appear plausible to him was not very large. To be sure, the conviction had been hard-won; as a good bourgeois, Freud had adopted it only after overcoming strong inner resistances to such a notion. Some of the teachers and colleagues he most admired—Charcot, Breuer, and his acquaintance Rudolf Chrobak, a prominent Viennese gynecologist—had broadly hinted that nervous disorders always involve, in Breuer's term, *secrets d'alcôve*. But Freud had promptly "forgotten" the casual observations they made, and the anecdotes they related, in

---

*While most victims of such assaults were girls, boys, too, as Freud knew, were not safe from them. In 1895, while his confidence in this theory was at its peak, he told Fliess that one of his neurotic patients "has given me the expected: (sexual fright, i.e., infantile abuse with *male* hysteria!)." (Freud to Fliess, November 2, 1895. *Freud–Fliess*, 153 [149].)

†Freud embodied his perception of complexity in the concept of "overdetermination," a term he first advanced in 1895: symptoms or dreams or other products of the unconscious mind are bound to have several causes, springing from heredity and environment, predisposition and traumas, and such products tend to condense a diversity of impulses and experiences into deceptively simple displays.

his presence. Early in 1886, during a reception at Charcot's house, he had overheard his host arguing in his lively way that a severely disturbed young woman owed her nervous troubles to her husband's impotence or sexual awkwardness. In such cases, Charcot exclaimed, it is always a genital thing, always: *"Mais, dans des cas pareils,"* he insisted, *"c'est toujours la chose génitale, toujours . . . toujours . . . toujours."* A year later, Chrobak referred an interesting woman patient to Freud. She was beset by apparently meaningless anxiety attacks, and Chrobak, sounding uncharacteristically cynical, attributed these attacks to her husband's inability to perform in bed. There was only one prescription that would be effective, he told Freud, a prescription her husband could never fill:

> "Penis normalis
> dosim
> repetatur!"

These offhand judgments, worldly-wise but in no way integrated into a general explanation of mental malfunctioning, worked silently in Freud until about 1893, when he was prepared to incorporate them into a theory of neuroses. We know that in a memorandum Freud sent Fliess in February of that year, he tersely announced his wish to assert, and test, the proposition that "neurasthenia can in fact *only* be a sexual neurosis." Certainly in the case histories he contributed to *Studies on Hysteria* he had intimated, if sometimes rather faintly, that his patients' symptoms had sexual origins.

As he began to reflect on the share of memory in the formation of nervous ailments, Freud pushed the mental or physical insult responsible for them back to his patients' early years. The "actual" neuroses—neuroses caused by current rather than remote experiences—were rapidly losing interest for him. "Have I already communicated the great clinical secret to you, orally or in writing?" he asked Fliess in October 1895, while he was still steeped in his project. "Hysteria is the consequence of a presexual *sexual scare.* Obsessional neurosis is the consequence of a presexual *sexual pleasure,* which later transforms itself into [self-]*reproach.*" Freud was by then dissatisfied with the vagueness of capacious diagnostic categories like neurasthenia and was beginning to classify the neuroses more precisely. But his word "presexual" suggests that the idea of infantile sexuality was still beyond his ken, though it was hovering on the horizon. " 'Presexual,' " he explained to Fliess, "means actually before puberty, before the release of sexual substances; the relevant events only take effect as *memories.*" Now these relevant events, as patient after patient remembered them for him, were sexual traumas—

whether the result of glib persuasion or of brutal assault—undergone in childhood.

By 1896, Freud was ready to say so in print. In a paper on the "neuro-psychoses of defense" written early in that year, he asserted on the basis of thirteen cases that those traumas causing hysteria *must belong to early childhood (the time before puberty), and their content must consist of an actual irritation of the genitals (proceedings resembling coitus)."* While obsessional neurotics appeared to have been precocious in their sexual activity, they too displayed hysterical symptoms; hence they too must have been first victimized as children. The childhood episodes that analysis uncovered, Freud added, were "grave," on occasion "down-right loathsome." The villains were above all "nursemaids, governesses, and other servants," as well as, regrettably, teachers and "innocent" brothers.

In the same year, on April 21, lecturing to the local Society for Psychiatry and Neurology on "The Etiology of Hysteria," Freud committed himself to this seduction theory before a select professional audience. His listeners were all experts on the twisted byways of erotic life. The great Richard von Krafft-Ebing, who had made sexual psychopathology his own, was presiding. Freud's lecture was a lively, highly skillful forensic performance. The stu-dent of hysteria, he said, is like an explorer discovering the remains of an abandoned city, with walls and columns and tablets covered with half-effaced inscriptions; he may dig them up and clean them, and then with luck the stones speak—*saxa loquuntur.* He expended all this rhetorical effort to persuade his incredulous listeners that they must seek the origin of hysteria in the sexual abuse of children. All eighteen of the cases he had treated, Freud noted, invited this conclusion. But his mixture of color-ful eloquence and scientific sobriety was wasted. The lecture, he told Fliess a few days later, "had an icy reception from the donkeys and, on Krafft-Ebing's part, the odd judgment: 'It sounds like a scientific fairy tale.' And this," Freud exclaimed, "after one has shown them the solution of a thousands-years-old problem, a source of the Nile!" Well, he added rude-ly, "they can all, euphemistically expressed, go to hell"—*sie können mich alle gern haben.* Even with Fliess, it seems, Freud did not let himself go entirely.

It was an evening Freud chose never to forget; the traumatic residue it left became a ground for low expectations, a justification of his pessimism. He perceived the atmosphere around him to be chillier than ever and was certain that his lecture had made him an object of ostracism. Some "password has been given out to abandon me," he reported to Fliess, "for everything round about me is falling away from me." He professed to be bearing his isolation "with equanimity," but the lack of new patients worried him. Yet he kept investigating, and for a time continued to accept as true, his patients' lurid recitals. He had, after all, thoroughly trained himself to listen to them. But gradually, the misgivings that assailed him grew irresistible. In May 1897, he dreamt of having "overly tender feelings" for his oldest daughter, Mathilde, and interpreted this erotic dream as the wish to find a "pater" as the cause of neurosis. This, he announced to Fliess, had quieted his "ever-stirring doubts" about the seduction theory. It is an odd, unconvincing reading, for the dream should have contributed to, rather than soothed, Freud's uneasiness. He knew perfectly well that he had not sexually assaulted Mathilde or his other daughters, and that a sexual desire is not identical with a sexual act. What is more, it was part of his scientific credo that wishing to see a theory confirmed is not the same as confirming it. But for the moment he took the dream as support for his favorite notion.

Freud's doubts did not gain the upper hand until the summer and early fall of 1897. Returning in mid-September from his summer vacation, "fresh, cheerful, impoverished," he confided to Fliess "the great secret" that had been "slowly dawning on me in the last few months. I no longer believe in my Neurotica"—his all-too-simple explanation of neuroses. This letter of September 21, 1897, is perhaps the most revealing in this revealing correspondence. In persuasive detail, Freud gave Fliess a "historical" account of why he had finally lost confidence in the seduction theory: He could not complete any of his analyses, either losing his patients midway or partly succeeding on other grounds. In addition, common sense had intervened to ruin his simplistic scheme; since hysteria was widespread, not even sparing the Freud household, it must follow that "in all cases, the *father* had to be accused of being perverse, my own not excluded." The Freud of the 1890s was not disposed to idealize his father as thoroughly as he idealized Fliess, but to include Jacob Freud among the child molesters struck him as absurd. Moreover, if paternal attacks were the sole sources of hysteria, such misconduct must be virtually universal, since there are bound to be fewer *cases* of hysteria than possible *causes* of it. After all, not all victims fall ill. "Such widespread perversion against children is scarcely probable." Besides, it is certain that "there are no marks of reality in the unconscious," and hence there is no way of distinguishing between truth on the one hand and emotionally charged fiction on the other. Freud was now prepared to apply the lesson of principled skepticism that his clinical experience had taught him. His patients' "revelations" were at least in part products of their imagination.

The collapse of his theory did not induce Freud to abandon his belief in the sexual etiology of neuroses or, for that matter, the conviction that some neurotics at least had been sexually victimized by their fathers. Like other physicians, he had come across such cases.* It is telling that in December 1897, nearly three months after he had presumably given up the seduction theory, he could still write that his "confidence in the father-etiology has risen a good deal." Less than two weeks later, he reported to Fliess that one of his woman patients had given him a horrifying account which he was disposed to believe: at the age of two, she had been bestially raped by her father, a pervert who needed to inflict bloody injuries to obtain sexual gratification. In fact, Freud did not definitively part with the theory for two years, and did not publicly register his change of mind for another six years after that. As late as 1924, almost three decades after he had worked his way out of what he penitently called "an error which I have repeatedly acknowledged and corrected since then," Freud insisted that not everything he had written in the mid-1890s on the sexual abuse of children deserved to be rejected: "Seduction has retained a certain significance for etiology." He explicitly noted that two of his early cases, Katharina and a "Fräulein Rosalia H.," had been assaulted by their fathers. Freud had no intention of exchanging one sort of credulity for another. Ceasing to believe everything his patients told him did not require him to fall into the sentimental trap of holding sober black-coated bourgeois incapable of revolting sexual aggression. What Freud repudiated was the seduction theory as a general explanation of how all neuroses originate.

This renunciation opened a new chapter in the history of psychoanalysis. Freud claimed to be anything but "upset, confused, weary," and wondered prophetically "whether this doubt merely represents an episode in the advance toward further discoveries?" He acknowledged that it pained him to lose "the expectation of eternal renown." It had been "so beautiful," as was the hope for "certain wealth, complete independence, travels, lifting the children above the severe cares that deprived me of my youth." Recalling this turning point much later, Freud wrote that when the seduction theory, which had been "almost fatal to the young science," had broken down "under its own improbability," his first response had been "a stage of complete perplexity." The "ground of reality had been lost." He had been too enthusiastic and a little naive.

---

*While the matter was treated with considerable reserve in the medical literature, sexual assaults on young girls by their fathers had been canvassed in public since the beginning of the nineteenth century. As early as 1821, the famous French psychiatrist Jean Étienne Esquirol had reported such a case, a father's attempt on his sixteen-year-old daughter, leading to the girl's breakdown and repeated attempts at suicide. (See "Suicide," in *Dictionnaire des Sciences Médicales*, by "A Group of Physicians and Surgeons," LIII [1821], 219–20. I owe this reference to Lisa Lieberman.)

But his dismay was short-lived. "At last came the reflection that, after all, one has no right to despond just because one has been deceived in one's expectations." This was characteristic for Freud. Aware that the world is not a hovering mother brimming over with supplies for her needy children, he accepted the universe. If the ground of reality had been lost, that of fantasy had been won. Krafft-Ebing had been almost right after all; what Freud had told his fellow physicians that April evening in 1896 had indeed been a fairy tale or, better, a collection of fairy tales his patients had first told him. But then, as Fliess had encouraged Freud to recognize, fairly tales enshrine buried truths. Freud's response to his liberation from the seduction theory was to take communications, whether from his patients or from himself, more seriously than before, but far less literally. He came to read them as coded messages—distorted, censored, meaningfully disguised. He listened, in short, with greater attention and finer discrimination than ever. It had been a strenuous and unsettling time, but the rewards were dazzling. "To be completely honest with oneself," he wrote, "is a good exercise." The way to his sustained self-analysis, to the recognition of the Oedipus complex and of unconscious fantasies now lay open.

SELF-ANALYSIS WOULD seem to be a contradiction in terms. But Freud's venture has become the cherished centerpiece of psychoanalytic mythology. Freud, analysts say, undertook a self-analysis beginning some time in the mid-1890s and engaged in it systematically from the late spring or early summer of 1897 on; and this act of patient heroism, to be admired and palely imitated but never repeated, is the founding act of psychoanalysis. "It is hard for us nowadays to imagine how momentous this achievement was," Ernest Jones has written, "that difficulty being the fate of most pioneering exploits. Yet the uniqueness of the feat remains. Once done it is done forever. For no one again can be the first to explore these depths."

Freud himself was rather less categorical. We know that he regarded *The Interpretation of Dreams* as part of his self-analysis, and his letters to Fliess abound with references to progress, and to impediments, in his continuous, pitiless self-probing. But at times he wondered. "My self-analysis," he told Fliess in November 1897, "remains interrupted. I have come to see why. I can analyze myself only with objectively gained knowledge (like a stranger)." The conclusion was gloomy: "True self-analysis is impossible, else there would be no illness." Yet Freud permitted himself an inconsistency that only the unprecedented nature of the work helps to explain. In the very letter in which he declared self-analysis impossible, he recalled how before the summer vacation he had told Fliess "that the most important patient for me was my own person, and after my vacation trip my self-analysis, of which then there was no trace, suddenly started." On later occasions, Freud would defend self-analysis as a way for the analyst to recognize, and thus neutralize, his own complexes. Yet he would argue at the same time that being analyzed by someone else is a markedly superior path to self-knowledge.* Interestingly enough, Freud did not consistently equate his self-scrutiny with a full analysis. In his popular *Psychopathology of Everyday Life*, he spoke of it in modest terms, calling it "self-observation." Looking back to 1898, he recalled how he "began in my forty-third year to turn my interest to the remains of my memory of my own childhood." This sounds less stringent, less exalted, certainly less formidable, than "self-analysis."

Freud's hesitations and modest circumlocutions are appropriate. No matter how one-sided, the psychoanalytic situation is a dialogue. The analyst, though largely a silent partner, offers interpretations that the analysand presumably could not have reached on his own. If he could have reached them, to speak with Freud, there would have been no neuroses. While the patient, swollen with grandiosity or bowed down with guilt feelings, distorts the world and his place in it, the analyst, neither praising nor condemning but tersely pointing out what the analysand is really saying, provides a therapeutic glimpse of reality. What is perhaps even more important, and quite impossible in self-analysis, is that the analyst—relatively anonymous and attentively passive—offers himself as a kind of screen onto which the analysand projects his passions, his love and hate, affection and animosity, hope and anxiety. This transference, on which so much of the curative work of the psychoanalytic process depends, is by definition a transaction between two human beings. Nor is it easy to imagine how the self-analyst could reproduce the regressive atmosphere that the analyst provides with his invisible presence, even tone, and long silences. The psychoanalyst, in short, is to his analysand what Freud elevated Fliess into being: the Other. How could Freud, no matter how bold or original, become his own Other?

Whatever we call it, Freud in the late 1890s subjected himself to a most thoroughgoing self-scrutiny, an elaborate, penetrating, and unceasing census of his fragmentary memories, his concealed wishes and emotions. From tantalizing bits and pieces, he reconstructed fragments of his buried early life, and with the aid of such highly personal reconstructions combined with his clinical experience, sought to sketch the outlines of human nature. He had

---

*In 1935, Freud forcefully reminded the psychiatrist Paul Schilder, with whom the psychoanalytic establishment had clashed before on the issue of training analyses, that those among the first generation of analysts who had not been analyzed "were never proud of it." In fact, "whenever it was possible" to be analyzed "it was done: Jones and Ferenczi, for instance, had long analyses." Speaking of himself, Freud suggested that "one might perhaps assert the right to an exceptional position." (Freud to Schilder, November 26, 1935. Freud Collection, B4, LC.)

no precedent for this work, no teachers, but had to invent the rules for it as he went along. Compared to Freud the explorer of his self, the most uninhibited autobiographers from Saint Augustine to Jean-Jacques Rousseau, however penetrating their insights and frank their revelations, had been somewhat reserved. Ernest Jones's hyperbole has much to commend it. Yet there are vital details of Freud's self-analysis that are likely to remain obscure. He doubtless conducted it every day, but did he take what free time he had in the evening, or did he analyze himself at slack times during consulting hours? Did he pursue his intense, often dismaying ruminations when he took his early afternoon walk to rest from his posture as the professional listener and to buy his cigars?

This much we know. The method Freud employed for his self-analysis was that of free association, and the material on which he principally relied was provided by his dreams.* To be sure, he did not confine himself to dreams; he also collected his memories, his slips of tongue or pen, his forgetting of lines of poetry or patients' first names, and allowed these clues to lead him from idea to idea through the "usual detour" of free association. But dreams were his most dependable and most abundant source for buried information. He had elucidated the core of his patients' neuroses in the mid-1890s principally by interpreting their dreams, and, he thought, "it was only these successes that put me in a position to persevere." Freud pursued his "self-analysis, whose necessity soon became clear to me, with the aid of a series of my own dreams which led me through all the events of my childhood." Though "masses of bristling riddles lie round about," he told Fliess, the "elucidation of dreams" seemed "the most solid" of resources. Not surprisingly, his self-analysis shaped the very dreams he then interpreted. He dreamt that "Old Brücke" had set him the strange assignment of dissecting his own lower body and read this highly condensed dream as referring to his self-analysis, connected as that was with the reporting of his own dreams and the uncovering of his own infantile sexual feelings.

Freud's letters to Fliess demonstrate that this was hard work, at once exhilarating and frustrating. "It is fermenting and simmering in me," he wrote in May 1897; he was only waiting for a new thrust forward. But insights did not come on command. In mid-June he confessed that he was bone lazy, intellectually at a standstill, vegetating in summery well-being: "Since the last thrust, nothing has stirred and nothing has changed." But he sensed great things about to burst out. "I believe," he wrote four days later, "I am in a

---

*Marie Bonaparte told Ernest Jones on December 16, 1953, that in Freud's self-analysis, "*predominantly* the analysis of his own dreams, as you point out so pertinently, was his firmest *stand.*" (Jones papers, Archives of the British Psycho-Analytical Society, London.)

cocoon, and God knows what kind of beast will crawl out." Having learned about resistance from his patients, he now experienced it in himself. "What has been going on in me, I still do not know," he confessed in early July. "Something from the deepest depths of my own neurosis has put up resistance against any progress in the understanding of the neuroses, and you have somehow been drawn into this." That Fliess should have obscurely become involved in Freud's difficulties made this pause all the more unpalatable. Yet "for some days, it seems to me, an emergence from this darkness has been in preparation. I notice that meanwhile I have made all kinds of progress in my work; in fact, now and then something occurs to me again." Never one to overlook the influence of the environment on the mind, Freud thought that the summer heat and overwork had helped to generate the momentary paralysis. Still, he was sustained throughout by the conviction that if he only waited and kept analyzing, buried material would swim to the surface of his consciousness.

But his self-confidence was shaky. "After having become very cheerful here," Freud wrote in August from the resort of Aussee, "I am now enjoying a period of bad humor." While he had been working at resolving his "little hysteria, much intensified by my work," the rest of his self-analysis had now come to a stop. He acknowledged that *this* analysis was "more difficult than any other," yet he was certain that "it must be done." It was an essential part of his work. Freud was right; his self-analysis was a necessary stage as he pressed on toward a theory of the mind. Gradually, his resistance crumbled. Late in September, back from vacation, Freud wrote Fliess that famous letter announcing the collapse of his faith in the seduction theory. By October, he had broken through to a heady mixture of self-knowledge and theoretical clarity. "For four days," he reported to Fliess in early October, "my self-analysis, which I consider indispensable for the clarification of the whole problem, has been continuing in dreams and has given me the most valuable explanations and clues." This is when he recalled the Catholic nurse of his infancy, his glimpse of his naked mother, his death wishes against his younger brother, and other repressed childhood memories. They were not all accurate, but as fantasies they proved indispensable signposts to self-knowledge.

As his resistance flared up, Freud continued to be harassed by short and painful interruptions. Then more memories came, more ideas. He felt (so he portrayed himself picturesquely in late October) as if he were being pulled forcibly through all his past as his thoughts made rapid connections: "Moods change like the landscapes before the traveler on a train." His practice was "hopelessly poor," and so he could live "only for the 'inner' work." He quoted Goethe's *Faust* to convey an impression of his mental state: beloved shades were emerging like an old, half-faded myth, bringing with them friendship and first love. "Also first scares and dissensions. Many a sad life's secret here goes back to its first roots; many prides and privileges become aware of their modest origins." There were the days, as he put it, when he dragged himself about because he had failed to fathom the meaning of a dream or a fantasy, and then came "the days when a flash of lightning illuminated the connections and lets me understand what had gone before as a preparation for the present." He found it all not only infinitely difficult but also exceedingly unpleasant; almost every day, his self-analysis cast up wicked wishes and discreditable acts. Still, he was buoyant as he shed one illusion about himself after another. He found it impossible, he told Fliess in early October 1897, to convey to him "any notion of the intellectual beauty of the work." Intellectual beauty: Freud always had something of an aesthetic response to the elegance of his findings and his formulations.

Everything now fell into place. He recognized that his remembered "infatuation with the mother and jealousy of the father" was more than a private idiosyncrasy. Rather, he told Fliess, the oedipal relationship of the child to its parents was "a general event in early childhood." He was sure, in fact, that it was an "idea of general value" that might explain "the gripping power of *Oedipus Rex*" and perhaps of *Hamlet.* Other startling discoveries crowded his days: the unconscious feeling of guilt, the stages of sexual development, the causal link between internally generated—"endopsychic"—myths and religious belief, the "family romance" in which so many children develop grandiose fantasies about their parents, the revelatory nature of slips and bungled actions, the power of repressed aggressive feelings, and (always on his mind) the intricate mechanisms of dream production. He even found a psychological explanation for addiction: it was displaced masturbation—an idea of peculiar relevance to him, with his irrepressible need for cigars.

DESPITE THIS RUSH of insights, most densely concentrated between the fall of 1897 and the fall of 1898, moments of dryness and discouragement still plagued him intermittently. Uncharacteristically, Freud, who had confessed that he had no head for wine—"any trace of alcohol makes me completely stupid"—now resorted to it freely. He sought "strength in a bottle of Barolo," called on "Friend Marsala" for help, and declared wine to be "a good friend." A glass or two allowed him to feel more optimistic than he did when wholly sober, but could not assuage his doubts for long. Besides, he was ashamed, he told Fliess, "to treat myself to a new vice." At times it was, he confessed, as though he were "parched; some spring within me is drying up and all feeling is so withered up. I don't want to describe too much; otherwise it would look too much like complaining."

Fortunately, his children continued to delight him as they grew up under his eyes, and he kept Fliess informed of Sophie's worrisome diarrhea, Oli's clever remarks, or Ernstl's scarlet fever. "Annerl is developing charmingly; she is of Martin's type, physically and mentally," runs one affectionate communiqué. "Martin's poetizing complete with self-irony is most amusing." Nor did he forget Fliess's interest in material that would substantiate his theories of biorhythmic cycles. Freud's eldest, Mathilde, was maturing rapidly, and in June 1899, with the precision Fliess looked for, Freud reported that she had begun to menstruate: "On June 25, Mathilde sealed her entry into womanhood, a little prematurely." But the strain of writing the dream book often made him gloomy. He would wonder if he was getting old—he was in his early forties—or perhaps undergoing some "periodic oscillations" in his moods. Such spells came upon him again and again, but they were short, and Freud had grown used enough to them to wait them out. He still needed Fliess as audience; to his infinite delight, Fliess continued to give him "the present of an Other," a "critic and reader" of the highest quality. He acknowledged that he could not do his work wholly without a public, but declared himself content with a public of one, content, he told Fliess, to be "writing only for you."

Yet Freud's dependence was on the verge of fading. One benefit of his self-analysis was that it gradually uncovered the tangled roots of his trust in his "daimon" from Berlin, and thus speeded his emancipation from the Other. He continued to share his thoughts with Fliess, sent him chapters of his dream book, and took his advice on matters of style and on protecting his subjects' privacy. He even allowed Fliess to veto a "sentimental" epigraph from Goethe. His submission to Fliess's editorial judgment proved costlier than this: at his insistence, and under protest, Freud deleted an important dream from the text. "A beautiful dream and no indiscretion," Freud wrote in resignation, "do not go together." But he continued to mourn it. Yet Freud's long labor with his masterpiece was about to come to term. "The time of gestation will soon be over," he told Fliess in July 1898. He was referring to Ida Fliess, his friend's wife, who was about to give birth, but the association with his own condition, his long, creative carrying time, was palpable. Fliess, the midwife of psychoanalysis, had done his duty and soon he could go.

Freud did not simply discard Fliess because he no longer needed him. As the true contours of Fliess's mind, his underlying mysticism and his obsessive commitment to numerology, dawned on Freud at last, and as Freud came to recognize Fliess's passionately held convictions to be hopelessly incompatible with his own, the friendship was doomed. In early August 1900, Freud met Fliess at the Achensee, near Innsbruck, an idyllic spot calculated to refresh and relax the summer tourist. But the two men quarreled violently. Each attacked the other at his most sensitive, most fiercely defended spot: the value, the very validity, of his work. It was their last "congress," the last time they saw one another. They continued to correspond for a while, ever more sparsely. Writing to Fliess in the summer of 1901, Freud once more gratefully recited his debts to him, but bluntly told him that they had drawn apart and that in personal as in professional matters "you have reached the limits of your perspicacity." Fliess had played a distinguished role in the prehistory of psychoanalysis, but as the history of psychoanalysis unfolded after 1900, his share in it was negligible.

THREE

Psychoanalysis

Freud first used the fateful term "psychoanalysis" in 1896, in French and then in German. But he had been working toward psychoanalysis for some time before that. Indeed, the famous analytic couch, a gift from a grateful patient, was part of his office furniture when he moved to Berggasse 19 in September 1891.* Originally under the influence of Breuer, he had shifted, as we have seen, from hypnosis to the cathartic talking cure, and he then went on gradually adapting Breuer's methods, until by the mid-1890s he was launched into psychoanalysis. Some of his most iconoclastic ideas, foreshadowed without a full recognition of their import, go back to his researches and clinical observations in the early 1890s. Freud worked them out, first with deliberate speed and then, from 1897 onward as his self-scrutiny yielded results, with accelerating tempo, scattering them across a handful of published papers and letter upon letter to Fliess. For more than three decades, Freud would tinker with his map of the mind, refine psychoanalytic technique, revise his theories of the drives, of anxiety, and of female sexuality, and invade art history, speculative anthropology, the psychology of religion, and cultural criticism. But by the time he published *The*

---

*Among some notes that Marie Bonaparte compiled for a Freud biography is the following undated entry, in French: "Madame Freud informed me that the analytic couch (which Freud would import to London) was given to him by a grateful patient, Madame Benvenisti, around 1890." (Ibid.)

Interpretation of Dreams at the end of 1899, the principles of psychoanalysis were in place. His *Three Essays on the Theory of Sexuality,* published in 1905, was the second cardinal text explicating these principles, but his dream book was the first, and Freud considered it the key to his work. *"The interpretation of dreams,"* he said emphatically, *"is the royal road to the knowledge of the unconscious in mental life."*

THE SECRET OF DREAMS

Freud's *Interpretation of Dreams* is about more than dreams. It is an autobiography at once candid and canny, as tantalizing in what it omits as in what it discloses. Even in its first edition, which is rather briefer than its successors, it offers a survey of fundamental psychoanalytic ideas—the Oedipus complex, the work of repression, the struggle between desire and defense—and a wealth of material from case histories. It provides, quite incidentally, sharply etched vignettes of the Viennese medical world, rife with rivalries and the hunt for status, and of Austrian society, infected with anti-Semitism and at the end of its liberal decades. It opens with an exhaustive bibliographical survey of the literature on dreams, and it concludes, in the difficult seventh chapter, with a comprehensive theory of the mind. The genre of Freud's masterpiece is, in short, undefinable.

Its argument, though, is lucidity itself. Yet Freud, a self-conscious stylist, had qualms about his manner of presentation. *The Interpretation of Dreams,* he confessed in the preface to the second edition, was "hard to read." His appraisals vacillated as he worked on it. "I am deep in the dream book, am writing it fluently," he told Fliess in early February 1898; and a few weeks later he reported that "the dream book," of which he had already written several chapters, "is turning out attractively." But in May he denigrated the chapter that Fliess was then reading as "stylistically still quite coarse and in some parts badly, that is lifelessly, presented."

His misgivings did not evaporate as his chapters neared publication. His effort was causing him "great agony," and he feared that the book would show this even if the dream materials themselves were unassailable. "What displeases me," he observed in September 1899, as he was reading proofs, "is the style, which was quite incapable of finding the noble, simple expression and lapsed into facetious, image-seeking circumlocutions." He gave vent to his disappointment with a joke borrowed from the satirical German weekly *Simplicissimus,* which he read and enjoyed regularly: "Conversation between two military comrades: 'Now, Comrade, have got yourself engaged, fiancée doubtless charming, beautiful, witty, graceful?'—'Matter of taste, *I* don't like her.' That's exactly my situation now." Goaded by his strong "feeling for form," his "appreciation of beauty as a kind of perfection," he feared that the "convoluted sentences of my dream book, squinting at ideas and strutting with their oblique words, have seriously offended an inner ideal" and indicated an "inadequate mastery of the material."

He was in fact anything but serene. The enigmatic motto from the seventh book of Virgil's *Aeneid,* which he chose after letting Fliess veto that "sentimental" one from Goethe, subtly intimates that he was both nervous and prepared to be angry. His own interpretation of *Flectere si nequeo Superos, Acheronta movebo* * was straightforward enough: the line tersely summarizes his fundamental thesis that wishes, rejected by the "higher mental authorities," resort to "the mental underworld (the unconscious)" to secure their aim.† But the truculent tone of the verse, spoken by an infuriated Juno after her fellow Olympians have frustrated her wishes, suggests more than this. It fits well into Freud's defiant mood. Reading proofs in September 1899, he predicted to Fliess that there would be an outraged outcry, a veritable "thunderstorm" over the nonsense, the foolishness, he had produced: "Then I'll really hear from them!" His dream book was going to leave the higher powers of Vienna unmoved; the unimaginative professors who had called his ideas a fairy tale, the bigoted bureaucrats who would not give him his professorship, were not likely to be converted to his views. No matter: he would raise the powers of hell against them.

FREUD'S DISPLEASURE WITH his presentation was as unjustified as his anticipation of a thunderstorm was unwarranted. But, as so often, it appears that Freud is not an impeccable judge of his own work. To be sure, the architecture of his dream book is distinctly sprawling, and the work was distended by material he added as edition followed edition. Stating his general theory of dreams at a brisk pace in the opening four chapters, pausing only over sample dreams and their interpretation, Freud grew more leisurely thereafter, allowing himself the luxury of expansiveness, as he detailed the varieties of dreams and pursued them from their immediate occasions to their origins in

---

*"If I cannot bend the higher powers, I will move the infernal regions."

†When Freud first mentioned the line in a letter to Fliess late in 1896, he told him that he intended to use it as a motto for the section on symptom formation in a book he was planning on the psychology of hysteria. (See Freud to Fliess, December 4, 1896. *Freud–Fliess,* 217 [205].)

distant causes. His sixth chapter, on the work done by dreams, was expanded in the later editions to become almost as long as the first five together. And the concluding chapter, the famous "philosophical" seventh, is austere, highly technical. But the solidity of his presentation and the elegance of his proofs remain unimpaired.

Freud shrewdly deployed his stylistic tactics to serve his message: the dream examples advance the argument, the anticipations of objections disarm criticism, and the conversational tone, like the literary allusions, lightens his reader's burden. Freud quoted with sovereign ease from Sophocles and Shakespeare, Goethe and Heine, Mozart and Offenbach and popular songs. His own master metaphor made *The Interpretation of Dreams* not a building but a guided tour: "The whole is laid out like the fantasy of a promenade. At the beginning, the dark forest of authors (who do not see the trees), hopeless, rich in wrong tracks. Then a concealed narrow pass through which I lead the reader—my model dream with its peculiarities, details, indiscretions, bad jokes—and then suddenly the summit and the view and the question: Please, where do you want to go now?" For all his laments over the "broken surfaces" of the text, all his doubts, Freud invited his audience to entrust itself to him as its cicerone.

Appropriately, Freud opened his *Interpretation of Dreams* with a provocative show of confidence: "In the following pages, I shall furnish proof that there is a psychological technique which permits the interpreting of dreams, and that with the application of that procedure every dream reveals itself as a meaningful psychical structure, which can be inserted at an assignable point into the mental activities of waking life." Freud asserted not just that dreams have meanings open to interpretation, but that they can be interpreted only if one follows his procedure. He was putting the reader on notice that he was about to launch on a work making large claims.

Freud underscored these claims by first canvassing, with patient thoroughness, the literature on dreams: philosophical treatises and psychological monographs, ancient and modern. In February 1898, as he knuckled down to the uncongenial work of studying his predecessors' writings on dreams, he had bitterly complained to Fliess about this inescapable but dismaying chore: "If one only didn't have to read, too! The little literature there is already disgusts me so much." He found doing his bibliographical survey "a horrible punishment." To make matters worse, he discovered as the months went by that there was far more reading to do than he had imagined. As late as August 1899, with some of the book already at the printer's, Freud was still grumbling. But he recognized that the introductory chapter stood as a shield in front of the rest; he did not want to hand the " 'scientists' "—he put the word into derisive quotation marks—"an ax to kill the poor book." The walk

Freiberg, in Moravia (now Příbor, in Czechoslovakia), Freud's birthplace, dominated by its church steeple and surrounded by the fields that Freud loved as a little boy and never forgot. *(Mary Evans/Sigmund Freud Copyrights, Wivenhoe)*

Schlossergasse 117, Freiberg, where Sigismund Schlomo Freud was born on May 6, 1856. *(Mary Evans/ Sigmund Freud Copyrights, Wivenhoe)*

Freud, about eight, with his father, Jacob, then nearly fifty, in a formal studio photograph taken after the family had settled in Vienna. *(Mary Evans/Sigmund Freud Copyrights, Wivenhoe)*

The Prater, Vienna's famous park, filled with rides and restaurants, to which Freud's parents often took him in the late 1860s. *(Bild-Archiv der Österreichischen Nationalbibliothek, Wien)*

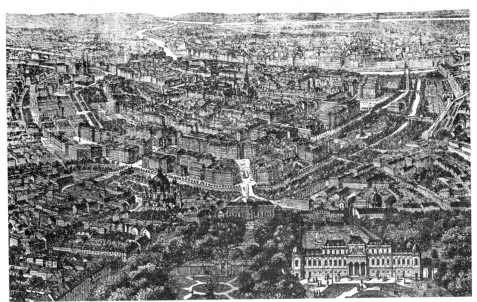

A bird's-eye view of Vienna in 1873, the year that Freud entered the University of Vienna. Lithograph. *(Direktion der Museen der Stadt Wien)*

Black Friday, a sketch by J. E. Hörwarter. It attempts to capture the excited scene in front of the stock exchange on May 9, 1873, after the great crash in the stock market. Many of the wildly gesticulating brokers bear the features that anti-Semites liked to attribute to all Jews. *(Bild-Archiv der Österreichischen National-bibliothek, Wien)*

The sixteen-year-old Freud with his adored mother, Amalia. *(Mary Evans/Sigmund Freud Copyrights, Wivenhoe)*

Samuel Hammerschlag, Freud's religion teacher at his Gymnasium and his fatherly, generous friend, with his wife, Betty. *(Mary Evans/Sigmund Freud Copyrights, Wivenhoe)*

The Freud family in 1876, with the twenty-year-old Freud standing in the center, facing the camera, and his half brother Emanuel turning his back on him. Also in the back row, left to right, are his sisters Pauline, Anna, Rosa, and Marie ("Mitzi"), and Amalia's cousin Simon Nathansohn. Freud's sister Adolfine ("Dolfi") and their parents are seated in the next row. The boy in the chair is probably Freud's brother Alexander. The other two children are unidentified. *(Mary Evans/Sigmund Freud Copyrights, Wivenhoe)*

The laboratory of the experimental station in Trieste, where Freud did research on the gonads of eels in the spring of 1876. *(Greti Mainx)*

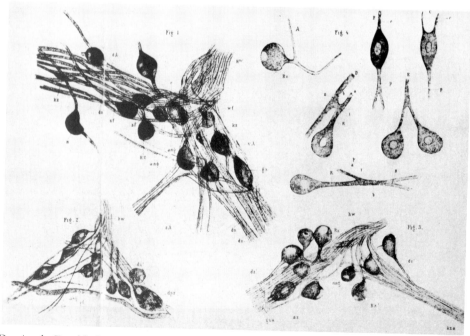

Drawings by Freud for his paper on the lamprey, which he described as "the lowest of the fishes." He wrote "On the Spinal Ganglia and Spinal Cord of the Petromyzon" in 1878, while working in Ernst Brücke's laboratory. *(Printed in* Sitzungsber. d.k. Akad. d. Wissensch. Wien—*Math.-Naturwiss. Kl.)*

Martha Bernays in 1880, about two years before meeting Freud. *(Mary Evans/Sigmund Freud Copyrights, Wivenhoe)*

Martha Bernays in 1884, at about the age of twenty-three. During their engagement, when Freud was passionately in love with her, he was convinced that photographs did not do her justice. *(Mary Evans/Sigmund Freud Copyrights, Wivenhoe)*

Minna Bernays, Martha Bernays's younger sister, who joined the Freud household in the mid-1890s. *(Mary Evans/Sigmund Freud Copyrights, Wivenhoe)*

The great German physiologist Ernst Brücke, later Ernst von Brücke, who had more influence on Freud than any other professor. (*Institut für Geschichte der Medizin der Universität, Wien*)

Hermann Nothnagel, professor of internal medicine at the University of Vienna, for whom Freud worked as a clinical assistant in 1882–83.

Theodor Meynert, professor of psychiatry at the University of Vienna, who at the time had an international reputation.

through the dark forest of authors in this chapter served to exhibit the essential poverty of existing theories on dreams. For every thesis, Freud complained, one could find a counterthesis. He did have appreciative words for some researchers. The German author F. W. Hildebrandt had perceived the outlines of the work of dreams in his study *The Dream and Its Utilization in Life*, published in 1875; the French archivist, ethnographer, and historian of magic Alfred Maury had performed some brilliant experiments on his own dream production and reported on them in *Sleep and Dreams* in 1878; the verbose but imaginative philosophy professor Karl Albert Scherner, whose main interest was aesthetics, had stumbled on the meaning of symbols and published his findings in a monograph of 1861, *The Life of Dreams.* Freud gracefully acknowledged that these and others had caught a trace of the truth. But none had it all. It was necessary to begin again.

Hence the second chapter, in which Freud launched on the method of dream interpretation, complete with the analysis of a model dream—the dream of Irma's injection. But before he felt ready to expound his method, Freud somewhat mischievously advertised the affinity of his findings to folk superstitions. After all, except for the unreadable Scherner, no modern investigator had valued dreams as susceptible to serious interpretation; such readings had been reserved to "lay opinion," to the uneducated masses obscurely sensing that dreams are legible messages.

They *are* messages, Freud agreed, but not the ones the lay public expects. They will not yield their meaning to the common method of assigning each dream detail a single, definite symbolic significance, or to the reading of the dream as a cryptogram to be decoded by means of a naive key. Freud flatly pronounced "both popular interpretative procedures" to be useless. In their place, he recommended Breuer's cathartic method, as elaborated and modified in his own practice: the dreamer must employ free association, abandoning his accustomed rational criticism of mental meanderings, to recognize his dream for what it is—a symptom. Taking each element of the dream separately (as in the old decoding method, thus exploited for scientific purposes) and using it as a starting point for free association, the dreamer or his analyst will eventually unravel its meaning. Freud claimed to have interpreted more than a thousand dreams of his own and of his analysands with this technique. What had emerged was a general law: *"The dream is a wish fulfillment."*

This formulation immediately raises a question, which Freud disposed of in the most succinct of chapters. Is wish fulfillment the universal law of dreams, or simply the reading appropriate to the dream of Irma's injection? Offering a sizable catalogue of instances, Freud insisted that it holds true for all dreams, whatever the indications to the contrary. Every apparent exception to this sweeping assertion appeared to Freud, on examination, to be yet another proof. Each was a subtle variation on a simple theme.*

ONE OF THE first dreams to give Freud a hint of his law antedated his dream of Irma's injection by almost five months. It was an amusing and fairly transparent "indolence dream"—*Bequemlichkeitstraum*—dreamt by a young, intelligent physician of his acquaintance, in fact Breuer's nephew. Disguised in *The Interpretation of Dreams* as "Pepi," he turns out to be someone who likes to sleep late. One morning, as his landlady tries to wake him and calls to him through the door, Pepi responds by dreaming that he is already at the hospital and hence does not need to get up. So he turns over and sleeps on. But, the objector will persist, many dreams do not seem to fulfill wishes at all. They may represent or arouse anxiety or develop a neutral, quite unemotional scenario. Why should such distressing or indifferent dreams count as instances of wish fulfillment? And why do they need to disguise their meaning? "When in scientific work the solution of a problem presents difficulties," Freud replied, "it is often a good thing to take up a second one, just as it is easier to crack two nuts against one another than singly." The solution lies in distortion, which furnishes the essential clue to the work the dreamer unconsciously performs as he dreams.

Preparing to explain distortion, Freud introduced a crucial distinction between the manifest dream and the latent dream thoughts. The former is what the individual dreams and recalls more or less fuzzily upon awakening; the latter, the latent dream thoughts, are hidden and will normally emerge, if at all, heavily veiled and in need of decoding. Children's dreams, which furnish an exception, are therefore paradoxically at once boring and informative: "The dreams of small children are frequently pure wish fulfillments," and hence "present no puzzles to be solved"; but they are "invaluable for the demonstration that dreams signify, in their innermost nature, the fulfillment of a wish." Quite nakedly, such dreams represent a forbidden piece of candy as eaten, a promised excursion as already taken. They require virtually no interpretation. To illustrate this point, Freud enlisted dreams of his small sons and daughters; in one charming instance Anna, the future psychoanalyst, makes her appearance by name. At the age of nineteen months, the little girl had vomited one morning and was kept fasting during the day. That night,

---

*Not until 1920, in an address to an international congress of psychoanalysts, did Freud allow an exception: the class of traumatic dreams, dreams that recall recent accidents or childhood traumas. And even they turned out not really to be an exception at all: traumatic dreams also fit into the wish-fulfillment theory of dreams in that they embody the wish to master the trauma by working it through. (See "Supplements to the Theory of Dreams" [1920], *SE* XVIII, 4–5.)

her parents heard her call out excitedly in her sleep, using her own name, as was then her habit, to mean that she was taking possession of something: "Anna F'eud, stawberry, wild stawberry, om'let, puddin." This "menu," Freud commented, "comprised about everything that must have appeared to her as a desirable meal."

With adults, on the other hand, dissimulation becomes second nature: politeness in everyday life and, dramatically, censorship of the press are the models that dreamers imitate as they cover their desires with innocuous-looking and virtually impenetrable masks. In short, the manifest dream is what the dreamer's inner censorship will permit to float to the surface of awareness: "We may thus assume as the originators giving dreams their shape, two psychical forces (currents, systems), of which one forms the wish brought to expression by the dream, while the other exercises censorship on this dream-wish and by this censorship compels a distortion of its utterance." The recognition that a dream consists of both manifest content and latent thoughts permits the interpreter to reach the conflicts that dreams embody and disguise.

These conflicts are usually fought out between the drives that want gratification and the defenses that want to deny it. But the dream can also exhibit contests of another kind: wishes may clash with one another. In 1909, in the second edition of *The Interpretation of Dreams,* probably piqued by objections to his theory, Freud added a telling instance of such an unconscious conflict; his patients, "in resistance against me," regularly produced dreams in which a wish was visibly frustrated. These "counter-wish dreams," as he called them, exhibited the wish to prove Freud wrong. But they did not make him doubt that he was right; even the anxiety dream, which appears as a spectacular refutation of Freud's theory, is nothing of the kind. It is a dream representing a wish produced in the unconscious but repudiated by the rest of the mind; hence the manifest dream is laden with anxiety.* Thus a little boy represses his sexual wish for his mother as wholly unacceptable, yet it persists in the unconscious and will emerge in one way or another, perhaps in an anxiety dream. What Freud proposed at this point, therefore, was not a retreat from his original formulation but an expansion of it: *"A dream is the (disguised) fulfillment of a (suppressed, repressed) wish."*

---

*Freud would elaborate on this tricky point in a long footnote he added in 1919 (see *Interpretation of Dreams, SE V,* 580–81n). His argument raises the inconvenient question of whether he claims to be in the right in every possible situation, so that his theory cannot be disproved: a dream that can be easily interpreted as a wish-fulfillment confirms his theory; an anxiety dream that seems to be the very opposite somehow fits into it as well. The explanation lies in Freud's view of the mind as a set of organizations in conflict with one another; what one segment of the mind wants, another is likely to reject, often very anxiously.

HIS FIRST GENERAL proposition complicated to his satisfaction, Freud set wish fulfillment aside and retraced his steps, approaching dream theory from "a new point of departure" for his "rambles" through "the problems of the dream." He now turned to its characteristic materials and sources. Having prepared the way by distinguishing between the manifest and the latent aspects of dreams, he proceeded to show that even though the two are meaningfully linked, they differ markedly. A dream invariably draws on recent materials, yet it leads upon interpretation to a most distant past; no matter how bland or bizarre its recalled scenario, it points toward issues of cardinal importance to the dreamer. "There are," Freud concluded pointedly, a little ominously, "no indifferent dream instigators; hence, too, no innocent dreams."

A woman patient of Freud's dreamt that she had put a candle into a candlestick, but because the candle had broken, it would not stand up properly. Her schoolmates told her she was clumsy, but her teacher said that it was not her fault. In the Freudian universe, a candle that cannot stand up evokes the image of a flaccid penis. This seems hardly novel now, but when Freud published this dream, and others like it, his erotic interpretations offended a shocked and defensive public as indications of an unseemly monomania. Undismayed, Freud, interpreting this dream, called its symbolism "transparent." After all, "a candle is an object that can excite the female genitals; when it is broken so that it cannot stand properly, this signifies the man's impotence." When Freud wondered out loud whether this properly brought up and carefully protected young analysand had any inkling of such uses for a candle, she enlightened him. She recalled that once, in a rowboat on the Rhine, she and her husband had been passed by another boat with students animatedly shouting out a song about the "Queen of Sweden who, with her shutters closed, . . . with Apollo candles." Because she had failed to hear, or understand, the missing word, which was "masturbates," her husband had explained it to her. Free association led from the "closed shutters" of the obscene verses to a bit of clumsiness which she had once perpetrated at boarding school and was now exploited in her dream to lend her sexual thoughts a harmless cloak. And "Apollo"? That was a brand name of candles, and connected this dream with an earlier one in which there had been something about the "virginal" Pallas Athene. "Truly," Freud said it again, laconically, "all of it far from innocent."

The immediate instigators of a dream, however, are in general harmless enough. Every dream, Freud maintained, exhibits "a point of contact with the events of the *previous day*. Whatever dream I take in hand, my own or someone else's, confirms this experience every time." These "day's residues," as he called them, frequently offer the easiest access to the interpretation of a dream. Take Freud's short dream about the botanical monograph, in which he saw before him an illustrated book he had written, with a dried plant specimen bound in each copy; the instigator of that dream had been a monograph on cyclamens he had seen in a bookstore window the morning before. Still, in nearly every instance, the dream ultimately borrows its essential ingredients from the dreamer's childhood days.

Earlier researchers like Maury had already noted that infantile material may push its way into the adult's manifest dream; recurrent dreams, first dreamt in childhood and returning years later to haunt the sleeper's nights, are another tribute to the agile acrobatics of human memory. But to Freud only the infantile material that interpretation can uncover, the material concealed in the latent dream thoughts, was truly absorbing. He found it so absorbing in fact that he devoted a whole section to it and recounted a number of his own dreams, complete with extensive, exceedingly intimate autobiographical revelations. He was prepared to demonstrate from his private memories that *"one finds the child with its impulses living on in the dream."* It is in these pages that Freud confessed to his ambitions in painful detail and related the story about the strolling poet at a Prater restaurant predicting a great political future for him. Here, too, Freud revealed his tormented, long-cherished and long-frustrated wish to visit Rome.

ONE OF THE most indiscreet autobiographical dreams Freud analyzed in *The Interpretation of Dreams* is his much-cited Count Thun dream. In his analysis he joined a circumstantial report on the day's residues that had unleashed the dream to an even more circumstantial interpretation. The day's residues of the dream about Count Thun show Freud in his most expansive, even bellicose mood. At the Western Station in Vienna, on his way to a summer vacation at Aussee, he watches Count Thun, the reactionary Austrian politician and, briefly, prime minister, at his haughtiest, and is filled with "all sorts of insolent and revolutionary ideas." He hums to himself Figaro's famous aria from the first act of *The Marriage of Figaro,* in which the commoner boldly challenges the count to a dance, and then associates it to Beaumarchais's stirring comedy that had served as the basis of Da Ponte's libretto for Mozart's opera. Freud had seen the play in Paris and, much to the point, recalled its hero's sturdy protest against the great gentleman who had taken the trouble to be born and had, it seemed, no other merit.*

---

*The words of the aria, as quoted by Freud, are: "Se vuol ballare, signor contino, / Se vuol ballare, signor contino, / Il chitarino le suonerò." Freud did not mention, though he may well have had in mind, Heinrich Heine, one of his favorite satirists. Heine had used these very lines as his motto to preface *The Baths of Lucca,* his devastating assault on Count Platen, the homosexual poet whom he imagined to be his enemy and at the center of a conspiracy against him.

This was the political Freud, the liberal bourgeois who thought himself as good as any count. But in uncovering the energy driving the Count Thun dream by tracing an elaborate network of associations, Freud was drawn back to long-forgotten childhood episodes. They were less political than the immediate instigators of the dream but just as much in character, and, indeed, constituted part of the foundation supporting his self-respecting political attitudes. The most significant of these episodes, already recounted, involved Freud, perhaps seven or eight, urinating in his parents' bedroom and being told by his father that he would never amount to anything. "It must have been a terrible blow to my ambition," Freud commented, "for allusions to this scene keep constantly recurring in my dreams and are regularly linked with enumerations of my achievements and successes, as though I wanted to say, 'You see, I have amounted to something after all.' "

Not every significant source of a dream need be traced all the way to infancy. His dream about the botanical monograph led Freud to think of his wife, to whom he brought flowers only too rarely, of his monograph on the coca plant, of a recent conversation with his friend Dr. Königstein, of his dream of Irma's injection, of his ambitions as a scientist, and also of the day long ago—he was five and his sister not yet three—when his father had given them a book with colored plates to tear up, a blissful and isolated memory from his earliest years.

HUNTING IN THE luxuriant jungles of childhood experience, Freud brought home some fascinating trophies, none so spectacular, or so controversial, as the Oedipus complex. He had first announced this momentous idea to Fliess in the fall of 1897.* Now, in *The Interpretation of Dreams,* he elaborated it without as yet using the name under which it has entered—indeed, dominated—the history of psychoanalysis. He introduced it, appropriately enough, in a section on typical dreams, among which those about the death of loved ones required some sober comment. Sibling rivalries, tensions between mothers and daughters or fathers and sons, death wishes against family members, all seem wicked and unnatural. They offend the most highly prized official pieties, but, Freud dryly observed, they are no secret to anyone. The Oedipus complex, embodied in myths, tragedies, and dreams no less than in daily life, is implicated in all these closet conflicts. It is driven into the unconscious, but is all the more consequential for that. The Oedipus complex is, as Freud would later put it, the "nuclear complex" of the neuroses. But, as he insisted from the first, "being in love with one and hating the other part of the

*See p. 100.

parental pair" is not the monopoly of neurotics. It is the lot, though less spectacularly, of all normal humans.

Freud's early formulations of the Oedipus complex were comparatively simple; he would considerably complicate them over the years. While the idea of the complex was soon strongly contested, his predilection for it steadily increased: he viewed it as an explanation of how neuroses originate, as a turning point in the developmental history of the child, as a marker differentiating male and female sexual maturation, even, in *Totem and Taboo,* as the deep motive for the founding of civilization and the creation of conscience. But in *The Interpretation of Dreams,* though the wider implications are not far to seek, the oedipal struggle has a more modest part to play. By accounting for those murderous dreams about the death of spouses or parents, it provides evidence for the theory that dreams represent wishes as fulfilled. Beyond that, it helps to explain why dreams are such odd productions; humans, all humans, harbor wishes they cannot allow to see the light of day in their uncensored form.

Every dream, then, is a piece of work, and hard work at that. If the pressure of wishes to reach consciousness were less severe, or if the need to resist that pressure were less urgent, the work would be easier. Serving as the guardian of sleep, the "dream work" has the function of converting unacceptable impulses and memories into a story harmless enough to blunt their edge and permit their utterance. The variety of dream work open to dreamers is virtually inexhaustible, since they have an infinity of day's residues and unique life histories at their disposal. But despite the appearance of planless crowded chaos, that work follows settled rules. The censor grooming the latent dream thoughts for their appearance in the manifest dream enjoys great leeway and exercises impressive ingenuity, but his instructions are terse, and the devices at his command few in number.

Freud devoted the longest chapter in the book to these instructions and devices. He regarded the dream interpreter as part paleographer, part translator, part code breaker. "The dream thoughts and the dream contents lie before us like two versions of the same contents in two different languages; or, better put, the dream contents appear to us as a transcription of the dream thoughts into another mode of expression, whose characters and syntactic laws we are supposed to become acquainted with by comparing the original with the translation." Varying the metaphor, Freud likened the dream to a rebus, a nonsensical-appearing picture puzzle that we learn to read only if we cease being astonished at its absurdity and "replace each picture with a syllable or a word."

The principal instruments in the tool kit of the dream work are condensation, displacement, and what Freud called "concern for representability."* These are not unique to dreams, but can be detected in the making of neurotic symptoms, slips of the tongue, and jokes. But it was in dreams that Freud first uncovered and described their work. He had found yet a fourth mechanism, "secondary revision," the neatening up of the confused dream story upon awakening, but he was uncertain whether to consider it an instrument of the dream work at all.

There is yet another way in which dreams convey their inner meaning—through symbols. Freud assigned only a marginal role to symbols; in the early editions of *The Interpretation of Dreams,* he mentioned them just in passing, and he later added a sizable section on them mainly under the prodding of Wilhelm Stekel and others among his first disciples. The sheer mechanical quality of symbol interpretation never ceased to disturb him. "I want to warn emphatically against overestimating the significance of symbols for dream interpretation," he wrote in 1909, and went on to caution against "restricting the work of dream translation to the translating of symbols and abandoning the technique of turning the dreamer's associations to good account." A year later, he categorically told his Swiss friend the pastor-psychoanalyst Oskar Pfister, "You have my full consent if you deal suspiciously with each new strong demand for a symbol"—*Symbolzumutung*—"until it thrusts itself upon you anew from experience." After all, "the best set of implements of ψA† is to know the singular dialect dictionary of the unconscious."

Freud's enumeration of the devices the dream work employs is thus pervaded by a certain irony. The interpretation of symbols had been the mainstay of dream books for centuries, and was to become a favorite parlor game among amateurs playing at psychoanalysis in the 1920s. Thus the very technique of reading dreams that Freud found most questionable established itself, after word of psychoanalysis had spread, as the technique many people found the most intriguing. It is not the only instance, as we shall see, of the kind of popularity that Freud deplored and thought he could do without.

THE FIRST OF the dream work's really significant implements, condensation, is explained by its name. Dream thoughts that flood into a dreamer's mind are infinitely richer than the manifest dream, which is "scanty, paltry, laconic in comparison." A handful of the associations the dreamer will produce may be new, but most of them arise from the dream itself. Each element of the

---

*In his popularization, *On Dreams* (1901), Freud listed "condensation, displacement, and dramatization" as the most important instruments available to the dream work. (*GW* II–III, 699/*SE* V, 685.)

†In their informal correspondence, Freud and his colleagues often used the abbreviation ψA for "psychoanalysis."

manifest dream's contents turns out to be overdetermined; it is represented in the latent dream thoughts several times. A person in a dream is a composite figure: Irma is a good instance—standing for several persons from whom she has borrowed features and characteristics. Comical made-up words or freshly minted neologisms, so frequent in dreams, are other instances of how condensation concentrates ideas with a kind of fanatical economy. Thus Freud's dream about the botanical monograph is a single scene, the briefest visual impression, but it contains and compresses the most diverse materials from several stages of Freud's life. Again, "Autodidasker," a word that Freud dreamt, proved to be a condensation of "author," "autodidact," and "Lasker," the name of a liberal German Jewish politician, to which Freud associated the name of the German Jewish Socialist Ferdinand Lassalle; these names led him through some devious byways into the mine field of erotic preoccupations, which is what this dream was really about. Lasker and Lassalle had both come to a miserable end over a woman: the first dying of syphilis, the second killed in a duel. Freud found another name concealed in "Autodidasker" as an anagram of "Lasker": that of his brother Alexander, known in the family as Alex; one wish this dream contained was Freud's wish that his brother might some day marry happily. The resourcefulness of condensation is nothing less than astonishing.

While condensation need not involve the censor, the work of displacement is his prize exhibit. It acts first to reduce the intensity of the passions bursting to express themselves, and then to transform them. Thus it enables these passions, however mutilated they often appear in their public guise, to escape the resistance censorship mobilizes. As a result, the real wishes animating a dream may never appear in it at all. That is obviously why dreamers seeking to understand their productions must associate as freely as they can let themselves, and why the analyst must deploy all his interpretative talents on what they tell him.

Since a dream is a picture puzzle with a crazy logic all its own, the dream interpreter needs to understand more than displacement and condensation. Concern for representability, too, plays its part. The categories one takes for granted in waking life have no place in a dream; it knows no causality, no contradiction, no identity. It represents thoughts as pictures, abstract ideas by concrete images: the notion that someone is superfluous may be conveyed by a flow of water spilling out of a tub. One dream element following another in time suggests the logical relation of cause and effect; the frequency with which a dream element appears graphically underscores its importance. Since the dream has no direct way of expressing negation, it does so by representing people, events, feelings, by their opposites. Dreams are punsters and tricksters; they make jokes or feign intellectual activity.

The space that Freud devoted to the stratagems available to the dream work was, then, wholly justified. Many dreams contain speeches, and these are almost invariably quotations, reproducing words the dreamer has heard somewhere. Yet the dream work enlists these very real speeches not to clarify the meaning of the dream, but to advance its devious effort to smuggle far from innocent materials past the censor. Again, dreams are often swamped by affects, which, Freud cautioned, the interpreter must not take literally, since the dream work is likely to weaken or exaggerate their force, disguise their real targets, or, as we have seen, turn them into their opposites. One of Freud's best-known instances, his *"Non vixit"* dream, illustrates the way of the dream both with words and with feelings. No wonder Freud called it "lovely." It was filled with friends, several of them dead. In the dream, one of these, Josef Paneth, fails to understand what Fliess has been saying, and Freud explains that this is because Paneth is not alive: *"Non vixit."* This, as Freud recognizes in the dream itself, is a mistake in the Latin, which means, of course, "He did not live," rather than "He is not living"—*Non vivit.* At that moment, Freud annihilates Paneth with a look; he simply melts away, as does Fleischl-Marxow. Each is nothing more than a *revenant,* an apparition that can be wished away at will, and the dreamer finds this thought delightful.

The source for Freud's dream-fantasy that he reduced Paneth to nothing with a piercing look is no mystery: this was the self-serving transformation of a humiliating scene in which his mentor, Brücke, had stared down Freud, the remiss assistant, and reduced him to nothing. But *"Non vixit"?* Freud finally traced the words to a speech not heard but seen: they appear, he recalled, on the pedestal of the monument to Emperor Josef II at the Imperial Palace in Vienna: *Saluti patriae vixit / non diu sed totus*—"For the well-being of his country he lived not long but wholly." Freud's dream borrowed these words to apply to another Josef, Josef Paneth, who had been his successor in Brücke's laboratory and had died young in 1890; evidently Freud was regretful about his friend's premature death, but also triumphant at having survived him. These were some of the affects Freud's dream reported and distorted; others, he added, were anxiety about his friend Fliess, who was about to undergo an operation, feelings of guilt over not rushing to Berlin to be with him, and irritation at Fliess for telling him to discuss the operation with no one, as though he, Freud, were by nature indiscreet and needed such reminders. The *revenants* in the dream brought Freud back to his childhood: they stood for friends and enemies of long ago. The pleasure in outliving others, the wish for immortality, underlay the petty feelings of superiority and the equally petty feelings of annoyance in which the *"Non vixit"* dream abounded. The whole scenario reminded him of an old story: one spouse, naive, egotistic, remarks to the other, "If one of us should die, I'll move to Paris." It should be clear by now why Freud thought that no dream can ever be interpreted exhaustively; its textures of associations are too rich, its devices too adroit, to permit the riddles they set to be wholly cleared up. But Freud never hesitated to assert that at the bottom of every dream there is a wish, at once infantile and what respectable society would probably call indecent.

A PSYCHOLOGY
FOR PSYCHOLOGISTS

 In the evolution of Freud's psychoanalytic thinking, *The Interpretation of Dreams* occupies the strategic center, and he knew it. That he should have chosen the dream as the most instructive exemplar of mental work is highly significant: dreaming is a normal, universal experience. Since Freud was also planning other studies of common and normal psychological processes at the time he was working on the dream book, he might well have selected a different point of departure. In the late 1890s, Freud had begun to gather the telling anecdotes about all sorts of slips and lapses that he would publish in 1901 under the suggestive title *The Psychopathology of Everyday Life*. Again, in June 1897, he told Fliess that he was starting a collection of "profound Jewish stories"; these, too, he would make into a book, in which he would canvass the relation of jokes to the unconscious. Both the most ordinary slips and the most unsophisticated jokes led him to the remotest regions of mind. But the dream was, for Freud, the privileged guide. At once commonplace and mysterious, bizarre yet open to rational explication, it ramifies to virtually every province of mental functioning. Accordingly, in the theoretical seventh chapter of his *Interpretation of Dreams*, Freud demonstrated its unsurpassed range of relevance in detail.

Freud's selection of materials for his book on dreams is also very revealing. As he noted in the preface to the first edition, the dreams of neurotics present special characteristics that might impair their representativeness and hence compromise the general application of his theory. That is why he sought out the dreams of his friends and his children, and dreams reported in literature, to say nothing of his own. In the end, he found some of his patients' contributions irresistible, but he overwhelmed them with instances drawn from what he liked to call normal people. He was determined not to let the road to psychoanalytic knowledge start in the specialized, constricted domain of his hysterical or obsessive analysands.

At the same time, while the materials his analysands provided might be unrepresentative, they did not seriously distort his investigations. That Freud should borrow from neurotics so freely was, of course, an obvious consequence of his daily occupation: they were available and they were interesting. But working out his theory of neuroses, Freud found that the neurotic throws such clear light on the normal largely because the two are really not so different from one another. Neurotics, and in their extravagant way psychotics, exhibit the traits of less troubled mortals in histrionic, but therefore all the more instructive ways. "A satisfactory general comprehension of neuropsychotic disturbances," Freud announced to Fliess in the spring of 1895, "is impossible if one cannot make connections to clear assumptions about normal mental processes." At the very time he was contemplating his "Project for a Scientific Psychology," he was also tormented by the enigma of the neuroses. In his own mind, these two inquiries were never—and could not be profitably—kept apart. It is not an accident that he should have enlivened his abstract theoretical memoranda with instances from his clinical cases. They were materials for a general psychology.

FREUD DID NOT always appreciate his analysands, however informative they might be. At times his long, exhausting hours with them made him feel swamped, and his therapeutic work seemed to be keeping him from the riddles of the universe. But his practice contradicts him: his clinical experience and his theoretical investigations usually fertilized each other. Freud liked to portray his medical career as a vast detour starting from an adolescent's passion for profound philosophical conundrums and ending with an old man's return to fundamental speculations after a long, unwanted exile among the doctors. In reality, "philosophical" questions were never far from his awareness, even after, in his drastic words, he had "become a therapist against my will." Looking back to his youth when he was forty, he told Fliess in 1896, "I knew no longing other than that for philosophical insight, and I am now in the process of fulfilling it, as I steer from medicine over to psychology." He could empathize with his friend in Berlin, who seemed to be going in the same direction. "I see," he wrote in a reflective New Year's letter on January 1, 1896, "how you, through the detour of being a physician, are reaching your first ideal, to understand humans as a physiologist, just as I most secretly nourish the hope of reaching my original goal, philosophy." However powerful his contempt for most philosophers and for their futile word games, he would pursue his own philosophical goals all his life. This inconsistency is more apparent than real. Freud gave "philosophy" a special meaning. In true Enlightenment fashion, he denigrated the philosophizing of metaphysicians as unhelpful abstractions. He was equally hostile to those philosophers who equate the reach of the mind with consciousness. *His* philosophy was scientific empiricism as embodied in a scientific theory of the mind.

The study of dreams led Freud directly to such high-flying aspirations. Since the dream is at bottom a wish in action, Freud found it necessary to undertake systematic, far-ranging forays into the very foundations of psychology. They alone might make the meaning of dream activity intelligible. Hence Freud's "shibboleths" of psychoanalysis, comprising the irreducible short catalogue that differentiates his psychology from that of others, do not make their appearance just in the rigorous analytical last chapter of the dream book. The principle of psychological determinism, the view of the mind as consisting of forces in conflict, the concept of the dynamic unconscious and the concealed power of passion in all mental activity, pervade its very texture.

It is a crucial point in Freud's theory that there are no accidents in the universe of the mind. Freud never denied that humans are exposed to chance; on the contrary, he insisted on it: "We like to forget that in fact everything in our life is chance, from our genesis out of the encounter of spermatozoon and egg onward." Nor did he deny that human choices are real; one aim of psychoanalytic therapy was precisely "to give the patient's ego *freedom* to decide one way or another." But neither Freud's "chance," nor his "freedom," is an arbitrary or random manifestation of spontaneity. In his view of the mind, every event, no matter now accidental its appearance, is as it were a knot in intertwined causal threads that are too remote in origin, large in number, and complex in their interaction to be readily sorted out. True: to secure freedom from the grip of causality is among mankind's most cherished, and hence most tenacious, illusory wishes. But Freud sternly warned that psychoanalysis should offer such illusory fantasies no comfort. Freud's theory of the mind is therefore strictly and frankly deterministic.

IT IS ALSO emphatically psychological and thus, for its time, revolutionary. Freud developed his program within the framework of contemporary psychology, but broke through that framework at point after decisive point. His most eminent colleagues in the field of psychiatry were neurologists at heart. In 1895, the year of Freud and Breuer's *Studies on Hysteria,* Krafft-Ebing published a monograph, *Nervousness and Neurasthenic States,* which illustrates the prevailing viewpoint to perfection. The little book is a brave attempt to bring some clarity into the confusion then current in the use of diagnostic terms. Krafft-Ebing defined "nervousness" as *"for the most part an innate pathological disposition, more rarely an acquired pathological change in the central nervous system.* " Heredity is the principal source of trouble: "The vast majority of individuals afflicted with a nervous disposition are nervous from their earliest years, on the basis of congenital influences." Krafft-Ebing saluted with grave, almost awed respect "the mighty biological law of heredity, which decisively intervenes in all of organic nature"; its influence on mental life, he thought, is undisputed and preeminent. Acquired nervousness, for its part, arises when the *"correct relationship between the accumulation and the expenditure of nerve force"* is disturbed. Lack of sleep, poor diet, alcoholic debauches, the "antihygienic" character of modern civilization, with its haste, its excessive demands on the mind, its democratic politics, its emancipation of women, all make people nervous. But acquired nervousness is, precisely like the congenital variety, a matter of "material, if extremely slight changes in the nervous system."

That graver malady "neurasthenia" is for Krafft-Ebing nervousness writ large, a "functional" disease in which mental life *"can no longer establish the balance between production and consumption of nerve force."* The mechanical metaphor is not an accident; Krafft-Ebing viewed neurasthenia as essentially the nervous system out of order. As with nervousness, the physician must seek the principal etiology of neurasthenia in heredity. The acquired sort can be traced to physiological causes, an unlucky set of traumas, or a destructive environment: a childhood illness due to a "neuropathic constitution," masturbation, or, once again, the excessive strains imposed on the system by modern life. Even when the instigator of neurasthenia turns out to be a psychological episode such as worry or mental stress, the ultimate disturbing element at work is neurological in nature. Krafft-Ebing was prepared to consider "sociological" factors, but their "predisposing cause," too, goes back to "a nervous constitution." The treatments Krafft-Ebing recommended naturally lean toward diet, medication, physiotherapy, electrotherapy, massages. As the preeminent specialist in the field of sexual aberration, he did not pass over what he called *Neurasthenia sexualis,* but he only glanced at it as a small part of the clinical picture, not as a cause.

In short, Krafft-Ebing treated psychological suffering largely as a matter of physiology. He had not moved in 1895 from the proposition he had advanced sixteen years earlier in his textbook on psychiatry: "Insanity is a brain disease." He was speaking for his profession. During the nineteenth century, the science of psychology had taken impressive strides, made stunning advances. But its position was paradoxical: it had emancipated itself from philosophy, as it had done earlier from theology, only to accept the imperious embrace of a new master—physiology. The idea that mind and body are linked by the most intimate ties had, of course, an age-old and honorable tradition behind it. "A man's body and his mind," Laurence Sterne had declared in the mid-eighteenth century, "with the utmost reverence to both I speak it, are exactly like a jerkin, and a jerkin's lining;—rumple the one,—you rumple the other." Nineteenth-century students of the mind subscribed to this proposition and went beyond it; they confidently specified which is the jerkin, which the lining. Mind, they argued, is dependent on body, the nervous system, the brain.

In 1876, the prominent American neurologist William Hammond, who was a specialist (among other things) in male and female impotence, expressed the overwhelming consensus of the experts. "The modern science of psychology"—he laid it down—"is neither more nor less than *the science of mind considered as a physical function.*" The emphatic italics are Hammond's. In England, the influential and prolific psychiatrist Henry Maudsley was no less emphatic. In 1874, speaking of insanity, he wrote, "It is not our business, it is not in our power, to explain *psychologically* the origin and nature of any of [the] depraved instincts" that the insane manifest. "The explanation, when it comes, will come not from the mental, but from the physical side." Psychologists and psychiatrists on the Continent had no quarrel on this issue with their English and American colleagues; early in the century, the distinguished French psychiatrist Jean Étienne Esquirol had defined "madness, mental alienation" as "an *ordinarily* chronic cerebral affection," and this definition retained its ascendancy to the end of the century and beyond, across Europe and the United States. In 1910, Freud told the "Wolf Man," one of his most famous patients, "We have the means to cure what you are suffering from. Up to now, you have been looking for the causes of your illness in the chamber pot." Looking back years later, the Wolf Man agreed, perhaps a little too emphatically: "In those days people tried to get at psychic states by way of the physical. The psychological was completely ignored."* There had been a few dissenters, like the English Quaker physicians who developed, around 1800, what they called "moral treatment" for their insane patients. They tried to repair the disorders of the miserable madmen and madwomen in their charge with moral suasion, mental discipline, and kindness rather than with drugs or physical abuse—and registered

---

*On March 6, 1917, the eminent American psychiatrist William Alanson White, one of the first to take a positive view of Freud, wrote to W. A. Robison, "If you are acquainted with the history of the care of the so-called insane in this country you will know the remarkable fact that it is only in the past few years that mental diseases have been treated as mental diseases. They have more usually been treated as evidences of physical disorder. We have been approaching the subject from a mental point of view for a long time, and in recent years have gone at it from a psychotherapeutic standpoint. We have followed Professor Freud's work and are using his psychoanalytic methods, without, however, dogmatizing about it or allying ourselves with any special cult." (Letter in Gerald N. Grob, ed., *The Inner World of American Psychiatry, 1890–1940: Selected Correspondence* [1985], 107.)

some successes. But practically all other neurologists, psychiatrists, and keepers of insane asylums worked on the assumption that the impact of the body on the mind is far more significant than that of the mind on the body.

Brilliant nineteenth-century researches into brain anatomy, which did much to map the complicated mechanisms of vision, hearing, speech, and memory, only served to support this neurological view of psychological processes. Even the phrenologists, curious, ultimately absurd as their ideas were, did their part in strengthening the grip of this view on educated opinion. While in the second half of the nineteenth century skeptical brain anatomists exploded the phrenological doctrine that each passion and each mental capacity has a highly specific location, they did not wholly reject the phrenologists' fundamental idea that mental functions originate in particular regions of the brain. The great Hermann Helmholtz and fellow scientists like his friend Emil Du Bois-Reymond further buttressed the authority of the materialistic view of the mind with their delicate experimental work on the speed and pathways of nervous impulses. The mind increasingly appeared as a little machine fueled by electrical and chemical forces that can be traced, diagrammed, and measured. With one discovery after another, a physiological substratum for all mental events seemed absolutely secure. Neurology was king.

As an admiring disciple of Brücke, who had brought the message of Helmholtz and Du Bois-Reymond to Vienna, Freud had been freely exposed to this view, and he never wholly abandoned it. Much in his practice spoke for it; his analytic patients had taught him that while many physical symptoms are hysterical conversions, some turn out to be really organic in nature.* One important reason why Freud was so attracted to the thesis that neuroses have their origins in sexual malfunctioning was that "after all, sexuality is not a purely mental affair. It also has a somatic side." Hence Freud was, as he told Fliess in 1898, "not at all disposed to keep the psychological dangling without the organic basis." Freud's subversion of the reigning orthodoxy was the outcome of a slow, not at all clearly planned change of mind. When he finally made his revolution, it consisted not of discarding the neurological theory but of reversing the accepted ranking in the mind–body interaction. He assigned primacy to the psychological dimension in mental work, not a monopoly.

Until Freud challenged the prevailing materialist consensus, there was relatively little dispute over the basically physical nature of the mental ma-

---

*That unfortunate seduction theory of the mid-1890s explicitly specified a physical trauma as the cause of all neuroses. And even after Freud felt compelled to jettison this theory, he never gave up the idea that there is often some somatic basis for mental events.

chine. As late as 1895, after all, Freud himself had offered his unfinished project as a "psychology for neurologists." But in addressing the question of just what causes this machine to break down, Freud joined a long-standing, inconclusive debate. While psychiatrists agreed by and large that mental ailments are nearly all manifestations of a lesion in the brain, they divided over the possible etiologies for that lesion. In the 1830s, Esquirol had still proffered an eclectic, rather indiscriminate catalogue of instigators. "The causes of mental alienation are as numerous as they are varied," he wrote. "Not only do climate, seasons, age, sex, temperament, profession, and manner of life influence the frequency, character, duration, crises, and treatment of insanity, but this malady is further modified by laws, civilization, morals, and the political condition of nations." By mid-century, though, that favorite candidate, heredity, had eclipsed though not eliminated the others. It retained the preeminent position for decades. Case histories provided massive—it seemed to many, conclusive—evidence that the mental patient is bound to be burdened with an abnormal family history. Krafft-Ebing's monograph on neurasthenia is wholly characteristic on this point. Freud, too, in his early case reports, gave room to details concerning the patient's "neuropathic" family; he carefully recorded the stay of a patient's mother in an insane asylum, or the severe hypochondria of a brother. Then psychology took the upper hand. By 1905, in his *Three Essays on the Theory of Sexuality,* he had reached the point where he could criticize his fellow psychiatrists for assigning far too much importance to heredity.

Freud's feelings about other presumed causes of mental distress were no less mixed. As Krafft-Ebing's study on neurasthenia attests, rival etiologies appeared to play second fiddle to tainted heredity but had their partisans in the literature. Few psychiatrists wholly ruled out sudden shocks or lingering illnesses—certainly for some years Freud did not—and many took particular interest in what they thought the pernicious side effects of modern culture. On this last diagnosis, in fact, Freud voted with the majority, though for reasons of his own. Like many other contemporary observers, he was persuaded that the urban, bourgeois, industrial civilization of his day markedly contributed to the nervousness which, he thought, was visibly on the rise. Yet while others held modern civilization responsible for nervousness by pointing to its haste, its bustle, its rapid communications and overburdening of the mental machinery, Freud blamed it rather for excessively restricting sexual behavior.

This deviation from the position of the majority is at the heart of Freud's own views on the origins of mental illness. He did not doubt that all the phenomena his fellow psychiatrists adduced had their share in the making of obsessional neuroses, hysterias, paranoia, and the rest of the dismal array. But he became persuaded that his profession had signally failed to probe their hidden nature. Above all, physicians had virtually all evaded the crucial role of sexuality and of the unconscious conflicts that this drive generates. That is why they had been pleased to exaggerate the importance of their patients' remote prehistory—their heredity—and assiduously overlooked that other, far more important prehistory—childhood—where these sexual conflicts arise. *The Interpretation of Dreams* is Freud's first comprehensive, though still far from complete, statement of these views, of his psychology for psychologists.

"WE SAW LITTLE of father during the summer holiday of 1899," Martin Freud recalled many years later. This was unusual, since Freud valued that time in the mountains with his children. That summer, though, racing to complete his book and beginning to read proofs, "he was absorbed in work which he could not neglect." But he freely discussed the book with his family, an exceptional procedure for him: "We had all been told about it, and he even encouraged us to tell him of our dreams: something we did with enthusiasm." As we have seen, some of the specimens Freud's children supplied proved publishable. "He even explained to us in simple language," Martin Freud went on, "what could be understood of dreams, their origin and meaning." The book he intended as a seminal contribution to general psychology could not remain an esoteric pursuit.

No doubt, some secretiveness was necessarily built into Freud's very enterprise. While he freely documented the instigating power of sexual desires and sexual conflicts in others, he refused to explore the libidinal origins of his own dreams with the same uninhibited freedom. But he paid a price for his ambivalence about quarrying his own past, and his own dreams, for raw material. Later, some of Freud's most alert readers, fellow analysts in the main, were struck forcibly enough by his partial reticence to remark on it. Karl Abraham asked Freud outright whether he had failed to complete his interpretation of the Irma dream on purpose; after all, sexual allusions seemed more and more obtrusive toward the end of Freud's account. In the confidential manner of the early analysts, Freud replied promptly and openly: "Sexual megalomania is concealed in it. The three women, Mathilde, Sophie, Anna, are the three godmothers of my daughters, and I have them all!" Carl G. Jung proved no less perceptive. Invited to offer comments for the forthcoming third edition of *The Interpretation of Dreams,* he objected to Freud's interpretations of his own and his children's dreams as superficial. He and his students, he added, "badly missed" the "(personal) essential meaning," the "libidinal dynamics" of such dreams as the Irma dream, and "the personal-

painful in your own dreams"; and he suggested that Freud use one of his patient's dreams "in which the ultimate true motives are uncovered mercilessly." Freud agreed and promised revisions in the text but no ultimate revelations: "The reader does not deserve to have me undress myself in front of him even more." In fact, none of the intriguing hints of his erotic past that his colleagues wanted him to pursue ever found their way into the later editions. One of the tensions pervading *The Interpretation of Dreams* is precisely the clash, largely underground, between self-revelation and self-protection. But Freud did not think that his unwillingness to undress himself further in any way compromised the exposition of his theory.

GIVEN THE CENTRALITY of determinism in Freud's thinking, it is only fitting that while he was studying dreams, he should also have been amassing materials on what he called the psychopathology of everyday life. The results did not surprise him: commonplace, "normal pathology" offered him literally uncountable instances of "accidents" that analysis showed to be anything but accidental. To misspell a familiar name, forget a favorite poem, mysteriously mislay an object, fail to send one's wife the usual bouquet of flowers on her birthday—these are all messages virtually begging to be decoded. They are clues to desires or anxieties the actor is not free to acknowledge even to himself. These findings confirmed Freud's unequivocal respect for the workings of causality. The diagnostic gain implicit in his conclusion is only too obvious. Inviting a scientific reading of apparently causeless and inexplicable events, it exhibits, using the most ordinary experiences as witnesses, the hidden order governing the human mind.

Freud appears to have become interested in the theoretical relevance of slips in late 1897, when he could not find an address he needed on a visit to Berlin. Listening to his own experience was nothing new for Freud, but in these years of self-analysis he was exceptionally sensitive to the slightest hint of the mind's shifty and circuitous ways. From the summer of 1898 on, he peppered his bulletins to Fliess with curious instances of his mundane psychopathology. "I have finally grasped a trifle long guessed at," he reported in August. He had "forgotten" the last name of a poet who had written a poem he knew well, and could demonstrate that he had repressed that name for private reasons he traced back to his childhood. Other instances soon followed, notably his inability to recall the name of Signorelli, the "great painter" who had painted the *Last Judgment* in Orvieto, and his substitution of names like Botticelli and Boltraffio. Upon analysis, Freud uncovered a complex web of associations and repressions, including a recent conversation about death and sexuality. "Now, to whom should I make this credible?"

Incredible or not, Freud found this instance of purposeful forgetting interesting enough to publish; it appeared late in 1898, complete with an intricate diagram, in a professional journal devoted to neurology and psychiatry.

Freud produced a still more outlandish example of the psychopathology of everyday life in the summer of 1899, while he was correcting the manuscript of *The Interpretation of Dreams*. No matter how hard to tried to improve the book, he wrote to Fliess, it would still contain "2,467 mistakes." The number seems, of course, wholly arbitrary: all that Freud meant to say was that his dream book would be disfigured by a great many errors. But for Freud there are no purely capricious actions in mental activity, and accordingly he analyzed the number in a postscript. In fact, Freud valued this bit of detective work enough to ask Fliess, a year later, to return the note describing it. It duly appeared, in his *Psychopathology of Everyday Life*, with an elaborate interpretation: Freud had read in the newspaper about the retirement of a general whom he had met while serving in the army. The item led Freud to calculate when he too might be retiring, and by combining various numbers that occurred to him, he decided he still had twenty-four years of work before him. Freud had reached his majority on his 24th birthday; his age at present was 43. Added together, these made 67; and 24 and 67, joined, accounted for the 2,467 he had casually thrown out in his letter to Fliess. The apparently uncaused number, in short, embodied a wish for another two decades or so of active life.

Freud completed the manuscript of *The Psychopathology of Everyday Life* in January 1901. By May, he was reading the first proofs on the book, cordially disliked it, and expressed the hope that others would dislike it even more strongly. More was in play here than the depressed mood that usually visited Freud when one of his writings approached publication; the book was deeply involved in his deteriorating relations with Fliess. His "Everyday Life," he told Fliess, "is full of references to you; manifest ones, for which you furnished the material, and concealed ones, for which the motif goes back to you. The motto is a present from you as well." All in all, Freud saw the book as testimony "to the role you have played for me until now."

That role had been even larger than Freud had been willing to admit and in a remarkable display of frankness, he now publicly exploited his injustice to Fliess as one more demonstration of the psychopathology of everyday life. At one of their meetings, Freud had informed Fliess, evidently with an air of discovery, that one could understand the neuroses only on the assumption that the human animal is endowed with a bisexual constitution. Fliess called Freud's attention to the fact that he, Fliess, had advanced that idea years before and that Freud had then wanted no part of it. Reflecting on Fliess's assertion during the following week, Freud finally recalled the episode, and recognized that Fliess was entitled to claim priority. But, he added, he had actually forgotten Fliess's communication until then. By repressing the earlier conversation, Freud had taken some unwarranted credit. Ruefully, he glossed his willful amnesia: it is hard to give up one's claim to originality.* In *The Psychopathology of Everyday Life,* Freud embedded this incident in a chapter on the forgetting of impressions and intentions. This placement concealed the emotional sting from the reader. But for the two friends, soon to be friends no more, the episode was disagreeable, even painful, in the extreme.

The world, of course, had no way of knowing this, and Freud's almost perverse wish that everyone dislike his *Everyday Life* was not realized. The book was not destined to remain the private property of a few specialists. It is almost wholly free of technical language; Freud crammed it with literally scores of anecdotes, compiling an entertaining anthology of motivated errors from his own experience and that of others, and saved his theoretical ideas on determinism, chance, and superstition for the last chapter. One of his most felicitous stories, which he found in his favorite newspaper, the *Neue Freie Presse,* concerns the president of the lower house of the Austrian parliament: anticipating a stormy session, he ceremoniously opened it with the declaration that the session was now closed. There was no mistaking the secret wish behind so blatant a slip. But Freud argued throughout the book that far less legible errors in thought, speech, or behavior pointed consistently to the same conclusion: the mind is ruled by laws. His *Psychopathology of Everyday Life* added nothing to the theoretical structure of psychoanalysis, and its critics complained that some of its examples were excessively far-fetched, or that the very concept of the Freudian slip is so loose that it does not permit scientific tests of verification. Even so, the book ranks as Freud's most widely read work; it enjoyed no fewer than eleven editions and transla-tions into twelve languages in his lifetime.†

THE PRINCIPAL REASON why the hidden order of the mind had escaped psychologists, Freud believed, was that so many mental operations, and the most consequential ones at that, are unconscious. Freud did not discover the unconscious; by the Age of the Enlightenment, some perceptive students of human nature had recognized the existence of unconscious mentation. One of Freud's favorite eighteenth-century German wits, Georg Christoph Lich-tenberg, had commended the study of dreams as the avenue to otherwise

---

*Freud later gave this type of "useful" forgetting the technical name "cryptomnesia."

†In light of Freud's determinism, psychoanalysts have justly pointed out that their technique of free association is misnamed. After all, the sequences of ideas and memories the analysand produces from the couch are of interest precisely because they are invisibly but indissolubly welded together.

inaccessible self-knowledge. Goethe and Schiller, whom Freud could quote by the hour, had sought the roots of poetic creation in the unconscious. The romantic poets, in England, France, and the German states alike, had paid tribute to what Coleridge called "the twilight realms of consciousness." In Freud's own lifetime, Henry James explicitly linked the unconscious with dreams; the narrator in his novella "The Aspern Papers" speaks of "the unconscious cerebration of sleep." Freud could discover very similar formulations in the memorable epigrams of Schopenhauer and Nietzsche. His particular contribution was to take a shadowy, as it were poetic, notion, lend it precision, and make it into the foundation of a psychology by specifying the origins and contents of the unconscious and its imperious ways of pressing toward expression. "Psychoanalysis was forced, through the study of pathological repression," Freud observed later, to "take the concept of the 'unconscious' seriously."

This linking of the unconscious and repression dates back to Freud's early days of psychoanalytic theorizing. Strands of conscious thought appear like chance clusters of discrete elements only because most of their associative connections have been repressed. In Freud's words, his theory of repression is the "keystone for the understanding of the neuroses"—and not of the neuroses alone. Most of the unconscious consists of repressed materials. This unconscious, as Freud conceptualized it, is not the segment of mind harboring thoughts temporarily out of sight and easily recalled; that is what he called the preconscious. Rather, the unconscious proper resembles a maximum-security prison holding antisocial inmates languishing for years or recently arrived, inmates harshly treated and heavily guarded, but barely kept under control and forever attempting to escape. Their breakouts succeed only intermittently and at great cost to themselves and to others. The psychoanalyst working to undo repressions, at least in part, is therefore bound to recognize the grave risks this poses, and to respect the explosive power of the dynamic unconscious.

Since the obstructions that resistance throws in the way are formidable, to make the unconscious conscious is at best very difficult. The desire to recall is countered by the desire to forget. This conflict, built into the structure of mental development practically from birth, is the work of culture, whether operating externally as police or internally as conscience. Fearful of unchecked passions, the world has found it necessary throughout recorded history to brand the most insistent human impulses ill-mannered, immoral, impious. From publishing books on etiquette to prosecuting nudity on beaches, from prescribing obedience to one's betters to preaching the incest taboo, culture channels, limits, frustrates desire. The sexual drive, like the other primitive drives, relentlessly pushes for gratification in the face of stringent, often excessive prohibitions. Self-deception and hypocrisy, which substitute good reasons for real reasons, are the conscious companions of repression, denying passionate needs for the sake of family concord, social harmony, or sheer respectability. They deny these needs, but they cannot destroy them. Freud liked the passage from Nietzsche that one of his favorite patients, the "Rat Man," quoted to him: " 'I did this,' says my Memory. 'I cannot have done this,' says my Pride and remains inexorable. In the end— Memory yields." Pride is the constraining hand of culture; memory the report on desire in thought and action. It may be that pride wins out, but desire remains humanity's most exigent quality. This brings us back to dreams; they exhaustively demonstrate man to be the wishing animal. That is what *The Interpretation of Dreams* is about: wishes and their fate.

FREUD WAS, OF course, not the first to assert the elemental power of passionate desires any more than he had been the first to discover the unconscious. Philosophers, theologians, poets, playwrights, essayists, and autobiographers had been celebrating, or lamenting, that power at least since the writing of the Old Testament. For centuries, too, as such names as Plato and Saint Augustine and Montaigne attest, men had probed the workings of the passions in their inner lives. In Freud's own time, in the salons and coffeehouses of Vienna, such self-examination had become commonplace. The nineteenth century was the psychological century par excellence. It was a time when confessional autobiographies, informal self-portraits, self-referential novels, intimate diaries and secret journals, grew from a trickle to a stream, and when their display of subjectivity, their purposeful inwardness, markedly intensified. What Rousseau in his painfully frank *Confessions* and the young Goethe in his self-lacerating and self-liberating *Sorrows of Young Werther* had sown in the eighteenth century, the decades of Byron and Stendhal, of Nietzsche and William James, reaped in the nineteenth. Thomas Carlyle perceptively spoke of "these Autobiographical times of ours." But this modern preoccupation with the self was by no means pure gain. "The key to the period," Ralph Waldo Emerson said late in life, "seemed to be that the mind had become aware of itself." With the "new consciousness," he thought, "the young men were born with knives in their brain, a tendency to introversion, self-dissection, anatomizing of motives." It was an age of Hamlets.

Many of these Hamlets were Austrians. Increasingly, their culture gave them license to reveal what was on their minds with exhibitionistic freedom. Late in 1896, the Viennese satirist Karl Kraus anatomized the reigning mood with mordant precision: "Soon one was done with consistent Realism, and Griensteidl"—a café much frequented by the literati—"stood under the sign of Symbolism. 'Secret nerves!' was the password now; one began to observe 'the condition of the soul' and sought to flee the commonplace distinctness of things. But one of the most important slogans was 'Life,' and every night one met to grapple with Life or, when things really got going, to interpret Life." Perhaps the most assertive artifact documenting such preoccupations was Alfred Kubin's drawing *Self-Consideration,* of 1902. It depicts a standing, half-naked, headless figure, seen from the rear, and on the ground, facing the viewer, a head rather too large to fit on that decapitated body, staring blindly, its open mouth revealing parted, terrible teeth.

This drawing looks like, but was not, an illustration for *The Interpretation of Dreams.* Freud had little interest in this excited, overstimulated Viennese world. Like everyone else in Vienna, he read the brilliant, unique periodical *Die Fackel,* a witty and devastating scourge of political, social, and linguistic corruption published and almost wholly written by Karl Kraus. What is more, he thought highly of Arthur Schnitzler's stories, novels, and plays for the perceptiveness with which they laid bare the inner, mainly the sensual, world of their characters. Schnitzler even invaded Freud's specialty with a quatrain describing dreams as "impudent wishes," as "cravings without courage" which, chased back into the corners of our minds, dare to creep out only at night:

> Träume sind Begierden ohne Mut,
> Sind freche Wünsche, die das Licht des Tags
> Zurückjagt in die Winkel unsrer Seele,
> Daraus sie erst bei Nacht zu kriechen wagen.

Freud expressed abiding pleasure in Schnitzler's work and told Schnitzler in a letter which was more than polite flattery that he envied him his "secret knowledge" of the human heart. But for the most part, as we have seen, Freud kept aloof from the modern poets and painters and café philosophers, and pursued his researches in the austere isolation of his consulting room.

One irresistible discovery, which forms a central theme in *The Interpretation of Dreams* and of psychoanalysis in general, was that the most persistent human wishes are infantile in origin, impermissible in society, and for the most part so adroitly concealed that they remain virtually inaccessible to conscious scrutiny. Freud likened these "alert, so to speak immortal, wishes in our unconscious" to the Titans of mythology; they bear the load of massive mountains that victorious gods piled on them, but at times they still convulsively lift their limbs. These are the buried forces that lie beneath all dreams. Freud described the daytime thought that instigates a dream as an entrepreneur with ideas and no capital; the capitalist, who provides the cash for the venture, is *"a wish from the unconscious."* These roles are not always sharply separated; the capitalist may himself become the entrepreneur. The point is that to be launched, a dream needs both an instigator and a source of energy.

This raises the question of why the capitalist should feel compelled to invest his surplus. The answer Freud provided recalls his abortive project of 1895: the human organism strives to reduce excitations, but it also activates memories in order to recall earlier pleasures, perhaps to secure their repetition. That is how wishes are born. They generate conflicts in the unconscious because, lacking moderation, they run counter to the commands of the cultural institutions among which the child grows up. But though repressed, they do not wither away: "unconscious wishes always remain active." In fact, Freud concluded, they are "indestructible. In the unconscious, nothing can be brought to an end, nothing is past or forgotten." But these wishes grow, as it were, sophisticated after a time. What Freud called the "primary process," the collection of primitive untamed mental energies lodged in the mind from the beginning, is still entirely under the sway of the pleasure principle: it wants gratification, heedlessly, downright brutally, with no patience for thought or delay. But with the years of development, the mind manages to superimpose a "secondary process" which takes account of reality; it regulates mental functioning less passionately and more efficiently by introducing thinking, calculating, the capacity to postpone satisfactions for the sake of enjoying them later. Freud warned against overestimating the influence of the secondary process; the primary process retains its persistent greed throughout life. Hence, as Freud put the matter laconically in the later editions of his dream book, the student of dreams must recognize that "psychical reality is a particular form of existence, which should not be confounded with *material* reality." Concluding his book on that note, Freud triumphantly vindicated the ambitious program with which he had started. If, he wrote hopefully in 1910, *The Interpretation of Dreams*, his "most significant work," would only "find recognition," it must place "normal psychology, too, on a new basis."

FROM ROME TO VIENNA:
A PROGRESS

Perhaps the most intriguing, certainly among the most poignant of the clues to his mind that Freud scattered through *The Interpretation of Dreams* is the theme of Rome, glittering in the distance as supreme prize and incomprehensible menace. It was a city that he had been avid to visit, but he found his desire strangely subverted by a kind of phobic prohibition. He took vacations in Italy more than once, but got no nearer to Rome than Lake Trasimeno, about fifty miles away. This was the place where Hannibal, too, had stopped short. In late 1897, he dreamt that he and Fliess might hold one of their "congresses" in Rome, and in early 1899, he played with the idea of meeting there at Easter. It struck him as a splendid idea, he wrote later that year, "to hear of the eternal laws of life first in the Eternal City." He studied the topography of Rome in what he called a torment of yearning, aware that there was something distinctly odd about his obsession. "By the way," he told Fliess, "my longing for Rome is deeply neurotic. It is connected with my schoolboy enthusiasm for the Semitic hero Hannibal." As we know, Freud interpreted his *Gymnasialschwärmerei* as an expression of his passionate wish to defy and defeat anti-Semites. To conquer Rome was to triumph in the seat—the very headquarters—of the Jews' most implacable enemies: "Hannibal and Rome symbolized for the youth the contrast between the tenacity of Jewry and the organization of the Catholic church." There was more to it even than that; his desire for Rome, he noted, stood as "cloak and symbol for several other hotly longed-for wishes." They were, he hinted, oedipal in nature; he recalled the ancient oracle given to the Tarquins that he who first kissed the mother would become the ruler of Rome.* A charged and ambivalent symbol, Rome stood for Freud's most potent concealed erotic, and only slightly less concealed aggressive wishes, and glanced at their secret history.

When Freud published *The Interpretation of Dreams,* he had still not conquered Rome. He found this appropriate somehow; it suited the sense of solitude and frustration that beset him in these tempestuous years of inner clarification and venturesome theorizing. The book had been long in the

---

*The psychoanalytic implication of that kiss (though Freud does not explicitly say so) is triumph over the father. There may be deeper mysteries still, and wider implications, but Freud does not provide enough fuel for secure speculation.

making, and he took its completion as a loss. For some time he was depressed, and in early October 1899, he endorsed Fliess's observation that it is "a painful feeling" to divest oneself of something that has been "very much one's particular property." After all his earlier self-criticism, he had come to like his forthcoming book, "certainly not well, but far better." Publishing it was all the more painful, he thought, "since it was not intellectual but emotional property that separated itself from me." The faint, still distant storm warnings that he might have to separate himself from Fliess, another cherished emotional property of these years, did not brighten his mood. Nor, for that matter, could he muster serenity when he got word that he had been passed over for a professorship—not for the first time. He sent one of the first two copies of his dream book to Fliess as a birthday present, and stoically steeled himself for the public's response: "I have become reconciled to the stuff long since and face its fortunes with—resigned expectancy."

Actually, while Freud's expectancy was real enough, his resignation was not. He was listless, moody, irritated with early readers of the dream book who pointed out minor slips instead of praising the whole. While the outcries of protest for which he was braced did not come, the first notice of *The Interpretation of Dreams,* which appeared fairly promptly in December, displeased him. It was simply "meaningless" as criticism, he told Fliess, and "unsatisfactory" as a review. The reviewer, one Carl Metzentin, partially redeemed himself in Freud's eyes only with a single word, "epoch-making." It was not enough. Freud found the attitude of the Viennese to his ideas "extremely negative," and tried to cheer himself up with the thought that he and Fliess were intrepid pioneers: "We are, after all, terribly far ahead." But his gloom did not abate. "I now have no strength at all for theoretical work. So, in the evening, I am terribly bored." Boredom is often a symptom of rage and anxiety, and probably was so for Freud, troubled maker of an undefinable masterpiece.

The new year brought no relief. In early January 1900, a review in *Die Zeit,* a widely read Viennese daily, struck him as "idiotic," as "little flattering and uncommonly uncomprehending." Another, in the *Nation,* by an acquaintance, the poet and playwright Jakob Julius David, was "kind and sensitive," if "somewhat vague." It did little to console him. "I find science ever more difficult. In the evening I'd like something that brightens things up, refreshes, and clears things away, but am always alone." This sounds suspiciously like a touch of self-pity. He seemed determined to feel himself surrounded by a void, and to anticipate nothing but misunderstanding and neglect: "I have been virtually cut off from the outside world," he reported in March 1900. "Not a little leaf has stirred to reveal that the *Interpretation of Dreams* has touched anyone's mind. Only yesterday I was surprised by a rather cordial article in the feuilleton of a daily newspaper, the *Wiener Fremdenblatt.*" Only good news surprised him now. "I give myself over to my fantasies, play chess, read English novels; everything serious remains banished. For two months not a line of what I am learning or surmising has been put into writing. Hence I live as a sybaritic philistine as soon as I am free of my trade. You know how constricted my indulgences are; I may not smoke anything good, alcohol does nothing for me at all, I am done begetting children, my contact with people has been cut off. Thus I vegetate, harmless, taking care to keep my attention diverted from the theme I work on during the day." He seemed exhausted.

The reasons for Freud's low spirits were in part financial, as his practice fluctuated. He called on his self-discipline, his hard-acquired mental balance, to rescue him, but he succeeded indifferently at best. "In general," he wrote on May 7, 1900, acknowledging Fliess's birthday greetings, "I am too sensible to complain—except for one weak point: the fear of poverty." He recognized "how much I have and how little one is entitled to if one considers the statistics of human misery." But at times his inability to understand, and to help, some of his more intractable analysands plunged him into despair, and when he was mired in that mood they became his tormentors. In the late winter days of 1900, longing for spring and sun, he spoke darkly of "catastrophe" and of "collapse"; he had been compelled to "demolish" all his "castles in the air." Still, he was doing his best to "muster a little courage to rebuild them again."

Public neglect and private desolation reinforced one another. He likened himself to Jacob wrestling with the angel; overmatched and out of breath, he had begged the angel to let him be. "It will be a just punishment for me," he predicted, in the most wildly inaccurate forecast he ever made, "that none of the undiscovered provinces of mental life which I was the first mortal to enter will ever bear my name or obey my laws." All he had got out of his duel with the angel was a limp, and he wallowed in this melancholy caricature of his premature decline. "Yes, I really am forty-four already," he wrote in May 1900, "an old, somewhat shabby Israelite." He took the same morose line with his family: thanking his nieces in Berlin for their good wishes on his birthday, he called himself "an old uncle." The year after, he resignedly observed that he had asked the family, obviously in vain, to "stop doing anything for the birthdays of the old ones," and described himself as a kind of elderly monument rather than "a birthday child." His age, even more than his shabbiness, would haunt him from then on.

Such eloquent elegies, invariably in the minor key, suggest how vulnerable Freud still was around 1900, for all his self-analysis. He evaded the risks of success by invoking the specter of failure. Freud must have known that the originality and the offensiveness of his ideas invited baffled silence or outraged disapproval; he might have taken both as so many involuntary compliments. But he was discontented with his reviewers, with his patients, with his friends, with himself. The birth of his "dream child" had indeed been hard.

FREUD FOUND IT disheartening that the completion of his treatise, from which he had expected so much, did so little to resolve his frustrations or relieve his sense of enforced solitude. In March 1900, he looked back with nostalgia to the previous summer, when "in feverish activity," he had completed the dream book. Then he had been foolishly "intoxicated once again with the hope that now a step toward freedom and ease had been taken. The reception of the book and the silence since have once again destroyed the budding relationship with my milieu." But gradually he came out of his depression. By September 1901, buoyed up by his self-analysis, he had at last overcome his long-standing inhibition and was visiting Rome, in the company of his brother Alexander. Like many northerners first entering Rome, like Gibbon, like Goethe, like Mommsen, he walked about wrapped in a daze of delight. Christian Rome disturbed him, modern Rome seemed promising and congenial, but it was ancient and Renaissance Rome that exhilarated him as he tossed a coin into the Trevi fountain, gloried in antique remains, stood fascinated before the *Moses* of Michelangelo.* The visit was, he said flatly, intending no hyperbole, a "high point" in his life.

Sending exuberant messages to his family every day, Freud wondered what had kept him so long from giving himself this supreme pleasure. Writing to his wife, "at noon, opposite the Pantheon," on September 3, he exclaimed, "So this is what I had been afraid of for years!" He found Rome charmingly hot, the Roman light magnificent. There was no need to worry about him, he reassured his wife two days later; the life he was leading was "splendid for work and pleasure, in which one forgets oneself and other things." Again, on September 6, still in Rome, he reported in his jaunty telegraphic manner, his cheer unabated, "This afternoon a few impressions off which one will live for years." Later, on his frequent visits to Italy, he would exclaim over the beauties of Venice and the landscape surrounding (if not the people of) Naples.† But Rome, "this divine city," would remain his undisputed favorite. Writing to his daughter Mathilde from Rome on one of these visits, he told her that he had not wanted to stay put at Fiesole, that lovely spot in the hills

---

*For the meaning of this sculpture, and of Moses, for Freud, see pp. 314–17.

†On September 1, 1902, Freud sent a postcard to his wife from Naples, in which he highly praised the beauty of the city's location, especially the view toward Vesuvius. But, he added, "the people are disgusting, look like galley slaves. Racket and filth here just as in the Middle Ages. Above all it's inhumanly hot." (Freud Museum, London.)

above Florence, "because I felt drawn to the austere seriousness of Rome." Indeed, "this Rome is a very remarkable city—many have already found it so."

Freud soon cashed in on the psychological opportunities that his conquest of Rome opened for him. His visit was at once emblem and instrument of a greater inner freedom, token of a new flexibility for social and political maneuver; it materially aided him to emerge from the ambiguous limbo, half gratifying and half dismaying, of his *"splendid isolation."* In the fall of 1902, Freud began to meet every Wednesday night at Berggasse 19 with a very small, very slowly growing number of physicians—there were only five at first—and a few interested laymen to discuss, under his undisputed chairmanship, case reports, psychoanalytic theory, and ventures into psychobiography.* A little more than half a year before, in February, he had at last secured the professorship he had coveted and deserved for years. From then on, Freud would never again be without social stature, public resonance, ardent followers, and closet controversies.

THE CONVOLUTED STORY of Freud's academic advancement throws a lurid light on the paths to preferment—at once labyrinthine and cozy—in the Austro-Hungarian empire. Originality was not necessarily an impediment, merit not necessarily a prerequisite. Only connections, known as *Protektion,* could guarantee professional progress. Freud had been a *Privatdozent* since 1885. Twelve long years later, in February 1897, two of his most influential senior colleagues, Hermann Nothnagel and Richard von Krafft-Ebing, proposed him for the rank of *Ausserordentlicher Professor*—Professor Extraordinarius. It was a position valued largely for the prestige (and higher fees) it promised, since the title carried neither salary nor membership in the professors' council of the medical faculty. No matter: a professorship, as Freud bluntly put it, "elevates the physician in our society into a demigod for his patients." Others of Freud's vintage were steadily rising in the professional hierarchy, but Freud remained a *Privatdozent.* The seven-man committee appointed to nominate him met in March 1897 and supported him unanimously. In June, the medical faculty endorsed the recommendation by a vote of 22 to 10. The Ministry of Education did nothing.

Watching silently, Freud witnessed the parade of promotion pass him by year after year. He was reluctant to step on the "slippery slope" of enlisting advocates who might deploy their connections to the higher bureaucracy. He thought the Austrian system of *Protektion* detestable. Nor did he think himself a desperate case who could not get on without it. He had, after all,

*See pp. 173–79.

every claim to consideration; his substantial monographs on aphasia and on infantile cerebral paralysis, one published in 1891, the other six years later, were impressive demonstrations of his competence in perfectly traditional domains of medicine. But there was no professorship for Freud—not in 1897, not in 1898 or 1899, not even in 1900, a year when Emperor Franz Josef confirmed a number of proposed promotions. Then, late in 1901, Freud veered about. Expressing disgust and recording conscious feelings of guilt, he moved from passivity to activity. The results were rapid and spectacular: on February 22, 1902, the emperor signed the decree giving Freud the title Professor Extraordinarius. It was a splendid occasion for the whole family; Freud's sister Marie quickly sent word to Manchester, and their half brother Phillip responded with delight about the good news concerning "our beloved brother Sigismund" and asked for further details about the promotion.

A letter from Freud to Fliess, one of his last in their correspondence, records those details in painful abundance. Fliess had congratulated Freud on being, finally, a *Herr Professor,* and had used terms like "recognition" and "mastery." In reply, Freud, driven by his "accustomed, injurious urge to sincerity," confessed a little wryly that he himself had stage-managed it all. After he had come back from Rome the previous September, he had found his practice much reduced, had felt, with the increasing estrangement from Fliess, more solitary than ever, and had recognized that simply waiting for the professorship might take up much of the rest of his life. "And I did want to see Rome again, take care of my patients, and keep my children in good spirits." All this together propelled him onto the slippery slope of seeking *Protektion.* "So, then I decided to break with strict virtue and to take appropriate steps, just like other mortals." For four years he had kept still; now he called on his old teacher Sigmund von Exner, professor of physiology, who rather gruffly advised him to neutralize hostile sentiments in the Ministry of Education and to "seek a personal counterinfluence." Accordingly, Freud mobilized his "old friend and former patient" Elise Gomperz, whose husband was Theodor Gomperz, the eminent classicist who had employed the young Freud to translate several essays for the German edition of John Stuart Mill. She intervened, only to discover that Freud would have to get Nothnagel and Krafft-Ebing to renew their earlier proposal. They did, but for the moment to no effect.

Then another friend and patient, the baroness Ferstel, socially even more elevated than Frau Professor Gomperz, took up Freud's cause. She maneuvered to be introduced to the minister of education and persuaded him to promise a professorship to "the physician who had given her back her health." The bribe, Freud reported, was a "modern painting" by Emil Orlik for the gallery the minister was planning to establish. If, Freud commented sardonically, "a certain Böcklin" (presumably more desirable than a mere Orlik) had been in Marie Ferstel's possession rather than in her aunt's, "I would have been appointed three months earlier." But Freud saved his most mordant sarcasms for himself. While the *Wiener Zeitung* had not yet published the appointment, he told Fliess, "the news that it is impending has rapidly spread from officialdom. The interest of the population is very large. Even now congratulations and gifts of flowers are raining down, as though the role of sexuality had suddenly been officially recognized by His Majesty, the significance of the dream confirmed by the Council of Ministers, and the necessity of the psychoanalytic therapy of hysteria accepted in Parliament by a two-thirds majority." He had finally learned "that this old world is ruled by authority as is the new by the dollar." Having made his first obeisance to that authority, he added, he could now hope for his reward. But he had been a fool, an ass, for having waited so passively: "In the whole business there is one person with very long ears, who is not sufficiently appreciated in your letter, that is: I." Clearly, "if I had taken these few steps three years ago, I would have been appointed three years ago, and spared myself quite a bit. Others are just as clever without first having to go to Rome." He made it sound almost as though he had gone to Canossa, barefoot, in the snow. Freud's pleasure in his new title was real enough, but that pleasure was compromised by discomfort over the inglorious stratagems he had employed to obtain what he should have had without them.

One thing is plain from the record: Freud's academic career was markedly—it seems deliberately—slowed down. A fair number of physicians were promoted from being *Privatdozent,* some even to full professorships, after five or four years, or even after only one. From 1885 on, during Freud's time of waiting, the average span between appointment to a *Dozentur* and appointment to a professorship was eight years. The great neurologist Julius von Wagner-Jauregg, who was appointed *Privatdozent* in 1885, Freud's year, secured his title as professor just four years later. Freud had to wait for seventeen. Apart from the handful who never secured a professorship at all, only four of the roughly one hundred aspirants who were appointed *Privatdozent* in the last fifteen years of the nineteenth century were held back longer than Freud. Exner was right; there was some tenacious prejudice against Freud in official circles.

Certainly anti-Semitism cannot be ruled out. While Jews, even those who refused the profitable refuge of baptism, continued to rise to positions of eminence in the Austrian medical profession, the spreading infection of anti-Semitism did not leave influential bureaucrats untouched. In 1897, when Nothnagel had informed Freud that he and Krafft-Ebing had proposed him for promotion, he had also warned him not to expect too much: "You know the further difficulties." Nothnagel was plainly hinting at the untoward atmosphere for Jews in the Vienna of the Lueger mayoralty. As we have seen, the anti-Semitism of the 1890s was more virulent, more open, than the anti-Semitism of the early 1870s, when Freud had encountered some of its manifestations as a student at the university. By 1897, securely entrenched, Lueger could manipulate Jew-hatred for political purposes of his own. That this atmosphere had effects on the professional careers of Jews in Austria was not a secret, but a commonplace. In his novel *The Road to the Open,* which deals with events around the turn of the century, Arthur Schnitzler has one of his Jewish characters, a physician, say to his son, who is protesting against the prevailing bigotry: "Personality and accomplishments will always prevail in the end. What harm can come to you? That you'll get your professorship a few years later than somebody else." That is just what happened to Freud.

But anti-Semitism was probably not the only reason why Freud languished in his preprofessorial limbo for so long. His scandalous theories on the origins of neuroses could scarcely have endeared him to those in the best position to smooth his way. Freud lived in a culture as intent on respectability as any and more avid for titles than most. Nor had it been so long ago—it was as recently as 1896—that he had delivered his lecture on the sexual etiology of hysteria, his "scientific fairy tale," before the Vienna Society for Psychiatry and Neurology. The motives for the government's reluctance to recognize and reward Freud's scientific merits were what he would have called "overdetermined"—complex and hard to fathom completely.

Freud's own motives, both for his patience and for his abrupt shift to vigorous tactics, are rather more transparent. He had always been intent on fame, but he craved fame unbought, the kind of recognition that is the sweetest of all: the reward of merit alone. He did not want to be like the man who arranges his own surprise birthday party lest the world forget the attention it owes him. But his frustrating wait in the antechambers of status eventually became too much for him. Realism triumphed over fantasies and over his exacting standards of conduct. He would have to take Vienna as it was. Freud had, of course, long known that a professorial title would open doors and improve his income substantially. But money worries alone would not have turned him into what he derisively called a "careerist"—a *Streber.* Such worries were, after all, old and familiar companions. Rather, Freud's new-found ability to gratify his wish to see Rome, to outdo his hero Hannibal, let him also take a somewhat more benign view of his other desires. Freud did not precisely decide to give his conscience a holiday; it was too securely entrenched to be dismissed. But he now found ways of forcing it to moderate its strenuous claims on his rectitude.

ALL THIS, AND MORE, emerges from Freud's confessional letter to Fliess. His tone, a mixture of defiance and apology, shows how much his new resoluteness cost him. As long as he was waiting, he told Fliess, "not a single fellow human would trouble himself about me." But after his conquest of Rome, his "pleasure in life and work had risen somewhat," and his pleasure "in martyrdom somewhat diminished." This must be one of the most revealing phrases Freud ever uttered about himself. His conscience was not just severe, it was punishing. Martyrdom was expiation for crimes committed, or rehearsed in fantasy, in his early years, whether it assumed the guise of poverty, solitude, failure, or untimely death. Freud was not exactly a moral masochist, but he took some pleasure in pain.

His habit of dramatizing his intellectual isolation testifies to this disposition. He was something of an advocate and something of a storyteller, both occupations that resort to painting in strong colors and stark outlines. He was, besides, something of a self-conscious hero, identifying with such world historic giants as Leonardo da Vinci and Hannibal, to say nothing of Moses; and these imaginative games, as serious as they were playful, lend his battle reports a certain magnificent simplicity. But while Freud's autobiographical accounts stylize his struggles, they capture an emotional truth: this is how the struggles felt to him. Even in late maturity, the scars continued to ache. In 1897, he joined the lodge "Wien" of B'nai B'rith, founded two years before, and began giving popular lectures to the brethren. Feeling "as though ostracized," he sought out a "select circle" of men who would welcome him "regardless of my audacity." Recalling these years always left him somber. "For more than a decade after my separation from Breuer, I had no adherents," he wrote a quarter century later. "I stood wholly isolated. In Vienna, I was shunned. Abroad, no one took notice of me." As for *The Interpretation of Dreams*, "it was hardly reviewed in the professional journals."

Each of these statements is somewhat misleading. Freud's estrangement from Breuer was gradual rather than abrupt, and was punctuated by moments of rapprochement. In any event, he was of course not wholly alone: Fliess, and to a lesser extent Minna Bernays, lent support during the most critical years of discovery. Nor was he really shunned in Viennese medical circles. Eminent specialists were prepared to recommend a maverick whose theories they found extravagant at best; as we have seen, Krafft-Ebing, who in 1896 had called his lecture on the origin of neuroses a fairy tale, proposed Freud for a professorship in the following year. Besides, while there was some delay, at home and abroad, in the notice given his dream book, it did have some appreciative, even enthusiastic reviewers. No doubt Freud had good reason for seeing himself as an exposed pioneer at work in dangerous terrain; learned journals labeled his ideas absurd, and called them more derisive names than that. But Freud hugged his loneliness tenaciously, discounting, even at times disregarding, the more cheering evidence. was as though by dwelling superstitiously on his travail and his impending demise, he would not provoke the jealous gods who resent nothing so much as smiling success. But superstition, as Freud himself had shown, is the anticipation of troubles through the projection outward of hostile and unpalatable wishes; and Freud's superstition points back to the unconscious conflicts bedeviling his childhood, back to his aggressive fantasies and his sibling rivalry, to say nothing of his fear of retribution for his wicked wishes.

In the late 1890s, with the death of his father, the progress of his self-analysis, and the accelerating pace of his psychoanalytic theorizing, Freud seems to have relived his oedipal conflicts with peculiar ferocity. Writing *The Interpretation of Dreams*, he was defying his surrogate fathers—the teachers and colleagues who had fostered him but whom he was now leaving behind.* Taking chances that seemed to be more extreme with every passing month, he was going his own way. That first visit to Rome in September 1901 put the stamp on his independence. Navigating through this murky atmosphere, at once challenging his own need for martyrdom and tasting it, Freud was ostentatiously paying his psychological debts.

But he was working, and work always restored him to himself. The year 1901 was very busy. Rather reluctantly, he wrote a digest of *The Interpretation of Dreams*, published that year as *On Dreams*. Retraversing ground he had already so arduously mapped bored and exasperated him. He took greater pleasure in finishing *The Psychopathology of Everyday Life*, which, as we know, was also published that year. Still more intriguing was the case of a hysteric, the famous "Dora"; he wrote up most of this case in January but then did not publish it until 1905.† The psychoanalysis of jokes, which also became the subject of a book published in 1905, occupied him intermittently. But best of all, somewhat to his bemused astonishment, his long-held scattered ideas about sexuality were beginning to add up to a comprehensive theory.

---

*Freud's "profound self-confidence," Ernest Jones has written, "had been masked by strange feelings of inferiority, even in the intellectual sphere"; he had tried to master them by elevating his mentors to an unassailable position, which then permitted him to remain dependent upon them. He "idealized six figures who played an important part in his early life," and Jones lists Brücke, Meynert, Fleischl-Marxow, Charcot, Breuer, and Fliess. But then, Jones insists, Freud's self-analysis brought him into "complete maturity" and made such constructions unnecessary. (*Jones* II, 3.) My own view is rather less categorical.

†See pp. 246–55.

A MAP FOR SEXUALITY

As Freud saw *The Interpretation of Dreams* through the press, some of his ideas about sexuality were stirring in him. "Things are working in the lowest floor, strange to say," he told Fliess in October 1899. "A theory of sexuality," he added prophetically, "may become the next successor to the dream book." Bleak as life seemed, Freud was steadily, slowly, rather dourly brooding on that successor. The following January, he could report that he was "collecting for the sexual theory and waiting until the piled-up material can be set aflame by a rousing spark." He would have to wait for some time. "At present," runs a bulletin of February 1900, "I have been deserted by luck; I no longer find anything useful."

In working toward a general theory of sexuality he followed the route to discovery that was most congenial, almost necessary, to him: Notions more or less inchoate, drawn from his patients, his self-analysis, and his reading, were floating about in his mind, and clamored, as it were, for coherence. Freud was never content with isolated observations; he felt an irresistible pressure to fit them into an orderly structure. At times he made rash raids into unknown territory from a very exiguous staging area of facts, only to fall back, sensibly enough, to wait for reinforcements. He trusted his preconscious to assist him. "In my work," he told Fliess in November 1900, "things have not exactly stopped, are probably going forward soundly on a subterranean level; but it is certainly not a time of harvest, of conscious mastery." Until he could see connections, he would live in a state of agitated suspense, barely held in check by the patience he had so painfully cultivated. Only the sense of closure brought relief.

WITH THE *Three Essays on the Theory of Sexuality,* that relief came as late as 1905. Like his other fundamental theoretical statements, his libido theory was slow to evolve. Freud the conventional bourgeois battled Freud the scientific conquistador every step of the way. His propositions on libido were little less scandalous to Freud than they were to most of his readers. Why had he "forgotten" those remarks by Charcot and Breuer and Chrobak about the ubiquitous presence of the "genital thing" in nervous disorders? Every such act of forgetfulness, as Freud himself amply documented in *The Psychopathology of Everyday Life,* was a resistance.

Yet Freud overcame this resistance earlier, and more completely, than most of the medical profession or the educated public. In the delicate domain of sexuality, he came to take emphatic pride in his iconoclasm, his ability to subvert middle-class pieties. Writing to the eminent American neurologist James Jackson Putnam, he confessed himself a reformer in this one area alone. "Sexual morality—as society, in its most extreme form, the American, defines it—seems to me very contemptible. I advocate an incomparably freer sexual life." He made this unequivocal declaration in 1915, but ten years before, responding to an inquiry concerning the reform of divorce law in the Austro-Hungarian empire—there was no divorce for Catholics then, only legal separation—Freud advocated "the granting of a greater measure of sexual freedom," condemned the indissolubility of marriage as contrary to "significant ethical and hygienic principles and psychological experiences," and added that most physicians vastly underestimate "the powerful sexual drive," the libido.

Freud's appreciation of this drive, and of its impact on normal as well as neurotic life, goes back, of course, to the early 1890s. He testified to that appreciation in paper after paper. Nor did his abandonment of the seduction theory in the fall of 1897 entail any retreat from his position. On the contrary, it enabled Freud to trace sexual longings and disappointments back to the child's fantasy life.* The experience of the Oedipus complex, another discovery of this period, was, significantly, an erotic experience.

Yet, while Freud reminded the world of what it did not want to hear, he was not the only one, or the first, to recognize the power of sexuality. Indeed, the Victorians, though normally circumspect, were far less prudish about the erotic than their slanderers—Freud among them—liked to charge. But it was the sexologists who took the lead. Krafft-Ebing published his *Psychopathia Sexualis* in 1886, and despite its carefully chosen esoteric title and the Latin into which its author cast the most titillating vignettes,† it became a publishing success, an instant classic in the scientific study of perversion. Krafft-Ebing's book, repeatedly revised and enlarged, opened a new continent to

---

*See pp. 93–96.

†Here is one instance. In "Observation No. 124," Krafft-Ebing recorded a report from a homosexual physician: "One evening I was seated at the opera next to an elderly gentleman. He courted me. I laughed heartily at the foolish old man and entered into his sport. Exinopinato genitalia mea prehendit, quo facto statim penis meus se erexit." Seeing in some alarm that after the old man grabbed his penis, he had an erection, the physician demanded to know what his neighbor had in mind. "He told me that he was in love with me. Since I had heard of hermaphrodites in the hospital, I thought I had to do with one of them here." The physician then became curious to see the old man's genitals: "Curiosus factus genitalia eius videre volui." But as soon as he saw the man's penis at its maximum erection, he took flight: "Sicuti penem maximum eius erectum adspexi, perterritus effugi." (Richard von Krafft-Ebing, *Psychopathia Sexualis* [11th ed., 1901], 218–19.) Anyone with a Gymnasium education could decipher this exposition without difficulty.

serious medical investigation; everyone, Freud included, was indebted to it. In the late 1890s, *Psychopathia Sexualis* was joined by the writings of Havelock Ellis, that courageous, enthusiastic, uninhibited, even garrulous compiler of reports on the glorious varieties of sexual behavior. By 1905, the year of Freud's *Three Essays on the Theory of Sexuality*, a small troop of sexologists was beginning to publish monographs and legal briefs on erotic themes hitherto confined to masculine jokes, pornographic novels, and papers in obscure medical journals.

In the *Three Essays*, Freud paid tribute to this literature. On the book's opening page, he credited the "well-known writings" of no fewer than nine authors, ranging from the pioneers Krafft-Ebing and Havelock Ellis to Iwan Bloch and Magnus Hirschfeld. He could easily have added others. Some of these experts on the erotic life were special pleaders, making the case for more tolerant attitudes toward what everyone then called "sexual inversion." But even the propagandists were not without pretensions to objective inquiry: Freud found Hirschfeld's *Yearbook for Intermediate Sexual Stages*, though he did not share its editor's sexual tastes, quite useful. While the most lyrical among the sexologists, such as Havelock Ellis, were vulnerable to prosecution, the literature they produced markedly enlarged the domain of the discussable. They put such secret matters as homosexuality and the perversions on the map for physicians and the general reading public alike.

Despite this heartening company, Freud continued to hang back for several years before he fully accepted infantile sexuality, a fundamental idea without which his libido theory would have remained seriously incomplete. Fliess, and a handful of other speculators before him, had already postulated the early origins of sexual life. As early as 1845, in a pamphlet on bordellos, an obscure provincial German physician named Adolf Patze observed in a footnote that "the sexual drive already manifests itself among little six-, four-, even three-year-old children." And in 1867, the far better known English psychiatrist Henry Maudsley ridiculed the notion that "the instinct of propagation" does not become "manifest till puberty." He found "frequent manifestations of its existence throughout early life, both in animals and in children, without there being any consciousness of the aim or design of the blind impulse. Whosoever avers otherwise," Maudsley added severely, "must have paid very little attention to the gambols of young animals, and must be strangely or hypocritically oblivious of the events of his own early life." There is no evidence that Freud was acquainted with Patze's brochure, but he did know the work of Maudsley, and after the mid-1890s he began to consider the idea of infantile sexuality, at least tentatively. In 1899, in his *Interpretation of Dreams*, he could still flatly observe in passing that "we extol the happiness of childhood, because it does not yet know sexual appetite." The sentence stands as a sober tribute to the tenacity of acceptable opinion, or its residues, in so fearless a researcher as Freud.* But in the same book, in his first published references to the Oedipus complex, Freud showed that he plainly considered children to be endowed with sexual feelings. And in the *Three Essays* there is no more hesitation. "Infantile Sexuality," the second essay, forms the centerpiece of the whole.

THERE ARE TIMES when Freud sounds rather too modest in his claims for the *Three Essays*. He was of two minds about its real importance. Thus in 1914, in the preface to the third edition, he cautioned his readers against excessive expectations: no complete theory of sexuality could be derived from these pages. It is indeed telling that the first of these three linked essays deals not with the vast expanse of "normal" erotic life, but with the more constricted field of "sexual aberrations." But gradually, as edition followed edition, Freud discovered the strategic uses of the *Three Essays* and its theories in his defense of psychoanalysis against its detractors. He used it as a kind of touchstone, separating those who truly accepted his libido theory from those who were unwilling to grant sexuality the prominent place he himself as-signed to it, or who had found it prudent to retreat from his scandalous ideas. In any event, the reader is entitled to claim more for the *Three Essays* than Freud himself was prepared to do. His sex book, opening in successive edi-tions ever more comprehensive vistas of the libidinal drives and their varied fates, forms an essential companion piece to his dream book, equal to it in stature if not in length. At moments, Freud himself came to think so. "The resistance to infantile sexuality," he wrote to Abraham in 1908, "strengthens me in my opinion that the three essays are an achievement of comparable value to the *Interpretation of Dreams.*"

THE FIRST ESSAY, as notable for its cool, clinical tone as for its range, exhibits without smirking or lamenting a richly diversified collection of erotic endow-ments and inclinations: hermaphroditism, homosexuality, pedophilia, sod-

*The passage about childish innocence, as Freud's English editors have observed, is "no doubt a relic from an early draft of the book." ("Editor's Note," *Three Essays, SE* VII, 129.) Goaded by Jung, who protested against the passage "on the basis of the *Freudian* theory of sex" (Jung to Freud, February 14, 1911. *Freud–Jung,* 433 [392]), Freud added a disclaimer in the edition of 1911, a mere footnote, but he kept the sentence intact. Freud's explanation to Jung—that *The Interpretation of Dreams* was an elementary introduction to dream theory and, published as it was in 1899, could not presuppose knowledge of ideas he did not publish until 1905—is singularly unconvincing. (See Freud to Jung, February 17, 1911. Ibid., 435–36 [394–95].) As I have noted, he had already largely accepted the idea of infantile sexuality in 1899; moreover, so few copies of his dream book were sold that he must have known that he was addressing specialists, who by 1911 would be familiar with his *Three Essays* and would have welcomed a revision.

omy, fetishism, exhibitionism, sadism, masochism, coprophilia, necrophilia. In a few passages, Freud sounds critical and conventional, but plainly his heart was not in censoriousness. After enumerating what he called "the most disgusting perversions," he described them neutrally, even approvingly; they have done "a piece of mental work" to which, "for all its atrocious success," one cannot deny the "value of an idealization of the drive." Indeed, "the omnipotence of love shows itself perhaps nowhere more strongly than in such aberrations as these."

Freud's point in compiling his catalogue was to reduce a bewildering array of erotic pleasures to order. He classified them into two groups—deviations from the normal sexual object and deviations from the normal sexual aim—and then inserted them into the spectrum of acceptable human conduct. As often before, he suggested that neurotics throw glaring light on more general phenomena by the very excesses in their sexual life. Here once again Freud's attempt to develop from his clinical materials a grand design for a general psychology emerges with striking clarity. Psychoanalysis discloses that "the neuroses in all their manifestations form an unbroken row all the way to health." Mischievously, he quotes the German psychiatrist Paul Julius Moebius to the effect that "we are all a little hysterical." All humans are innately perverse; neurotics, whose symptoms form a kind of negative counterpart to the perversions, only display this universal primitive disposition more emphatically than "normal" people. Neurotic "symptoms are the sexual activity of the patient." For Freud, then, a neurosis is not some outlandish and exotic disease, but rather the all too common consequence of incomplete development, which is to say, of unmastered childhood conflicts. Neurosis is a condition in which the sufferer has regressed to early confrontations; he is, in short, trying to dispose of unfinished business. With this formula, Freud has reached that touchiest of subjects—infantile sexuality.

PSYCHOANALYSIS IS A developmental psychology that underwent a marked development of its own. Freud did not offer his final assessment of psychological growth, its phases and its dominant conflicts, until the early 1920s, ably assisted by such younger analysts as Karl Abraham. In the first edition of the *Three Essays,* Freud was still quite summary on the sexual history of the human animal; he did not add the section on the growth of sexual organization until 1915. Yet he found a place in the first edition for discussion of the "erotogenic zones," those parts of the body—notably the mouth, the anus, and the genitals—that, in the course of development, become the focus of sexual gratification. In 1905, too, he dealt with what he called the "component drives." It was essential to Freud's theory from the outset that sexuality is not some simple, unitary biological force that springs into being fully formed at birth or for the first time at puberty.

Accordingly, in his essay on infantile sexuality, Freud threw a line from the turbulence of early childhood to the turbulence of adolescence across the relatively quiescent years of latency. Without claiming primacy of discovery, Freud took pleasure in pointing to the significance he attached to the manifestations of sexual passions in childhood. While acknowledging that the literature occasionally mentioned "precocious sexual activity" such as "erections, masturbation, and even coituslike actions," he noted that these were always presented as "curiosities, or as horrible instances of precocious depravity." No one before him, he observed with visible pride, had clearly recognized the ubiquity of "a sexual drive in childhood." He had written the second of the three linked essays on sexuality to repair that neglect.

Freud attributed the almost universal failure to recognize the sexual activity of children to prudery and propriety, but not to them alone. The latency period from about age five to puberty, that developmental phase in which youngsters make enormous intellectual and moral strides, pushes the expression of the child's sexual feelings into the background. What is more, an undefeatable amnesia covers the earliest years of childhood like a heavy blanket; the accepted view that sexual life starts at puberty had found welcome confirmation in the self-serving testimony of amnesiacs. But, characteristically, Freud directed his scientific curiosity at the obvious; everyone had been aware of this universal amnesia for a long time, but no one had thought to investigate it. What this uncannily effective forgetfulness blanks out, he argued, is the child's erotic experience, along with the rest of its agitated young life.

Freud did not maintain the absurdity that childhood sexuality manifests itself in precisely the same ways as that of the adult. Neither the child's physical, nor its psychological, state would permit this. Quite the contrary, infantile sexual emotions and desires take many and varied forms, not all of them palpably erotic: thumbsucking and other displays of autoeroticism, retention of feces, sibling rivalry, masturbation. With this last kind of play, the genitals of little boys and girls begin to be involved. "Among the erotogenic zones of the child's body there is one that certainly does not play the leading part, and cannot be the bearer of the oldest sexual impulses, but is destined to great things in the future." Freud is speaking, of course, about the penis and the vagina. "The sexual activities of this erotogenic zone, which belong to the sexual organs proper, are indeed the beginning of later, 'normal' sexual life." Those quotation marks around "normal" are eloquent: any part of the body, any conceivable object, can serve sexual gratification. Early violations, whether seduction or rape, will stimulate what Freud called, mellifluously, the child's "polymorphously perverse" inclinations, but the "aptitude" for such perversity is innate. What everyone is used to calling "normal" in sexual conduct is really the end point of a long, often disrupted pilgrimage, a goal that many humans never—and more of them only rarely—reach. The sexual drive in its mature form is an achievement.

THE YEARS OF puberty and adolescence, to which Freud devoted the last of his three essays, are the great testing time. They consolidate sexual identity, revive long-buried oedipal attachments, establish the dominance of the genitals for the attainment of sexual gratification. This primacy does not give the genitals an exclusive hold on sexual life; the erotogenic zones that served so well in early years continue to give pleasure, though they are reduced to the production of "fore-pleasure," which supports and enhances "end-pleasure." It is worth noting that for Freud this end-pleasure constitutes a new experience that arises only with puberty. For all his notorious stress on the lasting authority and diagnostic significance of childhood, Freud never discounted the experiences that men and women first encounter in adult life. It was only, as he once said, that adults speak eloquently for themselves, and that the time had come for a psychologist to act as an advocate for the early years, hitherto so cavalierly overlooked.

IN ITS FIRST edition, the *Three Essays on the Theory of Sexuality* was a small book of 80-odd pages, little more than a pamphlet, as tightly packed as a hand grenade and as explosive. By 1925, when it had reached its sixth edition, the last to appear in Freud's lifetime, it had grown to 120 pages. Some mysteries remained that it did not propose to solve: the definition of pleasure, the fundamental nature of the drives and of sexual excitation itself. Still, much had come clear in Freud's synthesis. Pushing the origins of sexual feelings back to the earliest years had enabled him to explain, on wholly naturalistic and psychological grounds, the emergence of such powerful emotional brakes as shame and disgust, of norms in matters of taste and morality, of such cultural activities as art and scientific research—including psychoanalysis. It had also laid bare the tangled roots of adult love. All is linked in Freud's universe: even jokes and aesthetic productions, and the "fore-pleasure" they generate, bear the imprint of the sexual drives and their adventures.

Freud's generous vision of libido made him into a psychological democrat. Since all humans share in the erotic life, all men and women are brothers and sisters beneath their cultural uniforms. Sexual radicals have reproached Freud for what they have called his genital ideology, for taking adult heterosexual intercourse with a tenderly loved partner and a modicum of foreplay as the ideal to which all humans should aspire. But since Freud uncoupled that ideal from monogamy, his ideology was deeply subversive for his time. He was no less subversive in his uncensorious, neutral stance on the perversions, for he was convinced that to be fixated sexually on early objects that had not been outgrown, whether this meant fetishism or homosexuality, was not a crime, not a sin, not a disease, not a form of madness or a symptom of decadence. This sounded a very modern, very unrespectable, in short a very unbourgeois note.

Yet Freud, one must insist, was not a pansexualist. He rejected the epithet with considerable acerbity, not because he was secretly a one-sided adulator of libido, but because, quite simply, he thought that his denigrators were wrong. In 1920, in his preface to the fourth edition of the *Three Essays,* he reminded his readers with a certain grim satisfaction that it had been the German philosopher Arthur Schopenhauer, not he, the rebel and outsider, who had "confronted mankind some time ago with the extent to which their aims and actions are determined by sexual impulses." This was a fact of cultural history that those critics who insisted that psychoanalysis "explains everything by sex" had conveniently forgotten. "May all those who look down upon psychoanalysis contemptuously from their superior vantage point let themselves be reminded how closely the expanded sexuality of psychoanalysis coincides with the *Eros* of the divine Plato." When it suited him, Freud, the positivist and principled anti-metaphysician, did not mind claiming a philosopher for an ancestor.

ELABORATIONS

1902-1915

FOUR

Sketch of an
Embattled Founder

AT FIFTY

 On May 6, 1906, Freud turned fifty. The years just past had been full of gratification, full of promise. Between late 1899 and mid-1905, he had published two key texts, *The Interpretation of Dreams* and *Three Essays on the Theory of Sexuality;* a technical study, *Jokes and Their Relation to the Unconscious;* a popular book on the psychopathology of everyday life; and the case history of "Dora," the first, still the most controversial, among his case histories. He had finally maneuvered to secure an appointment as *Ausserordentlicher Professor,* and with the finding of a few supporters among Viennese physicians, his sense of isolation in the profession had begun to abate. But if he believed for a moment that publishing two epoch-making books, receiving an honorific title, and gaining some followers would bring serenity, he was mistaken. His next years were no less agitated than the 1890s had been. Organizing the psychoanalytic movement would prove arduous, and absorbed much of Freud's best energy. The distractions never kept Freud from rethinking psychoanalytic theory and technique: the next decade and a half was a time for elaborations and for intimations of revisions to come. But he found that

[153]

the pressures of psychoanalytic politics often made irritating claims on his time.

To celebrate his fiftieth birthday, Freud's admirers presented him with a medallion showing his portrait in profile on one side and Oedipus solving the riddle of the Sphinx on the other. The inscription in Greek, drawn from Sophocles's *Oedipus Rex*, was plainly meant as a supreme compliment to Freud, the modern Oedipus: "He divined the famous riddle and was a most mighty man." Jones records that at the presentation, reading the legend, Freud "became pale and agitated." It was "as if he had encountered a *revenant.*" So he had. As a student at the university, strolling about the arcaded courtyard decorated with the busts of its departed luminaries, Freud had harbored the fantasy that one day his bust, too, would stand there, inscribed with the very words his followers had chosen for the medallion. It was emblematic of the impression Freud was beginning to make that his followers should so sensitively divine, and handsomely ratify, the most carefully guarded of his ambitions. At least a handful had recognized him, the explorer of the unconscious, as a giant among men.

Freud needed the accolade. His friendship with Fliess, long dying, had just expired in a final, unpleasant public flare-up, and the memories it evoked gravely afflicted him. After their violent quarrel in the summer of 1900, when Fliess had called the value of Freud's psychoanalytic researches into question, the two men had not met again. But, with lengthening intervals, their correspondence limped on through the next two years, as though their old cordiality had a residual momentum of its own.

Then, in the early summer of 1904, Fliess wrote Freud a testy letter. He had just come upon Otto Weininger's *Sex and Character,* published the year before. The book, a curious compound of biological-psychological speculation and fanciful cultural criticism, had quickly acquired the status of a cult object, not least because of Weininger's melodramatic suicide. At twenty-three, gifted, precocious, and mad, a convert from Judaism who loathed Jews no less than women, he had shot himself to death in Vienna in the Beethoven house. To Fliess's consternation, as he brusquely informed Freud, he had found in Weininger's book "my ideas on bisexuality and the nature of sexual attraction that follows from it—feminine men attract masculine women and vice versa." This was a thesis that Fliess thought he had virtually patented, and had imparted to Freud in confidence some years before. But he had not yet completely published it. Now, seeing it in print, he was sure that his old—his former—intimate must have indiscreetly transmitted the idea to Weininger, either directly or through Weininger's friend Hermann Swoboda, a psychologist who was one of Freud's patients.

As we have seen, the idea that one sex harbors elements of the other, and

Fliess's claim to priority in developing it, had made for some interesting difficulties between him and Freud some time before. Now, in 1904, confronted with a charge of indiscretion, Freud prevaricated. He admitted that he had told Swoboda about bisexuality in the course of treatment; that sort of thing, he wrote, comes up in all analyses. Swoboda must then have passed on the information to Weininger, who was at the time preoccupied with the problem of sexuality. "The late Weininger," he wrote Fliess, "was a burglar with a key he had found." He added that Weininger might well have picked up the idea elsewhere; it had, after all, figured in the technical literature for some years. Fliess was not placated. He had heard from a mutual friend that Weininger had shown Freud the manuscript of *Sex and Character,* and that Freud had advised Weininger not to publish such nonsense. But obviously Freud had failed to warn Weininger that he was about to commit intellectual burglary.

This reminder, accurate in every respect, prompted Freud to grant that there was more to this contretemps than he had allowed: Weininger *had* come to see him, but his manuscript had been very different from the book. Freud thought it a pity, he said severely—and, in his vulnerable position, rather imprudently—that Fliess should resume their correspondence only to raise such a petty incident. Intellectual robbery is after all easily done, but, he protested, he had always acknowledged the work of others, never appropriated anything that belonged to anyone else. This was not the best place or time for Freud to assert his innocence in the contentious arena of ideas competing for priority. But to forestall further disputes, he offered Fliess a look at the manuscript of his still-unfinished *Three Essays on the Theory of Sexuality,* so that Fliess might study the passages on bisexuality and have any offending ones revised. Freud even offered to postpone publishing the *Three Essays* until Fliess had brought out his own book. These were decent gestures, but Fliess chose not to take them up.

This was the end of the Freud–Fliess correspondence, but not the end of the quarrel. Early in 1906, Fliess finally published his treatise, ambitiously titled *The Course of Life: Foundation of Exact Biology,* which spelled out his theories of periodicity and bisexuality in exhaustive detail. At the same time, one A. R. Pfennig, a librarian and publicist (inspired, Freud charged, by Fliess), brought out a pugnacious pamphlet denouncing Swoboda and Weininger as plagiarists and accusing Freud of being the conduit through which they had secured access to Fliess's original property. What offended Freud most about this polemic was that it quoted from his private communications to Fliess. He struck back in a letter to Karl Kraus. While he soberly admitted the truth of Pfennig's contention that Weininger had come upon Fliess's theories indirectly through him, he criticized Weininger for failing to record his indebtedness. For the rest, he rejected Pfennig's—and hence Fliess's—accusations as miserable slanders.

This was one time when expressing his indignation did not bring relief; Freud found the controversy an unsettling experience. His offense was less his indiscretion in discussing bisexuality with Swoboda than his failure to be candid with Fliess about Weininger's visit. It may well have been, as Freud asserted, that the manuscript he had read and the book that had become such a fashionable best seller had little in common.* In any event, he had counseled Weininger not to publish it. Still, when it came to Fliess's share in Freud's discoveries, Freud displayed an impressive capacity for repressing inconvenient memories. For more than a decade, Fliess had been his closest, in critical respects his only, confidant, in whom he had invested his deepest emotions. Hence, in 1906 Freud found it impossible to master his final separation with serenity. Under these trying circumstances it was reassuring that he had followers willing to liken him to Oedipus.

FREUD AT FIFTY was intellectually fertile and physically vigorous, but he intermittently harassed himself with dark thoughts of decrepitude. When, in 1907, Karl Abraham visited Freud in Vienna for the first time, he regretted to see that "unfortunately, the old-age complex seems to oppress him." We know that at forty-four, Freud had already derisively called himself a shabby old Israelite. This concern became a constant refrain; in 1910, he wrote to a friend, "Let us anyhow note that I determined some time ago to die only in 1916 or 1917." But Freud's productivity and bearing belied this neurotic preoccupation. Though only of medium height—he was about five feet seven inches tall—he stood out in a crowd with his authoritative presence, neatly groomed appearance, and observant eyes.

Freud's eyes earned a great deal of comment. Fritz Wittels, who was close to Freud in these years, described them as "brown and lustrous," with a "scrutinizing expression." There were those who found them unforgettable. One was Max Graf, a cultivated Viennese musicologist with a strong interest in the psychology of the creative act, who first met Freud in 1900 and joined his inner circle soon after. He called Freud's eyes "beautiful" and "serious"— they "seemed to look at man from the depths." The English psychoanalyst Joan Riviere, who met him after the First World War, noted that while Freud was endowed with an "enchanting humor," his formidable presence was marked by "the forward thrust of his head and critical exploring gaze of

---

*The issue concerned Freud as late as 1938. He insisted that he had been "the first who read his [Weininger's] manuscript and—condemned it." (Freud to David Abrahamsen, March 14, 1938. Freud Collection, B3, LC.)

his keenly piercing eyes." If looking (as Freud once said) is a civilized substitute for touching, his penetrating glance, which missed very little, was most appropriate for him. He had, Wittels recalled, "the student's stoop." But this seems not to have diminished Freud's commanding air.

It was an air of power disciplined. Even Freud's mustache and pointed beard were subdued to order by a barber's daily attention. Freud had learned to harness his appetites—his volcanic emotions, his lust for speculation, and his restless energies—to the single-minded pursuit of his mission.* "I cannot imagine life without work as really comfortable," he wrote to his friend the Zurich pastor Oskar Pfister in 1910. "With me, fantasizing and working coincide; I find amusement in nothing else." His heroic effort at self-mastery in the service of concentrated work had chained him to a most precise timetable. Like the good bourgeois he was, and was not ashamed of being, "he lived," in his nephew Ernst Waldinger's words, "by the clock."

Even the variations animating Freud's daily life were built in: his card parties, his city walks, his summer vacations, were carefully programmed, largely predictable. Up by seven, he would see psychoanalytic patients from eight to twelve. Dinner was punctually at one: at the stroke of the clock, the household assembled around the dining-room table; Freud appeared from his study, his wife sat down facing him at the other end, and the maid materialized, bearing the soup tureen. Then came a walk to restore the circulation, perhaps to deliver proofs or buy cigars. Consultations were at three, and after that, he saw more analytic patients, often until nine in the evening. Then came supper, sometimes a short game of cards with his sister-in-law Minna, or a walk with his wife or one of his daughters, often ending up at a café, where they could read the papers or, in the summer, eat an ice. The rest of the evening belonged to reading, writing, and doing editorial chores on the psychoanalytic journals which, from 1908 on, disseminated Freud's ideas and complicated his life. To bed at one in the morning.

Freud gave his lectures at the university invariably on Saturday from five to seven and then proceeded just as invariably to his friend Leopold König-stein's house for his weekly game of tarock, an old card game for four, long popular in Austria and Germany. He could not do without his *"Tarockex-zess."* On Sunday mornings, he visited his mother; later in the day, he wrote the letters he had not had time to write during the week. Summer vacations, eagerly anticipated by the whole Freud clan, were a serious matter; plans for those months away from Vienna occupied a substantial portion of Freud's

---

*When Wittels, in his biography, described Freud as having a "volcanic nature," Freud noted the characterization in the margin with an exclamation point. (See p. 29 in Freud's copy of Wittels, *Sigmund Freud.* Freud Museum, London.)

correspondence. "I know," he wrote to Abraham in the spring of 1914, "how difficult the problem of summer is." In the bourgeois world that the Great War would largely shatter, the *Sommerproblem* was a matter demanding the most thoughtful attention. Freud often began making arrangements in the early spring to find the right spa for recuperation from his clinical labors, for the visits of intimates, and, when an important idea was at work in him, for weeks of solitude. When summer came, after months of his fatiguing analytic hours, the Freuds—the parents, the six children, and Aunt Minna—would settle in a quiet hotel in the mountains at Bad Gastein in Austria, or at Berchtesgaden in Bavaria, there to spend weeks together hunting mushrooms, gathering strawberries, going fishing, and taking hardy walks. For the last part of the summer—August and early September—Freud would go off with his brother Alexander, or a favored colleague like Sándor Ferenczi, to explore Italy. Once, in 1904, with his brother, he paid an unforgettable short visit to Athens; overwhelmed, he stood on the Acropolis and mused on how strange it felt to glimpse at last in reality what he had known for so long, and so well, from books alone.

In his famous study *The Protestant Ethic and the Spirit of Capitalism,* published in 1904 and 1905 while Freud was completing his *Three Essays,* the German sociologist Max Weber spoke bleakly of an iron cage in which modern man is confined as the victim of enforced punctuality, soul-destroying toil, and mindless bureaucracy. But Freud's rhythmic mode of life was the precondition, indeed the servant, of pleasure no less than of work. He did himself an injustice when he said that work alone gave him amusement. Visitors at Berggasse 19, and companions on his summer excursions, attest to Freud's unimpaired receptivity to fresh experience through his fifties and beyond. At times he would disconcert his guests by musing silently during a meal, leaving the conversation to his family. But more often he proved a genial host. After Abraham returned from visiting Freud in late December 1907, he wrote, still euphoric, to his friend Max Eitingon, "I had an extremely cordial reception in his home. He himself, wife, sister-in-law and daughter led me through Vienna, to art collections, café, the bookdealer Heller & to the antiquarian bookseller, etc. They were delightful days."

While Freud, for all his vitality, was not untouched by depression, he escaped prolonged gloomy ruminations. Looking back later on his visit to the United States in 1909, he commented, "I was only fifty-three years old then, felt youthful and healthy." When his son Martin sat down to write about these years, he remembered above all his "gay and generous father." Lapsing for precision into his native German, he reiterated that his father had *"ein froehliches Herz,* not perhaps perfectly translated as 'a merry heart.' " Anna Freud has confirmed her eldest brother's assessment: her father's real personality, she told Ernest Jones, did not fully emerge in his letters, for they were "always aimed at somebody, to inform them, or pacify them, or encourage, or to share problems and affairs." In general he was "even tempered, optimistic, and even gay," rarely ailing or losing a day's work from illness.*

The familiar Freud scowling from his photographs is no illusion; he found much to scowl about as he contemplated his fellow humans, and not just his dissident followers. But that was not all of him. Ernest Jones has made the useful point that Freud did not like being photographed; hence the formal pictures of him are more somber than the man. Only his sons, camera in hand, caught him off guard and captured a less formidable face. The Freud delighting in awesome mountain scenery, a particularly succulent mushroom, or a cityscape he had not seen before is as authentic as Freud the Newton of the mind, voyaging through strange seas of thought alone, or the forbidding founder staring down a heretic with his steely eyes.

Regularity did not mean rigidity. Indeed, his liking for informal organizations and no less informal arrangements with publishers and translators led to much confusion. But more than that, Freud found it possible to change his mind about some of his most cherished ideas. Except where such essential principles of psychoanalysis as infantile sexuality, the sexual etiology of neuroses, and the work of repression were concerned, he was open to promising theoretical and therapeutic departures, even eager for them. Improvisation held no terrors for him. His conversation, like his epistolary style, was a model of lucidity and vigor, abounding in original formulations. His fund of jokes, mainly pointed Jewish stories, and his unsurpassed memory for apt passages from poets and novelists, gave him the incomparable gift of relevant surprise in speech and writing alike. He was, by all accounts, a riveting lecturer, with a slow, clear, and energetic delivery. At the university each Saturday, he spoke, Wittels remembered, "without notes for nearly two hours, and his hearers were enthralled." Freud's "method of exposition was that of a German humanist, lightened by a conversational tone which he had probably acquired in Paris. No pomposity and no mannerisms." Even in the most technical discourse, his humor and his informality kept breaking through. He was, Wittels wrote, "fond of using the Socratic method. He would break off his formal exposition to ask questions or invite criticism. When objections were forthcoming, he would deal with them wittily and forcibly."

---

*On January 28, 1952, she wrote to Jones, after reading her father's letters to Abraham and Eitingon, "I was often struck by the fact that in these letters he complained about his health, whereas we never heard such complaints from him at home, on the contrary. Somehow I got the idea that this was a way of defending himself against the demands made on him from the outside." To be sure, she continued, "in the Fliess relationship where he was eager for the other's company," he did not employ this defensive maneuver. (Jones papers, Archives of the British Psycho-Analytical Society, London.)

Nor was Freud fixated on money, as would have been natural for one impecunious for so long, and prone to worry over his family's finances. Sounding rather rueful, he would forgo family pleasures, such as attending the Vienna debut of his niece Lilly Freud Marlé, a well-known diseuse, because he felt he could not afford the time. He was, he wrote her in apology, "a mere money-acquisition-machine," a "temporarily highly gifted day laborer." But he did not refrain from generosity to those who needed it. Around 1905—Freud was just nearing fifty—the young Swiss poet Bruno Goetz, then studying in Vienna, came to consult him for headaches that no remedy could alleviate. One of Goetz's professors had recommended Freud as a physician who might help, and, to smooth the way, had sent Freud some of Goetz's poems. Putting his visitor at ease, Freud elicited his life story, complete with intimate sexual details such as occasional youthful infatuations with sailors, and concluded that psychoanalysis was not indicated. He wrote out a prescription and, it seemed irrelevantly, got Goetz to talk about his poverty. "Yes," Freud said. "Severity against oneself has something good in it. But one mustn't overdo it. When did you eat your last steak?" Goetz admitted that it must have been about four weeks before. "I rather thought so," Freud replied, and then, Goetz remembered, becoming "almost embarrassed," offered him some advice on diet, and an envelope: "You must not be offended with me, but I am a grown doctor and you are still a young student. Accept this envelope from me and permit me to play your father just this once. A small honorarium for the pleasure you have given me with your verses and the story of your youth. Adieu, and call on me again some time. True, my time is heavily occupied, but half an hour or a whole one should turn up. *Auf Wiedersehn!*" When Goetz arrived at his room and opened the envelope, he found two hundred kronen in it. "I was," he recalled, "in so agitated a state I had to weep out loud." It was not the only time that Freud would support younger colleagues, even patients, with a well-placed gift, tactfully offered and gratefully accepted.

FREUD'S WAYS AS a father were consistent with his ways as a speaker, writer, and minor philanthropist. While much of the nineteenth-century domestic manner clung to him all his life, he was a bourgeois paterfamilias with a difference. Martha Freud, as everyone knew, made it her study to keep her husband's time and energies free for research and writing; practical domestic arrangements were in her competent and willing hands.*

But it was characteristic of his household that the Freud children were well behaved—well behaved, not cowed. Their mother was, as her eldest son

---

*For an important exception, after the First World War, see p. 384.

remembered, at once kind and firm. "There was no lack of discipline." The Freuds valued scholastic achievement without overemphasizing it; and indeed, the ruling code of good behavior did not inhibit rounds of jokes and high spirits. "I know," Martin Freud recalled, "that we Freud children did things and said things that other people found strange"; theirs was, he thought, a liberal upbringing. "We were never ordered to do this, or not to do that; we were never told not to ask questions. Replies and explanations to all sensible questions were always given by our parents, who treated us as individuals, persons in our own right." Here was psychoanalytic educational theory in sensible practice: modern openness reined in by middle-class decorum. Martha Freud testified that on her husband's "express wish," none of their three sons "followed in his footsteps."* But then their youngest child, their Annerl, became a psychoanalyst just the same: "With the daughter he could not prevent it." The history of Freud's later years shows that this was one defiance of his wishes that he warmly welcomed.

A touching episode in Martin Freud's adolescence illustrates his father's domestic style. One winter day, Martin was out skating with his older sister, Mathilde, and his younger brother Ernst, and the two boys, sailing along together, ran into an elderly bearded gentleman who wove about comically to regain his balance. Ernst made some rude, quite uncalled-for remarks about these awkward maneuvers, and a skilled figure skater who had observed the incident and mistook Martin for the culprit, skated by and slapped him. Martin Freud, imbued with boyish notions about honor and chivalry, took this as a profound humiliation. To make matters worse, the attendant confiscated his season ticket, and a fat, clumsy skater struggled over to him, introduced himself as a lawyer, and offered to represent him in court. This, Martin Freud recalled, "only added to my feeling of desperation": resorting to legal action would violate the medieval code to which he was then addicted. He indignantly refused. Mathilde did manage to get her brother's season ticket restored, and the Freud children, brimming over with the news, then rushed home to report. Martin alone was depressed by the course of events. "My whole future, it seemed to me, had been destroyed by this disgrace." He was sure that when the time came for his military service, "I could never be an officer. I might be a potato-peeler," or perhaps he would remain the lowly private who empties garbage pails and cleans latrines. He felt thoroughly dishonored.

Freud listened to this animated recital attentively, and once the children had calmed down, invited Martin to his study. Then he asked his son to tell

---

*It should be added that none of Freud's three sons seems to have shown any inclination, or talent, for Freud's vocation.

him the whole story again from beginning to end. Martin Freud, though remembering the rest of the incident in copious detail, could not recall later what his father had said to him; what he did recall was that the "soul-destroying tragedy" was reduced to "an unpleasant and meaningless trifle." Whatever Freud the father did for his son that evening, the point is that he was not too preoccupied, not too great a man or too strict a disciplinarian, to give his son the fond healing attention he thought was indicated.

As a typical bourgeois of his time and his northern culture, Freud was not very demonstrative. He was, his nephew Harry remembered, "always on very friendly terms with his children" but not "expansive"; rather, he was "always a bit *formal* and *reserved.*" Indeed, "it rarely happened that he kissed any of them; I might almost say, really never. And even his mother, whom he loved very much, he only kissed perforce at parting." Yet in 1929, in a letter to Ernest Jones, Freud spoke of "a fount of tenderness" within himself on which one could always count. He might not be inclined to parade such feelings—"but in my family they know better." It is likely that what he withheld from his boys he gladly gave to his girls; on one of his visits, Jones saw a Freud daughter, "then a big schoolgirl, cuddling on his lap." The tokens of Freud's affection, the subtle clues his bearing conveyed to his children, sufficed to create an emotional environment of warmth and substantial trust. "Grandfathers," he wrote to Jung in 1910, "are seldom harsh, and perhaps I have not been so even as a father." His children cheerfully substantiated this self-appraisal.

PLEASURES OF THE SENSES

Freud, then, was not a martinet. Nor was he an ascetic. His sexual activity seems to have tapered off early; we know that in August 1893, when he was only thirty-seven, he was living in sexual abstinence. But this was not the end of it all. Anna, his last child, was born in December 1895. The following year he informed Fliess, who was always looking for biological rhythms, that recurrently, every twenty-eight days, "I have no sexual desire and am impotent—which otherwise, after all, is not yet the case." And in 1897, he reported a dream to Fliess in which he was walking up a staircase with very few clothes on, being followed by a female. The accompanying affect was "not anxiety but erotic excitement."

True, as we have seen, in 1900 he had noted that he was "done begetting children." But there is some intriguing evidence that Freud was not yet done with sexual arousal, indeed with intercourse, and would not be done for another decade and more. In July 1915, he had a series of dreams which he promptly recorded and analyzed. One of these was about his wife: "Martha comes toward me, I am supposed to write something down for her—write into a notebook, I take out my pencil. . . . It becomes very indistinct." Interpreting the dream, Freud offered diverse day's residues to account for it, among these inevitably its "sexual meaning": the dream "has to do with successful coitus Wednesday morning." He was then fifty-nine. So when, this very year, Freud told James Jackson Putnam that he had "made very little use" of the sexual freedom he was advocating, he was essentially claiming an aversion to extramarital adventures. Like some of his dreams, some of his papers and casual comments whisper of luxuriant erotic fantasies persisting through the years. They may have been fantasies for the most part. "We cultured people"—*Kulturmenschen*—he told his followers with sardonic resignation when he was only fifty-one, "are all a little disposed to psychological impotence." Playfully, with more than a touch of melancholy, he suggested some months later that it would be useful to revive an antique institution: "an academy of love, where one would teach the *ars amandi.*" How much he practiced what he would have taught in such an academy remains his secret. But to make a special note of "successful coitus" in 1915 intimates that there must have been times when he suffered failure.

Freud's resignation was prompted in part by marked distaste for all known methods of birth control. We know that in the early 1890s, as he was exploring—in his patients and, it seems highly probable, in his own marriage—the sexual origins of the neuroses, he deplored the untoward psychological consequences of contraception. Except in the most favorable circumstances, he believed, the use of a condom is likely to produce neurotic malaise. *Coitus interruptus* and other means are no better; depending on the method employed, either the man or the woman is probably doomed to end up a victim of hysteria or of an anxiety neurosis. "If Freud had continued his own efforts in this direction," Janet Malcolm has observed, "he would have become the inventor of a better condom, not the founder of psychoanalysis." As it was, he exploited the difficulties resulting from the defects of contraceptives as so many clues to the workings of the human mind, including his own, at its most secretive. The memoranda he sent to Fliess on this delicate subject mention not himself but his patients and the ways his theory profited from their candid confessions. But his drafts, at once confident and impassioned, speak also of personal engagement. They subtly reverberate with his less than satisfactory sexual experience.

More subtly still, Freud's resignation appears to have been related to his expectation of an early demise. In 1911 he told Jung's wife, Emma, "My marriage has been amortized long since, now there is nothing more to do than—die." But Freud found abstention also a cause for some pride. In his paper on civilized sexual morality, published in 1908, he observed that modern civilization makes extraordinary demands on the capacity for sexual restraint, especially in those claiming a modicum of cultivation; it asks people to refrain from intercourse until they are married and then to confine their sexual activity to a single partner. Most humans, Freud was convinced, find such exactions impossible to obey, or obey them at exorbitant emotional cost. "Only a minority succeeds in mastery through sublimation, through the deflection of sexual instinctual forces to higher cultural aims, and then only intermittently." Most others "become neurotic or suffer damage in other ways."

But Freud did not think himself either neurotic or damaged; rather, he had no doubt that he had sublimated his instincts and was doing cultural work of the highest order. Yet the old Adam would not stay subdued: in his later years, Freud visibly enjoyed the admiration of good-looking women; the handsome and formidable Lou Andreas-Salomé was only the most striking of these. In 1907, writing from Italy at a time when he was presumably well on his way toward sublimating his erotic impulses, he told Jung that he had run into a young colleague of Jung's, who "seems to have provided himself with some female again. Such practice impedes theory." The incident led him to reflect on his own practice: "When I have wholly overcome my libido (in the common sense), I shall start on a 'Love life of Mankind.'" Apparently, in 1907 he had not yet overcome his libido—in the common sense.

FREUD, THEN, LONG remained hospitable to the pleasures of the senses. He expressed some sympathy for Horace's dictum *carpe diem*—"seize the day"—a philosophical defense of grasping the pleasure of the moment that appeals to "the uncertainty of life and the unfruitfulness of virtuous renunciation." After all, he confessed, "each of us has had hours and times in which he admitted that this philosophy of life is right." At such moments, we are apt to criticize the pitiless severity of moral teachings: "They only understand how to make demands without offering compensations."* Stern moralist though he was, Freud did not deny pleasure its innings.

*In a delightful little essay on transience, written, it is important to observe, during the senseless carnage that was the First World War, Freud argued that while all beauty is doomed to decay, this truth entails neither some mythical immortality nor mournful gloom: "If there is a flower that blooms only for one single night, its bloom does not appear to us on that account any less splendid." What matters is the emotion that beauty and perfection arouse at the very moment they do so. ("Vergänglichkeit" [1916], *GW* X, 359/"On Transience," *SE* XIV, 306.)

The objects that Freud amassed in his apartment across the years speak to the kind of sensual gratification that he, physician and family man, found both pleasing and acceptable. Berggasse 19 was a little world reflecting deliberate choices; it securely placed Freud in his larger culture both by what it contained and by what it, strikingly, did not contain. Freud was an educated middle-class burgher of his time; still, his attitude toward what his class professed to cherish and often cherished in actuality—art, music, literature, architecture—was not wholly predictable. Freud was far from insensitive to man-made beauty. In 1913, he was pleased to hear that Karl Abraham was enjoying the Dutch resort of Noordwijk aan Zee, where Freud had vacationed before. "The sunsets above all," he reminisced, "were glorious." But even more, he appreciated the works of man. "The small Dutch towns are enchanting. Delft is a little jewel." Painters and sculptors—and architects—gave him much visual enjoyment, more enjoyment even than landscapes.

Open to beauty or not, by and large Freud's tastes ran to the conventional. The things he chose to live with were uncompromising in their conservatism, their celebration of well-established traditions. He liked the kind of mementos most nineteenth-century bourgeois thought so indispensable to their well-being: photographs of family members and close friends, souvenirs of places visited and gladly remembered, etchings and pieces of sculpture that were, so to speak, legacies of the Old Regime in the arts—academic, unadventurous, all of them. The revolutions in painting, poetry, and music exploding all around him left Freud untouched; when they obtruded themselves on his notice, which was rarely, he energetically disapproved. One would not know from the pictures on Freud's walls that when he moved to Berggasse 19, French impressionism had been flourishing for some time, or that Klimt and Kokoschka and, later, Schiele were working in Vienna. Commenting with vehement distaste on a "most modern" portrait drawing of Karl Abraham, he told Abraham that he was horrified to see "how cruelly your tolerance or sympathy for modern 'art' must be punished." The sarcastic quotation marks around "art" are telling. Face to face with expressionism, Freud frankly admitted to Oskar Pfister, he was a philistine.

Appropriately, the furniture crowding the Freuds' apartment ignored all the experimental designs then transforming the living quarters of more up-to-date households in Vienna. The family lived amid solid Victorian comfort, with their embroidered tablecloths, plush-covered chairs, framed photographic portraits, and a profusion of oriental rugs. Their apartment breathes a wholly unapologetic eclecticism, reflected in an accumulation of objects that, far from obeying some decorator's program, speaks of the uncomplicated pursuit of domestic enjoyment over the years. The Freuds seem to have found this cluttered plenitude, which more austere tastes might have disdained as oppressive, most reassuring; it fulfilled the program for domesticity that Freud had laid down before he was married, and attests to prosperity finally achieved quite as much as to experiences fondly recalled. Indeed, both prosperity and memories stamp Freud's professional quarters—his consulting room and his private study—no less than the other rooms at Berggasse 19. His analysis of art was far more radical than his taste in beauty.

A VERY SIMILAR conflict pervaded Freud's attitudes toward literature. His treatises, monographs, and papers proclaim his wide reading, retentive memory, and exigent sense of style. As we know, he often resorted to his favorite German classics, notably Goethe and Schiller, and to Shakespeare, who set him fascinating riddles and whom he could recite at length in his near-perfect English. Wits like Heinrich Heine and more coarse-grained humorists like Wilhelm Busch supplied him with trenchant illustrations. But in choosing his favorites, he slighted the European avant-garde of his age; he knew his Ibsen, mainly as a courageous iconoclast, but he seems to have had little use for poets like Baudelaire or playwrights like Strindberg. Among the Viennese, who were in those days writing, painting, and composing in an atmosphere electric with irrepressible modernist impulses, Arthur Schnitzler alone, we have seen, secured Freud's unequivocal applause, for his penetrating psychological studies of sexuality in contemporary Viennese society.

This is not to say that Freud took no time to read novels and poems and essays for pleasure. He did, and his choices were catholic. When he needed to relax, notably when he was recuperating from operations, late in life, he indulged his taste for murder mysteries by such classic detective-story writers as Agatha Christie and Dorothy Sayers. Generally, to be sure, his reading matter was rather more elevated. In 1907, responding to a questionnaire from his publisher Hugo Heller asking for a list of ten "good" books, Freud named two Swiss writers, two French, two English, one Russian, one Dutch, one Austrian, and one American: Gottfried Keller and Conrad Ferdinand Meyer, Anatole France and Émile Zola, Rudyard Kipling and Lord Macaulay, Dmitri Merezhkovski, "Multatuli," Theodor Gomperz, and Mark Twain. These preferences were, like his preferences in art, relatively safe, a good deal less venturesome than might be expected from such a rebel. But they did at least display a modicum of rebelliousness. "Multatuli," the Dutch essayist and novelist Eduard Douwes Dekker, was something of a political and moral reformer; Kipling's *Jungle Book* could be read as an imaginative protest against the artificiality of modern civilization; and certainly Mark Twain was the most disrespectful of humorists.

Indeed, a few of Freud's favorites, such as Macaulay's resolutely optimistic essays on English culture from the seventeenth to the nineteenth century, and Gomperz's no less resolutely Whiggish history of ancient Greek philosophy, were somewhat subversive in their own way. They recall Freud's indelible debt to the thought of the eighteenth-century Enlightenment, its critical spirit and its hope for humanity, both as he directly experienced that thought through his reading of Diderot or Voltaire and as filtered through its nineteenth-century heirs. The governing theme of Macaulay's and Gomperz's work alike was the triumphant spread of light and reason across a world deeply shadowed by superstition and persecution. Freud, we know, liked to say that he was spending his life destroying illusions, but, for all his sturdy pessimism, he sometimes enjoyed playing with the illusion that progress is possible, and perhaps cumulative, in human affairs. It is noteworthy that when he was writing for publication, whether on the psychology of the individual, of groups, or of culture as a whole, he was rather less sanguine. When he was reading for pleasure, it seems, Freud permitted himself some of the wishful fantasies he sternly repressed during working hours.

Not surprisingly, Freud's literary verdicts were often downright political: one reason he prized Anatole France was that France displayed outspoken anti-anti-Semitism; one reason he granted Dmitri Merezhkovski, author of *The Romance of Leonardo da Vinci,* far more authority than he deserved was that Merezhkovski adulated a Renaissance artist whom Freud admired for his independence and his intellectual courage. But most of Freud's favorite writers were his favorites because they were gifted amateur psychologists. He could go to school to them, just as biographers or anthropologists, he thought, could go to school to him. This is not to reduce Freud to a consistent philistine, even though he aimed this epithet against himself. But the utilitarian streak in his tastes is undeniable. As he confessed in 1914, in his paper on Michelangelo's *Moses,* "I have often noticed that the subject matter of a work of art attracts me more strongly than its formal and technical properties, which, after all, the artist principally values. Indeed, I lack a proper understanding of many of the methods and some of the effects of art." Freud recognized the distinction between purely formal, aesthetic pleasure and the pleasure that the subject matter of art or literature can supply. But there he stopped, in part because he thought the ways of artists beyond comprehension. "Meaning is but little with these men, all they care about is line, shape, agreement of contours. They are given up to the Lustprinzip.''* In Freud, in sharp contrast, the reality principle asserted its predominance over the pleasure principle.

THIS PRACTICAL CAST of mind inevitably shaped Freud's rather distant and quizzical relationship to music. He made a point of proclaiming his ignorance in musical matters and admitted that he could not carry a tune. In his *Interpretation of Dreams,* he virtually boasted about his tone deafness: humming the challenge of Figaro to Count Almaviva in the first act of *The Marriage of Figaro,* he thought that "someone else would perhaps not have recognized the melody." Those compelled to hear him droning arias from Mozart operas confirmed that this was only too true. He did not seek out musicians, and, his daughter Anna tersely noted, he "never went to concerts." But he did enjoy opera or, rather, some operas. His daughters, searching their memories, could come up with five: Mozart's *Don Giovanni, The Marriage of Figaro,* and *The Magic Flute;* Bizet's *Carmen;* and Wagner's *Meistersinger.* The list is as safe as it is skimpy: no Claude Debussy, no Richard Strauss. Among Wagner's operas, the *Meistersinger* is certainly, after such early works as *The Flying Dutchman,* the most accessible. And *Carmen,* though it took some time to conquer Paris after its premiere there in 1875, quickly became a great favorite in the German-speaking lands. Brahms, Wagner, and Tschaikovsky, who agreed on little else, all thought Bizet's last opera a masterpiece; Nietzsche, who attended at least twenty performances of it, invoked its vitality and Gallic charm in his polemic against Wagner's heavy, decadent Teutonic music dramas; Bismarck, that well-informed amateur of music, boasted that he had heard it twenty-seven times. One did not have to be a votary of the avant-garde to enjoy these operas. Certainly Freud knew them well enough to quote them for his purposes: Figaro's aria, "Se vuol ballare, signor contino"; Sarastro's declaration to Princess Pamina in *The Magic Flute* that he cannot compel her to love him; Leporello impudently cataloguing Don Giovanni's conquests to Donna Elvira.

The appeal of opera to someone as unmusical as Freud is far from mysterious. Opera is, after all, music with words, song welded to dramatic action. Like most of his reading, it could offer Freud the pleasurable shock of

---

*Freud was a distinguished stylist and a pitiless critic of his own productions. His "self-criticism," he told Ferenczi, "is not an agreeable gift," but next to his courage, he thought it his best trait. It was this self-criticism that "has made a strict selection among my publication. Without it, I could have given the public three times as much." (Freud to Ferenczi, October 17, 1910. Freud–Ferenczi Correspondence, Freud Collection, LC.) This sounds rather extreme, but since Freud was in the habit of destroying his drafts and notes, it may actually be true. But it did not make him into a literary critic.

recognition; in its extravagant, often melodramatic way, opera grappled with the psychological issues that preoccupied Freud all his adult life: love, hatred, greed, betrayal. Beyond this, opera is also a spectacle, and Freud was particularly sensitive to visual impressions. That is why he looked at his patients as intently as he listened to them. What is more, opera depicts stirring moral conflicts issuing in satisfying moral resolutions; it presents highly verbal protagonists caught in the combat of good and evil. Of Freud's favorite five operas, all but *Carmen*—and most obviously *The Magic Flute* and the *Meistersinger*—enact the triumph of virtue over vice, an outcome that yields pleasure to the most sophisticated of listeners, in addition to providing information about the struggles raging in men's and women's minds.*

THE OPERA, AND for that matter, the theater, were rare diversions in Freud's life. In contrast, one of his regular, recurrent daily pleasures was food. Freud was neither gourmet nor gourmand; he had, we know, little tolerance for wine. But he liked his meals enough to consume them in quiet concentration. During the months in Vienna, the principal meal, the *Mittagessen,* served so promptly at one o'clock, consisted of soup, meat, vegetables, and dessert— "the usual three-course midday dinner, varied during appropriate seasons when, in springtime, we had an additional course in the way of asparagus." Freud was especially fond of Italian artichokes, of boiled beef—*Rindfleisch*— and of roast beef with onion, but he disliked cauliflower and chicken. He was fond of solid, satisfying *bürgerliche* fare, with not a touch of the refined French cuisine.

Instead, he saved whatever discrimination his palate possessed for his cigars. He was fatally addicted to them; when in the early 1890s Fliess—after all, a nose and throat specialist—proscribed them to clear up Freud's nasal catarrhs, Freud was in despair and pathetically pleaded for relief. He had begun smoking at twenty-four, at first cigarettes, but soon only cigars. He claimed that this "habit or vice," as he called it, greatly enhanced his capacity for work and his ability to muster self-control. Significantly, his father, "a heavy smoker" who "remained one until his eighty-first year," had been his model. Freud the cigar smoker was, of course, in sizable company in those days. For the weekly gatherings at his house the maid scattered ashtrays across the table, one for each guest. Late one Wednesday night, after one of these

---

*It should be noted that in Freud's particular favorite, *Don Giovanni,* this triumph is ambiguous in the extreme: the Don, who challenges the prevailing pieties of morality and religion, is sent to hell, but his pursuit of pleasure is so insouciant, and his conduct in face of condemnation and death so heroic, that the opera invites a more complex response than, say, the reconciliation enacted in *The Marriage of Figaro.* But in the absence of Freud's detailed comments on *Don Giovanni,* it is impossible to conjecture what the opera meant to him.

meetings had adjourned, Martin Freud got a glimpse—or, rather, a whiff—of the atmosphere. The room "was still thick with smoke and it seemed to me a wonder that human beings had been able to live in it for hours, let alone to speak in it without choking." When his nephew Harry was seventeen, Freud offered him a cigarette, and when Harry refused, his uncle told him, "My boy, smoking is one of the greatest and cheapest enjoyments in life, and if you decide in advance not to smoke, I can only feel sorry for you." It was a sensual gratification which Freud could not deny himself and for which he was to pay an extortionate price in pain and suffering. In 1897, we know, sharing an intuition he never developed into a paper, he told Fliess that addictions—and he explicitly included addiction to tobacco—are only substitutes for the "single great habit, the 'primal addiction,' " masturbation. But he was unable to translate this psychological insight into the decision to give up smoking.

IF FREUD'S HELPLESS love for cigars attests to the survival of primitive oral needs, his collecting of antiquities reveals residues in adult life of no less primitive anal enjoyments. What he once called his "partiality for the prehistoric" was, as he told his physician, Max Schur, "an addiction second in intensity only to his nicotine addiction." The consulting room where Freud saw his analysands, and his adjoining study, gradually became crowded to bursting with oriental rugs, with photographs of friends, with plaques. The glassed-in bookcases were laden with books and covered with objects; the walls carpeted with snapshots and etchings. The famous couch was a production in itself, piled high with pillows, supplied with a rug at its foot for patients to use if they were cold, and covered with a Persian rug, a Shiraz. But the most insistent presences in Freud's working rooms were the sculptures strewn over every available surface: they stood in serried ranks on bookshelves, thronged table tops and cabinets, and invaded Freud's orderly desk, where he had them under his fond eye as he wrote his letters and composed his papers.

It was this forest of sculptures that his visitors and his patients remembered most vividly. Hanns Sachs, a member of Freud's inner circle, observed that while Freud's collection was "still in its initial stages" when he first visited Berggasse 19 in 1909, "some of the objects at once attracted the visitor's eye." Upon entering analysis the following year, the Wolf Man also found Freud's ancient objects entrancing: "There was always a feeling of sacred peace and quiet" in Freud's "two adjoining studies"; he was reminded not of "a doctor's office but rather of an archeologist's study. Here were all kinds of statuettes and other unusual objects, which even the layman recognized as archeological finds from ancient Egypt. Here and there on the walls were stone plaques representing various scenes of long-vanished epochs."

This profusion had been lovingly amassed. Collecting antiquities was for Freud a lifelong avocation which he pursued with devotion and with system. When his old friend Emanuel Löwy, professor of archeology in Rome, and later in Vienna, was in town, he visited Freud and brought news from the ancient world. Freud for his part read about that world avidly when he found the time and followed excavations with an informed amateur's excitement. "I have made many sacrifices for my collection of Greek, Roman, and Egyptian antiquities," he told Stefan Zweig late in life, "and actually have read more archeology than psychology." This is genial hyperbole, no doubt: the focus of his organized curiosity was always the life of the mind, and the bibliographies attached to his writings display his mastery of the technical literature. But he enormously enjoyed his statuettes and fragments, the early purchases he could barely afford and, later, the gifts that friends and followers brought to Berggasse 19. In later years, as he looked around his consulting room from his comfortable upholstered armchair behind the couch, he could see a large picture of an Egyptian temple at Abu Simbel, a small reproduction of Ingres's painting of Oedipus interrogating the Sphinx, and a plaster cast of an antique relief, "Gradiva." On the wall opposite, above a glass cabinet filled with ancient objects, he had placed a picture of the Sphinx at Gizeh: another reminder of riddles—and of intrepid conquistadors like Freud who solve them.

So pointed a passion invites interpretation, and Freud was not reluctant to provide it. He told the Wolf Man that "the psychoanalyst, like the archeologist in his excavations, must uncover layer after layer of the patient's psyche, before coming to the deepest, most valuable treasures." But this weighty metaphor does not exhaust the significance of this addiction for Freud. His antique objects gave him sheer visual and tactile pleasure; Freud caressed them with his eyes or fondled them as he sat at his desk. At times, he took a new acquisition to the dining room to study and handled it there. And they were also emblems. They recalled friends who had taken the trouble to remember how fond he was of these artifacts, and they reminded him of the south: of sunny regions he had visited, those he hoped to visit, and those, too remote or too inaccessible, he despaired of visiting. Like so many northerners, all the way from Winckelmann to E. M. Forster, he loved Mediterranean civilization. "I have now adorned my room with plaster casts of the Florentine statues," he told Fliess late in 1896. "It was a source of extraordinary refreshment for me; I mean to get rich, in order to repeat these trips." Like Rome, his collection stood for obscure claims on life. "A congress on Italian soil! (Naples, Pompeii)," he exclaimed to Fliess in an access of longing after telling him about the Florentine plaster casts.

Even more obscurely, his antiques seemed reminders of a lost world to which he and his people, the Jews, could trace their remote roots. In August 1899, he announced to Fliess from Berchtesgaden that on the next rainy day he would "march" to his "beloved Salzburg," where he had recently "unearthed a few Egyptian antiquities. The things," he observed, "put me in high spirits and speak of distant times and lands." As he studied his prized possessions, he found, as he told Ferenczi many years later, "strange secret yearnings" rising up in him, "perhaps from my ancestral heritage—for the East and the Mediterranean and for a life of quite another kind: wishes from late childhood never to be fulfilled and not adapted to reality." It is no coincidence that the man in whose life history Freud took the greatest pleasure, and whom he probably envied more than any other, should have been Heinrich Schliemann, that celebrated digger and discoverer of Troy's mysterious, myth-laden antiquities. Freud thought the career of Schliemann so extraordinary because in discovering "Priam's treasure" he had found true happiness: "There is happiness only as fulfillment of a child's wish." It was precisely the kind of wish that, Freud felt in his mournful moods, had so rarely become reality in his own life.

But, as Freud told the Wolf Man, it is as a master metaphor for his life's work that his enduring partiality for antique objects acquires its most sweeping significance. *"Saxa loquuntur!"* he had exclaimed in 1896, in his lecture on the etiology of hysteria before his Viennese medical colleagues—"Stones speak!" At least stones spoke to him. In one exuberant letter to Fliess, he compared an analytic success he had just enjoyed to the discovery of Troy. With Freud's help a patient had found, buried deep underneath fantasies, "a scene from his primal period (before 22 months), which answers all requirements and into which all left-over riddles flow; it is everything at once, sexual, innocuous, natural, etc. I still scarcely dare to believe it properly. It is as if Schliemann had dug up Troy, considered legendary, once again." The metaphor never lost its efficiency for Freud: in his preface to the case history of Dora, he assimilated the problems presented by the "incompleteness of my analytic results" to those faced by "explorers fortunate enough to bring to the light of day after long burial the priceless though mutilated remnants of antiquity." He had done some restoring, but like "a conscientious archeologist" he had not "omitted to mention in each case where my reconstruction supplements the authentic." Three decades later, in *Civilization and Its Discontents,* in illustrating the "general problem of preservation in the mind," he employed a sweeping analogy with Rome as spread out before the modern tourist: a succession of cities whose fragments survive side by side or have been recovered by archeological excavation. Thus, in Freud's collection of antiquities, work and pleasure, early impulses and sophisticated adult sublimations, flowed into one. Still, the flavor of addiction remains. There is something poetic about the fact that at the first session of the Wednesday Psychological Society in the fall of 1902, the topic of discussion was the psychological impact of smoking.

THE WEDNESDAY PSYCHOLOGICAL SOCIETY

 Freud's Wednesday-night group was launched modestly and informally in the fall of 1902, when "a number of younger physicians gathered around me with the declared intention of learning, practicing, and disseminating psychoanalysis. A colleague who had experienced the beneficial effects of analytic therapy on himself gave the impetus." This is how Freud summarized the early history of the Society a decade or so later. It is symptomatic of his later annoyance with Wilhelm Stekel (or his discretion) that he failed to mention the name of this colleague, at whose suggestion the group began to meet. Stekel, an imaginative and prolific Viennese physician, had been in brief and for a time successful analytic treatment with Freud to alleviate symptoms of psychological impotence. That was one bond. Stekel's work on dream symbolism was another: as successive editions of *The Interpretation of Dreams* attest, with their explicit acknowledgment of Freud's debt to Stekel, Freud's relations with this adherent, as with some others, were mutually beneficial. Freud taught his early intimates far more than he learned from them, but he was open to their influence. In those early years, as Stekel put it in his autobiography with characteristic grandiloquence, he was "the apostle of Freud who was my Christ!"*

Had Freud lived to read this claim, he might have identified Stekel as

*When Freud read Wittels's biography of him and came upon his extravagant aside that Stekel deserved a monument, Freud noted in the margin, with visible irritation, "Too much Stekel." (See p. 47 in Freud's copy of Wittels, *Sigmund Freud*. Freud Museum, London.)

Judas; he came to judge Stekel with exceptional harshness. But in 1902, Stekel had fathered an idea whose utility Freud was quick to perceive. In fact, Freud found its timing most felicitous; whatever the shortcomings of the men who joined him every Wednesday night in his waiting room, in the early days they offered him the psychological echo he craved. They were, more or less, replacements for Fliess, and they supplied some of the applause he had expected to secure with his *Interpretation of Dreams.* At first, Freud noted a little wistfully later, he had had every reason to be satisfied.

However small the Wednesday Psychological Society at the outset, spirits were exuberant. Freud sent postcards inviting, in addition to Stekel, three other Viennese physicians: Max Kahane, Rudolf Reitler, and Alfred Adler. These formed the nucleus of what was to become, in 1908, the Vienna Psychoanalytic Society, the model for scores of such societies across the world. Kahane had, like Freud, translated a volume of Charcot's lectures into German, and had introduced Stekel to Freud and his writings. Reitler, who died prematurely in 1917, became the world's second analyst, after Freud, a practitioner whose work Freud cited with respect and whose interventions at the Wednesday-night sessions were marked by incisive, sometimes wounding, criticisms. Probably the most formidable recruit was Alfred Adler, a Socialist physician who had published a health book for the tailoring trade but was becoming increasingly interested in the social uses of psychiatry. The first sessions of the Wednesday-night group, Stekel proudly remembered, "were inspiring." There was "complete harmony among the five, no dissonances; we were like pioneers in a newly discovered land, and Freud was the leader. A spark seemed to jump from one mind to the other, and every evening was like a revelation."

Stekel's metaphors are commonplace, but his report captures the atmosphere; dissent and dissension were in the future. Certainly some of the early members found such theological terminology perfectly appropriate. "The gatherings," Max Graf recalled, "followed a definite ritual. First, one of the members would present a paper. Then, black coffee and cakes were served; cigars and cigarettes were on the table and were consumed in great quantities. After a social quarter of an hour, the discussion would begin. The last and the decisive word was always spoken by Freud himself. There was an atmosphere of the foundation of a religion in that room. Freud himself was its new prophet who made the heretofore prevailing methods of psychological investigation appear superficial." This was not language that Freud really appreciated. He liked to think of himself as more flexible, less authoritarian, than any "prophet" could be. But a certain sense of exaltation seems to have clung to the group, and after a few years it grew stifling enough to cause some, like Graf, to withdraw, much as they admired Freud.*

RECRUITMENT TO THE Wednesday Society was by unanimous consent, but that was, in the genial atmosphere of the first years, a mere formality. One member would introduce another; a few, but only a few, dropped out. By 1906, the year Freud turned fifty, membership stood at seventeen, and Freud could always count on a dozen for animated, increasingly aggressive talk. In October of that year, the style of the Wednesday Society changed subtly but distinctly. Upon starting its fifth year, the members decided to employ a paid secretary, Otto Rank, to record attendance, keep track of dues, and take extensive notes on each meeting.

Rank's notes record the group canvassing case histories, psychoanalyses of literary works and public figures, reviews of new psychiatric literature, and previews of forthcoming publications by members. There were confessional evenings: in October 1907, Maximilian Steiner, a dermatologist and specialist in venereal diseases, reported suffering all sorts of psychosomatic symptoms during a time of sexual abstinence, symptoms that disappeared as soon as he started an affair with the wife of an impotent friend. Again, in early 1908, Rudolf von Urbantschitsch, director of a sanatorium, entertained his fellow members with a paper drawn from his diary on "my years of development"— that is, his sexual development—"up to my marriage," in which he admitted to early masturbation and a certain taste for sadomasochism. Freud dryly observed in his closing comment that Urbantschitsch had offered the group a kind of present. It accepted the gift without blinking: the Wednesday Psychological Society took pride in that sort of scientific self-exhibition.

Some of the members who joined after 1902 were, and remain, obscure.

---

*In view of the persistent charge that Freud had founded a secular religion, it is worth noting that Ernest Jones found this criticism worth meeting head on. He calls one chapter of his autobiography "The Psycho-Analytical 'Movement,' " and observes that he put the word "movement" within "inverted commas—to pillory it, so to speak. . . . The word . . . is properly applied to activities, such as those of the Tractarian Movement, the Chartist Movement, and so many thousand others, characterised by the ardent desire to promulgate . . . beliefs that are accounted exceedingly precious. . . .

"It was this element that gave rise to the general criticism of our would-be scientific activities that they partook rather of the nature of a religious movement, and amusing parallels were drawn. Freud was of course the Pope of the new sect, if not a still higher Personage, to whom all owed obeisance; his writings were the sacred text, credence in which was obligatory on the supposed infallibilists who had undergone the necessary conversion, and there were not lacking the heretics who were expelled from the church. It was a pretty obvious caricature to make, but the minute element of truth in it was made to serve in place of the reality, which was far different." (Ernest Jones, *Free Associations: Memories of a Psycho-Analyst* [1959], 205.)

But a handful would contribute to the making of psychoanalytic history. They included Hugo Heller, bookseller and publisher, who ran a salon for intellectuals and artists and eventually added psychoanalytic titles to his list, and Max Graf, whose five-year-old son was to secure a measure of immortality as "Little Hans," one of Freud's most extraordinary cases. These were among the laymen, whom Freud particularly prized, worried as he always was that psychoanalysis might turn into a doctors' monopoly. But some of the physicians in the society were destined to assume dominant positions in the psychoanalytic movement in Austria and abroad. Paul Federn, rapidly developing into one of Freud's most trusted adherents in the Vienna Psychoanalytic Society, proved to be an original, influential theoretician; Isidor Sadger, an able analyst and rather provocative companion, introduced his nephew Fritz Wittels into the group; Eduard Hitschmann, who joined in 1905, six years later earned Freud's special gratitude for his popular exposition of psychoanalysis, which he tactfully identified in the title as Freud's creation—*Freud's Theories of the Neuroses*. Like Federn, Hitschmann showed himself, through all the vicissitudes the years would bring, a dependable lieutenant.

PERHAPS THE MOST astonishing recruit was Otto Rank. A trained machinist, short, unprepossessing, pursued for years by uncertain health, he escaped from the miseries of his impecunious and unhappy Jewish family by developing an inexhaustible appetite for learning. Far from being a typical autodidact, he was exceptional in his intelligence and his absorptive capacity. He read everything. Alfred Adler, his family physician, had introduced him to Freud's writings, and Rank devoured them. They dazzled him, seeming to offer the key to all the riddles of the world. In the spring of 1905, when he was twenty-one, he presented Freud with the manuscript of a small book, *The Artist*, a foray into the cultural application of psychoanalytic ideas. A little more than a year later, he was installed as secretary of the Wednesday Society. Freud took a paternal interest in him; affectionately, betraying just a touch of condescension, he called him "little Rank," employed him as an assistant for the revision of his writings, and benevolently smoothed his way through belated attendance at Gymnasium and the University of Vienna. In the Wednesday Society, Rank was no mere amanuensis: in October 1906, his first month there, he presented substantial excerpts from his forthcoming mountainous monograph on the incest motif in literature.

There were perhaps more losses during Rank's tenure than gains, though they were not of his making. The meetings grew testy, even acrimonious, as members sparred for position, vaunted their originality, or voiced dislike of their fellows with a brutal hostility masquerading as analytic frankness. In

early 1908, the group held formal discussions aimed at "reforming" procedures, and debated a proposal to abolish "intellectual communism"—*geistiger Kommunismus;* henceforth, each idea should be identified as its originator's private property. Freud proposed a compromise: let every member have
his contributions treated just as he wished, as a common possession or as his
own; he himself, he declared, still stood ready to put everything he had said
into the public domain.

Other members were less generous and less restrained. In December 1907,
on a typical evening, Sadger read a paper analyzing the nineteenth-century
Swiss poet Conrad Ferdinand Meyer in which he stressed Meyer's unrequited
love for his mother. Though this sort of oedipal analysis was congenial to the
intellectual habits of the group, Sadger's colleagues thought his presentation
crude. Federn professed himself outraged; Stekel expressed shock and protested against oversimplifications that could only damage the good cause.
Wittels came to his uncle's defense and frowned at these "personal eruptions
of rage and indignation." The dispute moved Freud, who had his own
reservations about Sadger's paper, to counsel moderation. When he thought
it necessary, he could be devastating, but Freud liked to hold back his big guns
for big occasions. In his response, nettled by the treatment he had received,
Sadger voiced disappointment; he had hoped for instruction and would carry
home nothing but a few words of abuse.

By 1908, such acerbic meetings were far from rare. All too often, vehemence made up for lack of penetration. But the disappointing showing of the
Wednesday Society was more than just a symptom of the pall that mediocrity
tends to spread over any group. The rubbing up of sensitive, often labile,
individuals against one another was bound to produce sparks of hostility.
What is more, the provocative subject matter of psychoanalytic inquiry,
rudely touching on the most heavily guarded spots in the human psyche, was
taking its toll and generating a pervasive irritability. After all, none of the men
who in those heroic, exploratory years tactlessly and confidently invaded the
most intimate sanctuaries of others, and their own, had been analyzed—
Stekel's treatment with Freud had been brief, far from complete. Freud, of
course, had analyzed himself, but by its very nature his self-analysis was
unduplicable. The others, most of whom could have used analysis, had not
enjoyed its benefits. Early in 1908, Max Graf sadly observed, "We are no
longer the fellowship we once were."

Not long before, Freud, still the undisputed authority over his restless
troops, had tried to take account of the changed conditions by proposing to
dissolve the informal group and reconstitute it as the Vienna Psychoanalytic
Society. This reorganization would give members who had lost interest or
were no longer in sympathy with Freud's aims an opportunity to resign

unostentatiously. It was a graceful expedient, no more; there was no way that Freud could compel the others to rise above their natural level. In December 1907, Karl Abraham was a guest at a meeting for the first time, and he shrewdly, pitilessly, recorded his impressions for his friend Max Eitingon: "I am not too thrilled by the Viennese adherents. I was at the Wednesday session. *He* is all too far ahead of the others. Sadger is like a Talmud-disciple; he interprets and observes every rule of the Master with orthodox Jewish severity. Among the physicians Dr. Federn made the best impression on me. Stekel is superficial, Adler one-sided, Wittels too much the phrasemonger, the others insignificant. The young Rank seems very intelligent, Dr. Graf just as much. . . ." In the spring of 1908, Ernest Jones saw for himself and agreed. He later recalled that visiting in Vienna and observing the Wednesday group for the first time, he was "not highly impressed" with Freud's Viennese adherents. From the cool distance of the outsider, they "seemed an unworthy accompaniment to Freud's genius, but in the Vienna of those days, so full of prejudice against him, it was hard to secure a pupil with a reputation to lose, so he had to take what he could get."

There were bright intervals: between 1908 and 1910, new members included Sándor Ferenczi from Budapest, the talented but severely neurotic jurist Victor Tausk, the schoolteacher and Social Democrat Carl Furtmüller, the witty lawyer Hanns Sachs. Their numbers were swelled by a stream of visitors who trooped to Vienna to make Freud's acquaintance and attend the Wednesday-night sessions: the "Swiss," psychiatrists and advanced medical students working in Zurich and elsewhere in Switzerland, came as early as 1907. Freud hailed them—Max Eitingon, Carl G. Jung, Ludwig Binswanger, Karl Abraham—as his most interesting new adherents. The following year, other visitors important for the future of psychoanalysis stopped by to meet Freud and his Viennese group: A. A. Brill, Freud's American apostle and translator; Ernest Jones, who was to become his most influential British supporter; and the pioneer of psychoanalysis in Italy, Edoardo Weiss.

Freud judged the contrast between these birds of passage and the Viennese regulars to be nothing less than painful. While he often let his fond wishes outrun his experience in judging people, he did not deceive himself about his local following. After one Wednesday-night meeting in 1907, visibly disenchanted, he said to the young Swiss psychiatrist Ludwig Binswanger, "So, now you have seen the gang!" There may have been a bit of subtle flattery in this succinct, derisive comment; Freud was courting his new Swiss supporters. But Binswanger, recalling the scene many years later, gave it a more charitable, probably more accurate, reading: it demonstrated to him just how isolated Freud still felt himself to be in the midst of this crowd. "All my Viennese," Freud told Abraham grimly in 1911, "won't amount to anything, except for little Rank." There were some promising personages among the Viennese: Rank, Federn, Sachs, perhaps Reitler, Hitschmann, even Tausk. But as the years went by, Freud increasingly invested his hopes abroad, with foreigners.

THE FOREIGNERS

 Four of these foreigners, Max Eitingon and Karl Abraham in Berlin, Ernest Jones in London, and Sándor Ferenczi in Budapest, were to carry the flag of psychoanalysis through years of arduous service to the cause—editing, debating, organizing, raising money, training candidates, making interesting, sometimes problematic clinical and theoretical contributions of their own. In sharp contrast to the dramatic collaboration and no less dramatic collision that marked Freud's relations with Jung, the association of these four men with Freud was, if at times somewhat tense, highly profitable to both sides.

Max Eitingon was the first of the "Swiss" to call at Berggasse 19. An affluent, generous, and self-effacing Russian Jew studying medicine in Zurich, he had written to Freud late in 1906, introducing himself as a "subassistant" at the Burghölzli Mental Hospital whose superiors, "Prof. Bleuler and Dr. Jung," had called his attention to Freud's writings. "Close study of them has persuaded me more and more of the astonishing range of your conception of hysteria and the great value of the psychoanalytic method." Freud, in his usual manner, did not delay exhibiting his delight at seeing a young man "attracted by the truth content of our teachings." In those days, Freud thought of himself as a "fisher of men," and did his best to live up to that biblical self-designation. In January 1907, Eitingon came to Vienna for a consultation concerning an intractable patient and stayed for two weeks. His friendship with Freud was launched, cemented by a handful of most unconventional analytic "sessions": Freud took Eitingon on walks through Vienna, and as they walked, Freud analyzed his new recruit. "Such," Ernest Jones later exclaimed, recalling the informality of those early days, "was the first training analysis!" In the fall of 1909, after some more ambulatory analytic strolls with Freud, Eitingon moved from Zurich to Berlin, securely Freud's "pupil." His practice grew slowly; occasionally he asked Freud to refer patients to him, and Freud obliged. In return, Eitingon deluged Freud with presents. "For three days," Freud wrote his Berlin pupil exuberantly in early 1910, "it has been raining works of D . . . in my house." Eitingon had been sending Freud one volume of Dostoevsky after another, calling particular attention to *The Possessed* and *The Brothers Karamazov*. The correspondence between the two grew affectionate and confidential. "I know you will remain faithful to me," Freud assured Eitingon in July 1914. "We are a little handful that includes none of the godly, but no traitors either." He never had reason to regret his faith in Eitingon, who became one of the most munificent patrons of psychoanalysis during Freud's lifetime.

EITINGON'S CLOSEST ALLY in Berlin, Karl Abraham, had to struggle for the financial independence that his lifelong friend could take for granted. Four years older than Eitingon, he was born in the port city of Bremen in 1877 into a Jewish family long settled in Germany. His father, a teacher of religion, was unusually broad-minded for his time; when Karl Abraham, about to take a position as a psychiatrist, informed him that he could no longer keep the Sabbath and other Jewish religious practices, the elder Abraham told his son to obey his own conscience. As a psychoanalytic watchdog, Abraham would sometimes show himself rather less tolerant than his father. His fellow analysts valued him as calm, methodical, intelligent, not given to speculation or effusions. Perhaps he was a little cool; Ernest Jones has described him as "emotionally self-contained." But Abraham's reserve permitted him to supply self-control and common sense to a movement badly in need of these qualities. He was, to quote Jones again, "certainly the most normal member of the group" around Freud. His cheerfulness became almost proverbial among his colleagues; Freud, who often warmed himself at Abraham's sunny forecasts, called him an incurable optimist.

Abraham came to psychiatry from medicine. He first met Freud in 1907, when he was thirty, and the encounter changed his life. For three years, he had worked at Burghölzli, the mental hospital near Zurich where Jung was chief resident physician, but after coming under Freud's sway, he ventured to open a private psychoanalytic practice in Berlin. It was a risky step for Abraham to take at a time, and in a country, wholly dominated by traditional psychiatry. Those Freud derisively called "the official rabble" of Berlin knew little about psychoanalysis and detested what they knew. "You must be having a hard fight of it in Berlin," Ernest Jones remarked to Abraham as late as 1911, from London, offering fraternal sympathy. For some years, in fact, Abraham was, as Freud noted with admiration, the only practicing psychoanalyst in the German capital. Abraham, always hoping against hope, needed little encouragement, but Freud, partly to keep up his own morale, cheered him on from Vienna: "It should turn out all right."

Sanguine as Abraham's temperament may have been, any slight sign of support was welcome. When, late in 1907, the Berlin psychiatrist Otto Juliusburger read a paper advocating psychoanalytic ideas, Freud wrote him a letter of thanks for his bravery. Buoyed up by such slender positive signs, Abraham founded the Berlin Psychoanalytic Society in August 1908, with a total of five members; besides himself, these included Juliusburger and the embattled sexologist Magnus Hirschfeld. From the beginning, Freud volunteered good advice: he urged Abraham not to allow the reigning distaste for Hirschfeld to prejudice him against that impassioned, far from disinterested partisan of homosexual rights.

Not all was psychoanalytic business between Freud and Abraham; the two, with their families, soon became close enough to visit back and forth, and Freud showed a paternal concern for the Abraham children.* In May 1908, he could gratefully inform Abraham, "My wife has reported to me a great deal about the cordial reception she found at your house." He showed himself pleased, but hardly surprised, to have made "a good diagnosis" concerning Abraham's hospitality.

After some difficult years, Abraham established himself as a sought-after therapist and the leading training analyst for the second generation of analytic candidates from two continents. In 1914, thanking him for his important paper on voyeurism, Lou Andreas-Salomé particularly praised Abraham's clarity of presentation and his willingness to follow the material rather than to impose dogma upon it. In the same year, Abraham was prominent enough to have the American psychologist G. Stanley Hall, president of Clark University, ask him for a photograph "to adorn our Seminary walls."

Success brought prosperity. By early 1911, Abraham could report to Freud that his practice had been "lively for a good long while," even "turbulent." He was doing analysis eight hours a day. But he perceived all this activity as a far from unambiguous blessing; it gave him, he observed regretfully in characteristic Freudian accents, "little time for science." By 1912, he had as many as ten analysands, and his practice had become even more "lucrative" than before. In the first six months of the year, he earned 11,000 marks, a very respectable sum, and he was planning to raise his fees into the bargain. "You see," he told Freud, "even in Berlin it is no longer a martyrdom to be your adherent." Abraham rarely had complaints, and when he did, they

---

*Abraham's widow recalled that "the Professor" took "great interest in the health and development of our children and also often reported about the events in his own family. When he visited us after the Haag Congress (1920), he gave us what was left of a sum, presented to him for his stay in Holland, & asked me to buy bycycles [sic] for our children as a Christmas present & so to gratify their hearts' desire." (Hedwig Abraham to Jones, April 1, 1952. Jones papers, Archives of the British Psycho-Analytical Society, London.)

concerned not his patients but his professional colleagues. "My practice," he wrote to Freud in the spring of 1912, "absorbs me," but he was moved to grumble that for a psychoanalyst interested in theory, "Berlin is only too sterile a soil." While the meetings of his psychoanalytic society were going well enough, "the right people are lacking." No matter: his relative intellectual solitude gave Abraham all the more incentive to do his own work.

Members of the psychoanalytic clan were almost universally endowed with overflowing vitality, but Abraham had more energy than most of the others. Some of his spirited activity, though, was an act of will; forced from childhood onward to contend with mild asthma and a somewhat frail constitution, he took up tennis, swimming, and, later, his favorite sport, mountain climbing. This was a popular form of exercise among many practitioners of Abraham's sedentary calling; even Freud, though less addicted to strenuous sports than some of his adherents, enjoyed long, sturdy mountain walks.

The determination that made Abraham into a mountain climber also fueled his professional work. He enlisted recruits, presided over meetings, and turned his attention to an impressive range of subjects; his bibliography includes surveys of current analytic literature, clinical studies, essays on applied psychoanalysis dealing with subjects as diverse as modern art and Egyptian religion. Even more consequential for the history of psychoanalysis were his important papers on the development of libido, which served to redirect Freud's own thinking in later years. Nor was he too busy to keep a trained eye on psychoanalytic politics in the storm centers, Vienna and Zurich. His exceptionally cheerful disposition, such a contrast to Freud's, was curiously combined with a wary attention to deviations among his fellow analysts and to the smallest cloud of defection on the horizon.

But though a good servant of the cause, Abraham was not servile to Freud. In fact, he maintained enough independence to drift into friendly relations with Fliess, whose break with Freud was no secret to him. Early in 1911, Fliess, learning that Abraham had discovered "Fliessian" cycles in one of his analysands, invited him to call. Abraham conscientiously reported this invitation to Freud, and Freud responded guardedly. "I do not see why you should not visit him," he wrote, and predicted that Abraham would "meet a very considerable, indeed fascinating, human being." The visit might give him an opportunity to "approach scientifically the piece of truth that is contained in [Fliess's] period doctrines." At the same time, Freud cautioned Abraham that Fliess would doubtless attempt to lure him away from psychoanalysis "and, as he believes, from me," to divert him into his own wake. Fliess, he went on bluntly, is "fundamentally a hard, wicked human being"; and he added for good measure, "I particularly warn you against his wife, clever-stupid, malicious, positive hysteric; in short: perversion not neurosis."

This warning did not prevent Abraham from cultivating Fliess's acquaintance. He acknowledged the caution, promised "to exercise the necessary prudence," and scrupulously kept Freud informed of his visits. Fliess, Abraham reassured Freud, was making no efforts to win him away from psychoanalysis or from its founder, and in any event had not struck him as fascinating in any way. But, with that touch of reserve that was his signature, he did not comment on Freud's disparaging characterization of Frau Dr. Fliess. Nor did he notify Freud, then or later, that he and Fliess were exchanging offprints. Freud no doubt exaggerated the danger to Abraham of associating with his former intimate. It is true that Fliess fulsomely acknowledged Abraham's offprints as though they offered psychoanalytic revelations that Freud himself had never been able to transmit: "Keep on opening our eyes!" But Fliess apparently made no effort to seduce Abraham into deserting Freud. And if he had tried, he would not have succeeded. Abraham was shrewd and self-possessed enough to resist such blandishments. At all events it is a mark of Freud's cordial feelings and unwavering trust that his intimacy with Abraham survived this provocation.

ERNEST JONES COULD not have been more different from Abraham. The two did find one another congenial, and through the stormy evolution of the international psychoanalytic movement, remained steadfast allies. They shared a fierce admiration for Freud, an addiction to work, and, far from trivial, a love of exercise; Abraham climbed mountains, and Jones, compact, brisk, bursting with vitality, preferred figure skating—in fact, found the time to write a learned treatise on the subject.* Emotionally, though, the two men inhabited quite different worlds. Volatile and provocative where Abraham was (or at least seemed) serene and sensible, repeatedly and at times embarrassingly embroiled in erotic adventures where Abraham was sober and monogamous, Jones was the most opinionated and, as Freud was happy to acknowledge, the most combative of adherents, an indefatigable letter writer, imperious organizer, and militant controversialist.

Ernest Jones discovered Freud not long after the publication of the case history of Dora in 1905. As a young physician specializing in psychiatry, he had been sorely disappointed by the failure of contemporary medical or-

---

*Jones first published his technical, though elegantly written and copiously illustrated, volume *The Elements of Figure Skating* in 1931; a revised and enlarged edition was issued in 1952. Sprinkled with carefully drawn diagrams displaying an astonishing variety of possible figures, and seemingly very remote from his professional concerns, the book exhibits Jones's irrepressible erotic impulse. "All art, however refined, disguised and elaborated its technique," he writes in the introduction, "takes its ultimate source in love for the human body and the desire to command it" (p. 15). And the book dwells with evident enjoyment on the pleasure that graceful motion and exhilarating, effortless-seeming gliding can provide.

thodoxy to explain the workings, and the malfunctioning, of the mind, and that disappointment facilitated his conversion. At the time he read about Dora, his German was still halting, but he "came away" from his reading "with a deep impression of there being a man in Vienna who actually listened to every word his patients said to him." It came as a revelation. "I was trying to do so myself, but I had never heard of anyone else doing so." Freud, he recognized, was that *"rara avis,* a true psychologist."*

After spending some time with Jung at Burghölzli learning more about psychoanalysis, Jones sought out Freud in the spring of 1908 at the Salzburg congress of psychoanalysts, where he heard Freud give a memorable address on one of his patients, the Rat Man.† Wasting no time, he followed up this meeting in May with a visit to Berggasse 19, where he was cordially received. After that, he and Freud saw one another often and bridged the gaps between meetings with long, frequent communiqués. Some years of distressing inner battles followed for Jones; he was besieged with doubts about psychoanalysis. But once sure of his ground, once fully persuaded, he made himself into the most energetic of Freud's advocates, first in North America, then in England, in the end everywhere.

That Jones started his campaign in behalf of Freud's ideas in Canada and the northeastern United States was not wholly a matter of free choice. The breath of scandal hangs over his early medical career in London: Jones was twice accused of misbehaving with children he was testing and examining.‡ Dismissed from his post at a children's hospital, he thought it prudent to move to Toronto. Once settled, he began lecturing on psychoanalysis to generally unreceptive audiences in Canada and the United States, and in 1911, he was active in founding the American Psychoanalytic Association. Two years later, in 1913, he was back in London, practicing psychoanalysis and organizing a small band of Freud's English followers. In November, he could triumphantly report to Freud that "the London Psycho-Analytic Society was duly constituted last Thursday, with a membership of nine."

Virtually the only gentile in Freud's intimate circle, Jones was at once outsider and insider. Storing up Jewish jokes and Jewish turns of phrase with

---

*He had first heard about Freud from his friend (later his brother-in-law) Wilfred Trotter, the brilliant surgeon and crowd psychologist. But it was the case of Dora that converted him.

†See pp. 261–67.

‡In his autobiography, Jones recounts these episodes in frank and reassuring detail and argues, plausibly enough, that the children in these incidents had projected their own sexual feelings upon him, an explanation that in the English medical atmosphere before the First World War naturally persuaded nobody. At the time of these incidents, Jones was already fully convinced that psychoanalysis was the only true depth psychology. (*Free Associations,* 145–52.)

his customary verve, he made himself into a kind of honorary Jew who fitted almost if not quite seamlessly into the relatively closed, defensive psychoanalytic culture in Vienna and Berlin. His papers, boxing the compass of analytic topics, including applied psychoanalysis, were marked more by lucidity and a certain dash than by originality—as he himself recognized when he described himself as feminine. "To me," he told Freud, "work is like a woman bearing a child; to men like you, I suppose it is more like the male fertilisation."* Original or not, Jones was the most persuasive of popularizers and the most tenacious of polemicists. "There are few men," Freud told him, not without admiration, "so fitted to deal with the arguments of others." Not least among the services he rendered was to conduct most of his vast correspondence with Freud in English. He had complained at the outset that he was "not familiar with Old German characters"—Freud's "Gothic" script— and so Freud, instead of just changing his handwriting, switched to English.† This quite incidentally compelled Freud to improve his mastery of his favorite foreign language.‡

By 1910, Jones's commitment to psychoanalysis was wholehearted, though occasionally a few remaining qualms still troubled him—and Freud little less. At least by that time he had become less opaque to his new psychoanalytic friends, for in the beginning he had struck them as hard to read and harder to predict. In the summer of 1908, Jung had observed to Freud, "Jones is a puzzling human being to me. I find him uncanny, incomprehensible. Is there a great deal to him, or too little? In any event, he is not a simple man, but an intellectual liar." Was he, Jung went on to ask, "too much of an admirer on the one hand, too much of an opportunist on the other?" Freud had no easy answer. "I thought you knew more about Jones than I could know," he

---

*Yet Jones was no mere blind follower; in the 1920s, he sturdily disagreed with Freud on the nature of female sexuality, just as he had earlier, during the Great War, disagreed with Freud about which side would triumph in the end.

†Except for his letters during the First World War, and the letters of the last years, Freud wrote to Jones in English. Unfortunately, Jones took the trouble to correct the large segments of Freud's letters that he quoted in his magisterial three-volume biography, so that Freud's occasionally stilted, and charmingly incorrect, formulations were "improved." I have restored all of Freud's original language, minor mistakes and all, without troubling to put *sic* after each of his slight deviations from the King's, or Queen's, English.

‡Jones, whose control of German after a time became as solid as Freud's control of English, perhaps more solid, had not asked Freud to write to him in English. Freud, however, shifted to English, and warned Jones, "You are responsible for my mistakes." (Freud to Jones, November 20, 1908. Freud collection, D2, LC.) On June 18, 1911, Jones apologized to Abraham for writing him in English, "but I am sure that your English is better than my German." However, to judge from later letters (for one instance, the long letter to Abraham of January 9 [1914], which is idiomatic and letter-perfect), Jones was a quick study. (Karl Abraham papers, LC.)

wrote in reply. "I found him a fanatic who smiles at me for being timid." But if he is indeed a liar, "he lies to the others, not to us." Whatever the truth about Jones, Freud concluded, certainly the "racial mixture in our band is very interesting to me. He is a Celt and hence not quite accessible to us, the Teuton and the Mediterranean man." Jones, though, proved an apt pupil, and was quite prepared to attribute his questioning of Freud's ideas to an irrational self-defense. "Shortly put," he told Freud in December 1909, "my resistances have sprung not from any objections to your theories, but partly from the influences of a strong 'Father-complex.'"

Freud was pleased to accept this explanation. "Your letters prove a continuous source of satisfaction to me," he told Jones in April 1910. "I wonder indeed at your activity, at the size of your erudition and at the recent sincerity of your style." Freud was glad, he wrote, that he had refused to "listen to the internal voices hinting at giving you up." Now, when all had come clear, "I trust we will walk and work a good bit together." Two years later, Freud recaptured the moment when he had decided that Jones was trustworthy after all. It had been in September 1909, after the two men had talked at length to each other at Clark University, in Worcester, Massachusetts. "I am very glad that you know how fond I am of you, and how proud of the high mental powers you have put into the service of ψA," he wrote to Jones. "I remember the first time when I got aware of this my attitude towards you, it was a bad one, when you left Worcester after a time of dark inconsistencies from your side and I had to face the idea that you were going away to become a stranger to us. Then I felt it ought not to be so and I could not show it otherwise than by accompanying you to the train and shaking hands before you went away. Maybe you understood me, in any case that feeling has proved true ever since and you have come out splendid at last."

From then on, there was no stopping Jones. In 1913, he went to Budapest for a brief training analysis with Sándor Ferenczi, and reported to Freud that the two were spending "much time together in scientific talks" and that Ferenczi was being "very patient with my eccentricities and changes of mood." Writing to Freud, Jones was never reluctant to be self-critical. In his turn, Freud adopted an avuncular, sometimes genially bullying posture toward Jones, who was twenty-three years his junior. He liked to encourage the younger man by praising him warmly and often. "You are performing big work," he wrote, and, "I enjoy the frequency of your letters and as you see I hasten to give you answering," and again, "I am very fond of your letters and papers." Freud did not begrudge the time he took to keep this important recruit lashed to the Cause.

From 1912 on, Freud analyzed Jones's attractive mistress Loe Kann, a morphine addict, whom everyone, including Freud, referred to as Jones's wife. Setting aside the sacred rule of confidentiality, he reported to Jones about her progress on the couch and the decreasing doses of morphine she was learning to live with.* At times, he would proffer Jones personal advice. Learning of yet another love affair in which Jones had entangled himself, Freud pleaded with him: "Will you do me the personal favour of not making marriage the *next step* in your life, but to put a good deal of choosing and reflection into the matter." A little later, donning the toga of that oratorical Roman patriot Cato the Elder reminding the senate of the enemy, Carthage, Freud sounded a sterner tone: "*Cet. censeo.* Be cautious with women and do not spoil your case this time." He disclaimed any "special motive" for his interference; he was "only pouring out my mind to you." Jones took it very well. Such confidential exchanges lent the two men's single-minded engagement with the psychoanalytic movement an aura of friendship. On the occasion of Jones's fiftieth birthday, Freud told him with his characteristic amalgam of sincerity and flattery, "I have always numbered you among my inmost family." His feelings of tenderness had first become manifest that day when he had accompanied Jones to the railroad station at Worcester. Whatever disagreements they might have had, or might still have, Freud suavely added, were family disagreements, nothing more.

IN POIGNANT CONTRAST, Sándor Ferenczi, the most vulnerable and complicated of the first psychoanalysts, was a far greater emotional drain on Freud. If Jones made Freud angry at times, Ferenczi could make him unhappy. For Ferenczi became, as Jones noted not without a twinge of envy, "the senior member" in the tight circle of Freud's professional confidants and "the one who stood closest" to him. Born in 1873 in Budapest, the son of a bookseller and publisher, he wrestled all his life with his insatiable appetite for love; as one of eleven children, with his father dying young and his mother busy with the store and her sizable brood, he felt from the start sadly deprived of affection. "As a child," Lou Andreas-Salomé, who came to know him well, put down in her diary, "he suffered under inadequate appreciation of his accomplishments." As an adult, he carried his neediness like a never-healing wound.

Ferenczi studied medicine in Vienna in the early 1890s, and settled down

*It was one of Jones's few published criticisms that Freud could be remarkably indiscreet: "Oddly enough, Freud was not a man who found it easy to keep someone else's secret. . . . He several times told me things about the private lives of colleagues which he should not have." (*Jones* II, 409.) In a letter to Max Schur, written after the second volume of his Freud biography had been published, Jones specified one instance of what he had in mind. Freud, he told Schur, had reported to him "the nature of Stekel's sexual perversion, which he should not have and which I have never repeated to anyone." (Jones to Schur, October 6, 1955. Jones papers, Archives of the British Psycho-Analytical Society, London.)

in his native city to practice as a psychiatrist. His first encounter with psychoanalytic ideas was unpromising; hastily leafing through Freud's *Interpretation of Dreams*, he rejected them as vague and unscientific. But then he learned of the experiments with psychoanalytic word association developed by Jung and his colleagues, and was won over to Freud, as it were, through the back door. The staff at Burghölzli would give their subjects clusters of words and then precisely measure the time it took them to respond with the first word that came to mind. Accordingly (his pupil and friend the Hungarian psychoanalyst Michael Balint recalled many years later), Ferenczi "bought a stop watch and no one was safe from him. Whomever he ran into in the Budapest coffeehouses—novelists, poets, painters, the hat-check girl, waiters, etc.—was subjected to the 'association experiment.'" Riding this hobbyhorse, Balint suggests, had one advantage: it induced Ferenczi to study the psychoanalytic literature with close attention. A careful reading of Freud's dream book persuaded him, and in January 1908 he wrote to Freud for an interview. Freud invited Ferenczi to call at Berggasse 19 on a Sunday afternoon.

The two men became friends rapidly; Ferenczi's speculative disposition intrigued Freud, who all his life at once felt the pressure of, and struggled against, the same bent in himself. Ferenczi developed psychoanalytic intuition into a high art; Freud could carry him along on his loftiest flights, only to find himself at times watching his pupil soar out of sight. Ernest Jones, writing as Ferenczi's colleague and analysand, described him as a man with "a beautiful imagination, perhaps not always thoroughly disciplined, but always suggestive." Freud found the suggestiveness irresistible and was for its sake willing to overlook the lack of discipline. "I was delighted with your occupation with riddles," he wrote Ferenczi at the beginning of their association. "You know the riddle advertises all the techniques that the joke conceals. A parallel study would indeed be instructive." Neither Freud nor Ferenczi ever pursued this promising conjecture, but they found much else to discuss: case histories, the Oedipus complex, homosexuality in women, the situation of psychoanalysis in Zurich and in Budapest.

By the summer of 1908, they were so close that Freud arranged to have Ferenczi stay at a hotel near his family in Berchtesgaden. "Our house is open to you. But you should keep your freedom." A year later, in October 1909, Freud headed his letters to Ferenczi "Dear Friend," a heartfelt salutation he reserved for a mere handful. But Ferenczi proved a problematic acquisition. His most powerful, and debatable, contributions to analysis were in technique. They were so powerful and so debatable in large part because they grew visibly from his extraordinary gift for empathy, his capacity for expressing and eliciting love. Unfortunately, Ferenczi's eagerness to give was only matched by, and the pendant to, his hunger to receive. In his relations with Freud, this meant boundless idealization and a craving for an intimacy that Freud, disillusioned after the calamitous fate of his affection for Fliess, was quite unwilling to grant.

Some faint hints of stresses to come emerged in the first year of their friendship: Freud found it necessary to chide his follower, gently, for straining "too anxiously" to confirm one of his conjectures about fantasies. More than once, Ferenczi put Freud under severe pressure to act as his confessor; he confided details of his love life, complicated as an eligible bachelor's often was, and complained of his loneliness in Budapest. A late-summer trip the two men took together to Sicily in 1910 proved less than wholly agreeable to Freud because Ferenczi exploited the occasion to try turning him into a loving father.

It was a role that Freud, for all his paternal streak, did not relish. He told Ferenczi that while he looked back at the time in his company with "warm and sympathetic feelings," he "wished that you had torn yourself from your infantile role to place yourself next to me as an equal companion—which you did not succeed in doing." A year later, Freud reluctantly, though with patient good humor, agreed to play the part that Ferenczi was imposing on him. "I gladly admit that I should prefer an independent friend," he wrote, "but if you make such difficulties, I shall have to adopt you as a son." And he closed, "Now farewell and calm yourself. With fatherly greetings." He followed up this charade by addressing Ferenczi in his next letter as "Dear Son," and glossed the salutation: "(Until you tell me to drop this form of address)." A week later, Freud was back to his usual "Dear Friend," but he had made his point.

Unwelcome and incurable as his dependency proved, Ferenczi's air-borne imagination, intense loyalty, and sheer brilliance, to say nothing of his work as a training analyst in Budapest, made Freud less irritable with his favorite Hungarian adherent than he would have been with anyone else quite that demanding. Freud eventually discovered in Abraham a private core of stiff reserve. "I see you were right," he told Ernest Jones in 1920. "Prussianity is very strong with Abraham." But there was no "Prussianity" in Ferenczi. Freud found Ferenczi a delightful companion for whose sake he cultivated the virtue of patience.

NEARLY ALL OF Freud's early recruits were plausible candidates for a career in psychotherapy. With a few exceptions, notably Sachs and Rank, they were physicians, and some of them, like Jung and Abraham and Eitingon, were already versed in the treatment of the mentally ill. Tausk, trained as a lawyer, active as a judge and a journalist, attended medical school once he decided to pursue the study of psychoanalysis seriously. But by their very nature, Freud's ideas attracted a number of laymen as well, much to his relief. He felt "intellectually isolated" in Vienna, he told an English correspondent in 1910, "despite my numerous medical pupils," and he thought it a consolation that in Switzerland, at least, "a number of nonmedical researchers" had become interested in "our work." Two of these amateurs among his followers, Oskar Pfister and Lou Andreas-Salomé, stand out: each was to be Freud's friend for a quarter century and more. They seem improbable associates for him, the one a pastor, the other a *grande dame* and collector of poets and philosophers. Freud's capacity to enjoy their visits and their letters, and his enduring fondness for them both, testify to his appetite for life, for variety, and for outposts beyond the confines of Vienna.

Pfister, a Protestant pastor in Zurich, had worked his way into a desperately earnest preoccupation with psychology years before he happened upon Freud's writings in 1908. Born in a Zurich suburb in 1873, the year that Freud entered medical school, he early came to detest disputes over theological dogma as squabbles over words. They grated on him as a supreme dereliction of the pastor's first duty, which is the cure of souls, the healing of spiritual misery. The psychological treatises he searched for an effective psychology of religion seemed to him quite as pointless as the theology he had been made to study at the seminary. Then he discovered Freud, and he felt, as he remembered, "as if old premonitions had become reality." Here was "no interminable speculation about the metaphysics of the soul, no experimenting with minute trifles while the great problems of life remain untouched." Freud had devised a "soul-microscope" which gave insight into the origins of mental functions, and into their development. For some time, he hoped to become a physician, just as his father, a liberal pastor, had done in order to help his parishioners. But Freud dissuaded him from studying medicine, and so Pfister became, and remained, the "analysis-pastor"—*Analysenpfarrer*—and Freud's good friend.

Pfister launched the acquaintance by sending Freud one of his early papers, on schoolboy suicides. "I have received a paper from your brave friend Pfister," Freud informed Jung in January 1909, "for which I shall thank him at greater length." Freud was inclined to see the irony: here was godless psychoanalysis being enlisted in the fight against sin. But he soon changed his quizzical tone; more than an ally to be used, Pfister turned out to be a companion to be enjoyed. There were moments during the first years of their friendship when some of Freud's closest associates, notably Abraham, wondered about Pfister's psychoanalytic orthodoxy and warned Freud against him. Freud was not persuaded: as far as he was concerned, Pfister's adherence was assured. For once, his often unreliable intuition about people proved well placed.

One reason why Freud could be so confident of Pfister was that he had abundant opportunity to observe him at close range. Pfister's first call at Berggasse 19, in April 1909, was a rousing success not merely with the head of the household, but with all the family. Pfister, Freud reported to Ferenczi, "is a charming fellow who has won all our hearts, a warmhearted enthusiast, half Saviour, half Pied Piper. But we parted as good friends." Anna Freud recalled that Pfister had seemed to her at first like "an apparition from an alien world"—but a welcome one. Unmistakably the pastor in his speech, his attire, his habits, he was a striking contrast to the other visitors who came to the Freuds' table and stayed to talk psychoanalytic shop. Unlike these single-minded admirers, Pfister did not neglect the children in favor of their famous father.* He was a tall, vigorous-looking man, with a "manly mustache" and "kind and searching eyes." He was also courageous; his undogmatic psychoanalytic Protestantism fell afoul of the Swiss theological establishment more than once, and for some years the danger that he would be deprived of his parish was very real. But, encouraged by Freud, he held his ground, aware that while he was performing valuable service to the psychoanalytic movement, the gift was reciprocated; years later he told Freud of his "vehement hunger for love," and added: "Without analysis I should have broken down long since."

Over fifteen years after his first visit to the Freuds, Pfister remembered it fondly; he had fallen in love, he wrote Freud, with "the cheerful-free spirit of your whole family." At the time, Anna, "who today already writes quite serious papers for the *Internationale Psychoanalytische Zeitschrift,* was still in short skirts, and your second son"—Oliver—"cut Gymnasium in order to introduce the boring, tail-coated pastor to the science of the Prater." Should someone ask him after the most agreeable place in the world, Pfister concluded, he would say, "Inquire at Professor Freud's."

Across the years, as Pfister employed psychoanalysis to help members of his flock, he and Freud canvassed their patients, and debated in unclouded amity the issues that divided them, notably religious belief. In Pfister's view,

---

*The visitors who stayed for a meal, Martin Freud recalled, "had little interest in the food they were offered and perhaps less in mother and us children. However, they always worked hard to maintain a polite conversation with their hostess and her children, most often about the theatre or sport, the weather not being a useful stand-by as it is in England on these occasions. Nevertheless, it could be seen quite easily that all they wanted was to get this social occasion over and done with and to retreat with father to his study to hear more about psychoanalysis." (Martin Freud, *Sigmund Freud: Man and Father* [1958], 108.)

Jesus, who had elevated love into the central tenet of his teaching, was the first psychoanalyst, and Freud not a Jew at all. "A better Christian," he told Freud, "never was."* Naturally Freud, who tactfully ignored this well-meaning compliment, could not think of himself as the best of Christians. But he was happy to see himself as the best of friends. "Ever the same!" he exclaimed to Pfister after they had known one another for more than fifteen years. "Courageous, honest, and benevolent! Your character will doubtless not change any more in my eyes!"

Lou Andreas-Salomé struck rather different chords in Freud's emotional life. Pfister was black-coated and transparent, Andreas-Salomé was spectacular and seductive. In her youth, she had been beautiful, with a high forehead, generous mouth, strong features, and voluptuous figure. In the early 1880s, she had been an intimate of Nietzsche's—how much of an intimate must remain uncertain because she steadfastly frustrated all inquiries into that part of her life—and she would become an intimate of Rilke's and of other distinguished men. In 1887, she had married Friedrich Carl Andreas, an orientalist in Göttingen, where she eventually settled. But, emancipated from bourgeois constraints, she took her lovers when and where she pleased. When she met Freud at the Weimar congress of psychoanalysts in 1911, which she attended as the companion of the Swedish psychoanalyst Poul Bjerre, she was fifty, still handsome and appealing. Her appetite for men, especially brilliant men, was unabated.

Freud once affectionately called Lou Andreas-Salomé a "muse." But "Frau Lou," as she liked to be called, was far more than the pliant female playing a supporting role to genius; she was a productive woman of letters in her own right, endowed with an impressive if eccentric intelligence and a no less impressive gift for absorbing new ideas. Once attracted to Freud's thought, she read her way through his writings; Abraham, who came to know her in Berlin in the spring of 1912, told Freud that he had never before "encountered such a comprehension of psychoanalysis." Half a year later, Freud was happy to report an inquiry from "Frau Lou Andreas-Salomé, who wants to come for some months to Vienna, solely to study psychoanalysis." As announced, she invaded Vienna in the fall, and conquered the psychoanalytic establishment without delay. By late October, Freud paid tribute to her formidable presence by calling her "a female of dangerous intelligence." A few months later he recognized, far less flippantly, that "her interests are

---

*When she came upon this letter many years later, Anna Freud sensibly found it beyond comprehension: "What in the world does Pfister mean here, and why does he want to dispute the fact that my father is a Jew, instead of accepting it?" (Anna Freud to Ernest Jones, July 12, 1954. Jones papers, Archives of the British Psycho-Analytical Society, London.)

really of a purely intellectual nature. She is a very considerable woman." It was a verdict Freud never felt compelled to revise.

Minutes of the Vienna Psychoanalytic Society meetings, which Frau Lou attended regularly, record her presence for the first time on October 30; the week before, Hugo Heller had given a paper on "Lou Andreas-Salomé as a writer." It is a measure of how quickly, and how thoroughly, she made herself at home in the Vienna circle that from November 27 on, Otto Rank recorded her among the guests simply as "Lou." Not all her involvements in Vienna were purely intellectual: she probably had a brief affair with the much younger Tausk, who was very attractive to women. Nor was her commitment to Freud at first absolute; at the beginning of her stay in Vienna, she toyed with Adler's ideas, then already in bad odor in the Freudian camp.* But Freud won her over; in November 1912, when she failed to attend one of his Saturday lectures, he noticed her absence and flattered her by telling her so. By the new year, the two had exchanged photographs, and before she left Vienna in the early spring of 1913, Freud had invited her to Berggasse 19 several times. To judge from her diary, these Sundays were happy occasions: Frau Lou had no monopoly on deploying the arts of seduction. Yet Freud genuinely liked the visitor he so assiduously wooed; as the years went by and she began to practice psychoanalysis in Göttingen, keeping up with Freud by sending him loving letters, he liked her more and more. Having followers like her and Pfister, to say nothing of Abraham, Ferenczi, and Jones, helped offset the strains of being a founder. His local followers were another, by and large far less pleasant matter. It is not that he had any cause for concern about the number of adherents in Vienna. What worried him, rather, was their quality and their reliability.

FREUD'S VIENNESE DISCIPLES were not alone in trying his patience. His adversaries in the psychiatric establishment in Germany and Austria, holding prestigious university chairs or running reputable mental hospitals, provided ample food for exasperation. Freud, we know, was inclined to paint his situation too starkly, but it was in reality stark enough; the resistance to psychoanalysis, whether through obtuse rejection, malicious gossip, or meaningful silence, was sustained and painful. To expect anything else would, of course, have been unrealistic; if Freud was right, eminent psychiatrists, most of them too old to change their ideas, would have to throw away the papers and textbooks they had written. But it was a disagreeable fact of Freud's life that some of his most obstinate critics were young. One of these, who lodged

---

*For Adler, see pp. 216–24.

in Freud's memory, was an *Assistent* in psychiatry who in 1904 published a book against psychoanalysis, taking as his target notions, like the seduction theory of neuroses, that Freud had already discarded. To make matters worse, he admitted that he had not even read *The Interpretation of Dreams*.

Corroborative evidence for such sublimely ignorant rejection came from across Europe and the United States. Congresses of specialists in mental disorders ignored Freud's ideas or applauded papers that denounced them as a farrago of unproved and fantastic assertions or (which seemed more enjoyable to the critics) as an unsavory bouquet of indecencies. After Freud published the *Three Essays on the Theory of Sexuality* in 1905, those disposed to accuse him of being a dirty-minded pansexualist had, of course, much ripe material for their misreadings. They called Freud a "Viennese libertine," psychoanalytic papers "pornographic stories about pure virgins," and the psychoanalytic method "mental masturbation." In May 1906, at a congress of neurologists and psychiatrists in Baden-Baden, Gustav Aschaffenburg, professor of neurology and psychiatry at Heidelberg, curtly dismissed the psychoanalytic method as wrong, objectionable, and unnecessary.

A few correspondents in Freud's camp kept him informed of such summary verdicts. In 1907, Jung, who had already done battle with Aschaffenburg in print and on the platform, reported to Freud that "Aschaffenburg has treated an obsessional neurotic, and when she wanted to start talking about sexual complexes, he forbade her to speak about them." In the same year, at a large international congress of psychologists, neurologists, and psychiatrists in Amsterdam—Aschaffenburg, too, was there—one Konrad Alt, director of a sanatorium in Saxony, launched, Jung told Freud, "terrorism against you, namely that he would never refer a patient to a physician of the Freudian persuasion for treatment—unscrupulousness—obscenity—etc. Most tremendous applause, and congratulations to the speaker on the part of Prof. Ziehen of Berlin." This address was followed, to general vehement approval, by more "asininities" against psychoanalysis.

When he sent these communiqués, Jung, histrionic and combative, was in the early flush of his filial devotion to Freud. But calmer spirits, like Karl Abraham, reported similar scenes elsewhere. In November 1908, Abraham addressed the Berlin Society for Psychiatry and Nervous Diseases on the delicate topic of neurosis and marriage among close relatives. Diplomatically, he made sure to stress the congruence of his views with those of the Berlin neurologist Hermann Oppenheim, who was in the audience; he avoided such provocative themes as homosexuality; and he mentioned Freud's name "not too often," for it still "works like the red rag" to the bulls assembled. The evening proved, Abraham thought, fairly successful. He held his listeners' attention, and some of the discussants showed themselves appreciative. Yet

Oppenheim, though polite, harshly and unequivocally objected to the very notion of infantile sexuality; while Theodor Ziehen—the man who had cheered the "terrorism" against Freud in Amsterdam—"mounted the high academic horse," denigrating Freud's writings as irresponsible, as nonsense. Then, after some reasonable interventions, one "careerist colleague" adopted the moralistic tone of a popular orator: Abraham had cited the love of the Swiss writer Conrad Ferdinand Meyer for his mother—the very topic that had caused a dispute in the Wednesday Society—and his critic complained that in talking of men's oedipal sexual attachments, Abraham had put "German ideals" at risk. But while Abraham found not a single wholehearted ally in the crowded assembly, privately he was told that his talk had been refreshing; it was good to hear something new for a change. He was left with the impression "that a whole number of colleagues went home at least *half* persuaded."

Freud cheered Abraham on by raking his adversaries with acidulous comments. "Some day," he wrote, "Z[iehen] will pay dearly for his 'nonsense.'" As for Oppenheim, he was, Freud said tartly, "too dense; I hope you will be able to do without him in the course of time." Infantile sexuality remained a provocative subject in Berlin, and Freud's name continued to release strong affects, well beyond 1909. In that year, Albert Moll, a respected Berlin sexologist, published a book on the sexual life of children that ran counter to all Freud had been saying on the subject for almost a decade. In print, in a note he added the following year to his *Three Essays,* Freud dismissed Moll's *The Sexual Life of the Child* as really inconsequential. In private, he responded with more gratifying vehemence. Moll, he told Abraham, "is not a physician but a shyster"—a *Winkeladvokat.* When Moll called on Freud in 1909, he was very rudely received; Freud reported to Ferenczi that he had nearly thrown his visitor out the door: "He is a repulsive, caustic, spiteful-pettifogging individual." Normally, Freud felt better after he had an opportunity to ventilate his rage; he preferred vocal opposition, no matter how obtuse, to silence. After 1905, the silence around psychoanalysis was definitively broken, and with controversy came followers, but emotion-ridden criticism continued to shadow the gently rising tide of approval. As late as 1910, Professor Wilhelm Weygandt, who had reviewed *The Interpretation of Dreams* in 1901, not very generously, could exclaim to the Hamburg Congress of Neurologists and Psychiatrists that Freud's theories were a matter not for discussion at a scientific gathering, but for the police.

Meanwhile, similar reports reached Freud from overseas. In April 1910, Ernest Jones complained about the professor of psychiatry in Toronto who had attacked Freud so venomously that "an ordinary reader would gather that you advocate free love, removal of all restraints, and a relapse into savagery!!!"

Three months earlier, Jones had sent Freud a detailed account of a meeting in Boston, attended by psychiatrists and neurologists. The great Harvard neurologist James Jackson Putnam, by that time Freud's most eminent recruit in the United States, had spoken warmly of psychoanalysis. But most of the others had been severe, even scathing. One lady had sought to disprove Freud's theory of dreams as egotistic productions by recounting some altruistic dreams of her own. Worse, the articulate and aggressive psychopathologist Boris Sidis "made a fierce general attack on you, made cheap fun of the 'mad epidemic of Freudism now invading America,' said your psychology took us back to the dark middle ages, & called you 'another of these pious sexualists.' " Evidently Freud's theories of sexuality were much on Sidis's mind. In the following year, he denounced psychoanalysis as "but another aspect of the pious quack literature on sexual subjects," and in 1914, he called it a "worship of Venus and Priapus" which encouraged masturbation, perversion, and illegitimacy.

Even meetings designed to explain and praise Freud could not do without their sour note. On April 5, 1912, the *New York Times* reported that the American neurologist Moses Allen Starr, who had briefly worked with Freud in Vienna during the 1880s, "created a sensation at a crowded meeting of the Neurological Section of the Academy of Medicine last night by denouncing the theories of Sigmund Freud," whom the *Times* described, getting things just a little wrong, as "the Viennese psychologist, whose conclusion that all the psychological life of human beings is based on the sex drive has gained considerable hold on American physicians." Starr told the astonished assembly, which had been addressed by Freud's most noted supporters, that "Vienna is not a particularly moral city," and that "Freud was not a man who lived on a particularly high plane. He was not self-repressed. He was not an ascetic," and, Starr thought, "his scientific theory is largely the result of his environment and of the peculiar life he led." In fact, Starr's Freud had diverted "into a frivolous vein the really serious new science of psychoanalysis." One of Freud's patients, who had visited New York, brought Freud the clipping from the *Times,* and he responded with a mixture of amusement and irritation. He professed to have no recollection of Starr, who claimed to have known him well, and asked Ernest Jones rhetorically, "Now what does this mean? Is wilful lying and calumny a usual weapon among American neurologists?" Not even favorably disposed journalists knew enough, or took the trouble, to be accurate. In March 1913, the *New York Times* printed a long and friendly article under the headline "Dreams of the Insane Help Greatly in Their Cure." It identified Freud as a professor in Zurich.

FIVE

Psychoanalytic Politics

JUNG: THE CROWN PRINCE

 Early in April 1906—Freud would be fifty the following month—Carl G. Jung sent Freud a copy of *Diagnostic Association Studies* which he had edited and which included an important paper of his own. He was beginning to enjoy a reputation as a clinical and experimental psychiatrist. Born in 1875 in the Swiss village of Kesswil, on Lake Constance, the son of a pastor, he had moved with his parents from one rural parish to another. Although he came to live near Basel after he was four, he was not exposed to the full impress of urban life until he entered Gymnasium in the city at the age of eleven. From his early childhood on, Jung was haunted by disconcerting dreams, and many decades later, when he wrote his highly subjective and episodic self-portrait, *Memories, Dreams, Reflections,* he would recall them as events of singular significance for his life. In that autobiography, as in some of the interviews to which he so gladly submitted, Jung liked to dwell on his rich and dream-filled inner life.

His inwardness was fostered by the discord between his parents and by his mother's moody instability. He further nourished his fantasy life with his wildly unsystematic, voracious reading. Nor did the theological environment in which he lived—most of the men in his family were pastors—serve to counteract his tendency to ruminate. He grew up convinced, with much justice, that he was different somehow from the boys growing up around him. At the same time, he had friends and enjoyed playing pranks. Early and late, Jung left the most contradictory impressions on those who knew him; he was sociable but difficult, amusing at times and taciturn at others, outwardly self-confident yet vulnerable to criticism. Later, as a famous, much-traveled psychiatrist and journalists' oracle, he appeared secure, even serene. But there were years, even after he had risen to international prominence, when he was beset by tormenting religious crises. Whatever his private conflicts, from his youth, Jung exuded a sense of power, with his large frame, sturdy build, strongly carved Teutonic face, and torrential eloquence. Ernest Jones, who first met him in 1907, saw him as "a breezy personality" endowed with "a restlessly active and quick brain." He "was forceful or even domineering in temperament," brimming over with "vitality and laughter"—surely "a very attractive person." This was the man whom Freud chose as his crown prince.

Unlike the rest of his family, Jung wanted to be a physician, and he started his medical training at the University of Basel in 1895. Yet, for all his scientific education, his preoccupation with the occult and his fascination with esoteric religions, to say nothing of his florid fantasy life, persisted through the years. Late in 1900, he joined the Burghölzli sanatorium, which served as the psychiatric clinic for the University of Zurich. He could not have chosen a better place. Under Eugen Bleuler's inspired directorship, Burghölzli was pushing its way to the forefront of research in mental illness. Physicians from many countries converged on it to observe, and its own staff physicians traveled abroad; in late 1902, Jung, much like Freud almost two decades before, spent a semester at that irresistible magnet to young psychiatrists, the Salpêtrière, where he heard Pierre Janet lecture on theoretical psychopathology.

Behind Jung stood his elusive, somewhat enigmatic chief, Eugen Bleuler, a commanding figure among the psychiatrists of his time. Bleuler, born a year after Freud, in 1857, had studied with Charcot in Paris and then returned to Switzerland. As a psychiatrist on the staff of several mental hospitals, he acquired impressive clinical experience. But he was far more than a clinician; an observant and imaginative researcher, he used his work with the insane for scientific purposes. In 1898, he was appointed Auguste Forel's successor as director of Burghölzli, and he turned that already reputable institution into a world-renowned center for research into mental illness. Following Charcot, he was among the pioneers reducing the exceedingly imprecise diagnoses of psychological malaise to order, and like Charcot, he proved an influential nomenclator. Some of his coinages, notably *schizophrenia, ambivalence,* and *autism,* permanently entered the psychiatric vocabulary.

For all of Burghölzli's international repute, Jung recalled his first years there as a time of dull and banal routine, a veritable assault on original thinking and creative eccentricity. Yet the place smoothed his way to psychoanalysis. Forel had already been acquainted with Breuer's and Freud's work on hysteria; now, shortly after Jung's arrival, Bleuler asked Jung to report to the staff on *The Interpretation of Dreams*. The book left its mark on Jung, who soon incorporated ideas from Freud's dream book, the early papers on hysteria, and, after 1905, the case history of Dora, into his own researches. Always a man of firm opinions, he appointed himself Freud's heated partisan, energetically defending psychoanalytic innovations at medical congresses and in his publications. His interest in Freud's theories intensified as he profitably applied them to schizophrenia (or dementia praecox, as it was still called), the psychosis in which he specialized and made his reputation. In the summer of 1906, in the preface to his much-praised monograph *On The Psychology of Dementia Praecox,* he singled out the "brilliant conceptions" of Freud, who had "not yet received his just recognition and appreciation." Jung confessed that at first he had "naturally made all those objections brought forward against Freud in the literature." But, he went on to say, he had come to the conclusion that the only legitimate way to refute Freud was to replicate his work. Failing that, one "should not judge Freud, else one acts like those famous men of science who disdained to look through Galileo's telescope." However, publicly insisting on his intellectual independence, Jung wondered if psychoanalytic therapy was really as effective as Freud claimed. Nor would he "attribute to the sexual trauma of youth the exclusive significance that Freud apparently does." It was a portentous reservation that would plague the Freud-Jung friendship throughout.

Still, in 1906, Jung maintained that "all these things are of secondary importance"; they "completely disappear before the psychological principles whose discovery is Freud's greatest merit." In the text he cited Freud repeatedly and with marked appreciation. But Jung was not content merely to polemicize in behalf of Freud's ideas; he also did innovative experimental work that buttressed Freud's conclusions. Thus in 1906, in a remarkable paper on word association, he offered ample experimental evidence to support Freud's theory of free association. Ernest Jones called that paper "great," and "perhaps his most original contribution to science."

Freud showed himself grateful for Jung's attentions and was, in his way, disarmingly frank. Thanking him for sending along the *Diagnostic Association Studies* which contained Jung's seminal article, he acknowledged that he had "naturally" liked Jung's own paper best. After all, Jung, "drawing on experience," had graciously insisted that Freud had "reported nothing but the truth from the hitherto unexplored regions of our discipline." The heady prospect of a respectable propagandist abroad, with access to interesting patients and interested physicians in a famous mental hospital, seemed to Freud almost beyond rational expectation. But he cannily warded off any suspicion that he might expect blind discipleship: "I count confidently on your often being in the position of corroborating me, and will also gladly see myself corrected."

In the fall of 1906, Freud repaid Jung's gift in kind with a copy of his just-published collection of papers on the theory of neuroses. In his letter of thanks Jung struck the posture of Freud's champion and missionary. He reported enthusiastically if prematurely that while Bleuler had at first vigorously resisted Freud's ideas, he was "now completely converted." Freud in his reply courteously translated these good tidings into a personal triumph for Jung: "I have taken great pleasure in your letter and the news that you have converted Bleuler." When it came to throwing graceful compliments at correspondents, Freud could at times rival the suavest of courtiers. He wasted no time: in the same letter he did not hesitate to cast himself in the part of an aging founder ready to hand on the torch to younger hands. Speaking of the egregious Professor Aschaffenburg and his intemperate attacks on psychoanalysis, he pictured the psychiatrists' debate over psychoanalysis as the struggle between two worlds; which of these was declining and which was on its way to victory would soon become apparent. Even if he should not live to see that triumph, "my pupils, I hope, will be there, and I hope, further, that whoever can bring himself to overcome inner resistance for the sake of truth will gladly count himself among my pupils and eradicate the residues of indecisiveness from his thought." The friendship between Freud and Jung was well launched.

ONCE INITIATED, THEIR friendship flourished mightily. In polite exchanges, the two discussed the place of sexuality in the genesis of neuroses, exchanged offprints and books, and traded vignettes from cases that particularly intrigued them. Jung was respectful, though never fawning. He hoped he did not misrepresent Freud; he attributed some of his qualms about psychoanalysis to his own inexperience, subjectivity, and lack of personal contact with Freud; he justified the prudent tone he adopted in his public defenses of Freud by invoking the craft of diplomacy. He sent bulletins he knew Freud would appreciate: "Your views are making rapid progress in Switzerland"; and again: "Personally I am enthusiastically partial to your therapy."

Freud accepted Jung's bouquets with fatherly expansiveness: "I find it extremely agreeable that you promise to trust me provisionally where your experience does not yet permit you to decide," but, hastening to soften his claim on Jung, "of course, only until it does permit you to do so." Freud portrayed himself as more flexible than the world thought him to be, and was pleased that Jung should have noticed this trait. "I have, as you well know, to deal with all the demons that can be let loose on an 'innovator'; not the tamest among these is the need to appear to one's own supporters as a self-righteous and incorrigible surly grumbler—which I really am not." With an ingratiating display of modesty, he concluded, "I have always remained persuaded of my own fallibility." He solicited Jung's views on a patient showing symptoms of what might be dementia praecox. He lauded Jung's writing, peppering his enthusiasm with shrewdly placed criticisms, and never forgot the Cause: "Quickly give up the error that your book on dementia praecox did not please me exceptionally well. The very fact that I offered criticism should prove that to you. For if it were not so, I should muster enough diplomacy to conceal it from you. It would, after all, be most unwise to affront you, the strongest aide who has joined me so far." With someone like Jung, Freud must have sensed, a measure of critical candor was a more astute form of flattery than unmitigated applause.

FREUD GENUINELY LIKED JUNG, had great hopes for him, and needed to idealize someone as he had idealized Fliess. No doubt Jung had his uses. But, whatever captious critics would soon charge, Freud did not just exploit him as a respectable gentile facade behind which Jewish psychoanalysts could do their revolutionary work. Jung was Freud's favorite son. Over and over, in his letters to his Jewish intimates, he praised Jung for doing "splendid, magnificent" work in editing, theorizing, or smiting the enemies of psychoanalysis. "Now don't be jealous," Freud prodded Ferenczi in December 1910, "and include Jung in your calculations. I am more convinced than ever that he is the man of the future." Jung guaranteed that psychoanalysis would survive after its founder had left the stage, and Freud loved him for it. What is more, there was nothing devious or secretive about Freud's intentions. In the summer of 1908, announcing to Jung that he planned to visit him, Freud told him that he looked forward to a thoroughgoing professional discussion, and disclosed his "egotistical intention, which I naturally confess frankly"; it was to "install" Jung as the analyst who would continue and complete "my work." But that was by no means all. "Besides, I am also very fond of you"—*habe ich Sie ja auch lieb.* But, he added, "I have learned to subordinate that element." The profit that Freud expected to realize from Jung was personal enough, for Freud identified himself with his creation, psychoanalysis. But as he covered Jung with flattering epithets and conspicuously favored him over his Viennese adherents, Freud was thinking about the prosperity of his movement more than about some narrow private benefit. As a "strong, independent personality, as a Teuton"—*Germane*—Jung seemed best equipped, Freud forthrightly told him, to enlist the sympathetic interest of the outside world in behalf of their great enterprise. Jung was not Viennese, not old, and, best of all, not Jewish, three negative assets that Freud found irresistible.

Jung, for his part, basked in Freud's beaming approval. "I thank you with all my heart for the proof of your confidence," he wrote in February 1908, after Freud had first addressed him as "Dear Friend." This "undeserved gift of your friendship signifies for me a certain high point of my life, which I cannot celebrate with noisy words." Freud had mentioned Fliess in his letter, and Jung, schooled as he was in psychoanalytic clue-hunting, could not allow that name to go by without making a pointed disclaimer; he found himself impelled to ask Freud "to let me enjoy your friendship not as that of equals but as that of father and son. Such a distance appears to me appropriate and natural." To be the appointed heir to Freud's magnificent legacy, and to be chosen by the founder himself, struck Jung as a call to greatness.

BOTH BUSY THERAPISTS unwilling to take time from pressing duties, Jung and Freud did not meet until early March 1907, almost a year after they had begun to exchange letters. Jung brought his wife Emma along to Berggasse 19, and his young colleague Ludwig Binswanger. The visit to Vienna was an orgy of professional talk, punctuated by a meeting of the Wednesday Psychological Society and by family meals. Martin Freud, who was present with the other children, recalled that Jung was full of himself and his case histories, full to bursting. He "never made the slightest attempt to make polite conversation with mother or us children but pursued the debate which had been interrupted by the call to dinner. Jung on these occasions did all the talking and father with unconcealed delight did all the listening." Jung recalled the discussion between himself and Freud as more evenly matched, if interminable. They talked, he remembered, for thirteen hours, virtually without stopping. Jung struck the Freuds as explosive with vitality and, Martin Freud wrote, endowed with "a commanding presence. He was very tall and broad-shouldered, holding himself more like a soldier than a man of science and medicine. His head was purely Teutonic with a strong chin, a small mustache, blue eyes and thin close-cropped hair." He appeared to enjoy himself enormously.*

Demanding as this first visit of the Swiss must have been, it had its relaxed side as well. Binswanger never forgot his host's cordial and fostering conversation and the "unconstrained, friendly atmosphere" that pervaded the occa-

---

*It was on this visit that Jung claims to have been told of an affair between Freud and his sister-in-law Minna Bernays.

sion from the beginning. Then all of twenty-six, Binswanger stood in awe of Freud's "greatness and dignity," but was neither frightened nor intimidated. His host's "distaste for all formality and etiquette, his personal charm, his simplicity, casual openness and goodness, and, not least, his humor," apparently banished all anxiety. At ease, the three men interpreted one another's dreams, shared walks and meals. "The flock of children conducted itself very quietly at table, although, here, too, a completely unconstrained tone dominated."

Freud declared that he was pleased with his visitors; Jung professed himself overwhelmed. His stay in Vienna, he wrote Freud soon after returning to Zurich, was an "event in the fullest meaning of the word" and had made a "tremendous impression" on him; his resistance to Freud's "enlarged conception of sexuality" was crumbling. Freud, in turn, reiterated what he had told Jung in Vienna: "Your person has filled me with confidence in the future." He himself was, he now knew, "as dispensable as anyone else," but, he added, "I am sure that you will not leave the work in the lurch." Was Freud that sure? Among Jung's dreams was one that Freud had interpreted as signifying that Jung wished to dethrone him.

Neither Freud nor Jung chose to take this dream as a disquieting augury. The pattern of their friendship, quickly set, seemed hewn in stone. They traded case reports like so many tokens of esteem, explored ways of extending psychoanalytic ideas to the study of the psychoses and of culture, and ridiculed the "imbecilic commonplaces"—the epithet is Jung's—of the academic psychiatrists who refused to see the truth of Freud's teachings. Though rapidly gathering clinical expertise and polemical exposure, Jung for years remained the student. "It is nice," Freud wrote him in April 1907, "that you ask me about so much even though you know that I can answer only a small part of it." Freud was not the only flatterer in this epistolary dialogue. Jung told Freud he was feasting on the riches Freud spread out before him, and "living on the crumbs that fall from the rich man's table." Freud demurred at this opulent oral metaphor and preferred to put the accent on Jung's value to him. About to go off on vacation in July 1907, he told Jung that news from him had "already become a necessity." In the following month he took occasion to reassure Jung, who was lamenting defects in his character: "What you call the hysterical in your personality, the need to make an impression on people and to influence them, is precisely what enables you to be a teacher and guide."

For all these cozy exchanges between ruler and crown prince, the potentially divisive debate over sexuality never quite faded away. Jung hung back while Abraham, in his last months at Burghölzli, showed himself more receptive to Freud's libido theory. This rival in his backyard aroused Jung's jealousy. Freud did not conceal from Jung that he was taken with Abraham because "he attacks the sexual problem directly." Yet jealousy and envy were emotional habits so close to the surface of Jung's mind that he did not bother to disguise, let alone repress, them. Early in 1909 he disarmingly informed Ferenczi that because Freud had praised a paper of Ferenczi's highly— something Freud had not always done for Jung—he, Jung, must dispose in this letter of "an ignoble feeling of envy." Still, Jung continued to profess nothing less than his "unconditional devotion" to Freud's theories and his "no less unconditional veneration" of Freud's person. He acknowledged that this "veneration" had a " 'religious'-enthusiastic" quality, a quality he found, "because of its undeniable erotic undertone," at once "repulsive and ridiculous." Once on the road to confession, Jung did not stop halfway: he attributed his powerful distaste for this quasi-religious infatuation to an incident in his childhood, when, "as a boy, I succumbed to a homosexual attack by a man I had formerly revered." Freud, at the time musing on his own homoerotic feelings for Fliess, took Jung's revelation in stride. A religious transference, he commented more sagely than he knew, can only end in apostasy. But he was doing his utmost to counteract it; he tried to persuade Jung that "I am unsuitable to be a cult object." The time would come when Jung would agree with Freud on this point.

IN HIS LETTERS to Abraham, which supply a sobering commentary on those he wrote to Jung, Freud spelled out the peculiar virtues of the Zurich connection without reserve. During his three years at Burghölzli, Abraham had got on with Jung, as appealing as he was brusque, but had harbored distinct misgivings about him. Once he had cut himself loose and was practicing in Berlin, he found occasion to irritate his old superior, notably when they met at psychoanalytic congresses. Freud, counseling the need for patience and cooperation, gently interpreted Abraham's rather cool attitude toward Jung as a harmless, almost inevitable, form of sibling rivalry. "Be tolerant," he enjoined Abraham in May 1908, "and don't forget that it is really easier for you," as a Jew, to accept psychoanalysis than it is for Jung, who, "as a Christian and the son of a pastor," can "find his way to me only against great inner resistances." Hence, "his adherence is all the more valuable. I almost said that only his appearance has saved psychoanalysis from the danger of becoming a Jewish national concern." Freud was persuaded that as long as the world perceived psychoanalysis as a "Jewish science," the burdens that its subversive ideas had to bear would only multiply. "We are and remain Jews," he wrote to a Jewish correspondent some time after; "the others will always simply exploit us and never understand or appreciate us." In a famous poignant outburst to Abraham, picking the most unmistakably Austrian- and gentile-sounding name he could think of, Freud summed up all the miseries of being Jewish: "Be assured, if my name were Oberhuber, my innovations would have found, despite it all, far less resistance."

In this self-protective spirit, Freud bluntly warned Abraham against "racial predilections." Precisely because the two of them, and Ferenczi in Budapest, understood one another so perfectly, such considerations must take a back seat. Their very intimacy should serve as a caution "not to neglect the Aryans, who are fundamentally alien to me." He had no doubt: "Our Aryan comrades are, after all, quite indispensable to us; otherwise, psychoanalysis would fall victim to anti-Semitism." It is worth repeating that despite this need for gentile supporters, Freud was not being simply manipulative when he encouraged Jung; he thought far better of Jung than Abraham ever did. At the same time, Freud did not discount the value, both professional and personal, of what he called in the jargon of the day the "racial kinship"— *Rassenverwandtschaft*—linking him and Abraham. "May I say that it is kindred Jewish traits that attract me in you?" Writing within the family, as Jew to Jew, Freud worried to Abraham about the "hidden anti-Semitism of the Swiss" and recommended a certain resignation as the only workable policy: "We must, as Jews, if we want to join in anywhere, develop a bit of masochism," even be prepared to hold still for a measure of injustice. And he reminded Abraham, incidentally displaying his complete innocence about the long tradition of Jewish mysticism, "In general, it is easier for us Jews, since we lack the mystical element."

To be happily free of the mystical element meant, in Freud's view, to be open to science, to have the only attitude suitable for an understanding of his ideas. Jung, the son of a pastor, harbored dangerous sympathies for mystics East and West, as so many Christians seemed to do. It was far better for a psychoanalyst to be godless—like Freud—whether a Jew or not. What mattered was the recognition that psychoanalysis is a science, to whose findings the religious origins of its practitioners are perfectly irrelevant. "There should be no distinct Aryan or Jewish science," Freud once declared to Ferenczi. But the realities of psychoanalytic politics made it imperative, Freud believed, to keep the religious differences among his adherents in mind. Hence he did his best to cultivate his Jewish and gentile followers alike. He fettered Jung to him with paternal affection, and Abraham with "racial" affinities, never losing sight of the Cause. In 1908, he was corresponding with Abraham and Jung on almost equal terms; his strategy seemed to be working well.

Certainly in these years, Freud had no doubt that Jung was firm in the faith. Jung said so often enough. "You may rest assured," he had written Freud in 1907, "that I shall never abandon a piece of your theory essential to me—I am far too committed for that." Two years later, he reassured Freud once again: "Not only for now but for all the future, nothing Fliess-like will happen." This was an emphatic, gratuitous vow that Freud, had he permitted himself to apply his own detective's techniques, could have taken as an ominous hint of Fliess-like things to come.

AMERICAN INTERLUDE

 In 1909, the year that Jung protested his unswerving loyalty, Freud obtained some unexpected relief from his political cares, and an even more unexpected distinction, far from home. On Friday evening, September 10, he stood in the gymnasium of Clark University, in Worcester, Massachusetts, to receive the degree of Doctor of Laws, *honoris causa.* The accolade came as a great surprise to Freud. He had his handful of followers in Vienna; recently, he had acquired adherents in Zurich, Berlin, Budapest, London, even New York. But these represented a small, embattled minority in the psychiatric profession; Freud's ideas still remained the property of the few, and a scandal to most.

But the president of Clark University, G. Stanley Hall, who orchestrated the festivities at which Freud received his honorary degree, was an enterprising psychologist who, far from fearing controversy, cultivated it. "Something of a kingmaker," Freud called him. Hall, an eccentric and an enthusiast, had done much to popularize psychology, especially child psychology, in the United States. In 1889, Hall had been appointed the first president of Clark University, which, munificently endowed, aspired to emulate Johns Hopkins University and to surpass Harvard in its graduate program. It was the ideal platform for Hall, more an indefatigable publicist and advocate of novel ideas than an original researcher. Alert, ambitious, and incurably eclectic, Hall quickly absorbed the new currents in psychology emanating from Europe. In 1899, he had imported the Swiss authority Auguste Forel, former director of the Burghölzli Mental Hospital, to report on the latest developments, and Forel had told his audience about Freud's and Breuer's work on hysteria. In succeeding years, other lecturers brought word to Clark of psychoanalysis in Vienna, and in 1904, in his bulky two-volume treatise *Adolescence,* Hall alluded more than once, with evident approval, to Freud's disreputable ideas about sexuality. Reviewing *Adolescence,* the noted educational psychologist Edward L. Thorndike sniffed at Hall's unprecedented frankness, and privately denounced the work as being "chock full of errors, masturbation and Jesus." The author, he said, "is a mad man."

This was the man who invited the controversial Freud to deliver a series of lectures. The occasion Hall chose was the twentieth-anniversary celebration of Clark's founding. He also invited Jung, then widely known as a specialist on schizophrenia and as Freud's most prominent adherent. "We believe," Hall wrote to Freud in December 1908, "that a concise statement of your own results and point of view would now be exceedingly opportune, and perhaps in some sense mark an epoch in the history of these studies in this country."

In his brief, improvised acknowledgment of his honorary degree, Freud proudly called the occasion "the first official recognition of our endeavors." Five years later, he was still under its pleasing impress. Using American generosity and open-mindedness as a stick with which to beat the Europeans, he characterized his visit to Clark as the "first time I was permitted to speak publicly about psychoanalysis." That he had delivered five lectures in German without losing his audience only heightened his appreciation of the event. Nor did he spare his European readers the tart reminder that "the introduction of psychoanalysis in North America took place with particular marks of honor." Freud admitted that he had not expected this: "We found to our great surprise that the unprejudiced men in that small but reputable university knew all the psychoanalytic literature," and employed it in their lectures. He added, tempering appreciation with the sort of ritual disparagement of America endemic among cultivated Europeans, "In prudish America one could, at least in academic circles, freely discuss and scientifically treat everything that is regarded as improper in ordinary life." A decade later, recalling the occasion in his autobiographical study, he observed that his American expedition had done a great deal for him. "In Europe I felt like someone excommunicated; here I saw myself received by the best as an equal. It was like the realization of an incredible daydream, as I stepped up to the lectern at Worcester." Clearly, then, "psychoanalysis was not a delusion any longer; it had become a valuable part of reality."

At first, Freud had felt unable to accept Hall's invitation. Scheduled for June, the ceremonies would have cut into his analytic year and thus reduced his income, always a touchy matter for him. He regretted having to refuse, he told Ferenczi, but "still, I find the demand to sacrifice so much money for the opportunity of giving lectures there too 'American.'" It was an uncharitable outburst: "America should bring in money, not cost money." And finances were not the only reason for Freud's reluctance to speak publicly in the United States. He feared that he and his colleagues would be ostracized once the Americans discovered "the sexual bedrock of our psychology." Yet the invitation intrigued him. When Hall was slow to respond to his letters, he fretted about the silence, though he quickly asserted, as if to protect himself against disappointment, that in any case he had no confidence in the Americans and feared "the prudery of the new continent." A few days later, changing his tune and sounding almost anxious, he wrote Ferenczi again: "No news from the U.S."

But Hall amended his proposal; he moved the festivities to September and substantially increased Freud's travel allowance. These gestures made it possible, Freud told Ferenczi, "indeed convenient, to accept the invitation." And he asked Ferenczi, as he had before, whether he might like to come along. Ferenczi did, very much so. As early as January, he had told Freud that he could afford the trip, and in March he began to think about "certain preparations for the oversea excursion," which included improving his "defective" English and doing some reading about the United States. As the weeks went by, Freud's excitement at the prospect, too, mounted visibly. "America dominates the situation," he reported in March, and, like Ferenczi, he set about preparing himself for the adventure by ordering books on the United States and "polishing" his English. It was likely to become "a great experience"; when he announced to Abraham that he would be lecturing in the United States, he burst out exuberantly: "And now the great news." In the manner of a prudent and experienced traveler, Freud began to inquire into passage, weighing various alternatives; he finally settled on the steamer *George Washington,* of the Norddeutsche Lloyd, since its schedule would allow for a week of sight-seeing in the United States before the visitors had to appear at Clark University. "We can do the Mediterranean in every other year. America will not come again so soon."

Freud was wryly aware of his ambivalence about this "travel adventure" and took it, he told Ferenczi, as "a veritable illustration of the profound words in the *Magic Flute:* 'To love I cannot compel you.' I do not care a bit for America, but look forward a great deal to our trip together."* He was happy, too, that Jung would be of the party: "It pleases me enormously for the most egotistical reasons," he let Jung know in June. But it also pleased him, he added, to see how much prestige Jung had already amassed in psychologists' circles.

While Freud dutifully took along some books about the United States on his summer vacation, he did not read them. "I want to let myself be surprised," he told Ferenczi, and he advised Jung to cultivate the same spontaneity. In the end, his single foray into the United States proved part holiday, part psychoanalytic progress. But it started with an ominous episode:

*For a detailed analysis of Freud's anti-Americanism, see pp. 562–70.

on August 20, the three travelers had lunch together in Bremen while waiting to board ship. Jung began to talk, and kept talking, about prehistoric remains being dug up in northern Germany. Freud chose to interpret this topic, and Jung's persistence, as a concealed death wish against him, and fainted. This was not the only time Freud would faint in Jung's presence. Yet pleasurable anticipation took over, and on the following day, Freud, Jung, and Ferenczi sailed from Bremen in good cheer. They beguiled the eight-day crossing with a pastime that was a great favorite among these early analysts: they analyzed one another's dreams. Among the memorable moments of the journey, Freud later told Ernest Jones, was discovering his cabin steward reading *The Psychopathology of Everyday Life.* To reach a lay audience had been, of course, one reason why Freud had written that book, and he was gratified by concrete evidence that it had indeed captured a wider public.

The trio set aside a week for New York, as Ernest Jones and A. A. Brill, the two psychoanalysts in the New World, showed them the city. Jones came down from Toronto to attend the distinguished guests. But their almost professional cicerone was Brill, who had lived in New York since 1889, when he had arrived from his native Austria-Hungary, alone, at the age of fifteen, with three dollars in his pocket. He knew the city—Manhattan, at least—inside and out. His flight from Europe had been a flight from his family: his father was uneducated and authoritarian, and his mother wanted him to become a rabbi. America saved him both from a career he did not want and from parents who "stifled" him. As an adolescent, he rejected his religious faith and his father's domestic dictatorship with equal determination, but, as Nathan G. Hale has justly put it, he "preserved the Jewish reverence for teachers and sages. He was seeking a guide, not a Top Sergeant."

Desperately poor but driven on by his will, Brill worked his way through New York University doing a variety of more or less menial jobs, including schoolteaching. After some years of scrimping, he later told Ernest Jones, he thought he had enough money to enter medical training at Columbia University, but could not raise the examination fees. "Appeal to the authorities for help or exemption was in vain; he had to stand on his own resources, and go back to his teaching for yet another year. He felt the hardship of it, but then said to himself: 'You have no one to blame but yourself; no one asked you to take up medicine.' And he went bravely onward." Jones could not suppress his admiration: "He might have been called a rough diamond, but there was no doubt about the diamond." By 1907, he had managed to save enough to spend a year at Burghölzli studying psychiatry. There he discovered Freud, and his discovery gave him his life's vocation. He decided that he would return to New York, train himself to become a spokesman for psychoanalysis, and make Freud's writings available in English. Now, in the late summer of

1909, he could, with enthusiasm and authority, repay some of his debt to Freud.

With the youthful appetite of the urban explorer intact, Freud proved indefatigable. He was not yet famous enough to be besieged by photographers or interviewers, and one of the New York morning papers could not even get his name right, dutifully recording the arrival of "Professor Freund of Vienna." This seems not to have troubled Freud in any way, busy as he was walking about New York. He got glimpses of Central Park and Columbia University, Chinatown and Coney Island, and took time to inspect his beloved Greek antiquities at the Metropolitan Museum. On September 5, the travelers were in Worcester. The others were put up at the Standish Hotel; Freud, obviously the principal guest, had been invited to stay at G. Stanley Hall's elegant house.

FREUD'S FIVE IMPROVISED lectures, each one talked out and rehearsed on a morning stroll with Ferenczi, were well received; his skill as a public speaker served him well with his American audiences. He opened the series with a generous tribute to Breuer as the true founder of psychoanalysis—a tribute which, on reflection, he came to regard as excessive—and offered a rapid history of his own ideas and techniques, coupled with cautions against over-drawn expectations from a science still so young. By the end of the third lecture, he had acquainted his listeners with the essential concepts of psycho-analysis: repression, resistance, dream interpretation, and the rest. In the fourth he tackled the delicate theme of sexuality, including infantile sexuality. He had never deployed his forensic skills to better purpose, adroitly playing the trump card of the American connection. The witness he called in his behalf was Sanford Bell, happily a fellow of Clark University. In 1902, three years before Freud's *Three Essays on the Theory of Sexuality,* Bell had published a paper in the *American Journal of Psychology* in which he had verified the phenomenon of infantile sexuality with numerous observations. There was something disarming about being unoriginal, and Freud exploited it to the full. He ended the series with a heady mixture of cultural criticism and applied psychoanalysis, and gracefully concluded with thanks for the opportunity to lecture and for the attention with which his listeners had followed him.

Freud had little reason to regret his visit; most of his later cavils sound farfetched, anything but generous or even rational. It is true that the American cuisine, the ice water no less than the heavy food, raised havoc with his already malfunctioning digestion. Certainly Freud was convinced that his stay in the United States had "markedly exacerbated" his intestinal complaint, and Jones was willing to play along. "I warmly hope," he wrote Freud some months after, "that your physical ailment is now a thing of the past. It is too bad that America should deal you a mean blow through its cooking." But Freud markedly overstated the adverse effect of American food, for he had long been beset by intestinal difficulties. And what is one to make of his statement that this visit to the United States had caused his handwriting to deteriorate? Even the faithful Ernest Jones felt compelled to conclude that at bottom Freud's anti-Americanism "actually had nothing to do with America itself."

In fact, virtually all of Freud's American reception, both by the people he met and by the press, was cordial; much of it was downright sensible. The headline in the *Worcester Telegram*—"All Types at Clark . . . Men with Bulging Brains Have Time for Occasional Smiles"—did, to be sure, exemplify popular journalism at its lowest level, but it was an exception. There were some in Freud's audience who thought his theories of sexuality quite shocking, and the press treated his fourth lecture, which canvassed that touchy topic, with becoming brevity and decorum. But Freud had no cause to feel slighted, let alone rejected, by his American listeners. What is more, leading figures in American psychology made the trip to Worcester especially to meet him. William James, America's most celebrated, most influential psychologist and philosopher, spent a day at Clark to hear Freud and take a walk with him. It was a walk Freud could not forget. James was already suffering from the heart disease that would kill him a year later. In his autobiographical study, Freud recounted how James suddenly stopped, handed Freud his briefcase, and asked him to walk on; he felt an attack of angina pectoris coming on and would catch up with Freud as soon as it was over. "Since then," Freud commented, "I have always wished for a similar fearlessness in face of the near end of life." Brooding on death as he had been doing for some years, he found James's courteous stoicism admirable, even enviable.

James had been following Freud's writings since 1894, when he had noticed Freud and Breuer's "Preliminary Communication" on hysteria. Now, with the large-mindedness that he normally brought to theories he found intriguing though unacceptable, he wished Freud and the Freudians well. As a professional student of religion, one who elevated religious experience to the level of higher truth, James was filled with qualms at what he thought the Freudians' programmatic, obsessive hostility to religion. But this did not erase his interest in their enterprise. Saying farewell to Ernest Jones in Worcester, he put an arm around his shoulder and told him, "The future of psychology belongs to your work." James strongly suspected Freud, "with his dream theory, of being a regular *halluciné.*" Still, he thought that Freud would "add to our understanding of 'functional' psychology, which is the real psychology." Again, just after the Clark conference, writing to the Swiss psychologist

Théodore Flournoy, he worried over Freud's "fixed ideas," confessed that he could do nothing with Freud's dream theory, and denounced psychoanalytic notions about symbolism as dangerous. But he expressed the hope that "Freud and his pupils will push their ideas to their utmost limits, so that we may learn what they are. They can't fail to throw light on human nature."

That was kind but tentative and a little vague. James thought rather better of Jung, whose sympathies for religion approached his own. No question, Jung's lectures at Clark on child psychology and on word-association experiments were less provocative than Freud's to the philosophical theology for which James spoke so eloquently. While Freud had not preached atheism at Clark, he was plainly committed to the kind of scientific convictions that rejected any claims for religious thinking in the pursuit of truth. But it was precisely such claims that James, elevating religion above science, had been making for years, most vigorously in his celebrated Gifford Lectures, *The Varieties of Religious Experience*, published a few years before, in 1902. In sharp contrast, James Jackson Putnam could give Freud wholehearted support, and proved far more effective a champion of psychoanalysis in the United States than James could ever be. Like James a professor at Harvard, Putnam was a neurologist who enjoyed an unmatched prestige among his colleagues. Hence it mattered that as early as 1904, treating hysterical patients at the Massachusetts General Hospital, he had declared the psychoanalytic method far from useless. His sympathetic reading of Freud had been the first real opening for analytic ideas in the American medical establishment. Somewhat to Freud's regret, Putnam always kept his independence and refused to exchange his philosophical orientation, which even gave room to a rather abstract divinity, for Freud's God-less positivism. But the Clark lectures, reinforced by his intensive discussions with Freud and his fellow visitors, persuaded Putnam that psychoanalytic theories and modes of treatment were essentially correct. In some ways, this conquest was the most lasting legacy of Freud's American interlude.

AFTER THE FESTIVITIES at Clark had adjourned, Freud, Jung, and Ferenczi spent several days at Putnam's camp in the Adirondacks, continuing their shop talk. On September 21, after two final days in New York, the three companions sailed on another German steamer, *Kaiser Wilhelm der Grosse*. They encountered some disagreeable stormy weather, but this did not keep Freud from analyzing Jung, much, Jung claimed, to his benefit. Eight days later, they docked at Bremen, America a vivid, rich, and complex memory. "I am very glad I am away from it, and even more that I don't have to live there," Freud wrote his daughter Mathilde. "Nor can I claim that I am returning greatly refreshed and rested. But it was extremely interesting and probably highly significant for our cause. All in all one can call it a great success." By early October, Jung, confessing a certain homesickness for Freud, was at work again in Zurich. Freud too was back in stride. He had come home a doctor of laws, with agreeable proofs that his movement was now a truly international affair.

After such gratifications, Vienna promised little but a letdown. Indeed, by early November, Freud's exasperation with his local followers had once again reached a high pitch. "I sometimes get so angry at my Viennese," he wrote to Jung, paraphrasing the Roman emperor Caligula for his purposes, "that I wish them a single rear end, so that I could thrash them all with one stick." A meaningful slip, though, betrayed Freud's suppressed uneasiness with Jung: instead of *ihnen*— "them"—he wrote *Ihnen*— "you"—thus intimating that it was Jung's rear end that deserved a caning. But the first serious disruption of analytic unity originated from a quarter right at home, in Vienna, and involved two of Freud's first associates—Wilhelm Stekel and Alfred Adler. Jung was a sympathetic bystander, firmly in Freud's camp.

VIENNA VERSUS ZURICH

 In a moment of extreme exasperation, one of many during these years, Freud once referred to Stekel and Adler as "Max and Moritz," those two proverbial bad boys in Wilhelm Busch's famous humorous tale about willful, cruel pranks and terrible retribution: "I am incessantly annoyed by these two." But the two, though friends and allies, were very different from one another and gave Freud very different causes for dismay and, eventually, for drastic action.

Stekel, for all his contributions to the organization of the Wednesday Psychological Society and to the theory of symbolism, had been something of an irritant from the beginning. He was intuitive and indefatigable, a prolific journalist, playwright, short-story writer, and author of psychoanalytic treatises. Though entertaining company, he alienated many with his boastfulness and his unscrupulousness in the use of scientific evidence. Avid to comment on whatever paper was being presented to the Society, he would invent a patient who fit into the discussion. " 'Stekel's Wednesday patient,' "

Ernest Jones recalls, "became a standing joke." It seemed that Stekel's imagination was too luxuriant to be kept in check. In one of his papers, he advanced the startling theory that names often have a subterranean influence on people's lives, and "documented" his contention by offering several of his analysands' names in evidence. When Freud remonstrated with him for violating medical discretion, Stekel reassured him: the names were all made up! No wonder Freud concluded, while he was still on good terms with him, that Stekel was "weak in theory and thought," though endowed with "a good flair for the meaning of the hidden and unconscious."

That was in 1908. Soon Freud became more dismissive, as he became infuriated by what he called Stekel's "moronic petty jealousies"—*schwachsinnige Eifersüchteleien.* In his final summing up, he characterized Stekel as "at first very meritorious, later wholly wayward."* That verdict was fairly severe, but compared to his private explosions, it was tame indeed; in his confidential letters, Freud called Stekel an impudent liar, an "uneducable individual, a *mauvais sujet,*" and even a "swine." He liked this pungent epithet so much that he tried it out in English: "that pig, Stekel," he called him in a letter to Ernest Jones, who, Freud thought, was giving Stekel too much credit. Many among the Viennese who did not descend to this sort of name calling agreed that Stekel was, though stimulating, quite irresponsible, often unintentionally amusing, and, when all was said, intolerable. Yet as late as 1911, he was still a member in good standing of the Vienna Psychoanalytic Society, gave papers, and participated in discussions. In April of that year, the Society even devoted an evening to comments—highly critical in the main—on Stekel's book *The Language of Dreams.* Intolerable as he may have been, for several years Stekel was tolerated.

WHILE OTHERS AMONG his Viennese followers were as irritating to Freud as Stekel, he had more than his followers to worry about. Around this time Freud became embroiled with Karl Kraus, a witty and dangerous adversary, after enjoying some years of friendly, if far from close relations with him. Kraus, never disrespectful of Freud himself, vehemently objected to then fashionable primitive applications of Freudian ideas to literary figures—including himself. One of these applications, by his former friend and collabora-

---

*In his unpublished autobiography, Fritz Wittels recorded that when he learned that there was to be a new printing of the "History of the Psychoanalytic Movement," he asked Freud to tone down this "spiteful" passage about Stekel's waywardness, and Freud agreed that while he could not suppress his criticisms, he could employ a "milder term." But in the end, *verwahrlost* remained. (Fritz Wittels, "Wrestling with the Man: The Story of a Freudian," 169–70. Typescript, Fritz Wittels Collection, Box 2. A. A. Brill Library, New York Psychoanalytic Institute.)

tor Fritz Wittels, which tried to diagnose his famous periodical, *Die Fackel*, as a mere neurotic symptom, particularly exasperated him, and he turned on psychoanalysis with a few pointed, at times vicious barbs. Loyal to his crew, disappointing as they were, Freud, who had almost as little use for the vulgarization of the psychoanalytic method as Kraus himself, denounced Kraus (in private) in the most unmeasured language. "You know the unbridled vanity and lack of discipline of this talented beast, K.K.," he wrote Ferenczi in February 1910. Two months later he confided to Ferenczi that he had guessed Kraus's secret: "He is a mad half-wit with a great histrionic talent," which enables him to mime intelligence and indignation. Such a verdict was the product of impulsive rage rather than sober judgment, and, however, poisonous and irrational Kraus's outbursts were, wildly off the mark.

But these were side issues. As the psychoanalytic movement gained momentum, Freud had influential and undecided foreign recruits to cultivate and keep in line. Freud's correspondence grew more international year by year, and increasingly resembled that of a general planning campaigns or a diplomat enlisting allies. Possibly the most unsettling, certainly the most consequential, of Freud's catches was Eugen Bleuler, Jung's eminent chief. For some time, Bleuler was a valued member of the Freudian clan. He was present in 1908 at a small international congress in Salzburg, the first of many, when a group calling itself "friends of psychoanalysis" from Vienna, Zurich, Berlin, Budapest, London, even New York, came together to hear papers by Jung, Adler, Ferenczi, Abraham, Jones—and, of course, Freud—and to foster closer cooperation. One promising result was the founding of the first psychoanalytic periodical, the *Jahrbuch für psychoanalytische und psychopathologische Forschungen*, with Bleuler and Freud as directors and Jung as editor. The masthead was the gratifying symbol of a working alliance between Vienna and Zurich and no less gratifying evidence of Bleuler's adherence to the Freudian cause.

Relations between Bleuler and Freud were perfectly amicable on the surface, if a little distant. But Bleuler, though much impressed with Freud's ideas, remained uncertain whether the emphasis on sexuality was really warranted. And this uncertainty, coupled with his uneasy sense that Freud was building up a tightly controlled political machine, made him waver in his attitude toward the establishment Freud was constructing. "This 'who is not for us is against us,' " he declared to Freud in 1911, upon resigning from the recently organized International Psychoanalytic Association, "this 'all or nothing' is in my opinion necessary for religious communities and useful for political parties. There I can understand the principle as such, but for science I consider it harmful." Freud might welcome such an open-minded, truly scientific posture in principle, but he felt too embattled to adopt it.* Hence he continued to cultivate Bleuler and at the same time to denounce him in letters to his intimates. "Bleuler," he confided to Ferenczi, "is insufferable."

WEARISOME AS FREUD might find Bleuler's conscientious uncertainties, he had graver matters to settle at home, notably the place of Alfred Adler in the Vienna Psychoanalytic Society. Freud's relations with Adler were more tangled than those with Stekel and, in the long run, more momentous. Adler was assertive and saturnine; his detractors in Freud's circle thought him humorless and avid for applause. Jones, for one, describes him as "sulky and pathetically eager for recognition." But those who knew him as a habitué of Vienna's cafés saw a different man—relaxed and full of jokes. Whoever the "real" Adler may have been, he secured an ascendancy among his colleagues second only to Freud's. Yet Freud did not fear, or treat, Adler as a rival. Rather, for some years, he extended him virtually unlimited intellectual credit. In November 1906, when Adler gave a paper on the physiological foundations of neuroses, Freud praised it warmly. He had little use for Adler's favorite term, *Minderwertigkeit*—"organ inferiority"—and would have preferred a more neutral term, like "a particular variability of organs." But for the rest, he found Adler's paper, like his work in general, helpful to him and significant. Other commentators that evening echoed Freud, all but Rudolf Reitler, who shrewdly sensed trouble in Adler's almost exclusive emphasis on the role of physiology and of heredity in the making of neuroses.

Undeterred by such mosquito stings, Adler continued to construct his psychology under the sheltering umbrella of Freud's psychoanalysis. Superficially, he and Freud seemed in broad agreement; both saw heredity and environment alike involved in the etiology of neuroses. In stressing the havoc that organ inferiority can wreak in human minds, Adler adopted a heavily biological orientation, yet this was a perspective that Freud did not wholly reject. At the same time, as a Socialist and social activist interested in the amelioration of humanity's lot through education and social work, Adler also assigned real importance to the environment in the shaping of minds. Freud, as we know, insisted emphatically on the impact of the child's world on psychological development—the role of parents, siblings, nurses, playmates, in the genesis of sexual traumas and unresolved conflicts. But Adler's view of the environment was not Freud's. In fact, Adler openly questioned Freud's

---

*"I have never fought against differences of opinion within the circle of ψa research," he once wrote to Lou Andreas-Salomé, "especially since I usually have more than one opinion about one issue—that is, before I publish one of them. But one must hold on to the homogeneity of the core, otherwise it is something else." (Freud to Andreas-Salomé, July 7, 1914. *Freud–Salomé*, 21 [19].)

fundamental thesis that early sexual development is decisive for the making of character. Refining and revising propositions he had advanced from the beginning of his turn to psychiatry, Adler forcefully if not stylishly evolved a distinctive family of ideas. His papers, his comments on the papers of others, his articles, and his first psychological monograph became quite unmistakably "Adlerian"; they all centered on his conviction that every neurotic seeks to compensate for some organic imperfection. However seriously Adler might take the external world, in his psychology he elevated biology into destiny. But none of this deprived Adler of sympathetic interest on the part of the small, still groping psychoanalytic community.

Organ inferiority remained an obsessive theme in Adler's talk and writings throughout his years in Freud's circle. He had first employed the term in 1904 in a short, hortatory article on the physician as educator, in which he cited the imperfection in some bodily organ as the cause of timidity, nervousness, cowardice, and other ills that beset children. He continually cautioned against overstating the impact of traumas on the mind. "One's constitution," he said, "finds its sexual traumas." The mind, detecting some physical or mental disability, attempts to compensate for it—at times successfully, but often enough, unsuccessfully. Adler, in short, essentially defined a neurosis as a failed compensation for inferiority feelings. He saw most of the crippling inadequacies the mind seeks to counteract, however, as inborn. For example, Adler thought that sadism, and the cluster of traits—orderliness, parsimony, obstinacy—that Freud called the anal character, could be shown to have hereditary roots. In a Wednesday Society discussion on the sexual enlightenment of children, Adler even rejected Freud's contention that such enlightenment, though perhaps no panacea, was a useful prophylactic against neuroses: "Infantile traumas have significance only in connection with the inferiority of organs."

WHILE MATTERS OF SUBSTANCE did much to divide Freud and Adler, psychoanalytic politics also entered, and served to exacerbate their disagreements. Writing to Abraham, Freud once observed, "Politics spoils the character." He had his problems with Stekel in mind, but he might well have been thinking about the effects of politics on himself. For Freud in politics was the true politician, more devious than in the rest of his conduct, and his struggles with Adler brought out all his latent gifts for navigating among contending forces and pursuing his program.

Freud seriously affronted Adler and his allies for the first time in the spring of 1910, during the international congress of psychoanalysts in Nürnberg and its aftermath, as he maneuvered to organize the psychoanalytic movement in accord with his long-range wishes. His later efforts to placate the egos he had bruised were no less political; they show Freud in his diplomatic, as distinct from his militant guise. The Nürnberg congress was something of a triumph. It gave Freud new energy. "With the Nürnberg *Reichstag,*" he wrote buoyantly to Ferenczi a few days after it adjourned, "the childhood of our movement has ended. That is my impression. I hope it will be followed by a rich and fair time of youth." But as Freud knew perfectly well when he made this assessment, the congress had also generated fierce resentments and open rebellion. Giving Jones the news from Nürnberg, he observed, "All are full of fresh hope and promise to work. I am retiring to the background as behoves an elderly gentleman (No more compliments pray!)." This was not wholly candid. It was in Nürnberg, after all, that Freud was thrown into the most emotional confrontation with fellow analysts in his entire career.

It all began with an address by Ferenczi. Acting as Freud's deputy at the congress, he presented Freud's proposals for an international psychoanalytic association: Jung was to be permanent president, and Franz Riklin, another Swiss psychiatrist and a relative of Jung's, was to serve as secretary. This was bitter enough medicine for Freud's earliest adherents to swallow, but Ferenczi exasperated them further by offering some gratuitous criticisms of the Vienna Psychoanalytic Society. Thinking back on the congress shortly afterward, Freud blamed himself no less than Ferenczi for "not sufficiently calculating the effect [of the proposals] on the Viennese." The self-criticism was certainly just; Freud should not have been surprised at their response. Not even the most tactful presentation could have concealed the implications of Freud's program: Vienna was in eclipse.

The Viennese analysts strenuously objected. Wittels recalled that they held a private meeting in the Grand Hotel "to discuss the outrageous situation. Of a sudden, Freud, who had not been invited to attend, put in an appearance. Never before had I seen him so greatly excited." In public, after all, Freud invariably gave the impression of perfect self-control. "He said: 'Most of you are Jews, and therefore you are incompetent to win friends for the new teaching. Jews must be content with the modest role of preparing the ground. It is absolutely essential that I should form ties in the world of general science. I am getting on in years, and am weary of being perpetually attacked. We are all in danger.'" Wittels's account, including Freud's characteristic appeal to his aging and his weariness—he was then not quite fifty-four—and the dramatic closing appeal, has the ring of truth. "Seizing his coat by the lapels, he said: 'They won't even leave me a coat to my back. The Swiss will save us—will save me, and all of you as well.'" In the end, a face-saving compromise was worked out: the term of Jung's presidency was limited to two years. But this did not alter the perception of the Viennese that Freud was callously neglecting them, his first followers, by courting his new recruits from Zurich.

They had a case. After all, since 1906, Freud had been conducting an increasingly intimate correspondence with Jung. Nor was it a secret that beginning in 1907, with visits from Jung and others from Zurich, affinity had ripened into friendship and, in Freud, into great expectations. The Nürnberg congress only hardened the uneasiness of the Viennese into grim certainty. Freud was perfectly clearheaded about his program. "I judged," he wrote in retrospect, "that the connection with Vienna was no recommendation for the young movement, but rather an obstacle to it." Zurich, at the heart of Europe, was far more promising. Besides, he added, adroitly translating his obsession with aging and dying into a reason for his stratagems, he was not getting any younger. The psychoanalytic cause, in need of authoritative guidance, should be entrusted to a younger man who could carry on after the founder was no longer in charge. After the way that "official science" had solemnly excommunicated and was consistently boycotting physicians who applied psychoanalysis in their practice, he had to work toward the day when there would be training institutes to guarantee the authenticity of the teaching and the competence of the taught. "It was this and nothing else that I wanted to achieve by the founding of the International Psychoanalytic Association."*

The Viennese were not persuaded that Freud's concerns were really justified and hence his organizational innovations really needed. Even the loyal Hitschmann worried that "taken as a race," the members of the Zurich contingent were "completely different from us Viennese." But early in April, when the Vienna Psychoanalytic Society held a post-mortem discussion on the congress just concluded, there was, though much grumbling, also much politeness. The compromise over the presidency, and the helpless recognition that Freud was after all still indispensable, had done something to lower the temperature. Freud did his part to calm emotions further; in an adroit gesture of appeasement, he nominated Adler to take his old place as the Society's presiding officer—*Obmann*—and proposed a new periodical, the monthly *Zentralblatt für Psychoanalyse*, to be edited jointly by Adler and Stekel. Suave in his turn, Adler first declared Freud's retirement from the presidency to be a "superfluous act," but then accepted the post and, with Stekel, the editorship of the new journal.

*In March 1911, in the midst of his final battle with Adler, Freud wrote Ludwig Binswanger, "When the realm I have founded is orphaned, no one but Jung should inherit it all. You see, my policy invariably pursues this aim, and my conduct toward Stekel and Adler fits into the same system." (Freud to Binswanger, March 14, 1911. Quoted in Ludwig Binswanger, *Erinnerungen an Sigmund Freud* [1956], 42.)

Freud interpreted all these displays of good will in his most sardonic vein. "The Viennese here," he confided to Ferenczi, "were, in the reaction after Nürnberg, very affectionate and absolutely wanted to found a republic with the Grand Duke at the head." Yet another compromise served to make everyone happy—more or less: while Adler was chosen *Obmann* by acclamation, a new post was invented, that of scientific chairman—*wissenschaftlicher Vorsitzender*—and Freud was named to it. Freud would later point to his conciliatory moves as proof that Adler's complaints of harassment were unfounded and irrational. But that was disingenuous. As Freud frankly told Ferenczi in the midst of working out his strategy, he was turning over the leadership of the Vienna group to Adler, "not from affection or satisfaction, but because he is, after all, the only real personage and because in this position he may be constrained to join in the defense of the common ground." If he could not persuade Adler, perhaps he could co-opt him.

BUT PSYCHOANALYTIC POLITICS, as we have seen, cannot wholly explain Freud's and Adler's tense coexistence and eventual parting. Organizational imperatives, unconscious conflicts, incompatibility of temper, and clashes of ideas fed one another until they reached their foreordained climax. It did not help matters that the two men should be opposites in almost every way. Contemporary partisans—on both sides—testify that Freud's and Adler's sartorial habits, personal styles, and therapeutic manners could not have been more unlike: Freud neat, patrician, and striving for clinical distance; Adler careless, democratic, and intensely involved. But in the end it was the clash of convictions that drove the two men apart; if, only a year after he had papered over their differences, Freud called Adler's position reactionary and questioned whether Adler was much of a psychologist at all, he was not doing so for tactical reasons or from sheer animosity.* Peace in Vienna was most desirable to Freud; by 1911, the Zurich connection was beginning to appear a little fragile. Yet the irreparable divergence between Adler's and Freud's thinking could not be in doubt—not by 1911. Indeed, Freud had had inklings of it for some years; he came to appreciate the gravity of Adler's departures only after long delay. As far back as June 1909, he had described Adler to Jung as "a theoretician, astute and original, but not oriented to the psycholog-

---

*Freud was in general disposed to discount rational or intellectual explanations for discord. He once observed that when differences of opinion make friendly relations impossible, "it is not the scientific differences that are so important; it is usually some other kind of animosity, jealousy or revenge, that gives the impulse to enmity. The scientific differences come later." (Joseph Wortis, *Fragments of an Analysis with Freud* [1954], 163.) Freud himself was, if anything, inclined to do the opposite—to make intellectual disagreements the ground for rather emotional quarrels.

ical; he aims past it to the biological." Yet he had immediately added that he thought Adler "decent" and "not likely to desert soon." If possible, he had concluded, "we must hold on to him." Two years later, such pacific tones were no longer possible to Freud: Adler, he told Oskar Pfister in February 1911, "has created for himself a world system without love, and I am in the midst of carrying out the revenge of the insulted goddess Libido on him."

When he drew this drastic conclusion, the showdown, a drawn-out affair, had been under way for some months. "With Adler," Freud told Jung in December 1910, "it is getting really bad."* Before then, Freud had oscillated between hopefully listening for Adler's contributions to his own thinking and uneasily worrying about Adler's depreciation of unconscious libidinal processes. But gradually his remaining hopes for Adler had waned. His impatience with what he called Adler's tactlessness and unpleasant behavior grew as his qualms about Adler's ideas intensified. One can see why Freud did not want to face these realities; late in 1910, there were times when such disputes, their impact on Freud only exacerbated by besetting uncertainties about teasing recruits like Bleuler, seemed like a doom to him. He was subject to bouts of fatigue and depression and confided to Ferenczi that the bickerings he had to endure in Vienna made him long for his old isolation: "I tell you, it was often more agreeable as long as I was alone."

It was not Freud who precipitated the crisis, though, but Hitschmann, among Freud's followers the most sympathetic to Adler. In November 1910, Hitschmann proposed that Adler rehearse his ideas in some detail to permit their thorough ventilation. Many of the members of the Society, after all, including Freud himself, had treated Adler's propositions as valuable supplements to psychoanalytic theories rather than as threatening substitutes for them. Adler readily complied and in January and February 1911, delivered two papers; the second of these, "Masculine Protest as the Core Problem of Neurosis," laid out his position so bluntly that Freud could not ignore it. Nor could he force it any longer into his own system of thought. He had remained silent after Adler's first talk; now he poured out his objections and his stored-up exasperation.

Freud's observations constitute a virtual counterpaper. To begin with, he called Adler's presentations so abstract as to be often incomprehensible. Moreover, Adler is given to presenting familiar ideas under new names: "One has the impression that somehow repression is concealed under 'masculine

---

*One trouble, as Freud admitted, was that Adler was arousing memories of Fliess.

protest' "; what is more, Adler "calls our old bisexuality 'psychical hermaphro-ditism,' as though it were something else."* But spurious, manufactured originality is the least of it: Adler's theory neglects the unconscious and sexuality. It is only "general psychology," at once "reactionary and retro-grade." While continuing to profess respect for Adler's intelligence, Freud charged that he was compromising the autonomous status of psychology by subjecting it to biology and physiology. "All these doctrines of Adler's," he grimly predicted, "will make a great impression and do psychoanalysis dam-age." Underlying Freud's vehemence was a persistent fear that his tough-minded ideas would win popularity only in Adler's watered-down version, which jettisoned such radical insights as the Oedipus complex, infantile sexuality, and the sexual etiology of neuroses. Freud regarded the acceptance of psychoanalysis in its Adlerian guise as a greater threat than forthright rejection.

Adler defended himself manfully, insisting that in his theories the neuroses were no less sexual in origin than in Freud's. But this apparent retreat could no longer camouflage their disagreement. The gladiators were in the arena, condemned to battle it out. Confronted with a split, several anguished mem-bers of the Society fled into denial: they professed to find no incompatibility between Freud and Adler. Stekel went so far as to praise Adler's views for deepening and developing "the facts we have discovered so far"; they "simply continue to build on Freud's foundations." But Freud was not interested in such forced compromises. If Stekel, he said dryly, finds no contradiction between the views of the two protagonists, "one is constrained to point out that two of the participants do find this contradiction, namely Freud and Adler."

The denouement was only a matter of time. Late in February 1911, Adler yielded up his post as presiding officer of the Vienna Psychoanalytic Society, and Stekel, the vice-president, "used the opportunity to demonstrate his friendship" for Adler and followed his example. By June, Freud had managed to pry Adler loose from the editorship of the *Zentralblatt*—Stekel continued as editor—and secured his resignation from the Society. Once angry, Freud stayed angry. He had long patiently listened to Adler, but no more. In this mood, he could not recognize that some of Adler's ideas, like his postulate of an independent aggressive drive, might be valuable contributions to psy-choanalytic thought. Rather, he bestowed on Adler the most damaging psy-

---

*The perceptive Ferenczi had noted this tendency of Adler's more than two years earlier. "Doubtless, Adler's doctrine of inferiority," he wrote Freud on July 7, 1908, "is not the last word in this contentious question; indeed, it is actually just a broader exposition of your idea of 'somatic compli-ance.' " (Freud–Ferenczi Correspondence, Freud Collection, LC.)

chological terms in his vocabulary. In August 1911, the told Jones that "as for the internal dissension with Adler, it was likely to come and I have ripened the crisis. It is the revolt of an abnormal individual driven mad by ambition, his influence upon others depending on his strong terrorism and sadismus." Freud, who as recently as 1909 had called Adler a decent fellow, persuaded himself not long after that Adler was suffering from paranoid delusions of persecution.* This was denunciation as diagnosis.

Adler's tone, certainly at first, was more temperate. In July 1911, reporting details of the dispute to Ernest Jones, he claimed "the best heads and the people of honest independence" for his side. He deplored what he called Freud's "fencer's postures" and insisted that while "like every author" he strove for recognition, "I have always stayed within moderate limits in that I could wait and never begrudged anyone being of a different opinion." Considerably stretching the length of time he had made propaganda for the Cause, he told Jones that he had tirelessly advocated psychoanalysis in Vienna "for fifteen years." If, he contended, "today Viennese clinical and intellectual circles take psychoanalytic research seriously and appreciate it, if it is not laughed at and ostracized—in Vienna—then I, too, have contributed my mite to that." Obviously he valued Jones's good opinion: "I do not want you to misunderstand me." Late in the summer, he grew more emphatic, and complained to Jones of "the nonsensical castration" that Freud planned to perform publicly, "before everyone's eyes." He thought that Freud's persecution of him was "in character." Freud was not alone in using psychological diagnosis as a form of aggression.

THE LONG SUMMER holiday suspended the contention for a time, but the crisis, ripened by Freud, reached its climax when the Vienna Psychoanalytic Society reconvened in the fall. "Tomorrow," Freud announced to Ferenczi early in October, "is the first session of the Society," and an attempt would be made to "force out the Adler pack." At the meeting, Freud announced that Adler and three of his most enthusiastic adherents had resigned and formed an Adlerian group, which, Freud declared, was "hostile competition." This formulation cut off all retreat. He insisted that membership in the new association was incompatible with membership in the Vienna Psychoanalytic

---

*In 1914, when Abraham read the manuscript of Freud's "History of the Psychoanalytic Movement," he objected to the word "persecutions": "A[dler] will defend himself against being called paranoid." But while Freud insisted that Adler had actually complained of being persecuted, he agreed to remove the term. When Freud's polemic was published, though, the word *Verfolgungen* reached cold print. (Abraham to Freud, April 2, 1914. *Freud–Abraham*, 165 [169]. See also Freud to Abraham, April 6, 1914. Ibid., 166 [170].)

Society and demanded that all those present choose between the two, within a week. In a final futile attempt to repair the irreparable, Carl Furtmüller, who was to become one of Adler's closest associates, presented the case against incompatibility at some length. But Freud, seconded by Sachs, Federn, and Hitschmann, was inexorable. When his views carried, six Adler partisans resigned from the Society. Freud was "a little tired from battle and victory," he reported to Jung with satisfaction after it was all over. "The whole Adler gang" was gone. "I was sharp but hardly unjust." He went on to inform Jung, with some annoyance, that "they have founded a society for 'free ψA,' in contrast to our unfree one, plan to put out a special journal." Still, the Adlerians continued to claim a right to membership in the Vienna Psychoanalytic Society, "naturally" hoping in their "parasitical" way, to exploit and misrepresent it. "I have made this symbiosis impossible." Freud and the Freudians had the Vienna Psychoanalytic Society to themselves. Only Stekel stayed on to remind Freud of unfinished work to be done.

Even more than Freud, Adler saw the break as largely a struggle over ideas. When the two were on the verge of parting, Freud at a private dinner pleaded with him not to desert the Society, and Adler asked rhetorically, "Why should I always do my work under your shadow?" It is hard to know whether the question was plaintive or defiant. Adler later chose to interpret his pained outcry as expressing the fear that he might "be made responsible for the Freudian theories in which he more and more disbelieved, while his own work was either misinterpreted by Freud and his followers or pushed to one side." It was not just that Freud rejected Adler; Adler rejected Freud no less vehemently—or came to see their break this way.

IN JUNE 1911, Freud had exclaimed to Jung, tersely and a little prematurely, "I have got rid of Adler at last." It was a shout of triumph. But in the deeper layers of Freud's mind apparently nothing was conclusive, nothing had been settled: instead of *endlich*—"at last"—Freud wrote, in a revealing slip, *endlos*—"endless." He seemed to be sensing trouble ahead. But he still had Jung by his side as his chosen successor. During the time of troubles in Vienna, the business of psychoanalysis—meetings, congresses, journals, to say nothing of Bleuler—had come to claim more and more space in his correspondence with Jung, though the exchange of case histories and communiqués from the war against the philistines did not die down. In successive congresses, and with voluminous psychoanalytic publications, Jung had consolidated his ascendancy, first acknowledged in 1910 when he had been elected president of the newly formed International Psychoanalytic Association. A year later, at the international congress held in Weimar in September 1911, not long after Adler's secession, Jung's position appeared unassailable. He was re-elected president, and Riklin secretary, by acclamation. Freud's intimate salutation, "Dear Friend," continued to introduce his frequent communications to Jung, as before. Yet only a month after the Weimar congress, in October, Emma Jung detected some strain between her husband and her husband's venerated mentor. "I have been tormented by the idea," she wrote to Freud, taking her courage in her hands, "that your relation with my husband is not quite as it could and should be." Freud told Ferenczi that he had answered the letter "affectionately and in great detail," but he claimed not to understand her message. For the moment, Frau Jung was more perceptive and more prescient than the protagonists. Something was wrong.

JUNG: THE ENEMY

 Looking back in enmity, Jung traced the roots of his break with Freud to an episode in the summer of 1909 on the *George Washington* as he, Freud, and Ferenczi headed for the United States. Jung—according to his account—had interpreted one of Freud's dreams as best he could without further details about Freud's private life. Freud had demurred at supplying them, looked at Jung suspiciously, and objected that he could not have himself analyzed; it would put his authority at risk. Jung recalled that this refusal had sounded the death knell of Freud's power over him. Freud, the self-proclaimed apostle of scientific candor, was placing personal authority above truth.*

Whatever really happened, Jung was chafing under Freud's authority, and, for all his protestations, was not disposed to continue tolerating it much longer. As late as July 1912, Freud wrote to Pfister that he hoped Jung would feel free to disagree with him "without a bad conscience." But that was just what Jung could not do. The rage, the sheer ferocity, pervading Jung's last letters to Freud testify to a very bad conscience indeed.

On occasion Jung would adduce more intricate causes for his parting from Freud. He suggested that Freud had refused to take seriously the lectures he had delivered in the United States and published late in 1912 as *The Theory of Psychoanalysis*. Indeed, "writing that book cost me my friendship with

*In a slightly different version, Jung, claiming to know of an affair between Freud and his sister-in-law, linked the dream Freud would not elucidate to his presumed infidelity. (See the bibliographical essay for chapter 2.)

Freud," he recalled, "because he couldn't accept it." But later he amended and complicated this diagnosis: that book was not so much the "real cause" as the "final cause" of the break, "because it had a long preparation." His whole friendship, he thought, had been in a sense a preparation for its angry denouement. "You know, from the beginning I had a *reservatio mentalis.* I couldn't agree with quite a number of his ideas," notably Freud's ideas on libido. This was reasonable enough: Jung's most besetting disagreement with Freud, which runs through the whole sequence of his letters like an ominous subtext, involved what he once gently called his inability to define libido— which meant, translated, that he was unwilling to accept Freud's definition. Jung steadily attempted to widen the meaning of Freud's term, to make it stand not just for the sexual drives, but for a general mental energy.

But Freud, infatuated with the dazzling thought that he had securely bestowed his legacy, was slow to recognize the persistence and pervasiveness of Jung's "mental reservation." And Jung, for his part, masked his true feelings for several years, even to himself. Freud remained "like Hercules of old," a "human hero and higher god." In November 1909, contrite about not writing more promptly after his return to Switzerland from their visit to Clark University, Jung submissively confessed to his "father" that he had sinned: *"Pater peccavi."* Two weeks later, he again appealed to Freud as the final authority, in his most filial style: "I often wish I had you in the vicinity. I often would have several things to ask you."

Until the breach became visible, in fact, Jung treated his disagreements with Freud's views as a personal flaw—his own. If he had some problem with them, this must be, "obviously," because he had "not yet adapted my position sufficiently to yours." The two continued their companionable exchanges and spent time alone together whenever they could find space in their crowded schedules. There was always much of substance to talk or write about. On January 2, 1910, Freud sent word to Jung that he was speculating about the source of man's need for religion in *"infantile helplessness."* This excited communiqué is a sign of Freud's trust in Jung; only the day before, he had confided to Ferenczi that his insight into the roots of religion had just come to him, around New Year's. Jung, for his part, mired in a domestic crisis produced by what he had called his "polygamous components," confidentially told Freud that he was ruminating about "the ethical problem of sexual freedom."

These private troubles made Freud a little apprehensive; they threatened to divert Jung's attention from the principal business, psychoanalysis. He pleaded with Jung to be patient. "You must stick it out longer, and lead our cause to its breakthrough." That was in January 1910. In the following month he reported to Ferenczi that things were "storming and raging again" in

Jung's "erotic and religious realm"; Jung's letters, Freud sensitively commented, sounded reluctant and distant. It was only some weeks later that
Freud was cheered to see Jung emerging from his "personal confusions," and
"rapidly made it up with him, since, after all, I was not angry but only
concerned." His equanimity apparently restored, Jung set about analyzing his
wife. Freud, to whom Jung reported this gross breach of technical rules, was
in a complaisant mood. He had recently assisted in Max Graf's analysis of
his own son, Little Hans, and thought that Jung might be successful with
his wife, even though he would doubtless find it impossible to surmount
his nonanalytic feelings completely.

When Jung was touchy, Freud was soothing. Thinking about the possible
application of psychoanalysis to the cultural sciences, an interest that Jung
enthusiastically shared, Freud expressed a longing for "students of mythology,
linguists, and historians of religion" to help in the work. "Otherwise we will
have to do it all ourselves." Somewhat unaccountably, Jung interpreted
Freud's fantasy as a criticism: "By this, I told myself, you probably mean that
I am unfit for *this* work." This was not at all what Freud had had in mind.
"Your being offended," he rejoined, was "music to my ears. I am quite
charmed that you yourself take this interest so seriously, that you yourself wish
to be this auxiliary army." When such strains emerged, Freud labored to
smooth them away. "Rest easy," he wrote his "dear son," and painted vistas
of great triumphs to come. "I leave you more to conquer than I could manage
myself, all of psychiatry and the approval of the civilized world, which is
accustomed to regard me as a savage!"

Through it all, Jung preserved the stance of the favorite son, loving, only
intermittently unruly. Early in 1910, on his way to the United States for a
profitable consultation that might make him late for the Nürnberg congress,
he sent Freud an apologetic boyish note from Paris: "Now, don't get cross
about my pranks!" He continued to proclaim the "feeling of inferiority
toward you which frequently overcomes me," and his uncommon pleasure at
one of Freud's appreciative letters: "I am, after all, very receptive to any
recognition the father bestows." At times, though, Jung's rebellious unconscious was irrepressible. Freud had been working on the studies that would
lead to *Totem and Taboo,* and, aware that Jung was interested in this sort
of speculative prehistory, he asked for some suggestions. Jung's reception of
this "very nice letter" was defensive; he thanked Freud warmly but quickly
added, "It is, though, very oppressive to me, if you too become involved in
this area, the psychology of religion. You are a dangerous competitor, if one
wants to speak of competition." Evidently, Jung needed to see Freud as a
competitor, though he blamed his flawed character—once again. He took
pride in promoting psychoanalysis, work that (he hoped Freud would agree)

was far more important than "my personal awkwardness and my offensiveness." Could it be, he asked anxiously, "that you distrust me?" He assured Freud that there was no cause; surely Freud would not object to Jung having his own views. Still, he insisted that he had "striven to change my opinions, following the judgment of the one who knows better. I would never have sided with you if heresy did not run in my blood a little." Some months after Freud's final break with Adler, Jung emphatically reaffirmed his loyalty: "I am not disposed to imitate Adler in the slightest."

Eager as he was to overlook these symptomatic disavowals, Freud could not find Jung's reassurances reassuring. But he tried, in his most delicate manner, to repair the slowly fraying fabric of their intimacy. He rejected Jung's severe self-diagnosis and substituted for "awkwardness" and "offensiveness" the far milder term "moods"; the only issue between them, he added, was Jung's intermittent neglect of his duties as president of the International Psychoanalytic Association. He reminded Jung, a little wistfully, "The indestructible foundation of our personal relationship is our engagement in ψA, but it was tempting to construct on this basis something beautiful, though more labile, an intimate solidarity—and should it not stay that way?" It was an appeal from the depth of Freud's being; scrupulously responding to all the issues Jung was raising, he declared himself in perfect accord with Jung's assertion of intellectual independence. Jung had quoted at him a long passage from Nietzsche's *Thus Spoke Zarathustra* to reinforce his plea for autonomy. "One poorly repays a teacher if one remains only the pupil," it began. "And why do you not want to pluck at my wreath?" Freud responded in some bewilderment, "If a third party should read this passage, he would ask me when I had undertaken to suppress you intellectually, and I would have to say: I do not know." Once again, somewhat poignantly, he tried to allay Jung's concerns: "Rest assured of the tenacity of my affective interest, and keep thinking of me in a friendly way, even if you write only rarely."

FREUD'S APPEAL WAS written in water. Jung, if he responded to it at all, read it as an attempt at seduction. By May 1912, he was embroiled with Freud in a dispute over the meaning of the incest taboo, behind which loomed that never-settled issue, sexuality. Freud's tone in that exchange was puzzled; he was desperately warding off the recognition that his friendship with Jung was doomed. But Jung sounded injured, like someone who has already broken with a friend and is now marshaling his reasons. It is no accident that the final rupture should have begun with a trivial incident.

In April 1912, Ludwig Binswanger, who had recently been appointed director of the sanatorium in Kreuzlingen, at Lake Constance, underwent an operation for a malignant tumor. Alarmed at the prospect of losing "one of his flourishing young men" to irrational death, Freud sent the invalid an anguished letter. He described himself as an "old man who must not complain if his life were to terminate in a few years (and who has decided not to complain)," and who found the news that Binswanger's life might be in danger "particularly painful." After all, Freud said, Binswanger was "one of those who is to continue my own life." There were times when Freud's secret wish for an immortality that his children or followers might secure for him rose to the surface of awareness. The wish had subtly influenced his relations with Jung, but it rarely found more poignant expression than when he thought that Binswanger might die.* Binswanger asked Freud to keep the news confidential, and Freud undertook a hurried visit to the patient, who was doing nicely.

Now, Jung's house at Küsnacht was only some forty miles from Kreuzlingen, but Freud, pressed for time, did not take the opportunity to stop by. Indifferent to Freud's busy schedule, Jung chose to be offended; he sent Freud a reproachful if guilt-ridden letter, attributing what he came to call the "Kreuzlingen gesture" to Freud's displeasure at his independent ways. In reply, Freud took the trouble to detail his movements without mentioning Binswanger's operation,† and reminded Jung that deep differences had never inhibited his visits before. "A few months earlier you would probably have spared me this interpretation." Jung's excessive sensitivity concerning the "Kreuzlingen gesture" made Freud wonder: "I find in this remark of yours an uncertainty in regard to my person."

FREUD'S UNEASINESS QUICKLY communicated itself to his intimates. In June, Ernest Jones was in Vienna; he saw Ferenczi, and took the occasion to canvass the threat of further dissension in the psychoanalytic camp. The emotional scars that Adler's departure had left on Freud and his adherents had not yet healed, and trouble with Jung now seemed as probable as it would be calamitous. Then Jones had one of those ideas that made psychoanalytic history: what was wanted, he thought, was a tight, small organization of loyalists, a clandestine "Committee," to rally around Freud as his dependable palace guard. The members of the Committee would share news and ideas with one another and undertake to talk over, in the strictest privacy, any desire "to depart from any of the fundamental tenets of psychoanalytical

---

*In the end, Binswanger would live on until 1966.

†He kept the matter from the others as well. "Over Whitsuntide," he wrote Abraham, "I spent two days in Konstanz as Binswanger's guest." (June 3, 1912. Karl Abraham papers, LC.) See also his letter to Ferenczi, in which he simply reported that he had spent a weekend at Binswanger's, without giving the real reason for his trip. (May 30, 1912. Freud–Ferenczi Correspondence, Freud Collection, LC.)

theory"—repression, the unconscious, or infantile sexuality. Ferenczi adopted Jones's proposal with enthusiasm, as did Rank. Much encouraged, Jones forwarded the suggestion to Freud, then recuperating from the year's work at the Karlsbad spa.

Freud took to the idea with a will. "What took hold of my imagination immediately, is your idea of a secret council composed of the best and most trustworthy among our men to take care of the further development of ψA and defend the cause against personalities and accidents when I am no more." He liked Jones's proposal well enough to claim, tentatively, paternity for himself: "You say it was Ferenczi who expressed this idea, but it may be my own, shaped in better times, when I hoped Jung would collect such a circle around himself composed of the official headmen of the local associations. Now I am sorry to say such a union had to be formed independently of Jung and of the elected presidents." Surely such a committee would "make living and dying easier for me." The first requirement, Freud thought, was that "this committee had to be *strictly secret*" in its existence and its actions. The membership should be small: Jones, Ferenczi, and Rank, the originators, were obvious candidates, as was Abraham. So was Sachs, "in whom my confidence is illimited in spite of the shortness of our acquaintance." Entering into the spirit of the proposal, he promised the utmost discretion.

The plan says much about the besetting insecurity of these first psy-choanalysts. Freud thought that "perhaps it could be adapted to meet the necessities of reality," but frankly recognized "a boyish perhaps a romantic element too in this conception." Jones had used the same charged language: "The idea of a united small body, designed, like the Paladins of Charlemagne, to guard the kingdom and policy of their master, was a product of my own romanticism." Actually, the Committee did work satisfactorily for some years.

THROUGH THE SUMMER OF 1912, Jung's insistence on being offended at the "Kreuzlingen gesture" remained on the agenda. Jung's anger fueled Freud's misgivings. The letter he had received from Jung, Freud told Jones in late July, "cannot but be construed into a formal disavowal of our hitherto friendly relations." He was sorry about that, not for personal but for professional reasons, and was "resolved to let things go and not to try to influence him more." After all, "ψA is no more my own affair but it concerns you and so many others besides as well." A few days later, he ruefully reported to Abraham, recalling Abraham's long-standing distrust of Jung, "I am occupied with events in Zurich, in which an old prophecy of yours, which I had wanted to ignore, is being confirmed." All his correspondence of these months shows Freud preoccupied with ways of ensuring his movement's future, which is to say, emotionally, his own: "I will certainly contribute nothing to a break, and hope that the businesslike community can remain intact." Sending Ferenczi Jung's letter about his failure to visit Küsnacht, Freud interpreted it as probably showing that Jung's neurosis must be active. He sadly conceded the failure of his effort at amalgamating "Jews and goyim in the service of ψA." Unfortunately, "They separate themselves like oil and water." The matter evidently preoccupied him; in the following month, he told Rank that he had hoped to achieve the "integration of Jews and anti-Semites on the soil of ψA." This remained Freud's goal even in adversity.

But Freud thought that Ferenczi would be pleased with the way he was taking it all: "emotionally quite detached and intellectually superior." In fact, Freud was less detached than he liked to show, though as late as September, he accepted Jones's prognosis that "there is no big danger of a separation between Jung and me." He wanted to be reasonable: "If you and the Zurich people bring about a formal reconciliation, I would make no difficulties. It would be a formality only, as I am not angry with him." But, he added, "my former feelings for him cannot be restored." Perhaps being on holiday in his beloved Rome made him more sanguine than he had any right to be.

But Jung gave Freud less and less reason for even a touch of optimism. In November, after he returned from a lecture tour in the United States, he wrote to Freud, cherishing his grievance. Speaking at Fordham (which Freud called "a little unknown university run by Jesuits") and elsewhere, Jung had thrown overboard most of the psychoanalytic baggage—childhood sexuality, the sexual etiology of neuroses, the Oedipus complex—and had openly re-defined libido. In his report to Freud, he cheerfully observed that his version of psychoanalysis had managed to win over many people who had hitherto been put off by "the problem of sexuality in neurosis." But, he went on, he stood on his right to speak the truth as he saw it. Still, though insisting once again that Freud's "Kreuzlingen gesture" had left a lasting wound, he hoped that friendly personal relations with Freud would continue. After all, he noted with a strenuous, momentary effort at graciousness, he owed Freud a great deal. But what he wanted from Freud was not resentment, but objective judgments. "With me this is not a matter of caprice, but of enforcing what I consider to be true."

JUNG'S LETTER WAS a truculent manifesto, a declaration of independence barely skirting rudeness. But it also reminded Freud that Zurich was not the only source of disagreeable news. "I hear," Jung noted, "that difficulties have broken out with Stekel." He added in his pugnacious tone that Stekel should be fired from the *Zentralblatt;* he had "already done enough damage with his indecent fanaticism for confession, not to say exhibitionism." Freud agreed with Jung, possibly for the last time. Through 1912, Stekel had continued to attend the meetings of the Vienna Psychoanalytic Society; in the early months of the year, he had prominently participated in a series of discussions on masturbation, and in October, he had been reconfirmed as editor of the *Zentralblatt*. But then he quarreled with Tausk, and the episode, the latest in a long string of provocations, drove Freud beyond the edge of patience. In his autobiography, Stekel was rather vague on Freud's break with him, and uncomplaining; perhaps, he conjectured, Jung had been working against him. Certainly Freud had favored the aggressive Tausk, whom Stekel considered an enemy. In fact, the final imbroglio was precipitated by Stekel's editorial management of the *Zentralblatt*. At first, as Freud gratefully acknowledged, he had been an "excellent" editor, in sharp contrast to Adler. But he soon treated the journal as his private preserve, and tried to keep Tausk's reviews from appearing in it. Freud felt he "could not allow" such highhandedness, and finally, in November 1912, he announced to Abraham that "Stekel is going his own way." He was greatly relieved: "I am so pleased about that; you cannot know what I suffered under the task of defending him against the whole world. He is an unbearable human being." Freud's growing conviction that Stekel was a "desperate shameless" liar made the break irreparable; Stekel, Freud told Jones, had told people in Zurich that there had been an attempt to "stifle the liberty of his mind" but had failed to mention his quarrels with Tausk or his claim that the *Zentralblatt* was "his own property." Freud, who had pronounced moral principles, saw such mendacity as frustrating all further collegial relations. Stekel, he thought, had degenerated into a preacher "in the pay of Adlerism."

BUT THE STEKEL AFFAIR could not divert Freud for long from the challenge that Jung's new tone threw out to him. Jung had been "Dear Friend"— *Lieber Freund*—to Freud for several years, but after his letter of mid-November, Freud drew the consequences. *"Lieber Herr Doktor,"* he headed his reply. "I greet you on your return home from America, no longer so affectionately as previously in Nürnberg—you have successfully weaned me of that— but still with enough sympathy, interest, and satisfaction in your personal success." He wondered out loud, though, whether that success had not been purchased at the cost of compromising the far-reaching insights of psychoanalysis. While he persisted in hoping for the survival of their good personal relations, Freud now allowed a note of irritation to enter his letters: "Your insistence on the 'Kreuzlingen gesture' is, to be sure, as incomprehensible as it is insulting, but there are things that cannot be settled in writing." Freud still wanted to talk with Jung, while his followers were ready to discard him.

On November 11, the day that Jung had reminded Freud of the "Kreuzlingen gesture" once more, Eitingon wrote Freud from Berlin, "Psychoanalysis is now old and mature enough to recover well from such processes of decomposition and elimination."

Late in November, the two protagonists took the occasion of a small psychoanalytic conference in Munich to sit down for an extended private talk about the Binswanger episode. It produced an apology from Jung and a rapprochement. "Result," Freud reported to Ferenczi, "the personal like the intellectual bonds will hold fast for years. No talk of separation, defection." This sanguine assessment was an almost desperate bit of self-deception, and it could not withstand the realities. Freud was growing wary, and much as he wanted to, could not quite trust this peaceful resolution. Jung reminded him, he told Ferenczi, of a drunk who incessantly screams, "Don't think I'm smashed!"

The reunion in Munich was marred by one of Freud's fainting spells—the second in Jung's presence. As in Bremen three years before, the scene was again the end of a luncheon; as before, there had been a spirited discussion between Freud and Jung, and Freud had again chosen to interpret what Jung said as revealing a death wish against him. In the discussion, Freud had reproached Jung and Riklin with publishing psychoanalytic articles in Swiss journals without mentioning his name. Jung defended the practice: after all, he said, Freud's name was well known. But Freud persisted. "I remember thinking, he was taking the matter rather personally," Jones, who was present, later recalled. "Suddenly, to our consternation, he fell on the floor in a dead faint. The sturdy Jung swiftly carried him to a couch in the lounge, where he soon revived." The incident had all sorts of hidden meanings for Freud, which he analyzed in letters to his intimates. Whatever physical causes might have lurked in the background—fatigue, headaches—Freud had no doubt that the principal agent in his fainting was a psychological conflict. In some obscure way, Fliess was mixed up in this attack, as before. Freud was still trying to settle his emotional accounts with his former friend. Jung, for his part, whatever he made of this startling moment, quickly put his evident relief at his reconciliation with Freud in writing. He was contrite, solicitous, once again the affectionate son. "Please," he wrote Freud on November 26, "forgive my mistakes, which I will not attempt to excuse or extenuate."

It was a false recovery. Jung was intent on being offended and chose to read compliments as insults. On November 29, Freud, writing to Jung, diagnosed his fainting episode as a migraine "not without psychic admixtures"; in short, "a piece of neurosis." And in the same letter, he praised Jung for having "solved the puzzle of all mysticism." But this struck Jung, who seemed to have forgotten the protestations of his previous letter, as an attack; once again, Freud was undervaluing his work. He seized on Freud's admission that he still harbored an unanalyzed piece of neurosis. It is that "piece," Jung announced, parading his "Helvetic boorishness," that kept Freud from appreciating his, Jung's, work to the full. Having for years used the term "father complex," and having supplied flamboyant evidence in his own conduct to support the theory, Jung now rejected it as Viennese name calling. He noted, with pain, that psychoanalysts were all too inclined to exploit their profession for purposes of denunciation.

Mustering a last remnant of forbearance, Freud did not cavil at Jung's "new style," agreed that it was distressing to see psychoanalysis misused, and suggested a "little household remedy": let "each of us occupy himself with his own neurosis more zealously than with that of his neighbor." In his response, Jung lowered his tone for a moment and informed Freud that he was preparing a scathing review of a new book by Adler. Freud approved, but reminded Jung of what divided them: Jung's "innovation" concerning the libido theory. This was too much for Jung's unconscious; in mid-December, in a short note, he made one of those slips that psychoanalysts live by. "Even Adler's accomplices," he wrote, "do not want to regard me as one of theirs." But instead of *ihrigen*—"theirs"—which the context called for, Jung unconsciously disavowed Freud by writing *Ihrigen*—"yours." Freud had caught himself in a very similar slip, hinting at his unconscious hostility to Jung, several years before.* Now, taking the mistake that was not a mistake as a clue to Jung's real feelings, and goaded beyond endurance, he did not resist the temptation of commenting on it. Rather maliciously, he asked Jung whether he could mobilize enough "objectivity"—it was one of Jung's favorite aggressive words—to consider the slip without anger.

Jung could not. In his most hectoring tone, he gave what Freud had once called his "healthy coarseness" free rein: "May I say a few serious words to you? I recognize my uncertainty toward you, but have the tendency to see the situation in an honest and absolutely decent way. If you doubt that, the problem is yours. I would like to call your attention to the fact that your technique of treating your pupils like your patients is a *blunder*. In that way you produce slavish sons or impudent rascals (Adler-Stekel and the whole impudent gang that is now giving itself airs in Vienna). I am objective enough to see through your trick." Having disavowed the father complex, he once again exhibited it to the full: Freud's way of detecting symptomatic actions, he continued, was a way of reducing everyone to the level of sons and daughters, all blushingly admitting their faults. "Meanwhile you are sitting

*See p. 213.

Freud at about the time he was appointed *Privatdozent*, in 1885. *(Freud Collection, LC)*

Freud and Martha Bernays in Wandsbek in 1885, the year before their marriage. *(Mary Evans/Sigmund Freud Copyrights, Wivenhoe)*

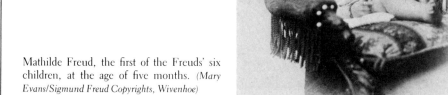

Mathilde Freud, the first of the Freuds' six children, at the age of five months. *(Mary Evans/Sigmund Freud Copyrights, Wivenhoe)*

Alexander, Freud's youngest sibling, with whom he got on famously. *(Mary Evans/Sigmund Freud Copyrights, Wivenhoe)*

Josef Breuer and his wife, Mathilde, Freud's intimate friends until the mid-1890s. *(Mary Evans/ Sigmund Freud Copyrights, Wivenhoe)*

André Brouillet, *La Leçon clinique du Dr Charcot*. Freud hung a reproduction of this painting in his consulting room. *(Mary Evans/Sigmund Freud Copyrights, Wivenhoe)*

Bertha Pappenheim, the famous hysteric "Anna O.," Breuer's patient between 1880 and 1882, who has the distinction of being, in a very real sense, the founding patient of psychoanalysis.

The hall of the Gesellschaft der Ärzte, the Vienna society of physicians, where Freud in 1886 gave a lecture on male hysteria. *(Bild-Archiv der Österreichischen Nationalbibliothek, Wien)*

Freud and his intimate of the 1890s, Wilhelm Fliess, the most important and most problematic friend Freud ever had. *(Mary Evans/Sigmund Freud Copyrights, Wivenhoe)*

A page of the important letter Freud sent to Fliess on September 21, 1897, explaining why he no longer found the seduction theory of neuroses convincing. *(Freud Collection, LC)*

The entrance to Berggasse 19, the house in which Freud and his family lived from September 1891 until June 1938, when they left for England after the Anschluss. *(Photograph © Edmund Engelman)*

The famous analytic couch, given to Freud about 1890. *(Photograph © Edmund Engelman)*

A glimpse of the antiquities—Freud's great and enduring passion—that crowded his consulting room and the adjoining study. *(Photograph © Edmund Engelman)*

Bellevue, the resort near Vienna where on July 24, 1895, Freud succeeded for the first time in interpreting a dream, more or less completely. *(Bild-Archiv der Österreichischen Nationalbibliothek, Wien)*

Freud in 1891, the year he published *On the Aphasias*. *(Mary Evans/Sigmund Freud Copyrights, Wivenhoe)*

Freud's father, Jacob, in his last years. *(Mary Evans/Sigmund Freud Copyrights, Wivenhoe)*

pretty on top, as father." Jung declared that he for one had no use for such servility. For a moment it seemed as though Freud was still willing to reason with Jung, as he watched his cherished plans for the future of psychoanalysis coming to pieces before his eyes. Drafting a reply, he noted that Jung's reaction to having his slip called to his attention was excessive, and defended himself against the charge of keeping his students in a condition of infantile dependence; on the contrary, he was criticized in Vienna for not being sufficiently concerned with analyzing them.

Freud's comment on Jung's overreaction invites a comment of its own. In their correspondence and their conversation, the psychoanalysts of the first generation employed an intrusive style that would have been wholly out of place in the discourse of other mortals. They fearlessly interpreted one another's dreams; fell on the others' slips of tongue or pen; freely, much too freely, employed diagnostic terms like "paranoid" and "homosexual" to characterize their associates and indeed themselves. They all practiced in their circle the kind of wild analysis they decried in outsiders as tactless, unscientific, and counterproductive. This irresponsible rhetoric probably served as relief from their austere labors in the psychoanalytic situation, a kind of noisy reward for keeping silent and being discreet most of the time. Freud played this game with the rest, even though he soberly warned his colleagues against abusing psychoanalysis as a weapon. Since, then, this slashing mode was irresistible, its coinage inflated, and its practice familiar, Freud was right to think that Jung's response to his interpretation of the slip was out of all proportion and hence highly symptomatic.

By late December, Freud finally recognized that the time for pointing out such niceties was over. He could no longer aspire to lofty statesmanship. "As regards Jung," he wrote Jones in a most revealing letter, "he seems all out of his wits, he is behaving quite crazy. After some tender letters he wrote me one of the utter insolence showing that his experience at Munich"—the "reconciliation" of November—"has left no trace with him." To react to Jung's revealing slip had been "a very slight provocation," after which "he broke loose furiously proclaiming that he was not neurotic at all." Still, Freud wanted no "official separation"; for the sake of "our common interest," that was undesirable. But he advised Jones to take "no more steps to his conciliation, it is to no effect." Jones, Freud was sure, could imagine what Jung had charged: "I was the neurotic, I had spoiled Adler and Stekel, etc. It is the same mechanism and the identical reaction as in Adler's case." It was the same and yet not the same; contemplating this latest, most consequential disillusionment, Freud could not suppress his dismay and drew a somewhat pathetic distinction with a complex pun: "To be sure, Jung is at least an 'Aiglon.' " We may read this epithet in conflicting ways, mirroring Freud's own contradictory feelings: "Aiglon," French for "little eagle," was a reference to Adler, whose name means "eagle" in German. But it also brought to mind Napoleon's son, "Napoleon II," who had been called *l'Aiglon*, and who had not lived to fulfill the mission his father had designed for him; just so had Jung, Freud's chosen successor, been the repository of expectations never to be realized. Jung's ambitions, which Freud had hoped to "force into my service," had proved unmanageable. He told Ernest Jones that Jung's letter had provoked in him a feeling of shame.

Freud also informed Jones that he had composed a "very mild answer" but had not sent it off, since Jung would "take so meek a reaction as a sign of cowardice and feel his importance the more." He still hoped against hope. Jung's "friendship is not worth the ink," he told Jones on January 1, 1913; but while he had "no need of his companionship myself," the "common interests" of the association and the psychoanalytic press should be kept in mind "as long as it shows possible." Two days later, in a letter to Jung that Freud did mail, he drew a heavy double line under the friendship that had promised so much. He found no way, he wrote, of replying to Jung's charges. "It is settled among us analysts that none of us needs to be ashamed of his piece of neurosis. But he who incessantly screams, in the midst of abnormal behavior, that he is normal awakens the suspicion that he lacks insight into his illness. Accordingly, I suggest to you that we give up our personal relations altogether." He added, permitting his distress to come through, "I lose nothing by this; for a long time, I have been tied to you emotionally by a thin thread, the lingering effect of disappointments experienced earlier." Fliess was still in Freud's mind. Certainly, by now the thread was torn beyond repair; Jung had become, in the privacy of Freud's intimate letters, nothing better than "outrageously insolent," had shown himself "the florid fool and brutal fellow he is." Jung accepted Freud's decision. "The rest," he wrote in reply, a little grandiloquently, "is silence."

But there was still more to be said. However widely his recently crystallized views diverged from Freud's, Jung was still known to the world as the most eminent spokesman for Freudian psychoanalysis after Freud. Moreover, as president of the International Psychoanalytic Association, he was the principal official personage in the international movement. Not without justice, Freud saw his own situation to be precarious in the extreme; there was a real danger that Jung and his followers, in control of the organizational and journalistic apparatus of psychoanalysis, might assert their power and expel the founder and his adherents. He was not alone in his concern. In mid-March 1913, Abraham circulated a proposal that in May the psychoanalytic groups in London, Berlin, Vienna, and Budapest call for Jung's resignation.

No wonder he headed his memorandum, intended only for a few, "Confidential!"

Freud was prepared for the worst. "According to news from Jones," he told Ferenczi in May 1913, "we must expect wicked things from Jung." Naturally, he added bitterly, "everything that strays from our truths has official applause on its side. It is quite possible that this time they will really bury us after they have so often sung us the dirge in vain." This, he added defiantly, "will change much in our fate, but nothing in that of science. We are in possession of the truth; I am as certain as I was fifteen years ago."

He was mobilizing all his self-confidence, spontaneous or cultivated, while Jung was rehearsing his differences with Freud on the lecture circuit. In July 1913, Jones sent Freud, without comment, the printed announcement of a "paper by Dr. C. G. Jung, of Zurich, entitled:—'PSYCHOANALYSIS,'" to be given before the Psycho-Medical Society in London. Jones and Freud must have found it ominous that the speaker was identified as "one of the greatest authorities on Psychoanalysis," especially since the following month, once again speaking in London, Jung bluntly restated the program he had first ventured to propose in New York ten months before: to free psychoanalysis from its exclusive emphasis on sexuality. In those London lectures, Jung for the first time called his revised doctrines not psychoanalysis, but "analytical psychology."

Freud's dream theory was another target of Jung's rethinking. Adopting a didactic, almost paternal tone that appeared to reverse their accustomed roles, Jung sent word to Berggasse 19 in July 1913 that Freud had evidently mistaken "our view." Jung was now speaking in the name of the Zurich group, just as Freud had long spoken for the Viennese. Freud's alleged misunderstanding involved the place that Jung assigned to current conflicts in dream formation. "We," Jung lectured him, "admit the correctness of the [Freudian] wish-fulfillment theory without cavil," but, regarding it as superficial, they had gone beyond it.

Patronizing Freud must have given Jung exquisite pleasure. He was hard at work constructing a psychology of his own; the ideas usually associated with Jungian analytical psychology all date from these years: the archetypes, the collective unconscious, the ubiquity of the uncanny, the sympathy with religious experience, the fascination with myth and alchemy. As a practicing psychiatrist and clinician who claimed to have learned most from his patients, Jung developed a psychology that naturally shows marked affinities with Freudian psychoanalysis. But the differences are fundamental. Thus for Freud, Jung's famous definition of libido was nothing better than a failure of nerve, a craven retreat from inconvenient truths about the sexual drives inhabiting the human animal. Jung's theory of the archetype, too, has no real counterpart in Freud's views. The archetype is a fundamental principle of creativity anchored in racial endowments, a human potentiality concretely manifested in religious doctrines, fairy tales, myths, dreams, works of art and literature. Its equivalent in biology is the "pattern of behaviour."

Apart from specific incompatibilities, Jung and Freud differed radically in their essential attitudes toward the scientific enterprise. It is noteworthy that they accused one another with equal vehemence of departing from scientific method and falling into mysticism. "I criticize in Freudian psychology," Jung wrote, "a certain narrowness and bias and, in 'Freudians,' a certain unfree, sectarian spirit of intolerance and fanaticism." Freud, Jung thought, had been a great discoverer of facts about the mind, but far too inclined to leave the solid ground of "critical reason and *common sense.*" Freud for his part criticized Jung for being gullible about occult phenomena and infatuated with oriental religions; he viewed with sardonic and unmitigated skepticism Jung's defense of religious feelings as an integral element in mental health. For Freud, religion was a psychological need projected onto culture, the child's feeling of helplessness surviving in adults, to be analyzed rather than admired. At a time when he was still on relatively good terms with Jung, Freud had already taxed him with making himself invisible behind a "religious-libidinal cloud." As the heir of the eighteenth-century Enlightenment, Freud had no use for systems of thought that blurred the irreconcilable differences and denied the unending war between science and religion.

The gulf dividing Freud and Jung on matters of substance was only widened by psychological conflicts between them. Taking deep satisfaction in developing his original psychology, Jung later asserted that he had not experienced his separation from Freud as an excommunication or an exile. It was a liberation for him. A Freudian interpretation will go far to illuminate Jung's most histrionic gestures in the short years of intimacy with his "father" in Vienna: the oedipal son had struggled free, at once suffering and inflicting suffering in the process. Jung had said it all in a letter to Freud on Christmas Day, 1909: "It is a hard lot to be compelled to work side by side with the creator." No doubt, what Jung got out of these years was more than a private quarrel and a broken friendship; he generated a psychological doctrine that was recognizably his own.

THE CORRESPONDENCE between Jung and Freud dwindled to occasional, formal business communications. Meanwhile, Freud was busy rescuing from the wreckage as much as he could. While he had in the past, especially in asides to Abraham, invited a "racial" reading of his conflict with Jung, he now vigorously resisted treating the conflict as a battle between Jew and gentile.

If the Swiss psychiatrist Alphonse Maeder, one of Jung's closer associates, preferred to see the struggle that way, Freud told the trusted Ferenczi, that was his privilege. But it was emphatically not Freud's view. "Certainly there are great differences with the Aryan spirit"—thus Freud outlined the argument that Ferenczi might adopt in response to Maeder. "Hence there would surely be different Weltanschauungen here and there." But "there should be no distinct Aryan or Jewish science. Their results should be identical; only their presentation might vary." Indeed, differences in results would only prove that "there must be something wrong." Ferenczi might well reassure Maeder, Freud added sarcastically, that "we have no desire to disturb their Weltanschauung and religion." He might also tell Maeder that Jung had apparently declared in the United States, "ψA is not a science but a religion." If that were so, it would explain the entire dispute. "But the Jewish spirit regrets that it cannot play along. A little mockery could do no harm." In the midst of these disheartening disputes, Freud found time to declare his fidelity to the austere discipline that the search for scientific objectivity imposed. Psychoanalysis as a science must be independent of all sectarian considerations, but independent also of all "Aryan patronage."

For all his weary pessimism, Freud tried to continue working with Jung— however frigid their cooperation. Harboring few illusions and only the most modest expectations, he attended the international congress of psychoanalysts in Munich in early September 1913. It was a more crowded affair than its predecessors, with some eighty-seven members and guests attending. But the atmosphere was prickly with partisanship, even though many of the participants had little inkling that the leadership was irreparably divided. The proceedings, Freud complained, were "fatiguing and unedifying"; Jung presided in "an unamiable and incorrect way." The vote on Jung's re-election demonstrated the bubbling up of widespread discontent: twenty-two of the participants abstained in protest, while fifty-two voted for the slate. "We parted"—thus Freud summed up the congress—"with no wish to see one another again." Lou Andreas-Salomé was there, and, comparing Freud and Jung, she judged the latter harshly. "A single look at these two," she wrote in her journal, "will reveal which of them is the more dogmatic, the more power-loving. Where with Jung a kind of robust gaiety, abundant vitality, spoke through his booming laughter two years ago, his seriousness now holds pure aggressiveness, ambition, mental brutality. Freud has never been so close to me as here: not only because of his break with the 'son' Jung, whom he loved, for whose sake he had, as it were, transferred his cause to Zurich, but precisely because of the manner of the break—as though *Freud* were carrying it through in narrow-minded stubbornness," an appearance that Jung had fabricated in defiance of the reality.

Jung did not leave the field quickly or quietly. In October—"playing injured innocence," as Freud put it—he resigned as editor of the *Jahrbuch*, brusquely citing "reasons of a personal nature" and "disdaining a public discussion." To Freud he explained, no less brusquely, that he had acted because he had learned from Maeder that Freud doubted his *"bona fides"*—whatever that meant. This, he said, made any further work together quite impossible. Freud, now wholly distrustful, thought Jung's resignation, with its obscure alibi, a mere ruse. "It is perfectly clear why he resigned," he told Jones. "He wanted me and Bleuler to fall off and have it all to himself." Sensing the need to act quickly, he "urgently" summoned Ferenczi to Vienna. Jung, whom he now saw as "brutal, insincere, sometimes dishonest," might negotiate with the publishers to secure control of the *Jahrbuch*. What was worse, Jung was still president of the organization in which Freud had invested so much.

Freud valiantly agitated to recapture both his periodical and his organization. It was unpalatable work, but he expressed confidence that, "as a matter of course," he and his followers would "never imitate Jung's brutality." The disclaimer would have been more telling if Freud had been less savage in his own correspondence. And his allies in Berlin and London were quite as scathing about the opposition. Ernest Jones dispatched urgent and outraged letters in his search for a winning strategy. "One is infuriated with Jung," he wrote to Abraham late in 1913, "until one discovers that he is simply crassly stupid, 'emotional stupidity,' as the psychiatrists term it." Freud's polemical style was evidently contagious. For some time, Jones counseled the dissolution of the International Psychoanalytic Association: "My chief reason for thinking it desirable to dissolve now is the ridiculousness of the situation; I should blush with shame for our former co-workers, to attend another congress" like the one in Munich the previous September. "Also the longer the Zurich school are allowed to identify themselves with Ps-A, the more difficult does it become to disown them. We must have a separation." His friend Abraham was just as emphatic. For him, the joining of Freudians and Jungians had been "an unnatural marriage" all along.

Freud was pleased, though hardly surprised, to have such energetic supporters in his corner. But his principal resource in those days was work on his "History of the Psychoanalytic Movement," a useful vessel to contain his rage. He envisioned it as a pamphlet setting out his version of the dissensions that had been plaguing the movement in the past few years. He first hinted at his intentions in early November 1913, in a note to Ferenczi: he was thinking about "a history of ψA with an outspoken critique of Adler and Jung." Two months later he could report, "I am working furiously at the history"; the adverb was appropriate as an indication of both his speed and his mood. The "History" was Freud's declaration of war. As he wrote it, furiously, he sent drafts to his intimates, and he came to call it affectionately the "bomb."

Even before the "bomb" was officially detonated, Freud was gratified to see his adversaries in Zurich making what he considered tactical mistakes. They were, he wryly concluded, working for him. Early in the spring of 1914, Jung gave Freud what he wanted: on April 20, he resigned as the president of the International Psychoanalytic Association. Two days later, the Berliners dispatched a joyous telegram to Berggasse 19: "On the news from Zurich cordial congratulations from Abraham, Eitingon." Jung's decision, Freud told Ferenczi, breathing easier, "has greatly eased the task."

The "bomb," which was dropped in mid-July, did the rest. It separated beyond cavil Freud and his adherents from those, like Jung, whom they no longer accepted as psychoanalysts. "I cannot suppress a hurrah," Freud wrote exultantly to Abraham. His exhilaration did not quickly dissipate. "So we are rid of them at last," he observed more than a week later, "the brutal holy Jung and his pious parrots"—*Nachbeter.* Reading the pamphlet just before publication, Eitingon was moved to unaccustomed eloquence and a salad of mixed metaphors. He had perused the "History," he told Freud, "with agitation and admiration." Freud's pen, which had in the past "as a plow broken our darkest and most fertile soil," had become "a keen blade" which he had wielded most deftly. "The hits strike home, and these scars will not fade" from "the no-longer-ours." The hyperbole was not misplaced. Just as Adler's departure had left the Vienna Psychoanalytic Society in the hands of Freud and the Freudians, so Jung's departure, far more significant, left the International Psychoanalytic Association a solid body for the discussion and dissemination of Freud's ideas. Whatever else the Jung affair produced, it helped to define publicly what Freud thought psychoanalysis really stood for.

IN RETROSPECT, FREUD's involvement with Jung appears like a new edition of earlier fateful friendships. Freud himself provided ammunition for such a reading: the names of Fliess and of other discarded allies flicker through his correspondence of these years. And Jung, as if infected by Freud's tormented allusions, meaningfully responded to them. As in earlier friendships, Freud rapidly, almost rashly, invested his affections, moved toward almost unreserved cordiality, and ended in irreparable, furious estrangement. In July 1915, when it was all over, he ranked Jung contemptuously among the "saintly converts." He had liked the man, he wrote, until Jung was visited "by a religious-ethical 'crisis,'" complete "with higher morality, rebirth," to say nothing of "lies, brutality and anti-Semitic condescension toward me." The only feeling Freud did not permit himself in this tempestuous alliance was indifference.

This emotional trajectory raises the question of whether Freud somehow needed to make his friends into his enemies. First Breuer,* then Fliess, then Adler and Stekel, now Jung, with other ruptures to come. It is understandable why one might see Jung as simply another Fliess. But this pairing in fact obscures more than it illuminates. Freud and Fliess were virtually of an age; there was a distance of nearly twenty years between Freud and Jung: when they began to correspond in 1906, Freud was fifty, Jung, thirty-one. Then too, for all his fatherly fondness, Freud never offered to Jung that final emblem of Germanic familiarity, the *du,* as he had to Fliess. At the summit of their intimacy, after Freud had anointed Jung crown prince of the psychoanalytic movement, their letters continued to preserve a measure of formality: Freud addressed Jung as "Dear Friend," but Jung never graduated beyond "Dear *Herr Professor.*" The stakes in Freud's friendship with Jung were as high as they had been with Fliess, but they were different stakes. Freud's situation had drastically altered; if he had embraced Fliess as his sole companion on an eccentric, daredevil expedition, he embraced Jung as the sturdy guarantor of a movement still embattled but enjoying growing support.

Moreover, Freud was not the victim of some obscure repetition compulsion. When he told Abraham in 1912, in the midst of battle, "I learn a bit more tolerance daily," he was doubtless seeing himself as rather more conciliatory than he was. Adler in 1911, or Jung in 1912, would not have recognized this genial self-portrait. Yet Freud did not enjoy lifelong, untroubled friendships merely with those who could never threaten his position in the psychoanalytic movement, men like the ophthalmologist Leopold König-stein and the archeologist Emanuel Löwy. More to the point, some of his closest professional associates, even though far from consistently "orthodox," felt nothing more than the occasional, quite bearable lash of Freud's frankly expressed disapproval. Paul Federn, Ernest Jones, and others among his most prominent adherents found themselves at odds with Freud on important issues of technique or theory without being banished as renegades or traitors. The Swiss psychiatrist Ludwig Binswanger, who wrestled all his life with the

---

*The estrangement of these two old friends was complete. On November 21, 1907, Breuer wrote to Auguste Forel, "Personally, I have now parted from Freud entirely." He added that "naturally" this had not been "a wholly painless process." Magnanimous as usual, he still regarded Freud's work as "magnificent: built upon the most laborious study in his private practice and of the greatest importance—even though," he felt constrained to add, "no small part of its structure will doubtless crumble away again." (Quoted in full in Paul F. Cranefield, "Joseph Breuer's Evaluation of His Contribution to Psycho-Analysis," *Int. J. Psycho-Anal.,* XXXIX [1958], 319–20.)

place of psychoanalysis in his psychiatric thinking and developed a highly individual existentialist psychology, remained on the most amicable footing with Freud across the decades. So did the Protestant pastor Oskar Pfister, for all of Freud's pugilistic contempt for religion.

Freud was exceedingly sensitive to the charge that he needed to break with his friends, so sensitive that he sought to disarm it in print. In his short autobiography of 1925, he contrasted those with whom he had fallen out, "Jung, Adler, Stekel, and a few others," with "a large number of persons," like "Abraham, Eitingon, Ferenczi, Rank, Jones, Brill, Sachs, Pastor Pfister, van Emden, Reik, and others," who had been faithfully working with him for about fifteen years, "for the most part in unclouded friendship."* When Freud told Binswanger that "independent doubt is for me sacred in everyone," he meant it, even if he sometimes forgot this humane scientific precept in the passion of combat.

*J. E. G. van Emden was a Dutch psychoanalyst whom Freud first met in 1910. For Theodor Reik, see pp. 490–92.

Six

Therapy and Technique

However irritating the weekly meetings at his apartment grew with the years, Freud continued to use them as a sounding board. Long before he published the case histories that soon became famous, he would report on his most interesting analysands to his followers. One memorable occasion stretched over two sessions. On October 30, 1907, and again a week later, on November 6, Freud spoke to the Wednesday Psychological Society on a patient then in analysis with him. "It is a very instructive case of obsessional neurosis (obsessional ideas)," Rank laconically reported him as saying, "concerning a 29-year-old young man (Dr. jur.)" This was the germ from which the case history of the Rat Man was to grow.

The following year, in April 1908, Freud addressed the international congress of psychoanalysts in Salzburg on the same case, while the Rat Man was still in treatment. He carried his dazzled audience with him. Ernest Jones, who had just met Freud, never forgot it. "Delivered without any notes," he wrote half a century later, Freud's presentation "began at eight o'clock and at eleven he offered to bring it to a close. We had all been so enthralled, however, at his fascinating exposition that we begged him to go on, and he did so for another hour. I had never before been so oblivious of the passage of time."

Jones was at one with Wittels in his admiration for Freud's lecturing style, and particularly struck by his conversational tone, his "ease of expression, his masterly ordering of complex material, his perspicuous lucidity, and his intense earnestness." This case history was, to Jones as to the others, "both an intellectual and an artistic feast." Fortunately, psychoanalytic politics did not preempt Freud's attention even in these turbulent times. Here were glimpses, and more than glimpses, from his laboratory.

Freud's laboratory was his couch. From the early 1890s on, Freud's patients had taught him much of what he knew, forcing him to refine his technique, opening breath-taking vistas to theoretical departures, substantiating or compelling him to amend—or even to drop—cherished conjectures. That is one reason why Freud set so much store by his case histories; they were a record of his education. Gratifyingly, they proved no less educational for others, effective and elegant instruments of persuasion.* When Freud described the case of the Rat Man as very instructive, he meant that it could serve as a pedagogic text for his adherents even more than for himself. Freud never spelled out why he selected the case histories of some patients for publication rather than others. Yet taken together, these histories map the broken terrain of neurotic suffering, and they hazard the most imaginative (and risky) reconstructions. Freud presents hysterics, obsessionals, and paranoiacs, a little phobic boy he saw only once during the treatment, and the psychotic inmate of a mental hospital whom he never saw at all. The subjects of some of these elaborate and intimate portraits, notably the case of Dora, have stepped out of their frame to become, rather like characters in memorable novels, actors in their own right—or at least witnesses in the interminable controversies surrounding Freud's moral character, competence as a therapist, and essential views of the human animal, male and female alike.

---

*Ernest Jones, as we have seen (pp. 183–84), was propelled into the psychoanalytic camp after reading Freud's case history of Dora. He was only the most conspicuous of Freud's adherents to be persuaded by one of these case histories. In retrospect, these classic clinical reports may appear more impressive as didactic than as clinical performances. In recent decades, psychoanalysts benefiting from hindsight and sophisticated diagnostic techniques have gone over them with care and have become convinced that the pathology of Freud's best-known analysands was usually more severe than Freud indicated. But as teaching devices they remain authoritative models for an age that seems to have forgotten how to write case histories.

A PROBLEMATIC DEBUT

 The young woman whom the world now knows as Dora first came to Freud's consulting room in the summer of 1898, when she was sixteen, and entered psychoanalytic treatment two years later, in October 1900. She abandoned it in December, after some eleven weeks, with most of the analytic work still to be done. As early as mid-October, Freud reported to Fliess that he had a "new case," an eighteen-year-old girl, "smoothly opening for the available collection of passkeys"—an erotic metaphor whose overtones he did not choose to explore.

In January 1901, after Dora's departure, he wrote up her history rapidly, recording its completion on January 25. "It is the subtlest I have written so far," he announced, indulging in a moment of self-congratulation. But he instantly subverted his exhilaration with predictions of general disapproval: he had no doubt that the paper would put people off even more than usual. "Anyhow," he added, with his characteristic mixture of self-assurance and stoical resignation, "one does one's duty and indeed does not write just for the day." In the end, he did not publish Dora's history until 1905. This delay provided him with a minor dividend: he could append the report of an interesting visit that his former patient paid him in April 1902, a visit that elegantly rounded out Freud's failure.

The reasons for this long gestation are not wholly transparent. Freud had strong incentives to publish Dora's history promptly. Since he saw it as the "fragment" of a case "grouped around two dreams," it was "really a continuation of the dream book"—*The Interpretation of Dreams* applied on the couch. It also offered a striking illustration of an unresolved Oedipus complex at work in the formation of Dora's character and of her hysterical symptoms. Freud adduced several explanations for the delay, notably medical discretion, but these seem a little lame. He was evidently disheartened by his friend Oscar Rie's critical reception of the manuscript, and no less by the decay of his most impassioned friendship. "I withdrew my last work from the printer," he told Fliess in March 1902, "because just shortly before I had lost my last audience in you." This response seems somewhat excessive: Freud must have known that the case had much to teach anyone interested in psychoanalysis. Moreover, it fitted the pattern of his clinical publications to perfection; Dora was a hysteric, the kind of neurotic who had been the mainstay of analytic attention since the mid-1890s—in fact since Breuer's Anna O. almost two decades earlier. No doubt the case had some peculiar, vaguely uncanny meaning for Freud; when he referred to it in retrospect, he consistently pushed it back from 1900 to 1899, a symptom of some unanalyzed preoccupation. Freud's reserve hints at intimate reasons why it disconcerted him and why he kept the manuscript on his desk.

One striking piece of evidence that Freud was not wholly at ease is the preface he attached to his report on Dora: it is unusually combative even for a writer not allergic to spirited controversy. He was offering the case, Freud wrote, to instruct a reluctant and uncomprehending public in the uses of dream analysis and its relation to the understanding of neuroses. Certainly its original title, "Dream and Hysteria," aptly sums up the points Freud wished to make with it. But the reception of his *Interpretation of Dreams* had shown him, he noted in a somewhat injured tone, how unprepared specialists were for his truths: "The new has always aroused bewilderment and resistance." In the late 1890s, he noted, he had been criticized for giving no information about his patients; now he expected to be criticized for giving too much. But the analyst who publishes case histories of hysterics must enter into details of the patients' sexual life. Thus discretion, the physician's supreme duty, clashes with the demands of science, which lives on uninhibited open discussion. But he defied any of his readers to identify Dora.

For all this heavy weather, Freud was not yet ready to start on the business at hand. He accused "many physicians" in Vienna of taking a prurient interest in the kind of material he was about to present, of reading "such a case history not as a contribution to the psychopathology of neuroses, but as a *roman à clef* designed for their entertainment." This was probably true, but Freud's somewhat gratuitous vehemence suggests that his involvement with Dora was more unsettling than he suspected.

THE MOST WORLDLY reader might have been astonished, even shocked, by the sexual entanglements among which young Dora lived. Perhaps only Arthur Schnitzler, whose disenchanted stories and plays sketched the intricate choreography of Vienna's erotic life, could have imagined such a scenario. Two families were performing a ballet of covert sensual self-indulgence draped in the most assiduous propriety. The protagonists were Dora's father, a prosperous and intelligent manufacturer who, suffering from the aftermath of tuberculosis and of a syphilitic infection he had contracted before his marriage, had been Freud's patient and had brought his daughter to him; her mother, to judge by all reports foolish and uncultivated, a fanatical, obsessive house cleaner; her older brother, with whom her relations were strained, and who would take his mother's side in domestic disputes, just as she, Dora, could be counted on to back her father.* The case was rounded out by the members of the K. family, to which Dora and her family had become very much attached: Frau K. had nursed Dora's father during one of his severe illnesses, and Dora had taken care of the young K. children. Despite the discord in Dora's household, the cast looked very much like two respectable, domestic, bourgeois families companionably helping one another out.

They were anything but that. When Dora was sixteen, growing into an engaging and good-looking young woman, she abruptly declared her detestation of Herr K., hitherto her affectionate older friend. Four years earlier, she had begun to show some signs of hysteria, notably migraines and a nervous cough. Now her afflictions intensified. Once attractive and lively, she acquired a repertory of disagreeable symptoms: beyond her cough a hysterical whisper (aphonia), intervals of depression, irrational hostility, even thoughts of suicide. She provided an explanation for her unhappy state: Herr K., whom she had long liked and trusted, had made a sexual advance to her during a walk; deeply offended, she had slapped him. Confronted with the charge, Herr K. denied it and went on the offensive: Dora cared about nothing but sex and was exciting herself with lubricious literature. Her father was inclined to take Herr K.'s word and dismissed Dora's accusations as a fantasy. But Freud, after he took Dora into analysis, was struck by certain contradictions in her father's story, and decided to reserve judgment. This was the most sympathetic moment in Freud's psychoanalytic relationship with Dora, which would be marred by mutual hostility and a certain insensitivity on the analyst's part. Freud proposed to wait for Dora's revelations.

They proved worth waiting for. Her father, it came out, had told the truth only about one thing: his wife brought him no sexual satisfaction. But while he was parading his ill health before Freud, he had actually compensated himself for his domestic frustrations by carrying on a passionate love affair with Frau K. The liaison did not remain a secret to Dora. Observant and suspicious, she became convinced that her adored father had refused to believe her anguished denunciation for his own scabrous reason: by selling her to Herr K., he could continue to sleep with Frau K. undisturbed. Yet there were still other erotic crosscurrents; penetrating to the truth of this illicit affair, Dora half consciously made herself its accomplice. Before she broke off her eleven-week analysis with Freud, he had discovered in her passionate

---

*"Thus," Freud placidly commented, "the usual sexual attraction had brought father and daughter on one side, mother and son on the other, closer together." ("Dora," GW V, 178/SE VII, 21.)

feelings for Herr K., for her father, and for Frau K., feelings she partially confirmed. Puppy love, incest, and lesbian desires were competing for pre-eminence in her anxious adolescent mind. At least this is how Freud read Dora.

Herr K.'s amorous proposition was, in Freud's judgment, in no way sufficient to account for Dora's florid hysterical symptoms, which had emerged even before she had grown resentful at her father's mean-spirited betrayal. Freud thought that not even an earlier traumatic incident that Dora disclosed to him could have caused her hysteria; rather, he saw her response as proof that the hysteria was already in existence when the incident occurred. When Dora was fourteen, a full two years before Herr K. had made his disputed advance, he had waylaid her in his office, suddenly embraced her, and kissed her passionately on the lips. She had responded to this assault with disgust. Freud interpreted that disgust as a reversal of affect and a displacement of sensations; the whole episode struck him as a perfect hysterical scene. Herr K.'s erotic advance, Freud flatly said, "was surely the situation that would call up in a fourteen-year-old innocent girl a distinct feeling of sexual excitement," caused in part by feeling the man's erect member against her body. But Dora had displaced her sensation upward, to her throat.

Freud was not insinuating that Dora should have yielded to Herr K.'s importunities at fourteen—or, for that matter, at sixteen. But he thought it only obvious that such an encounter should generate a measure of sexual arousal, and that Dora's response was a symptom of her hysteria. Such a reading follows naturally from Freud's posture as a psychoanalytic detective and a critic of bourgeois morality. Intent on digging beneath polite social surfaces, and committed to the proposition that modern sexuality was screened by an almost impenetrable blend of unconscious denial and conscious mendacity, particularly among the respectable classes, Freud felt virtually obliged to interpret Dora's vehement rejection of Herr K. as a neurotic defense. He had met the man and had found him, after all, an agreeable and handsome person. But Freud's inability to enter Dora's sensibilities speaks to a failure of empathy that marks his handling of the case as a whole. He refused to recognize her need as an adolescent for trustworthy guidance in a cruelly self-serving adult world—for someone to value her shock at the transformation of an intimate friend into an ardent suitor, to appreciate her indignation at this coarse violation of her trust. This refusal testifies also to Freud's general difficulty in visualizing erotic encounters from the woman's perspective. Dora wanted desperately to be believed, not to be thought a liar or a fantast, and Freud was willing to accept her story rather than her father's denials. But that was as far as he was prepared to go in seeing her side of the case.

HERR K.'S SEXUAL aggressions were not the only scenes in Dora's drama whose implications Freud failed to explore sympathetically. Almost on principle unwilling to accept Dora's qualms about his interpretations, he stood ready to read her denials as covert affirmations. In line with his practice at that time, much modified later, he offered immediate and energetic interpretations. Insisting that she was in love with her father, he took her "most emphatic contradiction" as proof that he was right in his conjecture. "The 'No' one hears from a patient after one has presented his conscious perception with a repressed thought for the first time only registers the repression and its decisive character and, as it were, measures its strength. If one takes this 'No' not as the expression of an impartial judgment, of which the patient is in fact not capable, disregards it, and continues the work, proofs will soon appear that 'No' in such a case signifies the desired 'Yes.' " Freud thus opened himself to the charge of insensitivity, and worse, of sheer dogmatic arrogance: though a professional listener, he was not listening now, but forcing his analysand's communications into a predetermined pattern. This largely implicit claim to virtual omniscience invited criticism; it suggested Freud's certainty that all psychoanalytic interpretations are automatically correct, whether the analysand accepts them or disdains them. "Yes" means "Yes," and so does "No."*

Freud's interpretations leave the impression that he viewed Dora less as a patient pleading for help than as a challenge to be mastered. Many of his interventions proved beneficial. Discussing her father's relationship with Frau K., Dora had insisted that it was a love affair, but also that he was impotent, a contradiction she resolved by telling Freud, candidly, that she knew one could secure sexual gratification in more than one way. Associating to her troublesome symptoms—her impaired speech and irritated throat—Freud told Dora that she must be thinking of oral sex, or, as he put it, delicately lapsing into Latin, of "sexual satisfaction *per os*," and she tacitly confirmed the validity of this interpretation by shedding her cough. But Freud's almost angry insistence that Dora endorse the psychological truths he was offering calls for an interpretation of its own. After all, by 1900, Freud was aware that

---

*Freud did not confront the perils of such a stance at that time; he would do so explicitly only years later. "If the patient agrees with us," he wrote in one of his last papers in 1937, paraphrasing some unnamed critic, "then [we are] right; but if he contradicts us, then that is only a sign of his resistance, which again puts us in the right. In this way we are always in the right against the helpless poor individual whom we are analyzing, no matter what attitude he may take toward our imputations." And he quoted the saying, in English, "Heads I win, tails you lose," as a condensation of what is generally thought to be psychoanalytic procedure. But actually, he demurred, this is not how analysts work. They are as skeptical of their analysands' assents as they are of their denials. ("Konstruktionen in der Analyse" [1937], *GW* XVI, 41–56/"Constructions in Analysis," *SE* XXIII, 257–69.)

resistance to unwelcome revelations are perfectly predictable, as the analyst probes into recesses the patient has kept carefully out of the sunlight for years, even if he did not yet recognize that to put pressure on a patient was a technical lapse. With later patients he would be less exigent, less overbearing, partly because of the lessons Dora taught him.

The vigorous and voluble interpretations Freud lavished on Dora have a dictatorial air about them. In the first of Dora's two revealing dreams, she had dreamt of a small jewel case which her mother wanted to save from a burning house over the protests of her father, who insisted on saving his children instead. Listening to her recital, Freud fastened on the jewel case that her mother seemed to value so highly. When he asked Dora for her associations, she remembered that Herr K. had given her just such a case, an expensive one. Now, the word *Schmuckkästchen,* Freud reminded her, stood for the female genitals. Whereupon Dora: "I knew that *you* would say that." Freud's response: "That is, *you* knew it.—The meaning of the dream is now becoming even more distinct. You said to yourself, 'The man is pursuing me, he wants to force his way into my room, my 'jewel case' is in danger, and if something unfortunate happens it will be Papa's fault.' That is why you took into the dream a situation expressing the opposite, a danger from which your Papa saves you. In this region of the dream in general everything is turned into its opposite; you will soon hear why. The secret, certainly, lies with your Mama. How does Mama come in here? She is, as you know, your former rival for the favor of your Papa." And Freud keeps up the pace for another page, emitting a very torrent of interpretations in which Dora's mother stands for Frau K. and Dora's father for Herr K.; it is Herr K. to whom she will hand her jewel case in return for his extravagant gift. "Thus you are prepared to give Herr K. as a present what his wife refuses him. Here you have the thought which has to be repressed with so much energy, which necessitates the conversion of all elements into their opposite. As I already told you before this dream, the dream confirms once again that you are reawakening your old love for Papa in order to protect yourself from your love for K. But what do all these efforts prove? Not only that you are afraid of Herr K.; you are even more afraid of yourself, of the temptation to yield to him. Thus you confirm how intense your love for him was."

Freud was not astonished at Dora's reception of this outpouring: "Naturally, Dora did not want to follow me in this piece of interpretation." But the question the interpretation raises is not whether Freud's reading of Dora's dream was correct or merely ingenious. What matters is his insistent tone, his refusal to take Dora's doubts as anything but convenient denials of inconvenient truths. This was Freud's share in the ultimate failure.

FAILURE, OF COURSE, both recognized and unrecognized, is the hallmark of this case, but—paradoxically—precisely this failure constitutes its ultimate significance for psychoanalytic history. Freud, we know, took it as a demonstration of the uses of dream analysis in psychoanalytic treatment and as confirmation of the rules which, he had discovered, govern dream construction. Moreover, it beautifully exhibited the complexities of hysteria. But one crucial reason why Freud finally published "Dora" was his inability to keep his troublesome patient in analysis.

In late December 1900, Freud worked on Dora's second dream, which satisfactorily confirmed his hypothesis that she had been unconsciously in love with Herr K. all along. But at the start of the next session, Dora blithely announced that this was her last. Freud took the unexpected announcement coolly, proposed that they use their final hour continuing to analyze, and interpreted for her, with new detail, her innermost feelings for the man who had insulted her. "She had listened, without contradicting as usual. She seemed moved, said farewell in the most amiable way with warm wishes for the New Year—and did not come back."

Freud interpreted her gesture as an act of revenge, animated by the neurotic desire to harm herself. She had left him at a moment when "my expectations of a successful termination of the treatment were at their highest pitch." He wondered out loud whether he might have kept Dora in treatment if he had theatrically exaggerated her importance to him and thus provided her with a substitute for the affection she craved. "I do not know." All he knew was, "I have always avoided playing a role, and contented myself with the unpretentious art of psychology." Then, on April 1, 1902, Dora returned for a visit, professedly to ask for help once again. Freud, observing her, was not convinced. Except for one period, she told him, she had been feeling much better. Having faced down both Frau and Herr K., she had secured confessions from them; her reports about them had been true. But for a couple of weeks she had been suffering from a facial neuralgia. Freud records that at this point he smiled: exactly two weeks before, the newspapers had announced his promotion to his professorship, and so he could read her facial pains as a form of self-punishment for having once slapped Herr K. and then transferring her rage onto him, her analyst. Freud told Dora he forgave her for depriving him of the opportunity to cure her completely. But he could not apparently quite forgive himself.

THE PERPLEXITY IN which Freud found himself as Dora dismissed him resembled his perplexity during the summer of 1897, as his seduction theory of neuroses had proved to be untenable. He had taken that earlier defeat as a foundation for far-reaching theoretical discoveries. Now he confronted this new defeat, explored its causes, and thus moved psychoanalytic technique forward a giant step. He frankly admitted that he had failed to "master the transference in time"; indeed, he had "forgotten to take the precaution of paying attention to the first signs of the transference." The emotional bond between analysand and analyst was only beginning to be understood when Freud worked with Dora. He had ventured some sketchy anticipations in *Studies on Hysteria*, and his letters to Fliess of the late 1890s show that he had already glimpsed, though far from wholly grasped, the phenomenon. Now, with Dora, for reasons of his own, he failed to build on what he had begun to understand. The case seems to have been the one that largely clarified the issue for him—but only after it was over.

The transference is the patient's way, sometimes subtle and often blatant, of endowing the analyst with qualities that properly belong to beloved (or hated) persons, past or present, in the "real" world. Freud now recognized that this psychological maneuver, "which seems destined to become the greatest obstacle to psychoanalysis," can also become "its most powerful auxiliary when it can be discovered and translated for the patient." But he had not discovered this while working with Dora, certainly not in time, and in her willful, somewhat unpleasant way, she had proved to him the costs of such neglect. By failing to observe her "infatuation" with him, which was only a substitute for the secret feelings she harbored for others, Freud had allowed her to exact on him the revenge she had wanted to visit on Herr K. "Thus she acted out an essential piece of her memories and fantasies instead of reproducing them in the treatment," and that inevitably led to the disruption of the analytic work.

This abrupt end hurt Dora, Freud thought; she had been, after all, on the road to recovery. But it also hurt Freud. "He who, like me, awakens the most wicked demons that he may fight them," he exclaimed in the most rhetorical passage of his recitation, "demons who dwell incompletely tamed in the human breast, must be prepared to suffer damage himself in this contest." But while he felt the injury, he could not clearly define it, for it touched him too closely. Freud could see that he had neglected to recognize Dora's transference onto him; but, worse, he had failed to recognize his transference onto Dora: the action of what he came to call countertransference had escaped his analytical self-observation.

As Freud later defined it, countertransference is an affect arising in the psychoanalyst "through the patient's influence on the analyst's unconscious feelings." Freud's continuing self-analysis had made self-scrutiny almost second nature to him, but the problematic influence of patients on the analyst never loomed large in his mind or in his technical papers.* He did not doubt, however, that countertransference is an insidious obstruction to the analyst's benevolent neutrality, a resistance to be diagnosed and defeated. It does to the psychoanalyst what unacknowledged bias does to the historian. The analyst—he sternly laid it down in 1910—"must recognize this countertransference in himself and master it," for "every psychoanalyst only gets as far as his own complexes and inner resistances allow." But as his conduct in the analytic sessions with Dora shows, he was far from invulnerable to her efforts at seduction and to her irritating hostility. That was one lesson of the case: Freud could be assailed by emotions that at times clouded his perceptions as a therapist.†

Yet this was the very case in which Freud proclaimed the sovereignty of the skilled observer who can glean information from the faintest movement, the slightest flicker. "He who has eyes to see and ears to hear," he wrote in a famous line, "becomes convinced that mortals can keep no secret. If their lips are silent, they gossip with their fingertips; betrayal forces its way through every pore."‡ As Dora lay before her analyst on the couch, dilating on her misery at home, recounting her adventures with the K. family, and trying to make sense of a dream, she played with her little purse, opening and closing it, pushing her finger into it over and over. Freud promptly interpreted her little gesture as a pantomime of masturbation. But Freud's emotional stake in Dora is harder to read than her gesture with the purse. "Of course," as he once confessed to Ernest Jones, "there is a great difficulty if not impossibility in recognising actual psychical processes" in one's own person.

It would be naive to insinuate that Freud was in love with this good-looking and difficult adolescent, however appealing she may have been to him at times. Rather, his principal feelings toward Dora seem to have been rather more negative. In addition to sheer interest in Dora as a fascinating hysteric, he showed a certain impatience, irritation, and in the end, undisguised disap-

---

*In recent years, some psychoanalysts have forcefully argued that they often find it profitable to enlist the unconscious feelings their analysands arouse in them to deepen their understanding of these analysands' minds at work. But this position would have found scant sympathy with Freud.

†By the mid-1920s, psychoanalytic institutes would expect candidates to uncover, and if possible master, their complexes and resistances by means of the didactic analysis that was by then an indispensable part of their training; seasoned practitioners, for their part, would consult a colleague if they had reason to believe that they were not listening to an analysand with the required clinical attitude. When Freud wrote "Dora," no such remedies were at hand.

‡Laurence Sterne, that psychological novelist before his time, had already said something very much like it a century and a half earlier: "There are a thousand unnoticed openings, continued my father, which let a penetrating eye at once into a man's soul; and I maintain it, added he, that a man of sense does not lay down his hat in coming into a room,—or take it up in going out of it, but something escapes, which discovers him." (*Tristram Shandy,* book VI, ch. 5.)

pointment. The rage to cure was upon him. It was a passion Freud would later deride as inimical to the psychoanalytic process. But with Dora he was in its grip. He was only too sure that he had access to the truth about Dora's twisted emotional life, but Dora would not accept that truth, even though he had proved to her the curative powers of cogent interpretations. Had he not exorcised her nervous cough by means of interpretation? He was right about her, knew he was right, and felt utterly frustrated that she should be so determined to prove him wrong. What is astonishing about the case history of Dora is not that Freud delayed it for four years, but that he published it at all.

Two Classic Lessons

 In pleasing contrast to the case of Dora, that of Little Hans was wholly gratifying to Freud. In the four years between the publication of the two case histories, much had happened in Freud's life. In 1905, he had published, in addition to "Dora," the epochal essays concerning the theory of sexuality and his psychoanalytic study of jokes. In 1906, the year he turned fifty, he had transformed the Wednesday Psychological Society by making Rank its secretary, broadened the base of the psychoanalytic movement by taking up contact with interested psychiatrists in Zurich, broken publicly with Fliess, and published his first major collection of papers on the neuroses. In 1907, he played host to Eitingon, Jung, Abraham, and other important adherents at Berggasse 19 for the first time. In 1908, the year Little Hans occupied his attention, he reorganized his Wednesday-night group as the Vienna Psychoanalytic Society, presided over the first international congress of psychoanalysts in Salzburg, and visited his beloved England for the second time in his life. In 1909, he went to Clark University for his only American visit, to lecture and receive an honorary degree, and inaugurated the *Jahrbuch für psychoanalytische und psychopathologische Forschungen*, with the history of Little Hans as the lead-off contribution to the first number. He was very pleased with it.

"I AM GLAD you see the importance of 'klein Hans,' " he wrote to Ernest Jones in June of that year. He too had seen the importance of this "Analysis of a Phobia in a Five-Year-Old Boy," he noted. "I never got a finer insight into a child's soul." Nor did Freud's affection for his youngest "patient" wane after the treatment was over; he remained "our little hero." The general idea Freud wanted to enforce with this case history was that Little Hans's "childhood neurosis" corroborated the conjectures which Freud's adult neurotic patients had encouraged him to explore: the "pathogenic material" that makes them suffer can be "traced back every time to the very infantile complexes that could be uncovered behind Hans's phobia." As we have seen, the history of Dora, with its exhaustive analysis of two dreams, had demonstrated the relevance of Freud's *Interpretation of Dreams* to the clinical setting and the sizable share of oedipal feelings in the making of hysteria. The report on Little Hans could serve as a pendant, illustrating the conclusions Freud had outlined in lapidary fashion in his second fundamental treatise, the *Three Essays on the Theory of Sexuality.* As usual, Freud the clinician and Freud the theorist never let one another out of sight.*

Freud had deliberately said little about technique in "Dora," and he said even less about it in "Little Hans." With good reason: while he had visited the little boy and taken him a present for his third birthday, he now worked almost exclusively through his father, who served as an intermediary. By its nature, then, however broad its theoretical implications, "Little Hans," with its most unorthodox technique, hardly commended itself as an exemplar. It must remain unique. The five-year-old in analysis was the son of the musicologist Max Graf, who had been for some years a member of Freud's Wednesday-night group. The boy's "beautiful" mother—it is Freud's word—had been Freud's patient, and together his parents were among the earliest adherents of psychoanalysis anywhere. They had agreed to raise their son according to Freudian principles, with as little coercion as possible; they were patient with him, took an interest in his chatter, recorded his dreams, and found his childish promiscuity in love entertaining. He was enamored of everyone: his mother, the daughters of a family friend, a boy cousin. Freud noted with undisguised admiration that Little Hans had developed into a "paragon of every wickedness!" When he began to show neurotic symptoms, his parents resolved, consistent with their principles, not to bully him.

At the same time, their psychoanalytic style of rearing their son did not protect the Grafs from falling into the dominant cultural evasions. When Little Hans was three and a half, his mother found him touching his penis and warned him that she would call the doctor to cut off his "wi-wi-maker." Again, when around this time his sister was born—"the great event in Hans's life"—his parents had nothing more original to offer by way of preparing him

---

*Freud also used material from the Little Hans case in two short related papers he published at this time, one on the sexual theories of children, the other on their sexual enlightenment.

than the legend of the stork. At this point Hans was more reasonable than his presumably enlightened parents. His investigations into the facts of life, especially into the process of birth, had made early and impressive progress, and in the course of his analysis, he let his father know in his shrewd little-boy way that he viewed the stork story with contempt. Later, when they partially enlightened him, they told him that babies grow inside their mothers and are then painfully pressed out the way a "lumf," as Hans called a turd, is pressed out. The tale only intensified the little boy's interest in "lumfs." But beyond displaying a certain precocity in his observations, his speech, and his erotic interests, Little Hans was growing up a cheerful, lovable bourgeois boy.

Then in January 1908, something unexplained and unpleasant happened. Little Hans developed a crippling fear that a horse would bite him. He grew afraid, too, that large dray horses pulling wagons might fall down, and he began to avoid the places where he might encounter them. Max Graf, father, hero, villain, and his son's private healer in one, began to interview his son and to interpret the meanings of Little Hans's phobias, reporting to Freud frequently and in detail. He was inclined to attribute the boy's anxieties to sexual overstimulation generated by his wife's excessive tenderness. Another of his suspicions, which Little Hans came to share, was that his masturbating was the source of those anxieties. But Freud, as usual willing to wait before offering a diagnosis, was not convinced. In accord with his early theorizing about anxiety, Freud conjectured that the trouble stemmed rather from Hans's "repressed erotic longing" for his mother, whom in his boyish way he kept trying to seduce.* His repressed erotic and aggressive wishes were transformed into anxiety, which then fastened on a particular object to be feared and avoided—this was the horse phobia.

Freud's way of attending to Little Hans's symptom was characteristic of his analytic style: he took reports about mental states seriously, no matter how absurd or apparently trivial they might appear. "A little boy's foolish anxious idea, one may say. But a neurosis never says anything foolish, any more than a dream. We always scold," Freud commented, frowning at his readers, "when we don't understand. That is to make things easy for oneself." In one of his few observations on technique in this account, Freud ventured to criticize Hans's father for pushing his son too hard: "He asks too much and investigates in accord with his own presuppositions instead of letting the little boy express himself." Freud had made that mistake with Dora, but now he knew rather better, and the emotional stakes were not quite so high—at least not for him. To follow Max Graf's method, he warned, is to make an analysis

*For Freud's theories of anxiety, see pp. 484–87.

"impenetrable and insecure." Psychoanalysis, as Freud had been saying since the 1890s, and usually remembered, is the art and science of patient listening.

Little Hans's phobia became more pervasive. He was reluctant to leave his house, but when he did, he sometimes felt compelled to look at horses. At the zoo, he would avoid the large animals, which he had liked before, but continued to take delight in the smaller ones. The penises on the elephants and giraffes evidently bothered him; Hans's preoccupation with genitalia— his own, his father's, his mother's, his little sister's, those of animals—was threatening to develop into an obsession. But Freud found it necessary to dispute Max Graf's obvious inference that his son was afraid of big penises. The conclusion to one conversation on Little Hans's favorite subject that his father recorded for Freud supplied an invaluable clue: "You were probably frightened"—the father is speaking—"when you saw the horse's big wi-wi-maker, but you need not be frightened of that. Big animals have big wi-wi-makers, little animals, little wi-wi-makers." Hans's reply: "And all people have wi-wi-makers. And my wi-wi-maker is growing with me when I get bigger; after all, it's attached." To Freud this was a clear signal that Little Hans was afraid of losing his own "wi-wi-maker." The technical term for that fear is castration anxiety.

AT THIS STAGE of the analysis the young patient and his father came to consult Freud, who now heard for the first time, and saw, material that greatly advanced the resolution of Little Hans's malaise. The threatening horses stood in part for Hans's father, who was equipped with a big black mustache just as the horses were with their big black muzzles. Hans, it turned out, was mortally afraid that his father was angry with him because he could not contain his overwhelming love for his mother and his obscure death wishes against his father. The biting horse was a stand-in for his angry father; the falling horse, for his dead father. Little Hans's fear of horses, then, was a sophisticated evasion, a way of coping with emotions he did not dare avow freely to himself or to anyone else.* He experienced his conflicts all the more painfully because he also loved the father whose rival he fancied himself to be, just as he harbored sadistic wishes against his mother in tandem with his passionate affection for her. The travail of Little Hans underscored for Freud

---

*The American psychoanalyst Joseph William Slap has offered an intriguing complementary (rather than contradictory) interpretation of Little Hans's fear of horses: In February 1908, in the second month of his neurosis, the little boy had his tonsils out (see "Little Hans," SE X, 29), and at this point his phobia grew worse. Shortly thereafter, he explicitly identified white horses as biting horses. On the basis of this and related evidence in Freud's history, Slap suggests that little Hans probably added his fear of the surgeon (with his mask and his white coat) to his fear of his mustachioed father. (Joseph William Slap, "Little Hans's Tonsillectomy," Psychoanalytic Quarterly, XXX [1961], 259–61.)

the ubiquitous working of ambivalence in mental life. Hans would punch his father and then kiss the spot he had hit. This was emblematic of a general human disposition; ambivalence is the rule in the oedipal triangle, not the exception.

From the moment that Freud kindly interpreted these realities to his five-year-old patient, Hans's phobia began to recede and his anxiety to disappear. He had distorted his unacceptable wishes and fears into symptoms. His way of dealing with bowel movements, the "lumfs" that came out, was characteristic of this defensive distortion: he thought about them inquisitively, but translated the pleasurable and exciting associations with his conjectures about them—babies are like so many "lumfs"—into unconscious shame and then into an overt expression of disgust. In the same way Hans's phobia, that source of troubling uneasiness, was the offspring of such activities as vigorously playing horse, which had once given him keen enjoyment. His case was a splendid illustration of defense mechanisms at work in the oedipal phase.

As Hans's analysis took hold, as he gained greater inner freedom, he could admit that he harbored death wishes against his little sister. He could also deal with, and talk about, his "lumf" theory and about the thought of being at once a mother and a father to his children, whom he would bear anally. These were tentative confessions, for he took them back as soon as he had made them. He wanted children, he said, and (in the same breath) he did *not* want children. But to admit to such feelings and such conjectures at all was a leap toward cure. Indeed, throughout his treatment, Little Hans showed extraordinary analytic acumen; he rejected his father's notions about his neurosis if they were offered at the wrong time or with intolerable intensity, and intelligently distinguished between thoughts and actions. He knew at age five that wishing and doing are not the same thing. Hence he could insist on his right to plead innocent in face of his most aggressive wishes. When he told his father that he thought—really, wished—that his little sister might fall into the bath water and die, the elder Graf interpreted the remark: "And then you would be alone with Mummy. And a good boy doesn't wish for that!" Little Hans, unfazed, rejoined, *"But he may think it."* When his father objected, "That isn't good," Hans had a ready response: *"If he thinks it, it's good just the same, so that one can write it to the Professor."* The Professor could not conceal his admiration: "Bravo, Little Hans! I could wish for no better understanding of psychoanalysis from any adult." The resolution of his oedipal conflicts was quite as inspiriting: he imagined his father married to *his* mother; thus he, Little Hans, could keep the elder Graf alive and at the same time marry his mother and have children with her.

The trail that Freud followed to expose the villain in Little Hans's psychological drama was far shorter, far less tortuous, than the trail would have been if Freud had been asked, a dozen or so years later, to analyze Big Hans: "The physician who treats an adult psychoanalytically, at last reaches through his work of uncovering psychical formations, layer by layer, certain hypotheses about the infantile sexuality in whose components he believes he has found the motive forces of all the neurotic symptoms of later life." With Little Hans, there was no need for such deep digging. If Freud, with evident satisfaction, claimed for the case "typical and exemplary significance," that was precisely because it condensed so perspicuously what analyses of adults were compelled to unravel in time-consuming labor.

One theory this unconventional psychoanalysis of a child exemplified was that of the Oedipus complex, which, we know, Freud had been able to complicate considerably since he had first broached the idea a decade or so earlier. Little Hans was no less informative about the work of repression, was in fact a veritable textbook case with his transparent self-protective maneuvers. A five-year-old, though he is well on his way toward erecting psychological defenses like shame, disgust, and prudery, has not yet consolidated them. Certainly, Freud suggested in his best anti-bourgeois manner, they are still far from being the steep and solid fortifications that will protectively hem in the adult, particularly in modern middle-class culture. This look at the history of repression in a growing child allowed Freud to say some sharp words in behalf of candor in the canvassing of sexual matters with the young. Hence the case study of Little Hans is more than a copious anthology of psychoanalytic propositions: it hints at the impact Freud's thinking would come to have outside the consulting room—though not yet in 1909, and not for some years after.

Freud was satisfied that the analysis of Little Hans had not had the dubious benefit of suggestion; the clinical picture made sense, the patient had assented to interpretations only when they fitted. Besides, Hans had conquered his anxieties and his phobia. In a short postscript added thirteen years later, in 1922, Freud triumphantly reported a visit from a "sturdy young man of nineteen," Little Hans grown up. Herbert Graf, later to become a well-known producer and director of operas, stood before him. Freud could not help gloating that the dire forecast of his critics had not been realized. They had predicted that the analysis would rob the little boy of his innocence and ruin his future. Freud could tell them that they had been proved wrong. Hans's parents had been divorced and had remarried, but their son had survived this ordeal, like that of his puberty, without apparent damage. What Freud found particularly interesting was his visitor's observation that when he looked at the case history, he felt he was reading about a complete stranger. It was rather like Martin Freud being unable to recall what his father had said to make him regain his self-respect after his humiliating confrontation at the skating rink.* Hans's comment was a reminder to Freud that the most successful analyses are the ones the analysand forgets after termination.

DORA WAS HYSTERIC, Little Hans phobic, the Rat Man, yet another of Freud's classic patients, was obsessive. He was most suitable, then, for inclusion in Freud's repertory of published case histories. We know that Freud thought the Rat Man's case very instructive, as instructive in its way as Dora's had been. But he liked him much better: it was Freud himself who referred to his famous patient informally, with a measure of affection, as the *Rattenmann*, or, in English, as the "man of the rats." The treatment started on October 1, 1907, and lasted rather less than a year, setting a pace that analysts of later generations would consider breath-taking rather than deliberate. But Freud claimed that it was enough to relieve the Rat Man's symptoms. Yet he could not defeat history. Looking back at the great slaughter of the First World War, he concluded somberly in a footnote added to the report in 1923, "The patient perished, like so many other valuable and promising young men, in the Great War."

The case had everything in its favor. Ernst Lanzer, a twenty-nine-year-old lawyer, struck Freud from the first meeting as clearheaded and shrewd. He was also entertaining; he told his analyst amusing stories and presented him with an apposite quotation from Nietzsche about the power of pride over memory which Freud happily quoted more than once.† Lanzer's obsessive symptoms were obtrusive and bizarre. Freud had discovered in his practice that obsessive neurotics can be interesting, with their self-contradictions and perverse logic. Rational and superstitious at once, they sport symptoms that conceal and reveal their origins, and are beset by maddening doubts. The Rat Man displayed this symptomatology more flamboyantly than most: as his treatment progressed, oscillating between the patient's communications and his analyst's interpretations, adult illness and infantile appetites, thwarted sexual needs and aggressive wishes, it became a model for the elucidation of obsessional neuroses as Freud then understood them.

They urgently called for such a model. As Freud noted in the introduction to this case history, obsessional neurotics are far harder to read than hysterics: the resistances they mobilize in the clinical setting are remarkable for their ingenious obstructiveness. For, while "the language of the obsessional neurosis" is often free of puzzling conversion symptoms, it is, so to speak, "only

*See pp. 161–62.
†See p. 129.

a dialect of the hysterical language." To compound the obscurities, an obsessional will simulate health as long as possible and seek out the psychoanalyst's help only when very sick indeed. All this, combined with the need for discretion, prevented Freud from making this case report complete. He could offer nothing more than "crumbs of insight" which were, he thought, in themselves perhaps not very satisfactory. "But the work of other investigators may link up with it." The year Freud wrote these words, after all, was 1909; by now there were other investigators on whom he thought he could count.

Apart from a handful of interesting deviations, the case history Freud published generally followed the process notes he made every night. In the introductory hour the patient presented himself and listed his complaints: fears that something terrible might happen to his father and to a young woman he loved; criminal impulses like the wish to kill people and retributive ones like the urge to cut his own throat with a razor; obsessive preoccupations, some of them centering on almost ludicrously insignificant matters such as repaying negligible debts. He then volunteered some details about his sexual life. When Freud asked why he had lit on this theme, the Rat Man acknowledged that he thought this would suit Freud's theories, of which he in fact knew virtually nothing. But after that, the Rat Man proceeded on his own.

Following this first hour, Freud acquainted the Rat Man with the "fundamental rule" of psychoanalysis: he would have to report everything, however frivolous or senseless, that came into his mind. Accordingly, the Rat Man started talking about a friend whose counsel he greatly appreciated, particularly when his impulses to commit murder or suicide troubled him most, and then he launched—"quite abruptly," Freud commented—into a recital of his sexual life in childhood. Like all early communications in the course of a psychoanalysis, this choice of initial topics—his male friend and his desire for women—had a significance that the analysis would gradually unravel. The topics the Rat Man chose pointed both to the episodic emergence of strong homosexual impulses in his childhood and adolescence and to even stronger, precociously developed, heterosexual passions.

In fact, it became quite obvious before long that the Rat Man's sexual activity had begun unusually early. He recalled pretty young governesses whom he had espied in seductive undress or whose genitals he had fondled. His sisters, too, had been of absorbing sexual interest to him; observing them, playing with them, was virtually incest accomplished. But soon the young Rat Man found his sexual curiosity, including the pressing wish to see women naked, undermined by the "uncanny feeling" that he must prevent such thoughts from arising lest, say, his father die. Thus in the opening phase of his treatment, the Rat Man threw a bridge from the past to the present: his father had died some years before, but his fear for him had somehow persisted. This uncanny feeling, first experienced when he was about six, yet still remaining extremely disturbing to him, was, the Rat Man told Freud, "the beginning of my illness."

But Freud had a different diagnosis: the events of his patient's sixth or seventh year were "not merely the beginning of his illness, but already that illness itself." In order to grasp "the complicated organization of his later illness," Freud thought, it was necessary to recognize that the six-year-old boy, that "little voluptuary," already displayed "a complete obsessional neurosis lacking no essential element, at once the nucleus and the prototype of his later disease."

This was a rich beginning. But the Rat Man kept up the pace; he recounted to Freud with deep emotion the event that had sent him into psychoanalysis. On military maneuvers he had heard a captain describe a particularly horrifying punishment practiced in the Orient. At this moment, dramatically interrupting himself, the Rat Man stopped, got off the couch, and pleaded with Freud to spare him the rest. Freud instead gave his patient a short lesson in technique. Disclaiming all inclinations to cruelty, he insisted that he could not give what was not at his disposal. "The overcoming of resistances is a law of the treatment." What he could do was to assist the Rat Man in finishing the story sentence by broken sentence: someone convicted of a crime was tied down, a pot with rats in it was turned upside down on his buttocks, and the rats would—here the Rat Man got up again in great agitation—bore their way into . . . "Into his anus," Freud supplied the decisive last word.*

Observing the Rat Man closely during this recital, Freud noticed in his patient's face "a very strange composite expression" which he could unriddle only as *"one of horror before a pleasure of his unknown to him."* It was a slight intimation, nothing more, which Freud filed away for later use. Whatever the Rat Man's concealed mixed feelings about the rat punishment might be, he told Freud that he visualized the young lady he adored, as well as his father, being subjected to it. Then, when such awful ideas invaded him, he would call elaborate obsessive thoughts and actions to his rescue.

These salvage operations resisted rational understanding and presented Freud with aesthetic as well as clinical puzzles of the first order. The Rat Man told Freud an involved, barely coherent, and it would seem trifling story about some money he owed a fellow officer, or perhaps a clerk at a post office, for a package containing some eyeglasses he had ordered. Freud glossed his conscientious account of his patient's absurd preoccupations and odd ideas

---

*Later psychoanalysts would have refrained and let the Rat Man flounder, and then would have interpreted his tormented hesitations.

by sympathizing with his audience: "I would not be surprised, if at this point the reader fails to follow me." Even Freud, intent above all on extracting meaning from the Rat Man's thoughts and ceremonies, found some of them "senseless and incomprehensible." But then, the Rat Man experienced his symptoms, whether inexplicable or ludicrous, as virtually unbearable. Freud appreciated this; still, at times they drove him almost to despair. With their extraordinary expenditures of energy on the unimportant, their seeming irrelevance and illegibility, and their repetitiveness, obsessive symptoms may become as boring as they are irrational.

Freud, the most literary of psychoanalysts, could not rest satisfied with serving up a dry case report or a collection of undigested observations; he wanted to reconstruct a human drama. But the material the Rat Man scattered with such abandon—material strange, copious, apparently pointless— threatened to elude Freud's control. He complained to Jung as he was completing his case history, "It is very hard for me, almost surpasses my arts of presentation, will probably be inaccessible to anyone except those closest to us. How botched our reproductions are, how miserably we pick apart these great art works of psychic nature!" Jung privately agreed. Writing to Ferenczi, he grumbled that while Freud's paper on the Rat Man was wonderful, it was also *very hard to understand. I will soon have to read it for the third time. Am I especially stupid? Or is it the style? I cautiously opt for the latter."* Freud would have blamed the subject matter instead.

In his bewilderment, Freud resorted to technique to provide a map to the maze. The point was not to set about rationally solving the puzzles that the Rat Man had set, but to let him pursue his own path—and to listen. Freud in fact converted the case history of the Rat Man into a small feast of psychoanalytic technique applied and explained; he repeatedly interrupted his account with brief excursions into clinical procedure. He instructed his patient in the difference between the conscious and the unconscious mind, the transience of the first and the endurance of the second, by pointing to the antiquities standing in his consulting room: "They were really only objects from tombs; their burial had meant preservation for them. Pompeii was only now being destroyed, since it had been uncovered." Again, after recounting how his patient had declared an interpretation plausible but unconvincing, Freud commented for his readers' benefit: "It is never the intention of such discussions to call forth conviction. They are only supposed to introduce the repressed complexes into consciousness, to kindle the conflict about them on the soil of conscious mental activity, and to facilitate the emergence of new material from the unconscious." In showing how he taught the Rat Man about psychoanalysis, Freud taught his readers no less.

The Rat Man called the "new material" about his father that he explored in response to Freud's interpretations his "train of thought"; it was harmless, he insisted, but connected somehow with a little girl he had loved when he was twelve. Freud was not content with such a vague, euphemistic formulation, so typical of the Rat Man's discourse. Rather, he interpreted this train of thought as a wish, a wish in fact, that his father might die. The Rat Man energetically protested: he was afraid of precisely such a calamity! he loved his father! Freud did not dispute that at all, but insisted that this love was accompanied by hatred and that these two powerful emotions had coexisted in the Rat Man from his earliest youth.

His UNDERSTANDING OF the Rat Man's fundamental ambivalence now beyond cavil, Freud could approach the enigma of his patient's obsessions. Patiently, he inched up to the episode in which the sadistic captain had described the oriental punishment and precipitated the Rat Man's current neurosis. Freud's notes on this case disclose that the Rat Man employed rats as symbols for many things: gambling, penises, money, children, his mother. The mind, Freud had always maintained, makes the most acrobatic, most improbable leaps, defying coherence and rationality, and the Rat Man amply confirmed this conviction. What appeared most far-fetched in the case, the ceremonies and prohibitions, turned out to be a compendium of the Rat Man's neurotic ideas, leading in subtle ways to unexplored regions in his mind. They were clues to his repressed and disavowed sadism, which explained his simultaneous horror of, and lascivious interest in, cruelty—the source of that strange mixed expression on the Rat Man's face that Freud had glimpsed at the very beginning of the treatment.

Exploring these hints, Freud now proposed a solution to the question of what the captain's story meant for the Rat Man. It revolved around his patient's conflicting feelings about his father. Freud found it highly significant that when, several years after his father's death, the Rat Man had first experienced the pleasures of sexual intercourse, a strange thought had forced itself into his mind: "But this is wonderful! For this one could murder one's father!" Freud found it no less significant that a few years before, just after the Rat Man's father had died, he had begun to masturbate, but had since managed to stop by and large, because the practice made him ashamed. By and large, but not completely: at some beautiful, elevating moments, such as reading a moving passage in Goethe's autobiography, he could not resist the urge. Freud interpreted this curious phenomenon as an instance of a "prohibition and the defiance of a command."

Stimulated by Freud's analytic construction, the Rat Man contributed a poignant, memorable incident dating from the time he was between three and four. His father had given him a thrashing for some sexual misdemeanor connected with masturbation, and in a burst of fury, he had begun to curse his father. But since he did not yet know any swear words, he had called him "all the names of things that occurred to him, and said, 'You lamp, you towel, you plate!' " Astonished, the father was moved to predict that his son would become either a great man or a great criminal, and never beat him again. With this memory out in the open, the Rat Man could no longer doubt that concealed behind his love for his father, there lurked an equally strong hatred. This was the ambivalence that governed the Rat Man's life, a tormenting ambivalence characteristic of all obsessional thinking, and was echoed in his relations with the woman he loved. These conflicting feelings, Freud concluded, "were not independent of one another, but soldered together in pairs. His hatred of his beloved was necessarily coupled with his attachment to his father and vice versa."

Freud pressed on with his solution. The Rat Man had not only fought his father but identified with him. His father had been a military man who greatly enjoyed telling anecdotes about his army career. What is more, he had been a "rat," a "gambling rat"—*Spielratte*—who had once run up a gambling debt that he could not afford to pay until a friend had opportunely lent him the money. Later, the Rat Man had reason to believe, his father, prosperous in civilian life, had been unable to repay his generous rescuer because he could not find his address. Freud's patient judged this youthful peccadillo of his father's very harshly, much though he loved him. Here was another link to his own peculiar compulsion to repay the minute sum someone had laid out on postage for him, and another link to rats as well. When, on maneuvers, he had heard the sadistic story of the rat punishment, it had awakened these memories, and remnants of his childhood anal eroticism no less. "In his obsessional deliriums," Freud noted, "he had made a veritable rat currency for himself." The story had dragged up from repression all the Rat Man's cruel sexual impulses. Once he had absorbed this cluster of interpretations and accepted it, the Rat Man approached closer and closer to the exit from the labyrinth of his neurosis. The "rat delirium"—the obsessive compulsions and prohibitions—disappeared, and with that the Rat Man had graduated from what Freud beautifully called his "school of suffering."

Despite the problems he set for his analyst, the Rat Man was something of a favorite with Freud from the beginning. There is a cryptic entry in Freud's notes for December 28 that attests to his feelings for his patient: *Hungerig und wird gelabt*—"Hungry and is refreshed."* Freud had invited

---

*The translation in the *Standard Edition* fails to reproduce the laconic quality of Freud's entry; nor does its prosaic "He was hungry and was fed" capture the archaic tenor of *hungerig* and the biblical resonance of *gelabt*. (See the editor's comment in Sigmund Freud, *L'Homme aux rats. Journal d'une analyse*, ed. Elza Ribeiro Hawelka [1974], 211n.)

his patient to a meal. This was a heretical gesture for a psychoanalyst: to gratify a patient by permitting him access to his analyst's private life, and to mother him by providing food in a friendly and unprofessional setting, violated all the austere technical precepts that Freud had been developing in recent years and was attempting to inculcate among his followers. But evidently Freud saw nothing wrong in thus setting aside his own rules. Indeed, despite these departures, Freud's account remains exemplary as an exposition of a classic obsessional neurosis.* It brilliantly served to buttress Freud's theories, notably those postulating the childhood roots of neurosis, the inner logic of the most flamboyant and most inexplicable symptoms, and the powerful, often hidden, pressures of ambivalent feelings. Freud was not masochist enough to publish only failures.

IN HIS OWN CAUSE:
LEONARDO, SCHREBER, FLIESS

 Most of Freud's writings bear the traces of his life. They are entangled, in important but often quite unobtrusive ways, with his private conflicts and his pedagogic strategies. *The Interpretation of Dreams* is an outpouring of self-revelations pressed into the service of science. The case of Dora is a public wrestling match between emotional needs and professional duties. "Little Hans" and "Rat Man" are more than just clinical documents; Freud drafted them to support the theories he had developed in his deeply subversive *Three Essays on the Theory of Sexuality.* To be sure, not all his decisions to publish one case rather than another were rooted in tormenting inner struggles or dictated by the pressures of psychoanalytic politics. The sheer fascination of the material also made its claims on him. Usually, Freud's personal needs, strategic calculations, and scientific excitement overlapped and reinforced one another. Certainly beneath the polished surfaces of the case histories of Schreber and the Wolf Man, published after "Rat Man," some unfinished, haunting psychological business was at work

*Later critics, reanalyzing the case, have faulted Freud for not paying enough attention to the Rat Man's mother and, given the patient's spectacular obsession with rats, his anal eroticism. Both appear somewhat more prominently in the process notes than in the text. At the beginning, as Freud explains his psychoanalytic procedure and sets his terms, the Rat Man says that he must consult his mother. (See Freud, *L'Homme aux rats,* ed. Hawelka, 32; and "Rat Man," *SE* X, 255.)

in him. The same holds true of his "Leonardo da Vinci and a Memory of His Childhood."

FREUD NEVER CONSIDERED his long paper on Leonardo da Vinci a case history, even though once, in great good humor, he playfully asked Ferenczi to "marvel" at his new and "illustrious" analysand. He thought of the paper, rather, as a scouting expedition for the massive invasion of cultural subjects he planned to undertake, weapons of psychoanalysis in hand. "The domain of biography, too, must become ours," he wrote Jung in October 1909, announcing triumphantly that "the riddle of Leonardo da Vinci's character has suddenly become transparent to me. That, then, would be the first step in biography." But it will emerge that this official description of the "Leonardo" as an exercise in psychoanalytic biography is incomplete.

While his essay on a childhood memory of Leonardo da Vinci turned out to be extremely controversial, Freud was, and remained, very fond of it, partly because he was very fond of Leonardo. He confessed that "like others I have succumbed to the attraction that proceeds from this great and mysterious man," and he quoted Jacob Burckhardt's admiring appraisal of this "universal genius, whose outlines one can only surmise, never fathom." Freud, we know, treasured Italy and visited it whenever he could, almost every summer. Leonardo was, among many, one important reason.

Freud had long been preoccupied with him. As early as 1898, he had offered Fliess, who was gathering material on left-handedness, "Leonardo, of whom no love affair is known," as "perhaps the most famous left-hander." Venturing into Leonardo's awesome and enigmatic presence gave Freud exquisite pleasure. Late in 1910, on his way to Italy from a Dutch seaside resort, he made a quick stop at the Louvre to get yet another look at Leonardo's canvas *The Virgin, Saint Anne, and the Christ Child.* To traffic with the great, even without presuming to be their equal, was one of the dividends Freud could draw from writing psychoanalytic biography.

IN NOVEMBER 1909, not long after his return from the United States, Freud complained to Ferenczi about his health, "which could be better," but immediately added, "My thoughts are, in so far as they can still make themselves heard, with Leonardo da Vinci and with mythology." In March 1910, he apologized to Ferenczi quite unapologetically for writing only a short letter: "I want to write on the Leonardo." That "Leonardo," he told Lou Andreas-Salomé almost a decade after its publication, in an access of nostalgia, was "the only beautiful thing I have ever written."

His predilection did not blind Freud to the risks he was taking. On first announcing his new, illustrious analysand to Ferenczi in November 1909, he protested that he had "nothing larger" in mind. In the same mood, he disparaged the paper to Ernest Jones: "You must not expect too much of Leonardo, who will come out in the next month. Neither the secret of the Vierge aux rochers nor the solution of the Monna Lisa puzzle. Keep your hopes on a lower level so it is likely to please you more." Again, he cautioned the German artist Hermann Struck that the "booklet" on Leonardo was a "half-fictional production"—*halbe Romandichtung*—and observed, "I would not want you to judge the certainty of our other investigations in accord with this pattern."

Some of the first readers of this little half-novel refused to accept Freud's appraisal of it, and he was grateful. "The L[eonardo] seems to please the comrades," he cheerfully observed in June 1910. It did, very much. "This analysis," Abraham wrote, fresh from reading the copy Freud had sent him, "is so elegant and perfect in its form that I know of nothing I could compare with it." Jung was, if anything, even more lyrical. "Leonardo," he told Freud, "is wonderful." Havelock Ellis, its first reviewer, showed himself, Freud was glad to see, "friendly as always." This reception enabled Freud to use the "Leonardo" as a touchstone to divide insiders from outsiders; it "pleases all friends," he told Abraham in the summer of 1910, "and will, I hope, arouse the abhorrence of all strangers."

The tone of the Leonardo paper itself is far less assertive; it is tentative, strenuously modest. Its very opening is a disclaimer: psychiatric research, Freud noted, has no intention of denigrating the great and of "dragging the sublime into the dust." But Leonardo, "already admired by his contemporaries as one of the greatest men of the Italian Renaissance," is human like everyone else, and "there is no one so great that it would be a disgrace for him to be subject to the laws that govern normal and pathological activity with equal severity." In the body of the paper Freud defended writing a pathography of Leonardo on the ground that ordinary biographers, "fixated" on their hero, succeed only in presenting a "cold, strange, ideal figure instead of the human being to whom we might feel ourselves distantly related." Freud assured his readers that his essay aimed solely at uncovering the determinants of Leonardo's "mental and intellectual development." If knowledgeable friends of psychoanalysis should accuse him of having "merely written a psychoanalytic novel, I should reply that I surely do not overestimate the certainty of these results."* After all, Freud conceded, reliable bio-

---

*As late as 1931, he wrote, "Once I dared to approach one of the very greatest, of whom unfortunately only too little is known, Leonardo da Vinci. I could at least make probable that *The Virgin, Saint Anne, and the Christ Child*, which you can visit in the Louvre daily, would not be comprehensible without Leonardo's peculiar childhood history." (Freud to Max Schiller, March 26, 1931. *Briefe*, 423.)

graphical materials for Leonardo were both sparse and uncertain. More playful than not, he was trying to put together a jigsaw puzzle with most of the pieces missing and some of the surviving ones virtually undecipherable.

THESE ARE THE opaque screens Freud put up in defense against captious critics. But they cannot conceal that the "Leonardo," for all the brilliance of its deductions, is a severely flawed performance. Much of the evidence Freud used to establish his portrait is inconclusive or tainted. The character sketch he drew of Leonardo remains a plausible likeness: Leonardo is the artist who has perpetual trouble finishing his work and who in his later years rejects art for science; he is the gentle repressed homosexual who has left the world one of the great enigmas of art, the Mona Lisa smile. But whatever plausibility Freud's portrayal possesses rests on grounds other than those he chose to stand on.

Freud's argument is perfectly straightforward. He proposed to view Leonardo and his work from two moments in his life: an adult experience and a childhood memory, the second evoked by the first.* The shaping experience Freud had in mind was that of painting the portrait of Mona Lisa, and he hoped to reconstruct and interpret the memory that the sittings aroused in Leonardo from whatever material he could uncover. Freud was lucky, with the luck of the well-prepared; he discovered the clue he was looking for amidst the vast morass of Leonardo's notebooks. In these crowded compilations, a jumble of caricatures, scientific experiments, designs of weapons and fortifications, musings on morals and mythology, and financial calculations, Leonardo adverted to his childhood only once, while ruminating on the flight of birds. Freud squeezed this rare find for all it was worth. Leonardo was recalling a strange and dreamlike encounter. "It seems"—so Freud rendered the passage—"that I was from the beginning destined to occupy myself so thoroughly with the vulture, for it comes to my mind as a very early memory that, as I was still in my cradle, a vulture came down to me, opened my mouth with its tail, and struck me many times against my lips with its tail." Freud was persuaded that this was a later fantasy rather than a literal recollection, a fantasy that, suitably examined, might provide access to Leonardo's emotional and artistic evolution.

Freud expended a good deal of erudition on the bird who had assaulted Leonardo in his cradle. In ancient Egypt, as Leonardo might well have known, the vulture was a hieroglyph for "mother." What is more, in Chris-

---

*Freud was following out some theoretical considerations he had developed not long before in a paper on the imaginative writer and daydreaming.

tian legend, also accessible to him, the vulture is a bird that exists only as a female; a poetic emblem for the virgin birth, it is impregnated by the wind. Now, Leonardo had been a "vulture-child that had had a mother but no father." This was Freud's poetic way of saying that Leonardo was illegitimate. Hence, Freud conjectured, Leonardo had in his earliest infancy enjoyed the exclusive and passionate love of his bereft mother. Such a love "must have been of the most decisive influence on his inner life." This meant that at the time the foundations of Leonardo's character were laid down, he was father-less: "The vehemence of the caresses to which his vulture fantasy points was only all too natural; the poor forsaken mother had to pour into her mother love caresses enjoyed as well as her yearning for new ones; she was impelled not merely to compensate herself for not having a husband, but also the child for not having a father who wanted to fondle him. So she took, in the manner of all unsatisfied mothers, her little son in place of her husband and robbed him of a piece of his masculinity through the all-too-early maturation of his eroticism." Thus, inadvertently, Leonardo's mother set the stage for his later homosexuality.

In the letter to Jung in which he first announced his solution to the Leonardo mystery, Freud added tantalizingly, giving no further details, "I recently encountered his likeness (without his genius) in a neurotic." That is one reason why he was so confident that he could reconstruct Leonardo's virtually undocumented youngest years: the vulture fantasy was, for him, heavily laden with clinical associations. As we have had occasion to notice before, Freud's couch and his desk were, physically and emotionally, very close to each other. He had no doubt that Leonardo's recollection represented at once the passive homosexual sucking on a penis and the infant blissfully sucking at its mother's breast.

It was, of course, a familiar principle of psychoanalysis, which Freud's patients had confirmed for him over and over, that the emotional entangle-ments of the first years and the passions of adult life are inescapably linked. In particular, "all our homosexual men," Freud noted, had displayed these consequential links in virtually identical ways: "In their earliest childhood, later forgotten," they had had "an intense erotic attachment to a female person, as a rule their mother, provoked and fostered by the excessive tender-ness of the mother herself, further buttressed by the recessiveness of the father in the child's life." Freud described this as one preliminary stage of homosexual development; it is succeeded by a stage in which "the boy represses his love for his mother by putting himself in her place, identifies himself with her, and takes his own person as a model in whose likeness he chooses his new love objects. Thus," Freud continued, "he has become homosexual; in fact he has slid back into autoeroticism, since the boys whom the growing youngster now loves are, after all, only substitute persons and renewals of his own childish person, boys whom he loves as his mother had loved him as a child." In short, psychoanalysts say that "he finds his love objects on the path of *narcissism,* since Greek myths call a youth Narcissus, whom nothing pleased so much as his own mirror image." This sentence marks a critical moment in the history of psychoanalysis: Freud here introduced, for the first time in his work, the concept of narcissism, an early stage of erotic self-love that he saw as occurring between the primitive autoeroticism of the infant and the object love of the growing child. Narcissism was soon to take a central place in his thinking.

That Leonardo was at first raised without a father, Freud thought, must have formed his character. But that character was shaped as well by another drastic intervention from the adult world. His father married shortly after Leonardo was born, and some three years later, Freud supposed, adopted his son and brought him to live in his house. Thus, Leonardo grew up with two mothers. Shortly after 1500, when he came to paint Mona Lisa, her ambiguous, misty smile recalled to him with oppressive vividness the two loving, lovely young women who, together, had presided over his childhood. The creative spark that makes art by leaping between experience and memory gave the portrait of the enigmatic, enticing Mona Lisa its immortality. Then, when Leonardo came to paint the sacred trio, *The Virgin, Saint Anne, and the Christ Child,* he painted his two mothers as he recalled them, or felt them, to have been—both the same age and subtly smiling the ineffable smile of La Gioconda.

None of this sleuthing, it is worth repeating, seduced Freud into claiming that he had discovered the secret of Leonardo's genius. But he believed that he had grasped the thread that would lead him to the core of Leonardo's character. Identifying with his father, the man who had begotten and then abandoned him, Leonardo would treat his "children" in precisely the same way: he would be passionate in the making, impatient with tedious detail, incapable of following inspiration through to the end. But by also rebelling against his father, Leonardo would find the way to science: he could thus trade obedience to authority for a superior loyalty—obedience to evidence. With an almost audible sigh of approval, Freud quoted Leonardo's "bold sentence which contains the justification for all free research: *'He who amidst the struggle of opinions calls upon authority, works with his memory rather than his reason.'* " Leonardo had energetically sublimated his sexual passions into the passion for independent scientific research. It is uncertain just when, and how intensely, Freud identified himself with Leonardo, but in quoting that proud maxim governing the nonconformist researcher, he was at one with his subject.

FREUD'S AFFECTION FOR this experiment in psychoanalytic biography was not wholly misplaced.* His schematic map of one royal road to homosexuality—intense, excessively prolonged oedipal attachment to the tender mother, regression to that stage, identification with the mother, love of other male adolescents as though they were he, the beloved son—retains all of its interest and much of its validity. Again, Freud's scattered observations on the defensive stratagem he called sublimation remain suggestive, even if they cannot resolve the taxing question of just how the mind enlists instinctual energies in the service of cultural pursuits like art or science. But when examined closely, the delicately woven fabric of Freud's argumentation begins to unravel. His assertion that Leonardo more or less originated the idea of depicting Saint Anne as youthful is untenable, even if Leonardo's *choice* of the convention of showing mother and daughter as being the same age may serve as a clue to his mental make-up. Again, Freud's conjecture that Leonardo's father took his son into his house only after a lapse of some three years has been put into doubt by some contrary evidence.†

This is vexing enough, but the most fragile strand in the texture of Freud's reasoning is the vulture fantasy. Freud had used German translations of Leonardo's notebooks that mistakenly rendered his *nibbio* as "vulture" rather than "kite." With this gaffe, first pointed out in 1923 but never acknowledged by Freud or by any other psychoanalyst during Freud's lifetime, the construct vulture-mother, with all its tremendous implications, stands discredited. The vulture was a creature much beloved in myth; the kite is only a bird. Leonardo's report of the bird that attacked him remains a vivid dramatization, perhaps recalling nursing, a homosexual encounter, or, more likely, a homosexual fantasy—perhaps condensing memories of all these. But the superstructure that Freud built on the mistranslation collapses into dust.

Taken together, these lapses considerably diminish the authority of Freud's character sketch. It was just as well that he made only modest claims for his favorite composition. Still, while it is exceedingly probable that the mistranslation making a vulture out of a kite had been called to Freud's attention, he never corrected it. Throughout his long career as a psy-

---

*The art historian Kenneth Clark, no Freudian, has accepted the "beautiful, and I believe profound, interpretation which Freud has put on" Leonardo's canvas of the sacred trio, and he sees, with Freud, "the unconscious memory" of Leonardo's two mothers in the women's faces. (Kenneth Clark, *Leonardo da Vinci: An Account of His Development as an Artist* [1939; rev. ed., 1958], 137.)

†Freud, it seems, disregarded a French study of Leonardo, which he owned and had marked up, that held that Leonardo's father had taken his illegitimate son into his house the year he married. Of course, Freud may have rejected that argument, but he was aware of it. (See Jack J. Spector, *The Aesthetics of Freud: A Study in Psychoanalysis and Art* [1972], 58.)

choanalytic theorist, Freud proved himself ready to revise far more important, long-held theories. But not his "Leonardo."

THERE WAS MORE than one reason for Freud's obstinate loyalty. No doubt, the paper on Leonardo offered him enticing professional rewards. Writing to Jung about the "analyzed" Leonardo, Freud noted, almost as an association, "I am inclining more and more toward esteeming theories of infantile sexuality, which I have treated, by the way, with criminal incompleteness." This was a gratuitous reminder to Jung that Freud was not inclined to compromise on the inflammatory and divisive issue of the libido. In this embattled decade, the making of polemical points, whether directed at open adversaries or at wavering supporters, was never far from the center of Freud's intentions.

Yet there were forces at work in Freud more elusive, less manifest: on December 2, 1909, the day after he reported on his researches into Leonardo to the Vienna Psychoanalytic Society, he wrote to Jung in mixed relief and self-criticism that he had not liked his lecture, but hoped that now he had delivered himself of it, his obsession would give him some respite. "Obsession" is a strong word, but Freud meant it almost literally. Without it he might not have written his psychoanalytic novel at all.

The secret energy animating this obsession left telltale marks on Freud's correspondence and conduct in these years. Its source was memories of Fliess, whom he thought he had done with forever—mistakenly. Recollections of his old intimate, now an intimate no longer, forced Freud to explore once again his affective economy; they gave his self-analysis much anguishing work to do.* In December 1910, he informed Ferenczi, "Fliess—you were so curious about that—I have now overcome." He added immediately, his association unmistakable, "Adler is a little Fliess redivivus, just as paranoid. Stekel, as appendix to him, is at least named Wilhelm." Freud saw Wilhelm Fliess everywhere, incorporated in others. Adler, he wrote to Jung, "awakens in me the memory of Fliess, an octave lower. The same paranoia." When he wrote this, he was already at work on the Schreber case, which would dazzlingly illustrate a thesis he had held for some time: the elemental agent in paranoia is disguised homosexuality. "My erstwhile friend Fliess," he had already told Jung in 1908, "developed a beautiful paranoia after he had disposed of his inclination, certainly not slight, toward me." Always prepared to translate

---

*"Freud was expressing [in the paper on Leonardo] conclusions which in all probability had been derived from his self-analysis and are therefore of great importance for the study of his personality. His letters of the time make it abundantly clear with what exceptional intensity he had thrown himself into this particular investigation." (*Jones* II, 78.)

private turmoil into analytic theory, Freud credited Fliess's conduct with leading him toward this insight, an insight that several of his patients had richly confirmed.

To call someone paranoid was, then, in the technical vocabulary Freud had developed, to call him a homosexual, at least a latent one; and it was remnants of unconscious homoerotic feelings that were bubbling up in Freud. Whatever he might tell Jung, he was laboring to analyze his sentiments for Fliess rather than Fliess's sentiments for him—to analyze and thus, if possible, to purge them. In the fall of 1910, warding off Ferenczi's exorbitant demands for intimacy, Freud cautioned him that "since the case of Fliess, with whose overcoming you just saw me occupied, this need has died out in me. A piece of homosexual charge has been withdrawn and utilized for the enlargement of my own ego. I have succeeded where the paranoiac fails." As he intimated to Jung, he found this "homosexual charge" far from overpowering. Late in September, in a letter from Rome, he complained about Ferenczi, "a very dear fellow, but a little awkwardly dreamy and infantile toward me," excessively admiring and passive. "He has let everything be done for him like a woman, and my homosexuality after all does not go far enough to accept him as one." Still, he recognized what he had once called a certain "androphile" element within himself.

Two years later, analyzing one of his much-discussed fainting attacks, he offered a no less unsparing self-diagnosis. As we know, in November 1912, in Munich, Freud fainted at a small private meeting of psychoanalysts, in Jung's presence. He thought an explanation particularly urgent because this was not the first episode of this sort. As he informed Ernest Jones, he had twice before, once in 1906 and once in 1908, "suffered from very similar though not so intense symptoms in the *same* room of the Park Hotel; in every case I had to leave the table." Then, again, he had fainted in 1909 in Jung's presence, in Bremen, just before boarding ship for the United States. Reflecting on this history, Freud let Ferenczi know that he was completely restored and had "analytically disposed of the fainting spell in Munich very well." These fits, he thought, "point toward the significance of deaths experienced very early." He was thinking of his little brother, who had died when Freud himself was less than two, and whose death he had greeted with such wicked relief.

But just the day before, writing to Ernest Jones, Freud had offered a more far-reaching explanation: he had been fatigued, slept little, smoked a great deal, was faced with the change in Jung's letters "from tenderness to overbearing insolence." More portentous was the fact that the room in the Park Hotel where he had three times suffered a spell of dizziness or fainting held an indelible association for him. "I saw Munich first when I visited Fliess during his illness," he wrote. "This town seems to have acquired a strong connection with my relation to this man. There is some piece of unruly homosexual feeling at the root of the matter." Jones felt close enough to Freud to express considerable interest in "your attack in Munich, especially so," he continued frankly, "as I had suspected a homosexual element, this being the sense of my remark in saying good-bye at the station that you would find it difficult to give up your feeling for Jung (meaning that perhaps there was some transference to him of older affects in you.)" Freud readily adopted Jones's formulation: "You are right in supposing that I had transferred to Jung homosex[ual] feelings from another part but I am glad to find that I have no difficulty in removing them for free circulation. We will have some good talk on this matter." Some of the emotions that Jung aroused, as Freud rightly saw, had been borrowed "from another part": Jung was, as Adler had been before him, Fliess redivivus. It is worth noting that Freud's visit to the ailing Fliess in Munich which had set up this chain of memories had taken place almost two decades earlier, in 1894. Freud's feelings for Fliess were nothing if not persistent.

They were also, as erotic feelings are likely to be, mixed. Examining the episode once again with Binswanger shortly thereafter, Freud reiterated that "suppressed feelings, this time against Jung, as formerly against a predecessor of his, naturally play the leading role." As his recollections continued to harass him, the only sentiments that Freud could now muster about Fliess, or his later surrogates, were the drastic antithesis of the affection he had once so lavishly expended on his Other from Berlin. His mind already exasperated by the conduct of Adler and of Stekel, Freud felt beleaguered by what he interpreted as Jung's death wishes against himself and by revivals of his own death wishes against his younger brother. But behind all these sentiments stood that stark ruin, not to be easily overlooked or quickly dismantled, his old passionate feelings for—and against—Fliess.

It was uncanny: Fliess kept reentering Freud's life in the most astonishing places. In 1911, Freud accounted for one of his most devastating headaches by resorting to a periodization he had learned from Fliess, counting from his birthday to the outbreak of his pains: "Since May 29 (May 6 + 23) I have been very low with a severe migraine." More than a year later, preoccupied with Jung, Freud found himself again drawing on his past history: "I have just come from 'Don Giovanni,' " he reported to Ferenczi. In the second act, during the Don's festive supper, the hired band plays the snatch of an aria from Mozart's *Marriage of Figaro* and Leporello remarks, "That music seems very familiar to me." Freud found "a good application to the current situation. Yes, this music, too, seems very familiar to me. I had experienced all this already before 1906"—that is, with Fliess in the last angry years of their friendship: "the same objections, the same prophecies, the same proclamations that I have now been got rid of." It would be giving Freud's unconscious feelings, especially his repressed feelings about Fliess, too much credit to make them entirely responsible for his papers on Leonardo and on Schreber. Certainly the fortuitous accumulation of intriguing paranoid patients coming into treatment participated in focusing his clinical and theoretical interests around 1910. Nor does Freud's borrowing from his continuing self-analysis in any way compromise the scientific value of his findings. Proclaiming he had overcome Fliess and showing that he had not, Freud exploited his unconscious to good purpose. He had been perfectly serious when he told Jung early in 1908, talking about what he was pleased to call Fliess's paranoia, "One must seek to learn something from everything." And *everything* included himself.

WHILE FREUD WAS reading the proofs of his "Leonardo" in the early spring of 1910, he was beginning to reflect on a new, hardly less singular case, that of the distinguished Saxon jurist and remarkable paranoiac Daniel Paul Schreber. Emotionally, chronologically, and in other ways, Freud's paper on Schreber is a pendant to his "Leonardo." Freud never saw either of these "analysands"; for Leonardo he had notes and paintings, for Schreber he had nothing more than an autobiographical memoir. Like Leonardo, Schreber was a homosexual, so Freud could continue to stay with a theme that deeply preoccupied him in those years. Like Leonardo, too, Schreber was a source of real pleasure. Affectionately, Freud called Schreber "wonderful," and jocularly proposed that he "should have been made a professor of psychiatry and director of a mental hospital."

When Freud stumbled on Schreber, he had been thinking about paranoia for some two years and more. In February 1908, he had told Ferenczi that he had just seen a woman patient afflicted with "a full-blown" case of it. She was, he thought, "probably beyond the bounds of therap[eutic] influence," but he felt entitled to take her into treatment: "At any event, one can learn from her."* Six weeks later, discussing the same patient, he reiterated his scientific creed of simultaneous engagement and detachment. He saw no prospect of therapeutic success, "but we need these analyses to arrive at last

---

*Sometime in April 1907, Freud had written Jung a kind of memorandum (reminiscent of the memoranda that he used to send Fliess in the 1890s) on paranoia; in it he did not yet dwell on the homosexual component of the disorder. (See *Freud-Jung*, 41–44 [38–40].)

at an understanding of all neuroses." The provocative mystery of paranoia absorbed him. "We still know too little about it," he told Ferenczi in the spring of 1909, "and must collect and learn."* Freud's consistent self-appraisal as a researcher more intent on science than on healing receives persuasive support from these injunctions. In the fall of the same year, Freud informed Abraham that he was in the midst of "thickest work" and had "penetrated a little more deeply into paranoia." By that time, the Schreber case had become another of Freud's obsessions, matching his earlier obsession with Leonardo.

With his fantastic symptoms displaying the ravages of his psychosis with striking clarity, Schreber was ideally suited to produce such strong reactions. Born in 1842 the son of Daniel Gottlob Moritz Schreber, an orthopedic physician, prolific author, and well-known educational reformer, he had traversed a distinguished career as a civil servant in the Saxon judicial system and, later, as a judge. In October 1884, he ran for the Reichstag as the joint candidate of the Conservative and National Liberal parties, which stood for Bismarckian law and order, but was resoundingly trounced by a Social Democrat who was a great local favorite. His first mental breakdown, which, like the others, he attributed to overwork, followed hard upon this defeat. He began to suffer from hypochondriacal delusions and spent some weeks in a mental hospital; by December, he was an inmate of the Leipzig Psychiatric Clinic. But he was discharged as cured in June 1885, and appointed to the bench in the following year. By 1893, clearly a man of demonstrated competence, he had risen to Saxony's highest court, where he was one of the presiding judges. But he began to complain of insomnia, attempted suicide, and late in November, he was back once more in the Leipzig clinic where he had been a patient some nine years earlier. It was this second, more tenacious mental illness, lasting until 1902, that he described in graphic detail in a mountainous memorandum, the *Memoirs of a Neuropath,* published as a book the following year. A final episode, again requiring hospitalization, darkened Schreber's last years. When he died in April 1911, Freud's case history of him was in galley proof.

Freud took the *Memoirs* of the wonderful Schreber—the only material he had—to Italy with him in the summer of 1910. He worked on the case in Rome and later, through the fall, back in Vienna. Among the "patients" whose histories Freud found worth recording, Daniel Paul Schreber probably

---

*Writing about symbol formation in dreams, which was the special province of Stekel, whom Freud had come to distrust, Freud noted in 1911 that it was "a dark matter. . . . We will have to observe there, and collect, for a long time." (Freud to Ferenczi, June 5, 1911. Freud–Ferenczi Correspondence, Freud Collection, LC.)

boasted the most spectacular symptoms. A paranoiac of heroic dimensions, he was, as his *Memoirs* sufficiently shows, an articulate commentator on his own condition and an eloquent advocate of his cause: he had written this massive apologia to secure his release from the mental hospital to which he was confined. His earliest readers among psychiatrists, notably Bleuler and Freud, picked over this plea for freedom, eloquent, circumstantial, baroque, logical with the logic of insanity, for nuggets attesting to a mind derailed. Schreber was nothing but a book to his psychoanalyst, but Freud thought he could learn to read it.

Freud's rather manic preoccupation with Schreber hints at some hidden interest driving him on: Fliess. But Freud was not just at the mercy of his memories; he was working well and derived much comic relief from Schreber, even sprinkling his intimate letters with neologisms from Schreber's book. These were the famous Schreberisms, fantastic coinages—"nerve contacts" and "soul murder" and being "miracled up"—imaginative, evocative, and eminently quotable. Freud's correspondents took their cue from him and replied in kind; Schreber's vocabulary became a kind of shorthand among insiders, so many tokens of recognition and intimacy. Freud and Jung and Abraham and Ferenczi gleefully used "soul murder" and the rest of Schreber's gems.

Still, Freud's work on Schreber was not untouched by anxiety. He was in the midst of his bruising battle with Adler, which, he told Jung, was taking such a toll "because it has torn open the wounds of the Fliess affair." Adler had "disturbed the otherwise calm feeling during my work on paranoia"—the Schreber paper. "I am not certain this time just how free I have been able to keep it from my own complexes." His suspicion that there were some subterranean connections was wholly warranted, though they were not precisely what Freud thought them to be. He blamed his memories of Fliess for interfering with his work on Schreber, but they were also a reason for his intense concentration on the case. To study Schreber was to remember Fliess, but to remember Fliess was also to understand Schreber. Had not both, Freud thought, been victims of paranoia? This was, no doubt, a highly tendentious reading of Fliess's mental history. But justified or not, Freud used the Schreber case to replay and work through what he called (in friendly deference to Jung, who had invented the term) his "complexes."

Jung, who later claimed to have drawn Freud's attention to Schreber, at first greeted his paper as "delicious and side-splitting" and "brilliantly written." But that was early in 1911, when Jung still professed himself Freud's faithful son. Later, Jung would declare himself sorely dissatisfied with Freud's reading of Schreber. No wonder: Freud's case history of Schreber buttressed psychoanalytic theories, especially about sexuality, and thus, like the Leonardo paper earlier, constituted an implicit criticism of Jung's emerging psychological system. "That passage in your Schreber analysis where you touch on the libido problem," Jung wrote to Freud late in 1911, was one of "the points where one of my mental paths crosses one of yours." A month later, Jung put his uneasiness more bluntly: the Schreber case had set up "a booming echo" in him, and revived all his old doubts about the relevance of Freud's libido theory to psychotics.

IN HIS *Memoirs*, Schreber elaborated an ambitious theory of the universe, complete with an intricate theology, and assigned to himself a messianic mission requiring a change of sex. God himself, it seemed, had inspired him to his work. With uncommon openness, which Freud found worth remarking on, Schreber did not deny his delusions, and the court that restored Schreber to freedom summarized them just as matter-of-factly: "He thinks himself called to redeem the world and restore it to its lost bliss" (a mental state that Freud explicitly identified with voluptuous feelings). "But he could do this only after he had first transformed himself from a man into a woman." Whatever amusement one could wring from such a picturesque program was undercut by Schreber's pathetic sufferings. There is something just a little callous about Freud and his correspondents trading comical Schreberisms; Schreber had undergone appalling mental anguish. He was haunted by frightening anxieties about his health, by horrifying physical symptoms, by the panicky fear of dying and of being tortured. At times he felt he was living without essential parts of his body, which had to be repeatedly restored to him by miracles. He was visited by distressing auditory hallucinations: voices mocked him by calling him "*Miss* Schreber," or professed astonishment that he should claim to be a superior judge, "who lets himself be f——."* Sometimes he spent hours in a stupor; often he wished for death. He had mysterious visions, trafficked with God and with devils. Delusions of persecution, that classic symptom of paranoia, also tormented him: more than anyone else, Dr. Flechsig, his former physician at the Leipzig Psychiatric Clinic, was stalking him—Flechsig was Schreber's "soul murderer." But then everyone, including God, was in the conspiracy against him. The God whom Schreber constructed was quite peculiar, as limited in his way as an exigent and most imperfect human being. He did not understand human beings, took Schreber

---

*Freud shook his head over the "shamefaced" attitude of the editors of Schreber's *Denkwürdigkeiten*, who could not bring themselves to spell out "fucked," as they later would not spell out "shit," in full. (See "Schreber," *GW* VIII, 252n/*SE* XII, 20n.)

for an idiot, and urged him to evacuate, repeatedly asking him, "Why don't you sh——?"

Freud did not miss the splendid opportunities for interpretation that every page of the *Memoirs* offered him. Schreber's frank anal and genital sensuality, his suggestive coinages, his transparent femininity, were all highly legible clues to the workings of his mind. For decades Freud had been persuaded that the craziest ideas of the most regressed psychotic are so many messages, rational in their own twisted way. In accord with this conviction, Freud chose to translate Schreber's confidences rather than to dismiss them. He read his world system as a coherent set of transfigurations designed to make the unbearable bearable: Schreber had invested his enemies, whether Dr. Flechsig or God, with such malign power because they had been so important to him. In short, Schreber had come to hate them so deeply because he had earlier loved them so much; paranoia was, for Freud, the mental ailment parading with unsurpassed vividness the psychological defenses of reversal and, even more, of projection.* The "core of the conflict in the paranoia of a man" is, as Freud put it in his case history, a "homosexual wish-fantasy *of loving a man.*" The paranoiac turns the declaration "I love him" into its opposite, "I hate him"; this is the reversal. He then goes on to say, "I hate him because he persecutes me"; this is the projection. Freud did not think himself paranoid; he had succeeded, as he told Ferenczi, in enabling his homoerotic emotions to serve his ego. But Schreber's spectacular transformation of love into hate had, he sensed, some muted application to himself.

The Schreber case history, though, and Freud's accompanying studies in paranoia, were not autobiography but science. As Freud's letters of these years amply testify, he insisted that his daring construction of how paranoia operates required much further empirical work with paranoid patients before it could be confirmed. But his general hypothesis, Freud was confident, correctly outlined the fatal sequence. According to Freud's scheme, the paranoiac reconstructs the world in order, almost literally, to survive. His remaking, which is desperately hard work, involves a regression to narcissism, the relatively primitive stage in childhood sexuality to which Freud had first called attention some months before in his paper on Leonardo da Vinci. He now ventured to sketch it in somewhat more fully. Having passed through

---

*Projection is the operation of expelling feelings or wishes the individual finds wholly unacceptable—too shameful, too obscene, too dangerous—by attributing them to another. It is a prominent mechanism, for example, in anti-Semites, who find it necessary to transfer feelings of their own that they consider low or dirty onto the Jew, and then "detect" those feelings in him. This is one of the most primitive among the defenses, and is easily observable in normal behavior, though far less prominent there than among neurotics and psychotics.

the opening stage in erotic development, a diffuse autoeroticism, the child concentrates its sexual drives to secure a love object. But the child begins by selecting itself, its own body, as that object, before seeking out someone else to love.

Freud was coming to see this intermediate narcissistic stage as an essential step on the road toward adult heterosexual love. As he came to argue, the principal steps include the primitive oral phase, followed by the anal, the phallic, and, later, the genital phase. The road is long, sometimes impassable; there are many, it seems, who never wholly free themselves from their child-like narcissistic self-involvement, and carry it into their later love life. Such people—and Freud called particular attention to them—may choose their own genitals as their love object and then move on to love others endowed with genitals like their own. This narcissistic fixation, as Freud called it, makes either for open homosexuality in adult life or for the sublimation of homosexual inclinations in passionate friendships or, on a larger stage, in the love of mankind. The road to maturation is not just long and perhaps impassable; it is also twisted and at times turns back on itself: those whose sexual development has taken the homoerotic direction may be swamped by waves of erotic excitement and will then feel compelled to retreat to an earlier, they believe safer, stage of sexual integration—to narcissism.

The psychoanalyst sees the most dramatic instances of such defensive regression in paranoiacs. They try to protect themselves by grossly distorting their perceptions and feelings with all sorts of outlandish fantasies. Schreber, for one, was pursued by the vision that the end of the world is near. Freud maintained that such terrifying fantasies are far from rare in those afflicted with paranoia; having withdrawn their love from others, and from the world as a whole, they project their "inner catastrophe" outward and become convinced that a universal doom is impending. Their great reconstructive work begins at this point: the world having been destroyed, "the paranoiac builds it up again, not more splendid, indeed, but at least so that he can once again live in it." In fact, *"What we take to be the pathological production, the delusional formation, is in reality the attempt at recovery, the reconstruction."*

The map that Freud drew of the paranoid process on the basis of a single document was a brilliant *tour de force*. Its strong outlines have been slightly redrawn by later research, but its authority remains substantially intact. With unprecedented lucidity, Freud demonstrated in the Schreber case how the mind deploys its defenses, what paths regression may take, and what costs ambivalence can impose. Some of the symbols, connections, and transformations that Freud detected in Schreber became obvious once he had pointed them out: the sun, about which Schreber developed lurid fantasies, symbolizing his father; the very similar identification of Dr. Flechsig, and even more significantly, of God, with the elder Schreber, who had also been a physician; the intriguing coupling of religiosity and lasciviousness in a man who had been irreligious and strait-laced most of his life; above all, the transmogrification of love into hatred. Freud's history of Schreber gave its readers perhaps as much intellectual pleasure as its author.

HAVING IDENTIFIED CHILDHOOD as the arena critical to the making of psychological conflict, Freud tried, a little halfheartedly, to inform himself about the environment in which young Schreber had grown up. He was aware that such added intelligence might have real utility, for Schreber's *Memoirs* had been bowdlerized by his family. "Thus I shall have to be satisfied," Freud wrote with evident dissatisfaction, "if I succeed in deriving the core of his delusional formation with some certainty from familiar human motives." He asked Dr. Arnold Stegmann, one of his German adherents, who lived not far from Schreber territory, "to ferret out all sorts of personal data about the old Schreber. It will depend on these reports how much I shall say about these things in public." The results of Stegmann's inquiries cannot have amounted to a great deal, for in his published case history, Freud stayed close to the text that his unknown analysand had provided. In his correspondence, however, he did venture some speculations. "What would you think," he asked Ferenczi rhetorically, teasingly borrowing his language from Schreber, "if the old doctor Schreber had performed 'miracles' as a physician? But apart from that was a domestic tyrant who yelled at his son 'and understood him as little as the lower God' of our paranoiacs?" And he added that he would welcome contributions to his Schreber interpretations.

It was a shrewd conjecture, but unfortunately, in the absence of confidential information, Freud did not follow it up. He did not even examine the published writings of "the old doctor," which would have proved as revealing to him as they had been popular in their time. Freud needed no research to establish that Dr. Schreber's tracts had made his name a household word. The elder Schreber had acquired a national reputation for advocating "the harmonious upbringing of youth," and for being "the founder of therapeutic gymnastics in Germany." For some years, he ran a reputable orthopedic clinic in Leipzig, but he was best known as the energetic promoter of what came to be called *Schrebergärten,* small plots for which cities set aside acreage to permit nostalgic urbanites to cultivate a vegetable garden, a few fruit trees, or just some restful green space of their own.

To deduce the formation of the younger Schreber's character from the psychological riches concealed in his father's writings would have supplied powerful corroboration for Freud's long-held thesis that the mind exercises extraordinary ingenuity in weaving mental representations out of materials picked from the outside world. Familiarity with the elder Schreber's monographs would have allowed Freud to add some nuances to his straightforward analysis of his priceless paranoiac. As it was, for whatever reason, Freud contented himself with reconstructing Schreber's melancholy efforts at regaining his shattered mental composure as the work of a good son loving his father with an impermissible homosexual love; in fact, Freud attributed Schreber's partial recovery precisely to the fact that his "father complex" had an "essentially positive coloration."

Freud's failure to penetrate Dr. Daniel Gottlob Moritz Schreber's character, and to follow up his guess that he might have been a domestic tyrant, was perfectly understandable. The elder Schreber seemed an excellent man. "Such a father was surely not unsuited to be transfigured into a god in the tender recollection of his son." What Freud did not know was that this worthy and admirable parent was more or less indirectly responsible for some of the most exquisite torments his son was forced to undergo. In his *Memoirs,* that son reported on a terrible *Kopfzusammenschnürungsmaschine,* a machine tying his head together. Though an integral element in his delusional system, this was a distorted version of a mechanical head straightener that Moritz Schreber had used to improve the posture of his children, including his son Daniel Paul. While precise details about the Schrebers' family life are skimpy, there is no doubt that Daniel Paul Schreber constructed much of his bizarre world of mechanical tortures from machinery to which he was subjected when he was a boy. The consequences of this discovery are hard to assess. Freud's essential diagnosis remains beyond dispute. But concealed behind the love which, Freud thought, Schreber bore his excellent father, there seems to have been a reservoir of silent resentment and impotent hatred that provided fuel for his suffering and his rage. His paranoiac constructions were caricatures of realistic grievances. Fascinating as Freud made Schreber, a fuller investigation would have made him more fascinating still.

In His Own Cause:
The Politics of the Wolf Man

 By the time Freud completed his account of Schreber in December 1910, he had been analyzing the Wolf Man, who would prove to be his most notable patient, for almost a year. When Sergei Pankejeff, a wealthy and handsome young Russian aristocrat, presented himself to Freud, he was in a pitiful psychological state; he seemed to have slipped beyond neurosis into a tangle of crippling symptoms.* Traveling in grand style with his own physician and attendant, he had undergone treatment after treatment, consulted expensive specialist after expensive specialist, to no avail. His health had collapsed after a gonorrheal infection when he was seventeen, and he was now, so Freud assessed him, "entirely dependent," unable to take care of himself—*existenzunfähig.*

Freud was no doubt particularly moved to take this desperate case by the knowledge that two eminent medical men whom he regarded as his enemies, Theodor Ziehen in Berlin and Emil Kraepelin in Munich, had given up on this interesting young man. After some years of taking a well-meaning if somewhat puzzled interest in psychoanalysis, Ziehen, then chief of psychiatry at the famous Charité hospital in Berlin, had turned into one of Freud's most vociferous detractors. Kraepelin, even more prominent than Ziehen for bringing order into psychiatric nosology, largely ignored Freud when he did not malign him for ideas he no longer held. At least until he assumed his chair in Berlin, Ziehen had echoed Freud's and Breuer's writings of the mid-1890s in his favorable comments on the art of psychiatric listening and the "abreaction" of the patient's feelings, but Kraepelin never found anything of value in Freud's ideas or clinical methods. These two specialists were among the most impressive representatives of German academic psychiatry in the days when Freud was establishing and elaborating his system of ideas. But they could not help the Wolf Man.

Freud thought that perhaps he might. "Consequent upon your impressive admonition to allow myself some rest," he informed Ferenczi in February 1910, "I have—taken on a new patient from Odessa, a very rich Russian with

*As with other cases, later analysts going over the material Freud left for them to study have come to think of the Wolf Man as more deeply disturbed than Freud's diagnostic term, "neurosis," would suggest.

compulsive feelings." After seeing him for some time in a clinic, Freud, once he had space in his regular schedule, invited him to become one of his patients at Berggasse 19. This is where the Wolf Man would discover the serenity and healing quiet of Freud's consulting room and, in Freud, an attentive and sympathetic listener who offered hope for recovery at last.

THE CASE HISTORY of the Wolf Man belongs in the series of papers that also includes Freud's papers on Schreber and on Leonardo. All of them were intended as clinical and theoretical contributions, but at the same time, whatever their merits and defects as psychoanalytic literature, they also served as agents for his own cause. Freud hoped that his clinical account of the Wolf Man would help him as efficiently as its predecessors, especially in confronting public rather than internal discord. As he pointedly observed on its first page, he had written it to combat Jung's and Adler's "twisted reinterpretations" of psychoanalytic verities. It was no accident that he should have written it in the fall of 1914; he saw this case history as the companion piece to his "History of the Psychoanalytic Movement," the rallying cry to loyalists that he had published earlier that year.

Freud paraded his aggressive intentions with his very choice of title: "From the History of an Infantile Neurosis." After all, he observed, Jung had chosen to single out "actuality and repression, Adler egoistic motives," a shorthand way of saying that for Jung, the memory of childhood sexuality is a later fantasy projected backward, while for Adler, early apparently erotic impulses are not sexual but aggressive in nature. Yet, Freud insisted, what these men were spurning as error "is precisely what is new in psychoanalysis and specifically belongs to it." By discarding Freud's insights, Jung and Adler had found it easy to reject "the revolutionary advances of uncomfortable psychoanalysis." That is why Freud chose to focus on the childhood neurosis of the Wolf Man rather than on the virtually psychotic condition of the twenty-three-year-old Russian who came to consult him in February 1910, as he was putting the finishing touches on his "Leonardo."

The Wolf Man impressed Freud as ideally suited to exhibit his "uncomfortable" theories, uncontaminated by craven compromises. Had he published the case promptly, he could have enlisted it in his campaign to clarify his differences with Jung and Adler. But the course of events thwarted his plans; the case report became a casualty of the First World War, which reduced psychoanalytic publications to virtual silence. When the paper finally appeared in 1918, the need for clinical confirmation was no longer quite so urgent. But Freud never ceased to think highly of the case, and it is easy to see why. The psychological turmoil agitating his patient seemed potentially so enlightening that Freud published tantalizing fragments while the analysis was still in progress, and asked other analysts to supply him with material that might throw light on early sexual experiences relevant to his remarkable patient.

The case reverberated with echoes from Freud's earlier histories. Like Dora, the Wolf Man supplied the master key to his neurosis in the form of a dream. Like Little Hans, he had suffered from an animal phobia in early childhood. Like the Rat Man, he was for a time propelled into obsessive ceremonies and neurotic ruminations. The Wolf Man provided some of Freud's recent theoretical interests, like the sexual theories of children or the development of character structure, with the authority of lived experience. Yet, while the analysis of the Wolf Man summed up much of the work Freud had been doing before he first saw him in 1910, it was also prophetic; it looked ahead to work he would do after its termination four years later.

The analysis began dramatically enough. Freud reported confidentially to Ferenczi after the first session that his new patient "confessed to me the following transferences: Jewish swindler, he would like to use me from behind and shit on my head." Plainly a promising but probably a difficult case. In fact, the emotional history that Freud painfully elicited from the Wolf Man was a harrowing tale of precocious sexual stimulation, devastating anxieties, specialized erotic tastes, and a full-fledged obsessive neurosis that had shadowed his childhood. When he was little more than three, his sister had initiated him into sexual games, playing with his penis. She was two years older, a willful, sensual, and uninhibited girl whom he admired and envied. But, viewing her as a rival rather than companion in childish erotic play, he had resisted her and instead sought to seduce his beloved nurse, his Nanya, by exhibiting himself before her and masturbating. Nanya grasped the meaning of his primitive display and solemnly warned him that children who did such things got a "wound" in that place. Her veiled threat took some time to sink in, as such threats do, but after he had observed his sister and a friend urinating and thus established for himself that some people have no penises, he began to be preoccupied with castration.

In terror, the little Wolf Man retreated to an earlier phase of sexual development, to anal sadism and masochism. He cruelly tortured butterflies and tortured himself no less cruelly with horrifying but exciting masturbatory beating fantasies. Having been rejected by his Nanya, he now, in true narcissistic fashion, chose his father as a sexual object; he longed to be beaten by him, and by indulging in screaming fits, he provoked—or, rather, seduced—his father into administering physical punishment. His character changed, and his famous dream about the silent wolves, which became the heart of his analysis with Freud, followed soon after, just before his fourth birthday. He dreamt that it was night time and he was in his bed, which stood (as it did in real life) facing the window. Suddenly the window opened, apparently on its own, and the terrified dreamer noticed that there were six or seven wolves sitting on branches of a big walnut tree. They were white and looked rather like foxes or sheep dogs, with their big, foxlike tails and their alert, pricked-up ears. "In great anxiety, evidently of being eaten by the wolves, I screamed and I woke up"—woke up, Freud recorded, in a state of anxiety. Half a year later his full-fledged anxiety neurosis was in place, complete with an animal phobia. He drove himself to distraction with childlike religious conundrums, compulsively practiced a variety of rituals, suffered attacks of ferocious rage, and grappled with his youthful sensuality, in which homosexual desires played a largely invisible part.

These traumatic childhood episodes prepared the way for the Wolf Man's neurotic sexual conduct. Some consequences of these dismaying experiences, obeying what psychoanalysts call the principle of delayed action, emerged as serious psychological difficulties only much later, in his early manhood; he did not experience the episodes as traumas until his mental organization was, as it were, ready for them. But they somehow shaped his taste in love: his compulsive quest for women with large buttocks who could satisfy his appetite for sexual intercourse from behind, and his need to degrade his love objects by desiring only servants or peasant girls.

Before Freud could even begin to think about repairing the torn fabric of the Wolf Man's erotic life, he felt it necessary to investigate his melodramatic recitals of those arousing and damaging childhood episodes involving his sister and his nurse. The Wolf Man insisted that they were authentic, but Freud naturally wondered. Yet even if they had occurred precisely as the Wolf Man reported them, they were insufficient, in Freud's view, to account for the severity of the Wolf Man's childhood neurosis. The causes of that prolonged misery remained obscure during years of treatment. Illumination gradually dawned with the analysis of his decisive dream, the dream that gave the Wolf Man his nickname.

This wolf dream stands second in the psychoanalytic literature only to the historic dream of Irma's injection, which Freud had analyzed some fifteen years before, in 1895. Precisely when the Wolf Man produced his dream for Freud is not certain; later he recalled, and Freud agreed, that it must have been near the beginning of his treatment; the dream was to be interpreted again and again across the years. In any event, after bringing the dream into his analysis, the Wolf Man, an artist by avocation, produced a drawing showing the wolves—there were only five in this version—perched on the branches of a large tree and looking at the dreamer.

Associating to this dream, dreamt some nineteen years before, the Wolf Man produced some tantalizing memories: his terror at the picture of a wolf in a book of fairy tales which his sister had kept showing him with evident sadistic pleasure; flocks of sheep kept in the neighborhood of his father's estate, most of whom had died during an epidemic; a story his grandfather had told him about a wolf who had his tail pulled off; fairy tales like "Little Red Riding Hood." These outpourings sounded to Freud like precipitates of a primitive, deep-seated fear of the father. The closely related fear of castration, too, apparently had its share in the making of this dream, as did the little boy's wish for sexual gratification from his father—a wish transformed into anxiety by the thought that to have it gratified would mean that he had been castrated, made into a girl. Yet not everything in the dream was wish and its effect, anxiety. The realistic impression it conveyed and the perfect stillness of the wolves, qualities to which the Wolf Man attached great importance, led Freud to suggest that a piece of reality had been reproduced, distorted in the manifest content of the dream. This conjecture was an application of Freud's rule that the dream work invariably transforms experiences or desires, often into their opposite. Those silent, unmoving wolves must mean that the young dreamer had actually witnessed an agitated scene. Cooperating in his passive, listless, intelligent way with Freud's unraveling, the Wolf Man interpreted the sudden opening of the window as the dream's way of saying that he had woken up to watch this scene, whatever it was.

At this point in his case history Freud thought it politic to pause for a comment. He was aware that the capacity for the suspension of disbelief among even his most uncritical followers had its limits. "I fear," he wrote, preparing to launch his sensational revelation, "that this is where my reader's trust will abandon me." What Freud was about to assert was that the dreamer had dredged up from the depths of his unconscious memory, suitably embroidered and heavily veiled, the spectacle of his parents engaging in sexual intercourse. There was nothing vague about Freud's reconstruction: the Wolf Man's parents had had sex three times running and at least once *a tergo*, a position giving the spectator a glimpse of both partners' genitals. This was fanciful enough, but Freud did not stop even here; he persuaded himself that the Wolf Man had witnessed this erotic performance at the age of one and a half.

Yet here Freud was assailed by a twinge of prudence and felt impelled to register doubts, not merely on his reader's behalf, but on his own. The tender age of the observer did not trouble him excessively; adults, he contended, regularly underestimate children's capacity to see, and to understand what they see. But he wondered whether the sexual scene he had so confidently sketched had really taken place or was a fantasy of the Wolf Man's, based on his observations of animals copulating. Freud was interested in the truth of the matter, but he firmly concluded that to decide this question was "not really very important." After all, "scenes of observing parental intercourse, of being seduced in childhood, and of being threatened with castration, are undoubtedly inherited property, but they can just as well be an acquisition through personal experience."* Fantasy or reality, the influence on a young mind would be quite the same. For the present, Freud left the matter open.

The question of reality and fantasy was, of course, not new for Freud. As we have seen, in 1897 he had jettisoned the theory that real events—the rape or seduction of children—alone cause neuroses in favor of a theory that assigned to fantasies the dominant role in the making of neurotic conflicts. Now once again he vindicated the formative influence of internal, largely unconscious mental processes. Freud did not maintain that psychological traumas emerge solely from baldly invented episodes. Rather, he saw fantasies as weaving fragments of things seen and heard and endured into a tapestry of mental reality. Near the conclusion of his *Interpretation of Dreams* he had argued that *"psychical* reality" is different from, but no less significant than, *"material* reality." It was a perspective that, as he analyzed the dream of the silent wolves in the trees, Freud found indispensable—for polemical almost as much as for scientific reasons. His insistence that the recall of a primal scene must have *some* basis in reality, whether in watching parents or animals or in early fantasies elaborated, was squarely directed against Jung: the point was that an adult neurosis originates in experiences acquired in childhood, however distorted and fantastic their later guise. The roots of neurosis, then, run deep rather than, as Jung would suggest, simply being smuggled in later. *"The influence of childhood,"* Freud said as emphatically as he could, *"already makes itself felt in the opening situation in the formation of the neurosis, in that it helps to determine, in a decisive way, whether and at what point the individual fails to master the real problems of life."*

ONE CRITICAL FAILURE in the adult Wolf Man's mastery of life's problems lay, as we have seen, in his consistently unhappy erotic attachments. It is no accident, indeed, that Freud should have been thinking about the theory of love during the years he was analyzing the Wolf Man and writing up his case. Freud wrote several papers on the subject after 1910, but never pulled them together into a book. "Everything has already been said," he once wrote, and he seems to have applied that weary, exhausted demurrer to love no less than

---

*We encounter here, and will encounter again, one of Freud's most eccentric and least defensible intellectual commitments: Freud accepted a version of the Lamarckian doctrine—most probably encountered in the writings of Darwin, who himself subscribed to that theory in part—that acquired characteristics (in this case, the "memory" of being seduced in childhood or being threatened with castration) can be inherited. Few reputable biologists of the time were willing to credit, and few analysts felt at all comfortable with, this thesis. But Freud stayed with it. See pp. 333, 368, and 647.

to other interesting matters of passion. Yet, given the principal place he assigned to sexual energies in the human mental economy, he could hardly afford to slight entirely this endlessly discussed, virtually undefinable theme. Year after year, he listened to patients whose affectional life had somehow gone wrong. Freud characterized "a completely normal attitude in love" as the confluence of "two currents," the *"tender* and the *sensual."* There are those who cannot desire where they love and cannot love where they desire, but this separation is a symptom of emotional development derailed; most people thus afflicted experience this split as a grievous burden. Yet such derailment is only too common, for love, like its rival, hate, emerges during the child's earliest days in primitive forms and is fated to undergo some elaborate vicissitudes in the course of maturation: the oedipal phase is, among other things, a time of experimentation and instruction in the domain of love. For once in tune with more respectable contemporary writers on the subject, Freud regarded tenderness without passion as friendship, passion without tenderness as lust. One principal aim of analysis is to provide realistic lessons in love and bring its two currents into harmony. With the Wolf Man, the prospects for such a happy resolution seemed for a long time exceedingly remote. His unresolved anal eroticism, his equally unresolved fixation on his father and his hidden wish to bear his father children, stood in the way of such a development—and of a favorable conclusion to his treatment.

THE WOLF MAN's analysis lasted almost precisely four and a half years. It would have lasted longer if Freud had not decided to employ a most unorthodox maneuver. He had found that the case "left nothing to be desired" in "fruitful difficulties." But for a time its difficulties were more conspicuous than its fruitfulness. "The first years of the treatment brought scarcely any change." The Wolf Man was courtesy itself but kept himself "unassailably entrenched" in an attitude of "submissive indifference. He listened, understood, and did not permit anything to touch him." Freud found it all very frustrating: "His unimpeachable intelligence was as if cut off from the instinctual forces that governed his conduct." The Wolf Man took untold months before he began to participate in the work of analysis; and then, once he felt the pressure of internal change, he resumed his gently sabotaging ways. He evidently found his illness too precious to exchange for the uncertain blessings of relative health. In this predicament, Freud decided to set a termination date—one year hence—for the analysis, and stick to it inflexibly. The risks were great, though Freud did not make his move until he felt sure that the Wolf Man's attachment to him was sufficiently strong to promise success.

    The stratagem worked; the Wolf Man came to see that Freud was "inexorable," and under this "pitiless pressure" he gave up his resistance, surrendering "his fixation on being ill." In rapid succession he now produced all the "material" Freud needed to clear up his inhibitions and relieve his symptoms. By June 1914, Freud regarded him, and the Wolf Man regarded himself, as more or less cured. He felt himself a healthy man and was about to marry.* It had been a most rewarding case for Freud, but, not surprisingly, what continued to interest him most was a matter of technique—his "blackmailing measure" designed to get the Wolf Man to work in the analytic hour. It was a tactic, Freud warned almost a quarter century later, apt to succeed only if utilized at the precisely right moment. For, he noted, "one must not extend the time limit after it has once been fixed; otherwise one has forfeited all credit from then on." It was one of Freud's boldest, and most problematic, contributions to psychoanalytic technique. Satisfied in retrospect, he concluded sonorously by citing with approval an old proverb: "The lion springs only once."

A HANDBOOK FOR TECHNICIANS

Each of Freud's major case histories was more or less explicitly a condensed course in psychoanalytic technique. The process notes that have partially survived for one case, that of the Rat Man, also document Freud's sovereign readiness to disregard his own rules. The meal Freud gave his best-known obsessive patient—who was hungry and was refreshed—has for decades stirred up comment in psychoanalytic circles, somewhat quizzical and slightly envious. But it was the rules Freud laid down for his craft, far more than his license in interpreting them for himself, that would make the difference for psychoanalysis.

*The future would compel Freud to add darker strokes to this buoyant appraisal of the Wolf Man's mental condition. In 1919, now a refugee from the Russian Revolution and in need of financial support (which Freud and some friends supplied), the Wolf Man briefly reentered analysis with Freud. Part of the Wolf Man's transference, Freud recognized and reported later, had not been cleared up. In the mid-1920s, under the pressure of a paranoid episode, he had some further intensive analysis, with Ruth Mack Brunswick. But he had become psychologically independent enough to marry, to face the loss of his family fortune with a certain mature resignation, and to hold a job. All his life, though, he was a suffering individual; he never realized his considerable talents, and seemed to invite disasters. To the end, he remained appreciative and admiring of Freud, basking a little in being the most famous patient of the most famous of healers.

Freud began discussing the psychotherapist's art very early, in 1895, in the case reports he included in the *Studies on Hysteria*. He would still be writing on technique in old age: his papers "Analysis Terminable and Interminable" and "Constructions in Analysis" were both published in 1937, when he was over eighty. Faustian in his ambitions though normally modest in his therapeutic expectations, Freud was never wholly contented, never wholly at rest. Near the end of his life he came to wonder whether chemical medication might not some day supersede the laborious procedure of putting the patient on the couch and instructing him to talk. But until that day, he thought, the analytic encounter would remain the most dependable road leading away from neurotic suffering.

The history of Freud's recommendations to therapists over forty years is a study in the cultivation of alert passivity. In the late 1880s, he had used hypnotism on his patients; in the early 1890s, he had tried to get them to confess what troubled them, and to stop evading the sore points, by rubbing their foreheads and interrupting their narratives. His report of resolving in a single session the hysterical symptoms of Katharina during his Alpine summer holidays in 1893 still smacks of a hubristic trust in his healing powers, while his intrusive interpretations to Dora reflect an authoritarian style he was on the verge of relinquishing. Certainly by 1904, when he wrote the short paper "Freud's Psychoanalytic Method" for Leopold Löwenfeld's *Psychic Obsessive Manifestations,* most of his characteristic ideas on technique were in place.

Yet in 1910, speaking at the Nürnberg congress, he gave voice in "The Future Chances of Psychoanalytic Therapy" to his new, chastened mood, which was to prove permanent. He warned his fellow analysts that they all still faced demanding, so far unsolved, technical puzzles, and cautioned them that "nearly everything" in the field of technique "still awaits its definitive determination and much is only now beginning to become clear." This included the analyst's countertransference on the analysand and the technical modifications that the widening repertory of psychoanalytic treatment was beginning to impose on its practitioners.

In the same year, Freud published an energetic short paper attacking what he called "wild" analysis. Considering the casual use—really, abuse—of psychoanalytic vocabulary that would become fashionable in the 1920s, "On 'Wild' Analysis" proved prescient. He recalled an awkward visit from an "elderly lady," a divorcée in her late forties, "fairly well preserved" and "evidently not yet finished with her womanliness." After her divorce, she had begun to suffer from anxiety states, only intensified following a visit to a young physician who had bluntly told her that her symptoms were caused by "sexual neediness." He had offered her a choice of three ways back to health: she could return to her husband, take a lover, or masturbate. None of these alternatives appealed to this "elderly lady." Yet, since her physician had named Freud as the discoverer of the dismal insights he had spread out before her, and suggested that Freud would confirm his diagnosis, she had come to him.

Instead of being flattered or grateful, Freud was irate. He recognized that patients, especially those harassed by nervous disorders, are not necessarily the most reliable of reporters. But even if the distraught lady before him had distorted, or invented, her doctor's unfeeling prescriptions, a word of warning seemed to him in order. To begin with, that amateurish medical psychotherapist had ignorantly assumed that analysts mean by "sexual life" exclusively coitus, rather than a far larger, far more differentiated domain of conscious feelings and unconscious urges. Freud conceded that his patient might perhaps be suffering from an "actual neurosis," a disorder caused by somatic factors—for her, the recent suspension of sexual activity—and if so, a recommendation for "a change in her somatic sexual activity" would have been natural enough. Most probably, though, her physician had misread her situation, and if he had, his prescription was worthless. But his technical errors were if anything graver than his diagnostic ones: it is a gross distortion of the psychoanalytic process to think that merely telling a patient what seems to be wrong, even if the diagnosis happens to be correct, will bring about a cure. Analytic technique must serve to overcome resistances. "Attempts to surprise the patient by brusquely communicating the secrets his physician has divined on a first visit during consulting hours are technically objectionable." What is more, they will "punish themselves" by subjecting the analyst to "the patient's hearty enmity": he will discover that he has lost whatever influence he had enjoyed. In short, before one ventures to offer analytic comments of any sort, one must know a great deal about "psychoanalytic precepts." They supply the place of that vague virtue, "physician's tact."

To forestall this sort of wild analysis and to codify what he had learned in his clinical practice, Freud published a series of papers on technique between 1911 and 1915. Moderate in tone as they were, they had a distinct polemical edge. "Your assent to the most recent technical article," Freud wrote to Abraham in 1912, "was very valuable to me. You are bound to have noticed my critical intentions." He had begun to think about writing on the subject some years earlier, while he was analyzing, or had just terminated, some of his most consequential cases. As usual, his clinical experience and his published writings fed on each other. "Except for Sunday," he told Ferenczi in late November 1908, "I barely get around to writing a few lines on a general methodology of psychoanalysis, of which so far 24 pages are done." It was going slowly, more slowly than the ever-enthusiastic Ferenczi expected;

two weeks later, Freud had managed ten more pages and thought that by Christmas, when Ferenczi was expected on a visit to Berggasse 19, he would be able to show him only a handful more. By February 1909, he planned to set the project aside until the summer holidays, and in June he could report to Jones only that "the essay on the technique is half finished, no leisure now to bring it to an end." But while his analytic work kept him from writing his papers on technique, it also provided him with invaluable material. "The pat[ients] are disgusting," he informed Ferenczi in October, "and give me an opportunity for new technical studies."

His plans for these studies grew more ambitious. In his address to the psychoanalytic congress in Nürnberg, Freud announced that he would "before long endeavor to deal with" interpretation, transference, and the rest of the clinical situation "in a 'General Methodology of Psychoanalysis.'" But Freud's "before long" grew into nearly two years. "When is your book on Methodik coming out?" Jones wondered later that year. "There must be many people eagerly awaiting that, both friends and foes." They would have to be patient; the first installment, "On the Handling of Dream Interpretation in Psychoanalysis," did not appear until December 1911. The other papers on technique, a round half dozen, straggled into print during the next few years. Other pressing work, and the demands of psychoanalytic politics, had intervened to slow Freud down. What is more, he was taking the assignment very seriously, and had done so from the outset. "I believe," he predicted to Ferenczi when he had committed no more than two dozen pages to paper, that the methodology "must become quite important to those who are already doing analyses." Time proved him right.

FREUD'S PAPER "On Beginning the Treatment," with its reassuring, reasonable tone, is representative of the series as a whole; he was offering flexible suggestions rather than ironclad edicts. The felicitous metaphor—chess openings—that he enlisted to elucidate the strategic initial moment in psychoanalysis is calculated to woo his readers; the chess player, after all, is not tied to a single, dictated line of procedure. Indeed, Freud observed, it is only just that the psychoanalyst should have some choices open to him: the histories of individual patients are too diverse to permit the application of rigid, dogmatic rules. Still, Freud left no doubt that certain tactics are plainly indicated: the analyst should select his patients with due care, since not every sufferer is stable enough, or intelligent enough, to sustain the rigors of the psychoanalytic situation. It is best if patient and analyst have not met before, either socially or in a medical setting—certainly one among his recommendations that Freud himself was most inclined to flout. Then, the patient duly chosen and a starting time set, the analyst is advised to take the initial meetings as an opportunity for probing; for a week or so, he should reserve judgment on whether psychoanalysis is in fact the treatment of choice.

Such provisional sessions are not like consultations; in fact, during these trial soundings, the psychoanalyst is bound to be even more silent than usual. Then, if he decides to drop the case, "one spares the patient the painful impression of a miscarried attempt at cure." Yet the experimental time for exploration is not over after these sessions. The symptoms of a patient who presents himself as a mild hysteric or obsessional neurotic may actually be masking the onset of a psychosis not amenable to analytic treatment. Especially in the early weeks, Freud warned, the analyst must not succumb to the heady illusion of certainty.

The trial period, then, is fully integrated into the analytic process: the patient lies on the couch with the analyst behind him, out of sight, listening intently. Those innumerable cartoons depicting that analyst in his chair, notebook on his lap or by his side, have perpetuated a misconception that Freud explicitly addressed in these early papers; he cautioned analysts against taking notes during the session, since doing so would only distract their attention. Besides, they could trust their memories to retain what they needed. He acknowledged that the couch and the invisible analyst were a heritage from hypnotism, and that he had a subjective reason for insisting on this arrangement: "I cannot stand being stared at eight hours a day (or longer) by others." Yet Freud also offered less subjective grounds for commending these "ceremonials": since he let his unconscious take over during the analytic hour, he did not want his patients to watch his facial expressions, lest they be unduly swayed by his responses.

Admittedly the analytic situation, that thoughtfully orchestrated state of deprivation, is stressful for the analysand. But that is precisely its unique virtue. "I know," Freud wrote, "that many analysts do it differently, but I do not know if it is the passion for doing it differently, or an advantage they have discovered in it, that has a larger share in this deviation." As for himself, he had no doubt: the psychoanalytic situation invites the patient to regress, to free himself from the constraints that ordinary social intercourse imposes. Whatever arrangements foster this regression—the couch, the analyst's silences and neutral tone—can only aid in the work of the analysis itself.

From the first day on, while the analysis is getting under way, analyst and analysand have practical, worldly matters to settle. As we know, psychoanalysis is professionally, almost proverbially, allergic to being shamefaced about anything. The very matters that nineteenth-century middle-class culture deemed too delicate for discussion, notably sex and money, are so laden with emotional freight that to veil them with decent silence or, perhaps even worse, with circumlocutions, is to cripple psychoanalytic inquiry from the start. The analyst must anticipate that the cultivated men and women visiting his consulting room will "treat matters of money as they do matters of sex, with the same inconsistency, prudishness, and hypocrisy." Freud acknowledged that money chiefly serves self-preservation and power, but insisted that "powerful sexual factors" are also implicated in attitudes toward it. Hence candor is of the essence. While the patient may not immediately recognize this, his own best interests and the self-interest of the analyst coincide in their practical negotiations. The patient agrees to lease a certain hour of the analyst's time and pays for it whether he avails himself of it or not. This, Freud observed, may seem rather grasping, downright ungenteel, for a medical man, but no other arrangement seems at all practicable. Special monetary favors imperil the analyst's livelihood; as Freud's letters to his intimates of these years attest, he rejoiced in the news that their practices were prospering. But Freud's dislike of financial compromises had more than the analyst's affluence in view; such compromises endanger the continuity and intensity of the patient's analytic involvement by encouraging resistance. If an analysand falls ill with an ailment that is authentically organic, the analyst should break off the analysis, dispose of the hour, and take the patient back, after his recovery, as soon as time is available.

To ensure continuity and intensity, Freud saw most patients six times a week. The exceptions were mild cases and those close to the end of treatment, for whom three days seemed sufficient. Even the interruption of Sunday exacts its price; that is why analysts, he wrote, speak jokingly of the "Monday crust." What is more, the analysis must necessarily stretch out over a substantial period; it is doing the analysand no favor to make a secret of the fact that his analysis may take several years. On this issue, as everywhere in the analytic situation, honesty with the patient is quite literally the best policy: "In general I consider it more honorable, but also more appropriate, to call his attention from the outset to the difficulties and sacrifices of analytic therapy, without necessarily trying to frighten him off; thus one deprives him of any right to claim later on that one had enticed him into a treatment whose extent and significance he had not known." In return, the analyst leaves the analysand free to break off the analysis at any time, a freedom of which some of his early patients, Freud said a little ruefully, had availed themselves all too readily. He could not forget Dora, and Dora had not been the only deserter from Freud's couch.

AMONG THE COMMUNICATIONS the analyst makes to his patient at the very outset, the "fundamental rule" is the one that is truly indispensable: he enjoins the analysand to yield himself up to free association, to say absolutely everything that comes to his mind. It is no doubt important for the analysand to keep his hours and pay his fees. But if he slights these obligations, his lapses can be analyzed. They are, as analysts like to say, grist for the mill. But a consistent failure to obey the fundamental rule must wreck the analysis. In his paper "On Beginning the Treatment," Freud was positively loquacious about this rule. It is true that he was aiming this paper, and its companions, at fellow analysts. "Who still remains outside," he told Ferenczi with respect to the "methodology" he proposed to write, "won't understand a single word of it." But he seems a little anxious even about his chosen audience, and hence rather emphatic, as though to make absolutely sure there will be no misunderstanding. The patient's talk with his therapist will not resemble any conversation he has ever carried on: he is supposed to dismiss from his discourse all order, syntax, logic, discipline, decorum, and considerations of style as irrelevant, in fact harmful. What the patient is most disinclined to mention is precisely what most urgently needs to be ventilated. Freud's key prescription for all analysands is absolute honesty—as impossible to enforce completely as it would be fatal to set aside.

The analysand's weapon in the campaign against his neurosis is talk; the analyst's weapon is interpretation, a very different sort of talk. For while the analysand's verbal activity must be as uninhibited as possible, the analyst's, in sharp contrast, must be thoughtfully dosed. In the strange enterprise that is psychoanalysis, half battle and half alliance, the analysand will cooperate as much as his neurosis lets him. The analyst for his part is, one hopes, not hampered by his own neurosis; in any event, he is required to deploy a highly specialized sort of tact, some of it acquired in his training analysis, the rest drawn from his experience with analytic patients.* It calls for restraint, for silence at most of the analysand's productions and comment on a few. Much of the time, patients will experience their analyst's interpretations as precious gifts that he doles out with far too stingy a hand.

Psychoanalytic interpretation is a subversive reading; it raises startling, often uncomfortable doubts about the ostensible messages the analysand thinks he is conveying. In short, the analyst's interpretation calls the analysand's attention to what he is really saying or doing. To interpret the silent, unmoving wolves in the Wolf Man's dream as distorted representations of a vigorous sexual act is to smoke out a memory, at once terrifying and thrilling, from its lair of repression. To interpret the Rat Man's obsessive ceremonies as signifying unconscious hatred of the persons he loves most is,

---

*The requirement that every prospective psychoanalyst must undergo a training analysis of his own did not appear in these papers, and almost none of the analysts to whom they were addressed had themselves been analyzed. The requirement is a development of the years following the First World War.

again, to drag what had been repressed into the light of day. The rewards of analysts' interpretations were by no means always so spectacular, but their purpose was always, at the least, to chip away at self-deception.

Deciding what to interpret, and when, is a subtle matter; the essential character of psychoanalytic therapy is bound up with it. In responding with irritation to wild analysis, Freud had already excoriated glib and hasty interpretations which, no matter how accurate, must bring an analysis to a premature, calamitous end. Now, addressing his colleagues directly in his paper "On Beginning the Treatment," Freud poured his scorn over such facile analysts, peacocks more intent on displaying their brilliance than on helping their patients: "It is not hard for a very practiced analyst to detect the patient's concealed wishes emerging audibly from his complaints and reports on his illness, but what a measure of complacency and thoughtlessness he must possess to tell a stranger unfamiliar with all psychoanalytic presuppositions, on the shortest of acquaintances, that he is incestuously fixated on his mother, that he harbors death wishes against his supposedly beloved wife, that he carries within himself the intention of cheating his boss, and so on! I have heard that there are analysts who boast of such instant diagnoses and rapid treatments, but I warn everyone against following such examples." The prudent psychoanalyst always pursues his therapeutic aims indirectly, first interpreting his analysand's resistance and then his transference. Extracting confessions of childhood crimes, imagined far more often than real, will follow.

Freud's discussion of resistance places the phenomenon squarely within the therapeutic context, where it obviously belongs. In *The Interpretation of Dreams* he had already defined it plainly: *"Whatever disturbs the progress of the work is a resistance."* Now, in his paper "The Dynamics of Transference," he stressed its perseverance: "Resistance accompanies the treatment at every step; every single association, every act of the patient's, must reckon with this resistance, represents a compromise between the forces aiming at cure and those opposing it." Clinical experience was teaching Freud and his fellow analysts how ingenious and indefatigable analysands' resistance could be, even in those most sincerely committed to analysis. Virtually anything, it seems, can serve it in the psychoanalytic hour: forgetting dreams, remaining silent on the couch, trying to convert the treatment into an intellectual discussion of psychoanalytic theory, holding back essential information, being consistently late, treating the analyst as an enemy. Defensive stratagems such as these are only the most obvious devices available to the forces of resistance. It may also disguise itself as compliance to the analyst's presumed wishes. The so-called good patient—the patient who dreams copiously, associates without hesitation, finds all interpretations brilliant, never shows up late for his hour, pays all his bills promptly—is a particularly intractable case precisely because his intentions are so difficult to unravel.

To resist efforts at cure must appear peculiarly irrational. The utility of resistance for masochists, who get their pleasure from pain, is easy to recognize, but it seems pointless for sufferers who have presumably come into analysis for relief from their symptoms. Their voluntary submission to the effort and expense and sheer unpleasantness of psychoanalytic treatment should vouch for the sincerity of their wish to get well. But the unconscious obeys different, scarcely fathomable laws of its own. A neurosis is a compromise enabling the neurotic to come to terms, however miserably, with repressed wishes and memories. To make the unconscious conscious, which is the announced aim of psychoanalytic therapy, is to threaten the patient with the reemergence of feelings and recollections that he believes are best buried. The argument that the neurotic will be better off recalling repressed material, no matter how distressing, carries rational conviction. And there are elements within the patient ready to make a compact with health; without them, no analysis would be possible. But these elements must do battle with an opposition wishing to leave well enough alone. The analyst seeks to mobilize, and ally himself with, the "normal" forces in the analysand's psyche. He is, after all, a dependable partner—the listener shocked by no revelation, bored at no repetition, censorious of no wickedness. Like the priest in the confessional, he invites confidences; unlike the priest, he never lectures, never imposes penances no matter how mild. Freud had this alliance in mind when he noted that the analyst should begin to reveal his patient's deeper secrets only after the analysand has formed a solid transference, a "regular rapport," with him.*

IT DID NOT escape Freud's attention that the transference is laden with contradictions. The case of Dora had already established for him that the emotional bond the patient tries to impose on the analyst, made up of bits and pieces from passionate, usually earlier, attachments to others, is at once the most intractable impediment to cure and its most effective agent. Now, in his papers on technique, notably "The Dynamics of Transference" and, even more, "Observations on Transference Love," he spelled out the paradoxical workings of transference in greater detail: it is the supreme weapon of resistance, and its nemesis.

These conflicting roles are not dialectical mysteries. Freud distinguished

---

*More recently, analysts have come to call this rapport a "working alliance," or a "therapeutic alliance," but it is not ancestor worship for them to reread Freud's papers on technique and conclude that they have been largely anticipated once again.

among three types of transference that emerge in the psychoanalytic situation: the negative, the erotic, and the sensible. The negative transference, a loading of aggressive, hostile feelings on the psychoanalyst, and the erotic transference, which turns the analyst into an object of passionate love, are both guardians of the resistance. But fortunately there is also a third type, the most rational, least distorted of all, which sees the therapist as a benevolent supportive ally in the struggle against neurosis. Once the first two of these transferences have been exposed, learned from, and disarmed by being brought into consciousness in the analytic hour—Freud called it "the battlefield of transference"—the last, most judicious transference can operate with relatively few obstructions to assist in the long, arduous process of cure. But this reasonable alliance with the analyst can hope to defeat the others only when it is intense enough, and the patient is ready to profit from the analyst's interpretations. "Our cures," Freud had told Jung late in 1906, "come about through the fixation of a libido governing in the unconscious (transference)." And this transference "provides the impulsion for comprehending and translating the unconscious; where it refuses to act, the patient does not take this trouble, or does not listen when we present the translation we have found. It is essentially a cure through love."

It all sounds very straightforward, but Freud was aware that this love is a most treacherous helper. The sensible transference is very vulnerable: only too often, the patient's warm feeling and active cooperation degenerate into erotic longing, serving not the resolution of the neurosis but its perpetuation. To put it bluntly, analysands are inclined to fall in love with the analyst, a fact of psychoanalytic life that promptly became the burden of bad jokes and sly insinuations. Freud thought such malicious gossip virtually inescapable; psychoanalysis offended too many pieties to remain immune from slanders. But real, embarrassing episodes were troubling enough to have Freud devote a separate paper to the matter. Written in late 1914, and published early the following year, "Observations on Transference Love" was the last of his papers on technique and, he thought, as he told Abraham, "the best and most useful in the whole series." Hence, he added sardonically, he was "prepared to see it call forth the strongest disapproval." Yet he wrote it largely to alert analysts to the dangers of transference love and thus to blunt such disapproval.

Transference love is at once distressing and comical, inescapable and devilishly hard to resolve. In ordinary medical practice, Freud wrote, three possible escape routes present themselves: patient and physician may marry; they may part; they may have a clandestine affair and continue the medical treatment. The first of these resolutions, Freud thought, is rare; the second, though common, is unacceptable to psychoanalysts because the ex-patient will only repeat her behavior with her next physician; the third is prohibited by both "middle-class morality and medical dignity." What the analyst must do, once he finds himself in the enticing spot of having his patient declare her love for him, is to analyze. He must show her that her infatuation only repeats an earlier, virtually always an infantile, experience. The patient's passion for her analyst is not an authentic love but a form of transference and of resistance.*

In this delicate situation, Freud said firmly, the analyst must resist all compromises, no matter how plausible or humane he may believe them to be. To argue with the patient, or to try deflecting her desire into sublimated channels, will prove ineffectual. The fundamental ethical position of the analyst, identical with his professional obligation, must remain his guide: "Psychoanalytic treatment is founded on truthfulness." Nor may the analyst yield to his patient's entreaties, even if he persuades himself that he is only trying to gain influence over her for the sake of speeding her cure. He would soon be disenchanted: "The patient would achieve her aim, he would never achieve his." This unacceptable solution reminded Freud of an amusing anecdote about a pastor and an insurance agent. On his deathbed, the agent, an unbeliever, is compelled to endure the ministrations of a divine, called in by his family in the desperate pious hope that in the presence of mortality the dying man will finally see the light of religious faith. "The conversation lasts so long that those waiting gather hope. At last the door of the sick chamber opens. The unbeliever has not been converted, but the pastor goes away insured."

The sobering recognition that his analysand's love is only a transference love will enable the analyst to keep his emotional, to say nothing of his physical, distance. "For the physician it represents a precious enlightenment and a useful warning against any countertransference lying in wait within him. He must recognize that the patient's infatuation is extorted by the analytic situation and cannot be ascribed to the merits of his person; that, in short, he has no reason whatever to be proud of such a 'conquest,' as one would call it outside analysis." The analyst in this situation, which is only a special case of the analytic situation in general, must deny the patient's clamor for gratification. "The cure must be carried through in abstinence; I mean by that not physical self-denial alone, nor the denial of every desire, for this perhaps no patient could tolerate. But I want to state the principle

---

*In this discussion Freud worked with a simplified model: a male analyst and a female patient. But the same rules hold for female analysts treating male patients and as well for analysts treating patients of the same sex. The ingenuity of the erotic transference is virtually limitless.

that one must permit neediness and yearning to remain as forces favoring work and change, and that one must beware of appeasing them with surrogates."

This blunt prescription was a firm, universal rule for the psychoanalyst at work. However tentative Freud might sound about many of his recommendations, on abstinence he was categorical. Yet on this crucial point, Freud's gift for vivid metaphor generated a certain amount of confusion and unleashed a debate on technique that has never died down. As a model, Freud offered his fellow analysts the surgeon, who "pushes aside all his affects and even his humane compassion and posits a single aim for his mental forces—to carry through the operation as correctly and effectively as possible." A therapist's ambition to provide spectacular cures is, after all, the lethal antagonist of such cures. The all-too-human wish to get close to the patient is no less damaging. Hence Freud felt justified in commending the surgeon's "coldness of feeling," which would ward off such understandable but unprofessional aspirations. To reveal intimate details of his inner life or family relationships is therefore a serious technical error: "The physician should be opaque to the patient and, like a mirror, show nothing but what is shown to him."

These frigid images state Freud's case with a chilling finality that some of his other texts, and even more his practice, partly invalidate. We have seen him bending his rules and at times breaking them, with a sovereign sense of mastery and in the interest of sheer humaneness. He remitted the fees of his analysands when they fell on hard times. He allowed himself cordial comments during the hour. He made friends with his favorite patients. He conducted, as we know, informal analyses in some astonishing settings; analyzing Eitingon during evening strolls through Vienna is only the most spectacular of his informal experiments. But in his papers on technique Freud allowed himself not a hint of such escapades.

There was, of course, no room for them in the handbook Freud was compiling for his colleagues. Everything that obstructs the analysis, he had written, is a resistance, and everything that distracts patients from following the fundamental rule is an obstruction. Even at best, patients introduce more than enough resistances of their own; there is no need for the analyst to add to them with tokens of affection, rational discussions of theory, or earnest aspirations in behalf of his analysands' self-development. To gratify patients by loving them, reassuring them, or just telling them one's vacation plans is to sustain the very habits of thought they have gone into analysis to overcome. It may sound callous, but the analyst must not permit pity for his suffering patients to overwhelm him; this very suffering is an agent in the curative process.* To take the shortcut of soothing reassurance is only to keep the neurosis in place. It is (one might say) offering Saint Sebastian aspirin to ease his pains. But to enlist as metaphors for the analyst's procedure the cool work of the surgeon, or the blank surface of the mirror, is to slight his partnership, at once taciturn and very human, with the unhappy being on the couch before him.

EVEN IF ANALYST and analysand scrupulously observe all of Freud's technical injunctions, the healing work of the analysis is always slow and never certain. Freud excluded from analytic treatment many types of mental disorder, notably the psychoses, on the ground that the psychotic cannot establish the necessary transference to the analyst. But even hysterics and obsessional neurotics, peculiarly suitable to analytic treatment, often showed snails' progress and dismaying relapses. Elusive memories, stubborn symptoms, an abiding affection for neurotic habits, proved potent obstructions to effectual interpretations and to the kind of transference that assists in the cure. The most trying obstructions to deal with were those transferences which induced the patient to repeat earlier conduct instead of remembering it. Clearly, Freud saw, the one quality the analyst can least afford is impatience. Clinical experience showed that for the analysand to know something intellectually is never good enough. But at long last the time may come when the patient, steadily relapsing, steadily forgetting insights painfully won, will begin to absorb, to "work through," his hard-won knowledge. "The physician," Freud suggested in his paper "Remembering, Repeating, and Working Through," has "nothing more to do than to wait and let things take their course, which cannot be avoided nor always be speeded up." Again, both partners in the analytic enterprise must cultivate patience: "This working through of the resistance may in practice become a wearisome task for the analysand and a trial of patience for the analyst. But it is that part of the work which has the greatest transforming impact on the patient" and which, indeed, distinguishes psychoanalysis from all those treatments that attempt to influence the patient by means of suggestion. The analyst is not simply passive in this important phase; if he finds sufficient compliance in his patient, he should manage to "give all the symptoms of the illness a new transference meaning, to replace his common neurosis with a transference neurosis." This transference neurosis is a unique sort of ailment, a disorder peculiar—and necessary— to the treatment. The analyst may rid the patient of it "by means of the

*As he put it not long after, addressing his colleagues at the Budapest congress in late September 1918: "We must see to it, cruel as it may sound, that the sufferings of the patient . . . do not come to an end prematurely." ("Wege der psychoanalytischen Therapie" [1919], GW XII, 188/"Lines of Advance in Psycho-Analytic Therapy," SE XVII, 163.)

therapeutic work." There follows a kind of coda, the phase of termination, on which Freud offered only a few sparse comments. It did, he knew, produce miseries of its own; he called them "leave-taking difficulties"—*Abschiedssch- wierigkeiten.* The analysis once well under way, the newly acquired knowl- edge worked through, and the transference neurosis sturdy enough, the desired end will come.

FOR ALL HIS CONCILIATORY and genial rhetoric, Freud presented these papers with an air of complete conviction, the air of a founder and seasoned practi- tioner. He was only setting out the methods he had found most efficient in his own practice; others might want to proceed in their own way. But despite these politic disclaimers, he left no doubt that he expected his recommenda- tions to assume commanding authority with his followers. The authority was earned; no one else could have written these papers, and his readers candidly admired, freely cited, and visibly profited from them. In 1912, Eitingon thanked Freud warmly for "Recommendations to Physicians Practicing Psy- choanalysis," a paper from which, he wrote, he "could learn a great deal." And Eitingon was in large company. Freud's series of papers on technique came to serve as an indispensable handbook for his profession. Justly so: they are as brilliant as anything he ever wrote. It is not that they are the last word on how to conduct an analysis; they are not even Freud's last word. Nor do they constitute an exhaustive or formal treatise. But taken together, as recom- mendations on how to manage the clinical encounter, on its opportunities and its pitfalls, they are so rich in sturdy analytical sense, so shrewd in anticipating criticisms, that they continue after all these years to serve as a guide to the aspiring, and a resource for the practicing, analyst.

One question they did not resolve, did not even address, was that of just how many analytic patients went away cured. This question was then, and has remained since, a most controversial issue. But in the years when he wrote these papers, Freud and his closest adherents thought that within the limits they themselves had set, the record of analytic successes compared favorably with the therapeutic efforts of their rivals. Nor did Freud permit whatever doubts he might harbor on this score to dim his confidence in his creation as an intellectual instrument for explaining the mind at work. That confi- dence was not just self-created. Gratifying echoes from the outside world were no longer so scarce as they had once been. By 1915, when Freud published the last in his series of papers on technique, he was far from being the isolated pioneer of the Fliess period or the first years of the Wednesday Psychological Society. And his studies of art and literature, of religion and prehistory, only strengthened his confidence that the writ of his psychology, so persuasively exhibited in his case histories, ran everywhere.

SEVEN

Applications and Implications

MATTERS OF TASTE

Freud's punishing schedule during these turbulent years raises the question just how he could find time for any private life at all. Between 1905 and 1915, deluged with clinical work, case histories, editorial chores, and the exhausting demands of psychoanalytic politics, he published papers on literature, law, religion, education, art, ethics, linguistics, folklore, fairy tales, mythology, archeology, war, and the psychology of schoolboys. Yet he punctually presented himself at one o'clock every day for the family's main meal, kept up with his weekly card game of tarock on Saturday night, unfailingly visited his mother on Sunday morning, took his walk in the evening, entertained visitors, and (though these were rare occasions) went to a Mozart opera.

Busy as he was, his growing notoriety made him increasingly the object of invitations to address or write for popular audiences, and some of these invitations he accepted. In 1907, he published, among other short essays, an "open letter to Dr. M. Fürst," the editor of a journal specializing in social hygiene, on "The Sexual Enlightenment of Children," in which he spoke out for candor. In the same year, he gave a genial talk on the place of daydreams in the creative work of the imaginative writer, the *Dichter*.* He spoke before a largely lay audience in the salon of Hugo Heller, his acquaintance and publisher, and therefore turned the talk into an accessible exposition of just how certain cultural artifacts are made. It was also his first attempt, apart from a few hints in *The Interpretation of Dreams*, to apply psychoanalytic ideas to culture.

For all its lightness of touch, this lecture, published the next year as "Creative Writers and Daydreaming," is a serious contribution to psychoanalytic aesthetics. The work of the unconscious, the psychology of wish fulfillment, and the long reach of childhood into later life are all central to its argument. Freud began innocently and tactfully enough by posing a question that is likely to interest all laymen: What are the sources from which writers draw their material? The answer, Freud noted, never seems satisfactory and, to deepen the mystery, even if it were satisfactory, this knowledge would not make the layman into a poet or playwright. He added, in his most self-effacing manner, that one might hope to find some preliminary enlightenment about the ways of the *Dichter* if one could discover some similar activity that is common to all humans. Piling up the prudent negatives, Freud expressed the hope that his approach might "turn out to be not unfruitful."

These apologies out of the way, Freud took one of his characteristic acrobatic leaps connecting one range of human experience with another. Parallel-hunting is a dangerous sport, especially if it presses inferences beyond their capacity, but valid parallels may discover hitherto unknown relationships and, even better, unsuspected causal connections. Freud's leap was of this last sort: every child at play, he argued, behaves like a *Dichter* "in that he creates his own world for himself or, more correctly put, transposes the things of his world into a new order that pleases him." In playing, the child is very much in earnest, but he knows that what he makes is an invention: "The opposite of play is not seriousness but—reality." The poet or novelist proceeds in very much the same way; he recognizes the fantasies he is elaborating to be fantasies, but that does not make them any less momentous than, say, the child's imaginary playmate. Children find play enjoyable, and since humans are most reluctant to forgo a pleasure they have once enjoyed, they find a substitute as adults. Instead of playing, they fantasize. These two activities are virtually mirrors of one another: both are actuated by a wish. But while children's play expresses the desire to be grown-up, adults find their fantasies childish. In that sense, play and fantasy alike reflect states of dissatis-

---

*The handy, untranslatable German term *Dichter* applies equally to the novelist, the playwright, and the poet.

faction: "One may say, the happy person never fantasizes; only the unsatisfied one does." In short, a fantasy is, like a wish expressed in play, "a correction of unsatisfying reality." The imaginative revisions that the grownup imposes on reality involve unrealized ambitions or unrealizable sexual desires; he keeps them concealed, because these are wishes that respectable society has banished from social, even familial, discourse.

This is where the *Dichter* finds his cultural task. Driven by his vocation, he gives utterance to his daydreams and thus broadcasts the secret fantasies of his less eloquent contemporaries. Like the dreamer at night, the creative daydreamer combines a powerful experience of his adult life with a reawakened distant memory, and then transforms into literature the wish that this combination has aroused. Like a dream, his poem or novel is a mixed creature of the present and the past, and of external no less than internal impulsions. Freud did not deny the imagination a share in the making of literary works, but saw these works principally as reality refashioned, beautifully distorted. He was no romantic celebrating the artist as the nearly divine maker; his reluctance to acknowledge the purely creative aspects of the writer's and painter's work is palpable.

Freud's analysis of literary creativity, then, is sober rather than rhapsodic; it concentrates on the psychological transactions between the creator and his childhood, between maker and consumer. Since at bottom all wishes are egotistic, their publication is likely to repel the audiences busy dreaming their own self-centered daydreams. The poet overcomes these resistances by "bribing" his readers or listeners with the "forepleasure" of aesthetic form, a forepleasure that promises greater pleasures to come and permits readers to view their own daydreams "without any self-reproach or shame." It is precisely in this act of bribery, Freud thought, that "the *Ars poetica* proper" consists. In his view, "the actual pleasure in an imaginative work emerges from a liberation of tensions in our minds." The artist (one might gloss Freud's essential argument) baits his hook with beauty.

DESPITE ALL HIS BURDENS, all his activity, Freud's regular routine continued to include, as it always had, traditional family pleasures, winters and summers alike. Until 1909, when Martin was admitted to the university and went off on his own, Freud spent precious vacation time with his wife, his sister-in-law, and all his children in the mountains. That same year, 1909, marked another milestone in Freud's family life; his daughter Mathilde, the eldest, was the first of his children to marry. For all the amusement and sheer pleasure she had given her father from the moment she was born in October 1887, she had also been a cause for anxious concern. An appendectomy in 1906, apparently botched, had left her in uncertain health: two years later she came down with a worrisome high fever that made her father suspect peritonitis, and two years after that, "brave as always," she had to undergo another serious operation. Her intermittent illnesses, somewhat heavy features, and sallow complexion wrought havoc with Mathilde's self-esteem; she worried out loud to her father that she might be unattractive. This gave Freud an opportunity for dispensing fond paternal reassurance. "I have long suspected," he wrote her in March 1908, when she was recuperating at a spa from her latest illness, "that, with all your usual reasonableness, you feel hurt that you are not beautiful enough and therefore will not appeal to any man." But, Freud told her, he had been watching her with a smile. "You seem beautiful enough to me." In any event she should remember that "for a long time now not the formal beauty of a girl but rather the impression of her personality has been decisive." He invited his daughter to look into the mirror; she would discover to her relief that her features were neither common nor repulsive. What is more—and this was the old-fashioned message her "loving father" wanted to convey—"the reasonable ones among the young men know, after all, what they should look for in a woman: sweet temper, cheerfulness, and the ability to make life pleasanter and easier for them." However anachronistic Freud's attitudes were beginning to appear, even in 1908, Mathilde Freud apparently found this letter bracing. At all events, the following February, at twenty-one, she married a fellow Viennese, a businessman twelve years her elder, Robert Hollitscher. Freud, then in the first glow of his friendship with Sándor Ferenczi, told Ferenczi that he would have preferred *him* as a son-in-law, but he never begrudged his daughter her choice: Hollitscher quickly became "Robert," a member of the Freud clan in good standing.

Four years later, in January 1913, Freud's second daughter, Sophie, also deserted him. Freud adopted her fiancé, the Hamburg photographer Max Halberstadt, with little delay. He had visited Halberstadt's studio and formed a favorable impression of his future son-in-law. In early July 1912, he still addressed him rather formally as "Dear Sir"—*Sehr geehrter Herr*—and told him a little sententiously that he was happy to see Sophie following her inclinations just as her older sister, Mathilde, had done four years before. Just two weeks later, Halberstadt had become "My dear Son-in-Law," though Freud still chose to address him with the distant *Sie*. Yet he was plainly pleased with the addition to his family. Halberstadt, Freud wrote Mathilde, complimenting her at the same time, was "evidently a very reliable, serious, tender, refined and yet not weak human being," and he thought it most likely that the Freuds would witness, for the second time, the rarity of a happy marriage among their children. By July 27, Halberstadt had become "Dear Max," and finally, two weeks after that, Freud admitted him to his inner family circle and called him *du.* Yet his sense of gain was faintly shadowed by a sense of loss. On a postcard that Freud sent his future son-in-law from Rome in September, he signed himself with "Cordial regards from a wholly orphaned father."*

BUT PSYCHOANALYSIS retained first claim on Freud's attention. Hanns Sachs, who came to know Freud at this time, exaggerated only slightly when he saw him "dominated by one despotic idea," a devotion to work that his family supported "with the greatest eagerness, without a grumble." His single-mindedness in these expansive days was perhaps greater than ever: the time to apply the discoveries of psychoanalysis outside the consulting room was at hand. "I am more and more penetrated by the conviction of the cultural value of ψA," Freud told Jung in 1910, "and I could wish for a bright fellow to draw the justified consequences for philosophy and society from it."† He still had moments of hesitation or uncertainty, though they were rare and becoming rarer. "I find it very hard," he wrote in the same year, responding to Ferenczi's extravagant New Year's greetings, "to comment on the value of my writings and their influence on the future formation of science. At times I believe in it, at times I have doubts." He added, in a phrase that was becoming a favorite with him, "The good Lord himself perhaps does not know it yet."

But while Freud might be proud, or even a little boastful, of his gift for self-criticism, the prospects for a psychoanalytic interpretation of culture made him euphoric. His next assignment, he was confident, lay right there. By 1913, summarizing the work of explanation outside the consulting room that psychoanalysis had already done, he outlined an ambitious program for further conquests. Psychoanalysis, he reported, is able to throw shafts of light on the origins of religion and morality, on justice and philosophy. Now the "whole history of culture" was only waiting for its psychoanalytic interpreter.‡

---

*When Sophie's first child was born, he greeted it with an exclamation of astonishment. "Last night," he wrote Ferenczi on a postcard on March 11, 1914, "around 3 o'clock a little boy as first grandchild! Very remarkable! An elderly feeling, respect before the wonders of sexuality!" (Freud–Ferenczi Correspondence, Freud Collection, LC.)

†In his enthusiasm, Freud wrote *Welt*—"world"—for *Wert*—"value"—a slight but suggestive slip intimating how far-reaching he thought his ideas to be.

‡What he told the maverick Flemish Socialist Hendrik de Man in 1925 had been his settled conviction for a decade and a half: "I have always been of the opinion that the extramedical applications of psychoanalysis are as significant as its medical ones; indeed, that the former might perhaps have a greater influence on the mental orientation of humanity." (Freud to Hendrik de Man, December 13, 1925. Archief Hendrik de Man, International Institute of Social History, Amsterdam.) This was the voice of the ambivalent physician, whose heart was elsewhere.

Some of Freud's papers on applied psychoanalysis were brief, inconclusive incursions into fields in which he did not profess to be an expert. He knew that he was neither archeologist nor historian, neither philologist nor lawyer. But then, as he noted with a mixture of asperity and satisfaction, professional practitioners of neighboring disciplines, whether from ignorance or timidity, seemed unwilling to avail themselves of the insights psychoanalysts were offering them. Their resistance was as adamant as the resistance of the psychiatric establishment, but it gave Freud welcome freedom of maneuver and permitted him to indulge the luxury of a tentative, often playful tone.

FREUD NEVER DOUBTED that the bright fellow who would draw the cultural consequences of psychoanalysis was himself. But he was delighted to have other advance men among the psychoanalysts joining him. Jung had long enjoyed dwelling on the psychoanalysis of culture, especially its occult side, as though he were satisfying a sensual appetite. In the early spring of 1910, he confessed to Freud that he was indulging himself "in the virtually auto-erotic enjoyment of my mythological dreams." He was so intent on gaining access to the secrets of mysticism "with the key of the libido theory," that Freud asked Jung "to return in good time to the neuroses. There," he added emphatically, "is the mother country in which we must first secure our domination against everything and everyone." For all his interest in applied psychoanalysis, Freud insisted on putting first things first.

But Karl Abraham and Otto Rank, though less mystical in disposition than Jung, were only marginally less excited. In 1911, Abraham published a small monograph psychoanalyzing the short-lived late-nineteenth-century Tyrolean painter Giovanni Segantini, then in high repute for his mystical peasant scenes. Abraham took no little pride in his pioneering effort, and in the following year added another contribution to applied psychoanalysis—a paper on the Egyptian pharaoh Amenhotep IV, the historic religious innovator who would later preoccupy Freud in his book on Moses and monotheism.* At the same time Rank, that omnivorous reader and facile writer, was spreading himself thin studying the psychology of the artist, the incest motif in literature, and the myths surrounding the birth of the hero.

In 1912, in association with Hanns Sachs, Rank founded *Imago*, a periodical specializing, as its masthead proclaimed, in the application of psychoanalysis to the cultural sciences. Originally, as Freud informed Ernest Jones, this

---

*Fliess, making himself agreeable to Abraham, as he liked to do, responded when he received an offprint of Abraham's paper on Amenhotep by telling the author that he would now "try to think through that personality once again in light of your conception." (Fliess to Abraham [postcard], October 12, 1912. Karl Abraham papers, LC.)

"new journal, not medical at all," was to be called *Eros and Psyche*. The name its founders finally adopted was a tribute to literature; it explicitly recalled a recent novel, *Imago*, by the Swiss poet Carl Spitteler, which had celebrated the power of the unconscious in a misty love story. Freud was at first concerned that even though *Imago* would be edited by "two bright and honest boys," it would "not have so easy a career as the other organs have met with." His worries proved unjustified. *Imago*, Freud could report in June 1912, "is doing surprisingly well"; the number of subscribers, 230, mainly from Germany, seemed to him exceedingly satisfactory, though the lack of interest in Vienna troubled him. The editors found psychoanalysts everywhere only too eager to contribute, and not least among their authors was Freud himself. He superintended the "two bright and honest boys," and sent them some of his boldest exploratory papers.

The nonclinical writings of the inner circle generated opportunities for round robins of good will and mutual congratulations. Freud welcomed Jones's weighty contribution to *Imago* on the symbolic significance of salt; Jones told Abraham that he had perused his "charming study" of Segantini "with the greatest interest"; Abraham for his part read Freud's *Totem and Taboo* "twice, with ever-increasing relish." Admittedly, some of the pathographies of artists and poets produced in the Vienna circle were naive and slapdash, and at times they aroused Freud's outspoken irritation. But whether well done or bungled, applied psychoanalysis was a cooperative venture almost from the start. Freud found this widespread interest agreeable, but he needed no urging from others to put culture on the couch.

The principles governing Freud's sorties into the domain of culture were few in number, easy to state, but hard to apply: all is lawful, all is disguised, and all is connected. Psychoanalysis, as he put it, establishes intimate links between "the psychological achievements of individuals and of society by postulating the same dynamic source for both." The "principal function of the mental mechanism" is to "relieve the person from the tensions which his needs create in him." He secures relief in part by "extracting satisfaction from the external world" or by "finding some other way of disposing of the unsatisfied impulses." Hence psychoanalytic inquiry into art or literature must be, like the inquiry into neuroses, a search for hidden wishes gratified or hidden wishes frustrated.

Equipped with these essentially simple principles, Freud traveled among the higher artifacts of culture, those privileged children of mind, covering an immense area. But in all his explorations, his focus always remained psychoanalysis. What mattered to him was less what he could learn from art history, linguistics, and the rest than what they could learn from him; he entered alien terrain as a conquistador rather than as a supplicant.* His paper on Leonardo was, as we have seen, an experiment in biography but at the same time a psychoanalytic investigation into the origins of homosexuality and the workings of sublimation. It was in this respect exemplary for all his other ventures into cultural analysis. Psychoanalysis, as he said, always remained his mother country.

FREUD ENJOYED SUCH excursions enormously. But his psychoanalytic preoccupation with the products of culture was not simply a refreshing holiday activity to beguile hours of leisure. The quality of compulsion so evident in his attitude toward case histories and theoretical investigations was also at work in his thinking about art and literature. He had, as we have seen, experienced the enigma of Leonardo and the more amusing puzzles posed by Schreber as so many obsessions to be gratified and discharged. The mysteries of *King Lear* and Michelangelo's *Moses* pursued him no less urgently. All his life, Freud felt under powerful pressure to penetrate secrets. When in 1909 Ernest Jones offered to send him his paper on Hamlet's Oedipus complex, Freud expressed great interest. Jones's paper was an extended footnote to Freud's famous pages in *The Interpretation of Dreams* on the guilt feelings aroused in Hamlet by love for his mother and hatred for his father, pages Freud recalled with evident pride: "When I wrote down what seemed to me the solution of the mystery I had not undertaken special research into the Hamlet literature but I knew what the results of our German writers were and saw that even Goethe had missed the mark." Freud found it a source of satisfaction, hard for a foreigner to appreciate, to have outdone the great Goethe himself.

Freud's earnest and driven researches, in short, were not wholly a matter of free choice. In June 1912, as his longed-for summer break was approaching, he told Abraham that "at present, my intellectual activity would be confined to the corrections for the fourth edition of my [Psychopathology of] Everyday Life if it had not suddenly occurred to me that the opening scene in Lear, the judgment of Paris, and the choice of caskets in the Merchant of Venice are really based on the same motif which I now must track down." He simply "must" track it down. No wonder he could describe his traffic with ideas in terms appropriate to suffering. "I am tormented today," he reported to Ferenczi in the spring of 1911, "by the secret of the tragic school, which will

---

*Reacting to Emil Ludwig's biography of Goethe, of which he thought very little, he wrote to Otto Rank, "The reproach one has raised against our ψA psychobiographies rather applies far more intensely to this [biography] as to all other nonanalytic ones." (Freud to Rank, August 10, 1921. Rank Collection, Box 1b. Rare Book and Manuscript Library, Columbia University.)

surely not withstand ψA." He never followed up this cryptic hint, and we may never know which tragic school he had in mind. His torment for once left him without compelling him to unravel it by strenuous intellectual work. But in general Freud's most powerful interests suspiciously resembled exigent pressures, unresolved tensions. "I have begun to study Macbeth, which has long been tormenting me," he wrote to Ferenczi in 1914, "without having found the solution thus far." Freud said more than once that he worked best when he was not feeling quite well; what he never commented on was that his necessary indispositions were at least in part the visible signs of thoughts struggling for expression.

A conundrum emerging in Freud's mind was like an alien irritant, the grain of sand in the oyster that could not be ignored and might in the end produce a pearl. Freud's view was that an adult's scientific curiosity is the belated elaboration of the child's search for the truth about the difference between the sexes and the mysteries of conception and birth. If so, Freud's own urgent inquisitiveness reflects an unusually strong need for illumination on these secrets. They baffled him all the more as he brooded on the notice-able disparity in his parents' ages and on the presence of brothers as old as his mother, to say nothing of a nephew older than himself.

PERHAPS NONE OF Freud's writings on art reveals their compulsive character more eloquently than his paper on the *Moses* of Michelangelo, published in 1914. Freud had stood fascinated before this over-life-size statue on his first trip to Rome, in 1901; he never ceased to find it baffling and splendid. No other work of art had ever impressed him quite so much. In 1912, on another of his holiday excursions to Rome, he wrote his wife that he was visiting Michelangelo's *Moses* daily and thought he might write "a few words" about him. As it turned out, he was very fond of the few words he did write, though he printed them in *Imago* as being "by * * *." Reasonably enough, Abraham wondered at the anonymity: "Don't you think that one will recognize the lion's claw?" But Freud persisted in calling the paper "a love child." In March 1914, just after "Moses" had come back from the printer, Freud still won-dered to his "dear Jones" whether "it may be better not to acknowledge this child before the public," and unacknowledged it remained for ten years. Yet he cherished it almost as much as the statue it analyzes. While Freud was in the midst of work on this paper, Ernest Jones was visiting Rome, and Freud wrote him with an access of longing, "I envy you for seeing Rome so soon and so early in life. Bring my deepest devotion to Moses and write me about him." Jones, sensitive to what was wanted, rose to the occasion. "My first pilgrimage the day after my arrival," he wrote to Freud, "was to convey your greetings to Moses, and I think he unbent a little from his haughtiness. What a statue!"

What intrigued Freud most about Michelangelo's massive statue was precisely that it should intrigue him so much. Whenever he visited Rome, he visited the *Moses,* most purposefully. "In 1913, through three lonely September weeks," he recalled, "I stood daily in the church in front of the statue, studied it, measured it, drew it, until that understanding came to me that I only dared to express anonymously in the paper." The *Moses* was ideally suited to pique Freud's curiosity; it had long generated admiration and conjecture. The monumental figure displays on its forehead the mythical horns representing the radiance that visited Moses's face after he had seen God. Michelangelo, given to the heroic, the outsize, depicted Moses as a vigorous, muscular, commanding old man, with a flowing river of a beard that he grasps with his left hand and with the forefinger of his right. He is seated, frowning, looking sternly to his left and holding the tablets of the law under his right arm. The problem that fascinated Freud was just what moment Michelangelo had chosen to depict. He was pleased to quote the art historian Max Sauerlandt to the effect that "no work of art in the world has been subjected to such contradictory judgments as this Pan-headed Moses. The very interpretation of the figure is open to complete contradictions." The tension in Moses's legs suggests an action begun or recently completed; but is Moses just rising or has he just sat down? This was the puzzle that Freud felt obliged to solve. Had Michelangelo portrayed Moses the eternal emblem of the lawgiver who has seen God, or was this Moses in a moment of rage at his people, ready to break the tablets he has brought from Mount Sinai?

In 1912, Freud brought a small plaster cast of the *Moses* home with him, but he was not yet ready to put his ideas on paper. Ernest Jones was helpfully complicating matters. "Jones sent me photos of a Donatello statue from Florence," Freud told Ferenczi in November, "which have rather shaken my point of view." The photographs raised the possibility that Michelangelo had carved his statue in obedience to artistic rather than emotional pressures. Late in December 1912, thanking Jones for his help, Freud asked, almost sheepishly, for a favor: "If I may trouble you for something more—it is more than indiscrete—let me say I want a reproduction—even by drawing of the remarkable lower contour of the tables running thus in a note of mine." He explained his meaning with an amateurish but serviceable little sketch showing the lower edges of the tablets of the law. Jones promptly complied; he knew how much such details mattered.

While he was contemplating his paper on the *Moses* and taking notes for it, Freud continued to vacillate. In August 1913, he sent Ferenczi a picture postcard from Rome showing Michelangelo's controversial statue, and in September he wrote to Ernest Jones, "I have visited old Moses again, and got confirmed in my explication of his position but something in the comparative material you collected for me, did shake my confidence which is not yet restored." Early in October he reported from Vienna that he had just returned, "still a little intoxicated from the beauty of the 17 days in Rome." But as late as February 1914, he was not yet sure: "In the Moses affair I am growing negative again."

As might be expected, Freud developed an interpretation all his own. Apart from the few who had read Michelangelo's statue as a monument to timeless grandeur, most art historians had understood it to represent the calm before the storm: coming upon the children of Israel worshiping the golden calf, Moses is about to explode in his wrath and smash the tablets. But Freud, closely investigating such details as the position of Moses's right hand and that of the tablets themselves, concluded that Michelangelo had intended to show Moses subduing his inner tempest, "not the introduction to a violent action but the remnants of a terminated movement." He was well aware that his interpretation contradicted the Scriptures; in his towering fury, the Book of Exodus records, Moses did break the tablets. But this authority could not shake Freud's ultimate conclusion: his *Moses* is a very human Moses, a man who is, like Michelangelo, given to outbursts of temper, and who is at this supreme moment manfully controlling himself. Hence Michelangelo "made his Moses for the Pope's mausoleum, not without reproach against the deceased, as an admonition to himself, raising himself with this self-criticism above his own nature."

This sounds very much as though Freud's reading of Michelangelo was a reading of himself. His life, it appears over and over, was a struggle for self-discipline, for control over his speculative impulses and his rage—rage at his enemies and, even harder to manage, at those among his adherents he found wanting or disloyal.* While he had been gripped by Michelangelo's *Moses* at first sight in 1901, he did not see the statue as an assignment for interpretation until 1912, when his association with Jung was going sour. And he drafted "The Moses of Michelangelo" in late 1913, just before he began to fashion his "History of the Psychoanalytic Movement," the "bomb" he planned to throw at Jung and Adler. In that polemic, he would keep his fury in check, just barely, the better to serve his cause.† But sorely tried as he felt,

*As we shall see later, this rage also had unconscious dimensions, most probably founded in his disappointment at being increasingly displaced from his privileged position as his mother's only child as Amalia Freud presented her first-born with sibling after sibling.

†"The winter of 1913–1914, following the unhappy Congress in Munich in the preceding September, was the worst time in the conflict with Jung. The *Moses* was written in the same month as the long

he was not at all certain whether he could muster the iron self-possession he had imputed to his favorite statue. In October 1912, he had written to Ferenczi, "In my mood, I compare myself rather with the historical rather than with the Moses of Michelangelo I have interpreted." The cardinal point of his exercise in art-historical detection, then, was to teach himself the virtue of imitating Michelangelo's restrained statesman rather than the impulsive leader of whose hot temper the Book of Exodus gives such eloquent evidence. Only some such biographical interpretation can account for Freud's daily visits to Michelangelo's statue, for his meticulous measuring, his detailed drawing, his perusal of monographs, all a little disproportionate to the results which had to be, at best, no more than a footnote in the psychoanalytic interpretation of art. But it was not only Freud the politician in search of self-discipline who spent all these hours on Michelangelo's *Moses*. It was also Freud the compulsive researcher, who was not at liberty to refuse the solicitations of a puzzle once it possessed him.

FREUD CONFINED HIS observations on aesthetics to papers and monographs. The "unriddling of the secrets of artistic creation" for which Max Graf pleaded in one of the Wednesday-night sessions late in 1907 remained a torso in Freud's writings. The failure was in large part personal. Freud's ambivalence about artists was, as we know, acute. "I have often asked myself in astonishment," he wrote to Arthur Schnitzler, thanking him for greetings on his fiftieth birthday, "whence you could have taken this or that secret knowledge, which I had acquired through laborious investigations." Nothing could be more gracious, and in letters of thanks one is not on oath. But for long years, the imaginative artist's apparently effortless psychological penetration had rankled in Freud. His was precisely the intuitive, untrammeled gift for speculation Freud felt it so necessary to discipline in himself.

To make the case more personal still, the artist's capacity to charm had aroused Freud's exasperation long ago, when he was courting Martha Bernays. As an edgy and imperious lover, consumed with jealousy of two young competitors, both in the arts, he had proclaimed that "there is a general enmity between artists and those engaged in the details of scientific work." He had noted with undisguised envy that poets and painters "possess in their

---

essays in which Freud announced the seriousness of the divergences between his views and Jung's ('Narcissism' and 'The History of the Psycho-Analytic Movement'), and there is no doubt that at the time he was feeling bitterly disappointed at Jung's defection. It cost him an inward struggle to control his emotions firmly enough to enable him to say calmly what he felt he had to say. One cannot avoid the pretty obvious conclusion that at this time, and probably before, Freud had identified himself with Moses and was striving to emulate the victory over passions that Michelangelo had depicted in his stupendous achievement." (*Jones* II, 366–67.)

art a master key to open with ease all female hearts, whereas we stand helpless at the strange designs of the lock and have first to torment ourselves to discover a suitable key to it." At times, Freud's comments on poets read like the revenge of the scientist on the artist. The tortoise is maligning the hare. That he had certain artistic ambitions of his own, as his literary style amply demonstrates, only made his envy of the artist all the more poignant.

But his letter to Schnitzler also shows that it was envy shot through with admiration. After all, while Freud at times described the artist as a neurotic seeking substitute gratifications for his failures in the real world, he also granted him uncommon analytical gifts. After analyzing *Gradiva*, a minor novella by the German playwright and novelist Wilhelm Jensen, first published in 1903, Freud sent the author a copy of his paper. Jensen courteously replied that he accepted Freud's interpretation, but made it quite clear that he had had no acquaintance with psychoanalytic thought before writing the tale. How then could he have "psychoanalyzed" the characters he had invented for his *Gradiva,* and plotted his novella as virtually an analytic cure? Freud solved the riddle he had set for himself by concluding that "we"—the writer and the analyst—"probably draw from the same source, work on the same object, each of us with a different method." While the analyst observes the unconscious of his patients, the writer observes his own unconscious and shapes his discoveries into expressive utterance. Thus the novelist and the poet are amateur psychoanalysts, at their best no less penetrating than any professional. Praise from Freud could hardly have been more heartfelt, but it was praise of the artist as analyst.

FRAGMENTARY AS FREUD'S analytic researches into high culture remain, they touch upon the three principal dimensions of aesthetic experience: the psychology of the protagonists, the psychology of the audience, and the psychology of the maker. These dimensions necessarily implicate and illuminate one another. Thus the psychoanalyst may read *Hamlet* as an aesthetic artifact whose hero, haunted by an unresolved Oedipus complex, invites analysis in himself; as a clue to the complexes of vast audiences, deeply moved as they recognize in his tragedy their own secret history;* and as oblique testimony to its author's own oedipal drama, to the unfinished emotional business with which he is still wrestling.† In short, the psychoanalytic investigation of

---

*"Every listener," Freud told Fliess in an important letter, "was once in embryo and in fantasy such an Oedipus." (Freud to Fliess, October 15, 1897. *Freud–Fliess,* 293 [272].)

†It had gone through his head in passing, Freud wrote to Fliess, to wonder whether traces of the unconscious Oedipus complex "may not also be at the bottom of *Hamlet.* I am not thinking of Shakespeare's conscious intention, but believe, rather, that a real event stimulated the poet to his portrayal, in that the unconscious in him understood the unconscious in the hero." (Ibid.)

Hamlet, a fictional character who has fascinated and puzzled so many of his later students, may account for his most obscure springs of action, for his uncanny power over centuries of admirers, and for his inventor's insight alike. Such an investigation promised a far more rounded, far more subtle reading than had been available to earlier interpreters, especially to formalist critics who (as Eitingon tersely put it) were wary of "contents and the powers that determine these contents."

Yet critics of Freud's aesthetics soon objected that psychoanalytic criticism normally suffers from precisely the reverse defect: a tendency to slight craftsmanship, form, style, in favor of contents. The psychoanalyst's determined search for concealed meanings in a poem or novel or painting is likely to seduce him into paying excessive attention to plot, narration, metaphor, and character, and to overlook the fact that cultural products issue from talented and trained hands and from a tradition that the artist obeys, modifies, or defiantly sets aside. Hence a satisfactory, rounded interpretation of a work of art or literature is likely to be far more untidy than neat psychoanalytic formulations suggest. But Freud was confident that "analysis allows us to suppose that the great, apparently inexhaustible wealth of the problems and situations the imaginative writer treats can be traced back to a small number of primal motifs, which stem for the most part from the repressed experiential material of the child's mental life, so that imaginative productions correspond to disguised, embellished, sublimated new editions of those childhood fantasies."

To draw from a work facile inferences about its creator was, therefore, a standing temptation for psychoanalytic critics. Their analyses of the makers of, and the audiences for, art and literature threatened to become, even in skillful and delicate hands, exercises in reductionism.* A Freudian may find it perfectly obvious that Shakespeare must have undergone the oedipal experience that he so absorbingly dramatized. Was he not human? When he was cut, did he not bleed? But the truth is that the playwright need not have fully shared the emotions he so grippingly portrays. Nor must these emotions, whether hidden or overt, necessarily awaken the same emotions in the audi-

---

*"Clinical analysis of creative artists," the psychoanalyst and art historian Ernst Kris once wrote in a salutary passage, "suggests that the life experience of the artist is sometimes only in a limited sense the source of his vision; that his power to imagine conflicts may by far transcend the range of his own experience; or, to put it more accurately, that at least some artists possess the particular gift to generalize from whatever their own experience has been." To find, say, Shakespeare in Falstaff or Prince Hal seems to be a "futile" quest, "and contrary to what clinical experience with artists as psychoanalytic subjects seems to indicate. Some great artists seem to be equally close to several of their characters, and may feel many of them as parts of themselves. The artist has created a world and not indulged in a daydream." (Ernst Kris, *Psychoanalytic Explorations in Art* [1952], 288.)

ence. Catharsis, as psychoanalysts had reason to know, works not to generate imitation but to make it superfluous: to read a violence-ridden novel or watch a sanguinary tragedy may purge rather than stimulate angry feelings. There are suggestions in Freud's writings—no more—that he had some glimpse of these complexities, but his views on art, while they opened fascinating vistas, also raised problems, little less fascinating.

IN GENERAL, WHAT made Freud's readers uneasy was less his ambivalence about the artist than his certainties about art. Probably the most controversial of his suggestions was that literary characters can be analyzed as though they were real persons. Most students of literature have been wary of such attempts: a personage in a novel or a drama, they have argued, is not a real human being with a real mind, but an animated puppet lent counterfeit life by its inventor. Hamlet had no existence before, or outside, the play that bears his name; to inquire into the states of mind that preceded his first speech, or to analyze his emotions as though he were a patient on the couch, is to confound the categories of fiction and reality. Quite undaunted, though, Freud boldly waded into this morass with his charming study of Jensen's *Gradiva*. He wrote it, he told Jung, "in sunny days," and the writing gave him "a great deal of pleasure. True, it brings us nothing new, but I believe that it allows us to enjoy our wealth." Freud's analysis beautifully illustrates what this sort of literary psychoanalysis can achieve and what hazards it encounters.

The patient-protagonist of *Gradiva*, Norbert Hanold, is a digger into the unknown, an archeologist. It is most likely Hanold's profession, and his special domain, Italy, that first attracted Freud to Jensen's tale. But *Gradiva* also had psychological implications to make it interesting to Freud. Hanold is the withdrawn, unworldly product of cool northern climes who will find clarity and a very Freudian cure through love in the sun-baked south, in Pompeii. He has repressed the memory of a girl, Zoë Bertgang, with whom he had grown up and to whom he had been affectionately attached. Visiting a collection of antiquities in Rome, he comes upon a bas-relief depicting a young, lovely woman with a distinctive gait. He calls her "Gradiva," which means "the woman who steps along," and hangs a plaster cast of the bas-relief in a "privileged place on the wall of his study." Freud would later install his own plaster cast of "Gradiva" in his consulting room.

The young woman's stance fascinates Hanold, for, as he does not yet recognize, she recalls to him the girl he had loved and then "forgotten" the better to pursue his isolated, and isolating, vocation. In a nightmare he sees "Gradiva" on the day of Pompeii's destruction, and he weaves an intricate network of delusions about her, mourning her passing as though she were his contemporary rather than just one victim among the thousands who died under the lava of Vesuvius nearly two millennia ago. His "whole science," Freud observed in the margin of his copy of Jensen's *Gradiva*, stands "in the service of f[antasy]." Under the impress of nameless feelings and inexplicable obsessions, Hanold ends up in Pompeii, where he encounters "Gradiva" and fancies himself back on that fatal day in 79 A.D. when Vesuvius erupted. But his vision is reality itself: she is, of course, the passion of his young years.

Hanold is wholly inexperienced with women—Freud comments in the margin on his "sex[ual] repression" and the "asexual atmosphere" in which he lives—but fortunately his "Gradiva" is as shrewd as she is beautiful. Zoë, the "source" of his malaise, also becomes the agent of its resolution; recognizing Hanold's delusions for what they are, she restores him to sanity, disentangling his fantasies from reality. By walking ahead of him in imitation of "Gradiva" on the plaque, she finds the key to his therapy: the young woman's unmistakable gait allows Hanold's repressed memories of her to enter consciousness.

This was psychoanalysis through archeology. One of the two passages in *Gradiva* that moved Freud to exclaim "beautiful"—*schön*—in the margin has the heroine retail a bit of wisdom that reminded him of his favorite metaphor. Hanold might find it strange, she says, "that someone must die first, in order to become alive." But, she adds, "for archeology that is doubtless necessary."* In his published paper on the novella, Freud made the metaphor explicit once more: "There is actually no better analogy for repression, which both makes something in the mind inaccessible and preserves it, than the burial that was the fate of Pompeii and from which the city could reappear through the work of the spade."† *Gradiva* demonstrates not just the triumph of repression but its unraveling as well; the young woman's cure of Hanold proves once again "the healing power of love." Reading the little book with pencil in hand, Freud made it plain that this love was at bottom sensual. "Erotic foot interest," he noted as Hanold observes Zoë's shoes; and next to the final paragraph, in which Jensen has Hanold asking Zoë to walk ahead of him and she complies with a smile, Freud put, "Erotic! Reception of fantasy; reconciliation."

Freud had some hesitations about his intrusive way with Jensen's fiction;

*As we know, he had likened his therapeutic technique to the excavation of a buried city as early as 1895, in discussing his patient Elisabeth von R. (*Studies on Hysteria, SE* II, 139.) The other passage in *Gradiva* that Freud praised as "beautiful" spoke to his vehement antireligious feelings: "If faith brought [Hanold] salvation, he put up with a considerable sum of incomprehensibilities at all points." (*Gradiva*, 140. Freud Museum, London.)

†Some three years later, Freud would explain the work of repression to the Rat Man with the same analogy.

he was, after all, analyzing and interpreting "a dream that had never been dreamt at all." He did his best to read Jensen's novella conscientiously: he carefully noted, as though he had another Dora on the couch before him, Hanold's three dreams and their consequences; he paid attention to subsidiary feelings at work in Hanold, such as anxiety, aggressive ideas, and jealousy; he observed ambiguities and double meanings; and he painstakingly traced the progress of the therapy as Hanold gradually learns to separate delusion from reality. Prudently, he concluded with a caution to himself: "But here we must stop, or we may really forget that Hanold, and the Gradiva, are only creatures of the writer."

Yet these hesitations did not stop Freud, nor, as we have seen, his followers; heedless of the perils ahead, psychoanalysts in those years saw no reason to refuse culture a place on the couch. It is true that their moves beyond clinical work with neurotics evoked some interest among aestheticians, literary critics, and reviewers of exhibitions, and generated earnest reappraisals in virtually all the specialized fields Freud had invaded. But while Freud chose to regard his talk on daydreaming and imaginative writers as "an incursion into terrain we have so far barely touched, in which one could settle down comfortably," most specialists came to think that Freud was making himself only too comfortable.

Freud's critics had some right to be anxious: the creative artist, that most cherished of human creatures, appeared in some psychoanalytic treatments as nothing better than an adroit and articulate neurotic duping a gullible world with his clever inventions. Freud's own analyses, though very ambitious, are scarcely appreciative. Freud did not merely dispute the "creativeness" of creative artists, he also circumscribed their cultural role. Shouting out society's secrets, they are little better than necessary licensed gossips, fit only to reduce the tensions that have accumulated in the public's mind. Freud saw the making of art and literature, as well as their consumption, as human pursuits much like others, enjoying no special status. It is no accident that Freud should have called the reward one obtains from looking or reading or listening by a name—forepleasure—he borrowed from the most earthy of gratifications. To his mind, aesthetic work, much like the making of love or war, of laws or constitutions, is a way of mastering the world, or of disguising one's failure to master it. The difference is that novels and paintings veil their ultimately utilitarian purposes behind skillfully crafted, often irresistible decorations.

Yet Freud was convinced that he could evade the trap of reductionism. Repeatedly and emphatically he took care to deny that psychoanalysis can shed any light on the mysteries of creativity. In his "Leonardo" he earnestly disclaimed any intention of making "the great man's achievement comprehensible" and declared himself ready to "concede that the nature of artistic achievement is indeed psychoanalytically inaccessible to us."* To inquire into "the laws of human mental life," especially among "outstanding individuals," is most appealing, but such investigations "are not intended to explain the genius of the poet." We are entitled to take these disclaimers at their face value. Freud candidly and finely calibrated his attitudes toward his publications, ranging all the way from dogmatic certainty to complete agnosticism. At the same time, though, however greatly he respected the awesome secret powers of creativity, Freud was prepared to claim a great deal for the psychoanalytic study of an artist's character and of his reasons for choosing certain themes or fastening on certain metaphors, to say nothing of his effect on his audiences. What Freud left behind, even among sympathetic readers, was the thought that to reduce culture to psychology seems no less one-sided than to study culture while leaving out psychology altogether.

APPEARANCES TO THE contrary, Freud did not take his view of the arts in order to discredit them wholly. Whether it is made of wit or suspense, of dazzling color or persuasive composition, the aesthetic mask hiding primitive passions provides pleasure. It helps to make life tolerable to maker and audience alike. Thus, for Freud, the arts are a cultural narcotic, but without the long-range costs that other drugs exact. The task of the psychoanalytic critic, then, is to trace the various ways in which reading and listening and seeing actually generate aesthetic pleasure, without presuming to judge the value of the work, its author, or its reception. Freud needed no one to tell him that the fruit need not resemble the root and that the garden's loveliest flowers lose none of their beauty because we are made aware that they grow from malodorous manure. But Freud was professionally committed to the study of roots. At the same time, if Freud chose to read *The Merchant of Venice* and *King Lear* as meditations on love and death, Shakespeare did not therefore become a matter of purely clinical interest to him. The Michelangelo who made the *Moses* was more than merely an interesting patient. Goethe did not lose stature as a *Dichter* in Freud's eyes even after he had psychoanalyzed a passage from Goethe's autobiography, *Poetry and Truth.* But the fact remains that with all his affection for literature, Freud was all his life more interested in truth than in poetry.

---

*In the late 1920s, in a much-quoted passage, he said it again: "Before the problem of the creative writer, analysis must lay down its arms." ("Dostojewski und die Vatertötung" [1928], *GW* XIV, 399/"Dostoevsky and Parricide," *SE* XXI, 177.)

FOUNDATIONS OF SOCIETY

Freud's application of his discoveries to sculpture and fiction and painting was audacious enough. But it pales before his attempt to dig down to the most remote foundations of culture. In his mid-fifties, he undertook nothing less: to determine the moment when the human animal took the leap into civilization by prescribing to itself the taboos indispensable to all ordered societies. Freud had long hazarded some hints at his intentions, in papers, prefaces, and laconic observations to his colleagues. With the passage of time, this intellectual play became more and more engrossing to him. In mid-November 1908, he told the Vienna Psychoanalytic Society, "The inquiry into the source of guilt feelings cannot be disposed of quickly. Undeniably, many factors are at work in it. What is certain is that guilt feelings come into being through the ruin of sexual impulses." Again, two weeks later, commenting on a paper by Otto Rank on myths clustering about the birth of the hero, he observed that the real protagonist in fiction is the ego. It rediscovers itself by going back to the time "when it was a hero through its first heroic deed: the rebellion against the father." The outlines of *Totem and Taboo,* four essays linked by a common theme, were forming in Freud's mind.

As Freud's correspondence attests, this work involved the usual fatiguing drudgery, passionately pursued. By mid-November 1911, he could tell Ferenczi, "I am again occupied from 8–8; but my heart is wholly with the Totem, with which I am getting on slowly." As usual, he canvassed the technical literature widely, but rather unwillingly, because he was fairly certain what he would find; pursuing his "totem work," he reported to Ferenczi, he was "reading fat books without real interest, since I already know the results." In important respects, he had leapt before he looked. At times, he had the visceral satisfaction of closure: "A few days ago," he wrote, again to Ferenczi, in early February 1912, "the totem-ambivalence question suddenly fitted, snapped shut with an audible 'click,' and since then I have been practically 'imbecilic.' "

His progress was dramatic enough. In March 1912, his speculative paper on the horror of incest, the first of the four essays, was published in *Imago.* That paper he told Ernest Jones in depreciation, "is by no means famous."*

---

*This use of "famous," one may note, is characteristic of Freud's occasional errors involving English cognates. He obviously had in mind *famos,* which is German colloquial for "wonderful" or "marvelous," but does not mean "famous."

Still he went forward. By May, he had completed the second essay and read it to the Vienna Psychoanalytic Society. He found the work so exacting that on occasion his English, usually so fluent, deserted him as he tried to convey his meaning with the necessary precision. "Now let me turn to science," he wrote to Jones in midsummer 1912, suddenly reduced to a mélange of two languages. "The true historical source of Verdrängung I hope to touch upon in the last of the 4 papers of which Taboo is the second in that to be called 'Die infant. Wiederkehr des Totemismus.' I may as well give you the answer now. Any internal (damn my English!)—Jede *innere* Verdrängungsschranke ist der historische Erfolg eines *äusseren* Hindernisses. Also: Verinnerlichung der Widerstände, die Geschichte der Menschheit niedergelegt in ihren heute angeborenen Verdrängungsneigungen." Then, his English recovered, Freud went on: "I know of the obstacle or the complication offered by the matter of Matriarchy and have not yet found my way out of it. But I hope it will be cleared away."*

He did not find the solution immediately. "I am all in omnipotence of thought," Freud wrote to Ferenczi in mid-December, working with his habitual obsessiveness on the third of the essays, and again, two weeks later, testifying to his absorption, "I have just been all omnipotence, all savage. That's how one must do it if one wants to get something done." By April 1913, he could report that he was writing out the "totem work," and in the following month he ventured an approving appraisal of the whole: "I am now writing on the Totem with the feeling that it is my greatest, my best, perhaps my last good thing."

He was not always quite so sure. Only a week later he sent a bulletin to Ferenczi: "Totem work ready yesterday," paid for with "a terrible migr[aine], (rarity with me)." But in June, the headache and most of the doubts were gone—for a time: "I have been easy and cheerful since the discharge of the totem work." In his preface to the book, he modestly declared that he was fully aware of its deficiencies. Some of these were necessitated by its pioneering nature, some by its attempt to appeal to the educated general reader and to "mediate between ethnologists, philologists, folklorists etc. on the one hand and psychoanalysts on the other."

Totem and Taboo is even more ambitious in its governing thesis than in its search for an audience; in sheer ingenuity, it outstrips even the conjectures of Jean-Jacques Rousseau, whose famous mid-eighteenth-century discourses on the origins of human society had been explicitly hypothetical. Rousseau

---

*The German passage reads in translation: " 'The infant[ile] return of totemism.' . . . Every *internal* repression barrier is the historical consequence of an *external* obstacle. So: internalization of resistances, the history of mankind deposited in the dispositions to repression today inborn."

had in so many words invited his readers to set the facts aside as he imagined the time when mankind stepped from precivilization to civilization. But unlike Rousseau, Freud invited *his* readers to accept his breath-taking guess as the analytic reconstruction of a long-buried, epoch-making prehistoric event. He had moved dangerously far from the intimate concreteness of his clinical inferences, but that did not slow him down.

FREUD'S *TOTEM AND TABOO* IS psychoanalysis applied, but it is also a political document. While the book was still in its early stages, in February 1911, Freud had told Jung, resorting to the weighty metaphor of generation, "For some weeks I have been pregnant with the germ of a larger synthesis, and will give birth to it in the summer." The pregnancy was, we know, far longer than Freud had anticipated, and there is a very understandable note of triumph in Freud's announcements to his friends in May 1913 that the book was essentially done. For Freud to give birth to a synthesis of prehistory, biology, and psychoanalysis was to anticipate, and to outdo, his "heir" and rival: the papers making up *Totem and Taboo* were weapons in Freud's competition with Jung. Freud was displaying in his own struggles an aspect of the oedipal wars often scanted—the father's efforts to best the son. Above all the last and most militant of his four papers, published after his break with Jung, was sweet revenge on the crown prince who had proved so brutal to him and so treacherous to psychoanalysis. The paper was due to appear in the August issue of *Imago* and, as Freud told Abraham in May, would "serve to cut off, cleanly, everything that is Aryan-religious." In September, Freud signed the preface to the book, with a flourish, in Rome, his queen of cities.

    Totem and Taboo leaves evidence on page after page that Freud's current combats reverberated with his past history, conscious and unconscious. Cultural anthropology and archeology were congenial preoccupations for him all his life, as those metaphors borrowed from archeology amply document. If Schliemann, realizing in adult life fantasies from childhood, was one of the few people Freud really envied, he saw himself for his part as the Schliemann of the mind. Once his travail was over, he paid it the tribute of a postpartum depression, not dissimilar to the one he had suffered after producing *The Interpretation of Dreams*. He began to feel uncertain of his case, a sure sign of his deep emotional engagement. Fortunately, the reward of applause from his loyal supporters was not long in coming; the approval of Ferenczi and Jones, Freud wrote in late June, "is the first pleasure dividend I can register after the completion of the work." When Abraham told Freud how thoroughly he had enjoyed "the Totem work" and how completely Freud had persuaded him, Freud promptly responded with unfeigned gratitude: "Your verdict on the Totem work was particularly important to me, since I had a period of doubt in its value after completing it. But the comments of Ferenczi, Jones, Sachs, Rank, were similar to yours, so that I have gradually regained my confidence." Publishing what he recognized to be scientific fantasies, he particularly welcomed Abraham's attempt to corroborate his work with "contributions, additions, inferences." He told Abraham that he was prepared for "nasty attacks," but that he would of course not allow them to disconcert him. One wonders how much of this was serenity recaptured, how much of it bravado.

THE INTELLECTUAL PEDIGREE of *Totem and Taboo* is impressive, somewhat tarnished in retrospect only by the passage of time and the increasing sophistication of the cognate disciplines that had fed Freud some of his most subversive conjectures. He had, he said, derived the first impulse for his investigations from Wilhelm Wundt's "nonanalytic" *Völkerpsychologie,* and from the psychoanalytic writings of the Zurich school, of Jung, Riklin, and the others. But he noted with some pride that while he had profited, he had also dissented, from them both. He had drawn as well on James G. Frazer, that prolific encyclopedist of primitive and exotic religions; on the eminent English biblical scholar W. Robertson Smith, for his writings on the totem meal; and on the great Edward Burnett Tylor, for his evolutionary anthropology;* to say nothing of Charles Darwin, for his picturesque surmises about the social condition of primitive man.

R. R. Marett, the first British anthropologist to review the English edition of *Totem and Taboo,* in early 1920, called it a "just-so story," a characterization that Freud found witty enough to acknowledge with some amusement. "Marett, the critic of T & T," he told Ernest Jones, "is well entitled to say, ψA leaves anthropology with all her problems as it found it before as long as he declines the solutions given by ψA. Had he accepted them he might have found it otherwise." But Marett's joke about the "just-so story," Freud thought, was "really not bad. The man is good, he is only deficient in phantasy." It was not a deficiency of which anyone would accuse Freud, not after *Totem and Taboo.* But Freud mingled boldness with prudence; after all, he observed in 1921, he had only advanced "a hypothesis like so many others with which prehistorians have attempted to light up the darkness of archaic

---

*Sounding much like Auguste Comte nearly a century before him, Freud postulated a sequence of three stages of thought, the animistic or mythological, the religious, and the scientific. (See *Totem and Taboo, SE* XIII, 77.) This scheme implies succession in time as well as a hierarchy of values. By the time Freud was writing, and certainly in the decades after the publication of *Totem and Taboo,* cultural anthropologists rejected this scheme, sometimes scornfully.

times." Surely, he added somewhat more confidently, "it is honorable to such a hypothesis if it shows itself suitable for creating coherence and understanding in ever new domains."

Freud did not rest his case on his formidable nonanalytic authorities alone. Without his clinical experience, his self-analysis, and his psychoanalytic theories, he would never have written *Totem and Taboo.* The ghost of Schreber, too, hovers over it, for in that case history of an exemplary paranoiac, Freud had investigated the relations of men to their gods as derivatives of their relations to their fathers. *Totem and Taboo* is, as Freud had told Jung, a synthesis; it weaves together speculations from anthropology, ethnography, biology, the history of religion—and psychoanalysis. The subtitle is revealing: *Several Congruences in the Mental Life of Savages and Neurotics.* The first of the essays, the shortest, on the horror of incest, ranges from Melanesians and the Bantu to boys in the oedipal phase and neurotic women living in Freud's own culture. The second explores current theories in cultural anthropology and connects taboo and ambivalence with the obsessive commands and prohibitions Freud had observed in his patients. The third essay examines the relevance of animism, at the time widely thought to be the primitive precursor of religion, to magical thinking and then links both of these to the child's wishful belief in the omnipotence of thoughts. Here, as throughout *Totem and Taboo,* Freud went beyond the contract he had made with his readers in its subtitle. He was interested in more than the congruence between what he called "primitive" and neurotic ways of thinking; he wanted to discover what light the primitive mind-set can shed on all thinking, even on "normal" thinking—and on history. He concluded that the mental style of "savages" reveals in the starkest contours what the psychoanalyst has been driven to recognize in his patients and, observing the world, in everyone: the pressure of wishes on thought, the utterly practical origins of all mental activity.

All this is imaginative enough, but in the last and longest of his four essays, in which Freud moved from taboo to totem, he launched his most ingenious flight. His critics thought it the reckless, fatal flight of Icarus, but for Freud it was, if not quite commonplace, far from intimidating. Totems are, after all, taboo—holy objects. They matter to the historian of culture because they dramatize what Freud had already canvassed in the opening essay—the horror of incest. The most sacred obligation imposed on tribes practicing totemism is that they must not marry members of their own totem clan, and in fact must shun all sexual contact with them. This, Freud observes, is "the famous and mysterious *exogamy,* linked to totemism."

Freud's rapid excursion through contemporary theories explaining the origins of totemism is not without some appreciative glosses. But after its detour through conjectures by Charles Darwin and Robertson Smith, his own explanation winds its way back to the analytic couch. Darwin had supposed that prehistoric man lived in small hordes, each governed by a domineering, sexually jealous male; Robertson Smith had hypothesized that the ritual sacrifice in which the totem animal is eaten is the essential ingredient in all totemism. Adopting the comparative strategy typical of his theorizing, Freud linked these unsubstantiated, quite insecure guesses to the animal phobias of neurotic children and then ushered the Oedipus complex, which had been hovering in the wings, to center stage. He enlisted none other than Little Hans, that intelligent and appealing five-year-old afraid of horses and in deep conflict about his father, as mediator between early-twentieth-century Vienna and the most distant, most obscure epochs in the human past. He added two other youthful witnesses to his own little favorite: a boy with a dog phobia studied by the Russian psychoanalyst M. Wulff, and a case that Ferenczi had communicated to him, "Little Arpad," who simultaneously identified with chickens and rejoiced in seeing them slaughtered. The behavior of these troubled youngsters helped Freud to interpret the totem animal as representing the father. This reading made it exceedingly likely to Freud that the whole "totemic system" would, "like the animal phobia of 'Little Hans' and the poultry perversion of 'Little Arpad,' have arisen from the conditions of the Oedipus complex."

The sacrificial meal, Freud argued, is a vital social cement; in sacrificing the totem, which is of the same substance as the men who eat it, the clan reaffirms its faith in, and identity with, its god. It is a collective act, drenched in ambivalence: the killing of the totem animal is an occasion for grief followed by rejoicing. Indeed, the festival, the sequel to the killing, is an exuberant, uninhibited saturnalia, a peculiar but necessary pendant to mourning. Once Freud had reached this stage in the argument, there was no stopping him; he stood ready to offer his historical reconstruction.

Freud had the grace to recognize that this reconstruction must appear fantastic to everyone, but to his mind it was perfectly plausible: The fierce, jealous father who dominated the horde and kept the women for himself drove away his sons as soon as they grew up. "One day the brothers who had been driven out got together, beat their father to death, and devoured him, and thus put an end to the patriarchal horde. United, they dared and managed to do what would have remained impossible for the individual." Freud wondered whether it was perhaps some cultural acquisition, like the capacity to handle a new weapon, that had given the rebellious brothers a certain sense of superiority over their tyrant. That they should have made a meal of the potent father they had killed, Freud thought, went without saying; that is how these "cannibal savages" were. "The violent primal father had surely been the envied and feared model for each of the fraternal troop. Now, in the act of devouring, they carried through their identification with him; each of them appropriated a piece of his strength." Its origins once understood, the totem meal, "perhaps the first festival of mankind," would turn out to be "the repetition and the commemoration of this memorable criminal act." This, according to Freud, is how human history must have originated.

He warned that vagueness must be inherent in any reconstruction of this prehistoric crime committed and celebrated: "It would be as nonsensical to strive for exactitude with this material, as it would be unreasonable to demand certainty." He "explicitly emphasized" that his breath-taking derivations should not be taken as evidence that he had overlooked the "complex nature of the phenomena"; all he had done was to "add another element to the sources, already known or still unknown, of religion, morality, and society." Yet, emboldened by his psychoanalytic reverie, Freud drew the most astonishing inferences. He supposed that the murderous band of brothers was "dominated by the same mutually contradictory feelings about the father" that psychoanalysts can demonstrate in "the ambivalence of the father complexes" haunting children and neurotics. Having at once hated the formidable father and loved him, the brothers were smitten with remorse, which showed itself in an emerging "consciousness of guilt." In death, the father became more powerful than he had ever been in his lifetime. "What he had previously prevented by his very existence," his sons "now prohibited to themselves in the psychological situation—'deferred obedience'—so familiar to us from psychoanalyses." The sons now, as it were, erased their act of parricide "by declaring the killing of the father-substitute, the totem, impermissible and renounced its fruits by denying themselves the women who had been freed." Thus, oppressed by their guilt, the sons established the "fundamental taboos of totemism, which had to correspond precisely with the two repressed wishes of the Oedipus complex"—the killing of the father and the conquest of the mother. In becoming guilty and acknowledging their guilt, they created civilization. All human society is constructed on complicity in a great crime.

This stark and grandiose conclusion invited yet another inference that Freud found irresistible: "An event like the elimination of the primal father by the band of brothers," he wrote, "must leave ineradicable traces in the history of mankind." Freud thought it demonstrable that such traces pervade all culture. The history of religion, the appeal of tragic drama, the exemplars of art, all point to the immortality of the primal crime and its consequences. But this conclusion, Freud admitted, depends upon two extremely controversial notions: the existence of a "collective mind which undergoes mental processes as though it were an individual," and the capacity of this mind to hand on "across many thousands of years" the sense of guilt first oppressing one murderous prehistoric band. In short, human beings can inherit the burden of conscience from their biological ancestors. This was sheer extravagance, piled upon the earlier extravagance of the claim that the primal murder had been a historical event. But reviewing the strenuous road he had traveled, Freud firmly stood by his improbable reconstruction. Primitives are not quite like neurotics; while the neurotic takes the thought for the act, the primitive acts before he thinks. Freud's peroration, quoting *Faust,* is so felicitous that it is tempting to wonder whether he had not gone all this distance in order to close his text with Goethe's famous line: "In the beginning was the act."

FOR FREUD, AS we have seen, the deed of the sons, that "memorable criminal act," was the founding act of civilization. It had stood at the beginning of "so much" in human history: "social organization, moral constraints, and religion." Without doubt, Freud found all these domains of culture of absorbing interest, as he undertook to explore the history of culture from his psychoanalytic vantage point. But the domain he listed last—religion—was, it seems, the one that engaged him most. To uncover its foundations in a prehistoric murder allowed him to combine his long-standing, pugilistic atheism with his new-found detestation of Jung. With the concluding essay of *Totem and Taboo,* we may recall, he hoped he could free himself from "everything that is Aryan-religious"; he would lay bare the roots of religion in primitive needs, primitive notions, and no less primitive acts. "In Ernst Barlach's tragic novel of family life, *Der Tote Tag,*" Jung wrote in criticism of Freud, "the mother-daemon says at the end: 'The strange thing is that man will not learn that God is his father.' That is what Freud would never learn, and what all those who share his outlook forbid themselves to learn."

But what Freud had learned, and was teaching in *Totem and Taboo,* though he formulated the matter more impiously, was that man *makes* a god of his father. Quoting James G. Frazer and Robertson Smith at some length, he led up to his account of the primitive parricide by noting that the earliest of religions, totemism, established taboos that could not be violated on the direst of penalties, and that subsequently the animal sacrificed in ancient sacred rites was identical with the primitive totem animal. That animal stood for the primitive god himself; the rite recalled, and celebrated, the founding crime in disguised form by reenacting the slaying and eating of the father. It "confesses, with a sincerity hardly to be exceeded, that the object of the act of sacrifice had always been the same, the same that is now worshiped as god—that is, the father." Religion, Freud had already suggested in some of his letters to Jung, was founded in helplessness. With *Totem and Taboo,* he complicated this suggestion by adding that religion arose as well from a rebellious act against that helplessness. Jung came to believe that to recognize God as man's father required a sympathetic understanding, and rediscovery, of the spiritual dimension. Freud took his findings in *Totem and Taboo* as further proof that such a demand was a retreat from science, a denial of the fundamental facts of mental life, in a word, mysticism.

Rather, the fact of life on which Freud most insisted in *Totem and Taboo,* and which organizes the book, is the Oedipus complex. In that complex, "the beginnings of religion, morality, society, and art converge." This, we know, was not a sudden or a new discovery for Freud; his first recorded hint at the oedipal family drama had come in 1897, in one of the memoranda he sent to Fliess concerning hostile wishes against parents. In the next few years, though it increasingly dominated his thinking, he referred to the concept rather sparingly. Yet it inevitably informed his thinking about his analysands; he briefly explicated it in the case history of Dora, and thought of Little Hans as a "little Oedipus." However, he did not plainly identify the "family complex" as the "Oedipus complex" until 1908, in an unpublished letter to Ferenczi; he did not call it *"the nuclear complex of the neuroses"* until 1909, in his case history of the Rat Man; and he did not employ the memorable term in print until 1910, in one of his short papers on the vicissitudes of love. By this time, Freud had learned to invest the emotional tension of ambivalence with considerable importance; this was one of the lessons that Little Hans had imparted. He now saw that the classic Oedipus complex, the little boy loving his mother and hating his father, was actually a rarity in this pure, simple form. But the very diversity of the complex only underscored, for Freud, its centrality in the human experience. "Every human newcomer has been set the task of mastering the Oedipus complex," Freud later said, summing up the argument he had been developing since the late 1890s. "Whoever cannot manage it falls prey to neurosis. The progress of psychoanalytic work has sketched the significance of the Oedipus complex ever more sharply; its recognition has become the shibboleth that separates the adherents of psychoanalysis from its opponents." Certainly it separated Freud from Adler and, even more decisively, from Jung.

As STUDENTS OF the human animal refined their methods and revised their hypotheses, the flaws compromising the argument of *Totem and Taboo* emerged more and more obtrusively—except to Freud's most uncritical acolytes. Cultural anthropologists demonstrated that while some totemic tribes practice the ritual of the sacrificial totem meal, most of them do not; what

Robertson Smith had thought the essence of totemism turned out to be an exception. Again, the conjectures of Darwin and others about the prehistoric horde governed autocratically by a polygamous and monopolistic male did not stand up well to further research, especially the kind of research among the higher primates that had not been available when Freud wrote *Totem and Taboo*. Freud's stirring portrayal of that lethal fraternal rebellion against patriarchy seemed increasingly implausible.

It came to appear all the more fantastic because it required a theoretical underpinning that modern biology discredited decisively. When Freud wrote *Totem and Taboo*, some responsible students of man were still ready to believe that acquired traits can be genetically handed on through the generations. The science of genetics was still in its infancy around 1913, and could accommodate the most varied conjectures about the nature of inheritance. Darwin himself, after all, though caustic in his references to Lamarck, had been something of a Lamarckian in hypothesizing that acquired characteristics may be inherited. But quite apart from the fact that Freud could legitimately lean on the remaining, though dwindling, prestige of this doctrine, he remained partial to it because he believed it would help to complete the theoretical structure of psychoanalysis.

Ironically, the historical reality of the primal crime was by no means essential to Freud's argument. Guilt feelings can be handed down by less fanciful, scientifically more acceptable mechanisms. Neurotics, as Freud himself pointed out in *Totem and Taboo*, fantasize about oedipal killings but never carry them out. If he had been willing to apply this clinical insight to his story of the primal crime as he employed other knowledge gleaned from the couch, he would have anticipated and disarmed the most devastating criticisms to which *Totem and Taboo* would be exposed. Presenting his stunning tale not as fact, but as a fantasy that has plagued the young through the centuries as they confront their parents, he could have dropped his Lamarckian thesis. The universality of family experience, of intimate rivalries and mixed feelings—in short, of the ubiquitous Oedipus complex—would have been sufficient to account for the recurrence of guilt feelings and to fit them perfectly into his theory of mind.* In the late 1890s, moving from reality to fantasy had saved Freud from the absurdity of the seduction theory of neurosis. But now, though he hesitated over his assertion and dutifully presented the evidence against it, he finally held fast: in the beginning was

*Psychoanalysts were not alone in suggesting such an alternative. As the American anthropologist Alfred L. Kroeber said in his reconsideration of *Totem and Taboo* in 1939 (he had first reviewed the book in 1920), "Certain psychic processes tend always to be operative and to find expression in human institutions." (*"Totem and Taboo* in Retrospect," *American Journal of Sociology*, LV [1939], 447.)

the act! It did not exactly increase the prestige of Freud's visionary construct that his account of the way the feeling of guilt arose should strikingly resemble, of all things, the Christian doctrine of original sin.

This obstinacy strongly contrasts with Freud's earlier doubts, to say nothing of his scientific ideal. What he wanted from the experts was corroboration; he pounced on their arguments when they sustained his own, disregarded them when they did not. He had drawn, he told Ferenczi in the summer of 1912, "the best confirmations for my Totem hypotheses" from Robertson Smith's book on the religion of the Semites. He feared that Frazer and his other authorities would not accept his solutions to the mysteries of totem and taboo, but this did not shake his confidence in conclusions to which he was already committed—did not shake it then or later.* There can be little question that his tenacity sprang from the same psychological source as his early doubts. His first readers suspected as much: both Jones and Ferenczi confronted him with the possibility that the painful reservations he expressed after publishing *Totem and Taboo* might have deeper personal roots than just uncomplicated, understandable author's anxiety. The two had read proofs of the book and were persuaded of its greatness. "We suggested he had in his imagination lived through the experiences he described in his book," Jones writes, "that his elation represented the excitement of killing and eating the father and that his doubts were only the reaction." Freud was disposed to accept this bit of intramural psychoanalysis but not to revise his thesis. In *The Interpretation of Dreams*, he told Jones, he had only described the wish to kill the father; in *Totem and Taboo* he had described the actual parricide, and "after all it is a big step from a wish to a deed." It is a step that Freud, of course, had never taken. But to represent the primal crime as a unique event casting an immortal shadow, rather than as a pervasive, all-too-human fantasy, allowed Freud to remain at some distance from his own oedipal struggles with his father; it allowed him to plead, as it were, for the acquittal that a rational world should grant the true innocents who only fantasize about committing parricide. In view of Freud's own showing that

---

*"I still hold fast to this construction today," he wrote near the end of his life. "I have repeatedly had to listen to vehement reproaches for not having changed my views in later editions of my book, after more recent ethnologists have rejected Robertson Smith's hypotheses unanimously and have in part brought forward other, quite differing theories. I must reply that I am fully acquainted with these supposed advances. But I have been persuaded neither of the correctness of these innovations nor of Robertson Smith's errors. A contradiction is not a refutation, an innovation not necessarily an advance." He concluded with an apology that suggests some unanalyzed component to his thinking on this point: "Above all, I am not an ethnologist, but a psychoanalyst. I had the right to pick out of the ethnological literature what I could use for my analytical work." (*Der Mann Moses und die monotheistische Religion. Drei Abhandlungen* [1939], GW XVI, 240/*Moses and Monotheism*, SE XXIII, 131.)

the world of mind is anything but rational, this is a somewhat pathetic attempt to flee the murderous implications of his oedipal aggressions.

Whatever the objective value of Freud's attempt to discover the foundations of religion in the Oedipus complex, then, it is highly plausible that some of the impulses guiding Freud's argument in *Totem and Taboo* emerged from his hidden life; in some respects the book represents a round in his never-finished wrestling bout with Jacob Freud. It was an episode, too, in his equally persistent evasion of his complicated feelings about Amalia Freud. For it is telling that in his reconstruction Freud said virtually nothing about the mother, even though the ethnographic material pointing to the fantasy of devouring the mother is richer than that for devouring the father. Ferenczi's Little Arpad, whom Freud borrowed as a witness for *Totem and Taboo*, wanted to make a meal of his *"preserved mother";* as he graphically put it, "One should put my mother into a pot and cook her, then there would be a preserved mother and I could eat her." But Freud chose to ignore this piece of evidence. Still, like so much else in Freud's work, *Totem and Taboo* productively translated his most intimate conflicts and his most private quarrels into material for scientific investigation.

MAPPING THE MIND

 Freud found his investigations of art, literature, and pre-history both enjoyable and important. They served to confirm his image of himself as the explorer who is the first to describe inhospitable, mysterious terrain that has baffled and frustrated all his predecessors. But his intellectual raids were neither digressions nor departures from his essential theoretical work. One preoccupation fed others. Case histories led him to questions of culture; reflections on literary creation sent him back to the Oedipus complex. For all the diversified calls on his time, Freud therefore never slighted what he considered his central task: to refine his map of the mind. While he was not aware of it at the time, he was also taking tentative steps to revise this map.

Among the theoretical papers he published between 1908 and 1914, three—on character, on the fundamental principles of the mind, and on narcissism—command particular attention. The first two in this trio are very short, the last not very long, but their succinctness is no measure of their significance. In "Character and Anal Erotism," Freud took off from his clinical experience to propose some general hypotheses about character formation. He had supposed as early as 1897 that excrement, money, and obsessional neurosis are somehow intimately linked; a decade later, he had suggested to Jung that patients who obtain pleasure from withholding their feces typically display the character traits of orderliness, stinginess, and obstinacy. Together these traits are, "as it were, the sublimations of anal eroticism." In his report on the Rat Man, Freud had offered further observations on this constellation. Now, in his paper on character marked by anal eroticism, drawing on a considerable number of his analytic patients, he ventured to generalize his conjecture. In psychoanalytic theory, character is defined as a configuration of stable traits. But this orderly grouping does not necessarily connote a persistent serenity; as a cluster of fixations to which the individual's life history has tethered him, character often stands as the organization of inner conflicts rather than their resolution.* What Freud was particularly interested in, and had already investigated in his *Three Essays on the Theory of Sexuality* three years before, was the part these traits play in the making of what he would soon call the ego. Like other papers of these years, "Character and Anal Erotism" offers both a summing up of ideas long held and a prospect of revisions to come.

WITH HIS "Formulations on the Two Principles of Mental Functioning," Freud threw his net of generalization wider still. Seeking a far larger catch than anal erotics, he aimed to gather in nothing less than the relation of the drives to developmental experience. He read the paper to the Vienna Psychoanalytic Society on October 26, 1910, but found the discussion unrewarding. "Dealing with these people is steadily becoming more difficult," he confided to Ferenczi the next morning. What one got was "a mixture of shy admiration and stupid contradiction." Undismayed, Freud plunged on. Once again, while restating ideas he had adumbrated in the mid-1890s and developed in the seventh chapter of *The Interpretation of Dreams*, he was at the same time looking ahead to future formulations.

The paper sharply distinguishes between two ways the mind works: the

---

*"Psychoanalytic characterology," Otto Fenichel wrote in his classic textbook of 1945, "is the youngest branch of psychoanalysis," because psychoanalysis began with "the investigation of neurotic symptoms, that is, with phenomena that are ego alien and do not fit into the 'character,' the customary mode of behavior." It was only when it "undertook the consideration of surface mental experiences" that psychoanalysis could "begin to understand that not only unusual and suddenly erupting mental states but also ordinary modes of behavior, the usual manner of loving, hating, and acting in various situations can be comprehended genetically as dependent on unconscious conditions." And only then is the systematic analytic study of character possible. (Otto Fenichel, *The Psychoanalytic Theory of Neurosis* [1945], 463.)

primary process, the first to emerge, is characterized by an inability to tolerate the modulation of wishes or any delay in their gratification. It obeys the pleasure principle. The other, the secondary process, which ripens with the course of maturation, develops the human capacity for thought and is thus an agent of judiciousness, of beneficial postponement. It obeys the reality principle—at least some of the time.

Every child must experience the enthronement of the reality principle as "a consequential step," one that life forces it to take. Once it has discovered that hallucinating the fulfillment of its desires is not enough to secure their real satisfaction, it begins to cultivate its gift for understanding and, if possible, manipulating and controlling, the outside world. This means, concretely, that the child learns to remember, to pay attention, to judge, to plan, to calculate, to treat thinking as an experimental form of action, to test reality. There is nothing easy, let alone automatic, about this secondary process: the heedless, imperious pleasure principle is slow to surrender its hold on the growing youngster and at intervals reasserts that hold. Indeed, the child, with its poignant conservatism, recalls pleasures once enjoyed and is unwilling to give them up even for the prospect of later, greater, more secure gratifications. The two principles therefore coexist uneasily, often in conflict.

Freud did not describe such conflict as inescapable and in fact surrendered momentarily to unaccustomed optimism: "In actuality, the replacement of the pleasure principle by the reality principle signifies not the deposition of the pleasure principle but only its safeguarding." The ultimate relationship between the two principles is bound to shift from issue to issue, but "external reality" acquires "increased significance" with the passage of time. Yet Freud recognized that the sexual drives are particularly resistant to education, since they may be gratified by autoerotic activity, in the person's own body. And the reluctance of these drives to accept the constraints of reality fertilizes the soil for later neuroses. This is why it is essential for culture to negotiate with the pleasure principle in the service of the reality principle, to make the *"pleasure-ego"* yield, at least in part, to the *"reality-ego."* This, too, is why consciousness has important work to do in mental functioning: to secure the hold of reality on the mind is principally its business. For, Freud reminded his readers, in the unconscious, in the dark realm of repression and fantasies, reality testing has no leverage. The only currency valid in that country, Freud noted in his best metaphorical manner, is *"neurotic currency."* Hence all the moments of truce cannot obscure the fact that mental life is, in Freud's judgment, a more or less continual warfare.

The paper on mental functioning dealt with the individual mind, chiefly the troubled commerce between its unconscious and its conscious domains. But implicitly, Freud was paving the way for a psychoanalytic social psychology. The forces propelling the child to traffic with the reality principle early, when its grasp on reason is still tentative and intermittent, are for the most part external—actions by authoritative others. The mother's temporary absence, the fatherly punishment, the inhibitions imposed on the child by anyone, whether nurse, older sibling, or schoolmate, are the great social No: they frustrate wishes, channel appetites, compel delays in gratification. After all, even that most intimate of experiences, the Oedipus complex, emerges and runs its course in an exquisitely social situation.

In 1911, the year he published this paper on the pleasure-ego and the reality-ego, Freud was fully persuaded that individual and social psychology are impossible to separate.* Three years before, he had already made the same point in an informal essay, " 'Civilized' Sexual Morality and Modern Nervousness." There he had suggested that what he saw as the prevalence of nervous malaise in his time sprang from the excessive self-denial that respectable middle-class society imposed on the sexual needs of ordinary humans. The unconscious, in short, cannot escape culture. His paper on the two principles of mental functioning, then, in company with the one on nervousness, subtly hinted at new departures.

THE JANUS-FACED CHARACTER of Freud's writings in the years before the First World War, aiming at summation and edging toward revision, is most spectacular in his subversive paper on narcissism—subversive, that is, of his own long-held views. In his characteristic style, Freud labeled it as introductory. This was not false modesty; he complained that writing the paper was unpalatable work and that he had difficulties containing his exploding thoughts within its framework. He was certain, though, that he could use it as a weapon in his crusade against his opponents: "The Narcissism will, I suppose, ripen during the summer," he wrote Ferenczi just before he left Vienna for the summer holiday of 1913; it was, to his mind, "the scientific settling of accounts with Adler."† By early October, just back from his "17 delicious days" in Rome, he could report that the paper was virtually ready. He told Ernest Jones that he "would be glad to talk it over" with him, as well as "with Rank and Sachs."

His adherents were only too anxious for whatever clarification Freud might have to offer; Jones has testified that they all found the essay "disturbing." Actually Freud himself was uneasy about it, more uneasy than usual. Giving

---

*Freud would discuss the relation of individual to social psychology in *Group Psychology and the Analysis of the Ego.* See p. 404.

†"On Narcissism" was a settling of accounts with Jung as well, though, as Abraham observed upon reading a draft of the paper, Freud could have emphasized the contrast between "Jung's therapy and psychoanalysis" even more strongly. (Abraham to Freud, April 2, 1914. *Freud–Abraham,* 165 [169].)

a gloomy cast to one of his favorite metaphors, he told Abraham in March 1914 that the essay "had been a difficult birth and shows all the deformations of such. Naturally I don't especially like it, but now I cannot offer anything else." Its completion brought him no relief but, on the contrary, disagreeable physical symptoms: headaches and intestinal troubles. Hence he was delighted to have Abraham reassure him that the paper was really brilliant and convincing—delighted, touched, but not wholly reassured. "I have a very strong feeling of serious inadequacy there." To be sure, during these months Freud was in a pugnacious mood; he was drafting his blast against Adler and Jung at the very time he was polishing his paper on narcissism. But something more elusive was stirring in him. He was standing on the verge of rethinking the psychology he had been planning merely to explain.

"On Narcissism" carries further, and suitably complicates, the ideas about mental development that Freud had launched some five years before. As early as November 1909, commenting on a paper by Isidor Sadger at the Vienna Psychoanalytic Society, he had suggested that narcissism, "the infatuation in one's own person (= in one's own genitals)," is "a necessary stage of development in the transition from autoeroticism to object love." As we have seen, he had first floated this proposition in print in his paper on Leonardo; he mentioned it again in his case history of Schreber, and once more, tersely though suggestively, in *Totem and Taboo.* * "Narcissism" was an appealing term that recalled one of Freud's prized Greek myths—of the beautiful youth who had died of self-infatuation; he had borrowed it, with acknowledgments, from the German psychiatrist Paul Näcke and from Havelock Ellis. Its explosive possibilities, though, did not emerge until the paper he devoted to it in 1914.

Freud had observed in *Totem and Taboo* that the narcissistic stage is never wholly overcome and that it appears to be a very general phenomenon. Now he spelled out the implications of his fragmentary thoughts. Originally the name "narcissism" was applied to a perversion: narcissists are deviants who can secure sexual satisfaction only by treating their own bodies as erotic objects. But, Freud observed, these perverts have no monopoly on this kind of erotic self-centeredness. After all, schizophrenics too withdraw their libido from the outside world and do not extinguish it; rather, Freud argued, they invest it in their own self. This was not all: psychoanalytic observers had also discovered massive evidence of narcissistic traits among neurotics, children,

---

*Tracing back evolving sexual energy—libido—to childhood, he had written there, psychoanalysts had been driven to divide its earliest stage, autoeroticism, into two. In the first, a set of independent, partial sexual drives seek primitive satisfaction in the body, while in the second the sexual drives, now unified, take the self as their object. It is this second phase that is properly the stage of *"narcissism."* (*Totem und Tabu, GW* IX, 109/*Totem and Taboo, SE* XIII, 89.)

and primitive tribes. In *Totem and Taboo* Freud had already added lovers to this growing list. He could not evade the conclusion that in this more comprehensive sense, narcissism is "not a perversion, but the libidinal complement to the egotism of the self-preservative drive." The word gained a rapidly enlarging sphere of signification, first at Freud's hands and then far more irresponsibly in general usage, much to its damage as a diagnostic term. When "narcissism" entered educated discourse in the 1920s and after, it came to be casually employed not just as a label for a sexual perversion or a developmental stage but also for a symptom in psychosis and for a variety of object relations. Some in fact exploited it as a handy term of abuse for modern culture or as a loose synonym for bloated self-esteem.

Even before this inflation of meanings had virtually ruined its precision, "narcissism" raised some inconvenient issues, which Freud showed some reluctance to address: "One resists the idea of leaving observation for sterile theoretical controversies." Yet, he added dutifully, one had an obligation to make "an attempt at clarification." This attempt compelled the recognition that the self can, and does, choose itself as an erotic object no less than it chooses others. There is, in short, an "ego-libido" as well as an "object-libido." The narcissistic type, under the sway of the ego-libido, loves what he is, what he once was, what he would like to be, or the person who had been part of his own self. But he is not a curiosity or a rare aberration: some narcissism, it seems, lies concealed in every closet. Even parental love, "moving, fundamentally so childlike," is "nothing other than the reborn narcissism of the parents." As Freud compiled his growing, somewhat tendentious list, he wryly acknowledged that the world seemed to be awash in narcissists—including women, children, cats, criminals, and humorists.*

It was only reasonable for Freud to wonder just what happens to all the narcissistic investment of early childhood. After all, having greatly enjoyed the self-love that seems so natural, the child is, as Freud always insisted, unable to give up this satisfaction, like others, without a struggle. The question propelled Freud into issues he would not fully resolve until after the war. In "On Narcissism," Freud argued that the growing child, confronted with criticisms from its parents, its teachers, or "public opinion," relinquishes narcissism by setting up a substitute to which it may then pay homage in place of its imperfect self. This is the famous "ego ideal," the censorious voices of the world made one's own. As a pathological aberration, it emerges

---

*The most offensive entry on that list is, of course, "women," as Freud acknowledged: "Perhaps it is not superfluous to assert, that" in describing woman as a narcissist, "I am far from any tendency to a denigration of woman." And he disclaimed the slightest inclination to tendentiousness of this sort. ("Narzissmus," *GW* X, 156/"Narcissism," *SE* XIV, 89.) But see pp. 501–22.

as the delusion that one is being watched—here is Schreber again—but in its normal form it is first cousin to what we call the conscience, which acts as the ego ideal's guardian.

Reading the paper, Abraham was particularly impressed with Freud's pages on the delusion of being watched, on the conscience, and on the ego ideal. But he had no immediate comment on Freud's modification of his theory of the drives. Yet this was the aspect of the paper that Ernest Jones found most unsettling. If there is an "ego-libido" as well as an "object-libido," what is to become of the distinctions on which psychoanalysts had hitherto relied? Here was the difficulty: Freud had long implied, and made explicit in 1910, the view that human drives may be sharply divided into two classes— the ego drives and the sexual drives. The former are responsible for the individual's self-preservation; they have nothing to do with the erotic. The latter press for erotic gratification and serve the preservation of the species. But if the self, too, can be erotically charged, then the ego drives must be sexual in character as well.

If this conclusion holds true, radical consequences for psychoanalytic theory must follow, for it palpably contradicts Freud's earlier formulation, according to which the ego drives are nonsexual. Were the critics who called Freud a pansexualist, a voyeur who detected sex everywhere, right after all? Freud had repeatedly, and vehemently, denied that. Or did Jung have a point when he defined libido as a universal force that indiscriminately pervades all mental effort? Freud professed to be unperturbed. Invoking the authority of his clinical experience, he pronounced the categories of ego-libido and object-libido which he had just introduced to be an "indispensable extension" of the old psychoanalytic scheme and insisted that there was nothing very new and certainly nothing at all troubling about them. His adherents were by no means so sure; more clearly than the author of the paper, they glimpsed its radical implications. "It gave," Ernest Jones recalls, "a disagreeable jolt to the theory of instincts on which psychoanalysis had hitherto worked." Freud's "On Narcissism" made Jones and his friends very nervous.

These conflicting appraisals reach down to the fundamentals of psychology as a science. Freud was never completely happy with his theory of the drives, whether in its early or its late form. In "On Narcissism" he lamented the "complete lack of a theory of the drives"—*Trieblehre*—that might provide the psychological investigator with a dependable orientation. This absence of theoretical clarity was in large part due to the inability of biologists and psychologists to generate a consensus on the nature of drives or instincts. Lacking their guidance, Freud constructed his own theory by observing psychological phenomena in the light of whatever biological information was available. To understand a drive one needs both disciplines, for it stands, in his words, at the border between the physical and the mental.* It is an urge translated into a wish.

At the time "On Narcissism" appeared, Freud still proclaimed himself more or less resigned to a classification of the drives into those aiming at self-preservation and those aiming at sexual satisfaction. Since the 1880s, we know, he had liked to quote the line from Schiller that love and hunger move the world. But he came to see that by reading narcissism as sexual self-love rather than just a specialized perversion, he had effectively ruined the simplicity of his old scheme. Try as he might, he could no longer maintain the clear separation between the two classes of drives that had served him for two decades: the fact is that love for the self and love for others differ only in their object, not in their nature.

By the spring of 1914, the need to reclassify the drives, and to make other equally unsettling adjustments in psychoanalytic theory, was becoming only too obvious. But with unexpected, ungracious suddenness the world intruded and for a time disrupted Freud's thoughts in the most spectacular, most brutal way imaginable. He had completed "On Narcissism" in March 1914 and published it in the *Jahrbuch* toward the end of June. Exhausted from a long hard year of political infighting and a crowded schedule of patients, Freud was looking forward to a long holiday in Karlsbad and to some time for work of his own. Within a month, though, he discovered that he had little time, and less taste, for exploring the subversive direction his thinking was taking. While Freud was edging toward great revisions, Western civilization was going mad.

THE END OF EUROPE

 On June 28, 1914, the Wolf Man took a long stroll through the Prater, musing about the instructive and in the end profitable years he had spent under Freud's care in Vienna. It was, he recalled later, "a very hot and sultry Sunday." He was about to terminate his analysis and to marry a woman of whom Freud approved; all seemed well, and he returned from his walk in a hopeful frame of mind. But he had scarcely got home when

*See p. 364.

the maid handed him an extra with stunning news: Archduke Francis Ferdinand and his consort had been assassinated at Sarajevo by young Bosnian militants. The event was a shocking commentary on that rickety anachronism, the Austro-Hungarian multinational empire, defiantly surviving into an age of feverish nationalism. The consequences of Sarajevo were not immediately clear. Writing to Ferenczi "under the impress of the surprising murder," Freud thought the situation unpredictable and observed that in Vienna, "personal sympathy" with the imperial house was small. Just three days before, Freud had signaled the appearance of his "History of the Psychoanalytic Movement" with an aggressive flourish to Abraham: "Now the bomb has exploded." It would, after Sarajevo, appear a very private, very paltry bomb indeed. The outbreak of the First World War was only six weeks away.

For the cultural historian, the impact of that catastrophe is something of a paradox. Most of the artistic, literary, and intellectual movements that would make the 1920s such an exciting, innovative decade had originated well before 1914: functional architecture, abstract painting, twelve-tone music, experimental novels—and psychoanalysis. At the same time, the war destroyed a world, forever. Looking back late in 1919 at the epoch before the great insanity, the English economist John Maynard Keynes pictured it as an age of stupefying progress. Most of the population, he wrote in a famous passage, "worked hard and lived at a low standard of comfort, yet were, to all appearances, reasonably contented with this lot. But escape was possible, for any man of capacity or character at all exceeding the average, into the middle and upper classes, for whom life offered, at a low cost and with the least trouble, conveniences, comforts, and amenities beyond the compass of the richest and most powerful monarchs of other ages."

Any observant social worker or principled radical could have told Keynes that this was far too benign a view of the creature comforts and social mobility open to the poor. But for the sizable middle classes, it was accurate enough. "The inhabitant of London could order by telephone, sipping his morning tea in bed, the various products of the whole earth, in such quantities as he might see fit, and reasonably expect their early delivery upon his doorstep; he could at the same moment and by the same means adventure his wealth in the natural resources and new enterprises of any quarter of the world, and share, without exertion or even trouble, in their prospective fruits and advantages." If he wished, this Londoner could taste similar pleasures abroad, "without passport or other formality." He "could despatch his servant to the neighboring office of a bank for such supply of the precious metals as might seem convenient," and then "proceed abroad to foreign quarters, without knowledge of their religion, language, or customs, bearing coined wealth upon his person, and would consider himself greatly aggrieved and much surprised at the least interference." Beyond that, "most important of all," Keynes concluded his nostalgic catalogue, "he regarded this state of affairs as normal, certain, and permanent, except in the direction of further improvement, and any deviation from it as aberrant, scandalous and avoidable." Militarism and imperialism, racial and cultural rivalries, and other troubles, "were little more than the amusements of his daily newspaper," and had no real influence on his life.

The very lyricism of this obituary for an extinct way of life documents how much devastation and despair the war would leave in its wake; in comparison, the world before August 1914 shone like a happy land of fantasies fulfilled. It was a time when Freud could dispatch a letter from Vienna to Zurich or Berlin on Monday and expect, without fail, a reply on Wednesday; a time when he could decide on the spur of the moment to visit France, or any other civilized country, without any preliminaries or formal documents. Only Russia, deemed an outpost of barbarism, required a visa from entering tourists.

During the relatively peaceful half century preceding August 1914, there had been militarists praying for war, generals planning for it, prophets of doom predicting it. But their voices were a distinct, if noisy, minority; when, in 1908, the brilliant English social psychologist Graham Wallas warned that "the horrors of a world-war" were a realistic danger, most of his contemporaries refused to credit his appalling fancy. True, the forming of hostile power blocs, with Britain and France confronting the Triple Alliance of Germany, Austria-Hungary, and Italy, was a menacing portent; the armaments race, especially the intensified naval rivalry of Britain and Germany, was another. It is true, too, that Kaiser Wilhelm craved what he called a place in the sun, and that meant a Germany competing for colonies with other great powers in Africa and the Pacific, and challenging Britain's traditional supremacy at sea. The Kaiser's blustering speeches and his loose talk about a fight to the death between the Teutonic and the Slavic races were additional reasons for nervousness. His rhetoric echoed an established, vulgarized interpretation of Darwin's teachings, which read them as a commendation of sanguinary struggles between peoples or "races" as a way to health, indeed as necessary to national survival.

What is more, from 1900 on, it was a commonplace to call the Balkans a tinderbox: the long agony of the Ottoman empire, which had been relaxing its hold on its African and Balkan dependencies for a century, tempted adventurous politicians into bellicose displays and rash expeditions. Moreover, the cheap daily press in the great metropolitan cities did its share by supplying dry kindling to feed the flames of chauvinist excitement. On

December 9, 1912, with the Balkans once again in an uproar, Freud commented to Pfister, in passing, that while all was well at home, "the expectation of war almost takes our breath away." On the same day, he reported to Ferenczi that "the war mood dominates our daily life." Yet the talk of confrontations in the making, and anxious armament to match, did not make a great war inevitable. Nor would the First World War in any way resemble, in its length and its cost, the fears—or hopes—of those who had predicted it.

There had long been persuasive arguments for peace, including that of sheer self-interest. The expanding network of world commerce made war a calamitous prospect for merchants, bankers, and industrialists. The lively traffic of art, literature, and philosophical ideas across frontiers had established a civilized international fraternity, in itself an informal agent of peace. Psychoanalysis was not the only cosmopolitan intellectual movement. One had hoped, Freud would write sadly, looking back, that the "educational element" of the compulsion to morality might do its work, and that "the splendid community of interests produced by trade and production would make a beginning of such a compulsion." The great powers, still tied to one another in the concert of Europe, worked to keep local wars local. They found a rather incongruous ally in the international Socialist movement, whose leaders confidently predicted that the machinations of malevolent warmongers would be frustrated by a strike of class-conscious proletarians everywhere. The wishes of pacific merchants and pacifist radicals proved pathetically wrong; during a few frenetic weeks, aggressive, downright suicidal forces were let loose that most had thought forever under control.

IN THE WEEKS FOLLOWING Sarajevo, Austrian politicians and diplomats took a hard line, their backs stiffened by German reassurances. Had he had access to their confidential dispatches, Freud could have read them as the utterances of anxious men feeling themselves under pressure to display their virility. They talked of violently hacking through the Gordian knot, doing away with the Serbians once and for all, the need to act now or never, the fear that the world might interpret a conciliatory Austrian policy as a confession of feebleness. Plainly, they felt it essential to escape the stigma of indecisiveness, effeminacy, impotence. On July 23, the Austrians confronted the Serbians with an imperious note, virtually an ultimatum; five days later, though the response had been prompt and placatory, Austria declared war.

The move was immensely popular in Austria. "This country," the British ambassador observed, "has gone wild with joy at the prospect of war with Serbia, and its postponement or prevention would undoubtedly be a great disappointment." At long last one could stand up straight. "There are really great rejoicings and demonstrations," Alexander Freud reported from Vienna to his brother Sigmund, who had been at Karlsbad for some two weeks. "But," he added, rather weakening the impression of general joy, "in general people are very dejected, since everyone has friends and acquaintances who are being called up." This did not keep him from a certain pugnacity. He was glad that, "despite all the misery," Austria had decided to act, and to defend itself. "Things couldn't have gone on like this." This stance, as Alexander Freud did not fail to note, was also his brother's at the time; Freud was suffering an unexpected bout of patriotism. "Perhaps for the first time in thirty years," he told Abraham late in July, "I feel myself an Austrian, and would like just once more to give this rather unpromising empire a chance."* He hailed the stiff Austrian attitude toward Serbia as courageous, and welcomed German support for his country's stand.

By no means all the diplomatic maneuvers of these days were parades of militancy and manliness; to the end, the British and French sought to cool tempers. To no effect: policy makers in the Central Powers—Austria-Hungary and Germany—had more devious, less pacific intentions. They schemed to keep Britain neutral and, what was more sinister, they tried to foist responsibility for the imbroglio on the Russians, whom they portrayed as intransigent and impulsive. Still, only a few believed that a great conflagration was in the offing, and Freud was not among them. If he had been, he would have insisted that his daughter Anna cancel the trip she was making to England in mid-July; and he would not have left Vienna about the same time and invited Eitingon with his new wife to visit him in Karlsbad in early August.

His mind was, as we shall see, on Anna, and on psychoanalysis, not on international politics: finding Ferenczi's emotional letters a strain, he told him frankly that he would stop corresponding for a while, to concentrate on work, "for which I cannot use sociability." Yet the world did not let him alone. "What do you say there about the chances for war and peace?" his daughter Mathilde inquired on July 23. He was evidently anticipating—or, perhaps more accurately, hoping for—a strictly limited conflict. "Should the war remain localized to the Balkans," he wrote to Abraham on July 26, "it won't be too bad." But with the Russians, he added, one never knew.

Freud's uncertainty echoed the general feeling of suspense. As late as July 29, he wondered out loud whether perhaps in two weeks the world would not look back at all this excitement half ashamed, or whether the long-threatened

---

*Almost three decades earlier, during his stay in Paris, Freud had presented himself as something of a patriot, making invidious comparisons between himself and light-headed Parisians. But even then his national allegiance had been far from unequivocal. He had declared himself to a French patriot, we will remember, as neither Austrian nor German, but as a Jew.

"decision of destinies" was now at hand. Abraham, as usual, remained sunny. "I believe," he wrote Freud on the same day, "that no great power will bring about a general war." Five days later, on August 3, Sir Edward Grey, Britain's foreign secretary, warned the Germans against the consequences that their violation of Belgian neutrality would bring. At dusk, Grey stood at the window of his office, gloomily watching with a friend the lamps being lit outside. "The lamps are going out all over Europe," he said, and memorably prophesied, "we shall not see them lit again in our lifetime."

In Vienna tension centered on what Britain would do. Italy had declared its neutrality, citing legalistic justifications for its failure to honor its obligations to the Triple Alliance. This move, Alexander Freud wrote his brother on August 4, had been expected. But now "everything depends on England's attitude; the decision will become known here tonight. Romantics maintain that England will not join in; a civilized people will not take the side of the barbarians, etc." An Anglophobe—unlike his brother—Alexander Freud was no romantic, at least on this point. "My good old hatred against English perfidy will probably turn out to be right; they won't be embarrassed to take the side of the Russians."* Perfidious or not, on that day, August 4, after Germany's invasion of Belgium was confirmed, Britain went to war. The old European order was gone.

THE WAR THAT ERUPTED in late July and spread in early August 1914 engulfed most of Europe and adjacent lands: the Austro-Hungarian empire, Germany, Britain, France, Russia, Rumania, Bulgaria, Turkey. The cause of the Allies would be strengthened later by the participation of Italy and the United States. Few suspected that the war would be a very extended affair; most observers, certainly in the camp of the Central Powers, predicted that the efficient German armies would reach Paris by Christmas. Alexander Freud's bleak prognosis of a long and costly conflict was something of a rarity. "No reasonable man doubts that in the end success will be on the side of the Germans," he wrote to his brother on August 4. "But how long it can last before the final success is won, what immense sacrifices in life, health, and fortune the business will cost, that is the question that no one dares to approach."

The most extraordinary thing about these calamitous events was less that they happened than how they were received. Europeans of all stripes joined

---

*The two brothers, who agreed on much, did not agree on England, which, as we know, Freud greatly admired. So did his son Martin. "The news that England is on the side of our opponents," he wrote his father two days after war had been declared, "was expected, but it remains a heavy blow to our feelings." And he added, "Do you have news of Annerl?" (Martin Freud to Freud, August 6, 1914. Freud Museum, London.)

in greeting the advent of war with a fervor bordering on a religious experience. Aristocrats, bourgeois, workers, and farmers; reactionaries, liberals, and radicals; cosmopolitans, chauvinists, and particularists; fierce soldiers, preoccupied scholars, and gentle theologians—all linked arms in their bellicose delight. The ideology triumphant was nationalism, even for most Marxists, nationalism driven to the highest pitch of hysteria. Some hailed the war as an opportunity to settle old scores; but, more sinister, for most it established their own nation's virtue and the enemy's viciousness. Germans liked to depict the Russian as an incurable barbarian, the Englishman as a canting shopkeeper, the Frenchman as a low sensualist; the English and the French in their turn suddenly discovered the German to be a malodorous amalgam of abject bureaucrat, woolly-minded metaphysician, and sadistic Hun. The European family of high culture was torn apart as professors returned honorary degrees from enemy countries and lent their scholarship to proving that their adversaries' claims to cultivation were only masks covering greed or the lust for power.

This was the primitive style of thinking that Freud would come to find so incredible. Orators, in prose and in verse, saluted the war as a rite of spiritual cleansing. It was destined to restore the ancient, almost lost heroic virtues, and to serve as a panacea for the decadence that cultural critics had long noted and deplored. The patriotic war fever attacked novelists, historians, theologians, poets, composers, on all sides, but perhaps most fervently in Germany and Austria-Hungary. The German poet Rainer Maria Rilke, a unique mixture of sophisticate and mystic, celebrated the outbreak of hostilities with "Five Songs," dated August 1914, in which he visualized the "most remote incredible God of War" rising again: "At last a God. Since we often no longer grasped the peaceable one, the Battle-God suddenly grasps us, flings the firebrand." Hugo von Hofmannsthal, that prolific Viennese aesthete, made himself into an assiduous official propagandist for the Austrian cause and boasted—or allowed others to boast in his behalf—of his military valor. Even Stefan Zweig, later a vociferous pacifist, had military ambitions in the early days of the war and until his shift to pacifism cheerfully served the Austrian propaganda machine, much as Hofmannsthal was doing. "War!" Thomas Mann exclaimed in November 1914, "it was purification, liberation we felt, and an enormous hope"; it "set the hearts of poets aflame" with a sense of relief: "How could the artist, the soldier in the artist, not praise God for the collapse of a peaceful world with which he was fed up, so exceedingly fed up!"*

---

*There were touches of this excitement even among those very few, like Arthur Schnitzler, who heroically refused to trade in their humanity for this easy, self-intoxicated patriotism. Fritz Wittels

As their scathing critic Karl Kraus delighted to point out, the writers who issued these frantic, almost demented-sounding calls to arms, struggled energetically and successfully to evade serving at the front. But this contradiction did not trouble, certainly did not silence, them. Their outbursts were a fitting climax to decades of irritation with what they and their avant-garde ancestors had been pleased to denounce as dull, safe, threadbare bourgeois culture; they epitomized a playful, sophisticated, irresponsible infatuation with unreason and purification and death. In the summer of 1914, this sort of talk swept across whole populations in a contagious war psychosis. It was a telling instance of how susceptible to collective regression presumably sensible and educated people can be.

AT FIRST, GERMAN and Austrian optimists, frenzied or not, drew ample support from the military communiqués. Toward the end of August, Abraham announced "dazzling news" to Freud. "German troops are scarcely 100 kilometers from Paris. Belgium is finished; England, on land, no less so." Two weeks later he reported that "we," in Berlin, "have been greatly reassured by the total defeat of the Russians in East Prussia. In the very next few days we hope for favorable news from the battles on the Marne." Once these have been won, "France is essentially finished." In mid-September, Eitingon exclaimed to Freud about the "incomparably splendid beginning in West and East," though he confessed that "the tempo seems to have slowed somewhat."

Like his followers, Freud too for a time indulged himself in partisan credulity, as cheerful, even triumphant bulletins kept pouring in from the front. But he never quite yielded to the irrational, quasi-religious exaltation of a Rilke or a Mann. In September, visiting his daughter Sophie Halberstadt to see his first grandson, Ernst, he discovered that his responses were once more regaining a certain complexity. "I am not in Hamburg for the first time," he wrote to Abraham, "but for the first time not as though I were in a foreign city." Yet, he confessed, he would "speak of the success of 'our' war loan and discuss the chances of 'our' battle of millions," and these quizzical quotation marks suggest a certain astonishment at himself.

While Freud was preparing for his journey to Hamburg, he wondered

---

recalled coming upon Arthur Schnitzler after that rare thing, an Austrian victory over the Russians, and was astonished to see this most astringent of writers moved and delighted: "He said to me, 'You know how much I hate almost everything in Austria, yet, when I heard that the danger of a Russian invasion was over, I felt like kneeling down and kissing this soil of ours.' " (Wittels, "Wrestling with the Man," 5.) This was not chauvinist excitement, but the kind of anti-Russian animus that nearly all Austrians, including Freud, shared.

whether he might be in Germany when "the news of a victory before Paris" arrived. Yet from the very beginning of hostilities, he was too much of a skeptic to abandon the analytic stance entirely. "One observes in everyone," he had noted in late July, "the most authentic symptomatic acts." Besides, his lifelong attachment to England got in the way of full-throated chauvinism. He would, he wrote to Abraham on August 2, support the war "with all my heart, if I did not know that England is on the wrong side." Abraham, too, found this line-up awkward, especially since among those on the wrong side was their good friend and indispensable ally Ernest Jones. "Is it a strange feeling for you, too," he asked Freud, "that he is among our 'enemies'?" Freud felt the strangeness keenly. "It has been generally decided," he told Jones in October, "not to regard you as an enemy!" As good as his word, he kept up his correspondence with Jones, the enemy who was no enemy, through neutral countries like Switzerland, Sweden, and the Netherlands, only making the gesture of switching to German.

NO DOUBT THE PRINCIPAL reason why Freud's zeal for his country soon began to fade was that the war came home to him from the start. Before it was over, all three of his sons had seen action, two of them a good deal of it. What is more, the outbreak of hostilities virtually ruined his practice; potential patients were drafted into the armed services or thought about the war more than about their neuroses. "These are hard times," he wrote as early as August 14, "our interests depreciated for the time being." In the spring of 1915, he estimated that the war had already cost him more than 40,000 kronen. Indeed, the war posed an acute danger to the very survival of psychoanalysis. The first casualty was the congress of psychoanalysts planned for Dresden in September 1914. Then, one after the other, Freud's followers were called up; most of them were physicians and hence eminently usable fodder for the military Moloch. Eitingon was drafted early; Abraham was detailed to a surgical unit near Berlin. Ferenczi was sent to the Hungarian hussars, in the provinces, for duty which turned out to be more boring than demanding; he had more time to himself than the other analysts in uniform. "You are now really the only one," Freud wrote Ferenczi in 1915, "who is working alongside us. The others are all militarily paralyzed."*

Yet the service to which the physicians among his followers were called was burdensome rather than dangerous; it gave them enough stolen leisure to respond to the ideas he poured out to them. Naturally it interfered with

---

*From early 1916 on, Ferenczi was even less paralyzed than before: transferred to Budapest as a part-time psychiatrist in a military hospital, he could resume some of his psychoanalytic activity. (See Michael Balint, "Einleitung des Herausgebers," in Sándor Ferenczi, *Schriften zur Psychoanalyse*, 2 vols. [1970], I, xiii.)

their analytic practice; nor could they keep up their writing and editing with the old efficiency. Freud cared enough about the future of psychoanalysis to report blithely that the nearsighted Hanns Sachs had been rejected for military service. Meanwhile his dependable amanuensis, Otto Rank, worked valiantly to stay out of the army, "defending himself like a lion," Freud told Ferenczi, "against the fatherland." The needs of psychoanalysis, like the news from his sons at the front, tested the limits of Freud's patriotism.

It was strained to those limits in 1915, if not before, when Rank was finally caught in the military dragnet; with the Austrian forces facing a new enemy, Italy, they could use even the unusable. He was made to serve for two years, miserably enough, as the editor of a newspaper in Kraków. Rank "is sitting tight as prisoner of the editorship of the *Krakauer Zeitung,* and is feeling pretty low," Freud reported to Abraham late in 1917. He found this tedious assignment for Rank nothing less than criminal waste.

Not surprisingly, there was little time, and less money, available for psychoanalytic journals; the *Jahrbuch* ceased publication, while *Imago* and the *Internationale Zeitschrift für Psychoanalyse* (founded in 1913) soldiered on, much reduced in size. The Vienna Psychoanalytic Society, which had for years faithfully assembled every Wednesday night, now convened once every two weeks and, from early 1916 on, once every three weeks or even more sporadically. There was, of course, no opportunity for mounting the international congresses of psychoanalysts which Freud and his followers considered the lifeblood of their science. In a glum Christmas letter to Ernest Jones during the first year of the war, Freud sketched a somber balance sheet and a no less somber forecast: "I do not delude myself: the springtime of our science has abruptly broken off, we are heading for a bad period; all we can do is to keep the fire flickering in a few hearths, until a more favorable wind makes it possible to light it again to full blaze. What Jung and Adler have left of the movement is now perishing in the strife of nations." Like everything else that was international, the psychoanalytic association now no longer seemed viable, and psychoanalytic periodicals were moribund. "Everything one wanted to cultivate and watch over one must now let grow rank and wild." He professed confidence in the long-run fortunes "of the cause to which you are devoting such a touching attachment." But the immediate future looked dark, hopeless. "I will not blame any rat when I see it leaving the sinking ship." Some three weeks later, he summed it all up tersely: "Science sleeps."

All this was troubling enough, but, far more important, Freud's children were not spared. His youngest daughter, Anna, who had gone to England on a visit in mid-July, was caught there by the outbreak of hostilities. With Jones's assiduous help, she managed to get home in late August by a circuitous route that included Gibraltar and Genoa. Freud's gratitude was eloquent. "I have not yet had the opportunity," he wrote Jones in October, "in these miserable times that impoverish us in ideal as in material goods, to thank you for the adroit and expedient way of sending my little daughter back to me, and for all the friendship behind it." It was a great relief.

Once the possible danger to his daughter was off his mind—it had never really been very acute—Freud had three grown sons to brood about. Each of them was eligible, and it turned out eager, for the army. Even in the first blush of his new-found sentiment for Austria, Freud had thought more protectively about his boys than about the needs of the Austro-Hungarian war machine. "My three sons are fortunately not affected," he confided to Abraham late in July 1914; the Austrian authorities had rejected two of them definitely, and exempted the third. He repeated the same good news, in virtually the same words, in a letter to Eitingon two days later, noting that his sons were "fortunately and undeservedly" safe.* But Martin, the eldest, volunteered early in August. "It would have been intolerable for me," he wrote his father, "to remain behind alone when all others are marching off." Besides, he added, serving on the eastern front would be "the best opportunity to give blunt expression to my aversion to Russia"; this way, as a soldier, he could cross the Russian frontier without the special permission that the czarist empire required of Jews. "By the way, since I have become a soldier," he told his father the next day, "I have been looking forward to the first military action as to a thrilling mountain climb." He need not have worried; he managed to secure admission to the artillery, in which he had served in peacetime, and was soon in battles on the eastern and southern fronts.

Oliver, Freud's second son, was rejected for service until 1916, but then did his part—generally remaining less exposed than his brothers—in a variety of engineering projects for the army. Ernst, the youngest, volunteered in October (rather late to see action, his comrades thought) and served on the Italian front. Freud's son-in-law Max Halberstadt, Sophie's husband, saw action in France, and in 1916 was wounded and invalided out. To judge from their decorations and promotions, the bravery and the gusto of these young men matched their rhetoric.† All Freud could do was to send his boys money and food packages, and hope for the best. "Our mood," he could still write to Eitingon early in 1915, "is not so brilliant as in Germany; the future seems to us unpredictable, but German strength and confidence has its influence."

---

*Late in 1912, when there were noisy rumors of war, Freud had already worried that "it may happen to me to have 3 sons at the front at the same time." (Freud to Ferenczi, December 9, 1912. Freud–Ferenczi Correspondence, Freud Collection, LC.)

†As it turned out, the Freud family was more fortunate than most; just one of its members—Hermann Graf, the only son of Freud's sister Rosa—died in action.

Yet the prospects for victory distinctly retreated to the margins of Freud's interest as he worried about the safety of his sons, his sons-in-law, his nephew. References to their military adventures provide a touching paternal counterpoint to the business matters that fill his letters. Freud rarely wrote to his associates, even to Ernest Jones, without reporting on how the soldiers in his family were faring. When they came home on leave, they would pose in uniform for family photographs, trim and smiling.

DESPITE ALL HIS ANXIOUS reservations, he continued to identify the cause of the Central Powers as his own, and was irritated by Jones's unfailing confidence in the eventual victory of the Allies. "He writes about the war like a real Anglo," Freud complained to Abraham in November 1914. "Sink a few more superdreadnoughts or carry through a few landings, otherwise their eyes won't be opened." The British, he thought, were animated by "an incredible arrogance." He warned Jones not to believe what the newspapers said about the Central Powers: "Don't forget that there is a lot of lying now. We are suffering under no restrictions, no epidemic, and are in good spirits." At the same time, he acknowledged that these were "miserable times." By late November, no longer sounding like a tendentious amateur strategist, he made a poignant declaration of measured despair to Lou Andreas-Salomé: "I have no doubt that humanity will get over this war, too, but I know for certain that I and my contemporaries will see the world cheerful no more. It is too vile." What Freud found saddest was that people were behaving precisely the way that psychoanalysis would have predicted. That is why, Freud told her, he had never shared her optimism; he had come to believe that mankind is "organically not fit for this culture. We have to leave the stage, and the great Unknown, he or it, will some day repeat such a cultural experiment with another race." His rhetoric is a little overcharged, but it records his dismay and mounting misgivings about his commonplace loyalty to the German-Austrian cause.

Nor did it take Freud long to begin wondering whether that cause, quite apart from whatever merit it might possess, had much of a future. The unimpressive performance of the Austrian armies against the Russians gave him pause. In early September 1914, after only a month of fighting, he had told Abraham, "Indeed, things seem to be going well, but there is nothing decisive, and we have given up the hope for a rapid disposition of the war" through overwhelming victories. "Tenacity will become the principal virtue." Soon even Abraham permitted a certain prudence to invade his letters. "At the front," he wrote to Freud in late October, "these are hard days. But on the whole one remains full of confidence." That was a new tone for Freud's "dear incurable optimist." In November, Abraham reported that the mood in Berlin "is at present very positively expectant." By this time, Freud had ceased being either positive or expectant. "There is no end in sight," he told Eitingon in early January 1915. "I continue to think," he wrote gloomily a little later that month, "it is a long polar night, and one must wait until the sun rises again."

His metaphor was pedestrian but only too apt. The war dragged on. Refusing to credit Ernest Jones's repeated well-meaning forecasts of an Allied victory, Freud clung to his tepid patriotism. In January 1915, thanking Jones for a New Year's greeting, he repeated an earlier caution: "I would be sorry to think that you too should believe all the lies spread against us. We are confident and are holding out." Intermittently, he recharged the fading batteries of his faith in the Germans' prowess by celebrating news of their exploits. In February 1915, he still hoped for the victory of the Central Powers and allowed himself a moment of "optimism." Three months later, the threatened defection of neutral Italy to the Allies troubled his hopes, but, as he told Abraham, "our admiration for our great ally grows daily!" In July, he attributed nothing less than his "increased capacity for work" to "our beautiful victories."

But by the summer of 1915, for all the extensive military operations on all fronts, the adversaries had long since reached a devastating stalemate, as bloody in its attrition as the fiercest battle. And battles, too, continued to exact their heavy price, as commanders ordered offensives no less costly than they were futile. "Rumors that there will be peace in May refuse to subside," Freud told Ferenczi in early April 1915. "Manifestly they arise from a deep urge, but they seem absurd to me." His habitual pessimism would no longer be denied. "If this war lasts another year, as is probable," he wrote to Ferenczi in July, "there should be nobody left over who had been present at its outbreak." Actually, it would last more than three years longer, taking a toll from which Europe never fully recovered.

FOR A DREAMER like Freud it was perhaps inevitable that Martin and Oliver and Ernst should invade his nocturnal life. During the night of July 8–9, 1915, he had what he called a "prophetic dream," which had as its manifest content "very clearly the death of my sons, Martin first of all."* A few days later, Freud discovered that on the very day he dreamt this dream, Martin was actually wounded at the Russian front—though, fortunately, only slightly on the arm. It made him wonder, as he sometimes did, whether reports about occult occurrences were not indeed worth investigating. Without ever declaring himself convinced, Freud had for some years taken a reserved, groping

---

*For another part of this important dream, see p. 163.

interest in such phenomena. The human mind, as he had good reason to know, was after all capable of such extravagant, unexpected tricks! But as the months went by and the war went on, Freud thought not so much about the strangeness of the mind as about the depths to which humanity could sink. The war seemed a piling up of distasteful symptomatic acts, a horrifying venture into collective psychosis. It was, as he had told Frau Lou, too vile.

Hence, in 1915, speaking for himself and other rational Europeans, Freud published a pair of papers on the disillusionment the war had generated and on the modern attitude toward death—an elegy for a civilization destroying itself. We had assumed, he wrote, that as long as nations existed on differing economic and cultural planes, some wars might be unavoidable. "But we dared to hope for something else," to hope that the leaders of the "great world-dominating nations of the white race" who were "occupied with the cultivation of world-spanning interests" would be able to settle "conflicts of interest in other ways." Jeremiahs had proclaimed war as man's lot. "We did not want to believe it, but how did we imagine such a war, if it should come?" It would be a gallant affair, sparing civilians, "a chivalrous passage at arms." This was a perceptive insight: most of those looking forward to the cleansing power of a great war had had in their minds a sanitary, romanticized version of battles fought long ago. In reality, Freud added, the war had degenerated into a conflict more bloody than any of its predecessors and had produced that "virtually inconceivable phenomenon," an outburst of hate and contempt for the enemy. Freud, a man astonished at very little, was astonished at the hideous spectacle of human nature at war.

Freud's papers on war and death show him coming to terms with these harrowing events. He began bleakly enough in the first paper, describing the sense of unease and uncertainty besetting so many of his contemporaries—and himself: the sketch he drew was at least in part a self-portrait. "Seized by the whirlwind of this wartime, tendentiously informed, lacking distance from the great changes that have already taken place or are beginning to take place, and without having wind of the future that is in the process of forming, we begin to be confused about the significance of the impressions that intrude upon us and the value of the judgments we form." These are indeed terrible times: "It seems to us as though never before has an event destroyed so many precious common possessions of humanity, confused so many of the clearest intellects, debased the highest so thoroughly. Science itself," Freud went on implacably, "has lost its dispassionate impartiality." He was saddened to see "her most deeply embittered servants" borrowing weapons from science. "Anthropologists feel it necessary to declare the adversary inferior and degenerate; psychiatrists, to proclaim the diagnosis of his mental or spiritual sickness." In this situation, the person who has not been caught up in warfare directly, and has "not become a small particle of the gigantic war machine," must feel at once bewildered and inhibited in his capacity for work. The predictable consequence is disappointment, disillusionment.

Freud judged that psychoanalysis might somewhat mitigate these feelings by putting them into perspective. They rest on a view of human nature that cannot withstand realistic examination. Elemental, primitive human impulses, neither good nor bad in themselves, seek expression, but are inhibited by social controls and internal brakes. This process is universal. But the pressure of modern civilization for taming the drives has been excessive, and so have its expectations of human behavior. At least, the war has deprived everyone of the illusion that humanity is originally good. In truth, our fellow citizens "have not sunk so low as we feared, because they had not at all risen so high as we had thought."

Freud's paper is an essay in consolation, an unwonted exercise for a stoic who refused to believe that psychoanalysis could, or should, traffic in that commodity. "My courage sinks to stand up before my fellow humans as a prophet," he would tell them sternly in *Civilization and Its Discontents,* "and I bow before their reproach that I do not know how to bring them consolation—for that is fundamentally what they all demand, the wildest revolutionaries no less than the most conformist pious believers." But that was in 1930. In 1915, he could have used a little consolation himself. For all his awareness that there might be a "biological and psychological necessity of suffering for the economy of human life," Freud could yet "condemn war in its means and aims, and yearn for the cessation of all wars." If the war has destroyed that hope, has exhibited that yearning to be an illusion, psychoanalytic realism might, he thought, help his readers to survive the war years less depressed, less despairing.

Freud's paper on death, somber as its subject may appear, also mentions the contributions of psychoanalysis to an understanding of the modern mind, and takes the calamities of the war as one more proof that psychoanalysis is close to the essential truth about human nature. Modern man, Freud argued, denies the reality of his own death and resorts to imaginative devices to mitigate the impact that the death of others might have upon him. That is why he finds the novel and the stage so agreeable: they permit him to identify with a hero's death while surviving him. "In the realm of fiction we find the plurality of lives we need."

Primitive man, too, finds his mortality unreal and unimaginable, but in one respect he is closer to hidden psychological realities than repressed, cultivated modern man can be: he openly rejoices at the death of enemies. It was only with the emergence of conscience in civilized societies that the injunction "Thou shalt not kill" could become a fundamental law of conduct. But modern man, much like primitive man, is at bottom, in his unconscious, nothing better than a murderer. Deny it as he will, aggressiveness lies concealed behind courtesy and kindliness. Still, aggression is not simply a liability; as Freud noted in a much-quoted passage, primitive aggression that is converted into its opposite by the defensive stratagem of reaction formation can serve civilization. "The strongest egotists as children can become the most helpful citizens, those most capable of self-sacrifice. Most enthusiasts for compassion"—*Mitleidsschwärmer*—"friends of humanity, protectors of animals, have evolved from little sadists and animal tormentors."

What the Great War has done, Freud concluded, has been to make these unpalatable truths highly visible by exposing cultivated evasiveness for what it is. The war has "stripped us of our later cultural superimpositions, and has let the primeval man within us into the light." This exposure may have its uses. It makes men see themselves more truthfully than before and helps them discard illusions that have turned out to be damaging. "We recall the old proverb *Si vis pacem, para bellum.* If you want to preserve peace, arm for war. It would be timely to paraphrase it: *Si vis vitam, para mortem.* If you want to endure life, prepare yourself for death." The time would come in the next few years when Freud could test his prescription on himself.

REVISIONS

1915–1939

EIGHT

Aggressions

COMPREHENSIVE AND MOMENTOUS THINGS

 Freud, like millions of others, experienced the Great War as a destructive, seemingly interminable disruption. But somewhat to his astonishment, for all his gloom, all his flare-ups of apprehension, those years of excitement and anxiety brought beneficial consequences for his work. He was seeing few patients, did only the lightest of editorial chores, and had no psychoanalytic congresses to attend. With nearly all of his followers in the army, he was lonely. "I often feel as alone as I did in the first ten years, when there was desert around me," he lamented to Lou Andreas-Salomé in July 1915. "But I was younger and still endowed with a boundless energy for endurance." He missed having patients, whose stimulus usually primed the pump of his theorizing and whose fees enabled him to perform his duties as a reliable provider. "My psychic constitution," he told Abraham late in 1916, "urgently requires the acquisition and the spending of money for my family as fulfillment of my father complex that I know so well." Yet the war years were far from barren. His unsought and unwelcome leisure simultaneously lowered Freud's morale and freed time for large-scale enterprises.

In November 1914, musing to Lou Andreas-Salomé about the war and the unfitness of the human animal for civilization, he had already hinted that he was busy "in secret" with "comprehensive and perhaps momentous things." It is highly probable that he was beginning to ruminate about producing an authoritative statement of fundamental psychoanalytic ideas. In December he told Abraham that if his low mood did not finally ruin his appetite for work, he might "ready a theory of neuroses with chapters on the fortunes of the drives, repression, and the unconscious." This laconic announcement contains in outline the substance of his secret plans. A month later, he lifted yet another veil when he wrote Frau Lou that his "depiction of narcissism" should "some day" be called *"metapsychological."** The connection he was making between narcissism and metapsychology was crucial. In his first thoughts on narcissism before the war, Freud had not yet walked through the door he had pushed open. Now he was getting ready to explore their larger implications.

Freud began to draft his "theory of neuroses," rapidly and energetically, early in 1915, writing what later became known collectively as his papers on metapsychology. The tortuous history of the book he was planning, even more than the segments that survive, suggests that he was working on something significant—or that something significant was working in him. In mid-February 1915, he asked Ferenczi to forward his "sheet on melancholy to Abraham directly"; the book was to contain a chapter on melancholia. As he had always liked to do, with Fliess above all, he was circulating drafts to his intimates. In early April, he reported to Ferenczi that he had completed two chapters, and attributed his "productivity probably to the splendid improvement in the activity of my bowels." Obviously, he did not exempt himself from the kind of analytic scrutiny he expended on others: "Whether I owe this to a mechanical factor, the hardness of the war-bread, or a psychological one, my necessarily changed relationship to money, I leave open." His mood held; late in April, he informed Ferenczi that "Drives, Repression, Unconscious," the first three chapters, were ready, and would be published that year in the *Internationale Zeitschrift für Psychoanalyse.* He did not think the "introductory" paper on the drives "very alluring," but for the most part

---

*As Freud worked with his coinage "metapsychology," which he had first used in a letter to Fliess on February 13, 1896 (*Freud–Fliess*, 181 [172]), he defined it more and more strictly, as a psychology that analyzes the workings of the mind from three perspectives: the dynamic, the economic, and the topographic. The first of these perspectives entails probing mental phenomena to their roots in conflict-ridden unconscious forces mainly originating in, but not confined to, the drives; the second attempts to specify the quantities and vicissitudes of mental energies; the third undertakes to differentiate distinct domains within the mind. Together, these defining perspectives sharply distinguished psychoanalysis from other psychologies.

professed himself content, and he announced the need for another paper, one that would compare dreams with dementia praecox. "It, too, is already drafted."

Several other papers followed promptly—one on Freud's old favorite theme, dreams, another a deceptively short study titled "Mourning and Melancholia." In both Freud amplified the fertile and disturbing train of thought he had broached in his paper on narcissism: they deal with the ways that libido can be withdrawn from external objects, in sleep and in times of depression. By mid-June, Freud could tell Ferenczi, "True, I am working morosely, yet steadily. 10 of the 12 articles are ready. 2 of them, however (consciousness and anxiety) in need of revision. I have just completed [the paper on] conversion hysteria; obsessive neurosis and synthesis of transference neurosis still lacking." At the end of July, he wrote confidently to Lou Andreas-Salomé that the "fruit" of these months would "probably be a book consisting of 12 essays, introduced by [a chapter on] drives and their fortunes." He added that "it has just been finished except for the necessary reworking." War or not, it seemed that Freud's book on metapsychology would be published before long.

As FREUD HAD TOLD Fliess in March 1898, metapsychology was designed to explicate that part of his psychology going beyond or, as he put it, "behind" consciousness. He quite obviously intended the term to have a polemical thrust: metapsychology was to rival, and to best, that grandiose and futile philosophical daydream, metaphysics. But when Freud had first used the word two years earlier, he had not yet determined its precise meaning. Metapsychology was, he wrote in December 1896, his "ideal and problem child." By early 1915, no less ideal but no longer so problematic and, for that matter, no longer a child, metapsychology seemed ready for definitive, formal presentation. The book, Freud wrote to Abraham in May, would be called *Preparatory Essays for Metapsychology,* and he would give it "to an uncomprehending world in calmer times." While Freud gave the impression of secure confidence, the title suggests some final hesitation, an attack of tentativeness. Freud, we know, was not a modest man; he frankly told Ferenczi, while he was engaged in writing these papers, "Modesty—I am enough of a friend to truth or, let us rather say, a friend to objectivity, to ignore this virtue." Defining his forthcoming book for Abraham, he classified it as "type and level of the VIIth chapter of *The Interpretation of Dreams.*" Yet he observed in the same letter, "I think on the whole it will be an advance." Evidently—the cautious title he was proposing only confirms this—he had some inkling that the book he was completing represented both a new departure and a return to past theorizing. It might be obsolete the moment it was published.

In fact, Freud's papers on metapsychology retain more than historical interest. Had he written them in the 1920s, he would have phrased a number of things differently, even seen a number of things differently. He would have added fresh material. But for all that remodeling, the house of psychoanalysis would have remained recognizable. Among the papers Freud eventually chose to publish, the first, on the drives, would probably have required the most thoroughgoing revision, for, as "On Narcissism" had made uncomfortably plain, his division of the drives into ego drives and sexual drives had proved untenable. Indeed, in his 1915 paper on the drives, Freud frankly admitted that his "arrangement" would likely require rethinking: "It cannot claim the significance of a necessary premise," but is "a mere auxiliary construction, which is to be retained only as long as it proves useful."

In that introductory paper, he essentially recapitulated the definition of a drive that he had given a decade earlier, in the *Three Essays on the Theory of Sexuality;* it is the "psychical representative" of "stimuli originating within the body, reaching the mind"—the "demand," in his much-quoted phrase, "for work imposed on the mind by its connection with the body." To trace the workings of a drive, he noted, still following the *Three Essays,* we may discriminate among its "pressure" (its incessant energetic activity), its "aim" (satisfaction, achieved by removing the stimulus), its "object" (which can be extraordinarily diverse, since almost anything, including one's own body and the lessons of pleasurable experiences may provide paths to satisfaction), and its "source" (the somatic processes from which stimuli arise, and which lie outside the competence of psychology). Freud took particular pains to comment on the mobility of the drives, especially the sexual ones: the history of love grandly attests to this mobility. Love, Freud reminded his readers, begins as narcissistic self-absorption, and then, climbing a complicated ladder of development, links up with the sexual instincts to provide a sizable repertory of gratifications. And hate, a pendant to love as its opposite and its companion, provides still more material for diversity. No wonder that ambivalence, the coexistence in the same person of love and hate for the same object, is the most natural and most common of conditions. Humans, it would seem, are destined to navigate among opposites: love and hate, love and indifference, loving and being loved. In short, the paper concludes, the fortunes of the drives are determined by "the three great polarities that dominate mental life": the tensions between activity and passivity, the self and the external world, pleasure and unpleasure. This part of the map Freud would not have to redraw.

TRACING THE VICISSITUDES of instinctual energies, Freud noted that their transformations enable them to secure partial satisfaction even when direct gratification is blocked by what he called, with tantalizing brevity, "modes of *defense* against the drives." In this paper on the drives, returning to some of his theorizing of the late 1890s, he listed some of these defensive tactics; later, he would elaborate upon and discriminate among them. But in another paper of 1915, "Repression," Freud chose to make that single name stand for them all. Even after the mid-1920s, when he revived the old term "defense" and reduced "repression" to a name for one of several mechanisms, repression remained to his mind the model of defensive activity. It was, in his emphatic pictorial language, the cornerstone, the foundation, on which the house of psychoanalysis rests—"its most essential part."

Freud was always very proud of this discovery. He believed that he had been the first to dig down to the bedrock of mental functioning; when Rank showed him a passage in Schopenhauer that anticipated him by decades, he dryly commented that he owed his originality to his "meager reading." In some ways, his *Unbelesenheit* only underscored how innovative he was, and he was particularly pleased to note that his insight had emerged from his favorite source of information—the analytic hour. Once he had translated his patients' resistance into words, he wrote, he had the theory of repression in his grasp.

As Freud used "repression" in 1915, then, the term stood for an array of mental maneuvers principally designed to exclude an instinctual wish from awareness. Why, Freud asked, should repression arise at all? Gratifying the demands of a drive is after all pleasurable, and it seems odd that the mind should deny itself satisfaction. Freud did not spell out the answer in any detail, but it is implicit in his view of the mind as a battleground. There are all too many prospective pleasures that turn into pain because the human mind is not a monolith. What it desperately wants, it often no less desperately scorns, or fears. The Oedipus complex in its various incarnations is the most telling instance of such domestic conflicts: the boy's desire for his mother comes to seem immoral, impermissible, laden with danger; his death wish against his father, another desire, threatens self-condemnation or other catastrophic consequences.

Freud offered only elusive glimpses of these theoretical issues. In his most concrete manner, he preferred to illustrate his general point with clinical instances. In one analysand suffering from anxiety hysteria, a mixed erotic longing for, and fear of, his father disappears from awareness and is replaced by an animal phobia. Another analysand, in treatment for a conversion hysteria, attempts to repress not so much her scandalous desires as the affects originally attached to them. Finally, an obsessional neurotic replaces hostile impulses directed against loved ones with all sorts of curious substitutes: excessive conscientiousness, self-reproaches, and preoccupations with trivia. In these striking examples, some of Freud's best-known patients—the Wolf Man, Dora, the Rat Man—take the stand to give their depositions.

A primitive form of repression arises early in infants' lives, and it subsequently branches out to include in its censorious work not just the impulse that is to be denied expression but its derivatives as well. Its strenuous operations, Freud emphasized, need to be repeated over and over: "Repression requires a continuous expenditure of energy." What has been repressed has not been wiped out. The old saying is wrong; out of sight is not out of mind. Repressed material has only been stored in the inaccessible attic of the unconscious, where it continues to luxuriate, pressing for gratification. Hence the triumphs of repression are at best temporary, always dubious. What has been repressed will return as a substitute formation or a neurotic symptom. That is why Freud saw the conflicts that beset the human animal as in essence unappeasable, perpetual.

IN "THE UNCONSCIOUS," the third and, significantly, the longest of his published papers on metapsychology, Freud mapped in some detail the arena in which most of these conflicts are fought out. Though his theory of the unconscious was one of Freud's most original contributions to general psychology, his view of the mind had a long and prestigious prehistory. Plato had envisioned the soul as two spirited winged horses, one noble and beautiful, the other coarse and insolent, pulling in divergent directions and virtually beyond their charioteer's control. With a rather different animus, Christian theologians taught that once Adam and Eve had fallen, humanity was torn between its duties to its divine creator and its carnal urges. Certainly, Freud's ideas about the unconscious were in the air in the nineteenth century and had already assumed some sophisticated guises.* Poets and philosophers had been speculating about the notion of mental activities beyond the reach of awareness; a century before Freud began to occupy himself with the unconscious, romantics like Coleridge could speak of "the twilight realms of consciousness," while Goethe, that romantic classicist, had found the idea of depths beyond depths in the psyche supremely attractive. In his *Prelude*, Wordsworth had celebrated the deep recesses in his heart as the realm in which he dwelt with pleasure. "I held unconscious intercourse with beauty," he wrote. "*Caverns* there were within my mind which sun / Could never penetrate." Some influential nineteenth-century psychologists, Johann Fried-

*See p. 128.

rich Herbart only the most eminent of them, made much of this idea. And among the philosophers whose influence Freud resisted but could hardly evade completely, Schopenhauer and Nietzsche repeatedly cautioned against overestimating the conscious at the expense of the unconscious forces in the mind.

What gave Freud's theory its unmatched explanatory range was that he assigned to the unconscious, with as much precision as is possible in this murky area, a stellar role in the making, and perpetuation, of psychological conflict. In 1915, he could not yet allocate unconscious mechanisms to their appropriate mental agencies; that had to wait until he completed his so-called structural system in the 1920s. He *could* unequivocally assert that since the psyche is subject to strict laws, the postulate of a secret mental domain is virtually required; this alone could account for such diverse phenomena as hypnotism, dreams, slips of the tongue and pen, symptomatic acts, self-contradictory and seemingly irrational behavior. The assumption of a dynamic unconscious, he argued, is more than merely justified, it is necessary.

To clarify, and make precise, what differentiates truly unconscious matters from those we happen not to have in mind at the moment, Freud restated a distinction he had already drawn in *The Interpretation of Dreams* between the preconscious and the unconscious. It is the latter, that untidy storehouse for the most explosive materials old and new, which preserves repressed ideas and affects, as well as the drives in their pristine form; the drives, Freud said flatly, can never become conscious without mediation or disguise. A strange place, that dynamic unconscious: laden to the brim with wishes, quite unable to entertain doubts, tolerate delay, or understand logic. Inaccessible as it may be to direct inspection, the psychoanalyst discovers its traces everywhere. In the metapsychological papers that he was so quickly turning out, Freud sought to establish its cardinal importance, beyond cavil, once and for all.

BUT IN SOME OBSCURE WAY, something was going wrong with his book. In mid-June 1915, he hinted to Ferenczi that he was not completely happy with the papers, that they lacked the proper finish. Two months later he wrote, again to Ferenczi, "The twelve articles are, as it were, ready." Freud's small reservation, "as it were"—*sozusagen*—is significant. He was revising, re-thinking, holding back, apparently unable to master some lingering dissatisfaction. The first trio of papers, on the drives, repression, and the unconscious, duly appeared as advertised, in 1915. But then, silence.

No doubt, Freud found stepping back from clinical detail to gain a comprehensive overview a hazardous enterprise. It reawakened his urge for untrammeled flights of thought; he found it virtually impossible to tame his lust for speculation. In April, after completing the paper on repression, he defined his writing—his "mechanism of production"—for Ferenczi's benefit as "the succession of boldly playing imagination and ruthlessly realistic criticism." But as spring went on, he silenced the criticism and gave his imagination free rein. In July he sent Ferenczi a draft of what he called a "phylogenetic fantasy," a fantasy carrying further the imaginative conjectures he had first rehearsed in *Totem and Taboo.* This was the twelfth and last of the metapsychological papers. It was nothing less than an attempt to show that modern desires and anxieties, passed on through the ages, are grounded in the childhood of humanity. One particularly sweeping implication of this Lamarckian fantasy* was embodied in Freud's proposal to plot the succession of neuroses onto a corresponding historical—or, rather, prehistorical—sequence. He was speculating that the relative ages at which moderns acquire their neuroses might recapitulate the course of events in the distant human past. Thus anxiety hysteria might prove to be a legacy from the ice age, when early mankind, threatened by the great freeze, had converted libido into anxiety. This state of terror must have generated the thought that in such a chilling environment, biological reproduction is the enemy of self-preservation, and primitive efforts at birth control must in turn have produced hysteria. And so on through the catalogue of mental distress. Ferenczi was supportive, indeed enthusiastic, but in the end, their joint speculation collapsed; as its incurable remoteness from empirical evidence became all too obvious, it lost all credibility. But while it lasted, Freud's phylogenetic fantasy at once elated and disturbed him.

NOT ALL OF FREUD'S time was occupied by theorizing and fantasizing, or by anxious reading of the newspapers and no less anxious waiting for news from his sons at the front. In the winter terms of 1915–16 and 1916–17, he delivered three series of general introductory lectures before sizable and growing audiences, with a view to publishing them. He spoke at his regular time, Saturday evening, and in his regular forum, the University of Vienna, aiming to acquaint "a mixed audience of physicians and laymen of both sexes" with the fundamentals of psychoanalysis. Among his most attentive listeners was his daughter Anna. He began with a short group of four lectures on slips, moved on to a more substantial series on dreams, and concluded with the longest series, on the theory of neuroses.

Freud had been acting as his own best popularizer for nearly two decades.

---

*During the war, as he told Abraham, he toyed with the possibility of enlisting Lamarck in the psychoanalytic cause by demonstrating Lamarck's idea of "need" to be nothing other than the "power of unconscious ideas over one's own body, of which we see remnants in hysteria, in short, 'the omnipotence of thought.' " (Freud to Abraham, November 11, 1917. *Freud–Abraham,* 247 [261–62].)

He had condensed his long, difficult *Interpretation of Dreams* into a lucid epitome, *On Dreams*. He had supplied chapters to collective volumes on psychiatry. He had contributed articles to encyclopedias. He had lectured on psychoanalysis to his fellow members of B'nai B'rith. In 1909, at Clark University, he had brilliantly distilled in five addresses the essence of his findings. But none of his ventures into the higher journalism proved so comprehensive and so prosperous as these introductory lectures. They were widely read and widely translated: perhaps 50,000 copies in German were sold in his lifetime, and there were at least fifteen translations, including Chinese, Japanese, Serbo-Croatian, Hebrew, Yiddish, and Braille. Freud, seasoned through years of experience, expended all his powers of persuasion on them. He lightened the intellectual burden on listeners and readers by skimming over the knottiest theoretical problems, deployed well-chosen anecdotes and apt quotations, genially anticipated objections, and admitted, here and there, his ignorance or fragmentary knowledge. The very sequence of the lectures was a cunning effort at seduction: by beginning with slips, Freud introduced his audiences to psychoanalytic ideas through ordinary, often amusing, mundane events; moving on to dreams, another mental experience familiar to all, he departed from the solid ground of common sense slowly, deliberately. He launched into a survey of the neuroses and of psychoanalytic therapy only after expounding the lawfulness of the mind and the ubiquity of the unconscious. Abraham was not alone in praising these performances for being "elementary" in the best sense—that is, for making only limited demands on their audiences; Freud's accomplished, utterly confident way of conveying his message would not, he thought, fail to be effective.

Abraham was right, but Freud was inclined to be very severe with these adroit recapitulations of his thought. He too had long called the lectures "elementary," but to him this meant that, certainly for knowledgeable readers like Lou Andreas-Salomé, they "contain absolutely nothing that could tell you anything new." Unjustly slighting their felicities and their innovative formulations, Freud found little to like in his presentations. They were, he wrote Frau Lou, "coarse stuff, intended for the multitude." It was the kind of stuff on which he would work, he told Abraham, when he was "very tired."

FATIGUE WAS A CONDITION about which Freud now complained a good deal. "The never-relaxing tension of the war years," he told Ferenczi as early as April 1915, "has an exhausting effect." In May 1916, he was sixty, and, thanking Max Eitingon for his congratulations, he pictured himself as entering the "age of dotage"—his *Greisenalter*. Abraham, the following spring, received an even more emphatic disclaimer. Sending greetings to Freud on his sixty-first birthday, he spoke glowingly of Freud's "freshness and delight in creativity"; in reply, Freud gently chided him for constructing an idealized image of him and repeated his plaint: "In reality I have become rather old, a little fragile and tired."

Yet Freud's weariness was periodically relieved by the intriguing turns the world continued to provide. The death of Emperor Franz Josef on November 21, 1916, after nearly sixty-eight years on the throne, stirred Freud very little; he was far more engaged with the good news he conveyed to Frau Lou two days later about his sons at the front: his "warriors" were well. A little later, Germany's unrestricted U-boat offensive, launched on February 1, 1917, enlisted his interest. Abraham had persuaded himself that this campaign might soon bring victory and peace, but Freud, rather less sanguine, preferred to give the submarines half a year to show their mettle. "If," he wrote Ferenczi in April, "September has not demonstrated the overwhelming effectiveness of the U-boats, Germany will see an awakening from illusion with terrible consequences." Six weeks after the Germans had let loose their submarines, Freud laconically noted in his family calendar, usually reserved for birthdays and anniversaries, "Revolution in Russia." The February Revolution had swept away the Romanov dynasty, and put into its place a provisional government full of liberal promises and in search of a separate peace.

In view of his alert involvement in the news, it is striking that in his *Introductory Lectures,* Freud should have virtually nothing to say about the war. It was as though by concentrating on his task of summarizing and popularizing, he might escape the daily burden for a time. But Freud did not wholly resist reminding his hearers that they were meeting under a looming cloud raining down death and destruction. "Look away from the individual to the great war that is still ravaging Europe," he said in an exceptionally rhetorical passage, "think of the excess of brutality, cruelty, and mendacity which is now allowed to spread itself over the civilized world." Could one in the light of these horrors hold only "a handful of unscrupulous and ambitious men" responsible for "loosing all these evil spirits"? Were "the millions of the led not partially guilty, too"? Could one dare to maintain that "the mental constitution of humanity" did not contain a measure of evil? The full import of the war for the remaking of Freud's thinking, especially on aggression, would not clearly emerge until some years later. But this forceful paragraph, almost irrelevantly injected into a lecture on dream censorship, attests how insistently human pugnacity was on Freud's mind during these years.

By 1917, he mainly longed for the slaughter to end. The entry of the United States into the war in April on the side of the Allies made prospects of a victory of the Central Powers all the more remote. In October, more pessimistic than ever, Freud declared the German submarine campaign a failure. To exacerbate his gloom, the war was increasingly leaving its mark on the home front. Life in Vienna was getting more and more difficult; food was scarce, fuel scarcer still. Hoarding and inflation in the cost of necessities made shortages all the more exasperating; and the official prices, already far too high, were of course greatly exceeded in the flourishing black market. Freud grumbled to his intimates, especially in winter, when he and his family did not have enough to eat and he sat in his unheated study trying to write, his fingers freezing. In January 1918, he dramatically headed a letter to Abraham, "*Cold tremor!*"—*Kältetremor!* Shipments of food from Ferenzci in Budapest and from friends in the Netherlands occasionally relieved the Freuds, but these were at best stopgaps.

In this dismal situation, Freud warily weighed rumors that he might be awarded the Nobel Prize. The latest recipient of the prize for physiology or medicine, the Austrian physician Robert Barany, had nominated him, but no prizes had been given for that category since 1914. Freud kept an eye out nevertheless. On April 25, 1917, he noted tersely in his calendar, "No Nobel Prize 1917." To be sure, in view of the resistance he expected, he would have been intensely surprised to be chosen. But Freud wanted that honor very much; he would have welcomed the recognition and could have used the money.

Certainly by 1917, after three years of war, nearly everything was calculated to irritate him. He kept up his morale by collecting bad jokes about the war, most of them untranslatable, primitive puns. One or two, scarcely worth rescuing, may survive into English. Here is one specimen: " 'Dear parents,' a Jew serving in the Russian army writes home, 'we are doing very well. We are daily retreating a few miles. God willing, I hope to be home on Rosh Hashana.' " But Ernest Jones continued to anger Freud with his predictions; when he suggested tactlessly in the fall of 1917 that German resistance was likely to prolong the war, Freud called that Jones's "authentic English manner." Admittedly, he wrote to Abraham in November 1917, "things are still very interesting." At the same time, though, he immediately added, "one ages quickly, and at times doubts arise whether one will live to see the end of the war, whether I shall see you again, etc." He was acting, in any event, as "though the end of all things were imminent," and had just decided to publish two more of his metapsychological papers. One thing that naturally aroused his interest was the Bolshevik revolution and Lenin's rise to power; it took Russia out of the war. News of the armistice between the Bolshevik regime and the Central Powers in December pleased him very much. So did the Balfour Declaration, promising a homeland to the Jews. By this time he had discarded all remaining illusions about the justice of "his" cause and the invincibility of German arms. "I judge the times most pessimistically," he wrote to Ferenczi in October. He took the view that "if there is no parliamentary revolution in Germany," the war would go on to a bitter end. Freud had believed that the Allied powers had lied about their war aims; he was now persuaded that his own side was no less mendacious. As he told Abraham late in 1917, he was on a war footing with writing and with much else, including "your dear German fatherland." The great German offensive in March 1918 left him cold: "I confess myself to be weary and sick of the struggle." He supposed that the idea of a German victory, which seemed still possible, might raise Abraham's spirits. But it did not raise his own. He was avid for creature comforts: "I have been a carnivore; perhaps the unaccustomed diet is contributing to my listlessness." Everyone, except perhaps the German high command, was feverishly waiting for peace to arrive, as President Woodrow Wilson's program, the Fourteen Points he had outlined to Congress and the world in January 1918, gave new hope for an end to the slaughter. Freud, too, had long looked ahead to the day of peace as an "ardently awaited date."

DURING ALL THIS TIME, Freud had been tantalizing his friends with references to his book on metapsychology. In the spring of 1916, thinking out loud to Lou Andreas-Salomé, he told her that "it cannot be printed before the end of the war." As usual, Freud dwelling on death dwelt on his own: "Life spans are incalculable," and he should much have liked to see the book in print. Interestingly enough, he made death a prominent theme in "Mourning and Melancholia," one of the two metapsychological papers he finally brought out late in 1917. More perhaps than anything else Freud wrote in these years, rivaling in this respect "On Narcissism," this paper hints at the revision in his thinking he would bring to fruition after the war.

Melancholia, Freud argued, resembles mourning in being marked by loss of interest in the outside world, persistent low spirits, indifference to work and love. But beyond that, melancholiacs load themselves down with self-reproaches, display low self-esteem, and in delusional ways anticipate some sort of punishment. They are in mourning, but in a particular way: they have lost an object to which they have been greatly attached and with which they identify. Freud had been saying for some years that virtually all sentiments of love are ambivalent, virtually all contain elements of rage and hostility. The melancholiacs' rage against themselves, their self-hatred and self-torment, are, then, enjoyable expressions of sadistic fury with the lost object. Sufferers from this disorder will resort to suicide, obviously the most extreme consequence of melancholia, only when their ego treats itself with unmitigated severity as a hated object. Years before Freud formally elevated aggression into a drive ranking with libido, he clearly perceived the power of aggressiveness—here directed against oneself.

This was one way that "Mourning and Melancholia" was prophetic. Freud's brief discussion of self-punishment was another. The self-abasement and self-denigration of melancholiacs, he wrote, are persuasive evidence that their ego has split off a part of itself. Their ego has created, as it were, a special mental agency designed to judge, normally to condemn. This, Freud noted, is an extreme, indeed morbid, form of what people commonly call the conscience. He had as yet no special name for this censorious agency, but there could be no doubt that it was intimately related to what he was then calling the ego ideal and would later explore under the name "superego."*

"Mourning and Melancholia," then, shows a Freud in transition. But what of the other seven papers, all written but not yet scheduled for publication? That rest, Freud told Ferenczi in November 1917, deserved suppression and silence: *Der Rest darf verschwiegen werden.* He had been dropping dark confidences to his trusted Abraham that this was somehow not a good time for the book. Nor did it seem to be getting better with the passing months. In the early summer of 1918, he protested a little mysteriously to Lou Andreas-Salomé, who had long been pressing him to publish these papers, that it was not just fatigue that held him back, but "also other indications." Whatever those indications were, they prevailed. At some point, while he was firing these intermittent salvos of hints and excuses, Freud put an end to his uncertainty by destroying the remaining papers.

It was, and is still, a puzzling gesture. Theoretical conundrums had not reduced Freud to silence before; difficulties in presentation had never held terrors for him. The war, of course, explains much. With his "warriors" Martin and Ernst daily in danger, Freud did not find the times propitious for originality. But then, Freud was not proposing to be original in his twelve chapters on metapsychology. Besides, he had more time on his hands than he liked or could use productively, and he had discovered that work, when he could flog himself to do it, was an anodyne. The book on metapsychology could have been a welcome escape from the newspapers. The real reasons for the collapse of his project lie concealed in the project itself.

The silent, eloquent drama of the book that was never finished lies in its timing above all. The foundations that Freud had intended to lay down definitively for his adherents and against his rivals were shifting in his hands.

---

*Freud discussed the self-punishing work done by this special, as yet unnamed agency in two other short papers of the time, both published in 1916: "Those Wrecked by Success," in which he showed that those who develop neurotic troubles at the moment of triumph are kept from enjoying that triumph by their punitive conscience; and "Criminals from a Sense of Guilt," in which he analyzed the neurotic need for punishment. In both papers, childish oedipal crimes, more imagined than real, turn out to be important instigators.

He was not undergoing a conversion; the shibboleths of psychoanalysis—the dynamic unconscious, the work of repression, the Oedipus complex, the conflicts between drives and defenses, the sexual origins of neuroses—remained intact. But much else had become open to question. The paper on narcissism was an early, florid symptom of important second thoughts, and the destruction of seven papers on metapsychology was in its way just as symptomatic. The Freud of the war years did not yet see very clearly what needed doing. As in the late 1890s, he was in one of his obscurely creative phases, in which agonizing was a sign of great things to come, dimly aware that (as he might have put it) he was pregnant once again.

UNEASY PEACE

All during the fall of 1918, Vienna was astir with rumors of peace. The secret talks Austrian diplomats had initiated in the spring of 1917 to secure a separate peace, behind Germany's back, had been clumsy and amateurish and had predictably come to nothing. But in early September 1918, after more than another year of costly fighting, the government in Vienna, facing hunger at home and almost certain defeat at the front, made a more far-reaching overture to the Allies. It proposed that the belligerents meet to negotiate an end to the war. Having barely faced down strikes and mutinies earlier in the year, Austria was now prepared to make extensive territorial concessions, though not to abandon the principle of the multinational empire. In mid-October, the Allied powers, on the way to victory, rejected the offer; the settlement the Austrians proposed did not go far enough. There was near chaos in the ministries; one historian has compared the situation to "the frantic and senseless knocking about of a drowning man." The sense of confusion infected the public. Freud, writing to Eitingon on October 25, found the times "frightfully thrilling. It is good," he added, "that the old should die, but the new is not yet here."

By this time, the theater of war had shrunk; though the slaughter went on unabated on the western front, fighting in the east was winding down. Russia had been definitively out of the war since early March, when the Central Powers, inexorable and vindictive, had imposed the draconian Treaty of Brest-Litovsk on the new, untried Soviet regime. Another minor triumph for the Central Powers came in May, when Rumania, long partially occupied by their troops, also made peace. On the other side, Bulgaria, which had veered between the belligerents before casting its lot with the Germans and Austrians in late 1915, was forced to conclude an armistice with the Allies in late September 1918. In the following month, after spectacular, almost legendary desert exploits in the Near East, the British forced Turkey, too, to submit.

Ultimately, it was not civilians' prayerful wishes, but Allied arms, coupled with the grandiose visions Woodrow Wilson had conjured up, that brought the Great War to an end. British and French and, later, American troops turned back the powerful German spring offensive in France. Early in June 1918, the Germans were stopped about forty miles from Paris, and in the middle of July, the great counteroffensive began. From then on there was no stopping the Allies. Toward the end of September, General Ludendorff, intent on keeping Allied troops off German soil at all cost, called for negotiations. The collapse of the Kaiser's forces, one of the most formidable war machines in history, was at hand—and so was peace.

In September, the month Ludendorff acknowledged the inevitable, Freud's spirits were further raised by an international congress of psychoanalysts, held in Budapest.* The last previous meeting had taken place in 1913, in Munich. Freud sorely needed the cheering reunions such a conclave promised; he had not seen Abraham for four years, since the outbreak of hostilities. In August he told Abraham that he had been "too furious and too starved" to answer his last letter—for that indefatigable letter writer a sure sign of exceedingly low morale. The congress, first planned for Breslau, convened in Budapest on September 28 and 29. It was necessarily much truncated and narrowed down in attendance; of the forty-two participants, two were Dutch, three German, thirty-seven from Austria-Hungary. Still, it was a congress. Freud delivered, not his usual free talk, but a formal lecture in which he sketched out departures in technique and called for the establishment of psychoanalytic clinics that would enable the poor to benefit from treatment. It was a festive occasion, complete with receptions and splendid accommodations; the analysts were put up at the elegant Gellert Hotel. A month later, Freud still savored the memory; with undisguised satisfaction, he recalled to Abraham "the beautiful Budapest days."

The congress was, as Ernest Jones has observed, the first "at which official

---

*During the summer of 1918, Freud had still another reason for being of good cheer. Anton von Freund, a rich brewer of Budapest, had responded to an operation for cancer with a neurosis, of which Freud seems to have relieved him. Grateful, and mindful that the cancer might still recur, von Freund arranged to subsidize a publishing house that would specialize in psychoanalytic publications and make Freud, and psychoanalysis in general, independent of other publishers. This was done, and it became one of Freud's chores to superintend the *Verlag*.

representatives of any Government were present, in this case of the Austrian, German and Hungarian Governments." The reason was a thoroughly practical one, "the increasing appreciation of the part played by 'war neuroses' in military calculations." The presence of official observers exemplifies, in its way, the strange dialectic of life and death in the history of psychoanalysis. The ideas of Freud, which in times of peace psychiatrists had been so reluctant to take seriously, now gathered prestigious support among physicians assigned to army hospitals and faced with shell-shocked soldiers. For some, the Great War had been a vast laboratory in which to verify psychoanalytic propositions. "Fate," the British psychiatrist W. H. R. Rivers said in 1917, "would seem to have presented us at the present time with an unexampled opportunity to test the truth of Freud's theory of the unconscious, in so far as it is concerned with the production of mental and functional nervous disorders." In the past, facing pressure from military authorities, psychiatrists had not resisted—indeed, by and large had shared—the facile notion that a soldier exhibiting the symptoms of a "war neurosis" must be malingering and should be unceremoniously sent back to the front, if not court-martialed. Yet a certain awareness grew, among physicians serving the Allies no less than the Central Powers, that, in Freud's words, "only the smallest proportion of war neurotics . . . were malingerers." The Budapest congress featured, topically enough, a symposium on the psychoanalysis of war neuroses, for which Ferenczi, Abraham, and Ernst Simmel prepared papers. Simmel, a German physician, was a particularly welcome recruit; he had discovered psychoanalysis in a psychiatric hospital for soldiers during the war. In the end, though, nothing came of the ambitious project, proposed by the delegates of the Central Powers in Budapest, for centers in which sufferers from war neuroses would be treated with purely psychological methods. The revolutions sweeping over the defeated nations intervened with irresistible speed.

FREUD'S LACONIC CALENDAR entries, punctuated with exclamation points, record the rush of events almost day by day. October 30: "Revolution Vienna & Budapest." November 1: "Traffic with Germany and Hungary interrupted." November 2: "Oli[ver] back. Republic in Bulgaria?" November 3: "Armistice with Italy. War over!" On November 4, he found time to think of his own affairs: "Nobel Prize set aside." November 6: "Revolution in Kiel." November 8: "Republic in Bavaria!! Traffic with Germ[any] interr[upted]." November 9: "Republic in Berlin. Wilhelm abdicates." November 10: "Ebert German Chancellor. Armistice conditions." November 11: "End of war. [Austria's] E[mperor] Karl renounces [throne]." November 12: "Republic and Anschluss with Germany"—the latter a little premature; the victors would not permit Austria and Germany to merge—"participated in panic." Four days later, on November 16: "Republic in Hungary." The "evil war dream" was over at last.

Other dreams, only little less nightmarish, were waiting in the wings. Martin, on the Italian front, had been out of touch with his family for some weeks; not until November 21 could Freud note in his calendar, "Martin in captivity since Oct[ober] 27." The Italians had taken his whole unit prisoner after hostilities were actually over. Nor could Freud extract any tranquility from the tense world of politics; the carnage that had put an end to the old Romanov dynasty would spare neither the Hohenzollern nor the Habsburg imperial houses. To Freud's rather grim satisfaction, the Austro-Hungarian empire was being dismantled. He had no illusions about its prospects for survival and, by that time, no regrets. In late October, before its fate was decided, he had already told Eitingon, "I weep not a single tear for *this* Austria or *this* Germany."

While Freud found it a relief to think that the new Germany would not turn Bolshevik, he predicted—correctly enough—that the collapse of the German empire, so long and so arrogantly led by that "incurable romantic" Wilhelm II, would drag bloody clashes in its wake. But he reserved his greatest fury for the dynasty under which he had lived all his life: "The Habsburgs have left behind nothing but a pile of muck." In late October, giving advice consistent with this scornful view, he urged Ferenczi, "a Hungarian patriot," to withdraw his libido from his fatherland and make it over, for the sake of mental balance, to psychoanalysis instead. He was trying to muster sympathy for the Hungarians, he said mischievously later that week, but discovered that he could not manage it. Among his associates, only Hanns Sachs could wring some humor from the revolution in Austria, which was far less sanguinary than revolutions elsewhere; Sachs imagined, for Jones's benefit, placards being put up reading, "The Revolution will take place tomorrow at two-thirty; in the case of unfavorable weather it will be held indoors."

There was in fact nothing amusing about the months after the conclusion of hostilities. Pitched battles between armies at the front were succeeded by pitched battles between radical and reactionary militants in the streets; months of disorder made the political future of Germany, of Austria, and of Hungary a prey to speculation and dismal prognoses. Eitingon wrote to Freud toward the end of November, "The old that had seemed quite solid had become so rotten that as it was removed, no signs of resistance became visible." In late December 1918, returning to English now that the war was over, Freud put his "dear Jones" on notice not to "expect me or any of ours in England next spring; it seems quite improbable that we should be able to travel in a few months, peace being put up until June or July." Writing to his proven friend, Freud felt free to include a request with his social report-age: "I am sure you cannot conceive what our condition here really is. But you should come over as soon as you can, have a look upon what was Aust-ria, and," he did not forget to mention, "bring my daughter's boxes with you."

In January 1919, Freud summed up the new situation tersely: "Money and taxes are now quite repulsive topics. Now we are really eating ourselves up. All four years of war were a joke compared to the bitter gravity of these months, and surely the next ones, too." Reflecting on the disordered political scene in Central Europe, Freud conceded to Jones that the warnings he had once rejected as British chauvinism had proved correct: "All your predictions about the war and its consequences have come true." Freud stood "ready to confess that fate has not shown injustice and that a German victory might have proved a harder blow to the interests of mankind in general." But this handsome acknowledgment did not ease the lot of Freud and his family. "It is no relief to have his sympathy placed on the winning side if one's wellbeing is staked on the losing one." And that well-being was being steadily under-mined. "We are all of us slowly failing in health and bulk." But then, Freud quickly added, he and his family were far from alone "in this town, I assure you. Prospects are dark."

Slow, contentious work on the peace treaties did not make these prospects any brighter. Convening in Paris in January 1919 to begin redrawing the map of Central Europe, the victorious nations were less united at the conference table than they had been in running the war. Britain's prime minister, David Lloyd George, proclaimed his determination to hang the Kaiser and to squeeze the Germans "until the pips squeak." He would be marginally more conciliatory once he sat down to negotiate, but Georges Clemenceau, his French counterpart, was implacable. It went without saying that Alsace-Lorraine, which had fallen to Germany in 1871, after the Franco-Prussian War, would be returned to France. The German Rhineland, rich in natural resources, offered the French other possible rewards. But the victors had to reckon with Woodrow Wilson, the self-intoxicated prophet from the west, who was orating his way across Europe with his dazzling message of self-determination, democracy, open diplomacy, and above all hope. He believed, he told his listeners in Manchester in a characteristic speech in December 1918, that "men are beginning to see, not perhaps the golden age, but an age which at any rate is brightening from decade to decade, and will lead us some time to an elevation from which we can see the things for which the heart of mankind is longing."

Others had less exalted visions of the future. Freud, for one, was growing uneasy about Wilson's prophecies and, even more, about his character; saviors were never among his favorites.* But at the beginning of Wilson's European mission Freud had been no less bewildered, and little less impressed, than most others. "Recently," he informed Abraham early in 1919, "I had a visit from an American on Wilson's staff." Clearly Freud had become a savant with an international reputation. "He came accompanied by two baskets of provisions and exchanged them against copies of [*Introductory*] *Lectures* and [*The Psychopathology of*] *Everyday Life.*" What is more, "he allowed us to have confidence in the President." The provisions, we know from Freud's American nephew Edward Bernays, included a box of his "beloved Havana cigars." No wonder that by April, Freud could sound positively serene in the midst of deprivation and uncertainty. "The first window opening in our cage," he wrote Ernest Jones. "I can write you directly and a closed letter." The wartime censorship had been terminated. What is more, Freud no longer felt so isolated. "I was extremely glad to hear," he added, "that five years of war and separation did not succeed in deteriorating your kind feelings for our crew." Still better, "psychoanalysis is flourishing I am glad to learn from everywhere."

IN THE COURSE OF 1919, a series of treaties officially ratified the collapse of the Central European empires. In June, the Germans were compelled to sign the Treaty of Versailles. It stripped them of Alsace-Lorraine, which went back to France; the small but strategic districts of Eupen and Malmédy, awarded to Belgium; their colonies in Africa and the Pacific, which were to become mandates under Allied supervision; and parts of the eastern provinces of Posen and West Prussia, from which, eked out with territory from Austria and Russia, the victors carved out a revived Poland. The new Germany was a geographic monstrosity, a country split in two, with East Prussia an island surrounded by Polish territory. Possibly even more damaging to the morale of the Germans was their signing of the notorious Article 231 of the peace treaty, which declared their country wholly responsible for causing the war.

The Austrians' turn came in September 1919, when they accepted an almost equally harsh treaty at St. Germain. They gave up what was to become a truncated Hungary as well as the Bohemian and Moravian lands soldered together into a new creation, independent Czechoslovakia. In addition, the Austrians signed away territories like the Trentino and South Tyrol, which went to Italy. To accommodate the southern Austrian province of Bosnia and Herzegovina, the busy mapmakers invented a Balkan concoction called Yugoslavia. As we know, the prospect of old Austria being broken up had given Freud considerable satisfaction almost a year before the Treaty of St. Ger-

---

*For Freud on Wilson, see pp. 553–62.

main made it official. His new homeland, explicitly prohibited from uniting with the German republic, was a curious construction, inviting the sour observation that Austria had become a hydrocephalic monster. Tired as the remark soon became, it was appropriate: one metropolis, Vienna, a city of two million, presided over a shrunken hinterland of just five million more. For months before the peace treaty was finally signed, the Allies had made their intentions plain. "Today we learn," Freud had noted in March 1919, that "we are not permitted to join Germany but must yield up South Tyrol. To be sure, I'm not a patriot, but it is painful to think that pretty much the whole world will be foreign territory."

Stefan Zweig, one of Freud's recent acquaintances, later remembered this postwar Austria precisely that way, as "an uncertain, gray, and lifeless shadow of the former imperial monarchy." The Czechs and the other nationalities had torn away their lands; what remained was a "mutilated rump, bleeding from all arteries." Cold, hungry, impoverished, German Austrians had to live with the fact that "the factories which had once enriched the land" were now in foreign territory, "the railways had shrunk to pathetic stumps," and "the national bank had been deprived of its gold." There was "no flour, no bread, no coal, no petroleum; a revolution seemed inescapable, or else some catastrophic solution." In those days, "bread tasted of pitch and glue, coffee was a decoction of roasted barley, beer a yellow water, chocolate colored sand, potatoes frozen." Lest they forget the taste of meat entirely, people raised rabbits or shot squirrels. Just as they had late in the war, profiteers ran a flourishing black market, and people returned to the most primitive barter to keep body and soul together. Anna Freud later confirmed Zweig's assessment. The bread, she recalled, was "mouldy" and there were "no potatoes to be had." At one point, Freud wrote a paper for a Hungarian periodical and asked to be paid not in money but in potatoes; the editor, who lived in Vienna, carried them to Berggasse 19 on his shoulders. "My father always referred to that paper as the 'Kartoffelschmarrn.'" In March 1919, Freud reported to Ferenczi that the government planned to "abolish meatless weeks, and replace them with meatless months. A foolish hungry joke!"

Freud could take these irritating and debilitating consequences of the war with more equanimity than many because one of his greatest anxieties, over his son Martin, had been happily dispelled. After he had been taken prisoner by the Italians late in October, Martin had for some time dropped from sight. Once word had come, almost a month later, that Martin was alive, though confined to a hospital, Freud made inquiries, sent money, and peppered his letters with little communiqués about his son the prisoner. In April 1919, he told Abraham that news from Martin was rare but not unpleasant, and in May he could inform his English nephew Samuel that while Martin was "still a prisoner" near Genoa, he "seems to be in good condition judging by his letters." He was set free some months later, "in excellent condition." Martin was fortunate; more than 800,000 Austro-Hungarian soldiers had died at the front or from sickness during the war.

The condition of Freud himself, and of his immediate family, though, was rather forlorn. Preoccupation with sheer survival came to dominate his life, and his correspondence, for two years and more. Food in Vienna was no less unpalatable or inadequate, heating materials were no less unobtainable, than they had been during the last two years of the war. The government tightly rationed all necessities; even milk was hard to come by. There were weeks when beef was available only to hospitals and to such public employees as firemen and streetcar conductors. Rice was offered as a substitute for meat, and sauerkraut was supposed to take the place of potatoes. Even those holding rationing coupons for soap could not find any in the stores. There was virtually no petroleum or coal to be had, and one stubby half candle was all a household could claim in January 1919. Tenderhearted individuals and organizations across the Western world, committees in country after country, responded to the desperate appeals of Austrian politicians and took up collections for Austrians. By early 1919, former enemies were sending wagonloads of essentials. But they were never enough. "Our nutrition is still, despite all the magnanimity of the Allies, scanty and miserable," Freud wrote in April 1919, "really a starvation diet"—*Hungerkost*. Infant mortality was rising at an alarming rate, as was tuberculosis. One Austrian authority, a physiologist named Durig, estimated that in the winter of 1918–19, the daily calorie intake per person would be 746.

Freud's letters frankly document the impact of the general misery on his own household. He was writing in a "bitterly cold room" and searched in vain for a usable fountain pen. As late as 1920, he was bedeviled by the paper shortage. Freud thought himself anything but querulous. "We have grown hungry beggars all of us here," he wrote to Ernest Jones in April 1919. "But you shall hear no complaints. I am still upright and hold myself not responsible for any part of the world's nonsense." But in what he liked to call his "cheerful pessimism," the pessimism was increasingly driving out the cheerfulness. Certainly Freud liked nothing less than being a beggar, but, busy surviving in postwar Vienna, he did not hesitate to disclose his precarious situation to others. He had never cultivated lip-biting asceticism, and now he was simply acquainting outsiders, obviously ill-informed, with his family's predicament. "If you press me to inform you," he scolded Jones a little indignantly in May 1919, "where and when we shall meet this summer or autumn, whether an ordinary congress should be held or a meeting of the comité instead, I cannot but infer that you know nothing of the conditions we live in and get no light on Austria by your papers." He had no idea when he could resume normal travel. "It all depends on the state of Europe in general and of this neglected unhappy corner in particular, on the signing of peace, on the improvement of our money, the opening of the borders etc." But he was not complaining!

There was in truth much to complain about. Despite all the consoling news about the spread of psychoanalysis, and all of Freud's resourcefulness and stoical posture, he felt compelled to admit that life was no joy. "We are passing through bad times," he told his nephew Samuel in the spring of 1919; "as you know by the papers, privations and uncertainty all around." A touching letter of thanks that Martha Freud wrote Ernest Jones in April 1919 shows just how extensive the privations were. Jones had sent her an "absolutely beautiful jacket," which, it turned out, not only suited her perfectly but "Annerl" as well; hence she and her youngest daughter would wear it alternately during the summer. In mid-May, though, Martha Freud came down "with a genuine grippe-pneumonia." The doctors advised Freud not to worry, but influenza was a most worrisome illness for those who, like Martha Freud, had to fight it undernourished, worn down with years of sheer coping under difficult circumstances. In truth the "Spanish influenza," often leading to lethal pneumonia, had been killing untold thousands since the previous winter. As early as the fall of 1918, Viennese schools and theaters were intermittently closed to reduce the risk of infection. All in vain, as wave upon wave struck vulnerable populations. Women were more susceptible than men, but men, too, died in appalling numbers. Before the influenza epidemic waned more than two years later, some 15,000 Viennese perished. But Martha Freud got over her influenza, though it proved tenacious; two weeks after she had come down with it, she was still "abed with a strong grippe, overcame a pneumonia but shows no good tendency to recover strength and has this very day begun to fever afresh." Not until early July could Freud report his wife fully restored.

IN THE SUMMER OF 1919, while his wife was recuperating in a sanatorium, Freud managed to spend a month in a favorite Austrian spa, Bad Gastein, accompanied by his sister-in-law Minna. He was a little apologetic about choosing such an expensive resort, but defended it on the ground that the cold season ahead made it necessary to store up as much recuperative strength as possible. "Who knows," he remarked to Abraham, "how many of us will weather the next winter, of which much evil is to be expected." Late in July he was glad to report to Jones that he had "nearly completely recovered from the scratches and bruises of this year's life." He was, at sixty-three, still resilient.

But once back in Vienna, Freud faced stark reality again. "Life is very hard with us," he wrote in October, replying to an inquiry from his nephew Samuel. "I do not know what the English papers tell you, may be they dont exaggerate. The scarcity of provisions and the deterioration of money are pressing mostly on the middle classes and on those who earn their livelihood by intellectual work. You must keep in view that all of us have lost ¹⁹⁄₂₀ of what we possessed in cash." An Austrian krone was worth less than a penny now and steadily dropping in value. Besides, "Austria (Deutsch-Oesterr.) never could produce as much as it wanted"; and Freud reminded his nephew that "not only the former provinces of the Empire but also our own countries are boycotting Vienna in the most reckless way, that industry has come to a dead stop by want of coal and materials, and that buying and importing from the foreign countries is impossible." The unfavorable balance of trade, the flight of capital, the need to import ever more expensive raw materials and foodstuffs, the precipitous decline in the production of goods for export in what remained of Austrian lands, produced a spiraling, devastating inflation. By December 1922, the Austrian krone, which had been five to the dollar before the outbreak of the war, was about 90,000 to the dollar. The collapse of the currency ended only after complex negotiations with international bankers and foreign governments.

SAMUEL FREUD, A PROSPEROUS merchant in Manchester, became the favorite recipient of Freud's purposeful jeremiads. The family, Freud told him, was "living on small diet. The first herring some days ago was a treat to me. No meat, not enough bred, no milk, potatoes and eggs extremely dear at least in crowns." Fortunately, his brother-in-law Eli, living in the United States, "has become a very rich man," and his help "has enabled us to save the existence of the female members of the family." The Freud clan, he added, "is dissolving rapidly." Two of his sisters, Dolfi and Pauli, and his mother, had been sent off to the spa of Ischl to spend the winter there under less stringent conditions. His sister-in-law Minna, unable to stand freezing Vienna, had escaped to Germany, which was marginally better off. Except for Anna, who "will be the only child left to us," his children were out of the house. Speaking of himself, Freud noted matter-of-factly, "You know I have a big name and plenty of work but I cannot gain enough and I am eating up my reserves." Responding to Samuel's "kind offer," he listed "the articles of food we need most: fat, corned beef, cocoa, tea, english cakes and what not."* Meanwhile, Max Eitingon in Berlin, rich and thoughtful, was lending

---

*His diet was of absorbing interest to Freud, not without reason. Late in 1919, he informed Eitingon that a "Mr. Viereck, journalist, politician, writer, a quite handsome fellow, even offered me 'food.'

him money; but that, Freud told him candidly, was a useless gesture as long as it was Austrian currency. He himself had "more than a hundred thousand" of worthless kronen. But Eitingon was also sending food—*Lebensmittel*—the "stuff of life," as the Germans felicitously call it. Nor did he forget, Freud gratefully acknowledged, coining a neologism for the occasion, the "stuff of work"—*Arbeitsmittel*—which is to say, cigars. They bolstered Freud for further endurance.

Indefatigably, Freud mobilized his relatives abroad to keep up the flow of supplies to Vienna. "Following Martha's direction," he asked his nephew Samuel early in 1920 to choose for him a "soft shetland cloth—pepper and salt or mouse-grey, or tête de nègre in colour—sufficient for a suit" appropriate "for spring and autumn." Freud continued to dispatch such commissions to England and America for several years. As late as 1922, he asked his family in Manchester to buy him some "strong boots" of the *"best* quality," since the pair he had bought in Vienna had fallen apart. He faithfully monitored all arriving shipments and checked their contents against the letters announcing their dispatch.

Such preoccupation with all these practical matters was psychologically necessary to Freud. Fascinating as political developments continued to be, they gave him no opportunity to assert even the slightest control over events. "The next months will be, I expect, full of dramatic movement," he predicted to Eitingon in May 1919. "But we are not spectators, not actors, in fact not even chorus, but merely victims!" He could hardly bear that. "I am very tired," he confessed to Ferenczi in the early summer of 1919, "more than that, malicious, corroded by impotent rage." To take care of his family was an escape from that impotence.

Freud showed himself a competent provider. Far from being the unworldly *Herr Professor* who made his wife relieve him of all domestic detail, he diligently compiled lists of goods, sent off itemized requests, recommended suitable packing materials—leakproof containers for food—and cursed the mails. During the months of revolution, when communications with foreign countries were for all practical purposes cut off, Freud realistically warned his patrons abroad that sending gifts to Vienna was extremely chancy. It was essential to relay packages through the English military mission in Vienna; ordinary food parcels only fed "the customs officials or the railway workmen." In late November 1919, Freud could report that "our condition has improved

---

I accepted with the observation that a diet of meat will certainly once again raise my capacity to produce." (The word "food" is in English. Freud to Eitingon, November 19, 1919. By permission of Sigmund Freud Copyrights, Wivenhoe.)

somewhat by gifts not sent but brought by friends from Holland and Switzerland, friends and pupils I should say." He was ready to find at least some consolation in these dismal days. "It is one of the good things of these miserable times," he told his Manchester nephew, "that connection between us has been reopened."

The undependability of foreign shipments was a continual irritant to him. On December 8, 1919, Freud informed his nephew that Martin had been married the day before, and added, virtually in the same breath, that a promised parcel had not arrived. He had little time for sentiment. "I have no hope it may still reach us." A few days later, thanking Samuel warmly for his concern—"you behave so friendly towards your poor relatives"—he urged him to mail nothing further until he had word that packages had actually got through to Vienna. "You seem not to be aware of the whole amount of governmental stupidity in D[eutsch] Oest[erreich]." Freud's English may have been a little formal, a little stiff, but it was pungent enough to supply him with eloquent, bitter epithets to characterize the German Austrian bureaucracy.

Denunciation was a form of action for Freud. One of his favorite German poets, Schiller, had once said that against stupidity the gods themselves contend in vain, but even the stupidity of Austrian officialdom did not reduce Freud to hopelessness. "None of your parcels did arrive," he informed Samuel in late January 1920, "but we hear they still may as the time of their travelling is often more than three months." He thought of everything. In October 1920, he reported that "three of your parcels have arrived," though "one of them absolutely stripped of its contents." At least Samuel Freud should not be the loser: "A deposition has been taken here at the post-office (Protokoll) and I have been advised to inform the dispatcher, so I hope you will get the assurance." As always, the wrapping mattered: "The two parcels happily landed were protected by sack-cloth, they brought a most welcome addition to our stores." But—there was always a but these days—"nearly all things in excellent condition, only the cheese being enveloped in paper had suffered by mould and affected the taste of some chocolate in sticks."

At times he gave vent to his exasperation. In May 1920, he wrote a blistering letter to the "Administration"—the American Relief Association in Vienna—complaining that a food package from the United States addressed to his wife (not then in town) had not been handed over to his son, "engineer O[liver] Freud," even though he had come "provided with power of attorney." The behavior of the agency seems rigid, but American relief officials had instituted the policy of delivering each package only to the actual addressee because too many so-called relatives had inundated their office with spurious identifications. Freud was not impressed by such excuses. Oliver "had been kept waiting, standing around from 2:30 to 5," and sent away without the parcel. "His time also has some value," so it would be demanding too much of him "to repeat the same experience several times more." Since only the addressee was allowed to pick up a package, "I appeal to you to inform me in what manner the intentions of the sender of this gift should be realized." Freud was not yet done. Furious, he boasted of his international stature: "I shall not fail to inform the public in America, where I am not unknown, about the inadequacy of your operation." The incident had an epilogue at once farcical and pathetic. The head of the relief agency, Elmer G. Burland, who had studied some of Freud's writings in college at Berkeley several years before, took delight in delivering the food package in person. He was treated with exquisite rudeness: Freud insisted that he speak to Oliver in English (even though Burland's German was by then first-rate) and had Oliver translate Burland's words into German (even though, it need hardly be pointed out, Freud understood every word). Freud then replied in German and had his son translate *his* words into English (even though Burland obviously needed no interpreter). This petty, calculated, stagy revenge was a measure of Freud's rage and frustration.

FREUD'S LETTERS OF these years suggest that he had to steal the time to continue thinking and writing. It is poignant to see him—the most independent of men, who really had other things to think about—engrossed in keeping himself and his family in essentials. But he did not remain a mere recipient for long. As soon as he could, he reimbursed Eitingon and began to pay for the stream of provisions he was so efficiently importing. In February 1920, he asked his nephew to "accept the inlaying cheque for £4 (payment of an English patient)"; five months later, he sent eight pounds, and in October he insisted, with a little air of triumph, "I thank you heartily for all your care and trouble but if these sendings are to continue you must give me the prize it costs you. I have somewhat recovered by the treatment of foreign patients and am in possession of a deposit of good money at the Hague."

By that time, the situation in Austria had eased a little and the Freuds' situation along with it. Stefan Zweig recalled the years between 1919 and 1921 as the hardest. But, after all, there had been not much violence, only some fairly sporadic looting. In 1922 and 1923, there was enough food to go around. The Austrian psychoanalyst Richard Sterba remembers that it took five years after the war's end "for the first *Schlagobers,* whipped cream, so essential to Austrians, to appear in the *'Kaffeehaus.'* " With food and fuel reappearing on the open market, "one was alive," in Zweig's words, "one felt one's powers." Freud, too, felt them. His clinical work, and the gifts his followers continued to send, ensured him an adequate living. "I am getting old, undeniably indolent and sluggish," he wrote to Abraham in June 1920, "also coddled and spoiled by the many presents of provisions, cigars, and money that people give me and that I must accept because otherwise I cannot live." By December 1921, life was again attractive enough to let him invite Abraham to stay at Berggasse 19; he baited his invitation with the tempting observation that the Freuds' guest room was not only far cheaper than a hotel, but heated.

Still, as we know, inflation was eating up those of Freud's savings that were in Austrian currency.* Nor were local politics any more appetizing. "With today's elections," Freud wrote to Kata Levy, a Hungarian friend and former analysand, in the fall of 1920, "the reactionary wave should be setting in here, too, after the revolutionary one had brought nothing pleasant. Which rabble is the worst? Surely always the one just on top." In politics, Freud was a man of the center, a position highly precarious and continuously imperiled during the unsettled postwar years. No wonder that when, in the summer of 1922, Eitingon invited him to settle in Berlin, Freud found the thought not unattractive. "For the eventuality that we must leave Vienna," he mused in a letter to Otto Rank, "because one can no longer live there and foreigners needing analysis no longer want to come, he is offering us a first shelter. If I were 10 years younger, I would weave all sorts of plans around this move."

The dislocations of the war had reduced most of Freud's offspring to dependents—his dependents. He was, he told Ernest Jones in the summer of 1919, "sending away all I can spare to my children at Hamburg bereft of their subsistence by the war. Of my boys only Oli the engineer has found some work for a time, Ernst is working at Munich for no salary and Martin whom we expect back in a few weeks would find himself on the street despite his many medals and decorations, if he had not an old father still at work." Nor was Oliver a dependable resource, for he was beset by neurotic difficulties that greatly troubled his father. Oliver, Freud confessed to Eitingon, "has often worried me." Indeed, "he needs therapy."

Freud's work was, no doubt, his financial salvation. The foreigners he was cultivating could pay him not merely in hard currency but also in hard cash. Writing to Leonhard Blumgart, a New York physician who wanted to enter

---

*It was also eating the savings of others. As late as January 20, 1924, Ferenczi wrote to Freud, "The devaluation of the Hung[arian] crown is proceeding rapidly; it will soon reach the Austrian low point. In the middle class, misery dominates; medical practice is almost at a total standstill. People have no money to be sick." (Freud–Ferenczi Correspondence, Freud Collection, LC.).

a training analysis in 1921, he specified "ten dollars for the hour (in real dollars, not checks)." He explained his reasons to the American psychiatrist and anthropologist Abram Kardiner, then his analysand: the ten dollars he charged for the analytic hour should be "paid in effective notes, not in checks which I could only change for crowns," which were losing value daily. Without the analysands from England and America, whom he called "this Entente people," he could not, he told Ernest Jones, "make the two ends meet." In contrast to "Entente people" endowed with dollars and pounds, patients from Germany or Austria were not so desirable: "I have 4 free hours now," he informed Jones early in 1921, "and would not like to feed on Central Power patients"—*Mittelmächtepatients.* He had "got the taste of Western valuta." As he told Kata Levy, "One can no longer make a living from Viennese, Hungarians, Germans." He regretted his bias and asked her to keep the matter confidential: "It is really no activity for a dignified old man. C'est la guerre." He was nothing if not candid about finances, just as, in his papers on technique, he had advised his colleagues to be.

With this shifting population of analysands, the principal language of Freud's practice now became English, which had long been a favorite with him. Just for that reason his shortcomings made him exasperated with himself—and with English. In the fall of 1919, he engaged a teacher "to polish up my English." But the results of his lessons did not satisfy him. "I am listening 4–6 hours daily to English or American talk," he noted in 1920, "and should have made better progress in my own English but I find it much harder to learn at 64 than at 16. I come up to a certain level and there I have to stop." Those analysands who mumbled their communications, or used current slang, gave him particular trouble. "I am anxious about my English," he told Ernest Jones, discussing two of the patients Jones had sent him, "both of them talking an abominable idiom." They made him "long for" the "distinguished correctness" of David Forsyth, an English physician who had worked for some time with Freud in the fall of 1919 and had earned Freud's gratitude with his refined vocabulary and clear enunciation.

His linguistic failures, far less damaging than he imagined them to be, became something of an obsession. "I listen and talk to Englishers 4–5 hours a day," he wrote to his nephew in July 1921, "but I will never learn their d——d language correctly." Shortly before, he had proposed to Leonhard Blumgart, ready to come to Vienna for his analysis, a little self-protective treaty: "It would be a great relief for me, if you talked German; if not, you should not criticize my English." Those English sessions made him so tired, he confessed to Ferenczi late in 1920, "that in the evening I am not useful for anything." This bothered him enough to make him dwell on it. He found the "5, sometimes 6 and 7 hours" that he was listening to, and speaking in, English so "strenuous," he told Kata Levy late in 1920, that he could no longer answer letters at night and left that chore to Sundays.

Yet the money Freud made from analytic work with his "Entente people" permitted him to do what he enjoyed more than getting—giving. For a man who had spent a lifetime worrying that his children might be destitute, he was remarkably free with his hard-earned funds. When, in the fall of 1921, Lou Andreas-Salomé accepted his invitation to visit him and his family at Berggasse 19—they had not seen one another for some time—Freud dared to broach a suggestion "connected with your trip, without fear of being misunderstood." In short, he offered her travel money should she need it. "I have become, through the acquisition of good foreign currency (Americans, Englishmen, Swiss), relatively *rich.*" Tactfully, he assured her that employing his resources that way would give *him* pleasure: "I too would like to get something out of this new wealth."* He was aware that her psychoanalytic practice in Göttingen brought her only skimpy returns. Through the early 1920s, very hard times for Germany, Freud saw to it that she was adequately supplied with American dollars, a continuing support she felt free to accept. In the summer of 1923, when he learned from a good source—his daughter Anna—that she was conducting as many as ten analyses a day, he reprimanded his "dearest Lou" paternally, forgetting his own heavy schedule through the years: "Naturally I consider this a badly veiled suicide attempt." He implored her to raise her fees and see fewer patients. And he sent her more money.

For his part, he was talking about cutting down his analytic hours; in 1921, he told Blumgart that he was accepting only "a very restricted number of pupils or patients," and mentioned six. But for some months in that year, weary as he was, he actually saw ten analysands. "I am an old man and have the good right to an undisturbed vacation," he wrote Blumgart, dwelling with a kind of masochistic pleasure, as he had for some years, on his advanced age. Quoting the German saying that art plays second fiddle to bread—*Die Kunst geht nach Brot*—he tersely told Jones that "business is devouring science." But he was not retiring. He was making important contributions to the future of psychoanalysis by superintending what he liked to call the "self-analysis" of future analysts. More important still, in the midst of turmoil around, and within, Freud completed the drastic revisions in his psychoanalytic system on which he had started half a decade before.

*In September 1922, Freud sent her 20,000 marks—inflated currency, but still a substantial sum. (Freud to Andreas–Salomé, September 8, 1922. Freud Collection, B3, LC.)

DEATH: EXPERIENCE AND THEORY

Freud's appetite for work, belying his professions of impending senility and dissolution, was not simply the visceral response to better food, new patients, and imported cigars. Work was also his way of coping with mourning. Ironically, with the coming of peace, Freud was forced to confront more than once what he had been almost wholly spared during the war—mortality. It made all his material discomforts appear trivial. Early in 1920, condoling with Ernest Jones on the death of his father, he asked, rhetorically, "Can you remember a time so full of death as this present one?" He thought it a "happy chance" that the elder Jones had died quickly, not having to hold out "until he got devoured piecemeal by his cancer." At the same time, he gently warned Jones of hard times ahead: "You will soon find out what it means to you." The event reminded Freud of mourning for his own father almost a quarter century before: "I was about your age when my father died (43) and it revolutioned my soul."

The first death in Freud's intimate circle, though, the appalling suicide of his disciple Victor Tausk, did not "revolution" his soul in the least. He took it with clinical, businesslike detachment. Tausk, after switching to psychoanalysis from a career in law and journalism, had rapidly distinguished himself in Vienna's analytic circles with a handful of important papers and brilliant introductory lectures that Freud singled out in his official obituary tribute. But Tausk's war experiences had been exceptionally wearing, and Freud publicly attributed his mental deterioration to the strains of his military service. More than exhaustion, though, had been working in him. A man of many women—he probably had, we recall, an affair with Lou Andreas-Salomé before the war—Tausk had been divorced, engaged to several women, and was now on the verge of marrying again. Long depressed, and increasingly distraught, he had asked Freud to take him into analysis, only to meet with a refusal. In previous years, Freud had generously supported Tausk, financially and emotionally, but now he sent him to Helene Deutsch, a young adherent who was herself in analysis with Freud. The result was a complex triangle which did not work out well: Tausk talked to Deutsch about Freud, and Deutsch talked to Freud about Tausk. In the end, Tausk's depression took the upper hand, and on July 3, 1919, with perverse ingenuity, he managed to hang and shoot himself at the same time. "Tausk," Freud notified Abraham three days later, "shot himself several days ago. You will recall his behavior at the Congress." In Budapest the previous September, Tausk had fallen ill with a rather spectacular vomiting attack. "He was crushed by his past and his last war experiences, was supposed to marry this week, could not pull himself together any more. For all his significant talent he was useless to us."

The "etiology" of Tausk's suicide, Freud told Ferenczi a few days later just as coolly, was "obscure, probably psychological impotence and the last act of his infantile battle with the ghost of his father." He confessed that "despite all appreciation of his gifts," he detected "no real sympathy" in himself. In fact, Freud waited almost a month before notifying Lou Andreas-Salomé of "poor Tausk's" end, repeating almost word for word what he had told Abraham. She was surprised at the news, but understood, and in fact largely shared, Freud's attitude; she had come to think of Tausk as somehow dangerous to Freud and to psychoanalysis. Freud told her, as he had the others, that Tausk had been useless to him. But, to judge from the way Freud jumped in this letter from Tausk's suicide to his own work, Tausk did have a certain posthumous utility: "I have now taken as my share of retirement property the theme of death, have stumbled onto an odd idea via the drives and must now read all sorts of things that belong to it, for instance Schopenhauer, for the first time." He would have a great deal to say about death soon, not as it came to Tausk or other individuals, but as a universal phenomenon.

However callous Freud may sound about his pathetic errant disciple, his response to another death, that of Anton von Freund, attests that his ability to feel loss had not atrophied. Von Freund had the recurrence of his cancer he had feared, and died in Vienna in late January 1920, at the age of forty. His lavish support of the psychoanalytic movement, most notably its publishing enterprises, was his monument. But von Freund was a friend to Freud, not just a benefactor to analysis; Freud visited him daily during his illness and kept Abraham, Ferenczi, and Jones informed of his irresistible dissolution. Writing the day after his friend died, Freud told Eitingon, "For our cause a heavy loss, for me a keen pain, but one I could assimilate in the course of the last months," when von Freund was visibly dying. "He bore his hopelessness with heroic clarity, did not disgrace analysis"—in short, he died as Freud's father had died and as he himself hoped to die.

THOUGH PREDICTABLE FOR some months, the loss of von Freund came as a shock. But the sudden death of Freud's daughter Sophie, his "dear, blooming Sophie," who died five days after von Freund of influenza complicated by pneumonia, was a far greater shock. She had been pregnant with her third child. Sophie Halberstadt was as much a victim of the war, which had left millions susceptible to infection, as a soldier killed at the front. "I do not know," Freud wrote to Kata Levy late in February, "whether cheerfulness will ever call on us again. My poor wife has been hit too hard." He was glad he had too much work "to mourn my Sophie properly." But in time he mourned her properly enough; the Freuds never quite got over this loss. Eight years later, in 1928, writing a letter of condolence to Ernest Jones's wife, Katharine, on the loss of her daughter, Martha Freud recalled the loss of her own: "It has now been eight years already since the death of our Sopherl, but I am always shaken up when something similar happens in the circle of our friends. Yes, I was then just as shattered as you are now; all security and all happiness seemed to me lost forever." And five years after that, in 1933, when the imagist poet Hilda Doolittle—H. D.—mentioned the last year of the Great War during an analytic hour with Freud, "he said he had reason to remember the epidemic, as he lost his favorite daughter. 'She is here,' he said, and he showed me a tiny locket that he wore, fastened to his watch-chain."

Freud helped himself with philosophical ruminations and psychoanalytic language. "The loss of a child," he wrote to Oskar Pfister, "seems a heavy narcissistic insult; what mourning there will be, will doubtless come later." He could not get over the "unconcealed brutality of our time," which made it impossible for the Freuds to join their son-in-law and his two small children in Hamburg. There were no trains. "Sophie," Freud wrote, "leaves two sons of six years and of thirteen months, and an inconsolable husband who will now dearly pay for the happiness of these seven years. That happiness was only between the two of them, not external: war, invasion, being wounded, dwindling away of their possessions, but they had remained brave and cheerful." And "tomorrow she will be cremated, our poor Sunday child!" He told Frau Halberstadt, the widower's mother, "Indeed, a mother is not to be consoled; and, as I am now discovering, a father hardly." Writing a heartfelt letter of condolence to the bereft widower, Freud spoke of "a senseless, brutal act of fate, which has robbed us of our Sophie." There was no one to blame, nothing to brood about. "One must bow one's head under the blow, as a helpless, poor human being with whom higher powers are playing." He assured Halberstadt that his feelings about him had not changed and invited him to regard himself as Freud's son as long as he wanted. And he signed himself, sadly, "Papa."

He sustained this reflective mood for some time. "It is a great unhappiness for us all," he wrote the psychoanalyst Lajos Levy, Kata Levy's husband, in Budapest, "a pain for the parents, but for us there is little to say. After all, we know that death belongs to life, that it is unavoidable and comes when it wants. We were not very cheerful even before this loss. Indeed, to outlive a child is not agreeable. Fate does not keep even to this order of precedence." But he was bearing up. "Do not worry about me," he assured Ferenczi. "I am, but for a bit more weariness, the same." Painful as Sophie's death had been to him, it would not change his attitude toward life. "For years I was prepared for the loss of my sons; now comes that of my daughter. Since I am the deepest of unbelievers, I have no one to accuse and know that there is no place where one can lodge an accusation." He was hoping for the soothing power of his daily routine, but "way deep down I sense the feeling of a deep narcissistic injury I shall not get over." He remained the most determined of atheists, wholly unwilling to trade his convictions for consolation. Rather, he worked. "You know of the misfortune that has befallen me, it is depressing indeed," he wrote to Ernest Jones, "a loss not to be forgotten. But let us put it aside for the moment, life and work must go on, as long as we last." He took the same line with Pfister: "I work as much as I can, and am grateful for the diversion."

Freud did work, and he was grateful. At the first postwar international psychoanalytic congress, held in The Hague in early September 1920, he gave a paper elaborating, and somewhat revising, his theory of dreams. It was a portentous appearance: he brought with him his daughter Anna, soon to become a psychoanalyst in her own right, and in his paper he adumbrated the idea of the repetition compulsion, which would loom large in the theory he was readying for publication. The Hague congress was a stirring reunion for Freudians who had been officially classified, just two years before, as mortal enemies. There was something touching about the meeting, as half-starved analysts from the defeated nations were fed and feted at luncheons and banquets by their generous Dutch hosts.* The English, Ernest Jones remembered, gave Freud and his daughter Anna a lunch, at which she made "a graceful little speech in very good English." It was a crowded and cheerful conclave: there were sixty-two members and fifty-seven guests. Few psychoanalysts had long succumbed to chauvinism, so American and English analysts found it perfectly natural to sit companionably with their German, Austrian, and Hungarian colleagues. True, in 1920 a meeting in Berlin would have been impossible, even though Abraham vigorously lobbied for it. With all their freedom from xenophobia, Anglo-American analysts still had hard feelings about the Germans. But only two years later, at Abraham's urging,

*For the Austrian, Hungarian, and German analysts, this congress forcefully recalled a world of abundance they had almost forgotten. Anna Freud remembered later that she and her father had little money. "But my father was, as always, most generous. He gave me a special sum every day to spend on fruit (bananas etc), which we had not had for years in Vienna, and he insisted that I buy new clothes for myself, making no limitations of what to spend: 'Whatever I need.' . . . I do not remember that he bought anything for himself—except cigars." (Anna Freud to Jones, January 21, 1955. Jones papers, Archives of the British Psycho-Analytical Society, London.)

the International Psychoanalytic Association chose Berlin as the site for its next congress, which went off without political recriminations. It was the last conclave Freud would attend.

DURING THE IMMEDIATE postwar years Freud's output was slim, measured by the number of words alone. He wrote papers on homosexuality and on that curious subject, telepathy—always intriguing to Freud. In addition, he published three short books, really brochures: *Beyond the Pleasure Principle* in 1920, *Group Psychology and the Analysis of the Ego** in 1921, and *The Ego and the Id* in 1923. Taken together, these writings amount to no more than perhaps two hundred pages. But their size is deceptive; they set out his structural system,† to which Freud remained faithful for the rest of his life. He had been evolving that system since the end of the war, while he was busy ordering cocoa and cloth from England and cursing his poor fountain pen. "Where is my [book on] metapsychology?" he asked Lou Andreas-Salomé rhetorically. "First of all," he told her more emphatically than he had before, "it remains unwritten." The "fragmentary nature of my experiences and the sporadic character of my ideas" did not permit him to offer a systematic presentation. "But," he added soothingly, "if I should live for another ten years, remain capable of working during that time, not starve, not be beaten to death, not be too exhausted by the misery of my family or of things around me—quite a lot of preconditions—then I promise to offer further contributions to it." The first of these would be *Beyond the Pleasure Principle*. This slim volume, and its two successors, demonstrate why he could not publish that much-announced, much-postponed book on metapsychology. He had complicated and modified his ideas too much. Not least of all, they had not had enough about death in them—or, more precisely, he had not integrated what they had to say about death into his theory.

IT IS TEMPTING TO READ Freud's late psychoanalytic system, with its stress on aggression and death, as a response to his grief of these years. At the time, Freud's first biographer, Fritz Wittels, said as much: "In 1920 [with *Beyond the Pleasure Principle*], Freud astonished us with the discovery that there is

---

*An infelicitous translation is worth noting here. Freud's German title is *Massenpsychologie und Ich-Analyse*. "Group," the term the editors of the *Standard Edition* chose for *Masse* (literally, "mass"), is far too tame. Freud himself, in a letter to Ernest Jones, spoke of his "Psychology of Mass" (Freud to Jones, August 2, 1920. In English. Freud Collection, D2, LC). If that term seemed too awkward, "crowd psychology" would have been nearer the mark than "group psychology."

†It is customary to call this postwar system the "structural" system and contrast it with the "topographic" system of the prewar years. There were, as these pages should make quite obvious, many connections and continuities between the two. Moreover, the names are linguistic accidents and purely conventional; both systems describe the topography and structure of the mind.

Freud's six children in 1899. Left to right: Sophie, Mathilde, Anna, Oliver, Martin, Ernst. *(Mary Evans/Sigmund Freud Copyrights, Wivenhoe)*

Freud and his wife, flanking his mother, during a summer holiday in Aussee in 1905. *(Mary Evans/Sigmund Freud Copyrights, Wivenhoe)*

Wilhelm Stekel, an early, vocal supporter, with whom Freud broke after 1910.

Alfred Adler, doubtless the most eminent and, next to Freud, most influential member of the Wednesday Psychological Society until their uneasy association came to an end in 1911.

Eduard Hitschmann, one of Freud's most dependable Viennese lieutenants.

Carl Gustav Jung, for some tempestuous years Freud's anointed crown prince and successor. *(Kurt Niehus, Baden, Switzerland)*

Oskar Pfister, a Protestant minister in Zurich who became an assiduous polemicist in behalf of psychoanalysis, especially its application in pedagogy and pastoral work.

Max Eitingon, a generous, dependable adherent to Freud's views, and a close friend, who founded the first psychoanalytic clinic in Berlin in 1920.

Freud at about fifty in a snapshot taken by one of his sons and hence less formidable than his other photographs. He is holding the inevitable cigar. *(Freud Collection, LC)*

The Pompeian relief known as "Gradiva," of which Freud had a plaster cast in his consulting room. The original is in the Vatican Museum. *(Alinari/Art Resources)*

Obverse of the medallion, by the sculptor Karl Maria Schwerdtner, given to Freud by his admirers on his fiftieth birthday. Students of slips note the misspelling of Freud's first name. *(Mary Evans/Sigmund Freud Copyrights, Wivenhoe)*

Reverse of the medallion, showing Oedipus solving the riddle of the Sphinx. *(Mary Evans/Sigmund Freud Copyrights, Wivenhoe)*

A formal group portrait taken at the third international congress of psychoanalysts, Weimar, September 1911. Freud is at the center. To his right, slightly below, is Sándor Ferenczi; to his left, stooping, is Carl G. Jung. Seated, fifth from the left, is Lou Andreas-Salomé. *(Mary Evans/Sigmund Freud Copyrights, Wivenhoe)*

Celebration of the Freuds' silver wedding anniversary, on September 14, 1911, with all the children, and Aunt Minna, on hand. Left to right: Oliver, Ernst, Anna, Sigmund and Martha Freud, Mathilde, Sophie, Minna Bernays, Martin. *(Freud Collection, LC)*

Sophie Freud with her mother on a summer holiday, about 1912. *(Mary Evans/Sigmund Freud Copyrights, Wivenhoe)*

Freud during a summer vacation in the Dolomites in 1913, with Anna, then seventeen, on his arm. *(Mary Evans/Sigmund Freud Copyrights, Wivenhoe/W. E. Freud)*

Leonardo da Vinci, *The Virgin, Saint Anne, and the Christ Child,* one of the paintings that Freud analyzed in "Leonardo da Vinci and a Memory of His Childhood." The original is in the Louvre. *(Cliché des Musées Nationaux—Paris)*

Michelangelo's powerful *Moses,* in the church of S. Pietro in Vincoli, Rome, the statue Freud analyzed in "The Moses of Michelangelo." *(Alinari/ Art Resource)*

Freud in 1909. *(Mary Evans/Sigmund Freud Copyrights, Wivenhoe)*

Freud in 1916, with his soldier sons Ernst, left, and Martin, at home on leave. *(Mary Evans/Sigmund Freud Copyrights, Wivenhoe)*

Freud with Sándor Ferenczi, then serving in the Hungarian army, in 1917. *(Mary Evans/ Sigmund Freud Copyrights, Wivenhoe)*

in everything living, in addition to the pleasure principle which, since the days of Hellenic culture, has been called Eros, another principle: What lives, wants to die again. Originating in dust, it wants to be dust again. Not only the life-drive is in them, but the *death-drive* as well. When Freud made this communication to an attentive world, he was under the impress of the death of a blooming daughter whom he lost after he had had to worry about the life of several of his nearest relatives, who had gone to war." It was a reductionist explanation, but most plausible.

Freud immediately took exception to it. In fact, he had anticipated Wittels by three years: in the early summer of 1920, he had asked Eitingon and others to testify, if necessary, that they had seen a draft of *Beyond the Pleasure Principle* before Sophie Halberstadt's death. Now, in late 1923, reading Wittels's biography, he admitted that this interpretation was "very interesting": had he been making an analytic study of someone else in these circumstances, he would have made such a connection "between my daughter's death and the train of thought advocated in my *Beyond* [*the Pleasure Principle*]. And yet," he added, "it is mistaken. *Beyond* was written in 1919, when my daughter was still healthy and flourishing." To clinch his point, he reiterated that he had circulated the virtually complete manuscript among his friends in Berlin as early as September 1919. "The probable is not always the true." He had solid support for his demurrer; Freud did not go beyond the pleasure principle because of a death in his family. Yet his perceptible anxiety to establish this point beyond cavil suggests that he was not just hoping to assure the universal validity of his new hypotheses. After all, he had often, and unapologetically, drawn general propositions about the workings of the mind from his own intimate experience. Was it an accident that the term "death drive"—*Todestrieb*—entered his correspondence a week after Sophie Halberstadt's death? It stands as a touching reminder of how deeply the loss of his daughter had distressed him. The loss can claim a subsidiary role, if not in the making of his analytic preoccupation with destructiveness, then in determining its weight.

The great slaughter of 1914 to 1918, with stark truths about human savagery revealed in combat and in bellicose editorials, had also forced Freud to assign enhanced stature to aggression. Lecturing at the University of Vienna in the winter semester of 1915, he had asked his auditors to think of the brutality, cruelty, and mendacity now spreading across the civilized world and to admit that evil cannot be excluded from basic human nature.* But in important ways, the power of aggression had been no secret to him well before 1914. Freud was the one, after all, who had revealed its workings

*See p. 370.

in himself, privately in his letters to Fliess and publicly in *The Interpretation of Dreams*. Without his printed confessions, Freud's death wishes against his little brother, his hostile oedipal feelings against his father, or his need for an enemy in his life might have remained known to him alone forever.* More generally, he had, as early as 1896, referred in print to the self-reproaches that haunt obsessional neurotics over *"sexual aggressions in childhood."* A little later, he had discovered that aggressive impulses are a powerful component in the Oedipus complex, and in his *Three Essays on the Theory of Sexuality* of 1905, he had suggested that "the sexuality of most men shows an admixture of *aggression."* True, in this passage he had regarded the aggression as confined to men, but that was a residue of parochialism requiring correction. On the presence of aggression everywhere, even in sexual life, even in women, he was clear-eyed a decade and more before the First World War. The war, he insisted with some justice over and over, had not created the interest of psychoanalysis in aggression; rather, it had only confirmed what analysts had been saying about aggression all along.†

What came to puzzle him, then, as it puzzled others, was only why he should have hesitated to elevate aggressiveness into a rival to libido. "Why have we ourselves," he asked later, looking back, "needed such a long time before we decided to recognize an aggressive drive?" A little ruefully he recalled his own defensive rejection of such a drive when the idea first appeared in the psychoanalytic literature, and "how long it took before I became receptive to it." He was thinking of a presentation by the brilliant Russian analyst Sabina Spielrein in the pioneering days of 1911 at one of the Wednesday-night meetings at Berggasse 19, and also of her pioneering paper of a year later, "Destruction as the Cause of Becoming."‡ In those years, Freud had simply not been ready.

---

*See esp. pp. 11 and 55.

†See Freud's letter of December 1914 to the Dutch poet and psychopathologist Frederik van Eeden. The war, Freud wrote, only confirmed what analysts had already learned "from a study of the dreams and mental slips of normal people, as well as from the symptoms of neurotics," namely that the "primitive, savage and evil impulses of mankind have not vanished in any individual, but continue their existence, although in a repressed state," and "wait for opportunities to display their activity." (Quoted in *Jones* II, 368.)

‡See her article "Die Destruktion als Ursache des Werdens," *Jahrbuch für psychoanalytische und psychopathologische Forschungen*, IV (1912), 465–503, in which she speculated on the work of destructive impulses contained in the sexual drives themselves. Sabina Spielrein was one of the most extraordinary among the younger analysts. A Russian, she had gone to Zurich to study medicine and, in desperate mental distress, went into psychoanalytic treatment with Jung. She fell in love with her analyst, and Jung, taking advantage of her dependency, made her his mistress. After a painful struggle, in which Freud played a minor but not admirable part, she freed herself from her involvement, and became an analyst. During her short stay in Vienna, she made regular contributions to discussions at the Wednesday-night sessions; later she returned to Russia, where she practiced psychoanalysis.

His delay no doubt had other causes as well. The very fact that Adler of all people championed the concept of male protest, however much it would differ from Freud's later definition, obstructed Freud's acceptance of a destructive drive. Similarly, Jung's claim that he had anticipated Freud by arguing that libido aims at death no less than at life was not calculated to hasten Freud's acceptance. Most likely, his halting recognition also had a personal dimension; it may have been one of the self-protective defensive maneuvers he mobilized against his own aggressiveness. He blamed modern culture for rejecting the blasphemous low appraisal of human nature which made aggression a fundamental drive. Perhaps. But his own hesitation reads rather like a piece of projection in which he attributed to others his own denials.

WHILE THE APPALLING daily display of human beastliness sharpened Freud's reformulations, his reclassification of the drives owed far more to problems internal to psychoanalytic theory. His paper on narcissism had, as we have seen, exposed the inadequacy of his early division of the drives into the sexual and the egotistic. But neither that paper nor its successors had supplied a more satisfactory scheme. Yet Freud had no intention of watering down libido into a universal energy, as he charged Jung had done. Nor did he wish to supplant libido with a universal aggressive force, which, he said, was Adler's fatal mistake. In *Beyond the Pleasure Principle*, he explicitly singled out Jung's *"monistic"* libido theory, and contrasted it unfavorably with his own *"dualistic"* scheme.

He would remain a firm dualist for clinical, theoretical, and aesthetic reasons. The cases of his patients amply confirmed his contention that psychological activity is essentially pervaded by conflict. What is more, the very concept of repression, that cornerstone of psychoanalytic theory, presupposes a fundamental division in mental operations: Freud separated the repressing energies from the repressed material. Finally, his dualism had an elusive aesthetic dimension. It is not that Freud was helplessly obsessed with the image of two infuriated swordsmen slashing at one another to the death; his analysis of the oedipal triangle, for one, shows him able to discard polarities when the evidence demands it. But the phenomenon of dramatic opposites seems to have given Freud a sense of satisfaction and closure: his writings abound in confrontations of active and passive, masculine and feminine, love and hunger, and now, after the war, life and death.

To be sure, the revisions Freud was making in his theories did not prevent him from rescuing the core of his prewar generalizations about mental struc-

---

She was not heard of after 1937. In 1941, after the Nazi invasion of the Soviet Union, she and her two grown daughters were cold-bloodedly shot to death by German soldiers.

ture and operations. As psychoanalysts complained at the time, and have complained since, Freud rarely spelled out the precise import of his self-corrections. He would not specify just what he had discarded, what modified, and what kept intact from his earlier formulations, but instead left the adjustment of apparently irreconcilable statements to his readers.* There could be no doubt, though, that the restatements he offered in *Beyond the Pleasure Principle* had kept intact the traditional psychoanalytic placement of thoughts and wishes according to their distance from awareness; the familiar trio of unconscious, preconscious, conscious retained its usefulness. Yet the new map of mental structure that Freud drew between 1920 and 1923 brought extensive, hitherto unsuspected provinces of mental function-ing and malfunctioning, like the sense of guilt, into the range of psy-choanalytic understanding. Perhaps most exciting of all was the access Freud's revisions provided to a region of the mind that analytic thought had hitherto grossly neglected, imprecisely named, and barely understood—the ego. With the ego psychology Freud elaborated after the war, he could approach ever closer the realization of an old ambition: to delineate a general psychology that would reach beyond its first restricted habitat, the neuroses, to normal mental activity.

BEYOND THE PLEASURE PRINCIPLE is a difficult text. The prose is as lucid as ever, though the compression of disturbing new ideas into the briefest com-pass offers obstacles to the reader's quick comprehension. More unsettling is Freud's yielding to flights of the imagination as uninhibited as any he had ever undertaken in print. The reassuring intimacy with clinical experience that marks most of Freud's papers, even at their most theoretical, seems faint here, almost absent.† To make matters more troubling still, Freud drove his familiar protestations of uncertainty to new lengths. "One might ask me," he wrote near the conclusion, "whether and how far I myself am persuaded by the hypotheses here brought forward. My answer would be that I am neither persuaded myself nor seek to recruit others to have faith in them. More correctly: I do not know how far I believe in them." He portrayed himself a little slyly as having followed a train of thought as far as it would

---

*There are some exceptions, and we shall discover one of these as we discuss his shift in the theory of anxiety in 1926. See pp. 486-87.

†Max Schur, whom no one can accuse of reading Freud unsympathetically, said flatly, "We can assume only that Freud's conclusions . . . are an example of *ad hoc* reasoning to prove a preformed hypothesis. . . . This way of thinking, which is so different from Freud's general scientific style, can be detected throughout *Beyond the Pleasure Principle."* (Max Schur, *The Id and the Regulatory Principles of Mental Functioning* [1966], 184.)

go, "merely from scientific curiosity, or, if you will, as an *advocatus diaboli,* who has not on that account sold himself to the devil."

At the same time, Freud professed himself satisfied that two of three recent advances in the theory of the drives—the enlargement of the concept of sexuality and the introduction of the concept of narcissism—are "direct translations of observation into theory." But the third, the stress on the regressive nature of the drives, essential to Freud's new dualism, seemed far less secure than the other two. Even here, to be sure, Freud claimed to be drawing on observed materials. "But perhaps I have overestimated their significance." Yet he thought that at least some consideration should be given to his "speculations," and consideration they have had, at times enthusiastic, more often quizzical. In the early spring of 1919, when he had completed a draft of the essay and was getting ready to send it to Ferenczi, he noted that he was "amusing" himself "a good deal" with this work. It was not an amusement in which his followers joined.

Beyond the Pleasure Principle opens with a commonplace then unchallenged in psychoanalytic theory: "The course of mental events is automatically regulated by the pleasure principle." On reflection, though, considering the unpleasure that so many mental processes seem to generate, Freud toned down this categorical assertion two pages later: "There exists in the mind a strong tendency toward the pleasure principle." With this reformulation, Freud approached the main business of his essay: he tried to show that there are fundamental forces in the mind which invalidate the pleasure principle in the most consequential way. He adduced in evidence the reality principle, that acquired capacity to postpone, and inhibit the impatient urge for, instant gratification.

By itself, this restatement makes no difficulties for the traditional psychoanalyst, nor does Freud's assertion that the conflicts working in all humans, especially as the mental apparatus matures, normally produce unpleasure rather than pleasure. But the handful of instances Freud then offered in support are neither familiar nor quite persuasive, even though he took them as proof, or at least impressive evidence, for the existence of hitherto unsuspected mental forces "beyond" the pleasure principle. One of his examples, though playful and scarcely conclusive, has become famous: the *fort-da* game that Freud had observed in his eighteen-month-old grandson, Sophie's elder son. Though much attached to his mother, little Ernst Wolfgang Halberstadt was a "good" boy who never cried when she left him briefly. But he played a mysterious game with himself; he would take a wooden spool tied round with a bit of string, throw it over the edge of his curtained crib, and sound out *o-o-o-o,* which his mother and grandfather understood to mean *fort*—

"gone." He would then pull the spool back and salute its reappearance with a happy *da*—"there." That was the whole game, and Freud interpreted it as a way of coping with an overwhelming experience: the little boy was moving from the passive acceptance of his mother's absence to the active reenactment of her disappearance and return. Or perhaps he was revenging himself on his mother—throwing her away, as it were, as though he no longer needed her.

This infantile game set Freud to wondering. Why should the little boy incessantly reenact a situation that was so disturbing to him? Freud hesitated to draw general conclusions from a single case, exemplifying the old humorous psychoanalytic injunction, Don't generalize from one case, generalize from two cases! But however fragmentary and puzzling the evidence he presented to his observant grandfather might be, Ernst Halberstadt raised the intriguing question whether the grip of the pleasure principle on mental life was really as secure as psychoanalysts had supposed.

Other pieces of evidence seemed rather more substantial, at least to Freud. In the course of psychoanalytic treatment, the analyst seeks to raise to awareness the unhappy, often traumatic, early experiences or fantasies which the patient has repressed. In a perverse way, the act of repressing and the analysand's resistance to undoing that repression obey the pleasure principle; it is more agreeable to forget certain things than to remember them. But in the grip of the transference, Freud observed, many analysands would return over and over to experiences that could never have been pleasurable. Now, it is true that their analysts had enjoined them to speak freely of everything in order to make the unconscious conscious; but something more tormenting seemed to be in play here, a compulsion to repeat a painful experience. Freud noticed one version of this monotonous, destructive replay of unpleasure in patients afflicted with a "fate neurosis," sufferers whose destiny it is to go through the same calamity more than once.

Freud, less inclined in this essay than in most of his other work to adduce clinical material, illustrated the fate neurosis by recalling a scene from Torquato Tasso's romantic epic *Jerusalem Delivered.* In a duel Tancred, the hero, kills his beloved Clorinda, who has confronted him disguised in an enemy's armor. After her burial, as Tancred penetrates an uncanny magic forest, he hacks away at a tree with his sword, only to have blood flowing from it. And he hears the voice of his Clorinda, whose bewitched soul has been imprisoned in that tree, accusing him of wounding his love once again. The behavior of sufferers from fate neurosis, and the repetitive preoccupations in analytic treatment of veterans suffering from war neuroses, were for Freud authentic exceptions to the reign of the pleasure principle. The repetition compulsion from which they arise neither recalls nor provides pleasure of any sort. Indeed,

Freud noted, patients who display this compulsion do their utmost to dwell on misery and injuries, and to force an interruption to the analysis before it is completed. They contrive to find evidence that they are despised. They discover ways of supplying realistic grounds for their jealous feelings. They fantasize about unrealistic plans guaranteed to leave them disappointed. It is as though they have never learned that all these compulsive repetitions bring no pleasure. There is something "demonic" about their activities.

That word "demonic" leaves no doubt about Freud's strategy. He saw the compulsion to repeat as a most primitive mental activity, displaying an "instinctual" character "to a high degree." The kind of repetition a child begs for—the retelling of a story exactly as it was told before, with no detail altered—is manifestly pleasurable, but the incessant replaying of horrifying experiences or childhood calamities in the analytic transference obeys other laws. It must spring from a fundamental urge independent of the appetite for pleasure and often in conflict with it. Freud thus reasoned himself into the discovery that some drives at least are conservative; they obey the pressure not for novelty and unprecedented experience, but, on the contrary, for the restoration of an earlier inorganic state of things. In short, *"The aim of all life is death."* The desire for mastery, along with other candidates for the status of a primitive drive with which Freud had experimented over the years, now fade into relative insignificance. All one can say is, "The organism wants only to die in its own fashion." Freud had arrived at the theoretical conception of a death drive.

Artfully disclosing his hesitations as he proceeded, Freud pronounced his portentous discovery dubious: "But let us reflect; it cannot be so!" It is unthinkable that life should be no more than a preparation for death. The sexual drives prove that truly it cannot be so: they are the servants of life. At the very least they lengthen the road to death; at best they strive for a kind of immortality. The mind, then, is a battleground. This proposition established to his satisfaction, Freud plunged into the thickets of speculative modern biology, even into philosophy, in search of corroborative evidence. One remembers what Freud had told his friend Lou Andreas-Salomé in the summer of 1919: he had stumbled onto a strange idea via the drives and was reading all sorts of things, including Schopenhauer. The result was his vision of two elemental pugnacious forces in the mind, Eros and Thanatos, locked in eternal battle.

Freud seemed a little uncertain in 1920 whether he really believed in the awesome picture of combat he had sketched, but he gradually committed himself to his dualism with all the energy at his command. He eloquently defended it, facing down his fellow analysts' resistance. "At the beginning," he recalled later, "I advocated the views here put forward only tentatively, but in the course of time they have acquired such a power over me that I can no longer think differently." In 1924, in his paper "The Economic Problem of Masochism," he employed the scheme quite casually, as though there were nothing controversial about it, and he retained it unaltered for the rest of his life. It informs the posthumous *Outline of Psychoanalysis*, published in 1940, no less than his *Civilization and Its Discontents* of 1930 or his *New Introductory Lectures on Psychoanalysis* of three years later. It was not a question, he wrote in 1937, of setting "an optimistic against a pessimistic theory of life. Only the collaboration and the conflict between both primal drives, Eros and death drive, explain the colorful variety of life's phenomena, never one of them alone." Yet, though he was convinced of his stern vision, he was not invariably dogmatic about it. "Naturally," he wrote Ernest Jones in 1935, rehearsing the conflict of life against death once again, "all this is groping speculation, until one has something better." No wonder if, for all of Freud's authority, not all the psychoanalytic movement followed his lead.

As they debated Freud's new theory of instinctual dualism, psychoanalysts were assisted by the distinction Freud drew between the silent death drive, working to reduce living matter to an inorganic condition, and showy aggressiveness, which one encountered, and could daily substantiate, in clinical experience. Practically without exception, they could accept the proposition that aggressiveness is part of the human animal's endowment: not only war and rapine, but hostile jokes, jealous slanders, domestic quarrels, sporting contests, economic rivalries—and psychoanalysts' feuds—confirm that aggression is loose in the world, fed in all probability by an inexhaustible stream of instinctual pressures. But for most analysts Freud's idea of a hidden primitive urge toward death, of a primary masochism, was something else again. They saw it bedeviled by problems with the evidence, whether drawn from psychoanalysis or from biology. In distinguishing the death drive from sheer aggression, Freud enabled his followers to uncouple the two, reject his epic vision of Thanatos confronting Eros, and yet retain the concept of the two warring drives.*

---

*Some of Freud's followers, notably the child analyst Melanie Klein and her school, proved more uncompromising on this issue than Freud himself. "The repeated attempts that have been made to improve humanity—in particular to make it more peaceable," Klein wrote in 1933, "have failed, because nobody has understood the full depth and vigour of the instincts of aggression innate in each individual." ("The Early Development of Conscience in the Child" [1933], in *Love, Guilt and Reparation and Other Works, 1921–1945* [1975], 257.) And by "instincts of aggression" she meant the death drive in all its elemental Freudian force. In sharp contrast, Heinz Hartmann, the most prominent among the ego psychologists who would greatly elaborate Freud's fragmentary structural theory of the 1920s, chose to concentrate on "the concept of drives which we actually encounter in clinical psychoanalytic theory," and to do without "Freud's other, mainly biologically oriented set

Freud was aware of the risks he was taking, and quite unrepentant. "In the work of my later years," he noted in his self-portrait of 1925, "I have given free rein to the long-suppressed inclination to speculation." Whether his new construction would prove useful, he added, remained to be seen. His ambition had been to settle some significant theoretical conundrums, but on the way, he acknowledged, he had gone "far beyond psychoanalysis." However uncomfortable his colleagues might be with such far-ranging excursions, Freud welcomed them as advances in his science and, quite incidentally, as proof that his intellectual vitality had not yet atrophied. "If scientific interest, which just now is asleep with me, gets aroused in the course of time," he told Ernest Jones in the fall of 1920, as *Beyond the Pleasure Principle* was being published, "I may still be able to bring some new contribution to our unfinished work." Greatly to his surprise, and even regret, the essay came to enjoy a certain favor. "For the *Beyond*," he reported to Eitingon in March 1921, "I have been punished enough; it is very popular, brings me masses of letters and encomiums. I must have made something very stupid there." He soon made it apparent that this little book was only the first installment in a larger enterprise.

EROS, EGO, AND THEIR ENEMIES

 Freud's vitality might be intact, but he was not a writing machine. He had to wait for inspiration to flow freely. "Here I am amidst the choice beauties of our Alps," he wrote Ernest Jones from Bad Gastein in August 1920, "pretty well worn out, waiting for the beneficial effects of radioactive water and delicious air. I have brought the material for the Psychology of Mass and the Analysis of the Ego with me, but my head obstinately refuses so far to take an interest in these deep problems." He had been working on them for some months, slowly, intermittently. But once his head was clear, he found work on his "Psychology of Mass" progressing quickly. By October, his disciples in Berlin were reading his draft, and early in 1921 he launched on the final revisions. "I am pretty full now," he wrote

of hypotheses of the 'life' and 'death instincts.' " ("Comments on the Psychoanalytic Theory of the Instinctual Drives" [1948], in *Essays on Ego Psychology: Selected Problems in Psychoanalytic Theory* [1964], 71–72.)

Jones in March, "and busy in rectifying the booklet on Mass-Psychology."
Characteristically, he had his doubts about the "booklet"; sending a copy of
it to Romain Rolland, he warded off criticism by self-criticism: "Not that I
consider this work particularly successful, but it points out a way from the
analysis of the individual to the understanding of society."

This, in a sentence, is the principal aim of Freud's *Group Psychology and
the Analysis of the Ego.* Freud had steeped himself in the essays and monographs that crowd psychologists from Gustave Le Bon to Wilfred Trotter had
been publishing for the last thirty years, and used them as stimuli for his own
train of thought. In the end, though, his own *Totem and Taboo* had a far
greater impact on his conclusions than Le Bon's *Crowd Psychology.* What
interested Freud was the question, What holds groups together, other than
the transparent rational motive of self-interest? His answer necessarily propelled Freud into social psychology. But what most arrests the attention in
his "Psychology of Mass" is Freud's liberal employment of psychoanalytic
propositions in the explication of social cohesion. "The contrast between
individual and social- or mass-psychology," he began, "which may appear to
us at first glance as very significant, on close examination loses much of its
sharpness." Indeed, "in the mental life of the individual, the Other enters
quite regularly as ideal, as object, as helper, and as adversary; hence individual
psychology is from the outset social psychology at the same time."

This assertion is sweeping but, from the psychoanalytic vantage point,
perfectly logical. True, he was prepared in the 1920s, as he had been in the
1890s, to recognize the impact of biological endowment on mental life. But
it is more to the point for his social psychology that in asserting the essential
identity of individual and social psychology, Freud made it plain that psychoanalysis, for all its uncompromising individualism, cannot explain the inner
life without recourse to the external world. From the moment of birth, the
infant is exposed to a bombardment of influences from others, influences that
widen and diversify during childhood. As the years pass, the child is subjected
to the shaping encouragement and disparagement, the praise and blame, the
enviable or distasteful example, of others. Character development, neurotic
symptoms, conflicts centering on love and hate, are compromise formations
between inner urges and outside pressures.

That is why, Freud was convinced, the social psychologist analyzing the
forces holding groups together must ultimately return to the study of individual mental qualities, precisely those qualities that had interested psychoanalysts for a quarter century. "The individual's relation to his parents
and siblings, his love object," Freud wrote, "his teacher and his physician,
that is to say all the relations which have so far been the principal subject of psychoanalytic research, could claim to be acknowledged as social

phenomena." Group behavior, to be sure, displays unmistakable characteristics of its own; Freud agreed with Le Bon that crowds are more intolerant, more irrational, more immoral, more heartless, above all more uninhibited, than individuals. But the crowd, as crowd, invents nothing; it only liberates, distorts, exaggerates, the individual members' traits. It follows that without the concepts developed by psychoanalysts for individuals—identification, regression, libido—no social-psychological explanation can be complete, or anything but superficial. In short, crowd psychology, and with it all social psychology, is parasitic on individual psychology; that is Freud's point of departure, to which he persistently held.

Freud's excursion into collective psychology, then, demonstrates in practice the universal relevance of psychoanalytic theory. On this point, Freud differed radically from earlier students of organizations, masses, and mobs. Crowd psychologists had been, by and large, amateurs, and tendentious amateurs at that—men with a mission. Hippolyte Taine, who had anatomized revolutionary crowds in his history of the French Revolution, was a literary critic, historian, and philosopher; Émile Zola, who had made crowds the principal actors in *Germinal*, his stirring novel about a miners' strike, was a pugnacious journalist and prolific writer of fiction; Gustave Le Bon, the most widely read of the crowd psychologists, had been an eclectic popularizer of contemporary science. Only the surgeon Wilfred Trotter could claim some professional competence in psychology; as Ernest Jones's intimate friend, later his brother-in-law, he made himself into a knowledgeable, far from uncritical reader of psychoanalysis.

All of these publicists had become fascinated by crowd psychology through observing what they thought the unbridled conduct of the modern mob. For Trotter, an Englishman writing about the "herd instinct" during the war, the mob was German. His "intelligent" book of 1916, *Instincts of the Herd in Peace and War*, Freud wrote with some regret, "had not quite escaped the antipathies loosened by the recent great war." Earlier, Zola, certainly no reactionary mourner for the vanished good old times, had depicted crowds of excited, often violent strikers as an inflammable mixture of menace and promise. His precursors and contemporaries had been less equivocal: they had written to warn rather than to celebrate; for them, the mass, especially when stirred up, was a vindictive, bloodthirsty, drunken, irrational modern phenomenon—democracy in action. Freud was no lover of what he once called "the stupid common folk"—*das blöde Volk;* his old-fashioned liberalism had an aristocratic tinge to it. Yet politics was not at all prominent in Freud's mind as he wrote his book on crowd psychology. He was applying psychoanalysis.

As a practicing psychoanalyst Freud saw groups, crowds, mobs, whether fleeting or stable, as held together by diffused sexual emotions—"aim-inhibited" libido—akin to the passions that unite families. "Love relationships (expressed neutrally, emotional ties) also constitute the essence of the crowd mind." These erotic bonds link the members of a group in two directions—vertically and horizontally, as it were. In "artificial crowds," Freud wrote, considering the church and the army in some detail, "each individual is bound libidinously on the one hand to the leader (Christ, commander-in-chief) and on the other hand to the other individuals in the crowd." The intensity of these double connections explains the individual's regression as he submerges himself in the crowd: here he may safely drop acquired inhibitions. It follows, for Freud, that just as erotic relationships make the crowd, the failure of these relationships will lead to its disintegration. Thus he dissented from social psychologists who hold panic responsible for the weakening of affectionate bonds within groups. Quite the contrary, Freud argued, it is only after libidinal ties have loosened that panic ensues.

These sublimated erotic alliances also explain why collectivities that bind their members with the chains of love are at the same time filled with hatred against outsiders. Whether experienced in the small family unit or in a larger group (which is really the family writ large), love is exclusive and haunted by feelings of hostility as its shadow. "According to the evidence of psychoanalysis, almost every intimate emotional relationship between two persons of any duration," such as marriage, friendship, or parenthood, "contains a sediment of negative, hostile feelings which escapes perception only in consequence of repression." Thus, Freud commented, never losing an opportunity to snipe at true believers, "a religion, even when it calls itself the religion of love, must be hard and loveless against those who do not belong to it."

Freud's *Group Psychology*, glancing at new ways of thinking about the mind in society, throws out suggestions that have not yet been fully explored. But the almost breathless brevity with which Freud touched on complex issues of social cohesion gives the study an air of improvisation. Its postscript, gathering together rather miscellaneous material Freud had failed to integrate into the body of the essay, emphasizes its tentative and transitional character. In many respects, Freud's *Group Psychology* looks back to such earlier studies as *Totem and Taboo* and *Beyond the Pleasure Principle*. But it also looks ahead. In an appreciative review published in 1922, Ferenczi singled out as particularly original Freud's comparison of infatuation with hypnosis. But, significantly, he thought that Freud's "second important innovation" lay in the field of individual psychology, in his *"discovery of a new developmental stage in the ego and in libido."* Freud was beginning to differentiate steps in the growth of the ego and to note its tense interaction with the ego ideal—the superego, as he soon came to call it. Freud's excursion into social psychology was a rehearsal for more definitive statements about the ego. But these were still two years away.

IN RETROSPECT, *The Ego and the Id*, published in 1923, appears as the inevitable climax of a reappraisal Freud had launched a decade before and accelerated after the war. But this is to impose a steady progress on his perception really beyond Freud's ken before the fact. In July 1922, he told Ferenczi that he was doing some speculative work, a continuation of *Beyond the Pleasure Principle*, and added prudently, "It will issue in a little book or in nothing at all." The following month he reported to Otto Rank, "I am mentally clear and in the mood for work. I am writing on something that calls itself the Ego and the Id." This would "become only a paper or even a little brochure, like the *Beyond* [*the Pleasure Principle*] whose continuation in fact it is." But, as was his style, Freud was waiting for inspiration to propel him forward. "It has progressed fairly far in draft, otherwise waits for moods and ideas without which it cannot be completed." Freud's casual and tentative announcements afford an exceptional glimpse into his working habits. He was writing the cardinal text of his last decades, yet he was uncertain when or how he would complete it, and no less uncertain whether it would be just a short paper or, perhaps, a companion piece for *Beyond the Pleasure Principle*.

While *The Ego and the Id* generated some puzzlement among analysts at first, it encountered little resistance and, for the most part, emphatic approval. This is not surprising; it matched, and deepened, their clinical experience and, with its tripartite division of the mind—id, ego, superego—offered an analysis of mental structure and functioning far more detailed and far more illuminating than its predecessors. Only Freud's announcement that *The Ego and the Id* stood "under the sponsorship of Groddeck" generated some mild protests.

Georg Groddeck, the self-styled "wild analyst," was the kind of maverick whom psychoanalysis was beginning to attract in uncomfortable numbers. He and his fellows threatened to compromise the reputation as sober, responsible medical men that analysts craved. Freud thought him inclined "to exaggeration, standardization, and a certain mysticism." Chief of his sanatorium at Baden-Baden, Groddeck had employed psychoanalytic concepts—infantile sexuality, symbolism, transference, resistance—as early as 1909, knowing of Freud only from hearsay. Then, in 1912, though no better informed, he had written a book in which he precipitously criticized psychoanalysis. His conversion came a year later, when he read *The Psychopathology of Everyday Life* and *The Interpretation of Dreams* and was overwhelmed. What he had paraded as his own ideas, others had thought before, and better. In an expansive letter to Freud in 1917, a long-delayed token of his "belated honesty," he confessed all of these missteps and concluded with the assurance that henceforth he would regard himself as Freud's pupil.

Freud was charmed, and, disregarding Groddeck's modest disclaimers, enlisted him in the ranks of the analysts. Groddeck's often provocative behavior did not weaken Freud's pleasure in him; he found something refreshing in his verve, his willingness to be original and outrageous. At times Groddeck pushed beyond the limits of his new colleagues' indulgence. He brought his mistress to the congress of psychoanalysts at The Hague in 1920, and opened the paper he read there with the long-remembered words "I am a wild analyst." He must have known that this was precisely what the analysts in the audience were struggling not to be, or not to appear. His paper seemed wild enough; it was a rambling exercise in free association about what would later be called psychosomatic medicine. Organic diseases, Groddeck maintained, even myopia, are simply physical expressions of unconscious emotional conflicts and hence are susceptible to psychoanalytic treatment. In principle, analysts had little quarrel with such a view, moderately expressed; after all, the conversion symptoms of hysteria, that classic neurosis of psychoanalytic practice, supported Groddeck's general position. But Groddeck spoke in the accents, ultimately unpersuasive, of the enthusiast, and he found only a few defenders—Freud among them. Later, Freud did inquire of Groddeck whether he had meant to have his talk taken seriously, and Groddeck assured him that he had.

Groddeck had other tricks up his sleeve. Early in 1921, he confirmed his status as the wild man of analysis by bringing out, with Freud's publishing house, a "psychoanalytic novel" called *The Seeker of Souls*. Rank had given the novel its felicitous title; Freud himself had read and enjoyed it in manuscript. So, a little later, had Ferenczi, who became Groddeck's close friend. "I am no literary critic," he wrote, reviewing the book in *Imago*, "and do not arrogate to myself a judgment on the aesthetic value of the novel. But I believe that it cannot be a poor book which succeeds, as this one does, in captivating the reader from beginning to end." Most of Freud's fellow analysts were more strait-laced: Ernest Jones disparaged it as "a racy book, with some bawdy passages"; Pfister was indignant. Psychoanalysts, the sworn enemies of gentility, were in their own way, it seemed, its victims and champions. Freud stood firm. He regretted to learn that Eitingon did not care for Groddeck. "He is a bit of a fantast," he admitted, "but an original fellow who has the rare gift of good humor. I should not like to do without him." A year later he was still, he told Pfister, "energetically defending Groddeck against your respectability. What would you have said as Rabelais's contemporary?" But Pfister was not so easily won over. He liked "fresh butter," he told Freud frankly in March 1921, "but Groddeck very often reminds me of rancid butter." After all, he knew the difference between Rabelais and Groddeck; the first was a satirist and did not pretend to be a scholar, while the latter was like a chameleon, oscillating between science and belles lettres. It was the mixture of genres that Pfister, and others, found so unsettling.

But Groddeck was more to Freud than simply a licensed jester who lightened the tone of an all-too-solemn profession. Around the time Groddeck published his *Seeker of Souls*, he began working on a book that would sum up his innovative teachings on psychosomatic medicine in language accessible to the common understanding; he cast them as a series of letters to a receptive woman friend. Whenever he had a batch of chapters done, he would send them to Freud, who was delighted with their fluency, their musical speech. "The five letters are charming," he told Groddeck in April 1921. They were more than charming; they were revolutionary. Interlarding his text with explicit anecdotes and speculations about pregnancy and birth, masturbation, love and hate, Groddeck returned over and over to the notion of an "It" that he had originated years before. This innocent-sounding term, borrowed from Nietzsche, was intended to cover a spectrum wider than the one psychoanalysts traditionally assigned to the domain of the unconscious. "I am of the opinion," Groddeck wrote in the second letter, "that man is animated by the Unknown. There is an It in him, something marvelous that regulates everything that he does and that happens to him. The sentence 'I live' is only conditionally correct; it expresses a little partial phenomenon of the fundamental truth: 'Man is lived by the It.'"

Freud had been thinking along similar, though far from identical, lines for some time. In April 1921, in his letter to Groddeck, he illustrated his tentative new view of the ego with a suggestive little diagram of mental structure, and commented, "The ego is in its depths also deeply unconscious and still flows together with the core of the repressed." That Freud inserted a revised version of this sketch in *The Ego and the Id* all of two years later is another indication of how long ideas sometimes germinated in him. But with these perceptions, the road to Freud's final view of the mind was open.

Yet Freud's "id" proved to be rather different from Groddeck's "It."* As early as 1917, Freud had told Lou Andreas-Salomé that Groddeck's " 'It' is more than our *Ucs*, not clearly delimited from it, but there is something real behind it." The differences between "It" and "id" became all the more

---

*Freud employed as his technical term a perfectly ordinary German word. Indeed, Freud's terms— *das Es, das Ich,* and *das Über-Ich*—literally translated, are "the It," "the I," and "the Over-I." But whatever the defects of the Latinate inventions of the *Standard Edition,* I have decided to stay with "id," "ego," and "superego," since across the years these three have lost their formidable and alienating quality.

visible in early 1923, when Groddeck published *The Book of the It,* and Freud his *The Ego and the Id* just a few weeks after. Reading Freud's succinct and definitive statement of his new position, Groddeck was a little disappointed and not a little irritated. He described himself to Freud, picturesquely, as the plow and Freud as the farmer who uses that plow. "In one thing we are in agreement, that we loosen the soil. But you want to sow and perhaps, if God and the weather permit it, to reap." In private he was less charitable and denounced Freud's book as "pretty" but "inconsequential." Fundamentally, he saw it as an attempt to take over ideas borrowed from Stekel and himself. "With all that, his Id has only limited value for the neuroses. He takes the step into the organic only secretly, aided by a drive of death or destruction taken from Stekel and Spielrein. The constructive aspect of my It he leaves aside, presumably to smuggle it in the next time." This was understandable, not wholly irrational, author's pique, and it suggests how hard it was for even a self-assigned disciple like Groddeck to sustain that role.

Freud for his part had no difficulty acknowledging the fertility of Groddeck's writings for his own thinking. The metaphors of plow and plowman were apt enough. But Freud insisted, and rightly, on the conflict between their conceptions. He had, to be sure, reiterated many times since the late 1890s that humans are buffeted by mental elements they do not know, let alone understand—elements they are not even aware of harboring. Freud's view of the unconscious and of repression was a forceful demonstration that psychoanalysis did not glorify reason as the undisputed master in its own house. But Freud did not accept Groddeck's dictum that we are lived by the It. He was a determinist, not a fatalist: there are forces inherent in the mind, concentrated in the ego, he believed, that give men and women mastery, however partial, over themselves and over the outside world. Sending Groddeck best wishes upon his sixtieth birthday, Freud captured the distance between the two of them in a playful sentence: "My Ego and my Id congratulate your It."*

More gravely, he dramatized that distance in the concluding paragraph of *The Ego and the Id:* "The id, to which we lead back in the end, has no means of showing the ego either love or hatred. It cannot say what it wants; it has not managed a unified will. Eros and the death drive struggle within it." One might represent the id "as though it stood under the domination of the mute but mighty death drives, which want to have peace and, following the hints

---

*This was, of course, also a graceful allusion to the titles of the books that the two men had published, just a month apart, three years earlier. But Freud's formula also tersely sums up the incompatibility of their ideas.

of the pleasure principle, bring Eros the troublemaker to rest. But we suspect that in this way we underestimate the role of Eros." Freud's account of Eros was a report on a struggle, not of a surrender.

SUNK IN HIS "familiar depression" after reading the proofs of *The Ego and the Id,* Freud denigrated it as "unclear, artificially put together, and nasty in its diction." He assured Ferenczi, "I am swearing to myself not to let myself get on to such slippery ice again." He thought that he had been in a steep decline since *Beyond the Pleasure Principle,* which had still been full of ideas and well written. As so often, he misjudged his own work; *The Ego and the Id* is among Freud's most indispensable texts. In the corpus of his writings, *The Interpretation of Dreams* and the *Three Essays on the Theory of Sexuality* must always hold pride of place, but whatever names Freud might call it, *The Ego and the Id* is a triumph of lucid mental energy. Freud's prewar protestations of being an old man, his tormented wrestling with personal loss, the sheer physical struggle to survive and help his family survive in postwar Vienna, should have furnished plentiful excuses for retirement. But what other discoverers would have left to their disciples, he felt obliged to do himself. If *The Ego and the Id* seems at all obscure, that is due to the extreme compression of his postwar work.

The preface to the little book has a reassuring air. Freud tells his readers that he is carrying further certain trains of thought started in *Beyond the Pleasure Principle,* now enriched with "diverse facts of analytic observation," and free of those borrowings from biology in which he had indulged before. Hence the essay "stands closer to psychoanalysis" than did his *Beyond.* He added that he was touching on theories that psychoanalysts had not worked on before, and that he had been unable to avoid "brushing against several theories advanced by nonanalysts or by former analysts in their retreat from analysis." But, he emphasized a little truculently, while he had always gladly recognized his obligations to earlier researchers, he felt no burden of gratitude now.

In the body of *The Ego and the Id,* Freud did find a place for crediting a "suggestion" by Groddeck, "an author who, from personal motives, protests in vain that he has nothing to do with severe, high science"—the suggestion that our mind *"is lived"* by "unknown, uncontrollable powers." To immortalize that insight, Freud proposed to follow Groddeck's nomenclature, though not quite his meaning, and to call a significant portion of the unconscious the "id." Groddeck might find this acknowledgment ungenerous. But Freud felt confident that his own work, with all his tentativeness, was highly original. It was "more of a synthesis than a speculation"—which, we might add, was all to the good.

Freud's work opens with a rehearsal of the known; that old psychoanalytic division between the conscious and the unconscious realms is absolutely fundamental to psychoanalysis. It is beyond question its "first shibboleth," not to be ignored: "In the end, the property of being conscious or not is the sole lantern in the darkness of depth psychology." Moreover, the unconscious is dynamic. It is no wonder that analysts first stumbled upon it through the study of repression: "The repressed is for us the prototype of the unconscious."

So far, Freud was on ground familiar to anyone acquainted with his thought. But he was using that ground only as a launching stage for his exploration of unknown terrain. Repression implies a repressing agent, and analysts have come to place that agent in "a coherent organization of mental processes," the ego. Yet the phenomenon of resistance, encountered in every psychoanalytic treatment, raises a difficult theoretical puzzle which Freud had identified years before; the patient who is resisting is often wholly unaware, or only dimly suspects in his neurotic misery, that he is obstructing the progress of his analysis. It follows that the ego, from which resistance and repression originate, cannot be wholly conscious. If it is not—Freud argued— the traditional psychoanalytic formula deriving neuroses from a conflict between the conscious and the unconscious must be defective. In his important paper on the unconscious, Freud had already intimated that his theory of neuroses required revision: "The truth is that not only the psychically repressed remains alien to consciousness, but also a part of the impulses dominating our ego." In short, "to the degree that we try to fight our way through to a metapsychological view of mental life, we must learn to emancipate ourselves from the significance of the symptom 'consciousness.' " This passage, written in 1915, stands as a reminder of how closely the old and the new were enmeshed in Freud's theorizing. But it was not until *The Ego and the Id* that he drew the full consequences of his insight.

Those consequences were drastic enough. Psychoanalysis now recognized that the unconscious does not coincide with the repressed; while everything that is repressed is unconscious, what is unconscious is not necessarily what has been repressed. "A part of the ego, too, God knows how important a part of the ego, can be unconscious, is surely unconscious." The ego began in the developing individual as a segment of the id, gradually differentiated itself, and was then modified by influences from the external world. Putting it rather too simply, "the ego represents what one may call reason and deliberation, in contrast to the id, which contains the passions." In the decade and a half left to him, Freud was not wholly consistent in deciding just what powers to assign to the ego and the id respectively. But he rarely doubted that normally the id holds the upper hand. The ego, he wrote in *The Ego and the Id,* in a famous analogy, "resembles the rider who is supposed to rein in the superior strength of the horse, with the difference that the rider does this with his own, the ego with borrowed strength"—borrowed from the id. Freud drove this analogy as far as it would go: "Just as there often remains nothing for the rider, if he does not want to be separated from the horse, but to lead it where it wants to go, so the ego, too, is accustomed to translating the will of the id into action as if that will were its own."

The id is not the ego's only troublesome adversary. We know that before the war in his paper on narcissism, and later in *Group Psychology,* Freud had recognized a special segment of the ego which critically watches over it. This he came to call the superego, and its elucidation occupied him throughout *The Ego and the Id.* The rider, the ego, is (one might say) not just desperately busy keeping a rein on his balky horse, the id, but is compelled at the same time to contend with a cloud of angry bees, the superego, swarming about him. We see the ego, Freud wrote, "as a poor thing, which is in threefold servitude and in consequence suffers under the menace of threefold dangers: from the external world, from the libido of the id, and from the severity of the superego." Exposed to anxieties corresponding to these dangers, the ego, for Freud, is a beleaguered, far from omnipotent negotiator earnestly trying to mediate among the forces that threaten it and that war with one another. It labors to make the id tractable to the pressures of the world and of the superego, and at the same time tries to persuade the world and the superego to comply with the id's wishes. Since it stands midway between id and reality, the ego is in danger of "succumbing to the temptation of becoming sycophantic, opportunistic, and mendacious, rather like a statesman who, with all his good insights, still wants to keep himself in the favor of public opinion." Yet this servile and pliant time-server controls the defense mechanisms, the ambiguous gift of anxiety, rational discourse, the ability to learn from experience. It may be a poor thing, but it is humanity's best instrument for coping with internal and external demands.

The implications of these metaphors are even more far-reaching than Freud then wholly recognized. Freud insisted that the ego is "first of all a bodily ego"; that is, it "is ultimately derived from bodily sensations." Yet it acquires not only much of its knowledge but much of its very shape from its commerce with the outside world—from its experiences with sights seen, sounds heard, bodies touched, pleasures explored. Freud did not explicitly pursue this line of inquiry in *The Ego and the Id,* though in his *Group Psychology* he had investigated some of the ego's involvements with external influences. In some of his last writings, though, he would take these ideas into larger domains.* His ego psychology served to transform the closet tragi-comedy of prewar psychoanalysis into a play with far wider reference—a richly costumed historical drama. The kind of analytic investigation into art, religion, politics, education, law, history, and biography that Freud found so fascinating was greatly eased by his perception of the ego as a rider who, however strenuous his double task of taming the id and appeasing the super-ego, keeps his eyes open to the surrounding countryside at the same time, and who, moreover, learns from experience as he gallops on.

To DEFINE THE EGO would have been enough for a single essay, but Freud went beyond his title. He should have called it, more accurately if less tersely, *The Ego, the Id, and the Superego.* For as we have already observed, in delineating the structure of the mind, Freud had to find a place for what he had been calling the ego ideal. If one uses conventional standards, he wrote, one will have to say that the "higher" one rises in the scale of mental activity, the closer one should approach consciousness. But it turns out quite differ-ently. As so often in *The Ego and the Id,* Freud appealed to clinical experi-ence. It teaches that some of the most elevated moral states, such as a sense of guilt, may never enter consciousness at all: "Not only what is lowest, but what is highest, too, in the ego can be unconscious." The strongest evidence in support of this assertion is that among some analysands "self-criticism and the conscience, which is to say, mental achievements valued extremely highly, are unconscious." In spite of their better judgment, therefore, psychoanalysts find themselves compelled to speak of an *"unconscious feeling of guilt."* Freud was confronting his readers with the superego.

The conscience and the superego are not quite the same thing. "The normal, conscious feeling of guilt (conscience)," Freud wrote, "offers inter-pretation no difficulties"; it is essentially "the expression of a condemnation of the ego by its critical judge." But the superego is a more intricate mental agency. Whether conscious or unconscious, it harbors the individual's ethical values on the one hand, and on the other, observes, judges, approves, or punishes conduct. In obsessional neurotics and melancholiacs, the resulting guilt feelings rise to awareness, but for most others they can only be inferred. Hence the psychoanalyst recognizes a relatively inaccessible source of tor-menting moral uneasiness which, precisely because it is unconscious, leaves only fragmentary, barely legible traces. The moral life of man, Freud sug-gested, reaches extremes much farther apart than moralists have commonly

*Psychoanalytically informed anthropologists, sociologists, and historians have been following up Freud's suggestions since the 1930s. They have felt licensed by Freud's new view of the ego as facing outward as well as inward, battling, bargaining, compromising with the environment no less than with the id and the superego.

believed. Hence the psychoanalyst can cheerfully endorse the apparent paradox that "normal man is not only much more immoral than he believes, but also far more moral than he knows."

Freud exhibited the phenomenon of unconscious guilt feelings by citing the example of patients in analysis whose symptoms become more severe when the analyst expresses hope for their eventual cure or praises the progress they are making. The better they seem to be, the worse they get. This is the notorious *"negative therapeutic reaction."* Freud insisted, as one would expect, that it is a mistake to dismiss this reaction as a kind of defiance, or as the patient's boastful attempt to show himself superior to his physician. Rather, one must read this rather perverse response as a serious, probably desperate message. The origin of the negative therapeutic reaction seemed to Freud beyond doubt: it stems from an unconscious feeling of guilt, from the desire for punishment. But it is quite beyond the patient's reach. "This sense of guilt is mute, it does not tell him that he is guilty; he does not feel guilty but ill."

In his *New Introductory Lectures on Psychoanalysis,* his last sustained statement of psychoanalytic theory, written a decade after *The Ego and the Id,* Freud lucidly summed up this analysis. Infants are not born with a superego, and its emergence is of great analytic interest. In Freud's view, the formation of the superego depends on the growth of identifications. Freud warned his readers that he was about to discuss a complicated issue, deeply enmeshed in the fortunes of the Oedipus complex. Those fortunes, to put it technically, involve the transformation of object choices into identifications. Children first choose their parents as objects of their love and then, forced to relinquish these choices as unacceptable, identify with them by taking their attitudes—their norms, injunctions, and prohibitions—into themselves. In short, having begun by wanting to *have* their parents, they end up wanting to *be* like them. But not precisely like them—they construct their identifications, as Freud put it, "not on the model of their parents but on that of the parental superego." In this way the superego becomes "the vehicle of tradition, of all the time-resistant valuations that have thus propagated themselves across generations." Hence the superego, at once preserving cultural values and attacking the individual it inhabits, becomes the agent of life and of death alike.

This is intricate enough, but matters are more intricate still: the superego, internalizing the parents' demands and ideals, consists of more than a mere residue of the id's earliest object choices, or of its identifications. It also includes what Freud called "an energetic reaction formation" against both. As before, in *The Ego and the Id* Freud explained his technical propositions in plain language: the superego "is not exhausted by the precept 'That (like the father) is how you *ought to be,*' but also embraces the prohibition 'That (like the father) you *may not* be—that is, you may not do everything he does; some things remain reserved to him.' " Retaining the impress of the father, the superego will produce a "conscience or, perhaps, the unconscious sense of guilt." In a word, the "ego ideal" turns out to be "the heir of the Oedipus complex." Thus man's "higher" nature and cultural achievements are explained by psychological means. This explanation, Freud intimated, had proved so elusive to philosophers or, for that matter, to other psychologists precisely because all of the id, most of the ego, and, indeed, most of the superego remain unconscious.*

AGED, DECREPIT, AND DECLINING—at least according to his own testimony— Freud had given the international psychoanalytic community much material for thought and for debate. He had changed a good deal, clarified much, but left some things uncertain. When in 1926 Ernest Jones sent him a paper on the superego, Freud acknowledged that "all the obscurities and difficulties you have marked out really exist." But he did not believe that Jones's semantic exercise provided the remedy. "What is needed is completely new investigations, accumulated impressions and experiences, and I know how hard these are to get." Jones's paper, he thought, "is a dark beginning in a knotty matter."

Much depended on how one chose to read *The Ego and the Id.* In 1930, Pfister told Freud that he had gone through the essay again, "perhaps for the tenth time, and was glad to see how you, since that work, have turned toward the gardens of humanity, after you had previously investigated only the foundations and the cloaca of their houses." That was a reasonable way of understanding Freud's new formulations, and partly warranted by his texts; Pfister, after all, was among Freud's many followers who did not believe in the "death drive." But a more somber interpretation was no less legitimate: Freud had, since his paper "Mourning and Melancholia," suggested that the superego, usually aggressive and punitive, often stood in the service of death more than in that of life. So the debate, far from being settled, went on.

*One further complication had to await Freud's reconsideration of the emotional development of boys and girls, to which he was beginning to devote his attention during these years. His conclusion, as we shall see, was that the superego differed considerably in the two sexes. See pp. 518–19.

NINE

Death against Life

INTIMATIONS OF MORTALITY

 In 1923, the year of *The Ego and the Id,* death visited Freud again, striking at one of his grandsons and making threatening flourishes at him. The calamities came as cruel surprises. Even if he intermittently complained about his stomach or his intestines, Freud continued to be vigorous enough during the working year. As in the past, he yearned for his lengthy summer vacation and liked to keep these months sacred; he reserved them for tramps in the mountains, cures at a spa, sight-seeing in Italy, and explorations of psychoanalytic theory. He rarely disrupted these holidays with analytic sessions, though he was now besieged by lucrative offers. In 1922, vacationing in Berchtesgaden, he "turned away the wife of a copper king," he told Rank, "who would certainly have covered the costs of my stay," as well as another American woman, "who would surely have paid $50 a day, since she was used to paying Brill $20 in New York for *half* an hour." He did not equivocate: "I will not sell my time here." His need for repose and recuperation, Freud told his friends more than once, was

urgent, and generally, "in the interest of rest and of making work possible," he stood firm.*

Despite his pleas, Freud's crowded schedule, like his undiminished output of letters and flow of important publications, attests to enviable reservoirs of energy and, on the whole, to sound health. But in the summer of 1922, he began to strike a rather more portentous note. In June, he told Ernest Jones that he had not felt tired "until now when the gloomy prospects of the political situation became obvious." By escaping Vienna, Freud escaped politics, the irreparable divisions between Austrian Socialists and Catholics and the ranting of political fanatics, at least for some time.† And indeed, in July, he could remark with palpable relief on the "delicious quiet" of his days at Bad Gastein; they were "free and fair," what with "the glorious air, the water, the Dutch cigars, and the good food, all resembling an idyll as closely as one can get in this Central European hell." But in August, writing to Rank from Berchtesgaden in strict confidence, he sounded less buoyant. Rank had inquired how he was, and Freud candidly responded by asking him to commit a pious deception: in writing to the others, he should describe Freud's health as just fine. Actually, he was anything but well. "That for some time now I have not felt quite certain of my health will not have escaped you." Freud had little inkling just how right he was to suspect his condition.

He soon had other reasons to feel doleful. In mid-August, his "best niece," Caecilie Graf, "a dear girl of 23," committed suicide. Pregnant and unmarried, she resolved her predicament by taking an overdose of veronal. In a loving and touching note to her mother, scribbled after she had taken the poison, she exonerated all others, including her lover, from blame. "I did not know," she wrote, "that dying is so easy and makes one so cheerful." Freud was "deeply shaken" by the event, he told Ernest Jones; nor did "the dark prospect of our country and all the uncertainties relating to the time" serve to allay his moodiness. But it was his own body that would betray him. In the spring of 1923, there was dismaying evidence that he might be suffering from cancer of the palate.

In mid-February 1923, Freud had detected what he called "a leukoplastic growth on my jaw and palate." A leukoplakia is a benign growth associated with heavy smoking, and Freud, in a panic that his physician might order him

___

*But at times he would break his resolution, especially when he was asked to analyze a "pupil"—a future analyst—rather than a "patient." Thus in 1928, he offered to analyze Philip Lehrman, an American physician, during the summer "on Mt. Semmering (2½ h. from Vienna) which with me is exceptional." (Freud to Lehrman, May 7, 1928. In English. A. A. Brill Library, New York Psychoanalytic Institute.)

†See pp. 446–47.

to give up his addiction, kept his discovery a secret from everyone for some time. But two months later, giving Ernest Jones the news in a half-reassuring, half-alarming letter on April 25, "after having lost a week or so by illness (operation)," he reported that the growth had just been removed. He had first noticed a painful swelling on his palate some years before, in late 1917. Ironically enough, it soon receded—after a patient had presented him with a much-desired box of cigars and he had lit up one of them. Now, in 1923, the growth had become too large and too persistent to be long neglected. "I was assured of the benignity of the matter but as you know nobody can guarantee its behaviour when it be permitted to grow further." Freud had been pessimistic from the start. "My own diagnosis had been epitelioma," a malignancy, "but was not accepted. Smoking," he added honestly, "is accused as the etiology of this tissue-rebellion." When he had finally felt ready to face the horrors of a cigarless future, he had consulted the dermatologist Maximilian Steiner, with whom he was on friendly terms. Steiner did ask him to give up smoking, but lied to Freud, trivializing the growth.

A few days later, on April 7, Felix Deutsch, who had been Freud's internist for some time, called on him, and Freud asked him to look at his mouth. "Be prepared," he warned his visitor, "to see something you won't like." Freud was right. "At the very first glance," Deutsch recalls, he saw that Freud's lesion was cancerous. But instead of pronouncing that dread word, or offering the technical diagnosis, epithelioma, to which Freud himself was inclined, Deutsch took refuge in the evasion "a bad leukoplakia." He advised Freud to stop smoking and to have the growth excised.

Freud was a physician surrounded by physicians. But he neither sought the opinion of an eminent specialist nor turned to an oral surgeon in whom he might have confidence. Instead, he chose Marcus Hajek, a rhinologist— another Fliess, one might say—although he had earlier expressed some skepticism about Hajek's competence. His choice—the mistake—was, as his daughter Anna said years later, Freud's alone. In the end, Hajek fully justified Freud's doubts. He knew the procedure he was recommending was merely cosmetic and really pointless, and casually performed the surgery in the outpatient department of his own clinic. Only Felix Deutsch accompanied Freud, and he did not stay through the operation; it was as though by treating the matter as a bagatelle he could wish away Freud's cancer. But something went terribly wrong on the operating table; Freud bled heavily both during and after the procedure and was made to lie down on a cot "in a tiny room in a ward of the hospital, since no other room was available." His only company was another patient, whom Anna Freud later described as a "nice, friendly" retarded dwarf.

The dwarf, in fact, may well have saved Freud's life. Martha and Anna

Freud had been asked to bring some necessities to the hospital, since Freud might have to spend the night. They found him blood-spattered, sitting on a kitchen chair. At lunchtime, no visitors were allowed in the ward, and they were sent home with the assurance that his condition was satisfactory. But when they came back in the early afternoon, they discovered that in their absence he had suffered an attack of copious bleeding. He had rung the bell for help, but the bell was out of order, so Freud, who was unable to make himself heard, was helpless. Fortunately, the dwarf rushed out to get the nurse, and with some difficulty the bleeding was brought under control.

After learning of this appalling episode, Anna Freud refused to leave her father. "The nurses," she recalls, "who did not have a good conscience about the failure of the bell, were very kind. They gave me black coffee and a chair and my father, the dwarf and I spent the night together. He was weak from loss of blood, half-drugged with medicines and in great pain." During the night, she and the nurse grew concerned over Freud's condition and sent for the house surgeon, but he refused to stir. In the morning, Anna Freud "had to hide while Hajek and his assistants made the usual rounds." Hajek showed no sign of contrition at his botched, nearly fatal performance, and later that day let Freud go home.

Since Freud could no longer keep the episode secret, he misled his correspondents, and to some measure himself, with sanguine bulletins. "I can report to you"—this to his "dearest Lou" on May 10, four days after his birthday—"that I can speak, chew, and work again; indeed, even smoking is permitted—in a certain moderate, cautious, so-to-speak petty-bourgeois way." The prognosis, he added, was good. Repeating the good news on the same day to Abraham, he proposed to "try your optimistic formula: many happy returns of the day and none of the new growth!" A little later, writing to his nephew in Manchester, he tried out an optimistic formula of his own: "Two months ago I had a growth removed from the soft palate which might have degenerated but had not yet."

Freud really knew better, even though no one had told him the truth. Hajek prescribed painful, futile X-ray and radium treatments, which Freud read as confirming his suspicion that his lesion was indeed cancerous. But the official deception went on; Hajek permitted Freud to take his usual summer holiday, though he did ask for frequent reports and a return visit in July for inspection of the scar. Freud went to Bad Gastein and then to Lavarone, across the Austrian border in Italy. But the summer brought no relief. His pains continued to make him so miserable that, at Anna's insistence, he asked Deutsch to come to Bad Gastein for a consultation. Deutsch did not delay, saw that a second, more radical operation would be required, but still withheld the whole truth from Freud.

DEUTSCH'S MISPLACED, KINDLY discretion, matched by that of the others, suggests a certain awe before the great man and a wishful unwillingness to accept his mortality. But Deutsch had other grounds for his inability to be candid. He worried that Freud's heart might not respond well to the truth. He had some hope that a second operation might eliminate all cause for alarm and let Freud live on without ever knowing that he had had cancer. But beyond that, Deutsch had been made uneasy by what he interpreted to be Freud's readiness for suicide; at their crucial meeting on April 7, Freud had asked Deutsch to help him "disappear from this world with decency" if he should be condemned to prolonged suffering. Informed openly that he had cancer, Freud might be tempted to make this implicit threat a reality.

As if this were not enough, Deutsch had, by the summer of 1923, yet one more reason for sparing his patient's sensibilities. Freud was in mourning for his beloved grandson Heinele, who had died in June. For some months the little four-year-old, the younger son of Freud's daughter Sophie, had been visiting in Vienna. The whole family adored him. "My little grandson here is the wittiest child of that age (4 y[ears])," the fond grandfather wrote Ferenczi in April 1923. "He is also correspondingly skinny and frail, nothing but eyes, hair, and bones." It was an affectionate report with sinister implications. "My eldest, Math[ilde], and her husband," Freud told friends in Budapest in early June, while the boy was dying, "have virtually adopted him and have fallen in love with him so thoroughly that one could not have predicted it. He was"—Freud, resigned, used the past tense—"indeed an enchanting fellow, and I myself know that I have hardly ever loved a human being, certainly never a child, so much as him."*

For a time, Heinele's high fever, headaches, and lack of specific symptoms had not permitted a diagnosis. But by June, miliary tuberculosis was a certainty, and this meant, in a word, that "the child is lost." As Freud was writing, Heinele lay in a coma, occasionally waking up, "and then he is again completely himself, so that it is hard to believe." Freud was suffering more than he would have thought possible. "I am taking this loss so badly, I believe that I have never experienced anything harder." He was working mechanically: "Fundamentally everything has lost its value."

He thought that his own illness intensified the shock he was feeling, but he felt worse about his grandson than about himself. "Don't try to live for ever," he wrote, quoting Bernard Shaw's preface to *The Doctor's Dilemma*, "you will not succeed." The end came on June 19. After Heinele, his "dear

*In 1896, when his father was near death, Freud had also used the past tense, a symptom that he had accepted the inevitable.

child" died, Freud, the man without tears, wept.* When in mid-July, Ferenczi, self-centered and a little obtuse, inquired why Freud had not congratulated him on his fiftieth birthday, Freud replied that he would not have
omitted this courtesy to a stranger. But he did not think he was exacting any
kind of revenge. "Rather, it is connected with my present distaste for life.
I have never had a depression before, but this now must be one." This is
a remarkable statement: since Freud had been recurrently afflicted with depressive moods, this bout must have been exceptionally severe. "I am still
being tormented in my snout," he told Eitingon in mid-August, "and obsessed by impotent longing for the dear child." He described himself as now
a stranger to life and a candidate for death. Writing to his cherished lifelong
friend Oscar Rie, he confessed that he could not get over the loss of the boy.
"He meant the future to me and thus has taken the future away with
him."

Or so it seemed to him in those days. Three years later, when Ludwig
Binswanger lost an eight-year-old son to tubercular meningitis and shared his
grief with Freud in a delicate letter, Freud responded with recollections of
1923. He was replying, he wrote, not with "a word of superfluous condolence,
but—yes, in fact only from an inner urge, because your letter has awakened
a memory in me—nonsense—which after all had never fallen asleep." He
recalled all his losses, especially the death of his beloved daughter Sophie, at
twenty-seven. "But," he added, "that I bore remarkably well. It was the year
1920, one was worn down from the misery of war, prepared for years to hear
that one had lost a son or even three sons. Thus, resignation to fate was well
prepared." But the death of Sophie's younger child had thrown him off his
balance. Heinele had stood in his mind "for all my children and other
grandchildren, and since then, since Heinele's death, I no longer care for my
grandchildren, but also take no pleasure in life. This is also the secret of the
indifference—people have called it bravery—toward the danger to my own
life." Empathizing with Binswanger, he found that his memories tore open
old wounds over and over. There was much vitality left in Freud, and much
affection. Yet Heinele would always remain his undisputed favorite. When
the little boy's older brother Ernst stayed with the Freuds in the summer of
1923 for two months, his grandfather at least, whatever the others might feel,
"did not find him a consolation to any amount."

---

*The psychotherapist Hilde Braunthal, who as a young student worked in Mathilde and Robert
Hollitscher's household, where Heinele spent his last months, thinks that Freud did not "see his
grandson too often. The Freuds lived around the corner of Hollitscher's. I often saw Freud on the
street walking with his dog. He looked very much absorbed in his thoughts." (Personal communication, January 4, 1986.) But even if he saw his grandson rarely, some of Freud's absorbing thoughts
seem to have been about him.

THIS, THEN, WAS Freud's situation in the summer of 1923 which Deutsch faced and could not face: Freud was vulnerable, mortal, like everyone else. Deutsch confided in Rank and, later, in Freud's palace guard, the Committee. That small group of Freud's intimates—Abraham, Eitingon, Jones, Rank, Ferenczi, Sachs—was then meeting in San Cristoforo, in the Dolomites, down a long hill from Lavarone, where Freud was staying. There was bad blood among them, and had been for some time, since the end of the war. The *Rundbriefe*, weekly circular letters they had begun to send around in October 1920, had not helped matters enough. The letters had been intended to keep Freud's closest adherents in Vienna, Budapest, Berlin, and London in steady touch with one another. "I am eager to learn," Freud had written to Ernest Jones when the letters were about to be launched, "how this institution will work. I expect it to prove very useful." But at about the same time, Jones had founded the *International Journal of Psycho-Analysis*, and his management of the journal had soured his relations with Rank. Jones resented what he interpreted as Rank's imperious interference with his editorial practice. Eager to minimize the Germanic contribution to psychoanalytic literature at a time when anti-German feeling was still running high, and just as eager to solicit American contributions, Jones had accepted several papers below the high standards the Viennese thought essential, and Rank did not hesitate to cavil at Jones's choices. Freud regarded such dissension as a threat to necessary peace. Dependent on Rank in matters of psychoanalytic business, he had praised Rank to Jones more than once, and gently chided Jones for his irritability. "I am nearly helpless and maimed when Rank is away," he wrote late in 1919; and, a little later, "in your remarks on Rank I noticed a harshness which reminded me of a similar mood regarding Abraham. You used kinder language even during the war. I hope nothing is wrong between you and ours." He faulted Jones for failing to control his passions and moods and hoped for better days.

But the irritations among the members of the Committee smoldered on. "Rank's hammer has once more fallen," Jones complained in a circular letter during the summer of 1922, "this time on London, and, as it seems to me, very unfairly." In contrast, there was a rapprochement between Jones and Abraham, who was growing disturbed by Rank's departures from orthodoxy in analytic technique. In the tight circle of seven, Freud was particularly close to Rank and Ferenczi, but he needed the others quite as much. Now, in the midsummer of 1923, beleaguered by sickness and bereavement, he hoped that at least a facade of amity could be restored in the warring Committee. "I am too old to give up old friends," he wrote shortly after. "If younger people would only think of that change in life they would find it easier to keep up good relations among themselves."

But for the moment at least Freud's hope that his younger adherents might adopt his pacific stance was unrealistic. On August 26, in an informative letter to his wife, Ernest Jones captured the atmosphere at San Cristoforo, at once angry and anxious. "The chief news is that F. has a real cancer, slowly growing & may last years. He doesn't know it & it is a most deadly secret." As for his quarrel with Otto Rank: the Committee had "spent the whole day threshing out the Rank-Jones affaire. Very painful, but I hope our relations will now be better." Yet he was aware that no improvement was in sight, for an unpleasant episode had exacerbated the tension. "I expect F[erenczi] will hardly speak to me, for Brill has just been there & told him I had said R[ank] was a swindling Jew." He partially disclaimed this bit of bigotry, insisting that it was greatly exaggerated—"stark übertrieben."

Whatever Jones had said, it must have been insulting enough.* Two days later, he reported, again to his wife, that the members of the Committee had spent "hours of talking & shouting till I thought I was in Bedlam." The group decided "that I was in the wrong in the Rank-Jones affaire, in fact that I am neurotic." He was the only gentile in the group, and felt it acutely. "A Jewish family council sitting on one sinner must be a great affair, but picture it when the whole five insist on analysing him on the spot & all together!" While he professed to be "English enough to take it all in good humour," and not to have become irritated, he admitted that the day had been quite an experience, an "Erlebnis."

In the midst of all this feuding, the Committee members had been shocked to learn of Freud's cancer. Their dilemma was acute. It was obvious that Freud needed radical surgery, but not so obvious how—and how much— he should be told. Freud had been planning to show Rome to his daughter Anna, and they were reluctant to spoil, or abort, that long-planned holiday. In the end, the physicians on the Committee—Abraham, Eitingon, Jones, Ferenczi—more or less prevailed, aided by good sense; they gravely urged Freud to return to Vienna for further surgery after his Italian excursion. Yet they still kept the full diagnosis from him; even Felix Deutsch could not bring himself to reveal the unvarnished truth. His ill-judged delicacy was to cost him Freud's confidence and his place as Freud's personal physician. He had failed to appreciate Freud's capacity for assimilating bad news, and his resent-

---

*On the basis of the fragmentary documentation now available, Jones's remark is impossible to reconstruct. In 1924, after Rank had drawn on himself not only Jones's wrath but that of all the others, including Freud, Freud ruefully acknowledged that Jones had been right about Rank all along. Writing to Abraham, Jones reproduced that part of Freud's letter to him and commented, "So even the part of my famous remark to Brill, which I had not the courage to defend at San Cristoforo, is at least justified (I am not of course referring to the erroneous addition to it made by Brill)." (Jones to Abraham, November 12, 1924. Karl Abraham papers, LC.)

ment at feeling patronized.* The members of the Committee, too, came to incur Freud's displeasure; when, years later, he discovered their well-meaning deception, he was furious. "With what right?" he exclaimed to Ernest Jones—*"Mit welchem Recht?"* In Freud's eyes, no one had the right to lie to him, not even from the most compassionate of motives. To tell the truth, however appalling, was the greatest kindness.

After the meeting of the Committee at which Deutsch reported on Freud's condition, Anna Freud joined the group for dinner, and in the evening, in the moonlight, she climbed up the hill to Lavarone with Deutsch and drew him out. Suppose she and her father had a particularly good time in Rome, she ventured, "half jokingly," might they not stay a while longer and not come home as planned? Appalled, Deutsch earnestly begged her not even to think of it. " 'You must do nothing of the kind,' " he said energetically, " 'on no account, promise me not to.' " That, Anna Freud commented long afterwards, "was plain enough."† Yet Freud's longed-for trip to Rome with his youngest daughter went forward. As he anticipated, she proved as observant in, and enthusiastic about, the city as he had always been. He reported to Eitingon from Rome on September 11 that "Anna is savoring it to the full, finds her way about brilliantly, and is equally receptive to all sides of Roman polydimensionality." After his return, he told Ernest Jones that in their "splendid time at Rome," his youngest daughter "did really show to her advantage."

Now at last the truth that Freud had long suspected was conveyed to him. On September 24 he stated it to his nephew in Manchester in somewhat veiled language: "I have not overcome the effects of my last operation in the mouth, have pains and difficulty in swallowing and am not yet sure of the future." Two days later, his position was clear enough. He set it out fully and freely to Eitingon: "I can today satisfy your need to have news of me. It has been decided that I must undergo a second operation, a partial resection of the upper jaw, since the dear new formation has emerged there. The operation will be performed by Professor Pichler," an eminent oral surgeon. He was the best possible choice, Felix Deutsch's recommendation. Hans Pichler, Freud told Eitingon, was "the greatest expert in these things; he will also

---

*Deutsch, Anna Freud observed years later, "had underrated" her father's "sense of independence and his ability to meet the truth." (Anna Freud to Jones, January 4, 1956. Jones papers, Archives of the British Psycho-Analytical Society, London.) "What my father did not forgive was the 'Bevormundung.' " (Anna Freud to Jones, January 8, 1956. Ibid.) After a time of strain, which Deutsch took very hard, Freud and Deutsch repaired their friendship. But Freud turned to other physicians for professional attention.

†Her own feeling about the episode was mixed: "I got an unforgettable trip to Rome out of it and I am grateful still." (Anna Freud to Jones, January 8, 1956. Ibid.)

make the prosthesis needed afterwards. He promises that I shall be able to eat and talk well in about four to five weeks."

Actually, there were two operations, performed on October 4 and 12. They were generally successful, but as drastic invasions they left Freud for some time unable to speak and to eat. He had to be fed through a nasal tube. Yet a week after his second operation, still in the hospital, he sent an irrepressible note, in telegram style, to Abraham: "Dear incorrigible optimist: Today tampon renewed, got up, still existing remnants stuck into clothes. Thanks for all the news, letters, greetings, newspaper clippings. Once I can sleep without an injection I shall soon go home." Nine days later he was discharged. But his wrestling match with death was not yet over.

THE MATCH PROVED grueling, and the adversary cunning and merciless. Freud prepared himself for the worst. At the end of October, considering that his "current condition" might prevent him from continuing to earn money, he wrote some codicils to his will, in the form of a letter to his son Martin. His principal concerns were for his wife and his daughter Anna: he asked that his children renounce their share in their "anyhow modest inheritance" in favor of their mother, and that Anna's dowry be increased to £2,000. Then, in mid-November, Freud took a very different step, understandable if less rational than the clarification of his will. He submitted to a minor operation on his testicles, called technically a "ligature of the vas deferens on both sides," identified with the controversial endocrinologist Eugen Steinach. The procedure had gained a certain vogue for supposedly aiding the restoration of fading sexual potency, but beyond that some authorities recommended it as a mobilization of the body's resources. Freud, who believed in the operation, hoped that it might serve to bar the recurrence of cancer and might even improve his "sexuality, his general condition and his capacity for work." After it was over, he was ambiguous about its effects, but at least some of the time he seems to have felt that it had actually made him feel younger and stronger.

More to the point, in the same month Pichler discovered some remaining cancerous tissue, and bravely told Freud that he needed another operation, to which Freud just as bravely submitted. Yet he acknowledged that the news was a grave disappointment. Clearly he had burdened his surgeon with magical expectations of omnipotence. He had, he told Rank in late November, "emotionally leaned on Prof. Pichler very much"; but this latest operation had brought a rude awakening and a "loosening of the homosex[ual] bond." Yet, however complicated his feelings toward his surgeon, the reality is that Pichler did not detect another cancerous growth until 1936.

Still, from 1923 on, Freud repeatedly developed benign or precancerous leukoplakias, which had to be treated or excised. Pichler was skillful and kind,

but the thirty or more minor operations he performed—some not so minor—
to say nothing of the scores of fittings, cleanings, and refittings of Freud's
prosthesis, were invasive and irksome procedures. Often they hurt him very
much.* The pleasure that continued smoking gave Freud, or, rather, his
incurable need for it, must have been irresistible. After all, every cigar was
another irritant, a little step toward another painful intervention. We know
that he admitted being addicted to cigars, and that he thought smoking
ultimately a substitute for that prototype of all addictions, masturbation.
Plainly there were depths to his mind that his self-analysis had never reached,
conflicts it had never been able to resolve. Freud's inability to give up smoking
vividly underscores the truth in his observation of an all-too-human disposition he called knowing-and-not-knowing, a state of rational apprehension that
does not result in appropriate action.

FREUD IN LATE 1923 was like an invalid athlete in need of drastic physical
rehabilitation. Once a masterly lecturer and brilliant conversationalist, he
trained himself to speak once again, but his voice never really recovered its
clarity and resonance. The operations also affected Freud's hearing; he complained of a "steady rushing sound," and gradually became almost deaf in his
right ear. Hence the couch was moved from one wall to another so that he
could listen with his left. Eating presented disagreeable difficulties, and for
the most part he now avoided dining in public. The prosthesis, the device
that kept the oral and the nasal cavities separate—Jones describes it as a huge
monstrous thing, "a sort of magnified denture"—was a torment to put in or
take out, often chafing and irritating, often enough painful. In the years that
remained to him, Freud changed that magnified denture more than once,
going to Berlin in the late 1920s to be fitted for yet another. Some measure
of discomfort rarely left him. Yet he refused to surrender to pathos; Freud
adjusted to his new condition with a certain jauntiness. "Dear Sam," he wrote
to Manchester in January 1924, dictating the letter to his daughter Anna, "I
am glad to let you know that I am rapidly recovering and was able to take
up my work with this new year. My speech may be impaired but both my
family and my patients say it is quite intellegible."

His hard-won psychoanalytic poise served him well. He had witnessed
deaths in the family, but fortunately births crowded in upon them. His three
sons were enlarging the Freud clan: Ernst "announced to us the birth of his

---

*The operations that Freud was compelled to undergo were of three types, as indicated by the way
they were performed: in Dr. Pichler's office, with local anesthesia; in the Sanatorium Auersperg with
local anesthesia and "sleep induced beforehand"; and in the sanatorium with general anesthesia.
(Anna Freud to Jones, January 8, 1956. Ibid.) In addition, Freud underwent regular examinations
in a little room fitted out next to his consulting room.

third son on the 24th of April," he informed Samuel Freud in the spring of 1924. "There are two more children on the way, Martin's second and Oliver's first (at Düsseldorf). So there is growth and decay in the family as in plants, a comparison you may find in the old Homer." In October 1924, Alix Strachey, a gifted and irreverent observer of the analytic scene, reported from Berlin to her husband James at home in London that Helene Deutsch "gave me the most glowing reports—as they all did—of Freud's health. It appears that he's once more installed in the chair at the Vereinigungen & talks away as usual & is in very high spirits." Five months later, early in 1925, she informed her husband that while Freud continued to have difficulties in speaking, "Anna says his general health leaves nothing to be desired."

ANNA

 Anna Freud's ascendancy over her father had been marked even before 1923; after his operations in that year, it was beyond dispute and beyond challenge. In April, following Freud's appalling day at Hajek's clinic, his daughter Anna, rather than his wife, had stayed with him through the night. This act sealed a shift in the Freuds' family constellation toward Anna as its emotional anchor.* The year before, in late March 1922, when Anna was away tending her brother-in-law Max Halberstadt and his two sons, Freud had informed Ferenczi that "our house is now desolate, for Anna, who by the nature of things dominates it more and more, has been in Hamburg for 4 weeks." Three weeks earlier, when she had been gone for only a week, Freud "certified" to her in an affectionate letter that "one misses you greatly. The house is very lonely without you and there's no complete substitute anywhere."

At heart, Anna would have preferred to stay with her father. She was most

---

*Her mother, though, retained firm control of domestic affairs. When Anna, away on a trip in 1920, wrote that she wanted to exchange one of her two rooms at Berggasse 19 for another, in order to work and live in two adjacent rooms, Freud, sympathetic to her proposal, advised her to consult her mother. He reported that her aunt Minna was willing to trade her room for one of Anna's, but that her mother did not want to hear of any drastic changes in the apartment: she was reluctant to spend money for new wallpaper, since she would really rather move to the suburbs. Such a move, Freud told Anna, was thoroughly impractical. Still, she must write to her mother directly. "I cannot force her," he wrote, "have always let her have her way in the house." (Freud to Anna Freud, October 12, 1920. Freud Collection, LC.) In the end, Anna prevailed.

anxious—had been anxious since her adolescence—to take care of him. In 1920 she had spent part of the summer in Aussee, helping to nurse the Freuds' old friend Oscar Rie during his convalescence from a serious illness. Rie had told his family nothing about his condition until he could keep it a secret no longer. His reserve and, she thought, misplaced considerateness made Anna think of her father, as she did in any event much of the time. She was determined not to let Freud adopt the same tight-lipped policy. "Promise me," she implored him, "that if you should fall ill some day and I'm not there, you will write me about it immediately, so that I can come?" Otherwise, she added, she would have no peace anywhere. She had wanted to broach the subject in Vienna, before she left for Aussee, but had in the end been too shy. Now, three years later, after her father's first operation, there was no room for shyness and she repeated her offer insistently. Freud, demurring mildly, complied. "I don't want to yield to your wish right away," he replied. "You should not prematurely take over the sad function of nursing old, ailing parents." He was writing from Vienna, where Hajek was examining his palate. But, he added, he was willing to make one concession: "You will be summoned by telegraph, immediately, if he should keep me in Vienna for any reason." Anna Freud, far more than Martha, was now in charge of him.

Quite naturally, then, in the summer of 1923 she appears to have been the first in the family to discover the truth about her father's cancer. And Freud's correspondence of this time amply documents how much she had come to mean to him. When, in mid-August, Freud reported to Oscar Rie on his wife and his sister-in-law, he confined himself to their health, but when he spoke of Anna, his tone changed. "She is flourishing and a great mainstay in all things." On that holiday she took with her father in Rome in September, a kind of last fling for him before his second operation, she showed herself, we know, much to her advantage.

Freud left no doubt that he was attached to all his children and concerned about them. We have seen that when his adolescent son Martin, humiliated at a skating rink, needed paternal reassurance, he was there, patient, unreproachful, responsive.* When his daughter Mathilde fell ill unexpectedly in the summer of 1912, he canceled a trip to London as a matter of course, much as he had been looking forward to another English visit. Again, he was visibly fond of his attractive "Sunday child" Sophie and, more discreetly, worried about the neurotic travail of his son Oliver.† During the war, as we know,

---

*See pp. 161–62.

†In the early 1920s, Oliver Freud was in analysis with Franz Alexander in Berlin. Some years later, writing to Arnold Zweig, Freud spoke appreciatively of Oliver's "extraordinary" gifts, and the range and reliability of his knowledge. "His character is faultless. Then the neurosis came over him and stripped off all the blooms." Being "unfortunately strongly inhibited neurotically," he had had "bad

he did not keep his fears for his sons at the front bottled up within himself, but sprinkled his letters with details on their whereabouts and their well-being as though these must be of absorbing interest to all his correspondents. "In a large family," he once philosophized to an analysand, the American physician Philip Lehrman, "one can always count on mishaps. Whoever has been assigned, like you, the role of general helper in the family—a role also familiar to me—has been provided with worries and interests for all his life." He could joke about a father's role—a little. "Too bad, as they say in your country," he wrote Lehrman, "that you get no peace in your family! But when does one of us Jews get left in peace by his family? Never, as long as he has not found eternal peace." Whatever the claims of his children on his emotions, Freud tried not to play favorites.

Yet with all his evenhandedness, Freud came to recognize that his last child, Annerl, was very special. "The little one," he observed to Ferenczi during the war, using a favorite diminutive for her, "is a particularly dear and interesting creature." She was, he came to admit, perhaps more dear, certainly more interesting, than her brothers and sisters. "You have turned out a little differently from Math[ilde] and Sophie," he told Anna in 1914, and "have more intellectual interests and will not be quite so satisfied with some purely feminine activity."

FREUD'S RECOGNITION OF Anna's unusual intelligence, and of her special place in his life, is mirrored in the particular tone—affectionate counsel laced with near-analytic interpretations—he adopted with her. It was a tone largely absent from his converse with his other children. In turn, Anna's claim to particular intimacy with her father was persistent and strong, and grew stronger. As a young girl, she was intermittently frail, and was repeatedly sent to health resorts for thorough rest, salutary walks, and some extra pounds to fill out her all too slender shape. Her letters of this period abound with news about a kilogram gained in one week, half a kilogram in another. And they are saturated with longing for her father. She was getting better, she reassured her "dear Papa" writing from a spa in the summer of 1910, when she was fourteen, "gaining weight and am already stout and fat." She was also, at this unripe age, motherly with her father: "Won't you upset your stomach again in the Harz Mountains?" She hoped that her brothers, "the boys," would watch over him, but left little doubt that she would take better care of him than they did. In general, she was relentlessly competitive with her siblings.

---

luck" in life. Freud found Oliver's problematic life, he told Zweig, a heavy burden to bear. (Freud to Arnold Zweig, January 28, 1934. By permission of Sigmund Freud Copyrights, Wivenhoe.)

"I, too, would very much like to travel alone with you, just as Ernst and Oli are doing now." And she showed a precocious interest in Freud's writings: she had asked her "very nice" Dr. Jekels to let her read "Gradiva," but he was willing to do so only if Freud gave his permission. She liked nothing better than the fond nicknames he bestowed on her: "Dear Papa," she wrote in the following summer, "it's been a long time since somebody called me 'Black Devil,' and I miss it very much."

Most of her ailments, such as back pains, struck her father as psychosomatic, accompanied as they were by brooding and by ruminations she herself severely criticized as pointless.* He encouraged her to inform him about her symptoms. She did not disappoint him; early in 1912, still miserable, she freely canvassed her state of mind with her father. She was neither sick nor well, she wrote him, and uncertain just what she was suffering from. "But somehow something comes out of me," and then she would become fatigued and worry about all sorts of things, including her idleness.† She longed to be reasonable, like her oldest sister, Mathilde. "I want to be a sensible human being or at least become one." But she had her bad days. "You know," she reminded her father, "I would not have written you all this, because I don't like to plague you." But, then, he had asked her to, and, she added in a postscript, "I could not write you any more because I don't know anything more myself, but I certainly don't keep any secrets from you." If only, she pleaded, he would write her again soon: "Then I will be sensible, if you help me a little."

Freud was only too willing to help. By 1912, now that Mathilde was married and Sophie was getting ready to follow her sister's example, Anna had become, as he liked to call her, his "dear only daughter." In November, when Anna had settled down to spend several months at the popular north Italian resort of Merano, he admonished her to relax and enjoy herself; once she had got used to laziness and sunshine, he told her, she would surely gain weight and feel better. For her part, Anna reminded her father how much she missed him. "I always eat as much as I can and am quite sensible," she wrote Freud from Merano. "I think about you a lot and greatly look forward to a letter from you when you have time to write." This was a constant theme; her father

---

*Some of these health problems, like difficulties with menstruation, persisted. "I am particularly happy," she wrote her father in 1920, "that I became unwell yesterday without any abnormal added medication, and tolerate it well this time." (Anna Freud to Freud, November 16, 1920. Freud Collection, LC.)

†This, too, was a persistent theme in her correspondence with her father. "Why is it that I am always so happy," she unhappily asked him in the summer of 1919, "when I have nothing to do? After all, I do like to work; or does it only seem that way?" (Anna Freud to Freud, August 2, 1919. Ibid.)

was *such* a busy man! When she offered to come home, he urged her to stay longer, even if that meant missing Sophie's wedding, which was scheduled for mid-January 1913. This was a shrewd therapeutic suggestion. Anna had confessed earlier that her "endless quarrels" with Sophie were "terrible" for her since she liked and admired Sophie who, however, had no use for her. Such bursts of self-denigration were, and long remained, characteristic of her. Not even her father, whose influence on her was often conclusive, could wholly persuade her otherwise.

But he tried. He had decided that Anna was old enough to absorb some psychoanalytic truths; she was, in any event, examining her own state of mind. Clearly, her sister's forthcoming wedding aroused powerful and conflicting emotions in her. She acknowledged that she wanted both to come home to see Sophie married and to stay away: on the one hand, she was glad she could rest luxuriously in Merano; on the other, she was sorry not to see Sophie before her sister left the parental home. But in any event, she was "far more sensible" than she had been. "You would be astonished how much, but from a distance you can't notice it. And to become as sensible as you think," she concluded with an almost audible sigh, "is much too hard, and I don't know if I will learn it." Such self-examinations gave Freud his opportunity. Her various aches and pains, he told her, were psychological in origin; they sprang from mixed feelings about Sophie's wedding and about Max Halberstadt, Sophie's future husband. "After all, you know you are a little odd." He was not disposed to blame her for her "age-old jealousy of Sophie," which seemed to him largely of Sophie's making. But, he thought, she had transferred that jealousy to Max, and that tormented her. And she was concealing something from her parents, "perhaps, too, from yourself." Gently, he urged her to "keep no secrets. Don't be bashful." He sounded much like an analyst advising his analysand to speak freely. But he concluded as a father: "After all, you should not forever remain a child, but acquire the courage of courageously looking life, and whatever it brings, in the eye."

IT WAS ONE THING for Freud to encourage Anna to grow up; it was quite another for him to *let* her grow up. She remained, for years, "the little one." The fond appellation "my dear only daughter," which he had playfully applied to her while Sophie was engaged, reappeared regularly after Sophie was married. Anna was, in March 1913, his "little, now only daughter," his "little only daughter" whom he took traveling to Venice that spring on a short holiday, which Anna breathlessly anticipated and immensely enjoyed. An Italian trip, "with you," she exclaimed, "makes it all the more beautiful than it would have been otherwise." Later that year, Freud confessed to

Ferenczi that his "little daughter" Anna had led him to thoughts of Cordelia, King Lear's youngest,* thoughts that generated a moving meditation on the role of women in a man's life and death, "The Theme of the Three Caskets," published in the same year. There is a charming photograph of Freud and Anna as a companionable pair taken in the Dolomites during this time: Freud in hiking outfit with jaunty hat, belted jacket, knickerbockers, and sturdy boots, a serene Anna on his arm, the simple aproned dirndl dress suiting her slim frame.

As late as the summer of 1914, when Anna was almost nineteen, Freud still called her "my little daughter" to Ernest Jones. But this time he had an ulterior motive. He was protecting Anna from Jones's amorous propensities. "I know from the best sources," he alerted her on July 17, as she prepared to set off for England, "that Dr. Jones has serious intentions of seeking your hand." He declared himself reluctant to interfere with the freedom of choice that her two older sisters had enjoyed. But since she had had as yet no proposals in her "young life," and lived "even more intimately" with her parents than had Mathilde and Sophie, Freud thought it right for her to make no major decisions without "being sure of our (in this case, my) consent beforehand."

Freud took good care to commend Jones as a friend and "very valuable co-worker." But, after all, "this might be a temptation the more for you." Hence he felt obliged to voice the two objections he saw to a match between Jones and his "only daughter." First, "it is our wish that you should not commit yourself or marry before you have seen, learned, lived a little more." Surely, she ought not to think of marriage for at least five years. And, Freud told Anna, speaking from the depths of his own painful memories of his long, frustrating wait for Martha Bernays, she ought to be spared a lengthy engagement. Second, Freud reminded her, Jones was thirty-five—which made him almost twice her age. Though doubtless a "tender, goodhearted" man who "would love his wife dearly and be very grateful for her love," he needed an older, worldly woman. Jones, Freud noted, had worked himself up from a "very simple family and from difficult life's circumstances"; he was largely wrapped up in science and "lacked the tact and the finer considerateness" that someone like Anna, a "spoiled," a "very young and somewhat reserved girl," had a right to expect from her husband. Indeed, Freud added, driving the knife in deeper, Jones was "far less independent and far more in need

---

*The theme of the youngest daughter never lost its attraction for Freud. In 1933, when Ernest Jones announced that his wife was pregnant, Freud replied, "If this should be a youngest, the youngest are, as you can see in my family, not exactly the worst." (Freud to Jones, January 13, 1933. Freud Collection, D2, LC.)

of moral support" than first impressions would suggest. And so, Freud concluded, Anna ought to be prudent, genial, and amiable with Jones, but avoid being alone with him.

Evidently, giving Anna these carefully pondered instructions did not allay Freud's anxiety. Five days later, on July 22, after she had landed in England, he gently, tersely, reiterated his earlier directives. She ought not to evade Jones's company; she should be as free and unembarrassed with him as possible, and put herself "on a footing of friendship and equality," which, he told Anna, is particularly easy to manage in England. Yet this second caution, too, failed to calm his worries. On the same day, he wrote Jones "a few lines," as he promptly notified Anna, "that will discourage any courting yet avoid all personal offense."

These "few lines" amount to a curious document. "Perhaps you know her not enough," Freud told Jones. "She is the most gifted and accomplished of my children, and a valuable character besides, full of interest for learning, seeing sights and getting to understand the world." This was nothing more than what he had already told Anna directly. But then Freud's tone shifted to what one can only call Victorian idealization. "She does not claim to be treated as a woman, being still far away from sexual longings and rather refusing man. There is an outspoken understanding between me and her that she should not consider marriage or the preliminaries before she gets 2 or 3 years older. I don't think she will break the treaty." This "treaty," we know, was imaginary; there was only Freud's firm suggestion to Anna that she postpone thinking seriously about men. No doubt his stratagem was neither farfetched nor unreasonable: Freud would tell others, and Anna herself, that she was emotionally younger than her age. More important, though, Freud was putting Jones on notice, not very subtly, to leave his daughter in peace. Yet to claim that Anna, a fully grown young woman, lacked any sexual feelings was to sound like a conventional bourgeois who had never read Freud. One might take this to be part of Freud's hint that for Jones to put his hands on Anna would be equivalent to child abuse—a veiled warning to which Jones, in view of the charges that had driven him from England in the previous decade, could only be extremely sensitive. But Freud's denial of his daughter's sexuality is transparently out of character; it reads like the surfacing of a wish that his little girl remain a little girl—*his* little girl.*

Anna's response to her father's entreaties added up to another exercise in low self-esteem. "What you write me about the regard I enjoy in the family,"

---

*The only comparable moment in Freud's writings, in which he denies his own insights with the same decisiveness, is the passage in *The Interpretation of Dreams* in which he speaks of the child's having no sexual feelings. (See p. 144.)

she wrote him from England, "would be very nice, but I cannot quite believe that it is true. For instance, I don't believe that it would make a great deal of difference at home if I were no longer around. I believe that I alone would sense the difference." Precisely how much Ernest Jones understood of this little drama, of which he was the involuntary protagonist, is hard to say. But in some ways he saw Freud's involvement with his last daughter very clearly. Anna, he replied to Freud, "has a beautiful character and will surely be a remarkable woman later on, provided that her sexual repression does not injure her. She is of course," he added, "tremendously bound to you, and it is one of those rare cases where the actual father corresponds to the father-imago." It was a perceptive observation, one that cannot have surprised Freud. But he was not prepared to accept its implications.

ANNA FREUD, AS WE KNOW, got through her English adventure safely. She returned home a month later after some intensive sight-seeing, some of it in Ernest Jones's company, unmarried and untouched. Her next few years— years of war, revolution, and slow reconstruction—read in retrospect like a rehearsal for a career as a psychoanalyst. But her route to becoming a Freudian was somewhat circuitous. She was trained as a teacher, passed her examinations, and worked, in her early twenties, in a girls' school. But it was plain that she was not destined to remain a teacher forever.

As a young girl, she recalled years later, she would sit outside her father's library at Berggasse 19 and "listen to his discussion with visitors. That was very useful." The straightforward study of her father's books was even more useful. During her long stay in Merano through the winter of 1912–13, she reported that she read "some" of them. "You must not be shocked about that," she wrote a little defensively. "After all, I am grown up now, and so it's no wonder that I am interested in them." She read on, asked her father to explain such technical terms as "transference," and in 1916 attended the second series of Freud's introductory lectures, on dreams, at the university. Those didactic performances did much to confirm her burgeoning ambition to become a psychoanalyst—like her father. In the following year, when she audited Freud's last series of lectures, on neuroses, she spotted among her fellow listeners Helene Deutsch wearing her white doctor's coat like a professional badge. Suitably impressed, she came home and told her father that, to prepare herself for an analyst's vocation, she wanted to go to medical school. Freud offered no objection to her long-range plans, but balked at her desire to become a physician; Anna Freud was neither the first nor the last among Freud's adherents whom he persuaded to follow a career as a lay analyst.

Seconded by a willing entourage, Freud now drew Anna increasingly into his professional family, and sometime in 1918, he took her into analysis. She was invited to the international congress of psychoanalysts in Budapest that year, but could not attend, prevented by her duties as a teacher. Two years later, when the analysts convened at The Hague, she was more fortunate, and accompanied her proud father to the scientific sessions and to congenial meals. Her letters match her increasing psychoanalytic sophistication. For some years, she had sent her father her most interesting, mainly frightening dreams; now she analyzed them and he responded with interpretations. She observed herself making slips of the pen. She was among the first to read her father's new publications.* She attended psychoanalytic meetings, and not in Vienna alone. Writing to her father from Berlin in November 1920, she offered some pointed, knowing appraisals of his followers and openly envied those, like "little Miss Schott," who were already analyzing children. "You see," she added in self-reproach, "everybody can do much more than I." By this time, she had given up her post as a teacher, with mixed feelings,† and was making herself into a psychoanalyst.

Her first "patients" were her nephews, her sister Sophie's orphaned little boys, Ernstl and Heinele. In 1920, she spent a good deal of time with them in Hamburg and, during the summer, in Aussee. Ernstl, now past six, whom her father liked far less than the winning, sickly Heinele, was her particular concern. She got him to tell her stories, and canvassed with him such grave mysteries as where babies come from and what death means. These informative confidential conversations enabled her to analyze the little boy's fear of the dark as a consequence of his mother's warning—really a threat—that if he continued "to play with his member, he would get very sick." Not all of Freud's family, it seems, obeyed Freud's pedagogic injunctions.

Anna did not stop with these tentative child analyses. She began to analyze the dreams of others, and in the spring of 1922, she wrote a psychoanalytic paper which she hoped to present as her entrance ticket to the Vienna Psychoanalytic Society—provided her father consented. That membership was something, she told him, that she desired very much. At the end of May her wish became reality. The paper, on beating fantasies, drew in part on her own inner life, but the subjective provenance of her argument made her contribution no less scientific. "My daughter Anna," her father, much pleased, informed Ernest Jones in early June, "gave a good lecture last

---

*On November 16, 1920, writing from Berlin, she reported to Freud, "I am reading your new work [*Beyond the Pleasure Principle*] with very great pleasure. I think the ego ideal is so congenial to me." (Freud Collection, LC.)

†In August she reported that "up to now, I have not regretted giving up the school for a minute." (Anna Freud to Freud, August 21, 1920. Ibid.) But in October she complained to her father that she was miserable, and missed her school. (See Freud to Anna Freud, October 25, 1920. Ibid.)

Wednesday." Two weeks later, having fulfilled that formal obligation, she became a full-fledged member of the Society.

After this, Anna Freud's reputation among Freud's intimates grew rapidly. As early as 1923, Ludwig Binswanger observed to Freud that his daughter's style was no longer distinguishable from his own. And in late 1924, Abraham, Eitingon, and Sachs wrote from Berlin to suggest that she be co-opted to the inner circle; she should "not merely work as her father's secretary," as she had done for years, but participate in their deliberations and, on occasion, in their meetings. To be sure, this was the kind of tribute which, the writers knew, would delight Freud. But the proposal also reflects the trust her father's most valued colleagues had come to place in Anna Freud's judgment.

WHILE FREUD ENCOURAGED his daughter's professional aspirations without reserve, he remained unreconciled to the shape of her private life. Her emotions were not stunted or forced to go underground; Anna Freud visibly enjoyed life and the pleasures of friendship. Her father recognized her need for companionship and schemed to foster it: when he invited Lou Andreas-Salomé late in 1921 to visit Berggasse 19, he did so principally for his daughter's sake. "Anna has a comprehensible thirst for friendships with women," he told Eitingon, "after the English Loe, the Hungarian Kata, and your Mirra have been carried off from her." Loe Kann, once Ernest Jones's mistress and Freud's analysand, had gone back to England. Kata Levy, having concluded her analysis with Freud, was living in Budapest. And Mirra, Eitingon's wife, was with her husband in Berlin. "She is, by the way, to my joy blooming and cheerful," Freud added; "only I could wish that she would soon find reason to exchange her attachment to her old father for a more durable one." Anna, he lamented to his nephew in England, "is a success in every respect except that she had not had the good luck to meet a man fit for her."

Freud's benevolent scheme of finding a worthy woman friend for his daughter worked beyond his fondest hopes. In April 1922, Anna went to Göttingen for an extended visit to her new friend—who was "really quite magnificent"—and resumed the confidential, quasi-analytical conversations she had initiated during Lou Andreas-Salomé's visit to Vienna the previous year. Their intimacy aquired mystical overtones; Anna claimed that without Frau Lou's help, given in "a strange and occult way," she would have been unable to write her paper on beating fantasies at all. Freud was elated with his success. "She is now deeply attached" to Frau Lou, Freud reported to Ernest Jones in June 1922, and the following month he expressed his gratitude to his "dear Lou" for her "loving" attitude toward "the child." Anna, he wrote, had for years wanted to know her better. And "if she is to amount to something—I hope she has some good aptitudes to start with—she needs influence and associations that will satisfy high demands. Inhibited through me on the male side, she has so far had a good deal of bad luck with her women friends. She has developed slowly," he added, "is younger than her years not only in looks." Holding back little, he let his conflicting desires rise to the surface: "Sometimes I urgently wish her a good man, sometimes I shrink from the loss." The two women, far apart in age but congenial in their psychoanalytic interests and at one in their admiration for Freud, soon were on intimate *du* terms, and their attachment lasted.

But the troubling reality of Anna's single status left Freud no peace. In 1925, he returned to it, again in a letter to Samuel Freud: "Last not least—Anna, we may well be proud of her. She has become a paedagogic analyst, is treating naughty American children[,] earning a lot of money of which she disposes in a very generous way helping various poor people, she is a member of the International ψA Association, has won a good name by literary work and commands the respect of her coworkers. Yet she has just passed her 30th birthday, does not seem inclined to get married and who can say if her momentary interests will render her happy in years to come when she has to face life without her father?" It was a good question.

AGAIN AND AGAIN, Anna let her father know how much he was in her fond thoughts. "You surely can't imagine how much I continually think of you," she wrote him in 1920. She watched over his digestion, or his stomach, with a mother's—or perhaps better, a wife's—solicitude. In mid-July 1922, she perceptively gathered from faint hints that he might be unwell. "What are your two papers about?" she asked him, and then moved, anxiously, to her main concern: "Are you not in a good mood, or does it only seem to me that way from your letters? Is Gastein not so beautiful as it was?" This was more than two weeks before Freud admitted to Rank in confidence that his health was uncertain. She earnestly defended his right to rest and recuperation even at the cost of coveted hard currency. "Don't let yourself be tormented by patients," she urged him, "and just let all millionairesses stay crazy, they don't have anything else to do." From 1915 on, years before her analysis and just as intensely during it, she recorded dreams for her father expressive of deep turmoil. Her "night life," as she called it, was often "uncomfortable," but even more often terrifying. "Most of the time now," she informed her father in the summer of 1919, "something bad happens in my dreams, about killing, shooting or dying." Something bad had been happening to her in her dreams for years. She dreamt, over and over, that she was going blind, which terrified her. She dreamt that she was compelled to defend a farm belonging to her

and her father, but as she drew her saber she discovered that it was broken
and she was ashamed before the enemy. She dreamt that Dr. Tausk's bride
had rented an apartment at Berggasse 20, across the street from the Freuds,
in order to shoot her father dead with a pistol. All these dreams invite
interpretations involving her passionate feelings for her father. But her most
transparent declaration to him, almost like a child's dream in its directness,
came in the summer of 1915. "Recently I dreamt," she reported, "that you
are a king and I a princess, that people want to separate us by means of
political intrigues. It was not pleasant and very agitating."*

Freud had massive evidence across the years that his daughter's tender,
wholly unclouded association with him might well cripple her ability to find
a suitable husband. Before he started to analyze her, he would respond to his
daughter's dream reports casually, almost flippantly. But he found it impossible to overlook her attachment to him. In 1919, he spoke to Eitingon, in
a light tone, of his Anna's "father complex." Yet, though he was a consummate student of family politics, he failed to appreciate fully how much he
must have contributed to his daughter's reluctance to marry. Others saw the
matter more clearly than he did. In 1921, when Freud's American "pupils"
wondered why Anna Freud, "quite an attractive girl," was not getting married, one of these analysands, Abram Kardiner, suggested an answer that
seemed to him obvious: "Well, look at her father," he told his friends. "This
is an ideal that very few men could live up to, and it would surely be a
comedown for her to attach herself to a lesser man." If Freud had fully
recognized the measure of his power over his daughter, he might have hesitated to psychoanalyze her.

This analysis was a most irregular proceeding, and Freud, like his daughter,
must have known that. It was a drawn-out affair. Begun in 1918, it continued
for more than three years, and was taken up again for another year in 1924.
Still, Freud never alluded to this analysis in public and only rarely in private,
and Anna Freud was no less discreet. She kept her analyst-father supplied
with dreams, which she now sometimes saved up, along with her tormenting
daydreams, the stories she told herself, for her analytic hours with him. But
she kept these intimate matters almost wholly to herself. In 1919, after a year
of analysis, taking the summer cure in rural Bavaria with a friend, Margaretl,
she repaid Margaretl's confidences about her medical treatments with a
confidence about her own. "I told her," she reported to her father, "that I

---

*She fully recognized the childlike nature of her dreams of these days. Three days before sending
this report, she had recounted a dream largely about coffee and whipped cream. This, she noted, was
virtually a "return" to the dream about "stawberry" she had dreamt at nineteen months and read
about later in *The Interpretation of Dreams*. (Anna Freud to Freud, August 3, 1915. Ibid.)

am in analysis with you." Naturally, Lou Andreas-Salomé shared the secret, as did Max Eitingon and, later, a mere handful of others. But it remained a closely held private affair.

No wonder. Freud's teachings on how the analyst should manage his analysand's transference and his own countertransference are unequivocal. His decision to put his daughter Anna on the couch appears like a calculated flouting of the rules he had laid down with such force and precision—for others. In 1920, writing to Kata Levy after her analysis with him was over, he expressed his gratification that he could now write her simply and warmly, "without the didactic rudenesses of analysis, without having to conceal my cordial friendship for you." And after Joan Riviere came to be analyzed two years later, having previously struggled through an analysis with Ernest Jones, Freud dashed off a stream of letters to Jones sternly reproaching him for his analytic conduct with her. She had fallen in love with Jones, and he had botched the transference relationship. "I am very glad," Freud wrote, "you had no sexual relations with her as your hints made me suspect. To be sure it was a technical error to befriend her before her analysis was brought to a close."

What, then, of the technical error that Freud was committing during this very period with his youngest daughter? Freud himself obviously did not think he had transgressed: in the early years of psychoanalysis, the rules he had propounded were casually applied and often violated; the ideal of analytic distance was still fluid and inchoate. Jung, in his Freudian phase, had tried to psychoanalyze his wife; Max Graf had analyzed his son, Little Hans, with Freud as consultant in the background; Freud had analyzed his friends Eitingon and Ferenczi, and Ferenczi, in turn, his professional colleague Ernest Jones. More: in the early 1920s, years after Freud, in his technical papers, had described the analyst's attitude toward his patient as akin to the cool professional demeanor of the surgeon, the pioneering child analyst Melanie Klein analyzed her own children. When the eldest son of the Italian psychoanalyst Edoardo Weiss, preparing to enter his father's profession, asked him to be his analyst, Weiss consulted Freud. In his reply, Freud called such an analysis a "delicate business." It all depended, he wrote, on the two persons involved and on their relationship to one another. With a younger brother it might be easier, with a son there would be special problems. "With my own daughter it turned out well."

Perhaps. But the analysis was, as Freud admitted, not easy, not even after he resumed it in 1924. He had cut down the number of his patients to six, but, as he wrote Lou Andreas-Salomé in May, had "undertaken a 7th analysis with special feelings: my Anna, who is unreasonable enough to cling to her old father." He was now completely candid with his dear Lou. "The child gives me enough worries: how she will bear the lonely life"—after Freud's death—"and whether I can drive her libido from the hiding place into which it has crawled." He admitted that "she has an extraordinary gift for being unhappy and yet probably not enough talent to let herself be stimulated to triumphant production by such unhappiness." He consoled himself that as long as Lou lived, his Anna "will not be left alone. But she is so much younger than the two of us!" For a time, in the summer of 1924, it looked as though the analysis would have to be broken off, but it went on. "What you say about Anna's chances in life," Freud told Lou Andreas-Salomé in August, "is wholly appropriate and thoroughly substantiates my fears." He knew that his daughter's continued dependency on him was, after all, "an impermissible lingering in a situation which should be only a preparatory stage." Yet she lingered. "Anna's analysis is continuing," Freud reported to his "dearest Lou" the following May. "She is not uncomplicated and does not easily find a way of applying to herself what she now sees so clearly in others. Her growth into an experienced, patient and sympathetic analyst is making excellent progress." But, he added, the whole trend of her life did not please him. "I am afraid that her suppressed genitality may some day play her a mean trick. I cannot free her from me, and nobody is helping me with it." Some time earlier he had put his dilemma as picturesquely and emphatically as he could: if she were to leave home, he wrote Lou Andreas-Salomé, he would feel as impoverished as he would if he had to give up smoking. Indeed, it is evident that Freud felt helplessly entangled—torn, weary of life—in his relationship to his favorite child. He was caught in his own needs and could not escape them. "With all these insoluble conflicts," he had confessed to Lou Andreas-Salomé as early as 1922, "it is a good thing that life at some time comes to an end."

Freud no doubt had every reason to be as proud of his "Annerl" as he was fond of her. But the emotional costs that attended her training as a psychoanalyst have never been calculated. Father and daughter, all the rest of his life, remained the closest of allies, virtually equal colleagues. When, in the late 1920s, her views on child analysis came under fire in London, Freud defended his daughter ferociously;* in turn, in her classic monograph on ego psychology and defense mechanisms, published in the mid-1930s, Anna Freud drew on her own clinical experience, but relied on her father's writings as the principal and authoritative source of her theoretical insights. She was possessive of her father, sensitive to any views that might even hint at criticism of his work,

_____
*See pp. 468–69.

jealous of others—siblings, patients, friends—who might cut into her prerogatives.* By the early 1920s the two had become, and they were to remain, intellectually and emotionally inseparable.

IN LATER LIFE, Freud liked to call his daughter Anna his Antigone. It will not do to press this affectionate name too far: Freud was an educated European speaking to other educated Europeans and had raided Sophocles in search of a loving comparison. But the meanings of "Antigone" are too rich to be wholly set aside. The name underscored Freud's identification with Oedipus, the bold discoverer of mankind's secrets, the eponymous hero of the "nuclear complex," the killer of his father and the lover of his mother. And there is more. It is a truism that Oedipus's children were all exceptionally close to him; having been fathered with his mother, they were his siblings as much as his offspring. But Antigone was preeminent among Oedipus's children. She was his gallant and loyal companion, just as Anna became her father's chosen comrade over the years. It is Antigone who, in *Oedipus at Colonnus,* leads her blind father by the hand, and by 1923, it was Anna Freud who was firmly installed as her wounded father's secretary, confidante, representative, colleague, and nurse. She became his most precious claim on life, his ally against death.

Anna Freud did not confine her work for her father to typing his letters when he was indisposed, or to reading his papers at congresses and ceremonies. From 1923 on, she tended his body in the most intimate way. Publicly, Freud credited others, too, with taking good care of him. "My wife and Anna have nursed me tenderly," he told Ferenczi after his first operation in the spring of 1923; "I need only mention," he wrote Samuel Freud in December, not long after the second set of operations, "that I owe whatever bodily power I save from this débâcle to the tender attentions of my wife and my two daughters." But his daughter Anna was Freud's nurse-in-chief.† When he had trouble inserting his prosthesis, he would call her for assistance, and at

---

*When Ernest Jones consulted Anna Freud during the writing of the Freud biography, she recalled her jealousy without reserve. "I wondered a bit about your mentioning Mrs. Riviere," analyst and brilliant translator, among "the women in his life. She must have played a part, since I remember being jealous of her (a sure sign!)." Again, when Jones mentioned Freud's having had "secretarial help" in 1909, she wondered who that could have been. Her aunt Minna? No: That would have been long before. Her sister Mathilde? Probably not. "I really do not know and it makes me quite jealous." (Anna Freud to Jones, February 14 and April 24, 1954. Jones papers, Archives of the British Psycho-Analytical Society, London.)

†In 1926, when he spent some weeks in a sanatorium because of a heart condition, he had a "sick nurse" in the next room, "who in the course of the day separates out into wife and daughter, but through the night will doubtless regularly remain the latter." (Freud to Eitingon, March 6, 1926. By permission of Sigmund Freud Copyrights, Wivenhoe.)

least once she had to struggle with the ungainly device for half an hour. Far from inspiring resentment or disgust, this physical closeness only tightened the bonds between father and daughter to the utmost. He became as irreplaceable for her as she had become indispensable to him.

Most of Freud's seductive maneuvers were, no doubt, unconscious. At times he was ingenuously frank concerning his ambivalent feelings about Anna's life with him. "Anna by the way is doing splendidly," he had told his "dear Max" Eitingon in April 1921. "She is cheerful, industrious and lively. I should like as much to keep her in my house as to know she has her own. If it's only the same to her!" More often, though, he continued to express misgivings about her unmarried state. "Anna is in splendid health," he wrote his nephew in December 1921, "and would be a faultless blessing where it not that she has lived through her 26th birthday (yesterday) while still at home." Like Sophocles's Antigone, Freud's Antigone never married. But this was not a foregone conclusion for Freud. Among his papers there is an envelope, probably dating from the mid-1920s, that clearly once held a gift of money, doubtless given to Anna Freud on her birthday. The front bears this legend: "Contribution to a dowry or to independence."

IT IS A MEASURE of their intimacy that Freud enlisted his youngest daughter in his experiments with telepathy. When he told Abraham in 1925 that Anna possessed "telepathic sensitivity," he was only half joking. As Anna Freud once aptly observed to Ernest Jones, "the subject must have fascinated, as well as repelled him." Jones testifies that Freud enjoyed telling stories of strange coincidences and mysterious voices, and magical thinking had something of a hold on him, though it was never secure. He had demonstrated that hold most dramatically in 1905, when he propitiated the gods during a dangerous illness of his daughter Mathilde by "accidentally" smashing one of his cherished antiquities. But what intrigued him most, inconclusive though he thought the evidence, was telepathy.

In a letter of 1921, Freud declared that he was not "among those who right off reject the study of the so-called occult psychological phenomena as unscientific, as unworthy, or even as dangerous." Rather, he described himself as a "complete layman and newcomer" in the field, but one who could not "get rid of certain skeptical materialistic prejudices." In the same year, he drafted a memorandum, "Psychoanalysis and Telepathy," for confidential discussion among the members of the Committee—Abraham, Eitingon, Ferenczi, Jones, Rank, and Sachs—in which he adopted the same stance. He noted a little mischievously that psychoanalysis had no reason to follow established opinion in the contemptuous condemnation of occult occurrences. "It would not be the first time that it lends support to the obscure but indestructible surmises of the common people against the knowing arrogance of the educated." Yet Freud readily acknowledged that much so-called research into the obscurities of mental phenomena was anything but scientific, while psychoanalysts, on the other hand, were "fundamentally incorrigible mechanists and materialists." As a scientist, Freud was unwilling to abet superstition and the flight from reason; but as a scientist, too, he stood ready to investigate phenomena that seemed uncanny and to defy mundane solutions. Nearly all such phenomena, he argued, are open to naturalistic explanations; amazing prophecies, astonishing coincidences, normally revealed themselves as projections of powerful wishes. Yet some occult experiences, particularly in the domain of thought transference, might prove authentic. In 1921, Freud declared himself willing to leave the matter open—but, at the same time, preferred to keep the issue confined to his innermost circle, lest the frank discussion of telepathy divert attention from psychoanalysis.

The following year, however, discarding some—though not all—of this prudence, Freud published a rather tentative article, intended as a paper for his colleagues in Vienna, on dreams and telepathy. Throughout, he declared himself agnostic. "From this lecture," he warned his audience, "you will learn nothing about the riddle of telepathy, not even be informed whether I believe in the existence of 'telepathy' or not." In his conclusion, he was quite as unforthcoming: "Have I awakened in you the impression that I am secretly disposed to take the part of the reality of telepathy in its occult sense? I should regret very much that it is so hard to avoid such an impression. For I really wanted to be completely impartial. I have every reason for this, for I have no opinion, I know nothing about it." One wonders why Freud published the paper at all; the dreams he reported in it did not prove the authenticity of telepathic communication and, in fact, supported a good measure of skepticism. Prophetic dreams or long-distance communications might be, after all, he said, nothing more than an activity of the unconscious. It is as though he simply wanted to keep the pot boiling. "The wish to believe," as Ernest Jones has justly put it, "fought hard with the warning to disbelieve."

Indeed, through the 1920s Freud cautioned his colleagues against taking too positive a stance on the matter. For one thing, the evidence was at best inconclusive. For another, there was danger in a psychoanalyst's openly accepting telepathy as worthy of serious investigation. Early in 1925, Ferenczi asked his intimate colleagues what they would say if he read to the next international congress of psychoanalysts a paper on the experiments in thought transference he had been conducting with Freud and Anna. Freud categorically objected. "I advise you against it. Don't do it."

Yet all these prudent precautions, which Freud always obeyed reluctantly if at all, slowly gave way. In 1926 he reminded Ernest Jones that he had long since harbored a "favorable prejudice in favor of telepathy" and had held back only to protect psychoanalysis from too close a proximity to occultism. But recently "the experiments that I have undertaken with Ferenczi and my daughter have gained such a persuasive power for me, that diplomatic considerations had to take a back seat."* He found telepathy fascinating, he added, because his preoccupation with it reminded him, though on a reduced scale, of "the great experiment of my life," when he had stood up against public obloquy as the discoverer of psychoanalysis. Then, too, he had had to disregard reigning respectable opinion. But, he reassured Jones, "if someone should reproach you with my Fall into Sin, you are free to reply that my adherence to telepathy is my private affair like my Jewishness, my passion for smoking, and other things, and the theme of telepathy—inessential for psychoanalysis." Anna Freud, who knew her father's mind better than anyone else, later minimized his will to believe. With telepathy, she told Ernest Jones, "he was trying to be 'fair,' i.e., not treat it as other people had treated psychoanalysis. I never could see that he himself believed in more than the possibility of two unconscious minds communicating with each other without the help of a conscious bridge." There is much in this defense, but she was being protective of her father, as she had long been, and did not cease to be.

WHILE FREUD FOUND his daughter a supportive, indeed necessary partner, his state of mind understandably fluctuated. Writing to Otto Rank in April 1924, he complained somewhat irritably that Abraham lacked all insight into his condition: "He hopes that my 'indisposition' will soon be overcome," and simply "will not believe that with me it is a new, reduced program of life and work." Freud admitted to Ernest Jones in September that he was doing some work, but it was "of a secondary order"—an autobiographical sketch. "There is no fresh scientific interest now aloof." Indeed, in May 1925, he described himself to Lou Andreas-Salomé as being gradually encrusted by insensibility. This was in the nature of things "a kind of beginning of becoming inorganic." The balance between the drives of life and death, with which he was then occupied, was gradually shifting toward death. He had just "celebrated" his sixty-ninth birthday. Yet eight years later, when he was seventy-seven, he could still impress his patient Hilda Doolittle with his vitality. "The Professor

*Unfortunately, Ferenczi gave no details of what these experiments were. Nor did Anna Freud. But much later, she reported to Ernest Jones that she and her father "acted out" certain "superstitions" while they were hunting for mushrooms, and that this "nonsense" was "such good fun at the time." She left no doubt, though, that these experiments had to do with "thought transference." (Anna Freud to Ernest Jones, November 24, 1955. Jones papers, Archives of the British Psycho-Analytical Society, London.)

told me a few days ago," H. D. noted in her journal, "that if he lived another fifty years, he would still be fascinated and curious about the vagaries and variations of the human mind or soul." Certainly, it was his curiosity that kept him at work even after his cancer operations—at work and thus alive. Not long after these operations, in mid-October 1923, he had hoped to be back analyzing in November, but Pichler's follow-up surgery made that date unrealistic. He did not begin seeing patients until January 2, 1924, and then "only" six of them a day. Soon he would add that seventh patient, Anna.

THE PRICE OF POPULARITY

 Early in 1925, reporting to Abraham, Anna Freud linked her father's health and that of his country in a telling metaphor: "Pichler wants, as he puts it, to *sanieren*"— rehabilitate—the prosthesis definitively, "and meanwhile" her father was "suffering under it, like Austria under *its* rehabilitation." She was referring to the recent *Sanierung* of the Austrian currency, which, though it seemed a rational and essential step to economic recovery, had saddled the country with high, in some regions catastrophic, unemployment.

The 1920s proved a stormy decade, in Austria as elsewhere, though not without sunny intervals. Central European countries labored to repair their shattered economies, with modest and intermittent success. They learned to live, more or less, with their truncated territories and their untried political institutions just as their erstwhile enemies hesitantly, often meanly, learned to live with them. The small Austrian republic was admitted to the League of Nations in 1920, six years ahead of Germany. This was a diplomatic triumph for Austria, one of the first for a defeated power, and also one of the last.

During these years, Austrians went through a hectic time of social experimentation undercut by political tension: the stalemate between "Red Vienna" and the Catholic provinces, between the Social Democratic and the Christian Social parties, was never wholly resolved. Powerful political groups agitated in parliament and in the streets; the pan-Germanic People's party, for one, volubly articulated its emotion-laden grievance, Austria's intolerable separation from Germany. Splinter parties—monarchists, National Socialists, and others—poisoned the political atmosphere with their incendiary rhetoric, provocative marches, and bloody clashes. While the Socialist city government of Vienna enacted an ambitious program of public housing, rent control, school construction, and poor relief, the Christian Social party, which controlled the rest of the country, distinguished itself less by a positive program than by its hatreds. It was intent on ejecting the Social Democrats from power, by force if necessary, and its members were drenched in an anti-Semitism mainly, though by no means wholly, concentrated against the hapless Jewish immigrants fleeing pogroms in Poland, Rumania, and the Ukraine.

While in retrospect the Weimar Republic in these years of recovery came to assume a golden haze of enviable cultural fertility, Austrians never even tried to manufacture so glowing a self-portrait. The legend to which they clung centered on the glittering culture of the prewar days in the Austro-Hungarian empire. Austria did make contributions to its time, but mainly to modern barbarism: one of its gifts to the world was Adolf Hitler. Born in 1889 in the small town of Braunau am Inn, he had been educated in the gutter politics of Vienna in the days of the anti-Semitic mayor Karl Lueger, to Hitler "the mightiest mayor of all time." It was in Vienna that he had absorbed his political "philosophy," a malignant brew of racial anti-Semitism, skillful populism, brutalized social Darwinism, and a vague yearning for "Aryan" dominion over Europe. Austria, the land so strenuously celebrated for its musical life, its sweet young things, its Sacher torte, and its largely mythical Blue Danube—actually not blue, but a muddy brown—provided Hitler with the notions, and the hints for political action, that he later loosed on the world from the larger staging area of Germany.

In 1919, in Munich, having been invalided out late in the war, Hitler joined an obscure group of nationalistic cranks imbued with anticapitalist notions; in the following year, when the group renamed itself the National Socialist German Workers' party—the Nazis, for short—Hitler's charismatic presence propelled him into leadership. He was a politician of a new breed, with an insatiable hunger for power, contemptuous of traditional ways, at once shrewd and fanatical. In 1922, Benito Mussolini, the most flamboyant of demagogues, had imposed his personal dictatorship, a squalid combination of bluff and force, on Italy. But Mussolini, in many respects the Nazis' model and teacher, could not compete with Hitler's deadly ability to shift between ruthlessness and opportunism, his gift for manipulating mass rallies and business leaders alike. History would judge Italian Fascism, however bombastic, corrupt, histrionic, and cold-blooded it was, as temperate compared to the

Nazi New Order of which Hitler dreamt from his most obscure days onward.*

Though uncannily adept at suiting his rhetoric to his audience, Hitler was never oblivious of his mortal enemies: liberal culture, democrats, Bolsheviks, and above all Jews. The putsch he staged in November 1923 at a beer hall in Munich failed ignominiously, but Hitler turned his debacle to good account: he spent some eight comfortable months in confinement in a fortress working on the book that became the bible of the Nazi movement, *Mein Kampf.* But as the Weimar Republic finally conquered inflation late in 1923, produced an unwonted measure of public order, and won renewed diplomatic respectability, Hitler found himself for some years little more than a minor orator on the fringe, though boasting some influential sympathizers and a devoted cadre of supporters.

The mid-1920s, then, were for Germany the age of Gustav Stresemann, the conciliatory foreign minister, rather than of Adolf Hitler, the rabid visionary. Stresemann set the tone as Germany rejoined the international community and attempted to work its way out of the mire of war reparations. Hitler's name does not appear in Freud's correspondence of those years; he was too unimportant. While there was still intermittent rioting in German streets, and while the Allies continued to press for the payment of reparations that Germany could ill afford, the novel, the film, the theater, the opera and operetta, the dance, painting, architecture, and sculpture flourished mightily. So did psychoanalysis. But Freud was not impressed by the Weimar Republic any more than by postwar Austria. In 1926, he told an interviewer, George Sylvester Viereck, "My language is German. My culture, my attainments are German. I considered myself German intellectually, until I noticed the growth of anti-Semitic prejudice in Germany and German Austria. Since that time, I prefer to call myself a Jew."

FREUD MIGHT HAVE found some solace as he turned from the larger world to contemplate the fortunes of psychoanalysis after the Great War. But he

---

*Fascist Italy proved something of an exception to the sweep of anti-Semitism in the new regimes until the late 1930s, when Mussolini, in Hitler's wake, introduced anti-Semitic legislation. Freud had one indirect contact with Mussolini, reported by the Italian analyst Edoardo Weiss: "As I was in the habit of doing," in 1933 "I brought a very sick patient to Freud for a consultation. The patient's father, who accompanied us, was a close friend of Mussolini's. After the consultation, the father asked Freud for a present for Mussolini, in which Freud was to write a dedication. I was in a very embarrassing position, for I knew that under these circumstances, Freud could not deny the request. The work he chose, perhaps with a definite intention, was 'Why War?,' " a brief published correspondence with Albert Einstein, in which Freud had confessed to pacifist sentiments. The dedication was "with the devoted greeting of an old man, who recognizes the cultural hero in the ruler," an allusion, Weiss notes, to Mussolini's *"large-scale archeological excavations,"* in which *"Freud was very much interested."* (Edoardo Weiss, "Meine Erinnerungen an Sigmund Freud," in *Freud–Weiss Briefe,* 34–35.)

remained wry and discontented. Writing to Pfister on Christmas Day, 1920, he reported that he had received some respectable works of psychoanalytic popularization from several countries and felt constrained to admit that "the cause progresses everywhere." But he immediately canceled his concession to optimism: "You seem to overestimate my pleasure in it. Whatever personal satisfaction one can draw from analysis I already enjoyed at the time when I was alone, and have, since the adhesion of others, been more annoyed than pleased." The increasing acceptance of psychoanalysis, he added, had not caused him to change his low opinion of people, an opinion dating from the days when they had flatly, obtusely, rejected his ideas. Perhaps, he wondered, his attitude was part of his own psychological history, a consequence of his early isolation: "Surely, in that time an incurable rift must have developed between me and the others." The year before, he had already told Eitingon that from the very beginning of his work, when he was quite alone, his "oppressive worry about the future" had been "what the human rabble" would make of psychoanalysis "when I'm no longer alive."

That sounds a little depressed and downright churlish. After all, he *was* propagating a highly technical set of ideas—ideas, moreover, most unpleasant, most scandalous. Psychoanalysis aimed at nothing less than the overthrow of reigning schools in psychology and psychiatry, to say nothing of the unwarranted self-esteem of ordinary men and women. In his *Introductory Lectures*, Freud had noted a little melodramatically that psychoanalysis had presented humanity with the third of three historic injuries to its megalomania. Copernicus had established that the earth is not the center of the universe; Darwin had invited mankind into the animal kingdom; now he, Freud, was teaching the world that the ego is largely the servant of unconscious and uncontrollable forces in the mind. Could one expect the world to understand, let alone welcome, such a message?

The propositions of psychoanalysis sounded in cold daylight improbable, even absurd, and the evidence in their behalf was remote and hard to assess; they required a leap of faith that many were unwilling to take. In 1919, when hungry postwar Vienna was humming with outlandish radical notions, psychoanalysis was hotly debated in the cafés. "The air," the philosopher Sir Karl Popper recalls, "was full of revolutionary slogans, ideas, and new and often wild theories." Karl Kraus's wicked, widely quoted aphorism that psychoanalysis is the disease whose cure it purports to be, was by then some years old, but it epitomized a fashionable and enduring response. Popper, for one—he was then all of seventeen—thought he had decisively refuted psychoanalysis, along with Adlerian psychology and Marxism: All these systems explained too much. They were so imprecise in their formulations that any event, any behavior, any fact whatever, could only confirm them. By proving absolutely everything, Popper argued, they proved absolutely nothing. And Popper was only the most sophisticated of many instant experts. In such a climate of opinion, with so much at stake, the tortuous progress of psychoanalysis should have been no surprise to Freud.

THE RECEPTION OF Freud in the coffeehouse, at the cocktail party, on the stage, was scarcely calculated to promote a sober understanding of his thought. His technical terms and fundamental ideas were misread, usually debased, to serve as common currency. "Psychoanalysis," one commentator, Thomas L. Masson, suggested in a characteristic review of four books on the subject in 1923, "is not only coloring our literature, but, as a natural result, is creeping into and influencing life in many other directions." Masson cited as an example of that influence the increased employment of psychoanalysis in business hiring practices, and expressed the hope that it would eventually "solve the problems raised by the Ku Klux Klan." But he quickly subverted this hope, though in somewhat deferential tones, with his conclusion that "we are frankly skeptical about its ultimate value." Most others moved to express an opinion on psychoanalysis during the 1920s were no less frank in their skepticism.

The popular press, newspapers and magazines alike, did its share to spread confusion and facile judgments by reducing Freud the man to a comical, often rather menacing caricature. The wider public in the unsettled postwar era found this caricature quite irresistible. Freud was the grave, bearded *Herr Professor,* complete with droll, heavy Central European accent, who had put sex on the map. His teachings, one heard, licensed the most uninhibited erotic self-expression. Even the few respectful reviewers who wrestled with his writings in the Sunday supplements declared themselves more baffled than enlightened by his work. One of them, Mary Keyt Isham, trying to make sense of Freud's *Beyond the Pleasure Principle* and *Group Psychology,* confessed in the book-review section of the *New York Times* that "the reviewer encounters many difficulties with Freud's works and in these two recent volumes more than ever," especially since they were attempting, Isham believed, to "present the results of his earlier investigations in a 'meta-psychological' form," which she misdescribed as a "newly invented discipline."

Few among the learned did anything to correct slanders about Freud or misinterpretations of psychoanalysis. Preachers, journalists, and pedagogues denounced his obscene notions and deplored his baleful influence. In May 1924, Dr. Brian Brown, author of *Power of the Inner Mind,* speaking at a symposium held at St. Mark's-in-the-Bowery in New York, characterized Freud's interpretations of the unconscious mind as "rotten." At the same symposium Dr. Richard Borden, director of the Speech Club at New York

University, manfully tried to explain such fundamental Freudian ideas as "Soul-Sickness, Libido, Complexes and the 'Old Adam,' " but Dr. Brown countered by warning that "Freud did not teach psychology." In fact, Freud's "idea was that there was an outer compartment where harmful ideas were hoarded, ready to rush into our consciousness. Furthermore, he resolved everything into sex." The old accusation that Freud was obsessed with sex seemed ineradicable.

A year after Dr. Brown called Freud's ideas rotten, Stephen S. Wise, the prominent New York Reform rabbi and advocate of Zionism, made the same charge in more refined language. Speaking to students at International House, he urged them to turn away from H. L. Mencken and rediscover the sweetness and light of Matthew Arnold. But, he went on, "a far more serious substitution of 'new gods for old' " than Mencken's cynicism was "the vogue of Freudianism." For Wise, as for many other anxious observers, Freud was the seductive prophet of raw instinct let loose. "I like to place Freud in juxtaposition to Kant," he declared. "To Kant's teaching of 'Thou must, thou shalt, thou canst,' " Freud "opposes the 'You may.' " Freudianism, Wise sonorously concluded, "is a digging down into the sewage of our moods and appetites, dreams and passions." Others were tempted into levity. In the summer of 1926, one ingenious divine, the Reverend John MacNeill of the Tenth Presbyterian Church of Philadelphia, told a conference at Stony Brook, "Every third person today is daft on the subject of psychoanalysis. If you want to get rid of them quickly, ask them to spell the word."

That sort of denunciation was typical of the time, and not just in the United States. In November 1922, Eitingon wrote Freud from his beloved Paris that psychoanalysis was struggling against noisy opposition there: "It is probably no coincidence that on the very day" a French translation of Freud's *Psychopathology of Everyday Life* appeared, "there should be an incendiary article on 'Freud et l'éducation,' in which a Professor Amar calls on the government to protect children from psychoanalysis. He is very angry, this Herr Amar." Anger, too, was a defense against Freud's message.

The discussion swirling around Freud's ideas, then, whether sympathetic or antagonistic, was often on an appallingly low level. In 1922, a writer in the London *Times,* reviewing Freud's *Introductory Lectures,* asserted that psychoanalysis had "fallen on evil days as the result of the excessive zeal of its apostles." It had begun as "a contribution to psychical science," but then had unfortunately become "a 'rage,'—that is to say it was feverishly discussed by people who had but a slight knowledge of its meaning." This was placing the blame a little tendentiously on Freud's followers alone. But the observation that psychoanalysis had become a kind of rage among those who had no knowledge of it was true enough. Freudianism, the Swedish physician Poul

Bjerre, whom Freud claimed as an adherent, wrote in 1925, "has agitated feelings" as though "it were a matter of a new religion and not a new area for research. Especially in America, the psychoanalytic literature has grown into an avalanche. *To be psyched*' has become fashionable." A year later, the eminent and prolific American psychologist William McDougall supported Bjerre's assessment: "In addition to the professional followers, a host of laymen, educators, artists, and dilettanti have been fascinated by the Freudian speculations and given them an immense popular vogue, so that some of the technical terms used by Freud have become embodied in the popular slang of both America and England."

The European continent was showing itself only marginally less susceptible to the seduction of the Freudian vocabulary and quite as ambivalent in its responses. "In the daily press," Abraham, Eitingon, and Sachs noted in a circular letter from Berlin in May 1925, "there is a good deal to read about Psa., mainly in a negative direction, but not always." They also had some good news: the courses offered by the Berlin Psychoanalytic Institute, founded in 1920, were attracting large audiences and a gratifying number of candidates. What was more, Abraham and his colleagues were "compensated for the frequently unfriendly atmosphere of the press" by the fact that Stefan Zweig had just dedicated a new book of biographical essays to Freud. And, not to forget an amusing item, one Friedrich Sommer had recently published a brochure, "The Measurement of Spiritual Energy," in which he had declared, "One day I became acquainted with Psa., and this then brought me closer to the Christian religion." In October, Abraham sent another bulletin: "One can report from Germany that the discussion of Psa. in the newspapers and periodicals is unceasing. We find it mentioned everywhere." It was only natural that "attacks are not lacking. But," he added soothingly, "without doubt interest has never been so strong as now." Yet much of the interest was no better informed than Friedrich Sommer had been when he took acquaintance with Freud's ideas as a means for getting closer to God.

This mixture of signals, mainly negative, also characterized the climate of opinion in Vienna. Elias Canetti, hardly an infatuated student of psycho-analysis, recalls that when he lived there in the mid-1920s, "there was hardly a conversation in which the name Freud did not surface." The "leading figures at the University still arrogantly rejected him," but the interpretation of "*slips* had become a kind of party game." The Oedipus complex was hardly less the rage: everybody wanted his own. The loftiest despiser of the mob did not mind having one. There were indeed many Austrians who found Freud's theories of aggression urgently relevant: "What one had witnessed of murderous cruelty was unforgotten. Many who had participated actively had now returned. They knew well of what—on orders—they had been capable, and greedily caught hold of all the explanations for the predisposition to murder that psychoanalysis offered them."

LIKE MOST DETRACTORS of Freud, many of his admirers had only the faintest notions about his distinctive message. Vagueness conquered all and not just among the half-educated: so learned a psychologist as Poul Bjerre could use the term "subconsciousness"—*Unterbewusstsein*—for "unconscious" in his popular exposition of psychoanalysis.* In a leaflet that the American publisher B. W. Huebsch produced in 1920 to advertise William Bayard Hale's "psycho-analytic study of Woodrow Wilson," *The Story of a Style,* one could read: "It may be astonishing to those who have not followed the rapidly-accumulating literature of psychoanalysis with what ingenuity the followers of Freud and Jung uncover the workings of the human mind and soul." This sort of imprecision was infinitely galling to Freud, and he sometimes took refuge in the old saying that while he could take care of his enemies, he needed protection from his friends.

He was not being quite fair. The greatest threats to the spread of psychoanalysis properly understood were the faddists and the profiteers. Some of those exploiting psychoanalysis were pure and transparent charlatans. As the *New York Times* properly noted in May 1926, "Most unfortunately for Freud's repute, his theories lend themselves with terrible ease to the uses of ignorance and of quackery." While Freud himself "has denounced these vagaries," his protests have had "little effect so far as the general public goes." This was only to be expected; the large and muddy pool of psychological healing invited self-appointed therapists to fish without a license. Ernest Jones notes, as one instance, the advertisement by an "English Psycho-Analytical Publishing Company," which read: " 'Would you like to earn £1,000 a year as a psycho-analyst? We can show you how to do it. Take eight postal lessons from us at four guineas a course!' "

Much of the excitement over Freud was far more harmless foolishness, calling less for indignation than for amusement at the human comedy in a democratic world. In the summer of 1924, the sensational murder trial of Nathan Leopold and Richard Loeb, with the redoubtable attorney Clarence Darrow in charge of the defense, made headlines across the United States.

---

*This was, and remains, a common and telling mistake. See for a physician contemporary of Bjerre's, W. Schmidt-Mödling, *Der Ödipus-Komplex der Freudschen Psychoanalyse und die Ehegestaltung des Bolschewismus* (n.d. [1928?]), 1; later in the same work he uses "unconscious" as a synonym for "subconscious." On the occasion of Freud's seventieth birthday two days before, the *New York Times* commented under the heading "Psychology Knows He Has Lived," that Freud's "theories of the subconscious" remained highly controversial. ("Topics of the Times," *New York Times,* May 8, 1926, 16.)

Colonel Robert McCormick, the imperious publisher of the *Chicago Trib-une*, had a telegram dispatched to Freud offering him the impressive sum of $25,000 "or anything he name come Chicago psychoanalyze" the two young killers. From wealthy and prominent families, apparently motivated only by the obscure urge to commit a perfect crime against a friend, Leopold and Loeb fascinated a public mystified by their gratuitous act and, in part uncon-sciously, tantalized by hints of homoerotic emotions at work. McCormick, aware that Freud was elderly and unwell, even offered to charter a steamer to bring the illustrious analyst to the United States. Freud declined. Later that year, Sam Goldwyn, already one of Hollywood's most powerful produc-ers, on his way to Europe, told a reporter of the *New York Times* that he would call on Freud, "the greatest love specialist in the world." His purpose: to offer Freud a fee markedly more lavish than Colonel McCormick's—the princely sum of $100,000. "Love and laughter are the two ideas uppermost in Samuel Goldwyn's mind in producing pictures," the reporter observed, and added that Goldwyn intended to prevail "upon the expert in psychoanalysis to commercialize his study and write a story for the screen, or come to America and help in a 'drive' on the hearts of this nation." After all, as Goldwyn put it, "there is nothing really so entertaining as a really great love story" and who better equipped to write, or advise on, such a story than Freud? "Scenario writers, directors and actors," Goldwyn thought, "can learn much by a really deep study of everyday life. How much more forceful will be their creations if they know how to express genuine emotional motivation and suppressed desires?" Freud was doing well enough on twenty dollars an hour, later twenty-five; still, he was getting on in years and always hungry for hard currency. This, then, as the saying goes, was an offer he could not refuse. Yet the *New York Times* headline of January 24, 1925, tersely reports a quite different outcome: "FREUD REBUFFS GOLDWYN. / Viennese Psychoanalyst is Not Interested in Motion Picture Offer." In fact, according to a Viennese boulevard paper, *Die Stunde,* claiming to base its story on an interview with Freud, he had responded to Goldwyn's request for an interview with a one-sentence letter: "I do not intend to see Mr. Goldwyn."

SUCH INCIDENTS ABUNDANTLY document that by the mid-1920s Freud had become a household name. The number of people who would read, let alone fully grasp, esoteric texts like *Beyond the Pleasure Principle* or *The Ego and the Id* was bound to remain small. Only a select minority could be expected to do Freud's teachings justice; unfortunately, most of those pronouncing on psychoanalysis in these years did not belong to that minority. Yet his name, and his photograph showing a stern, carefully dressed elderly gentleman with penetrating eyes and the inevitable cigar, became known to millions. But the

McCormick and Goldwyn episodes also show why all this irritated rather than elated him. "Popularity in itself is utterly indifferent to me," he had exclaimed to Samuel Freud late in 1920; it "must at the best be considered a danger for more serious achievement." His "actual popularity," he reiterated a year later, was a "burden" to him. This became a characteristic refrain in his letters; early in 1922, he voiced it again, this time to Eitingon: he found his popularity "repulsive." At best it was good for a derisive smile. "In England and America," he had told Eitingon a year before, "there is now a great Psa ballyhoo, which, however, I don't like and which brings me nothing but newspaper clippings and visits from interviewers. Still, though, it is amusing." It was fame, but not the fame he wanted.

Freud, we know, was not indifferent to public approval; after all, he insisted on the originality of his contributions to the science of the mind, contributions for which he expected recognition. But invasive reporters and ignorant newspapers articles, published rumors about his health, error-ridden summaries of his ideas, and the stream of letters pouring in on him—nearly all of which he felt compelled to answer—robbed him of time for scientific work and exposed him, and his cause, to a vulgarization he feared and abhorred. Yet sometimes he had to admit that his new visibility had its compensations. "I am considered a celebrity," he told his English nephew late in 1925. "The Jews all over the world boast of my name pairing me with Einstein." This boast was not his invention; nor did the pairing come from Jews alone. Speaking at the opening ceremonies of Hebrew University in Jerusalem in 1925, the elderly English statesman Lord Balfour linked Freud to Bergson and Einstein as one of the three men, all Jews, who had had the greatest beneficial influence on modern thought. This was praise from a source Freud strongly admired; late in 1917, as British foreign minister, Balfour had pledged his country's support for a Jewish homeland in Palestine, and Freud had hailed "the experiment of the English with the chosen people." His pleasure had not waned with the years. Acknowledging the report on Lord Balfour's speech, he asked Ernest Jones to forward an offprint of his "Autobiographical Study" in thanks for the "honorable reference."

In such a mood he could wax philosophical about his prominence. "After all," he told Samuel Freud, "I have no reason to complain and to look with fright at the near end of my life. After a long period of poverty I am earning money without hardship and I dare say I have provided for my wife." On one or two occasions an honor came his way that he could respect: in November 1921, the Dutch Society of Psychiatrists and Neurologists named him an honorary member, a distinction that gratified him. Well it might; this was the first formal recognition he had received since 1909, when Clark University had awarded him an honorary doctorate of laws. Voices continued to be heard that Freud was no better than a charlatan, but his reputation spread beyond the tight circle of committed Freudian analysts. He was beginning to correspond with luminaries, mainly famous writers: Romain Rolland, Stefan Zweig, Thomas Mann, Sinclair Lewis, and, from 1929 on, Arnold Zweig, who had made a name for himself with an antiwar novel, *The Case of Sergeant Grischa*, two years before. "Writers and philosophers who pass through Vienna," Freud informed his nephew in Manchester, "call on me to have a talk." Freud's days of isolation were only a dim memory.

ONE GRATIFICATION CONTINUED to elude him—the Nobel Prize. When, in the early 1920s, Georg Groddeck nominated him as others had nominated him before, Freud told Groddeck's wife, in resignation, that his name had been floated for years, always in vain. Some years later, in 1928 and again in 1930, Dr. Heinrich Meng, a young German psychoanalyst who had been analyzed by Paul Federn, mounted a well-orchestrated campaign in Freud's behalf. He collected an impressive outpouring of prestigious signatures; those responding included such prominent German admirers as the novelists Alfred Döblin and Jakob Wassermann, and also eminent foreigners—philosophers like Bertrand Russell, educators like A. S. Neill, biographers like Lytton Strachey, scientists like Julian Huxley, and many others only marginally less known to the educated public. Eugen Bleuler, too, though he had after some years' flirtation eluded Freud's wooing, joined the signatories. Even such improbable admirers as the Norwegian novelist and Nobel Prize winner Knut Hamsun and the German nationalist composer Hans Pfitzner, both later Nazi sympathizers, found it possible to subscribe to Meng's appeal. Protecting his own turf, Thomas Mann declared himself ready to add his signature—provided the prize in question was in medicine.* But this, as Meng knew, was precisely what was unobtainable: the psychiatrist whom the Swedish Academy consulted as its authority dismissed Freud as a fraud and a menace. Hence the only category open to him was literature. But Meng's evasive maneuver in this direction, too, failed, and so Freud joined a long list of stylists, from Proust to Joyce, Franz Kafka to Virginia Woolf, who never went to Stockholm.

Freud must have welcomed, but tried to discourage, all these well-meant

*One of the Nobel prize winners who refused to support Freud's candidacy was Albert Einstein, who wrote to Meng on February 15, 1928, that he could not offer any dependable opinion on the truth of Freud's teaching, "much less offer a verdict that should be authoritative for others." Moreover, Einstein cautioned, it seemed doubtful to him that a psychologist like Freud should really be eligible for the Nobel prize in medicine, "which is, I suppose, the only one that could be considered." (I owe this reference to Prof. Dr. Helmut Lück and Prof. Hannah S. Decker.)

efforts. Professing to be unaware of Meng's activities, he asked Ernest Jones rhetorically, "Who is fool enough to meddle in this affair?" The very vehemence of his question hints that had he been offered the prize, he would have grabbed it with both hands. In 1932, he reported to Eitingon that he was conducting a correspondence with Einstein, intended for publication, about the nature of war and the possibility of preventing it. But, he added, he did not expect to be awarded the Nobel Peace Prize for it. There is something wistful, even a little pathetic, about this remark. Yet he could not deny that he was leaving a deep impress on Western culture. And not only Western: in the 1920s, he began to correspond with the Indian physician Girindrasehkhar Bose. "I believe," said Stefan Zweig in 1929, trying to sum up Freud's influence, "that the revolution you have called forth in the psychological and philosophical and the whole moral structure of our world greatly outweighs the merely therapeutic part of your discoveries. For today all the people who know nothing about you, every human being of 1930, even the one who has never heard the name of psychoanalyst, is already indirectly dyed through and through by your transformation of souls." Zweig often let himself be carried away by his enthusiasms, but this appraisal is not far from the sober truth.

FORTUNATELY, AT LEAST some of the attention Freud garnered was not quite so lofty, and even rather amusing. The Hungarian playwright Ferenc Molnar, that wittiest of cosmopolitans, caricatured the popular caricatures of Freud's ideas in his plot summary for a proposed play, for which, he said, he had very good material: "How this is to be developed, I don't yet know, but the fundamental idea is quite simple, as in all great tragedies: Young man—happily married to his mother—discovers that she isn't his mother at all—shoots himself." In the late 1920s, in England, Ronald Knox, priest, translator of the Bible, and cultivated satirist, made gentle play with pseudo-psychoanalytic diagnoses; in one piece, he retold *Struwwelpeter*, that classic of German children's literature, in Freudian jargon. About the same time, in the United States, James Thurber and E. B. White lampooned the spate of sex books inundating American bookstores with *Is Sex Necessary? or, Why You Feel the Way You Do*. Among the mock-solemn chapters in this little book were "The Nature of the American Male: A Study of Pedestalism" and "What Should Children Tell Parents?" Freud, as their glossary of technical terms demonstrates, was much on their minds. They defined "Complex, Nuclear" as "Shock caused by discovery of a person of the opposite sex in his or her true colors; beginning of a general breakdown"; explained "Exhibitionism" as "Going too far, but not really meaning it"; and described "Narcissism" as "Attempt to be self-sufficient, with overtones." Helpfully, Thurber and White referred those who wanted to know the meaning of "Pleasure-

Principle" to "Libido," and under "Libido" noted, "Pleasure-Principle."
Some of this was puerile, but much presumably grave discourse was no more
responsible, and far more damaging, than such innocuous sallies.

Very early on, Freud had his responsible students, too, but their thoughtful
efforts at popularizing a dependable version of psychoanalysis were swamped
by notions about Freud that everybody accepted without taking the trouble
to read him. In 1912, studying "the Freudian psychology" with "a great deal
of enthusiasm," the young Walter Lippmann had told the English social
psychologist Graham Wallas that he felt about it "as men might have felt
about *The Origin of Species!*" Rereading William James after his discovery
of Freud left Lippmann "with a curious sense that the world must have been
very young in the 1880s." As he looked back on these heroic days, he recalled
that "serious young men took Freud quite seriously, as indeed he deserved
to be taken. Exploitation of Freud into a tiresome fad came later and generally from people who had not studied him and had only heard about him."

In self-defense, psychoanalysts made propaganda for Freud's ideas whenever they had the opportunity, addressing theologians and physicians and
writing articles they placed in more or less sophisticated periodicals. During
the 1920s, Oskar Pfister went on lecture tours in Germany and England,
bringing the Freudian message to his audiences and, in private conversations,
working on influential professors who might disseminate the Freudian truths
among their students. Pfister and other analysts also produced reliable, even
readable, aids to understanding: Pfister's exhaustive but accessible *The Psychoanalytic Method* was published in 1913 and appeared in an English
translation in New York four years later. It was not the first in the field: in
1911 Eduard Hitschmann had produced a far more concise exposition,
Freud's Theories of the Neuroses, soon translated into English. In 1920, G.
A. (later Sir Arthur) Tansley published *The New Psychology and Its Relation
to Life,* a gracefully written survey that went into seven printings in two years.
And in 1926, Paul Federn and Heinrich Meng edited a psychoanalytic
compendium "for the people," *Das Psychoanalytische Volksbuch,* for which
they enlisted a number of colleagues; the book covered the entire field of
psychoanalysis, including the analysis of art and culture, in some thirty-seven
short articles, which avoided technical terminology, translated foreign words,
and used homely instances to drive Freud's teachings home.

Freud might scoff, but all this labor was by no means wholly futile. In May
1926, newspapers and periodicals in country after country remembered
Freud's seventieth birthday with extensive appreciations, and some of these
turned out to be well informed. Perhaps the most intelligent was the civilized
tribute by the American essayist and biographer Joseph Wood Krutch, published in the *New York Times.* Freud, Krutch wrote, "father of the theory

of psychoanalysis," is "with the possible exception of Einstein, perhaps the most talked of scientist alive today." That welcome "scientist" was precisely the title Freud craved and rarely got. "There are of course, even today," Krutch conceded, "the behaviorists and other uncompromising anti-Freudians; but," he added, "it is safe to say that the influence of his chief conceptions is reflected more and more strongly in the writings of most of the important psychologists and psychiatrists." Krutch thought that just as Darwin and his ideas had penetrated modern culture, similarly "we are already making wide use of the Freudian conceptions, and in the course of time they will probably become, like the conception of evolution, a part of the mental equipment which every thinker takes for granted." When, at about the same time, a professor at Brown University worried that the psychological counseling the university was introducing might expose students to "mere analysis in the name of half-baked science," a *New York Times* editorial writer rebuked the skeptic: " 'Half-Baked,' " the headline of his paragraph proclaimed, "Seems Ill-Chosen."* Watching it all with sardonic distance, Freud observed to Arnold Zweig, "I am not famous, but I am 'notorious.' " He was only half right: he was both.

VITALITY: THE BERLIN SPIRIT

Even the pessimist Freud had to admit by the late 1920s that, with all their struggles and quarrels, psychoanalytic institutes were flourishing. In a retrospect of 1935, he pointed with pride to the "local groups in Vienna, Berlin, Budapest, London, Holland, Switzerland," to which new ones had been added "in Paris and Calcutta, two in Japan, several in the United States, most recently one each in Jerusalem and South Africa, and two in Scandinavia." No doubt, Freud triumphantly concluded, psychoanalysis had come to stay.

By the time Freud wrote this summary, several of the institutes had an

---

*This sort of work, it seemed, was never done, certainly not in the 1920s. Thus in the United States, in 1927, Philip Lehrman defended psychoanalysis at a meeting of the American Medical Association against the attacks of Morris Fishbein, the formidable editor of the *Journal of the American Medical Association*, whom he bravely—and rightly—called "misinformed." ("Presses the Value of Psychoanalysis / Dr. Lehrman Presents Present-Day Status of This Aid to the Mentally Ill," *New York Times*, May 22, 1927, sec. 2, 4.)

interesting history behind them. Abraham had transplanted the model of the
Vienna Psychoanalytic Society to Berlin back in 1908, scheduling regular
gatherings for discussions and papers in his apartment. This became the
nucleus for the Berlin chapter of the International Psychoanalytic Association, founded at the Nürnberg congress in 1910. In the United States, in
1911, physicians interested in psychoanalysis had organized themselves, not
without some tense moments, into two bodies, allies and rivals: the New
York Psychoanalytic Society and the American Psychoanalytic Association.
Two years after that, Ferenczi had established the Budapest Psychoanalytic
Society, which prospered briefly after the war, until the Bolshevik regime was
overthrown in the summer of 1919 and the anti-Semitic—and antipsy-
choanalytic—Horthy regime took over in February 1920. Budapest produced
some of the most conspicuous talents in the analytic profession: in addition
to Ferenczi, these included Franz Alexander, Sándor Radó, Michael Balint,
Geza Róheim, René Spitz, and others. The British Psycho-Analytical Society
was constituted in 1919, and the London Institute of Psycho-Analysis, principally animated by that tireless organizer Ernest Jones, was formally founded
late in 1924; the French, overcoming obstinate resistance from the medical
and psychiatric establishments, founded their psychoanalytic institute two
years after that.* The Italians followed suit in 1932; the Dutch, after lengthy
preliminaries, in 1933. Eitingon, who emigrated from Berlin to Palestine late
that year, one of the first analysts to leave Hitler's Germany, founded a
psychoanalytic institute in Jerusalem promptly after his arrival. Truly, as
Freud saw, psychoanalysis had come to stay.

IN THE 1920s, THE most vital of all these organizations was in Berlin. At the
outset, Abraham's society had been a brave, tiny band; some of the first
adherents (such as the sexologist Magnus Hirschfeld, who was interested only
in sexual liberation, not in psychoanalysis) dropped out. But by the first years
of the Weimar Republic, Berlin had established itself as the nerve center of
world psychoanalysis, despite the precarious political health of the young
republic, threatened by runaway inflation, political assassinations, sporadic
foreign occupation, and at times virtual civil war. In the light of this tumultu-
ous history, it is ironic that Berlin's analysts should profit from greater miser-

---

*There had been private, as it were unorganized, psychoanalytic activity in France for some years
earlier, as there had been in England before the founding of the British institute: on October 25,
1923, the French psychoanalyst René Laforgue had written to Freud, "Now that the psychoanalytic
movement has taken form in France and that the first successes have been obtained, I feel the need
to take closer contact with the Master of psychoanalysis and the Viennese school." (From the
Freud–Laforgue correspondence, tr. into French by Pierre Cotet and ed. André Bourguignon et al.,
in "Mémorial," *Nouvelle Revue de Psychanalyse*, XV [April 1977], 251.)

ies, and from persecutions, elsewhere. Hanns Sachs came to Berlin from Vienna in 1920; Sándor Radó and Franz Alexander, Michael and Alice Balint, finding life impossible in Horthy's Hungary, arrived soon after. Others, like Melanie Klein and Helene Deutsch, also went to Berlin to be analyzed and to analyze.

Alix Strachey, who had been Freud's analysand before she switched to Abraham, greatly preferred the pulsating, hectic atmosphere of Berlin to that of comparatively torpid Vienna. She also preferred Abraham to Freud as an analyst. "There is no doubt in my mind," she told her husband in February 1925, "that Abraham is the best analyst I could be working with." She was sure "that more psychological work," indeed, "has been done in these 5 months than was accomplished in 15 with Freud." She found this curious, but noted that others, like "Frau Klein," also thought Abraham a sounder analyst than Freud. Above all, she was taken with Berlin. Here psychoanalysts and candidates talked and debated and quarreled at meetings, at *Konditoreien,* even at parties. Digging into pastry and dancing through the night were not incompatible with earnest talk about oedipal attachments and castration fears. The psychoanalyst Rudolph Loewenstein, analyzed by Hanns Sachs, found the Berlin institute "cold, very German." But even he admitted that it boasted some fine technicians and inspiring teachers. For an analyst in the 1920s, Berlin had become the place to be.

For one thing, as the circular letters emanating from Berlin testify, the atmosphere in the city was growing ever less inhospitable to psychoanalysis. "This winter," Abraham, Sachs, and Eitingon reported in December 1924, "interest in Psa. has increased extraordinarily. Popular lectures are being organized by various groups." A number of outside speakers, including Pfister, came to give talks; his address to the Society for the Scientific Study of Religion, "generally good, only weak and maladroit in some places," received a "friendly reception before an audience of 150 persons, mainly theologians." Three months later, Abraham had some more "favorable news": he had just read a paper before the Berlin Society for Gynecology on the topic of gynecology and psychoanalysis. The auditorium at the university clinic had been packed. "At the outset," the physicians present, "in part so far very poorly informed, displayed the well-known smiling-skeptical attitude," but in the course of the evening they grew more favorable to the speaker. Soon after, in fact, the gynecological society asked Abraham for a copy of his paper, to be printed in the society's journal. "A sign," he exclaimed, "of success!"

BERLIN'S GREATEST ATTRACTION for psychoanalysts was Karl Abraham—reliable, confident, intellectual, a steady support to the young and the imaginative. What Freud had once called Abraham's "Prussianity" was, in the context of exuberant and excited Berlin, no drawback. There was also another magnet: the clinic that Ernst Simmel and Max Eitingon had established in 1920, financed with Eitingon's money. The founders credited Freud with the essential idea, and this was more than mere piety. Speaking at the Budapest congress of 1918, Freud had envisioned a future that, he admitted, might strike most of his listeners as fantastic. There was only a handful of analysts in the world and a great deal of neurotic misery, and much of that was concentrated among the poor, until now beyond analysts' reach. But "some day, the conscience of society will awaken and admonish it that the poor have just as much right to help for their minds as they already have to life-saving surgical help, and that neuroses threaten the health of the people no less than tuberculosis." Once this has been recognized, there will be public institutions employing psychoanalytically trained physicians to aid men who would other-wise succumb to alcoholism, women who threaten to break down under the burden of their privations, and children whose only choice seems to be delinquency or neurosis. "These treatments will be free of charge." Freud expected that it would be a long time before states came to accept these duties as urgent. "It is probable that it will be private philanthropy that will start such institutions, but some day it will have to come to this." It was a generous and, for the old-fashioned liberal Freud, a surprising vista.

The Berlin clinic "for the psychoanalytic treatment of nervous ailments" and its associated institute were the first realization of Freud's call to utopia. Looking back on the occasion of its tenth anniversary in a little Festschrift, members of the institute claimed some considerable achievements. With the institute's clinic and teaching facilities, Simmel wrote, Berlin's psychoanalysts had, in addition to their therapeutic and professional activities, engaged in the "psychoanalytic treatment of public opinion." The figures suggest that this self-praise was not just the fantasy of complacent celebrants pressing laurels on their own heads. Otto Fenichel, then a young analyst in Berlin, reported in a brief statistical overview that between 1920 and 1930, the institute had undertaken 1,955 consultations, of which 721 had led to psycho-analyses. Of these analyses, 117 were still continuing, 241 had been broken off, and 47 had to be written off as failures. Of the 316 other cases, 116 had shown improvement, 89 distinct improvement, and 111 had been cured. Claims for improvement and cure in psychoanalysis are notoriously inconclu-sive, but even if Fenichel's figures lack scientific certainty, they testify to a broadening of psychoanalytic activities unthinkable even a decade earlier. A total of ninety-four therapists had done the analyzing at the Berlin institute and clinic, and sixty of these were, or became, members of the International Psychoanalytic Association. In short, indigent neurotics coming for treatment were not simply turned over to candidates to be practiced on, but could count, at least part of the time, on being seen by a seasoned practitioner.

Meanwhile, the institute trained its candidates, and it was in Berlin in the 1920s that a program of study was carefully—its critics said, rigidly—worked out. It called for courses on the general theory of psychoanalysis, on dreams, on technique, on the transfer of analytic knowledge to the general practitioner, and on special topics such as the application of psychoanalysis to law, sociology, philosophy, religion, and art. As one might expect, though the institute's program was varied, Freud's works were required reading throughout. But while all students read Freud, not all became analysts: the institute drew a distinction between candidates and auditors. Candidates undertook the full training to pursue a career in psychoanalysis, while auditors—for the most part pedagogues, joined by a few interested laymen—expected to apply in their professions whatever analytic knowledge they managed to absorb.

The guidelines of the institute mandated a training analysis; this requirement was still controversial elsewhere, but in Berlin no one who had not been analyzed was to analyze anyone else. This training analysis was expected to take, the guidelines said, "at least a year"—a recommendation betraying a therapeutic optimism that now seems sheer frivolity. But even with such a short analysis, candidacy was a time of testing that corresponded, as Hanns Sachs put it, "to the novitiate in a church." Sachs's metaphor assimilating the institute to a religious institution was facile and unfortunate; it mirrored a common charge against psychoanalysis. But one can see why he used it. Freud would protest to Ernest Jones, "I am not fond of acting the Pontifex maximus." But he protested in vain.

Once the preeminence of the Berlin Psychoanalytic Institute became common knowledge among aspiring analysts, candidates flocked to it. Many of them were foreigners, British, French, Dutch, Swedish, American. They were delighted with the informality of the physical arrangements, astonished by the enthusiasm of the participants and by their inspiring seriousness. In time the graduates returned home from Berlin to launch practices or found institutes of their own. Charles Odier, one of the first among French psychoanalysts, was analyzed in Berlin by Franz Alexander; Michael Balint, who ended up in London, by Hanns Sachs; Heinz Hartmann, who later emigrated to New York, by Sándor Radó. The list of Karl Abraham's analysands reads like a roster of psychoanalytic eminence: the leading English analysts Edward and James Glover, Freud's analysand Helene Deutsch, who was to make her reputation with her writings on female sexuality, the articulate theoretical innovators Karen Horney and Melanie Klein, and that witty English observer, later to figure among Freud's translators, Alix Strachey.

BERLIN WAS ONLY the most spectacular of the centers in which psychoanalysis ensured its future. Freud continued to analyze in Vienna, concentrating more and more on apprentice psychoanalysts: such important followers as Jeanne Lampl-de Groot and Princess Marie Bonaparte, to say nothing of a whole contingent of Americans, were among Freud's "pupils" after the war.* More than six decades later, Jeanne Lampl-de Groot, her affection undimmed, recalled what Freud was like in April 1922, when she, the newly minted doctor, petite, musical, looking younger than her age, first presented herself at Berggasse 19. Freud was then almost sixty-six, and she found him a polite, "charming and considerate, old-fashioned" gentleman. When he asked her whether he or his daughters might be of assistance in getting her settled, she mentioned that she needed a piano. This prompted Freud to confess right off that he was unmusical, lest her later discovery of this flaw interfere with her analysis. Freud was, she added, "humane" and accessible, ungenerous only to "indecent people." When she told him that her beloved eldest sister, who had always been sturdy, had died of the Spanish influenza in five days during pregnancy, Freud responded by telling her about the death of his daughter Sophie. In the cordial correspondence they carried on after her return to the Netherlands, she soon became his "dear Jeanne." Not every analysand experienced Freud as quite so charming, but by the late 1920s the threads of his influence were woven across Europe and the United States in an intricate network.

PSYCHOANALYSIS SHOWED OTHER signs of robust health. Until the advent of the Nazis to power in 1933, the biennial international congresses of psychoanalysts were a fixture, eagerly awaited and faithfully attended. Freud, troubled by his prosthesis, no longer went, even though the decision to stay at home was hard for him. He postponed it as long as he could. "You are right to observe," he wrote to Abraham in March 1925, as preparations for the congress in Bad Homburg were going forward, "that I am making plans again, but when it comes to the point, my courage to carry them out leaves me. If, for example, around the time for the congress, I should feel no better with my prosthesis than I did last week, I should certainly not travel. So, make your arrangements without counting on me." He sent his daughter Anna in his place, and thus was present at least in spirit.

---

*Abram Kardiner, who was analyzed by Freud in 1921, recalls how Freud shifted from a six-day to a five-day week for his analysands. Faced with clamoring Americans who refused to be analyzed by anyone else, he consulted Anna Freud, "something of a mathematician," who suggested that he could see six if he gave them five hours each, whereas on his old schedule he could see only five of them. (A[bram] Kardiner, *My Analysis with Freud: Reminiscences* [1977], 17–18.)

As time went by and institutions became established, psychoanalytic periodicals sprouted in country after country, supplementing those founded before the First World War: the *Revue Française de Psychanalyse* in 1926, the *Rivista Psicanalisi* in 1932. No less heartening was the fact that Freud's writings were being made available in other languages. This meant a great deal to him: his correspondence of the 1920s is punctuated with expressions of intense interest in translations planned and comments on translations completed. *The Psychopathology of Everyday Life,* his most widely distributed book, appeared in twelve foreign languages during his lifetime; the *Three Essays on the Theory of Sexuality,* in nine; and *The Interpretation of Dreams,* in eight. The earliest versions were not always felicitous. A. A. Brill, who in the heroic days had something of a monopoly on translating Freud into English, was casual and at times fearfully inaccurate; for one thing, he did not know, or care about, the difference between "jokes" and "wit." Still, Brill gave the English-speaking world at least a glimpse, however uncertain, of Freud's theories even before the war: he published his translation of the *Three Essays on the Theory of Sexuality* in 1910, and of *The Interpretation of Dreams* three years later.*

Then translations began to improve: in 1924 and 1925, a small English team brought out Freud's *Collected Papers,* in four volumes.† This was the work of James and Alix Strachey and the incomparable Joan Riviere, that "tall Edwardian beauty with picture hat and scarlet parasol," whose renderings retained more of Freud's stylistic energy than any others. Freud was impressed. "The first volume of the 'Collection' has arrived," he exclaimed to Ernest Jones late in 1924. "Very handsome! And estimable!" He worried that some of his "antiquated" papers might not be the best introduction of psychoanalysis to the English public, but hoped for better things when the second volume, with the case histories, would appear a few weeks later. In any event, "I see that you have realized your intention of securing psycho-

---

*Freud had a sense of Brill's failings as a translator. In 1928, he hinted at them rather delicately in a letter to the aspiring Hungarian psychoanalyst Sándor Lorand: "Of my *Interpretation of Dreams* there is, as far as I know, only one *English* translation, that of Dr. Brill. It is, I suppose, best, if one wants to read the book at all, to read it in German." (Freud to Sándor Lorand, April 14, 1928. Freud Collection, B3, LC.)

†One obvious flaw in this translation was the substitution of esoteric neologisms for the plain German terms Freud preferred. A particularly egregious instance is "cathexis," now wholly domiciled in English and American psychoanalytic terminology. It renders Freud's *Besetzung,* a word from common German speech rich in suggestive meanings, among them "occupation" (by troops) and "charge" (of electricity). Freud's own solution, which he apparently never communicated to his translators, was ingenious and felicitous: in an early letter to Ernest Jones, he spoke of "interest (Besetzung)." (Freud to Jones, November 20, 1908. In English. Freud Collection, D2, LC.)

analytic literature in England, and congratulate you on this result, which I had scarcely dared to hope for any more." A year later he acknowledged receipt of the fourth volume with hearty thanks and the usual skepticism: "I won't be surprised if the book shows its influence only very slowly."

He was, as usual, more plaintive than necessary. This Englishing of Freud's writings was a momentous event in the diffusion of psychoanalytic ideas: the set of papers quickly established itself as the standard text for analysts unlettered in German. It contained nearly all of Freud's shorter publications from the mid-1890s right down to the mid-1920s: the essential papers on technique, the polemical history of the psychoanalytic movement, all the published papers on metapsychology and on applied psychoanalysis, the five great case histories—of Dora, Little Hans, the Rat Man, Schreber, the Wolf Man. Since many younger analysts in Britain or the United States did not have the talent, or did not take the trouble, to master German as Ernest Jones, the Stracheys, and Joan Riviere had done, to translate Freud and translate him well was a way of strengthening the bonds of the international psychoanalytic family.

As WE HAVE already plainly seen, that family was not a completely happy one. Some of the dissensions plaguing the movement from the early 1920s on were at bottom personal. Numerous analysts thought Groddeck too abrasive to be a useful public speaker at a congress—too abrasive and too indiscreet.* Ernest Jones resented Otto Rank, while Ferenczi thought Jones an anti-Semite. Freud was exasperated by news that Abraham was lending himself to the making of a film about psychoanalysis. Brill, enthroned in New York, tried everyone's patience by not answering letters. At meetings in London, Melitta Schmideberg, a child analyst, engaged in unseemly public controversy with the pioneering child analyst Melanie Klein, who was her mother.

But incompatible, fiercely defended views about psychoanalytic theory and technique were not simply masks for personal animosities, economic anxiety, or the understandable ambition to make one's mark in a highly competitive

---

*On March 15, 1925, the Berlin trio—Abraham, Sachs, and Eitingon—reported in their circular letter that Groddeck, who occasionally came to Berlin to lecture, had given a cycle of three talks in which he had called "unpleasant" attention to himself. In one of these, it seems, he had stopped after hearing an automobile honking in the street to offer his free associations to the noise. "According to a reliable report, for well over an hour he revealed all the most intimate details of his private life, which among other things included his wife, who was present; in doing this, he reveled continuously in the crassest expressions." One of the subjects he discussed, apparently, was his masturbatory activity. On April 13, Abraham and Eitingon added that an acquaintance had visited Groddeck in Baden-Baden and Groddeck had "spontaneously" told him of his free-associating in front of an audience. "A number of other details show that G. does with Psa. whatever suits him at the moment." (Both in Karl Abraham papers, LC.)

field. They sprang in part from conflicting readings of Freud's texts, and in part, too, from divergent clinical experiences that opened up new directions for analytic therapy and theory. These were opportunities for originality, and Freud was there to encourage them—always within limits.

The most innovative among the theorists of the 1920s was, without doubt, Melanie Klein. She had been born in Vienna, in 1882, but it was not until she moved to Budapest at twenty-eight that she discovered Freud. She read her way through the analytic literature, was analyzed by Ferenczi, and began to specialize in the analysis of children. Her young patients included her own sons and daughter, about whom she wrote some barely veiled clinical papers. It was a time when child analysis still appeared a highly problematic venture, but Ferenczi and later Abraham were fascinated by Klein's departures and defended them against quizzical fellow analysts. She needed this support badly, for she had no models to go on; Freud's analysis of Little Hans had been done, after all, largely at second hand.* By 1919, Klein began to publish the results of her clinical work with children, and in 1921, attracted by Abraham's openness to her ideas, she settled in Berlin, analyzing, arguing, publishing.

Alix Strachey came to know Melanie Klein well and liked her greatly; she went to coffeehouses and dances with her and wryly admired her flamboyance, her attractive erotic verve, her rhetorical presence. In one letter to her husband, James, she described a characteristic storm over Klein, larding her report, as was her habit, with comical bits of German. The letter is a vivid tribute to the contentiousness, but also the sheer intellectual stimulation, pervading Berlin's analytic culture: "Last night's Sitzung" of the Berlin Psychoanalytic Society, she wrote, had been very exciting. "Die Klein propounded her views & experiences on Kinderanalyse, & at last the opposition showed its hoary head—& it really was *too* hoary. The *words* used were, of course, psycho-analytical: danger of weakening the Ichideal, etc. But the *sense* was, I thought, purely anti-analysis: we mustn't tell children the terrible truth about their repressed tendencies, etc. And this, altho' die Klein demonstrated absolutely clearly that these children (from 2¾ upwards) were already wrecked by the repression of their desires & the most appalling *Schuld bewusstsein* (= too great, or incorrect oppression by the Ueberich.)" Alix Strachey went on to note that "the opposition consisted of Drs. Alexander & Radó, & was purely affective & 'theoretical'." After all, virtually no one outside "die Melanie" knew anything about children. Fortunately, one speaker after the other "rushed in" to "defend die Klein." In fact, everyone rallied to her & attacked the 2 swarthy Hungarians."

*See pp. 255–59.

The two instances Klein offered to support her argument at this intemperate meeting were, according to Alix Strachey, "specially brilliant." Indeed, "*if* die Klein reports correctly, her case seems to me to be quite overwhelming. She's going to Vienna to read her paper; & it is expected that she will be opposed by Bernfeldt & Eichhorn (?), those hopeless pedagogues, &, I fear, by Anna Freud, that open or secret sentimentalist." Alix Strachey's impulsive partisanship was a foretaste of debates to come after Melanie Klein moved to England in 1926 and charmed her astonished colleagues with her theories. "Well," Alix Strachey concluded her report, "it was most stimulating, & much more feeling was displayed than usual."*

It was true: wherever Melanie Klein went, feelings ran high. Even those who refused to follow her theoretical innovations were fascinated by the play technique she employed in psychoanalyzing children. Play, she energetically argued, was the best way, often the only way, to let the child's fantasies emerge for interpretation, whether they circled around curiosity about sexual intercourse, death wishes against siblings, or hatred of a parent. In Klein's hands, interpretation became a potent but, she insisted, ultimately beneficent weapon. In contrast to her critics, she was prepared to be as candid as humanly possible as she interpreted to her small patients the meaning of their fantasies. But she was more than an imaginative technician; her departures in clinical technique rested on, and in part engendered, departures in metapsychology. As she elaborated her system during her years in England, she postulated the emergence of the Oedipus complex and the superego far earlier than Freud thought possible. According to Klein, the internal world of the small child is a mass of destructive and anxious fantasies, redolent with unconscious images of mayhem and death. For Freud, the child is a selfish savage; for Klein, it is a murderous cannibal. If anyone took Freud's death drive with all its implications seriously, it was Melanie Klein.

Yet in her theorizing about infancy she was departing from the developmental schedule that Freud, and his analyst daughter, found most plausible. At first Freud assumed an agnostic posture. "The work of Melanie Klein has encountered much doubt and contradiction," he told Ernest Jones in 1925. "As for myself, I am not very competent to judge in pedagogic matters." Two years later, he had taken his stand. He insisted in a powerful letter to Jones that he had tried to be impartial between Melanie Klein and Anna Freud; on the one hand, Klein's most formidable adversary was after all his daughter, and on the other, Anna Freud's work was quite independent of his own. "One

---

*"Bernfeldt & Eichhorn" were Siegfried Bernfeld and August Aichhorn, two of the most promising of the younger generation in Vienna. The former later gathered important biographical material and published no less important biographical articles that served Ernest Jones in his life of Freud. The latter became well known for his psychoanalytic work with delinquent children.

thing I can reveal to you at any rate," he added, "Frau Klein's views on the behavior of the ego ideal in children seem wholly impossible to me and are in contradiction to all my presuppositions." He welcomed Klein's demonstration that children are "more mature than we used to think." But that, too, "had its limits and is in itself no proof."

Not surprisingly, the debate between Melanie Klein and Anna Freud stimulated larger conflicts, and no more surprisingly, Freud could not stay as neutral as he professed to be. But he ventilated his most impassioned irritation mainly in the privacy of his correspondence with Ernest Jones, where he allowed himself some rather tart language. He accused Jones of arranging a campaign against his daughter's way of analyzing children, defended her criticisms of Melanie Klein's clinical strategies, and resented the charge that she had been insufficiently analyzed. This last hit Freud in a sensitive spot; he thought such insinuations dangerous and impermissible. "Who, after all, has been sufficiently analyzed? I can assure you," he rejoined with some heat—to say nothing of private knowledge—"Anna has been analyzed longer and more thoroughly than, for example, you yourself." He denied that he was treating his daughter's views as sacred and immune from criticism; indeed, if anyone should try to close off Melanie Klein's avenues of expression, he would open them himself. But Klein and her allies were really very irritating: they went so far as to claim that in her analyses Anna Freud was evading the Oedipus complex on principle. He was beginning to wonder whether these attacks on his daughter were not really attacks on himself.

In print, though, Freud said little, except to comment briefly on Klein's views about the sense of guilt and, with approval, on her contention that the severity of the superego in no way corresponds to the severity of the treatment a child has experienced. This politic discretion shows Freud in the part of the elder statesman, the leader above the battle. Child analysis, he observed in a note he added to his "Autobiographical Study" in 1935, had received a powerful impetus through "the work of Frau Melanie Klein and of my daughter, Anna Freud." There were Kleinians at large from the early 1930s on, and their orientation was destined for a career of pervasive influence especially in Britain, Argentina, and some American analytic institutes. But Freud was concentrating his fire on other targets, reserving his energies for contentious issues that, he thought, needed his intervention more: the controversial redefinition of anxiety, the dispute over lay analysis, and that most troubling of questions, female sexuality. To participate actively in the debates these issues were engendering was one way of staying alive.

TEN

Flickering Lights on Dark Continents

The questions that preoccupied Freud from the mid-1920s on were not pure abstractions for him, but acquired their urgency from events in his personal life. They exhibit once again the continuous traffic in Freud's mind between private feelings and scientific generalizations—a traffic that reduced neither the intensity of his feelings nor their relevance to his science. Beneath the surface of his rational argumentation, there lurks Freud the disappointed father, the concerned mentor, the anxious son.

RANK AND THE CONSEQUENCES

 The last adherent Freud expected to give him trouble was his valued and, he thought, wholly dependable psychoanalytic son Otto Rank. But in 1923, Rank went through some distressing episodes that hinted at welling-up conflicts; in August, for one, at dinner with the Committee in San Cristoforo, Anna Freud witnessed an outburst she later described as

"hysterical hilariousness." Just as ominously, Rank began to espouse techniques and theoretical positions that would move him far from the ideas he had been steeped in for two decades and had done so much to propagate. Once the most orthodox of Freudians, he became a Rankian. After the war, Rank had shown himself such an agreeable aide—prompt, efficient, filial— that Freud wished there were a way to have multiple copies of him. But only a few years later, Freud could disparage Rank as "an impostor by nature"—a *Hochstaplernatur.* Freud's response was not limited to mere name calling: he assimilated, and worked through, this late and unexpected disappointment by proposing a fundamental revision in the psychoanalytic theory of anxiety. The essay he published in 1926 as *Inhibitions, Symptoms and Anxiety* displays his undiminished capacity for wringing profits from loss.

Freud's investment in Rank had been unstinted and of long duration. He had quickly recognized the talents of the young autodidact who came to visit him in 1905, manuscript of *The Artist* in hand. He had supported Rank's academic education, appointed him to take the minutes of the Wednesday-night group and encouraged his participation in the meetings, employed him as an editorial assistant, helped to finance his studies and his vacation trips. In 1912, with the delicacy he habitually mustered toward those less prosperous than himself, Freud invited Rank to accompany him as his guest on a visit to England and asked him to think of the invitation "as my thanks for your most recent splendid book." Most important, Freud strongly encouraged "little Rank" to train himself as a lay analyst and persistently demonstrated his confidence by appointing him to responsible positions: Rank figured as a founder and editor of *Imago* in 1912 and of the *Internationale Zeitschrift* a year later. When, in 1919, von Freund's munificent gift to the psychoanalytic cause made possible an analytic publishing house, the *Verlag,* Rank became one of its founders and its director. By that time, he had been an insider for some years. When the Committee, that tight praetorian guard around Freud, was formed in 1912, it was a matter of course that he should be a member.

Freud's attitude toward his young disciple was fond and paternal. He was inclined to worry about Rank. In December 1918, he wrote to Abraham about the young woman Rank had met during his wartime stint as an editor in Kraków and had married the month before: "Rank really seems to have done himself a good deal of harm with his marriage, a little Polish-Jewish wife whom no one finds congenial and who betrays no higher interests. Pretty sad and not quite comprehensible." It was one of those irresponsible summary judgments that Freud at times permitted himself and quickly discarded; he soon changed his mind about Beata Rank, an attractive and thoughtful young woman.* The following year, he thanked her in print for a useful suggestion she made for his paper on the "uncanny"; he came to welcome her contributions to the social life of his circle and in 1923 facilitated her application for membership in the Vienna Psychoanalytic Society. His capricious apprehension about Beata out of the way, Freud worried even more about Rank's career. He had after all advised him, as he had advised his daughter Anna and his friend Pfister, not to trouble with medical school for the sake of becoming a psychoanalyst. "I am never quite certain whether at the time I did right to hold you back from the study of medicine," he wondered in a letter to Rank in 1922. "I believe on the whole I was right when I think of my own boredom during my study of medicine." With an almost audible sigh of relief, he concluded that having seen Rank take his rightful place among analysts, he no longer found it necessary to justify that piece of advice.

Rank, to be sure, was not the recipient of unearned favors; he paid his way with strenuous service, unquestioning fidelity, and prolific publication. The mass and diversity of his activities—editing, writing, analyzing—made him stand out as exceptional amidst the early analysts, all noted for their long hours, hard work, and facile pens. Even Ernest Jones, who seriously disliked Rank, acknowledged him to be unsurpassed in his capacity for managing affairs. But this busy activity and this indispensability were tested, and destroyed, in the mid-1920s.

Freud was the last to grow suspicious of Rank. In 1922, when Rank and Ferenczi were writing a book on technique that other analysts would find extremely unsettling, Freud cheered them on. "Your alliance with Ferenczi," he wrote Rank, "has as you know my complete sympathy. The fresh daredevil initiative of your joint draft is really gratifying." He had always been afraid, Freud added, that he might be keeping those closest to him from taking up independent positions; now he was "pleased to see proofs to the contrary." The resulting book, *The Development of Psychoanalysis,* was published early in 1924; it contained much interesting material on technique, but hinted at a certain disregard of analysands' childhood experiences in the interest of shortening their analyses. Its therapeutic optimism ran counter to Freud's sense of the need for tedious, prolonged analytic work. About the same time, Rank published *The Trauma of Birth,* which he dedicated to Freud but which was potentially far more disturbing than his joint production with Ferenczi. It pointed to the birth trauma, and the fantasy of returning to the mother's

---

*Characteristically, Anna Freud's opinion of Beata Rank followed her father's. Speaking of Rank's "personality change," she told Ernest Jones, "I was inclined at one time to blame her for it, then it appeared as if she was the victim rather than anything else." (Anna Freud to Jones, February 8, 1955. Jones papers, Archives of the British Psycho-Analytical Society, London.)

womb, as far more important in the history of the mind than other, later traumas and fantasies. Yet Freud remained unperturbed.

FREUD'S TRANQUILITY WAS more than passive acceptance. Carefully cultivating his credulity, he did his utmost to minimize mounting indications that Rank might become another Adler—or Jung. He persisted in attributing the tensions among his followers to mere personal animosities. The others were not inclined to make light of them; only Eitingon, sanguine by nature and disposed to echo Freud's views, refused to take them seriously for some time. The issues dividing Rank and Abraham, he told Freud in January 1924, were, "to be sure, disagreeable, but far more trifling for the movement as a whole than the conflicts between R[ank] and Jones." In the same month, Freud reminded the Committee that he had after all accepted Rank's dedication of the birth-trauma book to him. Admittedly he had some problems with the hints at new techniques scattered by Rank and Ferenczi, and, even more, with Rank's theory of the birth trauma, but he hoped that the essential cordiality among colleagues would remain unimpaired. Early in February, he showed his astonishment at how grave a view Abraham was taking of Rank's and Ferenczi's recent publications. He was still reluctant to enter the debate. "I am making every effort," he told Eitingon, "not to abuse my authority to inhibit the independence of my friends and adherents. I do not demand that everything they produce be sure of my assent. Naturally this presupposes," he prudently added, "that they not leave the soil common to us, but this, after all, is hardly to be expected from R[ank] or from F[erenczi]." Rank showed some disappointment at Freud's response; he told Freud respectfully but frankly that it struck him as not wholly "unclouded" or free of misunderstandings. Still, he professed himself grateful for Freud's pacific stance.

By now, Abraham had mounted the barricades. In late February, he alerted Freud to a "worry that has only grown stronger in weeks of ever-renewed self-examination." He disclaimed any intention of organizing a hunting expedition against heretics. "Results of whatever kind reached in the legitimate-analytic way would never occasion severe misgivings." But this was something different. "I see signs of a calamitous development in which vital questions of psychoanalysis are involved. They force upon me to my deepest chagrin—not for the first time in my psychoanalytic career—the role of the warner." The ideas propagated by Rank and Ferenczi in their *Development of Psychoanalysis* and, even worse, by Rank alone in his *Trauma of Birth* struck Abraham as too wayward to be either ignored or condoned.

For the moment, at least, Freud refused to heed the alarm that Abraham was sounding from Berlin. In March, despite the impatient questions being

asked about all these "daredevil" initiatives, Freud could still write to Ferenczi, Rank's most consistent supporter in the inner circle, "My confidence
in you and Rank is unconditional. It would be sad if after 15 to 17 years of
living together one could find oneself still deceived." Rank's work, he added,
"has been invaluable, his person would be irreplaceable." He admitted to
skepticism about the brief analytic therapy that Rank and Ferenczi were
recommending; such therapy would, he thought, "sacrifice analysis to suggestion." But the growing gulf between Rank and the others distressed him. "I
have outlived the Committee that was designed to be my successor, perhaps
I shall still outlive the International Association. Let us hope that psychoanalysis will survive me." Fortunately, though, any resemblance of Rank to
Jung was superficial: "Jung was an evil fellow."

While Freud was being diplomatic, soothing, and patient, the protagonists
in the unfolding debacle appeared to be spoiling for combat. Ferenczi, angry
in Rank's behalf, denounced Abraham for his "unbridled ambitions and
jealousy"; they alone, he told Rank, could explain Abraham's "daring to
blacken" his and Rank's writings as "manifestations of defection." Freud was
deceiving himself when he continued to believe—or, rather, hope—that
Ferenczi did not share "Rank's embitterment against Abraham." But
through it all, Freud the old warrior, parading his ill-health and general
distaste for the friction around him, maneuvered to keep the peace, and Rank
within the family. The attempt was brave but futile. In mid-March, Rank
reported to Ferenczi confidentially on a talk with Freud. It had presented him
with some surprises. Freud was apparently working on a paper in which he
would criticize Rank's recent theories, but had shown himself evasive and not
even well informed. "Prof still has not read my book," or "only half of it."
He no longer seemed persuaded by some of Rank's arguments that he had
previously claimed to find impressive. Still, the meeting had been conciliatory: Freud had left it to Rank to decide when his forthcoming critique should
be published, or whether it should be published at all. But the dissension was
too fundamental to be easily contained, and so Freud proposed that the
members of the Committee meet to discuss all contentious questions. He
now admitted that he had come to be critical of Rank's newest writings. "But
I would like to hear what the threatening danger might be. I do not see it."
He would gradually be compelled to see.

DISCUSSING HIS *Trauma of Birth* with the members of the Vienna Psychoanalytic Society in early March, Rank told them that the book had grown
from a diary in which he had jotted down "impressions from analyses, in
aphoristic form. It was put together, as it were, like a mosaic." Nor, he added,
had he written it for analysts. But analysts found it significant enough to

debate it at length and criticize it vehemently. Later, Rank would argue that his central thesis, singling out the birth trauma as a decisive psychological event, was really an elaboration of Freud's own thinking—thinking, moreover, with which analysts had been acquainted for years. He had some warrant for his claim: in 1908, after Rank presented a paper on the myths that grow up around the birth of heroic figures, Freud had been recorded laconically as observing, "Act of birth as source of anxiety." A year later, listing a series of traumas afflicting children, Freud reminded the Vienna Psychoanalytic Society that "with anxiety one must keep in mind that the child has anxiety from the act of birth on." In 1909, too, in a note added to *The Interpretation of Dreams,* he had said it again, emphatically, in print: *"By the way, the act of birth is the first experience of anxiety and therefore source and model of the affect of anxiety."* That is why in the beginning Freud had found nothing inherently implausible about Rank's thesis.

In fact, that thesis was less a retreat from psychoanalytic thinking than a prophetic if rather one-sided anticipation of later developments in analytic theory. Rank was elevating the mother's role at the expense of the father's, and the prototypical anxiety of birth at the expense of the Oedipus complex. At first, Freud had thought that this might turn out to be a real contribution to his own thinking. When he accepted Rank's dedication of the book, he quoted a gracious line from Horace: *Non omnis moriar*—"I shall not wholly die." Indeed, in early March 1924, he suggested to Abraham, "Let us take the most extreme case: Ferenczi and Rank come out directly with the claim that we have been wrong to stop with the Oedipus complex, that the real decision in fact lies with the trauma of birth." If they are proved right, the origins of neuroses would have to be sought in a physiological accident rather than "our sexual etiology." In that case, analysts would certainly have to modify their technique. "What mischief would then occur? One could stay together under the same roof with complete peace of mind." A few years' work, he thought, would determine just who among the theorists had been right.

Freud's patience was reinforced by his fatherly feelings for Rank, but he was also speaking as a scientist ready to entertain the conjecture that his favorite discovery, the Oedipus complex, was not quite so critical to mental development as he had long believed. He reminded the members of the Committee, that "complete unanimity in all questions of scientific detail and on all newly broached themes" is not "possible among half a dozen people of differing nature." It was not even desirable. But very reluctantly, he grew less forbearing, not without accusing the "warners," notably Abraham, of hasty and tactless proceedings in their campaign against Rank. Unwilling to recognize the gravity of the situation, he blamed the messengers. He freely acknowledged that Rank was touchy, insensitive, clumsy and harsh in his way of expressing himself, and humorless. Doubtless, he had brought most of his current troubles on himself. But Freud also thought his colleagues had been less than kind to him. As the months went by, Freud took refuge in this Olympian neutrality and distributed blame with an even hand: "The animosity [Rank] partly had experienced from you and the Berlin people, and partly imagined," he told Ernest Jones in September 1924, "had a disturbing effect on his mind."

The psychoanalysts of the innermost circle, led by Freud, were engaged in an awkward dance of indecisive gyrations and unexpected reversals. But Abraham remained relentless. He feared that Ferenczi and, far worse, Rank, were caught in an act of "scientific regression." Some English psychoanalysts, notably Ernest Jones and the brothers Edward and James Glover, wholly agreed with Abraham: Rank was repudiating Freud's teaching about the father's role in psychological development. The doctrine of the birth trauma, Jones exploded to Abraham, was nothing less than a "flight from the Oedipus complex." Indeed, the members of the anti-Rank camp thought themselves now more consistent than the aging master, more Freudian than Freud. "It is not hard to make every allowance for him," Jones wrote, "when one considers all the factors, age, illness, and the insidious propaganda nearer home." It would be a pity if they should be alienated from "Prof" through "too great loyalty to his work." But if they had to choose between psychoanalysis and "personal considerations," Jones solemnly pronounced, surely psychoanalysis must come first.

They need not have worried too much. Freud was becoming increasingly quizzical about the value of Rank's new ideas. On reflection, he came to read Rank's emphatic, almost fanatical harping on the birth trauma as an intolerable abandonment of time-tested psychoanalytic insights, and his propaganda for short analyses as a symptom of the baneful rage to heal. By late March 1924, he could tell Ferenczi that while he had thought two-thirds of Rank's *Trauma of Birth* correct, he was now confining his approval to a mere one-third. Before long even that rather modest measure of agreement seemed excessive to him.

IN APRIL 1924, Rank went to the United States, and the struggle was kept alive by correspondence. He gave lectures, conducted seminars, analyzed patients, supervised aspiring analysts. It was his first visit to America, a heady, quite disorienting experience, and he was ill prepared to take it in his stride. Some American analysts were disconcerted by Rank's message. One of them, the psychiatrist Trigant Burrow, a curious amalgam of physician and crank and an inconstant supporter of psychoanalysis—Freud thought him a "muddled babbler"—warned Freud that Rank was propagating a dangerous heresy in the United States. Freud reassured him: "It is only an innovation in technique which deserves to be tried. It promises a shortening of the analysis; experience will show whether it can keep that promise." With all his private doubts, Freud could still muster a declaration of faith: "Dr. Rank is too close to me to let me anticipate his going in the same direction as others before him."

Rank had never before enjoyed such adulation as he received in America, never dreamt of all this influence, never seen so much money. He had things both ways: in his lectures, he made much of the fact that birth anxiety and short analytic therapy were Freud's ideas. At the same time, he left the impression that he was bringing sensational news to his astonished listeners. It was the mother, not the father, who mattered in the shaping of the human animal: *"Im Gegenteil, die Mutter!* On ze contrary, ze mozer!" He was official spokesman and daring revisionist at the same time, a position he found extraordinarily seductive.*

But Rank could not leave Vienna behind. Freud pursued him to the United States by letter, taking the trouble to inform him that his own six most recent analysands, five of whom were acquainted with Rank's ideas, had wholly failed to confirm the birth-trauma thesis. "I often worry about you a great deal," he declared in the old fatherly manner in July. He was not being hostile, not even covertly; earnestly he beseeched Rank not to let himself become inflexible: "Leave a retreat open to yourself." But Rank read Freud's almost desperate plea only as disapproval and a breakdown in communication. "Had I not known it all along," he wrote in his draft reply, "your letter of today would have made it plain beyond all doubt that an understanding is quite impossible." He did not mail this letter, but it reflects his injured feelings to perfection. At this point, Freud was more conciliatory than Rank. In a long letter written from his summer retreat in Semmering, he recounted important issues on which other analysts, including Jung in his psychoanalytic phase, had disagreed with him without incurring any disfavor. He did not want mere echoes; Ferenczi, indeed, "places, in my judgment, too great a value on complete agreement with me. I don't." And he assured Rank, "My feelings for you have been shaken by nothing."

But they had been shaken, and deeply so. His strictly limited optimism of the summer did not hold; Freud was moving closer to the anti-Rank sentiments of his intimates, all intent on closing the door to reconciliation. In

---

*The minutes of the New York Psychoanalytic Society disclose that Rank's presentations were received with earnest attention and caused lively discussion. He found vehement supporters and equally vehement detractors. (See minutes for May 27, October 30, and November 25, 1924. A. A. Brill Library, New York Psychoanalytic Institute.)

September, Eitingon wrote to Vienna with unaccustomed acerbity, "Our friend Rank is really riding very fast"—Eitingon resented talk of an anti-Rank "Berlin conspiracy." And by October, Anna Freud was firmly in the camp of the Berliners. "Anna spits fire," Freud wrote Eitingon that month, "when the name Rank is mentioned." Yet Freud was still vacillating, and sent contradictory messages. On the one hand, he did not yet want to give up on Rank the man. "I should like to separate his person from the trauma of birth," he told Abraham in mid-October, a little wistfully. On the other hand, a few days later, when Rank returned to Vienna and made a prompt call on Freud the first item on his agenda, Freud anticipated the meeting with considerable misgivings. "I nourish no illusions," he wrote Ernest Jones, "on the result of this interview." His inconsistency is a measure of his distress.

The Viennese found the new Rank very puzzling. "We cannot explain his behavior to ourselves," Freud informed Ernest Jones in November, "but this much is certain, he has cast all of us aside with great facility and prepared himself for a new existence, independent of us." To that end, he added, Rank had apparently felt it necessary to claim that Freud, for one, had treated him badly. "Confronted with his own unfriendly pronouncements, he dismisses them as gossip and invention." Freud now found Rank insincere, no longer credible. "I regret very much that you, dear Jones, have been right in the end to such an extent." He had been compelled to write such letters to Jones, and to Abraham, before.

Once back in Vienna, still intoxicated by his recent triumphs in the United States, Rank resigned his various official posts; barely home, he planned another trip overseas, again to America. His restlessness was understandable: his adversaries had succeeded in capturing his last ally, Ferenczi. "I was not surprised," Ernest Jones told his "dear Karl" Abraham in mid-November, "that Sandor should have proved himself loyal throughout." This, he commented, "is what one would have expected from him, for he is at least always a gentleman." But Rank was irresolution itself, depressed and guilt-ridden. In November, his wife took him to the train, on his way to the United States, only to have him turn up again at home soon after. "He runs around with a terribly bad conscience"—thus Freud sketched Rank for Lou Andreas-Salomé—with "a most miserable, embarrassed face," giving "the impression of someone who's had a thrashing." As Freud usually did in such contretemps, he firmly disclaimed all responsibility. He was so calm about Rank's defection, he noted, not only because he was growing old and indifferent, but mainly because he could not assign the slightest fault to himself. Rank was far more agitated. Late in November, he set off for America a second time, reached Paris, and turned back once more. By mid-December, in the grip of a mental crisis, torn between old allegiances and new opportunities, he was consulting Freud daily.

On December 20, in an astonishing circular letter, he spelled out his condition to his colleagues. He was contrite, apologetic, self-abasing; he recognized now, he told the Committee, that his behavior had been neurotic, governed by unconscious conflicts. Evidently, he had experienced "Professor's" cancer as a trauma, and failed both him and his friends. Anatomizing his travail, he fell back on traditional psychoanalytic wisdom and analyzed his deplorable mental state in the most orthodox Freudian terms: he had been acting out the Oedipus complex and the brother complex to boot. Among the recipients of this psychoanalyic confession, Ernest Jones, for one, was not convinced and not appeased. "I have honestly no feeling against Rank," he wrote confidentially to Abraham in late December, and professed himself happy to see Rank "regaining insight." But he was disposed to discount that as mere *"intellectual* insight." In short, Jones admitted, "I distrust Rank profoundly." It would be sheer blindness to overlook his earlier neurotic behavior, and expect the complete restoration of the old Rank. "The reality-principle has a way of revenging itself on the pleasure-principle sooner or later." Hence it was essential to keep him from reoccupying his old positions of responsibility.

Freud for his part was less exigent and welcomed Rank's *Rundbrief* as good news. "Although I know that you have been estranged from him for some time," he wrote Ernest Jones two weeks after receiving Rank's almost masochistic self-analysis, "I still expect from your insight and benevolence that you will draw a line under the account, forget the past and grant him new credit." He found it "gratifying" that he and his colleagues should not be compelled "to abandon one of us on the road as a fatal casualty or a marauder," and expected to see Rank bravely fighting once again alongside his comrades. Rank's recantation impressed him. "I cannot believe," he told the trusted Eitingon in January 1925, appraising Rank's earlier misbehavior, "that anything like it will ever occur again."

Freud's followers were not so disposed to forgive, let along forget. They shared Ernest Jones's suspicions to the full. On Christmas Day, the Berlin group—Eitingon, Sachs, Abraham—sent their "dear Otto" a letter welcoming him back to the fold. But the cordiality of their greeting did not conceal a certain sting; the three Berliners reminded Rank of his neurotic conduct, and strongly suggested that while he was busy revising his revisions in his return to psychoanalytic verities, he might do well to refrain from publishing. He could use that pause to subject himself to discussions and criticisms from his colleagues. A few days later, Ernest Jones followed the same line in an amicable but somewhat patronizing letter to Rank. He expressed pleasure at Rank's "clearer self-insight and the consequent desire to reestablish friend-ship." And, deftly skating over five years of wrangling and animosity, Jones assured his "dear Otto" that the friendship "has never been broken on my side," and that he greeted "unhesitatingly, therefore, your advances with full cordiality." Still, Jones thought a bit of severity indicated: words alone could not wipe out the past. Paraphrasing Goethe's famous line from *Faust,* with which Freud had concluded his *Totem and Taboo,* he observed, "In the end is the deed"—*Am Ende ist die Tat.* Rank's response to such unfriendly friendly messages—there were others like them—was to return to the United States early in January. He would not, could not, stay in Vienna. Freud, still patient, hoped that in his new American venture Rank would "make good the mischief he had made" during his first stay.

In fact, through the winter and spring of 1925, Freud struggled to return to his old attitude toward Rank. In March, after Rank had returned from his second excursion to the United States, Freud informed Abraham that he "once again extended" Rank his "full confidence." As late as July, Freud kept alive a flicker of trust in his unpredictable disciple. But the distasteful com-parisons that some of his adherents were making between Rank and Jung struck Freud, for all his wishful thinking, as sadly pertinent. Jung, too, had gone to the United States to give lectures in which he simultaneously pro-fessed his adherence to Freud and proclaimed his originality; Jung, too, had been afraid of his own courage and had apologized profusely to Freud for his aberrant conduct, only to take it all back later; Jung, finally, it seemed to Freud in retrospect, had profited greatly from his repudiation of Freud's uncompromising theories. Naturally, Rank was infuriated that anyone should liken him to Jung. To him and his few partisans, these suspicions and invidi-ous comparisons sounded like sheer name calling.

So, IN PART, they were. Rank was called disloyal, and worse, and became the target of wild analyses by his former friends. This was an old story. Even Freud, while still paternal with Rank, had been unable to resist diagnosing him as though he were an antagonist. He veered between seeing Rank as an oedipal son and a greedy entrepreneur. As early as November 1923, he had interpreted one of Rank's dreams to mean that "young David"—Rank—wanted to slay "boastful Goliath"—Freud. "You are the formidable David who, with his trauma of birth, will manage to invalidate my work." The following summer, Freud told Rank with robust candor that the theory of the birth trauma, which entailed the "elimination of the father," was an illegiti-mate translation of Rank's own miserable early years into grandiose theoreti-cal terms. Had he only been analyzed, Freud concluded, he would have worked through those early influences instead of building an ambitious structure on his neurosis. Then, in November, before Rank's public self-analysis, Freud harshly described Rank as someone "threatened by my illness and its dangers for his livelihood," who had "sought an isle of salvation" and found it in America. "It is really a case of the rat leaving the sinking ship." Struggling with a severely neurotic father complex, Rank had evidently found the dollar harvest that New York promised him quite irresistible. This was the hostile diagnosis of Rank to which Freud would in the end commit himself.

The psychoanalysts who had been pushing Freud to repudiate Rank did not cavil at such analytic abuse. Ernest Jones suggested to Freud that while the First World War had covered over Rank's "manifest neurosis" of 1913, that neurosis had "gradually returned in the form of a neurotic character." This entailed, above all, "denial of the Oedipus complex" and a "regression of hostility from the brother (myself) . . . to the father, presumably Freud." Abraham was, if anything, more scathing. Disclaiming any animosity, he pitilessly diagnosed "the neurotic process" in Rank as a development with a long prehistory. Rank, as Abraham saw him, had compensated for his negative feelings with overly conscientious work and a decreasing need for friendship. He had licensed himself to behave tyrannically, to become exceedingly touchy, and to cultivate his interest in money more and more openly. In short: "an unmistakable regression into the anal-sadistic."

These ventures into character assassination are instances of the kind of aggressive analysis that psychoanalysts, Freud in the vanguard, at once deplored and practiced. This, as we have had occasion to observe, was the way that analysts thought about others, and about themselves. Freud could attribute Jung's defection from psychoanalysis to "strong neurotic and egotistic motives." At the same time, he could judge himself only slightly less harshly, and admit that he was "egotistical enough" to use his ill-health as an alibi for staying away from analysts' quarrels. But if Freud did not direct such diagnoses against others alone, this does not make the abuse of psychoanalysis any the more valid or agreeable. It was endemic among analysts, a common professional deformation.

IN JUNE 1925, Freud had a momentary, strangely touching distraction from the Rank affair, which was moving inexorably toward its denouement. The fatherly friend of his thirties, Josef Breuer, with whom he had broken a quarter century before, had died at the age of eighty-three. Responding to Freud's graceful letter of condolence, Breuer's eldest son Robert must have assured Freud that his father had followed developments in psychoanalysis with a measure of sympathy—sympathy that Freud would have thought impossible—for Freud quickly wrote back, "What you say about the relation of your father to my later work was new to me and worked like balm on a painful wound that had never closed." As the letter attests, Freud had not, in all these years, quite worked through his estrangement from Breuer: the man who had supported him emotionally and financially, who had done so much, telling him about Anna O., to propel him toward his psychoanalytic discoveries, and whose kindnesses he had repaid with truculent discourtesy. Freud must have found it deeply gratifying to have been mistaken all along about Breuer's attitude, and to learn at long last that Breuer had kept watching him benevolently from afar—especially now that Rank was proving such a disappointment.

As the summer of 1925 went on, Freud had something to brood about far more important than Rank's defection: Karl Abraham's health. In early June, Abraham was writing Freud from bed. He had returned from lecturing in the Netherlands with apparent symptoms of bronchitis. It was given out that he had swallowed a fishbone which then lodged in his bronchial tubes. In actuality, he seems to have been suffering from undiagnosed lung cancer. In July, Abraham felt better and went off with his family for a restful summer holiday in Switzerland. By August, he was able to do some mild hiking in the mountains, and at the beginning of September he felt well enough to attend the international congress in Bad Homburg. It proved a strain on his weakened constitution, and Freud, who was steadily in touch, began to be concerned. "So it happened as I had feared," he wrote Abraham in mid-September. "The congress has exhausted you, and I can only hope that your youthfulness will soon overcome the disorder."

Reports from Berlin continued sanguine enough. In mid-October, Abraham sent around a reassuring circular letter: he was feeling fairly well. He noted, rather to Freud's displeasure, that he was under Fliess's care and praised his "extraordinary qualities as a physician." Fliess, he thought, was worth any three professors of internal medicine. "By the way," he added, "the whole course of my illness has confirmed his theory of periods in the most striking way." But the improvement did not hold. Attacks of fever, pains, gall-bladder trouble, indicated that the illness was grave. By early December, Freud was anxious in the extreme. "We are not in the mood to write a circular letter this month," he told Ernest Jones on December 13. "Abraham's illness keeps us all in suspense and we are very unhappy that the news should be so indefinite and sound so uncanny." Three days later, he informed Jones that Felix Deutsch had gone to see Abraham and had warned that "this week will be the critical period and [that] we ought to be prepared for the worst." Freud refused to give up hope: "It is a gloomy prospect, but as long as he is alive we may cling to the hope that his affection often gives a chance of recovery."

He did not feel well enough to go to Berlin, but expected that Ferenczi would make the trip and wondered if Jones's own health would permit him to go, too. Freud was denying the realities he saw before him. "I intentionally abstain from picturing the consequences if that fatal event occurs."

A few days later, on December 21, there seemed to be some room for optimism. "No news from Abraham today," Freud wrote Jones, but the most recent bulletin had "sounded reassuring." He took comfort in the thought that Alix Strachey, too, had recovered from an abscess of the lung, and that Abraham's heart was working well. But the postscript he added sounded very different. Deutsch had just called: he had left Abraham in satisfactory condition, free of fever, but had just learned that Abraham had relapsed and that his situation was desperate. Four days later, on Christmas Day, it was all over. Abraham was forty-eight.

Freud took Abraham's death very hard. The sensible organizer, the renowned training analyst, the indispensable optimist, the interesting theoretician, the loyal friend, was gone. "I can only repeat what you said," Freud wrote Ernest Jones on December 30. He must have been in virtual shock, for he was writing in German. "Abr[aham]'s death is perhaps the greatest loss that could strike us, and it has struck us. I used to call him in my letters, jokingly, my *rocher de bronze;* I felt secure in the absolute confidence that he inspired in me as in all others." He added that he was writing a short obituary notice and would apply to Abraham the famous praise that Horace had lavished on the man of integrity, free of vice: *Integer vitae scelerisque purus.* He meant it; the overblown declarations that a death normally evokes, he told Jones, "have always been particularly embarrassing to me; I have taken care to avoid them, but with this quotation I had the feeling of being truthful." The breathless obituary Freud wrote does indeed contain the line from Horace, and the no less sincere mournful assertion that with Abraham, the psychoanalytic movement was burying "one of the strongest hopes of our young science, still much attacked, a perhaps irretrievable part of its future." This catastrophe put the prospect of losing Rank into perspective.

RANK WENT HIS own way, shuttling for a time between Paris and New York before settling in the United States. Freud had other things on his mind: early in 1926, he had heart trouble—the flare-up of an old complaint—severe enough to send him to a sanatorium. In March, he told Eitingon coolly that he might be dying, but "the only fear I really have is of a prolonged invalidism without the possibility of working. More precisely: possibility of earning." Prosperous as he had become, providing for his family continued to be a worry to him. But by April, when Rank visited Freud for the last time, Freud was recovered, back at home, analyzing patients. Rank had not yet elaborated his final theories; they emerged two or three years later as he developed his concept of the will as the primary human force, as that part of the ego which masters the drives on one hand and the environment on the other. But by the spring of 1926, Rank had worked himself out of the Freudian camp. When he came to say farewell, Freud was done with him. "The gain from his illness," Freud judged, "in the form of material independence was very large." By June, he had drawn the final balance. "I cannot manage to work up any indignation against Rank," he confessed to Eitingon. "I leave him the right to go astray and, in return, to appear original. But it is plain that he no longer belongs to us."*

THE AFFAIR HAD been painful and long-drawn-out, but Freud, reflecting on Rank's maverick ideas, drew some important lessons. In the book that came out of it all, *Inhibitions, Symptoms and Anxiety,* he observed, "Rank's reminder that the affect of anxiety is, as I was the first to assert, a consequence of the birth process and a repetition of the situation then experienced, necessitated a fresh scrutiny of the problem of anxiety. But," he noted, "I could get nowhere with his conception of birth as trauma, of the anxiety state as a disposal reaction to it, of every fresh affect of anxiety as an attempt to 'abreact' the trauma more and more completely." Still, Freud felt constrained to confess, Rank had raised some interesting issues.

Freud was about to celebrate—or, rather, would balk at celebrating—his seventieth birthday, but the familiar pressure to solve problems had not deserted him. The little book embodying his new thoughts on anxiety promised fresh conundrums for psychoanalysts: they would have to assimilate another far-reaching theoretical revision. "That my most recent book would muddy the waters," Freud told Lou Andreas-Salomé with obvious satisfaction, "was predictable. After a while, things will clear up again. It does not hurt to have people notice that we do not yet have a right to dogmatic rigidity, and that we must stand ready to cultivate the vineyard over and over again." But, he added soothingly, "the proposed changes are not so very subversive, after all." In *Inhibitions, Symptoms and Anxiety,* as in his letter to Lou Andreas-Salomé, Freud's tactic was to acknowledge that he had abandoned an earlier theoretical position but to minimize the length traveled: "The

*Writing to Dr. Frankwood Williams, a member in good standing of the New York Psychoanalytic Society but an admirer of Rank's, Freud declared in his gruffest manner that Williams's description of himself as a psychoanalyst had surprised him: "I only knew of you that you had been a Rank enthusiast, and that I had not succeeded in a conversation with you to convince you that a few months' work with Rank has little to do with analysis in our sense and that R. has ceased to be an analyst. If you have not undergone a thorough transformation since then, I would have to dispute also your right to this name." (Freud to Frankwood Williams, December 22, 1929. Typescript copy, Freud Museum, London.)

conception of anxiety put forward in this essay diverges some distance from the one that had hitherto seemed justified to me." The words "some distance" signally fail to convey the import of the innovation he was introducing.

The book is aesthetically less satisfying than most of Freud's other writings. It strings together ideas instead of demonstrating their necessary connection. Some of its lasting contributions to psychoanalytic thinking, the passages on repression and defense, like those on anxiety, are scattered across the text and tucked away in one of the appendices. It is as though Freud had become impatient with the fatiguing task of renovating his analytic structure. He looks anxious to be done once and for all with the work of rebuilding. Many years before, Freud had laid it down that "a clear and unambiguous manner of writing teaches us that here the author is at one with himself," while, in contrast, "where we find a strained and tortuous expression," we recognize the presence of "an insufficiently settled, complicating thought or hear the stifled voice of the author's self-criticism." This was a literary detective's guide to the uses of style as clue. But in this instance the device does not work: Freud did not feel self-critical of his new ideas. Yet he does appear wearily indecisive about just how to order the sheer masses of his material. The very title, *Inhibitions, Symptoms and Anxiety,* a flat enumeration, demonstrates his uncertainty. The essay begins by distinguishing inhibitions from symptoms, though Freud was really far more interested in the nature of defense mechanisms and, even more, in anxiety; in fact, one American version was titled *The Problem of Anxiety.* Yet the essay is as crucial to his thought as it is disheveled.

While the name of Rank appears in it only a few times, Freud was carrying on a silent debate with him throughout. This was his way of dealing with his strayed disciple.* But a private settling of scores alone would not have made the book important. In fact, anxiety had forced itself on Freud's attention from the mid-1890s onward; his sense that it demanded not just clinical but theoretical consideration shows an astute alertness to phenomena that other investigators were neglecting. During the years when Freud began to think psychoanalytically, while he was writing his early papers on hysteria and anxiety neuroses, the psychiatric establishment had very little to say about anxiety. Textbooks and treatises mainly offered perfunctory physiological descriptions. D. Hack Tuke's authoritative *Dictionary of Psychological Medicine,* which summed up the professional wisdom around 1890, found room

*Rank talked back. In 1927, reviewing *Inhibitions, Symptoms and Anxiety* at length in an American professional journal, *Mental Hygiene,* he rehearsed once again the origins of the psychoanalytic concept of birth trauma and the differences between his and Freud's perceptions of the event and its consequences. (See E. James Lieberman, *Acts of Will: The Life and Work of Otto Rank* [1985], 263–67.)

for only the scantiest definition of anxiety: "Mental distress in expectation of some sorrow or trial. A condition of agitation and depression, with a sensation of tightness and distress in the praecordial region." That was all.

Freud thought that more needed to be said. Some of his earliest neurotic patients had displayed florid symptoms of anxiety, and since he was persuaded that all neuroses originate in sexual disorders, he was driven to the conclusion that anxiety, too, must have sexual roots. Its genesis, then, was in Freud's view not very mysterious, and the formula for it was simple: sexual excitement that remains undischarged is transformed into anxiety. "Undoubtedly," as Eugen Bleuler put it shortly after the First World War in his widely used *Textbook of Psychiatry,* anxiety is "connected in some way with sexuality, a fact we knew for a long time but which Freud first made clearer." One matter Freud clarified was that the emergence of anxiety is not simply a blind physiological process but draws on psychological mechanisms as well: repression, as he put it, causes anxiety. At this point of junction there emerges the intimate but not very conspicuous link between the two principal themes of *Inhibitions, Symptoms and Anxiety*—anxiety and defense mechanisms. But Freud did more than revise his first explanation of that relationship. He reversed it. Repression, he now said, does not create anxiety; rather, anxiety creates repression.

In this new theoretical formulation, Freud assigned to anxiety a task that neither he nor other psychologists had recognized before: the child, as it develops, learns to predict what Freud called danger situations and responds to their expected advent with anxiety. In other words, anxiety can work as a signal of possible future traumas. Thus Freud now saw anxiety not as a mere passive response, but as a piece of mental action.

Startling as this reversal may seem, Freud had been aware for decades that the serious study of anxiety was sure to produce complexities upon complexities. In some of his first psychoanalytic papers, he had already differentiated between neurotic and realistic anxiety and noted that anxiety attacks may be responses to inner pressures or to external dangers. In either event, anxiety springs up when the mind cannot handle the stimuli bombarding it. What remained was to define the nature, catalogue the sources, and perhaps discriminate the types, of anxiety. This became the assignment to which Freud devoted his essay of 1926. For Rank, we know, the experience of birth was really the only cause of anxiety that mattered; all later anxiety attacks were simply the mind's way of coping with that *Ur*-trauma. Freud, suspicious of simple schemes and single causes, read Rank's account as a tendentious exaggeration that privileged one aspect of the rich and varied anxiety experience over all the rest.

Anxiety, as Freud now defined it, is a painful affect accompanied by definite physical sensations. The trauma of birth is the prototype of all anxiety states; it evokes the response—pronounced physiological changes—that these later states will imitate. Freud had no doubt that the infant carries a certain preparedness for anxiety with it; the anxiety reaction is, in a word, innate. But small children suffer from many anxieties that cannot possibly be traced back to the experience of birth: fear of the dark, fear of the absence of those who minister to their needs. While Freud did not assign a precise timetable to them, he believed that each phase of mental development is shadowed by its own characteristic anxiety: the trauma of birth is followed by separation anxiety, which is succeeded in turn by the fear of the loss of love, castration anxiety, the feeling of guilt, and the fear of death. Thus the anxieties generated by a punishing superego emerge only after other anxieties have already done their work.

Freud did not hold that one type of anxiety replaces all the others. Quite the contrary, each may persist in the unconscious throughout life and be revived at any time. But all anxieties, early or late, share an urgent, highly uncomfortable sense of helplessness, of an inability to deal with overwhelming excitations—terrors, wishes, and emotions. To recapitulate, Freud's weightiest formulation was this: anxiety is a monitory report that there is danger ahead. Whether that danger is real or imagined, rationally appraised or hysterically overestimated, is irrelevant to the feeling itself; its sources vary enormously, its physiological and psychological effects are much the same.

In drastically rewriting his definition of anxiety, Freud moved from the particular to the general. He had first become interested in anxiety as he listened to his analysands; now, describing it as a signal guiding humans to navigate through the perils of life, he translated conclusions drawn from his specialized explorations in psychopathology into psychological laws applicable to everyone, neurotic or not. From Freud's perspective, the legend of innocent, intrepid Siegfried who set out to learn fear could be a metaphor for an ingredient essential to human maturation: one way of defining education is to see it as the process of discovering the uses of fear and learning to discriminate between what to be afraid of, what to avoid, and what to trust. Wholly without anxiety, humans would be defenseless against inner urges and external threats—indeed less than human.

FREUD'S SCATTERED OBSERVATIONS on the defenses in *Inhibitions, Symptoms and Anxiety* proved quite as fertile for psychoanalytic theory as the radical reversal of his ideas on anxiety, perhaps more fertile. But these observations gave his adherents much work in his lifetime and after, for Freud's pages on defense are little more than quickly sketched hints at large theoretical possibilities. This much Freud made perfectly plain in 1926: anxiety and defense have much in common. If anxiety is the sentinel on the tower sounding the alarm, the defenses are the troops mobilized to check the invader. Defensive maneuvers may be far harder to track down than anxiety, for they work almost entirely under the protective, scarcely penetrable cover of the unconscious. But like anxiety, the defenses are lodged in the ego; like anxiety, they are indispensable, all too human and all too fallible ways of managing. In fact, one of the most momentous things to be said about the defenses is that, from having been the assiduous servants of adaptation, they may turn into intransigent obstacles to it.

Freud acknowledged that he had long neglected the question just how the ego defends itself against its three adversaries: the id, the superego, and the world. "In connection with discussing the problem of anxiety," he wrote a little penitently, "I have once again taken up a concept—or, put more modestly, a term—which I employed exclusively at the beginning of my studies thirty years ago, and which I later dropped. I am speaking of 'defensive process.' I replaced it later by the term 'repression,' but the relation between the two remained indefinite." That was putting it mildly. Actually, Freud had first cleanly differentiated among various defense mechanisms and then confused the issue by making one of his favorite psychoanalytic concepts, repression, stand both for the mental technique of denying certain ideas access to consciousness and for all other ways of parrying unpleasurable excitations. He was now ready to correct this imprecision by returning to "the old concept of 'defense' " as a "general designation for all the techniques" the ego employs in the conflicts that may lead to neurosis, "while 'repression' remains the name of one certain method of defense."

The gains inherent in Freud's revival of his first formulations are striking. Repression retained for him its favored status among the stratagems of defense, and its historic place in psychoanalytic theory. But while most defensive tactics imitate repression in scheming to refuse psychological material access to awareness, they command resources of their own. Some of these Freud had described in earlier papers and in his case histories: the ego may defend itself against unacceptable instinctual impulses by regressing to an earlier phase of mental integration in which those impulses are masked and disarmed. The neurotic may labor to escape his hostile and destructive feelings against loved persons by converting his impermissible hatreds into exaggerated affection. This is not all; the mind has other defensive weapons at its disposal. Many of them, like projection, were already familiar to readers of Freud. Now, in *Inhibitions, Symptoms and Anxiety,* he added two tactics he had not mentioned before: "undoing" and "isolating." The first is a kind of "negative magic" which seeks to "blow away" not merely the consequences of an experience but the experience itself: what happened has miraculously never happened at all. The second, which Freud took to be the signature of obsessional neurotics, consists of an effort at fencing off obscene, terrifying, shameful fantasies or memories from the affects that really belong to them. Only the reinstitution of that old collective name "defense," Freud thought, could do justice to the many ways the mind protects itself against others, and against itself.

As with anxiety, so with the defenses, Freud's account drew much authority from observations he made from his favorite post—the easy chair behind his patient on the couch. In *Inhibitions, Symptoms and Anxiety*, he recalled once again, almost nostalgically, some of his most treasured cases: Little Hans, the Rat Man, the Wolf Man. He saw no reason to neglect these sources of information. After all, the resistances that analysands deploy to prevent change in their neurotic habits, to hold on to their suffering in preference to gaining painful insight, are defenses in action. But as Freud well knew, neurotics hold no monopoly on such stratagems; they merely exaggerate, in unmistakable, easily legible caricature, the practices of ordinary mortals. To give but one instance: isolation may be a specialty of obsessionals, but it is the neurotic counterpart of concentration; the withdrawal of attention from competing stimuli is a perfectly normal mental process designed to get work done. Thus, precisely like anxiety, the defenses are universal, essential to all humans. This is what brooding on *The Trauma of Birth* had taught Freud. In the very act of separating himself from Freud, Rank had served him better than he knew.

DOCTORS' DILEMMAS

 The rather shaggy appearance of Freud's book on defenses and anxiety, with its repetitions and formal infelicities, is conspicuous chiefly when measured against his usual performances. In any event, these defects did not herald a permanent loss of literary powers. For in 1926, the very year of *Inhibitions, Symptoms and Anxiety*, Freud published another small book, which manifested all his old stylistic verve, all his accustomed dry wit: *The Question of Lay Analysis*. It is a mixture of polemic and popularization that must rank, as a readable introduction to psychoanalysis, among

Freud's most pleasing efforts at persuasion. Freud chose, significantly, to make his argument in a dialogue, a literary form inviting informal exposition that he had used before more than once.

No doubt the genesis of the pamphlet in current debate stirred Freud to muster once again the confident pugnacity once so typical of him. Late in 1924, Freud was asked by a high Austrian medical personage to submit an expert opinion on the question of lay analysis, and he wrote to Abraham, full of optimism, that "in all such questions I hope the authorities will listen to me." The matter would prove far more intractable than this. Early the next year, municipal bureaucrats, apparently alerted by Wilhelm Stekel to the presence of lay analysts in Vienna, accused Theodor Reik of "unauthorized pursuit of medical practice." Reik, one of Freud's younger followers, duly appeared before the city magistrates and explained his procedures. Heated discussions, expert testimony, and legal wranglings followed, and Reik was ordered to stop analyzing. Instead, he consulted a lawyer, enlisted Freud's support, appealed the verdict, and for some time continued to practice. But the following spring, Reik was sued by an American patient, Newton Murphy, for quackery. Murphy, a physician, had come to Vienna to be analyzed by Freud; having no free hours, Freud had turned him over to Reik, with whom Murphy seems then to have worked for some weeks. The results must have been most unsatisfactory, for otherwise Murphy, obviously not hostile to psychoanalysis on principle, would not have taken Reik to court. Freud did not hesitate; *The Question of Lay Analysis,* written within a month, was the result.

Freud made no secret of the fact that his impulse for writing the pamphlet had come from events of the day: he patterned the figure of the sympathetic though unpersuaded interlocutor on the official with whom he had intervened, and who had asked his considered views on the case. Plainly, Freud was still himself. Pfister, to whom he sent a copy of *Lay Analysis,* exclaimed enthusiastically that nothing else Freud had written had been so easy, so comprehensible. "And yet everything gushes up from the depths." One might suspect Pfister, continuously embattled with Swiss medical psychoanalysts and proud to be one of Freud's "first lay pupils," of a certain bias. But the text of Freud's polemic bears him out.

FREUD FOUGHT FOR Reik as though he were fighting for himself. "I do not ask," he wrote to Paul Federn in March 1926, as the debate about lay analysis was raging in the Vienna Psychoanalytic Society, "that the members rally to my views, but I shall uphold them in private, in public, and before the courts." After all, he added, "the struggle for lay analysis must be fought through sometime or other. Better now than later. As long as I live, I shall balk at having psychoanalysis swallowed by medicine." In fact, Freud *was* fighting in his own cause: while Reik's travail in the Vienna courts now prompted Freud to commit himself to lay analysis in print, his interest in the issue was of long standing. Freud's awareness that he was more or less directly responsible for Reik's predicament must have intensified his vehemence and his tenacity.

The two men had met in 1911, after Freud had read Reik's doctoral dissertation on Flaubert's strange tale *The Temptation of Saint Anthony.* Reik never forgot that first encounter. "I had got into a fight with my professors," who disapproved of a student in literature and psychology writing a thesis along Freudian lines. A chance derogatory remark by one of his psychology professors had sent Reik to Freud's *Psychopathology of Everyday Life,* and after that he had hungrily swallowed everything of Freud's he could get his hands on, just as Otto Rank had done a few years before. He had sent the manuscript of his thesis to Freud, who was intrigued and invited Reik to come and see him. As he climbed the stairs at Berggasse 19, he recalled many years later, "I felt like a young girl going on a date, my heart was beating so fast." Then he entered the consulting room, where Freud worked "surrounded by the Egyptian and Etruscan figurines he loved so much." It turned out that Freud "knew Flaubert's book much better than I, and we discussed it at length."

Soon they were discussing graver matters. Reik had planned to attend medical school, but Freud "said no, he had other plans for me. He urged me to give my life to psychoanalysis and psychoanalytic research." As we know, Freud scattered this sort of advice rather freely. But with Reik, he did not confine himself to giving advice; he buttressed it with tangible support. For some years, he regularly sent the penniless Reik money and found him employment. And he introduced him into the Vienna Psychoanalytic Society, where Reik, never at a loss for words oral or written, soon made comments and gave papers. "He obviously has faults," Freud wrote to Abraham, who was, at Freud's urging, trying to smooth Reik's way in Berlin, "but he is a good, modest boy with strong devotion, firm convictions, and can write well." Another lay analyst was born, at Freud's own urging. And he survived the challenge to his practice. Headlines in the *New York Times* over the date line "Vienna, May 24, 1927" sum up the outcome of the case against Reik: "AMERICAN LOSES SUIT AGAINST FREUD / Psychoanalysis Discoverer Says It Can Do Good Regardless of Medical Science." Freud (who, whatever the headlines might proclaim, was of course not the defendant) was quoted as saying, "A medical man cannot practice psychoanalysis because he always has medicine in his mind, which is not necessary in cases where my treatment can effect good." The charges against Reik were dropped, and for the time, lay analysis was saved.

FREUD HAD FIRST addressed the risks attending nonphysicians in analytic practice some thirty years before, in 1895, in his famous dream of Irma's injection. He had dreamt that Irma, his patient, might perhaps be suffering from an organic ailment that he had diagnosed—or, rather, misdiagnosed—as a psychological symptom. This was the danger which opponents of lay analysis repeatedly cited as one of their main concerns. But Freud thought it a manageable problem. In 1913, supplying some prefatory remarks to a book by Pfister, he went on the offensive, flatly denying that psychoanalytic therapists need medical training. On the contrary: "The practice of psychoanalysis has far less need for medical schooling than for educational preparation in psychology and free human insight. The majority of physicians," he added, a little mischievously, "are not equipped for the work of psychoanalysis" and have, for the most part, failed dismally when they attempt it. Accordingly, it was only natural that some of Freud's most prominent adherents—from Otto Rank to Hanns Sachs, Lou Andreas-Salomé to Melanie Klein, to say nothing of the psychoanalyst in his house, his daughter Anna—should not be physicians. Besides, gifted younger recruits to the cause were coming along, teachers of literature like Ella Freeman Sharpe, pedagogues like August Aichhorn, art historians like Ernst Kris, who were proving themselves competent clinicians and imaginative theorists. Yet his early texts make plain that Freud's defense of lay analysts did not arise from the need for special pleading in their behalf. It followed naturally from what he perceived to be the essential nature of psychoanalysis. Freud had a high stake in lay analysis years before Theodor Reik came into conflict with the Austrian law.

FREUD'S ADVOCACY OF lay analysis was not a call to lighthearted and amateurish diagnoses; he consistently held that a potential analysand should first be examined by a physician. In fact he forcefully reiterated that point in *The Question of Lay Analysis.* It was possible, after all, that the physical symptoms an enthusiastic lay analyst might ascribe to hysterical conversion, just as he had done in his Irma dream, could turn out to be signs of a physical illness. But this apart, Freud thought, medical training was likely to be a handicap. All his life Freud was intent on preserving the independence of psychoanalysis from the doctors no less than from the philosophers.

It is true that after the war, four-fifths of his "pupils" were physicians, but he never tired of insisting that "physicians have no historical claim to a monopoly in analysis." An ill-equipped doctor playing at analysis is in fact nothing better than a quack. Of course, Freud added, it goes almost without saying that the nonphysician must be thoroughly versed in all the elements of psychoanalysis and must know something of medicine, but "it is unjust and inexpedient to compel a person who wants to liberate another from the torment of a phobia or an obsession to take the detour of medical study." In short, "we do not consider it at all desirable to have psychoanalysis swallowed up by medicine"—this was clearly a favorite metaphor for Freud—"and to find its final place of deposit in the textbook of psychiatry."

Freud was so intent on his case that he did not hesitate to question his opponents' motives; resistance to lay analysis, he charged, was really resistance to analysis in general. Considering the stature, and the arguments, of psychoanalysts on the other side of the question, this verdict seems facile and tendentious. While Freud had the better of the argument, at least intellectually, the opposition was not merely irresponsible or self-seeking. A quarter century later, wrestling with the issue from his British perspective, Ernest Jones would call it "a central dilemma in the psychoanalytical movement, one for which no solution has yet been found." Freud, wrote Jones, manfully laboring to be fair to all parties, "stood apart from the hurly-burly of the outer world, and it was appropriate for him to take long views and conjure up visions of the distant future." Of course, Freud had every right to indulge in fantastic schemes like a university for psychoanalysts in which nonphysicians would be introduced to biology and psychiatry. "But those of us in humbler stations of life were compelled to take shorter views and cope with more immediate contingencies." One might be captivated by Freud's grandiose program, Jones concluded, but meanwhile one had to deal with some mundane realities.

THESE REALITIES WERE too obtrusive to be ignored. Psychoanalysts felt under pressure to appease a public by no means wholly convinced by analysts' claims and had to handle their local medical and psychiatric establishments with tact, even at times a touch of servility. In 1925, the psychologist J. McKeen Cattell, then president of the American Association for the Advancement of Science, disparaged psychoanalysis as "not so much a question of science as a matter of taste, Dr. Freud being an artist who lives in the fairyland of dreams among the ogres of perverted sex." Cattell did not speak for everyone, but he had enough influential allies to threaten the aspirations of psychoanalysts to professional recognition.

Cattell's argument was lent added weight by the proliferation of quacks claiming to be analysts. In the year he made his derisive remarks, an American citizen named Homer Tyrell Lane was haled into a London court charged with being a "dangerous charlatan." He had been practicing in his office at

Gordon Square, a good address in Bloomsbury, consulting at two guineas an hour and lecturing on the "Philosophy of Individualism." While some eminent citizens, including the bishop of Lincoln, appeared as character witnesses for Lane, the prosecutor hinted darkly at "improper conduct with inmates of a girls' school with which he was connected." Lane was sentenced to a month in jail, but in the end, the sentence was quashed; he was fined forty shillings and made to promise to leave Britain within a month and never return. And Lane was described in court documents as a psychoanalyst.

Again in 1925, in Manhattan, the Reverend Charles Francis Potter, speaking on "psychoanalysis and religion" at the West Side Unitarian Church, warned that "quacks in psychoanalysis" had "mulcted" many. His solution was to call for the licensing of analysts. "It seems incredible but it is a fact," he said, "that while a physician has to have ten years or more in education and preparation before he can treat the bodies of men, an analyst who presumes to treat that more delicate organism, the human mind, can hang out his shingle and charge $25 a sitting after no more preparation than ten days' reading of Freud and Jung." This was precisely what psychoanalysts were afraid of—charlatans like Lane who got into the newspapers, detractors like Potter articulating the opinions, and hardening the resistance, of a larger public.

By the mid-1920s, therefore, analysts in France, Britain, and, most audibly, the United States, were heard to mutter that far too many self-appointed therapists were trying to live off, and managing to subvert, whatever prestige psychoanalysis had managed to amass. This situation was partly the analysts' doing. As one prominent American psychoanalyst, Smith Ely Jelliffe, told Ernest Jones in 1927, "The many 'cults,' " like "Christian Science, Mental Healing, Couéism, and innumerable other aspects of pseudo-medical practices," would never have become so prominent "if the 'doctor' had been on the job." Whoever was responsible for this clamorous chaos, real psychoanalysts must decisively distance themselves from all charlatans. Freud's foreign "pupils," going back home to practice, were beginning to think about the rewards of respectability and to construct professional establishments to safeguard them. In that enterprise, lay analysts were likely to figure as distracting, possibly embarrassing intruders.

FREUD HAD OTHER ideas. Precisely because he was a physician, he could afford to speak disinterestedly for the trained layman. But while he orchestrated a brave campaign, his victories were sporadic and limited. The question became highly contentious; it generated inconclusive debates in psychoanalytic journals and temporizing resolutions at psychoanalytic congresses through the 1920s and beyond. Institutes across the Western world had varying practices, but most either came to demand a medical degree as a prerequisite for admission, or surrounded the training of laymen with onerous restrictions. This was a question, for many the only question, on which psychoanalysts who deified Freud, and who appealed to his writings as sacred scriptures, flouted his wishes and risked his displeasure. A. A. Brill spoke for many of these edgy loyalists when he wrote in 1927, "Long, long ago I learned to accept what the master has offered even before I became convinced of it from my own knowledge, for experience taught me that whenever I thought a statement was far-fetched or incorrect I soon found that I was wrong; it was a lack of experience on my part that caused the doubt. However, for many years I have tried very hard to agree with the master on the question of lay analysis but I have not been able to accept his view." In arguing for that view, the "master" had been "brilliant" but ultimately unconvincing.

The issue was so highly charged that in 1927 Eitingon and Jones decided to organize an international symposium, to be published simultaneously in the *Internationale Zeitschrift* in German and in the *International Journal of Psycho-Analysis* in English. More than a score of participants, practically all the well-known analysts from half a dozen countries, articulated their positions in terse declarations or little essays. These offer no surprises, except perhaps one: Freud could not even hold his own local troops in line. Naturally, Theodor Reik, a little archly confessing that his position was scarcely disinterested, defended lay analysis, on the analogy of the psychological wisdom displayed by priests and poets. But other Viennese, among them some of Freud's oldest supporters, rejected this line of reasoning. Eduard Hitschmann, who had joined Freud's Wednesday-night group in 1905 and was now director of the psychoanalytic clinic in Vienna, said flatly, "I hold strongly to the legal standard laid down by the Minister of Health that psycho-analysis is a matter for the physician." Isidor Sadger, another of Freud's earliest adherents, was no less categorical: "I hold the view firmly and on principle that sick persons should be treated exclusively by physicians, and that any analysis of such persons by a lay analyst is to be avoided."

Even Felix Deutsch, though for his own reasons extremely anxious to please Freud, could do no better than cloud his real opinion with tortured definitions, and could not resist concluding that "the business of healing is an affair of the physician." Freud, to be sure, had his supporters among the symposiasts: some of the British psychoanalysts, among them Edward Glover and John Rickman, saw no harm in nonmedical therapists conducting analyses, provided one kept therapy "sharply distinct from diagnosis; the latter must be left to medically qualified persons." Britain, in fact, remained a country in which lay analysts continued to flourish: some 40 percent of its analysts, Jones recalls, were not physicians. Quite as heartening for Freud was the resolution passed by "The Hungarian Psycho-Analytical Society" in Budapest, affirming that lay analysis "was shown theoretically in Freud's book to be not only justified but, in the interest of the progress of our science even desirable, and, on the other hand, in practice 'lay analysis' in Hungary has not, so far as experience goes, up to the present resulted in any injury to patients." One contributor to the symposium, Hermann Nunberg, among the most talented of the younger Viennese, went so far as to tax the opponents of lay analysis with sheer selfishness. "I have the impression," he wrote, "that the resistance to the practice of psychoanalysis by laymen is not always sustained by purely theoretical considerations. It seems to me that other motives, such as medical prestige and motives of an economic nature, play a part. In our ranks, as elsewhere, the economic struggle finds its ideology." These were strong words, but they reflect Freud's views with fair accuracy.

In his own contribution, later printed as a postscript to *The Question of Lay Analysis,* Freud rehearsed the familiar arguments once more. In a nostalgic mood, he inserted an autobiographical reflection that has been much quoted: "Since my person is involved, I can offer anyone interested in such matters some insight into my own motives. After forty-one years of medical activity, my self-knowledge tells me that I have not really been a true physician. I became a physician through an enforced deflection from my original intention, and the triumph of my life lies in this: that I have once again found my initial direction after a great detour." He thought that his "sadistic disposition was not very strong, and so I did not need to develop its derivatives." Nor could he remember playing the doctor game: "Evidently my childish curiosity chose other paths. In my young years the need grew overwhelming to understand something of the riddles of this world and perhaps to contribute something to their solution." To study medicine had seemed to him the best way toward realizing his ambition. But from the outset his interests had centered on research in zoology, chemistry, and at last, physiology, "under the influence of von Brücke, the greatest authority that ever acted upon me." If he took up medical practice in the end, this was for financial reasons: Freud noted that his "material situation" had been "miserable." But—and this was, of course, the point of his excursion into his younger days—"I think that my lack of the correct medical disposition has not harmed my patients very much."*

---

*These chapters should have shown that this subjective self-appraisal requires two corrections: Freud did have accesses of humanitarian motivation, even if research ultimately remained for him a stronger interest than healing. And his description of his life's course as a long detour from his original plan ignores the kind of theoretical, even philosophical, work he managed to do not just in his late years, the 1920s and after, but as early as the 1890s.

Freud acknowledged that his report had doubtless done little to clarify the issue of lay analysis, and it is true enough that he made few converts to his position even if, as he modestly noted, he managed at least to moderate some extreme views. In letter after letter, to his intimates and to strangers alike, he complained about the bias of the doctors. "The physicians among the analysts," he wrote in October 1927, "have been only too inclined to engage in research closer to the organic, rather than in psychological research." A year later, in a letter to Eitingon, he declared himself more or less resigned to defeat; *Lay Analysis,* he wrote, "was a washout"—*ein Schlag ins Wasser.* He had wanted to create a communal feeling among analysts on this issue, but he had not succeeded: "I was, so to speak, a general without an army."

NOT UNEXPECTEDLY, FREUD discovered the true villains in the piece to be the Americans. Certainly American psychoanalysts were the most intransigent opponents of lay analysis anywhere. Writing for publication, Freud expressed his irritation with them rather more prudently than he did in his correspondence: "The resolution of our American colleagues against lay analysis," he wrote in the postscript to *Lay Analysis,* "governed essentially by practical motives, seems to me unpractical, for it cannot alter one of the elements that dominate the situation. It is virtually equivalent to an attempt at repression." And he asked in conclusion whether it would not be better to accept the existence of lay analysts and seek to train them as soundly as possible.

It was a rhetorical question to which he knew the answer. The Americans were a largely lost cause, and had been so more or less from the beginning. The New York Psychoanalytic Society, which A. A. Brill founded in February 1911, was an association of physicians. Its statutes recognized an associate membership, available to those "who take an active interest in psychoanalysis," but there was little question in the members' minds that physicians alone would be allowed to psychoanalyze patients. In 1921, lest there be any misunderstanding, Brill energetically underscored that point in the introduction to his popular *Fundamental Conceptions of Psychoanalysis;* unfortunately, he wrote, psychoanalysis has "attracted many charlatans and quacks who find in it a medium for the exploitation of the ignorant classes by promising to cure all their ailments." To be sure, all branches of medicine are afflicted with healers of this stripe, but this does not mean that one stands by silently in one's own specialty. "As I feel somewhat responsible for psychoanalysis in this country, I merely wish to say that whereas psychoanalysis is as wonderful a discovery in mental science as, let us say, the X-ray in surgery, it can be utilized only by persons who have been trained in anatomy and pathology."*

Brill's simile was, perhaps not consciously, a weapon in the war of nerves against lay analysts, and a warning to those thinking of treatment with one of them. In 1921, when Jelliffe, not yet in Brill's camp, supported lay analysts and employed nonmedical assistants, Brill reproved him sharply. Yet his strictures were talking past Freud's point: Freud had never envisioned turning analytic patients over to untrained therapists. The question had nothing to do with X rays or the surgeon's knife; rather, it was whether medical school provided the necessary, or the best, preparation for psychoanalytic practice.

The issue was dramatized in 1925, when Caroline Newton applied for candidacy in the New York Psychoanalytic Society. Civilized and well-informed, she had been in analysis with Freud for a time in 1921, and now, back in the United States, she was translating Rank's writings. She was, however, not a physician, which to the New York psychoanalytic establishment was a fatal defect. The society sent word of the affair to Abraham, then president of the International Psychoanalytic Association, without delay.† The New Yorkers, Abraham reported in a circular letter in March, had admitted Newton only as a guest and objected to her opening a practice and sending around testimonial cards. Furthermore, Abraham added, they wanted to amend the constitution of the international association to the effect that members of one society should not be automatically admitted to membership in others. He thought this a reasonable request, and so, hesitantly, did Freud. But Freud took the opportunity to castigate what he considered the characteristic self-centeredness of his American colleagues. "The claims of the Americans do seem to me to go too far," he wrote to Ernest Jones in September, "and to be dictated all too much by narrow-minded, egotistical interests."

The New York Psychoanalytic Society was not swayed by Freud's disap-

---

*Brill had in fact been largely anticipated by Isador Coriat, who had laid it down in 1917 in a brief catechism that the "practice of psychoanalysis" should be limited "to those thoroughly trained in the theory of psychoanalysis and in general psychopathology. For an untrained person to use psychoanalysis is as much to be deprecated as it is for someone to use radium who is ignorant of the physics of radio-activity or as dangerous as to attempt a surgical operation without a knowledge of anatomy." (Isador H. Coriat, *What Is Psychoanalysis?* [1917], 22.) By itself, this statement sounds a bit ambiguous, but Coriat speaks of "physicians" throughout.

†The minutes of the New York Psychoanalytic Society for February 24, 1925, record that guest privileges for Caroline Newton had been withdrawn, and the corresponding secretary was instructed to write Abraham that "it was essential for local and other reasons" to "restrict the attendance of our meetings to members of the profession"—which is to say, of course, the medical profession. (A. A. Brill papers, container 3, LC.)

proval. Startled and defensive, it responded to the Newton case by appointing an education committee that would screen all applicants in the future. The minutes of the society for October 27, 1925, note tersely that "after considerable debating the house arrived at the unanimous decision that it is opposed to laymen practising therapeutic psychoanalytic therapy." Bureaucratization, inevitable in maturing organizations, was in the air. In the same year, the analysts meeting in Bad Homburg founded an international training commission to establish standards of admission to psychoanalytic institutes and define methods of psychoanalytic training, both hitherto handled locally with sublime casualness. The training commission proved a mixed blessing; it generated squabbles with institutes anxious to preserve their autonomy. Still, it helped to formalize the requirements for the candidacy and the education of analysts.

Even if that training commission had never existed, the American analysts would still have known their own mind. "To be sure," Freud commented to Ernest Jones on the American stance in the fall of 1926, "fate will decide over the ultimate relation between ψA and medicine, but that does not imply that we should not try to influence fate, attempt to shape it by our own efforts." Yet on November 30, 1926, the New York Psychoanalytic Society adopted a resolution which was appended in the following year to the symposium on lay analysis and thus given international currency. "The practice of psycho-analysis for therapeutic purposes," it ran in part, "shall be restricted to physicians (doctors of medicine) who are graduates of recognized medical schools, have had special training in psychiatry and psycho-analysis and who conform to the requirements of the medical practice acts to which they are subject." Nothing could be more unequivocal.

Freud continued his efforts to influence the Americans, but for a time they seemed largely wasted. In the summer of 1927, Freud received a letter from Brill—the first, he told Ernest Jones sardonically, "in I do not know how many years"—in which Brill reassured Freud that "he and all of them 'shall remain absolutely loyal' " to him and his principles. Brill, Freud reported, had heard of his "intentions to drive the New York group from the association, and 'I should feel very sorry if anything like this should occur.' " Freud called this an imaginary grievance. He answered Brill "severely and sincerely," candidly telling him that he had been disappointed in the Americans. No less candidly, he told Brill that if they resigned, the International Psychoanalytic Association would lose nothing, whether in the domain of science, of economics, or of colleagueship. "Perhaps," Freud added, "he will now be offended, but he was that before, too. If he controls his sensitivity, which is the expression of a bad conscience, a good relationship can still result." In

1928, Freud told the Swiss analyst Raymond de Saussure that the Americans had established a Monroe Doctrine that would deny the Europeans all influence over their affairs. "In short, I have accomplished nothing with my book on lay analysis; they place their status interests above the analytic community and will not see the dangers to which they expose the future of analysis."

By early 1929, as the controversy did not die down, Freud wondered whether it might not make sense to separate from the American analysts peacefully and remain firm on the matter of lay analysis. Brill's uneasy feeling that Freud might want to force out the Americans was not just a fantasy without foundation. But at this point Brill developed the qualities of a statesman; unwilling to lead the Americans to a dubious independence, he made significant tactical concessions, agreeing that the New York Psychoanalytic Society should admit some nonphysicians to its ranks. "I am extraordinarily pleased," Freud wrote Ernest Jones in August 1929, after the analysts had met at Oxford, "that the congress went off in such conciliatory fashion, and brought an unmistakable approach of the New Yorkers to our point of view."* Brill, Freud gratefully noted, was taking up the good fight against "all the American medical quarter-, eighth-, sixteenth-analysts." Late in the year, the New York psychoanalysts, swayed by Brill's pacific efforts, grudgingly permitted lay analysts to work with children. "Brill's giving in on the question of American lay analysis," Ferenczi triumphantly observed in a circular letter in 1930, "has removed this problem from the agenda for the present." But on the analysis of adults the New Yorkers remained adamant for years. Freud's authority, however imposing, was not unlimited; his word was not law.

---

*As she had been doing for some years, Anna Freud once again represented her father at this international gathering. Freud advised her not to take Ernest Jones, or for that matter, "the whole congress," too seriously. "Treat Oxford as an interesting adventure, and anyhow be glad that you did not marry Jones." (Freud to Anna Freud, July 25, 1929. Freud Collection, LC.) To judge from her buoyant, humorous bulletins from the congress she took her father's advice. "More tradition than comfort," she wired home on July 27. "Stay the course!" (Freud Collection, LC.) Two days later, after reading a paper, she sent a second telegram: "Talk very successful. No disgrace to family. Mood good." (Ibid.) No doubt the thought that she had not married Jones contributed to her cheerfulness.

WOMAN, THE DARK CONTINENT

During the years when intramural dissension over the training and qualifications of analytic candidates threatened to disrupt the fragile unity of the Freudian movement, analysts also engaged in a debate over the psychology of woman. The discussion was on the whole polite, even good-tempered, but it went to the heart of Freud's theory, and the issue has continued to plague psychoanalysis. In the mid-1920s, Freud predicted that opponents would criticize his views on femininity as unfriendly to women's aspirations and biased in favor of men. His forecast would be realized, more fiercely than he imagined.

Much of later commentary has slighted the complexity of Freud's attitudes, which are an intricate amalgam of accepted commonplaces, tentative explorations, and unconventional insights. He said some deeply offensive things about women, but not all of his theoretical pronouncements and private opinions were antagonistic or patronizing. Nor were they at all doctrinaire; on female psychology Freud was at times almost agnostic. Late in 1924, attempting to resolve some puzzles about clitoral and vaginal sensitivity that Abraham had raised, Freud confessed that while the question greatly interested him, he knew "nothing whatever about it." In general, he admitted, perhaps a little too cheerfully, "the female aspect of the problem is extraordinarily obscure to me." As late as 1928, he told Ernest Jones that "everything we know of feminine *early development* appears to me unsatisfactory and uncertain." He had, he thought, sincerely tried to understand the "sexual life of the adult woman," but it continued to intrigue and puzzle him. It was something of "a *dark continent.*"

By then, two things at least seemed to him well established: "The first conception of sexual intercourse is an oral one—sucking on the penis as earlier at the mother's breast; and the giving up of clitoral onanism because of the inferiority of this organ, painfully recognized." That seemed a great deal, but "about everything else I must reserve my judgment." About the time that Freud confessed his bafflement to Ernest Jones, he told Marie Bonaparte that he had been doing research into "the feminine soul" for thirty years, with little to show for it. He asked, *Was will das Weib?*—"What does woman want?" This famous remark, of a piece with his description of woman as a dark continent, is an age-old cliché in modern guise: men for centuries had defended themselves against their obscure fear of woman's hidden power by describing the whole sex as unfathomable. But it is also a helpless shrug, a measure of his discontent with the gaps in his theory. What he had to say about femininity, he wrote as late as 1932, was "certainly incomplete and fragmentary"; should his readers want to know more, he advised them, they ought to "consult your own life's experience or turn to the poets, or wait until science can give you deeper and more coherent information." These public disclaimers were not just rhetorical devices; as we know, Freud punctuated his private correspondence with similar declarations of ignorance. When Freud was certain of something, he said so. But with woman he was not quite so sure.

The papers that Freud published on the psychology of woman between 1924 and 1933 dominated a debate which he had done much to start with some fragmentary comments in the early 1920s. In addition to Karl Abraham, the principals wrestling with his ideas included Ernest Jones, who was searching for a position of his own; the young German psychoanalyst Karen Horney, outspoken and independent-minded enough to challenge the master publicly on his own turf; and such loyalists as Jeanne Lampl-de Groot and Helene Deutsch, who both adopted Freud's final position with little cavil and only minor amendments. Unlike the debatable idea of a death drive, to which resistance remained strong, Freud's views on femininity largely carried the day among psychoanalysts: from the early 1930s onward, it was established as more or less canonical for his profession. Yet dissent flared up sporadically; proposals to revise Freud's postwar views on women never wholly ceased. The psychoanalytic revisionists were not angry at Freud, as feminists were to be, but his pronouncements made them uneasy.

FREUD'S WRITINGS ABOUT women are yet another demonstration just how overdetermined his ideas were: unconscious fantasies, cultural commitments, and psychoanalytic theorizing freely interacted in his mind. From his earliest days onward—to begin with the fantasies—Freud had been surrounded by women. His beautiful, dominant young mother shaped him more than he knew. His Catholic nurse had a somewhat mysterious share, abruptly terminated but indelible, in his infantile emotional life. His niece Pauline, about his own age, had been the first target of his youthful erotic aggressiveness. His five younger sisters arrived in rapid succession—the youngest, also a Pauline, was born when he was not yet eight—invading the exclusive attention he had enjoyed as an only child, and presenting themselves as inconvenient competitors no less than as rapt audiences. The one great love of his adult life, the passion for Martha Bernays that flooded him in his mid-twenties, struck him with unmitigated ferocity; it brought out a fierce possessiveness and subjected him to bouts of irrational jealousy. His sister-in-law Minna Bernays, who joined the Freud household in late 1895, was his valued companion in conversations, on walks, on trips. Freud could tell Fliess that women had never replaced the male comrade for him, but he was visibly susceptible to them.

Freud's professional life, too, was pervaded by women, historic figures, all of them, in the career of psychoanalysis. The first was the epoch-making Anna O., whom Freud borrowed, as it were, from her physician. She was followed by his hysterical patients of the early 1890s, who taught him much about the art of listening. Another teacher was Dora, the subject of the first among his five great published case histories, to whom he was indebted for lessons about failure, about transference and countertransference. And the two influential patrons who in the winter of 1901–2 schemed to secure a professorship for Freud were both women.

What is more, in later years, as the world's most famous psychoanalyst, he savored the companionship and admiration of handsome, interesting, accomplished disciples like Lou Andreas-Salomé and analysands like Hilda Doolittle. Some of his favorites among these women—Helene Deutsch, Joan Riviere, Jeanne Lampl-de Groot, Ruth Mack Brunswick, Marie Bonaparte, and, of course, his daughter Anna—left their stamp on the psychoanalytic profession. In 1910, when members of the Vienna Psychoanalytic Society were reviewing their bylaws, Isidor Sadger declared himself opposed to the admission of women, but Freud firmly disagreed; he would "see it as a serious inconsistency if we were to exclude women on principle."* Later, Freud did not hesitate to suggest that "female analysts" like Jeanne Lampl-de Groot and Helene Deutsch might dig more deeply than a male analyst like himself into woman patients' earliest years, "so gray with age, so shadowy"; after all, in the transference they served better as mother substitutes than a man ever could. Freud acknowledged, then, that in momentous aspects of analytic practice, women might be more competent than men. This was a substantial compliment, though not without a certain bite: a notable concession for a man with a reputation for unbending antifeminist prejudices and also a subtle expression of those very prejudices. The woman analyst, Freud was saying, succeeds best in doing the work for which biology has destined her—that of mother.

THIS POINT HAS almost unfathomable biographical implications. Among the women who meant most to Freud, his mother was, though not the most conspicuous, probably the most compelling. Her hold over Freud's inner life

---

*I should add that Adler, speaking just ahead of Freud, advocated admission of "female physicians and women who are seriously interested and want to collaborate." (April 13, 1910. *Protokolle*, II, 440.) The first woman member was Dr. Margarete Hilferding, elected April 27, 1910, by a vote of 12 to 2. (See ibid., II, 461.)

was as secure as that of his wife, his sister-in-law, even his daughter Anna— perhaps more decisive. It was Amalia Freud who had dazzled her first-born son when he was about four and got a glimpse of her, during a train trip, "nudam"; Amalia Freud whose love he craved and whose loss he feared. When he was a boy, probably just under ten, he had a famous anxiety dream about her which he duly reported and partially explicated in his *Interpretation of Dreams:* "It was very vivid and showed me my beloved mother with a peculiarly calm, sleeping facial expression, being carried into the room by two (or three) persons with birds' beaks and laid on the bed." He woke up screaming. Recalling this early dream, he had no difficulty detecting the sources for the figures carrying his mother: the birds' beaks were visual counterparts of the German vulgarism for sexual intercourse, *vögeln*—"to screw"—which derives from *Vogel,* the word for "bird"; the other source underlying Freud's construction of this earthy visual pun was an illustration showing bird-headed Egyptian deities in the family Bible over which he had pored as a little boy. His analysis of this dream revealed, then, among other matters best hidden, his boyish secret lust for his mother, a lust that set the most awesome religious taboos at defiance.

Freud's mother was bound to be desirable to her son, not just on his own theoretical showing, but in her handsome and obtrusive reality. She was by all accounts a formidable personage. Freud's son Martin, who remembered his grandmother well, described her as "a typical Polish Jewess, with all the shortcomings that that implies. She was certainly not what we would call a 'lady,' had a lively temper and was impatient, self-willed, sharp-witted and highly intelligent."* Freud's niece Judith Bernays Heller, who in her young years had spent much time with her maternal grandmother, amply supported her cousin's description: Amalia Freud, she wrote, was temperamental, energetic, and strong-willed, getting her way in small matters and large, vain of her appearance almost to her death at ninety-five, efficient, competent, and egotistical. "She was charming and smiling when strangers were about, but I, at least, always felt that with familiars she was a tyrant, and a selfish one." Yet—and this could only consolidate her power—she was no complainer and bore the hardships of Austrian life during and after the First World War, like the restrictions on her movements imposed by advancing age, with admirable

---

*It is characteristic of the contradictory attitudes that westernized Jews could hold about their Eastern European brethren that Martin Freud, speaking plainly about the "shortcomings" that "typical" Polish Jews display could, in the same article, refer with undisguised admiration to the courage of Eastern European law students in face of anti-Semitic riots in the law school at the University of Vienna. Here the "despised and spurned 'Polish Jews' resisted, with considerable physical toughness, the attacks of German and Austrian students, who greatly outnumbered them." (Martin Freud, "Who Was Freud?" in *The Jews of Austria: Essays on Their Life, History and Destruction,* ed. Josef Fraenkel [1967], 207.)

spirits. "She had a sense of humor, being able to laugh at, and at times even ridicule, herself." What is more, she visibly, and audibly, worshiped her first-born, calling him, as legend rightly has it, her "golden son." The presence of such a mother would be hard to escape, even after the most thorough-going self-analysis.

In fact there is no evidence that Freud's systematic self-scrutiny touched on this weightiest of attachments, or that he ever explored, and tried to exorcise, his mother's power over him.* Throughout his life as an analyst, he recognized the crucial importance of the mother for the child's development. He could hardly do less. "Whoever has been fortunate enough to evade the incestuous fixation of his libido does not wholly escape its influence," he wrote in 1905. "Above all a man looks for the memory picture of his mother as it had dominated him since the beginning of his childhood." Yet, almost deliberately evading this insight, Freud exiled mothers to the margins of his case histories. Dora's mother, beset by what Freud called a "housewife's psychosis," is a silent, minor actor in the family melodrama. Little Hans's mother, though to her husband's mind the cause of her son's neurosis with her seductive behavior, is subordinated to that husband, the auxiliary analyst who transmits Freud's interpretations. The Wolf Man's biological mother achieves only severely limited significance as a partner in the primal scene he had observed, or fantasized, as a little boy, though certainly mother substitutes contributed to his neurosis. The Rat Man's mother makes some fleeting appearances, mainly as the person whom the patient consults before he starts his analysis. And Schreber's mother might as well not have lived.

This summary reduction of the mother's role in the neurotic history of his patients in part reflected an unwelcome scantiness of information. Freud repeatedly deplored the way that the prized respectability of his time forced women patients into reticence, and hence made them less helpfully indiscreet than the men. It followed, as he observed in the early 1920s, that psychoanalysts knew a great deal more about the sexual development of boys than about that of girls. But Freud's professions of ignorance appear almost willful, as though there were some things about women that he did not want to know. It is telling that the only emotional tie Freud ever sentimentalized was the mother's love for her son. While every lasting intimate relationship, he wrote in 1921, whether in marriage, friendship, or the family, conceals a sediment of hostile feelings, there is perhaps "one single exception," the "relation of mother to son which, founded on narcissism, is undisturbed by later rivalry."

*Max Schur put the case I am making with due caution. "Altogether," he wrote to Ernest Jones, "there are many evidences of complicated pre-genital relationships with his mother which perhaps he never fully analysed." (Schur to Jones, October 6, 1955. Jones papers, Archives of the British Psycho-Analytical Society, London.)

He characterized this maternal affection for the son as "the most perfect, easily the most ambivalence-free of all human relationships." This sounds far more like a wish than a sober inference from clinical material.

Seeking to account for Freud's daring, independence, and unsurpassed productive curiosity, Ernest Jones singled out "undaunted courage" as "Freud's highest quality and his most precious gift. Whence could he have derived it other than from a supreme confidence in his mother's love?" The diagnosis seems to be supported by Freud's famous comment—he made it twice—that the young man who has been his mother's unquestioned favorite will develop a sense of triumphant self-esteem and, with that, the strength for success in later life.* But this, too, resembles a wish far more than a rational conviction or dependable self-appraisal. A mother's feelings about her son may well be less conflict-ridden than those of the son about his mother, but they are not free of ambivalence, of disappointment and irritation with the beloved offspring, even of downright animosity. It is highly probable that Freud was strenuously defending himself against the recognition that the tie to his mother was in any sense imperfect, that it might be unraveled even in the slightest by the love she bore his siblings, or tainted by an illicit desire he might harbor for her. He seems to have dealt with the conflicts that his complicated feelings toward his mother generated by refusing to deal with them.

Significantly, in his paper of 1931 on female sexuality, Freud speculated that perhaps a boy could keep his attachment to his mother intact and dispose of his ambivalence toward her by directing his hostility to his father. He prudently added that it would be wise not to rush to conclusions on this obscure point, and to await further study of pre-oedipal development. But this retreat should not obscure the insight his suggestion contains, not only for the emotional life of others but also for his own.

In the paper on femininity that he published two years later, Freud afforded a no less tantalizing glimpse into his inner life. Outlining the reasons why the little girl turns against her mother and to the father, however strong her first attachment has been, he argued that this shift is not simply a substitution of one parent for the other. Rather, it is accompanied by hostility, even hatred. The girl's most significant grievance "against the mother flares up when the next child appears in the nursery." This rival deprives the first-born of adequate nourishment, and "strange to say, even with an age difference of only eleven months, the child is not too young to take note of the circumstances." This comes close to Freud's own situation: only seven-

---

*See *Interpretations of Dreams*, *SE* V, 398n (note added in 1911); and "A Childhood Recollection from *Dichtung und Wahrheit*" (1917), *SE* XVII, 156.

teen months separated him from his younger sibling Julius, whose arrival he had greeted with rage and wicked death wishes.

"But the child," Freud went on, "begrudges the undesired intruder and rival not just the suckling but quite as much all other evidences of maternal care. It feels dethroned, despoiled, damaged in its rights, throws a jealous hatred upon the little sibling and develops a grudge against the faithless mother, which very often finds expression in an unpleasant change in its behavior." It becomes irritable, disobedient, and regresses in the control of its excretions. All this, Freud observed, is only too well known. "But we rarely form a correct perception of the strength of these jealous impulses, of the tenacity with which they persist, as well as of the magnitude of their influence upon later development." This is true all the more "since in the later years of childhood, this jealousy is steadily supplied with new nourishment and the whole shock is repeated with each new little sibling. Nor does it make much difference," he concluded, "if the child perhaps remains the mother's preferred favorite; the child's claims for love are immoderate, demand exclusiveness, admit no sharing." Freud professed here to be speaking of girls, but his portrait looks suspiciously like a self-portrait. Had he not described himself, in his letters to his fiancée, as jealous, exclusive, intolerant of competition? Freud, it seems, had good reason to find the subject of woman somewhat mysterious, even a little threatening.

No DOUBT FREUD was eased into side-stepping this unresolved, largely unconscious conflict because his masculine possessiveness matched his cultural conservatism. Freud was an unreconstructed nineteenth-century gentleman in his social, ethical, and sartorial style. He never adjusted his old-fashioned manners to a new age, nor his equally old-fashioned ideals, his ways of speaking and writing, his apparel, and—much of the time—even his spelling. He disliked the radio and the telephone. He thought contention over moral issues absurd, since what is decent or not, right or wrong, is after all perfectly obvious. In short, his adherence to an age that was becoming historical before his eyes never faltered. His letters and memoranda to Fliess and his case histories of the 1890s provide a small catalogue of traditional convictions—we have come to call them prejudices—about women. It is a husband's duty to protect his wife from explicit sexual details, even when they are cast in a medical form.* An intelligent and independent woman deserves praise because she is, in these respects, virtually as good as a man. Woman is by nature sexually passive. At the same time, he could question such popular platitudes, recognizing that much of women's erotic passivity was not natural, but

*See p. 62.

imposed by society. Freud saw the force of that old insight, as old as Defoe and Diderot and Stendhal, that whatever mental deficiencies one might discover among women were the consequence not of natural endowment but of cultural repression.

These and other notions about women, uneasily cohabiting and at times mutually contradictory, bedeviled his pronouncements through the years, with some of the ideas of male superiority occupying the foreground of his mind. In 1907, he could assert in "Gradiva" that man's role in love-making is inevitably that of aggressor. A dozen years later, he could ask Ferenczi to forward a letter to a lady from Budapest who had recently written to him, "but, as a genuine female"—*Frauenzimmer*—had "neglected to write her address in her letter, something that men always do." The little difference between the sexes loomed very large for him: writing to Ernest Jones about Joan Riviere, whom he admired, he commented, "In my experience you have not to scratch too deeply the skin of a so-called masculine woman to bring her femininity to the light." Freud's attitudes toward women were part of larger cultural loyalties, his Victorian style.*

THIS STYLE HAD never been monolithic. As usually employed, the global adjective "Victorian" is little better than a convenient, often disparaging, largely misleading cliché. It conjures up images of the Angel in the House: the docile female guarding the hearth, engrossed in child care and busy domesticity, while her masterful, far more highly sexed and aggressive husband is out struggling in the wicked world of business and politics. To divide the Victorians into two parties on the woman question, feminists and anti-feminists, is no more helpful than the name "Victorian" itself. It is true that on the woman question, tempers ran high and slogans were cheap. But the labels are far too facile to account for a richly articulated spectrum of views. There were antifeminists who wanted to withhold the vote from women but advocated their right to higher education, control over their own property, or equal access to the divorce court. There were feminists, presumably the antifeminists' adversaries, who took a very similar line. Freud, who did not conceal his wry distrust of the feminist movement, beautifully illustrates this confusion of alliances and positions. He might hold to the sweet, competent housewife as his ideal, but he never obstructed—on the contrary, he fostered—aspiring female psychoanalysts, and took their views seriously. Indeed, he undercut his comments on women, which ranged from frank puzzlement

*As late as 1938, he could write to Stefan Zweig in unmistakable nineteenth-century accents, "Analysis is like a woman who wants to be conquered but knows that she will be held in low esteem if she does not offer resistance." (Freud to Stefan Zweig, July 20, 1938. By permission of Sigmund Freud Copyrights, Wivenhoe.)

to lordly courtesy, by presiding over a profession in which women could rise to the top. He had acquired his convictions early and continued to find them perfectly satisfactory. But his conduct as the undisputed founder and leader of an international movement to which women made conspicuous and well-recognized contributions contradicted his rhetoric.

QUITE UNINTENTIONALLY, THEN, Freud became a participant in the sweeping campaign for women's rights in his lifetime. Since the mid-nineteenth century, across the Western world, feminists had labored to make inroads against legal, social, and economic handicaps. Shortly before the First World War militant English suffragettes resorted to passive disobedience, and at times to open violence, but most feminists continued to carry on their struggle, as they always had, with moderate demands and reasonable, if aggrieved language. The first full-fledged declaration of women's rights, voted in 1848 at a convocation in Seneca Falls, New York, was conciliatory in tone, almost timid: the call for universal suffrage was almost not broached at the convention, and once proffered, almost not passed. Those who thundered against feminists as uninhibited perverts bent on subverting the family and "natural" relations between the sexes could only have been driven by anxiety. In fact, to judge from the avalanche of cartoons, editorials, sermons, and broadsides against invasive, man-eating women and their henpecked, effeminate male supporters, a good number of nineteenth-century men must have been anxious in the extreme. Only a Freudian analysis can account for this outpouring of misogynistic sentiments in the decades after Seneca Falls in country after country.

While the feminists might appear menacing and while they bravely, noisily battled on, they confronted an opposition securely entrenched in church, state, and society. To injure their prospects further, by the late nineteenth century the movement had to deal with crippling, increasingly ferocious internal divisions over matters of strategy and final aims. Socialists among the feminists argued that only the demise of capitalism would bring the liberation of women; political tacticians insisted on universal suffrage as the entering wedge for all other reforms; more prudent feminists were content to concentrate on opening one door after the other, petitioning in behalf of women's access to medical school or the right to have their own bank account. And so, feminists secured change piecemeal, sporadically; it was never, anywhere, a record of easy victories. In their way, and making little of it, prominent woman analysts like Anna Freud and Melanie Klein were living embodiments of feminist aspirations, profiting from the lonely courage of an earlier generation—and from Freud's attitude.

In Freud's Austria, the pace of the feminist cause was more snail-like than elsewhere; frustration was piled on frustration. A law of 1867 had explicitly prohibited "female persons," lumped together with foreigners and minors, from engaging in any political activity; hence, feminist associations devoted to extending the ballot to women were by their very nature unthinkable. Even Austria's Socialists, who had grown into a mass movement in the late 1890s, were reluctant to make woman suffrage a conspicuous plank in their platform. While they demanded the removal of all laws that put women at a disadvantage, they were more interested in redressing their own traditional grievances: in 1898 their leader, Victor Adler, listed these as "economic exploitation, the lack of political rights, spiritual servitude."* Presumably, once these had been overcome, women too would be free. Hence Austrian women, when they organized at all, confined themselves to safe causes long identified with female concerns: education and charity. Few of them even dreamt of challenging the sections in the legal code of 1811 which officially appointed the husband "head of the family" and, in this capacity, the "director of the household," whose orders the wife must follow and enforce. This meant that while the nineteenth-century Austrian code treated women as real persons in law—some people congratulated them for being better off than women in France—it provided that without their husband's approval, they could not educate their children, superintend their household, go to court, or engage in commerce. In her authoritative survey of family law, published in 1907, Helene Weber called the Austrian regulations "predominantly German-patriarchal." The characterization was not too severe.

In this chilling legal and political climate, sustained as it was by dominant cultural attitudes, Austrian women ambitious for an education or for independence had to face down unsparing ridicule. Subtly, this atmosphere was nurtured by popular Austrian works of fiction, among which Arthur Schnitzler's poignant erotic stories were only the most accomplished. It was a literature bursting with sweet young things, usually of the lower classes—shop assistants, waitresses, dancers—as the delectable, pliant, often doomed victims of young officers, jaded bon vivants, or spoiled rich bourgeois who exploited them for their amusement. Stories, novels, and plays portrayed the *süsse Mädel* as a necessary safety valve for the middle-class or upper-class family: purveying the sexual pleasure that the respectable young woman dared not offer before she was married, and all too rarely afterwards, they rescued marriages from collapse or sex-starved males from neurosis. Actually, Schnitzler, at least, was not drawing a lighthearted portrait of gay and irresponsible

---

*By a curious twist of Austro-Hungarian law, a number of women voted in the provinces during the latter part of the nineteenth century—as property owners, not as women. Even radicals propagandizing in behalf of woman suffrage opposed this rather peculiar privilege. In any event, it did not apply in Vienna.

Vienna; he was offering a mordant critique of its cruelty, callousness, and hypocrisy. But superficial readers took such fiction as an exuberant endorsement of Vienna's preoccupation with wine, women, and song—above all, with women. This slander, against which Freud energetically protested, did nothing to improve the prospects for feminists in his country.

Middle-class women were largely unprepared to take up their own cause. In his autobiography, Stefan Zweig recalls that Viennese polite society assiduously protected its young women from all "contamination" and kept them "in a completely sterilized atmosphere" by censoring their reading, supervising their outings, and diverting them from erotic thoughts with lessons in piano, drawing, and foreign languages. They became "educated and overeducated" and were supposed to be "foolish and untaught, well-bred and unsuspecting, inquisitive and shy, uncertain and impractical, and predetermined by this unworldly education to be shaped and led in marriage by their husbands without a will of their own." There was far more to Austrian women in Freud's time than this. But Zweig, with his gift for hyperbole and striking antitheses, has caught one strand, and a colorful one, from a tangled texture of pressures and counterpressures.

One of these counterpressures was supplied by Austria's well-organized Socialist women, who had neither time nor inclination for the kind of erotic dalliance, at once thrilling and degrading, that was the meat of Vienna's storytellers and operetta librettists. Another came from a number of upper-bourgeois and liberal aristocratic women, many of them Jewish, who managed to secure a solid education, often abroad, and presided over literary salons where small talk was frowned on. Not all Viennese literati spent their free time in male preserves like their club or certain favorite coffeehouses. An educational reformer like Eugenie Schwarzwald, who obtained her doctorate in Zurich and then, in 1901, founded Vienna's best, and best-known, coeducational school, was doubtless exceptional in her devotion and her energy. But she exemplified the possibilities opening up to women, even Jewish women, at the time that Freud was beginning to be known for his psychoanalytic writings. In 1913, an English delegate on her way to the Women's International Congress in Budapest, a Mrs. de Castro, made a stop in Vienna for a preliminary meeting and reported on the effectiveness and liveliness of the feminists she met there. "I was struck by the fact," she wrote, "that so many of the leading spirits in the Viennese movement are evidently Jewesses. There is a very large and rich Jewish element in Vienna and they seem very enthusiastic supporters."

Freud, in short, had several contrasting models of woman available to him. He did not attend salons, but he could hear spirited discussions over woman's proper sphere in his own circle. Eminent medical professors like Karl Rokitansky and Theodor Billroth had spoken out against feminists' demands for improved secondary schooling, fearful that access to the university would be on the women's program next. On the other side, Theodor Gomperz, the no less eminent classicist, declared himself in favor of better education for women. Freud had no use for the silly females of Stefan Zweig's vivid caricature, and took pleasure in conversation and correspondence with some of the most cultivated women of his time. Lecturing to the brethren at B'nai B'rith in 1904, he explicitly took issue with Paul Julius Moebius's notorious contention that women are "physiologically feeble-minded"; four years later, he reiterated his objection to Moebius in print. The epithet remained lodged in his mind: as late as 1927, he still thought it useful to take explicit distance from the "general" view that women are suffering from " 'physiological feeble-mindedness,' that is, from a smaller intelligence than that of men. The fact is in dispute, its interpretation dubious." Freud conceded that one might show such an "intellectual atrophy" among women, but if so, it was the fault of society, which prevented them from occupying their minds with what interested them most—sexuality.

PERHAPS FREUD'S ULTIMATE judgment on women emerges incidentally, in a rather infelicitous context, in a reference to one of his dogs. Writing from Berlin to Lou Andreas-Salomé, he confessed that he missed his chow, Jo-Fi, "almost as much as a cigar; she is a charming creature, so interesting, also as a female, wild, instinctive, tender, intelligent, and yet not so dependent as other dogs can be." Women were also, he did not hesitate to admit, stronger than men; as far as health was concerned, he told Arnold Zweig in the summer of 1933, as he and his family watched the deterioration of the political climate in Germany and Austria with impotent rage, "the women stand up better" than the men. Freud did not find this surprising: "They are after all the more steadfast element; with justice, the male is biologically more likely to cave in"—*einfälliger*. Freud wanted only everything from women: strength, tenderness, wildness—and intelligence. But the patronizing, if affectionate, note in his voice suggests that the feminist movement would never win a recruit in him, despite all he was doing for it in his own profession.

He never changed from the position he took early, before the Vienna Psychoanalytic Society in 1908. Wittels had given a paper on "the natural position of woman," in which he had attacked "our contemporary god-damned culture" for forcing woman into the cage of monogamy, virtuous-ness, and an obsession with personal beauty. One consequence, Wittels concluded, was that "women regret not having been born men; so they try to become men (woman's movement)." People do not see how "senseless these aspirations are, not even the women." Commenting on the paper,

Freud, amused and intrigued, recalled once again the passage from John Stuart Mill on woman's earning power that he had criticized to his fiancée twenty-five years earlier, and added, "Anyway, women as a group do not profit from the modern woman's movement at all; at most a few."* That this movement should be most vocal and most successful in the United States (though progress there, too, was agonizingly slow) could hardly have commended it to Freud.

IN THE DEBATE over woman's nature and woman's place, the issue of female sexuality was touchy beyond all others. Throughout most of recorded history, few had doubted that woman is a passionate creature; the question was only whether she enjoys sexual intercourse more than man, or merely just as much. The early Christians pushed this question aside, sternly taking woman's undoubted erotic nature as a sign not of her humanity, but of her essential wickedness. Corrupted, she was also the great corrupter: the church fathers fiercely denounced Woman as the supreme source of sin. If Eve, in league with Satan, had not seduced Adam, humans would presumably be living in paradise still, engaging in sexual intercourse without lust. Whether one read these pious denunciations as a faithful account of man's earliest history in Eden, or rejected them as a childish fable, the perception of woman as a sexual being was hardly controversial.

All this was eventually to change, most conspicuously in the nineteenth century. William Acton, a fluent, smooth-talking English gynecologist whose books were widely read and translated, laid it down in 1857 that "the majority of women (happily for them) are not very much troubled with sexual feelings of any kind." While Acton's reputation among his colleagues was questionable, and dissent from his views articulate, he spoke for many, in Britain and elsewhere. As so often, denial proved the best defense: by refusing to grant woman any interest in sexuality at all, men could contain their hidden panic at the secret female appetite they feared. Perhaps the most striking instance of such denial is a book by a Berlin specialist, Otto Adler, who in 1904 sought to prove that *"the sexual drive (desire, urge, libido) of the woman is markedly smaller, in its first spontaneous origins as in its later manifestations, than that of the man."* The *Three Essays on the Theory of Sexuality,* which Freud

---

*It is interesting to see Freud's former friend Fliess also taking a traditional line. In his major work, *The Course of Life* (1906), he wrote, "In the mental life of woman the law of indolence dominates; while the man is keen on the new, woman opposes change: she receives passively and adds nothing of her own. . . . Feeling is her domain. Sympathy is her virtue. . . . The truly characteristic in the life of the healthy woman is that her sexual task forms the center to which everything is referred back. . . . Love of children is the distinctive mark of the healthy woman." (Quoted in the original German in Patrick Mahony, "Friendship and Its Discontents," *Contemporary Psychoanalysis,* XV [1979], 61n.)

published the following year, inhabits a different world. Adler, parading as a conscientious researcher, offered fifteen clinical vignettes to support his case for female frigidity. But in at least ten of these, his subjects displayed signs of intense, if somewhat wayward, sexual excitability: Adler managed to stimulate two of them to orgasm in his office, on the examination table. No wonder Adler's views, like those of Acton, encountered vocal detractors; many physicians, and some pastors as well, knew better. Even in the nineteenth century, writers depicting woman as endowed with erotic desire were never silenced or subdued; French novelists were not alone in seeing woman as highly sexed. Still, the figure of the inescapably frigid female received more attention than it deserved, then and after. She became a choice ingredient in a defensive antifeminist ideology in the nineteenth century and later proved a handy tendentious travesty that post-Victorians could use against their parents. Far more was involved than the technical question of how much, or whether, woman enjoys pleasure in bed: the sexually anesthetic female suited those who wanted to keep woman at home to concentrate on her domestic duties and, as Freud had once put it to his daughter Mathilde, make man's life more pleasant.

Freud's conservative attitudes did not prevent him, as we have seen, from taking it for granted that a woman is a sensual being, just like a man. The theory he developed in the early 1890s, that all neuroses originate in sexual conflicts, presupposes that women and men are equally susceptible to erotic stimuli. Again, in the drafts he sent Fliess at about that time, he attributed neurotic malaise to the use of contraceptives that compromise the gratification of the user, whether male or female. To be sure, Freud's psychoanalytic writings before the First World War hint at an assumption of male superiority. In one aside of 1908, he suggested that woman's sexual drive is weaker than man's. Moreover, Freud saw libido, that primitive, fundamental sexual energy, as masculine in nature. In 1905, in the first edition of his *Three Essays*, speaking of girls' autoerotic and masturbatory activities, he suggested tentatively that "the sexuality of little girls has a thoroughly masculine character." Again, in 1913, he described the seat of sexual pleasure in girls, the clitoris, as a male organ; their sexuality "often behaves like that of boys." At the same time he was fully aware, and repeatedly warned, that this vocabulary was imprecise and misleading: the terms "masculine" and "feminine" signify whatever each writer makes them signify. To call libido "masculine" means nothing more, he explicitly noted in 1915, than that it is "active." What mattered more in those years, and right through the war, was that Freud described the evolution of sexual life in boys and in girls as parallel, differentiated only by social pressures. As sexual beings, the way Freud then saw the matter, men and women are more or less mirrors of one another. In any event, these were technical issues, a subject for research rather than for polemics.

This is one reason why the intramural discussion of the 1920s over female sexuality did not become acrimonious. All participants saw it principally as an issue in psychoanalytic theory. But when Freud reexamined the comparative developmental schedules of boys and girls, his critics needed some self-control to keep controversy on this scientific level. For with his robust and caustic language, Freud put a match to inflammable material. On the vexed issue of woman, he moved to the right, subverting his own idea, so congenial to feminists, that human males and females have very similar psychological histories. Freud, however, was not concerned with politics, not even sexual politics. There was nothing in the climate of the 1920s and nothing in Freud's psychological biography to prompt the revisions that would make him propound his controversial, at times scurrilous, views on woman. They followed from his puzzling through of theoretical difficulties, in particular from new complications he introduced into his account of the Oedipus complex, its emergence, flowering, and decay.

BY THE EARLY 1920s, Freud seemed to have adopted the position that the little girl is a failed boy, the grown woman a kind of castrated man. In 1923, laying out the phases of human sexual history, he identified a phase, following the oral and the anal phases, which he called phallic. Little boys, like little girls, believe at first that everyone, even the mother, has a phallus, and disenchantment on this issue is bound to be traumatic. Man, then, the male, was Freud's measure. By this time Freud had abandoned his earlier manner of treating the sexual development of girls and boys as parallel. Varying Napoleon's famous saying about politics, he offered a provocative aphorism: "Anatomy is destiny."*

The most obvious evidence for that destiny, he thought, is the observable distinction between boys' and girls' genitalia. This makes for crucial differences in psychological development, especially in the career of the Oedipus complex in the two sexes. It followed for Freud that naturally the sequels to the decay of the Oedipus complex, notably the construction of the superego, must diverge as well. The boy acquires his superego after the threat of castration has destroyed his oedipal program of conquest; the girl, already "castrated," with fewer and weaker incentives for developing the exigent superego typical for the male, constructs hers from the fear of losing love.

By the following year, in 1925, Freud stood ready to be blunt about the

---

*He had already said this in 1912, in "On the Universal Tendency to Debasement in the Sphere of Love" (SE XI, 189), but there he was not referring to differences between men and women.

implications of his new conjectures. He did have the *savoir-faire*—or, more accurately, enough doubts—to show some qualms: "One hesitates to say out loud, but cannot resist the idea, that for woman the level of the ethically normal becomes different" from the level for man. "Her superego never becomes so inexorable, so impersonal, so independent of its emotional origins" as we demand it to be in the male. This peculiar thinness of woman's superego, Freud suggested, lends weight to the reproaches misogynists have leveled against the female character from time immemorial: "She shows less sense of justice than man, less inclination to submission to the great exigencies of life, is more often led in her decisions by tender or hostile feelings." It is a little ironic that Freud's daughter Anna should have been the one to read this paper of her father's at the international congress of psychoanalysts in Bad Homburg.

Freud declared himself hesitant to say all these things, but he said them nevertheless, said them with a kind of bravado suggesting his awareness that he was bound to offend some listeners and readers. But then, he never minded being offensive. It had not stopped him near the beginning of his career when he asserted the infantile origins of sexuality, nor would it stop him near the end when he called Moses an Egyptian. On the contrary, the sense of braving opposition acted on him as a stimulant, almost an aphrodisiac. He admitted that in most males the superego leaves much to be desired; he admitted, too, that his conclusions about woman's weaker superego required further confirmation. He had, after all, based his generalization on a mere handful of cases. But with all his tentativeness, Freud stood firm: one should not allow oneself to be distracted or disconcerted by "the protests of the feminists, who want to press a complete equality of the sexes in position and value."

He had still another reason for publishing what in earlier years he would have held back in order to amass additional material: he felt that he no longer had "oceans of time" before him. While he recognized that the point was touchy and that it deserved further exploration, he did not want to wait. He could have made a more respectable case, no doubt, if he had not appealed to his advanced age, or had refused to enlist the sheer shock value of his assertions in support of their validity. But Freud's antifeminist stance was not the product of his feeling old or wishing to be outrageous. Rather, he had come to see it as an inescapable consequence of men's and women's diverging sexual histories: anatomy is destiny. His comparative history of sexual development may be less than wholly compelling, but it calls on the logic of human growth as he redefined it in the 1920s. The psychological and ethical distinctions between the sexes, he argued, emerge naturally from the biology of the human animal and from the kinds of mental work that this implies for each sex. At the outset, the development of boys and girls is identical; Freud was not persuaded by the popular notion that little boys show aggressiveness and little girls, submission. On the contrary, males are often passive, females quite active, in their childish erotic ventures. Such sexual histories strongly support Freud's thesis of bisexuality, the idea that each gender displays some of the characteristics of the other.

But then, Freud went on, something happens. Perhaps at the age of three, or just before, girls face a task that boys are happily spared, and with that, male superiority begins to assert itself. All infants and toddlers, male and female, start out with the most profound attachment to the mother, the fount of life, the source of nourishment, care, and tenderness. The mother's power over the baby is unlimited at a time when the father's involvement is abstract, relatively remote. But as infants grow into children, the father assumes a more and more prominent role in their daily existence and their imagination, and eventually the ways that boys and girls cope with him diverge decisively. The boy's life grows stormy when he discovers his father to be an overwhelming rival for his mother's affection and attention; he feels as though he is being expelled from paradise. But the girl has far more difficult psychological work to do than her brother: his mother can remain the love of his life, even if the harsh realities of the family constellation compel his desire for her to undergo drastic retrenchment; but as we have seen, the girl finds herself obliged to transfer her principal erotic attachment from mother to father, and to manage traumatic moments that leave lasting, usually damaging, deposits in her mind.

The girl's ordeal, Freud argued, starts with penis envy. Discovering that she has no penis, that her genitalia are invisible and that she cannot urinate so impressively as boys, she develops feelings of inferiority and a capacity for jealousy far surpassing that of her brothers or her male friends. Boys, to be sure, must also wrestle with dismaying revelations: seeing a girl's genitals, they develop castration anxiety. What is worse, their father, so much more commanding than they can be, or their mother, catching them masturbating, may threaten to cut off their penis. After all, even a modern, liberal, psychoanalytically oriented couple like Little Hans's parents did not hesitate to caution their son that if he kept his hand on his wi-wi-maker, mother would call the doctor to cut it off. The girl, though, must deal not with fears but with reality, with her "mutilated" condition. Freud did not consider castration anxiety, the male's prerogative, a particularly enviable privilege. But it seemed to him that becoming afraid of losing what one has is less damaging than being sadly aware that one has nothing to lose.

It is after her narcissistic humiliation that the little girl rejects her mother, who has allowed her to be born so pathetically incomplete or may even have been responsible for taking her penis away. Then her childish love affair with her father begins. This crucial change in love object is painful and prolonged because, as Freud was to note in 1931 in his paper "Female Sexuality," the girl's pre-oedipal attachment to her mother is so intense. Freud took some pride in digging so far back into girls' infancy and thought this "insight" into the pre-oedipal phase, so hard to capture in analysis, a "surprise." The girl's passion for her mother is hard to detect because it is usually covered over by her later passion for her father. Borrowing a metaphor from archeology, as he liked to do, Freud compared this insight to the "discovery of the Minoan-Mycenean culture behind the Greek." The pre-oedipal phase is of particular importance for women, far more important than for men. By going back to this phase, Freud thought, we can completely clear up "many phenomena of female sexual life which were not really accessible to our understanding before."

The more visible psychological differentiation between the sexes, however, first appears a little later, in the oedipal phase; puberty, all appearances to the contrary, only underscores this differentiation, but does not originate it. The boy, faced with the threat of irreparable damage to his bodily integrity, retreats from his passionate love for his mother; the girl, recognizing her inferior physical state, turns to her father for consolation and replaces her wish for a penis with that for a baby. Freud put these contrasting sexual histories into the kind of definitive formula that was his specialty: *"While the Oedipus complex of the boy is destroyed by the castration complex, that of the girl is made possible and introduced by the castration complex."* Both boys and girls, in short, must navigate their way through two complexes, the castration and the Oedipus complex, but the sequence in which one gender encounters them is reversed for the other. Freud noted a little ruefully that having concentrated on boys in the past, psychoanalysts had assumed that these critical determinative events would follow the same line of development in girls. But recent work and more thinking had persuaded him that this is not how children's minds grow. The sexes are unlike, and woman is the greater sufferer from the difference.

These distinctive timetables explain Freud's readiness to deny woman's ability to develop a demanding superego. The boy's Oedipus complex is assaulted and smashed by the parental threat of castration. Then, much like a builder using stones from a demolished house, the boy incorporates broken remains of the complex into his ego and constructs his superego from them. But the little girl does not have such building blocks at hand. Freud supposed, radically oversimplifying the matter, that she must patch together her super-ego from the experiences of her upbringing and from her fear that she will lose her parents' love. This is far from persuasive. After all, the little boy, repressing his Oedipus complex, borrows strength to do so from his father, acting under "the influence of authority, religious teaching, education, reading." Influences of this sort, as both clinical and general observation demonstrate, work on the girl in the same way. Freud's lament for woman's superego was not illogical so much as it was partial: to the extent that psychoanalytic theory acknowledges the impact of external forces on the making of the mind, it can accommodate the idea of a very severe, even persecuting superego in women no less than in men. Culture, too, is destiny.

FREUD'S CASE FOR differential superego development was debatable enough. His argument concerning the seat of sexual pleasure proved more debatable still. The small child, as he put it, gives itself exquisite gratification by touching the phallus—that is to say, for the girl, the clitoris. But in adolescence, the pubertal young woman on the road to adult femininity adds to the pleasure she takes from her "masculine" organ by elevating "the vagina, derived from the cloaca, into the dominant erotogenic zone." Thus at this stormy time in her life, Freud argued, having already transferred her love from mother to father, the woman must engage in yet another laborious psychological shift, one that the young man need not confront. Freud was persuaded that, obliged to perform this additional assignment, the woman is only too likely to suffer erotic shipwreck. She becomes masochistic and humorless, gives up sex altogether, clings to her masculine traits, resigns herself to submissive domesticity. But to the extent that the grown woman secures sexual satisfaction at all, she does so principally through the vagina, using the clitoris at best as an adjunct to pleasure. If things were any different, she would need no man to give her erotic enjoyment.

Long before empirical investigations by sexologists and biologists raised damaging doubts about this developmental scheme, psychoanalysts expressed reservations about it. They did not yet have sufficient clinical or experimental information about the female orgasm to question Freud's thesis that in her sexual activity, the young woman graduates from clitoral to vaginal pleasure. Rather, dissenters like Karen Horney and Ernest Jones concentrated on woman's nature and refused to acquiesce in Freud's formula that femininity is essentially acquired by the successive renunciation of masculine traits. After all, in defining the clitoris as a residual penis, Freud was offering a dubious and highly tendentious analogy.

The critics had a point. In 1922, Horney valiantly stood up at the international congress of psychoanalysts in Berlin, with Freud in the chair, and suggested a revised version of penis envy. She did not deny its existence, but placed it within a context of normal female development. Penis envy does not create femininity, Horney said, but, rather, expresses it. Hence she rejected the idea that this envy necessarily leads women to the "repudiation of their womanhood." Quite to the contrary, "we can see that penis envy by no means precludes a deep and wholly womanly love attachment to the father." Horney was, from the Freudian perspective that dominated these congresses, behaving in the most correct manner possible: she respectfully cited the founder; she accepted the very idea of penis envy. She only speculated, a little dryly: perhaps it was "masculine narcissism" that had led psychoanalysts to accept the view that woman, after all half the human race, is discontented with the sex that nature has assigned to her. It seemed as though male analysts found this view "too self-evident to need explanation." Whatever the reasons, the conclusion psychoanalysts had drawn about woman, Horney argued, "is decidedly unsatisfying, not only to feminine narcissism but also to biological science."*

That was in 1922. Four years later, a year after Freud had published his provocative paper on the consequences of the anatomical distinction between the sexes, Horney became even more explicit about psychoanalysts' male bias. "In some of his latest works," she wrote, citing Freud's words for her own purposes, "Freud has drawn attention with increasing urgency to a certain one-sidedness in our analytical researches. I refer to the fact that till quite recently the minds of boys and men only were taken as objects of investigation." In view of Freud's well-known female patients, that was something of a misstatement, but Horney plunged ahead, undaunted: "The reason for this is obvious. Psychoanalysis is the creation of a male genius, and almost all those who have developed his ideas have been men." Hence it was only "right and reasonable" that psychoanalysis "should evolve more easily a masculine psychology." Borrowing some arguments from the German philosopher, sociologist, and cultural critic Georg Simmel, a rare resource for psychoanalysts, she described modern civilization as essentially masculine. Simmel had concluded not that the female is inferior but, rather, that current dominant views of her character were distorted. Listing the self-aggrandizing, highly subjective notions that little boys develop about themselves and their sisters, Horney pointed out that they matched, point for point, the positions on feminine development common among psychoanalysts. Talk about woman's natural masochism is as biased as the depreciation of motherhood, a gift of nature in which woman is obviously superior to man. It is a capacity, in fact, for

---

*In 1927, in her first paper, Jeanne Lampl-de Groot reported without comment that according to Horney, one reason why female sexuality continued to seem so mysterious was that "so far, analytical observations have been made principally by men." (Jeanne Lampl-de Groot, "The Evolution of the Oedipus Complex in Women," in *The Development of the Mind: Psychoanalytic Papers on Clinical and Theoretical Problems* [1965], 4.)

which boys envy girls. Often enough, Horney noted, penis envy is not an introduction to oedipal love but a defense against it. She did not deny that after their cruel disappointments, girls often turn away from sexuality altogether. But like boys, she insisted, girls undergo their oedipal experience first: she rejected as untenable Freud's famous differential formula concerning the sequence of the castration complex and the Oedipus complex. Indeed, she concluded, with a fair show of justice, reigning psychoanalytic theory about woman was self-serving—that is, it served the men who promulgated it. "The dogma of the inferiority of women had its origins in an unconscious male tendency."

All that was wicked and telling. What mattered to Horney, though, was not to score points but to establish a principle. Whatever Freud and the female analysts following him uncritically might hold, femininity is an essential endowment of woman. She is as worthy a creature as man, however hidden her genitalia, however arduous her work of transferring her love from mother to father. An analyst like Jeanne Lampl-de Groot might echo Freud's conclusions: "In the first years of her development as an individual" the "little girl behaves exactly like a boy, not only in the matter of masturbation but in other aspects of her mental life: in her love aim and object choice she is actually a little man." Horney could not agree.

Nor could Ernest Jones, who carried on an inconclusive correspondence with Freud on the subject of woman, and reiterated his dissent in three important papers. Freud, after publishing his paper on female sexuality, voiced the hope that Jones might rethink his position. The whole matter "is so important and still so unsettled that it really deserves to be worked on anew." But Jones could be as stubborn as Freud. In 1935, delivering a paper before the Vienna Psychoanalytic Society, he defended the "vigorous" Karen Horney and explicitly denied that woman is *"un homme manqué,"* a "permanently disappointed creature struggling to console herself with secondary substitutes alien to her nature." The "ultimate question," he concluded, is "whether a woman is born or made." He had no doubt that she is born.

JONES DEDICATED THE volume in which this paper first appeared to "Professor Freud, as a Token of the Author's Gratitude." But neither the arguments of Jones and of Horney, nor three long, carefully reasoned, and thoroughly documented papers by the brilliant young analyst Otto Fenichel, made any impression on Freud. Fenichel intended not so much to overthrow Freud's thesis as to complicate it: he accepted Freud's basic propositions, especially about the little girl's disillusionment with her mother and the need to shift her libido toward her father. But he demoted the girl's discovery of her "mutilation," and the phallic phase, as being, though important, far from decisive psychological experiences. " 'Oedipus complex' and 'castration-anxiety,' " he wrote, "are words: the psychic realities which they represent are infinitely various." But Freud was persuaded that his critics did not sufficiently distinguish between the inborn and the cultural aspects of female sexuality. In 1935, the very year Jones posed the ultimate question about woman, Freud summed up his case once again. Infantile sexuality had first been studied in males, and the complete parallelism between boys and girls had shown itself untenable; the little girl has to shift both in her sexual object and in her dominant genital zone. "From this, difficulties and possible inhibitions result, which do not apply to the man." This was Freud's bald last word on woman.

He might have said more. To call woman a dark continent was, as we have seen, to ally himself with a historic commonplace. All this popular wisdom about mysterious Eve hints at the fundamental, triumphantly repressed fear of woman that men have felt in their bones since time out of mind. Freud had an inkling of that fear: when Marie Bonaparte once observed, "Man is afraid of woman," he replied, "He's right!" In his student days, he had exclaimed to his friend Emil Fluss, "How wise our educators that they pester the beautiful sex so little with scientific knowledge!!" Women, he told Fluss, "have come into the world for something better than to become wise." But he had not rested content simply to accept the convenient darkness of the continent that is woman; he had sought to explore and to chart it. The map he produced had many white, empty spots and was misdrawn in ways researchers have come to recognize after his death. But he tried. His firm tone, which affronted many, his bland assumption that he was above any hint of tendentiousness, and his impolite attacks on feminists have not served him well. They have obscured the freshness of his ideas and the provisional character of his conclusions. He thought that analysts with feminist leanings would accuse him of male bias, while his supporters might turn this sort of reductionism against his opponents; such bellicose employment of analysis, he commented sagely, "leads to no decision." He refused to see that he had been bellicose enough himself. But then he did not want to spend all his energy on this limited, though significant, issue. From the late 1920s, he had been impatient to move on, and to allow other, even grander riddles to torment him, the riddles of religion and culture that had fascinated him since boyhood.

ELEVEN

Human Nature at Work

AGAINST ILLUSIONS

 For Freud, the relevance of psychoanalysis, whether carried on behind the couch or at the desk, was universal. True, the analytic situation provided a unique opportunity for generating and testing his hypotheses. Hermetic, highly professional, virtually unduplicable, that situation always remained for Freud an inexhaustible fount of information, a point of many departures.* But unlike most of the psychoanalysts who came after him, he saw each of his analytic investigations as equally instructive and

---

*Freud in fact respected, and quoted, some experimental verifications of his theories (note especially his comments on papers on dream formation by Otto Pötzl, to which he referred in the 1919 edition of *The Interpretation of Dreams, SE* IV, 181n.2). But in general he believed that the thousands of analytic hours he had spent with his analysands, to which one could add those thousands of hours spent by his adherents, provided sufficient proof of his ideas. This attitude, which has not wholly carried the day, was at the very least a tactical mistake.

When in 1934 the American psychologist Saul Rosenzweig sent Freud some experimental studies designed to test the validity of several psychoanalytic propositions, Freud replied politely but a little curtly that while he found such investigation interesting, he saw little value in it "because the wealth of dependable observations" on which psychoanalytic assertions rest "makes them independent of experimental verification. Still, it can do no harm." (Freud to Rosenzweig, February 28, 1934. Letter quoted in full in the original German in David Shakow and David Rapaport, *The Influence of Freud on American Psychology* [1964], 129n.)

equally significant. Teasing out the origins of civilization from scanty and speculative material was quite different from evaluating clinical data. But Freud was not embarrassed or apologetic about invading the domains of art or politics or prehistory, psychoanalytic instruments in hand. "My life's work," he said summarily in 1930, "has been directed at a single goal."

Not long before, he had dramatized this point with two widely read speculative essays: *The Future of an Illusion* of 1927, ambitious and controversial, and *Civilization and Its Discontents* of early 1930, no less ambitious and, if anything, more controversial still. But, giving way to his sour mood, Freud belittled these late incursions into culture with unsparing self-criticism. He disparaged *The Future of an Illusion* as "childish" and "feeble analytically, inadequate as self-confession." This sort of talk, a mixture of postpartum depression and a rather superstitious defensiveness, had become a habit with him. It never ceased to astonish Freud's associates. He had sounded a similar note decades before after sending *The Interpretation of Dreams* out into the world, and again, more recently, when he admitted to his "familiar depression" after reading proofs of *The Ego and the Id.* But his critique of *The Future of an Illusion* was exceptional in its vehemence. It verged on self-hatred. In October 1927, promising Eitingon a copy as soon as the proofs came back from the printer, he noted that "the analytic content of the work is very thin" and in other ways, too, "it is not worth very much."

He was feeling his age and the aftereffects of his cancer. His prosthesis was painful, and to make things worse, he suffered unpleasant episodes of angina. In March 1927, when Arnold Zweig offered to come and visit, Freud pressed him to make good his promise—without delay: "Don't wait too long with it, I'll soon be 71." In the same month, told he ought to rest in a sanatorium because he was looking unwell, he bitterly protested to Eitingon, "Life *for* health is something intolerable to me." Thoughts of his death were a familiar presence now. In the summer, inviting James and Alix Strachey to join other visitors in Semmering, he cautioned them as he had cautioned Zweig: "We may not have many chances more to meet."

Freud disliked parading his ill-health before the world, but to a handful of intimates he unbent a little, sending laconic bulletins enlivened with flashes of his old defiant comic touch. His letters to Lou Andreas-Salomé, among the most affectionate and affecting of his last years, chart his fluctuating health and corresponding moods. The two rarely saw one another now: she was living in Göttingen with her aged husband and traveling little; he was immured in or near Vienna. Their friendship continued to flourish because he respected her mind and enjoyed her company, even by mail. Moreover, she shared his great fondness for Anna, and was quite as stoical as her beloved Professor. Selflessly and thoughtfully, she tried to keep her illnesses to herself, forcing him, the professional reader of subtle clues, to guess at her condition from her phrasing and her silences. In May 1927, acknowledging Lou An-dreas-Salomé's congratulations on his seventy-first birthday, he found it won-derful that she and her husband could still enjoy the sun. "But with me, the grumpiness of old age has moved in, the complete disillusionment compa-rable to the congealing of the moon, the inner freezing." All his life, he liked to think, he had battled illusions; to acknowledge his inner temperature was part of his long warfare against lies, against bland surfaces, against taking wishes for realities. He was often cold now, even in warm weather.

There were moments when he could report holding up well. But they were precious exceptions, usually undercut by a hint at his decrepitude. In a letter of December 1927 to his "dear Lou," he began with a cheerful communiqué about his condition, but then immediately apologized for not replying to her long "chatter" sooner: "My slovenliness and indolence are gaining on me." For a man who had all his life taken pride in answering his mail promptly, and who interpreted any delay by his correspondents as a sign of disaffection, this was a sinister symptom. The realization that his body was simply refusing to serve him well spread gloom over his perception of *The Future of an Illusion*. When the French psychoanalyst René Laforgue, an occasional visi-tor in the 1920s, expressed delight with the essay, Freud, though pleased with the compliment, burst out, "This is my worst book!" Laforgue demurred, but Freud persisted: it was an old man's work. The authentic Freud had been a great man, but he was dead; how regrettable that Laforgue had not known him! Upset, Laforgue asked Freud what on earth he could mean. "The penetrating force has been lost" was his reply—*Die Durchschlagskraft ist verloren gegangen.*

FREUD'S SELF-LACERATION cannot obscure the fact that *The Future of an Illusion* was a book he had to write. "I do not know if you have guessed the secret link between *Lay Analysis* and *Illusion,*" he wrote a little tactlessly to Pfister. "In the first, I want to protect analysis from the doctors; in the second, from the priests." But the prehistory of his *Illusion* was far longer and far more intimate than that. Decades of principled atheism and of psychoanalytic thinking about religion had prepared him for it. He had been a consistent militant atheist since his school days, mocking God and religion, not sparing the God and the religion of his family. "For God's dark ways," he had told his friend Eduard Silberstein in the summer of 1873, when he was seventeen, "no one has yet invented a lantern." This obscurity did not make the deity any more attractive to Freud or, for that matter, any more plausible. When he instructed Silberstein that one was unjust to reproach religion with being metaphysical and lacking confirmation from the senses—

for, "rather, religion addresses the senses exclusively"—he was proffering not a serious thought but a culinary joke: "Even the God-denier who has the good fortune of belonging to a tolerably pious family cannot deny the holiday when he puts a New Year's morsel to his mouth. One could say that religion, moderately consumed, stimulates the digestion but, taken in excess, harms it."

This was the irreverent tone with which Freud felt most at home. As we know, for a few months at the university, under the influence of his admired philosophy professor Franz Brentano, he had toyed with philosophical theism. But his true disposition was, as he described it to his friend Silberstein, that of "a godless medical student." He never changed. "Neither in my private life nor in my writings"—thus he summed up his career as an atheist the year before he died—"have I ever made a secret of being an out-and-out unbeliever." All his life he thought that it was not atheism that needed explaining but religious belief.

As a psychoanalyst, he set about doing just that. Among some notes he wrote for himself in 1905 is this terse and suggestive entry: "Religion as ob[sessive] neurosis—Private religion." Two years later, he embodied this germ of an idea in a first exploratory paper, "Obsessive Actions and Religious Practices," an elegant, tantalizing attempt to bring religion and neurosis under one yoke. He had discovered blatant resemblances between the "ceremonies" and "rituals" so necessary to the obsessive neurotic and the observances that are an essential ingredient in every faith. Both sets of practices, neurotic and religious, he argued, involve the renunciation of impulses; both work as defensive, self-protective measures. "In view of these correspondences and analogies one might venture to regard obsessional neurosis as a pathological counterpart to religious formation, neurosis as an individual religion, religion as a universal obsessional neurosis."

With the years, Freud expanded this disenchanted analytic perspective on sacred things. In 1911, he told Ferenczi that he was ruminating "once again" about the "origins of religion in the drives," and thought that some day he might work out the idea in detail. *The Future of an Illusion* redeemed the promise he had made to himself. To demolish religion with psychoanalytic weapons, then, had been on Freud's agenda for many years. He insisted to Pfister that his views on religion did not "constitute part of the analytic set of dogmas. It is my personal attitude, which corresponds to that of many non- and pre-analysts and is surely not shared by many worthy analysts." But this was his way of sparing the feelings of a long-time trusted associate with whom he had been carrying on a good-natured feud about theology for two decades. The view of man implicit, and often explicit, in *The Future of an Illusion* is sustained by the body of his thought; Freud's conclusions may have been

far from unique, but his ways of reaching them were characteristic of psychoanalysis.

As so often, the timing of the essay had a highly personal dimension. In
October 1927, he announced to Pfister that the "brochure" about to appear
had "a good deal to do with you. I have been wanting to write it for a long
time but pigeonholed it out of consideration for you, until at last the urge
became too strong." It was easy to guess, he added, that the essay dealt "with
my absolutely negative attitude toward religion, in every form and dilution,
and although this cannot be news to you, I was afraid, and still am afraid,
that such a public confession will be embarrassing to you." Pfister responded
as expected—encouragingly: he would far rather read a sensible unbeliever
like Freud than a thousand worthless believers. But even if Pfister had betrayed some signs of uneasiness, or had been spoiling for a quarrel, Freud
would not—could not—have abandoned his plan. We have seen it before:
when an idea was working in him, it exerted almost painful pressure, relieved
only in the act of writing. Of all Freud's publications, *The Future of an
Illusion* is perhaps the most inevitable and the most predictable.

FROM ITS OPENING paragraphs, *The Future of an Illusion* makes large claims.
Its announced theme is religion, but it begins, significantly, with reflections
on the nature of culture; it reads like a rehearsal for *Civilization and Its
Discontents.* This gambit reveals Freud's perception of his assignment: by
embedding religion in the largest possible context, he makes it accessible, like
all human conduct, to scientific investigation. In short, his uncompromising
secularism, which he had in common with most contemporary psychologists
and sociologists of religion, denied matters of faith any privileged status, any
claim to exemption from analysis. He respected no sacred spots; saw no
temples that he, as a researcher, must not enter.

A century and a half before Freud, one of his intellectual ancestors, Denis
Diderot, had boldly asserted, "Facts may be distributed among three classes:
the acts of divinity, the phenomena of nature, and the actions of men. The
first belong to theology, the second to philosophy, and the last to history
properly speaking. All are equally subject to criticism." This is the air that
Freud's analysis of religion breathes—the critical spirit of the Enlightenment.
There was nothing mysterious or concealed about this intellectual legacy.
"Your substitute religion," his friend Pfister told him bluntly, "is in essence
the Enlightenment thought of the eighteenth century in proud, fresh, modern guise." Freud did not think he was advocating a substitute religion, but
he did not deny his indebtedness. "I have said nothing," he assured the
readers of *The Future of an Illusion,* "that other, better men have not said
before me far more completely, more vigorously, and more impressively." He

refused to mention the names of these "well-known" men, lest someone think he was trying to "place myself in their ranks." But they are easy to supply: Spinoza, Voltaire, Diderot, Feuerbach, Darwin.

Besides distinguished progenitors for his work on religion, Freud also had distinguished contemporaries. During the years he developed the psycho-analytic rationale for his pugnacious atheism, the scientific investigation of religion was flourishing among students of man and society. The researches of James G. Frazer and W. Robertson Smith into comparative and primitive religion had a very real impact on Freud's speculative writings, most notably *Totem and Taboo.* The work of Havelock Ellis that traced religious conversions back to the strains of adolescence or menopause, and religious excitement to sexual conflicts, was congenial to Freud's own. So were the somewhat earlier efforts of Jean Martin Charcot to reduce mysterious "supernatural" phenomena to natural causes. And after 1900, Max Weber and Émile Durkheim, the two most eminent sociologists of the day, published epoch-making studies on religion. Weber, in his classic collection of linked essays, *The Protestant Ethic and the Spirit of Capitalism,* published in 1904 and 1905, identified in certain religious sects, notably ascetic Protestants, a mental style conducive to the development of capitalism. Durkheim, like Weber intent on establishing the independence of sociology from psychology, treated religious beliefs as expressions of social organization. He insisted that he was directing all his researches, whether into suicide, education, or religion, toward social facts rather than individual mental events. Thus he wanted his much-discussed concept of "anomie"—the collapse or confusion of social norms that is a major contributor to disorientation and suicide—to be understood, and investigated, as a social phenomenon.* No doubt Weber and Durkheim were Freud's equals, in some ways his superiors, in relating the experience of religion to its manifestations in culture. But while categories such as Weber's "worldly asceticism" and Durkheim's "anomie" had powerful psychological implications, neither sociologist had explored these implications; neither had anchored religion quite so solidly in human nature as would Freud in *The Future of an Illusion.*

Still, Freud's own essay opens with a discussion of culture. In his terse definition, culture is a collective effort to master external nature and regulate the relations of humans to one another.† This means that everyone is necessarily exposed to disagreeable and difficult sacrifices, to postponements of

---

*Freud had read Durkheim's most sustained and influential work on religion, *The Elementary Forms of Religious Life* of 1912, and briefly discussed it among the "sociological theories." (*Totem und Tabu,* GW IX, 137/*Totem and Taboo,* SE XIII, 113.)

†In these pages I follow Freud's usage: "I disdain to separate 'culture' and 'civilization.' " (*Die Zukunft einer Illusion,* GW XIV, 326/*The Future of an Illusion,* SE XXI, 6.)

wishes and deprivations of pleasure, all for the sake of the common survival. Hence "every individual is virtually the enemy of culture," and coercion is indispensable. In some golden age, matters might be so arranged that neither force nor the suppression of drives would be needed. But that would be utopia. "One must reckon, I think," Freud maintained, "with the fact that all humans harbor destructive—that is, antisocial and anticultural—tendencies and that these are strong enough in a large number of persons to determine their behavior in human society."

Freud, the old-fashioned liberal defying the democratic temper of his day, drew a firm distinction between the mob and the elite. "The masses are indolent and unreasonable; they have no love for the renunciation of drives." One must face it: human beings "are not spontaneously fond of work, and arguments cannot prevail against their passions." This is the Freud who had told his fiancée in 1883 that the "psychology of the common man is rather different from ours." The *Gesindel*—the "rabble"—indulge their appetites, while those cultivated enough, like himself and Martha Bernays, husband their desires and suppress their natural urges. That derogatory epithet, *Gesindel,* was often under Freud's pen.* Yet Freud the superb despiser of the masses was no blind admirer of the existing social order. He found it only natural that the poor and deprived should hate and envy those who sacrifice far less; one could hardly expect them to internalize social prohibitions. "It goes without saying that a culture which leaves so large a number of participants unsatisfied and drives them to rebellion neither has the prospect of maintaining itself permanently, nor deserves it." But just or unjust, culture must resort to coercion to enforce its rules.

With all its palpable flaws, Freud added, culture has learned fairly well how to discharge its principal task, defending man against nature. It may do still better in the future. But this is not to say that "nature is already conquered." Far from it. Freud enumerated an alarming catalogue of nature's hostility to

---

*He used it early and late: as a schoolboy describing a family of Eastern European Jews he had encountered on a train (see p. 19) and as a man in his seventies reflecting on current Jew-hatred. "In the question of anti-Semitism," he told Arnold Zweig, "I have little inclination to seek for explanations, experience a strong inclination to surrender to my affects, and feel strengthened in my whole unscientific position that when all is said, on the average, all things considered, human beings are miserable rabble." (Freud to Arnold Zweig, December 2, 1927. *Freud–Zweig,* 11 [3].) Two years later, in 1929, he confessed to Lou Andreas-Salomé, "In my inmost depth, I am really convinced that my dear fellow humans—with a few exceptions—are rabble." (Freud to Andreas-Salomé, July 28, 1929. *Freud–Salomé,* 199 [182].) In 1932, Ferenczi noted in his private journal that Freud had once told him, "Neurotics are rabble, only good for sustaining us financially and to learn from their cases." (August 4, 1932, *Klinisches Tagebuch.* Typescript, with a few handwritten pages, Freud Collection, B 22, LC, catalogued as "Scientific Diary.") Ferenczi's recollection is not implausible. Had Freud not written him as early as 1909, "The pat[ients] are disgusting," and "give me an opportunity for new technical studies"? (See p. 295.)

man: earthquakes, deluges, storms, diseases, and—approaching closer to a pressing personal concern—"the painful riddle of death, against which so far no little medicinal herb has been found and probably none will be found. With these forces nature rises up against us, magnificent, cruel, implacable." This vengeful Nature, pitiless and unconquerable enemy, bringer of death, is a goddess far different from the supportive, embracing, erotic Mother Nature who, Freud remembered, had lured him as a young student, with his life before him, into medicine.* No wonder Freud concluded, the personal note unmistakable, that "as for humanity as a whole, so for the individual, life is hard to bear." Helplessness is the common lot.

AT THIS POINT Freud cunningly injected religion into his analysis. Cunningly, because by underscoring human helplessness he could link up the need for religion with childhood experiences. He thus maneuvered religion onto the home ground of psychoanalysis. Admittedly, religion is among the most prized possessions of mankind, along with art and ethics, but its origins lie in infantile psychology. The child fears the power of its parents but also trusts them for protection. Hence, growing up, it has no difficulty assimilating its sense of parental—chiefly paternal—power to ruminations about its place in the natural world, at once dangerous and promising. Like the child, the adult gives way to his wishes and embroiders his fantasies with the most fanciful decorations. They are at bottom survivals: the needs, the very vulnerability and dependence of the child, live on into adulthood, and therefore the psychoanalyst can contribute a great deal to the understanding of how religion came into being.† "Religious conceptions originated in the same need as all other achievements of culture, from the necessity of defending oneself against the crushing superiority of nature," and "from the urge to correct the painfully felt imperfections of culture."‡

This aphoristic analogy is neat, perhaps a little too neat. Its persuasiveness largely depends on the convictions the reader brings to the text. But in *The Future of an Illusion*, Freud left no doubt of *his* conviction that he was doing

---

*See p. 24.

†Freud knew, of course, that there are many different sorts of religions, and divergent attitudes toward belief within each culture, and that across the ages there have been distinct, drastic evolutions of religious thought and feeling. He was speaking in *The Future of an Illusion* principally about the religion of the modern common man, and he referred readers to his *Totem and Taboo* for a summary discussion of some of these evolutions in thought.

‡In *The Interpretation of Dreams*, he had already said flatly that all "the complicated mental activity" involved in the search for gratification "merely represents a *detour to wish-fulfillment* necessitated by experience. Thinking is after all nothing but a substitute for a hallucinatory wish." (*GW* II–III, 572/*SE* V, 567.)

more than just pointing out interesting resemblances. Men invent gods, or passively accept the gods their culture imposes on them, precisely because they have grown up with such a god in their house. Like the fantasies of the child facing the power of others and its own desires, and on the model of such fantasies, religion is fundamentally an illusion—a childish illusion. The psychological analysis of religious doctrines demonstrates that "they are not precipitates of experience or end results of thought; they are illusions, fulfillments of the oldest, strongest, most urgent wishes of mankind; the secret of their strength is the strength of these wishes." Freud was proud of these psychological arguments and singled them out as his unique contribution to the scientific study of religion. The idea that men make the gods in their own image might be as old as the ancient Greeks, but Freud added the claim that men make their gods in their father's image.

To unmask religious ideas as illusions is not necessarily to deny them all validity. Freud emphatically distinguished between an illusion and a delusion; the former is defined not by its contents but by its sources. "What remains characteristic of illusions is their derivation from human wishes." They may even come true; Freud adduced the pleasing instance of a bourgeois girl dreaming that she will meet a prince and marry him. It may happen and has happened. But religious illusions, such as the belief that the Messiah will come to found a golden age, are far less probable and approach delusive thinking. One might comment that Freud's own theories suggest that all thinking, including the most abstract and objective, can be shown to have nonrational sources; he himself, after all, had discovered the roots of scientific investigation in children's sexual curiosity. Nor have later psychoanalysts hesitated to call their continuing interest in their analysands' stories after a lifetime of clinical practice a sublimated voyeurism. The rule that the origins of an idea in no way determine its value—or lack of value—remains intact; certainly nothing Freud said in his papers on religion was designed to shake it. But what mattered to Freud was just how much influence these origins could retain. Sharply differentiating the scientific style of thought from the illusion-ridden style of religious thinking, he extolled the former as open to examination, demonstration, and disproof, and disparaged the latter as ostentatiously immune to all serious criticism. All thinking, including the most scientific variety, may be born as wishful thinking, but science is wishing disciplined—indeed, overcome—by the need for dependable verification and the kind of open atmosphere that alone permits convictions and beliefs to be refined, modified, and if necessary abandoned.

Freud therefore found it appropriate to spend as much time on religious proofs as on the foundations of religious beliefs. The devout, he observed, offer skeptics three defenses: the antiquity of their faith, the dependability of the proofs offered in the past, and the sanctity of belief, which by its very nature reduces any rational investigation to an act of impiety. Naturally, none of these impressed Freud. Nor did other defenses: the medieval view that the truth of religious doctrine is guaranteed by its very absurdity, and the modern philosophy of "as if," which holds that it is expedient for us to live as if we credited the fictions spread by the devout. The first struck Freud as virtually meaningless. If one absurdity, why not another? As for the second, it is a demand, he said derisively, that "only a philosopher could have advanced." They were not arguments; they were evasions. "There is no court higher than that of reason."

Freud was equally unpersuaded by the pragmatic claim for religion—that it has worked. Nor could he agree with contemporary radical polemicists that it is a conspiracy to keep the toiling classes submissive and undemanding by frightening them with prospects of hell and eternal damnation. Such exposés were too rationalistic for Freud's taste; they could not account for the potent grip of faith through the centuries. Moreover, history amply demonstrates, at least to his satisfaction, that while religion has made notable contributions toward taming mankind's wild drives, it has not invariably been a civilizing force, or even a force for order. Quite the contrary: in his own time, he observed, religion was not keeping the many from being unhappy in their civilization, and he thought there was good evidence that in earlier, more devout centuries men had not been any happier. "They were certainly not more moral." Indeed, "immorality has at all times found in religion a support no less than morality." The implication was only too transparent: since religion has made men neither happier nor better, irreligion can only be an improvement.*

Again the accents of Freud's predecessors, notably the philosophes in the Enlightenment, reverberate through these pages. Like their anticlerical, antireligious convictions, his too were unconquerable. Freud might differ from Voltaire or his heir, Feuerbach, on matters of political tactics or psychological diagnosis, but his ultimate verdict on religion was at one with theirs: it had failed. He might sturdily and sincerely attempt to differentiate between illusions and delusions. He might note, just as sincerely, that illusions can sometimes become reality. But as he warmed up to his inquiry into religion

---

*The best that Freud could say for religion is that it tames the individual and rescues him from solitude. As he put it in his case history of the Wolf Man: "We can say that in this case, religion has achieved everything for the sake of which it is introduced in the education of the individual. It tamed his sexual strivings by offering them a sublimation and a firm anchor; it weakened his familial connections and, with that, prevented a threatening isolation by opening for him a connection to the great community of mankind. The wild, cowed child became social, well-behaved, and educable." (Wolfsmann," *GW* XII, 150/"Wolf Man," *SE* XVII, 114–15.)

it became a polemic, and the distinction between illusions and delusions grew blurred.

IF, AS FREUD believed, religion had proved a failure, perhaps science might be a success. This hopeful conjecture is the pendant to Freud's critique of illusions past and present. Indeed, reflecting on the scientific way of thinking, Freud allowed himself to lapse into a tentative optimism unusual for him. Here is the Freud who admired Macaulay's historical writings, which steadfastly present the case for continuous progress in European history, and Gomperz's history of ancient Greek thought, which converts the great thinkers of the classical age into the makers of an antique Enlightenment. At least among the better-educated social strata, Freud suggested, reason has by and large conquered superstition; the higher critics have "gnawed away at the probative power of religious documents; natural science has shown up the errors they contain; comparative research has been struck by the fatal resemblance of the religious conceptions we revere to the mental products of primitive peoples and times."

Hence the expectation that secular rationalism would continue to make recruits seemed to him perfectly realistic. "The scientific spirit generates a certain posture toward matters of this world; before matters of religion it stops for a while, hesitates, at last there too crosses the threshold. In this process there is no holding back; the more the treasures of our knowledge become accessible to people, the more the defection from religious belief will spread, at first only from its obsolete, offensive vestments, but then from its fundamental presuppositions as well." This is the heart of Freud's argument: the very premises of science are incompatible with those of religion. He disdained all the bridges that modern historians had tried to build between the two, all the subtleties that modern theologians had spun. They were mere apologetics—in the disreputable sense of that word. "The warfare between science and religion," that militant slogan of the eighteenth century so fervently echoed in the nineteenth, continued to represent an axiomatic truth for Freud right into the middle of the twentieth. As he said more than once, in more than one text, religion was, quite simply, the enemy.*

*There is no record that Freud had read John W. Draper's rationalist manifesto of 1874, *History of the Conflict between Science and Religion,* or Andrew Dickson White's two-volume defense of free inquiry of 1896, *A History of the Warfare of Science with Theology in Christendom,* but their uncompromising titles (far more than their blander message) are reminders of how closely and characteristically Freud's rationalist stance resembles, and follows, nineteenth-century anticlerical thought—thought that had its roots in the eighteenth-century Enlightenment. His view of religion as the enemy was wholly shared by the first generation of psychoanalysts. The attempts of some later psychoanalysts to reconcile psychoanalysis with religion would never have found the slightest sympathy in Freud and his colleagues. In 1911, when Freud informed Ernest Jones that he was working

In joining the struggle against that enemy, Freud happily enlisted his psychology under the flag of science. "Psychoanalysis," he said in *The Future of an Illusion*, "is in reality a method of research, an impartial instrument, rather like the infinitesimal calculus." He clearly liked that definition; several years earlier he had told Ferenczi that "we," the psychoanalysts, "are and remain objective except for this: to investigate and to help." To be "objective"—*tendenzlos*—was to be scientific; hence psychoanalysis, too, could justly profess, or at least aspire, to be a science.* Given Freud's militancy, this profession was far from neutral. To define the sciences, including psychoanalysis, as untendentious was to advance a political claim, to assert that they are free of ideological, self-protective distortions.† If religion—from the most primitive sacrifice to the most elaborate theology—is infantile fear, awe, and passivity carried over into adult life, then science, as a psychoanalyst might put it, is an organized effort to get beyond childishness. Science disdains the pathetic effort of the believer to realize fantasies through pious waiting and ritual performances, through sending up petitions and burning heretics.

Freud had an inkling that atheism, too, might prove vulnerable to ideology: it might be used, to borrow psychoanalytic language again, as a defensive stratagem, the kind of reaction that is typical of the adolescent in rebellion against his father. Those who quarrel with God may be reenacting in the sphere of religion the oedipal battle they had failed to win at home. But Freud had no such quarrel; he would not fight with chimeras. His atheism, to his mind, was something better: the precondition to the unsparing and fruitful investigation of the religious phenomenon. Freud, we know, did not don the mantle of the social reformer. But as the modern heir of the philosophes he was persuaded that one office of science is to employ its insights in the relief of mental distress. Concealed in Freud's psychoanalytic critique of belief lies the hope that to discover and disseminate the truth about religion may help to free mankind of it.

---

on a psychoanalytic study of religion—he had in mind the essays that would become *Totem and Taboo*—Jones responded enthusiastically: "Obviously" the study of religion "is the last and firmest stronghold of what may be called the anti-scientific, anti-rational, or anti-objective Weltanschauung, and no doubt it is there we may expect the most intense resistance, and the thick of the fight." (Jones to Freud, August 31, 1911. By permission of Sigmund Freud Copyrights, Wivenhoe.)

*The most emphatic statement of this position may be found in his important paper on a world view, published as the last of the *New Introductory Lectures on Psychoanalysis* in 1933. See "The Question of a *Weltanschauung*," *SE* XXII, 158–82.

†*The Future of an Illusion* was also taken to be a political document in another way, not based on its advocacy of science in defiance of religion: in July 1928, Freud informed Ernest Jones (having had the news from Eitingon) that Soviet censors had prohibited translation of the book into Russian. (Freud to Jones, July 17, 1928. Freud Collection, D2, LC.)

To be sure, this hope, as Freud acknowledged in *The Future of an Illusion*, might turn out to be yet another illusion. But having raised the matter, he set it aside, since "in the long run, nothing can resist reason and experience." It may be that "our god *Logos* is perhaps not very omnipotent, can fulfill only a small part of what his predecessors had promised." It remains true that his devotees are prepared to give up a good portion of their childish wishes; their world would not collapse if they had to surrender still more of their dreams. The scientific method they practice and the presuppositions that govern their researches would permit them to amend their views in the light of better evidence. "No," Freud concluded in a famous paragraph, "our science is no illusion. But an illusion it would be to believe that we could get anywhere else what it cannot give us." This was his profession of a faith in science he had always held, rarely pronounced with such robust ebullience before, and never displayed again. Some years earlier, he had described himself to Romain Rolland as a man who had "spent a great part of my life destroying my own illusions, and those of mankind." Whether mankind at large would allow its illusions to be destroyed was quite another matter.

IN JANUARY 1928, someone Freud did not know, a typesetter named Edward Petrikowitsch identifying himself as "only a simple worker" who appreciated Freud's struggle against religion, sent Freud a clipping from the *St. Louis Post-Dispatch*. The story claimed that Freud's new book had caused a split among his followers and something of a sensation. Freud responded at once, politely and testily. He could not believe that his correspondent was anything but an educated man. Surely, Freud noted, he must be a European who had lived in the United States for a long time, and so "I may permit myself to wonder why you still believe anything you read in an American newspaper." He was partly right. Petrikowitsch, a trade unionist, freethinker, and socialist, had emigrated to St. Louis after the First World War. The article he had sent, Freud observed, "ascribed utterances to me that I never made." The fact was that "the public here has paid virtually no attention to my little work. I could say that nobody has given a hoot"—*es hat kein Hahn nach ihr gekräht.*

Actually, there were far more hoots about *The Future of an Illusion* than Freud was willing to concede as he wrapped himself in the worn and tattered mantle of a man to whom nobody pays any attention. Indeed, he himself knew better. The clipping that Petrikowitsch had sent Freud was a reprint of a story that had first appeared in the *New York Times* in late December 1927, under inflammatory and misleading headlines: "RELIGION DOOMED / FREUD ASSERTS / Says It is at Point Where It Must Give Way Before Science / HIS FOLLOWERS CHAGRINED / Master Psychoanalyst's New Book

Deplored for Dissention It is Expected to Cause."* This considerably over-dramatized the uproar that *The Future of an Illusion* was causing. Still, in April 1928, Freud told Eitingon that he had drawn upon himself "the most general displeasure." He was hearing "rumblings all around me with all sorts of muffled innuendoes." The book had not seriously divided his disciples, but it had made some of them nervous; religion remained, after all, a most delicate subject. "That Anna encountered resistance" to a paper she had given in Berlin, Eitingon reported to Freud in June, "had its cause in—*The Future of an Illusion,* on which she based herself, and against which here, now as before, there is a great deal of feeling, even if people do not want to make that clear to themselves." With all his mistakes and his distortions, the *Times* reporter in Vienna had caught some of this atmosphere.

Inevitably, Freud's analysis of religion—critics called it an assault—gener-ated replies and refutations.† Perhaps the most civilized among them was, as one might expect, Pfister's response, "The Illusion of a Future," published in *Imago.* It was courteous, reasoned, and most friendly. He had written it, Pfister noted, addressing Freud directly, "not against but for you, for whoever enters the lists for psychoanalysis battles for you." Plainly Freud did not object to the article, which he found to be a "kind riposte." In the riposte, Pfister had reversed roles with his old friend, for he convicted Freud, the inveterate pessimist, of unwarranted optimism. Knowledge, Pfister argued, does not guarantee progress. Nor can science, thin and antiseptic, ever take the place of religion; it cannot inspire moral values or enduring works of art.

Most of the reactions to Freud's brochure were not quite so civil. The Reform rabbi Nathan Krass, addressing his congregation at Temple Emanu-

---

*Freud's impatience with the dispatch is perfectly understandable. In addition to coarsening Freud's message, it teemed with mistakes. It called Freud "Sigismund," a name he had not used for more than half a century. It translated the title of Freud's work, in an amusing slip, as "The Future of an Allusion." It called Pfister "Pfiser," identified him, of all people, as "head of the Protestant Church in Zurich," and described the psychoanalytic journal *Imago,* in which, it informed readers of the *Times,* Pfister was about to respond to Freud, as a "Church magazine."

†One of the most curious "responses" was J. C. Hill, *Dreams and Education,* which its author, an English educator, sent to Freud. Hill's little book had been published in 1926, the year before *The Future of an Illusion,* but the author—who presented himself as a great admirer though "not a practicing psycho-analyst" and "not competent to express an opinion" (p. 1) on some of Freud's writings—thought it might serve as an answer. But it puzzled Freud considerably. In a series of simply written expository chapters filled with homely instances, Hill had applied what he understood of psychoanalytic ideas to "the study of normal conduct" (p. 1), notably of education. But then, wholly without any transition or preparation, he concluded with the assertion that the teacher who is willing to learn from Freud, "will realize, in short, the truth of Christianity" (p. 114). Freud acknowledged this gift with a few gracious if terse lines: "I got your booklet, read it with pleasure and satisfaction and trust it will make a strong impression on many people. There is only one point I cannot see: How is what you tell of ψA, to lead one to the truth of Christianity?" (Freud to Hill, February 18, 1928. In English. By permission of Sigmund Freud Copyrights, Wivenhoe.)

El on New York's Fifth Avenue, took the patronizing line of the expert putting the amateur in his place: "In this country we have grown accustomed to listening to men and women talk on all topics because they have done something notable in one field." He offered as one instance Edison, who "knows about electricity" and hence finds an audience for his "opinions of theology." Or someone who has made "a name for himself in aviation"—he had Lindbergh in mind, of course—"is asked to make speeches on everything under the sun." Krass's point needed little exegesis: "All admire Freud, the psychoanalyst, but that is no reason why we should respect his theology."

There is no record that Freud ever heard of Krass's strictures, but they were far from isolated. Some critics detected in Freud's analysis of religion a symptom of the pernicious relativism gnawing at the moral fiber of the modern world. In fact one anonymous commentator, writing in the conservative German monthly the *Süddeutsche Monatshefte,* lumped Freud's view of religion with what he called, a little picturesquely, the "pan-swinism" endemic to the age. And predictably, *The Future of an Illusion* provided anti-Semites in the academy with welcome ammunition. In 1928, Carl Christian Clemen, a professor of ethnology at the University of Bonn, took its appearance as an opportunity to deplore the disposition of psychoanalysis to discover sex everywhere. "One could explain this," he thought, "by the particular circles from which its advocates and perhaps, too, the patients it treats, principally hail." Another distinguished German professor, Emil Abderhalden, a versatile biologist and chemist, deplored the spectacle of "a Jew" venturing, wholly unauthorized as he was, "to offer a judgment on the Christian faith." To the extent that Freud was aware of such abuse, he treated it with contempt. Yet for his own part, more than ever convinced that his writings fell short of his self-imposed standards, he was saddened to think that he was no longer the Freud of a decade before.

FREUD FOUND LITTLE to enjoy in those days, least of all in himself. In April 1928, he told the Hungarian psychoanalyst István Hollós that he resisted dealing with psychotics: "Finally I confessed to myself that I do not like these sick people, that I am angry at them to feel them so far from me and all that is human." He thought this a "strange sort of intolerance"; and he added, in resignation, "In the course of time, I have ceased to find myself interesting, which is surely incorrect analytically." Yet he did find himself interesting enough to speculate about this failure of empathy. Might it be "the consequence of an ever more evident partisanship for the primacy of the intellect, a hostility toward the id? Or what else?"

Certainly the times were hardly propitious for asserting the primacy of the intellect. The unsavory spectacle of political demagogy and the precariousness of the world economy exhibited irrationality in the ascendant. When, again in April 1928, Fritz Wittels consulted Freud about accepting an invitation to lecture and teach psychoanalysis in the United States, Freud urged him to go. "You know the bleak economic conditions in Vienna and the improbability of a change soon." He seemed to hold himself personally responsible for the parlous situation of analysts looking for patients in the city, and the smaller the "personal influence" he could exert in behalf of his "younger friends," he told Wittels, the more "afflicted" he felt.

Yet, understandably enough, his infirmities—his discomfort in eating and speaking, and his pain—afflicted him even more grievously. They had emotional almost as much as physical repercussions. In July 1928, he confided to Ernest Jones "a little secret that should remain a secret." He was thinking of leaving Hans Pichler, the oral surgeon who had done so much for him since he had first operated on him in the fall of 1923. "This last year, I have suffered a great deal under Pichler's efforts to procure a better prosthesis for me, and the effect has been very unsatisfactory. So I have at last yielded to pressure from many sides to turn to someone else." Pichler himself had admitted being baffled, but Freud's conscience was bothering him: "It has not been easy for me, for fundamentally, after all, it is a desertion of a man to whom I already owe 4 years of life prolonged." But the situation had become intolerable. Pichler's notes on the case bear Freud out. "Everything bad," he wrote on April 16. "Pain at back [of the mouth], where swelling, sensitiveness and redness are found at posterior pharyngeal wall." A new prosthesis was not working well. "Prosthesis [number] 5 cannot be used," Pichler noted on April 24, "too thick and large"; an earlier prosthesis, number 4, Pichler added on May 7, "caused pressure" and "interfered badly with tongue." Hence Freud had been persuaded to try to find some relief from his "prosthesis misery" in Berlin, from the eminent Professor Schroeder. As a preliminary step, Schroeder sent an assistant to Vienna to take a look at the prosthesis, and at the end of August, Freud proceeded to Berlin for further work. It was all highly confidential. "Then word will be given out that I am visiting my children. So: discretion!"

The examinations, treatments, fittings, in Berlin proved intensely disagreeable, and Freud's sufferings were only exacerbated by his feelings of guilt toward Pichler and his doubts that a better prosthesis could be constructed. But he liked Schroeder and trusted him; in an access of optimism, he told his brother that he was in the best of hands. Almost as if to demonstrate how much better he felt, he took on two analytic patients whenever his condition permitted. To make life more tolerable still, he had brought his youngest daughter with him. "Anna is excellent as always," he wrote his brother. "Without her I would be totally lost here." She had rented a boat and was spending long hours rowing and swimming in the lake at Tegel, in the agreeable northwestern district of the city. His son Ernst, then living in Berlin, was a frequent and assiduous visitor, as were old friends like Sándor Ferenczi. In general, this medical excursion gave Freud grounds for cautious cheer; far beyond expectations, the new prosthesis was a marked improvement over its predecessors.

The device constructed for Freud in the fall of 1923 after his cancer operations had never fitted very well, and even when he was quite free of pain, which was not often, he was uncomfortable. Schroeder managed to reduce the intervals of pain, and ease some of the discomfort. But relief was neither permanent nor complete. "I disclose," Freud wrote his "dear Lou" in the summer of 1931, "that I have meanwhile experienced all kinds of disagreeable things with my prosthesis, which, as usual, has suspended my higher interests." While there were times when work made Freud forget his afflictions, more often his afflictions interfered with his work. During his stay in Berlin, Lou Andreas-Salomé had come to visit, and he had noticed, and could not forget, how he left the conversation to his daughter Anna. "The reason," he recalled later to his dear Lou, "was the observation that with my damaged hearing I could not grasp your low speech, and had to register the fact that you, too, found understanding the remnants of my speaking abilities troublesome. With all readiness for resignation, that is depressing and one falls silent." It was a cruel fate for that once-accomplished conversationalist. Attending international psychoanalytic congresses had been out of the question for Freud since the mid-1920s, and he took the loss of stimulation very hard. Some amateur movies made in 1928 by his American analysand Philip Lehrman show him looking gaunt, distinctly aged, as he promenades with his daughter Anna, sports with his dog, climbs into a train.

Late that year, Freud had a sudden reminder of a past he thought he had exorcised years before: Wilhelm Fliess died, and in December his widow wrote to ask for her late husband's letters. Freud could not oblige. "My memory tells me," he informed her, "that I destroyed the larger part of our correspondence some time after 1904." Some letters might have survived, and he promised to look further. Two weeks later, he reported that his search had turned up nothing; other letters, too, those from Charcot for example, were missing. He thought he had probably destroyed the lot. But the inquiry reminded him of his own side of the correspondence: "I would certainly like to hear that my letters to your husband, my intimate friend for long years, have found a fate that would protect them from any future utilization." The episode, though he did not comment on it, must have stirred up uncomfortable memories. They would return once more, no less uncomfortable, a decade later.

DURING THIS ANXIOUS and bruising time, Freud found distraction from an unexpected quarter—his chow, Lin Yug. For a couple of years, he had enjoyed watching his daughter Anna's Alsatian, Wolf, acquired to protect her on her long walks. Paternally, he entered into Anna's fondness for her dog. In April 1927, while she was on vacation in Italy, he telegraphed domestic news and concluded, "Affectionate regards from Wolf and family." Now he had a dog of his own. The donor was Dorothy Burlingham, an American who had come to Vienna in 1925. The mother of four young children, she was separated from her manic-depressive husband; once in Vienna, she went into analysis, first with Theodor Reik and then with Freud himself, and had her children analyzed as well. The treatment her children received induced her to take up child analysis as a profession. She soon became an intimate of the Freuds', being especially close to Anna; on that Italian vacation of 1927, it was Mrs. Burlingham who was Anna's traveling companion. The two, Anna assured her father, were enjoying "the most agreeable and most unalloyed comradeship." Freud, much taken with Dorothy Burlingham, called her "a quite congenial American woman, an unhappy virgin." Her gift could not have been better chosen: in June, Freud reported to Eitingon that he had "a charming Chinese bitch, a chow, which is giving us much pleasure." Lin Yug was a pet, but a responsibility as well: the lady who kept the kennel from which the chow came, Henrietta Brandes, sent Freud detailed instructions on how to take care of the animal. Late in June, she expressed her pleasure at hearing that Freud had made friends with his chow. From then on, Freud and a succession of chows, especially his Jo-Fi, were inseparable. The dog would sit quietly at the foot of the couch during the analytic hour.

All was not gloom, then. Freud continued to analyze and to watch the progress of the younger generation—at least some of it—with real gratification. His professional circle came to resemble a close-knit family. In 1927, Marianne Rie, a daughter of his old friend, colleague, and tarock partner Oscar Rie, married the art historian, later psychoanalyst, Ernst Kris; then a medical student, she was working toward a career as a child analyst in her own right.* In the same year, Heinz Hartmann, superbly trained as a physician, psychiatrist, and psychologist, and with an informed interest in philosophy, published his first book, *The Fundamentals of Psychoanalysis*, which foreshadowed the theoretical contributions to ego psychology he was destined to make later. Freud's daughter Anna, too, continued to consolidate her reputation among psychoanalysts. Her views on child development, which she

---

*Later, her sister Margarete married the analyst Hermann Nunberg, and both families established dynasties of psychoanalysts.

expounded in 1927 in her first book, *An Introduction to the Technique of Child Analysis,* clashed with those of Melanie Klein and caused animated, at times venomous, controversy in Viennese and London analytic circles.* The future of psychoanalysis seemed in good hands.

But while Freud looked upon his daughter's "splendid development" as an analyst with unalloyed pleasure, he confessed to Lou Andreas-Salomé in the spring of 1927 that he continued to worry about her emotional life. "You will not believe how little I contributed to her book, nothing but curtailing her polemic against Melanie Klein. Apart from that it is completely independent work." Yet "in other respects, I am less satisfied. Since the poor heart must absolutely have something, it clings to women friends, one taking the place of another." Anna needed worthy associates, and he wondered whether her latest intimate, Dorothy Burlingham, "the mother of her analytic children," would be any more acceptable to her than the others had been. He acknowledged, though, that his daughter was getting on extremely well with Mrs. Burlingham; a three weeks' Easter vacation she had taken with her at the Italian lakes had done her a great deal of good. But Freud's doubts persisted. "Anna," he wrote, again to his dearest Lou, in December, "is splendid and intellectually independent, but [has] no sexual life." And he asked, adverting once again to that old problematic point, "What will she do without her father?"

Apart from his daughter, Freud's most notable recruit of the 1920s was Princess Marie Bonaparte, the "energy devil," as Freud once fondly called her. She came by her title honestly—was, indeed, a walking wish-fantasy. As a great-granddaughter of Napoleon's brother Lucien and as the wife of Prince George—the younger brother of Constantine I, king of the Hellenes, and first cousin to Christian X, king of Denmark—she was a princess several times over. Though enviably rich and impeccably connected, she had never been content with the traditional round of empty ceremonial sociability that was thought suitable to royalty in a democratic age. Endowed with penetrating intelligence, a stranger to bourgeois inhibitions, and with a mind of her own, she had spent her young years in search of intellectual, emotional, and erotic satisfaction. She could not expect them from her husband, who disappointed her in bed and in conversation alike. Nor did she obtain them from her distinguished lovers, who included the statesman Aristide Briand, several times French prime minister, and the psychoanalyst Rudolph Loewenstein, a brilliant technician and theorist. In 1925, when René Laforgue mentioned "Princess George of Greece" to Freud for the first time, she was prey, as

*See pp. 468–69.

Laforgue diagnosed her, to a "quite pronounced obsessional neurosis," which, he added, had not impaired her intelligence but had "somewhat disturbed the general equilibrium of her psyche." She wanted Freud to analyze her.

If Freud was impressed by her resounding titles, he did not show it. He was ready to take her into analysis, he told Laforgue, provided "you can guarantee the seriousness of her intentions and her personal worth," and provided, too, she had German or English, since he no longer trusted his French. "For the rest," he added, the self-possessed bourgeois speaking, "that analysand must accept precisely the same obligations as all the other patients." Some delicate diplomatic negotiations followed: Laforgue described the princess as serious, conscientious, endowed with a superior mind, and so intent on a brief two-month analysis that she wanted two hours every day. Freud demurred, but then Marie Bonaparte, impatient of intermediaries, wrote him directly, and by July everything was settled. On September 30, 1925, she wrote to Laforgue from Vienna, "This afternoon I saw Freud."

The rest, as they say, is history. At the end of October, Freud triumphantly wrote to Eitingon about his "dear princess, Marie Bonaparte," to whom he was devoting two hours a day; she was, he observed, "a quite outstanding, a more than just half masculine female." Two weeks later, he could tell Laforgue, "the Princess is doing a very fine analysis and is, I think, very satisfied with her stay." Her analysis did not cure her frigidity, but it gave her a firm purpose in life and the fatherly friend she had never had. Back in Paris, she worked to organize the French psychoanalytic movement, diligently attending meetings and bolstering the cause munificently from her abundant resources. An indefatigable scribbler of diaries and journals, she took down Freud's comments to her in speaking detail, and she began to write psychoanalytic papers. Most rewarding perhaps of all was the change of her relationship with Freud from that of analysand to that of dependable friend and unstinting benefactor. She trustingly handed over to Freud her youthful notebooks, her "Bêtises," written in three languages between the ages of seven and nine; she corresponded with him, visited him as often as she could, bailed out the *Verlag*, the analytic publishing house, which was always hovering on the brink of bankruptcy, supplied him with choice antiquities, and gave him a love surpassed in his experience only by his daughter Anna's devotion. Her titles were part of her charm, no doubt, but they were not the source of Freud's fondness for her. For Freud she had, in a word, everything.

As the princess confided in him, he confided in the princess. In the spring of 1928, after she had told him that she was working on the problem of the unconscious and time, he revealed to her a strange, repetitive dream which, he said, he had failed to understand for years. He was standing before the gates of a beer garden, supported in some way by statues, but he could not get in and had to turn back. Freud told the princess that actually he had once visited Padua with his brother and had been unable to enter the grottos behind a very similar gateway. Years later, when he returned to Padua, he had recognized the place as the one in his dream, and this time he had managed to see the grottos. Now, he added, every time he found himself unable to unriddle an enigma, he would dream this dream again. Indeed, time and space were mysteries that Freud regretted he had been unable to solve so far. He was not disinclined to think that he might solve them yet.

CIVILIZATION:
THE HUMAN PREDICAMENT

 "Papa is writing on something," Anna Freud revealed to Lou Andreas-Salomé early in July 1929. Later that month, Freud confirmed the news from the Bavarian summer resort of Berchtesgaden. "Today I wrote down the last sentence, which completes the work as far as it is possible here—without library. It deals with culture, guilt feeling, happiness, and similar exalted things." He had just finished *Civilization and Its Discontents*. Some sort of pressure for work, he observed, was still alive in him. "What should I do?" he asked rhetorically. "One cannot smoke the whole day long and play cards; I no longer have staying power for walking, and most of what one can read no longer interests me. I wrote, and I passed the time with it quite agreeably."

An agreeable diversion, perhaps, but *Civilization and Its Discontents* struck Freud as no less discreditable than he thought its predecessor, *The Future of an Illusion*, had been: "I newly discovered the most banal truths as I worked." The little book, he confessed to Ernest Jones soon after its publication, consisted of "an essentially dilettantish foundation" on which "rises a thinly tapered analytic investigation." Surely a connoisseur of his writings, like Jones, "cannot have missed the peculiar nature" of this latest production. Freud could not then imagine that it would in fact prove to be one of his most influential writings.

Like *The Future of an Illusion*, its successor too concludes on a note of uncertain hope, though hope still further attenuated. *Civilization and Its Discontents* is Freud's most somber book, and also in some respects his most insecure. Repeatedly he stopped to protest that he felt, more than ever before, that he was telling people things they already knew, wasting his writing materials and, eventually, printers' time and printers' ink. To be sure, none of the leading ideas in *Civilization and Its Discontents* was new; Freud had adumbrated them in the 1890s in letters to Fliess, stated them briefly a decade later in his paper " 'Civilized' Sexual Morality and Modern Nervous Illness," rehearsed them most recently in *The Future of an Illusion.* But he had never analyzed them with such fierce concentration as now, never drawn out the implications of his thought so pitilessly. Originally, he had wanted to give the essay another title. "My work could perhaps be called," he wrote Eitingon in July 1929, "if it needs a title at all: Unhappiness in Culture"— *Das Unglück in der Kultur.* He added that the writing was not coming easily to him. Eventually he settled for *Unbehagen*—discontent, uneasiness, malaise—instead of *Unglück.* But whether he bluntly advertised his argument in the title or softened it slightly with a more benign-sounding circumlocution, Freud was treating human misery with deadly seriousness. As if on cue, the world provided spectacular confirmation just how appalling that misery could be. About a week before Freud sent the manuscript of *Civilization and Its Discontents* to the printer—on October 29, "Black Tuesday"—the New York stock market collapsed, and the reverberations of that event were quick and world-wide. What people soon came to call the Great Depression had begun.

As THOUGH TO accentuate the continuity between Freud's psychoanalysis of culture and his earlier psychoanalysis of religion, *Civilization and Its Discontents* opens with a meditation on belief. This point of departure, Freud observed, had been suggested to him by the French novelist Romain Rolland, a winner of the Nobel Prize for literature and an engaged pacifist. Freud and Rolland had been in cordial, mutually admiring correspondence since 1923, and when *The Future of an Illusion* appeared four years later, Freud had sent him a copy. In his response, Rolland professed general agreement with Freud's assessment of religion but wondered whether Freud had really discovered the true source of religious sentiment, a sentiment Rolland characterized as a pervasive and persistent "particular feeling." Others had confirmed its existence to him and he supposed that it must be shared by millions of people. It was a sensation of "eternity," a feeling of something boundless, as it were "oceanic." Purely subjective and in no way a guarantee of personal immortality, this must be "the source of religious energy" that churches had captured and channeled. Freud, who could not detect this feeling in himself, followed his customary procedure: he analyzed it. Most probably, he thought, it was a survival of very early ego-feeling originating in a time when the infant has not yet managed the psychological separation from the mother. Its value as the explanation for religion struck Freud as more than doubtful.

All this reads like a leisurely recapitulation of *The Future of an Illusion.* But Freud soon exhibited its relevance to the psychoanalysis of culture. We human beings, he argued, are unhappy: our bodies sicken and decay, external nature threatens us with destruction, our relations to others are sources of misery. Yet we all do our desperate utmost to escape that unhappiness. Under the sway of the pleasure principle, we seek "powerful diversions, which let us make light of our misery; substitute gratifications, which diminish it; intoxicating substances, which make us insensitive to it." Religion is just one of these palliative devices, no more effective, in many ways less effective, than others.

Freud pointedly noted that the most successful (or, better, the least unsuccessful) of these devices is work, especially professional activity freely chosen. "No other technique for the conduct of life fits the individual so firmly to reality." At the very least, "it ties him securely to a piece of reality, into the human community." As an addict to work, Freud spoke with some feeling. But unfortunately, he observed, returning once again to *The Future of an Illusion,* human beings do not prize work as a path to happiness. Generally they labor only under compulsion. And whether they try to escape their lot through work, love, drink, madness, the enjoyment of beauty, or the consolations of religion, they are bound to fail in the end: "Life, as it is imposed upon us, is too hard for us; it brings us too many pains, disappointments, insoluble tasks." Lest any doubt remain, Freud bluntly reiterated his point. It is as though "the intention that man should be 'happy' is not contained in the plan of 'Creation.'"

The pathetic human quest for happiness, and its foreordained failure, have generated an astonishing point of view: the hatred of civilization. While he rejected this "surprising hostility to culture," Freud thought he could explain it. It had a long history; Christianity, which put a low value on earthly life, was one of its most flamboyant symptoms. The voyagers who encountered primitive cultures during the age of exploration compounded that hostility by mistaking the life of these alien, seemingly uncivilized tribes as models of simplicity and well-being, a kind of reproach to Western civilization. More recently, advances in the natural sciences and technology have produced disappointment in their turn. This was not a mood Freud was disposed to share; the recognition that modern inventions have not secured happiness should produce one single conclusion: "Power over nature is not the only precondition for human happiness, just as it is not the only aim of cultural endeavors." Yet cultural pessimists belittle all scientific and technical advances. The invention of the railroad, they say, has only served to enable our children to move far away, and the only use of the telephone is to let us hear their voices. They even disparage the reduction of infant mortality as a dubious blessing. It has induced modern couples to practice contraception, and this has kept the total number of children as small as in previous centuries. Besides, it has made them neurotic. Unquestionably, "we do not feel comfortable in our present-day civilization."

Still, this uneasiness should not obscure the fact that throughout history, civilization has been a vast effort at subduing the forces of nature. Humans have learned the use of tools and of fire, tamed the waters and tilled the soil, invented powerful machines to lift and to transport, corrected visual infirmities with eyeglasses, aided their memory with writing, photography, the phonograph. They have found the time and energy to cultivate splendid useless things; to strive for order, cleanliness, and beauty; and to foster the most elevated capacities of the mind. Practically all the omnipotence they once attributed to the gods they have now engrossed for themselves. Freud condensed the case in a startling, deeply felt metaphor: man has become a "prosthetic god."*

Prostheses do not always work, and their malfunctioning may be disconcerting. But these failures fade before the unhappiness generated by the relationship of persons to one another: *homo homini lupus* — "man is as a wolf to other men." Hence mankind must be tamed by institutions. Here Freud linked up with the tough-minded political thought of Thomas Hobbes; lacking overpowering constraints, Hobbes had argued nearly three centuries before, mankind is bound to become enmeshed in perpetual civil war, with life solitary, poor, nasty, brutish, and short. Mankind had propelled itself into civilized human relations only by concluding a social contract that conferred the monopoly of coercion on the state. The Freud of *Civilization and Its Discontents* was writing in the Hobbesian tradition: the momentous step into culture had come when the community took power, when individuals eschewed the right to take violence into their own hands. The man who first flung an epithet at his enemy instead of a spear, Freud once observed, was the true founder of civilization. But while such a step was indispensable, it also set the stage for the discontents to which all societies are susceptible: it entailed the most drastic interference with the passionate desires of the individual, the suppression—and repression—of instinctual needs, which continue to fester in the unconscious and seek explosive utterance.

---

*Freud only enhanced the poignancy of this metaphor with his gloss that man "is quite magnificent when he puts on all his auxiliary organs, but they have not grown onto him and on occasion they still give him a good deal of trouble." (*Das Unbehagen in der Kultur,* GW XIV, 451/*Civilization and Its Discontents,* SE XXI, 92.)

FREUD'S DISTINCTIVE CONTRIBUTION to theorizing about politics lies in this vision of passions repressed by culture. This perspective lends *Civilization and Its Discontents* its power and originality: it is a briefly stated psychoanalytic theory of politics. Freud was not a political theorist any more than he was a historian of religion or an archeologist. He was a psychoanalyst bringing to bear the resources of his thought on the diverse manifestations of human nature. The greatest of political theorists all the way back to Plato and Aristotle had done precisely that. But Freud anchored his analysis of social and political life in a theory of human nature very much his own.

Looking back, he declared that such an analysis had been his aim for decades. "As early as the year 1912, at the height of psychoanalytic work," he noted in a late autobiographical comment, "I had made the attempt in *Totem and Taboo* to exploit the newly won analytic insights for an investigation of the origins of religion and morality." With *The Future of an Illusion* and *Civilization and Its Discontents* he had continued in this vein. "I recognized ever more clearly that the events of human history, the interactions between human nature, cultural development, and the precipitates of primeval experiences (as whose representative religion pushes to the fore), are only the reflection of the dynamic conflicts among the ego, id, and superego, which psychoanalysis studies in the individual—the same events repeated on a wider stage." He could not have stated the essential unity of his thought any more forcefully. And since *Civilization and Its Discontents* is part and parcel of his larger thought, it makes its full impact only against the background of Freud's psychoanalytic style of thinking. The essay outlines the shape of Freudian man in culture—any culture. He is man beset by his unconscious needs, with his incurable ambivalence, his primitive, passionate loves and hates, barely kept in check by external constraints and intimate feelings of guilt. Social institutions are many things for Freud, but above all they are dams against murder, rape, and incest.

Freud's theory of civilization, then, views life in society as an imposed compromise and hence as an essentially insoluble predicament. The very institutions that work to protect mankind's survival also produce its discontents. Knowing this, Freud was ready to live with imperfection and with the most modest expectations for human betterment. It is significant that when the First World War was over and the German empire had collapsed, he expressed his satisfaction at seeing the new Germany reject Bolshevism. Thinking about politics, he was a prudent anti-utopian. But to qualify Freud simply as a conservative is to miss the tension in his thought and to slight his implicit radicalism. He was no Burkean respecter of tradition; it follows from his thinking that timid traditionalism needs to be analyzed no less than ruthless idealism. What is old, Freud could have said with John Locke, is not therefore what is right. He was even willing to speculate that "a real alteration in the relation of mankind to property" was more likely than ethics or religion to bring some relief from modern discontents.

This did not make socialism any more appealing to Freud. He thought himself a radical social critic, we have observed more than once, in the domain of sexuality alone. But to invade that realm waving revolutionary manifestos was a profoundly subversive act: sexual mores, both as ideal and as practice, go to the quintessence of politics. To be a reformer of sexuality was to be a critic of bourgeois society as Freud perceived it, but also, even more, of the ascetic dictatorships tightening their grip on the world during Freud's last years. In fact, Freud's preoccupation with libido brought unexpected dividends for his social theory. The stark, widespread symptoms of sexual misery that had propelled Freud the physician into the study of neuroses served him well as he became engrossed in the study of religion and civilization: culture, we recall, is for him essentially the large-scale reflection of the dynamic conflicts inhabiting the individual. Hence Freud found the predicament of civilized humanity easy to state: men cannot live without civilization, but they cannot live happily within it. They are so constituted that serenity, a permanent peace between pressing passions and cultural constraints, is forever out of their reach. This is what Freud meant when he said that happiness is not in the plan of creation. At best, sensible human beings may arrange a truce between desire and control.

This dilemma pervades all dimensions of civilized life, even, and perhaps especially, love. Freud put the matter dramatically: Ananke, necessity, is not the only parent of civilization; Eros, love, is the other. Love—the erotic instinctual force that drives human beings to seek sexual objects outside themselves, or, in its aim-inhibited form, nurtures friendship—assists at the founding of such fundamental groupings of authority and affection as the family. But love, this parent of civilization, is also its enemy: "In the course of development, the relation of love to culture loses its unequivocal character. On the one hand, love resists the interests of culture; on the other hand, culture threatens love with severe restrictions." Love is exclusive; couples, and close families, resent outsiders as so many uninvited intruders. Women, who have increasingly become love's guardians, are particularly hostile to a civilization that corners the attention of their men and the service of their children. Civilization for its part seeks to regulate erotic passions and define legitimate love by setting up strict taboos.*

---

*Freud tentatively speculated that intrusive and domineering civilization may not be the only agent that cripples love; perhaps something in the very nature of sexual love itself works against its full satisfaction. But he dropped this bleak hint without developing it. (See ibid., 465/105.)

Throughout history, Freud thought, men have tried to evade this irreparable antagonism, largely by denying it. One good instance of such maneuvers is the injunction which Christianity has proudly claimed as its own: love your neighbor as yourself. This demand is in Freud's eyes as unrealistic as it is importunate. To love everybody is to love nobody very much. Moreover, one's neighbor is in general not worthy of one's love: "I must honestly confess that he has more claim to my hostility, indeed my hatred." The Christian call for universal love is so insistent and so sweeping precisely because it seems so urgently needed as a defense against human aggressiveness and cruelty. Man is not a gentle, loving, lovable creature, "but rather may count among his instinctual endowments a powerful portion of aggressive inclinations." No one who visualizes human nature at work, Freud said sternly, can deny this truth. And he put in evidence the atrocities of the Huns, the Mongols, the pious Crusaders, and the horrors of the First World War.

Freud's insistence on including aggressiveness among the human animal's essential endowments informs his critical comments on Russian Communism, the regime that some deluded intellectuals in his time persisted in calling, even after the Stalin purges, the Soviet experiment. To Freud's mind, whatever his unspecified quarrel with the property relations characteristic of capitalist society, the Communists' abolition of private property sprang from a misguided idealization of human nature. He did not presume to have an opinion on the economic consequences of the Soviets' attempt to establish Communism, but "I can recognize its psychological presuppositions as an untenable illusion." After all, since aggression "was not created by property," aggression would not be eliminated by its abolition. The truth is that aggressiveness is a source of a pleasure which, like other pleasures, human beings are extremely reluctant to give up once they have enjoyed it. "They do not feel comfortable without it." Aggressiveness serves as a complement to love: the libidinal ties that bind the members of a group in affection and cooperation are strengthened if the group has outsiders it can hate.

Freud called this convenient hatred "the narcissism of small differences." Men seem to find particular enjoyment, he observed, in hating and persecuting, or at least ridiculing, their immediate neighbors: the Spaniards, the Portuguese; the North Germans, the South Germans. The special mission of the Jewish people, scattered across the world, Freud mordantly added, seems to have been to serve as the favored target of such narcissism. The diaspora in which the Jews have lived for so long has won them the gratitude of their neighbors; it has given Christians for centuries an opportunity to vent their aggressions. "Unfortunately, all the massacres of Jews in the Middle Ages were not enough to make that age more peaceful and more secure for their Christian comrades." Still, one rewarding though obviously imperfect method for containing aggression is to concentrate it on a selected victim. That is what was happening in the Soviet Union, where the Bolsheviks' persecution of the bourgeoisie lent psychological support to the attempt at founding a new culture. "One only asks oneself uneasily," Freud commented dryly, "what the Soviets will do after they have exterminated their bourgeois."

THIS ANALYSIS, FREUD suggested, should make it easier to understand why human beings find it so hard to be happy in civilization: it imposes great sacrifices "not on sexuality alone, but also on mankind's aggressive inclinations." He next briefly rehearsed the complex, tortuous history of psychoanalytic drive theory, and acknowledged once again his long delay in recognizing the independent existence of a fundamental aggressiveness. Only here, with Freud's introduction of this subject, does it become fully apparent how solidly *Civilization and Its Discontents* is built on the instinctual dualism and the structural system that Freud had evolved a few years before. The great antagonists, love and hate, wrestle for control in man's social life quite as much as in his unconscious, and in very much the same way, with very much the same tactics. Visible aggressiveness is the outward manifestation of the invisible death drive. "And now, I think, the meaning of cultural development is no longer obscure to us. It must show us the battle between Eros and Death, the drive of life and the drive of destruction, as it is carried out in the human species. This battle is the essential content of life as such, and therefore cultural evolution is to be described, in short, as the life struggle of the human species. And it is this quarrel of the giants that our nursemaids are trying to appease with their hushaby-babys of Heaven!" The atheist in Freud was always glad of an opportunity to speak out.

But Freud's principal concern was how culture inhibits aggression. One way, the most remarkable, is through internalization, the forcing of aggressive feelings back into the mind, where they originated. This act, or series of acts, is the foundation of what Freud called the *Kultur-Über-Ich*—the "cultural superego." At first, the child fears authority, and is well behaved only to the extent that it calculates what punitive retribution to expect from its father. But once it has internalized adult standards of conduct, external threats become unnecessary; the child's superego will keep it in line. The struggle between love and hate, then, lies at the foundation of the superego, as it does of civilization itself; this psychological development of the individual is often replicated in the history of a society. Whole cultures can become guilt-ridden; the ancient Israelites supplied themselves with prophets to denounce them for their sinfulness and developed, from their collective sense of having transgressed against God, their excessively strict religion with its severe commandments.

It is all very paradoxical: children who are treated leniently often acquire exacting superegos; one can develop a sense of guilt for aggressions only imagined no less than for aggressions actually carried out. Whatever their origins, guilt feelings, especially the unconscious variety, are a form of anxiety. What is more, Freud defended once again his claim that not all experience emerges from the outside world. Innate endowment, including one's phylogenetic heritage, plays its part during the upheavals of the Oedipus complex in making the internal policeman that the individual and, with him, his culture, will carry about thereafter. Thus, introducing anxiety into his analysis of culture as well as of the individual superego, demonstrating the work of aggression as well as love, reflecting once more on the respective shares of endowment and environment in the growth of the mind, Freud wove together in *Civilization and Its Discontents* the principal strands of his system. The book is a grand summing up of a lifetime's thinking.

In the same way, Freud's concluding reflections, at once moving and robust, recall an old inner struggle. They show him yielding to his urge for speculation while cautioning against its excesses. The idea of the cultural superego, he suggested, should enable one to speak of neurotic cultures and to offer therapeutic recommendations for them as one does with a patient. But, he warned, one should approach this matter with the greatest delicacy; the analogy between the individual and his culture may be close and informative, but it is only an analogy. The disclaimer matters; it helped Freud define himself as a student, rather than a reformer, of society. He made perfectly plain that he had no wish to present himself as a physician to society, with prescriptions for its ills. "My courage sinks," he wrote in a much-quoted sentence, "to stand up before my fellow humans as a prophet, and I bow before their reproach that I do not know how to bring them consolation—for that is fundamentally what they all demand, the wildest revolutionaries no less passionately than the most conformist pious believers." In the end, he left the decisive question open: Will civilization be able to contain the human drive for aggression and destruction? Having taken the opportunity to laud modern technology, Freud now warned that it has put mankind's very survival at risk. "Men have now gone so far in the mastery of natural forces that with their help they could easily exterminate one another to the last man. They know this, hence a large part of their current unrest, their unhappiness, their mood of anxiety."

THOUGH INTENDED, AND working, as an analysis of man's uneasiness in modern culture, *Civilization and Its Discontents* mirrored Freud's own mood to perfection. Shortly after completing it, he had to go back to Berlin for another consultation on his prosthesis, and his heart again gave him a good deal of trouble. He was plagued by palpitations, and while they were officially pronounced harmless, they worried him. In his laconic diary, the *Kürzeste Chronik*, he recorded in November and December of 1929, "Neuralgia," "Heart–Intestines Attack," "Bad Heart Days." He also noted early in November, almost by the way, "Anti-Semitic riots," and a few days before, on October 31, matter-of-factly and without visible pathos, "Passed over for the Nobel Prize." Still, however cheerless life was for him, however cheerless his message in *Civilization and Its Discontents*, Freud could take comfort in his book's astonishing popularity; within a year, its first edition of 12,000, exceptionally large for a work of Freud's, was sold out.

One by-product was an unexpected revival of the debate among psychoanalysts over its bleakest intellectual prop, Freud's idea of the death drive. Ernest Jones, to whom he sent a copy with a cordial inscription, and who had already read the book in Joan Riviere's translation, gave wholehearted praise to Freud's views on civilization and the "theory of guilt." He agreed with Freud, too, that hostility is a central fact of life. "My only difference with your views still remains my uncertainty about the Todestrieb"; the death drive struck Jones as a leap from the reality of aggressiveness to an unwarranted generalization.* Freud responded more with assertions than with arguments: "I can no longer get along without the assumption of this fundamental [death] drive, either psychologically or biologically, and think one need not give up the hope that you will still find the way to it." When Pfister objected in his turn, preferring to see the "'death drive' as merely the subsiding of the 'life force,'" Freud took the trouble to reiterate his case in somewhat greater detail. He protested that he was not just translating his private gloom into psychoanalytic theory: if he doubted that humanity is called to "rise to greater perfection," if he found life "a continuous struggle between Eros and death drive," a struggle whose outcome seemed to him unpredictable, "I believe that I have not given expression to any of my constitutional temperament or acquired dispositions." He protested that he was neither a "self-tormentor" nor, for that matter, a "spiteful person"— Freud used the Austrian colloquialism *Bosnickel*—and would be delighted if he could see good things ahead for himself and for others, or a glorious future

---

*Jones's letter also throws some light on the emergence of the English title: "We are having a considerable discussion about the English title of 'Das Unbehagen' and should be glad to know if you have any suggestions to offer. The old English word 'dis-ease' would be admirable for it, but for obvious reasons is no longer possible. There is a rare word in English, 'unease.' I have also suggested 'malaise,' though I do not greatly like it. 'Discomfort' seems to be hardly strong enough: 'discontent' seems too conscious." (Jones to Freud, January 1, 1930. Typescript copy, Freud Collection, D2, LC.) Freud wanted "Man's Discomfort in Civilization," but the title finally chosen was suggested by the translator, Joan Riviere. (See "Editor's Introduction" to *Civilization and Its Discontents*, SE XXI, 59–60.)

for mankind. "But once again," he observed, "it seems a case of the conflict between illusion (wish fulfillment) and insight." What matters is "that mysterious reality which, after all, exists outside us," not what is agreeable or advantageous. The "death drive," he contended, was not his "heart's desire; it appears to me only as an inescapable assumption on biological as on psychological grounds." Hence "my pessimism appears to me as a result, the optimism of my adversaries as a presupposition." He might say that he had entered a "marriage of convenience" with his somber theories, while the others "live with theirs in a marriage of inclination." He wished them well: "I hope they will be happier with it than I."

Still, Freud concluded *Civilization and Its Discontents* with a flicker of optimism, though his cheering for the life drive in its duel with death seems far more a matter of duty than conviction. "And now one may expect that the other of the two 'heavenly powers,' eternal Eros, will make an effort to prevail in the battle with his equally immortal adversary." These were the last words he wrote for *Civilization and Its Discontents* in the summer of 1929. When the heavy sale of the book permitted a second edition, to be published in 1931, he took the occasion to add a portentous question. Chastened further by the darkening economic and political scene—Hitler's Nazi party had just won a stunning victory in the elections to the Reichstag in September 1930, increasing the number of its deputies from 12 to 107—he asked, "But who can foresee the prospects and the outcome?" Freud did not fully anticipate what was to come, but he had few illusions. "We are moving toward bad times," he told Arnold Zweig late that year; "I ought to ignore it with the apathy of old age, but I can't help feeling sorry for my seven grandchildren." Touched by pity for his family and anxiety for the world, Freud committed his final synthesis to paper.

THE UGLY AMERICANS

Not everything that Freud wrote in those years was memorable. Around 1930, he got himself entangled in a venture that resulted in an embarrassing production—a "psychological study" of Woodrow Wilson written with William Bullitt, an American journalist and diplomat. Bullitt had called on Freud in the mid-1920s to consult him about what he thought to be self-destructive behavior, and during one of their meetings told

Freud that he was writing a book about the Versailles treaty. He planned to concentrate on the leading participants, and Woodrow Wilson would be, of course, one of the protagonists.

He had obviously dropped the right name; when he mentioned Wilson, he recalled, "Freud's eyes brightened and he became very much alive." Bullitt had also caught Freud at the right time; Freud seemed to him depressed and ready to die, certain that "his death would be unimportant to him or to anyone else, because he had written everything he wished to write and his mind was emptied." Certainly, the savage things Freud was saying about his work during these years lend some plausibility to Bullitt's recollection. Freud had always needed patients to stimulate him, and now he could see only a few. When his practice was greatly reduced during the First World War, he had been miserable and felt empty, just as Bullitt remembered him feeling now. Admittedly, Woodrow Wilson was not an ideal patient: he was not on the couch. What is more, Freud had solemnly proclaimed that psychoanalysis, his creation, must not be employed as a weapon of aggression. But at his advanced age, with his infirm health, in his embittered mood, Freud was prepared to make an exception with Woodrow Wilson.

The harsh realities of the negotiations at Versailles had converted Freud's limited and fleeting hopes for Wilson into furious dissatisfaction. Freud was not disposed to forgive the American messiah for letting him down. Late in the summer of 1919, when Ernest Jones saw Freud again after the separation of the war years, Freud's opinion of Wilson had already soured. Jones had reasonably pointed out that no single individual could dominate the complicated forces at work after so disruptive a war and that Wilson could not dictate the peace. "Then," Freud retorted, "he should not have made all those promises." In 1921, he made some of his anger public, disparaging "the American president's Fourteen Points" as "fantastic promises" that had found too much credence.

But even though Freud had come to "detest" Wilson—it is his word—he was unwilling to compromise his psychoanalytic ideal of benevolent neutrality. In December 1921, William Bayard Hale, an American publicist who had once been Wilson's intimate and campaign biographer, sent Freud his book *The Story of a Style*. It was a malicious and devastating dissection of Woodrow Wilson's character—plainly the two men were no longer friends—using as evidence his former associate's style: the piled-up adjectives and incessant rhetorical questions, the whole arsenal of debatable oratorical devices. Freud replied that he would send a comment if one was warranted, but cautioned, "I may be possibly kept back by the consideration that Mr. Wilson is a living personality and not a product of poetical phantasy as the fair Gradiva was. In my opinion"—he laid it down once again—"psychoanalysis should never be used as a weapon in literary or political polemics, and the fact that I am conscious of a deep-going antipathy towards the President is an additional motive for reservation on my side."

Indeed, while Freud took wicked pleasure in *The Story of a Style,* he did not let the book corrupt his standards. At the outset, he informed Hale, he had been "prejudiced against it by your publisher advertising it as a 'psychoanalytic study,' "* which it plainly was not. Yet he found "the true spirit of psychoanalysis in it," and, Freud thought, this "higher and more scientific 'Graphologie' " had "opened up a new field of analytic research." The book might not be, as Hale had described it, a cool scientific study—Freud easily detected "deep passion behind your investigation"—but this, he reassured Hale, was nothing to be ashamed of. Still, Freud could not overcome his "objection that what you have done is a bit of vivisection and that psychoanalysis should not be practised on a living [historic] individual." Freud confessed that he had no positive sentiments left for Wilson: "As far as a single individual can be responsible for the misery of this part of the world, he surely is." Even so, self-denial must be the lot of the responsible psychoanalyst. One simply should not do long-distance analysis on a living public figure.†

Yet only eight years later, Freud chose to embark on an extended exercise in wild analysis. Bullitt proved an able agent of seduction from the straight path of psychoanalytic reserve and respect for complexity. Charming, impulsive, restless, from an old and affluent Philadelphia Main Line family, ready on short notice with memoranda outlining strategies for international peace or economic recovery, he had tried his hand at journalism before launching a career in the foreign service. He knew everybody; one of his fatherly friends was Colonel Edward M. House, Woodrow Wilson's closest adviser until the president brusquely broke with him at Versailles. After the war, Bullitt had worked on Wilson's staff, both during the peace negotiations at Versailles and on a secret mission to revolutionary Russia for Secretary of State Robert Lansing. But, piqued by Wilson's disregard of his recommendations and appalled, like so many others, at the Versailles debacle, he had resigned. Then he committed the one mortal sin in the diplomat's book: he went public with his disenchantment. In September 1919, he testified before the Senate Foreign Relations Committee that even Lansing was unhappy with the treaty. After this indiscretion, which instantly secured him international notoriety,

*For the advertisement in question, see p. 453.

†In this letter, Freud made a telling slip, suggesting that he was perhaps ready to forget his own injunctions. One should not practice psychoanalysis on a living historic subject, he said, "unless he submits to it against his own will." He meant, of course, to write something like "in accord with his own will."

Bullitt escaped to Europe, writing, traveling, cultivating his acquaintance with the great. By 1930, when he approached Freud about working with him on a psychological study of Wilson, the two, Bullitt later claimed, "had been friends for some years."

That intimacy was more imaginary than real. But Freud did lend himself to a clandestine project with Bullitt, who in his turn confided in only a few, among them Colonel House. Writing to House in July 1930, he measured Wilson's biographer, Ray Stannard Baker, against himself: he thought that Baker, who was proceeding majestically from volume to volume, "has the facts, but is so little of a psychologist & so unfamiliar with international affairs that he does not know which facts are important and his interpretations remain melodramatic." The invidious comparison is palpable; Bullitt *was* familiar with international affairs, and in league with a great psychologist. He planned to confer with Freud and do some indispensable research. "My plans are growing more definite," he wrote House. "After visiting F. and going through Prince Max of Baden's papers, I shall probably go to Moscow." Max of Baden, who had served as Germany's chancellor at the end of the war and initiated peace negotiations with the Allies, might have instructive information in his archives, and from Moscow beckoned Lenin's papers, to which Bullitt, never one to shy away from taxing and improbable assignments, hoped to get access.

Bullitt's trip to Moscow was to be a quixotic journey; his consultations with Freud were far less frustrating. Colonel House urged Bullitt on: "You are going to write a book that will not only be a credit to yourself and your friends but will be of benefit to the world." Bullitt replied that he was forwarding some material to "my friend in Vienna," and guaranteed Freud's discretion and wisdom: "He is as detached and scientific in his view of the whole of human life as any man can be." House had entreated Bullitt to tackle his sensitive subject in a moderate tone, and Bullitt promised to comply. "Understatement," he agreed, was the only style appropriate to a study of Wilson. In early September, Freud was ill, but expected to be "in shape to work" soon, and in midmonth, Bullitt could report that "Freud has fortunately recovered from his acute illness, and is for the moment in excellent shape & eager to start the job." Actually there was another worrisome delay: Pichler operated on Freud in mid-October, and on top of that, Freud had to contend with a bout of pneumonia. When Bullitt came to call on October 17, Freud's *Chronik* records, Freud had a fever. Not until October 26 could Bullitt send a triumphant note, marked "personal," to Colonel House: "Tomorrow F. and I go to work."

He added a calculating gloss; he had hurried to Vienna after reading Max of Baden's papers "because of the precarious condition of F.'s health." In short, it had occurred to Bullitt that Freud might not live to complete the project into which both men had plunged with such high emotion. But three days later, Freud noted, "Work taken up." Bullitt was buoyant—much too buoyant. "The work here is going splendidly," he wrote Colonel House in November; while it was "taking much longer than expected," he hoped to be done by mid-December. Freud for his part informed Arnold Zweig, a little mysteriously, that while he had wanted to publish nothing more, "I am again writing an introduction for something that someone else is doing. I may not say what it is; it is an analysis, too, but for all that highly contemporary, almost political." He concluded, almost visibly restraining himself, "You cannot guess what it is."

Writing the book was a slow affair; when Freud had been younger and working on his own, he had written far more rapidly. Yet Bullitt kept up a barrage of ebullient communiqués. In August 1931, he reported to Colonel House that "after three operations," Freud was "in excellent health" once more "and the first draft of the book is nearly completed." He was writing from his home in the United States, but planned to return to Vienna in November and settle there for a time; there should be "a finished manuscript by May"—that is, May 1932. "It is an immense task but a fascinating one." By mid-December 1931, he was settled in Vienna, with his daughter in school.

But Bullitt's mind was no longer wholly on the Wilson book; he found the atmosphere of the Great Depression pervasive, oppressive—and exhilarating. Seeing Austria "slowly sliding toward the abyss of stagnation and starvation," and the others not much better off, he was getting impatient; the international economic crisis, threatening a general political catastrophe, fascinated him. It seemed to call for his talents. But he and Freud persisted, doggedly and discreetly. Bullitt was reading new volumes of Baker's Wilson biography and thought them poor. And Colonel House kept prodding. "How are you and Prof. Freud getting along with your book?" he had asked Bullitt in December 1931. "I shall be eager to see it." Finally, in late April 1932, House had his answer. "The book is at last finished," Bullitt wrote him, "that is to say the last chapter has been written and it could be published if both F. and I were to die tonight." But by "finished" Bullitt did not mean that it was ready for publication. Each of the references would have to be rechecked; besides, the manuscript "still needs to be expurgated"—it was too long. What was wanted was a six months' rest to permit another round of editing with the kind of detachment not possible now. "But at least there is now a complete manuscript and I am beginning to think about politics again." In late November, Freud announced that he was expecting his "collaborator," and hoped to hear from him just when "the Wilson-book can be made public." It was complete, but in the end, *Thomas Woodrow Wilson* did not appear until 1967, the year of Bullitt's death.

THE BOOK AS IT was finally published presents some intriguing puzzles. There is no mystery about the delay; Bullitt waited until after the death of Woodrow Wilson's widow in 1961, and until his own political career was clearly at an end.* Nor can there be much doubt that Wilson invited psychoanalytic study: like all humans, he was a mass of contradictions, but his contradictions reached extremes. Wilson was brilliant and obtuse, purposeful and self-defeating, emotional and icy, combative and timid, an astute politician in one situation and an intransigent fanatic in another. As president of Princeton University between 1902 and 1910, he introduced notable reforms in the educational and social life of the university, but his obstinacy on small points and his imperiousness with colleagues and trustees alienated old friends and in the end overturned most of his plans. As governor of New Jersey, he kept what Freud and Bullitt would consider his unconscious bid for martyrdom in check; Wilson the man of high-minded principle showed himself a smooth opportunist, scoring spectacular legislative triumphs and breaking, ruthlessly, with the politicians who had brought him to office. But as president of the United States he reenacted, on a higher level, the pathetic spectacle of half-willed failure that had marred his tenure at Princeton. Having pushed through an impressive program of domestic reform, he began to court defeat and disaster after America's entrance into the war in 1917 cast him in a new role. His conduct during the tortuous peace negotiations was erratic and counterproductive. So was his exhausting speaking campaign back home, designed to sell the treaty to a skeptical country and a hostile Senate. In Europe he had made concessions that did violence to his fervently proclaimed and religiously held ideals, but afterwards, in the United States, he refused to countenance some trivial amendments that would have saved the treaty, with no disgrace to him.

Wilson's peculiar combination of contradictory traits emerged from unconscious conflicts so monumental that he found no way of placating, let alone resolving them. Freud's and Bullitt's fascination with this man is perfectly comprehensible; he had loomed over the recent history of two continents and had, they were certain, acted out his neuroses on a world stage. They were not unduly diffident about their knowledge of Wilson and thought they could "trace the main path of his psychic development." But they

---

*"The book to which you refer," Bullitt wrote to Ernest Jones in 1955, "has never been published. Personally I felt that it should not be published until after the death of Mrs. W. She is still alive!" (Bullitt to Jones, June 18, 1955. Jones papers, Archives of the British Psycho-Analytical Society, London.)

claimed neither omniscience nor comprehensiveness for their personality profile: "We shall never be able to achieve a full analysis of his character. About many parts of his life and nature we know nothing. The facts we know seem less important than those we do not know." In consequence, they refused to call their book a psychoanalysis of Wilson, but advertised it more modestly as "a psychological study based upon such material as is now available, nothing more."

The criticism that the book is incomplete therefore misses the point. But the charge of snide antagonism and mechanical psychologizing is justified. Throughout, the tone is scornful, as though Wilson's neuroses were somehow a moral failing. Throughout, too, the book draws just a single consequence from any particular emotional state, as though the authors had never heard of overdetermination. Alfred North Whitehead's famous injunction to scientists, Seek simplicity and distrust it, which could have been Freud's motto, finds no application here. *Thomas Woodrow Wilson* focuses on Wilson's repressed rage against his father, the Reverend Joseph Ruggles Wilson. "Hostility to the father"—the book puts it as a general rule—"is unavoidable for any boy who has the slightest claim to masculinity." While the authors did not deny Wilson his portion of manliness, they detected him in, and virtually accused him of, worshiping his father all his life. "He never grew beyond this father identification." It may be that "many little boys adore their fathers; but," they immediately added, "not many adore so intensely and completely as did Tommy Wilson." To put it bluntly, the Reverend Joseph Ruggles Wilson was Woodrow Wilson's God. Identifying himself with his father, Woodrow Wilson thus became imbued with the conviction that his mission in life was divine. "He had to believe that somehow he would emerge from the war as the Saviour of the World."

But this identification was complex. At times Woodrow Wilson was God; at times he was Christ. As the former he trumpeted the law; as the latter he expected to be mortally betrayed. Woodrow Wilson had a younger, submissive brother who greatly admired him but who, by his very arrival in the world, had become a competitor for parental love. In his adult life, Wilson reproduced this intimate drama, forever seeking out younger friends on whom he could lavish affection until they betrayed him. The pattern of his mind, then, was plain and simple. Wilson was the little boy forever craving love and fearing treachery, imitating his childhood patterns in whatever office he occupied, and subtly—sometimes not so subtly—soliciting destruction. More: the anger he could never express against his father festered in him until it emerged as monumental rage. What casual observers took to be Wilson's hypocrisy was actually an outsized gift for self-deception; his sanctimoniousness an inexhaustible reservoir of hidden hatred. As the end came, he was only an aged boy. "He loved and pitied himself. He adored his dead father in Heaven. He loosed his hatred of that same father on many men." And that was more or less all.

THE QUESTION REMAINS why Freud lent himself to this caricature of applied analysis. When the book finally appeared, sensitive reviewers argued on stylistic grounds that the short introduction, which bears Freud's signature, was the only part of the work that could be reliably assigned to him. It is terse, witty, and informative, while the rest of the book is repetitive, leaden, often sneering. The ideal of understatement, which Bullitt had told Colonel House would guide him, has fallen by the wayside. Nor is the piling up of short sentences in the text Freud's way with words. Again, the condescending references to Wilson, over and over, as "Tommy" resemble nothing else that Freud ever wrote. The kind of heavy-handed sarcasm in which the book abounds appears in Freud, when it appears at all, only in his most private correspondence. Freud's ideas are grossly simplified, pugnaciously stated, and coarsened out of all recognition. Yet according to Bullitt, the study was a true collaboration: each of the two authors drafted some chapters and thoroughly discussed his work with the other, signing each chapter and initialing in the margin changes made in the manuscript. Certainly Freud must be held responsible for the general intellectual framework of the book. What is more, he called Bullitt "my patient (and collaborator)" and acknowledged that he had done more than merely consult on the text. In 1934, asked for "my considered judgment about the person and the effectiveness of President Wilson," Freud told an American correspondent that he had "written an estimate of Wilson which is anything but favorable," but had been unable to publish it "because of particular personal complications."

The indications are that Freud balked at the manuscript that Bullitt showed him in London near the end of his life, but finally, weary, aged, and worrying about the future of psychoanalysis, the survival of his sisters, the ever-threatening cancer, gave his consent.* It is quite as likely that Bullitt chose to revamp the manuscript after Freud's death, introducing the infelicities and the mechanical applications of psychoanalytic categories of which reviewers and readers complained. But Freud shared Bullitt's animus against Wilson; he had, as we have noted, a powerful aversion to prophets and religious fanatics, and he saw in Wilson a melodramatic specimen of this

---

*I here agree with Anna Freud's verdict: "Why did my father finally consent after long (comprehensible) refusal? I believe it was after his arrival in London, and at the time other things were so much more important than the Bullitt-book." (Anna Freud to Schur, September 17, 1966. Max Schur papers, LC.)

infliction on humanity. He encountered in Wilson what the American histo-rian Richard Hofstadter has felicitously called "the ruthlessness of the pure in heart." Worse: Wilson's vain attempt to make the map of Europe conform to his exalted ideals, and to purify European politics, proved his ruthlessness to be empty bluster—the most hateful of combinations. In his introduction, Freud quoted a story about Wilson, as president-elect, telling a politician that his victory had been divinely ordained, and called attention to the fact that in the opposite camp the German kaiser had also professed to be "a chosen darling of Providence." Freud's dry comment: "No one gained thereby; respect for God was not increased."

But Freud's role in the *Woodrow Wilson* debacle cannot be wholly ex-plained as emotions recollected in irritation. One reason Freud chose to work with Bullitt was that their book might provide vital support to the ailing analytic publishing house. At the end of the 1920s, it was once again near bankruptcy, as so often before. Freud was deeply attached to the *Verlag* and repeatedly came to its rescue; he made generous contributions of his own, wrung timely munificence from wealthy admirers, and sent it some of his own writings, its most reliable drawing card, for publication. In 1926, he had presented the *Verlag* with 24,000 Reichsmarks, four-fifths of the sum his colleagues had collected to celebrate his seventieth birthday. The following year, he transferred to the publishing house a donation of $5,000 from an anonymous American benefactor.* Then, in 1929, Marie Bonaparte and other donors once again staved off a financial crisis. Freud called the publish-ing house his child, and did not wish to survive it. Its fate, he knew, heavily depended on the fortunes of politics in Germany: a triumph of what he called the "Hitlerei" would be devastating. But quite apart from that, it thirsted for financial support. The search for money, then, gave Freud a serious incentive for enthusiasm about the Wilson project. In 1930, it was obvious to him that a book on Woodrow Wilson would substantially bolster the sales of the *Verlag,* perhaps even save it.

Freud's confidence in Bullitt's assistance proved to be well grounded. "Bullitt," Freud told Eitingon late in 1931, "is here again to continue work on his analysis and on Wilson. Indeed, my hope remains that this book, and the Poe translation of the Princess"—the German version of Marie Bona-

---

*Reporting this transfer of funds, the *New York Times* said that the unknown donor had benefited from psychoanalysis—as had his wife and two children—and had released this statement: "Freud is undoubtedly the most important man of our age. Those of us who have money owe it to the culture of the world to see that Freud is supplied with all necessary funds to continue his scientific investiga-tions and educate those who will carry on in the future." ("Gives $5,000 to Aid Freud/Anonymous Donor has Profited by Psychoanalysis/$100,000 Sought," *New York Times,* May 18, 1927, 25.)

parte's substantial treatise on Edgar Allan Poe—"will help the *Verlag* over
the most difficult time of financial rehabilitation."* At last, early the following year, he could report important tangible results: an advance from Bullitt
of £2,500—about $10,000—on the American royalties. It was the advance
Bullitt sent him, far more than settlement of an old score with a disappointing
American idealist, that proved the principal benefit Freud derived from the
Wilson project. Then there was silence, as Bullitt turned to Democratic
politics in the United States and Freud contemplated demagogues close to
home who were far more pernicious than Wilson had ever been.

No doubt Woodrow Wilson's being an American gave Freud special
pleasure in venting his aggressive spleen. In his lofty contempt for the things
of this world, Wilson seemed simply the converse of the materialistic American epitomized by Colonel Robert McCormick and Sam Goldwyn, with their
naive faith in the power of the dollar. It is a commonplace of psychoanalytic
doctrine that the most dramatic divergencies may spring, like widely separated branches, from the same root. Whatever guise the American assumed,
saint or moneygrubber, Freud was ready to write him off as a most unattractive specimen in the human zoo.

Freud had given voice to his anti-American sentiments years before he set
foot in the United States: in 1902, giving way to a cynical mood, he had
compared his own Old World, "governed by authority," with the New,
governed "by the dollar." Later, though Americans had bestowed on Freud
his first handsome official honors, he never ceased taking pleasure in calling
them bad names. To be sure, he liked to recollect the honorary degree he had
received at Clark University in 1909, and found occasion to remind Europeans of it, pointedly. He had even, near the beginning of his career, considered emigrating to the United States. "33 years ago today," he reminisced
to Ferenczi on April 20, 1919, recalling the spring of 1886, the year he had
opened his medical practice and got married, "I stood as a freshly minted
physician before an unknown future, resolved to go to America if the three

---

*The travail of the *Verlag* became a continuous burden on Freud. In the fall of 1931, Martin Freud
took over as manager and did as well as he could, what with the miserable and steadily worsening
economic situation. Repeated infusions of funds from generous donors like Marie Bonaparte were
so many stopgaps. In 1932, Freud took another step: he wrote a series of "lectures" to be published
by the *Verlag;* though never actually delivered anywhere, they were presented as additions to the
introductory lectures he had delivered during the First World War. The *New Introductory Lectures
on Psychoanalysis* brought the old *Introductory Lectures* up to date, summed up his new thoughts
on female sexuality, and concluded with an important chapter on the Weltanschauung of psychoanalysis. In this last "lecture," Freud reiterated, more decisively—and incisively—than ever, his
conviction that psychoanalysis cannot formulate, and does not need, a world view of its own. It is,
quite simply, part of science.

months my supplies would last did not start out promisingly." He wondered whether it would not have been better if "fate had not smiled so amiably then." But such flashes of yearning for a career in the United States were exceptional; to hear him talk, the country and its denizens were hypocritical, uncultivated, shallow, enamored of money alone, and covertly anti-Semitic.*

Significantly, Freud's anti-Americanism emerged with particular virulence during his followers' excursions to the United States. Whenever Jung and, later, Rank or Ferenczi traveled there for lectures or analytic consultations, he viewed the trip as an invitation to defect from the Cause. It was almost as though he perceived the United States as a seductive rival, rich, alluring, powerful, in some primitive way superior to Europe, with its more austere attractions. America, Freud once told Arnold Zweig, savagely parodying self-satisfied American claims, is an "anti-Paradise." This was late in his life; some years before, he had confided to Jones, "Yes, America is gigantic, but a gigantic mistake." In short, he feared the United States as a country which induced his followers to commit gigantic mistakes.

These sentiments run through Freud's correspondence like an unpleasant, monotonous theme. They also exhibit some telling inconsistencies. As we know, in January 1909, negotiating with Clark University, he had found G. Stanley Hall's tight-fisted allowance for travel expenses "too 'American,'" which is to say, unduly preoccupied with the financial side of things. As far as he was concerned, "America should bring in money, not cost money." He liked to keep this crass formula under his pen. "What is the use of Americans, if they bring no money?" he asked Ernest Jones rhetorically late in 1924. "They are not good for anything else." This refrain was, as he knew only too well, one of his favorites. "I have always said," he repeated to Jones a year later, a little self-consciously, "that America is useful for nothing else but to supply money." During Rank's visit to the United States in 1924, Freud had made the same point in his most intemperate style; he had professed himself quite pleased to see that Rank had "found the only rational kind of conduct appropriate for a stay among these savages: to sell your life as dearly as possible." And he added, for good measure, "It has often seemed to me that analysis suits Americans as a white shirt suits a raven."† It is hardly necessary

*Freud told Eitingon in 1932 that Brill, trying to organize psychoanalysis in the United States, "has American anti-Semitism, latently gigantic, against him." (Freud to Eitingon, April 27, 1932. By permission of Sigmund Freud Copyrights, Wivenhoe.)

†It is interesting to note that Freud made these extreme formulations into favorite expressions. Thus on July 8, 1928, he wrote to Wittels that "the American and psychoanalysis are often so ill-adapted for one another that one is reminded of Grabbe's parable, 'as though a raven were to put on a white shirt.'" (Wittels, "Wrestling with the Man," 177–78.) And that startling epithet, "savages," was not a unique aberration either. On July 10, 1935, Freud wrote to Arnold Zweig, who had triumphantly reported that an American book club had selected one of his novels, "Is it not sad that we are

to point out that such an attitude displays the very moral defect Freud liked to find in Americans. But Freud felt no qualms; he was only exploiting the exploiters.

Freud's wry appreciation of American astuteness with money was just another expression of the same mercenary stance. "If you should get involved with America," he warned Pfister in 1913, "you will surely be swindled. In business matters they're way ahead of us!" Apparently unaware that he had hopelessly muddled his arrangements for the foreign rights to his writings, he was disposed to hold the Americans responsible for the confusions that resulted. "American publishers," he told one American correspondent in 1922, are "a dangerous sort of humans." In this same spirit he called Albert Boni and Horace Liveright, whose firm published a number of his early books in New York, "two crooks." What he wanted to extract from these resourceful savages was financial backing. "All its popularity in America," he lamented to Ferenczi in 1922, "has not procured analysis the benevolence of just *one* of the dollar uncles." The shortage of such *Dollaronkel* disappointed him and fed his prejudices.

IN DEALING WITH American analysands, as he increasingly did in the 1920s, Freud permitted himself an insensitivity he would have found uncivilized in others and, had he analyzed it, symptomatic in himself. He grew rather fond of some among the American physicians who came to Berggasse 19 for their training analyses and could expend unfeigned warmth on the few he liked. But his verdict on leading American analysts was often caustic. In general, he confided to Eitingon, these "by and large inferior" people were good mainly as subjects for studying "questions of technique." When, in 1921, Pfister reported to Freud that the eclectic American psychoanalyst Smith Ely Jelliffe was on his way to Berggasse 19, he added that "Yelliffe" had impressed him as "an adroit, clever man." Freud gave these appreciative adjectives a disparaging twist. Once before, he had called Jelliffe "one of the worst business-Americans—in plain speech: crook—Columbus ever discovered"; now he replied to Pfister that Jelliffe "is regarded as very smart—that is: crafty—very clever and not outstandingly decent." Clarence Oberndorf, an early enthusiast and long a dominant figure among American psychoanalysts, was, to Freud's mind, only "the worst" among them. "He appears to be stupid and arrogant." Freud confessed to Ernest Jones in 1921 that Oberndorf baffled him: "Why should a man who was considered so brilliant and successful, have taken up analysis unless his head or his heart had some part

materially dependent on these savages, who are not better-class human beings? After all we are in the same situation here." (By permission of Sigmund Freud Copyrights, Wivenhoe.)

in it." He wondered why American psychoanalysts, even the "better elements" among them, showed so little community spirit. "Brill," he added, out of patience with his most active advocate, "is behaving shamefully and has to be dropped." This was a hyperbolic threat on which he never acted, probably never planned to act.

Oblivious to their feelings, Freud would tell his American correspondents that their eccentricities or unexpected responses to analytic treatment must be national traits. "But you Americans are peculiar people," he wrote his analysand Leonhard Blumgart, after Blumgart had confessed that he had become engaged just when he would have to be separated from his future wife for six months. "None of you has ever found the right attitude toward your women." When another American analysand, Philip Lehrman, sent him a critical review of *Civilization and Its Discontents*, Freud acknowledged it with an uncivil comment: "It is of course precisely as stupid and ignorant as one can expect from an American journalist." A few months later, no more civilly, Freud voiced his somewhat astonished satisfaction at hearing that Lehrman and his family were doing well. It was, after all, depression time in the United States, "and what is the American without prosperity?" When he was in this mood, as he often was, he casually set aside his memories of such admirable Americans as William James and James Jackson Putnam.

Freud even found it possible to grumble that these miserable Americans could not stay sane when they were needed. In 1924, Freud's gifted analysand Horace Frink suffered a psychotic attack. Frink was, for Freud, one of the rare exceptions among Americans: he had thought highly of him and wanted him to head the psychoanalytic organization in the United States. But Frink's breakdown, which led to hospitalization, obviously upset this plan. Observing Frink's appalling mental condition, Freud treated this personal calamity as though it were a characteristic American failing. "My attempt at giving them a chief in the person of Frink which has so sadly miscarried is the last thing I will ever do for them," he swore, "had I to live the one hundred years you set down for the incorporation of ψA into Psychiatry." This callous outburst, to be sure, came in September 1924, while Freud was wrestling with the aftermath of his cancer. But the attitude underlying it was permanent.* In

---

*It is reasonable to conjecture that Freud's heartless denunciation of Frink was fueled in large part by unacknowledged, though largely conscious, feelings of guilt. To begin with, Freud had at first failed to perceive the potential for psychosis concealed behind Frink's neurotic difficulties, and then refused to take an early psychotic episode seriously. What is more, Freud had, with the best of will but a certain insouciant arrogance, compounded Frink's emotional turmoil by intervening in Frink's private life. In the course of his analysis, Frink had decided to divorce his wife in order to marry one of his patients, and Freud had encouraged him, and his intended wife, to pursue their plan. Yet when in 1923, a month after the divorce, Frink's first wife died, his mental health deteriorated disastrously. And a year later, his second marriage also collapsed. Not long before his death in 1936 at the age

1929, when Ernest Jones consulted him about an American proposal that he edit a source book of Freud's psychoanalytic writings for American audiences, Freud sent characteristic word: "Fundamentally the whole thing is, being authentically American, quite repellent to me. One can rely on it: if such a source book were available, no American would ever go to the original. Perhaps he would not do so without it, but take his information from the muddiest of popular sources."

Comments like these were not just reserved for private correspondence; Freud did not hesitate to put them into print. In 1930, writing a few words of introduction to a special number of the *Medical Review of Reviews*, edited by the American analyst Dorian Feigenbaum, he admitted that the presumed progress of psychoanalysis in the United States gave him only "clouded" satisfaction. Verbal assent was widespread but serious practice and financial support were rare; physicians and publicists alike were content with psychoanalytic slogans. They took pride in their *"broad-mindedness,"* which only demonstrated their *"lack of judgement."* Freud thought that "the popularity of the name of psycho-analysis in America signifies neither a friendly attitude to the thing itself nor any specially wide or deep knowledge of it." He thought so—and said so.

Some of Freud's aversion, then, was rooted in his anxiety over American impulsive receptiveness, coupled as it seemed to be with a most damaging lack of rigor and a no less damaging fear of sexuality, to say nothing of a counterproductive egalitarianism. As early as 1912, he had instructed Ernest Jones to keep James Jackson Putnam "warm," so that "America may be kept on the side of Libido." He thought then, and continued to think, that this would be ungrateful work, for among American psychoanalysts leadership was political and excellence went unrewarded. In the 1920s, he angrily denounced analysts in the United States for the way they managed their organization. "The Americans," he told Sándor Radó, "transfer the democratic principle from politics into science. Everybody must become president once, no one must remain president; none may excel before the others, and thus all of them neither learn nor achieve anything." When, in 1929, a group of American psychoanalysts—some of them Rankians—proposed to organize a congress and approached Freud about inviting his daughter, he demurred in his habitual impolite way. "I cannot hope that the congress—which I wish the greatest success—can mean very much for analysis," he told one of the organizers, Frankwood Williams. "It is being mounted following the American pattern

---

of fifty-three, his daughter Helen Kraft asked him what message to give Freud should she ever meet him. "Tell him he was a great man," Frink said, "even if he did invent psychoanalysis." (Helen Kraft, quoted in Michael Specter, "Sigmund Freud and a Family Torn Asunder: Revelations of an Analysis Gone Awry," *Washington Post*, November 8, 1987, sec. G, 5.)

of replacing quality with quantity." His anxieties were not wholly groundless, but they assumed unrealistic, almost nightmarish shapes in his jaundiced imagination.

Some of his grievances were more than sheer fantasies. His dyspepsia, for one, was real enough. After returning from Clark University in the fall of 1909, he had complained that his health was not what it should be, and he knew whom to hold responsible: "America has cost me a great deal." Late that winter he spent three weeks in Karlsbad for treatments designed to cure "my colitis earned in New York." When after the war he was having trouble with his prostate, he told Ferenczi that he found himself at times "in the most embarrassing situations as, for the first time 10 years ago, in America." He did not invent these ailments, but displaced his rage against them onto a single convenient target. And there were powerful professional irritants. The vigorous representations of the American psychoanalytic establishment against lay analysis did nothing to temper Freud's antipathy; they only proved to him that when Americans were not being naive and prudish, they were greedy and conventional. Their very manner of speech, Freud thought, should doom them. "This race," he once told his physician Max Schur, "is destined to extinction. They can no longer open their mouths to speak; soon they won't be able to do so to eat."

THE CONCLUSION IS inescapable that, slashing away at Americans wholesale, quite indiscriminately, with imaginative ferocity, Freud was ventilating some inner need rather than listening to his experience. Even the faithful Ernest Jones, we know, had to admit that Freud's anti-Americanism was not really about America at all.* Freud had some inklings that his feelings were less—or more—than wholly objective; in the 1920s, he even made fleeting efforts at diagnosing the mysterious Americans. Incensed at two psychoanalytic articles by American authors, he told Ernest Jones in 1921, "The Americans are really too bad." But, he added prudently, he would not "give a judgment why they are so without better opportunity for observation." He did venture the thought that "competition is much more pungent with them, not succeeding means civil death to every one, and they have no private resources apart from their profession, no hobby, games, love or other interests of a cultured person. And success means money. Can an American live in opposition to the public opinion, as we are prepared to do?"† Americans, it seemed, had unhappily

---

*See p. 211.

†In *Civilization and Its Discontents,* he retreated from firm judgments and proclaimed his willingness to "avoid the temptation of entering upon a critique of American culture," since he wished (he added gratuitously) to avoid employing American methods. (*Das Unbehagen in der Kultur, GW* XIV, 475/*Civilization and Its Discontents, SE* XXI, 116.)

wedded materialism to conformity. Three years later Freud took Rank's visit to the United States as the occasion for giving this diagnosis a crushing name: "Nowhere is one so overwhelmed by the senselessness of human doings as there, where even the pleasurable gratification of natural animal needs is no longer recognized as a life's goal. It is a crazy anal *Adlerei.*" Freud could do nothing more derisive than to burden Americans with the name of his most detested ex-disciple. To put it in technical terms, he saw Americans one and all as victims of an anal-sadistic retentiveness hostile to pleasure but conducive at the same time to the most aggressive conduct in business and politics. That was why American existence was marked by "haste." That, too, was why the nonutilitarian aspects of life, whether innocent hobbies or the higher reaches of culture, were unavailable to Americans.

Freud detected these manifestations of the American character everywhere. To begin with, probity was hard to come by. Freud meant to imply just this when he described his American nephew, Edward Bernays, the successful founder of the public-relations industry, as "an honest boy when I knew him. I know not how far he has become americanized." What is more, the United States offered a cold climate to lovers. This is the essential meaning of Freud's remark to Blumgart that American men had never established a right attitude toward their women. But worst of all, America was enslaved to that favorite product of anal adults, money. For Freud, the United States was, in a word, "Dollaria."

NONE OF THIS is original except for the psychoanalytic vocabulary; most of Freud's epithets were a century old, and many of them were commonplaces in the circles he frequented.* In 1927, the French psychoanalyst René Laforgue could describe an American referred to as "P." in a sentence Freud must have found congenial: "As an authentic American, P. has always thought that one could buy oneself analysts." In the same year, Ferenczi, leaving the United States after a long visit, worried that neurotic Americans, of whom there were all too many, needed far more, and far better, psychoanalytic treatment than they were getting. "I returned here after many years," he was quoted as saying, "to find the interest in psychoanalysis much

---

*Here is just one striking instance. In 1908, Ernest Jones told Freud, "Americans are a peculiar nation with habits of their own. They shew curiosity, but rarely true interest. . . . Their attitude towards progress is deplorable. They want to hear of the 'latest' method of treatment, with one eye dead on the Almighty Dollar, and think only of the credit, or 'Kudos' as they call it, it will bring them. Many eulogistic articles have been written on Freud's psychotherapy of late, but they are absurdly superficial, and I am afraid they will strongly condemn it as they hear of its sexual basis and realise what it means." (Jones to Freud, December 10 [1908]. By permission of Sigmund Freud Copyrights, Wivenhoe.)

greater than in Europe, but I have also found that this interest is somewhat superficial and that the deeper side is somewhat neglected."

Such opinions make it only too evident that Freud and his adherents were copying, often in so many words, the condescending pronouncements that cultivated Europeans had been uttering for years. And these in turn were largely echoing the views of their fathers and grandfathers who had been projecting on the Americans certain vices, some of them real and more of them trumped up, for a century. It had long been a favorite social game to decry the Americans' craze for equality, their no less pronounced craze for the new, and their materialism. As long ago as 1822, Stendhal had slandered them, in his witty study *Love,* as anti-imagination incarnate. They were, he thought, incapable of love: "In Boston one can leave a young girl alone with a handsome stranger, certain that she will be thinking only of the marriage portion of her future husband." The Americans, Stendhal reiterated in his novel *Lucien Leuwen,* though just and reasonable, "think of nothing but money and about the ways of accumulating it." A few years later, Charles Dickens, visiting the United States, was lionized beyond endurance and victimized by pirate publishers; his biting caricature in *Martin Chuzzlewit* is a triumph of indignation over empathy. Americans, we learn from that novel, preach liberty but are terrified of public opinion, cant about equality while they keep slaves, are snobbish and moneygrubbing. Most American conversation "may be summed up in one word—dollars. All their cares, joys, hopes, affections, virtues, and associations, seemed to be melted down into dollars." This charge, though a cliché by the time Freud began to write, retained its interest for European observers. In 1904, Sir Philip Burne-Jones condensed the old indictment in the title of his report on the United States—*Dollars and Democracy.* "And how they talk of money!" Burne-Jones exclaimed. "In snatches of conversation in the streets, the restaurants, and the cars," all one hears is " 'dollars-dollars-dollars.' " Freud had one advantage over Stendhal; at least he had, like Dickens and Burne-Jones, visited the United States. But his view of Americans was no better informed.

The question remains why Freud should so uncritically swallow this potent, but by his time musty, mixture of tendentious observation and unmitigated cultural arrogance. What happened was that his conformity and his radicalism oddly worked together to keep his anti-Americanism alive. As a conventional, faultless European bourgeois, he thought about Americans as others thought. Compared to this unthinking acceptance of current clichés, his realistic grounds for annoyance with Americans—messianic politics, resistance to lay analysis, to say nothing of American food—fade into insignificance. But at the same time, as a radical antibourgeois in his ideal of free sexual relations, he found Americans the very model of sexual hypocrisy. Freud the sexual reformer, it would seem, fashioned for himself a United States to represent in the most concentrated form the forces of cant he felt called upon to fight.

It is surely no accident that his earliest comments on Americans had centered precisely on their inability—as he saw it—to feel, or express, love. Some months before his visit to Clark University, he had told Ferenczi that he "feared the prudery of the new continent." Just after returning from Clark, he informed Jung that the Americans have "no time for libido." He never tired of this charge; he deplored "the strictness of American chastity," spoke derisively of "prudish" and of "virtuous" America. When, in 1915, in his famous letter to James Jackson Putnam, he denounced modern respectable sexual mores as contemptible, he made a point of saying that these mores were at their worst in the United States. Such a country would be obliged either to reject the uncomfortable, unconventional truths of psychoanalysis or to stifle them in its embrace. In *The Interpretation of Dreams* Freud had confessed, honestly enough, that all his life he had needed an enemy as much as a friend. Such a regressive need must drag a measure of oversimplification and sheer callousness in its train: the combatant, like the child, sharply divides his world into heroes and villains to sustain his morale and legitimate his cruelty. The America that Freud constructed stood as a gigantic collective manifestation of the enemy he said he could not do without.

For unhappy reasons of his own, Freud clung to this stark, monochromatic travesty even more desperately after the First World War than before. He found it galling to be "working for the dollar."* This dependency wounded his pride, but he found no way of escaping it. In the 1920s, Americans were pleading with him to take them into analysis, and Americans brought the hard currency he wanted and professed to despise. The conflicts this predicament aroused in him did not abate. As late as 1932, he confided to Eitingon, "My suspicion of America is unconquerable." In short, as his need for Americans grew, his animus against them grew with it. If in anatomizing Americans he was exhibiting human nature at work, he was also quite unwittingly exhibiting his own.

---

*Late in 1920, he wrote his daughter Anna that he had just rejected an invitation to spend six months in New York for $10,000. Half of that, Freud estimated, would have gone for his expenses. True, even $5,000 amounted to two and a half million Austrian kronen, but what with taxes and other outlays, he thought he could earn as much at home. "In other times," he observed angrily, "no American would have dared to make me such a proposition. But they're counting on our poverty"— Freud used the Hebrew term *Dalles*—"to buy us cheap." (Freud to Anna Freud, December 6, 1920. Freud Collection, LC.)

TROPHIES AND OBITUARIES

 During the years that Freud was working with Bullitt on the study of Woodrow Wilson, the cycle of public recognition and private afflictions accelerated. In late July 1930, he was informed that the city of Frankfurt had awarded him its coveted Goethe Prize. The citation was ceremoniously signed by the lord mayor of Frankfurt. "With the strict method of natural science," it began, rather fulsome in the way of these documents, "at the same time boldly interpreting the similes coined by imaginative writers, Sigmund Freud has opened access to the driving forces of the soul and thus created the possibility of recognizing the emergence and construction of cultural forms and of curing some of its illnesses. Psychoanalysis," it went on, "has not merely stirred up and enriched medical science, but the mental world of the artist and the pastor, the historian and the educator, as well." Reaching for language appropriate to the occasion, the citation called attention to the roots of psychoanalysis in Goethe's essay on Nature, to the "Mephistophelian" way that Freud had torn apart all veils and to his "Faustian" insatiability coupled with "reverence for the formative-creative forces slumbering in the unconscious." It concluded in subtle self-praise: so far Freud, the "great scholar, writer, and fighter," had been denied "every external honor." This was not wholly accurate; he had across the years received a few gratifying tokens of recognition. But in essence, the citation had a point; Freud had not exactly been overwhelmed with honors. In November 1930, he noted laconically in his *Chronik* once more, "Definitively passed over for Nobel Prize."

The Goethe Prize was therefore like a flash of sunlight in an overcast and thunderous sky. It diverted Freud's attention for a moment from his struggle with debilitating, maddening personal handicaps and his watch on the rapidly deteriorating world situation. He found the stipend attached to the award, 10,000 Reichsmark—some $2,500—a welcome supplement to his income. A little quizzical about being chosen, he thought that the lord mayor's being Jewish, though baptized, might have had something to do with it. Still, he was authentically pleased that the prize should bear the name of his beloved Goethe. Founded in 1927, it had previously been awarded to Stefan George, the celebrated poet and cult figure; Albert Schweitzer, missionary and biographer of Bach; and Leopold Ziegler, a philosopher of culture. Freud was in good company. He wrote a graceful short acceptance speech and proposed sending his daughter Anna to Frankfurt as his surrogate. He was too frail to travel, he told Dr. Alfons Paquet, secretary to the trustees of the fund awarding the prize, but thought that her reading his address could only improve the festivities: "My daughter Anna is certainly more agreeable to look at and listen to than I am." The occasion proved rewarding in more ways than one; Freud transmitted to Ernest Jones his daughter's impression that "the ceremonies," held on August 28, Goethe's birthday, "had been very dignified, and that people there expressed respect and sympathy for analysis."

The prize improved Freud's morale, but not by much and not for long. He feared that the welcome, conspicuous honor would draw unwelcome attention after it. "I believe," he wrote Ernest Jones at the end of August, "that this surprising episode will have no consequences either as far as the Nobel Prize or the general attitude toward analysis in Germany is concerned. On the contrary, I would not be surprised if the resistance did not thrust itself forward." This continued to trouble him. Two weeks later, he told Jones that foreign newspapers were printing alarming stories about the state of his health, and attributed these reports to his receipt of the Goethe Prize: "So they hasten to do me in."* But however envious others might be, the prize provided Freud with an opportunity he particularly enjoyed; he sent Lou Andreas-Salomé—in her late sixties, often ailing now, and not very prosperous—1,000 Reichsmark, with a note easing her into acceptance: "In this way, I can demolish a piece of the injustice committed in the granting of the prize." That he was still able to give made him feel more alive, perhaps even a little younger.

He needed that sort of consolation. The time for Freud's long-distance voyages of discovery was definitively over; those restorative trips he had taken with his brother Alexander, with Ferenczi, with Minna Bernays or his daughter Anna, to the sunny, classical Mediterranean world were now memories. To be within reach of his surgeon, Freud now chose summer resorts close to Vienna. A cigar was a festival, a stolen and choice pleasure, worthy of comment. In the spring of 1930, Freud reported to Ernest Jones from Berlin, where he was trying out a new prosthesis, that the previous month his "heart, stomach and intestines" had failed him so badly that he had briefly entered a sanatorium. Worst of all, he had developed "an absolute intolerance for cigars." Jones, only too well acquainted with Freud's addiction, sent a sympathetic reply, to which Freud responded hopefully a few days later: "Just yesterday I tried the timid first and, for the time being, the only cigar per day." During his working months in the city, he kept on analyzing fledgling

---

*As late as June 1931, he wrote Jones, "The conduct of my contemporaries has changed since the Goethe Prize to an admittedly reluctant recognition, only in order to show how little all this means. Somewhat like a bearable prosthesis which should not be the whole or main purpose of existence." (Freud to Jones, June 2, 1931. Dictated to Anna Freud. Freud Collection, D2, LC.)

analysts, though on a reduced schedule, while Dr. Pichler called often to inspect his palate for signs of recurrent malignant growths, and performed short, painful operations on suspicious-looking spots. Thanking Lou Andreas-Salomé for a loving letter on the occasion of his seventy-fourth birthday in May 1930, Freud lamented that he was paying a heavy price for whatever health he had left: "I have completely given up smoking, after it had served me for precisely fifty years as protection and weapon in the combat with life. So, I am better than before, but not happier." He signed himself her "Very Old Freud." It was a token of affection, like a cheerful, slightly tremulous wave of the hand.

MEANWHILE, THE RANKS around Freud were thinning. His old card partners, with whom he had played tarock every Saturday night, were disappearing. Leopold Königstein, the ophthalmologist who had been an intimate since his student days, died in 1924; Ludwig Rosenberg, another of his long-time physician friends, in 1928. Oscar Rie would follow soon after, in 1931. These men were among the handful with whom Freud had been on *du* terms. Among this cherished nonanalytic contingent, only the archeologist Emanuel Löwy, as enthusiastic as Freud about antiquities and of course better informed, remained to come for a visit and a long chat.

His family was not spared. In September 1930, Freud's mother died, at the ripe age of ninety-five. Freud had said farewell to her in late August, on the very day that a delegation from Frankfurt had arrived at Berggasse 19, the Goethe Prize diploma in hand. Amalia Freud had retained her energy, her zest for life, and her vanity until very late. Her death brought to the surface thoughts that Freud had pushed aside for a long time. Just the year before, when Eitingon's mother died, he had mused in his letter of condolence that "the loss of a mother must be something quite remarkable, not to be compared with anything else, and awaken excitations that are hard to grasp." He now felt, and tried to grasp, just such excitations. "Certainly there is no saying what such an experience may do in deeper layers," he mused to Ernest Jones, "but superficially I feel only two things: the growth in personal freedom I have acquired, since it was always an abhorrent thought that she would learn of my death, and secondly the satisfaction that she has at last the deliverance to which she had acquired the right in so long a life." He felt no grief, he added, and no pain, and had chosen not to attend the funeral. As he told his brother Alexander in extenuation, he was not as well as people thought, and besides, he did not like ceremonies. His daughter Anna represented him, as she had in Frankfurt some two weeks before. "Her significance for me," he wrote to Ernest Jones, "can hardly be increased." His dominant feeling about his mother's death was a sense of relief. He could now die.

In fact, Freud still had much living and suffering, and even some enjoying, ahead. In January 1931, David Forsyth, one of his English "pupils" for whom he had a high regard, invited him to deliver the Huxley Commemoration Lecture. It was a prestigious biennial affair, described by Forsyth as the "highest appreciation within our gift of the scientific work to which your life has been devoted." Thoughtfully he enclosed a list of the eminent men who had spoken on previous occasions. They included the great English surgeon Joseph Lister, ennobled for his introduction of antisepsis, and the famous Russian psychologist Ivan Petrovich Pavlov. Freud was perfectly aware how much this invitation meant. "It is a very great honor," he informed Eitingon, "and since R. Virchow, 1898, no German has received this call." For all his irascible, definitive-sounding disclaimers, remnants of his German identity were evidently still alive in him. But, deeply pained as he was to refuse, the invitation had come several years too late. He was simply not well enough to travel, nor articulate enough to lecture. Indeed, in late April, he was forced to undergo another painful operation, and it took a great deal out of him, physically and psychologically. He felt that he was where he had been in 1923 before his major operations, his life at risk. "This last illness," he confided to Ernest Jones soon after, "has terminated the security I enjoyed for 8 years." And he complained that he had lost much of his working strength. He was "weak, disabled and inhibited in my speech," he told Arnold Zweig, "not at all a pleasant remnant of reality." He did not get home from the hospital until May 5, the day before his seventy-fifth birthday.

THE NEXT DAY brought celebrations he had done his best, and utterly failed, to evade. They broke over him, he told Lou Andreas-Salomé, like a "flood." He could veto festivities, but not stop an avalanche of letters from friends and strangers, psychoanalysts and psychiatrists and admiring literati. Telegrams poured in from organizations and dignitaries, and Berggasse 19 was awash with flowers. A German congress of psychotherapists scheduled papers in his honor, and supporters in New York organized a festive banquet at the Ritz-Carlton, with speeches by William Alanson White and A. A. Brill, seconded by celebrities like Theodore Dreiser and Clarence Darrow. "Men and women recruited from the ranks of psychoanalysis, medicine and sociology," read the telegram the celebrants sent to Freud, "are assembling in New York to honor themselves by honoring on his 75th birthday the intrepid explorer who discovered the submerged continents of the ego and gave a new orientation to science and life." The mayor of Frankfurt, Alfons Paquet, Romain Rolland, all remembered the day. Albert Einstein wrote a particularly appreciative note: every Tuesday, he was reading Freud with a woman friend, and could not admire enough "the beauty and clarity" of his writings. "Apart from Schopenhauer," he graciously added, "there is no one for me who can, or could, write like that." Yet the victory of Freud's ideas over Einstein's skepticism was incomplete; being "thick-skinned," Einstein noted, he vacillated between "belief and unbelief." The Herzl Club greeted Freud "reverentially" as "the son of our people, whose seventy-fifth birthday is a day of joy and pride for all of Jewry," while Viennese institutions like the Psychiatric Neurological Clinic and the Association for Applied Psychopathology and Psychology sent their warmest greetings.

Freud took some of these tributes coolly, even resentfully. When he learned in March that to celebrate his seventy-fifth birthday the Society of Physicians proposed to make him an honorary member, he bitterly recalled the humiliations the Viennese medical establishment had visited on him decades before. In the privacy of a letter to Eitingon, he called the nomination repellent, a cowardly reaction to his recent successes; he thought he would accept it with a curt, distant acknowledgment. One letter of congratulation, though, may have amused him. It came from David Feuchtwang, chief rabbi of Vienna, who cozily claimed that "the author of *Future of an Illusion* is closer to me than he believes." This was the kind of closeness Freud could do without.

Gradually the floods receded and Freud worked his way through the mountain of messages, each requiring an answer. But there was still another celebration ahead, an honor that left him much more appreciative than he had been on his birthday, and unabashedly nostalgic. As the printed invitation proclaimed in slightly uncertain German, on Sunday, October 25, there was to be an "Unveiling of a Memorial Tablet at the Birth House of Profesor Dr. Sigmund Freud in PŘÍBOR-Freiberg, Moravia." He could not possibly attend, but the size and the quality of the Freud delegation—his children Martin and Anna, his brother Alexander, his loyal adherents Paul Federn and Max Eitingon—reflect the importance Freud ascribed to the occasion. The little town was bedecked with flags for the event, and once again, as so often in these years, Anna Freud spoke for her father. The letter she read is as eloquent as it is brief. Freud thanked the mayor and all those present for the honor they were bestowing on him while he was still alive, and while the world was still divided over the value of his work. He had left Freiberg when he was three and had returned, he recalled, at sixteen, as a schoolboy on vacation. He found it hard at seventy-five to put himself back into those distant years. But of one thing, he wrote, he could be sure: "Deep within me, covered over, there still lives that happy child from Freiberg, the first-born son of a youthful mother, who had received the first indelible impressions from this air, from this soil."

ON HIS SEVENTY-FIFTH birthday Freud had felt too wretched to see anyone outside his immediate family. One notable exception, perhaps the only exception, was Sándor Ferenczi, then in Vienna. Freud gave him about two minutes, a token of the special relationship that had bound the two men together for more than two decades. Ferenczi had been a faithful listener for Freud, afraid of no imaginative flights, and, what is more, himself the author of brilliant papers. Yet for some years there had been an appreciable cooling between them. The two never quarreled, but Ferenczi's insatiable demands for familiarity and reassurance, to say nothing of his smoldering resentment against the master he worshiped, had taken their toll. At times the friendship had given both almost as much pain as pleasure. As Freud's analysand, Ferenczi exploited the privilege of speaking and writing to him without reserve; Freud for his part often sounded like an uneasy, at times exasperated father. In 1922, Ferenczi had wondered out loud, practicing a bit of self-analysis, why he was not writing to Freud more often: "It is susceptible of no doubt that I, too, could not resist the temptation to 'make you a present' of the whole measure of overtender and oversensitive emotions appropriate to my physical father. The stage in which I now seem to find myself is a—badly delayed—weaning and the attempt to submit to my destiny." He thought that from now on he would be a more agreeable co-worker than he had been on the calamitous vacation trip to the south he had taken with Freud before the war.

Actually, Ferenczi was never wholly weaned of his dependence on Freud or of its consequent rage. One florid symptom of his ambivalence was an outpouring of flattery, which Freud did not appreciate. "It seems that you are—as always—right," Ferenczi had told Freud, characteristically, in 1915. Freud tried to parry this adulation by wishing that Ferenczi would idolize him just a little less. After the war, lamenting that he could hardly make ends meet despite doing analyses nine to ten hours a day, Ferenczi extravagantly admired Freud's "inexhaustible source of energy." On this occasion, Freud's response was blunter than usual: "Naturally I like to hear you going into raptures about my youth and productivity as you do in your letter. But then, when I turn to the reality principle, I know that it is not true." Late in the summer of 1923, writing from "the wonderful city of Rome," Ferenczi recalled the time when he and Freud had visited the city's "sacred places" together: "I count those days among the most beautiful of my life and think in gratitude of the incomparable guide you were to me." Ferenczi did not, could not, see that Freud was, as Freud once graphically put it, "no ψa superman" and wanted to be not a guide but a friend.

Unsettling as Ferenczi's bouquets were for Freud, his intermittent silences were even more disturbing. Once, very early in their friendship, during one of those silences, Freud sent a letter to Ferenczi consisting entirely of question marks between the salutation and the signature. It was a monitory gesture he might have repeated more than once. To be sure, at times Freud himself failed to keep up. "Our correspondence, once so lively, has gone to sleep in the course of the last few years," he wrote Ferenczi in 1922. "You write only rarely, and I reply even more rarely." But in general, Ferenczi was the silent one. In late June 1927, returning from his trip to the United States, Ferenczi visited London, but evidently neglected to stop off in Vienna, and Freud expressed mixed feelings about this. "That he is in no hurry to visit me," he wrote Eitingon, "is certainly not affectionate. But I am not hard to please. Some sort of effort at emancipation is probably involved." Yet Freud could not retain the distance of pure analysis. "When you get to be old enough," he added in some chagrin, "in the end you have everybody against you." Eitingon, too, did not like what he saw. "I must confess," he said, "that since my meeting with F[erenczi] here in Berlin, I have been, and am, fairly alarmed." In December, Freud voiced his concern for Ferenczi quite directly. "Dear Friend," he wrote, "What does your silence mean? I hope you are not ill. Send word before Christmas."

But Ferenczi did not help matters. Tormented as he was, he continued to vacillate between volubility and withdrawal. Thus, if on August 8, 1927, Freud could report to Eitingon, "We are now corresponding more briskly," a little more than two weeks later, things had changed. "The correspondence with Fer[enczi] has suddenly ceased again. Frankly," Freud confessed, "I don't quite understand him." One thing that Freud came to understand, or was at least willing to conjecture, was that Ferenczi's striking innovations in psychoanalytic technique, which Freud had at first welcomed and later deplored, were not purely professional departures but "an expression of inner dissatisfaction."

Ferenczi volunteered abundant evidence to sustain this tentative diagnosis. In 1925, in a telling letter, Ferenczi told Freud, "About my own health I cannot (with the greatest ill will) report anything sad." He seemed determined to be unwell. Early in 1930, he wrote Freud a long letter complaining of disturbing symptoms, including the fear of aging prematurely. In November of that year, Freud reported that he had had no news of Ferenczi and feared that "despite all our efforts, he is falling more and more into isolation." Ferenczi was fully alert to his condition. "You can well imagine," he told Freud in mid-September 1931, "how difficult it is to start again after so long a pause. But in the course of your life," he pleaded, mixing wishes with hopes, "you have encountered so much that is human that you will also understand, and forgive, such a state as this withdrawing-upon-oneself." He was immersed, he told Freud, in a "rather difficult internal and external and scientific work of purification," with no conclusive results as yet. Freud, delighted to hear from Ferenczi at all, replied without delay. "At last again a sign of life and of love from you!" he exclaimed with the old warmth. "After such a long time!" Freud frankly told Ferenczi he had "no doubt that you are, with these interruptions of contact, growing apart from me more and more. I say and hope: not growing estranged." But he took no responsibility for Ferenczi's disagreeable mood: "According to your own testimony, I have always respected your independence." But such independence, he implied, need not be bought at the price of separation.

While Freud, after years of benevolent watching, came to interpret Ferenczi's psychoanalytic departures as portentous, he thought it all the more necessary to assess them for their technical, as distinct from their symptomatic, significance. After all, Ferenczi had long been a prominent, highly visible member of the international psychoanalytic movement, an influential, original, and prolific author. "The interesting symbiotic relationship between nursing patient and teaching physician seems to be generally establishing itself," Ferenczi had disclosed to Freud as early as the summer of 1922. "I, for example, am taking mine along to Baden-Baden." By the late 1920s, he had moved far beyond this relatively innocuous way of managing his patients' transferences. While he did not fully disclose to Freud what he was doing in the analytic hour, Freud learned from Ferenczi's patients, such as Clara Thompson, just how actively their analyst was loving his analysands and letting them love him in turn.

Finally, late in 1931, Freud's mounting uneasiness about Ferenczi's experiments in affection with his patients conquered his oft-professed respect for Ferenczi's autonomy. "I have, as always, enjoyed your letter—its contents less," he told Ferenczi severely in a four-page communication devoted to a single subject, Ferenczi's psychoanalytic technique. Freud thought it unlikely that Ferenczi would change his mind about his innovations, but the path he had entered was, in Freud's judgment, "not fruitful." He was no prude, he assured Ferenczi, not constrained by bourgeois conventionality. But Ferenczi's way with his patients struck Freud as an invitation to disaster. "You have made no secret of the fact that you kiss your patients and let them kiss you." To be sure, a kiss may be perceived as harmless. People in the Soviet Union were very free with such salutations. "But that does not alter the fact that we are not living in Russia, and that with us a kiss signifies an unmistakable erotic intimacy." Accepted psychoanalytic technique was firm and unequivocal: patients "are to be denied erotic gratifications." Ferenczi's "motherly tenderness" departed from that rule. Freud thought that Ferenczi had two choices: he could conceal what he was doing, or publish it. The first course was dishonorable; the second invited extremists to go beyond Fe-

renczi's kisses to more intimate caresses. "Now imagine what the consequences would be if your technique were published." If Ferenczi was playing
the tender mother, he, Freud, playing the "brutal" father, could only warn
him, but he feared the warning would be futile, since Ferenczi seemed bent
on going his own way. "The need for defiant self-assertion, it seems to me,
is more powerful in you than you recognize." But at least, Freud concluded,
he had done his fatherly part.

Ferenczi responded at some length, in pacific tones. "I consider your
anxiety that I am developing into a second Stekel to be unfounded." The
technique he had evolved in the early 1920s, the so-called "active therapy"
designed to speed up analyses, had come to seem excessively ascetic; he had
instead attempted to "relativize" the "stiffness of prohibitions and avoid-
ances" in the analytic hour, creating an atmosphere that was "mild, passion-
less." He concluded that, having got over the pain that Freud's stern lecture
had caused him, he hoped that their disagreements would not interfere with
their "friendly personal and scientific concord."

Early in January 1932, Ferenczi began to keep what he called a "clinical
diary," a substantial, intimate, graphic collection of psychoanalytic vignettes,
theoretical and technical meditations, and asides on Freud at once astute and
disrespectful. This diary, which Ferenczi carried through the summer until
he had covered more than two hundred pages, amounts to a somewhat bleak,
often excited effort at honest reportage and self-analysis. He was continuing
his bruising discussion with Freud by other means, seeking to clarify his
procedures for himself and to discover his place, and rank, in the Freudian
army. Much of what Ferenczi wrote would have been no surprise to Freud;
much of it would have startled even him.

Ferenczi's journal opens with a denunciation of the classic analyst's "insensitivity," his "mannered way of greeting, formal request to 'say everything,'
his so-called free-floating attention." All these are shams. They insult the
patient, reduce the quality of his communications, and make him doubt the
reality of his feelings. The analytic attitude Ferenczi commended in sharp
contrast, and explored over and over in the coming months, sprang from the
analyst's "naturalness and sincerity." This attitude, which he had been cultivating for years, led Ferenczi to express "intense empathy" with his analysands, taking in stride all the problems such friendliness generated. He
noted—Freud's reproaches had not been imaginary—that some of his women
patients kissed him, an act that Ferenczi would permit and then analyze
"with complete lack of affect." However, there were occasions when "experiencing the sufferings of others, and my own, presses a tear from my eyes,"
moments of "emotion," he insisted, that one should not conceal from the
patient. There was nothing left in Ferenczi's practice of the cool, impersonal

analyst—the surgeon of the soul—of whom Freud had written so authoritatively before the First World War, even if Freud himself had shown more emotion than his icy metaphors implied.

Ferenczi's clinical diary amply documents that his aim was to make his analysands into full-fledged partners. He recommended, and practiced, what he called "mutual analysis." When a patient claimed the right to analyze him, Ferenczi would acknowledge the existence of his own unconscious and go so far as to disclose details of his past. He was, it must be said, somewhat uneasy about this procedure: it was not healthy for a patient to discover that a fellow patient was analyzing Ferenczi, or for Ferenczi to confess more than a patient could absorb. But he thought that "the humble acknowledgment to the patient of one's own weaknesses and one's own traumatic experiences, disappointments," would finally eliminate the patient's feelings of inferiority to, and distance from, the analyst. "Indeed, we grant patients the pleasure of being able to help us, of becoming, as it were, our analyst for a moment, which rightly raises their self-esteem."

This energetic flouting of traditional psychoanalytic technique was more than just technical in nature. Ferenczi's impassioned desire for emotional harmony, for virtual merging, with his analysands was part and parcel of his mystical sense of union with the universe, a kind of self-made pantheism. Freud had written that psychoanalysis confronted arrogant humans with the third of three narcissistic injuries: Copernicus had displaced humanity from the center of the world; Darwin had compelled it to recognize its kinship with the animals; he, Freud, had shown that reason is not master in its own house.* "Perhaps," Ferenczi glossed that famous passage, "a fourth 'narcissistic injury,' is in store for us: namely that even the intelligence of which we, as analysts, are still so proud is not our property, but must be recovered or regenerated through the rhythmical emanation of the ego into the universe, which alone is omniscient—therefore intelligent." Ferenczi offered such ruminations with some hesitation but was undeniably proud of them. "The daring suppositions concerning the contact of the individual with the whole universe must not merely be regarded from the standpoint that this All-knowing qualifies the individual for special attainments, but (and this is perhaps the most paradoxical thing that has ever been said) that such a contact could also have a humanizing effect on the whole universe." His "utopia" was "*elimination of impulses of hatred, an end to the bloody, vengeful-like chain of cruelties, progressive taming of all nature through control by insight.*" The future of psychoanalysis, Ferenczi speculated, might have a share in achieving this supremely desirable goal: a time when "all selfish

*See p. 449.

impulses in the world that go through a human brain are tamed." Ferenczi was perfectly aware that he was leaving well-trodden ground. In the midst of evolving his speculations, he acknowledged to Georg Groddeck, who had become his trusted friend, that his " 'scientific' imagination"—the ironic quotation marks around "scientific" are telling—"induced" him "on occasion to excursions beyond the unconscious to the so-called metaphysical."

Such woolly-minded, unworldly metaphysics by no means crippled Ferenczi's critical animus. In the privacy of his journal, he analyzed some of his master's weaknesses with a perceptiveness at once sharpened and distorted by long-borne, long-hidden resentments. He saw himself as the man whom Freud had "virtually adopted as his son, against all the technical rules he had himself laid down." Indeed, he recalled that Freud himself had told him that he, Ferenczi, was "the most consummate heir of his ideas."* But whether he or Jung was to be that heir, Freud seemed to have been convinced that once the son is ready to take his father's place, the father must die. Hence, Ferenczi thought, Freud could not allow his sons to grow up, but, as his hysterical attacks showed, was himself compelled to regress to childhood—to what Ferenczi called the "childish humiliation" Freud experienced when "he suppressed his American vanity." Pursuing this line of thought, Ferenczi came up with an original interpretation of Freud's anti-American sentiments: "Perhaps his contempt for Americans is a reaction to this weakness, which he could not conceal from us and from himself. 'How could I be so pleased with the American honors if I despise the Americans so?' "

Freud's fear of death, Ferenczi argued, showed that Freud the son had wished to murder his own father. And it had induced him to develop the theory of Oedipus, the parricide. In fact, Ferenczi believed, Freud's concentration on the father–son relationship had seduced him into exaggerations. No doubt Ferenczi, by his own confession so adoring, so tongue-tied in the presence of the master, so reluctant to contradict him, so overwhelmed by "crown-prince-fantasies," could speak with particular feeling about that relationship. But Ferenczi had a point. That concentration, he argued, had forced Freud's sexual theory into a "one-sided androphile direction," had forced him to sacrifice the interest of woman to that of man, and to idealize the mother. Ferenczi conjectured that witnessing the primal scene might have made Freud "relatively impotent." The son's wish for *the castration of the father, the potent one, a reaction to the humiliation he experienced, leads to the construction of a theory in which the father castrates the son.* " Ferenczi himself, as other passages in his clinical diary attest, was working to revise

---

*I have discovered no independent verification of this claim, though, as we know, at one time early in their friendship Freud had briefly fancied Ferenczi as a son-in-law. (See p. 309.)

Freud's theory of the Oedipus complex. He did not doubt the existence of infantile sexuality, but he was persuaded that adults, usually the parents, all too often artificially stimulated it, often by sexually abusing their children.

Ferenczi was not uncritical of his own slavish conduct before Freud. He had been slow to stand up to him, had fallen into radical extremes in his technical experiments. But now he was "in humaneness and naturalness," and full of good will, engaged to "work toward knowledge and, with that, as helper." Yet in his unsparing self-analysis, Ferenczi left no doubt that subordinating himself to Freud, fancying himself secretly as Freud's "grand vizier," had eventually produced the disappointing insight that his master "loves nobody, only himself and his work." The consequence: "ambivalence." It was only after he had freed his libido from Freud, Ferenczi concluded, that he had dared to embark on his " 'revolutionary' technical innovations"—such as "activity, passivity, elasticity, return to the trauma (Breuer)" as the cause of neuroses. But, poignant though this self-examination may have been, Ferenczi was deceived. Try as he might, he never wholly ceased to be Freud's imaginative, wayward, suffering son.

No WONDER THAT all of Ferenczi's efforts to minimize his differences with Freud, and Freud's efforts to keep the debate on a scientific level, could not prevent Freud from reading Ferenczi's clinical conduct as a concealed but transparent rebellion against him, the father. The long intervals between Ferenczi's letters were too telling to be ignored. "Isn't Ferenczi a cross to bear?" he asked Eitingon, rhetorically, in the spring of 1932. "Once again for months no news of him. He is insulted because we are not charmed by his playing mother and child with his female pupils." Late in the summer, he expressed his worry about Ferenczi even more fully, to Ernest Jones: "For three years now I have been observing his increasing alienation, his inaccessibility to warnings against his incorrect technical path, and, what is probably the decisive thing, a personal hostility toward me for which I have certainly given even less cause than in earlier cases." This was a menacing note: Freud was privately comparing Ferenczi to the other defectors. As he had with them, especially with Jung, Freud now perceived Ferenczi's hostility as a death wish against himself; perhaps Ferenczi was being so difficult "because I am still around." He was, Freud predicted in the summer of 1932, likely to go the way of Rank. It was a prospect that Freud did not relish.

Other contentious issues arising during these days, tense enough already, exacerbated the strains between the two. Ferenczi wanted to become president of the International Psychoanalytic Association, a post to which his long and devoted labors certainly entitled him. But Freud confessed himself ambivalent: holding the honorific post might just compel Ferenczi, he told him, to be cured of his isolation and his technical departures. But it would require Ferenczi to leave "the dream island where you dwell with your fantasy children" and rejoin the world. And that, Freud intimated, would be hard. Ferenczi took exception to this view of him: Freud should not take his expressions—" 'dream life,' 'daydreams,' 'crisis of puberty' "—to mean that something useful might not come of his "relative muddle." That was in May 1932. By mid-August, Ferenczi had decided, "after long tormented hesitation," to withdraw his candidacy. He was, he told Freud, too deeply engaged in rethinking his clinical procedures, which departed from accepted analytic practice; under these circumstances, it might be downright dishonest to accept the presidency.

Freud, back in the maelstrom of psychoanalytic politics, now prevaricated. Late in August, he protested that he regretted Ferenczi's decision and refused to accept Ferenczi's reasoning. But, he concluded, leaving himself a way out, Ferenczi must know his own feelings best. Two weeks later, after Ernest Jones had been chosen president of the International Psychoanalytic Association, Freud communicated to Jones somewhat different sentiments: "I was extremely sorry that Ferenczi's manifest ambition could not be gratified, but then there was not a moment's doubt that you alone could be appointed to the leadership." While this was not wholly candid either—Freud had his quiet reservations about Jones—the statement approximates Freud's actual opinion. His skepticism about Ferenczi was, after all, not new or sudden. "Ferenczi's turn is certainly a most regrettable event," he observed, but it had been in the making for three years. In some ways, one might amend Freud, it had been in the making far longer.

Ferenczi's "turn" included his rediscovery of what Freud had abandoned decades before—the seduction theory. His patients had supplied Ferenczi with evidence of infantile seduction and rape, not fantasized, but real, and he intended to explore their revelations in a paper he was writing for the international congress about to meet in Wiesbaden. On August 30, Ferenczi called on Freud and insisted on reading the paper to him. Of course, much of it was no news to Freud. But he was dismayed by Ferenczi's performance, as much by his conduct as by the substance of his remarks. Three days later, he dispatched a telegram to Eitingon with a curt verdict: "Ferenczi read paper out loud. Harmless, stupid, also inadequate. Impression unpleasant."

How unpleasant emerges from a long letter that Freud sent his daughter Anna on September 3, while the impress of the encounter was still fresh upon him. The Ferenczis, husband and wife, had come to call late in the afternoon. "She charming as ever; an icy cold emanated from him. Without further question or greeting, he began: I want to read you my paper. That's what he did and I listened, shocked. He has completely regressed to etiological views

I believed in, and gave up, 35 years ago: that the regular cause of neuroses is sexual traumas of childhood, said it in virtually the same words as I had used then." Ferenczi, Freud noted, was silent on the technique with which he had gathered this material. Had Freud had access to Ferenczi's clinical journal, he would have seen that Ferenczi was accepting at face value the testimony of some of his analysands, just as Freud had taken the word of his patients in the mid-1890s. "Right in the midst of it all," Freud went on, Ferenczi offered "observations on the hostility of patients and the need to accept their criticism and to acknowledge one's mistakes *before* them." This, of course, was the technique of mutual analysis, with which Ferenczi had been experimenting with increasing fervor for some time.

Freud was indeed appalled. Ferenczi's presentation, he told Anna, was "confused, obscure, artificial." Halfway through the recital, Brill came in, caught up on what he had missed, listened along with Freud, and whispered to him, "He is not sincere." That was Freud's pained conclusion as well. He elicited what he characterized as half-hearted, contradictory comments from Ferenczi on his departures from classic psychoanalytic formulations of the Oedipus complex, wondered how Ferenczi had managed to garner experiences unavailable to other analysts, and wondered, too, why he should have insisted on reading the paper out loud. "He does want to become president," Freud observed. The whole paper, he thought, innocuous as it was, could only hurt Ferenczi, but it would surely spoil the mood of the congress. "The same as with Rank but much sadder." He had already said the same thing to Eitingon in late August. There was to be sure little to surprise Freud—or his daughter—in Ferenczi's latest imaginative flight. "Now, after all," Freud noted in his report to Anna, "you have already heard the lecture in part and could judge for yourself." However vigorously Freud and his associates tried to dissuade Ferenczi from delivering his paper, Ferenczi persisted. He appeared in Wiesbaden, read the paper, and saw it published in the *Internationale Zeitschrift,* though not in an English translation in the *International Journal of Psycho-Analysis.* The acrimony over its message, and over the attempts that had been made to keep it from being read or published, did not die down for some time. All of this must have struck Freud much as had the letters from Fliess's widow more than four years earlier: as the revival of some old, traumatic affair he had thought he had disposed of once and for all.

Freud recognized that by no means all of Ferenczi's symptoms were neurotic messages from a disgruntled son. "Unfortunately," he wrote Ernest Jones in mid-September 1932, "it seems that with him the regressive intellectual and emotional development has a background of physical decay. His clever and courageous wife has had it conveyed to me that I should think of him as of a sick child." A month later, he informed Eitingon that Ferenczi's physician had diagnosed a "pernicious anemia." The physical, like the mental, condition of his passionate, once treasured friend troubled Freud exceedingly, and he was unwilling to precipitate a break. In December, Freud had what must have seemed a welcome diversion, a call away from present imbroglios to distant confessions. He read the French surrealist André Breton's just-published study, *The Communicating Vessels*, in which Breton noted—rightly—that in analyzing his own dreams Freud had shied away from the sexual motifs he had found in the dreams of others. Freud promptly denied the charge, and maintained that a full report on his dreams would have required unwelcome disclosures about his relations to his father. Breton would not accept this excuse, and the correspondence faded away.

In any event, nothing could keep Freud long from Ferenczi. In January 1933, responding to Ferenczi's cordial New Year's greetings, he recalled the "affectionate community of life, feelings, and interests" that had once united them, a community now invaded by "some psychological calamity." There was silence from Budapest, as Ferenczi wrestled with his illness. Then, in late March, conciliatory and self-critical, Ferenczi promised to interrupt his "childish pouting," and reported that his pernicious anemia had come back and that he was "slowly recovering from a kind of nervous breakdown." Alarmed, Freud responded a few days later in his most paternal manner; he urged Ferenczi, then already desperately ill, to take good care of himself. The thrashing out of their differences over technique and theory could wait. This was Freud's last letter to him; on the following day, he informed Eitingon that Ferenczi had suffered a "grave delusional outbreak," though he seemed to be getting over it. But the improvement was deceptive; Ferenczi dictated a letter on April 9, and on May 4 sent Freud a message through his wife, Gisela. On May 22, he died.

A FEW DAYS later, in an extraordinary reply to Ernest Jones's condolences, Freud mixed grief and analysis, giving analysis first place. "Our loss," he wrote, "is great and painful." Ferenczi had "taken a part of the old time with him"; another part would disappear once he, Freud, too departed from the scene. But the loss, he added, "was in fact not a new one. For years, Ferenczi was no longer with us, really no longer with himself. One can now estimate more easily the slow process of destruction to which he fell victim. Its organic expression was a pernicious anemia which soon linked up with grave motor disturbances." Liver therapy brought only the most limited improvement. "During the last weeks, he could no longer walk or stand at all. Simultaneously, there developed with uncanny logical consistency a mental degeneration which took the form of a paranoia." The latter had been inescapably directed against Freud. "At its center stood the conviction that I did not love him enough, did not want to appreciate his work, and that I had done his analysis badly." This in turn provided the key to Ferenczi's notorious clinical experiments. As Freud had been saying for some years, Ferenczi's "technical innovations were connected" with his feelings about him. "He wanted to show me how lovingly one should treat one's patients if one wants to help them. These were actually regressions to the complexes of his childhood, whose greatest injury was the fact that his mother did not love him, a middle child among 11 or 13, exclusively enough. And so he became a better mother himself, also found the children he needed." He had labored under the delusion that one of these, an American patient to whom he had devoted four to five hours daily, had upon her return to the United States influenced him across the ocean by means of vibrations; he fancied that she had analyzed and in that manner saved him.* "Thus he played both roles, was mother and child"; and he took her accounts of strange childhood traumas as truth. It was in such "aberrations," Freud concluded mournfully, "that his intelligence, once so brilliant, was extinguished. But," he concluded with a confidential coda, "we want to preserve his sad end as a secret between us."†

FERENCZI'S DEATH LEFT vacant a vice-presidency of the International Psychoanalytic Association, and Freud proposed Marie Bonaparte, not "only because one can show her off to the outside world," but because she "is a person of high intelligence, of masculine capacity for work, has done fine papers, is wholly devoted to the cause, and, as is well known, also in a position to lend material aid. She has now become 50 years old, will probably turn away increasingly from her private interests and steep herself in analytic work. I need not mention that she alone keeps the Fr[ench] group together." What was more, she was not a physician, and to invite a layman to fill so exalted

---

*Ernest Jones echoes Freud's account or, perhaps, relies on some independent source, which he does not document. Ferenczi, Jones writes, "related how one of his American patients, to whom he used to devote four or five hours a day, had analyzed him and so cured him of all his troubles." Moreover, she had done so telepathically, from across the Atlantic. (*Jones* III, 178.) Ferenczi's private diary for 1932 lends some color of plausibility to this description of his state of mind toward the end, but does not really sustain the charge. He reported there on one of his patients who was so "supersensitive" that "she can send 'telephonic news' across immensely long distances. (She believes in long-distance healing by means of concentrating her will and thought, but especially her sympathy.)" (July 7, 1932. *Klinisches Tagebuch*. Freud Collection, B22, LC.) But Ferenczi did not claim that *he* believed all this.

†In his life of Freud, Jones prints only the pious first portion of this letter (*Jones* III, 179), and omits the analytic portion. In consequence, what has remained largely a secret is that Jones's description of Ferenczi's mental state (which has been read as an expression of envious rivalry with an analyst who, he knew, stood closer to Freud than he did) is really an almost literal transcription of Freud's diagnosis.

a post would be "a definite demonstration against the undesirable arrogance of physicians, who like to forget that psychoanalysis is after all something other than a piece of psychiatry."

This letter to Jones reads like a little manifesto by an old man defying fate. During the last decade or so, Freud had suffered terrible losses: his daughter Sophie, his grandson Heinele, his tarock partners, his analytic followers from Abraham to Ferenczi and, in a different way, Rank. He had been struck by cancer. The world was out of joint, but that was no reason to stop analyzing. Nor was it a reason to reject the refuge of humorous distance. Freud rather resembled the bird stuck in birdlime in a famous poem by Wilhelm Busch, that comic versifier and illustrator whom Freud so much enjoyed quoting. As the bird tries in vain to extricate itself, a black tomcat, anticipating an easy meal, steals nearer and nearer; seeing its inevitable end approaching, the victim decides to spend its last moments singing lustily. "The bird, it seems to me," Busch sagely comments, "has a sense of humor"—*Der Vogel, scheint mir, hat Humor.* So did Freud, though he increasingly doubted that there was much point in making an effort.

TWELVE

To Die in Freedom

THE POLITICS OF DISASTER

 The public events that embittered Freud's last years made his gloomiest imaginings about human nature look pale. "Superfluous to say anything about the general situation of the world," he told Ernest Jones in April 1932. "Perhaps we are only repeating the ridiculous action of saving a bird cage while the house is burning down." Having few analysands, he spent the spring and summer working on the *New Introductory Lectures.* Despite all the political turmoil, the 1920s had, especially in mid-decade, enjoyed heady prospects of recovery. But these were specious, or in any event fragile and evanescent; the Great Depression, erupting in the fall of 1929, changed everything.

One of its most calamitous consequences was the meteoric rise of Hitler's Nazi party. In the Reichstag elections of 1928, it had had to be content with twelve seats; in the September elections of 1930, it was catapulted into sinister prominence with 107 seats, second only to the Social Democrats. What had happened was plain enough: Germany's new voters, and voters despairing of middle-class parties paralyzed by rising unemployment, bank failures, commercial bankruptcies, to say nothing of conflicting prescriptions, flocked to Hitler's standard. The Weimar Republic lingered on until January

1933, but after the elections of 1930 it was governed by Heinrich Brüning, a conservative Catholic, under emergency decrees. The country was on its way to join the totalitarian wave.

The brief and in the end tragic history of the Weimar Republic attests how much dry tinder, serviceable for new conflagrations, had been accumulating in the wake of the First World War. The Depression, far more destructive than the business cycles long endemic to modern capitalism, set the kindling aflame. The New York stock market collapsed on October 29, 1929, but "Black Tuesday" was far more a melodramatic symptom of underlying economic maladjustments than their cause. Hence the crash quickly left its imprint on vulnerable European economies, desperately dependent on American capital and American customers. The forbidding tariffs that the United States Congress passed in 1930, coupled with American inflexibility about collecting war debts, were signs that Europe's fragile financial structures could expect little help from that quarter. When in July 1931 President Hoover proposed a moratorium on war debts, it was too late. While vindictive and bungling politicians wrangled, investors saw their speculations collapse and millions of ordinary people their savings evaporate. Only someone like William Bullitt could find these disasters stimulating.

IN THE WORLD-WIDE calamity, Austrians were no better off than others, worse off than most. Beset by political unrest and economic hardship, they did not wait for the collapse of stock markets and banks to engage in bloody clashes. In July 15, 1927, pitched battles took place in Vienna between police and demonstrators. Several right-wing assassins, guilty beyond question of committing political crimes, had been acquitted by a complaisant jury, and this blatant miscarriage of justice brought the Social Democrats into the streets. The day's balance: eighty-nine dead and a disastrous weakening of the Socialists' moderate wing. "This summer is really catastrophic," Freud wrote to Ferenczi from Semmering, his vacation resort, "as though a large comet stood in the sky. Now we hear of a riot in Vienna, are almost all cut off and without deeper information as to what is going on there and what will become of it. It is a rotten affair."

Freud could not have chosen a better adjective. "Nothing has happened," he reassured his nephew in Manchester two weeks later, meaning that nothing untoward had happened to him or his family. But, he added, there were "bad social and material conditions in Vienna." When, a few years later, Austrian followers of Hitler began to import the German Nazis' terrorist tactics, the end of republican institutions was only a matter of time. "General conditions," Freud informed his nephew Samuel at the end of 1930, "are especially dreary in Austria."

Early in 1931, the veto of France, Italy, and other powers frustrated Austria's proposal for a customs union with Germany; their decision, ratified by the World Court in the fall, was yet another step into disaster for the Austrians. In May of that year, the Creditanstalt, Vienna's largest commercial bank, with strong ties to banks in other countries, was forced to report insolvency; it was saved from failure only through government intervention. But the withdrawal of confidence, and of assets, from the bank reverberated in neighboring economies, all tied into the international system like so many mountaineers roped together. "Public conditions, as you may know," Freud told his nephew in December 1931, "are going from bad to worse."

While Freud could not completely insulate himself from these dismaying events, he was protected from economic hardship by his solid income, most of it from foreign analytic "pupils" paying their fees in hard currency. Some members of his family were less fortunate. "All my three sons have their job," Freud noted in 1931, but his sons-in-law were not earning a living. "Robert [Hollitscher] does not make a penny in his business and Max [Halberstadt] is struggling wearily against the collapse of Hamburg life. They live by the allowance I can give them." Fortunately, he could afford it. He was not working full time any more, but his substantial fee, twenty-five dollars for an analytic hour, enabled him to support his extended family and save money at the same time.*

BY LATE 1931, Great Britain had gone off the gold standard, American banks were failing in appalling numbers, and everywhere unemployment had risen to fearful heights. In 1932, more than five and a half million were out of work in Germany, nearly three million in Britain. The index of production tells the alarming story in cold figures: if the index for 1929 is taken as 100, by 1932 it had dropped to 84 in Britain, to 67 in Italy, to 53 in the United States and in Germany. The human cost was incalculable. Personal tragedies—promising careers aborted, sudden poverty, educated men selling shoelaces or apples on street corners, proud bourgeois taking handouts from their relatives— became commonplace everywhere. In the courtyards of apartment houses in German cities, wandering bands, hoping for a few *Pfennige*, sang a lachrymose ditty about unemployment—*Arbeitslosigkeit.* Meanwhile in the United

---

*This fee was not necessarily firm. Freud, who at times treated patients without charge, was willing to make allowances for his patients' financial reverses. When the American Smiley Blanton came back into brief analysis with Freud in 1935, after having worked with him in 1929 and 1930, he asked whether the fee was still the same as before. Freud assented and then asked Blanton whether it would be convenient for him to continue paying it. "The tone of his voice and the implication of his manner was plainly that he would reduce the fee if I could not afford the usual sum of $25 an hour." (Smiley Blanton, *Diary of My Analysis with Sigmund Freud* [1971], 63–64.)

States, Bing Crosby gave mellow voice to the very unmellow refrain "Brother, can you spare a dime?" By October 1932, Yip Harburg's pathetic song had reached the Top Ten—evidently it spoke to an overwhelming preoccupation. The political consequences were quite predictable: economic misery generated the despairing search for panaceas. This was a time for the sellers of nostrums; as seductive orators flourished, the reasonable middle lost support.

Austria was spared nothing. A high rate of joblessness was not new for the country; from 1923 on, just under 10 percent of the labor force had been out of work. That average figure conceals some harsh realities: in pockets of the Austrian economy, such as the metal industry, as many as three workers in ten were looking for a job. But by the time the Creditanstalt nearly collapsed, Austrians recalled those statistics with some envy, for unemployment now mounted to unheard-of heights. In 1932, almost 470,000 people, nearly 22 percent of Austria's labor force, were out of work; and in February 1933, joblessness reached an unprecedented peak with 580,000, or 27 percent. With factories closing and social insurance pathetically inadequate, whole regions of the country were being deserted or were largely occupied by the unemployed and their families. Many succumbed to resignation after frantic and futile searches for work, and took to sitting about in parks and spending essential resources on drink, but a good number of the young, who graduated from school to the bread lines, became interested in the quack remedies that Austrian Nazis and their like tried to sell. "That you have not yet, at 60, bagged the dragon of unreason," Freud, watching all this, comforted Pfister in the spring of 1932, "should not offend you. I have at 76 not done any better with it, and it will withstand quite a few other battles. It is tougher than we are."

FROM LATE 1932 on, the Christian Social chancellor Engelbert Dollfuss governed under emergency legislation in Austria just as Brüning was doing in Germany; early the following year, the Germans provided him with a model for still more authoritarian rule. The Nazis demonstrated to the Austrians, and anyone else who was interested, just how to assassinate democracy. Hitler was appointed Germany's chancellor on January 30, 1933, and in the next few months he systematically rooted out political parties, parliamentary institutions, free speech and the free press, independent cultural organizations and universities, and the rule of law. From March 1933 on, Dollfuss followed Hitler part of the way: he governed without parliament. But the Nazi regime went much further; it opened concentration camps for political opponents and initiated government by mendacity, intimidation, proscription, and murder. Socialists, democrats, inconvenient conservatives, Jews, were "purged" from government posts and professorships, newspapers and publishing houses, orchestras and theaters. Racial anti-Semitism became government policy.

Among the first German Jews to leave their country—no longer theirs—were psychoanalysts, including Max Eitingon and Otto Fenichel, Erich Fromm and Ernst Simmel, and more than fifty others. Seeking refuge abroad, they found that in a world gripped by depression and a certain defensive xenophobia, they were not very welcome. So desperate had the times become that even some of the Dutch, usually immune to the bacillus of anti-Semitism, showed themselves susceptible to what one Dutch analyst, Westerman Holstijn, called "nazistic-narcissistic" regressions. Two of Freud's sons, Oliver and Ernst, who had settled in the Weimar Republic, also thought it wise to emigrate. For them, Freud wrote his nephew Samuel in Manchester, "life in Germany has become impossible." Oliver went to France for a time, Ernst to England to stay.

On May 10, 1933, the Nazis included Freud in their persecutions indirectly, in a spectacular burning of books. "The exclusion of 'Left,' democratic, and Jewish literature took precedence over everything else," the German historian Karl Dietrich Bracher has written. "The blacklists that were being compiled beginning in April, 1933," included the writings of German Social Democrats like August Bebel and Eduard Bernstein, of Hugo Preuss, the father of the Weimar constitution, of poets and novelists (both Thomas and Heinrich Mann were on the list), and of scientists like Albert Einstein. "The catalogue went back far enough to include literature from Heine and Marx to Kafka. The book burnings staged on May 10, 1933, in the public squares of cities and university towns symbolized the auto-da-fé of a century of German culture. Accompanied by torchlight parades of students and passionate orations of professors, but staged by the Propaganda Ministry, this barbaric act ushered in an epoch which Heinrich Heine had summed up by the prophetic words that there where one burns books, one ultimately also burns people." Psychoanalytic publications, Freud's books in the vanguard, were not missing from the great burning of culture.

These were "mad times," Freud exclaimed to Lou Andreas-Salomé four days after this theatrical event. His friends agreed, in tones as strong as his. "Last week," Pfister wrote to Freud late that month, "I was briefly in Germany and caught a disgust that I won't get rid of for a long time. Proletarian militarism smells even more rotten than the blue-blooded Junker spirit of the Wilhelmine era. Cowardly against others, it takes out its childish rage against defenseless Jews and even plunders libraries." Freud could still manage to be sardonic and amused. "What progress we are making," he said to Ernest Jones. "In the Middle Ages they would have burnt me; nowadays they are content with burning my books." This must have been the least prescient bon mot he ever made.

Life in Vienna went on more and more precariously, as the embrace of Austria by its powerful neighbors, Fascist Italy and Nazi Germany, tightened and became more threatening. Still, Freud's letters in the first year of Hitler's regime, though bleak and irate, were leavened with optimism. In March 1933—in one of his last letters to Freud—Ferenczi fondly, frantically, entreated Freud to get out of Austria. Freud would not hear of it. He was too old, he replied, too ill, too dependent on his physicians and on his comforts. Nor was it certain, he reassured himself and Ferenczi, "that the Hitler regime will also overwhelm Austria. It is indeed possible, but everyone believes that things here will not reach the height of brutality they have in Germany." He acknowledged that he was letting his judgment be swayed in part by emotions and rationalizations. But "there is, I suppose, no personal danger." He concluded firmly: "Flight would be justified, I believe, only if there were a direct danger to life." In April, in a long letter to Ernest Jones, he sounded rather the way many Germans had sounded about the Nazis the year before. Austrian Nazism, he suggested, would doubtless be contained by the other parties of the Right. As an old Austrian liberal, he understood that a dictatorship of right-wing parties would be exceedingly unpleasant for Jews. But he could not imagine discriminatory laws, since the peace treaties expressly forbade them and the League of Nations would surely step in. "And as for Austria joining Germany, in which case the Jews would lose all their rights, France and its allies would never allow that." Naturally, he remarked cautiously some weeks later, "the future still depends on what will develop from the German witches' cauldron." But like most of his contemporaries, he had not yet grasped the truth that the League, or France, or its allies, would prove exceedingly feeble once put to the test.

Writing to Ferenczi, he had spoken of rationalizations. It was the right word. While Hitler stopped short of launching an invasion of Austria so soon after taking power, he was stirring up Austrian Nazis and their paramilitary sympathizers. But for a time, at least, Mussolini served as Austria's protector against Nazi Germany's ambitions. Meanwhile the bulletins emanating from the Freud household, though displaying some concern, were pervaded by denial. The future, Freud told his nephew Samuel in the summer of 1933, was exceedingly murky. "You know from the papers (I am now a regular reader of the Manst. Guardian) how unassured our situation in Austria is. The only thing I can say is that we are determined to stick it out here to the last. Perhaps it may not come out too bad." He was analyzing five hours a day, he told the American poet Hilda Doolittle, a former analysand, in October 1933, and was quite pleased that their work together now showed results: "I am deeply satisfied to hear that you are writing, creating; that is why we dived into the depths of your unconscious mind, I remember." He expected to stay put. "I don't think I will come to London as your kind friends surmise—there may be no provocations to leave Vienna."

But there were provocations enough before long, and emigration increasingly presented itself to Freud as a possible course of action—presented itself only to be rejected. He did not relish the prospect of being a refugee: in early April 1933, he had asked Ferenczi to consider how unpleasant exile would be, whether in England or Switzerland. But a year later, he sounded less confident; he warned Pfister that if he did not come to Vienna soon, "we will hardly see one another again in this life." Air travel was now out of the question. He had tried it once, in 1930, but would not again. Besides, he added, "if I should be forced to emigrate, I would not choose Switzerland, which is notorious as especially inhospitable." In any event, everyone believed that what Austria could expect was "a moderate fascism, whatever that may be!"

A few days before Freud sent this letter, in mid-February, Chancellor Dollfuss had given a hint of what such a fascism might be; he repressed a Socialist-led political strike in Vienna with all the force at his command. He outlawed the Social Democrats and the small Communist party, arrested the Socialists' officials, had their leaders transported into camps. Some escaped abroad, others were imprisoned, a few executed. "Our bit of civil war wasn't pretty at all," Freud reported to Arnold Zweig. "One couldn't go out into the street without identification, the power broke down for a day, the thought that the water might fail was very discomfiting." A few days later, he recalled the same events for Hilda Doolittle: there had been a week of civil war, "not much personal suffering, just one day without electric light, but the 'Stimmung' was awful and the feeling as of an earthquake."

He pitied the victims, but rather frigidly. "No doubt," he told H. D., "the rebels belonged to the best portion of the population, but their success would have been very short-lived and brought about military invasion of the country. Besides they were Bolshevists and I expect no salvation from Communism. So we could not give our sympathy to either side of the combatants." He wrote caustically to his son Ernst, "Naturally, the victors are now the heroes and the saviors of sacred order, the others the impudent rebels." But he refused to condemn the Dollfuss regime too severely: "With the dictatorship of the proletariat, which was the goal of the so-called leaders, one cannot live either." The victors would of course now make all the mistakes in their power, and the future remained uncertain: "Either an Austrian fascism or the swastika. In the latter case, we should have to go." But the sanguinary events of February turned Freud's mind to *Romeo and Juliet,* and he quoted to Arnold Zweig, now uneasily settled in Palestine, Shakespeare's Mercutio: "A plague on both your houses."

Freud's neutrality was in part astute, in part imperceptive. A victory of the Left in Austria's "bit of civil war" might indeed have brought German troops pouring across the border. It is true enough as well that the Communists had participated in the February uprising and that the Social Democrats had never formally renounced their revolutionary program. But the share of the "Bolshevists" in the events of February 1934 was both honorable and minor, and the actions of the Social Democrats bore little resemblance to their radical rhetoric. Freud would have done the February disorders greater justice had he confined his condemnation to the suppressors and spared the suppressed.

ONE WAY OF mastering his feeling of impotence was, Freud found, to indulge in speculations about the political outlook. "Things can't go on like this," he predicted to Arnold Zweig in late February 1934. "Something is bound to happen." Like someone in a hotel room, he added, he was waiting for the second shoe to drop. The situation reminded him of "The Lady or the Tiger?" As he dimly and somewhat inaccurately remembered the story, a poor prisoner in a Roman arena waits to find out whether from a closed door there will emerge a tiger to devour him or a lady to marry him. Hitler might invade Austria; the local brand of fascists might take over; the Habsburg crown prince, Otto, who had not relinquished his claims to the throne, might restore the old regime. Pondering his course in the midst of all this turmoil, Freud allowed a note of pathos to creep into the letter: "We want to hold out here in resignation. After all, where should I go in my dependence and physical helplessness? And abroad is so inhospitable everywhere." He was forgetting all the offers of asylum in this moment of self-pity. But he acknowledged that if a "Hitlerian viceroy" were to govern Vienna, he would have to go, no matter where.

Freud's reluctance to leave Vienna became a refrain in his letters. He could not quite bring himself to foresee a Nazi viceroy in Austria, and his routine anchored him in his accustomed place. He was still analyzing and writing; was pleased to note that his works were being translated into such esoteric languages as Hebrew, Chinese, and Japanese; enjoyed the presents of antique statuettes that thoughtful friends brought him. He was receiving visitors at Berggasse 19. His uprooted sons, Ernst and Oliver, came to see him. Analysands and associates from across the world—Max Eitingon, Edoardo Weiss, William Bullitt, Marie Bonaparte, Jeanne Lampl-de Groot, Arnold

Zweig—stopped by. The calls of new admirers like H. G. Wells were important enough to be recorded in his *Chronik*. Compared with such a life, emigration could only be worse. In any event, Freud told Hilda Doolittle, "I know I am overdue and whatever I still have is an unexpected gift. Nor is it too painful a thought to leave this scene and set of phenomena for good. There is not much left to be regretted, times are cruel and the future appears to be disastrous."

During these dismal years, Hitler contributed to Freud's enjoyment just once, but then he gave Freud unmixed satisfaction. On June 30, 1934, Hitler had a number of his old comrades, whom he professed to fear as rivals and conspirators, routed out of bed and summarily shot. The most prominent of his victims was Ernst Röhm, leader of the brown-shirted Nazi militia, the S.A., and Röhm had company in sudden death, perhaps as many as two hundred others. Obligingly, the controlled Nazi press trumpeted the bloody purge as a necessary cleansing that rid the movement of homosexuals and power-mad schemers. For Hitler the result was undisputed dominance over his Third Reich. But Freud, rejoicing, saw only the immediate reality: Nazis killing Nazis. "Events in Germany," he wrote Arnold Zweig, "remind me by way of contrast of an experience in the summer of 1920. It was the first Congress in The Hague, outside our prison." For many Austrian, German, and Hungarian analysts this had been the first trip abroad since the war. "Even today it still does me good to recall how kind our Dutch colleagues were toward the starved and seedy Central Europeans. At the end of the Congress, they gave us a dinner of authentic Dutch sumptuousness, for which we were not allowed to pay anything. But we had forgotten how to eat it. As the hors d'oeuvres were handed around, they tasted good to us all, and then we were done, we could not take any more. And now the contrast! After the news of June 30, I had only one sentiment: What! After the hors d'oeuvres I should get up from table! And there is nothing more! I am still hungry."

Unfortunately, there was to be nothing more to satisfy Freud's appetite for revenge. In July 1934, Chancellor Dollfuss was murdered by Austrian Nazis in an abortive coup, abortive only because Mussolini was not yet ready to surrender Austria to the Germans. Hitler, poised for invasion but willing to wait, retreated. The Austrian republic would survive under emergency decrees, as it had done under Dollfuss, for four more years. "One's pent-up rage," Freud had written to Lou Andreas-Salomé in the spring of 1934, "uses one up, or whatever was left of one's earlier ego. And one does not form a new one at 78."

Defiance as Identity

Paradoxically, these were good years for Freud to be a Jew. He found hard times for Jews particularly suitable for proclaiming his "racial" loyalties, and these were hard times for Jews. The Depression and the political turmoil had put rational solutions at a discount and provided, especially in Central Europe, fertile soil for anti-Semites. But unlike Adler, who converted to Protestantism, or Rank, who had briefly turned to Roman Catholicism, Freud never rejected, or concealed, his ancestry. We know that in the autobiographical sketch he wrote in 1924, he noted explicitly, even a little truculently, that his parents had been Jews and that he, too, had remained a Jew. He made the same point, just as emphatically, two years later, when in May his brethren at B'nai B'rith lavishly celebrated his seventieth birthday. They organized a festive meeting filled with oratory, and devoted a special number of the *B'nai B'rith Mitteilungen* to their most famous member. In thanks, Freud recalled the early days after 1897, when he had joined B'nai B'rith: "That you are Jews could only be welcome to me, for I was a Jew myself, and it had always seemed to me not only undignified, but quite nonsensical, to deny it." When he was nearly eighty, he said it again: "I hope it is not unknown to you," he wrote to a Dr. Siegfried Fehl, "that I have always held faithfully to our people, and never pretended to be anything but what I am: a Jew from Moravia whose parents come from Austrian Galicia."

But in the poisonous atmosphere of the late 1920s and early 1930s he did more than refuse to deny his Jewish origins. He trumpeted them. Freud's attitude toward Judaism throughout his life reveals this largely unconscious strategy. In 1873, during his first year at the university, he had discovered that he was supposed to feel inferior because of his "race." His response was defiance: he saw no reason to bow to the verdict of the majority. Later, in 1897, it was when he felt virtually alone with his subversive discoveries that he joined a new local B'nai B'rith lodge and occasionally lectured there; once he found some like-minded physicians eager, and able, to absorb his ideas, he attended fewer meetings and gave fewer talks. Again, in 1908, struggling to keep his gentile Swiss recruits in line, he pleaded in letters to his Jewish intimates, Abraham and Ferenczi, for patience and tact, singling out the "racial" affinities that bound them together as essential ground for sympathetic cooperation at this critical moment.

Disturbing political developments had a very similar, if somewhat slower, effect on him. In 1895, after Franz Josef had refused to install the anti-Semitic politician Karl Lueger as mayor of Vienna even though the popular vote had gone his way, Freud celebrated by indulging in proscribed cigars. But the emperor could only postpone Lueger's accession to office, not prevent it; by 1897, the year Freud became a member of B'nai B'rith, Lueger had been installed. A dream Freud dreamt early in 1898, after seeing Theodor Herzl's play about anti-Semitism, *The New Ghetto,* reads like a virtual response to the political situation; he dreamt about "the Jewish question, the worry about the future of one's children, whom one could not give a homeland." Herzl is an interesting dream instigator. Freud, who was well acquainted with Herzl's message, watched the development of Zionism with benign interest, but did not become active in the movement.* Still, it is striking that he should allow Herzl, the eloquent champion of a Jewish homeland, to enter his dream life and help define his sense of what it meant to be a Jew in an anti-Semitic culture. But as we have seen, Freud's political education took some time. What is striking about his correspondence of the late 1890s, when the "Jewish question" became acute in Austria, is not how much Freud commented on politics, but how little. After the First World War, though, his defiant responses became more emphatic. We recall that interview of June 1926 in which, appalled by the burgeoning of political anti-Semitism, Freud displayed the importance of adversity for his Jewish identification by renouncing his German identification.†

---

*"Zionism," he wrote to J. Dwossis, in Jerusalem, who was translating some of his writings into Hebrew, "has awakened my strongest sympathies, which still attach me to it. From the beginning," he noted, he had been concerned about it, "something the present-day situation seems to justify. I should like to be mistaken about this." (Freud to Dwossis, December 15, 1930. Typescript copy, Freud Museum, London.) His most sustained comment on Zionism came in a letter to Albert Einstein. Apparently Einstein had asked Freud to make a public statement on the issue, and Freud refused: "Whoever wants to influence a crowd, must have something resounding, enthusiastic to say, and my sober appraisal of Zionism does not permit this." He professed his sympathy for the movement, declared that he was "proud" of "our" University of Jerusalem and took pleasure in the flourishing of "our" settlements. "On the other hand I do not believe that Palestine will ever become a Jewish state, and that the Christian or the Islamic world will ever be prepared to leave their shrines in Jewish hands. It would have seemed more comprehensible to me to found a Jewish fatherland on new, historically unencumbered soil." He was aware, he added, that such a "rational" attitude would never enlist "the enthusiasm of the masses and the resources of the rich." But he regretted to see the "unrealistic fanaticism" of his fellow Jews awakening the suspicions of the Arabs. "I can muster no sympathy whatever for the misguided piety that makes a national religion from a piece of the wall of Herod, and for its sake challenges the feelings of the local natives." (Freud to Einstein, February 26, 1930. Freud Collection, B3, LC.)

†See p. 448.

FREUD'S JEWISH IDENTIFICATION was emphatically secular. The intellectual and ethical gulf between those Jews who had themselves baptized and Freud, who disdained this road to acceptability, was unbridgeable, but the gulf between Freud and those who continued to practice the faith of their fathers was no less forbidding. Freud was as much an atheist as he was a Jew. In fact, he seems to have found the near veneration with which B'nai B'rith claimed him as its own a little embarrassing and quite amusing. "Altogether," he wrote to Marie Bonaparte in May 1926, after his seventieth birthday, "the Jews have celebrated me like a national hero, although my merit in the Jewish cause is confined to the single point that I have never denied my Judaism." It was a rather distant self-definition—his phrase, "the Jews," makes him seem a stranger even among those who believed themselves to be his brothers.

He would tirelessly reiterate this point, especially in his later years, as though he wanted no one to misconceive his position. "I adhere to the Jewish religion as little as to any other," he told one correspondent in 1929; he had said the same thing before and would say it again, to anyone who inquired. "The Jews," he wrote to Arthur Schnitzler as he had to Marie Bonaparte, "have seized upon my person from all sides and all places with enthusiasm, as though I were a God-fearing great rabbi. I have nothing against it, after I have clarified my position toward faith unequivocally. Judaism still means a great deal to me emotionally." In 1930, in his preface for a Hebrew translation of *Totem and Taboo,* he described himself once again as a man "wholly alienated from the religion of his fathers—as from every other," who "cannot participate in nationalist ideals and yet has never denied his affiliation with his people." When a devout American physician told Freud of the religious vision that had sent him to Christ, and urged him to study the matter that he, too, might find God, Freud demurred politely but firmly. God had not done that much for him, had sent him no inner voices, and he was therefore likely to remain in his last few years "an infidel Jew."

Freud underscored his infidelity by forgetting the little Hebrew he had ever known. As a schoolboy, he had studied religion with his admired teacher, later his friend and benefactor, Samuel Hammerschlag. But Hammerschlag, an inspired and inspiring classroom performer, had emphasized the ethical values and historical experience of the Jewish people at the expense of grammar and vocabulary. In his youth, Freud recalled, "our freethinking religion teachers set no store by their pupils' acquiring knowledge in the Hebrew language and literature." What is more, he had had no practice in the Hebrew language and saw no use for it. To be sure, on Freud's thirty-fifth birthday, his father had given him a Bible complete with an affectionate, flowery inscription in Hebrew, rhapsodizing over the spirit of God speaking to his seven-year-old son. It was, obviously enough, the gift of one Jew to another, but the gift of an enlightened, probably unobservant Jew.* In any event, Freud blamed his father, "who spoke the holy language as well as German or better," for letting him grow up "in complete ignorance of everything that concerned Judaism."† That Jacob Freud wrote the inscription in Hebrew did not imply that he expected his son to read it. Actually, Freud's inability to read Hebrew was a matter of some regret to him. In 1928, when he wrote to thank J. Dwossis for his translation of *Group Psychology and the Analysis of the Ego*, he said that he had relied on the assurances of an unnamed relative "who is master of our sacred old and now renewed tongue" that the translation was really excellent.‡

Freud's rigorous secularism did not permit the slightest trace of religious observance to survive in his domestic life. The Freuds studiously ignored even the companionable Jewish family holidays, like Passover, which Freud's parents had continued to celebrate despite their emancipation from tradition. Ruthlessly, Freud swept aside his wife's youthful orthodoxy, much to her pain and regret. "Our festivals," Freud's son Martin recalled, "were Christmas, with presents under a candle-lit tree, and Easter, with gaily painted Easter eggs. I had never been in a synagogue, nor to my knowledge had my brothers or sisters."§ Martin Freud joined Kadimah, a Zionist student organization,

---

*"If the dedication is analyzed as a Hebrew document it becomes apparent that Jacob Freud was neither a religious nor a nationalist Jew, but a member of the Haskala, a movement that saw Judaism as epitomizing the religion of enlightenment. No orthodox Jew would speak lightly about the Spirit of God speaking to a seven-year-old. Nor would any religious Jew see the Bible as belonging to mankind as a whole." (Martin S. Bergmann, "Moses and the Evolution of Freud's Jewish Identity," *Israel Annals of Psychiatry and Related Disciplines*, XIV [March 1976], 4.)

†In 1930, A. A. Roback, an American Yiddishist and psychologist, sent one of his books to Freud with an inscription in Hebrew. Freud, acknowledging the gift, observed that his father, though from a "Hassidic milieu," had been "estranged from his home-town associations for almost twenty years." He added, "I had such a non-Jewish upbringing that today I am not even able to read your dedication which is evidently in Hebrew characters. In later years I have often regretted this gap in my education." (Roback, *Freudiana* [1957], 57.)

‡A casual comment to Fliess in 1895 discloses that this was not a lacuna of which Freud complained only in his last years. Fliess had sent him an observation about anxiety in the naked Adam's feeling of shame before the Lord, and Freud, who found the comment "striking," told Fliess he would like to consult the passage and "ask a Hebrew [that is, someone who reads Hebrew] about the meaning of the language." (Freud to Fliess, April 27, 1895. *Freud–Fliess*, 128 [127].)

§This authoritative recollection invalidates the statement by Freud's nephew Harry that Freud was, though "thoroughly *antireligious . . . by no means an atheist.* He just did not think much of rites and dogmas and rebelled against every religious compulsion or religious obligation. He did not keep the high holidays and hardly ever went to the synagogue." (Richard Dyck, "Mein Onkel Sigmund," interview with Harry Freud in *Aufbau* [New York], May 11, 1956, 3.) If Freud went to the synagogue ever, it must have been for a memorial service for one of his friends. But there is no evidence that he ever did.

after the war, and his brother Ernst became active in editing a Zionist periodical, steps their father seems to have greeted with approval, or at least treated as his sons' business. But the ignorance of Freud's children about Jewish observances was as radical as his own. When Martin Freud got married, he had to go through a religious ceremony as required by Austrian law; all dressed up, he entered the sanctuary, and took off his top hat as a sign of respect for a holy place. The escort on his left, better informed, firmly jammed the hat back on Martin Freud's head. But the groom, unable to believe that one kept one's head covered during a religious ceremony, took it off again, whereupon his escort on the right repeated the gesture, putting Martin Freud's hat back on. This episode exemplifies the secularism that Freud fostered in his family. He was far more Jewish in the face of anti-Semites than he was at home.

At the same time, Freud believed that there was some elusive, indefinable element that made him a Jew. What tied him to Judaism, he wrote to the brethren at B'nai B'rith in 1926, was not faith, "for I was always an unbeliever, was brought up without religion though not without respect for the demands, called 'ethical,' of human culture." Nor was it national pride, which he thought pernicious and unjust. "But enough else remained to make the attraction of Judaism and of Jews so irresistible, many dark emotional powers, all the mightier the less they let themselves be grasped in words, as well as the clear consciousness of inner identity, the secrecy of the same mental construction." Freud might insist on his "clear consciousness" of Jewish identity, but these shadowy intimations obscure as much as they clarify. They invite intuitive assent but scarcely constitute rational analysis.

Yet they are a concrete consequence of Freud's belief in the inheritance of acquired characteristics; in some mysterious way his Jewishness, his identifying quality, had to be part of his phylogenetic inheritance. He never explored how this Lamarckian "racial" endowment worked in himself, but he was convinced it was there. In 1922, he exclaimed to Ferenczi that he was impatient with having to earn money, face a contemptible world, come to terms with his aging. "Strange secret longings," he wrote, were rising up within him, "perhaps from the heritage of my ancestors from the Orient and the Mediterranean, and for a life of quite another kind, wishes from late childhood unrealizable and ill-adapted to reality." These obscure yearnings continued to intrigue him. Ten years later, in 1932, he wrote to Arnold Zweig, who had just returned from Palestine, "And we hail from there (although one of us also thinks himself a German, the other not), our ancestors have perhaps lived there through half a millennium, perhaps a whole one (but that, too, only 'perhaps'), and it is impossible to say what we have taken along in blood and nerves (as one incorrectly puts it) as a heritage from life in that country." It was all very puzzling: "Oh, life could be very interesting if one only knew and understood more about it."

One may read Freud's passion for antiquities in the light of these puzzlements. No doubt it was richly overdetermined. But one of the unmistakable meanings of his statuettes and plaques was that they reminded him of a world he would never visit, yet he thought was somehow mysteriously his own. This is the message Freud wanted to convey in his preface to the Hebrew translation of *Totem and Taboo*: he had given up a great deal he had in common with other Jews, but what remained of his Jewishness was "still a great deal, probably the main thing." He could not express this "essence" in words, at least not yet. "Surely it will some day be accessible to scientific insight." This was Freud the researcher at work: his feeling of Jewish identity, enigmatic and beyond science for the present, had to be like Romain Rolland's oceanic feeling—a psychological phenomenon open in principle to investigation.

While the essence of Jewishness, or his personal Jewish identity, might resist analysis, Freud saw no obscurities in the implications of being a Jew in his society. A stranger to the faith of his fathers and resentful of powerful anti-Semitic elements in the Austria in which he must live and work, he felt doubly alienated. Freud saw himself, in short, as a marginal man and thought that this position gave him an inestimable advantage. Late in 1918, he concluded a cordial letter to Oskar Pfister with a pair of provocative questions: "Quite by the way, why did none of the devout create psychoanalysis? Why did one have to wait for a completely godless Jew?" Pfister, not at all disconcerted, replied that piety was not the same as the discoverer's genius and that most of the pious were incapable of such achievements. Besides, Pfister was disposed to see his friend Freud as neither godless nor Jewish: "A better Christian never was."

Freud did not comment directly on this well-meant, if dubious, compliment.* But he knew the answer to his own questions, and it differed decisively from Pfister's cheery and maladroit praise. As we know, his exclusion from "Austrianness" at the university had given him an early familiarity with being in opposition, and thus prepared the way for "a certain independence of judgment." In 1925, exploring the widespread resistance to psychoanalysis, he suggested that one cause must be that its founder was a Jew who had never made a secret of his origins. The year after that, in his letter to his fellow members of B'nai B'rith, he made this point somewhat more expansively. He

---

*Reading this letter some years later, Anna Freud exclaimed, with justice, "What in the world does Pfister mean here and why does he want to dispute the fact that my father is a Jew, instead of accepting it?" (Anna Freud to Ernest Jones, July 12, 1954. Jones papers, Archives of the British Psycho-Analytical Society, London.)

had discovered "that I owe only to my Jewish nature the two characteristics that had become indispensable on my difficult life's way. Because I was a Jew, I found myself free from many prejudices which limited others in the employment of their intellects, and as a Jew I was prepared to go into opposition." In his own way, and for his own purposes, Freud was willing to credit the anti-Semite's charge that Jews are bound to be cleverer than the majority.

The thesis is plausible but far from complete or, for that matter, conclusive. Other Jews, their position just as marginal as Freud's, had themselves baptized or went into business with their nominal Judaism intact, joined the Communist party or emigrated to America, and by and large showed themselves no smarter or more original than anyone else. On the other hand Darwin, to whom Freud is perhaps best compared, was securely at home in the English establishment and remained so even after he published his *Origin of Species*. There is something to Freud's observation that a devout Jew, or Christian, could never have discovered psychoanalysis: it was too iconoclastic, too disrespectful of religious faith and too disdainful of apologetics. Since Freud considered religious faith—all religious faith, including Judaism—as a subject of psychoanalytic study, he could approach it only from the perspective of the atheist. It is no accident that Darwin, too—though not marginal—should have been an atheist.

While it does not follow, then, that only a marginal man—in particular, a marginal Jew—could have done Freud's lifework, the precarious status of Jews in Austrian society did probably underlie the notorious fact that nearly all the first psychoanalysts in Vienna were Jewish. Their society permitted them to train as physicians but did not let them feel particularly welcome among the conventional medical elite. "I imagine," Ernest Jones wrote in his autobiography, reflecting about the Jewish phenomenon in psychoanalysis, "the reasons for this were mainly local ones in Austria and Germany, since, except to some slight extent in the United States, it is a feature that has not been repeated in any other country." He thought it obvious that in Vienna it was "easier for Jewish doctors to share Freud's ostracism, which was only an exacerbation of the life they were accustomed to, and the same was true of Berlin and Budapest, where anti-Semitism was almost equally pronounced."* In the face of social conservatism compounded by bigotry, the early psychoanalysts found a measure of toughness to be a highly adaptive quality.

Moreover, as we have seen, a mood of defiance pervaded Freud's temper.

---

*However, Jones, who had some primitive notions about national and racial qualities, goes on to generalize rather in Freud's way about the Jews' "aptness for psychological intuition, and their ability to withstand public obloquy," which, he thinks, "may also have contributed to this state of affairs." (*Free Associations*, 209.)

He took pleasure in being the leader of the opposition, the unmasker of shams, the nemesis of self-deception and illusions. He was proud of his enemies—the persecuting Roman Catholic Church, the hypocritical bourgeoisie, the obtuse psychiatric establishment, the materialistic Americans—so proud, indeed, that they grew in his mind into potent specters far more malevolent and far less divided than they were in reality. He likened himself to Hannibal, to Ahasuerus, to Joseph, to Moses, all men with historic missions, potent adversaries, and difficult fates. In a much-quoted early letter, Freud had told his fiancée, "One would hardly know to look at me, but already in school I was always a bold man of the opposition, was always where one could avow an extreme and, as a rule, had to atone for it." One evening, Breuer had told him "he had found out that there was hidden in me, beneath the cover of shyness, an immoderately bold and fearless person. I have always believed this, and simply never dared to tell it to anyone. I have often felt as though I had inherited all the obstinacy and all the passions of our ancestors when they defended their temple, as though I could throw away my life with joy for a great moment."

This, to be sure, was the outburst of a youthful lover posturing before the woman he wanted to marry. But Freud was like that, and remained like that, always. His exposed position as a Jew gave him ample opportunity to cultivate this stance; his even more exposed position as a psychoanalyst tested and hardened it across the years. But Freud was unique in his endowment no less than in the particular form of his family constellation and his mental development. In the end, unsatisfactory as it sounds, one comes back to Freud's own disclaimer that before creativity the psychoanalyst must put down his arms. Freud was Freud.

THE SPIRIT OF defiance that pressed Freud to proclaim his Jewishness in times of troubles also animates his last sustained work, *Moses and Monotheism*, though with a rather different target. Many of its apprehensive or infuriated readers would see it as an unfortunate reversal; with this speculative study of Moses, Freud seemed to be intent on wounding Jews instead of defending them. The work is a curious production, more conjectural than *Totem and Taboo*, more untidy than *Inhibitions, Symptoms and Anxiety*, more offensive than *The Future of an Illusion*. Its very form is peculiar. The book as finally printed late in 1938 consists of three closely linked essays of very unequal length: "Moses an Egyptian" is a rapid sketch covering a mere handful of pages; "If Moses Was an Egyptian . . ." is four times as long; the third essay, "Moses, His People and Monotheistic Religion," occupies a good deal more space than the first two put together. What is more, this concluding essay is equipped with two initial prefaces that largely cancel each other out and a third preface, to Part II, right in the middle, and is crowded with material deliberately repeated from the earlier papers. This is not senility; to read *Moses and Monotheism* is to participate in its making, in the internal and the political pressures acting on Freud during these years, and to catch echoes from earlier, less harrowing times.

The figure of Moses, Freud told Lou Andreas-Salomé in 1935, had haunted him all his life. All one's life is a long time, but a quarter century before, in 1909, he had indeed compared Jung to a Joshua who would take possession of the promised land of psychiatry while he, Freud, the Moses, was destined to glimpse it only from afar. The first fruit of Freud's preoccupation with Moses was his anonymous study of Michelangelo's famous statue in Rome, published in 1914.* Hence, when his obsession with Moses returned in the early 1930s, Freud found him an old, familiar, though far from comfortable companion. In an enigmatic letter to Arnold Zweig, he declared Moses to have been "a strong anti-Semite" who "made no secret of it. Perhaps," Freud speculated, "he really was an Egyptian. And surely he was right." The remark, virtually unique for Freud, underscores his bitter mood in those years; he detested any signs of abject Jewish self-hatred in others and did not suspect that he was in the slightest guilty of it himself. Plainly, Moses was for Freud a dangerous figure no less than an enticing one.

He began work on *Moses and Monotheism* in the summer of 1934, but kept it a fairly closely held secret; he told Eitingon of it, and Arnold Zweig. Late that year, Anna Freud reported to Lou Andreas-Salomé that her father had completed some "special work" in the summer, but did not disclose its contents. When Freud learned of his daughter's discreet indiscretion, he chose to tell his "dear Lou" that he had been wrestling with "the question what actually had created the special character of the Jew." Plainly, his preoccupation with Moses was part of that larger preoccupation, the mystery of Jewishness. His conclusion: "The Jew is a creation of the man Moses," who had been an Egyptian nobleman. Who this Moses was and how he had worked his way with the Jews he proposed to answer "in a kind of historical novel."†

---

*See pp. 314–17.

†In 1937, thanking Hans Ehrenwald for a copy of his book *On the So-called Jewish Spirit*, he confessed that "several years ago I began to pose the question to myself how the Jews had acquired the character peculiar to them," and that he "had not got very far." This much he had been driven to conclude: it had been "the first, so to speak embryonic experience of the people, the impact of Moses and the Exodus from Egypt, that had stamped Jews through the centuries." (Freud to Ehrenwald, December 14, 1937. Typescript copy, Freud Museum, London.)

Fascinating as Freud found his investigation, the genre he had fallen into was scarcely congenial. He did not think, he admitted to Eitingon, that historical novels were his forte; Thomas Mann was the one to write them. Besides, the historical evidence was inadequate. Yet, burdened with an "excess of leisure," he told Arnold Zweig, and "in view of the new persecutions," he had asked himself just "how the Jew came to be and why he had drawn this immortal hatred on himself." The formula "Moses created the Jew" had come easily enough. But the rest was giving him great difficulty. He already knew—this was at the end of September 1934—that he would organize the "stuff" into three divisions, "the first interesting in the manner of a novel, the second laborious and protracted." It was on the third that the enterprise threatened to founder, for it was to include a theory of religion which, he feared, he could not publish in the highly sensitive, strictly Catholic Austria of his day, ready at any moment to outlaw psychoanalysis. Still, he could not stop.

The first two brief parts of *Moses and Monotheism* are, if somewhat startling, only moderately subversive. The idea that Moses was an Egyptian had been suggested by respectable scholars for some decades. His name was Egyptian, and the story that the Egyptian princess had discovered the baby in the bulrushes sounded, at least to anticlericals, like a transparent alibi. In 1935, while Freud was pausing over the book, American audiences could hear in George Gershwin's folk opera *Porgy and Bess* the sardonic caution, "It ain't necessarily so, / De t'ings dat yo' li'ble / To read in de Bible, / It ain't necessarily so." And one of the things listed by the librettist Ira Gershwin was the convenient way the Egyptian princess had "found" Moses: "She fished him, she says, from dat stream." There is no evidence that Freud ever heard of *Porgy and Bess,* but the same skepticism about pious tales was far from unknown in Austria.

Nor were doubts about the Book of Exodus particularly new, or unique to Freud's time. Pious scholars, Jews and Christians alike, had found great difficulty making a coherent personage of Moses; they could not rationally account for his exclusion from the Promised Land or agree on the circumstances of his death. As long ago as the late seventeenth century, and well into the eighteenth, deists had made wicked sport with the miraculous tale about the children of Israel crossing the Red Sea and the no less miraculous tales of Moses's doings. In 1764, in his *Philosophical Dictionary,* Voltaire had adduced cogent reasons why Moses could not have written the Pentateuch (which, after all, records his death), and then raised a more radical question: "Is it really true that there was a Moses?" In 1906, the eminent German ancient historian Eduard Meyer, whose work Freud cited with respect, raised the same question and maintained that Moses was a legend rather than a real personage. Freud did not go that far; the historical existence of Moses was in fact the centerpiece of his theory. He did insist, though, as had Max Weber in his study of ancient Judaism, that Moses was not a Jew.

Freud was well aware that this hypothesis raises inconvenient questions about Moses the preacher of monotheism. The Egyptians, after all, had worshiped a veritable tribe of the most diverse deities. Freud thought he had the answer: there was a moment in Egypt's history, about 1375 B.C., when one pharaoh, Amenhotep IV, briefly introduced a rigorous, intolerant monotheism, the cult of Aton. This was the doctrine that Moses, a highly placed Egyptian noble, perhaps a member of the royal house, transmitted to the Jewish people, then in bondage. But at first his stern, demanding theology had fallen on stony ground; the deity they would adopt on their wanderings after their exodus from Egypt was Yahweh, a crude, vengeful, bloodthirsty "volcano-god." It would take centuries before the Chosen People finally accepted the teachings of another figure called Moses, an elevated monotheism laced with self-denying moral regulations. If this conjecture should prove correct, Freud noted dryly, many cherished legends would fall by the wayside: "No historian can regard the biblical report about Moses and the exodus as anything but a pious fiction, which a remote tradition has reworked in the service of its own biases." His reconstruction left "no room for a good number of show pieces of biblical narrative, such as the ten plagues, the passage through the Red Sea, the solemn legislation at Mount Sinai." The authors of the Bible had condensed all sorts of disparate figures, like the two men named Moses, and embroidered events out of all recognition.

Such iconoclasm presented no difficulties for Freud. But it seemed impossible to reconcile the primitive Yahweh worship of the ancient Hebrews with Moses's exacting doctrine. Here Freud found the support he sought in a monograph by the scholar Ernst Sellin who, in 1922, suggested that Moses had been murdered by the people he had led out of Egypt and that his religion had been abandoned after his death. For perhaps as long as eight centuries, Yahweh had remained the God of the Jewish people. But at last a new prophet, borrowing the name of Moses from the earlier reformer, had forced them to submit to the faith that the original Moses had tried to impose on them in vain. "And this is the essential result, the fateful contents, of the history of the Jewish religion." Sellin's conjecture about the murder of Moses was, Freud knew, exceedingly daring and not well documented, but it struck him as highly plausible, even probable. "The Jewish people of Moses were as little able to tolerate so spiritualized a religion, to find in its offerings satisfaction of their needs, as were the Egyptians of the 18th dynasty."

A Founder murdered by followers unable to raise themselves to his level but inheriting the consequences of their crime and eventually reforming under the pressure of their memories—no fantasy could be more congenial to Freud. He was, after all, the author of *Totem and Taboo,* which had postulated a very similar crime as the foundation of human culture. More poignantly, he saw himself as the creator of a subversive psychology who was now near the end of a long, embattled career that had been steadily obstructed by abusive enemies and craven deserters. The idea that there were those who wanted to murder him was, we know, only too familiar to him; had not Jung, and after him Rank, perhaps even Ferenczi, harbored such parricidal thoughts?

Then, near the end of 1934, Freud stopped in his tracks. He was grappling with some "inner misgivings" no less troubling than the "external dangers" posed by the Austrian authorities. To understand the true quality and authority of religious tradition, the influence of great men in history, the grip of religious ideas stronger than all material considerations, struck Freud as a vast and burdensome task; he feared that its very magnitude, which made it most attractive to him, might put it beyond his strength. Unfortunately, his "historical novel," he told Arnold Zweig in November, "cannot stand up to my own criticism. I am demanding more certainty and do not like to see the concluding, to me valuable, formulation of the whole, endangered by being mounted on a foundation of clay." Irritated with himself, he entreated his friend, "Leave me alone with Moses. That this probably final attempt to create something has run aground depresses me enough. Not that I have got away from it. The man, and what I wanted to make of him, pursues me incessantly." This pathetic appeal testifies that he could still be as obsessed with his work, at the age of seventy-eight, as he had been when he was a younger researcher. Nor did the obsession wane. In early May 1935, he reported to Arnold Zweig that he was neither smoking nor writing, but that " 'Moses' will not let my imagination go." The project, he confessed to Eitingon a few days later, "has become a fixation for me." He added, "I cannot get away from him and further with him." The man Moses was a guest to whom he could not show the door.

BUT MOSES WAS not Freud's only visitor; fortunately, Freud's obsession did not amount to monomania. He was reading as voraciously and as critically as ever,* and could still enjoy the sun, the flowers, and his holidays. "I am

---

*The popular English novelist James Hilton, whose work Freud admired, displeased him with his *The Meadows of the Moon* (1926)—"a complete failure"—and, in general, with his excessive output. "I am afraid he is too proliferous," Freud told Hilda Doolittle on September 24, 1934. (In English. Hilda Doolittle papers, Beinecke Rare Book and Manuscript Library, Yale University.)

sorry you never saw our house and garden here in Grinzing," he wrote to Hilda Doolittle in May 1935. "It is the nicest place we ever had, quite a daydream and only circa 12 minutes ride in the car from Berggasse. The harsh weather yet had the advantage of letting spring develop its splendour very slowly while in other years most of the flourishing was over when we came out. To be sure I am getting old and my ailments are increasing but I try to enjoy as much as I can and do work for 5 hours daily." After a pleasant summer spent mainly in Grinzing, he told her in November that he was still seeing five patients a day back "at Berggasse, a very comfortable prison." Harassed by his prosthesis, by politics, by Moses, he could still mobilize cheerful feelings, or at least write cheerful communiqués.

One occupation that kept Freud busy was following developments in institutes abroad. When Ernest Jones came to lecture in Vienna in the early spring of 1935, Freud showed himself deeply interested in the "startling novelties of English psychoanalysis" to which Jones had introduced "our people." Jones's "novelties" were principally his challenge to Freud's theory of the death drive and his championship of Melanie Klein's ideas. But Freud had said his last word on these subjects and was content to be the serene observer, commenting with unwonted mildness that in his judgment, the London Psycho-Analytic Society had "followed Frau Klein on a false path." Still, psychoanalysis was gaining converts, or at least gathering prestige. It gave Freud particular pleasure to be named "unanimously" an honorary member of England's Royal Society of Medicine around the time that Ernest Jones visited Vienna. "Since this cannot have happened because of my beautiful eyes," he told Jones with barely suppressed delight, "it must prove that respect for our psychoanalysis has made great progress in official English circles."

And then there was his mail. In the Nazi era, with his children and his fellow analysts scattered across the world, it was more international than ever. Ernst Freud and his family had settled in London, and Freud was gratified to hear that Hilda Doolittle, then living in London, was in touch with them. Oliver was still in France. Hanns Sachs in Boston, Ernest Jones in London, Jeanne Lampl-de Groot in Amsterdam, Max Eitingon in Palestine, all wrote faithfully and wanted, and fully deserved, answers.* What is more, as a famous man, he got letters from strangers, and a few moved him to long,

---

*Eitingon was bravely but a little desperately trying to feel at home in Palestine; he had founded a psychoanalytic institute upon his arrival, and though still something of a stranger, at least was not idle. "We analysts," he reported to Freud in the spring of 1935, "all have a great deal to do." The patients he and his colleagues were seeing were of a kind quite familiar to them; neither the Arabs nor the Orthodox Jews long settled in Palestine were likely analysands. (Eitingon to Freud, April 25, 1935. By permission of Sigmund Freud Copyrights, Wivenhoe.)

thoughtful replies. One of these, written in English to an American woman, sums up his long-held attitude toward homosexuality. It has been much quoted—justly: "I gather from your letter that your son is a homosexual. I am most impressed by the fact that you do not mention this term yourself in your information about him. May I question you why you avoid it?" Instead of belaboring his correspondent for typical American prudishness, he decided to be simply helpful. "Homosexuality is assuredly no advantage," he wrote, "but it is nothing to be ashamed of, no vice, no degradation, it cannot be classified as an illness; we consider it to be a variation of the sexual function, produced by a certain arrest of sexual development." This stance would not satisfy homosexuals intent on regarding their sexual tastes as an alternative adult way of loving. But at the time Freud wrote this letter, his views on homosexuality were still most unconventional and not widely shared, at least not in public. "Many highly respectable individuals of ancient and modern times have been homosexuals," he observed reassuringly, "several of the greatest men among them. (Plato, Michelangelo, Leonardo da Vinci, etc.) It is a great injustice to persecute homosexuality as a crime—and a cruelty, too. If you do not believe me, read the books of Havelock Ellis." Whether he could help his correspondent's son to change into a "normal" heterosexual was a difficult question, but he might bring the young man "harmony, peace of mind, full efficiency, whether he remains a homosexual or gets changed."*

Freud's defiant cast of mind, which had given point to his Jewish identity and, at the same time, permitted him to offend Jewish sensibilities, also shaped his subversive attitude toward respectable sexual mores and, for that matter, his decision to stay in Vienna in the face of rising danger. He told his anonymous American correspondent that if her son wanted to be analyzed, he would have to come to Vienna: "I have no intention of leaving here." Not that he was wholly blind to the threats ahead. "An anxious premonition tells us," he wrote Arnold Zweig in October 1935, "that we, oh the poor Austrian Jews, will have to pay a part of the bill. It is sad," he added, "that we even judge world events from the Jewish point of view, but how could we do it any other way!"

---

*In the Freud Collection there is a photocopy of this letter with a note at the bottom from "a grateful mother," turning the letter over to Alfred Kinsey: "Herewith I enclose a letter from a great and good man which you may retain." (Freud Collection, B4, LC.)

Finis Austriae

 Hitler was pressing the Jewish point of view on Freud, who was consumed with rage. So were Freud's intimates. "My personal physician Dr. Max Schur," Freud reported to Arnold Zweig in the fall of 1935, "a very able doctor, is so deeply indignant about the events in Germany that he is no longer prescribing German medicines." In his predicament, Freud found Moses to be more than an obsession; he was a refuge. Yet while thinking about Moses fascinated him, Freud was very skeptical about ever publishing his researches. "The 'Moses,' " he assured Stefan Zweig in November, "will never see the light of day." Writing to Arnold Zweig the following January about some archeological finds in Egypt, Freud refused to take them as an incitement to finishing his book. The fate of Moses, he said resignedly, is sleep. The very title of the enterprise, "The Man Moses: A Historical Novel," he told Ernest Jones, discloses "why I have not published this work and will not publish it." There was not enough historical material to make his reconstruction reliable, and besides, throwing doubt on the "Jewish-national legendary history" would only make an untoward sensation. "Only a few persons, Anna, Martin, Kris, have read the thing." But at least one could discuss Moses. When there seemed a chance of a visit from Zweig, then in Palestine, where he felt isolated and restless, Freud looked forward to the good talk they would have: "We will forget all misery and all criticism and fantasize about Moses." The visit was long delayed, but on August 18, 1936, Freud's *Chronik* records, "Moses with Arn. Zweig."

Pleasant as it was to talk with friends, the year 1936 also proved to be a time of repetitions and of ghosts. On May 6, Freud turned eighty, and the spectacle that had irritated and exhausted him on earlier occasions was now repeated. He liked recognition, but his mere birthday, even a large round number like eighty, was something to be not enjoyed but endured. Zweig's visit came shortly after he had survived the inescapable observances. At least he had succeeded in thwarting Ernest Jones's well-intentioned plan to issue a volume of celebratory essays. The psychoanalytic as much as the political situation was, he told Jones, wholly unpropitious for so festive an enterprise. But the congratulations that overwhelmed him had to be acknowledged, if only with a printed card of thanks. And he had to receive the distinguished visitors who called on him. Some of them—like Ludwig Binswanger and Marie Bonaparte, who tactfully stayed away on May 6 to leave Freud to himself and his family—were most welcome; others were obligations stoically borne. A month later, on June 5, Martha Freud wrote a niece, Lilly Freud Marlé, "Your poor uncle has slaved like a day laborer to get through only a fraction of the acknowledgments he owed."

Among the birthday tributes was a civilized congratulatory address written by Stefan Zweig and Thomas Mann and signed by 191 artists and writers. Thanking Stefan Zweig for it, Freud noted, "Although I have been uncommonly happy in my house, with wife and children and especially with a daughter who satisfies in rare measure all of a father's demands, I cannot reconcile myself to the wretchedness and helplessness of being old, and look forward to the transition into nonbeing with a kind of longing." Thomas Mann also celebrated Freud's eightieth birthday with a lecture, "Freud and the Future," of which he gave a private reading to the Freuds at Berggasse 19 on June 14. At the end of the month came the distinction he appreciated most, even more highly than his appointment to the Royal Society of Medicine: the still more exclusive Royal Society, forever identified with the luminous names of Newton and Darwin, elected him a corresponding member. A few days later, he rejoiced in a letter to Ernest Jones about the "very great honor" he had received. By comparison, the sparse and perfunctory accolades Freud's compatriots could think up for him amounted to nothing more than a studied insult.

THE SUPREME REALITIES dominating Freud's life, apart from the threat of Nazism, were his advanced age and his uncertain health. "I am an old man," he told Abraham Schwadron of the University Library at the Hebrew University in Jerusalem, "have obviously not much longer to live." Schwadron had asked Freud for his papers, but Freud had few papers to offer him. "I have a probably unjustifiable antipathy to personal relics, autographs, collections of handwriting specimens, and everything that springs from these. This goes so far that I have, for example, handed all my manuscripts before 1905 into the wastebasket, among them that of the *Interpretation of Dreams.*" Since then he had been persuaded to keep his manuscripts, but he did not like to occupy himself with them. "My daughter Anna Freud will inherit my books and writings."*

His daughter Anna continued to be what she had been for more than a decade: the center of his life. He gloried in her and worried about her, as he had for years. "My Anna is very good and competent," he proudly told Arnold

---

*In the will that Freud signed on July 28, 1938, and that was probated on December 1, 1939, with Martin, Ernst, and Anna Freud as executors, Freud took care of his widow and children with a generally even hand, but left his sister-in-law Minna £300, and Anna his antiquities and his books on psychology and psychoanalysis. (A. A. Brill papers, container 3, LC.)

Zweig in the late spring of 1936, but then his old worry came to the surface once again: "When a passionate woman almost wholly sublimates her sexuality!" He could never praise her enough. "The most enjoyable thing near me," he wrote Eitingon some months later, "is Anna's enjoyment in her work and her unchecked achievement." About his wife he reported more matter-of-factly: she was very well. On September 14, 1936, he and Martha Freud celebrated their golden wedding anniversary; but his old passion for Martha Bernays, Freud somewhat dryly told Marie Bonaparte, was now the dimmest of memories: "It was really not a bad solution of the marriage problem, and she is still today tender, healthy, and active."

Unlike his wife, Freud himself, though still active, was neither tender nor healthy. His eyes were as probing as ever, but his mouth had become a tight, thin line curved slightly downward, giving the impression of a disenchanted observer of mankind whose favorite form of humor was gallows humor. In mid-July 1936, Dr. Pichler operated on him again, as he had earlier that year, twice, and found a recurrence of the cancer; Freud did not consider himself released from being "gravely ill" until a week later. In December, Pichler operated once more, and on the twenty-fourth Freud recorded in his terse manner, "Christmas in pain."

A painful shock of a very different sort awaited him just a week later. For the last time, Wilhelm Fliess invaded his life. On December 30, 1936, Marie Bonaparte sent word that a bookseller from Berlin named Stahl had offered her Freud's letters to Fliess, as well as those long memoranda in which Freud had worked his way into psychoanalysis during the 1890s. Fliess's widow had sold them to him, and he was asking 12,000 francs, some $500.* Stahl, Marie Bonaparte told Freud, had had an offer from the United States but wanted to keep the collection in Europe. The princess had taken a look at one letter to confirm their authenticity. "After all," she told Freud, "I know your handwriting!"

Freud was appalled. When Fliess's widow had asked Freud to return her husband's letters, shortly after Fliess's death late in 1928, Freud, we will recall, had been unable to find them. But her request had caused him to worry about his own letters to Fliess. Their correspondence, he now told Marie Bonaparte, had been "the most intimate you can imagine. It would have been most awkward to have it fall into the hands of strangers." He offered to share the cost of the letters; clearly he wanted them destroyed. "I want none of them to come to the notice of so-called posterity." But Stahl, a man of some

---

*Writing to Ernest Jones in the mid-1950s, Marie Bonaparte recorded the sum she had paid for the letters: DM 1,200. (See Marie Bonaparte to Jones, November 8, 1957. Jones papers, Archives of the British Psycho-Analytical Society, London.)

probity, would sell the Freud letters only on condition that they not fall into the hands of the Freud family, precisely for that reason. Obviously, the Freuds' passion for privacy, quite in character for the nineteenth-century bourgeois they were, was no secret.

An affectionate duel now began: on one side Freud, anxious to secure the documents; on the other side the princess, just as anxious to keep them for "so-called posterity." In early January 1937, echoing Freud's attitude toward Fliess's widow, she reassured Freud that while the letters were still in Germany, they were at least "no longer in the hands of the 'witch.'" She volunteered not to read them, but proposed to deposit the letters in some safe library with the stipulation that they be kept from anyone's eyes "for eighty or a hundred years after your death." Perhaps, she argued, opposing her former analyst, Freud did not appreciate his greatness. "You belong to history of human thought like Plato, let us say, or Goethe." How much would have been lost if we did not have Eckermann's conversations with Goethe, or if the Platonic dialogues had been destroyed just to protect the reputation of Socrates, the pederast! "Something would be lost to the history of psychoanalysis, this unique new science, your creation, which is more important than even Plato's ideas," if these letters were to be destroyed just because of a few personal observations. She was writing this way, she assured him, because "I love you . . . and revere you."

Freud was relieved that she of all people should take possession of his letters to Fliess, but spurned her arguments and her comparisons, just as he had done a quarter century earlier when Ferenczi had persisted in likening him to Goethe. "With the very intimate nature of our relationship, these letters naturally dilate on just anything," he wrote; they involved business matters as well as personal ones. The former included "all the notions and wrong turnings concerning burgeoning analysis, [and] are in that case also quite personal." The princess listened respectfully, but was not persuaded. By mid-February, the collection was in her hands, and around the beginning of March, she was in Vienna, resisting Freud's importunate appeals face to face. Freud, still hoping that she would consent to have the letters burned, agreed to let her read them. Her response was not to his liking. She pointed out some of the most remarkable passages to Freud and then, defying the man she loved and revered, acting as the historian's true friend, deposited the letters in the Rothschild Bank in Vienna. A Jewish bank was not the wisest possible choice, but then, Hitler's absorption of Austria was not yet a foregone conclusion.

AT EIGHTY, FREUD was still capable of work, love, and hate. Early in 1937, he returned, in a sober professional mood, to issues of analytic technique. His long paper "Analysis Terminable and Interminable" is his most disenchanted pronouncement concerning the effectiveness of psychoanalysis. This bleakness was not new; Freud had never been a therapeutic enthusiast. But now, stressing the strength of the inborn drives and the resistance of the death drive and of character deformations to analytic influence, he found new reasons for assigning the curative powers of psychoanalysis the most modest scope. He even declared that a successful analysis does not necessarily prevent the recurrence of a neurosis. The paper read as though Freud were abandoning, or at least had come to question, the goal of therapy he had stated in a famous formulation only a few years earlier. The intention of psychoanalysis, he had written in the *New Introductory Lectures,* "is to strengthen the ego, to make it more independent of the superego, to enlarge its field of perception and to expand its organization so that it can appropriate new pieces of the id. Where id was, there ego shall be. It is cultural work rather like the draining of the Zuyder Zee." Now he was writing as though the gains to the ego were at best temporary. It would be too simple to attribute this plaintive view to the spectacle of contemporary events alone, but they played their part. Politics blighted everything.

"Analysis Terminable and Interminable" appeared in June 1937. In the same month, Freud was gratified to learn that he had outlived Alfred Adler. On a lecture tour in Britain, Adler had collapsed on a street in Aberdeen with a fatal heart attack. When Arnold Zweig displayed some sympathy at the news, Freud would have none of it. He had hated Adler for more than a quarter century, and Adler had hated him just as long, and as vocally. "For a Jewish boy from a Viennese suburb," Freud replied, "a death in Aberdeen, Scotland, is an unprecedented career and a proof of how far he had come. Truly, his contemporaries have richly rewarded him for his service in having contradicted psychoanalysis."* Freud had spoken to the point in *Civilization and Its Discontents* when he had said that he could not understand the Christian injunction to universal love, and that indeed many people were hateful; and among the most hateful in his view were those he thought had let him down and had made their fortune pandering to a public uncomfortable with his libido theory.

While Adler's demise gave Freud pleasure, or at least no pain, others gave him good grounds for worry. Some of those close to him were not faring well or aging gracefully. His sister-in-law Minna Bernays, still one of his favorite people, now seventy-two, was seriously ailing. His children, buffeted about by

---

*In his biography, Jones (III, 208) prints this portion of the letter, but misdates it by a year and translates Freud's term, *Judenbube,* as "Jew boy." There is no wholly satisfactory translation for the term, but Jones's solution has the wrong weight to it. Freud's reference to Adler is callous and snide, but not quite so disdainful or bigoted as "Jew boy" would imply.

the Hitler tide, were itinerants in search of a permanent home and a living. Only his daughter Anna was going from strength to strength. Whatever prestige she might have borrowed at first from her father's name and protection had long since given way to the authority she had acquired through her own psychoanalytic work with children, and her lucid papers. But sadly, Lou Andreas-Salomé, her friend and his, died in February 1937, at seventy-five, "a peaceful death in her little house in Göttingen." Freud had to learn of her death through the newspapers. "Was very fond of her," he mused to Arnold Zweig, "strange to say without a trace of sexual attraction." He remembered her in a terse but warm obituary. Eitingon, writing from Palestine, expressed Freud's feelings aptly: "Lou's death seems so strangely unreal. She seemed to us so independent of all time."

PREOCCUPIED THOUGH HE was with his personal life, Freud could not ignore the threat from Nazi Germany. Still clinging to the increasingly forlorn hope that he might die in Austria in relative peace, experimenting now and then with unwarranted sanguine predictions, Freud saw his illusions about Austria's continued independence fading away. His soothing denials melted before the undeniable realities: German rearmament, western reluctance to affront Hitler. It was not his prospects alone, but the prospects for psychoanalysis, that distressed him. As long ago as the summer of 1933, he had told Ernest Jones that he was "almost prepared to see that in the current world crisis our organization, too, will perish. Berlin is lost, Budapest devalued through the loss of Ferenczi; where they are heading in America is uncertain." Two years later, in September 1935, he urged Arnold Zweig not to postpone his planned trip to Europe: "Vienna must not become German before you visit me." His tone was jocular, his meaning was not. Zweig was still playing with the notion that Nazi rule over Germany might come to an end, and that the "brown" era might be followed by a monarchy covered with liberal whitewash. Freud, too, continued to harbor such fantasies, but with less and less conviction. As late as February 1936, he expressed the hope that he might live to see the collapse of the Nazi regime. This was a sign less of invincible naiveté than of the mixed, often unintelligible signals political observers were getting from Right and Left alike. He did not have the inestimable benefit of hindsight.

By mid-1936, though, Freud was sounding the bleakest possible note more often. "Austria's approach to National Socialism seems unstoppable," he wrote Arnold Zweig in June. "All the fates are conspiring with the rabble. I am waiting, with ever decreasing regret, for the curtain to fall for me." Less than a year later, in March 1937, he saw nothing but disaster ahead. "Our political situation seems to be clouding over more and more," he told Ernest

Jones. "The penetration of the Nazis can probably not be held up. The consequences for analysis, too, are baleful." He compared Vienna's situation now with its plight in 1683, when the Turks had been at the door. But then there had been relief—now one had little hope of that. Mussolini, who had so far protected Austria from the Germans, had apparently decided to give them a free hand. "I should like to live in England, like Ernst, and travel to Rome, like you." Writing to Arnold Zweig, he sounded no less portentous: "Everything around is growing ever darker, more threatening, and the awareness of one's own helplessness ever more importunate." Four years earlier, he had still been willing to pay tepid tribute to his countrymen. A right-wing dictatorship, he had told Ernest Jones, would make life disagreeable for Jews, but the League of Nations would intervene to prevent persecutions, and "besides: the Austrian is not partial to German brutality." Now he saw things with remorseless clarity, at least some of the time. "The government here," he commented in December 1937, "is different, but the people are the same, thoroughly at one with their brothers in the Reich in the worship of anti-Semitism. Our throat is being choked ever more tightly, even if we are not being strangled." The enthusiasm with which the Austrians would hail Hitler three months later cannot really have surprised him.

Austria's catastrophe had long been in the making and for some time virtually inescapable. In July 1936, Chancellor Kurt von Schuschnigg had committed his government to an accommodation with Nazi Germany—duly noted in Freud's *Chronik*. It included secret clauses undertaking to overlook the operations of the illegal Austrian Nazi party and to bring some of its leaders, like Arthur Seyss-Inquart, into the cabinet. The noose, then, to take Freud's metaphor, had been tightening for some time. In February 1938, Hitler bludgeoned Schuschnigg into appointing Seyss-Inquart minister of security and the interior. The Trojan horse was in place. Schuschnigg countered, in a brave but futile gesture, by calling a plebiscite on Austrian independence for March 13; everywhere, sidewalks and walls were scribbled over with pro-Schuschnigg slogans.

Freud saw the crisis as a final showdown whose devastating outcome was probable but not yet quite certain. "At present our government, upright and brave in its way," he wrote Eitingon in February 1938, "is more energetic in fending off the Nazis than ever before." But he did not venture to predict that its courage would keep the Germans out of Austria. Yet he and his family remained calm. "Vienna has been in panicky spirits," Anna Freud told Ernest Jones on February 20, adding, "We are not going along with the panic." Two days later, writing to his son Ernst, Freud hesitantly ventured to doubt that Austria would end up quite like Germany. "The Catholic Church is very strong and will offer strong resistance." Besides, "our Schuschnigg is decent, courageous and a man of character." Schuschnigg had invited a group of Jewish industrialists to assure them "that the Jews here have nothing to fear." Of course, if he were forced out of office, or if the Nazi invasion did take place, all hopes would be dashed.

But Freud still had no wish to escape. His flight would only "give a signal for the complete dissolution of the analytic group," and that was an eventuality he wanted to avoid. "I do not believe that Austria left to itself would degenerate into Nazism. That is a difference over against Germany that, as a rule, is neglected." It is a measure of how feeble a reed Freud was clinging to that he should put his fading hopes in a most improbable ally—the church. "Will it still be possible to find safety in the shelter of the Catholic Church?" he asked Marie Bonaparte on February 23. But he did not really believe it. "Who knows?" he asked in his school Spanish—*"Quien sabe?"* There is something pathetic about these last-minute attempts at self-reassurance; Freud had viewed the situation more realistically before.

Hitler's plans for the absorption of Austria into his Third Reich went on unabated; Schuschnigg's plebiscite was a tin shield against a machine gun. Germany's ambassadors sent word to Berlin from London and Rome that Hitler's annexation of Austria would provoke no resistance. Schuschnigg was bludgeoned into canceling the plebiscite. On March 11, after an ultimatum from Hitler, he resigned as chancellor in favor of Seyss-Inquart. Freud's verdict was laconic and precise: *"Finis Austriae."* The next morning, the new Austrian premier, obeying instructions from his masters in Berlin, invited German troops to cross the border.

ON THAT DAY, March 12, 1938, and on the next, Freud sat by his radio listening to the sound of Germans taking over Austria. He heard stalwart announcements of resistance, followed by collapse, the rejoicing on one side and then on the other. Sick as he felt with the aftereffects of an operation, political events drove the pains from his mind. His *Chronik* tersely notes the facts: Sunday, March 13, "Anschluss with Germany," and the next day, "Hitler in Vienna." The reign of terror began, an unsavory combination of the invaders' planned purges and spontaneous local outbursts of cruel sport— terror against Social Democrats, against inconvenient leaders of the old right wing, above all against Jews. Freud had understated the case against his fellow countrymen. Late in 1937, we know, he had characterized the Austrians as no less brutal than the Germans; in fact, they proved more adept than their Nazi models at savaging the helpless.

The bigotry and sadistic vengefulness it had taken many Germans five years to acquire, or to express, Austrians learned to act out in as many days.

Freud with his "Sunday child," Sophie, who died of influenza in 1920. (*Mary Evans/Sigmund Freud Copyrights, Wivenhoe/ W. E. Freud*)

Freud with Heinz ("Heinele"), left, and Ernst ("Ernstl") Halberstadt, his daughter Sophie's two sons. (*Mary Evans/Sigmund Freud Copyrights, Wivenhoe*)

Lou Andreas-Salomé, Freud's increasingly close friend during the last quarter century of his life. *(Mary Evans/Sigmund Freud Copyrights, Wivenhoe)*

Freud with the Committee, the small, tight group that formed around him in 1912. This 1922 photograph also includes Max Eitingon, who joined the original members in 1919. Standing, left to right, are Otto Rank Karl Abraham, Max Eitingon, and Ernest Jones. Seated, also left to right, are Freud, Sándor Ferenczi, and Hanns Sachs. *(Mary Evans/Sigmund Freud Copyrights, Wivenhoe)*

Freud in 1919, after the First World War, reunited with Ernest Jones. *(Mary Evans/Sigmund Freud Copyrights, Wivenhoe)*

Princess Marie Bonaparte—here shown with her chow, Topsy—Freud's friend, confidante, and benefactress, who provided vital help in the dangerous days after the Anschluss. *(Mary Evans/Sigmund Freud Copyrights, Wivenhoe)*

The German novelist Arnold Zweig, Freud's friend and correspondent in his last years, and the author of realistic fiction about the First World War that Freud much admired.

Freud about 1921, glowering at the photographer. *(Mary Evans/Sigmund Freud Copyrights, Wivenhoe)*

Freud with Anna in the fall of 1928, in Berlin to be fitted with a new prosthesis. *(Mary Evans/Sigmund Freud Copyrights, Wivenhoe)*

Freud in 1931, a year after publishing the most widely read of his essays, *Civilization and Its Discontents*. *(Mary Evans/Sigmund Freud Copyrights, Wivenhoe)*

Freud in 1932 at Hochroterd, a farmhouse not far from Vienna owned by his daughter Anna and her American friend Dorothy Burlingham. *(Mary Evans/Sigmund Freud Copyrights, Wivenhoe)*

Freud in 1937, with his sister Marie, to his right, his wife, and his brother Alexander. *(Mary Evans/Sigmund Freud Copyrights, Wivenhoe)*

A vivid instance of the way Jews were harassed in Austria after the Anschluss in mid-March 1938. A Jewish boy is being forced to write *Jud* —"Jew"—on a wall in Vienna, solemnly watched by his tormentors young and old. *(Dokumentationsarchiv des Österreichischen Widerstandes)*

Freud in his study in May 1938, waiting for permission to leave
Austria for England. *(Photograph © Edmund Engelman)*

Freud and Anna, on the train taking them to
France and freedom, some time during June 4–5,
1938. *(Mary Evans/Sigmund Freud Copyrights,
Wivenhoe)*

The burning of the chapel (*Zeremonienhalle*) at the Jewish cemetery in Graz, Styria, typical of the acts of barbarism perpetrated in hundreds of localities in Austria and in Germany on November 10, 1938, in what the Nazis billed as "spontaneous" protest against Jews. (*Dokumentationsarchiv des Österreichischen Widerstandes*)

Freud at work at his desk in London, in the summer of 1938. He is dressed complete with tie, the faultless bourgeois to the end. (*Mary Evans/Sigmund Freud Copyrights, Wivenhoe*)

Many Germans had given way under the relentless bombardment of propaganda, cowed by an exigent state, vigilant party, and controlled press; many Austrians needed no pressure at all. Only a little of this behavior can be explained, or excused, as enforced submission to Nazi terror. The mobs ransacking Jewish apartments and terrorizing Jewish shopkeepers did so without official orders and thoroughly enjoyed their work. The Austrian prelates, keepers of the Roman Catholic conscience, did nothing to mobilize whatever forces of sanity and decency still remained; with Theodor Cardinal Innitzer setting the tone, priests celebrated Hitler's accomplishments from the pulpit, promised to cooperate joyfully with the new dispensation, and ordered the swastika flag to be hoisted over church steeples on suitable occasions. These clerical testimonials to Hitler provide a devastating commentary on the mournful question Freud had asked just a few short weeks before, when he had wondered whether the powerful Catholic Church might not, in its own interest, stand against Hitler.*

Incidents in the streets of Austrian cities and villages right after the German invasion were more outrageous than those Hitler's Reich had yet witnessed. The obscene anti-Semitic slanders of such Nazi journals as the *Stürmer,* the regulations restricting Germany's Jews in their practice of the professions, the Nürnberg racial laws of late 1935, the villages proudly advertising that they were "clean of Jews"—*Judenrein*—were giving Germany's Jews a foretaste of hell. But they had suffered comparatively little of the kind of wholesale random violence that spread across Austria after the Anschluss: Austria in March 1938 was a dress rehearsal for the German pogroms of November. The popular German playwright Carl Zuckmayer, a liberal, happened to be in Vienna in those days and never forgot them. "The underworld had opened its gates and let loose its lowest, most revolting, most impure spirits. The city was transformed into a nightmare painting by Hieronymus Bosch," and the "air filled with an incessant, savage, hysterical screeching from male and female throats." For Zuckmayer all these people had lost their faces, "resembling distorted grimaces: some in anxiety, others in deceit, still others in wild, hate-filled triumph." He had witnessed some horrifying events in Germany, including Hitler's Beer Hall Putsch in November 1923 and the Nazis' accession to power in January 1933. But nothing could approach the scenes now playing themselves out in Vienna's streets. What was "unleashed here was the uprising of envy, of malevolence, of bitterness, of blind vicious lust for revenge."

---

*It is only fair to add that the Catholic policy of submissive collaboration with Austria's Nazi rulers went sour before the year was out, when the Nazi leadership was complaining about "political priests." But whatever resistance Austrian priests might have had to offer would of necessity have been feeble and futile.

A boycott of Jewish merchants in Vienna and other Austrian towns was the least of it. Yet the boycott was ugly enough, enforced by thugs in brown shirts or by marauding youths wearing the ubiquitous swastika armband, who would take savage reprisals against those who ignored or defied them. Armed with lists thoughtfully prepared for this opportunity, Austrian Nazis and their camp followers looted Jewish apartments and stores and synagogues. But even more appalling was the spontaneous violence. The sight of a defenseless Jew stimulated the imagination of Austrian mobs in town after town. Orthodox Eastern European Jews, conspicuous with their broad-brimmed hats, ear-locks, and flowing beards, were favorite targets, but others were not spared. As their tormentors yowled with pleasure, Jewish youngsters, women, old men alike were forced to rub out, with their bare hands or with toothbrushes, the slogans left over in the streets from the aborted Schuschnigg plebiscite. An English journalist witnessed one of these "rubbing parties"—*Reibpartien* —as they came to be called: "SA men dragged an elderly Jewish worker and his wife through the applauding crowd. Tears rolled down the cheeks of the old woman, and while she stared ahead and virtually looked through her tormentors, I could see how the old man, whose arm she held, tried to stroke her hand. 'Work for the Jews, at last work for the Jews,' howled the crowd. 'We thank our Führer, he has made work for the Jews!' " Other gangs, amid jeers and kicks, made Jewish schoolboys write "Jud" on walls, or perform humiliating gymnastics, or give the Hitler salute.

This was not a one-day outburst. An Associated Press dispatch from Vienna under a March 13 dateline reported that "beating of Jews and plundering of Jewish-owned stores increased today. Jews were disappearing from Vienna life. Few, if any, were to be seen on the streets or in the coffee houses. Some were asked to leave street cars." The reporter saw one man "beaten and left wounded on the street. Another, leaving a cafe, was beaten while his wife looked on helplessly. A Jewish woman who withdrew 40,000 schillings from a bank was arrested without charge." Meanwhile, "Nazis visited headquarters of the Makkabi Jewish sports organization, smashed some of the property and tore down the organization's insignia."

There were some who could not believe what they saw, and for whom the enchanting dream of Vienna, the charming city of gaiety on the Blue Danube, had not wholly died: "Jewish leaders expressed the opinion that anti-Semitism would be milder in Austria than in Germany." Actually, the opposite proved to be the case. In a dispatch under a March 15 dateline, a reporter commented, "Adolf Hitler has left behind him in Austria an anti-Semitism that is blossoming far more rapidly than ever it did in Germany." The reporter went on to describe scenes that had become all too familiar in the previous day or two to newspaper readers in the western world—rubbing parties and all the rest. And he observed that if Jews had a choice between an Austrian enjoying himself and a German following orders, the German was preferable: "The writer saw a woman in a fur coat near the Saechsischer Hotel, surrounded by six steel-helmeted Nazi guards with rifles, forced to go down on her knees and hopelessly try to remove the words 'Heil Schuschnigg!' painted in white enamel on the pavement. Yet even to these tormentors the Jews had cause to be grateful, despite the humiliations forced on them, because the guards did not otherwise mishandle them, as the mob seemed anxious to do." That mob, "in an extremely dangerous mood and bent on plunder," was scattered by steel-helmeted Nazi guards. "It is clear," the reporter mused, "that not only the Jews are going to be taught the price of Anschluss." A German Nazi from Berlin to whom this journalist spoke "expressed some astonishment at the speed with which anti-Semitism was being introduced here, which he said was going to make the plight of the Vienna Jews far worse than it was in Germany, where the change had come with a certain gradualness." What struck all the journalists reporting from Austria during these days was the general mood of celebration. "VIENNESE GO WILD; JAM NOISY STREETS," ran one headline on March 14. "Yelling, Singing, Flag-Waving Throngs Surge Through City, Giving Nazi 'Sieg Heil!' / YOUTHS ON THE MARCH / German Martial Airs Replace Waltzes in Coffee Houses—No Opposition Visible." For a time, as the German Nazis imported the stagy mass manipulation that had worked so well in their own country, Austria was on holiday.

The night side of the festivities was coercion and assassination. March 1938, in Vienna and elsewhere in Austria, became a time of organized political murder, and a time, too, of casual, improvised killing. The Jewish Social Democratic lawyer Hugo Sperber, something of a character, who had long been in his witty disheveled way a provocation to Austrian Nazis, was literally stomped to death. This incident was not unique: in April an engineer, Isidor Pollack, director of a chemical factory, was killed in the same way by S.A. men making what they called a search of his house. Other Austrian Jews, like the essayist, cabaret performer, and amateur cultural historian Egon Friedell, cheated the torturers and murderers of their prey; on March 16, as storm troopers were coming up the stairs to his apartment, Friedell jumped from a window to his death. This way out became an epidemic: on March 11, there had been two suicides in Vienna; three days later, the number had grown to fourteen, and eight among these were Jews. During the spring, some five hundred Austrian Jews chose to kill themselves to elude humiliation, unbearable anxiety, or deportation to concentration camps. The casualties were so conspicuous that in late March the authorities felt compelled to issue a denial of the "rumors of thousands of suicides since the Nazi accession to power." Flaunting the kind of mechanical exactitude that would characterize the Nazi murder machine throughout, the statement read, "From March 12 to March 22 ninety-six persons committed suicide in Vienna of whom only fifty were directly connected with the change in the political situation in Austria."

The thought of suicide even invaded the Freud household that spring. Freud's trusted physician Max Schur, who was close to the family during these desperate months, reports that when escape from Nazi Austria seemed hopeless, Anna Freud asked her father, "Wouldn't it be better if we all killed ourselves?" Freud's response was characteristic: "Why? Because they would like us to?" He might grumble that the game was not worth the candle and talk with longing for the curtain to fall, but he was not about to blow out the candle, or leave the stage, at the convenience of the enemy. The defiant mood that dominated so much of Freud's life was still stirring in him. If he had to go, he would go on his own conditions.

The new rulers accomplished Austria's integration into Hitler's Reich with rapid, ruthless efficiency. Their work literally meant *finis Austriae:* in less than a week, the Austrian army, laws, and public institutions were branches of their German counterparts, and the country was Austria no more but an eastern province of Germany, called "Ostmark" in a calculated archaism. Jewish judges, bureaucrats, industrialists, bankers, professors, journalists, musicians, were purged immediately; within a few weeks, the opera, the newspapers, the worlds of business, high culture, and the coffee house anxiously advertised themselves as "purely Aryan." Dependable Nazis were rewarded with all the posts of prominence and responsibility. There was virtually no resistance, nor even objections. But resistance would have been ineffective and irrational; what little opposition Austrians could muster, Heinrich Himmler and his elite black shirts, the S.S., took care to stifle with their time-tested methods. Those suspected of possibly rallying anti-Nazi forces, or even just thought to be in the way, were jailed, strangled, shot, shipped to the dreaded Dachau concentration camp in Bavaria. A handful escaped abroad only to discover that the rest of the world did not care to intervene in their behalf.

PARTLY SHIELDED BY his international reputation and his assiduous friends, Freud was spared most of the terror, though not all of it. On March 15, the day after recording Hitler's arrival in Vienna, Freud noted that there had been a "control" in his apartment and in the *Verlag.* Both the office of the psychoanalytic publishing house at Berggasse 7 and Freud's apartment at Berggasse 19 had been invaded by gangs of irregulars and brown shirts. They searched the files of the *Verlag,* and held Martin Freud prisoner all day, but failed to find some of the compromising documents stored in the office. This was a piece of good luck: Freud's will, kept there, would have revealed that he had funds abroad. At the apartment, the invaders stayed a long time; they were perhaps somewhat disconcerted by Martha Freud, that competent and courteous bourgeoise, but not disconcerted enough. Anna Freud took them to the safe in the apartment and opened it, for them to help themselves. The next visit from the Nazis, a week later, was to be less casual.

It was only too depressingly evident that there was no future for psychoanalysis in Vienna. Nor was Freud's own future clear by any means. He was enough of a celebrity not to go unnoticed: western newspapers reported that while the Palestine government had offered asylum to Freud, the new rulers of Austria would not grant him a passport. But Freud's *Chronik* records help at hand: "Jones," in the entry for March 16, and "Princess," the next day. The two represented connections—what the Austrians like to call *Protektion*—at their most impressive: Ernest Jones, with ties to members of the British cabinet, and Princess Marie Bonaparte, with her wealth, her pedigree, and her royal ties illustrious enough to give even the Gestapo pause. From Switzerland, Ludwig Binswanger sent an invitation in the kind of coded language that alert letter writers to Nazi-occupied territory had learned to use. "The purpose of my lines today," he wrote Freud on March 18, "is to tell you that I am inviting you at any time if you should wish a change of air." He assured Freud, "You can imagine that your Swiss friends are thinking of you, at all times ready to help." It was of even more consequence that William Bullitt, now American ambassador to France, closely watched over his old coauthor. The American consul general in Vienna, John Cooper Wiley, who had been appointed at Bullitt's instance, was on call as his agent in place. Freud was fortunate, too, in the gentile Austrians on whom he was so dependent, notably his surgeon, Hans Pichler, who continued to treat Freud as his patient as though nothing had changed in their world.

Still, there was no guarantee that even this formidable array of protectors would save Freud; intoxicated with victory upon victory, contemptuous of the pusillanimous western powers who craved peace and dreaded confrontation, the Nazis were inclined to make light of British or French or American protests. Memories of the First World War and its horrors haunted and virtually paralyzed Allied statesmen; these memories acted as so many agents of appeasement. Some of the rasher Nazi policy makers, like Himmler, were in fact urging that Freud and the whole gang of analysts still remaining in Vienna be put in prison, but they seem to have been restrained by Hermann Göring, supported by the German Foreign Office, counseling prudence. On March 15, Wiley cabled the American secretary of state, Cordell Hull, "Fear Freud, despite age and illness, in danger." Hull passed the message on to President Franklin Roosevelt, and noted on the following day that "in accordance with the President's instructions," he had requested the American ambassador in Berlin, Hugh Robert Wilson, "to take this matter up personally and informally with the appropriate German authorities"; Wilson was to try arranging for the Freud family to go to Paris, "where the President is informed friends are anxious to receive him." From then on, Freud's fate enlisted interest in the highest quarters of the American government, with the State Department—Cordell Hull, his powerful second in command, Sumner Welles, and the American ambassadors in Paris and Berlin—most closely involved. Wiley wired the secretary of state on March 17 that while Freud's passport had been confiscated, the "Vienna Police President" had promised "personal interest in case." Bullitt's energetic representations to the German ambassador to Paris, Count von Welczeck, that any mistreatment of Freud would scandalize the world, also did Freud's prospects no harm.

One of the most tenacious obstacles to the rescue of Freud was Freud himself. Ernest Jones, who had hastily flown to Vienna to be of assistance, has left an affecting account of his "heart to heart talk" with Freud shortly after March 15, in which Freud offered all sorts of reasons, some cogent but most of them farfetched, for wanting to remain in Vienna. He was too old; he was too feeble; he could not even climb up the steps to a railroad compartment; he would not get a permit to live anywhere. This last argument, Jones acknowledged, was unfortunately not without merit. In those days, he recalls, nearly every country, defensively looking at the unemployment figures and under pressure to keep out foreign competitors for jobs, was "ferociously inhospitable" to new immigrants. It is true—the world in the decade of Hitler was an ungenerous place: there were already too many people out of work, without adding more; and many liked to think that the horrendous stories of persecution in Nazi Germany and Nazi Austria were perhaps on a level with the imaginative propaganda tales that the allies had spread about German atrocities in the First World War. Besides, who needed more Jews?

After a long wrangle, Jones talked Freud round, overcoming Freud's final argument with an ingenious riposte. As he saw his arguments for remaining in Vienna beaten down one by one, Freud offered one "last declaration. He could not leave his native land; it would be like a soldier deserting his post." Jones was prepared: "I successfully countered this attitude by quoting the analogy of Lightoller, the second officer of the *Titanic.*" Lightoller had been blown to the surface when the boiler of the *Titanic* exploded as the ship was sinking. During the official interrogation, asked when he had left the ship, he responded, "I never left the ship, Sir; she left me." The anecdote "won his final acceptance." Reassured, Jones returned to England on March 20, to exploit his connections at home and obtain visas for the Freuds.

Freud made other difficulties. As Wiley cabled the secretary of state on

March 19, he wanted to bring out his whole family, including his in-laws, along with his physician and his physician's family—a total of sixteen persons. This, Bullitt promptly cabled to Wiley, was "entirely beyond any resources at my disposal," and he thought that Freud's caravan might even exceed Marie Bonaparte's resources. He offered $10,000, but "can not (repeat can not) be responsible for more." Wiley replied that Freud "plans to go to England. States only question involved is exit visa." This helped, and other assistance was at hand: "Princess here," Wiley reported to Bullitt. "Mrs. Burlington [Burlingham] also." The intrusive question of money receded into the background; to secure permission for the Freuds to leave became the principal issue.

A complicated telegraphic ballet now began in the diplomatic stratosphere. Jones mobilized his friends Sir Samuel Hoare, home secretary, and Earl De La Warr, lord privy seal, to procure residence permits for Freud and his family. Obtaining these was far from automatic, not even easy, but Jones's allies in the government promised to cooperate. Yet the rulers of Nazified Austria were still not done with the Freud family. On March 22, Wiley cabled to the secretary of state, "for Bullitt," that von Stein, the powerful "German Counsellor" in Vienna, had taken up the issue of "Freud's exit with Himler [sic]. I pointed out that Freud's age and health called for special treatment at frontier." But on the same day, at 2 P.M., Wiley wired to the same recipients, "Anna Freud just arrested." Freud noted in his *Chronik* where she had gone: "Anna at Gestapo."

The curt entry conceals Freud's agitation. When his daughter Anna was told she would have to appear at Gestapo headquarters at the Hotel Metropole, she and her brother Martin, who was expecting the same peremptory invitation, consulted Dr. Schur, wondering reasonably enough whether they might be tortured or, for that matter, would ever come out alive. "At their request," Schur recalls, he "supplied them with a sufficient amount of Veronal," and promised them that he would take care of their father as long as he could. That, Schur comments, was Freud's worst day.

No one would quarrel with this assessment. "I went to the Berggasse and stayed with Freud," Schur remembers. "The hours were endless. It was the only time I ever saw Freud deeply worried. He paced the floor, smoking incessantly. I tried to reassure him as well as I could." At the Gestapo, meanwhile, his daughter Anna never lost control. "She had been clever enough to sense," her brother Martin writes, "that her chief danger lay in being left waiting in the corridor and forgotten until the office closed. In that case, she suspected, she would be swept out with other Jewish prisoners and casually deported or shot." The details remain vague, but it appears that somehow mobilizing her influential friends, she managed to get herself interrogated. The Gestapo wanted to know about the international society to which she belonged, and she managed to persuade them that the International Psychoanalytic Association was a wholly unpolitical, purely scientific body. By seven in the evening, Wiley could cable the good news to the secretary of state, "for Bullitt," as always: "Anna Freud released."* In his relief, Schur records, her father allowed himself to show some emotion.

This event, even more than Ernest Jones's eloquence, convinced Freud that it was time to leave. "Two prospects survive in these trying times," he wrote a little after to his son Ernst, "to see you all together, and to die in freedom." But the price of freedom was submission to the kind of organized bureaucratic thievery in which the Nazis specialized. No one could legally leave Nazi Austria without an *Unbedenklichkeitserklärung*—a "certificate of innocuousness"—available only after the potential emigré had met all the financial obligations that the regime had ingeniously invented and multiplied. On March 13, the board of the Vienna Psychoanalytic Society had decided to recommend immediate emigration to its Jewish members and to reconvene wherever Freud eventually found a new home. The one gentile member, Richard Sterba, refused to preside over an "Aryanized" psychoanalytic establishment and chose to share his Jewish colleagues' exile.

This gave the Austrians the assets of the society, its library, and the property of the publishing house to confiscate. As mean in small matters as they were inhuman in large ones—a characteristic of all totalitarian regimes—the authorities now enlarged the list of their demands on the Freuds: they insisted on collecting the tax imposed on Jews for "fleeing" the country—the *Reichsfluchtssteuer*—and, in addition, they wanted to get their hands on the stock of Freud's collected works which Martin Freud had prudently sent off to Switzerland, that they might burn them. Characteristically, they billed Martin Freud for the transport of the books back to Austria. Freud did not have the funds on hand to meet these charges; his cash had been confiscated, as had his bank account. But Marie Bonaparte was there. She had stayed near the Freuds throughout March and early April, and then returned to Vienna later that month, paying what had to be paid. Her presence was invaluable. "I think our last sad weeks in Vienna from 11th March until the end of May," Martin Freud wrote later in gratitude, "would have been quite unbearable without the presence of the Princess." She

---

*Recalling the events of this day later, Anna Freud thought that "there may have been some intervention behind the scenes. At least there was a mysterious telephone call after I had been there a few hours and this promoted me from waiting in an outer hall-way to sitting in an inner room." (Anna Freud to Jones, February 20, 1956. Jones papers, Archives of the British Psycho-Analytical Society, London.)

brought not only her money and her cheer, but also her intrepidity: when the S.S. came to take Anna Freud to the Gestapo, the princess asked to be arrested as well.

Even Anna Freud, usually so self-possessed, sometimes gave way to discouragement. "In calmer times," she wrote to Ernest Jones on April 3, using the intimate *du*, "I hope to be able to show you that I understand in full measure what you are now doing for us." What mainly held up the issuance of exit visas, Wiley reported to Sumner Welles, was the "liquidation" of Freud's publishing house. Marie Bonaparte was indefatigable, but the endless errands to officials and authorities fell for the most part on Anna Freud's shoulders. "Between yesterday and today," she recounted to Ernest Jones in late April, "I was at the lawyer's 5 times and 3 times at the Amer[ican] consulate. Everything is going slowly." At times, her discouragement came through in her letters to London, and, disciplined and self-critical, she regretted such displays. "Usually," she virtually apologized to Ernest Jones on April 26, "I write late in the evening, when I have already used up a large supply of so-called 'courage,' and then perhaps I let myself go a little too much." She was worrying above all about her father. "What do we do if his health does not hold out? But that," she added pensively, "is among the things one better does not ask."

In fact, Freud's health was standing up to the strain remarkably well, but he was condemned to passivity, which he detested. To beguile the time, waiting for the new holders of power to learn their trade and complete their larcenous business, he sorted his books, his antiquities, and his papers. He weeded out titles he did not want and tried to throw away letters and documents, though Marie Bonaparte and Anna Freud managed to rescue some of them for posterity, fishing them out of the wastebasket. More enjoyably, he spent hours translating, with his daughter, Marie Bonaparte's slender memorial tribute to her chow, Topsy. He even found the energy to tinker a little—"an hour a day"—with his *Moses and Monotheism.* On May 6—it happened to be Freud's eighty-second birthday—Ambassador Wilson reported to the secretary of state from Berlin that the Gestapo official in charge of the Freuds' case saw only one obstacle to their departure: the settlement of Freud's debts to his publisher. But this single bit of business took more time than expected. Three days later, Freud wrote his son Ernst from "Vienna, while waiting to move to London," to thank him for his birthday greetings: "We are waiting more or less patiently for our affairs to be settled. In view of the little time we have left to live, I fret at the delay. Anna's youthful vigor and optimistic energy have fortunately remained unshaken. Otherwise life would be difficult to carry on at all." He added a gloss harking back to an old preoccupation, the differences between men and women: "In general women hold up better than men do."* At this point, Freud was wholly reconciled to emigration, and in mid-May, he acknowledged to Ernest Jones the most powerful among his incentives: "The advantage which the resettlement will bring Anna is worth all our little sacrifices. For us old folks (73, 77, 82)"—his sister-in-law, his wife, himself—"the resettlement would not have been worth while."

Work, even a little work, remained for Freud the best defense against despair. Nor did his sardonic sense of humor desert him entirely. Just before the authorities let the Freuds go, they insisted he sign a statement that they had not ill-treated him. Freud signed, adding the comment, "I can most highly recommend the Gestapo to everyone"—*Ich kann die Gestapo jedermann auf das beste empfehlen.* It is a curious act inviting some speculation. Freud was lucky the S.S. men reading his commendation did not perceive the heavy sarcasm lurking in it. Nothing would have been more natural than to find his words offensive. Why, then, at the moment of liberation, take such a deadly risk? Was there something at work in Freud making him want to stay, and die, in Vienna? Whatever the deeper reason, his "praise" of the Gestapo was Freud's last act of defiance on Austrian soil.

The trek to England had been under way for some time. Minna Bernays was the first member of the family to leave, on May 5; Martin Freud went nine days later; Mathilde Hollitscher and her husband Robert, ten days after that. On May 25, Anna Freud confessed to a feeling of unreality: "One would not be surprised if the whole affair continued this way for a hundred years. We are no longer quite here and not yet there at all." As late as May 31, she reported that the papers were still not in order. Freud, his wife Martha, and their daughter Anna still had to wait for the *Unbedenklichkeitserklärung.*

That passport to liberty finally arrived on June 2, and on the same day, Dr. Pichler examined Freud once again, finding little to worry about. Two days later, on Saturday, June 4, Freud left Vienna at last. His two final communications from Berggasse 19 were a brief note to Arnold Zweig and a postcard to his nephew Samuel, giving his new London address. In his *Chronik,* laconically recording these events, Freud made a slip, the kind of error he had taught the world to take seriously: he mistakenly dated his day of departure as Saturday, June 3, when it should have been June 4. Was this a subtle message from his unconscious, contradicting the revelation hidden behind his impolitic compliment to the Gestapo? Was he anxious to leave Vienna after all? Or was he perhaps, on the contrary, giving a sign that he

---

*Freud had made the same point earlier. "The women," he wrote Jones on April 28, "are the most effective." (Freud Collection, D2, LC.)

wanted in fact to postpone his departure? One can only speculate. Four weeks before, on May 10, he had noted, "Departure within two weeks?" No doubt he faced exile with deep, partly unconscious ambivalence. "The triumphant feeling of liberation," he would write in his first letter from London, "is mingled too strongly with mourning, for one had still very much loved the prison from which one has been released."

Almost poetically, the exodus did not go off without a hitch. Max Schur, who was to accompany Freud as his personal physician, "was clumsy enough" to need an appendectomy and could not join his patient until June 15. At Anna Freud's suggestion, a young pediatrician, Josefine Stross, accompanied Freud instead. Safety came, as Freud put it with grateful precision, at "2:45 A.M.," on June 5, when the Orient Express crossed into France at Kehl. "After the Rhine Bridge," Freud exclaimed, recalling the moment, "we were free!" Except for fatigue manifesting itself in his accustomed heart pains, he took the voyage well. The reception in Paris was cordial if a little noisy, with ebullient journalists and photographers at the station in search of pictures and interviews. But Bullitt, too, was there, as were Ernst and Harry Freud, hovering protectively, and so was Marie Bonaparte, who promptly whisked him away to her elegant house. There he spent a delightful, restful day. "Marie," he reported, "surpassed herself with tenderness and considerateness." Then the Freuds crossed over to England by the night boat. Arriving at Victoria Station on the morning of June 6, they were greeted by members of their family and by the Joneses, and taken off to a rented house in northwest London, near Regent's Park. As Jones drove the Freuds through the "beautiful city," they went past some of London's tourist sights—Buckingham Palace, Piccadilly Circus, Regent Street—and Freud identified them for his wife. Little had he dreamed he would end his life in London, as an exile.

DEATH OF A STOIC

Freud had come to England, as he had said, "to die in freedom." But his first letter from London attests that neither the anxieties and harassments he had recently endured, nor the cancer that had been his intimate enemy for fifteen years, nor his advanced age—he was now eighty-two—had obliterated his vitality, his gift for observation and the telling phrase, and his middle-class habits. "Dear Friend," he wrote to Max Eitingon in Jerusalem, "I have sent you little news during the last few weeks. In return, I am writing you the first letter from the new home, even before I have got new stationery." A whole bourgeois world, now receded into history, stands behind this observation: it was simply a matter of course— wasn't it?—that wherever one lived, even if it was a rented, furnished place such as 39 Elsworthy Road, one had stationery printed with one's address. But even without the new letterhead, Freud could rehearse for his old friend from Berlin the course of recent events: the straggling of the Freud family, complete with maid and physician and chow, from Vienna via Paris to England; Schur's untimely appendicitis; the impact of the strenuous trip on Freud's heart; the exemplary kindness of Marie Bonaparte; the charming location of his new residence, with its garden and pleasing view.

There was something defensive about this reportorial style, and Freud, the old psychoanalyst, knew it and said so. But his wife, no analyst, felt her new situation quite as clearly. If one were not incessantly thinking of those one had left behind, she wrote a niece in late June, "one could be perfectly happy." Four of Freud's sisters were still in Vienna. He had provided them with 160,000 schillings—well over $20,000—a substantial amount. Yet the fate of these funds, to say nothing of the fate of these old ladies, was uncertain under so brutal and unpredictable a regime as Austria's new order. Even the experiences that gave him relief, or made him happy, shook Freud. Too much had happened in the past few months; what now surrounded him presented too many surprises. He could not casually assimilate the sharp contrasts. Everything, he told Eitingon, was still dreamlike, unreal. "The emotional situation is hard to grasp, barely describable." His utter delight at living in this new world was slightly compromised by some of its small oddities, by the question just how much longer his heart would hold out, by the serious illness of his sister-in-law. Minna Bernays lay in bed on the floor above him; he had not yet been able to visit her. Not surprisingly, he was experiencing intervals of depression. "But the children, the authentic as well as the adopted ones, are behaving charmingly. Math[ilde] is showing herself as competent as Anna had been in Vienna"—the highest compliment available to him. "Ernst is really what he has been called, *a tower of strength;* Lux"—Ernst's wife—"and their children are worthy of him; the men, Martin and Robert, are carrying their head high once again. Should I be the only one who does not join them, who disappoints his family? And my wife has remained healthy and victorious."

He had been exceedingly lucky. The *Manchester Guardian,* which announced the Freuds' arrival in a cordial article on June 7, quoted Anna Freud as saying that "in Vienna we were among the very few Jews who were treated decently. It is not true that we were confined to our home. My father never went out for weeks, but that was on account of his health." Ernst Freud substantiated his sister's report: "The general treatment of the Jews has been abominable, but not so in case of my father. He has been an exception." Martin Freud added that his father "will stay in England because he loves the country and loves the people." That was at once diplomatic and sincere.

To be safe was exhilarating enough, but Freud had other grounds for elation. On June 28, he reported to Arnold Zweig with undisguised pride, three secretaries of the "R.S." had visited him, bringing "the sacred book of the [Royal] Society" for his signature. "They left a facsimile of the book with me, and if you were with me, I could show you the signatures from I. Newton to Charles Darwin. Good company!" The invitation to add his name to the names of these illustrious scientists was delight enough; the willingness of the Royal Society to bend its rules and take the Charter Book to him was an added note of welcome. They had done so only once before, for the king of England. But, Freud could not help adding, it was a strange place, this England; they even wanted him to change his signature. Here, he was told, only a lord signed himself with his last name alone. So, experimentally, Freud signed his letter to Arnold Zweig in a style he had abandoned more than forty years earlier: "Sigm. Freud."

What mattered far more than these petty oddities was the outpouring of kindness and sympathy Freud experienced in England. Famous personages and ordinary Englishmen, total strangers nearly all of them, gave Freud a reception genial and thoughtful almost beyond his capacity for acceptance. "We have become popular all of a sudden," he wrote Eitingon. "The manager in the bank says, 'I know all about you'; the chauffeur driving Anna observes, 'Oh, it's Dr. Freud's place.' We are choking in flowers." Perhaps most remarkable of all: "You may indeed once more write anything you want. Letters are not being opened." Two weeks later, answering a letter from his brother Alexander, who had managed to get out of Austria in March and was safe in Switzerland, Freud confirmed his euphoric, almost incredulous assessment. With all its idiosyncrasies, England is "a blessed, a happy land, inhabited by kindly, hospitable people; that at least is the impression of the first weeks." He was amazed to see that from the third day of his stay, letters bearing only such addresses as "Dr. Freud, London," or "Overlooking Regent's Park" had reached him. His wife was no less astonished. But all that mail could not be neglected. "And the letters!" Freud exclaimed in mock horror. "I have been working for two weeks like a writing-coolie to sort the chaff from the wheat," and to answer those deserving a reply. He had mail from friends and "surprisingly many from strangers who only want to express their joy that we have escaped and are now safe, and want nothing for it in return." Beyond these, as was to be expected, he was being plagued by "the horde of autograph hunters, fools, madmen, and the pious who send tracts and gospels, want to save my soul, show the way to Christ, and enlighten me about the future of Israel. And then the learned societies of which I am already a member, and the innumerable many Jewish 'associations' of which I am supposed to become an honorary member. In short, for the first time and late in life I have experienced what fame means."

In the midst of all these gratifications, Freud was suffering a little from a symptom he had years earlier identified as survivor guilt. He had noticed a real inhibition against answering his brother's letter, for he and his family were very well, almost too well. While Freud did not mention his sisters left in Vienna, they were plainly on his mind. And Freud was feeling the pangs of exile. "Perhaps you have omitted the one point that the emigrant feels so particularly painfully," he wrote to a former analysand, the Swiss psycho-analyst Raymond de Saussure, who had congratulated him on his escape. "It is—one can only say—the loss of the language in which one had lived and thought, and which one will never be able to replace with another for all one's efforts at empathy." He was even having trouble giving up his accustomed "Gothic script." It was ironic: "One has been told so often that one is not a German. And, indeed, one is glad oneself that one no longer needs to be a German." Still, these were manageable discomforts. For the time being at least, Freud was not dying but living in freedom, and enjoying it as much as his poor health, his twinges of guilt, and the world would let him.

FREUD'S RESPONSE TO the bracing effect of his reception was to go back to serious work, always a good sign. On June 21, just two weeks after landing in England, he noted in his *Chronik,* "Moses III started again." A week later, he told Arnold Zweig that he was working on the third part of the *Moses* with pleasure. Apparently it was a pleasure that few others shared. He had just received a letter, he went on, "from a young Jewish American, in which I am asked not to deprive my poor, unhappy fellow Jews of the sole consola-tion left them in their misery." Around the same time, the eminent Jewish orientalist Abraham Shalom Yahuda called on him to make the same plea. Freud had not even completed the manuscript of *Moses and Monotheism,* but the very prospect of its publication worried Jews eager to hold on to Moses in this time of terrible troubles. In 1937, Freud had published the first two essays in *Imago,* but a book available to the general public posed a far more powerful threat than two papers on Moses as an Egyptian in what was, after all, an obscure periodical for psychoanalysts.

From then on, anxious appeals, angry denunciations, contemptuous refuta-tions, and a scattering of applause became a leitmotiv. Freud was not moved, but professed to believe that what others called his obstinacy or arrogance was really a sign of modesty. He was not influential enough, he argued, to disturb the faith of a single believing Jew.* Passionately attached to his solution of the Moses question and the relevance of this solution to the history of the Jews, Freud was self-willed and surprisingly blind to its psychological implications for those who regarded Moses as their ancestral father. He had not always been so obtuse. In the opening sentences of the first essay, "Moses an Egyptian," he had faced the issue directly: "To deprive a people of a man it praises as the greatest among its sons is not something one does gladly or irresponsibly, especially if one belongs to this people oneself. But," he insisted, "one must not allow oneself to slight the truth in behalf of supposed national interests." He had found it painful enough to have Austrian politicians cow him into even temporary silence; he would not let fellow Jews do the same to him. So he went ahead working on his "Moses III"; it was an idea he must see through to the end. On July 17, he could triumphantly announce to his brother Alexander, "Have just written down the last sentence of my Moses III." Early the following month, his daughter Anna read a segment of this third part to an international congress of psychoanalysts in Paris.

While *Moses* absorbed most of his attention, Freud did not wholly neglect his other professional interests. Early in July, in one of his last letters to Theodor Reik, he showed that his old animus against Americans on the issue of lay analysis was still flourishing. Reik, who had, in a way, started the whole debate a dozen years earlier, was now settling in the United States. "What evil wind has blown you, of all people, to America?" Freud caustically asked him. "You should have known how amiably our colleagues there receive lay analysts, since for them, analysis is nothing else but one of the maidservants of psychiatry." He added, his animosity subduing his judgment, "Could you not have stayed in the Netherlands longer?" In the same month, he categorically denied that he had changed his mind about lay analysis and denounced the report as "a silly rumour." In fact, he wrote, "I have never repudiated these views and I insist on them even more intensely than before."

The dangers to psychoanalysis, whether in untrustworthy America or, far worse, in Nazi-dominated Central Europe, weighed on Freud's mind. The

---

*This remained a persistent theme in his disclaimers. "No one who seeks consolation in the holy Bible or in the prayers of the synagogue," he wrote as late as July 1939, "is in danger of loosing his faith by my preachings. I even think he will not come to learn, whatever it is I believe and defend in my books. Faith cannot be shaken by such means. I do not write for the people or the mass of believers. I just produce scientific stuff for the interest of a minority which has no faith to loose." (Freud to a Dr. Magarik, July 4, 1939. In English. Typescript copy, Freud Collection, Z3, LC. The spelling errors *may* be the transcriber's.)

Verlag in Vienna had been destroyed in March 1938, after the Anschluss; arrangements to have *Moses and Monotheism* printed had to be made with a publisher in Amsterdam. Now Hanns Sachs, who had sagely left Berlin for Boston in 1932, a year before Hitler's accession to power, wrote to propose a journal of applied psychoanalysis to succeed the defunct *Imago.* Freud was reluctant to give his approval to the scheme; he feared that it spelled the end of any effort to continue publishing psychoanalytic journals in German. "Your plan for a new, English-language *Imago* in America did not please me at first," he wrote to Sachs; he did not want to "let the light be extinguished completely in Germany." But Anna Freud and Ernest Jones persuaded him that his objections were groundless, and he proposed the name *American Imago,* which Sachs promptly adopted. A few days later, on July 19, Stefan Zweig, then in exile in England, brought Salvador Dali to call, and Freud, whose relation to the surrealists was equivocal, was much taken with "that young Spaniard, with his candid fanatical eyes and his undeniable technical mastery."

Three days later, on July 22, Freud started his *Outline of Psychoanalysis,* meticulously recording the date on the opening page. He drafted it with impatient speed, using abbreviations and omitting articles, and found his "vacation work," he wrote his daughter Anna, then in Paris at a conference, an "amusing occupation." Yet the *Outline* is a powerful, if succinct, statement of his mature views. In the five dozen pages he managed to write before he abandoned the manuscript, he summed up what he had learned about the mental apparatus, the theory of the drives, the development of sexuality, the nature of the unconscious, the interpretation of dreams, and psychoanalytic technique. Not all in this substantial fragment is pure summary: Freud dropped hints at new departures in his thought, especially about the ego. In one intriguing passage, he speculated that the time might come when chemical substances would alter balances in the mind and thus make psychoanalytic therapy, now the best available treatment for neuroses, quite obsolete. At eighty-two, Freud was still open to the future, could still entertain the thought of radical revisions in psychoanalytic practices. The *Outline of Psychoanalysis* looks like a highly condensed primer, but it is not for beginners; among Freud's "popularizations," it is by far the most difficult. With its comprehensiveness and its implicit warnings against letting psychoanalytic thinking ossify, it may stand as Freud's testament to the profession he had founded.

FREUD STOPPED WORK on the *Outline* in early September, when there were alarming signs that his malignancy was active once again. After anxious consultations with English physicians, the Freuds summoned Dr. Pichler from Vienna, and on September 8 he performed major surgery, which took over two hours, cutting through Freud's cheek for better access to the tumor. After the operation, Anna Freud reported promptly to Marie Bonaparte, with evident relief, "I am very glad that it is already today, and no longer yesterday." This operation proved to be Freud's last; he was now too frail to sustain anything more drastic than radium treatments, which were drastic enough.

Freud was allowed to go home from the clinic some days later, and on September 27 he moved into the house that had been prepared for him at 20 Maresfield Gardens, in Hampstead. It was commodious and agreeable, made still more agreeable by a lovely garden awash in flowers and shaded by tall trees. The fall was mild, and he spent much time outdoors, reading and resting in a swing couch. The house was arranged around his needs and wishes, to make him feel as much at home as humanly possible. The possessions he had had to ransom from the Nazis—his books, his antiquities, his famous couch—had finally arrived and were placed so that his two downstairs rooms broadly resembled his consulting room and the adjoining study at Berggasse 19. Paula Fichtl, the maid who had been with the Freud family since 1929 and had dusted his statuettes with supreme care in Vienna, now faithfully assigned them, as closely as she could from memory, the places they had once occupied. Among these cherished antiquities was the Greek krater, a gift from Marie Bonaparte, that had stood behind Freud's desk in Vienna and would one day hold his, and his wife's, ashes. Here at Maresfield Gardens, enveloped by his reconstituted old environment, Freud lived out the year he still had to live.

While the operation had sapped Freud's reserves of strength, he was alert enough to follow the events of the day. The international situation was steadily deteriorating, and the threat of war hung over the civilized world like a poisonous fog. On September 29, 1938, Neville Chamberlain and Édouard Daladier met Hitler in Munich and consented to have Germany swallow the "German" regions of Czechoslovakia in return for a dubious promise of pacific Nazi behavior in the future. On his return to England, Chamberlain was hailed by many as a savior and denounced by a few as a shameful appeaser. Writing to Freud, Arnold Zweig speculated whether the so-called peacemakers would understand "what a price they make others pay—until they pay it themselves." Munich bought the Allies a few months' time and, after the awakening, a reputation for treachery and cowardice, nothing more. The very name of the city where the prime ministers of Britain and France had sold Czechoslovakia to the Nazis became a synonym for abject surrender. Freud's comment on Munich in his *Chronik*, on September 30, was terse: "Peace."

He was not yet well enough to keep up with his correspondence. The first letter he sent from "Home," to Marie Bonaparte, was written on October 4, a whole week after he had moved in. The old obsessive promptitude that had been his signature was now gone; Freud had to husband his resources. In his letter he explained why. The operation, he told his princess, had been "the most severe since 1923 and has cost me a great deal." He had only energy enough for a short message: "I can hardly write, no better than speak or smoke"; he complained that he was terribly tired and weak. But for all that he was taking on three analytic patients. And once he had sufficiently recovered, he went back to his desk. Having abandoned the *Outline of Psychoanalysis,* he started another didactic essay, "Some Elementary Lessons in Psychoanalysis," on October 20. This, too, was fated to remain a fragment, and a very brief one. As he told Marie Bonaparte in mid-November, he was "still quite capable of work." But what he could do was strictly limited: "I can write letters, but nothing else." He was tantalized by one last fantasy. He wanted to seal his long-standing affection for England and, one supposes, his implacable rejection of Austria, by being naturalized as a British subject. But here his influential English friends and his impeccable connections failed him, and he died with that wish unrealized.

AN AIR OF FAREWELL hung over these fall days and months. Freud's last writings, published posthumously, read like so many valedictories. Aware of mortality, Freud urged his friends to come soon: when the celebrated French entertainer, the diseuse Yvette Guilbert, whom he had known and much liked for years, told him in October that she wanted to visit him the following May to celebrate his birthday, he was touched but concerned about the months of waiting: "At my age every postponement has a painful connotation." The stream of visitors, thoughtfully regulated by Martha and Anna Freud, slowed down but did not cease. Some, like Stefan Zweig, were old acquaintances; others, like H. G. Wells, were admirers of more recent vintage. His intimates were, of course, the most congenial visitors of all. Marie Bonaparte, who came often to stay at Maresfield Gardens, was virtually a member of the Freud family. Arnold Zweig, cut off from most of his accustomed sources of income, used an unexpected royalty check from the Soviet Union to finance a visit to Freud in September and stayed for several weeks. Saying farewell to Freud once again from Paris in mid-October, he recalled their long conversations, which, he wrote in fond apology, must have been exhausting.

During all this time, there were attempts to talk Freud out of publishing his book on Moses.* In mid-October, Charles Singer, an eminent historian

---

*In October, one correspondent from Palestine, Israel Doryon, suggested to Freud that he might have adopted the idea that Moses was an Egyptian from Josef Popper-Lynkeus, an Austrian physicist,

of science, delicately asked one of Freud's sons to convey the message that he would be wise to keep *Moses and Monotheism* in his desk, particularly since the English churches, bulwarks against anti-Semitism, would take the book as an attack on religion. His politic plea was as futile as Abraham Yahuda's earlier intervention had been. The book, Freud wrote Singer, faithfully expressing his lifelong commitment to science once again, would be "an attack on religion only in so far as, after all, every scientific investigation of a religious belief has unbelief as its presupposition." He professed himself dismayed at the response of Jews to his scientific speculations. "Naturally," he insisted, he did not enjoy offending them. "But what can I do about it? I have occupied my whole long life with standing up for what I considered to be the scientific truth, even when it was uncomfortable and disagreeable to my fellow men. I cannot close it with an act of disavowal." He intimated that there was not a little irony in all these requests for self-censorship: "One reproaches us Jews that in the course of time we have become cowardly. (We were once a courageous nation.) I have acquired no share in this transformation. Hence I must risk it."

In fact, far from abandoning his project, Freud was energetically pressing forward to secure an English translation—and promptly. Katharine Jones was working on it with her husband's assistance, but at the end of October, Ernest Jones sent disappointing word that the translation would not be completed before February or March of 1939. In a long, urgent reply, Freud did not conceal his consternation. He recognized that the Joneses' time was valuable, he wrote, and their conscientiousness great. But, after all, they had volunteered to take this burden upon themselves, and the postponement was disagreeable to him in more than one respect. He reminded Jones of his great age and uncertain life expectancy: "Above all, a few months mean more to me than to someone else"; it was a "comprehensible wish" to see the English version in print in his lifetime. Perhaps Jones could find someone else to translate a portion so that the book could be finished within two months. What is more, he called to Jones's attention "the impatience of the American publisher (Knopf NY), from whom we have already accepted payment."

This was not a subterfuge. Since the summer, Blanche Knopf had been in touch with Martin Freud about securing the American rights to *Moses and Monotheism*. With her husband, Alfred, Blanche Knopf was running a civi-

philosopher, and essayist whose sensitive work on dreams and other psychological issues Freud greatly admired. Doryon's suggestion, far from distressing Freud, greatly interested him. "Phenomena of so-called cryptomnesia"—an unconscious and guiltless borrowing of material—"have very frequently occurred with me, and have clarified the origins of apparently original ideas." He did not mind being unoriginal; his sole contribution, he wrote, had been his "little piece of psychoanalytic strengthening" of an old contention. (Freud to Doryon, October 7, 1938. Freud Museum, London.)

lized publishing house in New York, famous for its distinguished domestic authors, such as H. L. Mencken; its even more distinguished foreign list, including Thomas Mann; and its distinctive design. To appear under the Knopf imprint would indeed be desirable. In mid-November, Blanche Knopf called on Freud and made various suggestions for minor alterations, which Freud was not disposed to accept. It must have been a highly charged meeting: the slender, intense, self-assured American publisher making some "slight suggestions," attempting to persuade a stubborn Freud to revise a manuscript that had perhaps cost him more than any other. Freud offered to get out of the contract, but Blanche Knopf wisely refused, and in the end, the house of Knopf would publish *Moses and Monotheism* in the United States. During these negotiations, Freud was corresponding with his transla-tor J. Dwossis, in Jerusalem, about a translation of *Moses and Monotheism* into Hebrew. Much as he looked forward to the translation, Freud felt constrained to warn Dwossis that while the book would be a "continuation of the theme of *Totem and Taboo* as applied to the history of the Jewish religion," one should not overlook the inconvenient fact that "its contents are particularly suited to offend Jewish sensibilities, in so far as they do not submit themselves to science." Eager as he was for a translation, he did not fail to alert his translator that it might be risky.

THE FATE OF his *Moses* was immensely important to Freud, but the Nazis confronted him with events of far greater gravity. On November 10, Freud recorded in his *Chronik,* "Pogroms in Germany." The previous night, the Nazi regime had orchestrated a series of "spontaneous" demonstrations—sloganeering, window breaking, looting, and violence—and mass arrests. The excuse was the death of a German diplomat in Paris, shot by a desperate young Polish Jew, but the concerted action had been carefully prepared long before. Across the country, in small towns and large, some 7,000 Jewish stores were demolished; nearly all the synagogues in the country were burned to the ground; and perhaps 50,000 German Jews were transported to concentration camps. Extortionate collective fines, irrational and humiliating bureaucratic exactions, made emigration at once imperative and difficult. The end of Jewish life in Germany, already embittered by earlier racial laws and dis-criminatory regulations, was in sight, as German Jews desperately sought refuge in a world reluctant to receive them. The vandalism and the brutality of these "recent revolting events," which came to be known in black euphe-mism as *Kristallnacht*—the night of shattered windows—aroused in Freud memories of Vienna in March; they only "exacerbated the problem of what is to be done with the four old women between seventy-five and eighty," his sisters still living in Vienna. He asked Marie Bonaparte whether she could perhaps bring them to France, and she energetically tried to do so, but the bureaucracy, and the times, were against her.

These were matters of life and death. But they could not wholly divert Freud's attention from the mundane business that mattered to him, psychoanalytic business. This was just another distasteful set of problems the Nazis had visited upon his world. While psychoanalysis in Germany survived, more or less, under the aegis of the German General Medical Society for Psychotherapy, the so-called Göring Institute, headed by a cousin of Göring's, it was compelled to accommodate itself to Nazi racial ideology, use a purged vocabulary, and do without any of its Jewish practitioners. No independence of spirit, let alone research, could be expected from that quarter. In Austria, all traces of psychoanalysis had been obliterated. The Swiss, under the dubious leadership of Jung, who had been talking for some time about the difference between the Germanic and the Jewish unconscious, were hardly allies Freud could trust. In France, psychoanalysis remained embattled. It is true that the United States had been receiving an increasing number of German, Austrian, and Hungarian analysts, but Freud, we know, had little confidence in the Americans, and the lay analysts who streamed into New York and other large American cities constantly came up against regulations that prohibited them from practicing psychoanalysis. Hence, as he acknowledged to Ernest Jones, "the events of recent years have ordained that London has become chief place and center of the psychoanalytic movement." Under these circumstances, Freud was pleased to have an English publisher, John Rodker, found a house called the Imago Publishing Company to bring out a new and improved edition, in German, of his collected works. The German-language psychoanalytic journals that "political events in Austria" had kept from appearing also secured new life. Early in 1939, a periodical combining the old *Internationale Zeitschrift* and *Imago*, with Freud signing as editor, began publication in England.

Freud was still writing, a little—a brief comment on anti-Semitism published by an emigré journal Arthur Koestler was editing in Paris, and a letter to the editor of *Time and Tide* on the same subject. And still the visitors came. Toward the end of January 1939, his English publishers, Leonard and Virginia Woolf, owners of the Hogarth Press, were invited to tea at 20 Maresfield Gardens. Leonard Woolf was surprised into admiration. In his own right and as the husband of a socially prominent and internationally renowned novelist, he had consorted with celebrities all his life and was not easily impressed. But Freud, he remembered in his autobiography, "was not only a genius, but also, unlike many geniuses, an extraordinarily nice man." Woolf felt "no call to praise the famous men whom I have known. Nearly all famous men are disappointing or bores, or both. Freud was neither; he had an aura, not of fame, but of greatness." Tea with Freud was, Woolf thought, "not an easy interview. He was extraordinarily courteous in a formal, old-fashioned way—for instance, almost ceremoniously he presented Virginia with a flower. There was something about him as of a half-extinct volcano, something sombre, suppressed, reserved. He gave me the feeling which only a very few people whom I have met gave me, a feeling of great gentleness, but behind the gentleness, great strength."

Freud's family, Woolf observed, had turned his rooms at Maresfield Gardens into something of a museum, "for there were all round him a number of Egyptian antiquities he had collected." When Virginia Woolf speculated that perhaps if the Allied powers had lost the First World War there would have been no Hitler, Freud disagreed: "Hitler and the Nazis would have come and would have been much worse if Germany had won the war." Woolf concluded his account with a charming anecdote. He had read a newspaper story about a man convicted of stealing some books from Foyle's bookshop in London, among them a volume by Freud; the magistrate who fined him had said he wished he could sentence him to read all of Freud's works as punishment. Freud was amused by the story but also "deprecatory about it. His books, he said, had made him infamous, not famous. A formidable man." Virginia Woolf, as was her way, was more acerbic than her husband. Freud struck her as "a screwed up shrunk very old man: with a monkey's light eyes," inarticulate but alert. The other Freuds she thought socially and psychologically hungry in the extreme—as no doubt they were, in their situation as refugees. But even she could not deny that she had been in an unforgettable presence.

THE WOOLFS HAD tea with a man who was already very ill. Freud made only two entries in his *Chronik* for the month of January 1939, both of them recording moments of physical distress: "Lumbago" on the second of the month, "pains in bones" on the thirty-first. In fact, from the middle of the month onward, talk of his cancer invaded Freud's letters to an alarming extent. There were suspicious swellings near the cancerous lesions, and he was in ever greater pain. The man who disdained medications lest they cloud his mind now lived, as he had for some time, on minor painkillers like Pyramidon. In mid-February, Freud told Arnold Zweig that his "condition" was threatening "to become interesting. Since my operation in September I have been suffering from pains in the jaw which are growing stronger slowly but steadily, so that I cannot get through my daily chores and my nights without a hot-water bottle and sizable doses of aspirin." He was not certain whether it was a harmless episode "or a progress in the uncanny process against which we have been battling for 16 years." Marie Bonaparte, who was in constant touch, had consulted a French specialist in radium therapy, and there was some discussion of having Freud journey to Paris for medical treatment. Meanwhile, he added, no one knew, but he could "very well imagine that the whole is the beginning of the end which, after all, steadily lies in wait for us. Meanwhile I have these paralyzing pains." In late February, Dr. Antoine Lacassagne came over from Paris to examine Freud in Schur's presence, and he returned two weeks later to apply radium treatments. But the pains persisted.

Freud was still interested in the world, still sardonic, still writing to his closest friends, though his correspondence with many of them was drawing to an end. On February 21, Pfister reminded him, "How correctly you judged the German mentality on my last visit to Vienna! And how glad we must be that you have escaped a nation regressed to the sadistic father!" On March 5, in his last letter to Arnold Zweig, Freud gave some details of his afflictions and the continuing uncertainty of the physicians, and then suggested that Zweig might try his hand at analyzing a "Nazi-soul." But while the condition of the world remained interesting to Freud, his own condition necessarily had priority. A week later, in his usual restrained way, Freud vented some of his feelings to Sachs: the consulting physicians thought that a mixture of X-ray and radium therapy might be effective and would, he thought, "add some weeks or months of life." Freud was not sure it was worth the effort. "I don't deceive myself about the chances of the final result at my age. I feel tired and exhausted by all that they do to me. As a way to the unavoidable end it is as good as any other although I would not have chosen it myself."

By this time the verdict on his condition was in. A biopsy performed on February 28 was positive; the cancer was at work again, located so far back in his mouth that an operation was not indicated. For a time, X-ray treatments contained the growth, surpassing Schur's expectations, but the improvement proved only temporary. Yet through it all, Freud rejected the easy consolation of spurious hopes. "My dear Marie," he wrote to his princess in late April, "I have not written you for a long time, while you were bathing in the blue sea." Marie Bonaparte had been vacationing in St. Tropez. "I assume you know why, recognize it, too, from my handwriting." He confessed to her that he was "not doing well, my illness and the consequences of the treatment share in the cause, in a proportion unknown to me. One has tried to draw me into an atmosphere of optimism: the cancer is in shrinkage, the reaction manifestations are temporary. I do not believe it, and do not like being deceived." His psychoanalyst daughter was ever more indispensable to him: "You know that Anna is not coming to the meeting in Paris"—a congress of French-speaking psychoanalysts; "I am becoming less and less independent and more dependent on her." Once again, as so often these days, he wished for death. An illness "that would cut off the cruel process would be very desirable."

The letter is rich and revealing. It documents, once again, Freud's affection and need for his daughter and, at the same time, his detestation of dependence. And it underscores, once again, his sense that he had a right to the full truth about himself, no matter how discouraging. At least he could be confident that his personal physician, Max Schur, would not fail him in this respect as Felix Deutsch had done in 1923. Unfortunately, Schur was compelled to leave Freud for some critical weeks. Late in April, in a cruel quandary, he traveled to the United States to settle his wife and two small children, apply for his citizenship papers, and try to obtain his medical license. He was ridden with guilt, but Freud seemed to be feeling better after his X-ray treatments and Schur could not in good conscience delay his departure. He had received a visa for the United States and, citing the need to stay close to Freud, an extension until the end of April. But the American consular authorities, forced to follow an inflexible immigration law, would not extend the visa once more. Threatened with losing his right to immigrate to the United States for years, Schur decided to go and return as quickly as possible.

During these months, as before during the bleakest days in Nazi Austria, Max Schur established himself as a figure almost as central to Freud as his daughter Anna. Freud's repeated reference to him as his "personal physician" sounds almost regal, but he liked Schur and treated him as a trusted associate. So did Freud's children: we recall that it was Schur who supplied Martin and Anna Freud with the lethal drug he hoped they would not need to swallow. Schur had discovered Freud in 1915, when, as a young medical student, he listened with mounting excitement to the lectures later published as the *Introductory Lectures on Psychoanalysis.* While he chose to specialize in internal medicine, he kept up with psychoanalysis, and this persistent fascination, rare in an internist, had commended him to Princess Marie Bonaparte, who happened to consult him in 1927 and then, for more intensive treatments, in the following year. She urged Freud to take on Schur as his physician, and he did so in March 1929. He never regretted following her advice, and described himself as Schur's "docile patient, even when it is not easy for me." In fact, he rebelled against Schur on only two matters: he repeatedly complained that Schur's bills were too low; and—a more consequential act of disobedience—he disregarded Schur's advice to give up his beloved, necessary cigars. At their first meeting, Freud and Schur had settled the delicate matter of frankness, and Freud then broached an even more difficult issue: "Promise me also: when the time comes, you won't let them torment me unnecessarily." Schur promised, and the two men shook hands on it. By the spring of 1939, the time to keep this promise was almost ripe.

ONE OCCASION SCHUR'S necessary absence made him miss was Freud's eighty-third birthday. Marie Bonaparte came to 20 Maresfield Gardens, and stayed a few days. Yvette Guilbert, too, was present, as she had promised, and gave Freud her photograph signed with an adoring message: "With all my heart!"—*De tout mon coeur au grand Freud! Yvette Guilbert, 6 Mai 1939.* Then, on May 19, Freud had a real reason to celebrate. He triumphantly noted in his *Chronik,* "Moses in English." He had, as he had hoped, lived to see *Moses and Monotheism* published for the English-speaking world. But its appearance was not an unmixed blessing for him, or for his readers.

A look at the long essay completing the trio of papers on Moses serves to confirm the wisdom of Freud's earlier prudence. He did not lose sight of Moses and of his central question, What made the Jew what he is? But in that concluding essay on Moses and monotheism he generalized his inquiry to encompass all religion. He might well have called the book *The Past of an Illusion.* Indeed, despite all its personal digressions and asides, all its autobiographical references, *Moses and Monotheism* recalls certain persistent themes in his psychoanalytic work: the Oedipus complex, the application of that complex to prehistory, the neurotic ingredient in all religion, the relation of the leader to his followers.* Beyond these, the book touches on the only too sadly pertinent, apparently ineradicable phenomenon of anti-Semitism and on Freud's Jewish ancestry. Even one of the eccentric notions he had caught late in life makes a somewhat coy appearance as a footnote: his conviction that Edward de Vere, earl of Oxford, had really written Shakespeare's plays, a farfetched and somewhat embarrassing theory with which he would regale his incredulous visitors and no less incredulous correspondents.† But the identity of Shakespeare was quite incidental to his main concerns. Freud the incurable secularist was returning to the impious proposition he had maintained for decades: religion is a collective neurosis.

*In these years, Freud was engaged in a friendly dispute with Marie Bonaparte, who worshiped him, as to whether he was a great man or not. He decided that he was not, but that he had discovered great things.

†Freud pursued this chimera through some years, discussing it especially with Ernest Jones, who bravely tried to talk him out of his notion. He had been much impressed with Thomas Looney's *"Shakespeare" Identified* (1920), in which Shakespeare is "revealed" to be the earl of Oxford, and had read it twice. (See, among his letters, above all, Freud to Jones, March 11, 1928. Freud Collection, D2, LC.) Jones shrewdly connects this harmless mania with Freud's puzzled fascination with telepathy. Both, he suggests, support the view that things are not what they seem to be. (See *Jones* III, 428–30.)

Once Freud's complete argument was in print, it turned out that Christians had as good reasons as Jews to find *Moses and Monotheism* unpalatable, even scandalous. Freud interpreted the murder of Moses by the ancient Hebrews, postulated in the second essay, as a reenactment of the primal crime against the father, the crime he had analyzed in *Totem and Taboo*. A new edition of a prehistoric trauma, it constituted the return of the repressed. Hence the Christian tale of a spotless Jesus sacrificing himself for sinful mankind must conceal, "obviously in tendentious distortion," another such crime. Surely, Freud asked, sounding much like a relentless detective confronting a cornered criminal, "how should someone guiltless of the murder be able to take the guilt of the murderers upon himself by letting himself be killed? In historical reality such a contradiction did not exist. The 'redeemer' could be none other than the one chief culprit, the leader of the brother-band who had overpowered the father." Freud did not think it necessary to decide if such a shadowy crime had ever taken place, or such a chief rebel ever existed. In Freud's scheme of things, reality and fantasy were, after all, brothers if not twins. If the crime was only imagined, "Christ is the heir of a wishful fantasy that remained unfulfilled." But if it had really happened, he is the great criminal's "successor and reincarnation." Whatever the historical truth, the "Christian ceremony of Holy Communion" is a repetition of the ancient totem meal, though in its tender, worshipful version. Judaism and Christianity, then, though tied by many affinities, differ decisively in their attitude toward the father: "Judaism had been a religion of the father, Christianity became a religion of the son."

Freud's analysis, precisely in sounding so scientific and so dispassionate, is extremely disrespectful to Christianity. It treats the centerpiece of the Christian story as a gigantic, if unconscious deception. But Freud had more up his sleeve. A Jew, Saul of Tarsus—Paul—was the first to recognize obscurely the reason for the depression that had weighed on the civilization of his time: "We have killed God the father." It was a truth he could bear only in "the delusional guise of the glad tidings." In short, the Christian tale of redemption through Jesus, his life and fate, was a self-protective fiction hiding some terrible acts—or wishes.

Moses and Monotheism, to be sure, did not spare the Jews. They had never acknowledged the murder of the father. But the Christians had moved away from denial and admitted the murder—and thus had been saved. In the late 1920s, Freud had called religion, all religion, an illusion. Now he characterized Christianity as the most severe kind of illusion, blending into the madness of delusion. Not content with this insult to Christians, he added another: "In some respects," their religion "represented a cultural regression against the older, as is indeed regularly the case with the irruption or admission of new masses of people of a lower level. The Christian religion did not maintain the height of spirituality to which Judaism had risen." At their best, imbued with Moses's message that the children of Israel are God's chosen people, Jews had rejected "magic and mysticism," felt encouraged to cultivate their mental and spiritual qualities, and "blissful in the possession of the truth," treasured the mind and morality.

In this appraisal of historical Judaism, Freud the atheist Jew showed himself the true heir of his father, Jacob Freud, whose motto had simply been, "Think ethically and act morally." We know, Freud commented, "that Moses conveyed to the Jews the exalted feeling of being a chosen people; a new, valuable portion was added to the secret treasure of the people through the dematerialization of God. The Jews retained the tendency toward intellectual interests; the political misfortune of the nation taught it to value the sole possession that remained to it, its literature, at its true worth." Proud words to throw into the teeth of the Nazis' systematic slander, book burnings, and murderous concentration camps.

The conflicting attitudes of Jews and non-Jews toward the primal crime also help to explain for Freud the persistence of anti-Semitism, to which he devoted some trenchant pages. Whatever its origins, he suggested, Jew-hatred exhibits a depressing truth: Christians are not good Christians at all but rather, beneath a thin veneer, the polytheistic barbarians they have always been. Certainly one prominent ingredient in the enduring phenomenon of anti-Semitism was, in Freud's view, jealousy, sheer envy.

THIS SOMEWHAT BACKHANDED praise of Judaism did not placate Jewish scholars. At the beginning of June, a reviewer of Freud's *Moses and Monotheism* in *John O'London's Weekly*, Hamilton Fyfe, found the book "of the most vivid interest historically and spiritually." But he observed, not without cause, "What the author's fellow-Jews will say to it I dare not think!" They said a great deal, little of it complimentary. Anxious, and hence enraged, about what they foresaw as its probable consequences, they treated *Moses and Monotheism* with contempt or silence. Turning the weapons of psychoanalysis on its founder, they wondered why he should have tried to deprive the Jews of their Moses. Was it from a desire to flee Judaism in a final gesture? Was he, feeling the return of the repressed, doing his desperate best not to become like his father? Was it perhaps (and this was a favorite) that Freud grandiosely identified with Moses, the stranger who had given a great people its laws and marked its character forever? Later, Martin Buber, in his study of Moses, angrily confined his comments on Freud's book to one disdainful footnote, referring to it as a "regrettable" performance, "unscientific," and "based on groundless hypotheses."* J. M. Lask, writing in the *Palestine Review* of Jerusalem, called Freud, "with all respect to his deep learning and originality in his own field," an *"Am Haaretz"*—a boorish ignoramus. And Abraham Yahuda charged that Freud's words seemed to him like words "one of the most fanatical Christians" might utter "in his hatred of Israel."

But Christians were outraged in their own behalf.† Father Vincent McNabb, writing in the *Catholic Herald* of London, found "unquotable pages in *Moses and Monotheism,*" pages which "make us ask ourselves if their writer has not a sexual obsession." Father McNabb in fact moved from name calling to threats. "Professor Freud is naturally grateful to *'free, gener-ous England'* for the welcome it has given him," he wrote. "But if his frank championship of atheism and incest is widely recognised we wonder how long the welcome will remain in an England that still calls itself Christian." These were the accents that Freud, had he read the review, would have recognized from Austrian clerics in his Vienna days.

The letter-writing public, too, was vocal, even before *Moses and Monotheism* was published. A barrage hurtled toward Freud, as strangers from Palestine and the United States, South Africa and Canada, expressed their distaste for Freud's ideas with uninhibited freedom. One suggested that the sort of biblical criticism he employed was typical for impious Jews seeking to justify their desertion of the fundamental truths of the Jewish religion. Another voiced the hope that Freud would "not publish this book," since it would generate "irreparable harm" and only hand "a further weapon" to "Goebbels and the other beasts." Still another, an anonymous writer from Boston, berated Freud in some breathless paragraphs: "I read in the local press your statement that Moses was not a Jew. / It is to be regretted that you could not go to your grave without disgracing yourself, you old nitwit. / We have renegades like you by the thousands, we are glad we are rid of them and we

---

*Early in 1939, Max Eitingon had a long discussion with Martin Buber in Jerusalem, and reported to Freud that as soon as *Moses and Monotheism* appeared, Buber would have to write a refutation. As a "Jewish sociologist of religion," he had already found little to agree with in *Totem and Taboo;* nor had he accepted Freud's *Interpretation of Dreams,* which, to him, slighted the creative work of dreams. "It is clear," Eitingon commented, "that we now have in this country a great critic of psychoanalysis." (Eitingon to Freud, February 16, 1939. Freud Museum, London.) Freud replied testily on March 5, "Martin Buber's pious phrases will not harm the *Interpretation of Dreams* very much. The *Moses* is far more vulnerable, and I am prepared for the Jewish assault on it." (By permission of Sigmund Freud Copyrights, Wivenhoe.)

†A Marxist response is also of interest. Howard Evans in the *Daily Worker* of London, writing from his secure doctrinaire perspective, was willing to be somewhat indulgent with Freud: considering his "ideological limitations," one could hardly "expect this great bourgeois scientist to adopt a dialectical approach at the age of 83." (Review of *Moses and Monotheism,* *Daily Worker* [London], July 5, 1939. Freud Museum, London.)

hope soon to be rid of you. / It is to be regretted that the Gangsters in Germany did not put you into a concentration camp, that's where you belong." Others, writers and, later, reviewers, were marginally more polite, and a few even found Freud's ideas stimulating, or partly correct. One of these, one Alexandre Burnacheff, writing from Rio de Janeiro, told Freud that he was working on a similar book and that his own view "coincidates" with Freud's, and asked for a copy of the English edition of *Moses and Monotheism*, C.O.D.

Certainly the evidence on which Freud depended was far from solid; it was speculative at best, outmoded in part, unsettled in details. Freud's conjecture that the Hebrew word for "Lord," *Adonai,* might derive from the Egyptian monotheistic worship of Aton, a guess in which his own confidence was modest, seems improbable; his single-minded Lamarckianism, according to which historical events are transmitted in the unconscious from generation to generation, is no more trustworthy in *Moses and Monotheism* than in any of his earlier constructions. But the Freud who in his last years brooded on Moses the Egyptian and his later namesake was not a closet anti-Semite or a self-styled prophet leading his ungrateful followers toward the promised land of psychoanalytic truth, a land he should glimpse but never enter. He was the intellectual speculator unrestrained by clinical material, driven to give house room to conjectures of which he was enamored.

Such conjectures kept Freud in their grip despite persuasive voices testifying against them. The Freud who gave Moses to the Egyptians and had the ancient Hebrews murder him was the investigator who, contradicting dominant scholarly opinion, became convinced that the author of Shakespeare's plays could not possibly be some insignificant, ill-educated actor. Freud was, after all, the intrepid discoverer who had defied the scientific establishment and sided with the superstitious and the barely literate who believed that dreams have meaning. Had this receptive naiveté not produced one of the decisive break-throughs in the science of the mind? Just so with Moses: the speculative ventures of his old age were of a piece with earlier speculations. He was playing an intellectual game for high stakes, and enjoying it. But even if he had not enjoyed it, something within him would have compelled him to go on. He would have been unwilling to relinquish the thesis of Sellin's monograph of 1922, which provided the key to the riddle—the killing of Moses—even if its argument had been refuted conclusively; indeed, Freud was unshaken when told that Sellin had recanted. He held fast, while conceding that the "second Moses" was "wholly my invention." Earlier, in 1935, when he had temporarily ceased working on his study of Moses, he had likened his situation to one familiar to psychoanalysts: "When one has suppressed a certain theme" in a psychoanalysis, "nothing else comes up in its place. The visual field remains empty. So I remain fixated on the Moses I have put aside."

Some of this obsessive quality found its way into print. In one of his prefaces to the third part of *Moses and Monotheism*, written in London in June 1938, he declared himself happy to be in England; treated as a distinguished guest, he was breathing again now that the pressure of self-censorship had been removed, "so that I may speak and write—I had almost said, think—as I wish or must." *Wish or must:* he was a free man, but not free to stop writing about Moses. He had indeed been willing to suppress the last part of the book as long as he had lived in Vienna, "but it tormented me like an unlaid ghost." This is the Freud we know: the man who had sometimes been haunted by an idea for years. In the course of working through his compulsion, Freud said many interesting and many untenable things. He had conceived his *Moses and Monotheism* in defiance, written it in defiance, published it in defiance. This was the stance he thought proper to a discoverer at odds all his life with the "compact majority." And to his surprise the book did well. On June 15, 1939, he informed his "dear Marie" Bonaparte in what would be his last letter to her, "I gather that of the German 'Moses' some 1,800 copies have been sold." But in the body of Freud's work, his *Moses and Monotheism* remains something of an oddity, more extravagant in its way than *Totem and Taboo.* When he had first thought of it, he had planned to give it the subtitle "A Historical Novel." He would have done well to stay with his original intention.

IN EARLY JUNE 1939, while Max Schur was in the United States, frantically attempting to conclude his business there that he might return to his patient, Anna Freud reported to him some slight signs of improvement in her father's condition. Still, Freud's pains were severe, the prosthesis was hard to put in and take out, and the smell from his cancerous tissue, which had begun to ulcerate, was most disagreeable. When Schur returned to England on July 8, he found his patient altered for the worse. Freud was thinner and mentally less alert. He had trouble sleeping and spent most of his time resting. Friends came from afar for a last visit; Hanns Sachs managed a trip to London in July, and called on Freud daily for brief chats. "He looked very ill," Sachs recalls, "and incredibly old. It was evident that he pronounced every word at the cost of an enormous effort which nearly went beyond his strength. But these torments had not worn down his will." Freud still kept a few analytic hours whenever the pain did not torment him too much, and "still wrote his letters with his own hand when he was strong enough to hold the pen." He did not complain; rather, he spoke of analysis in the United States. When Sachs parted from Freud, aware how much Freud disliked emotional displays, he spoke lightly about travel plans. Freud, Sachs records, understood the gesture; he "pressed my hand and said: 'I know that I have at least *one* friend in America.'" A few days later, at the end of July, Marie Bonaparte came and stayed for a week, knowing she would never see him again. On August 1, in a decisive gesture of farewell to life, Freud officially closed his medical practice.

His last visitors, recording their impressions with a slight air of amazement—though they knew their Freud intimately—commented on Freud's unvarying courtesy: he inquired after others, and never showed signs of impatience or irritability. He would not be infantilized by his disease. On August 13, his nephew Harry said farewell. "When I replied to his question when I would be back from the United States, 'At Christmas,' a sad smile flashed around his mouth and he said, *'I don't believe that you will then still find me again.'*" A few days later, in a cordial short letter to the German poet Albrecht Schaeffer, he called himself "overdue," and quoted Schaeffer's own words back to him: he had nothing to do but "wait, wait."

Late that month, word reached his sisters in Vienna that "the beloved old man" was not well at all. "Anna," her aunt Rosa Graf noted in a letter, was said "to be doing incredible things in caring for her father." Writing a week before war broke out, she reported that the French visas, despite the "high protection" of her brother's good friend in Paris, had not yet arrived.* On August 27, Freud made the last entry in his *Chronik.* It concludes with the words "War panic."

The end was now near. Freud's ulcerated cancer wound continued to give off so fetid a smell that his chow would cringe from him and could not be lured to come near its master. Freud, Schur comments, "knew what it meant and looked at it with deep, tragically knowing eyes." He was tortured by pain, and relief from it was occasional, increasingly rare. Yet during his waking hours, Freud remained alert and followed events by looking at the newspapers. On September 1, the Germans marched into Poland, and Max Schur moved to Maresfield Gardens to be near Freud and be of assistance if there should be an air raid on London. On September 3, France and Britain entered the war they had worked so frantically to avert. On that day, Jones wrote Freud the warmest of tributes, reminding him that twenty-five years earlier, their respective countries had been on opposite sides, "but even then we

---

*Some weeks before, on August 2, 1939, Marie Bonaparte had written to the Greek consulate recommending that Rosa Graf be given a visa. (Freud Collection, B2, LC.) But neither French visa nor Greek ever arrived. Freud was fortunate that he died never knowing how his sisters would end: Adolfine perished of starvation at the Theresienstadt camp, while the other three were murdered, probably at Auschwitz, in 1942. (Martin Freud, *Freud,* 15–16.) His sister Anna, who had married Eli Bernays, Martha's brother, had emigrated to the United States many years earlier.

found a way to communicate our friendship to each other. Now we are near to each other and united in our military sympathies." And he expressed, for the last time, his "gratitude for all you have brought into my life."

The war came to Maresfield Gardens early in September, with an air raid alarm. Just to be sure, Freud's bed was moved to the "safe" part of the house, an operation, Schur records, that Freud observed "with a certain interest." He was already "far away," Schur adds. "The distance he had established" a year before, at the time of Munich, "was still more pronounced." But there were still flashes of his wit: when the two men heard a broadcast proclaiming this to be the last war, Schur asked Freud whether he believed it, and Freud replied dryly, "My last war." His bourgeois habits, too, continued to claim him. Schur notes that Freud had a wind-up watch and a seven-day clock, and to his death he wound them up as he had done all his life. "He commented to me," Schur remembers, "how fortunate he was, that he has found so many valuable friends." Anna had just left the room, which gave Freud the opportunity to tell Schur, "Fate has been good to me, that it should still have granted me the relationship to such a woman—I mean Anna, of course." The comment, Schur adds, was utterly tender, even though Freud had never been demonstrative with his daughter. She was always at hand, on duty round the clock. So were Schur, and Josefine Stross, affectionately known in the Freud family as "Fiffi," the young pediatrician who had accompanied the Freuds to England and remained close to them.

Freud was very tired now, and it was hard to feed him. But while he suffered greatly and the nights especially were hard, he did not get, and did not want, any sedation. He could still read, and his last book was Balzac's mysterious tale of the magical shrinking skin, *La Peau de chagrin.* When he had finished the book he told Schur, casually, that this had been the right book for him to read, dealing as it did with shrinking and starvation. It was the shrinking, Anna Freud thought, that seemed to speak particularly to his condition: his time was running out. He spent the last days in his study downstairs, looking out at the garden. Ernest Jones, hastily summoned by Anna Freud, who thought her father was dying, stopped by on September 19. Freud, Jones remembered, was dozing, as he did so much these days, but when Jones called out *"Herr Professor,"* Freud opened an eye, recognized his visitor, "and waved his hand, then dropped it with a highly expressive gesture that conveyed a wealth of meaning: greetings, farewell, resignation." He then relapsed into his doze.

Jones read Freud's gesture aright. Freud was saluting his old ally for the last time. He had resigned from life. Schur was agonized by his inability to relieve Freud's suffering, but two days after Jones's visit, on September 21, as Schur was sitting by Freud's bedside, Freud took his hand and said to him,

"Schur, you remember our 'contract' not to leave me in the lurch when the time had come. Now it is nothing but torture and makes no sense." Schur indicated that he had not forgotten. Freud gave a sigh of relief, kept his hand for a moment, and said, "I thank you." Then, after a slight hesitation, he added, "Talk it over with Anna, and if she thinks it's right, then make an end of it." As she had been for years, so at this juncture, Freud's Antigone was first in his thoughts. Anna Freud wanted to postpone the fatal moment, but Schur insisted that to keep Freud going was pointless, and she submitted to the inevitable, as had her father. The time had come; he knew and acted. This was Freud's interpretation of his saying that he had come to England to die in freedom.

Schur was on the point of tears as he witnessed Freud facing death with dignity and without self-pity. He had never seen anyone die like that. On September 21, Schur injected Freud with three centigrams of morphine—the normal dose for sedation was two centigrams—and Freud sank into a peaceful sleep. Schur repeated the injection, when he became restless, and administered a final one the next day, September 22. Freud lapsed into a coma from which he did not awake. He died at three in the morning, September 23, 1939. Nearly four decades earlier, Freud had written to Oskar Pfister wondering what one would do some day, "when thoughts fail or words will not come?" He could not suppress a "tremor before this possibility. That is why, with all the resignation before destiny that suits an honest man, I have one wholly secret entreaty: only no invalidism, no paralysis of one's powers through bodily misery. Let us die in harness, as King Macbeth says." He had seen to it that his secret entreaty would be fulfilled. The old stoic had kept control of his life to the end.

ABBREVIATIONS

Briefe: Sigmund Freud, *Briefe 1873–1939,* ed. Ernst and Lucie Freud (1960; 2d enlarged ed., 1968). English version, *Letters of Sigmund Freud, 1873–1939,* tr. Tania and James Stern (1961; 2d ed., 1975).

Freud–Abraham: Sigmund Freud, Karl Abraham, *Briefe 1907–1926,* ed. Hilda Abraham and Ernst L. Freud (1965). English version, *A Psycho-Analytic Dialogue: The Letters of Sigmund Freud and Karl Abraham, 1907–1926,* tr. Bernard Marsh and Hilda Abraham (1965).

Freud–Fliess: Sigmund Freud, *Briefe an Wilhelm Fliess 1887–1904,* ed. Jeffrey Moussaieff Masson, assisted by Michael Schröter and Gerhard Fichtner (1986). English version, *The Complete Letters of Sigmund Freud to Wilhelm Fliess, 1887–1904,* ed. and tr. Jeffrey Moussaieff Masson (1985).

Freud–Jung: Sigmund Freud, C. G. Jung, *Briefwechsel,* ed. William McGuire and Wolfgang Sauerländer (1974; third corr. printing, 1979). English version, *The Freud/Jung Letters: The Correspondence between Sigmund Freud and C. G. Jung,* ed. William McGuire and tr. Ralph Manheim (Freud's letters) and R. F. C. Hull (Jung's letters), (1974).

Freud–Pfister: Sigmund Freud, Oskar Pfister, *Briefe 1909–1939,* ed. Ernst L. Freud and Heinrich Meng (1963). English version, *Psychoanalysis and Faith: The Letters of Sigmund Freud and Oskar Pfister,* tr. Eric Mosbacher (1963).

Freud–Salomé: Sigmund Freud, Lou Andreas-Salomé, *Briefwechsel,* ed. Ernst Pfeiffer (1966). English version, Sigmund Freud, Lou Andreas-Salomé, *Letters,* tr. Elaine and William Robson-Scott (1972).

Freud–Zweig: Sigmund Freud, Arnold Zweig, *Briefwechsel,* ed. Ernst L. Freud (1968; paperback, ed., 1984). English version, *The Letters of Sigmund Freud and Arnold Zweig,* tr. Elaine and William Robson-Scott (1970).

GW: Sigmund Freud, *Gesammelte Werke, Chronologisch Geordnet,* ed. Anna Freud, Edward Bibring, Willi Hoffer, Ernst Kris, and Otto Isakower, in collaboration with Marie Bonaparte, 18 vols. (1940–68).

Int. J. Psycho-Anal.: International Journal of Psycho-Analysis.

Int. Rev. Psycho-Anal.: International Review of Psycho-Analysis.

J. Amer. Psychoanal. Assn.: Journal of the American Psychoanalytic Association.

Jones I, II, III: Ernest Jones, *The Life and Work of Sigmund Freud.* Vol. I, *The Formative Years and the Great Discoveries, 1856–1900* (1953); vol. II, *Years of Maturity, 1901–1919* (1955); vol. III, *The Last Phase, 1919–1939* (1957).

LC: Library of Congress.

Protokolle: Protokolle der Wiener Psychoanalytischen Vereinigung, ed. Hermann Nunberg and Ernst Federn, 4 vols. (1976–81). English version, *Minutes of the Vienna Psychoanalytic Society,* tr. M. Nunberg, 4 vols. (1962–75).

SE: Standard Edition of the Complete Psychological Works of Sigmund Freud, tr. under the general editorship of James Strachey in collaboration with Anna Freud, assisted by Alix Strachey and Alan Tyson, 24 vols. (1953–74).

Y-MA: Yale University Library, Manuscripts and Archives.

NOTES

PREFACE

p.xv *be about him:* Freud to Martha Bernays, April 28, 1885. *Briefe,* 144–45.

p.xv *"particular way":* "Eine Kindheitserinnerung des Leonardo da Vinci" (1910), *GW* VIII, 202/"Leonardo da Vinci and a Memory of His Childhood," *SE* XI, 130.

p.xvi *"not use it":* Freud to Arnold Zweig, May 31, 1936. *Briefe,* 445.

p.xvi *"candid than I":* *Traumdeutung* (1900), *GW* II–III, 126/*The Interpretation of Dreams, SE* IV, 121.

p.xvi *"such a man":* Freud to Fliess, February 1, 1900. *Freud–Fliess,* 437 (398).

p.xvii *"foremost pervert":* "The Pope's Secrets," distributed by Tony Alamo, Pastor, president of the Tony and Susan Alamo Christian Foundation, Alma, Arizona, n.d.

p.xvii *"sleep of mankind":* "Zur Geschichte der psychoanalytischen Bewegung" (1914), *GW* X, 60/"On the History of the Psycho-Analytic Movement," *SE* XIV, 21. He is quoting the nineteenth-century German dramatist Christian Friedrich Hebbel.

p.xvii *more unacceptable:* Freud to Stefan Zweig, April 14, 1925. By permission of Sigmund Freud Copyrights, Wivenhoe.

p.xvii *"aim of science":* Freud to Ferenczi, January 10, 1910. Freud–Ferenczi Correspondence, Freud Collection, LC.

p.xvii *"my métier":* Freud to Einstein, December 8, 1932. Freud Collection, B3, LC.

p.xix *"general amnesia":* "Eine Kindheitserinnerung aus *Dichtung und Wahrheit,*" (1917) *GW* XII, 17/"A Childhood Recollection from *Dichtung und Wahrheit,*" *SE* XVII, 148.

p.xix *"through every pore":* "Bruchstück einer Hysterie-Analyse" (1905), *GW* V, 240/"Fragment of an Analysis of a Case of Hysteria," *SE* VII, 77–78.

p.xx *"a few dates":* Freud to Edward Bernays, August 10, 1929. *Briefe,* 408.

CHAPTER ONE · *A Greed for Knowledge*

p.3 *"and of superstition":* "Der Wahn und die Träume in W. Jensens *Gradiva*" (1907), *GW* VII, 31 / "Delusions and Dreams in Jensen's *Gradiva,*" *SE* IX, 7.

p.4 *"on a new basis":* Freud to L. Darmstaeder, July 3, 1910. Freud Collection, B3, LC.

p.4 *"once in a lifetime":* *The Interpretation of Dreams* (3d [rev.] English ed., 1932), *SE* IV, xxxii.

p.4 *his wife Amalia:* Her name is nearly always given as "Amalie," and that is what people seem to have called her. But her gravestone in the Vienna cemetery, where she was buried with her husband, has "Amalia." (See photograph in Ernst Freud, Lucie Freud, and Ilse Grubrich-Simitis, eds., *Sigmund Freud: His Life in Pictures and Words* [1976; tr. Christine Trollope, 1978], 161.) Also, while her maiden name is usually spelled "Nathanson," and

[655]

appears on her marriage certificate that way, she liked to insist that the correct spelling was "Nathansohn." The Czechs who lived in Freiberg called it Příbor, and now that the town is in Czechoslovakia, that is its official name. The name was clearly a popular locution; Freud playfully used it at times in his schoolboy correspondence. (See Freud to Emil Fluss, September 28, 1872. *"Selbstdarstellung." Schriften zur Geschichte der Psychoanalyse*, ed. Ilse Grubrich-Simitis [1971; corr. ed., 1973], 110.)

p.5   *in 1873:* See Freud to Silberstein, June 11, 1872. Freud Collection, D2, LC. And see also Anna Freud to Ernest Jones, January 18, 1954. Jones papers, Archives of the British Psycho-Analytical Society, London.

p.5   *May 13, 1856:* In the contentious scholarship on Freud's early life, not even his birth date has escaped the speculative scrutiny of researchers; misled by an illegible entry of a local clerk, some have tried to foist an earlier date, March 6, on him. That would have been an interesting revision, since Jacob Freud married Amalia Nathansohn on July 29, 1855. But the documents, amply supported by the Freuds' family Bible, show that Freud and his bride seem to have obeyed the proprieties: the conventional date of the biographies, May 6, is correct.

p.5   *"into German Austria":* "Selbstdarstellung" (1925), *GW* XIV, 34 / "An Autobiographical Study," *SE* XX, 7–8.

p.5   *roots in Cologne:* From notes by Marie Bonaparte (in French) for a Freud biography, "given by Freud in April 1928." Jones papers, Archives of the British Psycho-Analytical Society, London.

p.5   *"companion in my misdeeds":* Freud to Wilhelm Fliess, October 3, 1897. *Freud–Fliess*, 289 (268).

p.6   *"'cause he beated me":* *Die Traumdeutung* (1900), *GW* II–III, 427–28 / *The Interpretation of Dreams*, *SE* V, 424–25.

p.6   *little rival?:* See *The Psychopathology of Everyday Life* (1901), *SE* VI, 51–52n (note of 1924).

p.6   *"remained a Jew":* "Selbstdarstellung," *GW* XIV, 34 / "Autobiographical Study," *SE* XX, 7.

p.6   *"that concerned Judaism":* Freud to J. Dwossis (in Jerusalem), December 15, 1930. Typescript copy, Freud Museum, London.

p.6   *"German or better":* Ibid.

p.7   *"art of reading":* Selbstdarstellung, 40 / "Autobiographical Study," *SE* XX, 8 (sentence added in 1935—the time Freud was particularly obsessed with Moses).

p.7   *"God Almighty does":* Freud to Fliess, October 15, 1897. *Freud–Fliess*, 291 (271).

p.7   *in sexual matters:* See Freud to Fliess, October 4, 1897. Ibid., 290 (269).

p.7   *being in jail:* Ibid., 292 (271–72).

p.7   *of two mothers:* See John E. Gedo, "Freud's Self-Analysis and His Scientific Ideas," in *Freud: The Fusion of Science and Humanism: The Intellectual History of Psychoanalysis*, ed. John E. Gedo and George H. Pollock (1976), 301.

p.8   *Freud was born:* See the pioneering researches of Josef Sajner: "Sigmund Freuds Beziehungen zu seinem Geburtsort Freiberg (Příbor) und zu Mähren," *Clio Medica*, III (1968), 167–80, and "Drei dokumentarische Beiträge zur Sigmund-Freud-Biographik aus Böhmen und Mähren," *Jahrbuch der Psychoanalyse*, XIII (1981), 143–52.

p.8   *"was worth remembering":* "Über Deckerinnerungen" (1899), *GW* I, 542 / "Screen Memories," *SE* III, 312.

p.8   *in a few days:* See "R. was my uncle," in *Interpretation of Dreams*, *SE* IV, 138–45.

p.8   *Josef Freud's schemes:* See Marianne Krüll, *Freud and His Father* (1979; tr. Arnold J. Pomerans, 1986), 164–66.

p.9   *"run off from my father":* "Über Deckerinnerungen," *GW* I, 542–43 / "Screen Memories," *SE* III, 312–13.

p.9   *"from this soil":* Freud to the mayor of Příbor, October 25, 1931. Typescript copy, Freud Collection, B3, LC / "Letter to the Burgomaster of Příbor," *SE* XXI, 259.

p.9   *"has been released":* Freud to Max Eitingon, June 6, 1938. *Briefe,* 462.

p.9   *"disgusting to me":* Freud to Fluss, September 18, 1872. *Selbstdarstellung,* 109.

p.9   *"that abominable steeple":* Freud to Martha Bernays, March 10, 1886. *Briefe,* 219.

p.10   *"hometown soil":* Freud to Fliess, March 11, 1900. *Freud–Fliess,* 442 (403).

p.10   *an anti-Semitic slander:* See "On the History of the Psychoanalytic Movement" (1914), *SE* XIV, 39.

p.10   *"with great respect":* Martin Freud, *Sigmund Freud: Man and Father* (1958), 10.

p.11   *"my friendships":* Freud to Fliess, October 3, 1897. *Freud–Fliess,* 288–89 (268).

p.11   *"tuberculous illness":* Anna Freud to Ernest Jones, May 29, 1951. Jones papers, Archives of the British Psycho-Analytical Society, London.

p.12   *"big strong man"?:* Traumdeutung, GW II–III, 202–3 / *Interpretation of Dreams, SE* IV, 197.

p.12   *"of the Catholic Church":* Ibid., 202 / 196.

p.12   The Robbers: See *Interpretation of Dreams, SE* V, 424.

p.12   *"move you to learning":* The Bible is on exhibition at the Freud Museum, London. See for this inscription, Ernst Freud et al., eds., *Sigmund Freud: His Life in Pictures and Words,* 134.

p.13   *"of the prophetess":* Traumdeutung, GW II–III, 198 / *Interpretation of Dreams, SE* IV, 192.

p.13   *"cabinet minister":* Ibid., 198–99 / 192–93.

p.13   *with that majority:* See Krüll, *Freud and His Father,* 147–51.

p.14   *not his playmates:* Anna Freud Bernays, "My Brother, Sigmund Freud," *American Mercury,* LI (1940), 336. Anna Bernays's reminiscences, filled as they are with mistakes, must be used with care.

p.14   *limited constitutionalism:* See, for this paragraph, above all Robert A. Kann, *A History of the Habsburg Empire, 1526–1918* (1974; corr. ed., 1977), 243–366 *passim.*

p.15   *"representative government":* Ilsa Barea, *Vienna* (1966), 244–45.

p.15   *"had any money":* Max Eyth, a Swabian poet and engineer visiting Vienna, to his parents, June 7, 1873. Quoted in Bernhard Zeller, ed., *Jugend in Wien: Literatur um 1900* (1974), 30.

p.16   *had been wiped out:* See Wolfdieter Bihl, "Die Juden," in *Die Habsburger Monarchie, 1848–1918,* ed. Adam Wandruszka and Peter Urbanitsch, vol. III, *Die Völker des Reiches* (1980), part 2, 890–96.

p.16   *"in his satchel":* Traumdeutung, GW II–III, 199 / *Interpretation of Dreams, SE* IV, 193.

p.16   *"anti-Semitic demonstrations":* Freud to Martha Bernays, June 2, 1885. By permission of Sigmund Freud Copyrights, Wivenhoe.

p.16   *irrevocable finality:* For this complex aspect of Lueger, see above all John W. Boyer, "Karl Lueger and the Viennese Jews," *Leo Baeck Yearbook,* XXVI (1981), 125–41; and John W. Boyer, *Political Radicalism in Late Imperial Vienna: Origins of the Christian Social Movement, 1848–1897* (1981).

p.16   *"the old school":* Freud to Arnold Zweig, November 26, 1930. *Freud–Zweig,* 33 (21).

p.17   *"enjoy equal rights":* Quoted in Zeller, ed., *Jugend in Wien,* 69.

p.17   *"forces of liberalism":* Dennis B. Klein, *Jewish Origins of the Psychoanalytic Movement* (1981), 4.

p.17   *queen of his heart:* See Joseph Samuel Bloch, *Der nationale Zwist und die Juden in Österreich* (1886), 25–26, and see also 18–21.

p.19   *Germany or overseas:* See Marsha L. Rosenblit, *The Jews of Vienna, 1867–1914: Assimilation and Identity* (1983), 13–45 *passim.*

p.19   *"a view of life":* Freud to Fluss, September 18, 1872. *Selbstdarstellung,* 107–8.

p.20   *total school population:* See Klein, *Jewish Origins,* 48.

p.20   *2 percent of the population:* This number includes only those Jews who were legal residents in the city; the actual number was doubtless larger. (See Rosenblit, *Jews of Vienna,* 17.)

p.20   *"venal press"*: Burckhardt to Friedrich von Preen, October 3, 1872. *Briefe,* ed. Max Burckhardt, 10 vols. (1949–86), V, 175.

p.20   *"judaized"*—verjudet: Burckhardt to Johann Jacob Oeri-Burckhardt, August 14, 1884. Ibid., VIII, 228.

p.20   *"take a position"*: Traumdeutung, *GW* II–III, 202 / *Interpretation of Dreams, SE* IV, 196.

p.21   *anxious and bitter:* Arthur Schnitzler, *Jugend in Wien* (1968), 78–81.

p.21   *adolescent hooligans:* Barea, *Vienna,* 305.

p.22   *"scarcely ever examined"*: "Selbstdarstellung," *GW* XIV, 34 / "Autobiographical Study," *SE* XX, 8.

p.22   *"heartfelt" talk:* Freud to Silberstein, June 11, 1872. Freud Collection, D2, LC.

p.22   *esa carta:* Freud to Silberstein, September 4, 1872. Ibid.

p.22   *conversation with her:* Ibid.

p.22   *suitably extinct:* See, for this dating, Freud to Silberstein, March 25, 1872, before his visit to Freiberg. There he referred to Gisela Fluss as "Ichth," and to her brother Emil as "Ichthyosaurus." (Freud Collection, D2, LC.) For a later use, see Freud to Fluss, September 18 and 28, 1872. (*Selbstdarstellung,* 109, 110.) In the earlier of these letters, Freud used the abbreviation "Ich."; indeed, as the earlier letter to Silberstein discloses, this code name had been familiar to both for a while.

p.22   *poignant encounters:* "Über Deckerinnerungen," *GW* I, 543 / "Screen Memories," *SE* III, 313.

p.23   *not least to him:* See Freud to Silberstein, September 4, 1872. Freud Collection, D2, LC.

p.23   *"friendship for the daughter"*: Ibid. Also in Ronald W. Clark, *Freud: The Man and the Cause* (1980), 25.

p.23   *in his dreams:* Traumdeutung, *GW* II–III, 221–22 / *Interpretation of Dreams, SE* IV, 216.

p.24   *"myself in medicine"*: "Selbstdarstellung," *GW* XIV, 34 / "Autobiographical Study," *SE* XX, 8.

p.24   *more than once:* See, in addition to his autobiography, a comment to his acquaintance Friedrich Eckstein, to whom he described this experience as "a decisive turnabout" in his "intellectual development." (Quoted in Friedrich Eckstein, *"Alte unnennbare Tage!" Erinnerungen aus siebzig Lehr- und Wanderjahren* [1936], 21.)

p.24   *not even by Goethe:* Students of Goethe now agree that the fragment was really written by an acquaintance of his, the Swiss writer Christoph Tobler. See the editorial note by Andreas Speiser in *Johann Wolfgang Goethe, Gedenkausgabe der Werke, Briefe und Gespräche,* ed. Ernst Beutler, 24 vols. (1949), XVI, 978.

p.24   *"take it back later"*: Freud to Fluss, March 17, 1873. *Selbstdarstellung,* 114.

p.24   *"willing to learn"*: Freud to Fluss, May 1, 1873. Ibid., 116.

p.24   *"Sigismund Freud / stud. jur."*: Freud to Silberstein, August 2, 1873. Freud Collection, D2, LC.

p.25   *unequivocal past experience:* See Fritz Wittels, *Sigmund Freud: His Personality, His Teaching, and His School* (1924; tr. Eden and Cedar Paul, 1924), 19. Freud first used the term "screen memory"—Deckerinnerung—in the paper of 1899 "Über Deckerinnerungen."

p.25   *"greed for knowledge"*: "Selbstdarstellung," *GW* XIV, 34 / "Autobiographical Study," *SE* XX, 8.

p.25   *"suppressed" himself:* Freud to Martha Bernays, February 2, 1886. *Briefe,* 208–9.

p.25   *"ruthlessly checked it"*: Jones I, 29.

p.25   *"in scientific inquiry"*: Freud to Marie Bonaparte, November 12, 1938. *Briefe,* 471.

p.26   *"philosophy and zoology"*: Freud to Silberstein, March 7, 1875. Freud Collection, D2, LC.

p.26   *"at natural objects"*: "Selbstdarstellung," *GW* XIV, 34 / "Autobiographical Study," *SE* XX, 8.

p.26   *"woven around us all"*: Freud to Fluss, September 28, 1872. *Selbstdarstellung,* 111.

p.26   *"wholly to yourself"*: Freud to Silberstein, August 17, 1872. Freud Collection, D2, LC.

p.26   *"for our self-knowledge"*: Freud to Fluss, June 16, 1873. *Selbstdarstellung,* 120–21.

p.26   *"remove them from the world":* Freud to Silberstein, September 9, 1875. Freud Collection, D2, LC.

p.27   *"task here, and significance":* Freud to Martha Bernays, August 28, 1883. *Briefe,* 54.

p.27   *circuitous journey:* See "Postscript" (1927) to *The Question of Lay Analysis: Conversations with an Impartial Person* (1926), *SE* XX, 253.

p.27   *"awakened to thinking":* "Nachschrift" (1935) to "Selbstdarstellung," *GW* XVI, 32 / "Postscript" to "Autobiographical Study," *SE* XX, 72.

p.27   *"compact majority":* "Selbstdarstellung," *GW* XIV, 34–35 / "Autobiographical Study," *SE* XX, 9.

p.28   *"minority opinions grown":* Freud to Silberstein, March 27, 1875. Freud Collection, D2, LC.

p.28   *triumphed over the "rabble":* Freud to Martha Bernays, December 16, 1883. *Briefe,* 84–85.

p.28   *his walking stick:* See Martin Freud, *Freud,* 70–71.

p.28   *"something like that":* Freud to Silberstein, July 11, 1873. Freud Collection, D2, LC.

p.28   *"philosophy from despair":* Freud to Silberstein, August 6, 1873. Ibid.

p.28   *"this man the most":* Freud to Silberstein, March 7, 1875. Ibid.

p.28   *"and perfidious judgments":* Ludwig Feuerbach, "Vorwort" to the second edition of *Das Wesen des Christenthums* (1843), iii. (It is omitted in the famous translation George Eliot made of this book, first published as *The Essence of Christianity* in 1854.)

p.29   *illusion at that:* Ibid., 408.

p.29   *"self-satisfied speculation":* Ibid., ix–xii.

p.29   *"the encyclopedic-methodological":* Feuerbach to Christian Kapp, November 1840. Quoted in Marx W. Wartofsky, *Feuerbach* (1977), 202.

p.29   geistiger Naturforscher: Feuerbach, *Wesen des Christenthums,* x.

p.29   *this "genius":* Freud to Silberstein, March 7, 1875. Freud Collection, D2, LC.

p.29   *"not yet a theist":* Freud to Silberstein, March 13–15, 1875. Ibid.

p.29   *"student and an empiricist":* Freud to Silberstein, November 8, 1874. Ibid.

p.30   *"devoted to pleasure":* Henry Hun, *A Guide to American Medical Students in Europe* (1883). Quoted in Sherwin B. Nuland, *The Masterful Spirit—Theodor Billroth,* The Classics of Surgery Library (1984), 9.

p.30   *"take as models":* "Selbstdarstellung," *GW* XIV, 35 / "Autobiographical Study," *SE* XX, 9.

p.31   *"the English disease":* Freud to Silberstein, August 6, 1873. Freud Collection, D2, LC.

p.31   *"drunkenness and conservatism":* Freud to Silberstein, September 9, 1875. Ibid.

p.31   *"influence" on his life:* Freud to Martha Bernays, August 16, 1882. *Jones* I, 178–79.

p.31   *"than ever of philosophy":* Freud to Silberstein, September 9, 1875. Freud Collection, D2, LC.

p.31   *biology in Trieste:* See *Jones* I, 37–38.

p.32   *all had failed:* "Beobachtungen über Gestaltung und feineren Bau der als Hoden beschriebenen Lappenorgane des Aals" (1877), in Siegfried Bernfeld, "Freud's Scientific Beginnings," *American Imago,* VI (1949), 165.

p.32   *"the tenderer sex":* Freud to Silberstein, April 5, 1876. Freud Collection, D2, LC.

p.32   *"at all to do with them":* Freud to Silberstein, n.d. [April 1876?], ibid.

p.32   *came to know well:* Selbstdarstellung, 41 / "Autobiographical Study," *SE* XX, 9–10.

p.33   *"worked upon me":* "Nachwort" to *Die Frage der Laienanalyse, GW* XIV, 290 / "Postscript" to *The Question of Lay Analysis, SE* XX, 253.

p.34   *"one-time youthful sinner":* Traumdeutung, *GW* II–III, 424–25 / *Interpretation of Dreams, SE* V, 421–22.

p.34   *"attraction and repulsion":* Bernfeld, "Freud's Scientific Beginnings," 169–74.

p.34   *"theological preconceptions":* Emil Du Bois-Reymond, "Über die Grenzen des Naturerkennens" (1872), in *Reden von Emil Du Bois-Reymond,* ed. Estelle Du Bois-Reymond, 2 vols. (1885; 2d enlarged ed., 1912), I, 461.

p.35   *"glad as a child":* Freud to Silberstein, January 24, 1875. Freud Collection, D2, LC.

p.35   *a great deal to Freud:* See Ernst Kris's introduction to Freud's letters to Fliess: "Einleitung zur Erstausgabe" (1950), in *Freud–Fliess,* 526.

p.35   *"scientific world view":* "Über eine Weltanschauung" (written in 1932), in *Neue Folge der Vorlesungen zur Einführung in die Psychoanalyse* (1933), *GW* XV, 197 / "The Question of a *Weltanschauung,"* in *New Introductory Lectures on Psycho-Analysis, SE* XXII, 181.

p.36   *"the great Darwin":* Zur Psychopathologie des Alltagsleben (1901), *GW* IV, 164 / *The Psychopathology of Everyday Life, SE* VI, 148.

p.36   *"torture humans":* Freud to Wilhelm Knoepfmacher, August 6, 1878. Typescript copy, Freud Collection, B3, LC.

p.36   *"far-off—conclusion":* Jones I, 50.

p.36   *"humane" with his patients:* "Qualifications Eingabe" (1886). Freud Museum, London.

p.37   *was his poverty:* See "Autobiographical Study," *SE* XX, 10.

p.37   *guise of loans:* See on this point *Jones* I, 60–61, quoting an unpublished letter from Freud to Martha Bernays of September 9, 1884.

p.38   *meeting and their marriage:* Ibid., 99.

p.38   *writer's block:* See Freud to Fliess, March 7, 1896. *Freud–Fliess,* 187 (177).

p.38   *stint in the army:* "The Enfranchisement of Women," first published in the *Westminster Review* of July 1851, was called, by John Stuart Mill himself, a joint work, written in collaboration with Harriet Taylor, whom he married that year. I accept Alice S. Rossi's judgment that the essay is mainly Harriet Taylor's work. See Rossi's edition of John Stuart Mill and Harriet Taylor Mill, *Essays on Sex Equality* (1970), 41–42.

p.39   *"for something else":* Freud to Martha Bernays, November 15, 1883. *Briefe,* 81–82.

p.39   *"nothing to kiss":* Freud to Martha Bernays, January 22, 1884. By permission of Sigmund Freud Copyrights, Wivenhoe.

p.40   *"breath and wild":* Freud to Martha Bernays, December 5, 1885. By permission of Sigmund Freud Copyrights, Wivenhoe.

p.40   *"beloved treasure":* See for one instance, Martha Bernays to Freud, New Year's Eve (December 31–January 1), 1885–86. By permission of Sigmund Freud Copyrights, Wivenhoe.

p.40   *kisses in return:* See Martha Bernays to Freud, June 4, 1885. By permission of Sigmund Freud Copyrights, Wivenhoe.

p.40   *"her well always":* Freud to Martha Bernays, January 22, 1884. By permission of Sigmund Freud Copyrights, Wivenhoe.

p.40   *deep repression:* "Über einige neurotische Mechanismen bei Eifersucht, Paranoia und Homosexualität" (1922), *GW* XIII, 195 / "Some Neurotic Mechanisms in Jealousy, Paranoia and Homosexuality," *SE* XVIII, 223–24.

p.40   *had become engaged:* Freud to Martha Bernays, June 19, 1882. *Briefe,* 20.

p.40   *"disposition to tyranny":* Freud to Martha Bernays, August 22, 1883. Ibid., 50.

p.41   *"without misgivings":* Freud to Martha Bernays, August 18, 1882. Ibid., 37.

p.41   *clinical assistant:* See *Jones* I, 63.

p.42   *"suppression lies open":* Traumdeutung, *GW* II–III, 488 / *Interpretation of Dreams, SE* V, 484.

p.42   *"head, cheeks, neck":* Freud to Martha Bernays, October 5, 1882. *Briefe,* 41.

p.42   *"myself far superior":* Freud to Martha Bernays, February 2, 1886. Ibid., 208.

p.42   *rival as protector:* Traumdeutung, *GW* II–III, 439 / *Interpretation of Dreams, SE* V, 437.

p.42   *still a medical student:* See *Interpretation of Dreams, SE* V, 437; and "Autobiographical Study," *SE* XX, 10.

p.42   *"crotchets and delusions":* Freud to Martha Bernays, August 29, 1883. *Briefe,* 58.

p.42   *"or understand you":* Freud to Martha Bernays, May 12, 1885. Ibid., 148.

p.42   *"those early years":* "Selbstdarstellung," *GW* XIV, 38–39 / "Autobiographical Study," *SE* XX, 14–15.

p.43   *withdrawal of morphine:* Freud to Martha Bernays, April 21, 1884. *Briefe,* 114.

p.43   *touching symptomatic slips:* "Selbstdarstellung," *GW* XIV, 38 / "Autobiographical Study," *SE* XX, 14; and a letter to a Professor Meller, November 8, 1934. Freud Museum, London. See also *Jones* I, 79.

p.43   *"congress at Heidelberg":* "Selbstdarstellung," *GW* XIV, 38–39 / "Autobiographical Study," *SE* XX, 15.

p.43   *properties of the drug:* Freud to Professor Meller, November 8, 1934. Freud Museum, London.

p.43   *"negligence at the time":* "Selbstdarstellung," *GW* XIV, 38–39 / "Autobiographical Study," *SE* XX, 15.

p.44   *"doses from it":* Freud to Martha Bernays, June 2, 1885. By permission of Sigmund Freud Copyrights, Wivenhoe.

p.44   *take some of the drug:* See Martha Bernays to Freud, June 4, 1885. By permission of Sigmund Freud Copyrights, Wivenhoe.

p.44   *early in 1885:* See Freud to Martha Bernays, January 7, 1885. *Briefe,* 138.

p.44   *"position, and reputation":* Freud to Martha Bernays, January 7, 1885. Ibid., 137.

p.45   *in the margin:* See p. 19 in Freud's copy of Wittels, *Sigmund Freud.* Freud Museum, London.

p.45   *"little princess":* Freud to Martha Bernays, August 22, 23, September 8, 1883. *Briefe,* 50, 52, 62.

p.45   *"too indolent":* Freud to Fliess, February 1, 1900. *Freud–Fliess,* 438 (398).

p.46   *"excess of interest":* Freud at the Wednesday Psychological Society, April 1, 1908. *Protokolle,* I, 338.

p.46   *"Schiller has said":* Freud to Martha Bernays, February 12, 1884. By permission of Sigmund Freud Copyrights, Wivenhoe.

p.46   *survival of the species:* See, for two instances, "Screen Memories," *SE* III, 316; and "The Psycho-Analytic View of Psychogenic Disturbance of Vision" (1910), *SE* XI, 214–15.

p.46   *"name of Charcot":* "Selbstdarstellung," *GW* XIV, 36 / "Autobiographical Study," *SE* XX, 11.

p.47   *"energetic advocate":* Freud to Martha Bernays, June 3, 1885. By permission of Sigmund Freud Copyrights, Wivenhoe.

p.47   *"great stir":* Fleischl-Marxow to Freud, n.d. [Anna Freud rightly gives the letter to June 1885]. Freud Collection, LC, uncatalogued.

p.48   *"aesthetic value":* Freud to Martha Bernays, October 19, 1885. *Briefe,* 176–78.

p.48   *"French lessons":* Freud to Martha Bernays, October 19, 1885. Ibid., 176. See also Freud to Martha Bernays, November 8, 1885. Ibid., 182–85.

p.48   *one franc fifty:* Freud to Martha Bernays, October 19, 1885. Ibid., 176.

p.48   *"only know where":* Freud to Minna Bernays, October 18, 1885. By permission of Sigmund Freud Copyrights, Wivenhoe.

p.48   *"mass convulsions":* Ibid. By permission of Sigmund Freud Copyrights, Wivenhoe.

p.48   *"Viennese colleague":* Freud to Martha Bernays, November 24–26, 1885. By permission of Sigmund Freud Copyrights, Wivenhoe.

p.48   *interpreted as "dishonest":* Freud to Martha Bernays, January 22, 1884. By permission of Sigmund Freud Copyrights, Wivenhoe.

p.48   *"terribly in Vienna":* Freud to Martha Bernays, December 5, 1885. By permission of Sigmund Freud Copyrights, Wivenhoe.

p.49   *"know for certain":* Freud to Martha Bernays, November 24, 1885. *Briefe,* 189.

p.49   *"teacher and pupil":* "Charcot" (1893), *GW* I, 28–29 / "Charcot," *SE* III, 17–18.

p.49   *naming the animals:* See ibid., 23 / 13.

p.49   *"brain tumor":* "Selbstdarstellung," *GW* XIV, 36–37 / "Autobiographical Study," *SE* XX, 12.

p.50   *erotic in nature:* Pierre Janet, *L'État mental des hystériques* (1892; 2d ed., 1911), 132–35.

p.50   *hidden in hypnosis:* "Selbstdarstellung," *GW* XIV, 52 / "Autobiographical Study," *SE* XX, 27.

p.50   *lend him money:* Freud to Martha Bernays, December 5, 1885. By permission of Sigmund Freud Copyrights, Wivenhoe.

p.51   *"boring it was":* Freud to Martha Bernays, February 2–3, 1886. *Briefe,* 209–10.

p.51   *facts from existing:* "Charcot," *GW* I, 23–24 / "Charcot," *SE* III, 12–13.

p.51   *"condition—a neurosis":* J. M. Charcot and Gilles de la Tourette, "Hypnotism in the Hysterical," in *A Dictionary of Psychological Medicine,* ed. D. Hack Tuke, 2 vols. (1892), I, 606.

p.52   *accepted or rejected:* "Vorrede des Uebersetzers," in Hippolyte Bernheim, *Die Suggestion und ihre Heilwirkung* (1888), iii–iv / "Preface to the Translation of Bernheim's *Suggestion,*" *SE* I, 75–76.

p.52   *"neuroses has come":* "Bericht über meine mit Universitäts-Jubiläums-Reisestipendium unternommene Studienreise nach Paris und Berlin" (written in 1886, first published in 1960), *Selbstdarstellung,* 130, 134 / "Report on my Studies in Paris and Berlin," *SE* I, 5–6, 10.

p.53   *"all my congratulations":* Inscribed, undated visiting card. Freud Collection, B3, LC.

p.53   *"from 1 to 2:30":* "Kleine Chronik," date line April 24, 1886, in *Neue Freie Presse,* April 25, 1886. Clipping in Freud Museum, London.

p.53   *"battle for Vienna":* Freud to Martha Bernays, May 13, 1886. *Briefe,* 225.

p.53   *suffer from hysteria?:* See "Autobiographical Study," *SE* XX, 15.

p.54   *"experiences of her life":* Quoted in Clark, *Freud,* 89.

p.54   *"really at home":* Freud to Emmeline and Minna Bernays, October 16, 1887. *Briefe,* 231.

p.54   *"already quite pretty":* Freud to Emmeline and Minna Bernays, October 21, 1887. Ibid., 232.

p.54   *Mathilde Breuer—"naturally":* Freud to Emmeline and Minna Bernays, October 16, 1887. Ibid., 231.

CHAPTER TWO · *The Theory in the Making*

p.55   *same person:* Traumdeutung, *GW* II–III, 487 / Interpretation of Dreams, *SE* V, 483.

p.55   *"impression on me":* Freud to Fliess, November 24, 1887. *Freud–Fliess,* 3 (15).

p.56   *"the alter":* Freud to Fliess, May 21, 1894. Ibid., 66 (73).

p.56   *"critical faculties":* Freud to Fliess, September 29, 1893. Ibid., 49 (56).

p.56   *"among Berlin physicians":* Abraham to Freud, February 26, 1911. *Freud–Abraham,* 106–7 (102).

p.56   *"me a monomaniac":* Freud to Fliess, May 21, 1894. *Freud–Fliess,* 67 (74).

p.57   *"every popular lunacy":* Freud to Fliess, June 30, 1896. Ibid., 203 (193).

p.57   *"nectar and ambrosia":* Freud to Fliess, July 14, 1894. Ibid., 81 (87).

p.58   *"entitled to accept it":* Havelock Ellis, *Studies in the Psychology of Sex,* 2 vols. (ed. 1900), II, 83.

p.58   *his life's span:* See Freud to Carl G. Jung, April 16, 1909. *Freud–Jung,* 242 (219).

p.58   *desire for immortality:* See Psychopathology of Everyday Life, *SE* VI, 260 and 260n.

p.58   *"Jewish mysticism":* Freud to Jung, April 16, 1909. *Freud–Jung,* 243 (220).

p.59   *"death deliria":* Freud to Fliess, April 19, 1894. *Freud–Fliess,* 63 (68).

p.59   *"in abstinence":* Freud to Fliess, August 20, 1893. Ibid., 47 (54).

p.59   *his admired Oliver Cromwell:* See Peter Gay, "Six Names in Search of an Interpretation: A Contribution to the Debate over Sigmund Freud's Jewishness," *Hebrew Union College Annual,* LIII (1982), 295–307.

p.59   *obsessive regularity:* See Martin Freud, *Freud,* 32–34, 38, 44–45.

p.59   *examining her husband:* Interview with Helen Schur, June 3, 1986.

p.60   *"good upbringing":* Martha Freud to Elsa Reiss, March 8, 1947. Freud Collection, B1, LC.

p.60   *stately matron:* See Freud to Fliess, July 10, 1893, and August 29, 1894. *Freud–Fliess,* 43, 90 (50, 95).

p.60   *"generous, and reasonable":* Freud to Martha Bernays, August 2, 1882. *Jones* I, 102.

p.60   *in February 1896:* Freud to Fliess, February 13, 1896. *Freud–Fliess,* 180 (172).

p.60   *"life from his path":* Martha Freud to Ludwig Binswanger, November 7, 1939. By permission of Sigmund Freud Copyrights, Wivenhoe.

p.61   *all these decades:* Martha Freud to Paul Federn, n.d. [early November? 1939]. By permission of Sigmund Freud Copyrights, Wivenhoe.

p.61   *"form of pornography":* René Laforgue, "Personal Memories of Freud" (1956), in *Freud As We Knew Him,* ed. Hendrik M. Ruitenbeek (1973), 342.

p.61   *were doing well:* Freud to Fliess, December 3, 1895. *Freud–Fliess,* 159 (153).

p.61   *"loneliness and privation":* Freud to Fliess, December 8, 1895. Ibid., 160 (154).

p.61   Verehrter Freund!: Freud to Fliess, August 29, 1888. Ibid., 9 (23).

p.61   Liebster Freund!: Freud to Fliess, July 21, 1890, and August 11, 1890. Ibid., 12, 14 (26, 27).

p.61   Geliebter Freund!: Freud to Fliess, August 20, 1893. Ibid., 46 (53).

p.61   *with Sie:* See Freud to Fliess, June 28, 1892. Ibid., 17, 23 (31, 35).

p.61   *"growing family":* "Selbstdarstellung," *GW* XIV, 41 / "Autobiographical Study," *SE* XX, 18.

p.62   *"language apparatus":* Zur Auffassung der Aphasien. Eine kritische Studie (1891), 18, 106, 107.

p.62   *therapeutic successes:* See "A Case of Successful Treatment by Hypnotism" (1892–93), *SE* I, 117–28.

p.62   *"something for them":* "Selbstdarstellung," *GW* XIV, 39 / "Autobiographical Study," *SE* XX, 16.

p.62   *"electrical apparatus aside":* Ibid., 40 / 16.

p.63   *"into prophylaxis":* Freud to Fliess, Draft B, enclosed in letter of February 8, 1893. *Freud–Fliess,* 27–32 (39–43).

p.63   *"nor palatable":* Ibid., 32 (44).

p.63   *"etiology of the neuroses":* "Selbstdarstellung," *GW* XIV, 47 / "Autobiographical Study," *SE* XX, 22.

p.64   *"once again":* Freud to Martha Bernays, July 13, 1883 ("2 A.M."). *Briefe,* 47–48.

p.64   *the first time:* See *Jones* I, 226.

p.64   *"married to Martha":* Freud to Martha Bernays, July 13, 1883. *Briefe,* 48.

p.64   *"the great man":* "Selbstdarstellung," *GW* XIV, 44 / "Autobiographical Study," *SE* XX, 19–20.

p.64   *"whole of psychoanalysis":* Breuer to Auguste Forel, November 21, 1907. The letter is quoted in full in Paul F. Cranefield, "Josef Breuer's Evaluation of His Contribution to Psycho-Analysis," *Int. J. Psycho-Anal.,* XXXIX (1958), 320.

p.64   *"cultivation and talents":* "Selbstdarstellung," *GW* XIV, 44 / "Autobiographical Study," *SE* XX, 20.

p.64   *she left school:* Josef Breuer, "Krankengeschichte Bertha Pappenheim" (1882), a report Breuer handed over to Robert Binswanger, chief of the Swiss sanatorium at Kreuzlingen, to which he referred her after he had "cured" her. Reprinted in Albrecht Hirschmüller, *Physiologie und Psychoanalyse im Leben und Werk Josef Breuers,* supplement 4 to *Jahrbuch der Psychoanalyse,* X (1978), 348–62. Quoted passages at 348.

p.65   *"fantastic talent":* Breuer, "Krankengeschichte Bertha Pappenheim," in Hirschmüller, *Physiologie und Psychoanalyse in Breuer,* 349.

p.65   *"astonishingly undeveloped":* "Selbstdarstellung," *GW* XIV, 47 / "Autobiographical Study," *SE* XX, 22.

p.65   *"chimney sweeping"*: Anna O. used these phrases in English. Breuer in Breuer and Freud, *Studien über Hysterie* (1895; 2d ed., unchanged, 1909), 23 / *Studies on Hysteria, SE* II, 30. (While the editors of the *Standard Edition* chose to translate the entire book, including Breuer's contributions, the editors of Freud's German *Gesammelte Werke* omitted Breuer's chapters. I am therefore citing the original German book, while referring the reader to the equivalent place in the *Standard Edition* for the English text.)

p.66   *"complete health"*: Ibid., 27, 32 / 35, 40–41.

p.66   *"possession of me"*: "Bertha Pappenheim über ihre Krankheit" (September 1882). Quoted in full in Hirschmüller, *Physiologie und Psychoanalyse in Breuer*, 369–70, quotation at 370.

p.66   *"interesting details"*: Breuer and Freud, *Studien über Hysterie*, 32 / *Studies on Hysteria, SE* II, 41.

p.67   *"not to my taste"*: Breuer to Forel, November 21, 1907. Quoted in Cranefield, "Breuer's Evaluation," 320.

p.67   *"to a colleague"*: Freud to Stefan Zweig, June 2, 1932. *Briefe*, 427–28. Freud said that he had confidence in what he called his "reconstruction" because Breuer's youngest daughter had read Freud's description and asked her father, who had confirmed it. But there is something wrong here: Freud thought that this very daughter had been born "shortly after the conclusion of that treatment, that too not without significance for deeper connections!" (*Briefe*, 428.) In his biography, Ernest Jones elaborated the story: Frau Breuer had become so jealous of her husband's attentions to this young and fascinating patient, that Breuer, in some panic, ended the treatment and took his wife to Italy for a second honeymoon, on which their youngest daughter was conceived (*Jones* I, 224–26). Freud seems to have believed something of the sort. But scholarly work by Henri Ellenberger and Albrecht Hirschmüller has shown that the chronology of the birth of Breuer's children simply does not match this account. Dora Breuer was born on March 11, 1882, three months before her father ended his treatment of Anna O., and in any event, he spent that summer not in Italy, but in Gmunden am Tramsee. (See Henri Ellenberger, "The Story of 'Anna O.': A Critical Review with New Data," *Journal of the History of the Behavioral Sciences*, VIII [1972], 267–79; and Hirschmüller, *Physiologie und Psychoanalyse in Breuer*, 47–48.)

p.67   *"demon 'But' "*: Quoted in Hirschmüller, *Physiologie und Psychoanalyse in Breuer*, 256.

p.68   *"writing is excellent"*: Freud to Minna Bernays, July 13, 1891. *Briefe*, 239.

p.68   *his "companion"*: Freud to Fliess, December 18, 1892. *Freud–Fliess*, 24 (36).

p.68   *"advancement in Vienna"*: Freud to Fliess, September 29, 1893. Ibid., 49 (56).

p.68   *"Breuer have ceased"*: Freud to Fliess, June 22, 1894. Ibid., 80 (86).

p.68   *needed to see him*: See Freud to Fliess, April 16, 1896, and June 4, 1896. Ibid., 191, 202 (181, 191).

p.68   *"neurotic insecurity"*: Freud to Fliess, January 22, 1898. Ibid., 322 (296).

p.68   *the real thing*: Breuer and Freud, *Studien über Hysterie*, 221 / *Studies on Hysteria, SE* II, 250–51.

p.68   *he was three*: See George H. Pollock, "Josef Breuer," in *Freud, Fusion of Science and Humanism*, ed. Gedo and Pollock, 133–63, esp. 141–44.

p.68   *"I don't"*: Freud to Fliess, November 8, 1895. *Freud–Fliess*, 154–55 (151). Hirschmüller conjectures that Breuer, more cautious than Freud, must have said, "I don't believe it all." (*Physiologie und Psychoanalyse in Breuer*, 234.)

p.69   *"worshiper of success"*: Freud to Fliess, May 16, 1900. *Freud–Fliess*, 453–54 (414).

p.69   *"felt his strength"*: Freud to Fliess, August 7, 1901. Ibid., 491 (447).

p.69   *"ordeal again"*: Breuer to Forel, November 21, 1907. Quoted in Cranefield, "Breuer's Evaluation," 319–20.

p.69   *"Nonsense!"*: See p. 33 in Freud's copy of Wittels, *Sigmund Freud*. Freud Museum, London.

p.69   *"instructor"*—Lehrmeisterin: Freud to Fliess, February 8, 1897. *Freud–Fliess*, 243 (229).

p.69   *"principal client"*: Freud to Fliess, August 1, 1890. Ibid., 12 (27).

p.69   *"prima donna"*: Freud to Fliess, July 12, 1892. Ibid., 18 (32).

p.70   *hypnotist Bernheim:* See Peter J. Swales, "Freud, His Teacher, and the Birth of Psychoanalysis," in *Freud, Appraisals and Reappraisals: Contributions to Freud Studies,* ed. Paul E. Stepansky, I (1986), 3–82.

p.70   *"pitying smile":* Studien über Hysterie, GW I, 162n / Studies on Hysteria, SE II, 105n (note added in 1924).

p.70   *"she had to say":* Ibid., 116 / 63.

p.71   *"psychoanalytic therapy":* The original German letter is quoted in full in Ola Andersson, "A Supplement to Freud's Case History of 'Frau Emmy v. N.' in Studies on Hysteria 1895," *Scandinavian Psychoanalytic Review,* II (1979), 5–15.

p.71   *"mainly from reminiscences":* Studien über Hysterie, GW I, 86 / Studies on Hysteria, SE II, 7.

p.71   *"bent backward":* Ibid., 198 / 137.

p.71   *"buried city":* Ibid., 201 / 139.

p.72   *"brisk dance":* Ibid., 212, 224, 226 / 148, 158, 160.

p.72   *marriage was happy:* "Memorandum for the Sigmund Freud Archives," unsigned but described as being by the youngest of Ilona Weiss's three daughters; dated January 11, 1953. Freud Museum, London.

p.73   *"criticism rest":* Studien über Hysterie, GW I, 168 / Studies on Hysteria, SE II, 111.

p.73   *"hovering" attention:* See, for instance, "Analysis of a Phobia in a Five-Year-Old Boy" ["Little Hans"] (1909), SE X, 23; and "Recommendations to Physicians Practising Psycho-Analysis" (1912), SE XII, 111.

p.73   *"case for me":* Freud to Fliess, August 20, 1893. *Freud–Fliess,* 48 (54).

p.73   *"not seen her again":* Studien über Hysterie, GW I, 193 / Studies on Hysteria, SE II, 133.

p.74   *"in a case history":* Ibid., 195n / 134n.

p.74   *"It is psychology.":* Freud to Fliess, May 25, 1895. *Freud–Fliess,* 130 (129).

p.74   *"individuals strong":* Freud to Fliess, October 16, 1895. Ibid., 149 (145).

p.74   *at the wedding:* Freud to Fliess, May 17, 1896. Ibid., 196 (187).

p.74   *of his "hen":* Freud to Fliess, May 21, 1894. Ibid., 66 (73).

p.74   *"second generation":* Freud to Fliess, November 22, 1896. Ibid., 215 (204).

p.75   *"very amusing":* Freud to Fliess, August 16, 1895. Ibid., 139 (136).

p.75   *"developing charmingly":* Freud to Fliess, February 23, 1898. Ibid., 328 (300).

p.75   *"stage of beauté":* Freud to Fliess, August 12, 1896. Ibid., 207 (196).

p.75   *"harmless poetitis":* Freud to Fliess, May 16, 1897. Ibid., 259 (244).

p.75   *"so many scares":* Freud to Fliess, April 12, 1897. Ibid., 250 (236).

p.76   *"grazing properly":* Freud to Fliess, March 27, 1899. Ibid., 382 (349).

p.76   *"demonstrate them":* Freud to Fliess, December 8, 1895. Ibid., 160–61 (154–55).

p.76   *"Your Brother Sigmund":* Freud to Minna Bernays, August 28, 1884. By permission of Sigmund Freud Copyrights, Wivenhoe.

p.76   *"My Treasure":* Freud to Minna Bernays, October 12, 1884. By permission of Sigmund Freud Copyrights, Wivenhoe.

p.76   *some of the way:* Interview with Helen Schur, June 3, 1986. Photographs in Ernst Freud et al., eds., *Sigmund Freud: His Life in Pictures and Words,* 99, 151, 193. And see the letters cited in appropriate places.

p.76   *"closest confidante":* Freud to Fliess, May 21, 1894. *Freud–Fliess,* 66 (73).

p.77   *as "mean":* Freud to Fliess, February 6, 1896. *Freud–Fliess,* 179 (170).

p.77   *gaining ground:* Adolf von Strümpell, "Studien über Hysterie." *Deutsche Zeitschrift für Nervenheilkunde,* VIII (1896), 159–61.

p.77   *did not smoke:* See Freud to Minna Bernays, April 17, 1893. Quoted in *Freud–Fliess,* 34n.

p.77   *"years in misery?":* Freud to Fliess, November 27, 1893. Ibid., 54 (61).

p.77   *"embarrassed and miserable":* Freud to Fliess, October 8, 1895. Ibid., 146 (141).

p.77   *not losing heart:* Freud to Fliess, October 15, 1895. Ibid., 147 (144).

p.77   *"become transparent":* Freud to Fliess, October 20, 1895. Ibid., 149 (146).

p.77   *"dubious to me":* Freud to Fliess, October 31, 1895. Ibid., 151–52 (148).

p.77   *still missing:* Freud to Fliess, November 8, 1895. Ibid., 153–54 (150).

p.78   *memorandum on migraine:* See ibid., 155–57 (142–44).

p.78   *afar for so long:* Freud to Fliess, May 25, 1895. Ibid., 130 (129).

p.78   *His "Psychology for Neurologists":* Freud to Fliess, April 27, 1895. Ibid., 129 (127).

p.78   *"does me good":* Freud to Fliess, May 25, 1895. Ibid., 130–31 (129).

p.78   *"hatched the Psychology":* Freud to Fliess, November 29, 1895. Ibid., 158 (152).

p.78   *adumbrated here:* The English editors of Freud's psychoanalytic writings were right to conclude that while the project is "ostensibly a neurological document," it "contains within itself the nucleus of a great part of Freud's later psychological theories." Indeed, "the *Project,* or rather its invisible ghost, haunts the whole series of Freud's theoretical writings to the very end." ("Editor's Introduction" to "Project for a Scientific Psychology," *SE* I, 290.)

p.79   *"graphic and consistent":* "Entwurf einer Psychologie" (1895), in *Aus den Anfängen der Psychoanalyse. Briefe an Wilhelm Fliess, Abhandlungen und Notizen aus den Jahren, 1887–1902,* ed. Ernst Kris, Marie Bonaparte, and Anna Freud (1950), 379 / "Project for a Scientific Psychology," *SE* I, 295.

p.79   *"for sheer pleasure":* Freud to Fliess, October 20, 1895. *Freud–Fliess,* 150 (146).

p.79   *"science like any other":* Abriss der Psychoanalyse (1940), *GW* XVII, 80 / Outline of Psychoanalysis, *SE* XXIII, 158.

p.79   *"mental apparatus":* Ibid., 108 / 182.

p.79   *called Newtonian:* See Robert C. Solomon, "Freud's Neurological Theory of Mind," in *Freud: A Collection of Critical Essays,* ed. Richard Wollheim (1974), 25–52.

p.80   *in the mind:* Jenseits des Lustprinzips (1920), *GW* XIII, 32 / Beyond the Pleasure Principle, *SE* XVIII, 31.

p.80   *"of Quantity":* "Entwurf," in, *Anfängen,* ed. Kris et al., 380 / "Project," *SE* I, 296.

p.80   *"from the stimulus":* Ibid., 381 / 297.

p.81   *"detailed interpretation":* Traumdeutung, *GW* II–III, 111n / Interpretation of Dreams, SE IV, 106n (note added in 1914).

p.81   *"candid than I":* Ibid., 126 / 120–21.

p.81   *engrossed him that day:* Freud to Fliess, July 24, 1895. *Freud–Fliess,* 137 (134). The crucial information in this and the following paragraphs is presented and interpreted in Max Schur, "Some Additional 'Day Residues' of 'The Specimen Dream of Psychoanalysis,' " in *Psycho-analysis—a General Psychology: Essays in Honor of Heinz Hartmann,* ed. Rudolph M. Loewenstein, Lottie M. Newman, Max Schur, and Albert J. Solnit (1966), 45–85. Schur's discussion needs to be supplemented with Didier Anzieu, *Freud's Self-Analysis* (1975; tr. Peter Graham, 1986), 131–56 and *passim;* and Jeffrey Moussaieff Masson, *The Assault on Truth: Freud's Suppression of the Seduction Theory* (1984), 205.

p.81   *"psychological processes":* Freud to Fliess, August 6, 1895. *Freud–Fliess,* 137 (134).

p.82   *"to Dr. Sigm. Freud":* Freud to Fliess, June 12, 1900. Ibid., 458 (417).

p.82   *"was not clean":* Traumdeutung, *GW* II–III, 111–12 / Interpretation of Dreams, *SE* IV, 107.

p.83   *"I am conscientious":* Ibid., 123 / 118.

p.83   *"doctor's conscientiousness":* Ibid., 125 / 120.

p.83   *a "composite":* Ibid., 298–99 / 292–93.

p.84   *"the strong sex":* Freud to Fliess, March 8, 1895. *Freud–Fliess,* 116–17 (116–17).

p.85   *"reproaching you":* Ibid., 117–18 (117–18).

p.85   *worst consequence:* See Freud to Fliess, April 11, 1895. Ibid., 125 (123–24).

p.85   *"of one's family":* Freud to Fliess, April 20, 1895. Ibid., 127 (125).

p.85   *"and yours":* Freud to Fliess, April 26, 1895. Ibid., 128 (127).

p.85   *"please you very much":* Freud to Fliess, April 16, 1896. Ibid., 191 (181).

p.85   *"from longing":* Freud to Fliess, April 28, 1896. Ibid., 193 (183).

p.85   *"wish-bleedings":* Freud to Fliess, June 4, 1896. Ibid., 202 (192).

p.85   *"brilliantly":* Ibid.

p.86   *"context of thought?" Traumdeutung, G W* II–III, 1 2 2 / *Interpretation of Dreams, SE* IV, 1 1 7.

p.86   *"beautiful and good":* Freud to Fliess, January 3, 1899. *Freud–Fliess,* 371 (339).

p.86   *"replace for me":* Freud to Fliess, May 7, 1900. Ibid., 452 (412).

p.86   *"comrade, the friend":* Freud to Fliess, August 7, 1901. Ibid., 492 (447).

p.87   *"to be satisfied":* Freud to Fliess, April 2, 1896. Ibid., 190 (180).

p.87   *"sturdily and alone":* Freud to Fliess, May 4, 1896. Ibid., 195 (185).

p.87   *"late in 1895":* Freud to Fliess, November 8, 1895. Ibid., 154 (150).

p.87   as *"repellent":* Freud to Fliess, July 15, 1896. Ibid., 205 (195).

p.88   *"and the like":* Freud to Fliess, June 30, 1896. Ibid., 203–4 (193).

p.88   *"decency and dignity":* Freud to Fliess, July 15, 1896. Ibid., 205–6 (194–95).

p.88   *"common human being":* Freud to Fliess, October 26, 1896. Ibid., 212 (201).

p.88   *"outlived himself":* Freud to Fliess, November 2, 1896. Ibid., 212–13 (202).

p.88   *somehow forbidden:* See "Brief an Romain Rolland (Eine Erinnerungsstörung auf der Akropolis)" (1936), *GW* XVI, 250–57 / "A Disturbance of Memory on the Acropolis," *SE* XXII, 239–48.

p.89   *"man's life": Traumdeutung, GW* II–III, x / *Interpretation of Dreams, SE* IV, xxvi.

p.89   *maternal relations:* See George F. Mahl, "Father-Son Themes in Freud's Self-Analysis," in *Father and Child: Developmental and Clinical Perspectives,* ed. Stanley H. Cath, Alan R. Gurwitt, and John Munder Ross (1982), 33–64; and Mahl, "Freud, *Father,* and *Mother:* Quantitative aspects," *Psychoanalytic Psychology,* II (1985), 99–113.

p.89   *"for this result": Studien über Hysterie, GW* I, 227 / *Studies on Hysteria, SE* II, 160.

p.89   *"only his own thoughts":* This statement is Freud's quotation of what Fliess said in one of his letters. (Freud to Fliess, August 7, 1901. *Freud–Fliess,* 492 [447].)

p.92   *"dosim / repetatur":* "Zur Geschichte der psychoanalytischen Bewegung" (1914), *GW* X, 52 / "On the History of the Psycho-Analytic Movement," *SE* XIV, 14–15.

p.92   *"sexual neurosis":* Freud to Fliess, February 8, 1893. *Freud–Fliess,* 27 (39).

p.92   *"effect as* memories": Freud to Fliess, October 15, 1895. Ibid., 147 (144).

p.93   *"resembling coitus":* "Weitere Bemerkungen über die Abwehr-Neuropsychosen" (1896), *GW* I, 380 / "Further Remarks on the Neuro-Psychoses of Defence," *SE* III, 163.

p.93   *"innocent" brothers:* Ibid., 382 / 164.

p.93   *invited this conclusion:* See "The Aetiology of Hysteria" (1896), *SE* III, 189–221 *passim.*

p.93   *alle gern haben:* Freud to Fliess, April 26, 1896. *Freud–Fliess,* 193 (184).

p.93   *"falling away from me":* Freud to Fliess, May 4, 1896. Ibid., 195 (185). Looking back in 1914, Freud spoke of a "void" that formed around him. ("Geschichte der psychoanalytischen Bewegung," *GW* X, 59 / "History of the Psycho-Analytic Movement," *SE* XIV, 21.)

p.94   *about the seduction theory:* Freud to Fliess, May 31, 1897. *Freud–Fliess,* 266 (249).

p.94   *fiction on the other:* Freud to Fliess, September 21, 1897. Ibid., 283, 284 (264).

p.95   *"a good deal":* Freud to Fliess, December 12, 1897. Ibid., 312 (286).

p.95   *obtain sexual gratification:* See Freud to Fliess, December 22, 1897. Ibid., 314 (288).

p.95   *six years after that:* For his public disavowal, see *Three Essays on the Theory of Sexuality* (1905), *SE* VII, 190–91 and 190–91n; and "My Views on the Part Played by Sexuality in the Aetiology of the Neuroses" (1906), ibid., 274.

p.95   *assaulted by their fathers: Studien über Hysterie, GW* I, 385n / *Studies on Hysteria, SE* III, 168n (note added in 1924).

p.95   *"of my youth":* Freud to Fliess, September 21, 1897. *Freud–Fliess,* 285 (265–66).

p.95   *"had been lost":* "Geschichte der psychoanalytischen Bewegung," *GW* X, 55 / "History of the Psycho-Analytic Movement," *SE* XIV, 17.

p.96   *"a good exercise":* Freud to Fliess, October 15, 1897. *Freud–Fliess,* 293 (272).

p.96   *"explore these depths": Jones* I, 319.

p.97   *"suddenly started":* Freud to Fliess, November 14, 1897. *Freud–Fliess,* 305, 301 (281, 279).

p.97   *"self-observation": Psychopathologie des Alltaglebens, GW* IV, 5 / *Psychopathology of Everyday Life, SE* VI, 1.

p.97   *"of my own childhood":* Ibid., 58 / 49.

p.98   *of free association:* Ibid., 153 / 138.

p.98   *"events of my childhood":* "Geschichte der psychoanalytischen Bewegung," *GW* X, 58–59 / "History of the Psycho-Analytic Movement," *SE* XIV, 20.

p.98   *of resources:* Freud to Fliess, July 7, 1897. *Freud–Fliess,* 273 (255).

p.98   *infantile sexual feelings: Traumdeutung, GW* II–III, 455–58 / *Interpretation of Dreams, SE* V, 452–55.

p.98   *thrust forward:* Freud to Fliess, May 16, 1897. *Freud–Fliess,* 258 (243).

p.98   *"nothing has changed":* Freud to Fliess, June 18, 1897. Ibid., 270 (252–53).

p.99   *"will crawl out":* Freud to Fliess, June 22, 1897. Ibid., 272 (254).

p.99   *momentary paralysis:* Freud to Fliess, July 7, 1897. Ibid., 272 (255).

p.99   *part of his work:* Freud to Fliess, August 14, 1897. Ibid., 281 (261).

p.99   *"explanations and clues":* Freud to Fliess, October 3, 1897. Ibid., 288 (268).

p.100   *"for the present":* Freud to Fliess, October 27, 1897. Ibid., 295 (274).

p.100   *"beauty of the work":* Freud to Fliess, October 3, 1897. Ibid., 289 (269).

p.100   *of Hamlet:* Freud to Fliess, October 15, 1897. Ibid., 293 (272).

p.100   *"completely stupid":* Freud to Fliess, April 16, 1896. Ibid., 192 (181).

p.100   *"bottle of Barolo":* Freud to Fliess, January 16, 1899. Ibid., 372 (340).

p.100   *for help:* Freud to Fliess, July 8, 1899. Ibid., 394 (359).

p.100   *"a good friend":* Freud to Fliess, June 27, 1899. Ibid., 391 (357).

p.100   *"new vice":* Freud to Fliess, December 5, 1898. Ibid., 368 (335).

p.100   *"like complaining":* Freud to Fliess, May 1, 1898. Ibid., 341 (312).

p.101   *"most amusing":* Ibid., 342 (313).

p.101   *"a little prematurely":* Freud to Fliess, June 27, 1899. Ibid., 391 (357).

p.101   *in his moods:* Freud to Fliess, May 1, 1898. Ibid., 341 (312).

p.101   *"only for you":* Freud to Fliess, May 18, 1898. Ibid., 342 (313).

p.101   *epigraph from Goethe:* See Freud to Fliess, July 17, 1899. Ibid., 396 (361).

p.101   *"do not go together":* Freud to Fliess, June 9, 1898. 344–45 (315).

p.101   *continued to mourn it:* See Freud to Fliess, June 20, 1898. Ibid., 346 (317).

p.101   *in July 1898:* Freud to Fliess, July 30 [1898]. Ibid., 351 (321).

p.102   *"your perspicacity":* Freud to Fliess, August 7, 1901. Ibid., 491–92 (447). When Marie Bonaparte showed Freud this letter in 1937, he described it as "very important." (Ibid., 490n [448n].)

CHAPTER THREE · *Psychoanalysis*

p.103   *in German:* See "Heredity and the Aetiology of the Neuroses" (1896), *SE* III, 151; and "Further Remarks on the Neuro-Psychoses of Defence" (1896), ibid., 162.

p.104   *"mental life": Traumdeutung, GW* II–III, 613 / *Interpretation of Dreams, SE* V, 608.

p.104   *"hard to read":* Ibid., ix / xxv.

p.104   *"it fluently":* Freud to Fliess, February 9, 1898. *Freud–Fliess,* 325 (298).

p.104   *"out attractively":* Freud to Fliess, February 23, 1898. Ibid., 327 (300).

p.104   *"lifelessly, presented":* Freud to Fliess, May 1, 1898. Ibid., 341 (312).

p.104   *"great agony":* Freud to Fliess, September 6, 1899. Ibid., 405 (369).

p.105   *"situation now":* Freud to Fliess, September 11, 1899. Ibid., 407 (371).

p.105   *"mastery of the material":* Freud to Fliess, September 21, 1899. Ibid., 410 (373–74).

p.105   *secure their aim:* Freud to Werner Achelis, January 30, 1927. *Briefe,* 389–90. In the same letter, Freud noted that he had taken the motto not from Virgil directly but from a book by the German Socialist Ferdinand Lassalle.

p.105   *"hear from them!":* Freud to Fliess, September 6, 1899. *Freud–Fliess,* 405 (369).

p.106   *"want to go now?":* Freud to Fliess, August 6, 1899. Ibid., 400 (365).

p.106   *"broken surfaces": Traumdeutung, GW* II–III, vii / *Interpretation of Dreams, SE* IV, xxiii.

p.106   *"of waking life":* Ibid., 1 / 1.

p.106   *"disgusts me so much":* Freud to Fliess, February 9, 1898. *Freud–Fliess,* 325 (299).

p.106   *"a horrible punishment":* Freud to Fliess, December 5, 1898. Ibid., 368 (335).

p.106   *"poor book":* Freud to Fliess, August 6, 1899. Ibid., 400 (365).

p.107   *"lay opinion":* Traumdeutung, *GW* II–III, 100 / *Interpretation of Dreams, SE* IV, 96.

p.107   *"wish fulfillment":* Ibid., 104, 126 / 99, 121.

p.108   *Breuer's nephew:* Freud reported it to Fliess on March 4, 1895. *Freud–Fliess,* 114–15 (114).

p.108   *sleeps on:* See *Interpretation of Dreams, SE* IV, 125.

p.108   *"than singly":* Traumdeutung, *GW* II–III, 141 / *Interpretation of Dreams, SE* IV, 135–36.

p.109   *"desirable meal":* Ibid., 132, 135 / 127, 130.

p.109   *"of its utterance":* Ibid., 149 / 143–44.

p.109   *"counter-wish dreams":* Ibid., 163 / 157.

p.109   *"(suppressed, repressed) wish":* Ibid., 166 / 160.

p.110   *"innocent dreams":* Ibid., 169, 189 / 163, 182.

p.110   *"far from innocent":* Ibid., 193–94 / 186–87.

p.110   *"experience every time":* Ibid., 170 / 165.

p.111   *morning before:* See ibid., 175–82, 287–90 / 169–76, 281–84.

p.111   *"in the dream":* Ibid., 197 / 191.

p.111   *no other merit:* Ibid., 214–24 / 208–18.

p.112   *"something after all":* Ibid., 221–22 / 216.

p.112   *"nuclear complex":* "Über infantile Sexualtheorien" (1908), *GW* VII, 176 / "On the Sexual Theories of Children," *SE* IX, 214.

p.113   *"parental pair":* Traumdeutung, *GW* II–III, 267 / *Interpretation of Dreams, SE* IV, 260.

p.113   *"or a word":* Ibid., 283–84 / 277–78.

p.114   *"concern for representability":* Ibid., 344 / 339.

p.114   *"good account":* Traumdeutung, *GW* II–III, 365 / *Interpretation of Dreams, SE* V, 359–60 (sentence added in 1909).

p.114   *"of the unconscious":* Freud to Pfister, November 6, 1910. By permission of Sigmund Freud Copyrights, Wivenhoe.

p.115   *marry happily:* Traumdeutung, *GW* II–III, 284, 304–8 / *Interpretation of Dreams, SE* IV, 279, 298–302.

p.116   *thought delightful:* Traumdeutung, *GW* II–III, 424–25 / *Interpretation of Dreams, SE* V, 421–22.

p.117   *"move to Paris":* Ibid., 425–26, 484–85, 489 / 423–24, 480–81, 485.

p.117   *"Jewish stories":* Freud to Fliess, June 22, 1897. *Freud–Fliess,* 271 (254).

p.117   *application of his theory:* See *Interpretation of Dreams, SE* IV, xxiii.

p.118   *"normal mental processes":* Freud to Fliess, May 25, 1895. *Freud–Fliess,* 130 (129).

p.118   *"over to psychology":* Freud to Fliess, April 2, 1896. Ibid., 190 (180).

p.118   *"goal, philosophy":* Freud to Fliess, January 1, 1896. Ibid., 165 (159).

p.119   *"egg onward":* "Eine Kindheitserinnerung des Leonardo da Vinci" (1910), *GW* VIII, 210 / "Leonardo da Vinci and a Memory of His Childhood," *SE* XI, 137.

p.119   *"way or another":* Das Ich und das Es (1923), *GW* XIII, 280n / *The Ego and the Id, SE* XIX, 50n.

p.120   *"in the nervous system":* Richard von Krafft-Ebing, *Nervosität und Neurasthenische Zustände* (1895), 4, 16, 9, 17.

p.120   *"nervous constitution":* Ibid., 37, 51, 53.

p.120   *electrotherapy, massages:* See ibid., 124–60.

p.120   *as a cause:* See ibid., 188–210.

p.120   *"brain disease":* Quoted in Erna Lesky, *The Vienna Medical School of the 19th Century* (1965; tr. L. Williams and I. S. Levij, 1976), 345.

p.121   *"rumple the other":* Laurence Sterne, *Tristram Shandy* (1760–67), book III, ch. 4.

p.121   "physical function": William Hammond, reviewing John P. Gray, *The Dependence of Insanity on Physical Disease* (1871), in *Journal of Psychological Medicine*, V (1876), 576. Quoted in Bonnie Ellen Blustein, " 'A Hollow Square of Psychological Science': American Neurologists and Psychiatrists in Conflict," in *Madhouses, Mad-Doctors, and Madmen: The Social History of Psychiatry in the Victorian Era*, ed. Andrew Scull (1981), 241.

p.121   "physical side": Henry Maudsley, *Responsibility in Mental Disease* (2d ed., 1874), 154. Quoted in Michael J. Clark, "The Rejection of Psychological Approaches to Mental Disorder in Late Nineteenth-Century British Psychiatry," in ibid., 271.

p.121   "cerebral affection": Jean Étienne Esquirol, *Des Maladies mentales considérées sous les rapports médical, hygiénique et médico-légal*, 3 vols. (1838), I, 5 (from a treatise of 1816 taken over into the larger later work).

p.121   "completely ignored": Quoted in Karin Obholzer, *The Wolf-Man Sixty Years Later: Conversations with Freud's Controversial Patient* (1980; tr. Michael Shaw, 1982), 30.

p.122   "somatic side": "Selbstdarstellung," *GW* XIV, 50 / "Autobiographical Study," *SE* XX, 25.

p.122   "organic basis": Freud to Fliess, September 22, 1898. *Freud–Fliess*, 357 (326).

p.123   "condition of nations": Esquirol, *Des maladies mentales*, I, 24.

p.123   *importance to heredity*: See *Three Essays on the Theory of Sexuality*, *SE* VII, 173.

p.124   "origin and meaning": Martin Freud, *Freud*, 67.

p.124   *Freud's account*: See Abraham to Freud, January 8, 1908. *Freud–Abraham*, 32 (18).

p.124   "have them all!": Freud to Abraham, January 9, 1908. Ibid., 34 (20).

p.125   "uncovered mercilessly": Jung to Freud, February 14, 1911. *Freud–Jung*, 433 (392).

p.125   "of him even more": Freud to Jung, February 17, 1911. Ibid., 435–36 (394–95).

p.125   *circuitous ways*: See editor's note in *Freud–Fliess*, 355.

p.125   *back to his childhood*: Freud to Fliess, August 26, 1898. Ibid., 354–55 (324).

p.125   "make this credible?": Freud to Fliess, September 22, 1898. Ibid., 357–58 (326–27).

p.126   *neurology and psychiatry*: See "The Psychical Mechanism of Forgetfulness" (1898), *SE* III, 289–97.

p.126   "2,467 mistakes": Freud to Fliess, August 27, 1899. *Freud–Fliess*, 404 (368).

p.126   *describing it*: See Freud to Fliess, September 24, 1900. Ibid., 467 (425).

p.126   *of active life*: See *Psychopathology of Everyday Life*, *SE* VI, 242–43.

p.126   *even more strongly*: See Freud to Fliess, May 8, 1901. *Freud–Fliess*, 485 (441).

p.126   "me until now": Freud to Fliess, August 7, 1901. Ibid., 492 (447).

p.127   *impressions and intentions*: See *Psychopathology of Everyday Life*, *SE* VI, 143–44. The abbreviated name of Fliess appears only in the earliest editions (1901 and 1904); hence the reference is bound to have made something of an impact on Fliess.

p.127   *was now closed*: See ibid., 59. He is quoting from an article by R. Meringer, "Wie man sich versprechen kann," *Neue Freie Presse*, August 23, 1900.

p.127   *in his lifetime*: See "Editor's Introduction" to *Psychopathology of Everyday Life*, *SE* VI, ix–x.

p.128   "cerebration of sleep": Henry James, "The Aspern Papers" (1888), in *Tales of Henry James*, ed. Christof Wegelin (1984), 185.

p.128   " 'unconscious' seriously": "Selbstdarstellung," *GW* XIV, 56 / "Autobiographical Study," *SE* XX, 31.

p.128   "of the neuroses": Ibid., 55 / 30.

p.129   "Memory yields": See "Bemerkungen über einen Fall von Zwangsneurose" (1909), *GW* VII, 407 / "Notes upon a Case of Obsessional Neurosis," *SE* X, 184. The quotation is from Nietzsche, *Beyond Good and Evil*, iv, 68.

p.129   "times of ours": Carlyle, *Sartor Resartus*, book II, ch. 2.

p.129   "anatomizing of motives": Quoted in Jerome Hamilton Buckley, *The Turning Key: Autobiography and the Subjective Impulse since 1800* (1984), 4.

p.130   "interpret Life": Kraus, "Die demolierte Literatur," manuscript of the draft in Zeller, ed., *Jugend in Wien*, 265–66.

p.130   *kriechen wagen:* Quoted in Amos Elon, *Herzl* (1975), 109.

p.130   *"secret knowledge":* Freud to Schnitzler, May 8, 1906. *Briefe,* 266–67.

p.131   *"from the unconscious":* Traumdeutung, *GW* II–III, 559, 566 / *Interpretation of Dreams, SE* V, 553, 561.

p.131   *"material reality":* Ibid., 583, 625 / 577, 620.

p.131   *"new basis":* Freud to Darmstaeder, July 3, 1910. Freud Collection, B3, LC.

p.132   *"congresses" in Rome:* See Freud to Fliess, December 3, 1897. *Freud–Fliess,* 309 (284–85).

p.132   *at Easter:* See Freud to Fliess, February 6, 1899. Ibid., 376 (344).

p.132   *"Eternal City":* Freud to Fliess, August 27, 1899. Ibid., 404 (368).

p.132   *torment of yearning:* See Freud to Fliess, October 23, 1898. Ibid., 363 (332).

p.132   *"hero Hannibal":* Freud to Fliess, December 3, 1897. Ibid., 309 (285).

p.132   *"longed-for wishes":* Traumdeutung, *GW* II–III, 202 / *Interpretation of Dreams, SE* IV, 196–97.

p.132   *ruler of Rome:* See ibid., 403n / 398n.

p.133   *"itself from me":* Freud to Fliess, October 4, 1899. *Freud–Fliess,* 414 (376, 377).

p.133   *"resigned expectancy":* Freud to Fliess, October 27, 1899. Ibid., 417–18 (380).

p.133   *"epoch-making":* Freud to Fliess, December 21, 1899. Ibid., 430 (392). See also editors' note in ibid., 430 (392).

p.133   *"terribly bored":* Ibid., 430, 431 (392).

p.133   *"uncommonly uncomprehending":* Freud to Fliess, January 8, 1900. Ibid., 433 (394).

p.133   *"always alone":* Freud to Fliess, February 1, 1900. Ibid., 437 (398).

p.134   *"during the day":* Freud to Fliess, March 11, 1900. Ibid., 441, 443 (402–3, 404).

p.134   *"human misery":* Freud to Fliess, May 7, 1900. Ibid., 452 (412).

p.134   *his tormentors:* See Freud to Fliess, March 11, 1900. Ibid., 442 (404).

p.134   *"rebuild them again":* Freud to Fliess, March 23, 1900. Ibid., 444 (405).

p.134   *"shabby Israelite":* Freud to Fliess, May 7, 1900. Ibid., 452–53 (412).

p.134   *"an old uncle":* Freud to [Margarethe, Lilly, and Martha Gertrude Freud] (postcard), May 20, 1900. Freud Collection, B2, LC.

p.134   *"a birthday child":* Freud to [Margarethe, Lilly, and Martha Gertrude Freud], May 8, 1901. Ibid.

p.135   *"dream child":* Freud to Fliess, March 23, 1900. *Freud–Fliess,* 444 (405).

p.135   *"with my milieu":* Freud to Fliess, March 11, 1900. Ibid., 442 (403).

p.135   *"high point":* Freud to Fliess, September 19, 1901. Ibid., 493 (449).

p.135   *"afraid of for years!":* Freud to Martha Freud (postcard), September 3, 1901. Freud Museum, London.

p.135   *"other things":* Freud to Martha Freud (postcard), September 5, 1901. Ibid.

p.135   *"live for years":* Freud to Martha Freud (postcard), September 6, 1901. Ibid.

p.135   *beauties of Venice:* See Freud to Minna Bernays (postcard), August 27, 1902. Ibid.

p.135   *"this divine city":* Ernest Jones to Freud from Rome, December 5 [1912], quoting Freud. By permission of Sigmund Freud Copyrights, Wivenhoe.

p.136   *"found it so":* Freud to Mathilde Freud, September 17, 1907. Freud Collection, B1, LC.

p.136   *"splendid isolation":* Freud to Fliess, May 7, 1900. *Freud–Fliess,* 452 (412). Freud used this phrase, in English, more than once.

p.136   *"for his patients":* Traumdeutung, *GW* II–III, 142 / *Interpretation of Dreams, SE* IV, 137.

p.136   *"slippery slope":* Freud to Elise Gomperz, November 25, 1901. *Briefe,* 256.

p.136   *Protektion detestable:* See K. R. Eissler, *Sigmund Freud und die Wiener Universität. Über die Pseudo-Wissenschaftlichkeit der jüngsten Wiener Freud-Biographik* (1966), 170.

p.137   *about the promotion:* Phillip Freud to Marie Freud, March 12, 1902. Freud Collection, B1, LC.

p.137   *to no effect:* Freud to Fliess, March 11, 1902. *Freud–Fliess,* 501–2 (455–56).

p.138   *"having to go to Rome":* Ibid., 502–3 (456–57).

p.138   *longer than Freud:* See Eissler, *Sigmund Freud und die Wiener Universität,* 181–85.

p.139   *"further difficulties"*: Quoted in Freud to Fliess, February 8, 1897. *Freud–Fliess*, 244 (229).

p.139   *"somebody else"*: Quoted in Eissler, *Sigmund Freud und die Wiener Universität*, 135.

p.139   *a Streber*: Freud to Elise Gomperz, November 25, 1901. *Briefe*, 256.

p.140   *"somewhat diminished"*: Freud to Fliess, March 11, 1902. *Freud–Fliess*, 501 (456).

p.140   *"of my audacity"*: Freud to members of B'nai B'rith (May 6, 1926). *Briefe*, 381. See also Hugo Knoepfmacher, "Sigmund Freud and the B'nai B'rith." Undated manuscript, Freud Collection, B27, LC.

p.140   *"professional journals"*: "Selbstdarstellung," *GW* XIV, 74 / "Autobiographical Study," *SE* XX, 48.

p.142   *"to the dream book"*: Freud to Fliess, October 11, 1899. *Freud–Fliess*, 416 (379).

p.142   *"rousing spark"*: Freud to Fliess, January 26, 1900. Ibid., 436 (397).

p.142   *"anything useful"*: Freud to Fliess, February 1, 1900. Ibid., 437 (398).

p.142   *"conscious mastery"*: Freud to Fliess, November 25, 1900. Ibid., 471 (429).

p.143   *"freer sexual life"*: Freud to Putnam, July 8, 1915. *James Jackson Putnam and Psychoanalysis: Letters between Putnam and Sigmund Freud, Ernest Jones, William James, Sándor Ferenczi, and Morton Prince, 1877–1917*, ed. Nathan G. Hale, Jr. (1971), 376.

p.143   *the libido*: Freud's responses to the inquiry launched by the Cultural-Political Society were published for the first time in full, in German, in John W. Boyer, "Freud, Marriage, and Late Viennese Liberalism: A Commentary from 1905," *Journal of Modern History*, L (1978), 72–102. Quoted passages at 100.

p.143   *liked to charge*: For documentation, see Peter Gay, *The Bourgeois Experience: Victoria to Freud*, vol. I, *Education of the Senses* (1984), and vol. II, *The Tender Passion* (1986).

p.144   *"well-known writings"*: *Drei Abhandlungen zur Sexualtheorie* (1905), *GW* V, 33n; see also 74n / *Three Essays on the Theory of Sexuality*, *SE* VII, 135n; see also 174n.

p.144   *"three-year-old children"*: Adolf Patze, *Ueber Bordelle und die Sittenverderbniss unserer Zeit* (1845), 48n. See Peter Gay, *Freud for Historians* (1985), 58.

p.144   *"own early life"*: Henry Maudsley, *The Physiology and Pathology of Mind* (1867), 284. See Stephen Kern, "Freud and the Discovery of Child Sexuality," *History of Childhood Quarterly: The Journal of Psychohistory*, I (Summer 1973), 117–41.

p.144   *"know sexual appetite"*: *Traumdeutung*, *GW* II–III, 136 / *Interpretation of Dreams*, *SE* IV, 130.

p.145   *from these pages*: See *Three Essays*, *SE* VII, 130.

p.145   *"to the* Interpretation of Dreams": Freud to Abraham, November 12, 1908. *Freud–Abraham*, 67 (57–58).

p.146   *"aberrations as these"*: *Drei Abhandlungen*, *GW* V, 59–60 / *Three Essays*, *SE* VII, 161.

p.146   *"activity of the patient"*: Ibid., 71, 63 / 171, 163.

p.146   *"component drives"*: Ibid, 67–69 / 167–69.

p.147   *"drive in childhood"*: Ibid., 73 / 173.

p.148   *but the "aptitude"*: Ibid., 88, 91 / 187, 191.

p.149   *"divine Plato"*: Ibid., 32 / 134.

CHAPTER FOUR · *Sketch of an Embattled Founder*

p.154   *for the medallion*: Jones II, 13–14.

p.154   *"vice versa"*: Fliess to Freud, July 20, 1904. *Freud–Fliess*, 508 (463).

p.155   *for some years*: Freud to Fliess, July 23, 1904. Ibid., 508 (464).

p.155   *intellectual burglary*: See Fliess to Freud, July 26, 1904. Ibid., 510–11 (465–66).

p.155   *his own book*: See Freud to Fliess, July 27, 1904. Ibid., 512–15 (466–68).

p.155   *letter to Karl Kraus*: See Freud to Kraus, January 12, 1906. *Briefe*, 265–66.

p.156   *"oppress him"*: Abraham to Eitingon, January 1, 1908. The letter is quoted in full in Hilda Abraham, *Karl Abraham. Sein Leben für die Psychoanalyse* (1974; tr. into German by Hans-Horst Henschen, 1976), 73.

p.156   *"1916 or 1917"*: Freud to Sándor Ferenczi, January 10, 1910. Freud–Ferenczi Correspondence, Freud Collection, LC.

p.156   *"from the depths"*: Max Graf, "Reminiscences of Professor Sigmund Freud," *Psychoanalytic Quarterly,* XI (1942), 467.

p.157   *"piercing eyes"*: Joan Riviere, "An Intimate Impression," *The Lancet* (September 30, 1939). Reprinted in *Freud As We Knew Him,* ed. Ruitenbeek, 129.

p.157   *"the student's stoop"*: Wittels, *Sigmund Freud,* 129.

p.157   *"in nothing else"*: Freud to Pfister, March 6, 1910. *Freud–Pfister,* 32 (35).

p.157   *"by the clock"*: Ernst Waldinger, "My Uncle Sigmund Freud," *Books Abroad,* XV (Winter 1941), 7.

p.157   *one in the morning:* See, for a most revealing catalogue of Freud's day's doings, Anna Freud to Jones, January 31, 1954. Jones papers, Archives of the British Psycho-Analytical Society, London.

p.157   *"Tarockexzess"*: Freud to Fliess, March 11, 1900. *Freud–Fliess,* 443 (404).

p.158   *"of summer is"*: Freud to Abraham, April 24, 1914. Karl Abraham papers, LC.

p.158   *from books alone:* See *Jones* II, 379–402; Martin Freud, *Freud, passim;* and "A Disturbance of Memory on the Acropolis: An Open Letter to Romain Rolland on the Occasion of his Seventieth Birthday" (1936), *SE* XXII, 239–48.

p.158   *to his family:* See the undated reminiscences of the psychoanalyst (and Freud's analysand) Ludwig Jekels, evidently in response to Siegfried Bernfeld's inquiries preparatory to the biography of Freud he never wrote. Siegfried Bernfeld papers, container 17, LC.

p.158   *"delightful days"*: Abraham to Eitingon, January 1, 1908. Quoted in Hilda Abraham, *Abraham,* 72.

p.158   *"youthful and healthy"*: "Selbstdarstellung," *GW* XIV, 78 / "Autobiographical Study," *SE* XX, 52.

p.158   *" 'a merry heart' "*: Martin Freud, *Freud,* 9, 27.

p.159   *from illness:* Anna Freud to Jones, June 16, 1954. Jones papers, Archives of the British Psycho-Analytical Society, London.

p.159   *than the man:* See *Jones* II, 415–16.

p.159   *"wittily and forcibly"*: Wittels, *Sigmund Freud,* 129–30.

p.160   *"day laborer"*: Freud to Lilly Freud Marlé, March 14, 1911. Freud Collection, B2, LC.

p.160   *"weep out loud"*: Bruno Goetz, "Erinnerungen an Sigmund Freud," *Neue Schweizer Rundschau,* XX (May 1952), 3–11.

p.161   *"our own right"*: Martin Freud, *Freud,* 32.

p.161   *"prevent it"*: Martha Freud to Elsa Reiss, January 17, 1950. Freud Collection, B1, LC.

p.162   *"meaningless trifle"*: Martin Freud, *Freud,* 40–43.

p.162   *"perforce at parting"*: Richard Dyck, "Mein Onkel Sigmund," interview with Harry Freud in *Aufbau* (New York), May 11, 1956, 3–4.

p.162   *"know better"*: Freud to Jones, January 1, 1929. *Briefe,* 402.

p.162   *"cuddling on his lap"*: *Jones* II, 387.

p.162   *"as a father"*: Freud to Jung, June 9, 1910. *Freud–Jung,* 361 (327).

p.162   *"yet the case"*: Freud to Fliess, December 17, 1896. *Freud–Fliess,* 229 (217).

p.162   *"erotic excitement"*: Freud to Fliess, May 31, 1897. Ibid., 266 (249).

p.163   *"begetting children"*: Freud to Fliess, March 11, 1900. Ibid., 443 (404).

p.163   *"Wednesday morning"*: Typescript copy, Freud Museum, London. The holograph original has not (yet) been found. The account of Freud's dreams and their analysis takes up five pages. It is titled "Dream of July 8 / 9, Th[ursday]. Fr[iday], upon Awakening." Freud sent part of this account, that dealing with a prophetic (but fortunately mistaken) dream about the death of his son Martin, then serving in the army, to Ferenczi on July 10, 1915. (Freud–Ferenczi Correspondence, Freud Collection, LC.) This letter strongly supports the authenticity of this somewhat mysterious memorandum.

p.163   *"very little use"*: Freud to Putnam, July 8, 1915. *James Jackson Putnam: Letters,* 376.

p.163   *"ars amandi":* Freud at the Wednesday Psychological Society, October 16, 1907, and February 12, 1908. *Protokolle,* I, 202, 293.

p.163   *"founder of psychoanalysis":* Janet Malcolm, *In the Freud Archives* (1984), 24.

p.164   *"do than—die":* Emma Jung quoted Freud to that effect in a letter to him of November 6 [1911]. *Freud–Jung,* 504 (456).

p.164   *"in other ways":* "Die 'kulturelle' Sexualmoral und die Moderne Nervosität" (1908), *GW* VII, 156 / " 'Civilized' Sexual Morality and Modern Nervous Illness," *SE* IX, 193.

p.164   *" 'life of Mankind' ":* Freud to Jung, September 19, 1907. *Freud–Jung,* 98 (89).

p.164   *"offering compensations":* Der Witz und seine Beziehung zum Unbewussten (1905), *GW* VI, 120 / *Jokes and Their Relation to the Unconscious, SE* VIII, 109.

p.165   *"little jewel":* Freud to Abraham, July 31, 1913. *Freud–Abraham,* 144 (145).

p.165   *"must be punished":* Freud to Abraham, December 26, 1922. Ibid., 309 (332). The epithet "most modern" is Abraham's, characterizing the aesthetic direction the painter who had done his portrait had recently adopted. (Abraham to Freud, January 7, 1923. Ibid., 310 [333].)

p.165   *a philistine:* See Freud to Pfister, June 21, 1920. *Freud–Pfister,* 80 (77).

p.166   *Dorothy Sayers:* See Anna Freud to Jones, undated typed comments on vol. III of Jones's biography of Freud. Jones papers, Archives of the British Psycho-Analytical Society, London.

p.166   *and Mark Twain:* See "Contribution to a Questionnaire on Reading" (1907), *SE* IX, 245–47.

p.167   *"effects of art":* "Der Moses des Michelangelo" (1914), *GW* X, 172 / "The Moses of Michelangelo," *SE* XIII, 211. Freud published this paper in *Imago* anonymously, and did not acknowledge authorship until ten years later.

p.168   *"Lustprinzip":* Freud to Jones, February 8, 1914. In English. Freud Collection, D2, LC.

p.168   *"recognized the melody":* Traumdeutung, *GW* II–III, 214 / *Interpretation of Dreams, SE* IV, 208.

p.168   *only too true:* See Anna Freud to Jones, May 29, 1951. Jones papers, Archives of the British Psycho-Analytical Society, London.

p.168   *"never went to concerts":* Anna Freud to Jones, January 23, 1956. Ibid.

p.168   *Wagner's Meistersinger:* See Anna Freud to Jones, May 29 and 31, 1951; and Marie Bonaparte to Jones (relaying a comment by Freud's eldest daughter, Mathilde), November 8, 1951. All in ibid.

p.168   *twenty-seven times:* See Mina Curtiss, *Bizet and His World* (1958), 426–30.

p.168   *to Donna Elvira:* For Figaro, see *Interpretation of Dreams, SE* IV, 208; for Sarastro, Freud to Ferenczi, August 9, 1909 (Freud–Ferenczi Correspondence, Freud Collection, LC); for Leporello, Freud to Fliess, May 25, 1897 (*Freud–Fliess,* 261 [245]).

p.169   *cauliflower and chicken:* Martin Freud, *Freud,* 33. See also Freud to Fliess, October 27, 1899. *Freud–Fliess,* 418 (381).

p.169   *been his model:* Freud to Victor Richard Rubens, February 12, 1929, in response to a questionnaire on smoking (Arents Collection, No. 3270, New York Public Library). This letter is quoted in full in the original German in Max Schur, *Freud, Living and Dying* (1972), 535, but is mistakenly said to be addressed to Wilhelm Fliess.

p.170   *"without choking":* Martin Freud, *Freud,* 110.

p.170   *"sorry for you":* Dyck, "Mein Onkel Sigmund," interview with Harry Freud, *Aufbau,* May 11, 1956, 4.

p.170   *masturbation:* Freud to Fliess, December 22, 1897. *Freud–Fliess,* 312–13 (287).

p.170   *"prehistoric":* Freud to Fliess, January 30, 1899. Ibid., 374 (342).

p.170   *"nicotine addiction":* Schur, *Freud, Living and Dying,* 247.

p.170   *"visitor's eye":* Hanns Sachs, *Freud: Master and Friend* (1945), 49.

p.171   *"long-vanished epochs":* "My Recollections of Sigmund Freud," in *The Wolf-Man by the Wolf-Man,* ed. Muriel Gardiner (1971), 139.

p.171   *"archeology than psychology":* Freud to Stefan Zweig, February 7, 1931. *Briefe,* 420–21.

p.171   *"most valuable treasures":* "My Recollections," in *The Wolf-Man,* ed. Gardiner, 139.

p.172   *Florentine plaster casts:* Freud to Fliess, December 6, 1896. *Freud–Fliess,* 226 (214).

p.172   *"times and lands":* Freud to Fliess, August 6, 1899. Ibid., 402 (366).

p.172   *"adapted to reality":* Freud to Ferenczi, March 30, 1922. Freud–Ferenczi Correspondence, Freud Collection, LC.

p.172   *"of a child's wish":* Freud to Fliess, May 28, 1899. *Freud–Fliess,* 387 (353).

p.172   *"Stones speak!":* "Zur Ätiologie der Hysterie" (1896), *GW* I, 427 / "The Aetiology of Hysteria," *SE* III, 192.

p.172   *"legendary, once again":* Freud to Fliess, December 21, 1899. *Freud–Fliess,* 430 (391–92).

p.172   *"the authentic":* "Bruchstück einer Hysterie-Analyse" ["Dora"] (1905), *GW* V, 169–70 / "Fragment of an Analysis of a Case of Hysteria" ["Dora"], *SE* VII, 12.

p.173   *archeological excavation:* See *Civilization and Its Discontents* (1930), *SE* XXI, 69–70.

p.173   *impact of smoking:* See *The Autobiography of Wilhelm Stekel: The Life Story of a Pioneer Psychoanalyst,* ed. Emil A. Gutheil (1950), 116.

p.173   *"gave the impetus":* "Geschichte der psychoanalytischen Bewegung," *GW* X, 63 / "History of the Psycho-Analytic Movement," *SE* XIV, 25.

p.173   *"was my Christ!":* Autobiography of Wilhelm Stekel, 106.

p.174   *to be satisfied:* See "History of the Psycho-Analytic Movement," *SE* XIV, 25.

p.174   *after Freud:* See *Jones* II, 7.

p.174   *"like a revelation":* Autobiography of Wilhelm Stekel, 116. For some of Reitler's early interventions, see *Protokolle,* I, 70–76, 105–6, 149, 167.

p.174   *"appear superficial":* Graf, "Reminiscences," 470–71.

p.175   *an impotent friend:* See October 9, 1907. *Protokolle,* I, 194.

p.175   *self-exhibition:* January 15, 1908. Ibid., 264–68.

p.176   *Theories of the Neuroses:* The book was translated into English by C. R. Payne and published under this title, with an appreciative introduction by Ernest Jones, in 1921. The original German title was *Freud's Neurosenlehre* (1911).

p.176   *motif in literature:* In the end Rank's book, *The Incest Motif in Literature and Legend,* did not appear until 1912.

p.177   *public domain:* See February 5, 1908. *Protokolle,* I, 284–85.

p.177   *words of abuse:* December 4, 1907. Ibid., 239–43.

p.177   *"we once were":* February 5, 1908. Ibid., 284.

p.178   *resign unostentatiously:* See Freud to Rank, September 22, 1907. Typescript copy, Freud Collection, B4, LC.

p.178   *"just as much":* Abraham to Eitingon, January 1, 1908. Quoted in Hilda Abraham, *Abraham,* 73.

p.178   *"what he could get":* Ernest Jones, *Free Associations: Memories of a Psycho-Analyst* (1959), 169–70.

p.178   *this crowd:* See Ludwig Binswanger, *Erinnerungen an Sigmund Freud* (1956), 13.

p.179   *"for little Rank":* Freud to Abraham, March 14, 1911. Karl Abraham papers, LC.

p.179   *"psychoanalytic method":* Eitingon to Freud, December 6, 1906. By permission of Sigmund Freud Copyrights, Wivenhoe.

p.179   *"of our teachings":* Freud to Eitingon, December 10, 1906. By permission of Sigmund Freud Copyrights, Wivenhoe.

p.179   *"fisher of men":* Freud used the resonant term *Menschenfischer,* recalling, of course, what Jesus said he would make his disciples (Matthew 4:19), in a letter of March 3, 1910, probably to John Rickman, an English physician who later became a psychoanalyst. Typescript copy, Freud Collection, B4, LC.

p.179   *"training analysis!":* Jones II, 32.

p.179   *Freud's "pupil":* Eitingon had already called himself Freud's "pupil" more than half a year before his move to Berlin. (Eitingon to Freud, February 5, 1909. By permission of Sigmund Freud Copyrights, Wivenhoe.)

p.179 *Freud obliged:* See Eitingon to Freud, February 9, May 5, and June 10, 1912. By permission of Sigmund Freud Copyrights, Wivenhoe.

p.180 *"in my house":* Freud to Eitingon, February 17, 1910. By permission of Sigmund Freud Copyrights, Wivenhoe.

p.180 *The Brothers Karamazov:* See Eitingon to Freud, February 10, 1910. By permission of Sigmund Freud Copyrights, Wivenhoe.

p.180 *"traitors either":* Freud to Eitingon, July 10, 1914. By permission of Sigmund Freud Copyrights, Wivenhoe.

p.180 *his own conscience:* See Hilda Abraham, *Abraham,* 41.

p.180 *around Freud:* Jones II, 159.

p.180 *"the official rabble":* Freud to Abraham, April 19, 1908. Karl Abraham papers, LC.

p.180 *fraternal sympathy:* Jones to Abraham, June 18, 1911. Ibid.

p.180 *"turn out all right":* Freud to Abraham, July 11, 1909. Ibid.

p.181 *homosexual rights:* See Freud to Abraham, April 19, 1908. Ibid.

p.181 *Abraham's hospitality:* Freud to Abraham, May 29, 1908. Ibid.

p.181 *dogma upon it:* See Andreas-Salomé to Abraham, November 6, 1914. Ibid.

p.181 *Seminary walls:* Hall to Abraham, January 2, 1914. Ibid.

p.181 *"good long while":* Abraham to Freud, February 26, 1911. Ibid.

p.181 *even "turbulent":* Abraham to Freud, March 9, 1911. Ibid.

p.181 *"time for science":* Ibid.

p.181 *"your adherent":* Abraham to Freud, July 24, 1912. Ibid.

p.182 *"absorbs me":* Abraham to Freud, April 28, 1912. Ibid.

p.182 *"sterile a soil":* Abraham to Freud, December 25, 1911. Ibid.

p.182 *"people are lacking":* Abraham to Freud, May 28, 1912. Ibid.

p.182 *mountain climbing:* See Hilda Abraham, *Abraham,* 39.

p.182 *"perversion not neurosis":* Freud to Abraham, February 13, 1911. Karl Abraham papers, LC. (*Freud–Abraham,* 105 [100–101], prints only part of this letter, omitting the characterization "wicked" and the warning against Frau Dr. Fliess.)

p.183 *"necessary prudence":* Abraham to Freud, February 17, 1911. Karl Abraham papers, LC.

p.183 *in any way:* See Abraham to Freud, February 26, 1911. *Freud–Abraham,* 106–7 (102).

p.183 *Frau Dr. Fliess:* See, for example, Abraham to Freud, April 9, 1911, where he mentions Fliess's referring a patient to him, but says not a word about Frau Fliess. Karl Abraham papers, LC.

p.183 *"opening our eyes!":* Fliess to Abraham, September 26, 1917. Ibid.

p.184 *"true psychologist":* Jones, *Free Associations,* 159–60.

p.184 *cordially received:* On May 13, 1908, Jones thanked Freud for his "kind reception" in Vienna. By permission of Sigmund Freud Copyrights, Wivenhoe.

p.184 *"membership of nine":* Jones to Freud, November 3, 1913. By permission of Sigmund Freud Copyrights, Wivenhoe. Not all these members, by the way, proved to be Freudians; several of them would prefer Jung.

p.185 *"male fertilisation":* Jones to Freud, June 19, 1910. By permission of Sigmund Freud Copyrights, Wivenhoe.

p.185 *"arguments of others":* Freud to Jones, April 28, 1912. Freud Collection, D2, LC.

p.185 *switched to English:* Jones to Freud, November 8 [1908]. By permission of Sigmund Freud Copyrights, Wivenhoe. See also Freud to Jones, November 20, 1908. In English. Freud Collection, D2, LC.

p.185 *"on the other?":* Jung to Freud, July 12, 1908. *Freud–Jung,* 181–82 (164).

p.186 *"Mediterranean man":* Freud to Jung, July 18, 1908. Ibid., 183 (165).

p.186 *" 'Father-complex' ":* Jones to Freud, December 18, 1909. By permission of Sigmund Freud Copyrights, Wivenhoe.

p.186   *"good bit together"*: Freud to Jones, April 15, 1910. In English. Freud Collection, D2, LC.

p.186   *"splendid at last"*: Freud to Jones, February 24, 1912. In English. Ibid.

p.186   *"changes of mood"*: Jones to Freud, June 3, 25, July 8 [1913]. By permission of Sigmund Freud Copyrights, Wivenhoe.

p.186   *"big work"*: Freud to Jones, February 22, 1909. In English. Freud Collection, D2, LC.

p.186   *"give you answering"*: Freud to Jones, June 1, 1909. In English. Ibid.

p.186   *"letters and papers"*: Freud to Jones, March 10, 1910. In English. Ibid.

p.187   *"into the matter"*: Freud to Jones, January 16, 1914. In English. Ibid.

p.187   *"case this time"*: Freud to Jones, February 8, 1914. In English. Ibid. *"Cet. censeo,"* as Jones would of course have known, are the opening words of Cato's celebrated oration proclaiming that Carthage must be destroyed: *Ceterum censeo Cartaginem esse delendam.*

p.187   *"mind to you"*: Freud to Jones, February 21, 1914. In English. Ibid.

p.187   *nothing more:* Freud to Jones, January 1, 1929. *Briefe,* 402.

p.187   *"closest"* to him: *Jones* II, 157.

p.187   *"his accomplishments"*: Lou Andreas-Salomé, *In der Schule bei Freud. Tagebuch eines Jahres, 1912 / 1913,* ed. Ernst Pfeiffer (1958), 193.

p.188   *" 'association experiment' "*: Michael Balint, "Einleitung des Herausgebers," in Sándor Ferenczi, *Schriften zur Psychoanalyse,* ed. Balint, 2 vols. (1970), I, xi.

p.188   *Sunday afternoon:* See Freud to Ferenczi, January 30, 1908. Freud–Ferenczi Correspondence, Freud Collection, LC. See also *Jones* II, 34–35.

p.188   *"always suggestive"*: Jones to Freud, July 8 [1913]. By permission of Sigmund Freud Copyrights, Wivenhoe.

p.188   *"be instructive"*: Freud to Ferenczi, February 11, 1908. Freud–Ferenczi Correspondence, Freud Collection, LC.

p.188   *"keep your freedom"*: Freud to Ferenczi, August 4, 1908. Ibid.

p.188   *a mere handful:* See, for example, Freud to Ferenczi, October 6, 1909. Freud–Ferenczi Correspondence, Freud Collection, LC. Freud addressed Abraham as "Dear Friend" a year later, in the summer of 1910. See his letter of August 22, 1910. *Freud–Abraham,* 97 (91).

p.189   *about fantasies:* Freud to Ferenczi, October 27, 1908. Freud–Ferenczi Correspondence, Freud Collection, LC.

p.189   *"succeed in doing"*: Freud to Ferenczi, October 2, 1910. Ibid.

p.189   *"fatherly greetings"*: Freud to Ferenczi, November 17, 1911. Ibid.

p.189   *"form of address"*: Freud to Ferenczi, November 30, 1911. Ibid.

p.189   *"Dear Friend"*: Freud to Ferenczi, December 5, 1911. Ibid.

p.189   *"strong with Abraham"*: Freud to Jones, August 2, 1920. In English. Freud Collection, D2, LC. "Prussianity" is one of the English coinages sprinkling Freud's letters to Jones.

p.190   *"our work"*: Freud to [Rickman?], March 3, 1910. Freud Collection, B4, LC.

p.190   *their development:* Oskar Pfister, "Oskar Pfister," in *Die Pädagogik der Gegenwart in Selbstdarstellungen,* ed. Erich Hahn, 2 vols. (1926–27), II, 168–70.

p.190   *studying medicine:* Years later, Pfister expressed his gratitude to Freud "for advising me, in 1912, against the study of medicine." (Pfister to Freud, June 14, 1927. By permission of Sigmund Freud Copyrights, Wivenhoe.)

p.190   *Freud's good friend:* Willi Hoffer, obituary of Pfister, *Int. J. Psycho-Anal.,* XXXIX (1958), 616. See also Peter Gay, *A Godless Jew: Freud, Atheism, and the Making of Psychoanalysis* (1987), 74.

p.190   *against sin:* Freud to Jung, January 17, 1909. *Freud–Jung,* 217 (195–96).

p.191   *"good friends"*: Freud to Ferenczi, April 26, 1909. Freud–Ferenczi Correspondence, Freud Collection, LC.

p.191   *their famous father:* Anna Freud, prefatory remark, dated 1962. *Freud–Pfister,* 10 (11).

p.191   *"searching eyes"*: Hoffer, obituary of Pfister, *Int. J. Psycho-Anal.*, XXXIX (1958), 616.

p.191   *"down long since"*: Pfister to Freud, November 25, 1926. By permission of Sigmund Freud Copyrights, Wivenhoe.

p.191   *"at Professor Freud's"*: Pfister to Freud, December 30, 1923. *Freud–Pfister*, 94–95 (90–91).

p.192   *"never was"*: Pfister to Freud, October 29, 1918. Ibid., 64 (63).

p.192   *"in my eyes!"*: Freud to Pfister, October 16, 1922. By permission of Sigmund Freud Copyrights, Wivenhoe.

p.192   *a "muse"*: "Lou Andreas-Salomé" (1937), *GW* XVI, 270 / "Lou Andreas-Salomé," *SE* XXIII, 297.

p.192   *"comprehension of psychoanalysis"*: Abraham to Freud, April 28, 1912. *Freud–Abraham*, 118 (115).

p.192   *"study psychoanalysis"*: Freud to Ferenczi, October 2, 1912. Freud–Ferenczi Correspondence, Freud Collection, LC.

p.192   *"dangerous intelligence"*: Freud to Ferenczi, October 31, 1912. Ibid.

p.193   *"considerable woman"*: Freud to Ferenczi, March 20, 1913. Ibid.

p.193   *October 30:* See October 30, 1912. *Protokolle*, IV, 104.

p.193   *"as a writer"*: October 23, 1912. Ibid., 103.

p.193   simply as *"Lou"*: See, for example, November 27, 1912. Ibid., 120. An exception is the entry for January 15, 1913, where she appears as "Frau Lou." Ibid., 138.

p.193   *telling her so:* See Freud to Andreas-Salomé, November 10, 1912. *Freud–Salomé*, 12 (11).

p.194   The Interpretation of Dreams: See "Autobiographical Study," *SE* XX, 48.

p.194   *and unnecessary:* See *Jones* II, 122, 115, 111.

p.194   *"speak about them"*: Jung to Freud, September 4, 1907. *Freud–Jung*, 92–93 (84).

p.194   *against psychoanalysis:* Jung to Freud, September 11, 1907. Ibid., 93–94 (84–85).

p.195   "half *persuaded*": Abraham to Freud, November 10, 1908. *Freud–Abraham*, 65 (55–56).

p.195   " *'nonsense'* ": Freud to Abraham, December 14, 1908. Karl Abraham papers, LC.

p.195   *"course of time"*: Freud to Abraham, March 9, 1909. Ibid.

p.195   *really inconsequential:* See *Three Essays*, *SE* VII, 174n, 180n.

p.195   *a* Winkeladvokat: Freud to Abraham, May 23, 1909. Karl Abraham papers, LC.

p.195   *"pettifogging individual"*: Freud to Ferenczi, April 26, 1909. Freud–Ferenczi Correspondence, Freud Collection, LC.

p.195   *not very generously:* See Wilhelm Weygandt, review of *Interpretation of Dreams* in *Centralblatt für Nervenheilkunde und Psychiatrie*, XXIV (1901), 548–49.

p.195   *for the police:* See *Jones* II, 109.

p.195   *"relapse into savagery!!!"*: Jones to Freud, April 20, 1910. By permission of Sigmund Freud Copyrights, Wivenhoe.

p.196   " *'pious sexualists'* ": Jones to Freud, January 2, 1910. By permission of Sigmund Freud Copyrights, Wivenhoe.

p.196   *"sexual subjects"*: Boris Sidis, "Fundamental States in Psychoneuroses," *Journal of Abnormal Psychology*, V (February–March 1911), 322–23. Quoted in Nathan G. Hale, Jr., *Freud and the Americans: The Beginnings of Psychoanalysis in the United States, 1876–1917* (1971), 297.

p.196   *and illegitimacy:* Boris Sidis, *Symptomatology, Psychogenesis and Diagnosis of Psychopathic Diseases* (1914), vi–vii. Quoted in ibid., 300.

p.196   *"science of psychoanalysis"*: "Attacks Dr. Freud's Theory / Clash in Academy of Medicine When Vienna Physician Was Honored," *New York Times*, April 5, 1912, 8.

p.196   *"American neurologists?"*: Freud to Jones, April 28, 1912. In English. Freud Collection, D2, LC.

p.196   *professor in Zurich:* "Dreams of the Insane Help Greatly in Their Cure," *New York Times*, Sunday, March 2, 1913, 10.

CHAPTER FIVE · *Psychoanalytic Politics*

p.198   *"a very attractive person"*: Jones, *Free Associations*, 165.

p.199   *creative eccentricity*: See William McGuire, Introduction to *Freud–Jung*, xv.

p.199   *"Freud apparently does"*: Carl G. Jung, *Über die Psychologie der Dementia Praecox. Ein Versuch* (1907), Introduction (dated July 1906), iii–iv.

p.199   *marked appreciation*: Ibid., iv. See also ibid., 38, 50n, 62.

p.199   *of free association*: See "Psychoanalysis and Association Experiments" (1906), translated by R. F. C. Hull and Leopold Stein in collaboration with Diana Riviere, in Carl G. Jung, *The Psychoanalytic Years*, ed. William McGuire (1974), 3–32.

p.199   *"contribution to science"*: Jones, *Free Associations*, 165.

p.200   *"myself corrected"*: Freud to Jung, April 11, 1906. *Freud–Jung*, 3 (3).

p.200   *"completely converted"*: Jung to Freud, October 5, 1906. Ibid., 5 (5).

p.200   *"from his thought"*: Freud to Jung, October 7, 1906. Ibid., 5–6 (5–6).

p.200   *"progress in Switzerland"*: Jung to Freud, November 26, 1906. Ibid., 10 (10).

p.200   *"partial to your therapy"*: Jung to Freud, December 4, 1906. Ibid., 11 (11).

p.201   *"my own fallibility"*: Freud to Jung, December 6, 1906. Ibid., 12–13 (12–13).

p.201   *might be dementia praecox*: See Freud to Jung, December 30, 1906. Ibid., 16–17 (16–17).

p.201   *"joined me so far"*: Freud to Jung, January 1, 1907. Ibid., 18 (17).

p.201   *enemies of psychoanalysis*: For at least three usages of the term *prächtig* for Jung in Freud's letters to Ferenczi, see his letters of January 18, 1909; May 17, 1909; and December 29, 1910. Freud–Ferenczi Correspondence, Freud Collection, LC.

p.201   *"man of the future"*: Freud to Ferenczi, December 29, 1910. Ibid.

p.202   *great enterprise*: Freud to Jung, August 13, 1908. *Freud–Jung*, 186 (168).

p.202   *"appropriate and natural"*: Jung to Freud, February 20, 1908. Ibid., 135 (122).

p.202   *"all the listening"*: Martin Freud, *Freud*, 108–9.

p.202   *without stopping*: See Carl G. Jung, *Memories, Dreams, Reflections* (1962; tr. Richard and Clara Winston, 1962), 146–47.

p.202   *"close-cropped hair"*: Martin Freud, *Freud*, 109.

p.203   *"tone dominated"*: Binswanger, *Erinnerungen*, 11.

p.203   *was crumbling*: Jung to Freud, March 31, 1907. *Freud–Jung*, 26 (25).

p.203   *"in the lurch"*: Freud to Jung, April 7, 1907. Ibid., 29 (27).

p.203   *dethrone him*: Binswanger, who recorded this episode, could not recall the contents of Jung's dream, only Freud's interpretation of it. (See Binswanger, *Erinnerungen*, 10.)

p.203   *of Freud's teachings*: Jung to Freud, May 24, 1907. *Freud–Jung*, 54 (49).

p.203   *"part of it"*: Freud to Jung, April 21, 1907. Ibid., 44 (40).

p.203   *"rich man's table"*: Jung to Freud, June 4, 1907. Ibid., 62 (56).

p.203   *"become a necessity"*: Freud to Jung, July 10, 1907. Ibid., 83 (75).

p.203   *"teacher and guide"*: Freud to Jung, August 18, 1907. Ibid., 85 (77).

p.204   *"problem directly"*: Freud to Jung, August 27, 1907. Ibid., 88 (79).

p.204   *"feeling of envy"*: Jung to Ferenczi, January 6, 1909. Carl G. Jung, *Briefe*, ed. Aniela Jaffé with Gerhard Adler, 3 vols. (1946–55; 3d ed., 1981), I, 26.

p.204   *"formerly revered"*: Jung to Freud, October 28, 1907. *Freud–Jung*, 105 (95).

p.204   *"cult object"*: Freud to Jung, November 15, 1907. Ibid., 108 (98).

p.204   *"Jewish national concern"*: Freud to Abraham, May 3, 1908. *Freud–Abraham*, 47 (34).

p.204   *"appreciate us"*: Freud to Sabine Spielrein, August 28, 1913. Typed transcript. By permission of Sigmund Freud Copyrights, Wivenhoe.

p.205   *"far less resistance"*: Freud to Abraham, July 23, 1908. *Freud–Abraham*, 57 (46).

p.205   *"alien to me"*: Freud to Abraham, October 11, 1908. Ibid., 64 (54).

p.205   *"victim to anti-Semitism"*: Freud to Abraham, December 26, 1908. Ibid., 73 (64).

p.205   *Abraham ever did*: See Freud to Abraham, July 20, 1908. Karl Abraham papers, LC.

p.205   *measure of injustice*: Freud to Abraham, July 23, 1908. *Freud–Abraham*, 57 (46).

p.205   *"mystical element"*: Freud to Abraham, July 20, 1908. Ibid., 57 (46).

p.205 *declared to Ferenczi:* Freud to Ferenczi, June 8, 1913. Freud–Ferenczi Correspondence, LC.

p.205 *"committed for that":* Jung to Freud, January 8, 1907. *Freud–Jung,* 21 (20).

p.206 *"Fliess-like will happen":* Jung to Freud, March 11, 1909. Ibid., 234 (211–12).

p.206 *Freud called him:* "Selbstdarstellung," *GW* XIV, 78 / "Autobiographical Study," *SE* XX, 51.

p.207 *"a mad man":* Thorndike to James Cattell, July 6, 1904. Quoted in Dorothy Ross, *G. Stanley Hall: The Psychologist as Prophet* (1972), 385.

p.207 *"in this country":* Hall to "Siegmund" Freud, December 15, 1908. Quoted in ibid., 386.

p.207 *"our endeavors":* See William A. Koelsch, *"Incredible Day Dream": Freud and Jung at Clark,* The Fifth Paul S. Clarkson Lecture (1984), unpaged.

p.207 *"ordinary life":* "Geschichte der psychoanalytischen Bewegung," *GW* X, 44, 70 / "History of the Psychoanalytic Movement," *SE* XIV, 7, 30–31.

p.207 *"part of reality":* "Selbstdarstellung," *GW* XIV, 78 / "Autobiographical Study," *SE* XX, 52.

p.207 *"of our psychology":* Freud to Ferenczi, January 10, 1909. Freud–Ferenczi Correspondence, Freud Collection, LC.

p.208 *"new continent":* Freud to Ferenczi, January 17, 1909. Ibid.

p.208 *"news from the U.S.":* Freud to Ferenczi, February 2, 1909. Ibid.

p.208 *"accept the invitation":* Freud to Ferenczi, February 28, 1909. Ibid.

p.208 *afford the trip:* See Ferenczi to Freud, January 11, 1909. Ibid.

p.208 *reading about the United States:* Ferenczi to Freud, March 2, 1909. Ibid.

p.208 *"a great experience":* Freud to Ferenczi, March 9, 1909. Ibid.

p.208 *"the great news":* Freud to Abraham, March 9, 1909. Karl Abraham papers, LC.

p.208 *"again so soon":* Freud to Ferenczi, April 25, 1909. Freud–Ferenczi Correspondence, Freud Collection, LC.

p.208 *"our trip together":* Freud to Ferenczi, July 25, 1909. Ibid.

p.208 *psychologists' circles:* Freud to Jung, June 18, 1909. *Freud–Jung,* 258 (234).

p.208 *"myself be surprised":* Freud to Ferenczi, July 25, 1909. Freud–Ferenczi Correspondence, Freud Collection, LC.

p.208 *same spontaneity:* See Freud to Jung, July 7, 1909. *Freud–Jung,* 264 (240).

p.209 of Everyday Life: See *Jones* II, 55.

p.209 *"stifled" him:* Brill to Smith Ely Jelliffe, December 4, 1940. Quoted in Hale, *Freud and the Americans,* 390.

p.209 *"Top Sergeant":* Ibid., 391.

p.209 *"the diamond":* Jones, *Free Associations,* 230–31.

p.210 *"Freund of Vienna":* Quoted in *Jones* II, 55–56.

p.210 *malfunctioning digestion:* On the ice water, see Anna Freud to Ernest Jones, March 10, 1954. Jones papers, Archives of the British Psycho-Analytical Society, London.

p.210 *intestinal complaint:* Freud to Pfister, March 17, 1910. By permission of Sigmund Freud Copyrights, Wivenhoe.

p.211 *"its cooking":* Jones to Freud, February 12, 1910. By permission of Sigmund Freud Copyrights, Wivenhoe.

p.211 *to deteriorate?:* See Freud to Jones, January 27, 1910. Freud Collection, D2, LC. See also *Jones* II, 59–60.

p.211 *"with America itself":* *Jones* II, 59.

p.211 *was an exception:* See Koelsch, *Incredible Day Dream,* unpaged.

p.211 *American listeners:* See Hale, *Freud and the Americans,* 3–23.

p.211 *"end of life":* "Selbstdarstellung," *GW* XIV, 78 / "Autobiographical Study," *SE* XX, 52.

p.211 *"to your work":* *Jones* II, 57.

p.211 *"the real psychology":* James to Mary W. Calkins, September 19, 1909. Quoted in Ralph Barton Perry, *The Thought and Character of William James,* 2 vols. (1936), II, 123.

p.212   *"on human nature":* James to Flournoy, September 28, 1909. *The Letters of William James,* ed. Henry James, 2 vols. (1920), II, 327–28.

p.212   *word-association experiments:* See Jung to Virginia Payne, July 23, 1949. Jung, *Briefe,* II, 159.

p.212   *to his benefit:* See Jung to Freud, October 14, 1909. *Freud–Jung,* 275 (250). See also Jung to Virginia Payne, July 23, 1949. Jung, *Briefe,* II, 158.

p.213   *"great success":* Freud to Mathilde Hollitscher, September 23, 1909. Freud Collection, B1, LC.

p.213   *in Zurich:* See Jung to Freud, October 14, 1909. *Freud–Jung,* 275 (250).

p.213   *a caning:* Freud to Jung, November 11, 1909. Ibid., 286 (260). Freud noted the slip in a marginal comment, but minimized its importance.

p.213   *"by these two":* Freud to Ferenczi, April 6, 1911. Freud–Ferenczi Correspondence, Freud Collection, LC.

p.214   *"standing joke":* Jones, *Free Associations,* 219.

p.214   *all made up!:* See ibid., 219–20.

p.214   *"hidden and unconscious":* Freud to Jones, November 20, 1908. In English. Freud Collection, D2, LC. This letter is quoted in full, but misdated 1909, in *Jones* II, 62.

p.214   Eifersüchteleien: Freud to Otto Rank, September 13, 1912. Rank Collection, Box 1b. Rare Book and Manuscript Library, Columbia University.

p.214   *"wholly wayward":* "Geschichte der psychoanalytischen Bewegung," *GW* X, 58 / "History of the Psychoanalytic Movement," *SE* XIV, 19.

p.214   *impudent liar:* See Freud to Jones, November 15, 1912. Freud Collection, D2, LC.

p.214   *"mauvais sujet":* Freud to Ferenczi, April 10, 1911. Freud–Ferenczi Correspondence, Freud Collection, LC.

p.214   *a "swine":* Freud to Ferenczi, October 17, 1912. Ibid.

p.214   *too much credit:* Freud to Jones, February 21, 1914. In English. Freud Collection, D2, LC.

p.214   The Language of Dreams: See April 26, 1911. *Protokolle,* III, 223–26. "talented beast, K.K.": Freud to Ferenczi, February 13, 1910. Freud–Ferenczi Correspondence, Freud Collection, LC. "histrionic talent": Freud to Ferenczi, April 12, 1910. Ibid.

p.215   *"it harmful":* Bleuler to Freud, December 4, 1911. Freud Collection, D2, LC.

p.216   *"is insufferable":* Freud to Ferenczi, November 30, 1911. Freud–Ferenczi Correspondence, Freud Collection, LC.

p.216   *"for recognition":* Jones, *Free Associations,* 169.

p.216   *making of neuroses:* November 7, 1906. *Protokolle,* I, 36–46.

p.217   *"its sexual traumas":* November 27, 1907. Ibid., 237.

p.217   *"inferiority of organs":* December 18, 1907. Ibid., 257.

p.217   *"spoils the character":* Freud to Abraham, January 1, 1913. Karl Abraham papers, LC.

p.218   *"time of youth":* Freud to Ferenczi, April 3, 1910. Freud–Ferenczi Correspondence, Freud Collection, LC.

p.218   *"compliments pray!":* Freud to Jones, April 15, 1910. In English. Freud Collection, D2, LC.

p.218   *"on the Viennese":* Freud to Ferenczi, April 3, 1910. Freud–Ferenczi Correspondence, Freud Collection, LC.

p.218   *" 'you as well' ":* Wittels, *Freud,* 140. For a more melodramatic but less plausible account, which has tears running down Freud's cheeks, see *Autobiography of Wilhelm Stekel,* 128–29.

p.219   *"International Psychoanalytic Association":* "Geschichte der psychoanalytischen Bewegung," *GW* X, 84–86 / "History of the Psychoanalytic Movement," *SE* XIV, 42–44.

p.219   *"from us Viennese":* April 6, 1910. *Protokolle,* II, 427.

p.219   *new journal:* Ibid., 425.

p.220   *"at the head":* Freud to Ferenczi, April 12, 1910. Freud–Ferenczi Correspondence, Freud Collection, LC.

p.220   *named to it:* See April 6, 1910. *Protokolle,* II, 422–30.

p.220   *unfounded and irrational:* "History of the Psychoanalytic Movement," *SE* XIV, 50.

p.220   *"common ground":* Freud to Ferenczi, April 3, 1910. Freud–Ferenczi Correspondence, Freud Collection, LC.

p.220   *intensely involved:* See Carl Furtmüller, "Alfred Adler: A Biographical Essay," in Alfred Adler, *Superiority and Social Interest: A Collection of Later Writings,* ed. Heinz L. and Rowena R. Ansbacher (1964; 3d ed., 1979), 345–48, particularly informative because Furtmüller was a strong partisan of Adler's.

p.221   *"hold on to him":* Freud to Jung, June 18, 1909. *Freud–Jung,* 259–60 (235).

p.221   *"Libido on him":* Freud to Pfister, February 26, 1911. *Freud–Pfister,* 47 (48).

p.221   *"getting really bad":* Freud to Jung, December 3, 1910. *Freud–Jung,* 415 (376).

p.221   *"as I was alone":* Freud to Ferenczi, November 23, 1910. Freud–Ferenczi Correspondence, Freud Collection, LC.

p.222   *"something else":* January 4 and February 1, 1911. *Protokolle,* III, 103–11, 139–49.

p.222   *"psychoanalysis damage":* February 1, 1911. *Protokolle,* III, 143–47.

p.222   *battle it out:* See ibid., 147–48.

p.222   *"namely Freud and Adler":* February 22, 1911. Ibid., 168–69.

p.222   *"his friendship":* Freud to Ferenczi, March 12, 1911. Freud–Ferenczi Correspondence, Freud Collection, LC.

p.223   *"and sadismus":* Freud to Jones, August 9, 1911. In English. Freud Collection, D2, LC.

p.223   *delusions of persecution:* See Freud to Jung, June 15 and July 13, 1911. *Freud–Jung,* 473, 479 (428, 434).

p.223   *for his side:* Adler to Jones, July 7, 1911. Jones papers, Archives of the British Psycho-Analytical Society, London.

p.223   *"misunderstand me":* Adler to Jones, July 10, 1911. Ibid. Adler was exaggerating the span of his loyalty to psychoanalysis: if his dating were right, he would have been a Freudian by 1896.

p.223   *"in character":* Adler to Jones, September 7, 1911. Ibid.

p.223   *"the Adler pack":* Freud to Ferenczi, October 5, 1911. Freud–Ferenczi Correspondence, Freud Collection, LC.

p.224   *"symbiosis impossible":* Freud to Jung, October 12, 1911. *Freud–Jung,* 493 (447).

p.224   *"pushed to one side":* Phyllis Bottome, *Alfred Adler: Apostle of Freedom* (1939; 3d ed., 1957), 76–77. Since Bottome was Adler's authorized biographer, and the incident scarcely redounds to Adler's credit, it bears the stamp of authenticity, even though it seems less than likely that Freud should have pleaded with Adler to remain.

p.224   *endlos—"endless":* Freud to Jung, June 15, 1911. *Freud–Jung,* 472 (428).

p.225   *"could and should be":* Emma Jung to Freud, October 30, 1911. Ibid., 499 (452).

p.225   *understand her message:* Freud to Ferenczi, November 5, 1911. Freud–Ferenczi Correspondence, Freud Collection, LC.

p.225   *above truth:* See Jung to Freud, December 3, 1912. *Freud–Jung,* 583–84, 584n (526, 526n). See also Jung, *Memories, Dreams, Reflections,* 158.

p.225   *"bad conscience":* Freud to Pfister, July 4, 1912. *Freud–Pfister,* 57 (56–57).

p.226   *"accept it":* "The Houston Films" (1957), an interview in *C. G. Jung Speaking: Interviews and Encounters,* ed. William McGuire and R. F. C. Hull (1977), 339.

p.226   *"number of his ideas":* "The 'Face to Face' Interview with John Freeman," on the BBC, 1959, in ibid., 433.

p.226   *"higher god":* Jung to Freud, December 14, 1909. *Freud–Jung,* 303 (275).

p.226   "Pater peccavi": Jung to Freud, November 15, 1909. Ibid., 289 (262).

p.226   *"to ask you":* Jung to Freud, November 30 / December 2, 1909. Ibid., 297 (270).

p.226   *"sufficiently to yours":* Jung to Freud, December 25 / 31, 1909. Ibid., 308 (280).

p.226   "infantile helplessness": Freud to Jung, January 2, 1910. Ibid., 312 (283–84).

p.226   *New Year's:* See Freud to Ferenczi, January 1, 1910. Freud–Ferenczi Correspondence, Freud Collection, LC.

p.226   *"polygamous components"*: Jung to Freud, March 7, 1909. *Freud–Jung,* 229 (207).

p.226   *"of sexual freedom"*: Jung to Freud, February 11, 1910. Ibid., 324 (294).

p.226   *"its breakthrough"*: Freud to Jung, January 13, 1910. Ibid., 316 (287).

p.227   *reluctant and distant:* Freud to Ferenczi, February 13, 1910. Freud–Ferenczi Correspondence, Freud Collection, LC.

p.227   *"only concerned"*: Freud to Ferenczi, March 3, 1910. Ibid.

p.227   *"all ourselves"*: Freud to Jung, December 19, 1909. *Freud–Jung,* 304 (276).

p.227   *"for* this *work"*: Jung to Freud, December 25, 1909. Ibid., 307 (279).

p.227   *"auxiliary army"*: Freud to Jung, January 2, 1910. Ibid., 311 (282).

p.227   *"as a savage!"*: Freud to Jung, March 6, 1910. Ibid., 331 (300).

p.227   *"my pranks!"*: Jung to Freud, March 9, 1910. Ibid., 333 (302).

p.227   *"father bestows"*: Jung to Freud, July 26 and August 29, 1911. Ibid., 482, 484 (437, 438).

p.227   *"speak of competition"*: Jung to Freud, November 14, 1911. Ibid., 509 (460).

p.227   *"blood a little"*: Jung to Freud, March 3, 1912. Ibid., 544 (491).

p.228   *"in the slightest"*: Jung to Freud, March 10, 1912. Ibid., 546 (493).

p.228   *"stay that way?"*: Freud to Jung, March 5, 1912. Ibid., 546 (493).

p.228   *"at my wreath?"*: Jung to Freud, March 3, 1912. Ibid., 544 (491). The passage is from *Also Sprach Zarathustra,* part I, section 3.

p.228   *"write only rarely"*: Freud to Jung, March 5, 1912. *Freud–Jung,* 545 (492).

p.229   *doing nicely:* Freud to Binswanger, April 14, 1912. Typescript copy, Freud Collection, D1, LC.

p.229   *to stop by:* On June 3, 1912, Freud noted in a letter to Abraham that there had not been enough time to visit Jung: "Not enough time for Zurich"—*Nach Zürich gings nicht mehr.* (Karl Abraham papers, LC.)

p.229   *independent ways:* Jung to Freud, June 8, 1912. *Freud–Jung,* 564 (509). Jung first used the term "Kreuzlingen gesture" in a letter to Freud on July 18, 1912. Ibid., 566 (511).

p.229   *"to my person"*: Freud to Jung, June 13, 1912. Ibid., 565–66 (510–11).

p.230   *infantile sexuality: Jones* II, 152.

p.230   *"of our acquaintance"*: Freud to Jones, August 1, 1912. In English. Freud Collection, D2, LC.

p.230   *"necessities of reality"*: Ibid.

p.230   *"this conception"*: Freud to Jones, August 10, 1912. In English. Ibid.

p.230   *"my own romanticism"*: Jones to Freud, August 7, 1912. By permission of Sigmund Freud Copyrights, Wivenhoe.

p.230   *"besides as well"*: Freud to Jones, July 22, 1912. In English. Freud Collection, D2, LC.

p.230   *"being confirmed"*: Freud to Abraham, July 29, 1912. Karl Abraham papers, LC.

p.231   *"remain intact"*: Ibid.

p.231   *"oil and water"*: Freud to Ferenczi, July 28, 1912. Freud–Ferenczi Correspondence, Freud Collection, LC.

p.231   *"soil of* ψA*"*: Freud to Rank, August 18, 1912. Rank Collection, Box 1b. Rare Book and Manuscript Library, Columbia University.

p.231   *"intellectually superior"*: Freud to Ferenczi, July 28, 1912. Freud–Ferenczi Correspondence, Freud Collection, LC.

p.231   *"cannot be restored"*: Freud to Jones, September 22, 1912. In English. Freud Collection, D2, LC.

p.231   *"run by Jesuits"*: Freud to Ferenczi, June 23, 1912. Freud–Ferenczi Correspondence, Freud Collection, LC.

p.231   *"to be true"*: Jung to Freud, November 11, 1912. *Freud–Jung,* 571–72 (515–16).

p.231   *"say exhibitionism"*: Ibid., 573 (516–17).

p.232   *editor of the* Zentralblatt: See October 9, 1912. *Protokolle,* IV, 99.

p.232   *considered an enemy:* See *Autobiography of Wilhelm Stekel,* 141–43.

p.232   *contrast to Adler:* Freud to Jones, August 9, 1911. In English. Freud Collection, D2, LC.

p.232   *"could not allow"*: Freud to Abraham, November 3, 1912. *Freud–Abraham,* 127 (125).

p.232   *"human being"*: Ibid. See also November 6, 1912. *Protokolle,* IV, 108–9n.

p.232   *"his own property"*: Freud to Jones, November 15, 1912. In English. Freud Collection, D2, LC.

p.232   *"the pay of Adlerism"*: Freud to Abraham, January 1, 1913. Karl Abraham papers, LC.

p.232   *"settled in writing"*: Freud to Jung, November 14, 1912. *Freud–Jung,* 573 (517).

p.233   *"and elimination"*: Eitingon to Freud, November 11, 1912. By permission of Sigmund Freud Copyrights, Wivenhoe.

p.233   *"I'm smashed!"*: Freud to Ferenczi, November 26, 1912. Freud–Ferenczi Correspondence, Freud Collection, LC.

p.233   *"soon revived"*: *Jones* I, 317.

p.233   *"or extenuate"*: Jung to Freud, November 26, 1912. *Freud–Jung,* 579 (522).

p.233   *"all mysticism"*: Freud to Jung, November 29, 1912. Ibid., 581–82 (524).

p.234   *of denunciation:* Jung to Freud, December 3, 1912. Ibid., 583–84 (525–26).

p.234   *"of his neighbor"*: Freud to Jung, [December] 5, 1912. Ibid., 587 (529).

p.234   *book by Adler:* See Jung to Freud, December 7, 1912. Ibid., 589–91 (531–32).

p.234   *the libido theory:* Freud to Jung, December 9, 1912. Ibid., 592 (532–33).

p.234   Ihrigen—*"yours"*: Jung to Freud, n.d. [written between December 11 and December 14, 1912]. Ibid., 592 (533).

p.234   *without anger:* Freud to Jung, December 16, 1912. Ibid., 593 (534).

p.234   *"healthy coarseness"*: Freud in conversation with Jones. (*Jones* II, 86.)

p.234   *"through your trick"*: Jung to Freud, December 18, 1912. *Freud–Jung,* 594 (534–35). Jung used the French term *truc.*

p.235   *such servility:* Ibid., 594 (535).

p.235   *analyzing them:* See Freud to Jung, December 22, 1912. Ibid., 596 (537).

p.235   *"an 'Aiglon' "*: Freud to Jones, December 26, 1912. In English. Freud Collection, D2, LC.

p.236   *"into my service"*: Freud to Ferenczi, January 23, 1912. Freud–Ferenczi Correspondence, Freud Collection, LC.

p.236   *feeling of shame:* See Freud to Jones, December 26, 1912. Freud Collection, D2, LC.

p.236   *"importance the more"*: Ibid.

p.236   *"shows possible"*: Freud to Jones, January 1, 1913. In English. Ibid.

p.236   *"experienced earlier"*: Freud to Jung, January 3, 1913. *Freud–Jung,* 598–99 (538–39)

p.236   *"brutal fellow he is"*: Freud to Ferenczi, December 23, 1912. Freud–Ferenczi Correspondence, Freud Collection, LC.

p.236   *"is silence"*: Jung to Freud (typed, signed postcard), January 6, 1913. *Freud–Jung,* 600 (540).

p.237   *"Confidential!"*: Typed memorandum, Karl Abraham papers, LC. It is undated, but on March 13 Jones wrote a detailed reply (ibid.), so it must have been mailed about March 10 or 11, 1913.

p.237   *"years ago"*: Freud to Ferenczi, May 8, 1913. Freud–Ferenczi Correspondence, Freud Collection, LC.

p.237   *"on Psychoanalysis"*: Mailed on July 4, 1913. Freud–Jones Correspondence, Freud Collection, D2, LC.

p.237   *beyond it:* Jung to Freud, July 29, 1913. *Freud–Jung,* 609–10 (548).

p.238   *"pattern of behaviour"*: See Jung to Henri Flournoy, March 29, 1949, in which "pattern of behaviour" is in English. Jung, *Briefe,* II, 151.

p.238   "common sense": Jung to J. H. van der Hoop, January 14, 1946. Ibid., 9.

p.238   *"religious-libidinal cloud"*: Freud to Jung, February 18, 1912. *Freud–Jung,* 537 (485).

p.238   *"the creator"*: Jung to Freud, December 25, 1909. Ibid., 307 (279).

p.239   *"do no harm"*: Freud to Ferenczi, June 8, 1913. Freud–Ferenczi Correspondence, Freud Collection, LC.

p.239   *"Aryan patronage"*: Freud to Ferenczi, May 4, 1913. Ibid.

p.239   *guests attending:* See *Jones* II, 102.

p.239   *irreparably divided:* See Jones, *Free Associations,* 224.

p.239   *"another again":* "Geschichte der psychoanalytischen Bewegung," *GW* X, 88 / "History of the Psychoanalytic Movement," *SE* XIV, 45.

p.239   *of the reality:* Andreas-Salomé, *In der Schule bei Freud,* 190–91.

p.240   *"injured innocence":* Freud to Abraham, November 2, 1913. *Freud–Abraham,* 150 (152).

p.240   *"public discussion":* Jung's statement in the *Jahrbuch,* reproduced in *Freud–Jung,* 612.

p.240   "bona fides": Jung to Freud, October 27, 1913. Ibid., 612 (550).

p.240   *"all to himself":* Freud to Jones, November 13, 1913. In English. Freud Collection, D2, LC.

p.240   *Ferenczi to Vienna:* Freud to Ferenczi, October 30, 1913. Freud–Ferenczi Correspondence, Freud Collection, LC.

p.240   *"sometimes dishonest":* Freud to Jones, January 8, 1914. In English. Freud Collection, D2, LC.

p.240   *"Jung's brutality":* Freud to Abraham, May 17, 1914. Karl Abraham papers, LC.

p.240   *"term it":* Jones to Abraham, December 29, 1913. Ibid.

p.240   *"a separation":* Jones to Abraham, January 14, 1914. Ibid.

p.240   *"unnatural marriage":* Abraham to Jones, January 11, 1914. Jones papers, Archives of the British Psycho-Analytical Society, London.

p.240   *"Adler and Jung":* Freud to Ferenczi, November 9, 1913. Freud–Ferenczi Correspondence, Freud Collection, LC.

p.241   *"at the history":* Freud to Ferenczi, January 12, 1914. Ibid.

p.241   *"Abraham, Eitingon":* Abraham and Eitingon to Freud (telegram), April 22, 1914. Karl Abraham papers, LC.

p.241   *"eased the task":* Freud to Ferenczi, April 24, 1914. Freud–Ferenczi Correspondence, Freud Collection, LC.

p.241   *exultantly to Abraham:* Freud to Abraham, July 18, 1914. *Freud–Abraham,* 178 (184).

p.241   Nachbeter: Freud to Abraham, July 26, 1914. Ibid., 180 (186).

p.241   *"no-longer-ours":* Eitingon to Freud, July 6, 1914. By permission of Sigmund Freud Copyrights, Wivenhoe.

p.242   "toward me": Freud to Putnam, July 8, 1915. *James Jackson Putnam: Letters,* 376.

p.242   *"tolerance daily":* Freud to Abraham, June 14, 1912. Karl Abraham papers, LC.

p.243   *"unclouded friendship":* "Selbstdarstellung," *GW* XIV, 80 / "Autobiographical Study," *SE* XX, 53.

p.243   *"sacred in everyone":* Freud to Binswanger, December 31, 1909. Quoted in Binswanger, *Erinnerungen,* 32.

CHAPTER SIX · *Therapy and Technique*

p.244   *"(Dr. jur.)":* November 6, 1907. *Protokolle,* I, 213. See also October 30 and November 6, 1907. Ibid., 212–23.

p.244   *"passage of time":* Jones, *Free Associations,* 166.

p.245   *"artistic feast":* Ibid.

p.246   *in October 1900:* Her real name was Ida Bauer, and her brother Otto was to become a leading Socialist politician in Austria.

p.246   *choose to explore:* Freud to Fliess, October 14, 1900. *Freud–Fliess,* 469 (427).

p.246   *"for the day":* Freud to Fliess, January 25, 1901. Ibid., 476 (433).

p.246   *"of the dream book":* Ibid.

p.246   *"audience in you":* Freud to Fliess, March 11, 1902. Ibid., 501 (456).

p.247   *unanalyzed preoccupation:* See "Editor's Note," *SE* VII, 5.

p.247   *"bewilderment and resistance":* "Bruchstück einer Hysterie-Analyse" ["Dora"] (1905), *GW* V, 164 / "Fragment of an Analysis of a Case of Hysteria" ["Dora"], *SE* VII, 11.

p.247   *"their entertainment":* Ibid., 165–66 / 9.

p.249   *against her body:* Ibid., 186 / 28.

p.249   *of her trust:* "Dora, no doubt, was in love with Mr. K. whom Freud found to be quite a presentable man. But I wonder how many of us can follow without protest today Freud's assertion that a healthy young girl would, under such circumstances, have considered Mr. K.'s advances 'neither tactless nor offensive.' " (Erik H. Erikson, "Psychological Reality and Historical Actuality" [1962], in *Insight and Responsibility: Lectures on the Ethical Implications of Psychoanalytic Insight* [1964], 169.)

p.250   *"the desired 'Yes' ":* "Dora," *GW* V, 219 / *SE* VII, 58–59.

p.250   *shedding her cough:* Ibid., 207 / 47–48.

p.251   *"love for him was":* Ibid., 231–32 / 69–70.

p.251   *"piece of interpretation":* Ibid., 232 / 70.

p.252   *"did not come back":* Ibid., 272–73 / 108–9.

p.252   *"art of psychology":* Ibid., 272 / 109.

p.253   *"of the transference":* Ibid., 282 / 118.

p.253   *of the analytic work:* Ibid., 281, 282–83 / 117, 119.

p.253   *"in this contest":* Ibid., 272 / 109.

p.253   *"unconscious feelings":* "Die zukünftigen Chancen der psychoanalytischen Therapie" (1910), *GW* VIII, 108 / "The Future Prospects of Psychoanalytic Therapy," *SE* XI, 144.

p.254   *"resistances allow":* Ibid., 108 / 144–45.

p.254   *"through every pore":* "Dora," *GW* V, 240 / *SE* VII, 77–78.

p.254   *pantomime of masturbation:* See ibid., 239–40 / 77.

p.254   *own person:* Freud to Jones, September 22, 1912. In English. Freud Collection, D2, LC.

p.256   *"child's soul":* Freud to Jones, June 1, 1909. In English. Ibid.

p.256   *"our little hero":* Freud to Jones, April 15, 1910. In English. Ibid.

p.256   *"behind Hans's phobia":* "Analyse der Phobie eines fünfjährigen Knaben" ["Der kleine Hans"] (1909), *GW* VII, 377 / "Analysis of a Phobia in a Five-Year-Old Boy" ["Little Hans"], *SE* X, 147.

p.256   *boy's "beautiful":* Ibid., 372 / 141.

p.256   *"every wickedness!":* Ibid., 252 / 15.

p.257   *legend of the stork:* Ibid., 245, 247 / 7–8, 10.

p.257   *trying to seduce:* Ibid., 260–61 / 25.

p.257   *"easy for oneself":* Ibid., 263 / 27.

p.258   *"impenetrable and insecure":* Ibid., 299 / 64.

p.258   *"it's attached":* Ibid., 269 / 34.

p.259   *"from any adult":* Ibid., 307, 307n / 72, 72n.

p.260   *"of later life":* Ibid., 243–44 / 6.

p.260   *"exemplary significance":* Ibid., 377 / 147.

p.260   *"man of nineteen":* "Nachschrift zur Analyse des Kleinen Hans" (1922), *GW* XIII, 431 / "Postscript," *SE* X, 148.

p.261   *as the* Rattenmann: See Freud to Jung, July 7, 1909. *Freud–Jung,* 263 (239).

p.261   *"man of the rats":* Freud to Jones, June 1 [1909]. In English. Freud Collection, D2, LC.

p.261   *"in the Great War":* "Bemerkungen über einen Fall von Zwangsneurose" ["Rattenmann"] (1909), *GW* VII, 463n / "Notes upon a Case of Obsessional Neurosis" ["Rat Man"], *SE* X, 249n (note added in 1923).

p.261   *and shrewd:* See "Rat Man" *SE* X, 158. The correct name of the Rat Man was first revealed in Patrick J. Mahony, *Freud and the Rat Man* (1986).

p.262   *"link up with it":* "Rattenmann," *GW* VII 382–83 / "Rat Man," *SE* X, 156–57.

p.262   *made every night:* The actual notes that survived cover only the first three and a half months of the case, beginning with the opening session of October 1, 1907, and ending on January 20, 1908. It is likely that Freud did not stop taking notes, and that the rest have been lost.

p.262   *life in childhood:* Ibid., 386 / 160.

p.263   *"of my illness":* Ibid., 384–87 / 158–62.

p.263   *"his later disease"*: Ibid., 388 / 162.

p.263   *decisive last word:* Ibid., 391–92 / 166.

p.263   "unknown to him": Ibid., 392 / 167.

p.264   *"and incomprehensible"*: Ibid., 394, 397 / 169, 173.

p.264   *"psychic nature!"*: Freud to Jung, June 30, 1909. *Freud–Jung*, 263 (238).

p.264   *"for the latter"*: Jung to Ferenczi, December 25, 1909. Jung, *Briefe*, I, 33.

p.264   *"had been uncovered"*: "Rattenmann," *GW* VII, 400 / "Rat Man," *SE* X, 176.

p.264   *"from the unconscious"*: Ibid., 404–5n / 181n.

p.265   *earliest youth:* Ibid., 400–401 / 178–79.

p.265   *children, his mother:* See the process notes, edited in full and faithfully transcribed (complete with notes and commentary), by Elza Ribeiro Hawelka: Sigmund Freud, *L'Homme aux rats. Journal d'une analyse* (1974), 230–34.

p.265   *"one's father!"*: "Rattenmann," *GW* VII, 423 / "Rat Man," *SE* X, 201.

p.265   *"of a command"*: Ibid., 426 / 204.

p.266   *"and vice versa"*: Ibid., 426–27, 454 / 205, 238.

p.266   *"currency for himself"*: Ibid., 433 / 213.

p.266   *"rat delirium"*: Ibid., 438 / 220.

p.266   *"school of suffering"*: Ibid., 429 / 209.

p.266   *"is refreshed"*: Freud, *L'Homme aux rats*, ed. Hawelka, 210 / "Rat Man," *SE* X, 303.

p.268   *"illustrious" analysand:* Freud to Ferenczi, November 10, 1909. Freud–Ferenczi Correspondence, Freud Collection, LC.

p.268   *"step in biography"*: Freud to Jung, October 17, 1909. *Freud–Jung*, 280 (255).

p.268   *"and mysterious man"*: "Eine Kindheitserinnerung des Leonardo da Vinci" (1910), *GW* VIII, 207 / "Leonardo da Vinci and a Memory of His Childhood," *SE* XI, 134.

p.268   *"never fathom"*: Ibid., 128, 128n / 63, 63n.

p.268   *"famous left-hander"*: Freud to Fliess, October 9, 1898. *Freud–Fliess*, 362 (331).

p.268   the Christ Child: See Freud to Abraham, August 30, 1910. *Freud–Abraham*, 98 (92).

p.268   *"and with mythology"*: Freud to Ferenczi, November 21, 1909. Freud–Ferenczi Correspondence, Freud Collection, LC.

p.268   *"write on the Leonardo"*: Freud to Ferenczi, March 17, 1910. Ibid.

p.268   *"have ever written"*: Freud to Andreas-Salomé, February 9, 1919. *Freud–Salomé*, 100 (90).

p.269   *"larger" in mind:* Freud to Ferenczi, November 10, 1909. Freud–Ferenczi Correspondence, Freud Collection, LC.

p.269   *"please you more"*: Freud to Jones, April 15, 1910. In English. Freud Collection, D2, LC.

p.269   *"with this pattern"*: Freud to Struck, November 7, 1914. *Briefe*, 317–18.

p.269   *in June 1910:* Freud to Ferenczi, June 7, 1910. Freud–Ferenczi Correspondence, Freud Collection, LC.

p.269   *"compare with it"*: Abraham to Freud, June 6, 1910. *Freud–Abraham*, 96 (90).

p.269   *"is wonderful"*: Jung to Freud, June 17, 1910. *Freud–Jung*, 364 (329).

p.269   *"friendly as always"*: Freud to Abraham, July 3, 1910. *Freud–Abraham*, 97 (91).

p.269   *"all strangers"*: Ibid.

p.269   *"equal severity"*: "Leonardo," *GW* VIII, 128 / *SE* XI, 63.

p.269   *"these results"*: Ibid., 202, 203, 207 / 130, 131, 134.

p.270   *"with its tail"*: Ibid., 150 / 82.

p.270   *"of his eroticism"* Ibid., 158–60, 186–87 / 90–92, 116–17.

p.271   *"in a neurotic"*: Freud to Jung, October 17, 1909. *Freud–Jung*, 281 (255).

p.272   *"mirror image"*: "Leonardo," *GW* VIII, 170 / *SE* XI, 100.

p.272   "than his reason": Ibid., 194 / 122.

p.273   *out in 1923:* See Eric Maclagan, "Leonardo in the Consulting Room," *Burlington Magazine*, XLII (1923), 54–57.

p.274   *"criminal incompleteness"*: Freud to Jung, November 21, 1909. *Freud–Jung*, 292–93 (266).

p.274   *some respite:* See Freud to Jung, December 2, 1909. Ibid., 298 (271).

p.274   *"at least named Wilhelm":* Freud to Ferenczi, December 16, 1910. Freud–Ferenczi Correspondence, Freud Collection, LC.

p.274   *"same paranoia":* Freud to Jung, December 3, 1910. *Freud–Jung,* 415 (376).

p.275   *richly confirmed:* Freud to Jung, February 17, 1908. Ibid., 134 (121).

p.275   *"paranoiac fails":* Freud to Ferenczi, October 6, 1910. Freud–Ferenczi Correspondence, Freud Collection, LC.

p.275   *"him as one":* Freud to Jung, September 24, 1910. *Freud–Jung,* 390 (353).

p.275   *element within himself:* Freud to Fliess, August 7, 1901. *Freud–Fliess,* 492 (447).

p.275   *"leave the table":* Freud to Jones, December 8, 1912. In English. Freud Collection, D2, LC.

p.275   *wicked relief:* Freud to Ferenczi, December 9, 1912. Freud–Ferenczi Correspondence, Freud Collection, LC.

p.276   *"root of the matter":* Freud to Jones, December 8, 1912. In English. Freud Collection, D2, LC.

p.276   *"affects in you":* Jones to Freud, December 23, 1912. By permission of Sigmund Freud Copyrights, Wivenhoe.

p.276   *"on this matter":* Freud to Jones, December 26, 1912. In English. Freud Collection, D2, LC.

p.276   *"leading role":* Freud to Binswanger, January 1, 1913. Quoted in Binswanger, *Erinnerungen,* 64.

p.276   *"severe migraine":* Freud to Ferenczi, June 1, 1911. Freud–Ferenczi Correspondence, Freud Collection, LC.

p.277   *"got rid of":* Freud to Ferenczi, December 31, 1912. Ibid.

p.277   *"something from everything":* Freud to Jung, February 17, 1908. *Freud–Jung,* 134 (121).

p.277   *"of a mental hospital":* Freud to Jung, April 22, 1910. Ibid., 343 (311).

p.277   *"learn from her":* Freud to Ferenczi, February 11, 1908. Freud–Ferenczi Correspondence, Freud Collection, LC.

p.278   *"of all neuroses":* Freud to Ferenczi, March 25, 1908. Ibid.

p.278   *"collect and learn":* Freud to Ferenczi, May 2, 1909. Ibid.

p.278   *"deeply into paranoia":* Freud to Abraham, October 24, 1910. *Freud–Abraham,* 101 (95). Freud added, courteously, that he was moving forward "on the path you have stepped onto." He was referring to Abraham's paper "Psychosexual Differences between Hysteria and Dementia Praecox" ("Die psychosexuellen Differenzen der Hysterie und der Dementia praecox," *Centralblatt für Nervenheilkunde und Psychiatrie,* New Series, XIX [1908], 521–33).

p.278   *case in Rome:* See Freud to Jung, September 24, 1910. *Freud–Jung,* 390 (353).

p.279   *"from my own complexes":* Freud to Jung, December 22, 1910. Ibid., 422–23 (382).

p.279   *attention to Schreber:* See a note by Jung in *Symbols of Transformation* (1952), quoted in *Freud–Jung,* 339n (307n).

p.279   *"brilliantly written":* Jung to Freud, March 19, 1911. Ibid., 449 (407).

p.280   *"one of yours":* Jung to Freud, November 14, 1911. Ibid., 509 (461).

p.280   *theory to psychotics:* Jung to Freud, December 11, 1911. Ibid., 521 (471).

p.280   *"man into a woman":* Quoted in "Psychoanalytische Bemerkungen über einen autobiographisch beschriebenen Fall von Paranoia (Dementia Paranoides)" ["Schreber"] (1911), *GW* VIII, 248 / "Psychoanalytic Notes on an Autobiographical Account of a Case of Paranoia (Dementia Paranoides)" ["Schreber"], *SE* XII, 16.

p.280   *"himself be f——":* See ibid., 252 / 20.

p.280   *"soul murderer":* See ibid., 245 / 14.

p.281   "*don't you sh——?":* See ibid., 259 / 25–26.

p.281   "loving a man": Ibid., 299 / 62.

p.281   *fatal sequence:* See ibid., 299–300 / 63.

p.282   "the reconstruction": Ibid., 308 / 71.

p.283   *"human motives":* Ibid., 272 / 37.

p.283   *"things in public"*: See Freud to Ferenczi, October 6, 1910. Freud–Ferenczi Correspondence, Freud Collection, LC.

p.283   *Schreber interpretations:* Ibid.

p.283   *"gymnastics in Germany"*: "Schreber," *GW* VIII, 286–87 / *SE* XII, 51.

p.284   *"positive coloration"*: Ibid., 315 / 78.

p.284   *"of his son"*: Ibid., 287 / 51.

p.285   *in December 1910:* See Freud to Abraham, December 18, 1910. *Freud–Abraham,* 102 (97).

p.285   existenzunfähig: "Aus der Geschichte einer infantilen Neurose" ["Wolfsmann"] (1918), *GW* XII, 29 / "From the History of an Infantile Neurosis" ["Wolf Man"], *SE* XVII, 7.

p.286   *"compulsive feelings"*: Freud to Ferenczi, February 8, 1910. Freud–Ferenczi Correspondence, Freud Collection, LC.

p.286   *psychoanalytic verities:* "Wolfsmann," *GW* XII, 29n / "Wolf Man," *SE* XVII, 7n. The translation "twisted reinterpretations" for *Umdeutungen* was suggested, the editors of the *Standard Edition* tell us, by Freud himself.

p.286   *that year:* Freud spoke of writing the case history in the winter of 1914–15, but he seems actually to have completed it in the fall of 1914.

p.286   *"uncomfortable psychoanalysis"*: Ibid., 82 / 53.

p.287   *"on my head"*: Freud to Ferenczi, February 13, 1910. Ibid. This passage is paraphrased a little genteelly in *Jones* II, 274, and is quoted by Jeffrey Moussaieff Masson in his review of Karin Obholzer, *Gespräche mit dem Wolfsmann. Eine Psychoanalyse und die Folgen* (1980), in *Int. Rev. Psycho-Anal.,* IX (1982), 117.

p.288   *state of anxiety:* See "Wolfsmann," *GW* XII, 54 / "Wolf Man," *SE* XVII, 29.

p.289   *at the dreamer:* For the drawing, see ibid., 55 / 30.

p.289   *"abandon me"*: Ibid., 63 / 36.

p.290   *"personal experience"*: Ibid., 131 / 97.

p.290   *mental reality:* See ibid., 84 / 55.

p.290   *"material reality"*: Traumdeutung, *GW* II–III, 625 / *Interpretation of Dreams, SE* V, 620.

p.290   *"problems of life"*: "Wolfsmann," *GW* XII, 83 / "Wolf Man," *SE* XVII, 54.

p.290   *into a book:* The first of these papers, "A Special Type of Choice of Object Made by Men," came out in 1910; the second, "On the Universal Tendency to Debasement in the Sphere of Love," in 1912, and a third, "The Taboo of Virginity," was read as a lecture in 1917, after the analysis of the Wolf Man had been terminated but before it had been published.

p.290   *"already been said"*: "Angst und Trieblehen," in *Neue Folge der Vorlesungen zur Einführung in die Psychoanalyse* (1933), *GW* XV, 115 / "Anxiety and Instinctual Life," in *New Introductory Lectures on Psycho-Analysis, SE* XXII, 107.

p.291   *"the sensual"*: "Über die allgemeinste Erniedrigung des Liebeslebens" (1912), *GW* VIII, 79 / "On the Universal Tendency to Debasement in the Sphere of Love," *SE* XI, 180.

p.291   *where they desire:* See ibid., 82 / 183.

p.291   *"governed his conduct"*: "Wolfsmann," *GW* XII, 32–33 / "Wolf Man," *SE* XVII, 10–11.

p.292   *his symptoms:* Ibid., 33–34 / 11.

p.292   *"only once"*: "Die endliche und die unendliche Analyse" (1937), *GW* XVI, 62 / "Analysis Terminable and Interminable," *SE* XXIII, 218–19.

p.293   *its practitioners:* "Die zukünftigen Chancen," *GW* VIII, 107–8 / "Future Prospects," *SE* XI, 144–45.

p.294   *come to him:* "Über 'wilde' Psychoanalyse" (1910), *GW* VIII, 118 / " 'Wild' Psychoanalysis," *SE* XI, 221.

p.294   *"physician's tact"*: Ibid., 122, 124 / 224, 226.

p.294   *"critical intentions"*: Freud to Abraham, June 14, 1912. Karl Abraham papers, LC.

p.294   *"pages are done"*: Freud to Ferenczi, November 26, 1908. Freud–Ferenczi Correspondence, Freud Collection, LC.

p.295   *handful more:* See Freud to Ferenczi, December 11, 1908. Ibid.

p.295   *summer holidays:* See Freud to Ferenczi, February 2, 1909. Ibid.

p.295   *"to an end":* Freud to Jones, June 1, 1909. In English. Freud Collection, D2, LC.

p.295   *"technical studies":* Freud to Ferenczi, October 22, 1909. Freud–Ferenczi Correspondence, Freud Collection, LC.

p.295   *" 'Methodology of Psychoanalysis' ":* "Die zukünftigen Chancen," *GW* VIII, 105 / "Future Prospects," *SE* XI, 142.

p.295   *"friends and foes":* Jones to Freud, November 6, 1910. By permission of Sigmund Freud Copyrights, Wivenhoe.

p.295   *"doing analyses":* Freud to Ferenczi, November 26, 1908. Freud–Ferenczi Correspondence, Freud Collection, LC.

p.296   *"attempt at cure":* "Zur Einleitung der Behandlung" (1913), *GW* VIII, 455 / "On Beginning the Treatment," *SE* XII, 124.

p.296   *by his responses:* Ibid., 467 / 133–34.

p.296   *"in this deviation":* Ibid., 467 / 134.

p.297   *attitudes toward it:* Ibid., 464 / 131.

p.297   *"had not known":* Ibid., 460, 462 / 127, 129.

p.298   *about this rule:* Freud discussed the fundamental rule in "On Beginning the Treatment," *SE* XII, 134–35, 135–36n; and in "Recommendations to Physicians Practising Psycho-Analysis," ibid., 112, 115.

p.298   *"word of it":* Freud to Ferenczi, November 26, 1908. Freud–Ferenczi Correspondence, Freud Collection, LC.

p.299   *"following such examples":* "Zur Einleitung der Behandlung," *GW* VIII, 474 / "On Beginning the Treatment," *SE* XII, 140.

p.299   *"is a resistance":* *Traumdeutung, GW* II–III, 521 / *Interpretation of Dreams, SE* V, 517.

p.299   *"those opposing it":* "Zur Dynamik der Übertragung" (1912), *GW* VIII, 368–69 / "The Dynamics of Transference," *SE* XII, 103.

p.300   *"rapport," with him:* "Zur Einleitung der Behandlung," *GW* VIII, 473 / "On Beginning the Treatment," *SE* XII, 139.

p.301   *"battlefield of transference":* Freud to Eitingon, February 13, 1912. By permission of Sigmund Freud Copyrights, Wivenhoe.

p.301   *"cure through love":* Freud to Jung, December 6, 1906. *Freud–Jung,* 13 (12–13).

p.301   *"strongest disapproval":* Freud to Abraham, March 4, 1915. *Freud–Abraham,* 204 (213).

p.302   *"medical dignity":* "Bemerkungen über die Übertragungsliebe" (1915), *GW* X, 307 / "Observations on Transference-Love," *SE* XII, 160.

p.302   *"away insured":* Ibid., 312, 314 / 164, 165.

p.303   *"with surrogates":* Ibid., 308, 313 / 160–61, 165.

p.303   *"shown to him":* "Ratschläge für den Arzt bei der psychoanalytischen Behandlung" (1912), *GW* VIII, 380–81, 384 / "Recommendations to Physicians Practising Psycho-Analysis," *SE* XII, 115, 118.

p.303   *informal experiments:* For Freud's analysis of Eitingon, see Freud to Ferenczi, October 22, 1909. Freud–Ferenczi Correspondence, Freud Collection, LC.

p.304   *"be speeded up":* "Erinnern, Wiederholen und Durcharbeiten" (1914), *GW* X, 136 / "Remembering, Repeating and Working-Through," *SE* XII, 155.

p.305   *"therapeutic work":* Ibid., 136, 134–35 / 155–56, 154.

p.305   *Abschiedsschwierigkeiten:* Freud to Eitingon, June 23, 1912. By permission of Sigmund Freud Copyrights, Wivenhoe.

p.305   *"learn a great deal":* Eitingon to Freud, June 18, 1912. By permission of Sigmund Freud Copyrights, Wivenhoe.

CHAPTER SEVEN · *Applications and Implications*

p.307 *"not unfruitful"*: "Der Dichter und das Phantasieren" (1908), *GW* VII, 213, 222/ "Creative Writers and Day-Dreaming,"*SE* IX, 143, 152.

p.307 *"but—reality"*: Ibid., 214/143–44.

p.308 *"unsatisfying reality"*: Ibid., 216/146.

p.308 *"in our minds"*: Ibid., 223/153.

p.309 *peritonitis:* See Freud to Abraham, January 19, 1908. Karl Abraham papers, LC.

p.309 *serious operation:* Freud to Pfister, March 17, 1910. By permission of Sigmund Freud Copyrights, Wivenhoe.

p.309 *"easier for them"*: Freud to Mathilde Freud, March 26, 1908. *Briefe*, 286–88.

p.309 *as a son-in-law:* See Freud to Ferenczi, February 7, 1909. Freud–Ferenczi Correspondence, Freud Collection, LC. See also *Jones* II, 55.

p.309 *years before:* Freud to Halberstadt, July 7, 1912. Freud Collection, B1, LC.

p.309 *distant Sie:* Freud to Halberstadt, July 24, 1912. Ibid.

p.309 *among their children:* Freud to Mathilde Hollitscher, July 24, 1912. Ibid.

p.309 *"Dear Max"*: Freud to Halberstadt, July 27, 1912. Ibid.

p.309 *him du:* Freud to Halberstadt, August 12, 1912. Ibid.

p.310 *"orphaned father"*: Freud to Halberstadt (postcard), September 17, 1912. Ibid.

p.310 *"a grumble"*: Sachs, *Freud: Master and Friend*, 68–69, 71.

p.310 *"society from it"*: Freud to Jung, July 5, 1910. *Freud–Jung*, 375 (340).

p.310 *"know it yet"*: Freud to Ferenczi, January 10, 1910. Freud–Ferenczi Correspondence, Freud Collection, LC.

p.310 *self-criticism:* See Freud to Ferenczi, October 17, 1910. Ibid.

p.310 *psychoanalytic interpreter:* "Das Interesse an der Psychoanalyse" (1913), *GW* VIII, 414–15/"The Claims of Psycho-Analysis to Scientific Interest," *SE* XIII, 185–86.

p.311 *advance men:* See Freud to Jung, October 17, 1909. *Freud–Jung*, 280 (255).

p.311 *"mythological dreams"*: Jung to Freud, April 17, 1910. Ibid., 340–41 (308).

p.311 *"everything and everyone"*: See Freud's report of this discussion to Ferenczi, December 29, 1910. Freud–Ferenczi Correspondence, Freud Collection, LC.

p.312 Eros and Psyche: Freud to Jones, March 10, 1910. In English. Freud Collection, D2, LC.

p.312 *by "two bright and honest boys"*: Freud to Jones, February 24, 1912. In English. Ibid.

p.312 *"met with"*: Freud to Jones, April 28, 1912. In English. Ibid.

p.312 *troubled him:* Freud to Abraham, June 14, 1912. Karl Abraham papers, LC.

p.312 *"greatest interest"*: Jones to Abraham, June 18, 1911. Ibid.

p.312 *"increasing relish"*: Abraham to Freud, June 29, 1913. *Freud–Abraham*, 141 (141).

p.312 *"unsatisfied impulses"*: "Das Interesse an der Psychoanalyse," *GW* VIII, 415/"The Claims of Psycho-Analysis to Scientific Interest," *SE* XIII, 185–86.

p.313 *"missed the mark"*: Freud to Jones, June 1, 1909. In English. Freud Collection, D2, LC.

p.313 *"track down"*: Freud to Abraham, June 14, 1912. Karl Abraham papers, LC. In 1913, Freud actually published in *Imago* a paper, "The Theme of the Three Caskets," interweaving these three themes.

p.314 *"withstand ΨA"*: Freud to Ferenczi, May 21, 1911. Freud–Ferenczi Correspondence, Freud Collection, LC.

p.314 *"thus far"*: Freud to Ferenczi, July 17, 1914. Ibid.

p.314 *quite so much:* See "The Moses of Michelangelo" (1914), *SE* XIII, 213.

p.314 *"words" about him:* Freud to Martha Freud, September 25, 1912. *Briefe*, 308.

p.314 *"lion's claw?"*: Abraham to Freud, April 2, 1914. Karl Abraham papers, LC.

p.314 *"love child"*: Freud to Edoardo Weiss, April 12, 1933. *Sigmund Freud–Edoardo Weiss*.

Briefe zur psychoanalytischen Praxis. Mit den Erinnerungen eines Pioniers der Psychoanalyse, introduction by Martin Grotjahn (1973), 84.

p.314   *"before the public":* Freud to Jones, March 19, 1914. In English. Freud Collection, D2, LC.

p.314   *me about him":* Freud to Jones, November 15, 1912. In English. Ibid.

p.315   *"a statue!":* Jones to Freud, December 5 [1912]. By permission of Sigmund Freud Copyrights, Wivenhoe.

p.315   *him so much:* See *Jones* II, 364.

p.315   *"in the paper":* Freud to Weiss, April 12, 1933. *Freud–Weiss Briefe,* 84.

p.315   *"contradictions":* "Der Moses des Michelangelo" (1914), *GW* X, 175/"The Moses of Michelangelo," *SE* XIII, 213.

p.315   *"point of view":* Freud to Ferenczi, November 3, 1912. Freud–Ferenczi Correspondence, Freud Collection, LC.

p.315   *of the law:* Freud to Jones, December 26, 1912. In English. Freud Collection, D2, LC. The mistakes—"indiscrete" for "indiscreet" and "tables" for "tablets"—are in the original, which, like Freud's other letters in English, I have left uncorrected.

p.315   *details mattered:* See *Jones* II, 365.

p.316   *controversial statue:* See Freud to Ferenczi, August 13, 1913. Freud–Ferenczi Correspondence, Freud Collection, LC.

p.316   *"yet restored":* Freud to Jones, September 21, 1913. In English. Freud Collection, D2, LC.

p.316   *"days in Rome":* Freud to Ferenczi, October [1?] 1913. Freud–Ferenczi Correspondence, Freud Collection, LC.

p.316   *"negative again":* Freud to Jones, February 8, 1914. In English. Freud Collection, D2, LC.

p.316   *"his own nature":* "Moses," *GW* X, 194, 199/*SE* XIII, 229, 234.

p.317   *"have interpreted":* Freud to Ferenczi, October 17, 1912. Freud–Ferenczi Correspondence, Freud Collection, LC. Jones, quoting this letter at *Jones* II, 367, misdates it October 10, 1912.

p.317   *"artistic creation":* December 11, 1907. *Protokolle,* I, 249.

p.317   *"laborious investigations":* Freud to Schnitzler, May 8, 1906. *Briefe,* 266–67.

p.318   *"key to it":* Quoted in *Jones* I, 111. This passage has been noted in Spector, *The Aesthetics of Freud,* 33.

p.318   *writing the tale:* See Freud to Jung, May 26, 1907. *Freud–Jung,* 57 (52). For Jensen's letters to Freud, see *Psychoanalytische Bewegung,* I (1929), 207–11.

p.318   *any professional:* "Der Wahn und die Träume in W. Jensens *Gradiva*" (1907), *GW* VII, 120–21/"Delusions and Dreams in Jensen's *Gradiva,*" *SE* IX, 92.

p.319   *"these contents":* Eitingon to Freud, December 23, 1909. By permission of Sigmund Freud Copyrights, Wivenhoe. Freud would have subscribed to this formulation.

p.319   *"childhood fantasies":* Freud to Stefan Zweig, September 4, 1926. By permission of Sigmund Freud Copyrights, Wivenhoe.

p.320   *"enjoy our wealth":* Freud to Jung, May 26, 1907. *Freud–Jung,* 57 (51).

p.320   *"of his study":* "Gradiva," *GW* VII, 35/*SE* IX, 10. I am using "Gradiva" for references to Freud's paper on Jensen's novella, and *Gradiva* for references to Freud's own copy of the novella, with his marginal comments, which is in the Freud Museum, London.

p.321   *"of f[antasy]":* Gradiva, at p. 7. Freud Museum, London.

p.321   *"sex[ual] repression":* Ibid., at p. 22.

p.321   *"asexual atmosphere":* Ibid., at p. 26.

p.321   *the "source":* Freud noted "source Zoë" at p. 7, ibid., and again later, complicating it with associations, at pp. 135, 136, 142.

p.321   *"doubtless necessary":* Ibid., 141.

p.321   *"of the spade":* "Gradiva," *GW* VII, 65/*SE* IX, 40.

p.321   *"power of love":* Ibid., 47/22.

p.321   *Zoë's shoes: Gradiva,* at p. 88. Freud Museum, London.

p.321   *"fantasy; reconciliation":* Ibid., at p. 151.

p.322   *"dreamt at all":* "Gradiva," *GW* VII, 31/*SE* IX, 7.

p.322   *their consequences:* See *Gradiva,* at pp. 11–12, 31, 76, 92, 96–97. Freud Museum, London.

p.322   *such as anxiety:* See ibid., at p. 13.

p.322   *aggressive ideas:* See ibid., at p. 94.

p.322   *and jealousy:* See ibid., at pp. 108, 112.

p.322   *double meanings:* See, above all, ibid., at pp. 58, 84.

p.322   *delusion from reality:* See ibid., *passim,* but esp. at pp. 124, 139.

p.322   *"of the writer":* "Gradiva," *GW* VII, 122/*SE* IX, 93.

p.322   *"down comfortably":* For this appraisal, see Freud to Jung, December 8, 1907. *Freud–Jung,* 114 (103).

p.323   *"inaccessible to us":* "Leonardo," *GW* VIII, 202, 209/*SE* XI, 130, 136.

p.323   *"of the poet":* Foreword to *Edgar Poe, eine psychoanalytische Studie,* the German edition (1934) of Marie Bonaparte, *Edgar Poe, étude psychanalytique* (1933).

p.324   *"sexual impulses":* November 11, 1908. *Protokolle,* II, 46.

p.324   *"against the father":* November 25, 1908, Ibid., 64.

p.324   *"on slowly":* Freud to Ferenczi, November 13, 1911. Freud–Ferenczi Correspondence, Freud Collection, LC.

p.324   *"the results":* Freud to Ferenczi, November 30, 1911. Ibid.

p.324   *"practically 'imbecilic' ":* Freud to Ferenczi, February 1, 1912. Ibid.

p.324   *"means famous":* Freud to Jones, February 24, 1912. In English. Freud Collection, D2, LC.

p.325   *Vienna Psychoanalytic Society:* See May 15, 1912. *Protokolle* IV, 95.

p.325   *"cleared away":* Freud to Jones, August 1, 1912. In English and German. Freud Collection, D2, LC.

p.325   *of the essays:* Freud to Ferenczi, December 16, 1912. Freud–Ferenczi Correspondence, Freud Collection, LC.

p.325   *"something done":* Freud to Ferenczi, December 31, 1912. Ibid.

p.325   *the "totem work":* Freud to Ferenczi, April 10, 1913. Ibid.

p.325   *"good thing":* Freud to Ferenczi, May 4, 1913. Ibid.

p.325   *"rarity with me":* Freud to Ferenczi, May 13, 1913. Ibid.

p.325   *"of the totem work":* Freud to Ferenczi, June 8, 1913. Ibid.

p.325   *"on the other":* "Vorwort" to *Totem und Tabu* (1913), *GW* IX, 3/"Preface" to *Totem and Taboo, SE* XIII, xiii.

p.326   *"in the summer":* Freud to Jung, February 12, 1911. *Freud–Jung,* 432 (391).

p.326   *"is Aryan-religious":* Freud to Abraham, May 13, 1913. *Freud–Abraham,* 139 (139).

p.326   *"completion of the work":* Freud to Ferenczi, June 26, 1913. Freud–Ferenczi Correspondence, Freud Collection, LC.

p.326   *persuaded him:* Abraham to Freud, June 29, 1913. *Freud–Abraham,* 141 (141).

p.327   *disconcert him:* Freud to Abraham, July 1, 1913. Ibid., 142 (142).

p.327   *from them both:* "Vorwort" to *Totem und Tabu, GW* IX, 3/"Preface" to *Totem and Taboo, SE* XIII, xiii.

p.327   *"deficient in phantasy":* Freud to Jones, March 8, 1920. In English. Freud Collection, D2, LC.

p.328   *"new domains":* *Massenpsychologie und Ich-Analyse* (1921), *GW* XIII, 136/*Group Psychology and the Analysis of the Ego, SE* XVIII, 122.

p.328   *"linked to totemism":* *Totem und Tabu, GW* IX, 129/*Totem and Taboo, SE* XIII, 105.

p.329   *"of the Oedipus complex":* Ibid., 160/132.

p.330   *"criminal act":* Ibid., 171–73/141–42.

p.330   *"demand certainty":* Ibid., 172n/142–43n.

p.330   *"morality, and society":* Ibid., 189n/157n.

p.330   *of the mother:* Ibid., 173/143.

p.330   *"history of mankind":* Ibid., 186/155.

p.331   *prehistoric band:* Ibid., 189/157–58.

p.331 *"was the act":* Ibid., 194/161.

p.331 *"constraints, and religion":* Ibid., 172/142.

p.331 *"themselves to learn":* Carl G. Jung, "Freud and Jung—Contrasts" (1931), in *Modern Man in Search of a Soul,* tr. W. S. Dell and Cary F. Baynes (1933), 140.

p.331 *"that is, the father":* Totem und Tabu, *GW* IX, 182/*Totem and Taboo, SE* XIII, 151.

p.332 *"art converge":* Ibid., 188/156.

p.332 *history of Dora:* See "Dora," *SE* VII, 56.

p.332 *"little Oedipus":* "Der kleine Hans," *GW* VII, 332/"Little Hans," *SE* X, 97.

p.332 *letter to Ferenczi:* Freud to Ferenczi, June 28, 1908. Freud–Ferenczi Correspondence, Freud Collection, LC.

p.332 *of the Rat Man:* "Rattenmann," *GW* VII, 428n/"Rat Man," *SE* X, 208n.

p.332 *vicissitudes of love:* See "A Special Type of Choice of Object Made by Men" (1910), *SE* XI, 171.

p.332 *"its opponents":* Drei Abhandlungen, *GW* V, 127n/*Three Essays, SE* VII, 226n (note added in 1920).

p.334 *of original sin:* Ernest Jones was perhaps the first to point this out, but not the last. (See *Jones* III, 311.)

p.334 *of the Semites:* Freud to Ferenczi, August 8, 1912. Freud–Ferenczi Correspondence, Freud Collection, LC.

p.334 *then or later:* See Freud to Jones, April 28, 1912. Freud Collection, D2, LC.

p.334 *"only the reaction":* Jones II, 354.

p.334 *"to a deed":* Quoted in ibid.

p.335 *"could eat her":* Ferenczi, "Ein kleiner Hahnemann" (1913), in *Schriften zur Psychoanalyse,* ed. Balint, I, 169. See also Derek Freeman, "Totem and Taboo: A Reappraisal," in *Man and His Culture: Psychoanalytic Anthropology after "Totem and Taboo,"* ed. Warner Muensterberger, (1970), 61.

p.336 *intimately linked:* See Freud to Fliess, December 22, 1897. *Freud–Fliess,* 312–14 (287–88).

p.336 *"anal eroticism":* Freud to Jung, October 27, 1906. *Freud–Jung,* 8–9 (8–9).

p.336 *this constellation:* See editor's note to "Character and Anal Erotism," *SE* IX, 168.

p.336 *developmental experience:* This fishing metaphor is borrowed from Freud. Writing to Otto Rank from the summer resort of Bad Gastein, where he was working through some important ideas, Freud said, "By the way, do not think that I will be accomplishing anything special during the vacations. The fisherman throws out his net; sometimes he catches a fat carp, often only a few little white fish." (Freud to Rank, July 8, 1922. Rank Collection, Box 1b. Rare Book and Manuscript Library, Columbia University.)

p.336 *"stupid contradiction":* Freud to Ferenczi, October 27, 1910. Freud–Ferenczi Correspondence, Freud Collection, LC. See also October 26, 1910. *Protokolle* III, 33–40.

p.337 *"consequential step":* "Formulierungen über die zwei Prinzipien des psychischen Geschehens" (1911), *GW* VIII, 232/"Formulations on the Two Principles of Mental Functioning," *SE* XII, 219.

p.337 *"its safeguarding":* Ibid., 235–36/223.

p.337 *passage of time:* Ibid., 232/220.

p.337 *"neurotic currency":* Ibid., 237–38/224–25.

p.338 *"accounts with Adler":* Freud to Ferenczi, June 17, 1913. Freud–Ferenczi Correspondence, Freud Collection, LC.

p.338 *"delicious days":* Freud to Jones, October 1, 1913. In English. Freud Collection, D2, LC.

p.338 *virtually ready:* See Freud to Ferenczi, October [1?] 1913. Freud–Ferenczi Correspondence, Freud Collection, LC.

p.338 *"Rank and Sachs":* Freud to Jones, October 1, 1913. In English. Freud Collection, D2, LC.

p.338 *essay "disturbing":* Jones II, 302.

p.339 *"anything else":* Freud to Abraham, March 16, 1914. *Freud–Abraham,* 163 (167).

p.339   *intestinal troubles:* See Freud to Abraham, March 25, 1914. Ibid., 164 (168).

p.339   *brilliant and convincing:* See Abraham to Freud, April 2, 1914. Ibid., 165 (169).

p.339   *"inadequacy there":* Freud to Abraham, April 6, 1914. Ibid., 166 (170–71).

p.339   *"object love":* November 10, 1909. *Protokolle,* II, 282.

p.339   *schizophrenics:* Freud had his own name for schizophrenics. "I intend to hold on to the name 'paraphrenics,' " he wrote to Ferenczi. (Freud to Ferenczi, July 31, 1915. Freud–Ferenczi Correspondence, Freud Collection, LC.) But in the end Bleuler's neologism, not Freud's, prevailed in the literature.

p.340   *"self-preservative drive":* "Zur Einführung des Narzissmus," (1914), *GW* X, 138–39/"On Narcissism: An Introduction," *SE* XIV, 73–74.

p.340   *"at clarification":* Ibid., 142/77.

p.340   *"of the parents":* Ibid., 156–58/90–91.

p.341   *of the drives:* See Abraham to Freud, April 2, 1914. *Freud–Abraham,* 165 (169).

p.341   *of the species:* See, for this terse statement, "The Psycho-Analytic View of Psychogenic Disturbance of Vision" (1910), *SE* XI, 211–18.

p.341   *"indispensable extension":* "Narzissmus," *GW* X, 143/"Narcissism," *SE* XIV, 77.

p.341   *"hitherto worked":* Jones II, 303.

p.341   *dependable orientation:* "Narzissmus," *GW* X, 143/"Narcissism," *SE* XIV, 78. As late as 1932, when he was done theorizing, Freud, at once sarcastic and patient, characterized the drives as, "so to speak, our mythology." They "are mythical beings, sublime in their indefiniteness." ("Angst und Triebleben," in *Neue Folge der Vorlesungen, GW* XV, 101 / "Anxiety and Instinctual Life," in *New Introductory Lectures, SE* XXII, 95.)

p.342   *move the world:* The earliest instance I have come across is in an unpublished letter to Martha Bernays of February 12, 1884, quoted on p. 46.

p.343   *Bosnian militants:* "Memoirs of the Wolf-Man," in *The Wolf-Man,* ed. Gardiner, 90.

p.343   *was small:* Freud to Ferenczi, June 28, 1914. Freud–Ferenczi Correspondence, Freud Collection, LC.

p.343   *"has exploded":* Freud to Abraham, June 25, 1914. *Freud–Abraham,* 175 (181).

p.343   *"other ages":* John Maynard Keynes, *The Economic Consequences of the Peace* (1920), 11.

p.344   *on his life:* Ibid., 11–12.

p.344   *realistic danger:* Graham Wallas, *Human Nature in Politics* (1908), 285.

p.345   *"breath away":* Freud to Pfister, December 9, 1912. *Freud–Pfister,* 59 (58).

p.345   *"daily life":* Freud to Ferenczi, December 9, 1912. Freud–Ferenczi Correspondence, Freud Collection, LC.

p.345   *"such a compulsion":* "Zeitgemässes über Krieg und Tod" (1915), *GW* X, 340/ "Thoughts for the Times on War and Death," *SE* XIV, 288.

p.345   *effeminacy, impotence:* For a bouquet of such declarations, see Fritz Fischer, *Griff nach der Weltmacht. Die Kriegszielpolitik des kaiserlichen Deutschland 1914/1918* (1961; 3d ed., 1964), *passim,* esp. 60–79.

p.345   *"great disappointment":* Quoted in Oron J. Hale, *The Great Illusion, 1900–1914* (1971), 300.

p.346   *"on like this":* Alexander Freud to Freud, July 29, 1914. Freud Museum, London.

p.346   *"empire a chance":* Freud to Abraham, July 26, 1914. *Freud–Abraham,* 180 (186).

p.346   *England in mid-July:* See Jones II, 169.

p.346   *in early August:* See Freud to Eitingon, July 10, 1914. By permission of Sigmund Freud Copyrights, Wivenhoe.

p.346   *"use sociability":* Freud to Ferenczi, July 22, 1914. Freud–Ferenczi Correspondence, Freud Collection, LC.

p.346   *on July 23:* Mathilde Hollitscher to Freud (postcard), July 23, 1914. Freud Museum, London.

p.346   *never knew:* Freud to Abraham, July 26, 1914. *Freud–Abraham,* 180 (186).

p.347   *now at hand:* Freud to Abraham, July 29, 1914. Ibid., 181 (186).

p.347 *"general war"*: Abraham to Freud, July 29, 1914. Ibid., 182 (188).

p.347 *"our lifetime"*: Viscount Grey of Fallodon, *Twenty-Five Years, 1892–1916*, 2 vols. (1925), II, 20.

p.347 *"of the Russians"*: Alexander Freud to Freud, August 4, 1914. Freud Museum, London.

p.347 *"dares to approach"*: Ibid.

p.348 *"the firebrand"*: Rainer Maria Rilke, "Fünf Gesänge: August 1914," in *Werke in drei Bänden*, ed. Ruth Sieber-Rilke and Ernst Zinn (1966), II, 86–87.

p.348 *military valor*: See Edward Timms, *Karl Kraus, Apocalyptic Satirist: Culture and Catastrophe in Habsburg Vienna* (1986), 289–95.

p.348 *"fed up!"*: Thomas Mann, "Gedanken im Krieg," *Neue Rundschau*, XXV (November 1914), 1475.

p.349 *"no less so"*: Abraham to Freud, August 29, 1914. *Freud–Abraham*, 187 (194).

p.349 *"essentially finished"*: Abraham to Freud, September 13, 1914. Ibid., 189 (196).

p.349 *"slowed somewhat"*: Eitingon to Freud, September 11, 1914. By permission of Sigmund Freud Copyrights, Wivenhoe.

p.349 *"of millions"*: Freud to Abraham, September 22, 1914. *Freud–Abraham*, 190 (197).

p.350 *"Paris" arrived*: Freud to Eitingon (postcard), September 15, 1914. By permission of Sigmund Freud Copyrights, Wivenhoe.

p.350 *"symptomatic acts"*: Freud to Abraham, July 26, 1914. *Freud–Abraham*, 180 (186).

p.350 *"wrong side"*: Freud to Abraham, August 2, 1914. Ibid., 184 (190).

p.350 *"our 'enemies'?"*: Abraham to Freud, August 29, 1914. Ibid., 188 (194).

p.350 *"as an enemy!"*: Freud to Jones, October 22, 1914. Transcribed in Jones's hand. Freud Collection, D2, LC.

p.350 *and the Netherlands*: See *Jones* II, 170.

p.350 *"the time being"*: Freud to Ferenczi (postcard), August 14, 1914. Freud–Ferenczi Correspondence, Freud Collection, LC.

p.350 *40,000 kronen*: See Freud to Ferenczi, April 8, 1915. Ibid.

p.350 *"militarily paralyzed"*: Freud to Ferenczi, July 31, 1915. Ibid.

p.351 *military service*: See Freud to Abraham. December 11, 1914. *Freud–Abraham*, 197 (205).

p.351 *"against the fatherland"*: Freud to Ferenczi, December 2, 1914. Freud–Ferenczi Correspondence, Freud Collection, LC. See also *Jones* II, 176.

p.351 *late in 1917*: Freud to Abraham, December 26, 1917. *Freud–Abraham*, 252 (267).

p.351 *"sinking ship"*: Freud to Jones, December 25, 1914. Transcribed in Jones's hand. Freud Collection, D2, LC. See also *Jones* II, 179.

p.351 *"Science sleeps"*: Freud to [Jones ? or Putnam ?], January 17, 1915. Typescript copy in Freud–Jones Correspondence, Freud Collection, D2, LC.

p.351 *of hostilities*: See Freud to Ferenczi, July 17, 1914, and (postcard) August 14, 1914. Freud–Ferenczi Correspondence, Freud Collection, LC. See also Freud to Eitingon (postcard), August 28, 1914. By permission of Sigmund Freud Copyrights, Wivenhoe. And see *Jones* II, 173.

p.352 *"behind it"*: Freud to Jones, October 22, 1914. Transcribed in a hand different from Jones's. Freud Collection, D2, LC.

p.352 *exempted the third*: Freud to Abraham, July 27, 1914. Karl Abraham papers, LC.

p.352 *"undeservedly" safe*: Freud to Eitingon, July 29, 1914. By permission of Sigmund Freud Copyrights, Wivenhoe.

p.352 *Required of Jews*: Martin Freud to Freud, August 17, 1914. Freud Museum, London.

p.352 *"thrilling mountain climb"*: Martin Freud to Freud, August 18, 1914. Freud Museum, London.

p.352 *food packages*: See, for instances of grateful acknowledgments, Martin Freud to Freud (postcards), September 13 and October 2, 1914; and Ernst Freud to Freud, November 20 and December 6, 1914, and March 19 [1915]. All in Freud Museum, London.

p.352 *"its influence"*: Freud to Eitingon, January 17, 1915. By permission of Sigmund Freud Copyrights, Wivenhoe.

p.353   *"incredible arrogance":* Freud to Abraham, November 25, 1914. Karl Abraham papers, LC.

p.353   *"miserable times":* Freud to Jones, October 22, 1914. Transcribed in a hand different from Jones's. Freud Collection, D2, LC.

p.353   *"another race":* Freud to Andreas-Salomé, November 25, 1914. *Freud–Salomé,* 22–23 (21).

p.353   *"principal virtue":* Freud to Abraham, September 3, 1914. *Freud–Abraham,* 188 (195).

p.353   *"full of confidence":* Abraham to Freud, October 28, 1914. Ibid., 193 (200).

p.353   *"incurable optimist":* Freud often referred to Abraham in this way. For one late instance, see Freud to Abraham, October 19, 1923. Ibid., 318 (342).

p.354   *"positively expectant":* Abraham to Freud, November 19, 1914. Ibid., 194 (202).

p.354   *early January 1915:* Freud to Eitingon (postcard), January 3, 1915. By permission of Sigmund Freud Copyrights, Wivenhoe.

p.354   *"rises again":* Freud to Abraham, January 25, 1915. *Freud–Abraham,* 201 (209).

p.354   *"holding out":* Freud to [Jones ? or Putnam ?], January 17, 1915. Typescript copy in Freud–Jones Correspondence, Freud Collection, D2, LC.

p.354   *of "optimism":* Freud to Abraham, February 18, 1915. *Freud–Abraham,* 203 (212).

p.354   *"grows daily!":* Freud to Abraham, May 4, 1915. Ibid., 212 (221).

p.354   *"beautiful victories":* Freud to Abraham, July 3, 1915. Ibid., 215 (225).

p.354   *"absurd to me":* Freud to Ferenczi, April 8, 1915. Freud–Ferenczi Correspondence, Freud Collection, LC.

p.354   *"at its outbreak":* Freud to Ferenczi, July 10, 1915. Ibid.

p.354   *"first of all":* Ibid. See also a memorandum, "Traum vom 8./9. Juli Dr. [Donnerstag] Fr. [Freitag] 3/4 2 [1:45 A.M.] beim Erwachen." Typescript copy, Freud Museum, London.

p.355   *destroying itself:* The papers were published in *Imago* under the collective title "Thoughts for the Times on War and Death."

p.355   *for the enemy:* "Zeitgemässes über Krieg und Tod," *GW* X, 324–29/"Thoughts for the Times on War and Death," *SE* XIV, 275–79.

p.356   *disappointment, disillusionment:* Ibid., 324–25/275.

p.356   *"we had thought":* Ibid., 336/285.

p.356   *"pious believers":* Das Unbehagen in der Kultur (1930), *GW* XIV, 506/*Civilization and Its Discontents, SE* XXI, 145.

p.356   *"of all wars":* "Zeitgemässes über Krieg und Tod," *GW* X, 325/"Thoughts for the Times on War and Death," *SE* XIV, 276.

p.356   *"lives we need":* Ibid., 344/291.

p.357   *"animal tormentors":* Ibid., 333/282.

p.357   *"yourself for death":* Ibid., 354–55/299–300.

CHAPTER EIGHT · *Aggressions*

p.361   *"for endurance":* Freud to Andreas-Salomé, July 30, 1915. *Freud–Salomé,* 35 (32).

p.361   *"know so well":* Freud to Abraham, December 18, 1916. *Freud–Abraham,* 232 (244).

p.362   *"momentous things":* Freud to Andreas-Salomé, November 25, 1914. *Freud–Salomé,* 23 (21).

p.362   *psychoanalytic ideas:* This is also the view of Barry Silverstein, " 'Now Comes a Sad Story': Freud's Lost Metapsychological Papers," in *Freud, Appraisals and Reappraisals,* ed. Stepansky, I, 144.

p.362   *"and the unconscious":* Freud to Abraham, December 21, 1914. *Freud–Abraham,* 198 (206).

p.362   *called "metapsychological":* Freud to Andreas-Salomé, January 31, 1915. *Freud–Salomé,* 29 (27).

p.362   *"Abraham directly":* Freud to Ferenczi, February 18, 1915. Freud–Ferenczi Correspondence, Freud Collection, LC. This was in all probability an early version (or perhaps a summary) of one of the papers on metapsychology that he would publish only in 1917.

p.362   *"leave open":* Freud to Ferenczi, April 8, 1915. Ibid. In this discussion, I am indebted to Ilse Grubrich-Simitis's essay "Metapsychologie und Metabiologie: Zu Sigmund Freuds Entwurf einer 'Übersicht der Übertragungsneurosen'," in her edition of a hitherto unpublished draft of the twelfth of the metapsychological essays, *Übersicht der Übertragungsneurosen* (1985), 83–119.

p.363   *"already drafted":* Freud to Ferenczi, April 23, 1915. Freud–Ferenczi Correspondence, Freud Collection, LC.

p.363   *"still lacking":* Freud to Ferenczi, June 21, 1915. Ibid.

p.363   *"necessary reworking":* Freud to Andreas-Salomé, July 30, 1915. *Freud–Salomé*, 35 (32).

p.363   *"behind" consciousness:* Freud to Fliess, March 10, 1898. *Freud–Fliess*, 329 (301–2).

p.363   *daydream, metaphysics:* See *Psychopathology of Everyday Life, SE* VI, 259.

p.363   *"problem child":* Freud to Fliess, December 17, 1896. *Freud–Fliess*, 228 (216).

p.363   *"calmer times":* Freud to Abraham, May 4, 1915. *Freud–Abraham*, 212 (221). See also "Editor's Introduction" to *Papers on Metapsychology, SE* XIV, 105.

p.363   *"this virtue":* Freud to Ferenczi, April 8, 1915. Freud–Ferenczi Correspondence, Freud Collection, LC.

p.363   *"be an advance":* Freud to Abraham, May 4, 1915. *Freud–Abraham*, 212 (221).

p.364   *"proves useful":* "Triebe und Triebschicksale" (1915), *GW* X, 216–17/"Instincts and Their Vicissitudes," *SE* XIV, 124.

p.364   *competence of psychology:* Ibid., 214–16/122–23.

p.364   *and unpleasure:* Ibid., 232/140.

p.365   *"against the drives":* Ibid., 219/127. In 1936, his daughter Anna would list and analyze the defense mechanisms he had scattered throughout his writings, and add some of her own. See Anna Freud, *The Ego and the Mechanisms of Defence* (1936; tr. Cecil Baines, 1937).

p.365   *"essential part":* "Geschichte der psychoanalytischen Bewegung," *GW* X, 54/"History of the Psycho-Analytic Movement," *SE* XIV, 16. I am indebted in this discussion to the comments of Freud's English editors in "Editor's Note" to "Repression," *SE* XIV, 143–44.

p.365   *"meager reading":* "Geschichte der psychoanalytischen Bewegung," *GW* X, 53/"History of the Psycho-Analytic Movement," *SE* XIV, 15. In his self-portrait of 1925 he repeated this claim: repression "was an innovation; nothing like it had ever been recognized in mental life." ("Selbstdarstellung," *GW* XIV, 55/"Autobiographical Study," *SE* XX, 30.)

p.365   *in his grasp:* See "Autobiographical Study," *SE* XX, 29.

p.366   *"of energy":* "Die Verdrängung" (1915), *GW* X, 253/"Repression," *SE* XIV, 151.

p.366   *charioteer's control:* See, for this image, Plato, *Phaedrus*, 246, 253–54.

p.366   *"realms of consciousness":* Quoted in Lancelot Law Whyte, *The Unconscious before Freud* (1960; paperback ed., 1962), 126.

p.366   *"never penetrate":* William Wordsworth, *The Prelude*, Book First, l. 562, and Book Third, ll. 246–47.

p.367   *proper finish:* See Freud to Ferenczi, June 21, 1915. Freud–Ferenczi Correspondence, Freud Collection, LC.

p.367   *"it were, ready":* Freud to Ferenczi, August 9, 1915. Ibid.

p.368   *"realistic criticism":* Freud to Ferenczi, April 8, 1915. Ibid.

p.368   *"phylogenetic fantasy":* Freud to Ferenczi, July 18, 1915. Ibid. See also Freud to Ferenczi, July 28, 1915; and Ferenczi to Freud, July 24, 1915. Ibid.

p.368   *mental distress:* See Freud to Ferenczi, July 12, 1915. Freud–Ferenczi Correspondence, Freud Collection, LC.

p.368   *"both sexes":* "Vorwort" to *Vorlesungen zur Einführung in die Psychoanalyse* (1916–17), *GW* XI, 3/"Preface" to *Introductory Lectures on Psycho-Analysis, SE* XV, 9.

p.368   *his daughter Anna:* See Anna Freud to Jones, March 6, 1917, in a postscript to a letter from her father. Freud–Jones Correspondence, Freud Collection, D2, LC. Further confirmation can be found in a later statement: "I accompanied my father on these occasions and listened to all of these Vorlesungen." (Anna Freud to Jones, November 10, 1953. Jones papers, Archives of the British Psycho-Analytical Society, London.)

p.369   *and Braille:* See "Bibliographische Anmerkung," *GW* XI, 484–85.

p.369   *to be effective:* See Abraham to Freud, January 2, 1917. *Freud–Abraham,* 232–33 (244–45).

p.369   *lectures "elementary":* See Freud to Andreas-Salomé, November 9, 1915. *Freud–Salomé,* 39 (35).

p.369   *"anything new":* Freud to Andreas-Salomé, May 25, 1916. Ibid., 50 (45).

p.369   *"for the multitude":* Freud to Andreas-Salomé, July 14, 1916. Ibid., 53 (48).

p.369   *"very tired":* Freud to Abraham, August 27, 1916. *Freud–Abraham,* 228 (239).

p.369   *"exhausting effect":* Freud to Ferenczi, April 8, 1915. Freud–Ferenczi Correspondence, Freud Collection, LC.

p.369   Greisenalter: Freud to Eitingon, May 8, 1916. *Jones* II, 188.

p.370   *"in creativity":* Abraham to Freud, May 1, 1917, *Freud–Abraham,* 224 (235).

p.370   *"fragile and tired":* Freud to Abraham, May 20, 1917. Ibid., 238 (251).

p.370   *"warriors" were well:* Freud to Andreas-Salomé (postcard), November 23, 1916. *Freud–Salomé,* 59 (53).

p.370   *victory and peace:* See Abraham to Freud, February 11, 1917. Karl Abraham papers, LC.

p.370   *"terrible consequences":* Freud to Ferenczi, April 30, 1917. Freud–Ferenczi Correspondence, Freud Collection, LC.

p.370   *"Revolution in Russia":* Prochaskas Familienkalender, 1917. Freud Collection, B2, LC.

p.370   *measure of evil?:* Vorlesungen zur Einführung, *GW* XI, 147/Introductory Lectures, SE XV, 146.

p.370   *campaign a failure:* See Freud to Ferenczi, October 9, 1917. Freud–Ferenczi Correspondence, Freud Collection, LC.

p.371   Kältetremor!: Freud to Abraham, January 18, 1918. *Freud–Abraham,* 253 (268).

p.371   *best stopgaps:* For the details in this paragraph, see esp. *Jones* II, 192.

p.371   *"No Nobel Prize 1917":* Prochaskas Familienkalender, 1917. Freud Collection, B2, LC.

p.371   *to be chosen:* See Abraham to Freud, December 10, 1916; and Freud to Abraham, December 18, 1916. Both in *Freud–Abraham,* 231–32 (243–44).

p.371   *" 'on Rosh Hashana' ":* Two sheets torn from a notebook, titled "Kriegswitze." Freud Collection, LC, uncatalogued.

p.371   *"English manner":* Freud to Abraham, October 5, 1917. *Freud–Abraham,* 244 (258). Jones's optimism had remained consistent throughout the war. As early as August 3, 1914, he had confidently written to Freud, "No one doubts here . . . that Germany and Austria will be badly defeated." (By permission of Sigmund Freud Copyrights, Wivenhoe.)

p.371   *metapsychological papers:* Freud to Abraham, November 11, 1917. *Freud–Abraham,* 246–47 (261). The two papers were "A Metapsychological Supplement to the Theory of Dreams" and "Mourning and Melancholia."

p.371   *to the Jews:* See Freud to Abraham, December 10, 1917. Ibid., 249 (264).

p.372   *a bitter end:* Freud to Ferenczi, October 9, 1917. Freud–Ferenczi Correspondence, Freud Collection, LC.

p.372   *"German fatherland":* Freud to Abraham, December 10, 1917. *Freud–Abraham,* 249 (264).

p.372   *"my listlessness":* Freud to Abraham, March 22, 1918. Ibid., 257 (272).

p.372   *"awaited date":* Freud to Andreas-Salomé, May 25, 1916. *Freud–Salomé,* 50 (45).

p.372   *book in print:* Ibid.

p.373   verschwiegen werden: Freud to Ferenczi, November 20[?] 1917. Freud–Ferenczi Correspondence, Freud Collection, LC.

p.373   *for the book:* See Freud to Abraham, November 11, 1917. *Freud–Abraham,* 246–47 (261).

p.373   *"also other indications":* Freud to Andreas-Salomé, July 1, 1918. *Freud–Salomé,* 92 (82).

p.374   *"a drowning man":* Kann, *History of the Habsburg Empire,* 481.

p.374   *"not yet here":* Freud to Eitingon, October 25, 1918. By permission of Sigmund Freud Copyrights, Wivenhoe.

p.375   *"too starved":* Freud to Abraham, August 27, 1918. *Freud–Abraham,* 261 (278).

p.375   *"Budapest days":* Freud to Abraham, October 27, 1918. Ibid., 263 (279).

p.376   *"military calculations":* Jones II, 197. See also Freud to Andreas-Salomé, October 4, 1918. *Freud–Salomé,* 92–93 (83–84).

p.376   *"nervous disorders":* W. H. R. Rivers, "Freud's Psychology of the Unconscious," a paper read before the Edinburgh Pathological Club on March 7, 1917, and printed in *The Lancet* (June 16, 1917). Quoted in Clark, *Freud,* 385.

p.376   *"were malingerers":* "Memorandum on the Electrical Treatment of War Neurotics," *SE* XVII, 213. The original five-page memorandum, "Gutachten über die elektrische Behandlung der Kriegsneurotiker von Prof. Dr. Sigm. Freud," dated "Vienna, February 23, 1920," has not been published.

p.377   *"Republic in Hungary":* Prochaskas *Familienkalender,* 1918. Freud Collection, B2, LC.

p.377   *"evil war dream":* Freud to Abraham, December 25, 1918. *Freud–Abraham,* 266 (283).

p.377   *"Oct[ober] 27":* Prochaskas *Familienkalender,* 1918. Freud Collection, B2, LC. Communications from Martin Freud to his family include one of November 8, 1918, marked "Prisoner of War Postcard"; one of November 14, reporting that he is still in the hospital, but better—this seems to have taken a week to reach Vienna; and one of December 24, 1918. (All in Freud Museum, London.)

p.377   *"this Germany":* Freud to Eitingon, October 25, 1918. By permission of Sigmund Freud Copyrights, Wivenhoe.

p.377   *in its wake:* Freud to Ferenczi, November 9, 1918. Freud–Ferenczi Correspondence, Freud Collection, LC.

p.377   *"pile of muck":* Freud to Ferenczi, November 17, 1918. Ibid.

p.377   *psychoanalysis instead:* Freud to Ferenczi, October 27, 1918. Ibid.

p.377   *not manage it:* See Freud to Ferenczi, November 7, 1918. Ibid.

p.377   *"held indoors":* Quoted in Jones II, 201.

p.377   *"became visible":* Eitingon to Freud, November 25, 1918. By permission of Sigmund Freud Copyrights, Wivenhoe.

p.378   *"boxes with you":* Freud to Jones, December 22, 1918. In English. Freud Collection, D2, LC. Most of Anna Freud's things were sent back, and did arrive safely. (See Freud to Jones, April 18, 1919. In English. Ibid.)

p.378   *"next ones, too":* Freud to Ferenczi, January 24, 1919. Freud–Ferenczi Correspondence, Freud Collection, LC.

p.378   *"are dark":* Freud to Jones, January 15, 1919. In English. Freud Collection, D2, LC.

p.378   *"is longing":* Quoted in George Lichtheim, *Europe in the Twentieth Century* (1972), 118.

p.379   *"in the President":* Freud to Abraham, February 5, 1919. *Freud–Abraham,* 267 (285).

p.379   *"Havana cigars":* Edward Bernays, "Uncle Sigi," *Journal of the History of Medicine and Allied Sciences,* XXXV (April 1980), 217.

p.379   *"from everywhere":* Freud to Jones, April 18, 1919. In English. Freud Collection, D2, LC.

p.380   *it official:* See Freud to Eitingon, October 25, 1918. By permission of Sigmund Freud Copyrights, Wivenhoe.

p.380   *"foreign territory":* Freud to Ferenczi, March 17, 1919. Freud–Ferenczi Correspondence, Freud Collection, LC.

p.380   *soul together:* Stefan Zweig, *Die Welt von Gestern. Erinnerungen eines Europäers* (1944), 259–66.

p.380   *"to be had":* Anna Freud to Jones, March 7, 1955. Jones papers, Archives of the British Psycho-Analytical Society, London.

p.380   *" 'Kartoffelschmarrn' ":* Ibid. *Kartoffel,* of course, means "potato"; *Schmarrn* is a kind of torn-up pancake, a delicacy in Austria and Bavaria. *Schmarrn* is also a slang term for "rubbish" or "nonsense."

p.380   *"hungry joke!":* Freud to Ferenczi, March 17, 1919. Freud–Ferenczi Correspondence, Freud Collection, LC.

p.380   *not unpleasant:* Freud to Abraham, April 13, 1919. *Freud–Abraham,* 269 (287).

p.381   *"by his letters":* Freud to Samuel Freud, May 22, 1919. In English. Rylands University Library, Manchester.

p.381   *"excellent condition":* Freud to Samuel Freud, October 27, 1919. In English. Ibid.

p.381   Hungerkost: Freud to Ferenczi, April 9, 1919. Freud–Ferenczi Correspondence, Freud Collection, LC.

p.381   *would be 746:* See quotation from *Reichspost,* December 25, 1918, in *Dokumentation zur Österreichischen Zeitgeschichte, 1918–1928,* ed. Christine Klusacek and Kurt Stimmer (1984), 124.

p.381   *"cold room":* Freud to Abraham, February 5, 1919. *Freud–Abraham,* 267 (284).

p.381   *fountain pen:* See Freud to Andreas-Salomé, February 9, 1919. *Freud–Salomé,* 100 (90).

p.381   *paper shortage:* See Freud to Abraham, June 4, 1920. Karl Abraham papers, LC.

p.381   *"world's nonsense":* Freud to Jones, April 18, 1919. In English. Freud Collection, D2, LC.

p.381   *the cheerfulness:* Freud to Max and Mirra Eitingon, May 9, 1919. Typescript copy. By permission of Sigmund Freud Copyrights, Wivenhoe.

p.382   *"borders etc.":* Freud to Jones, May 28, 1919. In English. Freud Collection, D2, LC.

p.382   *"all around":* Freud to Samuel Freud, May 22, 1919. In English. Rylands University Library, Manchester.

p.382   *during the summer:* Martha Freud to Jones, April 26, 1919. Freud Collection, D2, LC.

p.382   *not to worry:* Freud to Abraham, May 18, 1919. Karl Abraham papers, LC.

p.382   *Viennese perished:* See *Dokumentation,* ed. Klusacek and Stimmer, 156, 296–97.

p.382   *"fever afresh":* Freud to Jones, May 28, 1919. In English. Freud Collection, D2, LC.

p.382   *fully restored:* See Freud to Abraham, July 6, 1919. Karl Abraham papers, LC.

p.382   *"to be expected":* Ibid.

p.382   *"year's life":* Freud to Jones, July 28, 1919. In English. Freud Collection, D2, LC.

p.383   *"is impossible":* Freud to Samuel Freud, October 27, 1919. In English. Rylands University Library, Manchester.

p.383   *"and what not":* Freud to Samuel Freud, October 27, 1919. In English. Ibid.

p.384   *further endurance:* Freud to Eitingon, December 2, 1919. *Briefe,* 341–42.

p.384   *"spring and autumn":* Freud to Samuel Freud, February 22, 1920. In English. Rylands University Library, Manchester.

p.384   *fallen apart:* Freud to Samuel Freud, February 5, 1922. In English. Ibid.

p.384   *"merely victims!":* Freud to Max and Mirra Eitingon, May 9, 1919. Typescript copy. By permission of Sigmund Freud Copyrights, Wivenhoe.

p.384   *"impotent rage":* Freud to Ferenczi, July 10, 1919. Freud–Ferenczi Correspondence, Freud Collection, LC.

p.384   *"railway workmen":* Freud to Samuel Freud, October 27, 1919. In English. Rylands University Library, Manchester.

p.385   *"been reopened":* Freud to Samuel Freud, November 24, 1919. In English. Ibid.

p.385   *"still reach us":* Freud to Samuel Freud (postcard), December 8, 1919. In English. Ibid.

p.385   *"D[eutsch] Oest[erreich]":* Freud to Samuel Freud, December 17, 1919. In English. Ibid.

p.385   *"than three months":* Freud to Samuel Freud, January 26, 1920. In English. Ibid.

p.385   *"in sticks":* Freud to Samuel Freud, October 15, 1920. In English. Ibid.

p.385   *"your operation":* Freud to "Geehrte Administration," May 7, 1920. (This letter was brought to my attention by Dr. J. Alexis Burland.)

p.385   *no interpreter:* Dr. J. Alexis Burland, personal communication to the author, December 29, 1986.

p.385   *"English patient":* Freud to Samuel Freud, February 15, 1920. In English. Rylands University Library, Manchester.

p.385   *eight pounds:* See Freud to Samuel Freud, July 22, 1920. In English. Ibid.

p.385   *"at the Hague":* Freud to Samuel Freud, October 15, 1920. In English. Ibid.

p.386   *to go around:* See Zweig, *Die Welt von Gestern,* 279.

p.386   " 'Kaffeehaus' ": Richard F. Sterba, *Reminiscences of a Viennese Psychoanalyst* (1982), 21.

p.387   *"one's powers":* Zweig, *Die Welt von Gestern,* 279.

p.387   *"cannot live":* Freud to Abraham, June 21, 1920. *Freud–Abraham,* 291 (312).

p.387   *but heated:* See Freud to Abraham, December 9, 1921. Ibid., 304 (327).

p.387   *"just on top":* Freud to Kata Levy, October 18, 1920. Freud Collection, B9, LC.

p.387   *"this move":* Freud to Rank, September 8, 1922. Rank Collection, Box 1b. Rare Book and Manuscript Library, Columbia University.

p.387   *"still at work":* Freud to Jones, July 28, 1919. In English. Freud Collection, D2, LC.

p.387   *"needs therapy":* Freud to Eitingon, October 31, 1920. By permission of Sigmund Freud Copyrights, Wivenhoe.

p.388   *"not checks":* Freud to Leonhard Blumgart, April 10, 1921. A. A. Brill Library, New York Psychoanalytic Institute. Blumgart was to be president of the New York Psychoanalytic Institute from 1942 to 1945.

p.388   *"for crowns":* Freud to Abram Kardiner, April 10, 1921. In English. Quoted in A[bram] Kardiner, *My Analysis with Freud: Reminiscences* (1977), 15.

p.388   *"two ends meet":* Freud to Jones, March 8, 1920. In English. Freud Collection, D2, LC.

p.388   *"Western valuta":* Freud to Jones, January 28, 1921. In English. Ibid.

p.388   *la guerre:* Freud to Kata Levy, November 28, 1920. Freud Collection, B9, LC.

p.388   *"up my English":* Freud to Eitingon, October 12, 1919. By permission of Sigmund Freud Copyrights, Wivenhoe.

p.388   *"have to stop":* Freud to Samuel Freud, November 28, 1920. In English. Rylands University Library, Manchester.

p.388   *clear enunciation:* Freud to Jones, March 8, 1920. In English. Freud Collection, D2, LC.

p.388   *"language correctly":* Freud to Samuel Freud, July 25, 1921. In English. Rylands University Library, Manchester. The "d——d" sits a little oddly in a man who made a point of calling a spade a spade, but it is reminiscent of genteel usage in the nineteenth century, when Freud learned his English.

p.388   *"criticize my English":* Freud to Blumgart, May 12, 1921. In English. A. A. Brill Library, New York Psychoanalytic Institute.

p.388   *"useful for anything":* Freud to Ferenczi, November 28, 1920. Freud–Ferenczi Correspondence, Freud Collection, LC.

p.389   *chore to Sundays:* Freud to Kata Levy, November 28, 1920. Freud Collection B9, LC.

p.389   *"new wealth":* Freud to Andreas-Salomé, October 20, 1921. *Freud–Salomé,* 120 (109).

p.389   *to accept:* For one instance, see Andreas-Salomé to Freud [early September 1923]. Ibid., 139 (127). There are numerous others.

p.389   *fewer patients:* Freud to Andreas-Salomé, August 5, 1923. Ibid., 137 (124).

p.389   *mentioned six:* Freud to Blumgart, May 12, 1921. In English. A. A. Brill Library, New York Psychoanalytic Institute.

p.389   *ten analysands:* See Freud to Samuel Freud, December 4, 1921. Rylands University Library, Manchester.

p.389   *advanced age:* Freud to Blumgart, April 10, 1921. A. A. Brill Library, New York Psychoanalytic Institute.

p.389   *"devouring science":* Freud to Jones, November 18, 1920. In English and German. Freud Collection, D2, LC.

p.390   *"revolutioned my soul":* Freud to Jones, February 12, 1920. In English. Ibid. Actually, of course, Freud was forty, not forty-three, when his father died in 1896.

p.390   *obituary tribute:* See "Victor Tausk," *SE* XVII, 273–75. This obituary originally appeared in the *Internationale Zeitschrift für ärztliche Psychoanalyse,* V (1919), over the signature "Die Redaktion"—"The Editors."

p.391   *"useless to us":* Freud to Abraham, July 6, 1919. Karl Abraham papers, LC. In his typed reminiscences (p. 8), the psychoanalyst Ludwig Jekels reports that when he asked Freud why he did not take Tausk into analysis, Freud replied, "He is going to kill me!" (Siegfried Bernfeld papers, container 17, LC.)

p.391   *"sympathy" in himself:* Freud to Ferenczi, July 10, 1919. Freud–Ferenczi Correspondence, Freud Collection, LC.

p.391   *had told Abraham:* Freud to Andreas-Salomé, August 1, 1919. *Freud–Salomé,* 109 (98–99).

p.391   *and to psychoanalysis:* See Andreas-Salomé to Freud, August 25, 1919. Ibid., 109 (99). Picturesquely, she called Tausk a "frenzied soul"—*Seelenberserker*—"with a tender heart."

p.391   *"the first time":* Freud to Andreas-Salomé, August 1, 1919. Ibid., 109 (98–99).

p.391   *hoped to die:* Freud to Eitingon, January 21, 1920. Original German passage quoted in Schur, *Freud, Living and Dying,* 553.

p.391   *"blooming Sophie":* Freud to his mother, Amalia Freud, January 26, 1920. *Briefe,* 344.

p.391   *her third child:* This is what Freud told his analysand, later his friend, Jeanne Lampl-de Groot. (Interview by author with Lampl-de Groot, October 24, 1985.)

p.392   *"Sophie properly":* Freud to Kata Levy, February 26, 1920. Freud Collection, B9, LC.

p.392   *"lost forever":* Martha Freud to "Kitty" Jones, March 19, 1928. Jones papers, Archives of the British Psycho-Analytical Society, London.

p.392   *"his watch-chain":* H. D. [Hilda Doolittle], "Advent," in *Tribute to Freud* (1956), 128.

p.392   *"Sunday child!":* Freud to Pfister, January 27, 1920. *Freud–Pfister,* 77–78 (74–75).

p.392   *"father hardly":* Freud to "Mother" Halberstadt, March 23, 1920. Freud Collection, B1, LC.

p.392   *sadly, "Papa":* Freud to Max Halberstadt, January 25, 1920. *Briefe,* 343–44.

p.392   *"of precedence":* Freud to Lajos Levy, February 4, 1920. Freud Collection, B9, LC.

p.393   *"not get over":* Freud to Ferenczi, February 4, 1920. Freud–Ferenczi Correspondence, Freud Collection, LC.

p.393   *"as we last":* Freud to Jones, February 6, 1920. In English. Freud Collection, D2, LC.

p.393   *"for the diversion":* Freud to Pfister, January 27, 1920. *Freud–Pfister,* 78 (75).

p.393   *"very good English":* Jones III, 27.

p.393   *lobbied for it:* See Karl Abraham to Jones, January 4, 1920. Jones papers, Archives of the British Psycho-Analytical Society, London.

p.394   *be* Beyond the Pleasure Principle: Freud to Andreas-Salomé, April 2, 1919. *Freud–Salomé,* 105 (95).

p.395   *"gone to war":* Wittels, *Sigmund Freud,* 231. (While this book is dated 1924, we know from a letter that Freud sent Wittels immediately upon receiving it, on December 18, 1923, that it was completed in 1923. See *Briefe,* 363–64.)

p.395   *Halberstadt's death:* For example, on July 18, 1920, Freud wrote to Eitingon, "The *Beyond* is now finally finished. You will be able to confirm that it was half ready when Sophie lived and flourished." (By permission of Sigmund Freud Copyrights, Wivenhoe.) See also Freud to Jones, July 18, 1920. Typescript excerpt, Freud Collection, D2, LC.

p.395   *"always the true":* Freud to Wittels [December 1923?]. The holograph of this letter is not extant (at least I have not discovered it). But in the margin of a copy of Wittels's *Sigmund Freud,* now in the library of Ohio State University, which was clearly the working copy of the translators Eden and Cedar Paul, Wittels copied down the text of Freud's letter to him, and it is from this transcription that I am quoting. The translators inserted passages from this letter into the English edition. Wittels's marginal transcription of Freud's letter is at p. 231, while the English version is to be found on pp. 251–52.

p.395   *in his family:* In the fall of 1919, Freud published "The Uncanny," a curious paper, part lexicographical study, part psychoanalytic conjecture, which already contained some of the central concepts of *Beyond the Pleasure Principle,* notably that of the compulsion to repeat. And the ideas in that paper were not new to Freud even then. (See editor's note to "The 'Uncanny,' " *SE* XVII, 218.)

p.395   *Halberstadt's death?:* See Freud to Eitingon, February 8, 1920. By permission of Sigmund

Freud Copyrights, Wivenhoe. See also the discussion in Schur, *Freud, Living and Dying,* 328–33, esp. 329.

p.396   "in childhood": "Zur Ätiologie der Hysterie," *GW* I, 457/"The Aetiology of Hysteria," *SE* III, 220.

p.396   "admixture of aggression": *Drei Abhandlungen, GW* V, 57/*Three Essays, SE,* VII, 157.

p.396   "aggressive drive?": "Angst und Trieblében," in *Neue Folge der Vorlesungen, GW* XV, 110/"Anxiety and Instinctual Life," in *New Introductory Lectures, SE* XXII, 103.

p.396   "receptive to it": *Das Unbehagen in der Kultur, GW* XIV, 479/*Civilization and Its Discontents, SE* XXI, 120.

p.396   *pioneering days of 1911:* See November 29, 1911. *Protokolle,* III, 314–20.

p.396   "Cause of Becoming": For Freud's acknowledgment of Spielrein's contribution, see *Beyond the Pleasure Principle, SE* XVIII, 55n.

p.397   *than at life:* See, for one statement among many, Jung to J. Allen Gilbert, March 4, 1930. *Briefe,* I, 102.

p.397   "dualistic" *scheme: Jenseits des Lustprinzips* (1920), *GW* XIII, 56–57/*Beyond the Pleasure Principle, SE* XVIII, 53.

p.399   "to the devil": Ibid., 63–64/59.

p.399   *his "speculations":* Ibid. In *Beyond the Pleasure Principle,* Freud used that unpromising word "speculations" more than once.

p.399   *with this work:* Freud to Ferenczi, March 28, 1919. Freud–Ferenczi Correspondence, Freud Collection, LC.

p.399   "toward the pleasure principle": *Jenseits des Lustprinzips, GW* XIII, 3, 5/*Beyond the Pleasure Principle, SE* XVIII, 7, 9.

p.400   *psychoanalysts had supposed:* See ibid., 11–15/14–17.

p.400   *love once again:* See ibid., 21/22.

p.401   *about their activities:* Ibid., 20/21.

p.401   "its own fashion": Ibid., 36–41/35–39.

p.401   *kind of immortality:* Ibid., 41/39.

p.402   "think differently": *Das Unbehagen in der Kultur, GW* XIV, 478–79/*Civilization and Its Discontents, SE* XXI, 119.

p.402   "of them alone": "Die endliche und die unendliche Analyse," *GW* XVI, 88–89/"Analysis Terminable and Interminable," *SE* XXIII, 243.

p.402   "has something better": Freud to Jones, March 3, 1935. Freud Collection, D2, LC.

p.403   "far beyond psychoanalysis": "Selbstdarstellung," *GW* XIV, 84/"Autobiographical Study," *SE* XX, 57.

p.403   "our unfinished work": Freud to Jones, October 4, 1920. In English. Freud Collection, D2, LC.

p.403   "stupid there": Freud to Eitingon, March 27, 1921. By permission of Sigmund Freud Copyrights, Wivenhoe.

p.403   "these deep problems": Freud to Jones, August 2, 1920. In English. Freud Collection, D2, LC.

p.403   *the final revisions:* See *Jones* III, 42–43.

p.404   "on Mass-Psychology": Freud to Jones, March 18, 1921. In English. Freud Collection, D2, LC.

p.404   "understanding of society": Freud to Rolland, March 4, 1923. *Briefe,* 360.

p.404   "the same time": *Massenpsychologie und Ich-Analyse* (1921), *GW* XIII, 73/*Group Psychology and the Analysis of the Ego, SE* XVIII, 69.

p.405   "as social phenomena": Ibid.

p.405   "recent great war": Ibid., 130/118.

p.405   *das blöde Volk:* Freud to Andreas-Salomé, November 22, 1917. *Freud–Salomé,* 75 (67).

p.406   "in the crowd": *Massenpsychologie, GW* XIII, 100, 104/*Group Psychology, SE* XVIII, 91, 95.

p.406   "belong to it": Ibid., 110, 107/101, 98.

p.406   "and in libido": Ferenczi, "Freuds 'Massenpsychologie und Ich-Analyse.' Der individual-psychologische Fortschritt" (1922), in *Schriften zur Psychoanalyse,* ed. Balint, II, 123–24.

p.407   *"nothing at all":* Freud to Ferenczi, July 21, 1922. Freud–Ferenczi Correspondence, Freud Collection, LC.

p.407   *"cannot be completed":* Freud to Rank, August 4, 1922. Rank Collection, Box 1b. Rare Book and Manuscript Library, Columbia University.

p.407   *"of Groddeck":* Ibid.

p.407   *"certain mysticism":* Freud to Andreas-Salomé, October 7, 1917. *Freud–Salomé,* 71 (63).

p.408   as *Freud's pupil:* Groddeck to Freud, May 27, 1917. *Georg Groddeck–Sigmund Freud: Briefe über das Es,* ed. Margaretha Honegger (1974), 7–13.

p.408   *"a wild analyst":* Quoted in Carl M. and Sylva Grossman, *The Wild Analyst: The Life and Work of Georg Groddeck* (1965), 95.

p.408   *that he had:* See Groddeck to Freud, September 11, 1921. *Briefe über das Es,* 32.

p.408   *it in manuscript:* See Freud to Groddeck, February 7 and 8, 1920. Ibid., 25–26.

p.408   *"beginning to end":* Ferenczi, "Georg Groddeck, *Der Seelensucher.* Ein psychoanalytischer Roman" (1921), *Schriften zur Psychoanalyse,* ed. Balint, II, 95.

p.408   *"bawdy passages":* Jones III, 78.

p.408   *"do without him":* Freud to Eitingon, May 27, 1920. By permission of Sigmund Freud Copyrights, Wivenhoe.

p.408   *"Rabelais's contemporary?":* Freud to Pfister (postcard), February 4, 1921. *Freud–Pfister,* 83 (80–81).

p.409   *belles lettres:* Pfister to Freud, March 14, 1921. By permission of Sigmund Freud Copyrights, Wivenhoe.

p.409   *in April 1921:* Freud to Groddeck, April 17, 1921. *Briefe über das Es,* 38.

p.409   " *'by the It' ":* Groddeck, *Das Buch vom Es. Psychoanalytische Briefe an eine Freundin* (1923; rev. ed., 1979), 27.

p.409   *"of the repressed":* Freud to Groddeck, April 17, 1921. *Briefe über das Es,* 38–39.

p.409   *"real behind it":* Freud to Andreas-Salomé, October 7, 1917. *Freud–Salomé,* 71 (63).

p.410   *"to reap":* Groddeck to Freud, May 27, 1923. *Briefe über das Es,* 63.

p.410   *"next time":* Groddeck to his second wife, May 15, 1923. Ibid., 103.

p.410   *"congratulate your It":* Freud to Groddeck, October 13, 1926. Ibid., 81.

p.411   *"role of Eros": Das Ich und das Es* (1923), *GW* XIII, 289/*The Ego and the Id, SE* XIX, 59.

p.411   *and well written:* Freud to Ferenczi, April 17, 1923. Freud–Ferenczi Correspondence, Freud Collection, LC.

p.411   *gratitude now: Ich und Es, GW* XIII, 237/*Ego and Id, SE* XIX, 12.

p.411   *unconscious the "id":* Ibid., 251/23.

p.411   *"than a speculation":* Ibid., 239/12.

p.412   *"first shibboleth":* Ibid., 239/13.

p.412   *"of depth psychology":* Ibid., 245/18.

p.412   *"prototype of the unconscious":* Ibid., 241/15.

p.412   *"symptom 'consciousness' ":* "Das Unbewusste" (1915), *GW* X, 291/"The Unconscious," *SE* XIV, 192–93.

p.412   *"contains the passions": Ich und Es, GW* XIII, 244, 252–53/*Ego and Id, SE* XIX, 18, 25.

p.413   *"were its own":* Ibid., 253/25.

p.413   *"of public opinion":* Ibid., 286–87/56.

p.413   *"from bodily sensations":* Ibid., 255/26, 26n. The explanatory note was first printed, in English, in the translation of 1927, with Freud's authorization. No German version appears to exist.

p.414   "feeling of guilt": Ibid., 254–55/26–27.

p.415   *"than he knows":* Ibid., 280–82/50–52.

p.415   *"guilty but ill":* Ibid., 278–80/49–50.

p.415   *"across generations":* "Die Zerlegung der psychischen Persönlichkeit," in *Neue Folge der Vorlesungen, GW* XV, 73/"The Dissection of the Psychical Personality," in *New Introductory Lectures, SE* XXII, 67.

p.416   *"of the Oedipus complex": Ich und Es, GW* XIII, 262–64/*Ego and Id, SE* XIX, 34–36.

p.416   *"knotty matter":* Freud to Jones, November 20, 1926. In English. Freud Collection, D2, LC.

p.416   *"of their houses":* Pfister to Freud, September 5, 1930. *Freud–Pfister,* 147 (135).

p.416   *in the "death drive":* Pfister to Freud, February 4, 1930. Ibid., 142 (131). For Freud's vigorous defense of his position, see his reply, February 7, 1930. Ibid., 143–45 (132–34).

CHAPTER NINE · *Death against Life*

p.418   *stood firm:* Freud to Rank, August 4, 1922. Rank Collection, Box 1b. Rare Book and Manuscript Library, Columbia University.

p.418   *"became obvious":* Freud to Jones, June 25, 1922. In English. Freud Collection, D2, LC.

p.418   *"Central European hell":* Freud to Rank, July 8, 1922. Rank Collection, Box 1b. Rare Book and Manuscript Library, Columbia University.

p.418   *"escaped you":* Freud to Rank, August 4, 1922. Ibid.

p.418   *"girl of 23":* Freud to Jones, August 24, 1922. In English. Freud Collection, D2, LC.

p.418   *"so cheerful":* Caecilie Graf to Rosa Graf, "Dear Mother," August 16, 1922. Typescript copy, Freud Collection, LC.

p.418   *his moodiness:* Freud to Jones, August 24, 1922. In English. Freud Collection, D2, LC. Shaken as he was, he was not upset enough to silence his sarcastic tongue. He called his sister Rosa, whose sole surviving child Caecilie had been, "a virtuoso of despair." (Freud to Ferenczi, August 24, 1922. Freud–Ferenczi Correspondence, Freud Collection, LC.)

p.419   *been removed:* Freud to Jones, April 25, 1923. In English. Freud Collection, D2, LC.

p.419   *one of them:* Freud to Ferenczi, November 6, 1917. Freud–Ferenczi Correspondence, Freud Collection, LC. Anna Freud copied out the relevant passages in a letter to Max Schur, August 20, 1965. Max Schur papers, LC.

p.419   *"tissue-rebellion":* Freud to Jones, April 25, 1923. In English. Freud Collection, D2, LC.

p.419   *growth excised:* Schur, *Freud, Living and Dying,* 350. For the material on which I have mainly relied in these paragraphs, see the bibliographical essay for this chapter.

p.419   *Freud's alone:* See Anna Freud to Jones, January 4, 1956. Jones papers, Archives of the British Psycho-Analytical Society, London. In view of Anna Freud's disinclination to criticize her father, this is a significant piece of testimony.

p.419   *"was available":* Deutsch, "Reflections," 280.

p.419   *retarded dwarf:* Anna Freud to Jones, March 16, 1955. Jones papers, Archives of the British Psycho-Analytical Society, London.

p.419   *Freud's life:* This is Ernest Jones's reasonable speculation. (*Jones* III, 91.)

p.420   *"usual rounds":* Anna Freud to Jones, March 16, 1955. Jones papers, Archives of the British Psycho-Analytical Society, London. Jones's account (*Jones* III, 90–91) follows Anna Freud's report virtually word for word; so does Clark, *Freud,* 440, which is based on Jones's and Deutsch's secondhand accounts.

p.420   *was good:* Freud to Andreas-Salomé, May 10, 1923. *Freud–Salomé,* 136 (124).

p.420   *"new growth!":* Freud to Abraham, May 10, 1923. *Freud–Abraham,* 315 (338). The last part of the sentence ("many happy returns . . .") is in English.

p.420   *"had not yet":* Freud to Samuel Freud, June 26, 1923. In English. Rylands University Library, Manchester.

p.421   *prolonged suffering:* From the notes Felix Deutsch made after his visit of April 7, 1923, when Freud showed him his lesion. Quoted in Gifford, "Notes on Felix Deutsch," 4.

p.421   *"hair, and bones":* Freud to Ferenczi, April 17, 1923. Freud–Ferenczi Correspondence, Freud Collection, LC.

p.421 *"much as him"*: Freud to Kata and Lajos Levy, June 11, 1923. *Briefe*, 361–62.

p.421 *"its value"*: Ibid.

p.421 *"not succeed"*: Ibid., 361. The quoted sentence is in English in Freud's letter.

p.422 *"dear child"*: Freud to Ferenczi (postcard), June 20, 1923. Freud–Ferenczi Correspondence, Freud Collection, LC.

p.422 *tears, wept: Jones* III, 92.

p.422 *"must be one"*: Freud to Ferenczi, July 18, 1923. Freud–Ferenczi Correspondence, Freud Collection, LC.

p.422 *"the dear child"*: Freud to Eitingon, August 13, 1923. By permission of Sigmund Freud Copyrights, Wivenhoe.

p.422 *"away with him"*: Freud to Rie, August 18, 1923. Freud Museum, London.

p.422 *"my own life"*: Freud to Binswanger, October 15, 1926. Quoted in Binswanger, *Erinnerungen*, 94–95.

p.422 *"to any amount"*: Freud to Samuel Freud, September 24, 1923. In English. Rylands University Library, Manchester.

p.423 *"very useful"*: Freud to Jones, October 4, 1920. In English. Freud Collection, D2, LC.

p.423 *late in 1919:* Freud to Jones, December 11, 1919. In English. Ibid.

p.423 *"you and ours"*: Freud to Jones, December 23, 1919. In English. Ibid.

p.423 *for better days:* See Freud to Jones, January 7, 1922. Ibid.

p.423 *"very unfairly"*: Jones to the Committee, August 1922. Rank Collection, Box 1b. Rare Book and Manuscript Library, Columbia University.

p.423 *"among themselves"*: Freud to Jones, September 24, 1923. In English. Freud Collection, D2, LC.

p.424 *"übertrieben"*: Jones to Katharine Jones, August 26, 1923. Jones papers, Archives of the British Psycho-Analytical Society, London.

p.424 *"Erlebnis"*: Jones to Katharine Jones, August 28, 1923. Ibid.

p.425 *"welchem Recht?"*: *Jones* III, 93.

p.425 *"plain enough"*: Anna Freud to Jones, January 8, 1956. Jones papers, Archives of the British Psycho-Analytical Society, London.

p.425 *"polydimensionality"*: Freud to Eitingon, September 11, 1923. By permission of Sigmund Freud Copyrights, Wivenhoe.

p.425 *"to her advantage"*: Freud to Jones, September 24, 1923. In English. Freud Collection, D2, LC.

p.425 *"of the future"*: Freud to Samuel Freud, September 24, 1923. In English. Rylands University Library, Manchester.

p.426 *"five weeks"*: Freud to Eitingon, September 26, 1923. Quoted in the original German in Schur, *Freud, Living and Dying*, 554. See also Freud to Jones, September 26, 1923, in which he stated the case virtually word for word as he did to Eitingon. (Freud Collection, D2, LC.)

p.426 *October 4 and 12:* I am here following Schur, *Freud, Living and Dying*, 362.

p.426 *"soon go home"*: Freud to Abraham, October 19, 1923. *Freud–Abraham*, 318 (342).

p.426 *increased to £2,000:* Freud to "Dear Martin!" signed "Cordially, Papa." October 30, 1923. Freud Museum, London. Except for the signature, the letter is not in Freud's hand.

p.426 *"both sides"*: *Jones* III, 98–99. See also Sharon Romm, *The Unwelcome Intruder: Freud's Struggle with Cancer* (1983), 73–85.

p.426 *"capacity for work"*: Max Schur, "The Medical Case History of Sigmund Freud," an unpublished manuscript, dated February 27, 1954. Max Schur papers, LC.

p.426 *younger and stronger:* Interview with Helen Schur, June 3, 1986.

p.426 *"homosex[ual] bond"*: Freud to Rank, November 26, 1923. Rank Collection, Box 1b. Rare Book and Manuscript Library, Columbia University.

p.427 *"rushing sound"*: Freud to Eitingon, March 22, 1924. By permission of Sigmund Freud Copyrights, Wivenhoe.

p.427 *with his left:* For a sketch of the two positions of the couch, before Freud's operation and after, see Anna Freud to Jones, January 4, 1956. Jones papers, Archives of the British Psycho-Analytical Society, London.

p.427 *"magnified denture"*: Jones III, 95.

p.427 *"quite intellegible"*: Freud to Samuel Freud, January 9, 1924. In English. Rylands University Library, Manchester.

p.428 *"old Homer"*: Freud to Samuel Freud, May 4, 1924. In English. Ibid.

p.428 *"high spirits"*: Alix Strachey to James Strachey, October 13 [1924]. *Bloomsbury/Freud: The Letters of James and Alix Strachey, 1924–1925,* ed. Perry Meisel and Walter Kendrick (1985), 72–73.

p.428 *"be desired"*: Alix Strachey to James Strachey, March 20 [1925]. Ibid., 224.

p.428 *two sons:* See Anna Freud to Jones, April 2, 1922. By permission of Sigmund Freud Copyrights, Wivenhoe.

p.428 *"for 4 weeks"*: Freud to Ferenczi, March 30, 1922. Freud–Ferenczi Correspondence, Freud Collection, LC.

p.428 *"substitute anywhere"*: Freud to Anna Freud, March 7, 1922. Freud Collection, LC.

p.429 *been too shy:* Anna Freud to Freud, August 4, 1920. Ibid.

p.429 *"for any reason"*: Freud to Anna Freud, July 21, 1923. Ibid.

p.429 *"in all things"*: Freud to Rie, August 18, 1923. Freud Museum, London.

p.430 *"all his life"*: Freud to Lehrman, March 21, 1929. A. A. Brill Library, New York Psychoanalytic Institute.

p.430 *"eternal peace"*: Freud to Lehrman, January 27, 1930. Ibid. The phrase "Too bad" is in English.

p.430 *"interesting creature"*: Freud to Ferenczi, September 7, 1915. Freud–Ferenczi Correspondence, Freud Collection, LC.

p.430 *"feminine activity"*: Freud to Anna Freud, July 22, 1914. Freud Collection, LC.

p.431 *his permission:* Anna Freud to Freud, July 13, 1910. Ibid.

p.431 *"it very much"*: Anna Freud to Freud, July 15, 1911. Ibid.

p.431 *"me a little"*: Anna Freud to Freud, January 7, 1912. Ibid.

p.431 *"only daughter"*: Freud to Anna Freud, July 21, 1912. Ibid. For another example of Freud's use of this phrase, see Freud to Anna Freud, February 2, 1913. Ibid.

p.431 *feel better:* See Freud to Anna Freud, November 28, 1912. Ibid.

p.431 *"time to write"*: Anna Freud to Freud, November 26, 1912. Ibid.

p.432 *stay longer:* See Anna Freud to Freud, December 16, 1912. Ibid. See also Freud to Anna Freud, January 1, 1913. Ibid.

p.432 *use for her:* Anna Freud to Freud, January 7, 1912. Ibid.

p.432 *"will learn it"*: Anna Freud to Freud, December 16, 1912. Ibid.

p.432 *"in the eye"*: Freud to Anna Freud, January 5, 1913. Ibid.

p.432 *"now only daughter"*: Freud to Pfister, March 11, 1913. *Freud–Pfister,* 61 (61).

p.432 *"little only daughter"*: Freud to Abraham, March 27, 1913. *Freud–Abraham,* 137 (136).

p.432 *"been otherwise"*: Anna Freud to Freud, March 13, 1913. Freud Collection, LC.

p.433 *Lear's youngest:* Freud to Ferenczi, July 7, 1913. Freud–Ferenczi Correspondence, Freud Collection, LC.

p.433 *"my little daughter"*: Freud to Jones, July 22, 1914. In English. Freud Collection, D2, LC.

p.433 *"consent beforehand"*: Freud to Anna Freud, July 17, 1914. Freud Collection, LC.

p.434 *alone with him:* Ibid.

p.434 *manage in England:* Freud to Anna Freud, July 22, 1914. Ibid.

p.434 *"personal offense"*: Freud to Anna Freud, July 24, 1914. Ibid.

p.434 *"understand the world"*: Freud to Jones, July 22, 1914. In English. Freud Collection, D2, LC.

p.434 *Anna directly:* See Freud to Anna Freud, July 22, 1914. Freud Collection, LC.

p.434 *"break the treaty"*: Freud to Jones, July 22, 1914. In English. Freud Collection, D2, LC.

p.435 *"the difference"*: Anna Freud to Freud, July 26, 1914. Freud Collection, LC.

p.435   *"father-imago"*: Jones to Freud, July 27, 1914. By permission of Sigmund Freud Copyrights, Wivenhoe.

p.435   *"very useful"*: Anna Freud to Joseph Goldstein, October 2, 1975. Quoted in Joseph Goldstein, "Anna Freud in Law," *The Psychoanalytic Study of the Child,* XXXIX (1984), 9.

p.435   *"interested in them"*: Anna Freud to Freud, January 31, 1913. Freud Collection, LC.

p.435   as *"transference"*: See Anna Freud to Freud, July 30, 1915. Ibid.

p.435   *at the university*: See Anna Freud to Freud, August 28, 1916. Ibid.

p.435   *lay analyst*: I owe this account to Dr. Jay Katz, who had it from Anna Freud herself.

p.436   *duties as a teacher*: See Anna Freud to Freud, September 13, 1918. Freud Collection, LC.

p.436   *with interpretations*: See Anna Freud to Freud, July 24 and August 2, 1919. Ibid.

p.436   *of the pen*: See Anna Freud to Freud, July 28, 1919. Ibid.

p.436   *"more than I"*: Anna Freud to Freud, November 12, 1920. Ibid.

p.436   *death means*: See Anna Freud to Freud, July 4, 1921. Ibid.

p.436   *"get very sick"*: Anna Freud to Freud, August 4, 1921. Ibid.

p.436   *dreams of others*: See Anna Freud to Freud, August 9, 1920. Ibid.

p.436   *desired very much*: See Anna Freud to Freud, April 27, 1922. Ibid.

p.436   *inner life*: For evidence, see the forthcoming biography of Anna Freud by Elisabeth Young-Bruehl, parts of which she summarized at a meeting of the Muriel Gardiner Program in Psychoanalysis and the Humanities, Yale University, January 15, 1987.

p.437   *"last Wednesday"*: Freud to Jones, June 4, 1922. In English. Freud Collection, D2, LC.

p.437   *from his own*: Binswanger to Freud, August 27, 1923. By permission of Sigmund Freud Copyrights, Wivenhoe.

p.437   *their meetings*: Abraham, Eitingon, and Sachs to Freud, November 26, 1924. Karl Abraham papers, LC.

p.437   *"durable one"*: Freud to Eitingon, November 11, 1921. By permission of Sigmund Freud Copyrights, Wivenhoe.

p.437   *"fit for her"*: Freud to Samuel Freud, March 7, 1922. In English. Rylands University Library, Manchester.

p.437   *fantasies at all*: Anna Freud to Freud, April 30, 1922. Freud Collection, LC. See also Anna Freud to Freud, April 27 and July 15, 1922. Ibid.

p.437   *June 1922*: Freud to Jones, June 4, 1922. In English. Freud Collection, D2, LC.

p.438   *"from the loss"*: Freud to Andreas-Salomé, July 3, 1922. Freud Collection, B3, LC.

p.438   *attachment lasted*: In 1930, in an affectionate postscript to one of her father's letters, Anna Freud ended, "I kiss you many times. Your Anna." (Freud and Anna Freud to Andreas-Salomé, October 22, 1930. Ibid.)

p.438   *"her father?"*: Freud to Samuel Freud, December 19, 1925. In English. Rylands University Library, Manchester.

p.438   *in 1920*: Anna Freud to Freud, August 9, 1920. Freud Collection, LC.

p.438   *"as it was?"*: Anna Freud to Freud, July 18, 1922. Ibid.

p.438   *"else to do"*: Anna Freud to Freud, July 20, 1922. Ibid.

p.438   *"uncomfortable"*: Anna Freud to Freud, July 23, 1915. Ibid.

p.438   *"shooting or dying"*: Anna Freud to Freud, August 5, 1919. Ibid.

p.438   *terrified her*: Anna Freud to Freud, July 12, 1915. Ibid.

p.439   *before the enemy*: Anna Freud to Freud, July 27, 1915. Ibid.

p.439   *a pistol*: Anna Freud to Freud, July 24, 1919. Ibid.

p.439   *"very agitating"*: Anna Freud to Freud, August 6, 1915. Ibid.

p.439   *attachment to him*: See, for a humorous "interpretation" of Anna Freud's king-princess dream, Freud to Anna Freud, July 14, 1915. Ibid.

p.439   *"father complex"*: Freud to Eitingon, December 2, 1919. By permission of Sigmund Freud Copyrights, Wivenhoe.

p.439   *"lesser man"*: Kardiner, *My Analysis with Freud,* 77.

p.439   *in 1924*: Again I am indebted to Elisabeth Young-Bruehl, for her talk at a meeting of the

Muriel Gardiner Program in Psychoanalysis and the Humanities, Yale University, January 15, 1987.

p.439 *hours with him:* See Anna Freud to Freud, August 5, 1918, and November 16, 1920. Freud Collection, LC.

p.440 *"analysis with you":* Anna Freud to Freud, July 24, 1919. Ibid.

p.440 *"friendship for you":* Freud to Kata Levy, August 16, 1920. Freud Collection, B9, LC.

p.440 *"to a close":* Freud to Jones, March 23, 1923. In English. Freud Collection, D2, LC. See also, among many other letters, Freud to Jones, June 4 and 25, 1922. In English. Ibid.

p.440 *"turned out well":* Freud to Weiss, November 1, 1935. *Freud–Weiss Briefe,* 91.

p.440 *"two of us!":* Freud to Andreas-Salomé, May 13, 1924. Freud Collection, B3, LC.

p.441 *"preparatory stage":* Freud to Andreas-Salomé, August 11, 1924. Ibid.

p.441 *"me with it":* Freud to Andreas-Salomé, May 10, 1925. Ibid.

p.441 *up smoking:* See Freud to Andreas-Salomé, March 13, 1922. Ibid.

p.441 *"to an end":* Freud to Andreas-Salomé, March 13, 1922. Ibid.

p.442 *his Antigone:* This point has been noted by, among others, Uwe Henrik Peters, in his *Anna Freud. Ein Leben für das Kind* (1979), 38–45.

p.442 *spring of 1923:* Freud to Ferenczi, May 10, 1923. Freud–Ferenczi Correspondence, Freud Collection, LC.

p.442 *"my two daughters":* Freud to Samuel Freud, December 13, 1923. In English. Rylands University Library, Manchester.

p.443 *half an hour:* See *Jones* III, 95, 196.

p.443 *"same to her!":* Freud to Eitingon, April 24, 1921. By permission of Sigmund Freud Copyrights, Wivenhoe. Freud addressed Eitingon as "Dear Max" for the first time on July 4, 1920, and kept it up after that. After some hesitation, he had come to regard Eitingon as virtually a member of his family. (See Freud to Eitingon, January 24, 1922. By permission of Sigmund Freud Copyrights, Wivenhoe.) Eitingon was probably the only member of his professional family with whom Freud was never very angry, or angry for long.

p.443 *"still at home":* Freud to Samuel Freud, December 4, 1921. In English. Rylands University Library, Manchester.

p.443 *"to independence":* Freud Collection, LC.

p.443 *"telepathic sensitivity":* Freud to Abraham, July 9, 1925. *Freud–Abraham,* 360 (387).

p.443 *"repelled him":* Anna Freud to Jones, November 24, 1955. Jones papers, Archives of the British Psycho-Analytical Society, London.

p.443 *never secure:* See *Jones* III, 380–81.

p.443 *cherished antiquities:* See ibid., 382.

p.443 *"materialistic prejudices":* Freud to Nandor Fodor, July 24, 1921. Typescript copy, Siegfried Bernfeld papers, container 17, LC.

p.444 *"and materialists":* "Psychoanalyse und Telepathie" (written 1921, published 1941), *GW* XVII, 28–29/"Psycho-Analysis and Telepathy," *SE* XVIII, 178–79.

p.444 *"'telepathy' or not":* "Traum und Telepathie" (1922), *GW* XIII, 165/"Dreams and Telepathy," *SE* XVIII, 197.

p.444 *"nothing about it":* Ibid., 191/220.

p.444 *"to disbelieve":* *Jones* III, 406.

p.444 *"Don't do it":* Freud to Ferenczi, March 20, 1925. Freud–Ferenczi Correspondence, LC. See also Ferenczi to "Dear Friends," February 15 and March 15, 1925, and Ferenczi to Freud, February 16 and March 16, 1925. Ibid.

p.445 *"for psychoanalysis":* Freud to Jones, March 7, 1926. Typescript copy, Freud Collection, D2, LC. In the early 1930s, in one of his *New Introductory Lectures* Freud alluded to telepathy with somewhat less reserve.

p.445 *"conscious bridge":* Anna Freud to Jones, November 24, 1955. Jones papers, Archives of the British Psycho-Analytical Society, London.

p.445 *"life and work":* Freud to Rank, April 10, 1924. Rank Collection, Box 1b. Rare Book and Manuscript Library, Columbia University.

p.445   *"now aloof"*: Freud to Jones, September 25, 1924. In English. Freud Collection, D2, LC.

p.445   *toward death:* Freud to Andreas-Salomé, May 10, 1925. *Freud–Salomé,* 169 (154).

p.446   *"or soul"*: H. D., "Advent," in *Tribute to Freud,* 171.

p.446   *"rehabilitation"*: Anna Freud to Abraham, March 20, 1925, in a long postscript to a letter her father had dictated to her. Karl Abraham papers, LC.

p.448   *"myself a Jew"*: George Sylvester Viereck, *Glimpses of the Great* (1930), 34. This interview was also published separately three years earlier, in 1927.

p.448   *"and the others"*: Freud to Pfister, December 25, 1920. *Freud–Pfister,* 81–82 (79).

p.449   *"longer alive"*: Freud to Eitingon, November 23, 1919. By permission of Sigmund Freud Copyrights, Wivenhoe.

p.449   *in the mind:* See *Introductory Lectures, SE* XVI, 284–85.

p.449   *"wild theories"*: Karl R. Popper, "Philosophy of Science: A Personal Report" (1953), in *British Philosophy in the Mid-Century: A Cambridge Symposium,* ed. C. A. Mace (1957), 156–58.

p.450   *"ultimate value"*: Thomas L. Masson, "Psychoanalysis Rampant," *New York Times,* February 4, 1923, sec. 3, 13.

p.450   *"invented discipline"*: Mary Keyt Isham, review of *Beyond the Pleasure Principle* and *Group Psychology and the Analysis of the Ego, New York Times,* September 7, 1924, sec. 3, 14–15.

p.451   *"into sex"*: "Critics Make Freud Symposium Target / Dr. Brian Brown Calls His Interpretation of the Unconscious Mind 'Rotten.' / Discussion at St. Mark's / Dr. Richard Borden Explains Soul-Sickness, Libido, Complexes and the 'Old Adam,' " *New York Times,* May 5, 1924, 8.

p.451   *"dreams and passions"*: "Dr. Wise Attacks Modern Writers / Tells Students at International House to Abandon Mencken for the Classics / Regrets Freudian Vogue / Declares War Has Lost for Religion the Faith and Loyalty of Millions," *New York Times,* March 16, 1925, 22.

p.451   *"spell the word"*: "Declares Freud Devotees / Can't Spell Psychoanalysis," *New York Times,* August 27, 1926, 7.

p.451   *"this Herr Amar"*: Eitingon to Freud, November 10, 1922. By permission of Sigmund Freud Copyrights, Wivenhoe.

p.451   *"of its meaning"*: "Mind Cure. / Professor Freud's Lectures," London *Times,* April 15, 1922, 17.

p.452   *"become fashionable"*: Poul Bjerre, *Wie deine Seele geheilt wird! Der Weg zur Lösung seelischer Konflikte,* tr. from the Swedish by Amalie Brückner (1925), 163.

p.452   *"America and England"*: William McDougall, *An Outline of Abnormal Psychology* (1926), 22. Quoted in Carl Christian Clemen, *Die Anwendung der Psychoanalyse auf Mythologie und Religionsgeschichte* (1928), 2–3.

p.452   *"Christian religion"*: Abraham, Eitingon, and Sachs to "Dear Friends," May 16, 1925. Karl Abraham papers, LC.

p.452   *"strong as now"*: Abraham to "Dear Friends," October 17, 1925. Ibid.

p.453   *"offered them"*: Elias Canetti, *Die Fackel im Ohr. Lebensgeschichte 1921–1931* (1980), 137–39.

p.453   *exposition of psychoanalysis:* Bjerre, *Wie deine Seele geheilt wird!,* 163.

p.453   *"mind and soul"*: William Bayard Hale papers, box 1, folder 12. Y-MA.

p.453   *"public goes"*: "Topics of the Times," *New York Times,* May 8, 1926, 16.

p.453   *" 'guineas a course!' "*: *Jones* III, 48n.

p.454   *young killers:* Quoted in ibid., 103.

p.454   *Freud declined:* See ibid.

p.454   *"suppressed desires?"*: "To Ask Freud to Come Here," *New York Times,* December 21, 1924, sec. 7, 3. See also *Jones* III, 114; and Clark, *Freud,* 461.

p.454   *"see Mr. Goldwyn"*: Quoted in *New York Times,* January 24, 1925, 13. See also *Jones* III, 114; and Clark, *Freud,* 462. The original of Freud's presumed letter has not turned up.

p.455   *"serious achievement":* Freud to Samuel Freud, November 5, 1920. In English. Rylands University Library, Manchester.

p.455   *"burden" to him:* Freud to Samuel Freud, December 4, 1921. In English. Ibid.

p.455   *popularity "repulsive":* Freud to Eitingon, January 24, 1922. By permission of Sigmund Freud Copyrights, Wivenhoe.

p.455   *"it is amusing":* Freud to Eitingon, February 17, 1921. By permission of Sigmund Freud Copyrights, Wivenhoe.

p.455   *"me with Einstein":* Freud to Samuel Freud, December 19, 1925. In English. Rylands University Library, Manchester.

p.455   *on modern thought:* See *Jones* III, 109–10.

p.455   *"chosen people":* Freud to Abraham, December 10, 1917. *Freud–Abraham,* 249 (264).

p.455   *"honorable reference":* Freud to Jones, June 9, 1925. Dictated to Anna Freud. Freud Collection, D2, LC.

p.455   *"for my wife":* Freud to Samuel Freud, December 19, 1925. In English. Rylands University Library, Manchester.

p.455   *gratified him:* See the certificate sent Freud by the Nederlandsche Vereeniging voor Psychiatrie en Neurologie after its meeting of November 17, 1921. Freud Museum, London. And see *Jones* III, 82 (giving the date, however, as December rather than November).

p.456   *"have a talk":* Freud to Samuel Freud, December 19, 1925. In English. Rylands University Library, Manchester.

p.456   *always in vain:* Freud to Emmy Groddeck, December 18, 1923. Groddeck, *Briefe über das Es,* 70–71.

p.456   *was in medicine:* See Mann to Meng, September 8, 1930. A. A. Brill Library, New York Psychoanalytic Institute.

p.457   *"in this affair?"* Freud to Jones, February 18, 1928. In English. Freud Collection, D2, LC.

p.457   *Prize for it:* See Freud to Eitingon, August 18, 1932. Quoted in *Jones* III, 175.

p.457   *Girindrasehkhar Bose:* See *Bose–Freud Correspondence* (n.d. [1964?]), a brochure published in Calcutta. Freud Collection, B9, LC.

p.457   *"of souls":* Stefan Zweig to Freud, December 8, 1929. By permission of Sigmund Freud Copyrights, Wivenhoe.

p.457   *"shoots himself":* Quoted in Friedrich Torberg, *Die Erben der Tante Jolesch* (1978; 2d ed. 1982), 26–27.

p.457   *Freudian jargon:* Ronald A. Knox, "Jottings from a Psycho-Analyst's Note-Book," in *Essays in Satire* (1928), 265–76.

p.458   *noted, "Pleasure–Principle":* James Thurber and E. B. White, *Is Sex Necessary? or, Why You Feel the Way You Do* (1929), 190–93.

p.458   *"in the 1880s":* Lippmann to Wallas, October 30, 1912. Quoted in Ronald Steel, *Walter Lippmann and the American Century* (1980), 46.

p.458   *"heard about him":* Lippmann to Frederick J. Hoffman, November 18, 1942. *Public Philosopher: Selected Letters of Walter Lippmann,* ed. John Morton Blum (1985), 429.

p.458   *among their students:* See Pfister to Freud, October 24, 1921; December 23, 1925; May 6 and October 21, 1927. By permission of Sigmund Freud Copyrights, Wivenhoe.

p.459   *"takes for granted":* Joseph Wood Krutch, "Freud Reaches Seventy Still Hard at Work/Father of Psychoanalysis Continues to Expand and Alter the Theories That Have Made Him a Storm Centre," *New York Times,* May 9, 1926, sec. 9, 9.

p.459   *"Ill-Chosen":* "Topics of the Times," *New York Times,* May 10, 1926, 20.

p.459   *"am 'notorious' ":* Freud to Arnold Zweig, December 20, 1937. *Freud–Zweig,* 164 (154). The word "notorious" is in English.

p.459   *come to stay:* "Nachschrift 1935" to "Selbstdarstellung," *GW* XVI, 34/"Postscript (1935)," to "Autobiographical Study," *SE* XX, 73. (In the English version, "Russia," accidentally omitted in the German original, was added with Freud's permission.)

p.461   *than Freud:* Alix Strachey to James Strachey, February 9, 1925. *Bloomsbury/Freud,* 184.

p.461   *"very German"*: "The Reminiscences of Rudolph M. Loewenstein" (1965), 19–25. Oral History Collection, Columbia University.

p.461   *"mainly theologians"*: Abraham, Eitingon, and Sachs to "Dear Friends," December 16, 1924. Karl Abraham papers, LC.

p.461   *to the speaker:* Abraham, Eitingon, and Sachs to "Dear Friends," March 15, 1925. Ibid.

p.461   *"of success!"*: Abraham and Sachs to "Dear Friends," April 13, 1925. Ibid.

p.462   *Eitingon's money:* See Phyllis Grosskurth, *Melanie Klein: Her World and Her Work* (1986), 94.

p.462   *essential idea:* See Ernst Simmel, "Zur Geschichte und sozialen Bedeutung des Berliner Psychoanalytischen Instituts," in *Zehn Jahre Berliner Psychoanalytisches Institut (Poliklinik und Lehranstalt),* ed. Deutsche Psychoanalytische Gesellschaft (1930), 7–8.

p.462   *"come to this"*: "Wege der psychoanalytischen Therapie" (1919), *GW* XII, 192–93/ "Lines of Advance in Psycho-Analytic Therapy," *SE* XVII, 167.

p.462   *"public opinion"*: Simmel, "Zur Geschichte," in *Zehn Jahre Berliner Psychoanalytisches Institut,* 12.

p.462   *been cured:* See Otto Fenichel, "Statistischer Bericht über die therapeutische Tätigkeit 1920–1930," in ibid., 16.

p.463   *seasoned practitioner:* See ibid., 19.

p.463   *"least a year"*: "Anhang: Richtlinien für die Lehrtätigkeit des Instituts," following Karen Horney, "Die Einrichtungen der Lehranstalt, A) Zur Organisation," in ibid., 50.

p.463   *"in a church"*: Hanns Sachs, "Die Einrichtungen der Lehranstalt, B) Die Lehranalyse," in ibid., 53.

p.463   *"Pontifex maximus"*: Freud to Jones, June 4, 1922. In English. Freud Collection, D2, LC.

p.463   *inspiring seriousness:* See, for example, Gregory Zilboorg, "Ausländisches Interesse am Institut, A) Aus Amerika," in *Zehn Jahre Berliner Psychoanalytisches Institut,* 66–69; and Ola Raknes, "Ausländisches Interesse am Institut, B) Aus Norwegen," in ibid., 69–70.

p.464   *daughter Sophie:* Interview by author with Jeanne Lampl-de Groot, October 24, 1985.

p.464   *"dear Jeanne"*: See, for example, Freud to Lampl-de Groot, August 28, 1924. Freud Collection, D2, LC.

p.464   *"counting on me"*: Freud to Abraham, March 3, 1925. Dictated to Anna Freud. Karl Abraham papers, LC.

p.465   *and "wit"*: Thus in 1916, when he translated Freud's book on jokes, *Der Witz und seine Beziehung zum Unbewussten,* he rendered the title as *Wit and Its Relation to the Unconscious.*

p.465   *"scarlet parasol"*: Katharine West, *Inner and Outer Circles* (1958). Quoted in Paula Heimann, "Obituary, Joan Riviere (1883–1962)," *Int. J. Psycho-Anal.,* XLIV (1963), 233.

p.466   *"for any more"*: Freud to Jones, November 16, 1924. Dictated to Anna Freud. Freud Collection, D2, LC.

p.466   *"very slowly"*: Freud to Jones, December 13, 1925. Dictated to Anna Freud. Ibid.

p.467   *"swarthy Hungarians"*: Alix Strachey to James Strachey, December 13 [really 14, 1924]. *Bloomsbury/Freud,* 131–32.

p.468   *"than usual"*: Ibid., 132–33.

p.468   *"pedagogic matters"*: Freud to Jones, July 22, 1925. Dictated to Anna Freud. Freud Collection, D2, LC.

p.469   *"presuppositions"*: Freud to Jones, May 31, 1927. Dictated to Anna Freud. Ibid.

p.469   *"no proof"*: Freud to Jones, July 6, 1927. Ibid.

p.469   *"you yourself"*: Freud to Jones, September 23, 1927. Ibid.

p.469   *attacks on himself:* See Freud to Jones, September 23 and October 9, 1927. Ibid.

p.469   *has experienced:* See *Civilization and Its Discontents, SE* XXI, 130n, 138n.

p.469   *"daughter, Anna Freud"*: "Selbstdarstellung," *GW* XIV, 96n/"Autobiographical Study," *SE* XX, 70n.

CHAPTER TEN · *Flickering Lights on Dark Continents*

p.471   *"hysterical hilariousness"*: Anna Freud to Jones, January 8, 1956. Jones papers, Archives of the British Psycho-Analytical Society, London.

p.471   *copies of him:* See Freud to Ferenczi, July 18, 1920. Freud–Ferenczi Correspondence, Freud Collection, LC.

p.471   Hochstaplernatur: Freud to Eitingon, July 2, 1927. By permission of Sigmund Freud Copyrights, Wivenhoe.

p.471   *"splendid book"*: Freud to Rank, August 18, 1912. Rank Collection, Box 1b. Rare Book and Manuscript Library, Columbia University. He had in mind Rank's bulky study of the incest theme in literature.

p.471   *"quite comprehensible"*: Freud to Abraham, December 25, 1918. Karl Abraham papers, LC.

p.472   the *"uncanny"*: See "The 'Uncanny' " (1919), *SE* XVII, 230n.

p.472   *of advice:* Freud to Rank, July 8, 1922. Rank Collection, Box 1b. Rare Book and Manuscript Library, Columbia University.

p.472   *"to the contrary"*: Freud to Rank, September 8, 1922. Ibid.

p.473   *"R [ank] and Jones"*: Eitingon to Freud, January 31, 1924. By permission of Sigmund Freud Copyrights, Wivenhoe.

p.473   *remain unimpaired:* See Freud to "Dear Friends," January 1924. Photocopy of typescript copy, Rank Collection, Box 1b. Rare Book and Manuscript Library, Columbia University.

p.473   *"or from F[erenczi]"*: Freud to Eitingon, February 7, 1924. By permission of Sigmund Freud Copyrights, Wivenhoe.

p.473   *pacific stance:* Rank to Freud, February 15, 1924. Rank Collection, Box 1b. Rare Book and Manuscript Library, Columbia University.

p.473   *"of the warner"*: Abraham to Freud, February 21, 1924. *Freud–Abraham,* 324 (348–49).

p.474   *"evil fellow"*: Freud to Ferenczi, March 20, 1924. Typescript copy, Rank Collection, Box 1b. Rare Book and Manuscript Library, Columbia University.

p.474   *"of defection"*: Ferenczi to Rank, March 18, 1924. Ibid.

p.474   *"against Abraham"*: Freud to Ferenczi, March 26, 1924. Typescript copy, ibid.

p.474   *published at all:* Rank to Ferenczi, March 20, 1924. Ibid. Actually, the circular letters Freud wrote during this time strongly suggest that he had fully grasped Rank's message.

p.474   *"not see it"*: Freud to "Dear Friends," February 25, 1924. Ibid.

p.474   *it for analysts:* March 5, 1924. Vienna Psychoanalytic Society, minutes for 1923–24, kept by Otto Isakower. Freud Collection, B27, LC.

p.475   *"source of anxiety"*: November 25, 1908. *Protokolle,* II, 65.

p.475   *"of birth on"*: November 17, 1909. Ibid., 293.

p.475   *"affect of anxiety"*: *Traumdeutung, GW* II–III, 406n / *Interpretation of Dreams, SE* V, 400–401n.

p.475   *"wholly die"*: Freud to Rank, December 1, 1923. Rank Collection, Box 1b. Rare Book and Manuscript Library, Columbia University.

p.475   *had been right:* Freud to Abraham, March 4, 1924. *Freud–Abraham,* 328 (352–53).

p.475   *even desirable:* Freud to "Dear Friends," January 1924. Rank Collection, Box 1b. Rare Book and Manuscript Library, Columbia University.

p.476   *kind to him:* See esp. Freud to Ferenczi, March 26, 1924. Typescript copy, ibid.

p.476   *"on his mind"*: Freud to Jones, September 25, 1924. In English. Freud Collection, D2, LC.

p.476   *"scientific regression"*: Abraham to Freud, February 26, 1924. *Freud–Abraham,* 326 (350–51).

p.476   *must come first:* Jones to Abraham, April 8, 1924. Karl Abraham papers, LC.

p.476   *mere one-third:* See Freud to Ferenczi, March 26, 1924. Typescript copy, Rank Collection, Box 1b. Rare Book and Manuscript Library, Columbia University.

p.477 *"muddled babbler"*: Freud to Sándor Radó, September 30, 1925. Dictated to Anna Freud. Freud Collection, B9, LC.

p.477 *"others before him"*: Freud to Burrow, July 31, 1924. Trigant Burrow papers, series I, box 12. Y-MA.

p.477 *"ze mozer!"*: Quoted in E. James Lieberman, *Acts of Will: The Life and Work of Otto Rank* (1985), 235.

p.477 *"open to yourself"*: Freud to Rank, July 23, 1924. Rank Collection, Box 1b. Rare Book and Manuscript Library, Columbia University.

p.477 *"quite impossible"*: Rank to Freud, August 7, 1924. Ibid. The letter he did mail, though very similar, does not contain this decisive passage. (August 9, 1924. Ibid.)

p.477 *"shaken by nothing"*: Freud to Rank, August 27, 1924. Ibid.

p.478 *"Berlin conspiracy"*: Eitingon to Freud, September 2, 1924. By permission of Sigmund Freud Copyrights, Wivenhoe.

p.478 *"is mentioned"*: Freud to Eitingon, October 7, 1924. By permission of Sigmund Freud Copyrights, Wivenhoe.

p.478 *little wistfully:* Freud to Abraham, October 17, 1924. *Freud–Abraham,* 345 (371).

p.478 *"this interview"*: Freud to Jones, October 23, 1924. In English. Freud Collection, D2, LC. For instances of Freud preparing himself to give up on Rank around this time, see Freud to Eitingon, September 27 and November 19, 1924. By permission of Sigmund Freud Copyrights, Wivenhoe.

p.478 *"such an extent"*: Freud to Jones, November 5, 1924. Dictated to Anna Freud. Freud Collection, D2, LC.

p.478 *"always a gentleman"*: Jones to Abraham, November 12, 1924. Karl Abraham papers, LC. See also circular letter to "Dear Friends" from Berlin, November 26, 1924. Ibid.

p.478 *"had a thrashing"*: Freud to Andreas-Salomé, November 17, 1924. *Freud–Salomé,* 157 (143).

p.478 *fault to himself:* See Freud to Jones, November 16, 1924. Dictated to Anna Freud. Freud Collection, D2, LC.

p.479 *to boot:* Rank to the Committee, December 20, 1924. Quoted in Lieberman, *Rank,* 248–50.

p.479 *of responsibility:* Jones to Abraham, December 29, 1924. Karl Abraham papers, LC.

p.479 *alongside his comrades:* Freud to Jones, January 6, 1925. Dictated to Anna Freud. Freud Collection, D2, LC.

p.479 *"ever occur again"*: Freud to Eitingon, January 6, 1925. By permission of Sigmund Freud Copyrights, Wivenhoe.

p.479 *from his colleagues:* Eitingon, Sachs, and Abraham to Rank, December 25, 1924. Rank Collection, Box 1b. Rare Book and Manuscript Library, Columbia University.

p.480 *ist die Tat:* Jones to Rank, January 3, 1925. Ibid.

p.480 *first stay:* Freud to Jones, January 6, 1925. Dictated to Anna Freud. Freud Collection, D2, LC.

p.480 *"full confidence"*: Freud to Abraham, March 3, 1925. Karl Abraham papers, LC.

p.480 *unpredictable disciple:* See Freud to Eitingon, July 16, 1925. By permission of Sigmund Freud Copyrights, Wivenhoe.

p.480 *sadly pertinent:* See Abraham to Freud, February 26, 1924. *Freud–Abraham,* 326 (350–51). Freud himself had hesitantly drawn such a comparison. See Freud to Ferenczi, March 20, 1924. Rank Collection, Box 1b. Rare Book and Manuscript Library, Columbia University.

p.480 *"invalidate my work"*: Freud to Rank, November 26, 1923. Rank Collection, Box 1b. Rare Book and Manuscript Library, Columbia University.

p.481 *on his neurosis:* Freud to Rank, July 23, 1924. Ibid.

p.481 *quite irresistible:* Freud to Andreas-Salomé, November 17, 1924. *Freud–Salomé,* 157 (143).

p.481 *"presumably Freud"*: Jones to Freud, September 29, 1924. Quoted in Vincent Brome, *Ernest Jones: Freud's Alter Ego* (English ed., 1982; American ed., 1983), 147.

p.481   *"anal-sadistic":* Abraham to Freud, October 20, 1924. *Freud–Abraham,* 347 (373).
p.481   *"egotistic motives":* Freud to Abraham, March 4, 1924. Ibid., 327 (352).
p.481   *analysts' quarrels:* Freud to Abraham, March 31, 1924. Ibid., 331 (355).
p.482   *"had never closed":* Freud to Robert Breuer, June 26, 1925. Quoted in full in Albrecht Hirschmüller, " 'Balsam auf eine schmerzende Wunde'—Zwei bisher unbekannte Briefe Sigmund Freuds über sein Verhältnis zu Josef Breuer," *Psyche,* XLI (1987), 58.
p.482   *Freud from bed:* See Abraham to Freud, June 7, 1925. *Freud–Abraham,* 355 (382).
p.482   *"overcome the disorder":* Freud to Abraham, September 11, 1925. Ibid., 367 (395).
p.482   *"striking way":* Abraham to "Dear Friends," October 17, 1925. Karl Abraham papers, LC.
p.482   *"sound so uncanny":* Freud to Jones, December 13, 1925. Dictated to Anna Freud. Freud Collection, D2, LC.
p.483   *"event occurs":* Freud to Jones, December 16, 1925. In English. Ibid.
p.483   *working well:* Freud to Jones, December 21, 1925. Dictated to Anna Freud. Ibid.
p.483   *"being truthful":* Freud to Jones, December 30, 1925. Ibid.
p.483   *"of its future":* "Karl Abraham" (1926), *GW* XIV, 564 / "Karl Abraham," *SE* XX, 277. First published in the *Internationale Zeitschrift für Psychoanalyse,* XII (1926), 1.
p.483   *"of earning":* Freud to Eitingon, March 19, 1926. By permission of Sigmund Freud Copyrights, Wivenhoe.
p.484   *"very large":* Freud to Eitingon, April 13, 1926. By permission of Sigmund Freud Copyrights, Wivenhoe.
p.484   *"belongs to us":* Freud to Eitingon, June 7, 1926. By permission of Sigmund Freud Copyrights, Wivenhoe.
p.484   *"more completely":* Hemmung, Symptom und Angst (1926), *GW* XIV, 194 / *Inhibitions, Symptoms and Anxiety, SE* XX, 161.
p.484   *"after all":* Freud to Andreas-Salomé, May 13, 1926. *Freud–Salomé,* 178 (163).
p.485   *"justified to me":* Hemmung, Symptom und Angst, *GW* XIV, 193 / *Inhibitions, Symptoms and Anxiety, SE* XX, 160–61.
p.485   *"author's self-criticism":* Psychopathologie des Alltagslebens, *GW* IV, 112 / *Psychopathology of Everyday Life, SE* VI, 101.
p.486   *"praecordial region":* D. Hack Tuke, ed., *A Dictionary of Psychological Medicine,* vol. I, 96.
p.486   *"made clearer":* Eugen Bleuler, *Textbook of Psychiatry* (1916; 4th ed., 1923; tr. A. A. Brill, 1924), 119.
p.487   *done their work:* See *Inhibitions, Symptoms and Anxiety, SE* XX, 139.
p.488   *"method of defense":* Ibid., 195–96/163.
p.489   *belong to them:* Ibid., 149–52/119–21.
p.490   *"listen to me":* Freud to Abraham, November 28, 1924. Karl Abraham papers, LC.
p.490   *"medical practice":* Quoted in a long letter from Reik to Abraham, April 11, 1925. Karl Abraham papers, LC.
p.490   *continued to practice:* See ibid.
p.490   *"first lay pupils":* Pfister to Freud, September 10, 1926. *Freud–Pfister,* 109 (104). Pfister's principal opponent was Emil Oberholzer, president of the Swiss Society for Psychoanalysis until 1927, whom Freud, taking Pfister's side, called "a stubborn fool whom one best leaves alone." (Freud to Pfister, February 11, 1928. By permission of Sigmund Freud Copyrights, Wivenhoe.) See also, among Pfister's accounts of Swiss psychoanalytic affairs, above all Pfister to Freud, February 16, 1925. (Ibid.)
p.491   *"swallowed by medicine":* Freud to Federn, March 27, 1926. Typescript copy. By permission of Sigmund Freud Copyrights, Wivenhoe.
p.491   *"it at length":* Quoted in Erika Freeman, *Insights: Conversations with Theodor Reik* (1971), 86–87.
p.491   *"psychoanalytic research":* Quoted in ibid., 87. Reik recalled the same point in his long letter to Abraham, April 11, 1925. Karl Abraham papers, LC.

p.491   *"can write well":* Freud to Abraham, February 15, 1914. Karl Abraham papers, LC. See also Freud to Abraham, March 25, May 17, and July 15, 1914. Ibid.

p.492   *"effect good": New York Times,* May 25, 1927, 6.

p.492   *they attempt it:* "Geleitwort" (1913), *GW* X, 450 / "Introduction to Pfister's *The Psycho-Analytic Method," SE* XII, 330–31.

p.493   *"of psychiatry": Die Frage der Laienanalyse. Unterredungen mit einem Unparteiischen* (1926), *GW* XIV, 261, 282–83 / *The Question of Lay Analysis: Conversations with an Impartial Person, SE* XX, 229, 247–48.

p.493   *"distant future": Jones* III, 287, 289.

p.493   *and psychiatry:* See *Lay Analysis, SE* XX, 246.

p.493   *mundane realities: Jones* III, 289.

p.493   *"perverted sex":* Quoted in John C. Burnham, "The Influence of Psychoanalysis upon American Culture," in *American Psychoanalysis: Origins and Development,* ed. Jacques M. Quen and Eric T. Carlson (1978), 61.

p.494   *"of Individualism":* "American Accused As London 'Charlatan' / Bow Street Police Recommend Deportation for Homer Tyrell Lane, Psychoanalist [*sic*], 'Individualist,' " *New York Times,* March 18, 1925, 19.

p.494   *never return:* "Imprisons Psychoanalyst / London Magistrate Sentences H. T. Lane of Boston," *New York Times,* March 25, 1925, 2. See also "London Court Fines American Alienist / And He Must Leave Country / Letters From Women Signed 'God' and 'Devil' Read," *New York Times,* May 15, 1925, 22.

p.494   *"Freud and Jung":* "Pastor Rakes Quacks in Psychoanalysis / Many Mulcted by Fakers, Warns Rev. C. F. Potter— / Would License Teachers," *New York Times,* March 30, 1925, 20.

p.494   *"on the job":* Jelliffe to Jones, February 10, 1927. Quoted in John C. Burnham, *Jelliffe: American Psychoanalyst and Physician* (1983), 124.

p.495   *ultimately unconvincing:* "Discussion on Lay Analysis," *Int. J. Psycho-Anal.,* VIII (1927), 221–22.

p.495   *"for the physician":* Ibid., 246.

p.495   *"to be avoided":* Ibid., 274.

p.495   *"of the physician":* Ibid., 251.

p.495   *"qualified persons":* Rickman, in ibid., 211.

p.495   *were not physicians: Jones* III, 293.

p.496   *"injury to patients":* The Hungarian Psycho-Analytical Society, "Discussion on Lay Analysis," *Int. J. Psycho-Anal.,* VIII (1927), 281.

p.496   *"finds its ideology":* Ibid., 248.

p.496   *"patients very much":* "Nachwort" to *Laienanalyse, GW* XIV, 290–91 / "Postscript" to *Lay Analysis, SE* XX, 253–54.

p.497   *extreme views:* See Freud to Jones, May 31, 1927. Dictated to Anna Freud. Freud Collection, D2, LC.

p.497   *"psychological research":* Freud to "Sehr geehrter Herr Kollege," October 19, 1927. Freud Collection, B4, LC.

p.497   *"without an army":* Freud to Eitingon, April 3, 1928. By permission of Sigmund Freud Copyrights, Wivenhoe.

p.497   *soundly as possible:* "Nachwort" to *Laienananalyse, GW* XIV, 295–96 / "Postscript" to *Lay Analysis, SE* XX, 258.

p.497   *"interest in psychoanalysis":* Constitution of the New York Psychoanalytic Society, adopted March 28, 1911. Quoted in Samuel Atkin, "The New York Psychoanalytic Society and Institute: Its Founding and Development," in *American Psychoanalysis,* ed. Quen and Carlson, 73.

p.498   *"anatomy and pathology":* A. A. Brill, *Fundamental Conceptions of Psychoanalysis* (1921), iv.

p.498   *reproved him sharply:* See Brill to Jelliffe, May 1, 1921. Quoted in Burnham, *Jelliffe,* 118.

p.498   *a time in 1921:* See Freud to Leonhard Blumgart, June 19, 1921. A. A. Brill Library, New

York Psychoanalytic Institute. It emerges from this letter that Newton had already been in analysis with Blumgart before coming to Vienna.

p.498 *reasonable request:* See Abraham, Sachs, and Eitingon to "Dear Friends," March 15, 1925. Karl Abraham papers, LC.

p.498 *"egotistical interests":* Freud to Jones, September 25, 1925. Dictated to Anna Freud. Freud Collection, D2, LC.

p.499 *"psychoanalytic therapy":* Minutes of the New York Psychoanalytic Society for October 27, 1925. A. A. Brill Library, New York Psychoanalytic Institute.

p.499 *"own efforts":* Freud to Jones, September 27, 1926. In English. Freud Collection, D2, LC.

p.499 *"are subject":* "Discussion on Lay Analysis," *Int. J. Psycho-Anal.,* VIII (1927), 283.

p.499 *"still result":* Freud to Jones, September 23, 1927. Freud Collection, D2, LC. The passages shown in single quotes, obviously repeated directly from Brill's letter, are in English.

p.500 *"of analysis":* Freud to de Saussure, February 21, 1928. Freud Collection, Z3, LC.

p.500 *of lay analysis:* See *Jones* III, 297–98.

p.500 *"point of view":* Freud to Jones, August 4, 1929. Freud Collection, D2, LC.

p.500 *"sixteenth-analysts":* Freud to Jones, October 19, 1929. Ibid.

p.500 *"for the present":* Ferenczi to "Dear Friends," November 30, 1930. Freud Collection, LC.

p.501 *"obscure to me":* Freud to Abraham, December 8, 1924. *Freud–Abraham,* 350 (376).

p.501 *"and uncertain":* Freud to Jones, February 22, 1928. Freud Collection, D2, LC.

p.501 *"dark continent":* Laienanalyse, GW XIV, 241 / *Lay Analysis,* SE XX, 212. The phrase "dark continent" is in English in the original.

p.501 *"my judgment":* Freud to Jones, February 22, 1928. Freud Collection, D2, LC.

p.501 *"woman want?":* Undated remark to Marie Bonaparte. Quoted in *Jones* II, 421, translation of phrase slightly changed from Jones's version.

p.502 *"coherent information":* "Die Weiblichkeit," in *Neue Folge der Vorlesungen zur Einfüh-rung in die Psychoanalyse* (1933), GW XV, 145 / "Femininity," in *New Introductory Lectures on Psycho-Analysis,* SE XXII, 135. Although dated 1933, this volume was actually published in December 1932.

p.503 *"on principle":* April 13, 1910. *Protokolle,* II, 440.

p.503 *man ever could:* "Über die weibliche Sexualität" (1931), GW XIV, 519 / "Female Sexuality," SE XXI, 226–27.

p.504 *under ten:* For the dating, which contradicts Freud's own assignment of the dream to his "seventh or eighth year," see William J. McGrath, *Freud's Discovery of Psychoanalysis: The Politics of Hysteria* (1986), 34; and Eva M. Rosenfeld, "Dreams and Vision: Some Remarks on Freud's Egyptian Bird Dream," *Int. J. Psycho-Anal.,* XXXVII (1956) 97–105.

p.504 *woke up screaming: Traumdeutung,* GW II–III, 589–90 / *Interpretation of Dreams,* SE V, 583.

p.504 *"highly intelligent":* Martin Freud, "Who Was Freud?" in *The Jews of Austria: Essays on Their Life, History and Destruction,* ed. Josef Fraenkel (1967), 202.

p.505 *"ridicule, herself":* Judith Bernays Heller, "Freud's Mother and Father: A Memoir," *Commentary,* XXI (1956), 420.

p.505 *"golden son":* There is a picture postcard Amalia sent to her son (no date) showing her sitting in front of an Alpine backdrop, with the inscription "My golden son." (Freud Museum, London.)

p.505 *"of his childhood": Drei Abhandlungen, GW V, 129 / Three Essays,* SE VII, 228.

p.505 *"housewife's psychosis":* "Dora," GW V, 178 / *SE* VII, 20.

p.505 *not have lived:* "Reading these cases, I could not help wondering about the discrepancy in Freud's presentations of his patients' fathers and mothers. Why is it always the father who becomes the central part of the child-parent relationship, regardless of whether the child is male or female? . . . Perhaps these portrayals were bound up with Freud's self-analysis, or, more specifically, with his preoccupation at that time with the relationship between himself and his father. Whatever the reason, the 'oedipal mother' in Freud's early work is a static figure, a Jocasta who unknowingly plays out her destiny while Laius springs back to life." (Iza S. Erlich, "What Happened to Jocasta?" *Bulletin of the Menninger Clinic,* XLI [1977], 283–84.)

p.505   *"later rivalry":* Massenpsychologie, *GW* XIII, 110n / Group Psychology, *SE* XVIII, 101n.

p.506   *"human relationships":* "Die Weiblichkeit," in *Neue Folge der Vorlesungen, GW* XV, 143 / "Femininity," in *New Introductory Lectures, SE* XXII, 133. He had said much the same thing a little earlier, when he wrote that aggression "forms the fundamental sediment of every tender and amorous relation among humans, perhaps with the single exception of a mother with her male child." (*Das Unbehagen in der Kultur, GW* XIV, 473 / *Civilization and Its Discontents, SE* XXI, 113.)

p.506   *"mother's love?":* Jones II, 433.

p.506   *pre-oedipal development:* See "Female Sexuality," *SE* XXI, 235.

p.506   *"of the circumstances":* "Die Weiblichkeit," in *Neue Folge der Vorlesungen, GW* XV, 131 / "Femininity," in *New Introductory Lectures, SE* XXII, 122–23.

p.507   *death wishes:* Ernest Jones (*Jones* I, 7) and Robert D. Stolorow and George E. Atwood ("A Defensive-Restitutive Function of Freud's Theory of Psychosexual Development," *Psychoanalytic Review,* LXV [1978], 217–38), have asserted that Freud was in fact *eleven* months old when his brother Julius was born. If so, of course, this would greatly enhance the emotional relevance and evidentiary value of Freud's reference to "eleven months" in his paper on femininity. To be sure, Freud may have believed this: Jones offers no documentation for his flat assertion, and it is plausible to conjecture that he had the information from Freud himself. The facts, however, are somewhat different: Freud was born on May 6, 1856; Julius was born in October 1857 and died on April 15, 1858. (See "Chronology," in Krüll, *Freud and His Father,* 214. For these details, Krüll cites the researches of Josef Sajner.)

p.507   *"no sharing":* "Die Weiblichkeit," in *Neue Folge der Vorlesungen, GW* XV, 131 / "Femininity," in *New Introductory Lectures,* SE XXII, 123.

p.507   *medical form:* See Freud to Fliess, Draft B, enclosed in letter of February 8, 1893. *Freud–Fliess,* 27 (39).

p.507   *good as a man:* See "Frau Emmy von N.," in Breuer and Freud, *Studies on Hysteria, SE* II, 103.

p.507   *sexually passive:* See Freud to Fliess, Draft K, enclosed in letter of January 1, 1896. *Freud–Fliess,* 176–77 (169).

p.508   *imposed by society:* See Freud to Fliess, Draft G, n.d. [the editors give it to January 7, 1895]. Ibid., 101 (101).

p.508   *that of aggressor:* See "Gradiva," *SE,* IX, 38.

p.508   *"men always do":* Freud to Ferenczi, January 12, 1919. Freud–Ferenczi Correspondence, Freud Collection, LC.

p.508   *"to the light":* Freud to Jones, March 23, 1923. In English. Freud Collection, D2, LC.

p.509   *after country:* I have tried to offer such an analysis in *Education of the Senses,* vol. I of *The Bourgeois Experience;* see esp. ch. 2, "Offensive Women and Defensive Men."

p.510   *"spiritual servitude":* Quoted in Erika Weinzierl, *Emanzipation? Österreichische Frauen im 20. Jahrhundert* (1975), 37.

p.510   *"German-patriarchal":* Helene Weber, *Ehefrau und Mutter in der Rechtsentwicklung. Eine Einführung* (1907), 343. See also Richard J. Evans, *The Feminists: Women's Emancipation Movements in Europe, America and Australasia 1840–1920* (1977), 92–98.

p.511   *"of their own":* Zweig, *Die Welt von Gestern,* 79, 81.

p.511   *"enthusiastic supporters":* Quoted in Juliet Mitchell, *Psychoanalysis and Feminism: Freud, Reich, Laing and Women* (1974; paperback ed., 1975), 419.

p.512   *"feeble-minded":* Freud's lecture of April 16, 1904, is summarized in Klein, *Jewish Origins of the Psychoanalytic Movement,* 159.

p.512   *Moebius in print:* See " 'Civilized' Sexual Morality and Modern Nervous Illness," *SE* IX, 199.

p.512   *most—sexuality:* Die Zukunft einer Illusion (1927), *GW* XIV, 371 / *The Future of an Illusion, SE* XXI, 48.

p.512   *"dogs can be":* Freud to Andreas-Salomé, May 8, 1930. *Freud–Salomé,* 205 (188).

p.512   *einfälliger:* Freud to Arnold Zweig, August 18, 1933. By permission of Sigmund Freud Copyrights, Wivenhoe.

p.512   *"even the women":* March 11, 1908. *Protokolle,* I, 329.

p.513   *"most a few":* Ibid., 331.

p.513   *"of any kind":* William Acton, *The Functions and Disorders of the Reproductive Organs, in Childhood, Youth, Adult Age, and Advanced Life, Considered in their Physiological, Social, and Moral Relations* (1857; 3d ed., 1865), 133.

p.513   *"that of the man":* Otto Adler, *Die mangelhafte Geschlechtsempfindung des Weibes. Anaesthesia sexualis feminarum. Dyspareunia. Anaphrodisia* (1904), 124.

p.514   *weaker than man's:* See " 'Civilized' Sexual Morality and Modern Nervous Illness," *SE* IX, 191–92.

p.514   *"masculine character":* Drei Abhandlungen, *GW* V, 120 / *Three Essays, SE* VII, 219.

p.514   *"that of boys":* "Die Disposition zur Zwangsneurose" (1913), *GW* VIII, 452 / "The Disposition to Obsessional Neurosis," *SE* XII, 325.

p.514   *it is "active":* Drei Abhandlungen, *GW* V, 121n / *Three Essays, SE* VII, 219n (note added in 1915).

p.515   *called phallic:* See "The Infantile Genital Organization (An Interpolation into the Theory of Sexuality)" (1923), *SE* XIX, 141–45.

p.515   *"is destiny":* "Der Untergang des Ödipuskomplexes" (1924), *GW* XIII, 400 / "The Dissolution of the Oedipus Complex," *SE* XIX, 178.

p.515   *losing love:* See ibid.

p.516   *"hostile feelings":* "Einige psychische Folgen des anatomischen Geschlechtsunterschieds" (1925), *GW* XIV, 29–30 / "Some Psychical Consequences of the Anatomical Distinction between the Sexes," *SE* XIX, 257–58. The debate over Freud's ideas on female sexuality continues, both within psychoanalytic circles and outside them. James A. Kleeman, a leading expert (himself an analyst) critical of Freud, has nevertheless observed, "What is remarkable about Freud's ideas on early sexuality, derived as these were largely from the analyses of adults, is that so many of them have withstood the test of time." (James A. Kleeman, "Freud's Views on Early Female Sexuality in the Light of Direct Child Observation," in *Female Psychology: Contemporary Psychoanalytic Views,* ed. Harold P. Blum [1977], 3.) For a detailed canvass of the controversy and the literature, see the bibliographical essay for this chapter.

p.516   *"position and value":* "Einige psychische Folgen," *GW* XIV, 30 / "Some Psychical Consequences," *SE* XIX, 258.

p.516   *"time" before him:* Ibid., 20 / 249. The phrase quoted is in English in Freud's original.

p.518   *"behind the Greek":* "Weibliche Sexualität," *GW* XIV, 519 / "Female Sexuality," *SE* XXI, 226.

p.518   *than for men:* See ibid., 523, 529, 531–33 / 230, 235, 237–39.

p.518   *"understanding before":* Ibid., 523 / 230.

p.518   "the castration complex": "Einige psychische Folgen," *GW* XIV, 28 / "Some Psychical Consequences," *SE* XIX, 256.

p.519   *"education, reading":* Das Ich und das Es, *GW* XIII, 263 / *The Ego and the Id, SE* XIX, 34.

p.519   *"erotogenic zone":* "Die Disposition zur Zwangsneurose," *GW* VIII, 452 / "The Disposition to Obsessional Neurosis," *SE* XII, 325–26.

p.520   *"attachment to the father":* Karen Horney, "On the Genesis of the Castration Complex in Women," in *Feminine Psychology,* a collection of Horney's papers, ed. Harold Kelman (1967), 52–53. The paper was first published in German, in 1923, and then appeared in English in *Int. J. Psycho-Anal.,* V, part 1 (1924), 50–65.

p.520   *"biological science":* Ibid., in *Feminine Psychology,* ed. Kelman, 38.

p.520   *"masculine psychology":* Horney, "The Flight from Womanhood: The Masculinity-Complex in Women as Viewed by Men and by Women," in *Feminine Psychology,* ed. Kelman, 54. The paper was published in German in 1926, and appeared in English in *Int. J. Psycho-Anal.,* VII (1926), 324–39.

p.520   *common among psychoanalysts:* See ibid., in *Feminine Psychology,* ed. Kelman, 57–58.

p.521   *"unconscious male tendency":* Ibid., 62.

p.521   *"a little man":* Jeanne Lampl-de Groot, "The Evolution of the Oedipus Complex in Women," in *The Development of the Mind: Psychoanalytic Papers on Clinical and Theoretical Problems* (1965), 9.

p.521   *"worked on anew":* Freud to Jones, January 23, 1932. Freud Collection, D2, LC.

p.521   *"born or made":* Ernest Jones, "Early Female Sexuality" (1935), in *Papers on Psycho-Analysis* (4th ed., 1938), 606, 616.

p.521   *"Author's Gratitude":* Dedication in Jones, *Papers on Psycho-Analysis.*

p.522   *psychological experiences:* See Otto Fenichel, "The Pregenital Antecedents of the Oedipus Complex" (1930), "Specific Forms of the Oedipus Complex" (1931), and "Further Light upon the Pre-oedipal Phase in Girls" (1934), in *The Collected Papers of Otto Fenichel,* ed. Hanna Fenichel and David Rapaport, 1st Series (1953), 181–203, 204–20, and 241–88. Freud took note of the first of these papers in his "Female Sexuality" (*SE* XXI, 242).

p.522   *"infinitely various":* Fenichel, "Specific Forms of the Oedipus Complex," in *Collected Papers,* 1st Series, 207.

p.522   *"apply to the man":* "Selbstdarstellung," *GW* XIV, 64n / "Autobiographical Study," *SE* XX, 36 (note added in 1935). "We deal with only one libido, which acts in a masculine way," Freud wrote to the German psychoanalyst Carl Müller-Braunschweig on July 21, 1935. (Quoted in full in the original German, and translated, in Donald L. Burnham, "Freud and Female Sexuality: A Previously Unpublished Letter," *Psychiatry,* XXXIV [1971], 329. I have partially retranslated the sentence.)

p.522   *"He's right!":* Journal of Marie Bonaparte. Quoted in *New York Times,* November 12, 1985, sec. C, 3.

p.522   *"to become wise":* Freud to Emil Fluss, February 7, 1873. *Selbstdarstellung,* 111–12.

p.522   *"to no decision":* "Weibliche Sexualität," *GW* XIV, 523n / "Female Sexuality," *SE* XXI, 230n.

CHAPTER ELEVEN · *Human Nature at Work*

p.524   *clinical data:* See "Postscript" to *Lay Analysis, SE* XX, 257.

p.524   *"single goal":* "Ansprache im Frankfurter Goethe-Haus" (1930), *GW* XIV, 547 / "Address Delivered in the Goethe House at Frankfurt," *SE* XXI, 208.

p.524   *"self–confession":* Freud to Ferenczi, October 23, 1927. Freud–Ferenczi Correspondence, Freud Collection, LC.

p.524   *of The Ego and the Id:* Freud to Ferenczi, April 17, 1923. Ibid.

p.524   *"worth very much":* Freud to Eitingon, October 16, 1927. By permission of Sigmund Freud Copyrights, Wivenhoe.

p.524   *"soon be 71":* Freud to Arnold Zweig, March 20, 1927. *Freud–Zweig,* 10 (2).

p.524   *"intolerable to me":* Freud to Eitingon, March 22, 1927. By permission of Sigmund Freud Copyrights, Wivenhoe.

p.524   *"more to meet":* Freud to James Strachey, August 13, 1927. In English. By permission of Sigmund Freud Copyrights, Wivenhoe.

p.525   *"inner freezing":* Freud to Andreas-Salomé, May 11, 1927. *Freud–Salomé,* 181 (165).

p.525   *"gaining on me":* Freud to Andreas-Salomé, December 11, 1927. Ibid., 188 (171).

p.525   *verloren gegangen:* Laforgue's account of this episode is quoted in Clark, *Freud,* 471.

p.525   *"from the priests":* Freud to Pfister, November 25, 1928. *Freud–Pfister,* 136 (126).

p.525   *"invented a lantern":* Freud to Silberstein, August 6, 1873. Freud Collection, D2, LC.

p.526   *"harms it"*: Freud to Silberstein, September 18, 1874. Ibid.

p.526   *"godless medical student"*: Freud to Silberstein, November 8, 1874. Ibid.

p.526   *"out-and-out unbeliever"*: Freud to Charles Singer, October 31, 1938. *Briefe*, 469.

p.526   *"Private religion"*: Freud Collection, LC, uncatalogued.

p.526   *"universal obsessional neurosis"*: "Zwangshandlungen und Religionsübungen" (1907), *GW* VII, 138–39 / "Obsessive Actions and Religious Practices," *SE* IX, 126–27.

p.526   *idea in detail*: Freud to Ferenczi, August 20, 1911. Freud–Ferenczi Correspondence, Freud Collection, LC.

p.526   *"worthy analysts"*: Freud to Pfister, November 26, 1927. *Freud–Pfister*, 126 (117).

p.527   *"embarrassing to you"*: Freud to Pfister, October 16, 1927. Ibid., 116 (109–10).

p.527   *worthless believers*: Pfister to Freud, October 21, 1927. Ibid., 117 (110).

p.527   *"subject to criticism"*: Denis Diderot, "Fait," in the *Encyclopédie* (1756). Reprinted in his *Oeuvres complètes*, ed. Jules Assézat and Maurice Tourneux, 20 vols. (1875–77), XV, 3.

p.527   *"modern guise"*: Pfister to Freud, November 24, 1927. *Freud–Pfister*, 123 (115).

p.528   *"their ranks"*: *Die Zukunft einer Illusion, GW* XIV, 358 / *The Future of an Illusion, SE* XXI, 35.

p.529   *"in human society"*: Ibid., 326–27, 328 / 6, 7.

p.529   *"against their passions"*: Ibid., 328–29 / 7–8.

p.529   *natural urges*: Freud to Martha Bernays, August 29, 1883. *Briefe*, 56.

p.529   *"nor deserves it"*: *Die Zukunft einer Illusion, GW* XIV, 333 / *The Future of an Illusion, SE* XXI, 12.

p.530   *"hard to bear"*: Ibid., 336–37 / 15–16.

p.530   *"imperfections of culture"*: Ibid., 343 / 21.

p.531   *"of these wishes"*: Ibid., 352 / 30.

p.531   *"from human wishes"*: Ibid., 353 / 31.

p.532   *"could have advanced"*: Ibid., 351 / 29.

p.532   *"that of reason"*: Ibid., 350 / 28.

p.532   *"less than morality"*: Ibid., 361 / 37–38.

p.533   *"peoples and times"*: Ibid., 361–62 / 38.

p.533   *"presuppositions as well"*: Ibid., 362 / 38.

p.534   *"infinitesimal calculus"*: Ibid., 360 / 36.

p.534   *"and to help"*: Freud to Ferenczi, April 20, 1919. Freud–Ferenczi Correspondence, Freud Collection, LC.

p.535   *"had promised"*: *Die Zukunft einer Illusion, GW* XIV, 378–79 / *The Future of an Illusion, SE* XXI, 54.

p.535   *"cannot give us"*: Ibid., 380 / 56.

p.535   *"those of mankind"*: Freud to Rolland, March 4, 1923. *Briefe*, 359.

p.535   *of a sensation*: Petrikowitsch to Freud, draft of letter of January 1, 1928. Leo Baeck Institute, New York. See also Fred Grubel, "Zeitgenosse Sigmund Freud," *Jahrbuch der Psychoanalyse*, XI (1979), 73–80.

p.535   *ihr gekräht*: Freud to Petrikowitsch, January 17, 1928. Quoted in ibid., 78.

p.536   *"Expected to Cause"*: *New York Times*, December 27, 1927, 6 (dateline "Vienna, December 26").

p.536   *"muffled innuendoes"*: Freud to Eitingon, April 3, 1928. By permission of Sigmund Freud Copyrights, Wivenhoe.

p.536   *"clear to themselves"*: Eitingon to Freud, June 19, 1928. By permission of Sigmund Freud Copyrights, Wivenhoe.

p.536   *"battles for you"*: Oskar Pfister, "Die Illusion einer Zukunft. Eine freundschaftliche Auseinandersetzung mit Prof. Dr. Sigmund Freud," *Imago*, XIV (1928), 149–50.

p.536   *"kind riposte"*: Freud to "Dear Friends," February 28, 1928. Circular letter dictated to Anna Freud. Jones papers, Archives of the British Psycho-Analytical Society, London.

p.537   *"respect his theology"*: Nathan Krass, January 22, 1928, as reported in "Psychoanalyzing a Psychoanalyst," *New York Times*, January 23, 1928. Quoted in Clark, *Freud*, 469–70.

p.537   *modern world:* See, for example, Emil Pfennigsdorf, *Praktische Theologie*, 2 vols. (1929–30), II, 597.

p.537   *to the age:* "Psychoanalyse und Religion," *Süddeutsche Monatshefte*, XXV (1928). Quoted in A. J. Storfer, "Einige Stimmen zu Sigm. Freuds 'Zukunft einer Illusion,'" *Imago*, XIV (1928), 379.

p.537   *"principally hail":* Clemen, *Die Anwendung der Psychoanalyse auf Mythologie und Religionsgeschichte*, 127–28.

p.537   *"the Christian faith":* Emil Abderhalden, "Sigmund Freuds Einstellung zur Religion," *Ethik*, V (1928–29), 93.

p.537   *"Or what else?":* Freud to Hollós, April 10, 1928. Freud Museum, London.

p.538   *"of a change soon":* Freud to Wittels, April 20, 1928. Ibid. (Wittels quotes the complete letter—in a rather clumsy translation—in his unpublished autobiography, "Wrestling with the Man: The Story of a Freudian," 176. Typescript, Fritz Wittels Collection, Box 2. A. A. Brill Library, New York Psychoanalytic Institute.)

p.538   *"afflicted" he felt:* Freud to Wittels, July 11, 1928. Quoted in translation in Wittels, "Wrestling with the Man," 176–77. Ibid.

p.538   *"someone else":* Freud to Jones, July 1, 1928. Freud Collection, D2, LC.

p.538   *being baffled:* See summary of Pichler's notes for May 8, 1928, in *Jones* III, 141.

p.538   *become intolerable:* Freud to Jones, July 1, 1928. Freud Collection, D2, LC.

p.538   *"pharyngeal wall":* Pichler, notes for April 16, 1928. Quoted in "Extract of Case History," *Jones* III, 479.

p.538   *"thick and large":* Pichler, notes for April 24, 1928. Ibid.

p.538   *"badly with tongue":* Pichler, notes for May 7, 1928. Ibid.

p.538   *"prosthesis misery":* Freud to Andreas-Salomé, May 9, 1928. *Freud–Salomé*, 191 (174).

p.538   *"discretion!":* Freud to Jones, July 1, 1928. Freud Collection, D2, LC.

p.538   *best of hands:* Freud to Alexander Freud, September 28, 1928. Ibid., B1, LC.

p.539   *of the city:* Freud to Alexander Freud, September 24, 1928. Ibid. See also Freud to Alexander Freud, September 4, 1928. Ibid.

p.539   *"higher interests":* Freud to Andreas-Salomé, n.d. [shortly before July 10, 1931]. *Freud–Salomé*, 212 (194).

p.539   *"falls silent":* Freud to Andreas-Salomé, May 9, 1929. Ibid., 196 (179).

p.539   *into a train:* These movies are included in "Sigmund Freud, His Family and Colleagues, 1928–1947," a group of movies ed. Lynne Weiner. A. A. Brill Library, New York Psychoanalytic Institute.

p.539   *look further:* Freud to Ida Fliess, December 17, 1928. By permission of Sigmund Freud Copyrights, Wivenhoe.

p.539   *"future utilization":* Freud to Ida Fliess, December 30, 1928. By permission of Sigmund Freud Copyrights, Wivenhoe.

p.540   *"Wolf and family":* Freud to Anna Freud (telegram), April 12, 1927. Freud Collection, LC.

p.540   *"unalloyed comradeship":* Anna Freud to Freud, n.d. [spring 1927]. Ibid.

p.540   *"unhappy virgin":* Freud to Andreas-Salomé, May 11, 1927. Freud Collection, B3, LC.

p.540   *"much pleasure":* Freud to Eitingon, June 22, 1928. By permission of Sigmund Freud Copyrights, Wivenhoe.

p.540   *with his chow:* See Brandes to Freud, June 11 and 26, 1928. Freud Museum, London.

p.540   *analytic hour:* See Joseph Wortis, *Fragments of an Analysis with Freud* (1954), 23.

p.541   *deal of good:* Freud to Andreas-Salomé, May 11, 1927. Freud Collection, B3, LC.

p.541   *"her father?":* Freud to Andreas-Salomé, December 11, 1927. Ibid.

p.541   *fondly called her:* Freud to Ferenczi, October 23, 1927. Freud–Ferenczi Correspondence, Freud Collection, LC.

p.542   *to analyze her:* Laforgue to Freud, April 9, 1925. From the Freud–Laforgue correspondence, tr. into French by Pierre Cotet and ed. André Bourguignon et al., in "Mémorial," *Nouvelle Revue de Psychanalyse*, XV (April 1977), 260. Some of the passages I quote here have also been used in Celia Bertin, *Marie Bonaparte: A Life* (1982), 145–50.

p.542   *"the other patients":* Freud to Laforgue, April 14, 1925. "Mémorial," 260–61.

p.542   *hours every day:* See Laforgue to Freud, May 1, 1925. Ibid., 261.

p.542   *"I saw Freud":* Quoted in Bertin, *Marie Bonaparte*, 150.

p.542   *"masculine female":* Freud to Eitingon, October 30, 1925. By permission of Sigmund Freud Copyrights, Wivenhoe.

p.542   *"with her stay":* Freud to Laforgue, November 15, 1925. "Mémorial," 273.

p.542   *seven and nine:* See five notebooks, softbound in black leatherette, with entries dated between November 22, 1889, and July 21, 1891. In English, French, and German. Freud Museum, London.

p.543   *solve so far:* See notes by Marie Bonaparte for a possible biography of Freud, "given me by Freud in April 1928." In French. Jones papers, Archives of the British Psycho-Analytical Society, London.

p.543   *in July 1929:* Quoted in Andreas-Salomé to Freud, July 14, 1929. *Freud–Salomé,* 198 (181).

p.543   *"quite agreeably":* Freud to Andreas-Salomé, July 28, 1929. Ibid., 198 (181).

p.543   *"as I worked":* Ibid.

p.543   *latest production:* Freud to Jones, January 26, 1930. Freud Collection, D2, LC.

p.544   *printers' ink:* See *Civilization and Its Discontents, SE* XXI, 117.

p.544   *easily to him:* Freud to Eitingon, July 8, 1929. By permission of Sigmund Freud Copyrights, Wivenhoe. See "Editor's Introduction" to *Civilization and Its Discontents, SE* XXI, 59–60.

p.544   *and channeled: Das Unbehagen in der Kultur, GW* XIV, 421–22 / *Civilization and Its Discontents, SE* XXI, 64.

p.545   *"insensitive to it":* Ibid., 432 / 75.

p.545   *"insoluble tasks":* Ibid., 432 / 75.

p.545   *"of 'Creation' ":* Ibid., 438n, 434 / 80n, 76.

p.546   *"present-day civilization":* Ibid., 445–47 / 87–89.

p.546   *"prosthetic god":* Ibid., 451 / 91–92.

p.546   homini lupus: Ibid., 471 / 111. This saying is originally derived from Plautus.

p.547   *"wider stage":* "Nachschrift 1935" to "Selbstdarstellung," *GW* XVI, 32–33 / "Postscript" to "Autobiographical Study," *SE* XX, 72.

p.547   *reject Bolshevism:* See Freud to Ferenczi, November 17, 1918. Freud–Ferenczi Correspondence, Freud Collection, LC.

p.548   *from modern discontents: Das Unbehagen in der Kultur, GW* XIV, 504 / *Civilization and Its Discontents, SE* XXI, 143.

p.548   *"severe restrictions":* Ibid., 462 / 103.

p.549   *"aggressive inclinations":* Ibid., 469–70 / 110–11.

p.549   *of human nature:* See ibid., 504 / 143.

p.549   *"without it":* Ibid., 473 / 113–14.

p.549   *"small differences":* Ibid., 474 / 114. As indicated in a note to Freud's text (see ibid., 475n / 114n), he had coined the term somewhat earlier, and used it in a paper of 1918, "The Taboo of Virginity," and in *Group Psychology and the Analysis of the Ego* (1921).

p.550   *"their bourgeois": Das Unbehagen in der Kultur, GW* XIV, 474 / *Civilization and Its Discontents, SE* XXI, 114–15.

p.550   *"of Heaven!":* Ibid., 474, 481 / 115, 122.

p.550   *"cultural superego":* Ibid., 502–6 / 141–44.

p.551   *"mood of anxiety":* Ibid., 506 / 145. I have already quoted the first of these passages on p. 356.

p.552   *"Bad Heart Days": Kürzeste Chronik,* November 11 and 14, December 7–10, 1929. Freud Museum, London.

p.552   *"Nobel Prize":* November 7 and October 31, 1929. Ibid.

p.552   *was sold out:* See *Jones* III, 148.

p.552   *unwarranted generalization:* Jones to Freud, January 1, 1930. Typescript copy, Freud Collection, D2, LC.

p.552   *"way to it":* Freud to Jones, January 26, 1930. Ibid.

p.552   *" 'life force' ":* Pfister to Freud, February 4, 1930. *Freud–Pfister*, 142 (131).

p.553   *"it than I":* Freud to Pfister, February 7, 1930. Freud Museum, London.

p.553   *"the outcome?":* Das Unbehagen in der Kultur, *GW* XIV, 506 / Civilization and Its Discontents, *SE* XXI, 145.

p.553   *"seven grandchildren":* Freud to Arnold Zweig, December 7, 1930. *Freud–Zweig*, 37 (25).

p.553   *self-destructive behavior:* See Will Brownell and Richard N. Billings, *So Close to Greatness: A Biography of William C. Bullitt* (1987), 123.

p.554   *"was emptied":* William Bullitt, "Foreword" to Freud and Bullitt, *Thomas Woodrow Wilson: A Psychological Study* (1967; paperback ed., 1968), v–vi.

p.554   *"those promises":* Jones III, 16–17.

p.554   *much credence:* Massenpsychologie, *GW* XIII, 103 / Group Psychology, *SE* XVIII, 95.

p.554   *come to "detest":* Freud to William Bayard Hale, January 15, 1922. In English. William Bayard Hale papers, box 1, folder 12. Y-MA.

p.555   *"on my side":* Freud to Hale, January 3, 1922. In English. Ibid.

p.555   *" 'psychoanalytic study' ":* Freud to Hale, January 15, 1922. In English. Ibid.

p.555   *plainly was not:* When Ernest Jones reviewed the book, he hailed it as "a remarkable and original study," but agreed with Freud that it was not psychoanalysis. (*Int. J. Psycho-Anal.*, III [1922], 385–86.)

p.555   *"he surely is":* Freud to Hale, January 15, 1922. In English. William Bayard Hale papers, box 1, folder 12. Y-MA.

p.555   *public figure:* See Freud to Hale, January 20, 1922. In English. Ibid.

p.556   *"for some years":* Bullitt, "Foreword" to *Thomas Woodrow Wilson*, v.

p.556   *"go to Moscow":* Bullitt to House, July 29, 1930. Colonel E. M. House papers, series I, box 21. Y-MA.

p.556   *"to the world":* House to Bullitt, July 31, 1930. Ibid.

p.556   *study of Wilson:* Bullitt to House, August 4, 1930. Ibid.

p.556   *"to work" soon:* Bullitt to House, September 3, 1930. Ibid.

p.556   *"start the job":* Bullitt to House, September 20, 1930. Ibid.

p.556   *had a fever:* Kürzeste Chronik, October 17, 1930. Freud Museum, London.

p.556   *"go to work":* Bullitt to House, October 26, 1930. Colonel E. M. House papers, series I, box 21. Y-MA.

p.556   *"F.'s health":* Ibid.

p.557   *"Work taken up":* Kürzeste Chronik, October 29, 1930. Freud Museum, London.

p.557   *done by mid-December:* Bullitt to House, November 23, 1930. Colonel E. M. House papers, series I, box 21. Y-MA.

p.557   *"what it is":* Freud to Arnold Zweig, December 7, 1930. *Freud–Zweig*, 37 (25).

p.557   *"fascinating one":* Bullitt to House, August 17, 1931. Colonel E. M. House papers, series I, box 21. Y-MA.

p.557   *much better off:* Bullitt to House, December 13, 1931. Ibid.

p.557   *"eager to see it":* House to Bullitt, December 28, 1931. Ibid.

p.557   *"politics again":* Bullitt to House, April 29, 1932. Ibid.

p.558   *"be made public":* Freud to Eitingon, November 20, 1932. By permission of Sigmund Freud Copyrights, Wivenhoe.

p.559   *"nothing more":* Freud and Bullitt, *Thomas Woodrow Wilson*, 59–60.

p.559   *"claim to masculinity":* Ibid., 69.

p.559   *"this father identification":* Ibid., 86.

p.559   *"did Tommy Wilson":* Ibid., 83.

p.559   *"of the World":* Ibid., 228.

p.560   *"on many men":* Ibid., 338.

p.560   *all recognition:* According to a memorandum by Alick Bartholomew, an editor at Houghton Mifflin, which published the book, Anna Freud declared that the published book had
become "a kind of parody by thoughtlessly repeating phrases like 'passively toward his
father' and 'identification with Jesus Christ.' The repetition of psychoanalytic formulae
became an incantation." (Quoted in Brownell and Billings, *So Close to Greatness,* 349.)
In August 1965, after rereading the work, she put it just as forcefully: "B[ullitt]'s application of the analytic interpretations given to him are impossible, childish, and clumsy,
almost ridiculous." (Anna Freud to Schur, August 10, 1965. Max Schur papers, LC.)

p.560   *"and collaborator":* Freud to Eitingon, July 25, 1931. By permission of Sigmund Freud
Copyrights, Wivenhoe.

p.560   *"personal complications":* Freud to Paul Hill, November 16, 1934. Paul Hill Collection,
Hoover Institution Archives, Stanford University. (I owe this reference to Juliette George.)

p.561   *"pure in heart":* Richard Hofstadter, *The American Political Tradition and the Men Who
Made It* (1948), 248.

p.561   *"was not increased":* Freud, "Introduction" to *Thomas Woodrow Wilson,* xiii–xiv.

p.561   *his seventieth birthday:* See *Jones* III, 124.

p.561   *financial crisis:* See ibid., 144.

p.561   *to survive it:* See Freud to Pfister, Easter 1932. By permission of Sigmund Freud Copyrights, Wivenhoe.

p.561   *would be devastating:* Freud to Jones, September 12, 1932. Freud Collection, D2,
LC.

p.562   *"financial rehabilitation":* Freud to Eitingon, November 15, 1931. By permission of Sigmund Freud Copyrights, Wivenhoe.

p.562   *American royalties:* See *Kürzeste Chronik,* January 18, 1932. Freud Museum, London.
Writing to Eitingon, Freud mistakenly used a dollar sign in conveying the news. This was
clearly a slip, for Freud asked Eitingon right after, "How much is this in dollars?" (Freud
to Eitingon, January 19, 1932. By permission of Sigmund Freud Copyrights, Wivenhoe.)

p.562   *"by the dollar":* Freud to Fliess, March 11, 1902. *Freud–Fliess,* 503 (457).

p.563   *"so amiably then":* Freud to Ferenczi, April 20, 1919. Freud–Ferenczi Correspondence,
Freud Collection, LC.

p.563   *"anti-Paradise":* Freud to Arnold Zweig, March 5, 1939. *Freud–Zweig,* 186 (178).

p.563   *"gigantic mistake":* Jones, *Free Associations,* 191.

p.563   *"not cost money":* Freud to Ferenczi, January 10, 1909. Freud–Ferenczi Correspondence,
Freud Collection, LC.

p.563   *"for anything else":* Freud to Jones, September 25, 1924. In English. Freud Collection,
D2, LC.

p.563   *"to supply money":* Freud to Jones, December 21, 1925. Dictated to Anna Freud. Ibid.

p.563   *"suits a raven":* Freud to Rank, May 23, 1924. Rank Collection, Box 1b. Rare Book and
Manuscript Library, Columbia University.

p.564   *"ahead of us!":* Freud to Pfister, March 11, 1913. By permission of Sigmund Freud
Copyrights, Wivenhoe.

p.564   *"sort of humans":* Freud to "Miss Downey," March 1, 1922. Freud Collection (to be
placed in series B), LC.

p.564   *"two crooks":* Freud to Rank, August 6, 1924. Rank Collection, Box 1b. Rare Book and
Manuscript Library, Columbia University.

p.564   *"dollar uncles":* Freud to Ferenczi, March 30, 1922. Freud–Ferenczi Correspondence,
Freud Collection, LC.

p.564   *"questions of technique":* Freud to Eitingon, November 11, 1921. By permission of
Sigmund Freud Copyrights, Wivenhoe.

p.564   *"clever man":* Pfister to Freud, July 21, 1921. By permission of Sigmund Freud Copyrights,
Wivenhoe.

p.564   *"ever discovered":* Freud to Abraham, August 24, 1912. Karl Abraham papers, LC.

p.564   *"outstandingly decent"*: Freud to Pfister, July 29, 1921. By permission of Sigmund Freud Copyrights, Wivenhoe.

p.565   *"share in it"*: Freud to Jones, December 9, 1921. In English. Freud Collection, D2, LC.

p.565   *"to be dropped"*: Freud to Jones, March 18, 1921. In English. Ibid.

p.565   *"toward your women"*: Freud to Blumgart, November 28, 1922. A. A. Brill Library, New York Psychoanalytic Institute.

p.565   *"American journalist"*: Freud to Lehrman, January 27, 1930. Ibid.

p.565   *"without prosperity?"*: Freud to Lehrman, October 5, 1930. Ibid.

p.565   *"ΨA into Psychiatry"*: Freud to Jones, September 25, 1924. In English. Freud Collection, D2, LC.

p.566   *"of popular sources"*: Freud to Jones, January 4, 1929. Ibid. Reproduced in Jones's slightly different translation in *Jones* III, 143.

p.566   *and said so:* "Introduction to the Special Psychopathology Number of *The Medical Review of Reviews*" (1930), *SE* XXI, 254–55. The words in italics are in English in Freud's original.

p.566   *"side of Libido"*: Freud to Jones, December 26, 1912. In English. Freud Collection, D2, LC.

p.566   *"achieve anything"*: Freud to Radó, September 30, 1925. Ibid., B9, LC.

p.567   *"quality with quantity"*: Freud to Frankwood Williams, December 22, 1929. Typescript copy, Freud Museum, London.

p.567   *was real enough:* See *Jones* II, 59–60.

p.567   *"a great deal"*: Freud to Ferenczi, November 21, 1909. Freud–Ferenczi Correspondence, Freud Collection, LC.

p.567   *"earned in New York"*: Freud to Jones, March 10, 1910. In English. Freud Collection, D2, LC.

p.567   *"ago, in America"*: Freud to Ferenczi, April 20, 1919. Freud–Ferenczi Correspondence, Freud Collection, LC.

p.567   *"do so to eat"*: Quoted in Schur to Jones, September 30, 1955. Max Schur papers, LC.

p.567   *"prepared to do?"*: Freud to Jones, April 12, 1921. In English. Freud Collection, D2, LC.

p.568   *"anal Adlerei"*: Freud to Rank, May 23, 1924. Rank Collection, Box 1b. Rare Book and Manuscript Library, Columbia University.

p.568   *by "haste"*: "Die endliche und die unendliche Analyse," *GW* XVI, 60 / "Analysis Terminable and Interminable," *SE* XXIII, 216.

p.568   *"become americanized"*: Freud to Jones, March 8, 1920. In English. Freud Collection, D2, LC.

p.568   *"Dollaria"*: Freud to Pfister, August 20, 1930. *Freud–Pfister*, 147 (135).

p.568   *"oneself analysts"*: Laforgue to Freud, July 8, 1927. "Mémorial," 288.

p.569   *"somewhat neglected"*: "Warns of Danger in American Life / Dr. Ferenczi of Budapest Sees Need for Psychoanalysis to Treat Neurotics / Sails after Lecture Tour / Associate of Dr. Freud Trained Psychoanalysts Here to Carry on His Work," *New York Times*, June 5, 1927, sec. 2, 4.

p.569   *"future husband"*: Stendhal, *De l'amour* (1822), ed. Henri Martineau (1938), 276.

p.569   *"accumulating it"*: Stendhal, *Lucien Leuwen* (posthumously published), ed. Anne-Marie Meininger, 2 vols. (1982), I, 113.

p.569   *"down into dollars"*: Charles Dickens, *Martin Chuzzlewit* (1843), ch. 16.

p.569   *" 'dollars-dollars-dollars' "*: Philip Burne-Jones, *Dollars and Democracy* (1904), 74. (I owe this reference to C. Vann Woodward.)

p.570   *"the new continent"*: Freud to Ferenczi, January 17, 1909. Freud–Ferenczi Correspondence, Freud Collection, LC.

p.570   *"time for libido"*: Freud to Jung, October 17, 1909. *Freud–Jung*, 282 (256).

p.570   *"American chastity"*: Freud to Jones, September 21, 1913. In English. Freud Collection, D2, LC.

p.570   *of "prudish"*: Freud to Dr. Samuel A. Tannenbaum, April 19, 1914. Ibid., B4, LC.

p.570   *of "virtuous":* Freud to Jones, May 11, 1920. In English. Ibid., D2, LC.

p.570   *in the United States:* See Freud to Putnam, July 8, 1915. *James Jackson Putnam: Letters,* 376.

p.570   *"for the dollar":* Freud to Pfister, November 3, 1921. *Freud–Pfister,* 86 (83).

p.570   *"is unconquerable":* Freud to Eitingon, July 21, 1932. By permission of Sigmund Freud Copyrights, Wivenhoe.

p.571   *"external honor":* Citation for the Goethe Prize, signed "Landmann," lord mayor of Frankfurt. Typescript copy, Freud Collection, B13, LC. See also letter from Dr. Alfons Paquet, secretary to the trustees of the fund, to Freud, July 26, 1930, informing him of the award. (*GW* XIV, 545–46n.)

p.571   *"for Nobel Prize":* Kürzeste Chronik, November 6, 1930. Freud Museum, London.

p.571   *do with it:* See Freud to Eitingon, August 26, 1930. By permission of Sigmund Freud Copyrights, Wivenhoe.

p.571   *beloved Goethe:* See *Jones* III, 151.

p.572   *"to than I am":* Freud to Paquet, August 3, 1930. *GW* XIV, 546 / *SE* XXI, 207.

p.572   *"sympathy for analysis":* Freud to Jones, August 30, 1930. Freud Collection, D2, LC.

p.572   *"itself forward":* Ibid.

p.572   *"to do me in":* Freud to Jones, September 15, 1930. Ibid.

p.572   *"of the prize":* Freud to Andreas-Salomé, October 22, 1930. *Freud–Salomé,* 207 (190).

p.572   *"for cigars":* Freud to Jones, May 12, 1930. Freud Collection, D2, LC.

p.572   *"cigar per day":* Freud to Jones, May 19, 1930. Ibid.

p.573   *"Old Freud":* Freud to Andreas-Salomé, May 8, 1930. *Freud–Salomé,* 205 (187–88).

p.573   *diploma in hand:* See Kürzeste Chronik, August 24, 1930. Freud Museum, London.

p.573   *"hard to grasp":* Freud to Eitingon, December 1, 1929. By permission of Sigmund Freud Copyrights, Wivenhoe. See also Freud to Abraham, May 29, 1918. *Freud–Abraham,* 259 (275). And see Schur, *Freud, Living and Dying,* 314–15, 423–24.

p.573   *attend the funeral:* Freud to Jones, September 15, 1930. Freud Collection, D2, LC. The phrase "there is no saying" is in English.

p.573   *like ceremonies:* See Freud to Alexander Freud, September 10, 1930. Ibid., B1, LC.

p.573   *"hardly be increased":* Freud to Jones, September 15, 1930. Ibid., D2, LC.

p.574   *Ivan Petrovich Pavlov:* Forsyth to Freud, January 7, 1931. Freud Museum, London.

p.574   *"received this call":* Freud to Eitingon, January 18, 1931. By permission of Sigmund Freud Copyrights, Wivenhoe. See also Freud to Jones, February 12, 1931. Freud Collection, D2, LC.

p.574   *"for 8 years":* Freud to Jones, June 2, 1931. Ibid.

p.574   *"remnant of reality":* Freud to Arnold Zweig, May 10, 1931. By permission of Sigmund Freud Copyrights, Wivenhoe.

p.574   *seventy-fifth birthday:* See Kürzeste Chronik, May 5, 1931. Freud Museum, London.

p.574   *like a "flood":* Freud to Andreas-Salomé, May 9, 1931. *Freud–Salomé,* 210 (193).

p.574   *"science and life":* Quoted in *Jones* III, 158.

p.575   *"belief and unbelief":* Einstein to Freud, April 29, 1931. Freud Collection, B3, LC.

p.575   *"all of Jewry":* Dr. M. Bernhard, president of the Herzl Club, and Dr. Wilhelm Stein, secretary, to Freud, May 5, 1931. Freud Museum, London.

p.575   *warmest greetings:* All in Freud Museum, London.

p.575   *distant acknowledgment:* See *Jones* III, 155.

p.575   *"than he believes":* Feuchtwang to Freud, April 7, 1931. Freud Museum, London.

p.575   *"Freiberg, Moravia":* Printed invitation to the festival at Příbor on October 25, 1931. Ibid.

p.575   *"from this soil":* Freud to the mayor of Příbor, October 25, 1931. Typescript copy, Freud Collection, B3, LC / "Letter to the Burgomaster of Příbor," *SE* XXI, 259. I have already quoted this passage on p. 9.

p.576   *about two minutes:* See *Jones* III, 157.

p.576   *before the war:* Ferenczi to Freud, May 15, 1922. Freud–Ferenczi Correspondence, Freud Collection, LC.

p.576   *in 1915:* Ferenczi to Freud, October 14, 1915. Ibid.

p.576   *a little less:* See for one instance Freud to Ferenczi, April 8, 1915. Ibid.

p.576   *"source of energy":* Ferenczi to Freud, March 20, 1922. Ibid.

p.576   *"is not true":* Freud to Ferenczi, March 30, 1922. Ibid.

p.576   *"were to me":* Ferenczi to Freud, September 3, 1923. Ibid.

p.576   *"ψa superman":* Freud to Ferenczi, October 6, 1910. Ibid.

p.577   *and the signature:* Freud to Ferenczi, June 28, 1909. Ibid.

p.577   *"even more rarely":* Freud to Ferenczi, July 21, 1922. Ibid.

p.577   *"everybody against you":* Freud to Eitingon, June 30, 1927. By permission of Sigmund Freud Copyrights, Wivenhoe.

p.577   *"fairly alarmed":* Eitingon to Freud, August 10, 1927. By permission of Sigmund Freud Copyrights, Wivenhoe.

p.577   *"before Christmas":* Freud to Ferenczi (postcard), December 18, 1927. Freud–Ferenczi Correspondence, Freud Collection, LC.

p.577   *"more briskly":* Freud to Eitingon, August 8, 1927. By permission of Sigmund Freud Copyrights, Wivenhoe.

p.577   *"understand him":* Freud to Eitingon, August 26, 1927. By permission of Sigmund Freud Copyrights, Wivenhoe.

p.577   *"inner dissatisfaction":* Freud to Ferenczi, September 18, 1931. Freud–Ferenczi Correspondence, Freud Collection, LC.

p.577   *"anything sad":* Ferenczi to Freud, February 6, 1925. Ibid.

p.577   *aging prematurely:* See Ferenczi to Freud, February 14, 1930. Ibid.

p.577   *"into isolation":* Freud to Eitingon, November 3, 1930. By permission of Sigmund Freud Copyrights, Wivenhoe.

p.578   *results as yet:* Ferenczi to Freud, September 15, 1931. Freud–Ferenczi Correspondence, Freud Collection, LC.

p.578   *"your independence":* Freud to Ferenczi, September 18, 1931. Ibid.

p.578   *"to Baden-Baden":* Ferenczi to Freud, August 17, 1922. Ibid.

p.579   *fatherly part:* Freud to Ferenczi, December 13, 1931. Ibid.

p.579   *"scientific concord":* Ferenczi to Freud, December 27, 1931. Ibid.

p.579   *"and sincerity":* January 7, 1932, *Klinisches Tagebuch.* Typescript, with a few handwritten pages, Freud Collection, B22, LC, catalogued as "Scientific Diary."

p.579   *"intense empathy":* March 17, 1932. Ibid.

p.579   *"lack of affect":* January 7, 1932. Ibid.

p.579   *from the patient:* March 20, 1932. Ibid.

p.580   *of his past:* January 7, 1932. Ibid.

p.580   *"their self-esteem":* March 20, 1932. Ibid.

p.580   *"therefore intelligent":* February 14, 1932. Ibid.

p.581   *"control by insight":* June 28, 1932. Ibid.

p.581   *"are tamed":* Ibid.

p.581   *"so-called metaphysical":* Ferenczi to Georg and Emmy Groddeck, March 3, 1932. Sándor Ferenczi and Georg Groddeck, *Briefwechsel 1921–1933,* ed. Willi Köhler (1986), 85.

p.581   *"'Americans so?'":* August 4, 1932, *Klinisches Tagebuch.* Freud Collection, B22, LC.

p.581   *the parricide:* Ibid.

p.581   *"crown-prince-fantasies":* Ibid.

p.581   *"castrates the son":* Ibid.

p.582   *abusing their children:* See April 5, and July 26, 1932. Ibid.

p.582   *"as helper":* August 4, 1932. Ibid.

p.582   *cause of neuroses:* July 7, 1932. Ibid.

p.582   *"female pupils":* Freud to Eitingon, April 18, 1932. By permission of Sigmund Freud Copyrights, Wivenhoe.

p.582   *"still around":* Freud to Jones, September 12, 1932. Freud Collection, D2, LC.

p.582   *way of Rank:* See Freud to Eitingon, August 24, 1932. By permission of Sigmund Freud Copyrights, Wivenhoe.

p.583   *would be hard:* Freud to Ferenczi, May 12, 1932. Freud–Ferenczi Correspondence, Freud Collection, LC.

p.583   *"relative muddle":* Ferenczi to Freud, May 19, 1932. Ibid.

p.583   *accept the presidency:* Ferenczi to Freud, August 21, 1932. Ibid.

p.583   *feelings best:* See Freud to Ferenczi, August 24, 1932. Ibid.

p.583   *for three years:* Freud to Jones, September 12, 1932. Freud Collection, D2, LC.

p.583   *"Impression unpleasant":* Freud to Eitingon (telegram), September 2, 1932. By permission of Sigmund Freud Copyrights, Wivenhoe.

p.584   *"before them":* Freud to Anna Freud, September 3, 1932. Freud Collection, LC.

p.584   *"much sadder":* Ibid. Brill's words, "He is not sincere," are in English in Freud's letter. It is noteworthy that Ernest Jones's account of this meeting (*Jones* III, 172–73) follows this letter in the closest detail.

p.584   *in late August:* See Freud to Eitingon, August 24, 1932. By permission of Sigmund Freud Copyrights, Wivenhoe.

p.584   *"for yourself":* Freud to Anna Freud, September 3, 1932. Freud Collection, LC. This last sentence disposes of the insinuation by Jeffrey Moussaieff Masson that Freud had condemned Ferenczi's ideas unheard, in a letter to Eitingon on August 29, the day before Ferenczi read his paper to Freud in Vienna. (See Masson, *The Assault on Truth,* 170–71.) Obviously, Freud, like his daughter, had been thoroughly acquainted with Ferenczi's newest notions for some time.

p.585   *"sick child":* Freud to Jones, September 12, 1932. Freud Collection, D2, LC.

p.585   *"pernicious anemia":* Freud to Eitingon, October 20, 1932. By permission of Sigmund Freud Copyrights, Wivenhoe.

p.585   *faded away:* See Spector, *The Aesthetics of Freud,* 149–55.

p.585   *"psychological calamity":* Freud to Ferenczi, January 11, 1933. Freud–Ferenczi Correspondence, Freud Collection, LC.

p.585   *"nervous breakdown":* Ferenczi to Freud, March 27, 1933. Ibid.

p.585   *theory could wait:* See Freud to Ferenczi, April 2, 1933. Ibid.

p.585   *getting over it:* Freud to Eitingon, April 3, 1933. By permission of Sigmund Freud Copyrights, Wivenhoe.

p.586   *"secret between us":* Freud to Jones, May 29, 1933. Freud Collection, D2, LC.

p.587   *"piece of psychiatry":* Freud to Jones, August 23, 1933. Ibid.

p.587   *hat Humor:* Wilhelm Busch, "Es sitzt ein Vogel auf dem Leim," in *Kritik des Herzens* (1874), *Wilhelm Busch Gesamtausgabe,* ed. Friedrich Bohne, 4 vols. (1959), II, 495.

Chapter Twelve · *To Die in Freedom*

p.588   *"burning down":* Freud to Jones, April 26, 1932. Freud Collection, D2, LC.

p.588   *the spring:* See Freud to Jones, June 17, 1932. Ibid.

p.589   *"rotten affair":* Freud to Ferenczi, July 16, 1927. Freud–Ferenczi Correspondence, Freud Collection, LC.

p.589   *"conditions in Vienna":* Freud to Samuel Freud, August 3, 1927. In English. Rylands University Library, Manchester.

p.589   *"dreary in Austria":* Freud to Samuel Freud, December 31, 1930. In English. Ibid.

p.590   *"bad to worse":* Freud to Samuel Freud, December 1, 1931. In English. Ibid.

p.590   *"give them":* Ibid.

p.591   *"than we are":* Freud to Pfister, May 15, 1932. By permission of Sigmund Freud Copyrights, Wivenhoe.

p.592   *regressions:* Holstijn to Karl Landauer, September 1933. Quoted in Karen Brecht et al., eds., *"Hier geht das Leben auf eine sehr merkwürdige Weise weiter. . . ."* Zur Geschichte der Psychoanalyse in Deutschland (1985), 57.

p.592   *"become impossible":* Freud to Samuel Freud, July 31, 1933. In English. Rylands University Library, Manchester.

p.592   *"burns people":* Karl Dietrich Bracher, *The German Dictatorship: The Origins, Structure, and Effects of National Socialism* (1969; tr. Jean Steinberg, 1970), 258.

p.592   *"mad times":* Freud to Andreas-Salomé, May 14, 1933. *Freud–Salomé,* 218 (200).

p.592   *"plunders libraries":* Pfister to Freud, May 24, 1933. *Freud–Pfister,* 151 (139).

p.593   *"burning my books":* Quoted in *Jones* III, 182.

p.593   *"danger to life":* Freud to Ferenczi, April 2, 1933. Freud–Ferenczi Correspondence, Freud Collection, LC.

p.593   *"allow that":* Freud to Jones, April 7, 1933. Freud Collection, D2, LC.

p.593   *"witches' cauldron":* Freud to Jones, July 23, 1933. Ibid.

p.593   *"too bad":* Freud to Samuel Freud, July 31, 1933. In English. Rylands University Library, Manchester.

p.594   *"leave Vienna":* Freud to Hilda Doolittle, October 27, 1933. In English. Hilda Doolittle papers, Beinecke Rare Book and Manuscript Library, Yale University.

p.594   *"may be!":* Freud to Pfister, February 27, 1934. By permission of Sigmund Freud Copyrights, Wivenhoe.

p.594   *"very discomfiting":* Freud to Arnold Zweig, February 25, 1934. *Freud–Zweig,* 76 (65).

p.594   *"an earthquake":* Freud to Hilda Doolittle, March 5, 1934. In English. Quoted in full in "Appendix" to H. D., *Tribute to Freud,* 192.

p.594   *"the combatants":* Ibid.

p.595   *"have to go":* Freud to Ernst Freud, February 20, 1934. Freud Collection, B1, LC.

p.595   *"your houses":* Freud to Arnold Zweig, February 25, 1934. *Freud–Zweig,* 77 (65). The quotation from Shakespeare is in English.

p.595   *matter where:* Ibid., 76–77 (65).

p.596   *his* Chronik: See *Kürzeste Chronik,* June 5, 1933. Freud Museum, London.

p.596   *"be disastrous":* Freud to Hilda Doolittle, March 5, 1934. In English. Quoted in full in "Appendix" to H. D., *Tribute to Freud,* 192.

p.596   *"still hungry":* Freud to Arnold Zweig, July 15, 1934. *Freud–Zweig,* 96–97 (86).

p.596   *"at 78":* Freud to Andreas-Salomé, n.d. [May 16, 1934]. *Freud–Salomé,* 220 (202).

p.597   *"deny it":* Freud to the members of B'nai B'rith, n.d. [May 6, 1926]. *Briefe,* 381.

p.597   *"Austrian Galicia":* Freud to Fehl, November 12, 1935. Typescript copy, Freud Collection, B2, LC.

p.598   *proscribed cigars:* See Freud to Fliess, November 8, 1895. *Freud–Fliess,* 153 (150).

p.598   *"give a homeland":* Traumdeutung, *GW* II–III, 444/*Interpretation of Dreams, SE* V, 442.

p.599   *"my Judaism":* Freud to Marie Bonaparte, May 10, 1926. *Briefe,* 383.

p.599   *in 1929:* Freud to Isaac Landman, August 1, 1929. Typescript copy, Freud Collection, B3, LC.

p.599   *"me emotionally":* Freud to Schnitzler, May 24, 1926. Sigmund Freud, "Briefe an Arthur Schnitzler," *Neue Rundschau,* LXVI (1955), 100.

p.599   *"with his people":* "Vorrede zur hebräischen Ausgabe von *Totem und Tabu*" (written 1930, published 1934), *GW* XIV, 569/"Preface to the Hebrew Edition of *Totem and Taboo,*" *SE* XIII, xv.

p.599   *"an infidel Jew":* Quoted in "A Religious Experience" (1928), *SE* XXI, 170. The phrase is in English in Freud's original.

p.599   *"and literature":* "Brief an den Herausgeber der *Jüdischen Presszentrale Zürich*" (1925), *GW* XIV, 556/"Letter to the Editor of the *Jewish Press Centre in Zurich,*" *SE* XIX, 291.

p.600   *"concerned Judaism":* Freud to Dwossis, December 15, 1930. Typescript copy, Freud Museum, London.

p.600   *really excellent:* Freud to Dwossis, September 20, 1928. Typescript copy, Freud Museum, London. In 1930, he referred to his ignorance of Hebrew in print in his preface to Dwossis's

Hebrew translation of *Totem and Taboo* (*SE XIII*, xv); and in 1938, he repeated this disclaimer: "Unfortunately I cannot read Hebrew." (Freud to Dwossis, September 11, 1938. Freud Museum, London.)

p.600   *"or sisters":* Martin Freud, "Who Was Freud?" in *The Jews of Austria*, ed. Fraenkel, 203.

p.601   *sons' business:* See Ernst Freud to Siegfried Bernfeld, December 20, 1920. Siegfried Bernfeld papers, container 17, LC. See also Avner Falk, "Freud and Herzl," *Contemporary Psychoanalysis*, XIV (1978), 378.

p.601   *hat back on:* See Martin Freud, "Who Was Freud?" in *The Jews of Austria*, ed. Fraenkel, 203–4.

p.601   *"mental construction":* Freud to the members of B'nai B'rith n.d. [May 6, 1926]. *Briefe*, 381.

p.601   *"to reality":* Freud to Ferenczi, March 30, 1922. Freud–Ferenczi Correspondence, Freud Collection, LC.

p.602   *"more about it":* Freud to Arnold Zweig, May 8, 1932. *Freud–Zweig*, 51–52 (40).

p.602   *"scientific insight":* "Vorrede zur hebräischen Ausgabe," *GW* XIV, 569/"Preface to the Hebrew Edition," *SE* XIII, xv.

p.602   *"godless Jew?":* Freud to Pfister, October 9, 1918. *Freud–Pfister*, 64 (63).

p.602   *"Christian never was":* Pfister to Freud, October 29, 1918. Ibid., 64 (63).

p.602   *"of judgment":* "Selbstdarstellung," *GW* XIV, 35/"Autobiographical Study," *SE* XX, 9. See also p. 27, above.

p.602   *his origins:* See "The Resistances to Psycho-Analysis" (1925), *SE* XIX, 222.

p.603   *"into opposition":* Freud to the members of B'nai B'rith, n.d. [May 6, 1926]. *Briefe*, 381–82.

p.603   *"equally pronounced":* Jones, *Free Associations*, 208–9.

p.604   *"great moment":* Freud to Martha Bernays, February 2, 1886. *Briefe*, 208–9.

p.605   *all his life:* See Freud to Andreas-Salomé, January 6, 1935. *Freud–Salomé*, 224 (205).

p.605   *from afar:* See Freud to Jung, January 17, 1909. *Freud–Jung*, 218 (196–97).

p.605   *"was right":* Freud to Arnold Zweig, August 18, 1933. By permission of Sigmund Freud Copyrights, Wivenhoe.

p.605   *its contents:* Quoted in Andreas-Salomé to Freud, January 2, 1935. *Freud–Salomé*, 221 (203).

p.605   *"historical novel":* Freud to Andreas-Salomé, January 6, 1935. Ibid., 222–23 (204).

p.606   *was inadequate:* See Freud to Eitingon, November 13, 1934. By permission of Sigmund Freud Copyrights, Wivenhoe.

p.606   *outlaw psychoanalysis:* Freud to Arnold Zweig, September 30, 1934. *Freud–Zweig*, 102 (91–92).

p.606   *"was a Moses?":* Voltaire, "Moses," in *Philosophical Dictionary* (1764; tr. Peter Gay, 1962), 2 vols. continuously paginated, II, 400n.

p.607   *real personage:* See Martin Buber, *Moses: The Revelation and the Covenant* (1946; paperback ed. 1958), 7.

p.607   *cult of Aton:* Karl Abraham had already treated this pharaoh and his religious innovation in an important paper of 1912, which Freud curiously failed to mention in *Moses and Monotheism*. The paper is "Amenhotep IV: A Psycho-Analytical Contribution towards the Understanding of His Personality and the Monotheistic Cult of Aton," conveniently available in Abraham's *Clinical Papers and Essays in Psycho-Analysis*, tr. Hilda C. Abraham and D. R. Ellison (1955), 262–90.

p.607   *"volcano-god":* *Der Mann Moses und die monotheistische Religion. Drei Abhandlungen* (1939), *GW* XVI, 133 /*Moses and Monotheism: Three Essays*, *SE* XXIII, 34.

p.607   *"Mount Sinai":* Ibid., 132/33.

p.607   *after his death:* See Ernst Sellin, *Mose und seine Bedeutung für die israelitisch-jüdische Religionsgeschichte* (1922).

p.607   *"18th dynasty":* *Der Mann Moses*, *GW* XVI, 148 / *Moses and Monotheism*, *SE* XXIII, 47.

p.608   *Austrian authorities:* Freud to Arnold Zweig, December 16, 1934. *Freud–Zweig,* 108–9 (98).

p.608   *"of clay":* Freud to Arnold Zweig, November 6, 1934. Ibid., 108 (97).

p.608   *"me incessantly":* Freud to Arnold Zweig, December 16, 1934. Ibid., 108 (98).

p.608   *"imagination go":* Freud to Arnold Zweig, May 2, 1935. Ibid., 117 (106).

p.608   *"further with him":* Freud to Eitingon, May 12, 1935. By permission of Sigmund Freud Copyrights, Wivenhoe.

p.609   *"5 hours daily":* Freud to Hilda Doolittle, May 19, 1935. In English. Hilda Doolittle papers, Beinecke Rare Book and Manuscript Library, Yale University.

p.609   *"comfortable prison":* Freud to Hilda Doolittle, November 3, 1935. In English. Ibid.

p.609   *"our people":* Freud to Hilda Doolittle, May 19, 1935. In English. Ibid.

p.609   *"false path":* Freud to Jones, May 26, 1935. Freud Collection, D2, LC.

p.609   *"English circles":* Ibid.

p.609   *touch with them:* See Freud to Hilda Doolittle, n.d. [November 16 or 17], 1935. Hilda Doolittle papers, Beinecke Rare Book and Manuscript Library, Yale University.

p.610   *"gets changed":* Freud to Mrs. N. N., April 9, 1935. In English. *Briefe,* 438.

p.610   *"leaving here":* Ibid.

p.610   *"other way!":* Freud to Arnold Zweig, October 14, 1935. By permission of Sigmund Freud Copyrights, Wivenhoe.

p.611   *"German medicines":* Ibid.

p.611   *"light of day":* Freud to Stefan Zweig, November 5, 1935. By permission of Sigmund Freud Copyrights, Wivenhoe.

p.611   *is sleep:* See Freud to Arnold Zweig, January 20, 1936. *Freud–Zweig,* 129 (119).

p.611   *"read the thing":* Freud to Jones, March 3, 1936. Freud Collection, D2, LC.

p.611   *"about Moses":* Freud to Arnold Zweig, February 21, 1936. *Freud–Zweig,* 133 (122).

p.611   *"with Arn. Zweig":* *Kürzeste Chronik,* August 18, 1936. Freud Museum, London.

p.611   *now repeated:* For Freud's attempts to avoid celebrations, commemorative volumes, and the like, see Freud to Jones, July 21, 1935, and March 3, 1936. Freud Collection, D2, LC. See also *Jones* III, 200–201.

p.611   *an enterprise:* See Freud to Jones, July 21, 1935. Freud Collection, D2, LC. See also *Jones* III, 200–201.

p.612   *"he owed":* Martha Freud to Lilly Freud Marlé, June 5, 1936. Freud Collection, B2, LC.

p.612   *"kind of longing":* Freud to Stefan Zweig, May 18, 1936. By permission of Sigmund Freud Copyrights, Wivenhoe.

p.612   *on June 14:* See *Kürzeste Chronik,* June 14, 1936. Freud Museum, London.

p.612   *corresponding member:* See *Kürzeste Chronik,* June 30, 1936. Ibid.

p.612   *had received:* Freud to Jones, July 4, 1936. Freud Collection, D2, LC.

p.612   *"and writings":* Freud to Schwadron, July 12, 1936. Freud Museum, London.

p.613   *"her sexuality!":* Freud to Arnold Zweig, June 17, 1936. By permission of Sigmund Freud Copyrights, Wivenhoe.

p.613   *very well:* Freud to Eitingon, February 5, 1937. By permission of Sigmund Freud Copyrights, Wivenhoe.

p.613   *"and active":* Freud to Marie Bonaparte, September 27, 1936. Quoted in *Jones* III, 209.

p.613   *"gravely ill":* *Kürzeste Chronik,* July 23, 1936. Freud Museum, London.

p.613   *"in pain":* *Kürzeste Chronik,* December 24, 1936. Ibid.

p.613   *"your handwriting!":* Marie Bonaparte to Freud, December 30, 1936. Quoted in the introduction to *Freud–Fliess,* xviii.

p.613   *"so-called posterity":* Freud to Marie Bonaparte, January 3, 1937. Ibid., xviii–xix.

p.614   *"revere you":* Marie Bonaparte to Freud, January 7, 1937. Ibid., xix–xx.

p.614   *"quite personal":* Freud to Marie Bonaparte, January 10, 1937. Ibid., xx.

p.615   *therapeutic enthusiast:* See "Editor's Note" to "Analysis Terminable and Interminable," *SE* XXIII, 212.

p.615   *"The Zuyder Zee":* "Die Zerlegung der psychischen Persönlichkeit," in *Neue Vorlesun-*

gen, GW XV, 86/"The Dissection of the Psychical Personality," in *New Introductory Lectures, SE* XXII, 80.

p.615   *"contradicted psychoanalysis":* Freud to Arnold Zweig, June 22, 1937. By permission of Sigmund Freud Copyrights, Wivenhoe.

p.616   *"sexual attraction":* Freud to Arnold Zweig, February 10, 1937. By permission of Sigmund Freud Copyrights, Wivenhoe.

p.616   *warm obituary:* See "Lou Andreas-Salomé" (1937), *SE* XXIII, 297.

p.616   *"all time":* Eitingon to Freud, February 24, 1937. By permission of Sigmund Freud Copyrights, Wivenhoe.

p.616   *"is uncertain":* Freud to Jones, August 23, 1933. Freud Collection, D2, LC.

p.616   *"you visit me":* Freud to Arnold Zweig, September 23, 1935. *Freud–Zweig,* 121 (111).

p.616   *whitewash:* See Arnold Zweig to Freud, November 22, 1935. Ibid., 124 (113–14).

p.616   *Nazi regime:* See Freud to Arnold Zweig, February 21, 1936. Ibid., 132 (122).

p.616   *"fall for me":* Freud to Arnold Zweig, June 22, 1936. Ibid., 142–43 (133).

p.617   *"like you":* Freud to Jones, March 2, 1937. Freud Collection, D2, LC.

p.617   *"more importunate":* Freud to Arnold Zweig, April 2, 1937. *Freud–Zweig,* 149 (139–40).

p.617   *"German brutality":* Freud to Jones, April 7, 1933. Freud Collection, D2, LC.

p.617   *"being strangled":* Freud to Arnold Zweig, December 20, 1937. *Freud–Zweig,* 163 (154).

p.617   *out of Austria:* Freud to Eitingon, February 6, 1938. By permission of Sigmund Freud Copyrights, Wivenhoe.

p.617   *"with the panic":* Anna Freud to Jones, February 20, 1938. Jones papers, Archives of the British Psycho-Analytical Society, London.

p.618   *would be dashed:* Freud to Ernst Freud, February 22, 1938. Freud Collection, B1, LC.

p.618   *"Quien Sabe?":* Freud to Marie Bonaparte, February 23, 1938. *Jones* III, 217.

p.618   *"Finis Austriae":* Kürzeste Chronik, March 11, 1938. Freud Museum, London.

p.618   *"Hitler in Vienna":* Kürzeste Chronik, March 13 and 14, 1938. Ibid.

p.619   *"lust for revenge":* Carl Zuckmayer, *Als wär's ein Stück von mir. Horen der Freundschaft* (1966), 71.

p.620   " *'work for the Jews!' ":* G. E. R. Gedye, of the London *Daily Telegraph.* Quoted in Dieter Wagner and Gerhard Tomkowitz, *"Ein Volk, Ein Reich, Ein Führer!" Der Anschluss Österreichs 1938* (1968), 267.

p.620   *Hitler salute:* For details and documentation, see Herbert Rosenkranz, "The Anschluss and the Tragedy of Austrian Jewry, 1938–1945," in *The Jews of Austria,* ed. Fraenkel, 479–545.

p.620   *"organization's insignia":* "Vienna Jews Beaten; Stores Plundered / Offices of Societies and Papers Occupied by Nazis—Arrests Made on Money Charges," *New York Times,* March 14, 1938, 2.

p.620   *"than in Germany":* Ibid.

p.621   *"certain gradualness":* "Jews Humiliated by Vienna Crowds / Families Compelled to Scrub Streets, Though German Guards Drive Off Mob / Nazis Seize Big Stores / Total of Arrests Enormous—Austria German District as Ministries Are Absorbed," *New York Times,* March 16, 1938, 3 (Associated Press dispatch).

p.621   *"Opposition Visible":* New York Times, March 14, 1938, 3 (Associated Press dispatch, dateline "March 13, 1938").

p.621   *stomped to death:* See Friedrich Torberg, *Die Tante Jolesch, oder Der Untergang des Abendlandes in Anekdoten* (1975; paperback ed., 1977), 154–67, esp. 155.

p.621   *of his house:* See Raul Hilberg, *The Destruction of the European Jews* (1961; 2d ed., 1981), 61.

p.621   *these were Jews:* See Wagner and Tomkowitz, *'Ein Volk, Ein Reich, Ein Führer!,'* 341.

p.621   *concentration camps:* See Martin Gilbert, ed., *The Macmillan Atlas of the Holocaust* (1982), 22. Of the 60,000 Jews who could not get out of Austria, some 40,000 were murdered.

p.622   *"situation in Austria":* Quoted in "Jews Scrub Streets in Vienna Inner City / Forced to

Remove Crosses of Fatherland Front," *New York Times,* March 24, 1938, 7 (Associated Press dispatch, dateline "March 23, 1938").

p.622   *"like us to?":* Schur, *Freud, Living and Dying,* 499.

p.622   *in the* Verlag: *Kürzeste Chronik,* March 15, 1938. Freud Museum, London.

p.623   *help themselves:* See Anna Freud to Ernest Jones, n.d. Jones papers, Archives of the British Psycho-Analytical Society, London. This account contradicts the popular story that Martha Freud asked them to sit down and then offered them the contents of the cash box.

p.623   *him a passport:* See "Aid for Freud Offered / Palestine Will Grant Entry to Professor Neumann Also," *New York Times,* March 23, 1938, 5 (dateline "Jerusalem, March 22, 1938"). See also "Freud Forbidden to Go / Can't Get Passport, Member of Dutch Group Inviting Him Says," *New York Times,* March 30, 1938, 4 (dateline "The Hague, March 29, 1938").

p.623   *the next day: Kürzeste Chronik,* March 16 and 17, 1938. Freud Museum, London.

p.623   *"ready to help":* Binswanger to Freud, March 18, 1938. By permission of Sigmund Freud Copyrights, Wivenhoe.

p.623   *counseling prudence:* This is the interpretation of Max Schur, which I find persuasive; see Schur, *Freud, Living and Dying,* 496.

p.623   *"in danger":* In this instance, and in succeeding paragraphs, I am quoting from photocopies of the original telegrams, by permission of Sigmund Freud Copyrights, Wivenhoe. See also Clark, *Freud,* 505–11, drawing on documents in the Public Record Office and the Foreign Office in London, and the National Archives in Washington. Clark's reading of these documents and mine are in close agreement.

p.624   *new immigrants:* Jones III, 220.

p.624   *"final acceptance":* Ibid., I, 294.

p.625   *"Anna at Gestapo": Kürzeste Chronik,* March 22, 1938. Freud Museum, London.

p.625   *worst day:* Schur, *Freud, Living and Dying,* 498. See also Anna Freud to Schur, April 28, 1954. Max Schur papers, LC, and Martin Freud, *Freud,* 214.

p.625   *"as I could":* Schur, *Freud, Living and Dying,* 498.

p.626   *scientific body:* Martin Freud, *Freud,* 212–13.

p.626   *"die in freedom":* Freud to Ernst Freud, May 12, 1938. *Briefe,* 459. The phrase "to die in freedom" is in English.

p.626   *to confiscate:* See Jones III, 221.

p.626   *back to Austria:* "The Nazi official who organized this business showed a strange sense of humour when he debited father's account with the quite considerable cost of the books' transportation to their funeral pyre in Vienna." (Martin Freud, *Freud,* 214.)

p.627   *arrested as well:* Ibid. It is worth noting that Freud, ever scrupulous, paid back these sums as soon as he was able to do so.

p.627   *"doing for us":* Anna Freud to Jones, April 3, 1938. Jones papers, Archives of the British Psycho-Analytical Society, London.

p.627   *"going slowly":* Anna Freud to Jones, April 22, 1938. Ibid.

p.627   *"does not ask":* Anna Freud to Jones, April 26, 1938. Ibid.

p.627   *wastebasket:* See McGuire, introduction to *Freud–Jung,* xx note.

p.627   Moses and Monotheism: Freud to Jones, April 28, 1938. Freud Collection, D2, LC.

p.628   *"than men do":* Freud to Ernst Freud, May 9, 1938. Photocopy of holograph courtesy Dr. Daniel Offer. (I owe this reference to George F. Mahl.)

p.628   *"been worth while":* Freud to Jones, May 13, 1938. Freud Collection, D2, LC.

p.628   beste empfehlen: Martin Freud, *Freud,* 217.

p.628   *"there at all":* Anna Freud to Jones, May 25, 1938. Jones papers, Archives of the British Psycho-Analytical Society, London.

p.628   *not in order:* See Anna Freud to Jones, May 30 and 31, 1938. Ibid.

p.628   *London address:* See Freud to Arnold Zweig, June 4, 1938. *Freud–Zweig,* 168 (160). And see Freud to Samuel Freud, June 4, 1938. In English. Rylands University Library, Manchester.

p.628   *June 4:* See *Kürzeste Chronik* at the relevant dates. Freud Museum, London. Up to that fateful day of departure, the dates in the *Chronik* are perfectly correct; but "Saturday, June 3" follows upon "Thursday, June 2." Freud did not correct the wrong dating until the middle of the following week: thus, the first entry about London reads "Monday, June 5," when it should be "June 6"; then, by Thursday, the date is recorded correctly: "Thursday, June 9."

p.629   *"two weeks?":* Kürzeste Chronik, May 10, 1938. Ibid.

p.629   *"been released":* Freud to Eitingon, June 6, 1938. *Briefe,* 462.

p.629   *"clumsy enough":* Ibid., 461.

p.629   *Freud instead:* See Anna Freud to Jones, May 25, 1938. Jones papers, Archives of the British Psycho-Analytical Society, London.

p.629   *"2:45 A.M.":* Kürzeste Chronik, June 3, 1938. Freud Museum, London. As previously noted, Freud's entries for this period are incorrectly dated. Saturday was June 4, not June 3. And of course by 2:45 A.M., strictly speaking, the day was Sunday, June 5.

p.629   *"beautiful city":* Freud to Eitingon, June 6, 1938. *Briefe,* 461–62.

p.629   *for his wife:* See *Jones* III, 228.

p.630   *"new stationery":* Freud to Eitingon, June 6, 1938. *Briefe,* 461.

p.630   *"perfectly happy":* Martha Freud to Lilly Freud Marlé and her husband, Arnold, June 22 [1938]. Freud Collection, B2, LC.

p.630   *"and victorious":* Freud to Eitingon, June 6, 1938. *Briefe,* 461–63.

p.631   *"loves the people":* "Prof. Freud / In London After Sixty Years / Well But Tired," *Manchester Guardian,* June 7, 1938, 10.

p.631   *"Sigm. Freud":* Freud to Arnold Zweig, June 28, 1938. *Freud–Zweig,* 173 (164). The word "signatures" is in English. Half a century before, he had signed himself "Dr. Sigm. Freud" in his early letters to Fliess.

p.631   *"being opened":* Freud to Eitingon, June 6, 1938. *Briefe,* 463. The quoted passages are in English.

p.631   *reached him:* Freud to Alexander Freud, June 22, 1938. Ibid., 463–64.

p.631   *less astonished:* "Already in the second week," she wrote, "letters without any indications more concrete than 'Freud, London,' arrived without fail." (Martha Freud to Lilly Freud Marlé and her husband, Arnold, June 22, 1938. Freud Collection, B2, LC.)

p.632   *"fame means":* Freud to Alexander Freud, June 22, 1938. *Briefe,* 464.

p.632   *"to be a German":* Freud to de Saussure, June 11, 1938. Freud Collection, Z3, LC.

p.632   *"started again":* Kürzeste Chronik, June 21, 1938. Freud Museum, London.

p.632   *"their misery":* Freud to Arnold Zweig, June 28, 1938. *Freud–Zweig,* 172 (163).

p.632   *same plea:* See *Jones* III, 234.

p.633   *believing Jew:* See Freud to Arnold Zweig, June 28, 1938. *Freud–Zweig,* 172 (163).

p.633   *"national interests":* Der Mann Moses, *GW* XVI, 103/Moses and Monotheism, *SE* XXIII, 7.

p.633   *"Moses III":* Freud to Alexander Freud, July 17, 1938. Freud Collection, B1, LC. See also *Kürzeste Chronik,* July 17, 1938. Freud Museum, London.

p.633   *"Netherlands longer?":* Freud to Reik, July 3, 1938. Typescript copy, Siegfried Bernfeld papers, container 17, LC. The letter is quoted in a different translation in Theodor Reik, *The Search Within: The Inner Experience of a Psychoanalyst* (1956), 656.

p.633   *"than before":* Freud to Jacques Schnier, July 8, 1938. In English. Siegfried Bernfeld papers, container 17, LC.

p.634   *promptly adopted:* Freud to Sachs, July 11, 1938. Quoted in Sachs, *Freud: Master and Friend,* 180–81.

p.634   *"technical mastery":* Freud to Stefan Zweig, July 20, 1938. Quoted in full in *Jones* III, 235.

p.634   *"amusing occupation":* Freud to Anna Freud, August 3, 1938. Freud Collection, LC.

p.635   *"longer yesterday":* Anna Freud to Marie Bonaparte, September 8, 1938. Quoted in Schur, *Freud, Living and Dying,* 510.

p.635   *"pay it themselves"*: Arnold Zweig to Freud, November 8, 1938. *Freud–Zweig*, 179 (170).

p.635   *"Peace"*: *Kürzeste Chronik*, September 30, 1938. Freud Museum, London.

p.636   *analytic patients*: Freud to Marie Bonaparte, October 4, 1938. *Briefe*, 467.

p.636   *"nothing else"*: Freud to Marie Bonaparte, November 12, 1938. Ibid., 471.

p.636   *"painful connotation"*: Freud to Yvette Guilbert, October 24, 1938. Ibid., 468. The word "connotation" is in English.

p.637   *been exhausting*: See Arnold Zweig to Freud, August 5 and October 16, 1938. *Freud–Zweig*, 176, 178 (167–68, 169–70).

p.637   *"risk it"*: Freud to Singer, October 31, 1938. *Briefe*, 469–70.

p.637   *"accepted payment"*: Freud to Jones, November 1, 1938. Freud Collection, D2, LC.

p.638   *"slight suggestions"*: Blanche Knopf to Freud, November 15, 1938. Freud Museum, London.

p.638   *in the United States*: See Blanche Knopf to Martin Freud, September 19, 27, 1938; Blanche Knopf to Freud, November 15, December 9, and 22, 1938, and January 16, March 31, and April 28, 1939. All in Freud Museum, London. The book was published in the United States in mid-June 1939.

p.638   *"themselves to science"*: Freud to Dwossis, December 11, 1938. Typescript copy. Freud Museum, London.

p.638   *"Pogroms in Germany"*: *Kürzeste Chronik*, November 10, 1938. In English. Freud Museum, London.

p.639   *them to France*: Freud to Marie Bonaparte, November 12, 1938. *Briefe*, 471. For some months, at least, his sisters were paid the monthly sum he had left for them. See Freud to Anna Freud, August 3, 1938. Freud Collection, LC.

p.639   *"psychoanalytic movement"*: Freud to Jones, March 7, 1939. Freud Collection, D2, LC.

p.639   *collected works*: See *Jones* III, 233.

p.639   *"events in Austria"*: *Internationale Zeitschrift für Psychoanalyse und Imago*, XXIV (1939), nos. 1 / 2 (combined issue), title page.

p.640   *"great strength"*: Leonard Woolf, *Downhill All the Way* (1967), 166, 168–69.

p.640   *"formidable man"*: Ibid., 169.

p.640   *unforgettable presence: The Diary of Virginia Woolf*, ed. Anne Olivier Bell, vol. V, *1936–1941* (1984), 202.

p.640   *thirty-first*: *Kürzeste Chronik*, January 2 and 31, 1939. Freud Museum. London.

p.640   *like Pyramidon*: See Anna Freud to [Pichler?], September 20, 1938. Max Schur papers, LC.

p.641   *"paralyzing pains"*: Freud to Arnold Zweig, February 20, 1939. *Freud–Zweig*, 183–84 (175–76).

p.641   *radium treatments*: See Marie Bonaparte's handwritten copy of a letter from Dr. Lacassagne to her, dated November 28, 1954, noting that he had examined Freud on February 26, 1939, and had assisted in applying radium on March 14. (Enclosed in letter from Marie Bonaparte to Jones, n.d. Jones papers, Archives of the British Psycho-Analytical Society, London.)

p.641   *"sadistic father!"*: Pfister to Freud, February 21, 1939. By permission of Sigmund Freud Copyrights, Wivenhoe.

p.641   *"Nazi-soul"*: Freud to Arnold Zweig, March 5, 1939. *Freud–Zweig*, 186–87 (178).

p.641   *"it myself"*: Freud to Sachs, March 12, 1939. Quoted in Sachs, *Freud: Master and Friend*, 181–82.

p.642   *"very desirable"*: Freud to Marie Bonaparte, April 28, 1939. *Briefe*, 474–75.

p.642   *quickly as possible*: See Schur, *Freud, Living and Dying*, 522–25.

p.642   *"personal physician"*: One such reference, for example, is in Freud to Marie Bonaparte, April 28, 1939. *Briefe*, 474.

p.642   *March 1929*: See Freud to Marie Bonaparte, March 6, 1929: "I have engaged Schur as it were as our house physician." (Quoted in Jones to Schur, October 9, 1956. Max Schur papers, LC.)

p.642   *"easy for me":* Freud to Schur, June 28, 1930. *Briefe,* 415. For Schur's relations with Freud, see his *Freud, Living and Dying,* esp. his introduction and ch. 18.

p.642   *too low:* See Freud to Schur, January 10, 1930, January 10 and July 26, 1938. Max Schur papers, LC.

p.643   *hands on it:* Quoted in Schur, *Freud, Living and Dying,* 408.

p.643   *6 Mai 1939:* See Ernst Freud et al., eds., *Sigmund Freud: His Life in Pictures and Words,* 315.

p.643   *"Moses in English":* Kürzeste Chronik, May 19, 1939. Freud Museum, London.

p.643   *Jewish ancestry:* See *Moses and Monotheism, SE* XXIII, 90.

p.643   *incredulous correspondents:* See ibid., 65n.

p.644   *"of the son":* Der Mann Moses, GW XVI, 193–94/*Moses and Monotheism, SE* XXIII, 87–88.

p.644   *"glad tidings":* Ibid., 244/135.

p.645   *"Judaism had risen":* Ibid.

p.645   *mind and morality:* Ibid., 194, 191–92 / 88, 85–86.

p.645   *"act morally":* Quoted in Anna Freud Bernays, page proofs of "Erlebtes" (1933), 5. Freud Collection, B2, LC.

p.645   *"true worth":* Der Mann Moses, GW XVI, 222–23/*Moses and Monotheism, SE* XXIII, 115.

p.645   *always been:* See ibid., 198/91.

p.645   *"not think!":* Hamilton Fyfe, review of *Moses and Monotheism, John O'London's Weekly,* June 2, 1939.

p.646   *"groundless hypotheses":* Buber, *Moses,* 7n.

p.646   *boorish ignoramus:* J. M. Lask, review of *Moses and Monotheism, Palestine Review* (Jerusalem), IV (June 30, 1939), 169–70.

p.646   *"hatred of Israel":* Quoted in *Jones* III, 370.

p.646   *"itself Christian":* Father Vincent McNabb, O.P., review of *Moses and Monotheism, Catholic Herald* (London), July 14, 1939.

p.646   *Jewish religion:* See N. Perlmann (from Tel Aviv) to Freud, July 2, 1939. Freud Museum, London.

p.646   *"other beasts":* S. J. Birnbaum (a barrister in Toronto) to Freud, February 27, 1939. Ibid.

p.647   *"you belong":* Unsigned letter to Freud, May 26, 1939. Ibid. For other opinions, see *Jones* III, 362–74.

p.647   *C.O.D.:* Alexandre Burnacheff to Freud, July 4, 1939. Freud Museum, London.

p.647   *"wholly my invention":* Freud to Rafael da Costa, May 2, 1939. Typescript copy, Freud Museum, London.

p.648   *"put aside":* Freud to Arnold Zweig, June 13, 1935. *Freud–Zweig,* 118 (107).

p.648   *"wish or must":* "Vorbemerkung II," in *Der Mann Moses, GW* XVI, 159/"Prefatory Note II," in *Moses and Monotheism, SE* XXIII, 57.

p.648   *"unlaid ghost":* "Zusammenfassung und Wiederholung," in ibid., 210/"Summary and Recapitulation," in ibid., 103.

p.648   *"been sold":* Freud to Marie Bonaparte, June 15, 1939. Quoted in the original German in Schur, *Freud, Living and Dying,* 567.

p.648   *most disagreeable:* See Anna Freud to Schur, June 9, 1939. Max Schur papers, LC.

p.649   *" 'friend in America' ":* Sachs, *Freud: Master and Friend,* 185–87.

p.649   *medical practice:* See *Kürzeste Chronik,* August 1, 1939. Freud Museum, London.

p.649   *" 'me again' ":* Dyck, "Mein Onkel Sigmund," interview with Harry Freud, *Aufbau,* May 11, 1956, 4.

p.649   *"wait, wait":* Freud to Schaeffer, August 19, 1939. Dictated to Anna Freud. Isakower Collection, LC.

p.649   *yet arrived:* Rosa Graf to Elsa Reiss, n.d. [August 23, 1939]. Freud Collection, B2, LC.

p.649   *"War panic":* Kürzeste Chronik, August 27, 1939. Freud Museum, London.

p.649   *"knowing eyes"*: "The Medical Case History of Sigmund Freud," dated February 27, 1954. Max Schur papers, LC.

p.650   *"into my life"*: Jones to Freud, September 3, 1939. By permission of Sigmund Freud Copyrights, Wivenhoe.

p.650   *with his daughter:* "The Medical Case History of Sigmund Freud." Max Schur papers, LC.

p.650   *close to them:* Schur dealt with Freud's last days in "The Problem of Death in Freud's Writings and Life," his lecture on May 19, 1964, in the prestigious Freud Anniversary Lecture Series, under the auspices of the New York Psychoanalytic Institute. In the same year, Anna Freud commented on the lecture, "Shouldn't Dr. Stross, too, appear in it? She was quite indispensable, on the trip and in the last nights which she wholly shared." (Anna Freud to Schur, October 12, 1964. Max Schur papers, LC.)

p.650   *running out:* See Anna Freud to Jones, typed comment on vol. III of Jones's biography, n.d. Jones papers, Archives of the British Psycho-Analytical Society, London.

p.650   *into his doze:* Jones III, 245–46. Important details, like Anna Freud's summons, are from a letter Jones sent to Max Schur, February 21, 1956. (Max Schur papers, LC.) In fact, Jones thought that Freud actually lapsed into unconsciousness and did not wake up again. Schur's account in "The Medical Case History of Sigmund Freud" contradicts this. (Ibid.)

p.651   *"end of it"*: Ibid.

p.651   *"Macbeth says"*: Freud to Pfister, March 6, 1910. *Freud–Pfister*, 33 (35).

p.651   *to the end:* The principal source for my pages on Freud's last days is Max Schur's unpublished memorandum "The Medical Case History of Sigmund Freud," dated February 27, 1954. (Max Schur papers, LC.) He intended this for the Freud archives—the Freud Collection, LC—and as an *aide-mémoire* for Ernest Jones, then working on his biography of Freud. One use to which Schur later put this memorandum was as a basis for his Freud Lecture of 1964, "The Problem of Death in Freud's Writings and Life." (For an abstract, by Milton E. Jucovy, see *Psychoanalytic Quarterly*, XXXIV [1965], 144–47.) There are six or more drafts of this lecture in the Schur papers—Schur seems to have agonized over these pages as he had not agonized over anything else all his life. I have supplemented Schur's memorandum with an agreeable and most fruitful interview with Helen Schur (June 3, 1986) and correspondence with her, and, mainly to confirm some details, with a letter from Freud's nephew Harry, dated September 25, 1939, written from New York to his aunts in Vienna and based, Harry Freud says in the letter, on "partly direct, partly telegraphic information from friends." (Freud Collection B1, LC.) I found immensely useful several letters from Anna Freud to Ernest Jones, notably one of February 27, 1956, containing significant details. (Jones papers, Archives of the British Psycho-Analytical Society, London.) A few discrepancies remain, to be partly attributed, I think, to the high emotions with which the participants experienced, and later recalled, these moving events.

     My own account departs in apparently minor but actually significant details from Max Schur's *published* account (*Freud, Living and Dying,* 526–29) and the Jucovy abstract of Schur's 1964 Freud Lecture. In the lecture, Schur said—untruthfully: "On September 21st he [Freud] indicated to his doctor that his suffering no longer made any sense and *asked for sedation. Given morphine for his pain,* he fell into a peaceful sleep and then lapsed into a coma and died at three o'clock on the morning of September 23rd." (Jucovy abstract of Schur's Freud Lecture, p. 147, italics mine.) Later biographers, having no other usable report at hand—Schur, after all, was the most authoritative and eloquent witness—have simply followed his published version and his Freud Lecture. (See, for one instance, Clark, *Freud,* 526–27.)

     In writing his classic biography, Ernest Jones was at first skittish about all the "morbid" detail, but then liberally used Schur's memorandum, closely paraphrasing and at times virtually quoting it. Anna Freud reported to Schur that Jones was hanging back about Freud's severe ailments, but, she commented, "the illness, with all its horrifying details, was at the same time the highest expression of his attitude toward life." (Anna Freud to Schur, September 2, 1956. Max Schur papers, LC.) Anna Freud had wanted Jones to use

Schur's memorandum as the last chapter in his biography, but he decided, with justice, to paraphrase and quote it extensively instead (see *Jones* III, 245–246); he did thank Schur warmly in the preface (see ibid., xii–xiii). The differences between Schur's memorandum and Jones's pages are subtle but worth noting: while Schur, lawyerlike, does not make any explicit comment on this delicate point, Jones firmly (and inaccurately, following Schur's Freud Lecture) says that Schur, when Freud asked for his help now that life had become only torture, "pressed his hand and promised he would give him *adequate sedation.*" (*Jones* III, 246, italics mine.) Again, Jones says that on September 22, Schur "gave Freud a third of a grain of morphia"; this is a dose of 0.0216 gram, virtually identical with the one specified by Schur in *Freud, Living and Dying* (p.529), where he says he gave Freud "a hypodermic of two centigrams of morphine." But while Jones mentions only one injection, Schur mentions two even in the published report: "I repeated this dose after about twelve hours." (Ibid.) And in the introduction Schur wrote for his unpublished memorandum, he notes that in what he intended to publish, he would distort the dosage and omit one conversation between Freud and himself. Writing to Anna Freud on April 7, 1954, he offered a different list, indicating that the "correct version (dosage, more than one injection) has been handed over to the [Freud] Archive." (Carbon copy, Max Schur papers, LC.)

In my own text I have drawn mainly on this "correct version": the dose was three centigrams rather than the two he mentions in his book, and Schur may have administered three rather than two injections. As Schur made clear in a letter to Anna Freud on March 19, 1954, he had consulted a lawyer concerning the question of euthanasia and had, in response, watered down his report. (Carbon copy, ibid.) As Jerome H. Jaffe and William R. Martin make clear in their "Opioid Analgesics and Antagonists," in *Goodman and Gilman: The Pharmacological Basis of Therapeutics*, ed. Alfred Goodman Gilman, Louis S. Goodman, and Alfred Gilman (1941; 6th ed., 1980), the physicians' bible on the use and effects of drugs, one centigram is a normal dose for patients in pain: "10 mg is generally considered to be an optimal initial dose of morphine and provides satisfactory analgesia in approximately 70% of patients with moderate-to-severe pain" (p. 509). While "subsequent doses may be higher," the authors nowhere recommend more than two centigrams (p. 509; see also 499). While the severely ill and very elderly—and Freud was, of course, both—may absorb the drug very slowly and be able to tolerate more than a patient in better repair, three centigrams is in all probability a virtually lethal dose for anyone.

Another distortion in Schur's published version of Freud's last days, one he perpetrated out of respect for Anna Freud's desire for privacy, was to minimize her role. In one draft of his Freud Lecture, Schur omits the "tell Anna" episode altogether. This, too, deserves comment: the published version has *Sagen Sie es der Anna*—"Tell Anna about this." (Schur, *Freud, Living and Dying,* 529.) Jones, following Schur faithfully, has "Tell Anna about our talk." (*Jones* III, 246.) But the unpublished memorandum has *Besprechen Sie es mit der Anna*, which means "discuss it," or "talk it over," with Anna. This version appears to be authentic; it is made particularly plausible by what Freud said next, according to Schur: "and if she think it's right, then make an end of it." It is worth conjecturing that, innocent as she was in the great denouement, well-meaning and justified as Schur's actions may have been, she bore a heavy burden of guilt for her eventual acquiescence in the decision to put her father out of his misery. She fought against it, Schur recalls in his memorandum, but then sadly resigned herself. This reading of the situation has dictated my treatment in the text: I see Freud's end as a stoic suicide, carried out in his behalf, since he was too weak to act himself, by his loyal and loving physician and reluctantly acquiesced in by his no less loyal and even more loving daughter.

Bibliographical Essay

General

The secondary literature on Freud is vast, rapidly growing, almost out of control. Some of this avalanche is revealing, much of it useful, more of it provocative; an astonishing share is malicious or downright absurd. I have not tried for completeness in this essay, but have concentrated rather on the works I found informative on matters of fact, interesting in their interpretations, or worth debating. I have written it, that is to say, to give reasons (briefly) why I have adopted, or failed to adopt, one position or another, and to indicate from whom I have learned most.

The best German edition of Freud's psychoanalytic writings is *Gesammelte Werke, Chronologisch Geordnet,* ed. Anna Freud, Edward Bibring, Willi Hoffer, Ernst Kris, and Otto Isakower, in collaboration with Marie Bonaparte, 18 vols. (1940–68). Though very valuable, it is not flawless: it is not quite complete; its running heads are not as helpful as they might be; the editorial notes and the indexes to individual volumes are skimpy. Most troubling of all, the *Gesammelte Werke* does not differentiate among the various editions of such much-revised works of Freud's as *The Interpretation of Dreams* and *Three Essays on the Theory of Sexuality.* This differentiation is supplied by the handy *Studienausgabe,* ed. Alexander Mitscherlich, Angela Richards, and James Strachey, 12 vols. (1969–75). The *Studienausgabe* has limitations of its own; it omits some minor papers and Freud's autobiographical writings and its arrangement is not chronological but topical. But the editorial apparatus, based on the English *Standard Edition,* is copious.

The international authority of that *Standard Edition of the Complete Psychological Works of Sigmund Freud,* tr. under the general editorship of James Strachey in collaboration with Anna Freud, assisted by Alix Strachey and Alan Tyson, 24 vols. (1953–74), is deservedly assured, whatever new and better translations may be offered sometime in the future. It is a heroic enterprise. Where necessary, it offers variorum texts; it wrestles with intractable material (such as the German jokes Freud quotes in his book on jokes); and it introduces each work, even the slightest paper, with indispensable bibliographical and historical information. The translations have been quite controversial—and not unjustly: shifts in tenses, rebarbative translations like "anaclitic" and "cathexis" for technical terms for which Freud used ordinary, highly suggestive German words have provoked severe criticisms. The most severe (and, I think, cranky) of those is Bruno Bettelheim, *Freud and Man's Soul* (1983), which argues in essence that the translators have ruined Freud's argument and that anyone reading Freud only in Strachey's English cannot understand Freud's concern with man's soul. Far soberer, and more reasonable, are the papers by Darius G. Ornston; see esp. "Freud's Conception Is Different from Strachey's," *J. Amer. Psychoanal. Assn.,* XXXIII (1985), 379–410; "The Invention of 'Cathexis' and Strachey's Strategy," *Int. Rev. Psycho-Anal.,* XII (1985), 391–99; and "Reply to William I. Grossman," *J. Amer. Psychoanal. Assn.,* XXXIV (1986), 489–92. The *Standard Edition* can now be used in conjunction with S. A. Guttman, R. L. Jones, and S. M. Parrish, *The Concordance to the Standard Edition of the Complete Psychological Works of Sigmund Freud,* 6 vols. (1980). The most vigorous translations into English, capturing Freud's virile and witty German speech better than any other, can be found in vols. I–IV of *Collected Papers* (1924–25), mainly tr. by the brilliant Joan Riviere. Vol. V, ed. James Strachey, appeared in 1950. No wonder this edition, which contains virtually all of Freud's shorter papers and his case histories, remains the favorite of older American psychoanalysts.

Occasional rare finds enlarge the corpus of Freud's psychoanalytic writings. We owe the most exciting recent discovery, one of the missing metapsychological papers (see text, pp. 367–68 and 373–74), to Ilse Grubrich-Simitis, who has also beautifully edited and introduced it: Sigmund Freud, *A Phylogenetic Fantasy: Overview of the Transference Neuroses* (1985; tr. Axel and Peter T. Hoffer, 1987). An edition of Freud's voluminous and, for the biographer, important prepsychoanalytic writings has long been in preparation and would be a desideratum.

Much of Freud's enormous correspondence has been published. A mouth-watering chronological selection is *Briefe 1873–1939*, ed. Ernst and Lucie Freud (1960; 2d enlarged ed., 1968; English version, *Letters of Sigmund Freud, 1873–1939*, tr. Tania and James Stern, 1961, 2d ed., 1975). Most other editions present the letters correspondent by correspondent. These editions vary exceedingly in merit and must be used with care. Among the most authoritative is Sigmund Freud, C. G. Jung, *Briefwechsel*, impeccably ed. William McGuire and Wolfgang Sauerländer (1974; English version, *The Freud/Jung Letters: The Correspondence between Sigmund Freud and C. G. Jung*, ed. William McGuire and tr. Ralph Manheim [Freud's letters] and R. F. C. Hull [Jung's], also 1974). A third printing of the German edition (1979) has some corrections, mainly in the notes. Hull's renderings do Jung no favor: he raises Jung's already rather coarse language to heights of vulgarity. For example, he renders Jung's *"schmutziger Kerl,"* which is essentially "dirty fellow," as "slimy bastard" (Jung to Freud, June 2, 1910, 359 [325]). Another instance: Jung wrote Freud, according to Hull, that the psychiatrist Adolf Albrecht Friedländer, a vehement critic of psychoanalysis, has been "puking again" (April 17, 1910, 339 [307]); what Jung actually wrote, *"Friedländer hat sich wieder übergeben,"* is far more accurately rendered as "Friedländer has thrown up again." Freud's all-important letters to his "Other," Wilhelm Fliess (a collection for which the word "indispensable" is for once absolutely just), raise smaller difficulties. The American edition, *The Complete Letters of Sigmund Freud to Wilhelm Fliess, 1887–1904*, ed. and tr. Jeffrey Moussaieff Masson (1985), is extremely valuable, for all its minor interpretative vagaries. But the edition of the original German letters, *Briefe an Wilhelm Fliess 1887–1904*, which appeared later (1986), also ed. Masson, assisted by Michael Schröter and Gerhard Fichtner, is superior in its annotations and also contains Ernst Kris's long, fascinating introduction to the selection that first appeared in 1950. For an interesting if limited set of letters, see Martin Grotjahn, ed., *Sigmund Freud as a Consultant: Recollections of a Pioneer in Psychoanalysis* (1970), which contains letters from Freud to the Italian analyst Edoardo Weiss, with comments by the latter. The German edition is *Sigmund Freud–Edoardo Weiss. Briefe zur psychoanalytischen Praxis. Mit den Erinnerungen eines Pioniers der Psychoanalyse* (1973). H. D. [Hilda Doolittle], *Tribute to Freud* (1956) contains, as an appendix, several letters from Freud to her; the complete collection is at the Beinecke Library at Yale. Freud's schoolboy letters to his friend Emil Fluss (not yet translated into English) have been carefully edited by Ilse Grubrich-Simitis in her fine edition of Freud's "self-portrait": Sigmund Freud, *"Selbstdarstellung." Schriften zur Geschichte der Psychoanalyse* (1971; corr. ed., 1973), 103–23. (This edition contains the complete version of Freud's autobiography; the version in *GW*, which I usually cite as "Selbstdarstellung," omits a few sentences, which I quote from *Selbstdarstellung.* The volume also includes several documents in addition to Freud's letters to Emil Fluss.) For Freud's letters to his even closer friend Eduard Silberstein, long being prepared for scholarly publication, I used the originals in the Library of Congress. As this volume went to press, they had not yet appeared in print. I have also consulted, with profit, the careful transcriptions by William J. McGrath for his book on Freud's younger years, *Freud's Discovery of Psychoanalysis: The Politics of Hysteria* (1986). (For an appraisal of that book, see the essay for chapter 1, below.) See also Heinz Stanescu, "Unbekannte Briefe des jungen Sigmund Freud an einen rumänischen Freund," *Zeitschrift des Schriftstellerverbandes des RVR*, XVI (1965), 12–29.

The editions of Freud's other epistolary exchanges, precisely because the letters can be so extraordinarily revealing, offer a rather more disheartening picture. A selection from Freud's important correspondence with his favorite and most dependable disciple in Berlin is presented in Sigmund

Freud, Karl Abraham, *Briefe 1907–1926*, ed. Hilda Abraham and Ernst L. Freud (1965; English version, *A Psycho-Analytic Dialogue: The Letters of Sigmund Freud and Karl Abraham, 1907–1926*, tr. Bernard Marsh and Hilda Abraham, 1965). This edition tantalizingly lists the total number of letters the two exchanged and the number of those printed, but does not indicate *which* letters have been excised; the editors also cut paragraphs, sentences, at times single words, from the printed text without indicating the omissions with suspension points. They do equip each letter that has cuts with an asterisk—not much help. Ernst Pfeiffer, editor of Sigmund Freud, Lou Andreas-Salomé, *Brief-wechsel* (1966; English version, Sigmund Freud, Lou Andreas-Salomé, *Letters*, tr. William and Elaine Robson-Scott, 1972), at least uses suspension points to show omissions, but excludes some of the most important letters (notably those touching on Anna Freud, in the Freud Collection, LC) entirely. Ernst L. Freud and Heinrich Meng, editors of Sigmund Freud, Oskar Pfister, *Briefe 1909–1939* (1963; English version, *Psychoanalysis and Faith: The Letters of Sigmund Freud and Oskar Pfister*, tr. Eric Mosbacher, 1963) employ suspension points to mark the places where they have wielded their editorial scissors, but they drop many significant (certainly the most intimate) letters between these friends. Omissions also compromise the value of Sigmund Freud, Arnold Zweig, *Briefwechsel*, ed. Ernst L. Freud (1968; paperback ed., 1984; English version, *The Letters of Sigmund Freud and Arnold Zweig*, tr. William and Elaine Robson-Scott, 1970), which makes some drastic cuts without specifying them. Ludwig Binswanger made his own selection of his epistolary exchanges with Freud, complete with commentary, in *Erinnerungen an Sigmund Freud* (1956). See also F. B. Davis, "Three Letters from Sigmund Freud to André Breton," *J. Amer. Psychoanal. Assn.*, XXI (1973), 127–34. Other highly instructive correspondences (notably Freud–Jones and Freud–Ferenczi, at present available only in archives) are in the process of being edited for publication. The Freud–Eitingon correspondence also would repay publication. So would the exchanges between Freud and Anna Freud, to say nothing of those between him and his fiancée Martha Bernays, of which Ernst Freud has published only an alluring selection of some ninety-three. Many hundreds more lie under lock and key at the Library of Congress, and a number of unpublished ones (that I could consult) at Sigmund Freud Copyrights. Ernest Jones prints numerous and extensive excerpts from Freud's letters in his three-volume biography, but, as I noted in the text, he was induced by Anna Freud to correct "the most disturbing mistakes" of her father's English letters on the ground that he was very sensitive about his somewhat less than complete mastery of the language. (Anna Freud to Ernest Jones, April 8, 1954. Jones papers, Archives of the British Psycho-Analytical Society, London.) I have quoted Freud's English precisely as he wrote it, restoring his minor mistakes and imaginative, delightful coinages.

Obviously, Freud's autobiographical statements, open and concealed, are of inestimable importance, both for what they disclose and for what they refuse to disclose. His "Autobiographical Study," published in 1925, is doubtless the most important of these documents. Freud's reminiscences in *The Interpretation of Dreams* (1900) virtually all dredged up as he analyzed his own dreams, are of course invaluable, and have been widely cited. They must be read, if possible, with what else we know about him. The same holds true of the revelations that he scattered in such papers as "Screen Memories" (1899) and *The Psychopathology of Everyday Life* (1901).

I shall explore the many biographical studies covering particular parts of Freud's life in the sections on the relevant chapters. The classic biography of Freud remains, for all its evident and much-criticized flaws, Ernest Jones, *The Life and Work of Sigmund Freud*, 3 vols. (1953–57; one-volume abridgment by Lionel Trilling and Steven Marcus, 1961). Jones knew Freud intimately and through many years of combat (with others and, to a lesser degree, with Freud himself). As a pioneering psychoanalyst and by no means slavish follower of Freud, Jones was extremely well informed on all the technical issues. And he could comment with confidence on Freud's family life no less than on the infighting within the analytic establishment. Though rather graceless in style and (more important) unfortunately disposed to separate the man and the work, Jones's biography contains many astute judgments. The most serious charge against him has been that of malice against other followers of Freud, a supposedly unconquerable jealousy that led him to be scathing about such rivals as Ferenczi. There is something in this criticism, but less than is commonly thought. Indeed, Jones's final verdict on Ferenczi, which heavily hints that in his last years Ferenczi was subject to psychotic episodes, and to which strong exception has been taken, largely echoes the opinion that Freud expressed in an unpublished letter to Jones. His life of Freud remains indispensable.

There are many other lives, in many languages. The earliest of them all, which Freud did not much like and criticized in a letter to the author, was Fritz Wittels, *Sigmund Freud: His Personality, His Teaching, and His School* (1924; tr. Eden and Cedar Paul, 1924). The most usable recent biography is Ronald W. Clark, *Freud: The Man and the Cause* (1980), based on much diligent research, reasonable in judgment, and particularly full on Freud's private life, but fairly skimpy and heavily dependent on others in its treatment of Freud's work. A picture biography, well annotated and using quotations from Freud as captions, is Ernst Freud, Lucie Freud, and Ilse Grubrich-Simitis, eds., *Sigmund Freud: His Life in Pictures and Words* (1976; tr. Christine Trollope, 1978); it includes a dependable biographical sketch by K. R. Eissler. Max Schur, *Freud, Living and Dying* (1972), by the physician who was Freud's private doctor during his last ten years and later became a psychoanalyst, is invaluable for its private revelations and judicious, well-informed judgments. I shall cite it repeatedly. Among shorter biographies, O. Mannoni, *Freud* (1968; tr. from the French by Renaud Bruce, 1971) is perhaps the most informative. J. N. Isbister, *Freud: An Introduction to His Life and Work* (1985) is typical of the denigratory school, uncritically drawing upon the biographical speculations and reconstructions of Peter J. Swales. Steven Marcus's review of this book, "The Interpretation of Freud," *Partisan Review* (Winter 1987), 151–57, is devastating, and justly so. Ludwig Marcuse, *Sigmund Freud. Sein Bild vom Menschen* (n.d.) is an informal mixture of essay and biography. Gunnar Brandell, *Freud: A Man of His Century* (1961; rev. ed., 1976; tr. from the Swedish by Iain White, 1979) tries to enlist Freud among such Naturalists as Zola and Schnitzler; see also Louis Breger, *Freud's Unfinished Journey: Conventional and Critical Perspectives in Psychoanalytic Theory* (1981), which reads Freud as at the junction of nineteenth- and twentieth-century cultures. Helen Walker Puner, *Freud: His Life and His Mind* (1947), one of the early lives, is fairly hostile and neither very scholarly nor very reliable; it was influential enough to have Jones explicitly take it to task in the first two volumes of *his* biography.

Then there is Paul Roazen. His *Freud and His Followers* (1975) pays particular attention to Freud's entourage, and includes much usable material. A maddening mixture of hard digging, extensive interviewing, snap judgments, and uncertain tone, it must be used cautiously. Reviewing the book for the *Times Literary Supplement* (March 26, 1986, 341), Richard Wollheim shrewdly characterized it, and a whole school: "Professor Roazen has many criticisms to make of Freud. Freud, he tells us on different occasions, was cold, snobbish, excessively interested in money, indifferent to his family: he never fed his children bottles nor did he once change their diapers; he was a respecter of persons but not of the truth, over-controlled, resentful, narrow-minded, authoritarian. Yet alongside all these different criticisms, and there are few that do not surface on one page or another, there is one reiterated eulogy: Freud was a great man, we must not forget to praise him for his bravery and his genius. Freud has as a good a friend in Professor Roazen as ever Brutus found in Mark Antony." Precisely. In sharp contrast, the best study of Freud's thought in my judgment is Richard Wollheim's own compact, precise, illuminating *Freud* (1971). I must admit, too, that Roazen is justified in complaining about the protective way that Freud's family and adorers have withheld some of the most intriguing material or sought to "correct" his image for posterity; see his "The Legend of Freud," *Virginia Quarterly Review*, XLVII (Winter 1971), 33–45.

Naturally, many of these writings explicitly or implicitly assess Freud's character; so do other works I shall mention in their appropriate places. *Jones* should be singled out for "The Man," part 3 of vol. II, a brave attempt at a coherent estimate, which is valuable but (as I try to show in the text) overrates Freud's serene "maturity" and misreads Freud's relations with his mother, which were, I believe, far less secure than Jones believed. Jones, *Sigmund Freud: Four Centenary Essays* (1956) is, naturally, very admiring, but not without its insights. Philip Rieff, *Freud: The Mind of the Moralist* (1959; rev. ed., 1961) is an elegant extended essay eminently worth reading. Among innumerable other appraisals, I single out John E. Gedo, "On the Origins of the Theban Plague: Assessments of Freud's Character," in *Freud, Appraisals and Reappraisals: Contributions to Freud Studies*, ed. Paul

E. Stepansky, I (1986), 241–59. Hanns Sachs, *Freud: Master and Friend* (1945) is slight in volume but intimate in information; admiring but not sycophantic, it "feels" right. *Freud and the Twentieth Century*, ed. Benjamin Nelson (1957) contains a series of brief and sometimes illuminating appraisals and appreciations by Alfred Kazin, Gregory Zilboorg, Abram Kardiner, Gardner Murphy, Erik H. Erikson, and others. Lionel Trilling, *Freud and the Crisis of Our Culture* (1955), his Freud Lecture for 1955, somewhat revised and expanded, is a brilliant, civilized ruminative defense. Ilse Grubrich-Simitis, who has done invaluable editing of Freud texts, has a particularly sensitive "Einleitung" to her edition of Freud's "Selbstdarstellung" (cited above), 7–33. Richard Sterba, who knew the old Freud in Vienna, has some touching words of appreciation, "On Sigmund Freud's Personality," *American Imago*, XVIII (1961), 289–304.

The debate over the scientific status of Freud's ideas has been so prolonged (and at times venomous) that I can cite only a few titles here. The most discriminating, most careful, and to my mind most satisfactory study is Paul Kline, *Fact and Fantasy in Freudian Theory* (1972; 2d ed., 1981). See also Seymour Fisher and Roger P. Greenberg, *The Scientific Credibility of Freud's Theories and Therapy* (1977), a wide-ranging and well-informed survey, somewhat less positive than Kline; it should be supplemented with the same authors' anthology, *The Scientific Evaluation of Freud's Theories and Therapy* (1978), which fair-mindedly includes a spectrum of views. Helen D. Sargent, Leonard Horwitz, Robert S. Wallerstein, and Ann Appelbaum, *Prediction in Psychotherapy Research: A Method for the Transformation of Clinical Judgments into Testable Hypotheses*, Psychological Issues, monograph 21 (1968) is technical and sympathetic. *Empirical Studies of Psychoanalytic Theories*, ed. Joseph Masling, 2 vols. (1983–85) contains much fascinating material on the work done by such psychoanalytic experimenters as Hartvig Dahl. The most formidable among the skeptics, who has made the credibility of Freudian science (or lack of it) into an obsessive concern for a decade, is the philosopher Adolf Grünbaum; he has summed up his researches in *The Foundations of Psychoanalysis: A Philosophical Critique* (1984). It is taken seriously, but ably questioned, in Marshall Edelson, "Is Testing Psychoanalytic Hypotheses in the Psychoanalytic Situation Really Impossible?" *The Psychoanalytic Study of the Child*, XXXVIII (1983), 61–109. See also Edelson, "Psychoanalysis as Science, Its Boundary Problems, Special Status, Relations to Other Sciences, and Formalization," *Journal of Nervous and Mental Disease*, CLXV (1977), 1–28; and Edelson, *Hypothesis and Evidence in Psychoanalysis* (1984). The debate over Grünbaum, with an abstract of the book, a series of comments, and the author's reply, is presented in "Précis of *The Foundations of Psychoanalysis: A Philosophical Critique,"Behavioral and Brain Sciences*, IX (June 1986), 217–84. A searching, critical, but by no means unsympathetic extended analysis of Grünbaum's book is Edwin R. Wallace IV, "The Scientific Status of Psychoanalysis: A Review of Grünbaum's *The Foundations of Psychoanalysis,"Journal of Nervous and Mental Disease*, CLXXIV (July 1986), 379–86. One incidental benefit of Grünbaum's polemic is that it disposes of Karl Popper's argument, long thought (by many) irrefutable, that psychoanalysis is a pseudoscience, since its propositions cannot be disconfirmed. For this argument, see esp. Popper, "Philosophy of Science: A Personal Report," in *British Philosophy in the Mid-Century: A Cambridge Symposium*, ed. C. A. Mace (1957), 155–91; this essay is also included in Popper, *Conjectures and Refutations: The Growth of Scientific Knowledge* (1963; 2d ed., 1965), 33–65. Other instructive assessments of psychoanalytic claims to scientific validity include a series of lectures by Ernest R. Hilgard, Lawrence S. Kubie, and E. Pumpian-Mindlin, *Psychoanalysis as Science*, ed. E. Pumpian-Mindlin (1952); these are quite positive. B. A. Farrell, *The Standing of Psychoanalytic Theory* (1981) is far more critical, as is Barbara Von Eckardt, "The Scientific Status of Psychoanalysis," in *Introducing Psychoanalytic Theory*, ed. Sander L. Gilman (1982), 139–80. For some revealing papers on Freud by philosophers, see the anthology *Freud: A Collection of Critical Essays*, ed. Richard Wollheim (1974; 2d ed., enlarged, *Philosophical Essays on Freud*, ed. Wollheim and J. Hopkins, 1983). Paul Ricoeur, *Freud and Philosophy: An Essay on Interpretation* (tr. Denis Savage, 1970) is a highly disciplined study by the leading advocate of psychoanalysis as hermeneutics. A challenging (as they say) reading of Freud's thought, it deserves close attention, but Ricoeur's Freud is not my Freud. For comments on Freud as a child of the Enlightenment, see Peter Gay, *A Godless*

Jew: Freud, Atheism, and the Making of Psychoanalysis (1987), esp. ch. 2; and Ilse Grubrich-Simitis, "Reflections on Sigmund Freud's Relationship to the German Language and to Some German-Speaking Authors of the Enlightenment," *Int. J. Psycho-Anal.*, LXVII (1986), 287–94—brief but valuable comments on papers by Didier Anzieu and Ernst A. Ticho delivered at the International Psychoanalytic Congress in Hamburg in 1985.

A definitive census of Freud's books is not yet available, but Harry Trosman and Roger Dennis Simmons, "The Freud Library," *J. Amer. Psychoanal. Assn.*, XXI (1973), 646–87, offers a valuable preliminary assessment.

CHAPTER ONE · *A Greed for Knowledge*

Freud's ancestry, his father's background and mysterious second wife, as well as his early days in Freiberg and Vienna, have been exhaustively canvassed in Marianne Krüll, *Freud and His Father* (1979; tr. Arnold J. Pomerans, 1986), a book based on much patient, at times somewhat speculative, investigation; Krüll depends, as must all students of those years in Freud's life, on the pioneering researches of Josef Sajner: "Sigmund Freuds Beziehungen zu seinem Geburtsort Freiberg (Příbor) und zu Mähren," *Clio Medica*, III (1968), 167–80, and "Drei dokumentarische Beiträge zur Sigmund-Freud-Biographik aus Böhmen und Mähren," *Jahrbuch der Psychoanalyse*, XIII (1981), 143–52. Wilma Iggers provides background material on Bohemia in her anthology, *Die Juden in Böhmen und Mähren: Ein historisches Lesebuch* (1986). Didier Anzieu, *Freud's Self-Analysis* (2d ed., 1975; tr. Peter Graham, 1986) is an important, enormously detailed (if in minor points debatable) study of Freud's early life as mirrored in the dreams he chose to recount and analyze in *The Interpretation of Dreams*. Another very clear view into Freud's intimate early life is provided by Alexander Grinstein, *On Sigmund Freud's Dreams* (1968; 2d ed., 1980). The reminiscences of Freud's sister Anna Freud Bernays, *Erlebtes* (privately printed, ca. 1930) and "My Brother, Sigmund Freud," *American Mercury*, LI (1940), 335–42, have been much quoted, since they recount vivid episodes from Freud's childhood (such as his objections to his sisters' piano lessons) that are both picturesque and impossible to come by (and hence to verify) elsewhere. Unfortunately, her writings must be used with the greatest caution, since a number of the facts that *can* be independently checked, like her father's age at his marriage, turn out to be wrong. Judith Bernays Heller, "Freud's Mother and Father," *Commentary*, XXI (1956), 418–21, is brief but evocative. And see Franz Kobler, "Die Mutter Sigmund Freuds," *Bulletin des Leo Baeck Instituts*, V (1962), 149–71, which is as informative as the limited evidence will permit. For his first years, there is also Siegfried and Suzanne Cassirer Bernfeld, "Freud's Early Childhood," *Bulletin of the Menninger Clinic*, VIII (1944), 107–15. Marie Balmary, *Psychoanalyzing Psychoanalysis: Freud and the Hidden Fault of the Father* (1979; tr. Ned Lukacher, 1982) is imaginative enough to be of some interest even to those who, like me, find no rational basis for her speculation that Freud's mother was pregnant before her marriage to Freud's father (a claim that works only if—a most improbable *if*—Freud was born on March 6, not May 6, 1856, the conventional, and I think correct, date); Balmary also asserts that Jacob Freud's second wife, Rebecca, about whom we know nothing at present, committed suicide by jumping from a train. With Freud, fiction seems to replace fact with ease. Kenneth A. Grigg, " 'All Roads Lead to Rome': The Role of the Nursemaid in Freud's Dreams," *J. Amer. Psychoanal. Assn.*, XXI (1973), 108–26, brings together material relevant to the Catholic nurse whom the toddler Freud loved. P. C. Vitz, in "Sigmund Freud's Attraction to Christianity: Biographical Evidence," *Psychoanalysis and Contemporary Thought*, VI (1983), 73–183, has amassed an abundant number of Roman Catholic themes in Freud's early life but has not, I think, successfully demonstrated his attraction to Christianity.

Freud's uncle Josef Freud, the dealer in counterfeit currency, whom Freud mentions in his "R. was my uncle" dream in *The Interpretation of Dreams*, is ably, if briefly, discussed, with valuable archival documentation, in Krüll, *Freud and His Father*, 164–66. Krüll rightly criticizes Renée Gicklhorn's angry and malicious pamphlet *Sigmund Freud und der Onkeltraum. Dichtung und Wahrheit* (1976) for unfounded speculations. More evidence concerning Jacob Freud's involvement (like that, possibly, of his sons Emanuel and Philipp, by 1865 settled in Manchester) would be welcome. See also Leonard Shengold's interesting exploration, "Freud and Joseph," in *The Unconscious Today: Essays in Honor of Max Schur*, ed. Mark Kanzer (1971), 473–94, which takes off from Freud's uncle Josef to comment incisively on Freud's encounters with other Josephs, and on Freud's character formation generally.

For Freud's intellectual and emotional development during his years at school, at the university, and in medical practice, down to the discovery of psychoanalysis in the 1890s, see, of course, *The Interpretation of Dreams*, passim, and the early pages of his "Autobiographical Study." Anzieu, *Freud's Self-Analysis* is particularly informative. There is abundant good material (with often unhackneyed illustrations) in Ernst Freud et al., eds., *Sigmund Freud: His Life in Pictures and Words;* and see *Jones* I, which relies extensively on the pioneering researches of Siegfried Bernfeld. In addition to the article cited just above, these include "Freud's Earliest Theories and the School of Helmholtz," *Psychoanalytic Quarterly*, XIII (1944), 341–62, a most influential paper; "An Unknown Autobiographical Fragment by Freud," *American Imago*, IV (1946–47), 3–19; "Freud's Scientific Beginnings," *American Imago*, VI (1949), 163–96; "Sigmund Freud, M.D., 1882–1885," *Int. J. Psycho-Anal.*, XXXII (1951), 204–17; and, with Suzanne Cassirer Bernfeld, "Freud's First Year in Practice, 1886–1887," *Bulletin of the Menninger Clinic*, XVI (1952), 37–49. A. Pokorny's almost unobtainable history of Freud's school (I discovered it in the Siegfried Bernfeld papers, container 17, LC), *Das erste Dezennium des Leopoldstädters Communal- Real- und Obergymnasiums (1864–1874). Ein historisch-statistischer Rückblick* (n.d., evidently 1874) shows (p. 44) that while in 1865 there were 32 Jews in that Gymnasium, by 1874 there were 335; the number of Roman Catholics had risen only from 42 to 110, and that of Protestants from 1 to 3. Dennis B. Klein, *Jewish Origins of the Psychoanalytic Movement* (1981) has instructive pages on Freud's schooling (and early Jewish allegiances). McGrath, *Freud's Discovery of Psychoanalysis* is an impressive scholarly study (particularly valuable on Freud's time at the university and his studies with Brentano), somewhat undercut by the untenable thesis that Freud developed psychoanalysis as a "counterpolitics," defiantly chosen, McGrath strongly suggests, because in anti-Semitic Vienna the political career Freud wanted was closed to him. (This thesis was first broached by McGrath's mentor Carl Schorske in an influential but to my mind eccentric article, "Politics and Patricide in Freud's *Interpretation of Dreams,*" *American Historical Review*, LXXVIII [1973], 328–47, reprinted in his *Fin-de-Siècle Vienna: Politics and Culture* [1980], 181–207.) That notion apart, one can learn much from McGrath's book. For background to Freud's translations from Mill, see Adelaide Weinberg, *Theodor Gomperz and John Stuart Mill* (1963). There is also much of interest in Théo Pfrimmer, *Freud lecteur de la Bible* (1982), with a long section on the young Freud at home and thoughts on the role of religion in the making of his mind.

Of the ample collection of biographical studies in *Freud: The Fusion of Science and Humanism: The Intellectual History of Psychoanalysis*, ed. John E. Gedo and George H. Pollock (1976), the following are particularly pertinent to this chapter: Gedo and Ernest S. Wolf, "From the History of Introspective Psychology: The Humanist Strain," 11–45; Harry Trosman, "Freud's Cultural Background," 46–70; Gedo and Wolf, "The 'Ich.' Letters," 71–86; Gedo and Wolf, "Freud's *Novelas Ejemplares,*" 87–111; Julian A. Miller, Melvin Sabshin, Gedo, Pollock, Leo Sadow, and Nathan Schlessinger, "Some Aspects of Charcot's Influence on Freud," 115–132. S. B. Vranich, "Sigmund Freud and 'The Case History of Berganza': Freud's Psychoanalytic Beginnings," *Psychoanalytic Review*, LXIII (1976), 73–82, makes an interesting (somewhat extravagant) claim for Freud's role as a "psychoanalyst" in his adolescent identification with Cipio, one of the dogs in Cervantes's *Coloquio de los perros*. For Freud's youthful "calf love" for Gisela Fluss, see the thoughtful paper by K. R. Eissler, "Creativity and Adolescence: The Effect of Trauma on Freud's Adolescence," *The Psychoanalytic Study of the Child*, XXXIII (1978), 461–517. Heinz Stanescu has published an early poem of Freud's in "Ein 'Gelegenheitsgedicht' des jungen Sigmund Freud," *Deutsch für Ausländer: Informationen für den Lehrer* (1967), 13–16.

Freud's Vienna has been dissected in Ilsa Barea, *Vienna* (1966), a disillusioned, sobering historical essay on the city falsely known as the world headquarters of gaiety, waltzes, and the Beautiful Blue Danube. Arthur Schnitzler's posthumous autobiography, *My Youth in Vienna* (1968; tr. Catherine Hutter, 1970), is laden with trenchant, quotable observations. Robert A. Kann, *A History of the*

Habsburg Empire, 1526–1918 (1974; corr. ed., 1977) sets the city into its Austrian and long-range historical context. A. J. P. Taylor, *The Habsburg Monarchy, 1809–1918: A History of the Austrian Empire and Austria-Hungary* (1941; 2d ed., 1948) is vintage Taylor: amusing, racy, opinionated. David F. Good, *The Economic Rise of the Habsburg Empire, 1750–1914* (1984) is a sensible monograph. William M. Johnston's full *The Austrian Mind: An Intellectual and Social History, 1848–1938* (1972) soberly surveys leaders of culture (economists, lawyers, and political thinkers as well as musicians and artists); Johnston's abundantly illustrated picture book, *Vienna, Vienna: The Golden Age, 1815–1914* (1981; preceded by Italian version, 1980) attractively displays much familiar but also much unfamiliar material. See also the fascinating catalogue of an exhibition in the Schiller-Nationalmuseum, Marbach: *Jugend in Wien: Literatur um 1900*, ed. Ludwig Greve and Werner Volke (1974). In a sizable literature on politics, Richard Charmatz, *Adolf Fischhof. Das Lebensbild eines österreichischen Politikers* (1910) is, if old-fashioned, particularly informative. There is much to be learned from Joseph Roth's beautiful novel about the empire in decline, *Radetzkymarsch* (1932). Allan Janik and Stephen Toulmin, *Wittgenstein's Vienna* (1973), a sophisticated compendium of Viennese intellectual life, is to my mind excessively eager to construct connections among disparate groups. In contrast, for Freud's detachment from most of this Vienna, see the fine article by George Rosen, "Freud and Medicine in Vienna," *Psychological Medicine*, II (1972), 332–44, conveniently accessible in *Freud: The Man, His World, His Influence*, ed. Jonathan Miller (1972), 21–39. Most of the other short essays in Miller's well-illustrated volume are rather skimpy. See also Rupert Feuchtmüller and Christian Brandstätter, *Markstein der Moderne: Österreichs Beitrag zur Kultur- und Geistesgeschichte des 20. Jahrhunderts* (1980) and the early chapters of David S. Luft, *Robert Musil and the Crisis of European Culture, 1880–1942* (1980).

Schorske, *Fin-de-Siècle Vienna* is a collection of elegant essays; the best of these, far more defensible than the one on Freud, is "The Ringstrasse, Its Critics, and the Birth of Modern Urbanism" (24–115). See also in this connection William J. McGrath's first book, *Dionysian Art and Populist Politics in Austria* (1974). John W. Boyer, *Political Radicalism in Late Imperial Vienna: Origins of the Christian Social Movement, 1848–1897* (1981) impressively sets out, with scholarly thoroughness, the political situation in which Freud lived down to his early forties. Kirk Varnedoe, *Vienna 1900: Art, Architecture and Design* (1986) is a splendidly illustrated exhibition catalogue which, in its text, rightly refuses to idealize the painters and designers of the period or to establish between them and Freud links which were not there.

There is much reliable modern scholarship on the Jews in Vienna. See above all the authoritative, concise monograph by Marsha L. Rosenblit, *The Jews of Vienna, 1867–1914: Assimilation and Identity* (1983) and John W. Boyer, "Karl Lueger and the Viennese Jews," *Leo Baeck Yearbook*, XXVI (1981), 125–41. I have learned from Steven Beller, *"Fin de Siècle* Vienna and the Jews: The Dialectic of Assimilation," *Jewish Quarterly*, XXXIII (1986), 28–33, and am also indebted to Beller's unpublished manuscript, "Religion, Culture and Society in Fin de Siècle Vienna: The Case of the Gymnasien," which he let me read in the summer of 1986. See also Wolfdieter Bihl, "Die Juden," in *Die Habsburger Monarchie, 1848–1918*, ed. Adam Wandruszka and Peter Urbanitsch, vol. III, *Die Völker des Reiches* (1980), part 2, 890–96. On Jewish liberalism, including Freud's, see Walter B. Simon, "The Jewish Vote in Austria," *Leo Baeck Yearbook*, XVI (1971), 97–121. A moving collection, in both German and English, of essays about Vienna's Jews—reminiscences, memoirs, papers on the Jewish share in the city's professional life, on the history of the community and its extermination—is *The Jews of Austria: Essays on Their Life, History and Destruction*, ed. Josef Fraenkel (1967); inevitably uneven, this collection at its best lights up more than a century of Jewish life. It includes a revealing essay by Martin Freud on his father, with some comments on his mother: "Who Was Freud?" 197–211. While Martin Freud's affectionate, humorous, and eminently usable *Sigmund Freud: Man and Father* (1958) is particularly relevant to chapter 4, it also offers good material on Freud's youth. See also, for miscellaneous information, Johannes Barta, *Jüdische Familienerziehung. Das jüdische Erziehungswesen im 19. und 20. Jahrhundert* (1975); the reminiscences of Friedrich Eckstein, *"Alte unnennbare Tage!" Erinnerungen aus siebzig Lehr- und Wanderjahren* (1936); and those of Sigmund Mayer, *Ein jüdischer Kaufmann 1891 bis 1911. Lebenserinnerungen* (1911). Mayer, *Die Wiener Juden. Kommerz, Kultur, Politik* (1917; 2d ed., 1918) is personal, mournful, but revealing on the late nineteenth century. Peter G. J. Pulzer, *The Rise of Political Anti-Semitism in Germany and Austria* (1964) is an excellent, terse survey; ch. 4, "Austria, 1867–1900," is particularly relevant here.

For Freud's debts to the thought and thinkers of his time, see the papers by Lucille B. Ritvo, esp. "Darwin as the Source of Freud's Neo-Lamarckianism," *J. Amer. Psychoanal. Assn.*, XIII (1965), 499–517; "Carl Claus as Freud's Professor of the New Darwinian Biology," *Int. J. Psycho-Anal.*, LIII (1972), 277–83; "The Impact of Darwin on Freud," *Psychoanalytic Quarterly*, XLIII (1974), 177–92; and, with Max Schur, "The Concept of Development and Evolution in Psychoanalysis," in *Development and Evolution of Behavior*, ed. L. R. Aronson et al. (1970), 600–619. Freud's acquaintance Friedrich Eckstein reports on Freud's shift from law to medicine in his *"Alte unnennbare Tage!"* For Brentano's influence on Freud, see—in addition to McGrath, *Freud's Discovery of Psychoanalysis*—Philip Merlan, "Brentano and Freud," *Journal of the History of Ideas*, VI (1945), 375–77, and Raymond E. Fancher's more extensive "Brentano's *Psychology from an Empirical Standpoint* and Freud's Early Metapsychology," *Journal of the History of the Behavioral Sciences*, XIII (1977), 207–27. The standard English-language study on Feuerbach is Marx W. Wartofsky, *Feuerbach* (1977); for Freud's reading in that thinker, see Simon Rawidowicz, *Ludwig Feuerbachs Philosophie. Ursprung und Schicksal* (1931), 348–50. Peter Amacher, *Freud's Neurological Education and Its Influence on Psychoanalytic Theory*, Psychological Issues, monograph 16 (1965) is sound but could have been longer. Larry Stewart, "Freud before Oedipus," *Journal of the History of Biology*, IX (1976), 215–28, is fairly slight. More substantial is Rudolf Brun, "Sigmund Freuds Leistungen auf dem Gebiet der organischen Neurologie," *Schweizer Archiv für Neurologie und Psychiatrie*, XXXVII (1936), 200–207.

For Freud's teachers in medical school, see (in addition to Rosen's liberating article "Freud and Medicine in Vienna") Erna Lesky's monumental *The Vienna Medical School of the 19th Century* (1965; tr. L. Williams and I. S. Levij, 1976), to which every student of Vienna's medicine must be indebted; Dora Stockert Meynert, *Theodor Meynert und seine Zeit: Zur Geistesgeschichte Österreichs in der zweiten Hälfte des 19. Jahrhunderts* (1930); Ernst Theodor Brücke, *Ernst Brücke* (1928); and Sherwin B. Nuland, *The Masterful Spirit—Theodor Billroth*, The Classics of Surgery Library (1984), 3–44. Julius Wagner-Jauregg, *Lebenserinnerungen*, ed. and completed by L. Schönbauer and M. Jantsch (1950), has a few vivid glimpses of Freud.

The best collection of materials on the controversial cocaine episode is *Cocaine Papers by Sigmund Freud*, ed. Robert Byck (1974), with notes by Anna Freud; it contains Freud's publications on the subject and a thorough, dependable introduction. See also Siegfried Bernfeld, "Freud's Studies on Cocaine, 1884–1887," *J. Amer. Psychoanal. Assn.*, I (1953), 581–613. Hortense Koller Becker, "Carl Koller and Cocaine," *Psychoanalytic Quarterly*, XXXII (1963), 309–73, carefully details the share of Freud's friend in the discovery of cocaine as an anesthetic. Peter J. Swales, "Freud, Cocaine, and Sexual Chemistry: The Role of Cocaine in Freud's Conception of the Libido" (privately printed, 1983) has some characteristic speculations. And see Jürgen vom Scheidt, "Sigmund Freud und das Kokain," *Psyche*, XXVII (1973), 385–430. E. M. Thornton, *Freud and Cocaine: The Freudian Fallacy* (1983) is a model in the literature of denigration; it attempts to persuade the reader that Freud, "a false and faithless prophet" (p. 312), originated psychoanalysis in the haze of a cocaine psychosis; the author claims that "the 'unconscious mind' does not exist, that his theories were baseless and aberrational and, greatest impiety of all, that Freud himself, when he formulated them, was under the influence of a toxic drug with specific effects on the brain" (p. 1).

For Charcot, see A. R. G. Owen's rather skimpy *Hysteria, Hypnosis and Healing: The Work of J.-M. Charcot* (1971). Georges Guillain, *J.-M. Charcot, 1825–1893: His Life—His Work* (1955; tr. Pearce Bailey, 1959) is far more substantial but concentrates on Charcot's early neurological work somewhat at the expense of his later studies on hysteria. For these, Mark S. Micale (whose dissertation on Charcot and male hysteria [Yale, 1987] is authoritative) has already published "The Salpêtrière in the Age of Charcot: An Institutional Perspective on Medical History in the Late Nineteenth Century," *Journal of Contemporary History*, XX (1985), 703–31. See also the article by Miller et al., "Some Aspects of Charcot's Influence on Freud."

CHAPTER TWO · *The Theory in the Making*

For Freud's fateful friendship with Fliess, *Freud–Fliess* is naturally a princely source. Max Schur, who in the 1960s had access to then unpublished portions of the correspondence, has sagacious comments in *Freud, Living and Dying.* Schur's pathbreaking article "Some Additional 'Day Residues' of 'The Specimen Dream of Psychoanalysis,' " in *Psychoanalysis—a General Psychology: Essays in Honor of Heinz Hartmann,* ed. Rudolph M. Loewenstein, Lottie M. Newman, Schur, and Albert J. Solnit (1966), 45–85, is, despite its innocuous title, explosive: in elucidating the dream of Irma's injection, it throws rather lurid light on Freud's infatuation with Fliess. K. R. Eissler, "To Muriel M. Gardiner on Her 70th Birthday," *Bulletin of the Philadelphia Association for Psychoanalysis,* XXII (1972), 110–30, is a thoughtful and in the best sense suggestive essay on Freud and Fliess. See also Edith Buxbaum, "Freud's Dream Interpretation in the Light of His Letters to Fliess," *Bulletin of the Menninger Clinic,* XV (1951), 197–212. Frank J. Sulloway's extensive *Freud, Biologist of the Mind: Beyond the Psychoanalytic Legend* (1979) suffers from some overkill, presenting itself as a great unmasking document but bringing the essentially old news that Freud's theory had a biological background; however, chaps. 5 and 6, analyzing Freud's dependence on Fliess and what Sulloway calls "nineteenth-century psychophysics," have much of value. Patrick Mahony, "Friendship and Its Discontents," *Contemporary Psychoanalysis,* XV (1979), 55–109, meticulously examines Freud in the 1890s, with particular attention to the German material. Erik H. Erikson, "The Dream Specimen of Psychoanalysis," *J. Amer. Psychoanal. Assn.,* II (1954), 5–56, principally examines the Irma dream, but also comments on the Freud–Fliess association. Peter J. Swales, "Freud, Fliess, and Fratricide: The Role of Fliess in Freud's Conception of Paranoia" (privately printed, 1982) goes so far as to intimate that Freud may have tried to murder Fliess during their last "congress" in 1900. George F. Mahl, "Explosions of Discoveries and Concepts: The Freud–Fliess Letters," ch. 4 of *A First Course in Freud,* as yet unpublished, meticulously and dependably canvasses this correspondence. The deterioration of the Freud–Fliess friendship left traces in the inscriptions that Fliess put into his books. In 1897, when he sent Freud his substantial monograph *Die Beziehung zwischen Nase und weiblichen Geschlechtsorganen. In ihrer biologischen Bedeutung dargestellt,* he wrote, "Seinem teuren Sigmund, innigst, d. V.*";* five years later, in 1902, he sent his *Über den ursächlichen Zusammenhang von Nase und Geschlechtsorgan* with the far cooler inscription *"Seinem lieben Sigmund!" Teuer* is a very affectionate term—"dearest" perhaps renders it best—and *innigst* means something like "most affectionately"; but *lieb* is a commonplace form of address—"dear," as in "Dear Sir." (These inscribed copies are in the Freud Museum, London.)

For Martha Bernays Freud, see the biographies of her husband, notably *Jones* I, and the unpublished fragments of letters I quote in the text. A short article by Martin Freud's wife, Esti D. Freud, "Mrs. Sigmund Freud," *Jewish Spectator,* XLV (1980), 29–31, evokes the "serenity" (p. 29) for which Martha Freud had a certain (but not completely uncontroverted) reputation. Peter Gay, "Six Names in Search of an Interpretation: A Contribution to the Debate over Sigmund Freud's Jewishness," *Hebrew Union College Annual,* LIII (1982), 295–307, suggests something of Freud's domestic authority. Among studies of Stefan Zweig (on whom Martha Freud commented so scathingly), D. A. Prater, *European of Yesterday: A Biography of Stefan Zweig* (1972) provides the necessary background.

By far the most authoritative study of the case of "Anna O.," and of Breuer in general, is Albrecht Hirschmüller's exhaustive (but not exhausting) dissertation, *Physiologie und Psychoanalyse im Leben und Werk Josef Breuers,* supplement 4 to *Jahrbuch der Psychoanalyse,* X (1978); it satisfactorily sets right faulty conjectures and dubious interpretations, puts Breuer securely on the map of Freud scholarship, and explores Freud's medical world. The documents concerning Anna O.'s medical history and those by Anna O. herself are fascinating. Hirschmüller argues instructively with Julian A. Miller, Melvin Sabshin, John E. Gedo, George H. Pollock, Leo Sadow, and Nathan Schlessinger, "The Scientific Styles of Breuer and Freud and the Origins of Psychoanalysis," and with Pollock, "Josef Breuer," both in *Freud, Fusion of Science and Humanism,* ed. Gedo and Pollock, 187–207, 133–63. Paul F. Cranefield, "Josef Breuer's Evaluation of His Contribution to Psycho-Analysis," *Int. J. Psycho-Anal.,* XXXIX (1958), 319–22, reproduces and analyzes an interesting 1907 letter from

Breuer to Auguste Forel, which throws retrospective light on his earlier attitudes. Henri Ellenberger, "The Story of 'Anna O.': A Critical Review with New Data," *Journal of the History of the Behavioral Sciences*, VIII (1972), 267–79, persuasively corrects Jones's misreading and Freud's misremembering of the case. Hirschmüller has also dug up a fascinating case history of a severe hysteric, "Nina R.," referred to the Bellevue sanatorium at Kreuzlingen by Freud and Breuer: "Eine bisher unbekannte Krankengeschichte Sigmund Freuds und Josef Breuers aus der Entstehungszeit der 'Studien über Hysterie,' " *Jahrbuch der Psychoanalyse*, X (1978), 136–68. For the admirable later career of Anna O. (Bertha Pappenheim) as a leading Jewish feminist and social worker, see Ellen Jensen, "Anna O., a Study of Her Later Life," *Psychoanalytic Quarterly*, XXXIX (1970), 269–93. Richard Karpe, "The Rescue Complex in Anna O's Final Identity," *Psychoanalytic Quarterly*, XXX (1961), 1–24, connects her neurosis with her later achievement. Lucy Freeman, *The Story of Anna O.* (1972), is a popular treatment. But see the excellent historical study by Marion Kaplan, *The Jewish Feminist Movement in Germany: The Campaign of the Jüdischer Frauenbund, 1904–1938* (1979), which has important material on Bertha Pappenheim's career.

For Freud's study on the aphasias, a rather neglected text, see the useful, if perhaps too compressed, paper by E. Stengel, "A Re-evaluation of Freud's Book 'On Aphasia': Its Significance for Psycho-Analysis," *Int. J. Psycho-Anal.*, XXXV (1954), 85–89. One of Freud's early hysteric patients, "Frau Cäcilie M.," has been studied in rewarding detail by Peter J. Swales, "Freud, His Teacher, and the Birth of Psychoanalysis," in *Freud, Appraisals and Reappraisals*, ed. Stepansky, I, 3–82. See also Swales's essay on "Katharina": "Freud, Katharina, and the First 'Wild Analysis,' " typescript of a lecture, with added materials (1985). Ola Andersson, "A Supplement to Freud's Case History of 'Frau Emmy v. N.' in Studies on Hysteria 1895," *Scandinavian Psychoanalytic Review*, II (1979), 5–15, includes biographical material. See also Else Pappenheim, "Freud and Gilles de la Tourette: Diagnostic Speculations on 'Frau Emmy von N.,' " *Int. Rev. Psycho-Anal.*, VII (1980), 265–77, which suggests that this patient may not have been a hysteric at all, but instead may have been suffering (as Freud, too, conjectured for a time) from Gilles de la Tourette's syndrome.

Freud's "Psychology for Neurologists," abandoned incomplete, was first published in *Aus den Anfängen der Psychoanalyse. Briefe an Wilhelm Fliess, Abhandlungen und Notizen aus den Jahren 1887–1902*, ed. Ernst Kris, Marie Bonaparte, and Anna Freud (1950; English version, *The Origins of Psychoanalysis*, tr. Eric Mosbacher and James Strachey, 1954). In his introduction to this first, severely truncated edition of the Fliess letters, Kris deals with the place of the project in Freud's thought. The project is conveniently available in English, under the title "Project for a Scientific Psychology," in *SE* I, 283–397. It has been beautifully appreciated in Wollheim, *Freud*, esp. ch. 2. Isabel F. Knight argues in "Freud's 'Project': A Theory for *Studies on Hysteria,*" *Journal of the History of the Behavioral Sciences*, XX (1984), 340–58, that the project was designed as a critique of Breuer's theories. John Friedman and James Alexander, "Psychoanalysis and Natural Science: Freud's 1895 *Project* Revisited," *Int. Rev. Psycho-Anal.*, X (1983), 303–18, an important essay, suggests that Freud was at this early date trying to free himself from the constraints of late-nineteenth-century scientific discourse. See also, on Freud's "Newtonianism," Robert C. Solomon, "Freud's Neurological Theory of Mind," in *Freud: A Collection of Critical Essays*, ed. Wollheim, 25–52.

The discussion over Freud's so-called seduction theory has been muddied by Jeffrey Moussaieff Masson, *The Assault on Truth: Freud's Suppression of the Seduction Theory* (1984), which argues— preposterously—that Freud abandoned that theory because he could not tolerate the isolation from the Vienna medical establishment to which his radical ideas had condemned him. One wonders why, if Freud had been made so anxious, he then proceeded to publicize even more unsettling theories, such as those on infantile sexuality and the ubiquity of perversion. In fact, the reasons Freud gave in his letter to Fliess of September 21, 1897 (*Freud–Fliess*, 283–86 [264–67]) are (*pace* Krüll) good and sufficient. Moreover, Freud never disputed the depressing truth that the seduction or the rape of young girls—and boys—whether attempted or consummated, was only too real an event. He could point to patients (including Katharina) of his own. The standard accounts of Freud's attitude toward his seduction theory, given in *Jones* I, esp. 263–67, and by other writers, stand up.

For Freud's self-analysis, especially as it relates to his father, see the materials already listed in the essay for chapter 1, notably *The Interpretation of Dreams;* Krüll, *Freud and His Father;* Anzieu,

Freud's Self-Analysis; and Grinstein, *On Sigmund Freud's Dreams.* And see also George F. Mahl, "Father-Son Themes in Freud's Self-Analysis," in *Father and Child: Developmental and Clinical Perspectives,* ed. Stanley H. Cath, Alan R. Gurwitt, and John Munder Ross (1982), 33–64; and Mahl, "Freud, *Father* and *Mother:* Quantitative Aspects," *Psychoanalytic Psychology,* II (1985), 99–113, both of which bring precision to a murky area. Schur's extensive comments in *Freud, Living and Dying* are indispensable. *Freud and His Self-Analysis,* ed. Mark Kanzer and Jules Glenn (1979) brings together some interesting papers, but is a little miscellaneous.

Did Freud have an affair with his sister-in-law Minna Bernays? The first to have made this charge was apparently Carl G. Jung, in private (it is reported) and then in 1957 in an interview with his friend John M. Billinsky, who published it in 1969: "Jung and Freud (the End of a Romance)," *Andover Newton Quarterly,* X (1969), 39–43. The relevant passage occurs in Jung's account of his first visit to Berggasse 19, in 1907: "Soon I met Freud's wife's younger sister. She was very good-looking and she not only knew enough about psychoanalysis but also about everything that Freud was doing. When, a few days later, I was visiting Freud's laboratory, Freud's sister-in-law asked if she could talk with me. She was very much bothered by her relationship with Freud and felt guilty about it. From her I learned that Freud was in love with her and that their relationship was indeed very intimate. It was a shocking discovery to me, and even now I can recall the agony I felt at the time. Two years later Freud and I were invited to Clark University in Worcester, and we were together every day for some seven weeks. From the very beginning of our trip we started to analyze each other's dreams. Freud had some dreams that bothered him very much. The dreams were about the triangle—Freud, his wife, and wife's younger sister. Freud had no idea that I knew about the triangle and his intimate relationship with his sister-in-law. And so, when Freud told me about the dream in which his wife and her sister played important parts, I asked Freud to tell me some of his personal associations with the dream. He looked at me with bitterness and said, 'I could tell you more, but I cannot risk my authority' " (p. 42).

What is one to make of this? Jung, as many of his contradictory autobiographical comments suggest, was a less than reliable reporter. The story about Freud's refusal to help interpret one of his own dreams aboard ship may be true enough; Jung repeated it more than once in Freud's lifetime, once in a letter to Freud (Jung to Freud, December 3, 1912. *Freud–Jung,* 583–84, 584n [526, 526n]), and Freud never denied it. But in other respects this particular account is exceedingly odd. Freud, of course, did not have a "laboratory." His consulting room was next door to his study, and Jung might have been referring to either of these rooms, but the expression remains a strange one. Moreover, while such judgments are of course highly subjective, I submit that the photographs we have do not show Minna Bernays to have been "very good-looking." She may indeed have been to Freud's taste, but it seems highly implausible that Jung, who had an eye for feminine beauty and was himself sexually quite active during these years, beyond the bounds of marriage, would really have found her so. Schur, who admittedly knew Minna Bernays only in relatively advanced age, found her quite unattractive (interview with Helen Schur, June 3, 1986). Again, it seems quite improbable that Minna Bernays would have confided such an intimate matter to a total stranger—a man whom she had just met and who was alien to her in religion and culture and professional interests. To be sure, she might conceivably have seen an outsider, especially one who would soon depart again, as precisely the right person to confide in. But I find it virtually impossible to visualize the scene.

More recently, Peter J. Swales has made the same claim, offering confident conjectures as demonstrated fact, in "Freud, Minna Bernays, and the Imitation of Christ" (an unpublished 1982 lecture, photocopy courtesy Mr. Swales); and "Freud, Minna Bernays, and the Conquest of Rome: New Light on the Origins of Psychoanalysis," *New American Review: A Journal of Civility and the Arts,* I (Spring/Summer 1982), 1–23. Swales utilizes what I should call the "Bernfeld way of reading," a fruitful but risky method. Siegfried Bernfeld, who intended to write a biography of Freud and amassed a great deal of material, read certain of Freud's texts, notably his paper "Screen Memories" (1899), as disguised autobiographical revelations. It was thus that he discovered Freud's adolescent infatuation with Gisela Fluss. To be sure, perfectly plausible, and sometimes correct, inferences can be drawn from many of Freud's statements (*The Psychopathology of Everyday Life* is a particularly rich source of indirect self-revelations); put together until they tell a coherent story, they may take on a weight they would not have individually. Swales does this sort of thing well, and the psychoanalytic technique of digging beneath manifest surfaces virtually invites it. Concentrating on material from Freud's "Screen Memories," *The Interpretation of Dreams*, and *The Psychopathology of Everyday Life*, Swales constructs a sequence of events in Freud's life which he takes to prove that Freud did indeed have an affair with his sister-in-law. When a statement that Freud makes concerning someone else may well apply to himself, Swales accepts it as evidence; when a statement fails to fit, he accuses Freud of disguising the material, or of brazen deception. He may, of course, be right: the dream work, a mixture of revelation and concealment, proceeds somewhat in this way, and any clever storyteller knows that one most effective tactic is to mingle truth with fiction. So, Freud *may* have had an affair with Minna Bernays.

Ernest Jones's pertinent comments hint, not so much perhaps that Jung's story is necessarily true, but that it had been circulating and seemed persuasive enough (at least to some) to deserve explicit refutation. Certainly, Jones is emphatic enough on the matter to cause the suspicious to wonder whether he is not being a little defensive. Thus he calls Freud "monogamic in a very unusual degree," a man who "always gave the impression of being an unusually chaste person—the word 'puritanical' would not be out of place" (*Jones* I, 139, 271). In his criticism of Puner's biography of Freud he feels impelled to say a few words on Freud's "married life, since various strange legends seem to be in vogue about it. . . . His wife was assuredly the only woman in Freud's love life, and she always came first before all other mortals. . . . [As for Minna Bernays,] her caustic tongue gave rise to many epigrams that were cherished in the family. Freud no doubt appreciated her conversation, but to say that she in any way replaced her sister in his affections is sheer nonsense" (*Jones* II, 386–87). Clark, too (see his *Freud*, 52), has considered the evidence, notably the Jung interview, and rejects it as highly improbable.

The Freud Collection at the Library of Congress includes a packet of letters between Freud and Minna Bernays that are being scrutinized before being released; at this writing they are (maddeningly) not yet available. Given the incompleteness of the evidence (another instance of how the restrictive policy of Freud's guardians, either denying or slowing down access to important materials, nourishes rumors), one cannot be dogmatic—at least, I cannot be. Freud wrote some passionate letters to Minna Bernays while he was engaged to her sister, but this, rather than offering support to the Jung-Swales theory, seems to me to make it all the less probable. If dependable independent evidence (as distinct from conjecture and clever chains of inferences) should emerge that Freud did indeed have an affair with his sister-in-law and actually (as Swales has argued in some detail) took her to get an abortion, I shall revise my text accordingly. Meanwhile, I must accept the established, less scandalous view of Freud as correct.

CHAPTER THREE · *Psychoanalysis*

For the making of *The Interpretation of Dreams*, the *Freud–Fliess* letters are, of course, beyond compare. See also, once again, for detailed explorations of his dreams that Freud uses in the book, Anzieu, *Freud's Self-Analysis* and Grinstein, *On Sigmund Freud's Dreams*. In addition, Freud's dream theory is examined in Fisher and Greenberg, *Scientific Credibility of Freud's Theories*, ch. 2 (a good, full discussion), and in *Jones* I and in other biographical studies I have already listed. For the reasons given in the essay for chapter 1, I cannot accept McGrath's "political" interpretation of Freud in *Freud's Discovery of Psychoanalysis*, but I have found many of his readings of Freud's dreams to be subtle. See also Ella Freeman Sharpe, *Dream Analysis* (1937; 2d ed., 1978), an elegant text by an eminent English lay analyst; Bertram D. Lewin's suggestive Freud Lecture, *Dreams and the Uses of Regression* (1958); several early papers by Ernest Jones, conveniently collected in his *Papers on Psycho-Analysis* (3d ed., 1923) and together interesting as indications of how dream interpretation penetrated the psychoanalytic profession: "Freud's Theory of Dreams" (1910), 212–46; "Some Instances of the Influence of Dreams on Waking Life" (1911), 247–54; "A Forgotten Dream" (1912), 255–65; "Persons in Dreams Disguised as Themselves" (1921), 266–69; and "The Relationship between Dreams and Psychoneurotic Symptoms" (delivered in 1911), 270–92.

More recent papers include a survey by D. R. Hawkins, "A Review of Psychoanalytic Dream Theory in the Light of Recent Psycho-Physiological Studies of Sleep and Dreaming," *British Journal of Medical Psychology*, XXXIX (1966), 85–104, and a rewarding paper by Leonard Shengold, "The Metaphor of the Journey in 'The Interpretation of Dreams,'" *American Imago* XXIII (1966), 316–31. A short, readable, and eclectic essay by the analyst Charles Rycroft, *The Innocence of Dreams* (1979), surveys the recent literature, not confining itself to psychoanalytic work. Research on dreams goes on; one intriguing theory, admittedly very tentative (and explicitly critical of Freud's), is presented in Francis Crick and Graeme Mitchison, "The Function of Dream Sleep," *Nature*, CCCIV (1983), 111–14, which proposes that REM sleep is designed to remove "undesirable modes of interaction in networks of cells in the cerebral cortex." See also James L. Fosshage and Clemens A. Loew, eds., *Dream Interpretation: A Comparative Study* (1978), and Liam Hudson, *Night Life: The Interpretation of Dreams* (1985), in which this psychologist offers an interpretative scheme of his own. One other profitable item in the literature Freud's dream book has generated, Walter Schönau, *Sigmund Freuds Prosa. Literarische Elemente seines Stils* (1968), has some interesting and to my mind convincing material (pp. 53–89) on the mottos that Freud rejected, and the one he used, for *The Interpretation of Dreams*. Erikson, "The Dream Specimen of Psychoanalysis," is an interesting long paper on the Irma dream. See also A. Keiper and A. A. Stone, "The Dream of Irma's Injection: A Structural Analysis," *American Journal of Psychiatry*, CXXXIX (1982), 1225–34. Other useful essays on Freud's dreams are the brief paper by Leslie Adams, "A New Look at Freud's Dream 'The Breakfast Ship,'" *American Journal of Psychiatry*, CX (1953), 381–84; the deservedly well-known paper by Eva M. Rosenfeld, "Dream and Vision: Some Remarks on Freud's Egyptian Bird Dream," *Int. J. Psycho-Anal.*, XXXVIII (1956), 97–105; and once again, Buxbaum, "Freud's Dream Interpretation in the Light of His Letters to Fliess" (cited in the essay for chapter 2).

The genre of autobiography, which flourished uncommonly in the nineteenth century, and to which Freud's program in its own unique way belongs, is attracting an increasing number of scholars. I here briefly mention only a handful of the most interesting recent titles: Jerome Hamilton Buckley, *The Turning Key: Autobiography and the Subjective Impulse since 1800* (1984), from which I have learned a good deal; William C. Spengemann, *The Forms of Autobiography: Episodes in the History of a Literary Genre* (1980), which covers some nineteenth-century examples in the last chapter; Linda H. Peterson, *Victorian Autobiography: The Tradition of Self-Interpretation* (1986), which is more concentrated; A. O. J. Cockshut, *The Art of Autobiography in Nineteenth and Twentieth Century England* (1984), full of sage comment; and Avrom Fleishman, *Figures of Autobiography: The Language of Self-Writing* (1983).

Quite directly to Freud's work. For Freud's own ideas in those years, we have the valuable study by Kenneth Levin, *Freud's Early Psychology of the Neuroses: A Historical Perspective* (1978). There is no historians' consensus on nineteenth-century mental science, or on madhouses. These topics have been attracting a great deal of attention and stirred a good deal of debate recently, not least thanks to Michel Foucault's (to my mind, if stimulating, generally baleful) radical revisionism; I particularly have in mind Foucault's influential *Madness and Civilization: A History of Insanity in the Age of Reason* (1961; tr. Richard Howard, 1965). Lancelot Law Whyte, *The Unconscious before Freud* (1960; paperback ed., 1962) is a brief but helpful survey. Far more comprehensive is Henri F. Ellenberger, *The Discovery of the Unconscious: The History and Evolution of Dynamic Psychiatry* (1970), a rather swollen but thoroughly researched nine-hundred-page volume, with long chapters on the early history of psychology, and on Jung, Adler, and Freud. Though far from elegant, though opinionated and not always reliable in its quick judgments (such as its verdict that Freud was the quintessential Viennese), it is a rich source of information. Robert M. Young, *Mind, Brain and Adaptation in the Nineteenth Century: Cerebral Localization and Its Biological Context from Gall to Ferrier* (1970) is a minor modern classic. There is a fine anthology, *Madhouses, Mad-Doctors, and Madmen: The Social History of Psychiatry in the Victorian Era*, ed. Andrew Scull (1981); with no wish to single out some contributions at the expense of others, I may say that I learned most from William F. Bynum, Jr., "Rationales for Therapy in British Psychiatry," 35–57, and Michael J. Clark, "The Rejection of Psychological Approaches to Mental Disorder in Late Nineteenth-Century British Psychiatry," 271–312. Another fascinating anthology, which shows Foucault's impact but resists sensationalism, is *The Anatomy of Madness: Essays in the History of Psychiatry,* vol. I, *People and Ideas,* and vol. II, *Institutions and Society,* ed. Bynum, Roy Porter, and Michael Shepherd (1985). Raymond E. Fancher, *Pioneers of Psychology* (1979) lucidly, though economically, lays out the field from René Descartes to B. F. Skinner. J. C. Flugel, *A Hundred Years of Psychology: 1833–1933* (1933) covers a wide field necessarily in the tersest manner. See also Clarence J. Karier, *Scientists of the Mind: Intellectual Founders of Modern Psychology* (1986), with even-handed chapters on ten modern psychologists from William James to Otto Rank, not forgetting Freud, Adler, and Jung. Gerald N. Grob, ed., *The Inner World of American Psychiatry, 1890–1940: Selected Correspondence* (1985) is well chosen and annotated. And see Kenneth Dewhurst, *Hughlings Jackson on Psychiatry* (1982), an excellent short monograph; and *Essays in the History of Psychiatry,* ed. Edwin R. Wallace IV and Lucius C. Pressley (1980), a useful collection of pieces on George M. Beard (by Eric T. Carlson) and others. Steven R. Hirsch and Michael Shepherd, *Themes and Variations in European Psychiatry: An Anthology* (1974) have dug up, among other material predating the First World War, papers by Emil Kraepelin, Karl Bonhoeffer, and others. Barry Silverstein, "Freud's Psychology and Its Organic Foundations: Sexuality and Mind-Body Interactionism," *Psychoanalytic Review,* LXXII (1985), 203–28, fruitfully pursues the proposition that the impact of Freud's neurological education should not be overstated, and that psychoanalysis, though it does not give up mind-body interaction, insists on the independence of the mental. For a fascinating modern attempt by an analyst to link psychoanalytic with neurological theories, see Morton F. Reiser, *Mind, Brain, Body: Toward a Convergence of Psychoanalysis and Neurobiology* (1986). And see R. W. Angel, "Jackson, Freud and Sherrington on the Relation of Brain and Mind," *American Journal of Psychiatry* (1961), 193–97. Anne Digby, *Madness, Morality and Medicine: A Study of the York Retreat, 1796–1914* (1986) is a fine specialized study that should be a model to others. Equally exemplary are the writings of Janet Oppenheim, notably "The Diagnosis and Treatment of Nervous Breakdown: A Dilemma for Victorian and Edwardian Psychiatry," in *The Political Culture of Modern Britain: Studies in Memory of Stephen Koss,* ed. J. M. W. Bean (1987), 75–90; and her monograph, *The Other World: Spiritualism and Psychical Research in England, 1850–1914* (1985).

K. R. Eissler, *Sigmund Freud und die Wiener Universität. Über die Pseudo-Wissenschaftlichkeit der jüngsten Wiener Freud-Biographik* (1966) is the authoritative study, superseding all others, of Freud's slow rise to a professorship; it proves in a spirited polemic against two Austrian researchers, Joseph and Renée Gicklhorn, that Freud's promotion to professor *was* held up for years.

The most searching, extremely negative examination of Freud's thesis that the mental order is revealed in ordinary slips of the tongue and related symptomatic acts is Sebastiano Timpanaro, *The Freudian Slip: Psychoanalysis and Textual Criticism* (1974; tr. Kate Soper), which is worth wrestling with, though I do not find it convincing.

Freud on sexuality has been explored probably even more than Freud on dreams. For an examination of respectable nineteenth-century sexuality, norms, and realities, of which Freud was a part as well as a critic, see Peter Gay, *Education of the Senses* (1984) and its companion volume, *The Tender Passion* (1986), vols. I and II of *The Bourgeois Experience: Victoria to Freud;* these portray the "Victorian" bourgeoisie as far less hypocritical or repressed than its critics have claimed. See also the revealing, wide-ranging essay by Stephen Kern, "Freud and the Discovery of Child Sexuality," *History of Childhood Quarterly: The Journal of Psychohistory,* I (Summer 1973), 117–41; it should be read in conjunction with Kern, "Freud and the Birth of Child Psychiatry," *Journal of the History of the Behavioral Sciences,* IX (1973), 360–68. And see Sterling Fishman, "The History of Childhood Sexuality," *Journal of Contemporary History,* XVII (1982), 269–83, useful but slighter than Kern. There is a survey of contemporary medical opinion in K. Codell Carter, "Infantile Hysteria and Infantile Sexuality in Late Nineteenth-Century German-Language Medical Literature," *Medical History,* XXVII (1983), 186–96. Freud's view of marriage is discussed in John W. Boyer, "Freud, Marriage, and Late Viennese Liberalism: A Commentary from 1905," *Journal of Modern History,* L (March 1978), 72–102, which includes an important statement of Freud's in the original German.

CHAPTER FOUR · *Sketch of an Embattled Founder*

For my sketch of Freud at fifty, I have drawn on all the obviously relevant biographies, monographs, and reminiscences previously mentioned; on his correspondence, published and unpublished; and on Anna Freud's important letters to Ernest Jones (in Jones papers, Archives of the British Psycho-Analytical Society, London) and the unpublished recollections of Freud's analysand the psychoanalyst Ludwig Jekels (in Siegfried Bernfeld papers, container 17, LC). Jones, Schur, Sachs, and above all Martin Freud, are particularly indispensable. For Freud's apartment, the photographs by Edmund Engelman in *Berggasse 19: Sigmund Freud's Home and Offices, Vienna 1938* (1976) are evocative. These photographs, taken in May 1938, show Freud's consulting room as he rearranged it after he became partly deaf in one ear. See also my introduction to that collection, "Freud: For the Marble Tablet," 13–54, and the revised version, "Sigmund Freud: A German and His Discontents," in *Freud, Jews and Other Germans: Masters and Victims in Modernist Culture* (1978), 29–92. Rita Ransohoff's captions to Engelman's pictures are only moderately helpful; a professional catalogue of Freud's possessions, especially his antiquities, is a desideratum. See also the thoughtful comments of an early intimate, Max Graf, "Reminiscences of Professor Sigmund Freud," *Psychoanalytic Quarterly*, XI (1942), 465–77; Ernst Waldinger, "My Uncle Sigmund Freud," *Books Abroad*, XV (Winter 1941), 3–10; and an interview by Richard Dyck with another nephew, Harry Freud: "Mein Onkel Sigmund," *Aufbau* (New York), May 11, 1956, 3–4. Bruno Goetz, "Erinnerungen an Sigmund Freud," *Neue Schweizer Rundschau*, XX (May 1952), 3–11, is short but charming and touching. Excerpts from a number of these reminiscences, as well as many others, have been diligently collected in *Freud As We Knew Him*, ed. Hendrik M. Ruitenbeek (1973), a very comprehensive anthology. For the context of Freud's musical taste (especially for opera), I have sampled the vast literature; I single out Paul Robinson's fascinating and persuasive *Opera and Ideas from Mozart to Strauss* (1985), which argues that music *can* convey ideas. For Karl Kraus, see esp. Edward Timms, *Karl Kraus, Apocalyptic Satirist: Culture and Catastrophe in Habsburg Vienna* (1986), a scholarly biography that carefully corrects widespread misreadings of Freud's relations with Vienna's most celebrated literary gadfly.

For Freud's early adherents, see Franz Alexander, Samuel Eisenstein, and Martin Grotjahn, eds., *Psychoanalytic Pioneers* (1966), a rich but uneven anthology containing material unavailable elsewhere. The biographical comments in the four volumes of the *Protokolle* of the Vienna Psychoanalytic Society concerning Freud's circle are far from uninformative though too brief. Lou Andreas-Salomé, *In der Schule bei Freud. Tagebuch eines Jahres, 1912/1913*, ed. Ernst Pfeiffer (1958) is vigorous and perceptive. One of the most important among the Viennese, Otto Rank, has had more than one admiring biography: Jesse Taft, *Otto Rank* (1958) and the full study by E. James Lieberman, *Acts of Will: The Life and Work of Otto Rank* (1985), which sets the accents somewhat differently from the way I am setting them in this chapter and later. For the early days of the movement in Vienna and elsewhere, Ernest Jones's autobiography, *Free Associations: Memories of a Psycho-Analyst* (1959), is terse, opinionated, and informative.

The "foreigners" can use fuller treatment than they have so far received. There is no biography of Pfister, but his autobiographical statement, "Oskar Pfister," in *Die Pädagogik der Gegenwart in Selbstdarstellungen*, ed. Erich Hahn, 2 vols. (1926–27), II, 161–207, is a good start. Nearly the complete Freud–Pfister correspondence is at the Sigmund Freud Copyrights, Wivenhoe, and, in conjunction with the Pfister papers in the Zentralbibliothek, Zurich, would make the basis for a biography. See meanwhile Willi Hoffer's obituary of Pfister, *Int. J. Psycho-Anal.*, XXXIX (1958), 615–16, as well as Gay, *A Godless Jew*, ch. 3. The biography of Karl Abraham by his daughter Hilda Abraham, *Karl Abraham: An Unfinished Biography* (1974), is a valiant and incomplete first effort (its German version, *Karl Abraham. Sein Leben für die Psychoanalyse*, tr. into German by Hans-Horst Henschen, 1976, contains some important letters of Abraham's quoted in the original); far more needs to be done. Ernest Jones, a fascinating and documented figure, deserves better than Vincent Brome, *Ernest Jones: Freud's Alter Ego* (English ed., 1982; American ed., 1983); its principal virtues are reports of interviews with Jones and abundant quotations of texts from the archives, but it lacks critical judgment and is downright perfunctory. The papers published on the occasion of the centenary of Jones's birth, *Int. J. Psycho-Anal.*, LX (1979), are expectably admiring but do include some nuggets: Katharine Jones, "A Sketch of E. J.'s Personality," 171–73; William Gillespie, "Ernest Jones: The Bonny Fighter," 273–79; Pearl King, "The Contributions of Ernest Jones to the British Psycho-Analytical Society," 280–87; and Arcangelo R. T. D'Amore, "Ernest Jones: Founder of the American Psychoanalytic Association," 287–90. Binswanger, *Erinnerungen*, already cited for the letters of Freud's it quotes with abandon, also has Binswanger's own responses. There is all too little on the handsome, elegant, and brilliant Joan Riviere, but we have two affectionate obituaries by James Strachey and Paula Heimann, in *Int. J. Psycho-Anal.*, XLIV (1963), 228–30, 230–33. Perhaps the most severe lacuna is a full biography of Ferenczi (or, for that matter, a history of the Budapest institute). The best sources now are Michael Balint's fond, well-informed "Einleitung des Herausgebers," in Sándor Ferenczi, *Schriften zur Psychoanalyse*, ed. Balint, 2 vols. (1970), I, ix–xxii; and Ilse Grubrich-Simitis, "Six Letters of Sigmund Freud and Sándor Ferenczi on the Interrelationship of Psychoanalytic Theory and Technique," *Int. Rev. Psycho-Anal.*, XIII (1986), 259–77, well annotated and commented upon.

Hannah S. Decker, *Freud in Germany: Revolution and Reaction in Science, 1893–1907* (1977), is a model monograph on the early reception of Freud in Germany; it revises oversimplifications in Freud's and Jones's references to this reception without falling into the trap of revisionism for its own sake. Similar monographs on Freud's early reception elsewhere would be desirable.

For Otto Weininger, about whom a sizable literature has collected, I found particularly instructive Hans Kohn's pamphlet *Karl Kraus. Arthur Schnitzler. Otto Weininger. Aus dem jüdischen Wien der Jahrhundertwende* (1962); the relevant pages of Johnston, *The Austrian Mind*, esp. 158–62; Paul Biro, *Die Sittlichkeitsmetaphysik Otto Weininger. Eine geistesgeschichtliche Studie* (1927); and Emil Lucka, *Otto Weininger, sein Werk und seine Persönlichkeit* (1905; 2d ed. 1921).

A note on Eitingon: On January 24, 1988, the *New York Times Book Review* published an article by Stephen Schwartz, identified as "a fellow at the Institute of Contemporary Studies in San Francisco," which makes extremely serious charges against Max Eitingon. Schwartz links Eitingon to an international network of artists and intellectuals who, chiefly in the 1930s, served Stalin's murderous policy across the western world—in France, Spain, the United States, Mexico—helping to orchestrate, or participating in, the abduction and assassination of those whom Stalin or his secret police wanted eliminated. The allegations came at a most awkward time for me. I had never heard or read anything of the kind about Eitingon, and the chapters of my biography were past page proofs; only this bibliographical essay, at the printer's, allowed me an opportunity to comment. I thought I had learned a good deal about Eitingon in the course of writing this book, and the notion that he might have been among those ready to set aside their independence and their humanity to lend themselves to Stalin's murder machine seemed preposterous. But I was not disposed to take Schwartz's charges lightly, even though his account of Eitingon does not inspire confidence. (Schwartz, among other misstatements, calls Eitingon, "from 1925 to 1937," Freud's "factotum and shield against the world. Abraham was dead, Ferenczi and Rank were alienated from the master, and Sachs and Jones were unsuited to the role Dr. Eitingon carried out so well, attending to the ailing Freud with continuous kindnesses. He was a virtual social secretary to the old man." Readers of this biography will know that this is absurd: Eitingon saw Freud a few times at most in those years, either on a rare visit to Vienna or during Freud's even rarer visits to Berlin. As Freud's *Chronik* reveals, after Eitingon emigrated to Palestine at the end of 1933, he came to Berggasse 19 once a year.)

Still, however uninformed Schwartz, or the research assistant he acknowledges, may be about the life of the psychoanalytic establishment, this ignorance does not by itself disprove his case. And although there was not the slightest hint in Eitingon's letters to Freud of any possible sympathies with the Bolsheviks, I did not therefore automatically acquit him. After all, had Eitingon really been a Soviet agent, he would not have revealed that fact to his intimates—especially not to Freud, whose aversion to Bolshevism, and even to Socialism, was well known. But if Schwartz's charges proved true, it was incumbent on me to reveal that appalling fact to the readers of this biography, however marginal Eitingon may be to its central concerns.

I therefore decided to investigate the matter as thoroughly as time permitted. I consulted Wolfgang Leonhard, one of the world's most eminent specialists on Soviet iniquity. He had never heard of Max Eitingon, and could not find anything about him in his extensive specialized library. In addition, I went through a sizable literature on the Soviet secret police at home and abroad, including such classic texts as Robert Conquest, *Inside Stalin's Secret Police: NKVD Politics, 1936–1939* (1985) and a number of other monographs in English, French, and German. Though teeming with the names and activities of Soviet agents, none of these books so much as mentioned Max Eitingon. Beyond that, I paid particular attention to the two sources on which Schwartz relied, John J. Dziak, *Chekisty: A History of the KGB* (1988) and Vitaly Rapoport and Yuri Alexeev, *High Treason: Essays on the History of the Red Army, 1918–1938*, ed. Vladimir G. Treml and Bruce Adams, and tr. Adams (1985). Schwartz's first allegation is that Eitingon had participated in the kidnapping of a White Russian, General Yevgeni Karlovich Miller, in Paris in 1937, collaborating in this venture with the well-known Russian folk singer Nadezhda Plevitskaya and her husband, Nikolay Skoblin, both members of a special unit of the Soviet secret police. In addition, Schwartz hints darkly at another crime. "There is evidence," he writes, "that Dr. Max Eitingon was instrumental in preparing the 1937 secret trial in which the highest leaders of the Soviet Army, including the chief army commissar and eight generals, fell before the Stalinist execution machine." That secret trial, I should note, involved the sinister cooperation of NKVD agents with such prominent Nazi officials as Reinhard Heydrich, who conspired to decimate the leadership of the Soviet Army. While Schwartz does not document this accusation beyond asserting that there is evidence, he cannot resist concluding, "And, not to put too fine a point on it, it is not pleasant to imagine an associate of Freud in league with a henchman of Heydrich." Admittedly, it is not pleasant. But is it true?

Since Schwartz offers no corroboration for his second assertion, I concentrated my inquiries on the first. This is how he summarizes the findings of Dziak's *Chekisty:* "Mr. Dziak reports that one of the group's key agents in the kidnapping of General Miller was none other than a close personal associate of Sigmund Freud and a pillar of the psychoanalytic movement, Dr. Max Eitingon . . . the brother of Leonid Eitingon." Leonid, I should note, was a mysterious figure, also called by at least one source Naum Ettingon; he appears to have been a high official in the NKVD and a mastermind in the murder of Trotsky in 1940. "In his book," Schwartz writes, "Mr. Dziak concludes that it was Dr. Max Eitingon who recruited Skoblin and Plevitskaya into the special unit [of Stalin's assassins]." Toward the end of his article, Schwartz sounds far less categorical: "It may be argued that his [Max Eitingon's] own participation, over all, must have been slight. . . ." But this partial disclaimer cannot repair the damage done by his earlier indictments. In fact, however, Dziak is far more prudent than Schwartz makes him out to be. Dziak mentions Max Eitingon only three times in his book more or less in passing and notes that "Marx [*sic!*] *apparently* was linked to General Skoblin and his wife Plevitskaya" (p. 100, italics mine). While Plevitskaya's "financial connection" with Max Eitingon "*apparently* involved significant financial support," Dziak is not at all sure, for "whether the money came from the Eitingon family or from Soviet sources is unclear" (p. 101, italics mine). Indeed, "Mark Eitingon's name came up in the trial [of Plevitskaya] but not Naum's. Yet a Soviet *dissident source* claims it was *Naum* who organized and ran the Miller abduction" (p. 102, italics mine). And in an endnote, Dziak, showing real restraint in face of the paucity of dependable material, remarks resignedly that "there is considerable confusion over the activities of the two Eitingon brothers" (p. 199). This does not clear Max Eitingon's name but it raises crucial doubts about his involvement.

Schwartz's use of his other principal source is no less wayward. This is how he paraphrases the conclusions of Rapoport and Alexeev: they "declare flatly . . . that Dr. Eitingon . . . was the control agent for Skoblin and Plevitskaya." In fact, they do nothing of the sort. "Plevitskaya's superior in the NKVD was the legendary Naum Ettingon [*sic*]. Her contact and bagman," they write, "was Ettingon's brother Mark [*sic*]." They note further that "for many years he [Max Eitingon] was the generous patron of Nadezhda Plevitskaya. She said at her trial that 'he dressed me from head to foot.' He financed the publication of her two autobiographical books." These skimpy facts lead them to speculate: "It is unlikely that he did so only for the love of Russian music. It is more likely that he acted as messenger and finance agent for his brother Naum" (p. 391). Whatever else we may say of these conjectures, they sound far less conclusive than Schwartz's confident insinuations.

In the end, virtually all the allegations against Max Eitingon lead back to a book by B. Prianishnikov, *Nezrimiaia pautina (The Invisible Web),* published by the author in Russian in the United

States in 1979. Prianishnikov reprints substantial excerpts from the defendants' testimony at Plevit-skaya's trial in Paris after the kidnapping of General Miller. This is, for obvious reasons, a problematic source: it is extremely hard to fathom just what someone on trial will find it advantageous to testify. This granted, all that emerges from the testimony is a set of innocuous-sounding assertions: Plevits-kaya knew Max Eitingon well; he had often given her presents; he was very generous with his money (something that readers of this biography will be able to confirm); she had never "sold" her sexual favors to anyone for money or gifts (and certainly not to Max Eitingon); he was in fact a clean, decent man uninterested in gallant adventures. Indeed, so clean was his reputation that when a French interrogator alluded to Max Eitingon, a Russian witness corrected him to say that the person in question was Max's brother.

None of this, to be sure, guarantees Max Eitingon's innocence. The fact that he had a brother who, on better grounded evidence, was a senior official in the Soviet secret police says very little if anything about his possible role in these scurvy affairs. We can establish from Freud's correspondence with Eitingon and with Arnold Zweig, who became very friendly with the Eitingons during the exile they shared in Palestine, that Eitingon spent most of his time in Jerusalem attending to his analytic practice and to the business of organizing a psychoanalytic institute there. We know, too, from Freud's *Chronik*, that Eitingon was in Europe during the summer of 1937. None of this amounts to a great deal. It is certainly not enough to require a reevaluation of Eitingon's character. To be sure, almost by definition, uncovering the activities of a clandestine operative is a formidable enterprise. But the almost uniform silence about Max Eitingon in the literature is not without significance. At times, when the dog fails to bark in the night, this only means that the dog is safely asleep. It may be, of course, that Schwartz in a forthcoming book, or some of the researchers to whom he alludes, have as yet unpublished materials that will point to Eitingon's guilt. But until that evidence is published and analyzed, I conclude that Schwartz's findings are unsubstantiated.

CHAPTER FIVE · *Psychoanalytic Politics*

There is no biography of Jung anywhere near comparable to Jones's life of Freud. The principal reason is the difficulty in gaining access to important documents. Jung's imaginative, very inward autobiogra-phy, *Memories, Dreams, Reflections* (1962; tr. Richard and Clara Winston, 1962), is well titled, emphasizing as it does dreams. Like many autobiographies, it is more revealing than the author meant it to be. No less revealing is the substantial collection of Jung's pronouncements, *C. G. Jung Speaking: Interviews and Encounters*, ed. William McGuire and R. F. C. Hull (1977), which amplifies, modifies, and sometimes contradicts his autobiography. There are, meanwhile, some fairly informative lives, mainly by those who knew and enormously admired him. Liliane Frey-Rohn, *From Freud to Jung: A Comparative Study of the Psychology of the Unconscious* (1969; tr. Fred E. and Evelyn K. Engreen, 1974) is typical of this literature. Note among other lives E. A. Bennet, *C. G. Jung* (1961), which is terse; and by an intimate, Barbara Hannah, *Jung: His Life and Work, A Biographical Memoir* (1976), which stresses—and shares—Jung's mysticism. Ellenberger, *Discovery of the Unconscious*, ch. 9, is very thorough. Robert S. Steele, *Freud and Jung: Conflicts of Interpretation* (1982) repays reading. Aldo Carotenuto, *A Secret Symmetry: Sabina Spielrein between Jung and Freud* (1980; tr. Arno Pomerans, John Shepley, and Krishna Winston, 1982; 2d ed. with additional material, 1984), lavishly using documents, throws a lurid and disagreeable light on Jung as it tells the story of Jung's brilliant patient (and mistress)—a story in which Freud does not come off particularly well either.

Jung's work is readily accessible in comprehensive editions in both German and English. For the years of Jung's association with Freud, see esp. the papers collected in Jung, *Freud and Psychoanalysis* (1961; corr. ed., 1970), vol. IV of the *Collected Works;* and Jung, *The Psychoanalytic Years*, ed. William McGuire (1974), drawn from vols. II, IV, and XVII. I have already noted McGuire's admirable edition of the all-important Freud–Jung correspondence. In the growing monographic literature, I found the "contextual approach" of Peter Homans, *Jung in Context: Modernity and the Making of a Psychology* (1979) particularly thoughtful. Ernest Glover, *Freud or Jung?* (1956) is a partisan Freudian—though to my mind defensible—polemic. On the other hand, Paul E. Stepansky,

"The Empiricist as Rebel: Jung, Freud and the Burdens of Discipleship," *Journal of the History of the Behavioral Sciences*, XII (1976), 216–39, is in my judgment, though careful and intelligent, too partisan to Jung. K. R. Eissler, "Eine angebliche Disloyalität Freuds einem Freunde gegenüber," *Jahrbuch der Psychoanalyse*, XIX (1986), 71–88, offers a carefully reasoned defense of Freud's conduct toward Jung in 1912. Andrew Samuels, *Jung and the Post-Jungians* (1984) follows the fate of Jung's ideas beyond Jung's death, from a Jungian perspective. Among the many reviews of the Freud–Jung correspondence, I single out as most instructive Hans W. Loewald, "Transference and Counter-Transference: The Roots of Psychoanalysis," *Psychoanalytic Quarterly*, XLVI (1977), 514–27, conveniently accessible in Loewald, *Papers on Psychoanalysis* (1980), 405–18; Leonard Shengold, "The Freud/Jung Letters: The Correspondence between Sigmund Freud and C. G. Jung," *J. Amer. Psychoanal. Assn.*, XXIV (1976), 669–83; and D. W. Winnicott, in *Int. J. Psycho-Anal.*, XLV (1964), 450–55. On the vexed question of the break between Freud and Jung, see Herbert Lehman, "Jung contra Freud/Nietzsche contra Wagner," *Int. Rev. Psycho-Anal.*, XIII (1986), 201–9, which attempts to fathom Jung's state of mind. See also the intelligent essay by Hannah S. Decker, "A Tangled Skein: The Freud-Jung Relationship," in *Essays in the History of Psychiatry*, ed. Wallace and Pressley, 103–11.

Freud's visit to the United States can profitably repay further study. William A. Koelsch, "*Incredible Day Dream*": Freud and Jung at Clark, The Fifth Paul S. Clarkson Lecture (1984) is brief and popular but authoritative, based on thorough knowledge of the archival material. Nathan G. Hale, Jr., *Freud and the Americans: The Beginnings of Psychoanalysis in the United States, 1876–1917* (1971), a fine, detailed study (for Freud at Clark, see esp. part I) sets the visit into its context. So does Dorothy Ross, *G. Stanley Hall: The Psychologist as Prophet* (1972), a very full and responsible biography.

The prolific Stekel tells his side of his break with Freud (or Freud's break with him) in the posthumously published *The Autobiography of Wilhelm Stekel: The Life Story of a Pioneer Psychoanalyst*, ed. Emil A. Gutheil (1950). Fritz Wittels's unpublished autobiography, "Wrestling with the Man: The Story of a Freudian" (typescript, Fritz Wittels Collection, Box 2, A. A. Brill Library, New York Psychoanalytic Institute), is far kinder to Stekel than Freud let himself be. For the long-continued canvass of masturbation in the Vienna Psychoanalytic Society, in which Stekel still took part, see esp. Annie Reich, "The Discussion of 1912 on Masturbation and Our Present-Day Views," *The Psychoanalytic Study of the Child*, VI (1951), 80–94. The best life of Adler is Phyllis Bottome's authorized biography, *Alfred Adler: Apostle of Freedom* (1939; 3d ed., 1957); it is anecdotal, not very searching, and, not surprisingly, shows its subject in the most favorable light possible. Paul E. Stepansky, *In Freud's Shadow: Adler in Context* (1983) is far more sophisticated; it meticulously analyzes the Freud–Adler relationship, including the decisive split, but (watch Stepansky's adjectives) is inclined to give Adler the benefit of most doubts in the controversy. Ellenberger, *Discovery of the Unconscious*, has a substantial chapter (ch. 8) using, among other unpublished materials, a manuscript by an assiduous Adler researcher: Hans Beckh-Widmanstetter, "Kindheit und Jugend Alfred Adlers bis zum Kontakt mit Sigmund Freud." Adler's writings are readily available in English and German paperback editions; for informative biographical details, see the introductory essay by Heinz L. Ansbacher on Adler's growing influence, and the biographical study by Carl Furtmüller, both in *Alfred Adler, Superiority and Social Interest: A Collection of Later Writings*, ed. Heinz L. and Rowena R. Ansbacher (1964; 3d ed., 1979). Freud's own account, "On the History of the Psycho-Analytic Movement" (1914), *SE* XIV, 1–66, is fiery and partisan, and must be read as a polemic, but it remains most enlightening. Jones's autobiography, *Free Associations*, also has revealing pages on these years and combats. Walter Kaufmann's comprehensive study, *Discovering the Mind*, vol. III, *Freud versus Adler and Jung* (1980) sets Freud's great disputes into a larger context.

CHAPTER SIX · *Therapy and Technique*

The literature on Freud's published case histories is understandably almost unmanageable. Quite as understandably, the "Dora" case, with its irresistible implications for feminist and literary interpreters, has generated the largest and most impassioned literature; what follows is therefore merely a representative selection. For psychoanalysts' papers, see esp. Jules Glenn, "Notes on Psychoanalytic Concepts and Style in Freud's Case Histories" and "Freud's Adolescent Patients: Katharina, Dora and the 'Homosexual Woman,' " both in *Freud and His Patients*, ed. Mark Kanzer and Glenn (1980), 3–19, 23–47; the same volume also contains worthwhile pieces by Melvin A. Scharfman, "Further Reflections on Dora," 48–57; Robert J. Langs, "The Misalliance Dimension in the Case of Dora," 58–71; Kanzer, "Dora's Imagery: The Flight from a Burning House," 72–82; and Isidor Bernstein, "Integrative Summary: On the Re-viewings of the Dora Case," 83–91. See also the special issue of *Revue Française de Psychanalyse*, XXXVII (1973), with no fewer than seven papers devoted to this single case; Alan and Janis Krohn, "The Nature of the Oedipus Complex in the Dora Case," *J. Amer. Psychoanal. Assn.*, XXX (1982), 555–78; and Hyman Muslin and Merton Gill, "Transference in the Dora Case," *J. Amer. Psychoanal. Assn.*, XXVI (1978), 311–28. Thoughtful work on the same case, from a historian's perspective, has been done in Hannah S. Decker, "Freud and Dora: Constraints on Medical Progress," *Journal of Social History*, XIV (1981), 445–64; and in her ingenious "The Choice of a Name: 'Dora' and Freud's Relationship with Breuer," *J. Amer. Psychoanal. Assn.*, XXX (1982), 113–36. Felix Deutsch's well-known (I should hope notorious) and gratuitously nasty follow-up, describing a middle-aged Dora in the most unfeeling way, "A Footnote to Freud's 'Fragment of an Analysis of a Case of Hysteria,' " *Psychoanalytic Quarterly*, XXVI (1957), 159–67, is a document in analysis as aggression. Arnold A. Rogow, "A Further Footnote to Freud's 'Fragment of an Analysis of a Case of Hysteria,' " *J. Amer. Psychoanal. Assn.*, XXVI (1978), 331–56, a more good-tempered follow-up to Deutsch, addresses the familial context of Dora's life. See also the brilliant (if, I think, somewhat harsh) comments in Janet Malcolm, *Psychoanalysis: The Impossible Profession* (1981); she suggests (pp. 167–68) that the pseudonym "Dora" echoed the name of the mythical creature who brought evil into the world with her "box."

In *Dora's Case: Freud—Hysteria—Feminism*, ed. Charles Bernheimer and Claire Kahane (1985) is a provocative anthology of essays mainly by literary critics; the papers are of extremely varying merit, and their authors have very different axes to grind. Not without interest, the book contains two lengthy introductions by the editors, and sizable excerpts from Steven Marcus, "Freud and Dora: Story, History, Case History" (originally published in *Partisan Review*, [Winter 1974], 12–108, and reprinted in his *Representations* [1975], 247–309). Marcus, insisting on reading the case history as a species of literature, is partly responsible for the heavy burden of often arbitrary interpretations "Dora" now has to bear. One object lesson from this anthology is Toril Moi, "Representation of Patriarchy: Sexuality and Epistemology in Freud's Dora," 181–99. The author quotes Freud as saying that he had brought to light "the priceless though mutilated relics of antiquity" (*SE* VII, 12), and makes much of Freud's adjective: " 'Mutilated' is [Freud's] usual way of describing the effect of castration, and 'priceless' . . . means just what it says: price-less, without value. For how can there be value when the valuable piece has been cut off?" (p. 197). This is absurd even in English, but Moi has used only the translation from the *Standard Edition*, unwilling (or unable?) to look up the German. Yet in the original, Freud used *unschätzbaren*, and there is no way that anyone can legitimately read this as "without value." It means "inestimable," or, if you will, "beyond price," the highest praise a German adjective can bestow.

Little Hans has received far less attention. Joseph William Slap, "Little Hans's Tonsillectomy," *Psychoanalytic Quarterly*, XXX (1961), 259–61, has an interesting hypothesis complicating Freud's interpretation of Hans's phobia. Martin A. Silverman offers "A Fresh Look at the Case of Little Hans," in *Freud and His Patients*, ed. Kanzer and Glenn, 95–120, with a full bibliography on infantile experience. See also, in the same volume, Glenn's interesting paper "Freud's Advice to Hans' Father: The First Supervisory Sessions," 121–34.

The most sustained exploration of Freud's case history of the Rat Man, his family and his neurosis, and of the differences between Freud's process notes and the published case history, is Patrick J. Mahony, *Freud and the Rat Man* (1986). Elza Ribeiro Hawelka has made a meticulous transcription of the full German text of Freud's process notes (the much-used English text in *SE* X, 253–318, is neither complete nor completely reliable), adding a facing French translation, notes, and commentaries: Freud, *L'homme aux rats. Journal d'une analyse* (1974). The holograph manuscript of those notes, with annotations that look much like Freud's later handwriting, is in LC, among still unsorted materials. The rather sparse underlinings and marginalia suggest that Freud possibly wanted to return to this case, but no other manuscript on the Rat Man has come to light. Elizabeth R. Zetzel offers some interesting psychoanalytic second-guessing in "1965: Additional Notes upon a Case of Obsessional Neurosis: Freud 1909," *Int. J. Psycho-Anal.*, XLVII (1966), 123–29, to be read in conjunction with the article directly following: Paul G. Myerson, "Comment on Dr. Zetzel's Paper," 130–42. See also in *Int. J. Psycho-Anal.* Samuel D. Lipton, "The Advantages of Freud's Technique As Shown in His Analysis of the Rat Man," LVIII (1977), 255–73, and his follow-up, "An Addendum to 'The Advantages of Freud's Technique As Shown in His Analysis of the Rat Man,' " LX (1979), 215–16; as well as Béla Grunberger, "Some Reflections on the Rat Man," LX (1979), 160–68. As before, contributions to *Freud and His Patients*, ed. Kanzer and Glenn, are of interest, here notably Judith Kestenberg, "Ego Organization in Obsessive-Compulsive Development: The Study of the Rat Man, Based on Interpretation of Movement Patterns," 144–79; Robert J. Langs, "The Misalliance Dimension in the Case of the Rat Man," 215–30; and Mark Kanzer, "Freud's Human Influence on the Rat Man," 231–40. One of the earliest comments came in Ernest Jones's paper "Hate and Anal Erotism in the Obsessional Neurosis" (1913), in Jones, *Papers on Psycho-Analysis* (3d ed., 1923), 553–61.

For Freud's paper on Leonardo da Vinci, Meyer Schapiro, "Leonardo and Freud: An Art-Historical Study," *Journal of the History of Ideas*, XVII (1956), 147–78, is, in a word, indispensable. K. R. Eissler's response, *Leonardo da Vinci: Psycho-Analytic Notes on the Enigma* (1961) ranges widely and offers some brilliant comments, but is an instance of Eisslerian overkill—a 350-page book attempting to dissect an article of approximately 30 pages. From the library on Leonardo, I single out Kenneth Clark, *Leonardo da Vinci: An Account of His Development as an Artist* (1939; rev. ed., 1958), short, lucid, well-informed, and sympathetic. The first to call attention to Freud's mistake about the "vulture" was Eric Maclagan, "Leonardo in the Consulting Room," *Burlington Magazine*, XLII (1923), 54–57. Edward MacCurdy, ed., *The Notebooks of Leonardo da Vinci* (1939), is most useful.

The authoritative study of Schreber, diligently correcting earlier work, is the thesis by Han Israëls, *Schreber, Father and Son* (1980; tr. from the Dutch by the author, 1981; further modified in the French version, *Schreber, père et fils*, tr. Nicole Sels (1986). One particular virtue of Israëls's work is that it places Schreber in his family environment. His book has, however, not wholly antiquated a series of pioneering articles by William G. Niederland, three of them included in *Freud and His Patients*, ed. Kanzer and Glenn, 251–305, and all collected in *The Schreber Case: Psychoanalytic Profile of a Paranoid Personality* (1974). These demonstrate that some of Schreber's "inventions," such as the machines torturing him, bore a strong resemblance to devices his father strapped him into when he was a boy. Between Israëls and Niederland, both the substantive and the polemical aspects of the case are covered sufficiently—and impressively.

Patrick J. Mahony has dealt as thoroughly with the Wolf Man, in *Cries of the Wolf Man* (1984), as he has with the Rat Man, paying particular attention to Freud's style. (Mahony has also written a separate study of that style, *Freud as a Writer* [1982].) Among psychoanalysts' papers reviewing the case, the most interesting is William Offenkrantz and Arnold Tobin, "Problems of the Therapeutic Alliance: Freud and the Wolf Man," *Int. J. Psycho-Anal.*, LIV (1973), 75–78. Harold P. Blum, "The Borderline Childhood of the Wolf Man," *J. Amer. Psychoanal. Assn.*, XXII (1974), 721–42, conveniently accessible in *Freud and His Patients*, ed. Kanzer and Glenn, 341–58, suggests that this famous analysand was rather more disturbed than Freud diagnosed him to be. This volume also has a fine paper by Mark Kanzer, "Further Comments on the Wolf Man: The Search for a Primal Scene," 359–66. Ruth Mack Brunswick, who analyzed the Wolf Man for a time in the 1920s, reports on him in "A Supplement to Freud's History of an Infantile Neurosis" (1928), conveniently reprinted in *The Wolf-Man by the Wolf-Man*, ed. Muriel Gardiner (1971), 263–307. This fascinating volume also contains the Wolf Man's reminiscences, including his account of Freud, and Gardiner's report on the Wolf Man's later years. J. Harnik began a discussion, worth following up, criticizing Brunswick's dealings with the Wolf Man: "Kritisches über Mack Brunswicks 'Nachtrag zu Freud's "Geschichte einer infantilen Neurose," ' " *Int. J. Psycho-Anal.*, XVI (1930), 123–27; Brunswick's reply, directly following, is "Entgegnung auf Harniks kritische Bemerkungen," 128–29. This in turn provoked Harnik's "Erwiderung auf Mack Brunswicks Entgegnung," *Int. J. Psycho-Anal.*, XVII (1931), 400–402, which is directly followed in the same issue by Brunswick's final word, "Schlusswort," 402. Karin Obholzer, *The Wolf-Man Sixty Years Later: Conversations with Freud's Controversial Patient* (1980; tr. Michael Shaw, 1982) records some interviews with the very elderly Wolf Man which are of quite limited value and must be read with caution.

Most later psychoanalysts' papers and books on psychoanalytic technique can be safely read as commentaries on Freud's classic papers, though the best among them, of course, do not lack a certain originality and introduce refinements on Freud's pioneering expositions. Among those I have found most instructive—I am slighting a number of important shorter papers—are Edward Glover, *Technique of Psycho-Analysis* (1955), lucid and vigorous; Karl Menninger, *Theory of Psychoanalytic Technique* (1958), enviably succinct; and the splendid essay by Leo Stone, an expanded Freud Lecture, *The Psychoanalytic Situation: An Examination of Its Development and Essential Nature* (1961). Ralph R. Greenson, *The Technique and Practice of Psychoanalysis*, vol. I (1967), the only volume to appear, is a thorough, highly technical textbook, with an instructive treatment of the working alliance; it is mainly intended for candidates in psychoanalytic institutes. I have learned much from Loewald's series of elegant (subtly revisionist) papers grouped together under the subtitle "The Psychoanalytic Process," in his *Papers on Psychoanalysis*, most notably "On the Therapeutic Action of Psychoanalysis," 221–56; "Psychoanalytic Theory and the Psychoanalytic Process," 277–301; "The Transference Neurosis: Comments on the Concept and the Phenomenon," 302–14; "Reflections on the Psychoanalytic Process and Its Therapeutic Potential," 372–83; and the stimulating, original "The Waning of the Oedipus Complex," 384–404. Sándor Ferenczi's controversial papers on technique are available in the two-volume *Schriften zur Psychoanalyse*, ed. Balint; in English, the volume *Further Contributions to the Theory and Technique of Psycho-Analysis* (1926; 2d ed., 1960) makes many of them easily available. Also among the most valuable papers on technique are Rudolph M. Loewenstein's short survey, "Developments in the Theory of Transference in the Last Fifty Years," *Int. J. Psycho-Anal.*, L (1969), 583–88; and several contributions by Phyllis Greenacre, collected in her *Emotional Growth: Psychoanalytic Studies of the Gifted and a Great Variety of Other Individuals*, 2 vols., continuously paginated (1971), esp. "Evaluation of Therapeutic Results: Contributions to a Symposium" (1948), 619–26; "The Role of Transference: Practical Considerations in Relation to Psychoanalytic Therapy" (1954), 627–40; "Re-evaluation of the Process of Working Through" (1956), 641–50; and "The Psychoanalytic Process, Transference, and Acting Out" (1968), 762–76, to name only the most significant. Janet Malcolm's witty and wicked *Psychoanalysis: The Impossible Profession* has been praised by psychoanalysts (with justice) as a dependable introduction to analytic theory and technique. It has the rare advantage over more solemn texts of being funny as well as informative.

CHAPTER SEVEN · *Applications and Implications*

Freud's writings on aesthetics are scattered. "Delusions and Dreams in Jensen's *Gradiva*" (1907), *SE* IX, 3–95, is, after a few hints in letters to Fliess and *The Interpretation of Dreams*, his first venture in psychoanalysis applied to the unriddling of a literary text. (Incidentally, Wilhelm Jensen's letters to Freud regarding *Gradiva* are to be found in *Psychoanalytische Bewegung*, I (1929), 207–11.) "Creative Writers and Day-Dreaming" (1908), *SE* IX, 141–53, was an influential early text, a finger exercise never developed into a theory. See also Freud's moving reading of two famous scenes, one in *King Lear*, the other in *The Merchant of Venice*, in "The Theme of the Three Caskets" (1913), *SE* XII, 291–301. His first incursion into the biography of an artist is, of course, "Leonardo da Vinci and a Memory of His Childhood" (1910), *SE* XI, 59–137, a daring, in important ways flawed, exploration. (Much is to be learned about this famous paper from the fine article by Schapiro, "Leonardo and Freud: An Art-Historical Study," already cited.) Freud's next venture, published anonymously, was "The Moses of Michelangelo" (1914), with a "Postscript" (1927), *SE* XIII,

211–38. (Amid a sizable literature, there are some particularly weighty comments on that statue in Erwin Panofsky, *Studies in Iconology: Humanistic Themes in the Art of the Renaissance* [1939], ch. 6; see also the observations in Robert S. Liebert, *Michelangelo: A Psychoanalytic Study of His Life and Images* [1983], ch. 14. Another controversial paper of Freud's is "Dostoevsky and Parricide" (1928), *SE* XXI, 175–96, attacked a little too savagely (but not without reason) by Joseph Frank in "Freud's Case-History of Dostoevsky," the appendix to his *Dostoevsky: The Seeds of Revolt, 1821– 1849* (1976), 379–91.

The most satisfactory general analysis of Freud's complex attitude toward the arts, from which I have learned a good deal, is Jack J. Spector's precise and perceptive *The Aesthetics of Freud: A Study in Psychoanalysis and Art* (1972). See also Harry Trosman, *Freud and the Imaginative World* (1985), esp. part II. Among earlier art critics dealing with Freud, the most interesting is probably Roger Fry, who, in *The Artist and Psycho-Analysis* (1924) criticized Freud for unduly minimizing the aesthetic pleasure residing in the formal aspects of art—a criticism to which Freud would have assented.

Many psychoanalysts among Freud's earliest adherents did not resist the temptation to psychoanalyze poets and painters (sometimes to Freud's chagrin). Among the most notable, and most praised, of their efforts is Karl Abraham's early essay *Giovanni Segantini*, subtitled *Ein psychoanalytischer Versuch* (1911). In "Methodik der Dichterpsychologie," a paper given at the Wednesday Psychological Society on December 11, 1907, the musicologist Max Graf, who was for some years close to Freud, attempted in a fascinating proposal to win his colleagues away from traditional pathographies of artists and writers. (See *Protokolle*, I, 244–49.) While he never published this paper, Graf did publish *Aus der inneren Werkstatt des Musikers* (1911) and *Richard Wagner im "Fliegenden Holländer". Ein Beitrag zur Psychologie des künstlerischen Schaffens* (1911), the latter first given as a talk to the Wednesday Society. In the preface, Graf gratefully paid tribute to his "uninterrupted exchange of views with Professor Freud." Eduard Hitschmann, for many years a member of the psychoanalytic inner circle in Vienna, wrote a number of "psychoanalyses" of poets and novelists, groping efforts rather than definitive researches. A number of these are available in English in Hitschmann, *Great Men: Psychoanalytic Studies*, ed. Sydney G. Margolin, with assistance of Hannah Gunther (1956). Ernest Jones, venturing into literary analysis, took off from a few pregnant pages in *The Interpretation of Dreams* in a paper of 1910 (continuously enlarged until it became the book *Hamlet and Oedipus* in 1949). The essay has been severely, and I think excessively, criticized for its presumed reductionism—it has the modest aim of elucidating only why Hamlet hesitates to kill Claudius—but Jones's controversial treatment retains its interest. Otto Rank was indefatigable in his psychoanalysis of literary figures and themes. The manuscript he carried on his first visit to Freud was published as *Der Künstler* (1907; 4th enlarged ed., 1918). His *The Myth of the Birth of the Hero* (1909; tr. F. Robbins and Smith Ely Jelliffe, 1914) is probably his most enduring essay. (A sophisticated companion piece, drawing on materials first published in the 1930s, is Ernst Kris and Otto Kurz, *Legend, Myth, and Magic in the Image of the Artist: A Historical Experiment* [1979].) But the most compendious of his ventures, which Freud apparently thought well of, is Rank's bulky study of the incest theme in poetry, prose, and myth, *Das Inzest-Motiv in Dichtung und Sage* (1912; 2d ed., 1926). Among Rank's many other papers, perhaps the most interesting is his long essay "Der Doppelgänger," *Imago*, III (1914), 97–164 (English version, *The Double*, tr. Harry Tucker, 1971). It also appears in a useful collection of papers from *Imago: Psychoanalytische Literaturinterpretationen*, ed. Jens Malte Fischer (1980); equipped with a substantial introduction, this anthology also includes papers (among others) by Hanns Sachs and Theodor Reik. The latter, as I recount in the text, introduced himself to Freud with a thesis on Flaubert, subsequently published as *Flaubert und seine "Versuchung des Heiligen Antonius". Ein Beitrag zur Künstlerpsychologie* (1912). One influential text in "applied analysis" has been Marie Bonaparte's psychobiography, *The Life and Works of Edgar Allan Poe: A Psycho-Analytic Interpretation* (1933; tr. John Rodker, 1949); it is somewhat rigid and mechanical, but spirited. After a decade in the United States, Hanns Sachs, that cultivated Central European, published a collection of papers on art and beauty, *The Creative Unconscious: Studies in the Psychoanalysis of Art* (1942), which has been unjustly neglected: in particular, ch. 4,

"The Delay of the Machine Age," is a suggestive piece of conjectural history from a Freudian perspective.

Not surprisingly, psychoanalysts (and psychoanalytically trained lay people) have actively continued to play in this field. A small sampling must do. To begin with the analysts: Gilbert J. Rose's meaty *The Power of Form: A Psychoanalytic Approach to Aesthetic Form* (1980) studies the complex interaction of the primary and the secondary process in the arts. The imaginative British psychoanalyst D. W. Winnicott has touched on aesthetic experience in a number of his papers, most excitingly perhaps in "Transitional Objects and Transitional Phenomena" (1953), conveniently available in a version he calls a "development" in his *Playing and Reality* (1971), 1–25. That collection also contains his important paper "The Location of Cultural Experience" (1967), 95–103. William G. Niederland, "Psychoanalytic Approaches to Artistic Creativity," *Psychoanalytic Quarterly*, XLV (1976), 185–212, repays close reading, as does his earlier "Clinical Aspects of Creativity," *American Imago*, XXIV (1967), 6–34. Robert Waelder's Freud Lecture, *Psychoanalytic Avenues to Art* (1965) is rich in suggestions beyond its brief text. John E. Gedo, *Portraits of the Artist: Psychoanalysis of Creativity and Its Vicissitudes* (1983) is a collection of essays attempting to approach the secrets of the creative artist. From many psychoanalysts' efforts at full-scale psychobiography, I single out Liebert, *Michelangelo* (cited above), not uncontested yet most interesting; and Bernard C. Meyer, *Josef Conrad: A Psychoanalytic Biography* (1967).

As for the "amateurs": Meredith Anne Skura, *The Literary Use of the Psychoanalytic Process* (1981) is a sophisticated analysis taking four principal themes of psychoanalysis—case history, fantasy, dream, transference—as possible models for literary criticism. I have also learned much from Elizabeth Dalton, *Unconscious Structure in "The Idiot": A Study in Literature and Psychoanalysis* (1979), a brief, daring essay which attempts (successfully, I think) to treat characters in Dostoevsky's novel as psychologically coherent beings. Ellen Handler Spitz, *Art and Psyche: A Study in Psychoanalysis and Aesthetics* (1985) examines the presence of the artist in his work, its psychological implications, and the artist's relations to his audience. Among the most precisely targeted and stimulating studies on this last issue—reception of the work of art—are those of Norman N. Holland, esp. *Psychoanalysis and Shakespeare* (1966); *The Dynamics of Literary Response* (1968); and *Poems in Persons: An Introduction to the Psychoanalysis of Literature* (1973). Richard Ellmann, "Freud and Literary Biography," *American Scholar*, LIII (Fall 1984), 465–78, is at once critical and, as expected, immensely intelligent.

The Practice of Psychoanalytic Criticism, ed. Leonard Tennenhouse (1976) collects a number of fairly recent articles, largely from *American Imago*; *Literature and Psychoanalysis*, ed. Edith Kurzweil and William Phillips (1983) starts with Freud and moves into modern analytic criticism, including a classic piece by Lionel Trilling, "Art and Neurosis," previously published in Trilling, *The Liberal Imagination: Essays on Literature and Society* (1950), 160–80. See also the theoretical statement by Simon O. Lesser, *Fiction and the Unconscious* (1957), to be complemented with the collection of Lesser's papers, *The Whispered Meanings*, ed. Robert Sprinch and Richard W. Noland (1977).

Philosophers have not neglected this field. See esp. Richard Wollheim, *On Art and the Mind* (1974) and the anthology *Philosophical Essays on Freud*, ed. Wollheim and Hopkins (already cited). Richard Kuhns, *Psychoanalytic Theory of Art: A Philosophy of Art on Developmental Principles* (1983) draws on ego psychologists like Heinz Hartmann and object-relations theorists like D. W. Winnicott for a stimulating integration of all the dimensions of artistic productivity. In *Art and Act: On Causes in History—Manet, Gropius, Mondrian* (1976), I have attempted to place artistic creation within the network of private, craft, and cultural experience. *Freud for Historians* (1985), my effort to persuade my fellow historians that psychoanalysis should be productively, and can be safely, employed in my profession, has, as far as I can see, largely fallen on stony ground. On the encouraging side I single out Peter Loewenberg, *Decoding the Past: The Psychohistorical Approach* (1983), a series of papers on theory and application (most of them antedating my own work) by a historian trained in psychoanalysis. The opening chapter, "Psychohistory: An Overview of the Field," 9–41, ably surveys the territory, while subsequent chapters exemplifying the psychoanalytic approach include several on Austrian history: "Theodor Herzl: Nationalism and Politics," 101–35; "Victor and Friedrich Adler: Revolutionary Politics and Generational Conflict in Austro-Marxism," 136–60; and "Austro-Marxism and Revolution: Otto Bauer, Freud's 'Dora' Case, and the Crises of the First Austrian Republic," 161–204, a paper of particular relevance to this biography. Saul Friedländer, *History and Psychoanalysis: An Inquiry into the Possibilities and Limits of Psychohistory* (1975; tr. Susan Suleiman, 1978), is a model of rational argumentation.

For *Totem and Taboo*, Edwin R. Wallace IV, *Freud and Anthropology: A History and a Reappraisal* (1983) offers an excellent judicious survey. Alfred L. Kroeber's famous two reviews of Freud's book (the second less scathing than the first) deserve rereading: "*Totem and Taboo*: An Ethnologic Psychoanalysis," *American Anthropologist*, XXII (1920), 48–55; and "*Totem and Taboo* in Retrospect," *American Journal of Sociology*, LV (1939), 446–57. So does the witty treatment by R. R. Marett, "Psycho-Analysis and the Savage," *Athenaeum* (1920), 205–6. Suzanne Cassirer Bernfeld, "Freud and Archeology," *American Imago*, VIII (1951), 107–28, is an abundant source from which others have drawn. The most convincing recent attempt to rescue Freud's central argument (though not the historical reality of the primal crime) is Derek Freeman, "Totem and Taboo: A Reappraisal," in *Man and His Culture: Psychoanalytic Anthropology after "Totem and Taboo,"* ed. Warner Muensterberger (1970), 53–78. Sandor S. Feldman, "Notes on the 'Primal Horde,' " in *Psychoanalysis and the Social Sciences*, ed. Muensterberger, I (1947), 171–93, is a relevant companion piece. See also Robin Fox, "*Totem and Taboo* Reconsidered," in *The Structural Study of Myth and Totemism*, ed. Edmund Leach (1967), 161–78. I must mention the brilliant essay by Melford E. Spiro, *Oedipus in the Trobriands* (1982), a psychoanalytically informed anthropologist's refutation of Malinowski's skepticism about the applicability of Freud's ideas to the Trobriand Islanders—based entirely on Malinowski's own materials.

Because Freud never fully developed the idea of character—that organized cluster of habits and fixations—there has been a disposition to return to his early statements, to the short important paper "Character and Anal Erotism" (1908) and to the trio of papers published eight years later under the collective title "Some Character-Types Met With in Psychoanalytic Work," *SE* XIV, 309–33, the three types being "The 'Exceptions,' " "Those Wrecked by Success," and "Criminals from a Sense of Guilt." An interesting expansion on Freud's definition of "exceptions" is Edith Jacobson, "The 'Exceptions': An Elaboration of Freud's Character Study," *The Psychoanalytic Study of the Child*, XIV (1959), 135–54; and a no less interesting commentary on the same paper of Freud's is Anton O. Kris, "On Wanting Too Much: The 'Exceptions' Revisited," *Int. J. Psycho-Anal.*, LVII (1976), 85–95. In view of Freud's failure to pull the material together, Otto Fenichel's fairly systematic comments are particularly welcome. See above all, "Psychoanalysis of Character" (1941), in *The Collected Papers of Otto Fenichel*, ed. Hanna Fenichel and David Rapaport, 2d Series (1954), 198–214. See also the relevant chapters in Fenichel's substantial, far from outdated work *The Psychoanalytic Theory of Neurosis* (1945), notably "Digression about the Anal Character," 278–84, and "Character Disorders," 463–540. In this connection, David Shapiro's terse essay *Neurotic Styles* (1965) has helpful things to say. So does P. C. Giovacchini, *Psychoanalysis of Character Disorders* (1975).

This is not the place to rehearse the debates about narcissism that have been agitating psychoanalysts in recent years. Sydney Pulver, "Narcissism: The Term and the Concept," *J. Amer. Psychoanal. Assn.*, XVIII (1970), 319–41, presents a clarifying survey. Among the numerous clinical and theoretical studies on narcissistic disorders by Otto F. Kernberg, see esp. *Borderline Conditions and Pathological Narcissism* (1975). Two papers by Heinz Kohut in *The Psychoanalytic Study of the Child*—"The Psychoanalytic Treatment of Narcissistic Personality Disorders," XXIII (1968), 86–113, and "Thoughts on Narcissism and Narcissistic Rage," XXVII (1972), 360–400—are still experimental and tentative, having been written before Kohut turned his particular reading of narcissism into an ideology. And see R. D. Stolorow, "Toward a Functional Definition of Narcissism," *Int. J. Psycho-Anal.*, LVI (1975), 179–85; and Warren Kingston, "A Theoretical and Technical Approach to Narcissistic Disorders," *Int. J. Psycho-Anal.*, LXI (1980), 383–94. Arnold Rothstein, *The Narcissistic Pursuit of Perfection* (1980) reviews and seeks to redefine the concept. Among discussions of the issue by "classical" analysts, certain papers by Heinz Hartmann are particularly pertinent here, esp.

"Comments on the Psychoanalytic Theory of the Ego" (1950) and "The Development of the Ego Concept in Freud's Work" (1956), in *Essays on Ego Psychology: Selected Problems in Psychoanalytic Theory* (1964), 113–41, 268–96. The well-known monograph by Edith Jacobson, *The Self and the Object World* (1964) is no less important.

Oron J. Hale, *The Great Illusion, 1900–1914* (1971) dependably synthesizes recent historiography on the atmosphere before Armageddon. Walter Laqueur and George L. Mosse have edited an interesting collection of essays, moving from country to country, *1914: The Coming of the First World War* (1966). On the war psychosis that gripped presumably cosmopolitan and intelligent professional people on all sides, including in some measure Freud, see the well-documented, sobering essay by Roland N. Stromberg, *Redemption by War: The Intellectuals and 1914* (1982); it can be read in tandem with Robert Wohl, *The Generation of 1914* (1979). For the First World War, on which whole libraries have been written, it should suffice to name a few dependable texts: B. H. Liddell-Hart, *The Real War, 1914–1918* (1930); Corelli Barnett, *The Swordbearers: Supreme Command in the First World War* (1964); and René Albrecht-Carrié, *The Meaning of the First World War* (1965). Fritz Fischer, *Griff nach der Weltmacht. Die Kriegszielpolitik des kaiserlichen Deutschland 1914/1918* (1961; 3d ed., 1964) caused a storm among German historians with its fierce critique of German war aims, and its violation of German taboos against frankly exploring the causes of the war; it is a salutary text, particularly useful in this chapter for its collection of bellicose, "manly" statements by diplomats. It can be read in connection with Hans W. Gatzke, *Germany's Drive to the West* (1950).

CHAPTER EIGHT · *Aggressions*

For the history of the unconscious from a nonpsychoanalytic perspective, see, once again, Whyte, *The Unconscious before Freud* and the far more extensive Ellenberger, *Discovery of the Unconscious.* For psychoanalytic comments on the unconscious, see amidst a large literature, above all Edward Bibring, "The Development and Problems of the Theory of the Instincts," *Int. J. Psycho-Anal.*, XXII (1934), 102–31; Bibring, "The Conception of the Repetition Compulsion," *Psychoanalytic Quarterly*, XII (1942), 486–516; Robert Waelder, "Critical Discussion of the Concept of an Instinct of Destruction," *Bulletin of the Philadelphia Association for Psychoanalysis*, VI (1956), 97–109; and several influential papers by the ego psychologist Heinz Hartmann, collected in his *Essays on Ego Psychology.* These include "Comments on the Psychoanalytic Theory of Instinctual Drives" (1948), 69–89; "The Mutual Influences in the Development of Ego and Id" (1952), 155–81; and (already cited) "Comments on the Psychoanalytic Theory of the Ego" and "The Development of the Ego Concept in Freud's Work," a particularly helpful historical essay. Hartmann also joined his fellow ego psychologists Ernst Kris and Rudolph M. Loewenstein in "Comments on the Formation of Psychic Structure" (1946), in their *Papers on Psychoanalytic Psychology* (1964), 27–55. The terse study by Max Schur, *The Id and the Regulatory Principles of Mental Functioning* (1966) has much of value. David Holbrook, ed., *Human Hope and the Death Instinct: An Exploration of Psychoanalytic Theories of Human Nature and Their Implications for Culture and Education* (1971), though in no way hostile to psychoanalysis, brings together papers devoted to escaping from destructiveness and in search of a humanist conscience.

On death as it touched Freud—both as an idea and as a threat—Schur, *Freud, Living and Dying* is magisterial. For Freud's recognition of the aggressive drive, so long delayed (though the drive was not wholly disregarded), see the survey by Paul E. Stepansky, *A History of Aggression in Freud* (1977). It may be supplemented with Rudolf Brun, "Über Freuds Hypothese vom Todestrieb," *Psyche*, VII (1953), 81–111. From the avalanche of papers on this subject, I select some outstanding contributions: Otto Fenichel's important paper "A Critique of the Death Instinct" (1935), in *Collected Papers*, 1st Series (1953), 363–72; two papers in *The Psychoanalytic Study of the Child*, III/IV (1949): Anna Freud, "Aggression in Relation to Emotional Development: Normal and Pathological," 37–42, and Beata Rank, "Aggression," 43–48; Heinz Hartmann, Ernst Kris, and Rudolph M. Loewenstein, "Notes on the Theory of Aggression" (1949), in their *Papers on Psychoanalytic Psychology*, 56–85; René A. Spitz, "Aggression: Its Role in the Establishment of Object Relations," in

Drives, Affects, Behavior: Essays in Honor of Marie Bonaparte, ed. Rudolph M. Loewenstein (1953), 126–38; T. Wayne Downey, "Within the Pleasure Principle: Child Analytic Perspectives on Aggression," *The Psychoanalytic Study of the Child,* XXXIX (1984), 101–36; Phyllis Greenacre, "Infant Reactions to Restraint: Problems in the Fate of Infantile Aggression" (1944), in her *Trauma, Growth, and Personality* (1952), 83–105; Albert J. Solnit, "Aggression," *J. Amer. Psychoanal. Assn.,* XX (1972), 435–50; and—to me most important—Solnit, "Some Adaptive Functions of Aggressive Behavior," in *Psychoanalysis—A General Psychology,* ed. Loewenstein, Newman, Schur, and Solnit, 169–89. Among those who, in contrast to most other analysts, take Freud's doctrine of the death drive seriously, K. R. Eissler has been the most persuasive—or least unpersuasive—in "Death Drive, Ambivalence, and Narcissism," *The Psychoanalytic Study of the Child,* XXVI (1971), 25–78, a spirited defense of Freud's controversial idea. Alexander Mitscherlich examines it from the perspective of psychoanalytic social psychology in "Psychoanalysis and the Aggression of Large Groups," *Int. J. Psycho-Anal.,* LII (1971), 161–67. For one eminent psychoanalyst's profoundly skeptical view of the possibility of treating aggression as a single entity, see Leo Stone, "Reflections on the Psychoanalytic Concept of Aggression," *Psychoanalytic Quarterly,* XL (1971), 195–244, a most unsettling piece.

There is for obvious reasons little material on Freud's "lost" metapsychological papers. One brilliant essay is Ilse Grubrich-Simitis, "Trauma or Drive; Drive and Trauma: A Reading of Sigmund Freud's Phylogenetic Fantasy of 1915," the Freud Lecture delivered in New York on April 28, 1987, not yet published at this writing. In her essay on Freud's twelfth metapsychological paper, which she discovered, deciphered, and published as *A Phylogenetic Fantasy,* Grubrich-Simitis suggestively connects the high-flying theorizing of Freud's phylogenetic fantasy with the lifelong battle in his thinking between the trauma theory and the drive theory of neuroses. This view is congruent with the Freud I present in this book: a man engaged in a titanic subterranean struggle between the urge to speculate and the need for self-discipline. There are also usable conjectures in Barry Silverstein, " 'Now Comes A Sad Story': Freud's Lost Metapsychological Papers," in *Freud, Appraisals and Reappraisals,* ed. Stepansky, I, 143–95. (I should also like to call attention to the anti-metapsychological school of psychoanalytic thought, which chooses to stress Freud's clinical thinking instead. Among the most original, but to my mind in the end unpersuasive, essays in this vein are the papers of George S. Klein, notably "Two Theories or One?" in his *Psychoanalytic Theory: An Exploration of Essentials* [1976], 41–71, to be read in conjunction with other papers in that volume. Merton M. Gill and Philip S. Holzman have collected some suggestive papers from this perspective in *Psychology versus Metapsychology: Psychoanalytic Essays in Memory of George S. Klein* [1976].)

For the end of the war and its immediate aftermath among the defeated Central Powers, the best account is F. L. Carsten's scholarly study, *Revolution in Central Europe, 1918–1919* (1972), which draws on unpublished sources as well as printed material and has extensive chapters on Austria. John Williams, *The Other Battleground: The Home Fronts, Britain, France and Germany 1914–1918* (1972) goes beyond its title with comments on Austria on the way to defeat. Otto Bauer, *Die österreichische Revolution* (1923) is an account by a Socialist participant. Modern scholarship is soberly and economically presented in *Österreich 1918–1938. Geschichte der Ersten Republik,* ed. Erika Weinzierl and Kurt Skalnik, 2 vols. (1983); note esp. Wolfdieter Bihl, "Der Weg zum Zusammenbruch—Österreich-Ungarn unter Karl I. (IV.)," 27–54; Karl R. Stadler, "Die Gründung der Republik," 55–84; and Fritz Fellner, "Der Vertrag von St. Germain," 85–106. Also of particular significance in this volume are Hans Kernbauer, Eduard März, and Fritz Weber, "Die wirtschaftliche Entwicklung," 343–79; Ernst Bruckmüller, "Sozialstruktur und Sozialpolitik," 381–436; and Erika Weinzierl, "Kirche und Politik," 437–96. One of these authors, Karl R. Stadler, can be read in English: *The Birth of the Austrian Republic* (1966). The memoir by Anna Eisenmenger, *Blockade: The Diary of an Austrian Middleclass Woman, 1914–1924* (tr. anon., 1932) is moving. Also worth reading in this connection is Ottokar Landwehr-Pragenau, *Hunger. Die Erschöpfungsjahre der Mittelmächte 1917/18* (1931). *Aufbruch und Untergang. Österreichische Kultur zwischen 1918 und 1938,* ed. Franz Kadrnoska (1981) is an illuminating pendant, containing essays on the theater and the circus, caricatures and movies, painters and festivals; Ursula Kubes's article " 'Moderne Nervositäten' und die Anfänge der Psychoanalyse," 267–80, is particularly relevant here. Walter Goldinger, *Ge-*

schichte der Republik Österreich (1962) is a sober survey. Among reminiscences, see esp. Bertha Zuckerkandl, *Österreich intim. Erinnerungen 1892–1942,* ed. Reinhard Federmann (1970). Christine Klusacek and Kurt Stimmer, eds., *Dokumentation zur österreichischen Zeitgeschichte, 1928–1938* (1982) offers well-chosen snippets on all aspects of Austria's history during this decade. Jacques Hannak, *Karl Renner und seine Zeit. Versuch einer Biographie* (1965) is an exhaustive biography of the Socialist politician and theorist, with extensive quotations from documents. Peter Csendes, *Geschichte Wiens* (1981) is a skimpy survey. *The Jews of Austria,* ed. Fraenkel, is indispensable once more in a number of its selections. A. J. May has a useful essay, "Woodrow Wilson and Austria-Hungary to the End of 1917," in *Festschrift für Heinrich Benedikt,* ed. H. Hantsch et al. (1957), 213–42. Wilson is also the subject of Klaus Schwabe, *Woodrow Wilson, Revolutionary Germany, and Peacemaking 1918–1919: Missionary Diplomacy and the Realities of Power* (1971; tr. Rita and Robert Kimber, 1985). Three biographies already cited are valuable for this epoch: Timms, *Karl Kraus, Apocalyptic Satirist;* Luft, *Robert Musil and the Crisis of European Culture,* and Prater, *European of Yesterday: A Biography of Stefan Zweig.*

Victor Tausk's suicide has been the subject of envenomed controversy. First canvassed in Paul Roazen's tendentious study, *Brother Animal: The Story of Freud and Tausk* (1969), which makes Freud the villain of the piece, it was re-canvassed by K. R. Eissler in a characteristic reply (very indignant and very circumstantial), *Talent and Genius: The Fictitious Case of Tausk Contra Freud* (1971), and re-re-canvassed by Eissler in *Victor Tausk's Suicide* (1983).

Freud's testimony on war neuroses before the Vienna courts has been discussed in K. R. Eissler's very thorough *Freud as an Expert Witness: The Discussion of War Neuroses between Freud and Wagner-Jauregg* (1979; tr. Christine Trollope, 1986). See also Eissler, "Malingering," in *Psychoanalysis and Culture,* ed. George Wilbur and Warner Muensterberger (1951), 218–53. The recognition of analysts that soldiers' psychological traumas were grist for their mill gained wide publicity with some papers at the international congress of psychoanalysts in Budapest in 1918; see Sándor Ferenczi, Karl Abraham, Ernst Simmel, and Ernest Jones, *Psycho-Analysis and the War Neuroses* (1919; tr., probably by Ernest Jones, 1921). Freud's "Introduction" to that volume, and his "Memorandum on the Electrical Treatment of War Neurotics," written in 1920 and published in 1955, are conveniently accessible in *SE* XVII, 205–15. One pioneer in this work, in Germany, was Ernst Simmel, whose *Kriegsneurosen und psychisches Trauma* (1918) was influential; another pioneer, in England, was M. D. Eder; see his *War-Shock. The Psycho-Neuroses in War: Psychology and Treatment* (1917).

Details on Freud's way of living in hungry, cold Vienna after 1918 are abundant in his correspondence with his intimates in Budapest, Berlin, and London, as well as with his nephew Samuel in Manchester. See also the short article by another nephew, Edward L. Bernays, "Uncle Sigi," *Journal of the History of Medicine and Allied Sciences,* XXXV (April 1980), 216–20. I have profited from an illuminating paper on the impact of war and "social reality" on Freud's thinking of these years: Louise E. Hoffman, "War, Revolution, and Psychoanalysis: Freudian Thought Begins to Grapple with Social Reality," *Journal of the History of the Behavioral Sciences,* XVII (1981), 251–69. Stefan Zweig, *Die Welt von Gestern. Erinnerungen eines Europäers* (1944), esp. the chapter "Heimkehr nach Österreich," has much vivid—perhaps, as usual, a little too vivid—detail. For a sober corrective to Zweig's fluent hyperbole, see again Prater, *European of Yesterday: A Biography of Stefan Zweig,* esp. ch. 4, "Salzburg and Success, 1919–1925." The autobiographical text by Richard F. Sterba, *Reminiscences of a Viennese Psychoanalyst* (1982) is slight. A[bram] Kardiner, *My Analysis with Freud: Reminiscences* (1977), though far from thorough, conveys something of what it was like to be a foreign "pupil" of Freud's after the war.

For Groddeck, see esp. Carl M. and Sylva Grossman, *The Wild Analyst: The Life and Work of Georg Groddeck* (1965), short and popular, but with a full bibliography of Groddeck's writings. Sándor Ferenczi reviewed Groddeck's novel, *Der Seelensucher,* in 1921 (see *Schriften zur Psychoanalyse,* ed. Balint, II, 94–98). The appreciation by Lawrence Durrell, "Studies in Genius: VI. Groddeck," *Horizon,* XVII (June 1948), 384–403, is interesting. Groddeck's main book on the It is available in English: *The Book of the It* (1923; tr. M. E. Collins, 1950). Margaretha Honegger has edited a small selection of his correspondence with Freud and others: *Georg Groddeck–Sigmund Freud. Briefe über das Es* (1974).

For Freud's social psychology, see esp. Sándor Ferenczi, "Freuds 'Massenpsychologie und Ich-Analyse.' Der individualpsychologische Fortschritt" (1922), in *Schriften zur Psychoanalyse*, ed. Balint, II, 122–26; and Philip Rieff, "The Origins of Freud's Political Psychology," *Journal of the History of Ideas*, XVII (1956), 235–49. Robert Bocock suggestively treats Freud as a sociologist in *Freud and Modern Society: An Outline and Analysis of Freud's Sociology* (1976). Incidentally, there is an annotated manuscript of Freud's *Massenpsychologie und Ich-Analyse*, a real find, in the Rare Book and Manuscript Library, Columbia University.

CHAPTER NINE · *Death against Life*

For Freud's battle with cancer, Schur, *Freud, Living and Dying*, esp. chaps. 13–16, is once more authoritative, to be supplemented—and at points corrected!—by his unpublished memorandum, "The Medical Case History of Sigmund Freud," dated February 27, 1954, Max Schur papers, LC. Anna Freud's letters to Schur and Ernest Jones add both precision and poignancy. Sharon Romm, *The Unwelcome Intruder: Freud's Struggle with Cancer* (1983) has medical details and information about Freud's physicians, surgeons, and operations that are largely unobtainable elsewhere. I am indebted to a well-informed unpublished manuscript by Sanford Gifford, "Notes on Felix Deutsch as Freud's Personal Physician" (1972), which is sympathetic to Deutsch's plight, but unsentimental. Deutsch's own "Reflections on Freud's One Hundredth Birthday," *Psychosomatic Medicine*, XVIII (1956), 279–83, is also of help. Again my interview with Helen Schur, June 3, 1986, proved invaluable. On Freud's grandson Heinele, I was aided by a private communication from Hilde Braunthal, who as a young student worked in Mathilde and Robert Hollitscher's home, where Heinele lived in his last months. H. D. [Hilda Doolittle], *Tribute to Freud* has some backward glances from the 1930s to the 1920s. George Sylvester Viereck's interview of 1926, published in 1927 separately and then in *Glimpses of the Great* (1930), has characteristic quotations but must be used with caution.

There are evocative and amusing passages about the popularity of Freud in the Austria of the 1920s in Elias Canetti, *Die Fackel im Ohr. Lebensgeschichte 1921–1931* (1980), esp. 137–39. For America, the glimpses in Ronald Steel, *Walter Lippmann and the American Century* (1980) can be supplemented by some of Lippmann's letters, skillfully edited by John Morton Blum, in *Public Philosopher: Selected Letters of Walter Lippmann* (1985). Alfred Kazin, *On Native Grounds: An Interpretation of Modern American Prose Literature* (1942; paperback ed., 1956) has passing comments on Freud's impact in the 1920s, as does Richard Weiss, *The American Myth of Success, from Horatio Alger to Norman Vincent Peale* (1969). Martin Wangh, ed., *Fruition of an Idea: Fifty Years of Psychoanalysis in New York* (1962) is thin and rather self-congratulatory; what is wanted is a fully documented history of the New York Psychoanalytic Institute. An earlier study by someone who was there, C. P. Oberndorf, *A History of Psychoanalysis in America* (1953) is highly personal but useful. David Shakow and David Rapaport, *The Influence of Freud on American Psychology* (1964) takes the story beyond Hale's fine *Freud and the Americans*. A good companion to Hale is John C. Burnham, *Psychoanalysis in American Medicine, 1894–1918: Medicine, Science, and Culture* (1967). There is also good material in Burnham, *Jelliffe: American Psychoanalyst and Physician* (1983), which includes Jelliffe's correspondence with Freud and Jung, edited by William McGuire. And see John Demos, "Oedipus and America: Historical Perspectives on the Reception of Psychoanalysis in the United States," *The Annual of Psychoanalysis*, VI (1978), 23–39, which is reflective and enlightening. (For titles touching on lay analysis in the United States, see the essay for chapter 10, next.)

Uwe Henrik Peters, *Anna Freud: A Life Dedicated to Children* (1979; tr. anon., 1985) bravely but pretty ineffectually soldiers on without help from Anna Freud's papers, as have other biographical efforts; we shall have to wait until the authoritative biography by Elisabeth Young-Bruehl comes along. She shared some of her researches in a talk at the Muriel Gardiner Program in Psychoanalysis and the Humanities, Yale University, January 15, 1987; in several conversations; and in a letter to me of May 17, 1987. Some of the memorial papers devoted to Anna Freud, in *The Psychoanalytic Study of the Child*, XXXIX (1984), help to round out the portrait of a reserved and fascinating person. See esp. Joseph Goldstein, "Anna Freud in Law," 3–13; and also Peter B. Neubauer, "Anna

Freud's Concept of Developmental Lines," 15–27; Leo Rangell, "The Anna Freud Experience," 29–42; Albert J. Solnit and Lottie M. Newman, "Anna Freud: The Child Expert," 45–63; and the evocation by Robert S. Wallerstein, "Anna Freud: Radical Innovator and Staunch Conservative," 65–80. The lecture by Anna Freud's niece, Sophie Freud, *The Legacy of Anna Freud* (1987), is personal and moving. Kardiner, *My Analysis with Freud* has a few arresting comments. Anna Freud's unpublished letters, especially to Max Schur and Ernest Jones, and Freud's unpublished letters to Ernest Jones and—even more—to his indispensable friend and confidante Lou Andreas-Salomé, help the biographer along further. (For Andreas-Salomé, see her autobiographical writings, most notably her *Lebensrückblick* [1951], and Angela Livingstone, *Lou Andreas-Salomé* [1984], which depends on some unpublished materials.) The most rewarding resource for Anna Freud, however, is of course the unpublished correspondence between herself and her father, in the Freud Collection, LC.

For psychoanalysis in Berlin, see the revealing (and highly amusing) correspondence between the Stracheys: *Bloomsbury/Freud: The Letters of James and Alix Strachey, 1924–1925*, ed. Perry Meisel and Walter Kendrick (1985). In addition, see the extremely instructive Festschrift, *Zehn Jahre Berliner Psychoanalytisches Institut (Poliklinik und Lehranstalt)*, ed. Deutsche Psychoanalytische Gesellschaft (1930), with informative short reports by Ernst Simmel, Otto Fenichel, Karen Horney, Hanns Sachs, Gregory Zilboorg, and others on all aspects of the institution, its rules, its students, its patients, and its program. Melanie Klein, who first made her mark in Berlin, remains extraordinarily controversial, and the life by Phyllis Grosskurth, *Melanie Klein: Her World and Her Work* (1986), though very full and based on extensive research in the Klein papers, has not stilled the debate. I have learned much from the book, but I dissent from Grosskurth's rather low estimate of Anna Freud. Hanna Segal, an eminent Kleinian, has written two very helpful brief surveys: *Introduction to the Work of Melanie Klein* (1964) and *Klein* (1979).

For Freud's impact in France, see Sherry Turkle's brief but meaty *Psychoanalytic Politics: Freud's French Revolution* (1978), which describes the emergence of a characteristically French psychoanalytic culture. The exchanges between Freud and René Laforgue, tr. into French by Pierre Cotet and ed. André Bourguignon et al., in "Mémorial," *Nouvelle Revue de Psychanalyse*, XV (April 1977), 236–314, are instructive as well. So is the very ample account in Elisabeth Roudinesco, *La bataille de cent ans. Histoire de la psychanalyse en France*, vol. I, *1885–1935* (1982) and vol. II, *1925–1985* (1986). See also Ilse and Robert Baraude, *Histoire de la Psychanalyse en France* (1975). Psychoanalysis in France is, of course, bound up with Marie Bonaparte. Celia Bertin, *Marie Bonaparte: A Life* (1982) is unfortunately fairly insubstantial, especially on Bonaparte's ideas and her work of organizing psychoanalysis in France. There is room for a better biography.

Analysands reporting on Freud include Hilda Doolittle [H. D.], Kardiner, and the late Jeanne Lampl-de Groot (in a cordial, fascinating, often moving interview with me on October 24, 1985). For H. D., see the full life by Janice S. Robinson, *H. D.: The Life and Work of an American Poet* (1982), to be supplemented by Susan Stanford Friedman, "A Most Luscious 'Vers Libre' Relationship: H. D. and Freud," *The Annual of Psychoanalysis*, XIV (1986), 319–43. The book by that "experimental" analysand Joseph Wortis, *Fragments of an Analysis with Freud* (1954), records some striking interventions by Freud but is ultimately unsatisfactory, since Wortis was not really interested in being analyzed. On Freud's acquaintances and correspondents in those years, two articles by David S. Werman in *Int. Rev. Psycho-Anal.* shed much light: "Stefan Zweig and His Relationship with Freud and Rolland: A Study of the Auxiliary Ego Ideal," VI (1979), 77–95, and "Sigmund Freud and Romain Rolland," IV (1977), 225–42. There is in addition an essay by David James Fisher, "Sigmund Freud and Romain Rolland: The Terrestrial Animal and His Great Oceanic Friend," *American Imago*, XXXIII (1976), 1–59. Mary Higgins and Chester M. Raphael, eds., *Reich Speaks of Freud: Wilhelm Reich Discusses His Work and His Relationship with Sigmund Freud* (1967) has some tantalizing (if dubiously reliable) comments on Freud's later years, including K. R. Eissler's long interview with Reich. Albrecht Hirschmüller has published a pair of revealing letters from Freud to Josef Breuer's son on the occasion of Breuer's death: " 'Balsam auf eine schmerzende Wunde'—Zwei bisher unbekannte Briefe Sigmund Freuds über sein Verhältnis zu Josef Breuer," *Psyche*, XLI (1987), 55–59.

On the vexed issue of Freud's interest in the occult, more work might perhaps be done. Nandor

Fodor, *Freud, Jung, and Occultism* (1971) is far from conclusive. On the other hand, *Jones* III, 375–407, is very full and fair.

CHAPTER TEN · *Flickering Lights on Dark Continents*

For Otto Rank, in addition to the lives already cited—Lieberman, *Rank* and Taft, *Otto Rank,* both biographical labors of love—see Esther Menaker, *Otto Rank: A Rediscovered Legacy* (1983), which reads Rank as an ego psychologist and responds to some of Ernest Jones's criticisms of his work and character. Rank and Ferenczi's study, *The Development of Psychoanalysis* (1924; tr. Caroline Newton, 1925) has been reprinted more than once. Rank's most popular book, *The Trauma of Birth* (1924; tr. anon., 1929) remains available. There is also a selection from his voluminous writings: Philip Freund, ed., *The Myth of the Birth of the Hero and Other Writings* (1959), mainly on art and myth. The most prominent of Rank's enthusiasts was the late sociologist Ernest Becker, as his *The Denial of Death* (1973) and *Escape from Evil* (1975) attest.

On anxiety, the "Editor's Introduction" to *Inhibitions, Symptoms and Anxiety, SE* XX, 77–86, is particularly helpful. Far more extensive is the three-part survey by Allan Compton, "A Study of the Psychoanalytic Theory of Anxiety," which appeared in *J. Amer. Psychoanal. Assn.:* "I. The Development of Freud's Theory of Anxiety," XX (1972), 3–44; "II. Developments in the Theory of Anxiety since 1926," XX (1972), 341–94; and "III. A Preliminary Formulation of the Anxiety Response," XXVIII (1980), 739–74. Otto Fenichel has, as usual, several interesting papers on the topic, notably "Organ Libidinization Accompanying the Defense against Drives" (1928), *Collected Papers,* 1st Series, 128–46; "Defense against Anxiety, Particularly by Libidinization" (1934), *Collected Papers,* 1st Series, 303–17; and the particularly original "The Counter-Phobic Attitude" (1939), *Collected Papers,* 2d Series, 163–73. Phyllis Greenacre's persuasive two-part paper "The Predisposition to Anxiety" (1941), in *Trauma, Growth, and Personality,* 27–82, traces the disposition back to uterine existence. See also Ishak Ramzy and Robert S. Wallerstein, "Pain, Fear, and Anxiety: A Study in Their Interrelations," *The Psychoanalytic Study of the Child,* XIII (1958), 147–89; René A. Spitz, "Anxiety in Infancy," *Int. J. Psycho-Anal.,* XXXI (1965), 138–43, to be added to the fascinating material in Spitz, *The First Year of Life* (1965); Clifford Yorke and Stanley Wiseberg, "A Developmental View of Anxiety: Some Clinical and Theoretical Considerations," *The Psychoanalytic Study of the Child,* XXXI (1976), 107–35; Betty Joseph, "Different Types of Anxiety and Their Handling in the Analytic Situation," *Int. J. Psycho-Anal.,* LIX (1978), 223–28; and the article directly following: Leo Rangell, "On Understanding and Treating Anxiety and Its Derivatives," 229–36. Max Schur, "The Ego in Anxiety," in *Drives, Affects, Behavior,* ed. Loewenstein, 67–103, is a minor classic. For a rather individual treatment of the theme, see the important text by Silvan Tomkins, *Affects, Imagery, Consciousness,* vol. II, *The Negative Affects* (1963), esp. 511–29. There are some revealing (at times vehement) discussions about Rank's maverick ideas in the minutes of the New York Psychoanalytic Society, in the A. A. Brill Library, New York Psychoanalytic Institute.

Theodor Reik's reminiscences (studded with quotations from Freud's letters to him) offer many interesting details: *The Search Within: The Inner Experience of a Psychoanalyst* (1956) is a vast compendium; his earlier *From Thirty Years with Freud* (tr. Richard Winston, 1940) is more economical and more pointed. Erika Freeman prompted Reik to reminisce; see her *Insights: Conversations with Theodor Reik* (1971). The great symposium on lay analysis, organized by Max Eitingon and Ernest Jones, appeared (in its English guise) in *Int. J. Psycho-Anal.,* VIII (1927), 174–283, 391–401. The full story of the American attitude toward lay analysts has not been written, and in view of its great historical interest, remains a desideratum. On lay analysis, the minutes of the New York Psychoanalytic Society are unfortunately very skimpy. For now, see above all, *American Psychoanalysis: Origins and Development,* ed. Jacques M. Quen and Eric T. Carlson (1978). In Oberndorf, *History of Psychoanalysis in America,* see esp. ch. 9, "Status of Psychoanalysis at the Beginning of the Third Decade," and ch. 10, "Stormy Years in Psychoanalysis under New York Leadership," which are vigorous, subjective, and all too brief. Once again Hale, *Freud and the Americans*, though it reaches only to 1917, sets the stage very well; Burnham, *Jelliffe*, too, is helpful on this issue.

Jones III, 287–301, offers a fair-minded general conspectus covering the controversy on lay analysis, remarkably informative for all its terseness. No one can accuse K. R. Eissler of terseness; his *Medical Orthodoxy and the Future of Psychoanalysis* (1965) is expansive, crippled by self-indulgent digressions, but in parts illuminating. Some recent contributions include Lawrence S. Kubie, "Reflections on Training," *Psychoanalytic Forum*, I (1966), 95–112; Shelley Orgel, "Report from the Seventh Pre-Congress Conference on Training," *Int. J. Psycho-Anal.*, LIX (1978), 511–15; Robert S. Wallerstein, "Perspectives on Psychoanalytic Training Around the World," *Int. J. Psycho-Anal.*, LIX (1978), 477–503; and Newell Fischer, reporting on a panel discussion of the American Psychoanalytic Association, "Beyond Lay Analysis: Pathways to a Psychoanalytic Career," *J. Amer. Psychoanal. Assn.*, XXX (1982), 701–15. Harald Leupold-Löwenthal, "Zur Geschichte der 'Frage der Laienanalyse,' " *Psyche*, XXXVIII (1984), 97–120, has some added materials.

Much, indeed most, of the literature that has gathered round Freud's views on female development, specifically sexuality, is polemical; the issue has been almost completely politicized. Fortunately, analysts, male and female, have kept their heads. There are two responsible surveys of the history of Freud's ideas by Zenia Odes Fliegel: "Feminine Psychosexual Development in Freudian Theory: A Historical Reconstruction," *Psychoanalytic Quarterly*, XLII (1973), 385–408, ably followed up by "Half a Century Later: Current Status of Freud's Controversial Views on Women," *Psychoanalytic Review*, LXIX (1982), 7–28; both provide excellent bibliographical information. A comprehensive anthology, *Female Psychology: Contemporary Psychoanalytic Views*, ed. Harold P. Blum (1977) contains a generous sampling of papers from *J. Amer. Psychoanal. Assn.* Among the most rewarding, for me, are James A. Kleeman, "Freud's Views on Early Female Sexuality in the Light of Direct Child Observation," 3–27, at once critical and appreciative of Freud's ideas; Eleanor Galenson and Herman Roiphe, "Some Suggestive Revisions Concerning Early Female Development," 29–57, a very interesting paper; Samuel Ritvo, "Adolescent to Woman," 127–37, which persuasively takes up the story beyond childhood; William I. Grossman and Walter A. Stewart, "Penis Envy: From Childhood Wish to Developmental Metaphor," 193–212, another pointer toward revision within psychoanalysis; Roy Schafer, "Problems in Freud's Psychology of Women," 331–60, a perceptive analysis of some fundamental issues; Daniel S. Jaffe, "The Masculine Envy of Woman's Procreative Function," 361–92, which deals with the other side of penis envy; and Peter Barglow and Margret Schaefer, "A New Female Psychology?" 393–438, which severely examines recent non-, semi-, and pseudo-psychoanalytic literature, to excellent effect. Nearly all of these papers supply extensive bibliographies. Other significant papers by authors represented in the anthology include Kleeman, "The Establishment of Core Gender Identity in Normal Girls. (a) Introduction; (b) Development of the Ego Capacity to Differentiate," *Archives of Sexual Behavior*, I (1971), 103–29; and Galenson and Roiphe, "The Impact of Early Sexual Discovery on Mood, Defensive Organization, and Symbolization," *The Psychoanalytic Study of the Child*, XXVI (1971), 195–216, which can be supplemented (and contrasted) with their "The Preoedipal Development of the Boy," *J. Amer. Psychoanal. Assn.*, XXVIII (1980), 805–28. For a clear-headed summary of material that has appeared since the 1977 anthology, see Shahla Chehrazi, "Female Psychology: A Review," *J. Amer. Psychoanal. Assn.*, XXXIV (1986), 141–62. See also the highly instructive short paper by Iza S. Erlich, "What Happened to Jocasta?" *Bulletin of the Menninger Clinic*, XLI (1977), 280–84, which pertinently asks about the mothers in Freud's case histories. And see Jean Strouse, ed., *Women and Analysis: Dialogues on Psychoanalytic Views of Femininity* (1974).

Most prominent among the classic psychoanalytic texts that follow the Freudian reading of women's sexual development, though not without some cavils, are Marie Bonaparte, *Female Sexuality* (1951; tr. John Rodker, 1953), which first appeared as three articles in *Revue Française de Psychanalyse*, in 1949; Helene Deutsch, *The Psychology of Women*, 2 vols. (1944–45); and Ruth Mack Brunswick, "The Preoedipal Phase of Libido Development" (1940), in *The Psychoanalytic Reader*, ed. Robert Fliess (1948), 261–84. Jeanne Lampl-de Groot's papers, available in her collection *The Development of the Mind: Psychoanalytic Papers on Clinical and Theoretical Problems* (1965), state

Freud's views with particular lucidity: "The Evolution of the Oedipus Complex in Women" (1927), 3–18; "Problems of Femininity" (1933), 19–46; review of Sándor Radó, "Fear of Castration in Women" (1934), 47–57; and an important contribution on the question of a very early stage—in the male—"The Preoedipal Phase in the Development of the Male Child" (1946), 104–113. See also Joan Riviere, "Womanliness as a Masquerade" (1929), in *Psychoanalysis and Female Sexuality*, ed. Hendrik M. Ruitenbeek (1966), 209–20.

For Abraham on this issue, see, in addition to his correspondence with Freud, his paper "Manifestations of the Female Castration Complex" (1920), in *Selected Papers of Karl Abraham* (1927), 338–69. Jones's most significant papers, all in *Papers on Psycho-Analysis* (4th ed., 1938), are "The Early Development of Female Sexuality" (1927), 556–70; "The Phallic Phase" (1933), 571–604; and "Early Female Sexuality" (1935), 605–16.

Karen Horney's papers are easily available in English. The ones that made her a force, collected in her *Feminine Psychology*, ed. Harold Kelman (1967), are "On the Genesis of the Castration Complex in Women" (1924), 37–53; "The Flight from Womanhood: The Masculinity-Complex in Women as Viewed by Men and Women" (1926), 54–70; "The Dread of Women: Observations on a Specific Difference in the Dread Felt by Men and by Women Respectively for the Opposite Sex" (1932), 133–46; and "The Denial of the Vagina: A Contribution to the Problem of the Genital Anxieties Specific to Women" (1933), 147–61. This collection of her papers also has some other relevant texts. *The Adolescent Diaries of Karen Horney* (1980) are touching and revealing; Marcia Westkott, *The Feminist Legacy of Karen Horney* (1986) discusses her ideas in context. The new biography by Susan Quinn (which the author let me read in manuscript), *A Mind of Her Own: The Life of Karen Horney* (1987), is a full treatment that does justice to her private life.

This is not the place to discuss the feminist protest against Freud's "phallocentric" views, interesting as it is; the article by Barglow and Schaefer (cited above) vigorously, indeed bellicosely, defends the psychoanalytic perspective. The most rewarding and responsible contribution, which tries to take into account, but also to rise above, "sexual politics" and Freud's "male chauvinism," is a study by a trained psychotherapist and active feminist, Juliet Mitchell, *Psychoanalysis and Feminism* (1974). Mary Jane Sherfey, *The Nature and Evolution of Female Sexuality* (1972) is a rational attempt to revise Freudian theory on the basis of modern biology. K. R. Eissler, "Comments on Penis Envy and Orgasm in Women," *The Psychoanalytic Study of the Child*, XXXII (1977), 29–83, tries to take recent feminist and psychoanalytic literature into account. For aspects of the fascinating history of women's sexuality, and attitudes toward love in nineteenth-century Europe, far from irrelevant to Freud's views, see Gay, *The Bourgeois Experience*, vol. I, *Education of the Senses*, and vol. II, *The Tender Passion*. From a vast literature, I single out only Helene Weber, *Ehefrau und Mutter in der Rechtsentwicklung. Eine Einführung* (1907), which has a section on Austria, as does Richard J. Evans, *The Feminists: Women's Emancipation Movements in Europe, America and Australasia 1840–1920* (1977). The best brief history of Austrian women in the current age is Erika Weinzierl, *Emanzipation? Österreichische Frauen im 20. Jahrhundert* (1975), an introduction. A longer history would be welcome.

On the touchy topic of Freud and his mother, in addition to *Jones, passim*, and McGrath, *Freud's Discovery of Psychoanalysis*, see Eva M. Rosenfeld, "Dreams and Vision: Some Remarks on Freud's Egyptian Bird Dream," *Int. J. Psycho-Anal.*, XXXVII (1956), 97–105; and Robert D. Stolorow and George E. Atwood, "A Defensive-Restitutive Function of Freud's Theory of Psychosexual Development," *Psychoanalytic Review*, LXV (1978), 217–38, an important paper that treats Freud's relations to Amalia Freud much as I do. The authors use, profitably, Tomkins's *Affect, Imagery, Consciousness*. Donald L. Burnham has published a late letter of Freud's to the German psychoanalyst Carl Müller-Braunschweig: "Freud and Female Sexuality: A Previously Unpublished Letter," *Psychiatry*, XXXIV (1971), 328–29.

Much hitherto unpublished material is revealed for the first time in *Arnold Zweig, 1887–1968. Werk und Leben in Dokumenten und Bildern*, ed. Georg Wenzel (1978).

CHAPTER ELEVEN · *Human Nature at Work*

I have already noted that more work on Ferenczi would be most desirable. For his last years (as for the earlier ones) the Freud–Ferenczi Correspondence, Freud Collection, LC, is, of course, fundamental. Michael Balint offers some important if cursory comments in *The Basic Fault: Therapeutic Aspects of Regression* (1968), esp. ch. 23, "The Disagreement between Freud and Ferenczi, and Its Repercussions." Ferenczi's correspondence with the good friend of his later life Georg Groddeck, *Briefwechsel 1921–1933* (1986), is illuminating. Masson, *Assault on Truth* has a persuasive-sounding but wholly unreliable chapter, "The Strange Case of Ferenczi's Last Paper," on Ferenczi's late relations with Freud. Thus Masson cites, as an instance of Freud's strong positive feelings for Ferenczi, the way he "often addressed him as 'dear son' " (p. 145). In fact I encountered that salutation only once, and then Freud used it in exasperation at Ferenczi's inability to grow up. (See Freud's letters to Ferenczi, November 30 and December 5, 1911. Freud–Ferenczi Correspondence, Freud Collection, LC.) Again, Masson's claim that Ferenczi's insistence on reviving the seduction theory "cost him the friendship of Freud" (p. 148) is contradicted by the facts. The clinical diary of Ferenczi's that I quote in the text from the manuscript in the Freud Collection, LC, is in the process of being published by S. Fischer Verlag, Frankfurt am Main: Judith Dupont, ed., *"Ohne Sympathie keine Heilung." Das klinische Tagebuch von 1932* (1988).

There is no full treatment of Freud's anti-Americanism. Hale, *Freud and the Americans*, gives the background up to 1917. For one of Freud's earliest and most serious American supporters, see, again, Steel, *Walter Lippmann*. (Martin J. Wiener, *Between Two Worlds: The Political Thought of Graham Wallas* [1971], has some interesting comments on Lippmann.) Burnham, *Jelliffe*, is again helpful. The most thorough biographical study of Bullitt is Will Brownell and Richard N. Billings, *So Close to Greatness: A Biography of William C. Bullitt* (1987), which I had the opportunity of reading in manuscript. It cannot, however, fully resolve the mysteries surrounding the Freud-Bullitt study of Woodrow Wilson. Trying to reconstruct the making of that book, I made use of Bullitt's letters to Colonel House (in Colonel E. M. House papers, series I, box 21, Y-MA). Beatrice Farnsworth, *William C. Bullitt and the Soviet Union* (1967) concentrates on Bullitt's early diplomatic missions but fortunately goes beyond its title. William Bayard Hale, *The Story of a Style* (1920), the book that Freud enjoyed but would not publicly endorse, is a dissection of Wilson by means of his stylistic devices. For an American's review of that book, which gave its author a good chance to savage Wilson, see H. L. Mencken, "The Archangel Woodrow" (1921), in *The Vintage Mencken*, ed. Alistair Cooke (1955), 116–20.

Orville H. Bullitt, who saw the manuscript of *Thomas Woodrow Wilson* in 1932 while he was staying with his brother William, confirms that Freud and Bullitt had indeed signed each of the chapters. Around 1950, he saw it again and noticed no changes. (See Orville Bullitt to Alexander L. George, December 6, 1973, courtesy Alexander George.) Dr. Orville Horwitz, a cousin, who was also thoroughly familiar with the manuscript in the 1930s, agrees. (Telephone conversation with Dr. Horwitz, May 31, 1986.) On the other hand, the style of the book does not support these recollections: more than one reviewer has justly noted that while the introduction is unquestionably Freud's, the text simply lacks his humor and subtlety of formulation and expression. Thus Max Schur wrote to Miss M. Legru at Houghton Mifflin on January 19, 1968, "The study of the manuscript revealed clearly that only the introduction, although not submitted in his handwriting (Freud had written *all* his manuscripts and letters in longhand) had all the unmistakeable earmarks of Freud's style and reflected his analytical point of view. We [Schur, Ernst Freud, and Anna Freud] had to conclude that this was a preserved transcript of Freud's original contribution. As to the rest of the book, it must have been written by Mr. Bullitt who applied as well as he could *(not questioning at all his good faith)* from memory and notes he had taken during and after his meetings with Freud, the analytical formulations given to him by the latter." (Courtesy Helen Schur.) Freud himself told Arnold Zweig in December 1930, "I am again writing an introduction for something that someone else is making; I am not allowed to say what it is, it's also an analysis, but a highly contemporary one, almost political." (Freud to Arnold Zweig, December 7, 1930. *Freud–Zweig*, 37 [25].)

The least awkward way of resolving these contradictions, I believe, is to assume that Bullitt revised the manuscript after Freud's death. At one point Anna Freud took a different view. "You know how little I like Bullitt," she wrote Max Schur on October 24, 1966. "But that is not the kind of thing which he would do." (Max Schur papers, LC.) On the other hand, she wrote Schur on November 6, 1966, "I am absolutely certain that my father wrote his own Foreword. This is his style and his way of thinking and I would be ready to swear to it at any time./ I am equally certain, and equally ready to swear to it that none of the later chapters have been written by my father, neither wholly nor in part. Firstly, it is not his style; secondly, he has never in his life used repetitions which are used in this book ad nauseam; thirdly, he has never denigrated or made ridiculous any subject under analysis which is done in the book." No doubt, she added, her father had "suggested analytic interpretations to Bullitt, for him to use, never imagining that they would be used in this clumsy way." (Max Schur papers, LC.) It is plain from some of Anna Freud's letters to Jones in the mid-1950s that she did not see the manuscript of the Wilson study during her father's lifetime. (See Anna Freud to Jones, April 16 and April 25, 1955. Jones papers, Archives of the British Psycho-Analytical Society, London.) Bullitt himself wrote Jones on July 22, 1955, that the book "was the result of much combat. Both Freud and I were extremely pig-headed: somewhat convinced that each of us was God. In consequence, each chapter: indeed each sentence: was the subject of an intense debate." In June 1956, again writing to Jones, Bullitt added, "I visited London twice [in 1939] in order to discuss with him [Freud] certain changes which I considered essential. We agreed on the wording of those changes and I made them. But I have felt that his death precluded further alterations." (Both in Jones papers, Archives of the British Psycho-Analytical Society, London.) Perhaps Anna Freud had the best judgment of the matter: "There is no doubt about it that my father over-estimated Bullitt. I never did. But in matters of this kind, my father was not guided by anybody." (Anna Freud to Max Schur, November 6, 1966. Max Schur papers, LC.) But the manuscript remains inaccessible.

On the Horace Frink case, see Michael Specter, "Sigmund Freud and a Family Torn Asunder: Revelations of an Analysis Gone Awry," *Washington Post*, November 8, 1987, sec. G, 1, 5. The Frink papers, in the Alan Mason Chesney Medical Archives, The Johns Hopkins University, shed further light.

Among the studies of Freud's religiosity, Reuben M. Rainey's dissertation, *Freud as Student of Religion: Perspectives on the Background and Development of His Thought* (1975), is not without interest. On Freud's Jewishness, his son Martin's article "Who Was Freud?" in *The Jews of Austria*, ed. Fraenkel, 197–211, is indispensable. A. A. Roback, *Freudiana* (1957), which includes "unpublished letters from Freud, Havelock Ellis, Pavlov, Bernard Shaw, Romain Rolland et alii," is more irritating than informative. I have freely drawn in this chapter on my *A Godless Jew*, which canvasses the issues more fully than I had the opportunity to do here. (For titles on Freud's Jewishness, see the essay for chapter 12, next.)

Works appraising *Civilization and Its Discontents* include Paul Roazen's survey, *Freud: Political and Social Thought* (1968), which has several pages on human nature in politics. For an interesting canvass of the social (and political) implications of Freud's thought from a Freudian perspective, see J. C. Flugel, *Man, Morals and Society: A Psycho-Analytical Study* (1945). R. E. Money-Kyrle, *Psychoanalysis and Politics: A Contribution to the Psychology of Politics and Morals* (1951) is a terse but meaty essay from the same perspective. "Politics and the Individual," in Rieff, *Freud: The Mind of the Moralist*, is a fine chapter. Heinz Hartmann's considerably expanded Freud Lecture, *Psychoanalysis and Moral Values* (1960), a sophisticated defense of the superego and (largely implicitly) of Freudian social and political theory, repays close reading. Also on the superego, see Michael Friedman, "Toward a Reconceptualization of Guilt," *Contemporary Psychoanalysis*, XXI (1985), 501–47, which canvasses post-Freudian rethinking, including Melanie Klein, and such object-relations theorists as W. R. D. Fairbairn and D. W. Winnicott. The eminent American sociologist Talcott Parsons studied the social bearing of Freud's ideas in several significant papers, notably "The Superego and the Theory of Social Systems" (1952), collected, along with papers on the father taboo and the incest taboo, and on character and society, in *Social Structure and Personality* (1964). Bocock, *Freud and Modern Society* is again useful. I have attempted to give an instance of how the historian may link psychoanalytic ideas to culture in "Liberalism and Regression," *The Psychoanalytic Study of the Child*, XXXVII (1982), 523–45.

CHAPTER TWELVE · *To Die in Freedom*

The great economic—eventually political—catastrophe that started in the fall of 1929 and triggered the events of the 1930s is best encapsulated in John A. Garraty, *The Great Depression* (1986), a fine comparative study including comments on Austria. For Freud's life in Austria between 1933 and 1938, see esp. the *Freud–Zweig* correspondence and some of Freud's later letters to Lou Andreas-Salomé and to Max Eitingon (in Palestine after 1933). Schur, *Freud, Living and Dying* is necessarily *the* indispensable eye witness for Freud's months under Hitler. Clark, *Freud*, esp. ch. 23, "An Order for Release," is based in part on diplomatic documents—neglected by other biographers—which I used independently. Dr. Josefine Stross, who was (literally) close to Freud from May 1938 to his death, kindly enlarged my knowledge of Freud in those months (esp. in letters of May 12 and June 19, 1987). Detlef Berthelsen, *Alltag bei Freud. Die Erinnerungen der Paula Fichtl* (which I saw in proof, to be published in 1988) offers many exceedingly intimate details of the Freud household that emerged from the reminiscences of a servant who worked for the Freuds from 1929 on and accompanied them to London. The "revelations" include the maidenly Fichtl's shock at a glimpse of Freud's penis; the whole, unchecked recollections of an aged servant, is not a document to be trusted implicitly. Carl Zuckmayer's autobiography, *Als wär's ein Stück von mir. Horen der Freundschaft* (1966), esp. 64–95, vividly records his experiences in Austria—Vienna and elsewhere—in March 1938. For Austria at the time of the Anschluss, I have discussed the best titles in the essay for chapter 8; see esp. contributions by Kadrnoska, Goldinger, Zuckerkandl, Klusacek and Stimmer, Hannak, Csendes, and Weinzierl and Skalnik. One other chapter in the volume the last two have edited, *Österreich 1918–1938*, should be mentioned: Norbert Schausberger, "Der Anschluss," 517–52. Additional helpful titles are *Dokumentation zur Österreichischen Zeitgeschichte, 1938–1945*, ed. Christine Klusacek, Herbert Steiner, and Kurt Stimmer (1971), the first two sections of which contain rich (and appalling) material on the Anschluss and on Austria as "Ostmark" to the outbreak of the Second World War; Christine Klusacek, *Österreichs Wissenschaftler und Künstler unter dem NS-Regime* (1966), a laconic, eloquent listing of persecuted scientists (including Freud) and artists and their fates; Dieter Wagner and Gerhard Tomkowitz, *"Ein Volk, Ein Reich, Ein Führer!" Der Anschluss Österreichs 1938* (1968), journalistic but dependable and including some telling photographs of Jews being mistreated in March 1938; see also, once again, some of the papers in *The Jews of Austria*, ed. Fraenkel, esp. Herbert Rosenkranz, "The Anschluss and the Tragedy of Austrian Jewry, 1938–1945," 479–545, with terrifying statistics and no less terrifying reminiscences. And see T. Friedmann, ed., *"Die Kristall-Nacht." Dokumentarische Sammlung* (1972), which documents the barbaric attacks on synagogues, community centers—and Jews themselves—in November 1938. Raul Hilberg, *The Destruction of the European Jews* (1961; 2d ed., 1981), though controversial in its general thesis of Jewish passivity, is impeccable in its scholarship. There are other relevant statistics on Austrian Jewry under Hitler in Martin Gilbert, ed., *The Macmillan Atlas of the Holocaust* (1982). As the text shows, the daily stories filed by reporters in Vienna, mainly in the *New York Times*, the *Manchester Guardian*, and the London *Daily Telegraph*, are rich evidence for events.

German psychoanalysis and psychiatry under Hitler are vividly documented in Karen Brecht et al., eds., *"Hier geht das Leben auf eine sehr merkwürdige Weise weiter. . . ." Zur Geschichte der Psychoanalyse in Deutschland* (1985), a sobering, informative catalogue. It should be supplemented with Geoffrey Cocks, *Psychotherapy in the Third Reich: The Goering Institute* (1985), scholarly, and effectively revisionist, though more inclined to see a certain survival of psychoanalysis under the Nazis than, in my judgment, the evidence can fully support. In the vast literature on Nazi Germany, Karl Dietrich Bracher, *The German Dictatorship: The Origins, Structure, and Effects of National Socialism* (1969; tr. Jean Steinberg, 1970) retains most of its authority.

Freud's Jewishness continues to invite more and more comment. For my own views, see again my *A Godless Jew*. I have argued part of my case in "Six Names in Search of an Interpretation," also already cited. Justin Miller, "Interpretation of Freud's Jewishness, 1924–1974," *Journal of the History of the Behavioral Sciences*, XVII (1981), 357–74, comprehensively surveys the literature of half a century. An important early essay attempting to place Freud is Ernst Simon, "Sigmund Freud, the Jew," *Leo Baeck Yearbook*, II (1957), 270–305, which should be read in conjunction with Peter

Loewenberg, " 'Sigmund Freud as a Jew': A Study in Ambivalence and Courage," *Journal of the History of the Behavioral Sciences*, VII (1971), 363–69. Martin S. Bergmann, "Moses and the Evolution of Freud's Jewish Identity," *Israel Annals of Psychiatry and Related Disciplines*, XIV (March 1976), 3–26, to which I am indebted, exhaustively canvasses Freud's comments on the subject and has interesting observations on Freud's father's religiosity. Marthe Robert, *From Oedipus to Moses: Freud's Jewish Identity* (1974; tr. Ralph Manheim, 1976) is an impressive and subtle interpretation, though perhaps overplaying Freud's identification with Moses, the murdered prophet. Stanley Rothman and Phillip Isenberg, "Sigmund Freud and the Politics of Marginality," *Central European History*, VII (1974), 58–78, ably dispels tendentious misreadings. The same authors' "Freud and Jewish Marginality," *Encounter* (December 1974), 46–54, also helps to puncture Schorske, "Politics and Patricide in Freud's *Interpretation of Dreams*" (already cited). Henri Baruk, "La signification de la psychanalyse et le Judaïsme," *Revue d'Histoire de la Médicine Hébraique*, XIX (1966), 15–28, 53–65, rather critical of Freud, effectively disposes of such farfetched notions as the idea that Freud was deeply influenced by the Kabbalah, as maintained (with no convincing evidence) in David Bakan, *Sigmund Freud and the Jewish Mystical Tradition* (1958). (Among Bakan's most effective critics is Harry Trosman, in his already cited *Freud and the Imaginative World*, which in addition has interesting comments on Freud's Jewish identity.) A. A. Roback, *Jewish Influence in Modern Thought* (1929) is in the same problematic league as Bakan, but contains some letters of Freud's to the author. See also, again, Roback, *Freudiana*. Sander Gilman, *Jewish Self-Hatred: Anti-Semitism and the Hidden Language of the Jews* (1986), though devilishly ingenious on self-hatred, strikes me as eccentric. *Judaism and Psychoanalysis*, ed. Mortimer Ostow (1982) provides a varied menu of papers, including a chapter from Rabbi Richard Rubinstein's provocative study *The Religious Imagination* (1968). However, I prefer the sober analyses of Bergmann, Rothman and Isenberg, and even Robert. Jewish humor should not be neglected as a possible clue to Freud's Jewish identity. Kurt Schlesinger, "Jewish Humor as Jewish Identity," *Int. Rev. Psycho-Anal.*, VI (1979), 317–30, is a useful effort. Theodor Reik has made the subject his own, most prominently in *Jewish Wit* (1962). See also Elliott Oring, *The Jokes of Sigmund Freud: A Study in Humor and Jewish Identity* (1984), short, suggestive, a little humorless. "Mein Onkel Sigmund," the interview (already cited) of Richard Dyck with Freud's nephew Harry, who denies that his famous uncle was an atheist, must be used with some skepticism. Avner Falk, "Freud and Herzl," *Contemporary Psychoanalysis*, XIV (1978), 357–87, examines Freud's Jewishness from the perspective of his acquaintance with Herzl's ideas.

Many of the titles just cited, principally Bergmann, "Moses and the Evolution of Freud's Jewish Identity" and Robert, *From Oedipus to Moses*, have much to say on Freud's *Moses and Monotheism*. I add Rieff, *Freud: The Mind of the Moralist*, ch. 6, "The Authority of the Past"; and two titles by Edwin R. Wallace IV: *Freud and Anthropology* and "The Psychodynamic Determinants of *Moses and Monotheism*," *Psychiatry*, XL (1977), 79–87. See also the careful discussion in "Freud and the Religion of Moses," ch. 5 of W. W. Meissner, *Psychoanalysis and Religious Experience* (1984); and see F. M. Cross, "Yahweh and the God of the Patriarchs," *Harvard Theological Review*, LV (1962), 225–59. Some interesting speculations about why Freud failed to mention Abraham's early paper (1912) on Amenhotep IV, so relevant to Freud's intellectual excursion into ancient Egypt, are presented in Leonard Shengold, "A Parapraxis of Freud's in Relation to Karl Abraham," *American Imago*, XXIX (1972), 123–59.

Several eye-witness accounts give the flavor of the last year and a half of Freud's life. The Woolfs' responses to tea with Freud at 20 Maresfield Gardens early in 1939 are striking—and somewhat contrasting in tone: see Leonard Woolf, *Downhill All the Way* (1967), 95–96, 163–69; and *The Diary of Virginia Woolf*, ed. Anne Olivier Bell, assisted by Andrew McNeillie, vol. V, *1936–1941* (1984), 202, 248–52. Hanns Sachs has described his farewell to Freud in *Freud: Master and Friend*, ch. 9, "The Parting"; and Jones has also described *his* farewell, in *Jones* III, ch. 6, "London, The End."

For Freud's famous letter to an anonymous American mother on her homosexual son, see the instructive article by Henry Abelove, "Freud, Male Homosexuality and the Americans," *Dissent* (Winter 1986), 59–69.

There is, in addition to the usual obituaries, an all-too-brief retrospect on Max Schur in the *American Psychoanalytic Association Newsletter*, III (December 1969), 2.

For my treatment of Freud's last days, see the final end note to chapter 12.

A postscript: In the course of my work, I came upon an intriguing but, I thought, rather suspect account of an episode that supposedly took place at Berggasse 19 after the Anschluss. Barbara Hannah, in her adoring "biographical memoir" *Jung: His Life and Work* (already cited), reports (pp. 254–55) that not long after the Nazis invaded Austria in mid-March 1938, Franz Riklin, Jr., son of Jung's long-time associate Franz Riklin, "was chosen by some exceedingly rich Swiss Jews to go into Austria *at once*, with a very large sum of money, to do all he could to persuade leading Jews to leave the country before the Nazis had time to start persecuting them." The younger Riklin, then nearly thirty and at the start of his medical career, thought he had been chosen for this delicate mission because of his self-possession and his "exceedingly Teutonic appearance." In general, he was *"exceedingly* successful in carrying out his mission," but not at the Freuds'. Riklin's father had strongly urged his son to persuade Freud to leave Austria promptly "and to take advantage of the most unusual facilities which he could offer." But when the younger Riklin went to see Freud "and explained the situation to him," Freud disappointed him by saying sternly, "I refuse to be beholden to my enemies." Riklin explained the situation as well as he could and insisted that neither his father nor Jung had any animosity toward Freud. But Freud only reiterated his uncompromising stand. Still, Hannah concludes, the Freuds were very cordial with the messenger, and even asked him to dinner.

Thus far Hannah. She offers no documentation of this startling story, but since she knew the younger Riklin intimately, and often met him at the Jungs', it seems more than likely that Riklin was the source on which she drew. Yet her account has its improbable aspects: those "exceedingly rich Swiss Jews" must have known that the persecution of Jews in Austria had begun the minute the Nazis marched into the country. More important, the suggestion that Swiss Jews should have chosen as their emissary the son of one of Freud's most famous enemies does not ring true. Only Freud's sturdy and uncompromising refusal seems to be in character. So I set the report aside.

Then, last year, when the text of this biography was already in print, Dr. Robert S. McCully (now a professor of psychology, and in the mid-1960s, on the psychiatric faculty of Cornell University Medical College in New York City and in training at the local Jung Institute) partly corroborated and significantly corrected Hannah's account. When the younger Riklin lectured in New York, McCully met him and heard the story of his mission to Vienna in detail. As he remembers Riklin's account, it was not rich Swiss Jews but Jung and the older Riklin who put together $10,000 from their own funds, and they wanted this money to go to Freud alone. When Riklin arrived at Berggasse 19, Anna Freud opened the door part way but would not let him into the apartment and told him that her father would not receive him. Then Freud came to the door and said just what Hannah quotes him as saying: "I refuse to be beholden to my enemies." The hostility of the Freuds, Riklin recalled to McCully, was such that he left and returned to Zurich, the money still in his money belt. (See Robert S. McCully, "Remarks on the Last Contact Between Freud and Jung," a letter to the editor, *Quadrant: Journal of the C. G. Jung Foundation* [New York], XX [1987], 73–74.)

Dr. McCully (whom I have consulted) has a very clear memory of Riklin's report, and his version sounds at once more plausible than Hannah's and more interesting. It would put Jung into a new light. According to his letter, Dr. McCully can only wonder "how Miss Hannah came upon her description of this event," but does feel certain Franz Riklin, Jr., (now deceased) neither saw her manuscript nor was consulted" (p. 73). As I have noted, there is little doubt in my mind that however garbled Hannah's account may be, her informant must have been Riklin himself. I have every reason to credit Dr. McCully's account of his conversations with Riklin, and (as I have also noted), Freud's curt response sounds very much like him. But in the absence of independent documentation—after all, I only had two reports on reports—I decided not to recall the last chapter from the printer to insert this fascinating tale into my text. Yet it deserves to be recorded. Perhaps, once access to the Jung papers has been granted, it may be elevated into a historical fact.

ACKNOWLEDGMENTS

This book has been in the making for a long time, far more than the two and a half short and intense years I took to write it. My interest in Freud goes back to graduate school in the late 1940s, and I made that interest central to my work as a historian when, in the mid-1970s, I was accepted as a candidate in the Western New England Institute for Psychoanalysis. Candidacy gave me an unsurpassed opportunity to make myself at home in the world of psychoanalysis. But, while this proved invaluable in the writing of this biography, I have relied on my historian's professional distance to preserve me from the idealization that Freud thought the biographer's inescapable fate.

Thinking of the striking disparity between the time of writing and the years of incubation, I am reminded of Whistler's famous remark during the libel action he took against Ruskin for calling a picture of his a pot of paint flung in the public's face. Ruskin's counsel put one of Whistler's mistiest nocturnes on exhibit and asked him how long it had taken him to paint *that*. Whistler's memorable reply: "All my life." Now, "all my life" is hyperbole, certainly when applied to the making of this biography of Freud. But there were times during the writing when I felt I had never done anything else. Fortunately, I enjoyed the sustained and sustaining support of archivists, librarians, friends, and colleagues. Strangers, too, seeking me out after a lecture or sending me unsolicited material after reading about my project, took a welcome, helpful interest.

Indeed, one great facilitator of dialogue—giving real meaning to that much-overworked word— one on which I have come to rely, and have had occasion to mention in my other books, proved itself once again: the formal lecture that elicits questions, comments, sometimes spirited dissent, and a few times an unpublished letter. Since 1985, I have been speaking to a variety of audiences about my biography in progress, about matters of substance in Freud's life, about the relation of psychoanalysis to history and biography, about the politics of the public perception of Freud now current. I have invariably enjoyed, and usually profited from, these occasions. In 1985, I talked at Clark University on Freud's tastes in literature, and at the Indiana Historical Society and the American Psychological Association on the relationship between psychoanalysis and the historian, a subject I also canvassed, with varying emphases, at Rice University, Houston, and in a large public lecture at Groningen, in the Netherlands. In 1986, I continued this series of presentations at several more or less informal forums at Yale: at the Hillel Foundation and a Yale alumni reunion, before the graduate students of my department and a group of students in the school of architecture, and in a full-fledged lecture to the Friends of the Medical Library. That year, I also spoke at the State University of New York, Stony Brook; at Ohio University, Athens, Ohio; at the Boston Psychoanalytic Society; at the University of California at San Diego (a cheerful and moving celebration honoring the distinguished career of H. Stuart Hughes); at a luncheon at the Southern Historical Association meeting at Charlotte, North Carolina; and—a particularly delightful and rewarding occasion—at the Hebrew Union College in Cincinnati, where I spent a week lecturing on Freud, the godless Jew. In 1987, I spoke at the Chicago Institute for Psychoanalysis, at a workshop for psychoanalysis and the social sciences at the University of Chicago, as the second George Rosen Lecturer at the Beaumont Club at the medical school of my university, and, finally, to my fellow fellows at the Humanities Center at Yale. As I have noted, it has all been extremely stimulating and valuable—at least to me. Owing so much to the people in these audiences, and feeling under the deepest obligation also to a great many others, I can only hope that I have overlooked or slighted no one in these acknowledgments.

I am, to begin with, immensely grateful to Ronald S. Wilkinson, Manuscript Historian at the Manuscript Division of the Library of Congress. In charge of the largest and most valuable treasure-trove of Freud materials anywhere, he shared without reserve his knowledge of his holdings, and of holdings elsewhere; generously and imaginatively, he eased my search for elusive documents. Mark Paterson, director of Sigmund Freud Copyrights at Wivenhoe, near Colchester, cordially made all his rich Freud materials available to me. He was ably assisted by two archivists, Celia Hirst and Jo Richardson. David L. Newlands, who was, while I was writing this book, Curator of the Freud Museum, 20 Maresfield Gardens, Hampstead, London, made me welcome, and Steve Neufeld of the Museum saved me unnumbered hours of work by supplying invaluable information and by discovering some rare gems. Pearl H. M. King, Honorary Archivist at the Archives of the British Psycho-Analytical Society, also in London, gave me permission to explore, and use, the riches of the Ernest Jones papers, which allowed me to reconstruct Jones's biography of Freud in the making, while Jill Duncan, Executive Officer at the Archives, was responsive to my inquiries and tracked down some important letters for me. Two librarian-archivists, Ellen Gilbert and, after her, David J. Ross, received me kindly at the A. A. Brill Library of the New York Psychoanalytic Institute, and steered me through its intriguing holdings, mainly (but not solely) the papers of Freud's American analysands. Kenneth A. Lohf, Librarian for Rare Books and Manuscripts at Columbia University, helped me with the Otto Rank Collection, as did Rudolph Ellenbogen. Glenise A. Matheson, Keeper of Manuscripts at the John Rylands University Library, Manchester, England, was most forthcoming about the revealing correspondence between Freud and his nephew Samuel. Judith A. Schiff, Chief Research Archivist at Manuscripts and Archives, Yale University Library, was (as always) helpful, this time chiefly with the Colonel E. M. House papers. Alan S. Divack, Assistant Archivist at the Leo Baeck Institute, New York, supplied me with several unpublished letters. Bernard McTigue, Curator of the Arents Collection at the New York Public Library, made available to me an important letter of Freud's on his smoking habits (previously published but misidentified). I also thank Elena S. Danielson, Assistant Archivist at the Hoover Institution on War, Revolution, and Peace for sending me a letter of Freud's to Paul Hill. A. M. J. Izermans of the International Institute of Social History in Amsterdam gave me permission to print part of a Freud letter to Hendrik de Man. Sally Leach of the Harry Ransom Humanities Research Center at the University of Texas, Austin, was helpful in tracking down some correspondence between Blanche Knopf and the Freuds. As always, I found the historical library of the Yale Medical Library (Ferenc A. Gyorgyey in charge) cordiality itself.

I am most grateful to those who volunteered unpublished material or information about little-known events in Freud's life. J. Alexis Burland sent me a fascinating letter that Freud wrote to his father shortly after the First World War, and supplied the background for it. Anton O. Kris and his sister, Anna K. Wolff, graciously presented me with several letters from Freud to Ernst Kris and Oscar Rie, and added useful anecdotal information. Sanford Gifford sent me his revealing unpublished manuscript on Felix Deutsch, containing valuable, hitherto unknown material. Willi Köhler, my editor at S. Fischer Verlag, Frankfurt am Main, sent me some important material in advance of publication. Josefine Stross, who was close to the Freuds in Freud's last years, reminisced instructively without violating her physician's obligation to confidentiality.

The late Jeanne Lampl-de Groot, an analysand of Freud's and an eminent Dutch psychoanalyst, overcame her skepticism about yet another Freud biographer to grant me a memorable interview in her home in Amsterdam on October 24, 1985. Helen Schur, not skeptical even from the start, did the same on June 3, 1986. She did more: she searched her memory and her safe to come up with letters both to and from her husband that throw sharp light on Freud's last years. The Max Schur papers at the Library of Congress, which I was fortunate enough to be the first to examine, further enriched chapters 11 and 12. Ingeborg Meyer-Palmedo of S. Fischer Verlag took the trouble to send me the corrected version of the Freud–Edoardo Weiss correspondence. I want also to record my particular gratitude to Ilse Grubrich-Simitis—psychoanalyst, editor, author—for her letters, her conversation, and her immense considerateness in furnishing me with galley proofs of vital texts (such as the Freud–Fliess letters in the original German) long before they became generally available. As she knows, her Freud is my Freud, but she did much to clarify that Freud for me.

Indeed, I enjoyed that kind of benefit over and over, as friends provided me with the stimulus of good talk and good correspondence. Janet Malcolm, whose witty and accurate books on psychoanalysis have educated the uninformed and delighted the knowledgeable, has been a pure pleasure as what the Germans call a conversation-partner. The Katwans, Jackie and Gaby, were wonderful. Iza S. Erlich, a practicing psychoanalyst and valued friend with whom I have been talking Freud for well over a decade, sent me an eye-opening paper of her own and pointed the way to those of others. Elise Snyder proved a loyal accomplice, not least (though not only) in opening doors for me. Over the years, Susanna Barrows has made my life as a scholar both easier and far more agreeable. Peter Loewenberg, who has long been magnanimous toward me and my work, explored theoretical issues, sent offprints, and provided leads to sources of information. Juliette L. George and her husband, Alexander, considerably enriched my grasp on the Freud-Bullitt study of Woodrow Wilson. Jay Katz told me good, true stories about Anna Freud that I could use. Joseph Goldstein proved a mainstay and, I must say, made me feel better about psychoanalysts. So did Albert J. Solnit, my colleague and friend, to whom I owe a sizable debt for well-placed encouragement, precise information, and timely access to elusive materials. Ernst Prelinger and I have had rewarding discussions about Freud for a decade and more; he has left his mark on this book. My friend the late Richard Ellmann, whose great biography of James Joyce was a spur to me, and whose presence I sorely miss, clarified several obscure points. Martin S. Bergmann showed me the manuscript of his psychoanalytic-historical study of love, sent me valuable offprints, and, with Marie Bergmann, has kept up a running conversation on Freud. Several analysts attached to the Western New England Institute for Psychoanalysis whom I may claim as more than casual acquaintances—James Kleeman, Richard Newman, Morton Reiser, Samuel Ritvo, Paul Schwaber, Lorraine Siggins—earned my thanks by providing information, printed materials, and (invaluable to a document hunter in sensitive terrain) tactical counsel. Phyllis Grosskurth and I peacefully debated our differing appraisals of Anna Freud. William McGuire patiently shared with me his scholarly information on Jung, Ferenczi, Spielrein, and others. I have profited from my conversations with Ivo Banac, John Demos, Hannah S. Decker, and David Musto. Stanley A. Leavy helped me to obtain Ernest Jones's monograph on ice skating. My friends C. Vann Woodward and Harry Frankfurt proved good listeners, or good skeptics, when I needed these responses. As always the Webbs, Bob and Pattie, to whom I have been affectionately bound for thirty years, made my stays in Washington, D.C., a real pleasure. So did Joe and Millie Glazer. And far beyond the call of duty for the seasoned editor she is at Yale University Press, my old friend Gladys Topkis superbly understood the needs of an author, even when he is doing a book for another publisher.

I also thank (for volunteering information, answering questions, and sending offprints or books) Henry Abelove, Ola Andersson, Roger Nicholas Balsiger, Hortense K. Becker, Steven Beller, Edward L. Bernays, Gerard Braunthal, Hilde Braunthal, Paul Brooks, Robert Byck, Edward T. Chase, Francis Crick, Hana Davis, Howard Davis, George E. Ehrlich, Rudolf Ekstein, Jason Epstein, Avner Falk, Max Fink, David James Fisher, Sophie Freud, Alfreda S. Galt, John E. and Mary Gedo, Robert Gottlieb, Henry F. Graff, Fred Grubel, Edwin J. Haeberle, Hendrika C. Halberstadt-Freud, Hugh R. B. Hamilton, John Harrisson, Louise E. Hoffman, Margo Howard, Judith M. Hughes, Orville Hurwitz, Han Israëls, Alice L. Kahler, Marie Kann, Mark Kanzer, Jonathan Katz, John and Robert Kebabian (who identified the rug on Freud's couch), George Kennan, Paul Kennedy, Dennis B. Klein, W. A. Koelsch, Richard Kuisel, Nathaniel S. Lehrman, Harry M. Lessin, E. James Lieberman, Arthur S. Link, Murray Louis, H. E. Lück, John Maass, Patrick J. Mahony, Henry Marx, Robert S. McCully, Frank Meissner, Graeme Mitchison, Melvin Muroff, Peter B. Neubauer, Lottie M. Newman, Fran H. Ng, Sherwin B. Nuland, R. More O'Ferrall, Daniel Offer, Alice Oliver, Darius Ornston, Peter Paret, Alan P. Pollard, Susan Quinn, Robert Rieber, Ana-Maria Rizzuto, Paul Roazen, Arthur

Rosenthal, Rebecca Saletan, Perdita Scheffner, Josef and Eta Selka, Leonard Shengold, Michael Shepherd, Barry Silverstein, Roszi Stein, Leo Steinberg, Riccardo Steiner, Paul E. Stepansky, Anthony Storr, Peter J. Swales (who, though doubtless aware of my quizzical attitude toward his biographical reconstructions, liberally supplied me with copies of his writings and other hard-to-get materials), John Toews, Don Heinrich Tolzman, Edwin R. Wallace IV, Robert S. Wallerstein, Lynne L. Weiner, David S. Werman, Dan S. White, Jay Winter, Elisabeth Young-Bruehl (who generously shared some of her findings on Anna Freud with me), and Arthur Zitrin.

My colleague William Cronon deserves a paragraph of his own. Without his painstaking, relaxed but enthusiastic instruction, often time-consuming but never grudgingly given, and without his rescue operations at critical times, I should never have mastered the intricacies of my IBM-XT word processor, and this book would have been delayed for incalculable months.

Former students—especially Carl Landauer, Mark Micale, and Craig Tomlinson—and present students like Andrew Aisenberg, Patricia Behre, John Cornell, Robert Dietle, Judith Forrest, Michèle Plott, and Helmut Smith, have patiently given me equal time on Freud and supplied valuable comments of their own. I also want to thank my undergraduate assistants James Lochart and Rebecca Haltzel for their fine support.

I feel singularly fortunate in the ways that W. W. Norton has managed this long, by no means uncomplicated manuscript. Donald S. Lamm, in addition to discharging his manifold duties as head of the publishing house, acted as my editor. I am glad he did; for all my considerable experience with the printed word, I had never written a biography, and Don taught me much about clarity and chronology that I had been aware of far more dimly before. Amy Cherry acted as conduit and buffer—splendidly in both roles. Esther Jacobson is a demon of a copy editor; the flicker of flags fluttering at the right margins of my manuscript was a reminder that, careful as I and my first readers had been, it was possible and desirable to exercise still greater care. It is a measure of my gratitude to her these hundreds of pages later, that we are still speaking cordially to one another.

ALL THIS ABOUNDING cheer makes it seem positively churlish for me to strike a less harmonious note. But I find it necessary to alert readers to gaps in this biography for which I am not responsible, gaps I tried in vain to close, with more strenuous eloquence, and more pleading letters, than I care to recall. While the right to permit publication of Freud's words rests with Sigmund Freud Copyrights, Ltd, the right to consult the bulk of the unpublished Freud material is granted by The Sigmund Freud Archives, Inc., of New York. This institution was founded by Dr. Kurt R. Eissler, who for a long time directed it with a firm hand. He has now been succeeded by Dr. Harold P. Blum. Dr. Eissler gathered innumerable documents that would otherwise have remained scattered or might have been lost; he also interviewed scores of Freud's analysands, colleagues, friends, and acquaintances, and deposited this vast and invaluable material with the Manuscript Division of the Library of Congress. For his diligence and assiduity in this largely one-man operation, he has earned the gratitude of all scholars doing research on Freud and on the history of psychoanalysis. But his policy was, with certain stated exceptions, to keep Freud material closed for decades; he set many of the dates (not always to the pleasure of the donors) at which the restrictions are to be lifted, and these reach well into the twenty-first century, often beyond the life span of the scholars now at work. Dr. Eissler has freely and frequently expressed the view that anything—I mean *anything*—that Freud had not intended for publication should not be published. On more than one occasion I have taken the opportunity to argue in behalf of a more liberal position. Several years ago, when I debated the issue with Dr. Eissler at a meeting of the Committee on History and Archives of the American Psychoanalytic Association (of which I have been a member for several years), he voiced the opinion that even the publication of the Freud–Jung correspondence had done Freud a disservice, since it had been used to denigrate Freud. My counterargument was simplicity itself: bad history or bad biography can be driven out only by better history or better biography, and these can be written only if documents are accessible to scholars. The addiction to secrecy to which Dr. Eissler was—and is—so passionately committed could only encourage the festering of the most outlandish rumors about the man whose reputation he was trying to protect. I also commented on the palpable contradiction of a discipline devoted to the greatest possible candor, psychoanalysis, showing itself before the world as secretive, not to say devious. Obviously, my arguments did not impress him. I have been corresponding with Dr. Eissler on this vexed issued for almost twenty years now, and have been asking for material he controls ever since the writing of this biography became a possibility. But the results have always been the same for me—total defeat.

Perhaps the most significant casualty of Dr. Eissler's policy has been the collection of letters that Freud and his fiancée exchanged during the five long years of their engagement, a time when they were separated more than they were together. Since they wrote to one another practically every day, each must have written about a thousand letters. These so-called *Brautbriefe* would show the young Freud at work or in love in the early 1880s as intimately as the letters to Fliess show psychoanalysis in the making in the 1890s. At a meeting of the Committee on History and Archives in December 1986, Dr. Blum called this correspondence the greatest collection of love letters in the history of Western culture. One can only respond, How does he know? In 1960, Ernst and Lucie Freud edited a sizable (but still very fragmentary) selection of Freud's correspondence, containing nearly a hundred of these letters. (See above, p. 743.) This number was not increased in the second edition, of 1968. Repeated attempts on my part to gain access to the remaining letters were repulsed by Dr. Eissler, politely but definitively. In consequence, I have had to depend on a handful of unpublished letters I managed to obtain (including several from Martha Bernays to Freud) to eke out those that have been published.

The current policy of The Sigmund Freud Archives, Inc., under the leadership of Dr. Blum, offers greater hope by being less predictable. Early in my work, I was granted access to the complete Freud–Abraham correspondence (in the Manuscript Division of the Library of Congress as the Karl Abraham papers), as well as the complete series D of the Freud Collection, which includes as its prize most of Freud's letters to Ernest Jones. On July 17, 1986, the *New York Review of Books* published a letter from Dr. Blum, writing as "Executive Director," noting that "all papers and documents under the ownership and control of The Sigmund Freud Archives which are in the process of publication or have already been published will be open to all scholars on the basis of equal access," and promising "to release all letters and documents from restriction, as soon as possible, consistent with legal and ethical standards and obligations." The *only* material to be kept from readers, Dr. Blum has said emphatically and repeatedly, and confirmed in correspondence with me, would be sentences or paragraphs that directly identify, or make it possible to identify, a patient. My suggestion that scholars be given access to all hitherto restricted material after signing a rigorous statement, to be devised by the Library of Congress, making each user promise not to publish, or use in any way, specified passages or letters that might disclose the identity of a patient, was rejected in favor of having each still-closed letter read by some trusted person appointed by The Sigmund Freud Archives, who could then mark whatever passages should be kept from the public. This procedure has shown itself slow and clumsy in the extreme. It is only fair to note that much Freud material is open to scholars; some of it has been accessible for years, and more is being made accessible year after year. But it is, of course, precisely the materials still being withheld that are—or by their very character appear to be—of greatest interest to the historian.

BUT TO RETURN to sunnier ground. As with my earlier books, so once again I leaned heavily on informed readers. My former student, now good friend, Hank Gibbons, a historian deeply sensitive to the demands of intellectual history, gave me genial and highly valued counsel on matters small and large, especially large. Dick and Peggy Kuhns carefully went over this manuscript with the trained eye of the psychoanalytically schooled philosopher and psychologist, respectively; their readings, combined with the splendid conversations we have been carrying on for years about Freud and psychoanalysis, have left a deep imprint on the book. Jerry Meyer, my classmate at the Western New England Institute for Psychoanalysis, a practicing analyst and a cultivated reader, paid particularly close attention to the technical and medical issues involved in this biography, and contributed to whatever clarity it may boast. And I want to express my particular gratitude to George Mahl, an experienced psychoanalyst and seasoned teacher, who disinterestedly took time off from a book of his own on Freud to give this text the most meticulous of readings; his superb familiarity with the history of psychoanalysis, his unfailing respect for precision, and his kindly though always tough-minded way of correcting slips and offering improvements and felicitous reformulations, have left me with a debt that seems impossible to discharge. My wife, Ruth, played her accustomed role of final reader with virtuosity and tact. I thank all my readers, hoping that the finished work will prove worthy of the time and care they have bestowed on it.

P.G.
Hamden, Connecticut
December 1987

INDEX